Perspectives on Behavior in Organizations

Second Edition

Edited by

J. Richard Hackman
Yale University

Edward E. Lawler III
University of Southern California

Lyman W. Porter
University of California, Irvine

McGraw-Hill Book Company

New York St. Louis San Francisco Auckland Bogotá Hamburg
Johannesburg London Madrid Mexico Montreal New Delhi
Panama Paris São Paulo Singapore Sydney Tokyo Toronto

This book was set in Times Roman by Black Dot, Inc. (ECU).
The editors were Patricia S. Nave and Barry Benjamin;
the production supervisor was Diane Renda.
New drawings were done by ECL Art Associates, Inc.
The cover was designed by Anne Canevari Green.
R. R. Donnelley & Sons Company was printer and binder.

PERSPECTIVES ON BEHAVIOR IN ORGANIZATIONS

67890 DODO 89876

ISBN 0-07-025414-1

Library of Congress Cataloging in Publication Data
Main entry under title:

Perspectives on behavior in organizations.

1. Organizational behavior—Addresses, essays,
lectures.   I. Hackman, J. Richard.   II. Lawler,
Edward E.   III. Porter, Lyman W.
HD58.7.P47   1983   658.4   82-175
ISBN 0-07-025414-1   AACR2

Contents

2

DEVELOPMENT OF INDIVIDUAL-ORGANIZATION RELATIONSHIPS

3

DESIGN OF WORK AND REWARD SYSTEMS

4

INTERPERSONAL AND GROUP PROCESSES

Preface

Knowledge about behavior in organizations has been expanding at a rapid rate. This book provides some perspectives on that knowledge, with special emphasis on factors that affect the lives of those who work in organizations. Each of the articles included here describes some important aspect of behavior in organizations, analyzes why things happen the way they do, or provides some guidelines for managing and changing organizations.

The book does not include articles that report the details of specific research projects, nor does it delve into the complexities of organizational research methodology. Instead, our attempt has been to provide a general and informative overview of current thinking about behavior in organizations, including ideas about how organizations can be changed for the better.

The book is primarily intended for students—particularly those enrolled in junior-senior and beginning graduate-level courses in organizational behavior, organizational psychology, and management. We also believe that the book can be informative for the practicing manager. No extensive background in the behavioral sciences is assumed.

The organization of the book roughly follows that of our textbook (*Behavior in Organizations*, by L. W. Porter, E. E. Lawler, and J. R. Hackman, also published by McGraw-Hill), and we hope that this book will be useful in supplementing and updating that one. In selecting the materials reprinted here, however, we had in mind students in a wide variety of courses on organizations—not just those in which our own text is used. We hope these students also find the perspectives presented here helpful in rounding out their understanding of organizational behavior.

The readings are grouped into six parts. Part One provides some introductory perspectives, and considers the nature of individuals and organizations as a point of departure for exploring other issues in organizational behavior. Then, in Part Two, we examine the development of relationships between individuals and organizations—how each party chooses the other, adapts to the other, and develops continuing relationships. Part Three addresses the design and management of work in organizations, with special emphasis on how jobs are structured and on how work performance is assessed, evaluated, and rewarded.

The readings in Part Four deal with interpersonal and group processes that pervade organizational life and powerfully affect what happens there. In Part Five, we cover intergroup and structural factors that affect behavior in organizations—including material on how organizations themselves are designed. Finally, in Part Six, questions of leadership and organizational change are addressed. Included here are normative articles that provide ideas about how organizations *should* function, as well as readings that explore the dynamics of leadership and change processes.

We are indebted to many people for their help in completing this book. Nearly one-quarter of the book consists of articles written especially for inclusion here or in the first edition of this book. Our special thanks go to these colleagues, and to others who were generous in giving us permission to reprint articles they had published elsewhere. Finally, we wish to acknowledge the faithful and expert work of Susan Majcher in preparing these materials for the publisher.

J. Richard Hackman
Edward E. Lawler III
Lyman W. Porter

Part One

Individuals and Organizations

Chapter 1

Introduction

This book is about behavior in organizations. Its very existence assumes that the behavioral sciences can be helpful in understanding and influencing what transpires in work organizations.

That assumption is controversial. It can be argued, for example, that behavior in organizations is merely the tail of the economic dog, wagging in ways that may *seem* meaningful and orderly, but that are not useful for changing what transpires in organizations. Or it can be argued that organizational behavior is best understood as a reflection of the enduring capabilities and dispositions of individual organization members—the characteristics they bring with them to the organization and that they take with them when they leave. In this view, understanding organizational behavior involves little more than understanding the people who make up the organization—and changes in organizations would best be carried out simply by changing the people who work there. Or it even can be argued that what happens in organizations is basically unpredictable, that anarchy and accident rather than design and

planned change better characterize organizational behavior. In this view, it would be better for the field of organizational behavior to be a purely descriptive undertaking rather than a social science that aspires to inform and guide the behavior of managers and other organization members.

When you have finished this book, you should be in a position to decide for yourself how useful the behavioral sciences actually are for understanding, predicting, and changing what happens in organizations. The three readings in this chapter may help provide a framework for use in making that assessment.

We look first at the managerial role. Managerial behavior is generally viewed as a key factor in understanding organizations, and we devote an entire chapter in the book (Chapter 13) to questions of managerial leadership and effectiveness. Yet there also are many unfounded myths about what managers actually *do* at work, and the first reading, by Mintzberg, destroys some of these myths. Based on detailed studies of how managers spend their time at work, Mintzberg shows that traditional conceptions of what managers do (and what writers about management often assert that they *should* do) are far removed from the realities of their life at work. Mintzberg offers an alternative framework for characterizing the managerial role, and offers some new ideas about what may be key to managerial effectiveness. His ideas provide a healthy measure of realism for considering how and when managers can actually use behavioral science knowledge about organizations.

The next article, by Peters, extends this line of thinking even further. Peters argues that the most frequently cited change tools used by managers (such as altering organizational structures or inventing new organizational processes) are largely ineffectual. Instead, he proposes that there are great opportunities for change embedded in the daily message-sending and message-receiving activities of senior managers—opportunities that can be exploited to energize and redirect even massive, lumbering businesses and government agencies. Peters subtitles his article "An Optimistic Case for Getting Things Done." It also is a provocative and nontraditional view about how change actually happens in organizations, and it provides a perspective well worth keeping in mind as one reads and evaluates behavioral science findings about organizational behavior.

The last article in this section, by Lorsch, focuses explicitly on how the behavioral sciences can be made more useful in managing organizations. Lorsch argues that "universal" theories (that is, managerial prescriptions that are supposed to be useful in all managerial situations) rarely fit the *specific* situation in which they are applied well enough to make much of a difference. Managers need to recognize that the easy solutions do not work and to become more intelligent consumers of behavioral science knowledge. This, he says, will involve outright rejection of most universal theories. It also will require managers to take an explicitly diagnostic stance as they assess organizational problems and decide upon ways to deal with them. And, finally, it will require managers to be more conscientious in keeping themselves and their staffs up to date about behavioral science theories and tools that can be applied to various kinds of organizational problems. We hope that this book will be of use to both students and managers in responding to Lorsch's challenges.

Reading 1

The Manager's Job: Folklore and Fact
Henry Mintzberg

If you ask a manager what he does, he will most likely tell you that he plans, organizes, coordinates, and controls. Then watch what he does. Don't be surprised if you can't relate what you see to these four words.

When he is called and told that one of his factories has just burned down, and he advises the caller to see whether temporary arrangements can be made to supply customers through a foreign subsidiary, is he planning, organizing, coordinating, or controlling? How about when he presents a gold watch to a retiring employee? Or when he attends a conference to meet people in the trade? Or on returning from that conference, when he tells one of his employees about an interesting product idea he picked up there?

The fact is that these four words, which have dominated management vocabulary since the French industrialist Henri Fayol first introduced them in 1916, tell us little about what managers actually do. At best, they indicate some vague objectives managers have when they work.

The field of management, so devoted to progress and change, has for more than half a century not seriously addressed *the* basic question: What do managers do? Without a proper answer, how can we teach management? How can we design planning or information systems for managers? How can we improve the practice of management at all?

Our ignorance of the nature of managerial work shows up in various ways in the modern organization —in the boast by the successful manager that he never spent a single day in a management training program; in the turnover of corporate planners who never quite understood what it was the manager wanted; in the computer consoles gathering dust in the back room because the managers never used the fancy on-line MIS some analyst thought they needed. Perhaps most important, our ignorance shows up in the inability of our large public organizations to come to grips with some of their most serious policy problems.

Somehow, in the rush to automate production, to use management science in the functional areas of marketing and finance, and to apply the skills of the behavioral scientist to the problem of worker motivation, the manager—that person in charge of the organization or one of its subunits—has been forgotten.

My intention in this article is simple: to break the reader away from Fayol's words and introduce him to a more supportable, and what I believe to be a more useful, description of managerial work. This description derives from my review and synthesis of the available research on how various managers have spent their time.

In some studies, managers were observed intensively ("shadowed" is the term some of them used); in a number of others, they kept detailed diaries of their activities; in a few studies, their records were analyzed. All kinds of managers were studied— foremen, factory supervisors, staff managers, field sales managers, hospital administrators, presidents of companies and nations, and even street gang leaders. These "managers" worked in the United States, Canada, Sweden, and Great Britain. [A brief review of the major studies that I found most useful in developing this description, including my own study of five American chief executive officers, is informative.]

A synthesis of these findings paints an interesting picture, one as different from Fayol's classical view as a cubist abstract is from a Renaissance painting. In a sense, this picture will be obvious to anyone who has ever spent a day in a manager's office, either in front of the desk or behind it. Yet, at the same time, this picture may turn out to be revolutionary, in that it throws into doubt so much of the folklore that we have accepted about the manager's work.

I first discuss some of this folklore and contrast it with some of the discoveries of systematic research —the hard facts about how managers spend their time. Then I synthesize these research findings in a description of ten roles that seem to describe the essential content of all managers' jobs. In a concluding section, I discuss a number of implications of this synthesis for those trying to achieve more effective management, both in classrooms and in the business world.

SOME FOLKLORE AND FACTS ABOUT MANAGERIAL WORK

There are four myths about the manager's job that do not bear up under careful scrutiny of the facts.

1

Folklore *The manager is a reflective, systematic planner.* The evidence on this issue is overwhelming, but not a shred of it supports this statement.

Fact *Study after study has shown that managers work at an unrelenting pace, that their activities are characterized by brevity, variety, and discontinuity, and that they are strongly oriented to action and dislike reflective activities.* Consider this evidence:

• Half the activities engaged in by the five chief executives of my study lasted less than nine minutes, and only 10% exceeded one hour.[1] A study of 56 U.S. foremen found that they averaged 583 activities per eight-hour shift, an average of 1 every 48 seconds.[2] The work pace for both chief executives and foremen was unrelenting. The chief executives met a steady stream of callers and mail from the moment they arrived in the morning until they left in the evening. Coffee breaks and lunches were inevitably work related, and ever-present subordinates seemed to usurp any free moment.

• A diary study of 160 British middle and top managers found that they worked for a half hour or more without interruption only about once every two days.[3]

• Of the verbal contacts of the chief executives in my study, 93% were arranged on an ad hoc basis. Only 1% of the executives' time was spent in open-ended observational tours. Only 1 out of 368 verbal contacts was unrelated to a specific issue and

could be called general planning. Another researcher finds that "in *not one single case* did a manager report the obtaining of important external information from a general conversation or other undirected personal communication."[4]

• No study has found important patterns in the way managers schedule their time. They seem to jump from issue to issue, continually responding to the needs of the moment.

• Is this the planner that the classical view describes? Hardly. How, then, can we explain this behavior? The manager is simply responding to the pressures of his job. I found that my chief executives terminated many of their own activities, often leaving meetings before the end, and interrupted their desk work to call in subordinates. One president not only placed his desk so that he could look down a long hallway but also left his door open when he was alone—an invitation for subordinates to come in and interrupt him.

• Clearly, these managers wanted to encourage the flow of current information. But more significantly, they seemed to be conditioned by their own work loads. They appreciated the opportunity cost of their own time, and they were continually aware of their ever-present obligations—mail to be answered, callers to attend to, and so on. It seems that no matter what he is doing, the manager is plagued by the possibilities of what he might do and what he must do.

• When the manager must plan, he seems to do so implicitly in the context of daily actions, not in some abstract process reserved for two weeks in the organization's mountain retreat. The plans of the chief executives I studied seemed to exist only in their heads—as flexible, but often specific, intentions. The traditional literature notwithstanding, the job of managing does not breed reflective planners; the manager is a real-time responder to stimuli, an individual who is conditioned by his job to prefer live to delayed action.

2

Folklore *The effective manager has no regular duties to perform.* Managers are constantly being told to spend more time planning and delegating, and less time seeing customers and engaging in negotiations. These are not, after all, the true tasks of the manager. To use the popular analogy, the good manager, like the good conductor, carefully orchestrates everything in advance, then sits back to

[1]All the data from my study can be found in Henry Mintzberg, *The Nature of Managerial Work* (New York: Harper & Row, 1973).

[2]Robert H. Guest, "Of Time and the Foreman," *Personnel*, May 1956, p. 478.

[3]Rosemary Stewart, *Managers and Their Jobs* (London: Macmillan, 1967); see also Sune Carlson, *Executive Behaviour* (Stockholm: Strombergs, 1951), the first of the diary studies.

[4]Francis J. Aguilar, *Scanning the Business Environment* (New York: Macmillan, 1967), p. 102.

enjoy the fruits of his labor, responding occasionally to an unforeseeable exception.

But here again the pleasant abstraction just does not seem to hold up. We had better take a closer look at those activities managers feel compelled to engage in before we arbitrarily define them away.

Fact *In addition to handling exceptions, managerial work involves performing a number of regular duties, including ritual and ceremony, negotiations, and processing of soft information that links the organization with its environment.* Consider some evidence from the research studies:

• A study of the work of the presidents of small companies found that they engaged in routine activities because their companies could not afford staff specialists and were so thin on operating personnel that a single absence often required the president to substitute.[5]

• One study of field sales managers and another of chief executives suggest that it is a natural part of both jobs to see important customers, assuming the managers wish to keep those customers.[6]

• Someone, only half in jest, once described the manager as that person who sees visitors so that everyone else can get his work done. In my study, I found that certain ceremonial duties—meeting visiting dignitaries, giving out gold watches, presiding at Christmas dinners—were an intrinsic part of the chief executive's job.

• Studies of managers' information flow suggest that managers play a key role in securing "soft" external information (much of it available only to them because of their status) and in passing it along to their subordinates.

3

Folklore *The senior manager needs aggregated information, which a formal management information system best provides.* Not too long ago, the words *total information system* were everywhere in the management literature. In keeping with the classical view of the manager as that individual perched on the apex of a regulated, hierarchical system, the literature's manager was to receive all

his important information from a giant, comprehensive MIS.

But lately, as it has become increasingly evident that these giant MIS systems are not working—that managers are simply not using them—the enthusiasm has waned. A look at how managers actually process information makes the reason quite clear. Managers have five media at their command—documents, telephone calls, scheduled and unscheduled meetings, and observational tours.

Fact *Managers strongly favor the verbal media—namely, telephone calls and meetings.* The evidence comes from every single study of managerial work. Consider the following:

• In two British studies, managers spent an average of 66% and 80% of their time in verbal (oral) communication.[7] In my study of five American chief executives, the figure was 78%.

• These five chief executives treated mail processing as a burden to be dispensed with. One came in Saturday morning to process 142 pieces of mail in just over three hours, to "get rid of all the stuff." This same manager looked at the first piece of "hard" mail he had received all week, a standard cost report, and put it aside with the comment, "I never look at this."

• These same five chief executives responded immediately to 2 of the 40 routine reports they received during the five weeks of my study and to four items in the 104 periodicals. They skimmed most of these periodicals in seconds, almost ritualistically. In all, these chief executives of good-sized organizations initiated on their own—that is, not in response to something else—a grand total of 25 pieces of mail during the 25 days I observed them.

An analysis of the mail the executives received reveals an interesting picture—only 13% was of specific and immediate use. So now we have another piece in the puzzle: not much of the mail provides live, current information—the action of a competitor, mood of a government legislator, or the rating of last night's television show. Yet this is the information that drove the managers, interrupting their meetings and rescheduling their workdays.

Consider another interesting finding. Managers

[5]Unpublished study by Irving Choran, reported in Mintzberg, *The Nature of Managerial Work*.

[6]Robert T. Davis, *Performance and Development of Field Sales Managers* (Boston: Division of Research, Harvard Business School, 1957); George H. Copeman, *The Role of the Managing Director* (London: Business Publications, 1963).

[7]Stewart, *Managers and Their Jobs*; Tom Burns, "The Directions of Activity and Communication in a Departmental Executive Group," *Human Relations 7,* no. 1 (1954): 73.

seem to cherish "soft" information, especially gossip, hearsay, and speculation. Why? The reason is its timeliness; today's gossip may be tomorrow's fact. The manager who is not accessible for the telephone call informing him that his biggest customer was seen golfing with his main competitor may read about a dramatic drop in sales in the next quarterly report. But then it's too late.

To assess the value of historical, aggregated, "hard" MIS information, consider two of the manager's prime uses for his information—to identify problems and opportunities[8] and to build his own mental models of the things around him (e.g., how his organization's budget system works, how his customers buy his product, how changes in the economy affect his organization, and so on). Every bit of evidence suggests that the manager identifies decision situations and builds models not with the aggregated abstractions an MIS provides, but with specific tidbits of data.

Consider the words of Richard Neustadt, who studied the information-collecting habits of Presidents Roosevelt, Truman, and Eisenhower:

It is not information of a general sort that helps a President see personal stakes; not summaries, not surveys, not the *bland amalgams*. Rather . . . it is the odds and ends of *tangible detail* that pieced together in his mind illuminate the underside of issues put before him. To help himself he must reach out as widely as he can for every scrap of fact, opinion, gossip, bearing on his interests and relationships as President. He must become his own director of his own central intelligence.[9]

The manager's emphasis on the verbal media raises two important points:

First, verbal information is stored in the brains of people. Only when people write this information down can it be stored in the files of the organization —whether in metal cabinets or on magnetic tape— and managers apparently do not write down much of what they hear. Thus the strategic data bank of the organization is not in the memory of its computers but in the minds of its managers.

Second, the manager's extensive use of verbal media helps to explain why he is reluctant to delegate tasks. When we note that most of the manager's important information comes in verbal form and is stored in his head, we can well appreciate his reluctance. It is not as if he can hand a dossier over to someone; he must take the time to "dump memory"—to tell that someone all he knows about the subject. But this could take so long that the manager may find it easier to do the task himself. Thus the manager is damned by his own information system to a "dilemma of delegation"—to do too much himself or to delegate to his subordinates with inadequate briefing.

4

Folklore *Management is, or at least is quickly becoming, a science and a profession.* By almost any definitions of *science* and *profession,* this statement is false. Brief observation of any manager will quickly lay to rest the notion that managers practice a science. A science involves the enaction of systematic, analytically determined procedures or programs. If we do not even know what procedures managers use, how can we prescribe them by scientific analysis? And how can we call management a profession if we cannot specify what managers are to learn? For after all, a profession involves "knowledge of some department of learning or science" (*Random House Dictionary*).[10]

Fact *The manager's programs—to schedule time, process information, make decisions, and so on— remain locked deep inside their brains.* Thus, to describe these programs, we rely on words like *judgment* and *intuition,* seldom stopping to realize that they are merely labels for our ignorance.

I was struck during my study by the fact that the executives I was observing—all very competent by any standard—are fundamentally indistinguishable from their counterparts of a hundred years ago (or a thousand years ago, for that matter). The information they need differs, but they seek it in the same way—by word of mouth. Their decisions concern modern technology, but the procedures they use to make them are the same as the procedures of the

[8]H. Edward Wrapp, "Good Managers Don't Make Policy Decisions," HBR September-October 1967, p. 91; Wrapp refers to this as spotting opportunities and relationships in the stream of operating problems and decisions; in his article Wrapp raises a number of excellent points related to this analysis.

[9]Richard E. Neustadt, *Presidential Power* (New York; John Wiley, 1960), pp. 153–154; italics added.

[10]For a more thorough, though rather different, discussion of this issue, see Kenneth R. Andrews, "Toward Professionalism in Business Management," HBR March–April 1969, p. 49.

nineteenth-century manager. Even the computer, so important for the specialized work of the organization, has apparently had no influence on the work procedures of general managers. In fact, the manager is in a kind of loop, with increasingly heavy work pressures but no aid forthcoming from management science.

Considering the facts about managerial work, we can see that the manager's job is enormously complicated and difficult. The manager is overburdened with obligations; yet he cannot easily delegate his tasks. As a result, he is driven to overwork and is forced to do many tasks superficially. Brevity, fragmentation, and verbal communication characterize his work. Yet these are the very characteristics of managerial work that have impeded scientific attempts to improve it. As a result, the management scientist has concentrated his efforts on the specialized functions of the organizations, where he could more easily analyze the procedures and quantify the relevant information.[11]

But the pressures of the manager's job are becoming worse. Where before he needed only to respond to owners and directors, now he finds that subordinates with democratic norms continually reduce his freedom to issue unexplained orders, and a growing number of outside influences (consumer groups, government agencies, and so on) expect his attention. And the manager has had nowhere to turn for help. The first step in providing the manager with some help is to find out what his job really is.

BACK TO A BASIC DESCRIPTION OF MANAGERIAL WORK

Now let us try to put some of the pieces of this puzzle together. Earlier, I defined the manager as that person in charge of an organization or one of its subunits. Besides chief executive officers, this definition would include vice presidents, bishops, foremen, hockey coaches, and prime ministers. Can all of these people have anything in common? Indeed they can. For an important starting point, all are vested with formal authority over an organizational

unit. From formal authority comes status, which leads to various interpersonal relations, and from these comes access to information. Information, in turn, enables the manager to make decisions and strategies for his unit.

The manager's job can be described in terms of various "roles," or organized sets of behaviors identified with a position. My description, shown in Figure 1-1, comprises ten roles. As we shall see, formal authority gives rise to the three interpersonal roles, which in turn give rise to the three informational roles; these two sets of roles enable the manager to play the four decisional roles.

Interpersonal Roles

Three of the manager's roles arise directly from his formal authority and involve basic interpersonal relationships.

1 First is the *figurehead* role. By virtue of his position as head of an organizational unit, every manager must perform some duties of a ceremonial nature. The president greets the touring dignitaries, the foreman attends the wedding of a lathe operator, and the sales manager takes an important customer to lunch.

The chief executives of my study spent 12% of their contact time on ceremonial duties; 17% of their incoming mail dealt with acknowledgments and requests related to their status. For example, a letter to a company president requested free merchandise for a crippled schoolchild: diplomas were

[11]C. Jackson Grayson, Jr., in "Management Science and Business Practice," HBR July–August 1973, p. 41, explains in similar terms why, as chairman of the Price Commission, he did not use those very techniques that he himself promoted in his earlier career as a management scientist.

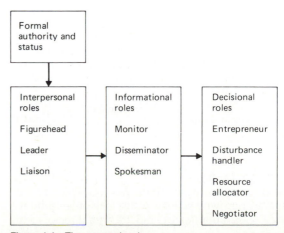

Figure 1-1 The manager's roles.

put on the desk of the school superintendent for his signature.

Duties that involve interpersonal roles may sometimes be routine, involving little serious communication and no important decision making. Nevertheless, they are important to the smooth functioning of an organization and cannot be ignored by the manager.

2 Because he is in charge of an organizational unit, the manager is responsible for the work of the people of that unit. His actions in this regard constitute the *leader* role. Some of these actions involve leadership directly—for example, in most organizations the manager is normally responsible for hiring and training his own staff.

In addition, there is the indirect exercise of the leader role. Every manager must motivate and encourage his employees, somehow reconciling their individual needs with the goals of the organization. In virtually every contact the manager has with his employees, subordinates seeking leadership clues probe his actions: "Does he approve?" "How would he like the report to turn out?" "Is he more interested in market share than high profits?"

The influence of the manager is most clearly seen in the leader role. Formal authority vests him with great potential power; leadership determines in large part how much of it he will realize.

3 The literature of management has always recognized the leader role, particularly those aspects of it related to motivation. In comparison, until recently it has hardly mentioned the *liaison* role, in which the manager makes contacts outside his vertical chain of command. This is remarkable in light of the finding of virtually every study of managerial work that managers spend as much time with peers and other people outside their units as they do with their own subordinates—and, surprisingly, very little time with their own superiors.

In Rosemary Stewart's diary study, the 160 British middle and top managers spent 47% of their time with peers, 41% of their time with people outside their unit, and only 12% of their time with their superiors. For Robert H. Guest's study of U.S. foremen, the figures were 44%, 46%, and 10%. The chief executives of my study averaged 44% of their contact time with people outside their organizations, 48% with subordinates, and 7% with directors and trustees.

The contacts the five CEOs made were with an incredibly wide range of people: subordinates; clients, business associates, and suppliers; and peers—managers of similar organizations, government and trade organization officials, fellow directors on outside boards, and independents with no relevant organizational affiliations. The chief executives' time with and mail from these groups is shown in Figure 1-2. Guest's study of foremen shows, likewise, that their contacts were numerous and wide ranging, seldom involving fewer than 25 individuals, and often more than 50.

As we shall see shortly, the manager cultivates such contacts largely to find information. In effect, the liaison role is devoted to building up the manager's own external information system—informal, private, verbal, but, nevertheless, effective.

Informational Roles

By virtue of his interpersonal contacts, both with his subordinates and with his network of contacts, the manager emerges as the nerve center of his organizational unit. He may not know everything, but he typically knows more than any member of his staff.

Studies have shown this relationship to hold for all managers, from street gang leaders to U.S. presidents. In *The Human Group*, George C. Homans explains how, because they were at the center of the

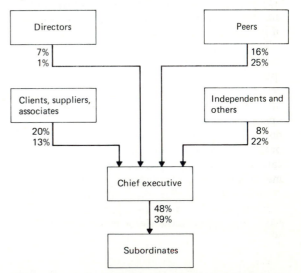

Figure 1-2 The chief executive's contacts. *Note:* The top figure indicates the proportion of total contact time spent with each group, and the bottom figure, the proportion of mail from each group.

information flow in their own gangs and were also in close touch with other gang leaders, street gang leaders were better informed than any of their followers.[12] And Richard Neustadt describes the following account from his study of Franklin D. Roosevelt:

> The essence of Roosevelt's technique for information-gathering was competition. "He would call you in," one of his aides once told me, "and he'd ask you to get the story on some complicated business, and you'd come back after a couple of days of hard labor and present the juicy morsel you'd uncovered under a stone somewhere, and *then* you'd find out he knew all about it, along with something else you *didn't* know. Where he got this information from he wouldn't mention, usually, but after he had done this to you once or twice you got damn careful about *your* information."[13]

We can see where Roosevelt "got this information" when we consider the relationship between the interpersonal and informational roles. As leader, the manager has formal and easy access to every member of his staff. Hence, as noted earlier, he tends to know more about his own unit than anyone else does. In addition, his liaison contacts expose the manager to external information to which his subordinates often lack access. Many of these contacts are with other managers of equal status, who are themselves nerve centers in their own organization. In this way, the manager develops a powerful data base of information.

The processing of information is a key part of the manager's job. In my study, the chief executives spent 40% of their contact time on activities devoted exclusively to the transmission of information; 70% of their incoming mail was purely informational (as opposed to requests for action). The manager does not leave meetings or hang up the telephone in order to get back to work. In large part, communication *is* his work. Three roles describe these informational aspects of managerial work.

1 As *monitor,* the manager perpetually scans his environment for information, interrogates his liaison contacts and his subordinates, and receives

unsolicited information, much of it as a result of the network of personal contacts he has developed. Remember that a good part of the information the manager collects in his monitor role arrives in verbal form, often as gossip, hearsay, and speculation. By virtue of his contacts, the manager has a natural advantage in collecting this soft information for his organization.

2 He must share and distribute much of this information. Information he gleans from outside personal contacts may be needed within his organization. In his *disseminator* role, the manager passes some of his privileged information directly to his subordinates, who would otherwise have no access to it. When his subordinates lack easy contact with one another, the manager will sometimes pass information from one to another.

3 In his *spokesman* role, the manager sends some of his information to people outside his unit—a president makes a speech to lobby for an organization cause, or a foreman suggests a product modification to a supplier. In addition, as part of his role as spokesman, every manager must inform and satisfy the influential people who control his organizational unit. For the foreman, this may simply involve keeping the plant manager informed about the flow of work through the shop.

The president of a large corporation, however, may spend a great amount of his time dealing with a host of influences. Directors and shareholders must be advised about financial performance; consumer groups must be assured that the organization is fulfilling its social responsibilities; and government officials must be satisfied that the organization is abiding by the law.

Decisional Roles

Information is not, of course, an end in itself; it is the basic input to decision making. One thing is clear in the study of managerial work: the manager plays the major role in his unit's decision-making system. As its formal authority, only he can commit the unit to important new courses of action; and as its nerve center, only he has full and current information to make the set of decisions that determines the unit's strategy. Four roles describe the manager as decision maker.

1 As *entrepreneur,* the manager seeks to improve his unit, to adapt it to changing conditions in the environment. In his monitor role, the president is

[12]George C. Homans, *The Human Group* (New York: Harcourt, Brace & World, 1950), based on the study by William F. Whyte entitled *Street Corner Society,* rev. ed. (Chicago: University of Chicago Press, 1955).
[13]Neustadt, *Presidential Power,* p. 157.

constantly on the lookout for new ideas. When a good one appears, he initiates a development project that he may supervise himself or delegate to an employee (perhaps with the stipulation that he must approve the final proposal).

There are two interesting features about these development projects at the chief executive level.

First, these projects do not involve single decisions or even unified clusters of decisions. Rather, they emerge as a series of small decisions and actions sequenced over time. Apparently, the chief executive prolongs each project so that he can fit it bit by bit into his busy, disjointed schedule and so that he can gradually come to comprehend the issue, if it is a complex one.

Second, the chief executives I studied supervised as many as 50 of these projects at the same time. Some projects entailed new products or processes; others involved public relations campaigns, improvement of the cash position, reorganization of a weak department, resolution of a morale problem in a foreign division, integration of computer operations, various acquisitions at different stages of development, and so on.

The chief executive appears to maintain a kind of inventory of the development projects that he himself supervises—projects that are at various stages of development, some active and some in limbo. Like a juggler, he keeps a number of projects in the air; periodically, one comes down, is given a new burst of energy, and is sent back into orbit. At various intervals, he puts new projects on-stream and discards old ones.

2 While the entrepreneur role describes the manager as the voluntary initiator of change, the *disturbance handler* role depicts the manager involuntarily responding to pressures. Here change is beyond the manager's control. He must act because the pressures of the situation are too severe to be ignored: strike looms, a major customer has gone bankrupt, or a supplier reneges on his contract.

It has been fashionable, I noted earlier, to compare the manager to an orchestra conductor, just as Peter F. Drucker wrote in *The Practice of Management*:

The manager has the task of creating a true whole that is larger than the sum of its parts, a productive entity that

turns out more than the sum of the resources put into it. One analogy is the conductor of a symphony orchestra, through whose effort, vision and leadership individual instrumental parts that are so much noise by themselves become the living whole of music. But the conductor has the composer's score; he is only interpreter. The manager is both composer and conductor.[14]

Now consider the words of Leonard R. Sayles, who has carried out systematic research on the manager's job:

[The manager] is like a symphony orchestra conductor, endeavouring to maintain a melodious performance in which the contributions of the various instruments are coordinated and sequenced, patterned and paced, while the orchestra members are having various personal difficulties, stage hands are moving music stands, alternating excessive heat and cold are creating audience and instrument problems, and the sponsor of the concert is insisting on irrational changes in the program.[15]

In effect, every manager must spend a good part of his time responding to high-pressure disturbances. No organization can be so well run, so standardized, that it has considered every contingency in the uncertain environment in advance. Disturbances arise not only because poor managers ignore situations until they reach crisis proportions, but also because good managers cannot possibly anticipate all the consequences of the actions they take.

3 The third decisional role is that of *resource allocator*. To the manager falls the responsibility of deciding who will get what in his organizational unit. Perhaps the most important resource the manager allocates is his own time. Access to the manager constitutes exposure to the unit's nerve center and decision maker. The manager is also charged with designing his unit's structure, that pattern of formal relationships that determines how work is to be divided and coordinated.

Also, in his role as resource allocator, the manager authorizes the important decisions of his unit before they are implemented. By retaining this power, the manager can ensure that decisions are interrelated; all must pass through a single brain. To

[14]Peter F. Drucker, *The Practice of Management* (New York: Harper & Row, 1954), pp. 431–432.
[15]Leonard R. Sayles, *Managerial Behavior* (New York: McGraw-Hill, 1964), p. 162.

fragment this power is to encourage discontinuous decision making and a disjointed strategy.

There are a number of interesting features about the manager's authorizing others' decisions. First, despite the widespread use of capital budgeting procedures—a means of authorizing various capital expenditures at one time—executives in my study made a great many authorization decisions on an ad hoc basis. Apparently, many projects cannot wait or simply do not have the quantifiable costs and benefits that capital budgeting requires.

Second, I found that the chief executives faced incredibly complex choices. They had to consider the impact of each decision on other decisions and on the organization's strategy. They had to ensure that the decision would be acceptable to those who influence the organization, as well as ensure that resources would not be overextended. They had to understand the various costs and benefits as well as the feasibility of the proposal. They also had to consider questions of timing. All this was necessary for the simple approval of someone else's proposal. At the same time, however, delay could lose time, while quick approval could be ill considered and quick rejection might discourage the subordinate who had spent months developing a pet project.

One common solution to approving projects is to pick the man instead of the proposal. That is, the manager authorizes those projects presented to him by people whose judgment he trusts. But he cannot always use this simple dodge.

4 The final decisional role is that of *negotiator*. Studies of managerial work at all levels indicate that managers spend considerable time in negotiations: the president of the football team is called in to work out a contract with the holdout superstar; the corporation president leads his company's contingent to negotiate a new strike issue; the foreman argues a grievance problem to its conclusion with the shop steward. As Leonard Sayles puts it, negotiations are a "way of life" for the sophisticated manager.

These negotiations are duties of the manager's job; perhaps routine, they are not to be shirked. They are an integral part of his job, for only he has the authority to commit organizational resources in "real time," and only he has the nerve center information that important negotiations require.

The Integrated Job

It should be clear by now that the ten roles I have been describing are not easily separable. In the terminology of the psychologist, they form a gestalt, an integrated whole. No role can be pulled out of the framework and the job be left intact. For example, a manager without liaison contacts lacks external information. As a result, he can neither disseminate the information his employees need nor make decisions that adequately reflect external conditions. (In fact, this is a problem for the new person in a managerial position, since he cannot make effective decisions until he has built up his network of contacts.)

Here lies a clue to the problems of team management.[16] Two or three people cannot share a single managerial position unless they can act as one entity. This means that they cannot divide up the ten roles unless they can very carefully reintegrate them. The real difficulty lies with the informational roles. Unless there can be full sharing of managerial information—and, as I pointed out earlier, it is primarily verbal—team management breaks down. A single managerial job cannot be arbitrarily split, for example, into internal and external roles, for information from both sources must be brought to bear on the same decisions.

To say that the ten roles form a gestalt is not to say that all managers give equal attention to each role. In fact, I found in my review of the various research studies that

> . . . sales managers seem to spend relatively more of their time in the interpersonal roles, presumably a reflection of the extrovert nature of the marketing activity:
>
> . . . production managers give relatively more attention to the decisional roles, presumably a reflection of their concern with efficient work flow;
>
> . . . staff managers spend the most time in the informational roles, since they are experts who manage departments that advise other parts of the organization.

Nevertheless, in all cases the interpersonal, informational, and decisional roles remain inseparable.

[16]See Richard C. Hodgson, Daniel J. Levinson, and Abraham Zaleznik, *The Executive Role Constellation* (Boston: Division of Research, Harvard Business School, 1965), for a discussion of the sharing of roles.

TOWARD MORE EFFECTIVE MANAGEMENT

What are the messages for management in this description? I believe, first and foremost, that this description of managerial work should prove more important to managers than any prescription they might derive from it. That is to say, *the manager's effectiveness is significantly influenced by his insight into his own work.* His performance depends on how well he understands and responds to the pressures and dilemmas of the job. Thus managers who can be introspective about their work are likely to be effective at their jobs. . . .

Let us take a look at three specific areas of concern. For the most part, the managerial logjams —the dilemma of delegation, the data base centralized in one brain, the problems of working with the management scientist—evolve around the verbal nature of the manager's information. There are great dangers in centralizing the organization's data bank in the minds of its managers. When they leave, they take their memory with them. And when subordinates are out of convenient verbal reach of the manager, they are at an informational disadvantage.

1

The manager is challenged to find systematic ways to share his privileged information. A regular debriefing session with key subordinates, a weekly memory dump on the dictating machine, the maintaining of a diary of important information for limited circulation, or other similar methods may ease the logjam of work considerably. Time spent disseminating this information will be more than regained when decisions must be remade. Of course, some will raise the question of confidentiality. But managers would do well to weigh the risks of exposing privileged information against having subordinates who can make effective decisions.

If there is a single theme that runs through this article, it is that the pressures of his job drive the manager to be superficial in his actions—to overload himself with work, encourage interruption, respond quickly to every stimulus, seek the tangible and avoid the abstract, make decisions in small increments, and do everything abruptly.

2

Here again, the manager is challenged to deal consciously with the pressures of superficiality by giving serious attention to the issues that require it, by stepping back from his tangible bits of information in order to see a broad picture, and by making use of analytical inputs. Although effective managers have to be adept at responding quickly to numerous and varying problems, the danger in managerial work is that they will respond to every issue equally (and that means abruptly) and that they will never work the tangible bits and pieces of informational input into a comprehensive picture of their world.

As I noted earlier, the manager uses these bits of information to build models of his world. But the manager can also avail himself of the models of the specialists. Economists describe the functioning of markets, operations researchers simulate financial flow processes, and behavioral scientists explain the needs and goals of people. The best of these models can be searched out and learned.

In dealing with complex issues, the senior manager has much to gain from a close relationship with the management scientists of his own organization. They have something important that he lacks—time to probe complex issues. An effective working relationship hinges on the resolution of what a colleague and I have called "the planning dilemma."[17] Managers have the information and the authority; analysts have the time and the technology. A successful working relationship between the two will be effected when the manager learns to share his information and the analyst learns to adapt to the manager's need. For the analyst, adaptation means worrying less about the elegance of the method and more about its speed and flexibility.

It seems to me that analysts can help the top manager especially to schedule his time, feed in analytical information, monitor projects under his supervision, develop models to aid in making choices, design contingency plans for disturbances that can be anticipated, and conduct "quick-and-dirty" analysis for those that cannot. But there can be no cooperation if the analysts are out of the mainstream of the manager's information flow.

3

The manager is challenged to gain control of his own time by turning obligations to his advantage and by

[17]James S. Hekimian and Henry Mintzberg, "The Planning Dilemma," *The Management Review,* May 1968, p. 4.

turning those things he wishes to do into obligations. The chief executives of my study initiated only 32% of their own contacts (and another 5% by mutual agreement). And yet to a considerable extent they seemed to control their time. There were two key factors that enabled them to do so.

First, the manager has to spend so much time discharging obligations that if he were to view them as just that, he would leave no mark on his organization. The unsuccessful manager blames failure on the obligations; the effective manager turns his obligations to his own advantage. A speech is a chance to lobby for a cause; a meeting is a chance to reorganize a weak department; a visit to an important customer is a chance to extract trade information.

Second, the manager frees some of his time to do those things that he—perhaps no one else—thinks important by turning them into obligations. Free time is made, not found, in the manager's job; it is forced into the schedule. Hoping to leave some time open for contemplation or general planning is tantamount to hoping that the pressures of the job will go away. The manager who wants to innovate initiates a project and obligates others to report back to him; the manager who needs certain environmental information establishes channels that will automatically keep him informed; the manager who has to tour facilities commits himself publicly.

The Educator's Job

Finally, a word about the training of managers. Our management schools have done an admirable job of training the organization's specialists—management scientists, marketing researchers, accountants, and organizational development specialists. But for the most part they have not trained managers.[18]

Management schools will begin the serious training of managers when skill training takes a serious

[18]See J. Sterling Livingston, "Myth of the Well-Educated Manager," HBR January–February 1971, p. 79.

place next to cognitive learning. Cognitive learning is detached and informational, like reading a book or listening to a lecture. No doubt much important cognitive material must be assimilated by the manager-to-be. But cognitive learning no more makes a manager than it does a swimmer. The latter will drown the first time he jumps into the water if his coach never takes him out of the lecture hall, gets him wet, and gives him feedback on his performance.

In other words, we are taught a skill through practice plus feedback, whether in a real or a simulated situation. Our management schools need to identify the skills managers use, select students who show potential in these skills, put the students into situations where these skills can be practiced, and then give them systematic feedback on their performance.

My description of managerial work suggests a number of important managerial skills—developing peer relationships, carrying out negotiations, motivating subordinates, resolving conflicts, establishing information networks and subsequently disseminating information, making decisions in conditions of extreme ambiguity, and allocating resources. Above all, the manager needs to be introspective about his work so that he may continue to learn on the job.

Many of the manager's skills can, in fact, be practiced, using techniques that range from role-playing to video-taping real meetings. And our management schools can enhance the entrepreneurial skills by designing programs that encourage sensible risk taking and innovation.

No job is more vital to our society than that of the manager. It is the manager who determines whether our social institutions serve us well or whether they squander our talents and resources. It is time to strip away the folklore about managerial work, and time to study it realistically so that we can begin the difficult task of making significant improvements in its performance.

Reading 2

Symbols, Patterns, and Settings: An Optimistic Case for Getting Things Done

Thomas J. Peters

What tools come to mind when you think about changing an organization? If you came up through the ranks in the 1950s and 1960s, the answer is quite likely to be divisionalizing and developing a strategic planning system. Shifting the organizational structure and inventing new processes are still options for change. But increasingly thorny and overlapping international, competitive, and regulatory problems call for increasingly complex responses—and such responses are getting increasingly difficult to devise and problematical in their application.

It is reasonable to propose, however, that an effective set of change tools is actually embedded in senior management's daily message sending and receiving activities, and that these tools can be managed in such a way as to energize and redirect massive, lumbering business and government institutions. The tools will be characterized as symbols (the raw material), patterns (the systematic use of the raw material), and settings (the showcase for the systematic use).

It is not suggested that these tools merely be added to the traditional arsenal of formal change instruments—primarily structure and process. Rather, it will be argued that historically effective prescriptions are losing some of their impact, and their formal replacements—such as the matrix structure—have comparatively little leverage. Moreover, the typical top management is seldom around for much more than five or six years—too little time in which to leave a distinctive and productive stamp on a large, history-bound institution solely by means of the available formal change alternatives. Hence effective change may increasingly depend on systematic use of the informal change mechanisms, derived from coherent daily actions.

The author wholeheartedly acknowledges the help of Anne Hartman Peters in the preparation of this article, along with the thoughtful comments of Anthony G. Athos, Harold J. Leavitt, and Eugene J. Webb.

PESSIMISM: FROM RATIONAL MEN TO GARBAGE CANS

Many leading organizational researchers seem to imply "You'll never get much done." James March describes organizations as "garbage cans," in which problems, participants, and choices circle aimlessly around, connecting—with resultant decisions—only occasionally. Other colorful metaphors or contrived terms have sought to convey similar images of confusion: for example, "organizational seesaws" (William Starbuck), "organized chaos" (Igor Ansoff), "loosely coupled systems" (Karl Weick). The theory of resource dependency developed by Jeffery Pfeffer and Gerald Salancik depicts the typical executive as having but a single course for inducing stable outcomes: Diversify to cope with uncertainty by reducing dependence on any one source of supply or market segment. The common message seems to be one of nearly unrelieved pessimism: It is a confusing, messy world.

It would be hard to quarrel with the researchers' descriptions of the complexity and ambiguity of real life in organizations. The trouble is that most of them fail to address in any but the most general terms the question of whether (and how) one can operate in such a world.

In the face of such pessimism, I argue that actually senior management has an array of underutilized tools at hand to help it come to grips with organizational complexity. In the words of British researcher Rosemary Stewart, ". . . managers tend to exaggerate the amount of choice that they have while failing to appreciate the nature of some of the choices that are available to them."

It may be well to begin by briefly examining the origin of the pessimistic views. Herbert Simon, the most noted analyst of organizational complexity, coined the term *satisficing* in 1957 to suggest that organizations seek satisfactory rather than optimal solutions to problems.

Simon and his successors were reacting to decades of management and organization theorizing in search of reliable management prescriptions. The quest for certainties in management began at least as early as Frederick Taylor's time and motion studies and soon expanded to a search for highly rational principles of management—for example, optimal spans of control and rules of delegation. After the Hawthorne experiments, a competing form of prescriptive certainty, based on an opposite set of assumptions about human nature, emerged. Enhancing participation in decision making became a substitute panacea.

When Simon and his successors revolted against the quest for certainty, their line of attack (based on descriptions of ambiguity in managerial settings) was not surprisingly marked by a refusal to develop prescriptions for the management of change. Their complex models in general provide little comfort for the struggling executive. It is in fact commonplace in organizational behavior articles to dismiss most practical advice as "not contingent enough." The contingency theorists correctly assert that different organizational solutions work in different settings. In practice, this frequently seems to imply that every solution is unique, hence the search for generally useful principles is essentially futile.

Carefully reading the work of the leading architects of complexity, one can, however, unearth the rudiments of some practical prescriptions for beleaguered managers. Almost as an aside, for example, Michael Cohen and James March in *Leadership and Ambiguity,* a study of university presidents, offer "eight basic tactical rules for those who seek to influence the course of decisions." The sorts of rules that Cohen and March propose (see Figure 2-1) have a particularly startling property: Although, as the authors demonstrate, some such tools as these may be the most effective change vehicles available in today's environment, they are too "trivial" to be at the forefront of most managers' minds—one reason, perhaps, why they have not been explored.

The author's research has focused on what many audiences have called the "theory of the small win." Patterns of consistent, moderate size, clear-cut outcomes—patterns of small wins—are a special subclass of managerial activity patterns influencing future change. The effectiveness of these patterns was first validated in laboratory experiments with M.B.A. graduates. In addition, patterns of small wins were repeatedly noted in the literature of business and politics. Successful executives in both the private and public sectors apparently often attend to manageable situations where the value of their own persistence and ability to control intermediate events maximizes their influence on subsequent outcomes. Strings of these controlled successes are used over time to shape and manage attention and perceptions, thereby affecting the course of interactions and outcomes.

During the past year, several colleagues and I have been testing similar change techniques in a handful of large American and European corporations. The results so far obtained by sensitive application of these "mundane tools"—as practical alternatives to ponderous weapons such as structural overhauls—have been impressive enough to give grounds for cautious optimism. Based on these experiences, I will propose in the following pages a simple set of change instruments whose practical value seems to warrant trial and application on a broader scale.

A FRAMEWORK FOR THINKING ABOUT CHANGE

In the minds of senior managers, what does it mean to induce effective change? Surely speed of effect and control over outcomes would be near the top of any list of criteria. Consider the typology derived from these two dimensions:

Category 1: High control, low speed.
Category 2: High control, high speed.
Category 3: Low control, high speed.
Category 4: Low control, low speed.

Our revised view of organizational change may be considered in the framework of this categorization. First, some historical change tools will be assigned to each category; next, the apparently decreasing effectiveness of several tools will be discussed; last, some alternative change levers will be suggested.

Historically, the most regularly considered tools for change have been formal processes, structure, and human resource development programs. The first two of these levers have been at the forefront of organization change in the past; the third has never attained its purported full potential.

The modern planning system is the most typical formal process. Its roots go back decades. Planning,

Rule	Interpretation
1. Spend time	Spending time exerts, in itself, a "claim" on the decision-making system.
2. Persist	Having more patience than other people often results in adoption of a chosen course of action.
3. Exchange status for substance	One of the most effective way to gather support for programs is to reward allies with visible tokens of recognition.
4. Facilitate opposition participation	Often those outside the formal decision centers overestimate the feasibility of change; encouraged to participate, they will often become more realistic.
5. Overload the system	Bureaucracies chew up most projects, but on the other hand, some sneak through; merely launching more projects is likely to result in more successes.
6. Provide garbage cans	Organizations endlessly argue issues; to induce desired outcomes, put "throw-away" issues at the top of agendas (to absorb debate) saving substantive issues for later.
7. Manage unobtrusively	Certain actions can influence the organization pervasively but almost imperceptibly; moreover, the resulting changes will persist with little further attention.
8. Interpret history	By articulating a particular version of events, the leader can alter people's perception of what has been happening; whoever writes the minutes influences the outcome.

Figure 2-1 Rules for managing change.

as managers generally think of it today, received its major impetus during World War II. Strategic planning systems burgeoned in the 1960s; General Electric and Texas Instruments, among others, have attributed much of their continuing success to the planning revolution. Planning tends to affect organizational outcomes over a period of years, as experience and skill accumulate at many levels within the organization. Historically, then, planning systems are perhaps the most important and typical change tool in Category 1 (high control, low speed).

Structural solutions, especially decentralization and divisionalization, have commonly been employed for strategically realigning increasingly complex organizations into manageable, typically product-line-oriented chunks. Having reached its highwater mark in the United States in the years after World War II, decentralization spread to Europe in the 1960s in response to the U.S. multinational invasion. The vast majority of major business enterprises today are organized on the divisional principle—or some variation thereof, for example GE's recent sectoral reorganization. Working out the problems of divisionalization took years in many cases, but noticeable change more often than not came quickly and was generally in the hoped-for direction. Thus it seems fair to consider this historical solution as the leading candidate for Category 2 (high control, high speed) change tools.

An obvious candidate for Category 4 (low control, low speed) change appears to be human resource development, particularly typified by bottom-up team building. Numerous organizations, under a wide range of circumstances, have noted the benefits of team building. By and large, however, organizational development, no matter what its form, seems not to have had the hoped-for impact. Chief executives are frequently unaware of ongoing experiments in their own organizations. Few corporations with stable, energetic cultures attribute much of their success to formal application of behavioral science techniques.

TRADITIONAL TOOLS: WHAT'S HAPPENED

Meanwhile, something rather disturbing has been happening to the traditional, controlled-change tools. In effect, they have largely been migrating to the low-speed, low-control category. Left with no obvious set of replacement tools, the senior manager may well adopt the pessimistic view noted earlier.

Over time, government and competitive pressures requiring recentralization along various dimensions have nibbled away at the decentralization principle until most organizations today are a hodgepodge of centralized and decentralized activities. The matrix structure, which has arisen in response to these conflicting demands, has as often as not multiplied rather than resolved coordination problems. Even the foremost advocates of the matrix, for example Paul Lawrence and Jay Galbraith, point to imposing lists of pathologies leading to failures—or at least significant delay in implementation.

Similarly, strategic planning systems are no longer viewed as a panacea by many executives. Their greatest value often came soon after they were put in place: They provided novel perspectives on the business. Now, in many large organizations, the strategic planning system has become a rather routine and highly politicized part of the bureaucracy. It is seldom the font of new directions or the spearhead of rapid adaptation to changing economic or political conditions.

SOME SPECULATIONS

My thesis in this article is that there are a variety of practical controlled change tools appropriate to today's complex and ambiguous organization settings. Most have been around a long time and need only to be consciously packaged and managed. Some are rather new. Few have been thought of as major instruments for achieving organizational redirection. Almost all are associated with the informal organization.

Figure 2-2 arrays some of these change tools along the previously noted dimensions of controllability and speed of change, and Figure 2-3 presents some mundane change tools. By briefly assessing the

reasons for the failure or obsolescence of the conventional tools and their successors (shown here as having drifted to the low-control, low-speed category), a very general rationale for the nature of the new change-tool candidates can be developed. Then each new category of tools can be assessed in turn.

There are at least two reasons why the conventional solutions have failed to achieve their full promise or have declined in effectiveness. One is that none of them takes time explicitly into account. In the case of structural solutions, management typically miscalculates in two different ways. On the one hand, it grossly underestimates the growing time lag between changed structure and changed behavior. On the other hand, it overestimates their durability under growing environmental pressures and consequently tends to leave them in place long after they have outlived their effectiveness.

The second reason for the weakness of conventional solutions is over- or underdetermination. Several solutions seem to rest on an overestimation of managers' ability to determine the best way to accomplish great purposes—overdetermination. For example, complex planning systems, multiple project teams, and the matrix structure proceed from the implicit assumption that effective organizing flows from figuring out the correct wiring diagram—an assumption increasingly at odds with today's organizational tasks. Koppers' chief executive officer, Fletcher Byrom, recently remarked, "Of all the things that I have observed about corporations, the most disturbing has been a tendency toward overorganization, producing a rigidity that is intolerable in an era of rapidly accelerating change."

At the other end of the spectrum—

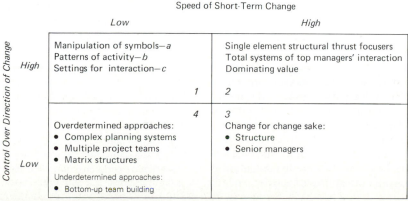

Figure 2-2 Speculation about current change tools.

a—Symbols:	Calendars
	Reports
	Agenda
	Physical settings
	Public statements
	Staff organization
b—Patterns:	Positive reinforcement
	Frequency and consistency of behavior
	Implementation/solution bias
	Experimenting mode
c—Settings:	Role of modeling
	Location
	Agenda control
	Presentation format
	Questioning approaches
	Deadline management
	Use of minutes

Figure 2-3 Mundane tools.

underdetermination—bottom-up team building has been based on the opposite presumption: Overall organizational purposes can be largely ignored; seeding effective new behavior patterns at the bottom of the organization or in the ranks of middle management will somehow eventuate in desirable organizational performance levels.

The proposed "new" change tools partially address both issues. First, they explicitly take time into account, recognizing both that change typically comes slowly as the result of the application of many tools and that the organizational focus of prime importance today is temporary and will almost certainly have changed substantially four or five years hence. Second, they are tools of the experimenter: That is, they neither assume an ability to fix organizational arrangements with much precision—the failing of overdetermination—nor do they ignore purposiveness—the failing of underdetermination.

OBSESSION WITH THE MUNDANE

Cell 1 of Figure 2-2 (high control, low speed change), the realm of what my colleagues and I have come to call "mundane tools," reflects the notion that the management of change—small or large—is inextricably bound up with the mundane occurrences that fill an executive's calendar.

By definition, managing the daily stream of activities might be said to consist of the manipulation of symbols, the creation of patterns of activity, and the staging of occasions for interaction. The mundane tools are proposed as direct alternatives to structural manipulation and other grand solutions to strategic organization needs. Conscious experimentation with these tools can provide a sound basis for controlled, purposive change.

Manipulation of Symbols

Because they have so often been applied by the media to the performances of politicians intent on reshaping or repairing an image, the terms *symbolic behavior* and *symbol manipulation* have lately acquired something of a pejorative connotation: symbol vs. substance. In a much more basic sense, however, symbols are the very stuff of management behavior. Executives, after all, do not synthesize chemicals or operate lift trucks; they deal in symbols. And their overt verbal communications are only part of the story. Consciously or unconsciously, the senior executive is constantly acting out the vision and goals he is trying to realize in an organization that is typically far too vast and complex for him to control directly.

What mundane tools might best aid the executive interested in effecting change through symbol manipulation? To signal watchers, which includes nearly everyone in his organization, there is no truer test of what he really thinks is important than the way he spends his time. As Eli Ginsberg and Ewing W. Reilley have noted:

> Those a few echelons from the top are always alert to the chief executive. Although they attach importance to what he says, they will be truly impressed only by what he does.

Is he serious about making a major acquisition? The gossip surrounding his calendar—Has he seen the investment banker?—provides clues for senior and junior management alike.

As reported in *Fortune*, Roy Ash's early activities after assuming the reins at Addressograph-Multigraph suggest mastery of the calendar and other mundane tools:

> Instead of immediately starting to revamp the company, Ash spent his first several months visiting its widely scattered operations and politely asking a lot of searching questions. . . . His predecessors had always sum-

moned subordinates to the headquarters building, which had long lived up to its official name, the Tower. Rather than announcing his ideas, Ash demonstrated them. He left his office door open, placing his own intercom calls to arrange meetings, and always questioned people in person, not in writing. Then he removed some of the company's copying machines "to stop breeding paperwork." Spotting a well-written complaint from an important customer in Minneapolis, Ash quickly flew off to visit him. As he now explains, "I wanted the word to get around our organization that I'm aware of what's going on." Ash's next dramatic step to reshape company attitudes will be moving its headquarters to Los Angeles . . . he justifies the move primarily on psychological grounds. "We must place ourselves in a setting where—partly through osmosis—we get a different idea of our future." For much the same reason, he wants to change the corporation's name, too.

Calendar behavior includes review of reports and the use of agenda and minutes to shape expectations. What kinds of questions is the executive asking? Does he seem to focus on control of operating costs, quality, market share? How is his memory about what was "assumed" last month? Last quarter? What kinds of feedback is he giving? What sorts of issues get onto his agenda?

Other symbolic actions include the use of physical settings and public statements. By attending operating meetings in the field, the top man can provide vital evidence of his concerns and the directions he wants to pursue. By touching or ignoring a particular theme, a public statement—boilerplate to a skeptical outsider—can lead to a rash of activity. In a talk to investment bankers, a president devoted a paragraph to new departures in an R&D area that had previously been underfunded. Almost overnight, a wealth of new proposals began bubbling up from a previously disenchanted segment of the labs.

Last, his use of his personal staff—its size, their perquisites, how much probing he allows them to do—will indicate, not only the chief executive's style of doing business, but the direction of his substantive concerns as well.

The executive's ability to manage the use of symbols is at the heart of the case for optimism. Literally at his fingertips, he has powerful tools—his day-timer and phone—for testing the possibilities of change and, over time, substantially shifting the focus of the organization.

Patterns of Activity

Success or failure in exploiting these simple tools is seen in the pattern of their use. Richard E. Neustadt in *Presidential Power* maintained:

> The professional reputation of a President in Washington is made or altered by the man himself. No one can guard it for him; no one saves him from himself. . . . His general reputation will be shaped by signs of pattern in the things he says and does. These are the words and actions he has chosen, day by day.

In short, the mundane tools that involve the creation and manipulation of symbols over time have impact to the extent that they reshape beliefs and expectations. Frequent, consistent, positive reinforcement is an unparalleled shaper of expectations—and, therefore, inducer of change.

Patterns of positive reinforcement can be applied in at least two ways: (1) use of praise and design of positive reinforcement schemes for individuals (or groups), and (2) allowing the bad to be displaced by the good, instead of trying to legislate it out of existence.

The White House, for example, has historically made meticulous use of the tools of praise. Selecting the attendees for major events and controlling the use of various classes of presidential letters of praise is a key activity controlled by very senior staff and the President himself.

Along the same lines, a research vice-president, responsible for about 2,000 scientists, has his executive assistant provide him with a sample of about 50 reports produced each month. He sends personal notes to the authors, often junior, of the best half-dozen or so.

Without touching on the complex ramifications of reinforcement theory, these instances merely support the point that senior managers are signal transmitters, and signals take on meaning as they are reiterated. Moreover, there is ample evidence that giving prominence to positive efforts and exposing them to the light of day induces constructive change far more effectively than trying to discourage undesired activities through negative reinforcement. As an associate of mine succinctly observed, "It's a hell of a lot easier to add a new solution than attack an old problem." An example illustrates the point in a broader context:

The information system unit of a multibillion-dollar conglomerate had a disastrously bad reputation. Rather than "clean house" or develop better procedures, the vice-president/systems installed, with some fanfare, "Six Programs of Excellence." Six reasonably sizable projects—out of an agenda of over 100—were singled out for intensive management attention. The effort was designed to build, from the inside out, a reputation for excellence that would gradually increase user confidence and group motivation alike.

Frequency and consistency are two other primary attributes of effective pattern shaping. A pattern of frequent and consistent small successes is such a powerful shaper of expectations that its creation may be worth the deferral of ambitious short-term goals:

In one large company, the top team wished to establish a climate in which new product development would be viewed more favorably by all divisional managers. Rather than seeking an optimal product slate the first year—with the attendant likelihood of a high failure rate—the top team instead consistently supported small new product thrusts that gradually "made believers out of the operators."

Since consistency becomes a driving force in inducing major change over time, the executive committed to change ought to be constantly on the lookout for opportunities to reinforce activities, even trivial activities, that are congruent with his eventual purpose. He scours his in-basket for solutions—bits of completed action—to be singled out as exemplars of some larger theme. Support of completed actions typically generates further actions consistent with the rewarded behavior. The executive who keeps on testing tools to produce this result will find that by varying his patterns of reinforcement he can substantially influence people's behavior over time, often several levels down in the organization. (Figure 2-4 offers advice to pattern shapers based on my research.)

Settings for Interaction

The third class of mundane tools is settings. Senior management's development of a symbolic pattern of activities occurs somewhere. These are some of the setting variables that can directly reinforce or attenuate the impact of the symbolic message:

Presence or Absence of Top Managers Psychologists now agree on the high impact of modeling behavior—the most significant finding of the last decade, according to many. The senior

---

— The world is a stream of problems that can be activated, bound in new ways, or bypassed.

— His associates are pattern watchers and are acutely aware of his and their impact, over time, on each other.

— Above all, timing is important.

— An early step in analyzing a situation is careful assessment of the levers he does or does not control.

— Most change occurs incrementally, and major change typically emerges over a long period of time.

— Much of the change induced in subordinates results from consciously acting as a model himself.

— Frequent rewards—directed at small, completed actions—effectively shape behavior over time.

— Good questioning, focusing on the short term, helps him and his subordinates learn about system responses to small nudges one way or another.

— Creating change in organizations is facilitated by unusual juxtaposition of traditional elements with small problem-making subunits that seed changes.

— Long-term goals are of secondary importance since control of change follows from learning about multiple, small, real-time adjustments.

— Consistency in delivering small, positive outcomes is an efficient and effective way to manipulate others' perceptions when attempting to induce change.

— Patience, persistence, self-control, and attention to the mundane are often keys to achieving small, consistent outcomes.

— Surprise should usually be avoided in an attempt to present stable expectations to peers, subordinates, and bosses.

— It is possible approximately to calculate the opportunity value of others' and one's own time, thus substantially increasing the ability to pick change opportunities.

— Adding new solutions is often better than tackling old problems; that is, as much or more change and learning can ensue from the effective implementation of new solutions as from time-consuming efforts to over-come typically deep-seated resistance to old problems.

Figure 2-4 Guiding assertions for the pattern shaper.

executive's presence and his minor actions can bring to life and rather precisely shape an institutional point of view—about investment, competitive response, the importance of tight controls. The careers of top executives abundantly reflect their intuitive awareness of this point.

Location of Groups and Meetings Moving a meeting or a staff unit or a new activity is often a dramatic signal that something new is afoot. At one company, the previously isolated top team began holding meetings in the field, thus signaling a sincere intent to make decentralization work after three previous failures.

Agenda Control Since agenda directly symbolize priorities, agenda management can be a potent change tool. A division's top team changed its basic approach to management by suddenly devoting more than half its meeting time to issues of project implementation, previously a relatively minor item on its agenda. To cope with the new questions they were getting from the top, managers throughout the organization were soon following suit.

Attendance Who attends which meetings, and who presents material, can signal new approaches to management and new substantive directions. When one company president decided to force his vice-presidents, instead of junior staff, to present reviews and proposals, the atmosphere of his meetings perceptibly changed. All at once, heated battles between analytic guns-for-hire over numerical nuances were replaced by sober discussion of the issues.

Presentation/Decision Memorandum Formats Format control can shift managers' focus to new issues and fundamentally reshape the process of organizational learning. One management team vastly improved its approach to problem solving by meticulously starting every decision presentation with an historical review of "the five key assumptions." At a second major corporation, the chief executive brought to life his major theme—focus on the competition—by requiring all decision documents to include much greater depth of competitive analysis.

Questioning Approaches Among the clearest indicators of the direction or redirection of interest are the sorts or questions the top team consistently asks. Accounts of the working methods of Roy Ash, Harold Geneen, and others stress their unique questioning style and its pervasive effect on the issues the organization worries about. For instance, *Forbes* describes how A. W. Clausen of the Bank of America shifted concern from revenue to profit: "Ask an officer, 'How's business,' and you'd immediately hear how many loans he's made. I tried to leave my stamp by making everyone aware of profit."

Approaches to Follow-up Effective use of minutes, ticklers, and history can become the core of top management's real control system. Genuine accountability was introduced into a lax management organization by introducing a "blue blazer" system that made follow-up a way of life. In tracking issues, whenever operating executives' proposals had been modified by staff, the impact of the changes was explicitly noted. This put the staff and its contribution on stage. Accountability was further substantially sharpened by revamping a previous forecast-tracking procedure to highlight assumptions and outcomes.

Professor Serge Muscovici has asserted that:

> Social status, leadership, majority pressure . . . are not decisive factors in social influence. A minority can modify the opinions and norms of a majority, irrespective of their relative power or social status, as long as, all other things being equal, the organization of its actions and the expression of its opinions and objectives obey the conditions . . . of consistency, autonomy, investment, and fairness.

Fairness takes on added meaning on the context of mundane management tools, intended as they are to shape expectations, over time, through minor shifts of emphasis. To be effective, the management of expectations must be unfailingly honest, realistic, and consistent. Violation of this property, especially if perceived as intentional, automatically destroys the effectiveness of patterned symbolic manipulation.

Richard Neustadt captures the essence of the use of mundane tools:

> [Franklin D. Roosevelt] had a strong feeling for a cardinal fact in government: That Presidents don't act on policies, program, or personnel in the abstract; they

act in the concrete as they meet deadlines set by due dates, act on documents awaiting signatures, vacant posts awaiting appointees, officials seeking interviews, newsmen seeking answers, audiences waiting for a speech.

Note that the tools he mentions are all at hand. Though rarely disruptive or threatening, they have the potential to revolutionize an organization's ways of thinking and doing over time—particularly if, instead of being used intuitively and implicitly, they are consciously packaged and managed.

MAJOR CHANGE VIA TEMPORARY FOCUS

Big bureaucracies are run largely on inertia. Salesmen make their calls, products roll off the line, and checks get processed without any intervention by senior management. The task of today's slate of top managers, then, might well be viewed as time-bound: "How do we make a distinctive, productive difference over the next four years?" Or, "How do we leave our mark?"

It has been suggested above that certain prescriptions—undertaking structural shakeups or introducing new formal processes—are less effective than they once were in altering corporate perspectives. Constructing temporary systems to redirect the organization's attention and energies may be a better way to coax along institutional change. The high-impact devices proposed for this purpose are a natural extension of the mundane tools just discussed, in that in and of themselves they act as strong signals (or accumulations of symbols) of attention to new corporate directions.

Major—but limited—shifts in emphasis have been accomplished by public and private bureaucracies through three kinds of temporary focusing mechanisms: single-element focusers, systems of interaction, and dominating values. Each of these focusing mechanisms is discussed below.

Single-Element Focusers

To begin with, single-element focusers have been used time and again as a strategic signaling and implementing device. Consider how General Motors, a massive bureaucracy by any definition, recently adapted more swiftly than any other major automobile maker to the need to downsize its entire product line:

The project center [says *Fortune*] was probably GM's single most important managerial tool in carrying out that bold decision. . . . It has eliminated a great deal of redundant effort, and has speeded numerous new technologies into production. Its success . . . rests on the same delicate balance between the powers of persuasion and coercion that underlines GM's basic system of coordinated decentralization.

Some other business examples of single-element focusers similarly wrested the attention of major organizations—temporarily—to something new:

Harris Corporation created an interdivisional technology manager to oversee transfer of technology—Harris's "main strategic thrust"—between previously isolated groups.

Product family managers—three to five senior men with small staffs—were introduced as a means of wrenching the attention of two huge functional bureaucracies toward the marketplace; the creation of these high-visibility positions was thought to be a clearer, more efficient signal of strategic redirection than a major structural shift. Similarly, the establishment of just one job, executive vice-president for marketing, at White Consolidated is credited with sprucing up the long-stagnant sales of White's newly acquired Westinghouse appliance group.

ITT's product group managers are a free-wheeling band of central staff problem-solvers and questioners who have brought a common market-based orientation to a highly diversified conglomerate.

An oil company's central technology staff (a roving group of top-ranking geologists and engineers) has markedly upgraded exploration and production quality.

In surveying these and other instances of success, some common threads can be identified (see Figure 2-5). Most important of these is singleness of focus. That is, the single-element focuser should not be confused with multiple-team project management. Its effectiveness rests on achieving a limited, temporary focus on one, or at most two, major new items. Note, also, that the structural manifestations tend to be about half staff, half line. On one hand, the focusing element often has the look of a traditional staff unit, but its manager, as the unmistakable agent of the top team's highest priority, visibly intrudes on operating managers' territory.

Kenneth Arrow, the Nobel laureate economist, describes an analogous approach to galvanizing mas-

Success Characteristic	Related Failure Mode
— Focus: limited number of "devices," no more than two and preferably one.	— Use—usually simultaneously—of many devices (e.g., teams, meetings) dilutes attention and can become just a bureaucratic encumbrance.
— Focus within focus: The limited device must, moreover, have a limited agenda and not take on everything at once.	— Limited devices charged with turning the world around in 12 months are likely to fail (i.e., a failure of expectation).
— Incumbent: Manned with a very senior contender(s) for the top.	— Selection of good men, but not those recognized as members of "the top ten" or sure-fire top ten contenders.
— Startup: Either a pilot element (e.g., one product family manager of an eventual set of five) or a "pilot decision," (e.g., a visible output—perhaps a decision—by the new event/process) will affect acceptance.	— Groups/processes invented, but no clear sign of early progress or shift of emphasis.
— Need: A clear-cut, agreed-upon business need for the element exists.	— The new element's agenda is not clear and/or is not viewed as urgent.
— CEO role: CEO is reinforcer of project *and* lets it make its mark.	— CEO nonsupporter or a supporter but preempts the new role by continuing to play the game by the old rules.
— Conscience systems—formal or informal—to "watch" the top team and ensure that actions are being taken consistent with the purpose of the shift.	— Element "implemented," but top team regularly takes decisions inconsistent with purpose.
— Implementation duration: Even though single device, implementation should be expected to take a couple of years at least.	— Since it is only a simple new element, put it in place and let it go.

Figure 2-5 Attributes of single-element focusing devices.

sive government institutions into acting on new agenda: "Franklin D. Roosevelt . . . saw the need of assigning new tasks to new bureaus even though according to some logic [such a task] belonged in the sphere of an existing department." Congressional Budget Office Deputy Director Robert Levine summarizes the thesis this way:

> Since it seems impossible . . . to change overall public bureaucratic systems substantially either by changing their direction at the top by devices like program budgeting, or by changing their culture à la organization development, it may be useful to look for a third class of solutions . . . specifically, trying to treat bureaucratic units as if they were competing business units. . . . Even if it worked very well, this would be less well than program budgeting or organization development if they worked well. But the contention here is that in the real world this alternative concept is substantially more likely to work.

System of Interaction

Attention-directing organization elements are only the first of the three high-impact focusing mecha-

nisms to be considered here. The second is the construction of a coherent system of senior management interaction, again with the purpose of shifting management attention either to some new direction or to some new method of reaching overall consensus. Under some circumstances, this second mechanism might even be preferred to the first. On the one hand, a system of forums has perhaps less symbolic impact than a single high-visibility element. On the other hand, however, such a system does directly manipulate the agenda of senior managers.

Systems of forums designed to turn top management's eyes to new horizons range from one company's five "management forums"—a formal system of interaction designed to force regular discussion of strategic issues—to a president's regular informal breakfast meetings where senior executives, free of their staffs and the attendant bureaucratic insulation, engage in untrammeled discussion of key issues.

One particularly striking class of forums is special operating or strategic review sessions. Texas Instruments, ITT, and Emerson Electric, among others, focus top-management direction setting in regular sessions where—as everyone in the organization knows—"things get done" or "the buck stops." Another notable example is cited by *Fortune:*

> One of the enduring questions of management, a subject of constant concern and endless analysis, is how a large corporation can best monitor and direct operations spread over many industries and throughout many parts of the world. A number of companies have sought the answer in ponderous and elaborate management mechanisms. . . . But there is at least one large company whose top management continues to rely on plain, old-fashioned, face-to-face contact. Richard B. Loynd, the president and chief operating officer of Eltra Corp. . . . visits each of Eltra's thirteen divisions as many as eight times a year, and puts managers through formal grillings that last several hours at a time. The people at Eltra call this the "hands-on" management technique. Loynd says: "I think I spend more time with our operating people than the president of any other major company."

Invariably, like the single-element focusers, these systems are temporary in nature. Since most of them tend to become rigid and lose their unique value in the course of time, they need to be modified at intervals. One executive reports:

> The monthly breakfast meeting finally got the chairman and his operating presidents away from staff. For two years these sessions, preliminary to the regular monthly review, became the real decision-making/enervating forum. But then the staffs caught on. One by one, *they* began coming to breakfast.

Dominating Value

The discussion of change mechanisms has had a consistent undercurrent. The three classes of mundane tools have been presented as apparently trivial signaling devices for redirecting organizational attention and energy over time toward a theme, while the first two major change tools have been characterized as just larger-scale or agglomerated devices for the same purpose.

One final tool, which may be labeled the *dominating value,* addresses the role and utilization of the theme itself. It is, on the one hand, more delicate than the other tools, in that its use demands consummate political commitment-building skills and a shrewd sense of timing. In another sense it is more robust than the others, in that, if handled effective-

ly, it can generate substantial, sustained energy in large institutions. For the senior manager, therefore, thinking about and acting on the value management process is, although imprecise, extremely practical.

Business researchers have coined various terms for an effective, predominant institutional belief. Richard Normann calls it a business idea or growth idea. He devotes an entire book, *Management and Statesmanship,* to documenting a case for the power of an effective, simply articulated business idea and describing the unique role and leverage of top management in indirectly guiding the process of belief establishment and change. He argues that "the interpretation of ongoing and historical events and the associated adjustment and regulation of the dominating idea is probably the most crucial of the processes occurring in the company."

Some other recent scholarly work, well-grounded in the leading edge of social science findings, provides a corroborating point of view. Andrew Pettigrew's anthropological study of the creation of organization culture is representative:

> One way of approaching the study of the entrepreneur's relationship with his organization is to consider the entrepreneur as a symbol creator, an ideologue, a formulator of organizational vocabularies, and a maker of ritual and myth. Stylistic components of a vision, which may be crucial, might include the presence of a dramatically significant series of events, rooting the vision back into history, and thus indicating the vision was more than a fad. Visions with simple, yet ambiguous content expressed in symbolic language are not only likely to be potent consciousness raisers, but also flexible enough to sustain the ravages of time and therefore the certitude of events. Visions contain new and old terminology perhaps organized into metaphors with which it is hoped to create new meanings. Words can move people from a state of familiarity to a state of awareness. Some people have the capacity to make words walk. I suspect this is one of the unexplored characteristics of successful entrepreneurs.

Louis Pondy, in "Leadership is a Language Game," quite similarly equates leadership effectiveness with the capacity to achieve what he calls "language renewal."

Roy Ash puts the same notion in more concrete terms:

At a sufficiently high level of abstraction, he says, "all businesses are the same." Ash's plans for testing that theory are summed up in the notes that he continually pencils on yellow legal pads. One of the most revealing of these notes says: "Develop a much greater attachment of everybody to the bottom line—more agony and ecstasy." As he sees it, the really important change in a company is a process of psychological transformation.

If one combs the literature for the lessons extracted by business leaders, the crucial role of a central belief emerges. The biographies of Cordiner at GE, Vail at AT&T, Greenewalt at Du Pont, and Watson at IBM all stress the quest to give operational force and meaning to a dominant, though imprecise, idea. Such accounts may be dismissed as self-serving, but it would seem a bit more cynical than even these times call for to write off the extraordinary consistency of so many closing statements.

Among active business leaders, the pattern of evidence is repeated. Richard Pascale, for example, has described the management style of several particularly effective chief executive officers. He notes the recurrence of a simple, over-arching theme captured in a few words: for example, Harold Geneen's ceaseless "search for the unshakable facts," reflected in all kinds of organizational arrangements from structural contrivances—his controllers reporting to the chief executive and his intrusive product group managers—through interaction mechanisms—the famed ITT monthly review sessions. Further examples dot the business press:

- *A. W. Clausen at Bank of America:* "Stay around Tom Clausen for about 15 minutes and he'll talk about laying pipe," says *Forbes.* "That's his shorthand for anticipating events and readying a response. Subordinates lay pipe to Clausen when they tell him about potential problems; he lays the pipe the other way when he sketches his expectations. The expression isn't especially catchy, the process isn't particularly glamorous. But it does help to explain why Bank of America isn't facing huge loan losses—and this big, slow-moving tortoise seems perfectly able to keep up with the flashier, more dynamic hares."
- *John DeButts at AT&T* incessantly uses the term "the system is the solution." The concept, professed by DeButts in every setting from management meetings to television commercials, is aimed at starting the process of shifting the massive million-person Bell System's focus to the market place.
- *Tom Jones at Northrup, Fortune* notes, has been particularly successful at gaining more than a fair share of defense contracts—largely, he believes, by bringing to life the theme "Everybody at Northrup is in marketing."
- *Walter Spencer at Sherwin Williams,* according to *Forbes,* spent his five years as CEO working to introduce a "marketing orientation" into a previously manufacturing-dominated institution. Says Spencer: "When you take a 100-year old company and change the culture of the organization, and try to do that in Cleveland's traditional business setting—well, it takes time; you just have to keep hammering away at everybody. . . . The changeover to marketing is probably irreversible now. It's not complete, but we've brought along a lot of young managers with that philosophy, and once you've taken a company this far, you can't go back."

When the scholarly research and the anecdotal evidence are drawn together, some characteristic attributes of an effective dominating value can be discussed:

It is both loose and tight. That is, it connotes a clear directional emphasis—focus on the competition, stand for quality, become low-cost producer—but ample latitude for supporting initiatives.

It must, almost always, emerge rather than be imposed. Though it may be crystallized in a succinct phrase, it usually represents the end product of time-consuming consensus-building processes that may have gone on for a year or more.

Just as it cannot be imposed by fiat, it cannot be changed at will. Typically, a major shift in the dominant belief can be brought about only when an important change is perceived to be at hand. The process of gaining commitment requires so much emotional commitment and institutional energy that it can be repeated only infrequently.

It has a reasonably predictable life cycle. Beginning with a great deal of latitude, it becomes progressively less flexible over time—though never approaching the rigidity of a quantified goal.

It may be a definition or characterization of the past, meant primarily to mark the end of a period and provide the energy to start a search for new modes of organizational behavior. For example, one might choose to label the past five years as "the era of tight control" in order to suggest that something now coming to an end should be replaced with something new, as yet unspecified.

It imposes choices. Despite the general nature of most effective beliefs, they do require management to face up to the limits of the organization's capacities. Of course, any huge enterprise does a bit of everything, but, for example, a choice to stress controls, if effectively implemented, is likely also a choice not to push harder for new products.

It can be anything from a general management principle to a reasonably specific major business decision. At the management-principles end, it can become a commitment to something like "fact-based analysis." At the business-decision end, it can be a commitment to a revised position for a key product line. In the middle are hybrids such as "enhanced focus on competition."

It suggests movement (e.g., toward becoming the industry quality leader or dominating a particular market niche), thus implying some sort of tension or imbalance. Few leaders have been noted for achieving balance. Most have been known for going from somewhere to somewhere else.

Figure 2-6 gives a graphic portrayal of the essentials of the process I have been discussing. It depicts a five- to nine-year cycle of strategic transition marked by the tightening, executing, loosening, and redirecting search for an operational dominating value.

CHANGE FOR CHANGE'S SAKE

At least one significant tool remains to be considered: namely, change for its own sake.

This is the device assigned, in Figure 2-2, to Cell 3

(low-control, high-speed change). Sometimes things are such a muddle that significant change for its own sake is a good bet to produce, on balance, a more desirable outcome than any directionally managed program.

In *The Economist,* Norman McRae recently observed:

> . . . the most successful companies have been those restless enough to be unsure what their management styles should be. Successful big American corporations today will often centralize their policy making, and get a significant initial gain in effectiveness; but then, as time passes, will find that this does not work because the central planners do not know what is really going on out in the field. So these corporations will then decentralize, and get a significant initial gain in effectiveness. This constant reorganization is in fact very sensible, and is a main reason why I judge that big American corporations are still the most efficient day-to-day business operators in the world.

A somewhat less radical dose of the same medicine is the rather arbitrary reshuffling of top team member responsibilities, even when it results in a seemingly less rational match of skills to tasks. A fresh juxtaposition of perspectives, per se, is often of value.

At least one word of warning about high-early impact, low-control prescriptions is in order. The secret of their success is novelty. Routine reorganizing or all-too-regular shakeups of top team assignments all too readily evoke the sense of déjà vu. "Nobody on the top team has been in the same job for more than 15 months," remarks an executive of a

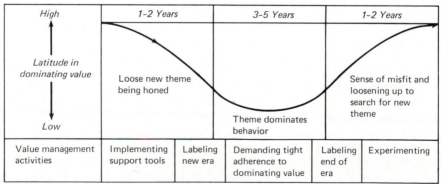

Figure 2-6 Five- to nine-year cycle of strategic transition.

high-technology company. "Of course, all they do is trade bureaucratic barbs. That's all they've got. No one sees the results of his own initiatives."

Although it certainly merits much more discussion, the analysis of this last class of tools must necessarily be cut short at this point.

IN CONCLUSION: LIMITS AND OPTIMISM

The purpose of this essay has been twofold: first, to provide a simple classification of change tools and some speculative hypotheses in support of the case for pessimism about the old favorites among them; second, to suggest that for the alert senior manager, today's organizational garbage cans are still full of powerful change tools—tools that he uses intuitively, and therefore not systematically, but which nevertheless are numerous and potentially powerful enough to justify a measure of optimism.

A limited measure, to be sure. Even with a mastery of all the change tools reviewed here, today's senior manager is unlikely to be able to develop real consensus, commitment, and change in more than a single new direction. Richard Neustadt's metaphor captures the essence of his role:

Presidential power is the power to persuade. Underneath our images of Presidents-in-boots, astride decisions, are the half-observed realities of President-in-sneakers, stirrups in hand, trying to induce particular department heads . . . to climb aboard.

As he tries to coax his senior colleagues aboard, the senior executive has at his command a variety of settings—settings in which he can experiment, implement, and build patterns to provide a general conception of what's possible. He can, with luck and to a limited extent, grasp control of the signaling system to point a general direction and mark out limited areas of expected new institutional excellence. By adroitly managing agenda, he can nudge the day-to-day decision-making system, thus simultaneously imparting new preferences and testing new initiatives.

And some day, in retrospect, he may be able to see himself as an experimenter who attempted to build consensus on a practical (and flexible) vision of what was possible over a five-year time horizon, and through incessant attention to the implementation of small, adaptive steps, eventually made that vision a reality.

If so, he should be well content.

Reading 3

Making Behavioral Science More Useful

Jay W. Lorsch

Since World War II management thought and practice have undergone great change. The computer has revolutionized information processing and, along with operations research and other quantitative techniques, has improved management decision making. New methods of market and consumer research also provide better information on which to base decisions. All these developments mean better tools for obtaining and analyzing information for more effective management.

During the same period the behavioral sciences—anthropology, psychology, social psychology, and sociology—have also contributed many potential ideas and theories to management. Unlike the first set of management tools, these ideas have focused not only on how decisions are made, but also on how employees from top management levels to the factory floor implement them. Thus these ideas should be of use to every manager: how to communicate effectively; how to give performance evaluations to employees; how to resolve conflicts between individuals or between one department and another; how to design organization structures, measurement systems, and compensation packages; how to introduce changes in organization, procedures, and strategy.

In spite of their potential for wide application, however, these ideas have been only sparingly used. Surely, General Foods, Volvo, and Procter & Gamble have introduced innovations in some factory organizations, and some management organizations have done so as well, but how many other company managements have failed to use the available knowledge? Further, why have the companies that have claimed success in one location or division been so reluctant to apply the ideas in other appropriate places?

One obvious reason seems to be the confusion, skepticism, and controversy about the relevance of these ideas in the minds of many managers. For example: Is participative management a suitable style for all managers? Can job enrichment be applied in a unionized factory? Will managers set realistic goals with a management by objectives program? Has laboratory training improved managerial effectiveness? And, ultimately, some hardheaded manager always asks, "What does all this psychological mumbo-jumbo contribute to the bottom line?" The list of such questions may seem endless, but, equally discouraging, the answers the experts provide often seem unpersuasive and even contradictory.

Another facet of the situation, however, concerns me even more. The behavioral sciences occasionally burst with enthusiasm about certain ideas. Job enlargement, T-Groups, creative thinking, participative leadership, and management by objective are cases in point. Each set of ideas or each technique becomes almost a fad with strong advocates who tout its early successes. Then, as a growing number of companies try the ideas or techniques and as reports of failure and disappointment mount, the fad quickly dies. This often repeated pattern has caused many managers to lose interest in trying other behavioral science ideas which could help them.

In this article, I explore why so much heat and confusion have arisen around these behavioral science ideas and why, consequently, they have had such a limited impact on management practice. Because this is a matter of applying knowledge developed in the academic world to the problems of practicing managers, I am addressing both managers and academics. What can managers do themselves to make better use of the behavioral sciences? What

can they demand from academics to get more practical knowledge? What can the academics working in this field do to provide more knowledge practitioners can use?

LURE OF THE UNIVERSAL THEORY

One major reason for the difficulties in applying behavioral science knowledge has been the interpretation that such ideas are applicable to all situations. From their earliest attempts to apply these ideas, both behavioral scientists developing the knowledge and managers applying it have at one time or another maintained the universality of the ideas. For example, Rensis Likert's participative-management ("Systems 4" Management) model was a call by a behavioral scientist for a universal application of ideas regardless of industry, company size, or geographic location.[1]

Over the past few years, Likert's voice has been joined by many other behavioral scientists who assume that their theories are also universally appropriate. Many of these theories were derived from studies carried out during and after World War II. The data from these studies were interpreted as supporting, for example, the notion that all employees have strong needs for group membership at work and, consequently, the universal superiority of participative management. Researchers were not concerned whether these ideas were more appropriate in one setting than in another, with different groups of employees, with different jobs, and so forth.

Along with this search for the universal went a tendency to invent specific techniques for applying the theories, which it was argued would lead to improved results in all situations. Examples are management by objectives, autonomous work groups, laboratory training, job enrichment, and participative leadership.

By now many managers have tried these techniques, and their attempts have led to numerous difficulties stemming from the variable conditions existing in different companies. For example, a basic premise underlying management by objectives is that if people set their own goals, they will be

[1]Rensis Likert, *New Patterns of Management* (New York: McGraw-Hill, 1961).

committed to them. Because of the nature of the business or of the technology, however, in some situations employees can have little or no real voice in setting goals.

To illustrate, consider the case of the back office of a large bank, where managers down to first-line supervisors were directed to become involved in an MBO program. The quantity, schedule, and quality of their work, however, were imposed on them by the work flow from other groups in the bank and by their customers' requests, rather than being set by the managers themselves. Moreover, upper managers trying to meet strategic goals set their cost targets. These lower-level managers had little or no leeway in which to choose their own goals. As a result, they soon saw the management by objectives program as a sham.

Another example of a situation not fitting a theory occurs when a manager's personality is not consistent with what is demanded of a participative leader. As Harry Levinson and Abraham Zaleznik, among others, have indicated, although personality development is a life-long process, a 35-year-old's character is generally stable and is unlikely to change in radically new directions.[2] Since one's style of dealing with others is closely linked to one's personality makeup, it is not surprising that some managers are comfortable with one way of managing subordinates and some with another.

To illustrate my point: Companies have faced a major difficulty in introducing autonomous work groups and similar techniques. These techniques require supervisors to involve their subordinates more heavily in decision making, and many of these managers find it difficult to adjust to this new "participative" style. Not only have they spent many years managing in a different way, but also they consciously or unconsciously chose to be foreman because their personalities were suited to the traditional, more directive role.

Such situational problems are a primary reason that so many of these techniques are flashes in the pan. They are applied successfully in a few companies where conditions are right and receive attention and publicity. Without considering the differences, managers, consultants, and academics alike decide the technique can be applied to other situations. Because conditions are not right, the second-generation attempts are often failures, and the enthusiasm dies.

EACH SITUATION IS UNIQUE

Neither universal theories nor the resulting techniques have been the only behavioral science ideas available to managers. Another set of ideas is built on the premise that the organization can be viewed as a social system. This approach developed out of the Hawthorne studies by Elton Mayo, F. J. Roethlisberger, and William Dickson.[3]

In this well-known study, it was learned that worker behavior is the result of a complex system of forces including the personalities of the workers, the nature of their jobs, and the formal measurement and reward practices of the organization. Workers behave in ways that management does not intend, not because they are irresponsible or lazy but because they need to cope with their work situation in a way that is satisfying and meaningful to them. From this perspective, what is effective management behavior and action depends on the specifics in each situation.

Although many scholars, including Roethlisberger and Mayo themselves, elaborated on these ideas and taught them at many business schools, managers never gave them the attention they gave to the universal ideas. Interestingly enough, many saw the central significance of the Hawthorne studies as being either the *universal* importance of effective interpersonal communication between supervisors and workers or the so-called "Hawthorne Effect." The latter is the notion that any change in practice will *always* lead to positive results in the short run simply because of the novelty of the new practice.

In essence, this world-renowned study, which its authors saw as proving that human issues need to be viewed from a "social system," or situational perspective, was interpreted by others as a call for universal techniques of "good human relations."

---

[2]Harry Levinson, *The Exceptional Executive* (Cambridge, Mass.: Harvard University Press, 1968); Abraham Zaleznik, *Human Dilemmas of Leadership* (New York: Harper & Row, 1966).

[3]Elton Mayo, *The Human Problems of an Industrial Civilization* (New York: Viking Press, 1960); F. J. Roethlisberger and William Dickson, *Management and the Worker* (Cambridge, Mass.: Harvard University Press, 1939).

(For Roethlisberger's comments on this, see *The Elusive Phenomena.*)[4]

Of course, stating that one should *always* take a situational perspective could be seen as a universal prescription itself. My concern is not with universal ideas, such as this and others which I shall mention shortly, which seem to hold generally true. Rather, it is with techniques invented under a specific set of conditions, which have not been more widely tried but which their advocates argue have universal application.

Why these social-system concepts did not catch on is a matter of conjecture, but one reasonable explanation is that managers naturally prefer the simplest apparent approach to a problem. When faced with the choice between the complex and time-consuming analysis required to apply such situation-

[4]F. J. Roethlisberger, *The Elusive Phenomena*, ed. George. F. F. Lombard (Boston: Division of Research, Harvard Business School, 1977).

al ideas and the simpler, quicker prescriptions of universal theories and techniques, most managers seem to prefer the simpler universal approach. The human tendency to follow the fads and fashions also adds to the appeal of these techniques. If competitors are trying T-groups for management development, shouldn't we? If the company across the industrial park is using MBO, shouldn't we as well?

In spite of the rush to simple popular solutions in the last decade, some behavioral scientists have become aware that the universal theories and the techniques they spawned have failed in many situations where they were inappropriate. These scholars are trying to understand situational complexity and to provide managers with tools to analyze the complex issues in each specific situation and to decide on appropriate action. Examples of these efforts are listed in *Exhibit 3-1*.

These behavioral scientists do not all agree on what variables are important to understand. At this stage, people conceptualize the issues and define the

Author	Publication	Major focus
Fred E. Fiedler	*A Theory of Leadership Effectiveness* (New York: McGraw-Hill, 1967).	Leadership of a work unit
John P. Kotter	*Organizational Dynamics* (Reading, Mass.: Addison-Wesley, 1978).	Organizational change
Edward E. Lawler	*Pay and Organizational Effectiveness: A Psychological View* (New York: McGraw-Hill, 1971).	Employee motivation
Paul R. Lawrence and Jay W. Lorsch	*Organization and Environment* (Division of Research, Harvard Business School, Harvard University, 1967.)	Organizational arrangements to fit environmental requirements
Harry Levinson	*Men, Management and Mental Health* (Harvard University Press, 1962).	Employee motivation
Jay W. Lorsch and John Morse	*Organizations and Their Members* (New York: Harper and Row, 1975).	Organizational arrangements and leadership in functional units
Edgar H. Schein	*Career Dynamics: Matching Individual and Organizational Needs* (Reading, Mass.: Addison-Wesley, 1978).	Life stage careers, and organizational requirements
Robert Tannenbaum and Warren H. Schmidt	*"How To Choose A Leadership Pattern"* (HBR May-June 1973).	Leadership
Victor H. Vroom and Phillip W. Yetton	*Leadership and Decision-Making* (University of Pittsburgh Press, 1973).	Leadership behavior for different types of decisions.
Joan Woodward	*Industrial Organization: Theory and Practice* (Oxford University Press, 1965).	Organizational design

Exhibit 3-1   Examples of situational frameworks.

variables and the important relationships among them in many different ways. Also, the "theories" they have developed often throw light on a limited set of applications.

All these behavioral scientists focusing on situational theories, however, share two fundamental assumptions. First, the proper target of behavioral science knowledge is the complex interrelationships that shape the behavior with which all managers must deal. Harold J. Leavitt, in his well-known text *Managerial Psychology,* presents a diagram (see *Exhibit 3-2*) that illustrates clearly the basic set of relationships.[5] Behavior in an organization results, he writes, from the interaction of people's needs, their task requirements, and the organization's characteristics. He uses two-headed arrows to both suggest this complex interdependence and indicate that behavior itself can influence the other forces over time.

Although Leavitt's was an early and, from today's perspective, a simplified view of the relationships involved, it captures the essential issues in situational theories and is very close to the Roethlisberger and Dickson conception.

The second assumption that behavioral scientists focusing on situational theories seem to share is that, at this juncture, they cannot hope to provide a

grand and general theory of human behavior in organizations. Rather, what the behavioral sciences can, and should, provide are what L. J. Henderson called "walking sticks" to guide the managers along complex decision-making paths about human affairs.[6] In this case, by walking sticks I mean conceptual models for understanding the complexity of the human issues a manager faces.

Such models represent the product these scholars have to offer managers. Universal prescriptions or techniques are like a mirage. Each situation is unique and the manager must use these conceptual models to diagnose it. With an understanding of the complex and interrelated causes of behavior in the organization, the manager can use his or her intellect and creative ability to invent a new solution or to judge what existing solutions might fit the situation.

An Applied Example

The case of a major insurance company illustrates how a situational walking stick can help managers. Like many of its competitors, the top management of this company was concerned about the high rate of turnover among its younger professional staff. The managers felt that they did not understand the causes of this turnover and were unwilling to accept the conclusion that their competitors reached—namely, that the basic cause was low pay. Instead, they used an in-house consultant to help them diagnose the causes of their problem.

This consultant used a relatively simple situational model—the concept of the psychological contract—as a framework for diagnosing the causes of the problem.[7] From this perspective, the relationship between a group of employees and the company is seen as an implicit, as well as explicit, contract.

While this contract is not binding in the legal sense, it is of psychological importance. Employees have certain expectations about what they are to get from their work in the company—both economically and psychologically. If these expectations are not met, the employees become dissatisfied, and ultimately can express themselves by walking out the door.

[5]Harold J. Leavitt, *Managerial Psychology* (Chicago: University of Chicago Press, 1958), p. 286.

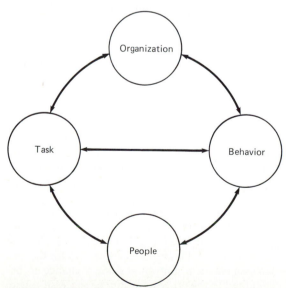

Exhibit 3-2   Basic forces shaping behavior.

[6]L. J. Henderson, *On The Social System: Selected Writings* (Chicago, Ill.: University of Chicago Press, 1970).
    [7]The concept of the psychological contract was first developed by Harry Levinson et al. in *Men, Management and Mental Health* (Cambridge, Mass.: Harvard University Press, 1966).

With these ideas in mind, the consultant, through a series of interviews in offices that had varying levels of turnover, sought the answers to two basic questions: What did the employees expect from the company? And how well were these expectations being met?

He learned that these young employees considered their current salary level relatively unimportant. More important to them were future career opportunities, the chance to do their jobs with minimum interference from above, and immediate supervisors who cared about their progress and tried to facilitate their learning. Furthermore, the consultant found that staff turnover was much lower in offices where managers were meeting expectations than where they were not.

From this diagnosis, top management developed an approach to improve the skills of its middle managers in meeting the expectations of its younger staff. By discovering the basic causes of its turnover problem, the company avoided the trap its competitors with identical problems fell in of mistakenly relying on salary increases as a way of trying to buy the loyalty of its younger staff.

Potential of Situational Theories

The insurance company case illustrates the greatest potential the behavioral sciences have for managers at present. They can provide situational theories to analyze, order, understand, and deal with the complex social and human issues managers face. By their nature the universal theories make simplified assumptions about the human and business factors involved in a situation.

For example, many universal theories do not recognize that not all employees have the same career expectations. Yet we now know that while older managers may be more interested in jobs that enable them to develop subordinates and build the organization for the future, younger persons, such as the professionals just mentioned, are at a stage of life where advancement is usually critical.[8]

Similarly, different business tasks do not all lend themselves to similar leadership styles or reward schemes; running a production shop may require directive leadership, but managing a group of professional underwriters for an insurance company may require employee involvement in decisions.

Even though they neither provide ready-made solutions nor solve all classes of human problems, the situational theories are tools to understand the variety and complexity of these problems. The manager has to select the theory that seems most relevant to his or her specific problem, analyze the situation according to it, develop his or her own action alternatives, and choose among them.

A hospital laboratory provides a useful analogy. It is full of diagnostic tools, but the doctor has to make the choice of the appropriate ones. Then, he makes a diagnosis and decides on the appropriate treatment. So it will be for managers. The behavioral sciences can provide conceptual frameworks for analyzing problems. They will indicate what data are required, in some cases how best to collect them, how the problem areas are related to each other, and the outcomes with which the managers will be concerned. With this analysis the managers can then use their experience, intuition, and intellect to decide which actions make sense.

From this description, the analytical process may seem difficult and time-consuming. How true this is will depend to some extent on the complexity of the problem and the experience that a manager has in applying these tools. A manager with experience can apply them with the same ease and skill a physician displays in using his diagnostic tools. Applying these tools to complex and infrequently encountered issues, however, may require some expertise beyond the scope of a typical line manager—a problem I shall deal with shortly.

The trend toward more situational theories signifies only a decline in emphasis on universal theories and the techniques they have spawned, not that these theories and techniques should or will disappear. Undoubtedly, on a limited number of issues, such generalizations are useful guides to actions. The problem for a manager is to identify those issues where a universal theory is helpful, and not confuse them with issues where the solution depends on the situation.

For example, certain maxims about interpersonal communication seem to be generally useful in conducting performance appraisal interviews. And it seems clear that it is absolutely necessary for the top management of a unit undergoing a change to be committed to the process for it to be successful. Use

[8]See Daniel Levinson et al., *The Seasons of A Man's Life* (New York: Alfred Knopf, 1978); or Edgar H. Schein, *Career Dynamics* (Reading, Mass.: Addison-Wesley, 1978).

of such valid generalizations from the behavioral sciences should continue and expand.

But the application of techniques and universal principles that are inappropriate in a variety of situations must decline. Because of the tendency toward fads in both managers and academics, I am not naive enough to think that the misapplications of universal theories will suddenly end. My hope is that the increasing availability and use of situational theories will gradually make universal ideas less attractive. As managers become more sophisticated diagnosticians, they will be less likely to try an idea or a technique simply because it is a fad.

Managers need also to recognize a number of current difficulties in using situational theories and must, with the help of those who are developing these ideas, seek solutions to them. In essence, in the behavioral science market they must act as consumers who influence the end product, and in their companies they must, among other things, act as teachers so that they and their associates are prepared to use these tools.

THE MANAGER AS A CONSUMER

If a manager, acting as a consumer, begins to explore the relevant literature, what is he likely to find? To what extent are the situational theories in a useful, usable form? Unfortunately, much needs to be done to make many of these tools more widely applicable. As managers become informed and demanding consumers, I hope they can influence behavioral scientists to take steps to overcome the current problems.

The Tower of Babel

One difficulty with today's situational tools is that each scholar (or group of scholars) has developed his or her own language and methods and makes interpretations based on his or her values, assumptions, and research about individual behavior. Also, in the same way physical scientists and engineers have done, each set of scholars, not surprisingly, prefers its own ideas and rejects those "not invented here." Understandably, communication among behavioral scientists and their communication with managers is confused. Different scholars use different labels to mean the same thing. Because no one relates his ideas to those of others, an academic Tower of Babel develops.

Managers and scholars alike find it difficult to understand what one label means in one model as compared to another or how the ideas developed by one group relate to those developed elsewhere. Clearly, what managers and academics can and must do is judge future studies more carefully and explicitly to determine whether they are related to each other. In this way, we will be able to see the parallels and differences in various theories and will be able to make more informed decisions about their relevance to particular problems. Similarly, such action should gradually reduce much of the variation in language and terminology that characterizes the behavioral sciences.

Lack of Parsimony

Many of these concepts are so complex that managers need to learn how to define the concepts and their relationships before they can apply them. All this takes time and, naturally, makes these ideas less appealing to the busy line executive. By their preference for complex and elegant theories that greatly exceed the needs of most managers, academics have compounded the problem. Rather than worrying about how to help managers, many academics seem preoccupied with impressing their colleagues. In my own experience, moreover, it is the relatively simple concepts that managers find most useful.

As consumers of knowledge, managers can and should reject those theories that are too complex and seek those simple enough to be understood and implemented by intelligent managers. But academics must strive to develop such theories, what Sheldon has called "friendly" models.[9] By this, he means theories that are not so complex as to intimidate potential users, yet are complete enough to enable them to deal with the real human complexities they face.

One way to ensure such a balance is for managers to encourage and for academics to conduct more research focusing on managerial issues. Experience in medicine and space technology, for example, has demonstrated anew the axiom that research leading to a productive and practical payout will also likely lead to important theoretical results. Certainly, encouraging the design of research programs that tie

[9]Alan Sheldon, "Friendly Models," *Science, Medicine, and Man,* Vol. I, 1973, p. 49.

real managerial concerns to theoretical behavioral science issues should also lead to gains in knowledge complete enough to be useful and simple enough to use.

Managers should also look for research that clarifies the conditions where findings are relevant and where they are not. In this manner, the distinction between situationally relevant ideas and universally applicable ones should be clearer. This, in turn, should reduce some of the misuses of behavioral science and also discourage academics from developing techniques in a vacuum.

An Aside to Academics

Although HBR readers are primarily practitioners, much of my preceding argument has particular relevance to my academic colleagues. Managers can only influence us indirectly by their reactions as consumers. The responsibility for the changes in the development of knowledge for which I am calling lies directly with academics. Yet, in many centers of behavioral science research, researchers are more concerned with proving a minor but neat conceptual point or resolving a measurement issue than with tackling issues that have clear practical application. Disciplinary traditions, the promotion criteria in most universities, and the acceptance standard for most relevant publications place more emphasis on theoretical elegance and methodological perfection than on practical use of knowledge.

It will, therefore, require more than just pressure from consumers to make the necessary changes in our approach to knowledge-building. It is going to require dedication and courage from the behavioral scientists who believe, as I do, that our tools are still too little used.

THE MANAGER AS MANAGER

If academics can be encouraged to move in such directions, the manager's job will be easier. He or she will gradually acquire simpler conceptual tools that are relevant to real problems, specific about the range of situations to which they apply, and related to each other.

Even today, however, a few such conceptual tools exist. The issue for managers is how to select the specific set of tools relevant to a particular type of problem. To help in this regard, in *Exhibit 3-3* I compare the conceptual tools from *Exhibit 3-1* as to

their major focus, the type of management or organizational issues for which they are most relevant, and some of the key questions managers must be able to answer to use these tools.

In examining *Exhibit 3-3*, bear in mind some caveats. First, the list represents my personal choices. It is not exhaustive. It is based on my own and some of my colleagues' experiences in helping managers deal with these problems. Second, many of these tools are relatively new and still somewhat crude. Although, in some cases, fairly sophisticated and validated techniques have been developed for answering the key questions, in others the manager will have to rely on his or her own knowledge and judgment of the situation. Third, in such a compact article, it is obviously not possible to define the variables in each conceptual framework or state the relationships among them. For this the reader will have to refer to the original works listed in *Exhibit 3-1*.

By using tools such as these, managers will be forced to be more diagnostic. They will have to approach human problems with the same analytical rigor they devote to marketing or financial issues. This approach means less acceptance of the latest fad in management practice, whether it be management by objective, job enrichment, office of the president, sensitivity training, or whatever. Instead, managers can use these tools to identify problems and diagnose their causes. Then they can invent their own solutions or even examine what other companies are doing to see what might be relevant to their situation. In this process, managers should not ignore their intuitive hunches and past experience. Accordingly, this more rigorous analysis should be compared with such insights to arrive at the best possible judgments.

Need for Education

Because these situational tools require more skill, knowledge, and time, line managers may need help and support in the longer run to realize their full potential. Education and training, in both university courses and company management-development programs, can and should aim at giving managers knowledge about these tools and the skills necessary to apply them. Such programs will have to provide not only content, but also, and equally important, practice in using these tools for analysis and problem solving.

Exhibit 3-3 table — columns (Issues): Leadership, Management selection, Career planning, Measurement and performance feedback, Compensation, Job design, Division and coordination of activities, Organizational change.

Framework	Major focus	Leadership	Management selection	Career planning	Measurement and performance feedback	Compensation	Job design	Division and coordination of activities	Organizational change	Diagnostic questions
Fiedler	Leadership of a work unit	●	●				●			What is the preferred leadership style of the relevant manager(s) on a continuum from permissive, passive, considerate, to controlling, active, and structuring? What is the quality of leader relations with the members of the subordinate group(s)? How well-defined and structured are the activities being performed by subordinates? How much positional authority does the leader(s) have?
Kotter	Organizational change				●			●	●	Is management concerned with short-term, moderate-term, or long-term change? If *short-term*, what is the current state of the organization's human and financial resources, its organization process and structure, its technology, and its external environment? If *moderate-term*, how well are the organization's resources, structure, and process aligned with each other and the external environment and the goals of management? If these are not well aligned, what changes have caused this? If *long-term*, are major changes likely in top management, in the organization's human and financial resources, its structure and processes, or its technology and external environment, which would make one or two of these elements out of line with the other? How maleable are the other elements so that a new alignment can be created? Is the organization inventing resources to achieve sufficient flexibility to adapt to such major changes?
Lawler	Employee motivation				●	●	●			What do the relevant individuals expect to get as rewards for their behavior on the job? How valuable are these rewards to these individuals? How hard do these individuals believe it will be to achieve the results expected of them?
Lawrence and Lorsch	Organizational arrangements to fit environmental requirements				●			●		How different are the organizational practices, traditions, and the goals and time horizons of members of various organization units? To what extent are these differences consistent with the different activities each unit is performing (e.g., selling products versus manufacturing them versus designing them)? To what extent is it necessary for these units to work collaboratively and to what extent can they perform activities independent of each other? Do the existing mechanisms for dividing and coordinating work (e.g., authority structure, coordinating rules, cross-unit committees, rewards, and measurement) facilitate the necessary division of work and coordination?
Levinson et al	Employee motivation			●	●	●	●			What is the psychological contract between the relevant individuals and the company? What does each party expect to receive from the other? How well is each party living up to its part of the contract?
Lorsch and Morse	Organizational arrangements and leadership in functional units	●	●		●		●			What is the nature of the unit's tasks? How certain are they? What goals do members have to work toward? How quickly is feedback about results available? What are members' shared psychological predispositions in terms of working together versus alone, preference for close supervision or not, preference for clear and predictable activities or for ambiguous ones? How well does existing leadership style, unit structure, measurement, and job design fit the unit task and members' predisposition?
Schein	Life stage, careers, and organizational requirements		●	●						At what stage of life is (are) the relevant individual(s)? Where are these people in their careers? What are their underlying career interests? What are the key dimensions of jobs available now and in the future? What are future personnel requirements for these jobs?
Vroom and Yetton	Leadership behavior for different types of decisions	●	●							Who among the boss and his subordinates have information to make a high-quality decision? Is the problem well-defined or not? Is acceptance of decisions by subordinates critical to implementation? Do subordinates share the organizational goals to be attained in making these decisions? Is conflict among subordinates likely in seeking solutions?

Exhibit 3-3 Situational frameworks and their applications.

In calling for management education, I am not suggesting that line managers can or should develop knowledge of or skill in applying a broad range of these ideas. Rather, as *Exhibit 3-1* shows, they should gain understanding about those concepts which are relevant to the problems they regularly encounter. For example, concepts that focus on understanding leadership issues with a small group of workers (e.g., Fiedler's) would be of value to first-level supervisors.

At the general manager level, concepts that enhance understanding of multiple-unit organizations would be more relevant (e.g., Lawrence and Lorsch). This is not to say that some of these tools will not have utility at many organizational levels. For example, managers concerned with compensation issues might find Lawler's ideas useful whether their subordinates are salesmen, blue collar workers, or general managers.

Role of Staff

In the long run, along with educational programs, corporations will need to develop staff specialists with a broader range of knowledge about the behavioral sciences. These specialists, whatever their titles —organization development agent, human resources expert, organization designer, behavioral scientist—should be able to apply their wider and deeper behavioral science knowledge to a broader range of issues.

Their role would be analogous to what market research analysts, cost analysts, and so on, perform. Their job should be first to help managers decide what concepts will be most useful in understanding the problems they face, to design studies to gather data, to analyze them, and to work with their line colleagues to develop solutions. Again, academics have an important contribution to make. They can develop courses and programs to educate the professionals to staff these functions.

Awareness of One's Values and Style

To use these tools effectively, both line and staff managers will need to be aware of their own values and their own preferred management styles. Without such awareness, one can easily and unwittingly confuse one's own sense of what is right or appropriate with what the situation seems to require and objective analysis seems to suggest. With self-knowledge about one's values and preferences, one

can at least be explicit when making choices between what a situation requires and one's own preferences.

Achieving such self-awareness is not easy. It requires a willingness to be introspective and cognizant of one's limits as well as one's strengths, one's preferences as well as one's dislikes. Such probing is difficult for many managers; yet it is something that a number of seasoned, mature, and successful managers achieve. With this self-understanding, they are better able to comprehend their relationships with others around them. These same qualities must also be put to work to apply behavioral science knowledge effectively.

TOOLS ARE AVAILABLE NOW

Based on what you have read here, you may conclude that it is better to defer trying these situational tools until they have been improved, expanded, and refined. No doubt such improvements are needed. But if managers use the best of the existing situational tools now, in spite of their shortcomings, they will no doubt achieve improved effectiveness in dealing with the complex human problems of management.

The need for solving these human problems has never been more pressing. The increased size of organizations makes this so, as do the inflationary pressures on personnel costs and the rate of change in the environment of many companies. Additionally, demands from many employees for a more rewarding organizational life are growing. These situational tools offer a virtually untapped resource to provide more effective management of the human assets of most companies.

To use these tools will not be easy, and managers will have to make efforts at many levels: to be more critical consumers of behavioral science knowledge; to become more analytic and diagnostic; to gradually build educational programs and staff resources for developing skill and knowledge in using these tools; and, finally, to become more self-aware, so they can discriminate between their own preferences, current fads, and what will be most effective in their particular situations.

These efforts will be difficult, but to defer doing these things is to neglect these new and valuable tools that the behavioral sciences are making available, and this would be a tragic waste.

Chapter 2

The Nature of Individuals

Understanding and predicting human behavior in organizations requires knowledge about the nature of individuals. Individuals are, after all, the basic building blocks that make up even the largest and most complex organizations. There is a vast amount of research-based knowledge about individuals in organizations. Much is known, for example, about how individuals' characteristics (such as their personalities and their special talents) affect their behavior at work. While that material is interesting and useful for developing a robust understanding of behavior in organizations, we have not included it here. Instead, we have selected articles that emphasize the *processes* by which individuals perceive, construe, and respond to the people and events that make up their organizational experiences.

The first article, by Hamilton, examines what is known about how people perceive other people, form impressions of them, and make attributions about why they act as they do. Since much of what

we do in organizations depends on our views of other people—including our evaluations of them and our private explanations for their public behavior—it is incumbent on any student of organizational behavior to have a good grasp of the basic processes of person perception.

Yet making sense of people and events in organizations is not simply a matter of responding to what is "out there." As Weick points out in the second article in this chapter, people often actually create (or "enact") the very environments they seem to be responding to. Weick points out the importance of enactment processes for understanding life in organizations, and provides insight into the means by which this ubiquitous phenomenon takes place. Of special interest is the role of social relationships in making sense of one's organizational experiences. Weick shows how people routinely collaborate with other people, often without even being aware of it, to develop a shared view of the world that can powerfully shape (and sometimes limit) their work behavior.

The third reading examines motivational processes in organizations. Why is it that some people in organizations work very hard, while others seem to do as little as possible? Why do people sometimes arrive late for work or miss work entirely? What are the "levers" available to managers to try to influence employee motivation to work? Nadler and Lawler present the "expectancy theory" of motivation to address questions such as these. This theory, which focuses on the cognitive processes by which people choose how they will behave, offers considerable help both in understanding why people at work behave as they do and in developing managerial strategies for dealing with motivational problems and opportunities in organizations.

The final article in the chapter, by Lawler, examines people's *feelings* about their work and their organizational life. Lawler shows how overall satisfaction can be understood in terms of the difference between the kinds of outcomes a person feels he or she *should* be receiving and what is *actually* received. It turns out that an important factor influencing the "should receive" part of the equation is what one perceives that *other* people are getting—once again reinforcing the interdependence between individual and social processes in understanding organizational behavior.

Reading 4

Person Perception
David L. Hamilton

At one time or another, we have all heard someone say about a friend, "I liked him from the moment we met." Or "I knew right away that we would get along." Or even "It was love at first sight." These comments all reflect our immediate reactions to persons we meet, and indicate that our first perceptions of a person can provide us with some sense of what the person is like and how our relationship with him is likely to develop. While our initial reactions to persons often do not possess the degree of certainty reflected in the above quotations, we do develop first impressions of others with remarkable ease and quickness. Given that the way we perceive people is likely to influence our interpretation of their behavior and even the course of our future interactions with them, the task of understanding the person perception process takes on considerable significance. In this chapter we will discuss some of the theoretical ideas and research approaches that have developed as social psychologists have investigated this process. Virtually all of these ideas and approaches take off from the information-processing perspective, since we will be concerned primarily with how people understand the others around them.

Some of the language or terminology we use in referring to our perceptions of others suggests that such perception is a highly elusive process that should be difficult to study experimentally. For example, we sometimes refer to "having a sense of" what a person is like. Such vague characterizations of what it is like to "know" a person imply that this process may be beyond the reach of rigorous scientific investigation. On the contrary, social psychologists have learned a considerable amount about this process. This research has focused on the cognitive processes involved in the acquisition of information about others and in making judgments about them.

This information-processing approach rests on the assumption that one's perceptions of another person are based on the information available about the person *and* how one uses this information. When you first meet someone, your initial reactions are based on whatever fragmentary information is available about the person. This information may be limited to physical characteristics—Chris is tall, attractive, and well dressed. Despite the surface nature of this information, you are likely to use it to make a number of inferences about Chris. For example, considerable research has shown that perceivers make more favorable inferences about the personality characteristics of physically attractive than physically unattractive stimulus persons (Berscheid & Walster, 1974). Similarly, a person's sex and race are immediately obvious to any observer, who uses his own race and sex stereotypes to assume certain things about the person. Thus, you as a perceiver would go beyond the information available and make inferences about what else is likely to be true about Chris. This phenomenon occurs regularly in the person perception process. Whether these inferences are valid or invalid is irrelevant here. They are "true" for the perceiver and hence will have an important bearing on his perceptions of a person. But the perceiver doesn't make just *any* inferences. What is the nature of this process, and what determines the kind of inferences made? This is one of the questions we will consider in this chapter.

As you get to know Chris better, you obviously will acquire a good deal more information about her. You will learn about her "style" of interacting with people, how she spends time, her interests and aspirations, and perhaps even her concerns and insecurities. All of this information will, of course, alter, modify, and shape your perceptions of Chris. In other words, the acquisition of new information about a person can modify and/or elaborate the perceiver's conception of what she is like and can influence the judgments made about her. The processes involved in the development of such impressions have been studied extensively by social psychologists, and the findings of this research will also be discussed in this chapter.

In our perceptions of others, we attempt to gain

an understanding of what the person is like, to "make sense" of the information we acquire about him. Often this requires that the perceiver consider the question of *why* a person behaved in a particular manner. Suppose that you know that another student in one of your classes worked extremely hard on a term paper. Does this mean that the student is intrinsically interested in the subject matter of the course, or does it mean that he is "hungry" for an "A" in order to protect his sterling grade point average? How you answer this question may considerably influence your perceptions of this person. To ask "Why?" is to seek an explanation for the causes of a person's behavior. Later in this chapter we will consider recent research concerned with how perceivers answer this question.

As we consider several topics which have been the foci of investigation in person perception research, one theme will persist throughout the chapter. This theme is central to the cognitive, or information-processing, orientation reflected in virtually all person perception research: The perceiver, rather than being a passive recipient of information about others, is an active processor of information and hence contributes herself in significant ways to the overall person perception process. Most of the information we acquire about others—whether we obtain it from observation of their behavior, by hearsay from a third party, or through other means—can be construed or interpreted in various ways. The perceiver actively imposes some interpretation on this information, and only then does the information take on some meaning for the person perception process. For example, suppose you learn that Kathy has helped her friend Joanne on a take-home exam on which they were supposed to work individually. Kathy's behavior can be interpreted in several ways. You might view it as an act of kindness, in which Kathy provided assistance to a friend in need. Alternatively, you might interpret the same behavior as an act of dishonesty. How you interpret the behavior—that is, as reflecting Kathy's kindness or dishonesty—will influence your perceptions of Kathy in substantially different ways. In either case, the behavior is the same, but the interpretation that you impose on it has quite different implications for your impression of Kathy. Thus, the meaning of that behavior is something that you, the perceiver, have determined.

The importance of this interpretive process for person perception is demonstrated in an experiment by Duncan (1976). In this study subjects watched a videotape of two male stimulus persons engaged in a discussion of possible solutions to a human relations problem. The subjects, who were led to believe they were watching a "live" interaction in another room over closed circuit television, were told that their job would be to assist the experimenter in coding interpersonal behaviors. To do this, they were given a coding sheet listing a set of categories of different types of behavior, and were instructed, each time the experimenter gave a signal, to code the behavior which had just occurred according to this category system. The last signal and the only one of interest in the study, was given immediately after the discussion had become rather heated and one of the actors had given the other a mild shove. At this point the screen went blank and the experiment ended. There were actually four versions of the stimulus tape in which the same behavior sequence was shown but in which the race—black or white—of the two actors (protagonist and victim) was varied. Subjects, all of whom were white, used four different categories in coding the shoving incident; these categories were "playing around," "dramatization," "aggressive behavior," and "violent behavior." How this behavior was interpreted and categorized was almost totally a function of the protagonist's race. The results of the study are shown in Table 4-1, where it can be seen that if the protagonist was white, the shove was interpreted as an act of playfulness or dramatization. In contrast, if the protagonist was black, the shove was interpreted as aggressive or violent behavior. Apparently the subjects' stereotypic expectancies about blacks and whites led them to interpret the same behavioral act in quite different ways.

However, once a behavior has been interpreted and categorized in a particular way, its meaning for the perceiver has been determined and it will influence one's perceptions of the actor accordingly. Thus the perceiver has had an active role in determining his or her perceptions of another person's behavior.

COGNITIVE STRUCTURES IN PERSON PERCEPTION

We have seen that as perceivers we are active contributors to the perception process. We actively process the information we receive in terms of our existing ideas and conceptions. This suggests that perceivers have certain cognitive structures which they use in organizing and interpreting the stimulus

Table 4-1   Category Use in Codings of Shoving Incident

Behavior category (in percent)

Race protagonist	Victim	Playing around	Dramatizes	Aggressive behavior	Violent behavior
White	White	18.75	43.75	25.00	12.50
White	Black	25.00	37.50	25.00	12.50
Black	White	3.13	6.25	15.63	75.00
Black	Black	0.00	6.25	25.00	68.75

Adapted from Duncan (1976).

world. The study by Duncan described above illustrates this point: Subjects apparently had different expectancies about blacks and whites based on their stereotypic conceptions of these groups; and these expectancies influenced the way the subjects interpreted the behavior of individual members of these groups. The stereotypes and the expectations which followed from them were in the heads of the perceivers. In the first part of this chapter we will be concerned with the nature of the cognitive structures which a perceiver brings to the perception process and how the structures may influence one's perceptions of others.

Implicit Personality Theories

Social psychologists interested in person perception have recognized the importance of the perceiver's cognitive structures for quite some time. More than 25 years ago Bruner and Tagiuri (1954) introduced the idea that perceivers, through their observation of and interaction with others, develop intuitive notions about the nature of personality and about what aspects of personality are and are not likely to coexist in the same person. That is, much like "real" personality theorists, naive observers of human behavior develop expectations and make inferences about "what goes with what" in the personalities of others. This pattern of beliefs and expectancies is referred to as the perceiver's *implicit personality theory*.

Suppose, for example, you know only that Joe Arbuthnot is talkative. From this one piece of information you might infer that Joe is also likely to be friendly, outgoing, and popular, but is probably not shy or moody. Notice that these are inferences which you believe are likely to be true of Joe, even though you have no information regarding them. In fact, these inferences may not be valid. We all know people who talk a lot and are not particularly

friendly, who talk so much that their popularity is lessened, and who we perceive as moody simply because they always tell us about their ups and downs. Nevertheless, we make such inferences and they may be quite accurate. The point here is that, in inferring Joe's other qualities, we have gone beyond the information available and have assumed on the basis of what is known to be true that certain other things are also true.

Evidence Indicating the Importance of Implicit Personality Theories

If people have implicit personality theories, then these cognitive structures should have some influence on their perceptions of persons and the inferences they make about them. Is there evidence that implicit personality theories have any impact on the way we think about and perceive others? In this section we will consider research findings that bear on this question.

One type of evidence indicating the importance of implicit personality theories was presented earlier in this chapter. In our consideration of inferences you might make about Joe Arbuthnot if you know only that he is talkative, we noted that certain kinds of inferences (he is also outgoing and popular, but probably not moody) are more likely to be made than others, even though it is not difficult to think of persons who would violate these expectations. The fact that one readily makes these inferences can be explained only by recognizing that some cognitive structure exists in the perceiver, and these inferences represent the influence of the perceiver's implicit personality theory on the perceptual process. That is, Joe is no longer perceived simply as talkative, but as also possessing other attributes which may influence our subsequent perceptions of, and even our interactions with, him.

Another phenomenon commonly found in the

trait inferences people make also illustrates this point. An evaluative bias, or *halo effect*, occurs in our inference process, so that knowing something favorable about a person will lead us to infer other desirable qualities. This may be most dramatically seen in the large number of inferences about personality characteristics perceivers commonly make on the basis of a person's physical attractiveness. A large number of studies have indicated that physically attractive stimulus persons are perceived as being "more sexually warm and responsive, sensitive, kind, interesting, strong, poised, modest, sociable, and outgoing than persons of lesser physical attractiveness" (Berscheid & Walster, 1974, p. 169). In our inferences about others, good qualities beget other good qualities; undesirable characteristics beget other undesirable characteristics.

While the halo effect is clearly an instance of a perceiver going beyond the information given, in many cases such inferences may represent fairly accurate expectations learned over the course of one's interaction with other people. True, we can think of talkative people who aren't popular, but perhaps most talkative persons we have known have been popular. The fact that a perceiver is going beyond the information available doesn't mean that all his inferences are invalid. On the other hand, as inferences based on physical attractiveness suggest, in some cases implicit personality theories can result in judgments which are unlikely to be generally true. We know of no evidence that physically attractive persons are more likely to be kind or sensitive than less attractive persons.

We have suggested that a person's perceptions of others are not totally determined by the stimulus information available but are in part a function of her implicit personality theory. The question naturally arises of which is more important— (1) the available information about the person's behavior and personality or (2) the perceiver's cognitive framework, in which the information is processed and interpreted?

This point is addressed in a study by Dornbusch, Hastorf, Richardson, Muzzy, and Vreeland (1965). These experimenters had children at a summer camp give free descriptions of some of their tentmates. From a content analysis of these descriptions, an extensive listing of the various content categories used by the children was developed. The investigators then determined the degree of overlap in the categories contained in three pairs of descriptions. Three types of comparisons were made: (1) In comparisons between one child's descriptions of two different persons the descriptions come from the same perceiver and describe different target persons. (2) In comparisons between two children's descriptions of the same other person the descriptions come from different perceivers and describe the same target person. (3) In comparisons between descriptions of different persons by different perceivers neither the perceiver nor the target person was the same. This third comparison was included to determine the amount of overlap in the categories used in two descriptions that might be expected because subjects came from a common culture. The results showed the greatest amount of overlap when the two descriptions came from the same child (comparison 1). The overlap in descriptions of the same child by two different perceivers (comparison 2) only slightly exceeded the baseline overlap attributed to common culture (comparison 3). Based on subjects' free descriptions of others, these results provide strong evidence that perceivers consistently use a common set of cognitive categories in their thoughts and perceptions of others.

SCHEMAS IN PERSON PERCEPTION

The research on implicit personality theories has shown that perceivers have well-developed concepts about the nature of personality, and that perceivers' expectations about what aspects of personality are likely to coexist can influence their inferences about other persons. Much of this research has focused on the structure of implicit personality theories: the development of methods for identifying the major dimensions of implicit personality theory, the assessment of individual differences in cognitive structures, and the investigation of the relationship between the perceiver's personality and his implicit personality theory constructs. Given that we have these cognitive structures, it becomes important to determine how they influence our cognitive processing of information about persons. In this section we will consider some recent research concerned with this question.

The question of how cognitive structures influence the processing of information became an active and important area of investigation in the 1970s. Research focused on the role of schemas in the encoding, representation, and retrieval of information. While there is no single, generally accepted definition of the term "schema," there is general agreement that a schema is a cognitive structure which consists of the person's knowledge and beliefs pertaining to some stimulus domain. In person perception, a schema may be thought of as representing the perceiver's generalized concept of the network of traits and behaviors likely to be associated with some personality content. For example, one's schema for an extroverted person (Cantor & Mischel, 1977) may include one's expectations that such a person would be outgoing, talkative, adventurous, and perhaps uninhibited, as well as that such a person would be likely to engage in such behaviors as being an active participant in class discussions, telling jokes at parties, and seeking thrills. Such a schema might also include other ingredients, such as situations in which extroverted behavior is likely to be observed (social gatherings as opposed to a library) and occupational preferences (salesperson as opposed to accountant). A schema, then, represents the perceiver's generalized knowledge and beliefs, abstracted from previous experience, regarding a specific domain of content. Similar to our description of implicit personality theories, a schema represents a set of expectations the perceiver considers likely to be true, given some limited information about a person. A schema, however, is a narrower concept in that it pertains to a specific content domain (such as extroversion). Thus, we can think of one's implicit personality theory as consisting of the set of schemas one has about the personality and behavior of others.

How do these person schemas influence the processing of information about others? In this section we will consider the effect of schemas on (1) what information about another person is encoded, (2) how this information is organized, (3) how this information is interpreted and what inferences are drawn from it, and (4) what information is available for later retrieval.

Influence of Schemas on Encoding

Given the enormous number of sights and sounds which surround us at any moment and to which we might respond, it is obvious that we as perceivers cannot possibly attend to all of the diverse stimuli impinging on us at any given time. Our perception must be selective. This means that in our perceptions of others, some but not all of the information available will be encoded. Several factors can influence which aspects of the stimulus information a perceiver will attend to. One of these factors is the schema he is using while processing the information.

The influence of schemas on information encoding has been demonstrated by Zadney and Gerard (1974). In this experiment subjects watched a videotape of two persons having a conversation as they moved about in a living room. In the course of the videotape the actors handled a number of objects in the room, some of which were valuable (an expensive ring, some credit cards) and some of which were related to the use of drugs (a waterpipe, a roach clip). Subjects were given one of three different sets of instructions before watching the videotape. One group was told that the persons in the tape had come to a friend's apartment to burglarize it. A second group was told that the persons were in a friend's apartment because they had heard that there was going to be a drug raid, and they wanted to remove incriminating evidence. The third group was told that the persons were simply waiting for their friend to arrive home. After they watched the videotape, subjects were asked to write down as many of the objects in the living room as they could remember. The three different sets of instructions presumably would activate different schemas in the perceivers, schemas which would influence the subjects' attention to and interpretation of details of the actors' behavior. For example, if the subject thought that the stimulus persons' intent was to burglarize the apartment, their attention would likely be drawn to aspects of the stimulus sequence most related to a theft (for example, the expensive ring). The results of the study showed that subjects tended to recall more of the items congruent with the perceived intent of the actors. For example, subjects given the burglary instruction recalled more theft-related objects than did subjects given the drug raid instructions. Thus, the instructions regarding the actors' intent provided subjects with a schema or frame of reference which they could use in selecting and interpreting the various aspects of the behavior sequence.

Influence of Schemas on Organization and Representation

Information that is encoded into memory is not passively stored as isolated bits of knowledge. Rather, the perceiver organizes the information into a meaningful framework. The schemas used in processing information about others can provide a meaningful context in which information is organized and stored.

This process is shown in research reported by Hamilton, Katz, and Leirer (1980). Subjects in their experiment read a series of 16 sentences, each sentence describing a single behavior. The 16 sentences contained 4 items in each of 4 categories of content. For example, some of the behaviors reflected social or interpersonal activities ("went to a movie with friends"), others were concerned with athletic activities ("jogs every morning before going to work"), and still others represented the other types of personality content. Half of the subjects were told that the experiment was concerned with memory and that their task was to try to remember as many of the sentences as possible. The other half of the subjects were told that the experiment concerned impression formation processes and that their task was to form an impression of a person described by the sentences. The latter instructions would presumably make the content themes reflected in the items more salient to the subjects in the impression formation condition and would lead this group to process the items in terms of schemas related to the content themes. The 16 items were presented in random order. Subjects were later asked to recall as many of the items as they could. In recalling the items, subjects in the impression formation, but not in the memory, condition tended to group the items according to the four categories of personality content. Thus, the impression formation instructions activated schemas relevant to understanding persons, and these schemas were used in organizing and storing the descriptive items.

Influence of Schemas on Inferences and Interpretation of Information

We have just indicated that information acquired about another person is selected, encoded, and represented in memory within the framework of the schemas being used by the perceiver while the information is being processed. These schemas—the perceiver's accumulated knowledge and beliefs pertaining to some domain of content—also provide the context in which the perceiver interprets the meaning of the acquired information and makes further inferences based on it. Going beyond the information available and filling in the gaps by making inferences from the information available constitutes another important role played by these knowledge structures in the perception of one's social world.

These points are well illustrated in a study reported by Bower (1977). Subjects in this experiment read a series of five brief paragraphs, each paragraph describing the behavior of Nancy in a different situation. For example, one paragraph described Nancy making a cup of coffee; another gave a brief description of her visit to a doctor's office; the third paragraph was concerned with a class lecture Nancy attended; the fourth described a shopping trip to the grocery store; and the fifth reported on a cocktail party that Nancy attended. Half of the subjects simply read the series of paragraphs describing these five neutral episodes. The other half of the subjects, before reading the paragraphs, read the following three-sentence lead-in: "Nancy woke up feeling sick again, and she wondered if she really were pregnant. How would she tell the professor she had been seeing? And the money was another problem" (Bower, 1977, p. 9). Subjects commonly interpreted this material to mean that Nancy was afraid she was pregnant as a result of having an affair with a college professor, that she was wondering how to inform him, and was worried about the cost of an abortion. Subjects read the series of paragraphs either with or without the introductory information about Nancy and returned the next day. They were then asked to recall the information in the paragraphs. The activation of a "pregnancy schema" about Nancy in subjects who received the three-sentence lead-in to the paragraphs had a substantial effect on their recall of the information. The episodes described in the paragraphs were interpreted in light of Nancy's presumed pregnancy and the problems it would create. For example, one paragraph stated that Nancy had awakened feeling sick, a statement which was often interpreted as indicating the morning sickness often associated with early pregnancy. Similarly, ambiguously described "procedures" during Nancy's visit to a doctor's office were recalled as relating to pregnancy tests. Similar interpretive distortions occurred in the subjects' recall of the other stimulus paragraphs. Such intrusions and distortions emanating from the interpretive framework suggested by the lead-in material were much more common in this condition than for those subjects who read only the five stimulus paragraphs. Thus, when information about a person is processed in terms of a particular schema, the information will be interpreted and its meaning determined according to the knowledge and beliefs contained in the schema. The schema will also be used as a basis for drawing further inferences and expanding upon the actual information available.

Influence of Schemas on Retrieval

We have seen that activation of a particular schema can influence what information about a stimulus person is encoded and how this information is interpreted. In addition, schemas can influence what information is retrieved from memory and how this information is interpreted in the retrieval process. This influence is clearly demonstrated in a study by Snyder and Uranowitz (1978). Subjects read a lengthy case history describing events in the life of a woman named Betty K. The narrative portrayed Betty's life historically, describing her childhood, her homelife and her relationship with her parents, her social life in high school and college, her education, and her choice of a career. All subjects read the identical case history. Three groups of subjects were then established by information provided after they had read this material. Some of the subjects were told that Betty was currently living a lesbian life-style, others learned that she was living a heterosexual life-style, and the third group learned nothing at all about her current life-style. The effect of this manipulation on subjects' recall of factual information about Betty's life was then assessed, using a questionnaire that asked factual questions about actual events in Betty's life. The subjects' newly acquired knowledge about Betty's sexual life-style had a substantial influence on their asnwers to these questions. Subjects who had learned that Betty was living a lesbian life-style "remembered" various events in her life in a manner consistent with their stereotypic schemas about lesbians, whereas those who had learned that she was living a heterosexual life-style recalled these same events in a different manner. Thus, information which made a particular schema salient influenced the retrieval of information about various aspects of the person's life.

We have seen, then, that schemas can influence the way in which a perceiver will encode, organize,

store, and reconstruct or retrieve information about another person. The studies described in this section again portray the perceiver as an active contributor to the overall person perception process. Schemas represent the perceiver's previously acquired knowledge, beliefs, and expectations about personality and about the nature of social behavior. The nature of the perceiver's schemas will influence the way in which information about others is processed and hence will influence her perceptions of those persons.

IMPRESSION FORMATION

When we meet a stranger for the first time, we begin to form an impression of him almost immediately. To be sure, such an initial impression may be tentative. Nevertheless, very early in our interactions with a person we develop a sense of whether we like or dislike him, and some conception of the person's personality begins to emerge. In this section we will discuss the nature of this impression formation process. This research has focused on two questions: (1) How do we organize and integrate the diverse items of information available about a person into an overall impression? (2) How is this information combined in making judgments about the person?

Development of First Impressions

Research on impression formation began with a classic paper published in the 1940s by Solomon Asch (1946). Asch, whose thinking reflected the tenets of Gestalt psychology, believed that an impression of a person is an organized, integrated conception of the person's personality. One forms an impression of the whole person; that is, the person is seen as an integrated unit, not as a composite of several parts. An impression is not a collection of individual pieces of information that one accumulates about another person. Rather, the items of information interact with each other and become integrated into a total picture of the person. Because of this interaction among the elements contributing to an impression, the meaning of any given piece of information—its role or its function within the overall impression—depends on the context of other information of which it is a part. Thus, the same trait attribute may mean different things in different persons, because other information known about the person may result in differing interpretations of the meaning of the trait. For example, in a person who is "intelligent," "insightful," and "clever," the attribute "clever" may imply that this person is creative and sees new solutions to problems. In contrast, in a person who is "devious," "untrustworthy," and "clever," the attribute "clever" may have quite different connotations, implying that this person is selfish and manipulative. Thus, the meaning of any item of information will be determined in part by the other information known about the person. Finally, Asch argued that certain aspects of the information known about a person are central to the resulting impression. He referred to these components as "central traits" to indicate the large influence that they have on the overall impression.

Asch's views (1946) on the nature of impressions and how they develop are intuitively appealing and have stimulated considerable research. Some of his hypotheses and observations have received empirical support, while others have been opened to alternative interpretations. In this section on impression formation we will discuss some of the issues that have been investigated, the research strategies that have been employed, and some of the findings that have accumulated as a result of this effort.

Asch (1946) developed a very simply methodology for studying the impression formation process empirically. He presented a list of traits which supposedly described a person, and asked subjects to form an impression of the person. He then had subjects complete two tasks. First, he had them write a paragraph describing their impression of the stimulus person. Second, he gave them a list of 40 trait adjectives and asked them to place a check mark next to the attributes which they believed described the stimulus person. By systematically varying certain aspects of the trait list, Asch could determine the influence of such manipulations on the impressions formed by the subjects.

In perhaps his best-known experiment, Asch (1946) sought to demonstrate that the attributes "warm" and "cold" had the status of central traits in the development of an impression. In this study two groups of subjects were given a list of trait attributes which described a hypothetical stimulus person. For one group, the stimulus person was described as

being "intelligent, skillful, industrious, warm, determined, practical, and cautious." The stimulus list was the same for the other group, except that the attribute "cold" was substituted for "warm." Asch found that the two groups of subjects formed quite different impressions of the stimulus person. The paragraphs describing their impressions were dramatically different in these two conditions, as was the pattern of trait adjectives that subjects checked as being characteristic of the stimulus person. For example, the "warm" stimulus person was more likely to be considered good-natured and popular, while the "cold" person was perceived as irritable, moody, and unsociable. Thus, the manipulation of the "warm-cold" variable within the stimulus list had a substantial impact on the subjects' impression. To demonstrate that not all attributes qualify as "central" traits, Asch repeated this experiment using the same trait list in the stimulus descriptions but substituting "polite" and "blunt" for "warm" and "cold." In this case, the impressions formed by the two groups were quite similar, indicating that the manipulation of "polite" versus "blunt" in these stimulus descriptions had relatively little impact. Thus, Asch argued that certain central traits can constitute the core or organizational focus of the impressions we develop of another person.

An important aspect of Asch's theoretical ideas about the impression formation process is the notion that the impression becomes organized through the interaction of the traits. According to Asch, the meaning of an item of information will be influenced by the meaning of the perceiver's other information about the person. Asch attempted to demonstrate this process in the following way. To one group of subjects he read the following description of a hypothetical person: "intelligent, industrious, impulsive, critical, stubborn, and envious." To another group of subjects he read these same adjectives, presenting them in the reverse order. In the first case, the series of adjectives begins with highly desirable characteristics and proceeds to characteristics which are less desirable. In the second case the evaluative sequence of traits is just the opposite. If our impressions are based solely on objective information available about a person, then impressions of Asch's hypothetical person should be the same, since the identical adjectives were presented to both groups. However, as Asch predicted, the impressions formed by the two groups of subjects were strikingly different. Subjects in the first group had a much more favorable impression of the stimulus person than did subjects in the second group. Asch explained this finding in terms of the influence of the early information of the interpretation of items appearing later in the list. The first few items "set the tone" for the developing impression and influenced the perceived connotations of the later information. Thus, the order in which information is presented can have a substantial influence on the impression formed. A *primacy effect* occurs when the information appearing early in the sequence has a greater effect on the final impression than does later information. A *recency effect* occurs when the information presented late in the sequence has greater influence on the resulting impression. Such order effects are commonly found in studies of impression formation.

Asch's interpretation of order effects rests on the assumption that the meaning of a particular trait will be influenced by the context of other information about the person. Information we learn about another person is often open to alternative interpretations. For example, to say that a person is "daring" could imply that he is courageous and willing to take risks, or that he is reckless and unconcerned with safety. Similarly, to describe a person as "proud" may imply that she is confident and poised, or that she is conceited and egotistical. Asch contended that the interpretation of the trait will be a function of the other information known to be true of the person. Support for this hypothesis has been obtained in several studies (Wyer, 1974; Zanna & Hamilton, 1977). Individual facts that we learn about a person, and the inferences we make from these facts, do not remain isolated from each other but are organized into an integrated impression of the person.

Information Integration in Judgments of Others

A second line of research on impression formation processes has been concerned not with how information about a person becomes cognitively organized but with how the perceiver combines the information in making a judgment about the person. Suppose you knew that a person was trustworthy, friendly, witty, and lazy, and you were asked how much you would like this person. To answer this

question, you would have to combine several different items of information into a single judgment. The process by which perceivers integrate several disparate pieces of information into a single judgment has been the topic of considerable research.

Several researchers have proposed that simple mathematical models can be used to predict such judgments. Most prominent among these scientists has been Norman Anderson, who argues that our judgments of liking for others can be predicted from the average of our evaluations of each of the individual traits describing a person. According to this approach, each item of information known about a person has a *scale value*, which reflects its position on the dimension on which the judgment will be made. For example, in judging one's liking for another person, each trait item would have a scale value reflecting the trait's likableness. Consider the person described above as trustworthy, friendly, witty, and lazy. Assume that there is a 10-point scale of likability, such that the higher the scale value the more likable the trait. In this example highly likable attributes such as trustworthy and friendly might have scale values of 9, witty might have a value of 7, and an undesirable characteristic such as lazy might have a value of 3. Anderson proposes that your liking for this person can be predicted from an average of the scale values of these individual traits. That is,

$$\frac{9 + 9 + 7 + 3}{4} = 7$$

Suppose now that you are asked to judge your liking for a second person who is described as intelligent, outspoken, moody, and dogmatic. Assume that these traits have scale values of 9, 5, 4, and 2, respectively, on the likability scale. The average of these scale values is 5. This averaging process would predict that your liking for the first person would be higher than your liking for the second person. If we presented a variety of such stimulus persons to a sample of subjects and obtained their ratings of each person, the degree of congruence between the model's predictions and the obtained judgments could be determined. In this way the adequacy of the model could be evaluated.

Models of this kind are quite simple, both mathematically and in terms of the processes they represent. Nevertheless, such models have been quite useful in generating a considerable amount of research on the judgment process. In particular, a substantial number of studies have shown an averaging model to be quite successful in predicting judgments of this kind (cf. Anderson, 1974).

Differential Weighting of Information

The examples given thus far have assumed that each stimulus item was of equal importance to the perceiver in making a likableness judgment. That is, in determining the predicted values from a particular model, the scale values of the individual items have simply been averaged or summed. It is clear, however, that in any judgment some kinds of information will be more important than others. Consider again the trustworthy, friendly, witty, and lazy person we have already described. How important is it for your judgment that the person is lazy? If you were considering how much you would like this person as a potential roommate, laziness would be considerably less important than the knowledge that the person is trustworthy, friendly, and witty. On the other hand, if you were judging how much you would like this person as a co-worker on an important project, the fact of laziness might be of paramount importance. Thus, the weight given to this attribute would differ in the two judgment contexts. The *weight* attached to a stimulus item reflects the importance of the attribute for the particular judgment being made. Several variables have been found to influence the manner in which perceivers differentially weight stimulus information in the judgment process—such as the amount of negative information (it counts more heavily than positive information), the order in which information is received (early items count more), the uniqueness of the information, and its salience for the judgment being made.

ATTRIBUTION PROCESSES

In discussing implicit personality theories earlier in this chapter, we pointed out that as perceivers we have intuitive conceptions about the nature and organization of personality, and that these conceptions provide the basis for our expectations and inferences regarding which traits and characteristics are likely to "go together" in the personalities of others. In this sense we are all informal personality theorists.

The conceptual ideas and research to be discussed in this section also assume that perceivers function as informal theorists. Rather than focusing on the organization of personality characteristics, we will consider the perceiver as a theorist who attempts to explain causes of behavior. The underlying premise is that when a perceiver observes another person engage in some action, she will attempt to determine why the person behaved in that way. Perceivers are like intuitive psychologists (Ross, 1977) in that they attempt to understand the causes of the behavior they observe. Of course, perceivers do not undertake this task systematically; and in many cases their judgments regarding the causes of a behavior are made with little, if any, conscious thought. Like many other judgments, attributions of causality may become routine and fairly automatic.

Why would the perceiver be concerned with understanding the causes of the behaviors she observes? Here again, the perceiver as intuitive theorist is similar to the formal theorist. An important purpose for both is to be able to predict the behavior of other persons. To the extent that we can understand the causes of a person's behavior—why the person responded in a particular way in a particular situation—our ability to predict his future behavior in similar situations will be increased.

Theories of Attribution Processes

Heider's Naive Psychology While most empirical research on attribution processes has been conducted within the last ten years, Fritz Heider was writing on the topic over 35 years ago (Heider, 1944), and his *The Psychology of Interpersonal Relations* (Heider, 1958) was perhaps the single most important impetus to the development of this research area.

Heider's theorizing is often referred to as "naive psychology" because of its emphasis on the phenomenology of the perceiver in his attempt to understand the causes of behavior. Heider begins with the perceiver's perception of some action performed by another person; he then considers the inferences the perceiver would make in analyzing the possible causes of the person's behavior. Heider makes a fundamental distinction between two classes of forces which influence behavioral outcomes—personal forces and environmental forces. *Personal forces* are characteristics of the actor which will influence his performance of some behavior, such as his ability and his motivation to complete a task. *External forces* are environmental factors (such as the degree of difficulty of a task) which can facilitate or inhibit the completion of some behavior. Heider argues that in the naive analysis of causality, the perceiver attempts to assess the strength of these factors. Heider refers to one important consideration as the *perception of can*. Here the perceiver attempts to determine whether the actor has sufficient ability to perform the task, given its difficulty; hence the perception of can concerns the relationship between a personal force and an environmental force. A person's effective completion of the performance implies that her ability level was adequate for that task. The extent to which this fact has important implications for the actor's ability is a function of the task difficulty. If the task were extremely difficult, then its successful completion would be highly informative about the actor's ability. In contrast, successful performance of a task which almost anyone could easily do would provide little basis for strong attributions regarding the person's ability. Under such easy conditions, failure to complete the task would be more informative about the actor's ability.

Ability alone, however, is not sufficient for the successful completion of a task. Therefore, a second consideration noted by Heider is the *perception of trying;* this is the person's motivation to complete the task and, according to Heider, involves two components: intention and exertion. The perception of trying involves inferring the actor's intent to perform the action and the amount of effort she invests in the behavior. If either ability or trying are absent, then the person is unlikely to successfully complete the task. Successful performance, on the other hand, requires the presence of both; hence, observation of such behavior provides the perceiver with the basis for making inferences about several dispositional variables, namely, the person's ability, intentions, and effort.

Suppose that you observe a person successfully complete the task of changing a tire on a car. In Heider's view, the perceiver's naive analysis of causality begins with the assessment of can and of trying. Successful performance by the actor provides the basis for the perceiver's inference of sufficient ability, given the level of task difficulty: The actor has the skill to change a tire. Ability alone, however, is not sufficient to explain an actor's performance

of this behavior. A person may have the ability to change a tire, but choose not to do so. Consequently, understanding the person's behavior also involves an analysis of her motivation, or the perception of trying. Since successful performance is seen as requiring both sufficient ability and motivation, the actor's completing the job of changing the tire provides the basis for inferring that she intended to perform the behavior and was willing to expend some effort in doing so.

Failure to complete a task, on the other hand, may be due to a number of possible causes. In this case, the perceiver's assessment of can may lead him to infer that the task is a difficult one (changing a tire does require some knowledge and a moderate amount of strength), which the actor did not have the ability to perform (perhaps she never learned how to change a tire). If the task is not seen as overly difficult, the perceiver may infer either that the actor did not intend to perform the task or that she did intend to but was unwilling to expend the necessary effort.

Exactly how the perceiver resolves this question and attributes causality to one or another factor has important implications. As we noted at the outset, the purpose of conducting this causal analysis, according to Heider, is to facilitate the perceiver's ability to anticipate and predict the future behavior of the actor. To the extent that the person's behavior is attributed to personal forces (abilities, dispositions, intentions, motives), the perceiver has inferred characteristics of the actor which, if valid, would increase his ability to anticipate the actor's behavior in similar situations. On the other hand, if the actor's behavior is attributed to environmental forces, the behavior will be seen as caused by situational conditions which may or may not arise in the future, and hence will be less informative regarding likely future behavior. Thus, Heider states that the perceiver conducting this intuitive analysis will be oriented towards identifying personal or dispositional characteristics which will facilitate prediction of the actor's future behavior.

Kelley's Covariation Model of Attribution As just noted, one of Heider's important insights was the distinction between internal attributions—in which an actor's behavior is explained in terms of her dispositional characteristics—and external attributions—in which situational influences are perceived as causing the actor's behavior. Harold Kelley (1967) has proposed a theory to account for how the perceiver uses relevant information in making an attribution as to whether an observed behavior was internally or externally caused. Kelley proposed that in making attributions the perceiver looks for *covariation* between possible causes and the observed effect. That is, he seeks regularities so that when a particular causal condition is present, the behavior occurs; and when that condition is absent, the behavior does not occur. Kelley identified three kinds of information the perceiver may examine in performing this analysis: (1) *entities,* or the stimulus objects towards which the behavior is directed; (2) *persons;* and (3) *time and modality,* or the various occasions and situations in which the behavior may have occurred.

Suppose that our friend Bob tells us that he enjoyed a wonderful meal at Alfredo's Italian Restaurant. What may we infer from this statement? Should we interpret it as reflecting a characteristic of Bob, that he likes Italian restaurants? Or should we attribute Bob's enjoyment to an external cause and infer that Alfredo's is a particularly good Italian restaurant? Kelley suggests that in making such attributions, a perceiver will determine the extent to which the behavior of interest—enjoying a dinner in a restaurant—covaries with each of the three kinds of information noted above.

First, we may consider Bob's reaction to similar entities, that is, the extent to which he has enjoyed dinner in other Italian restaurants. If Bob raves about dinner every time he goes to an Italian restaurant, we may infer that he loves Italian food no matter where or how it's cooked. He'd enjoy Mario's microwave pizza just as much as Alfredo's veal marsala! On the other hand, if Bob has not had this reaction after eating in other restaurants, his behavior is distinctive to the meal he had at Alfredo's. Kelley refers to the extent to which a person's response is distinctive to a particular entity as *distinctiveness information.* Second, we may think about other times Bob has eaten at Alfredo's restaurant. That is, when he has eaten at Alfredo's in the past, has he also enjoyed the meal on those occasions, or was last night the first night he has reacted in this way? Kelley calls this *consistency information,* as it refers to the consistency of the same actor's behavior to the same entity across time.

Third, we may consider the behavior of other persons in response to the same entity. Have other people we know who have eaten at Alfredo's Italian Restaurant also enjoyed their meals there? If no one else has had the same reaction as Bob, then this behavior is idiosyncratic to Bob. On the other hand, if everyone enjoys their meals at Alfredo's, we may infer that it is indeed a good restaurant. This Kelley refers to as *consensus information.* According to Kelley's model, the perceiver analyzes and integrates these three kinds of information in making causal attributions.

McArthur (1972) conducted an experiment to test these ideas. Subjects read a series of simple descriptions of hypothetical events. For each event, McArthur provided information regarding the distinctiveness, consistency, and consensus aspects of the behavior. One stimulus event consisted of the statement "John laughed at the comedian." Following this statement, three additional statements conveyed either high or low distinctiveness, high or low consistency, and high or low consensus information. For example, high distinctiveness was conveyed by the statement "John doesn't laugh at most other comedians." That is, John's behavior was distinctive to this comedian. Low distinctiveness was conveyed by the statement "John almost always laughs at comedians." Similarly, high or low consistency information was conveyed by the statement that "In the past John has almost always laughed at this comedian" or "In the past John has almost never laughed at this comedian." Finally, consensus information informed the subjects of how other persons reacted to this comedian. High consensus was conveyed by the statement "everyone else laughed at the comedian," whereas low consensus information was conveyed by the statement "hardly anyone else laughed."

After subjects had read these statements, they were asked to indicate on rating scales the likely cause or reason for the event described in the stimulus item. They rated the extent to which the response or behavior was due to something about the actor (an internal or dispositional attribution) and the extent to which the behavior was due to something about the stimulus entity (an external or situational attribution).

McArthur found that person or dispositional attributions were most likely to be made under conditions of low distinctiveness (John laughs at almost any comedian), high consistency (John has almost always laughed at this comedian in the past), and low consensus (almost no one else laughed at this comedian). A situational attribution (the comedian caused John to laugh) was most likely to occur when all three types of information were high. That is, if John does not laugh at most comedians (high distinctiveness), if he almost always laughs at this comedian (high consistency), and if everyone laughed at this comedian (high consensus), the information suggests that this is indeed a good comedian. In this case, the perceiver has little basis for making inferences about John, but understands John's behavior as being due to the good performance of the comedian.

So far, we have discussed the three types of information—distinctiveness, consistency, and consensus—as if they were equally important in determining a perceiver's causal attributions. In fact, some kinds of information may have more impact than others. For example, one might intuitively suspect consensus information to be particularly influential, since it provides information about how a number of people have responded in the same situation and thus reveals whether the actor conforms to or deviates from the typical response of most people in the situation. Using the data from her experiment, McArthur (1972) was able to determine the relative importance of each of the three kinds of information for making causal attributions. She found that distinctiveness information was the most important, while (in contrast to the intuitive hypothesis I just made) consensus information had the least impact on attributional judgments. Why consensus information should be "underused" by perceivers is unclear at this point, but it is interesting to note that of the three types of information, consensus information is the only one that does not focus on the actor. In other words, consensus information deals with the context in which the actor's behavior occurred. It tells us not about John, but about how others reacted to the same stimulus entity John was responding to. In contrast, distinctiveness and consistency information both provide information about the actor's behavior. This finding suggests that perceivers who are making attributional judgments may be more influenced by information about the actor than by information about the context in which the actor's behavior took place. This theme will reappear later in our discussion of attribution processes.[1]

[1]Another influential model for understanding these phenomena, "corespondent inference theory," has been developed by E. E. Jones and his colleagues (Jones & Davis, 1965). For a discussion of this model, see pp. 206–208 of the chapter from which this reading was excerpted.

Causal Attributions of Actors and Observers

In some of the research discussed above, we have encountered evidence that perceivers may be more heavily influenced by information about a person's behavior than by information about the situational conditions under which the behavior occurred. This tendency was evident in McArthur's study (1972), where information about the target person's behavior (distinctiveness and consistency information) was more influential than information about how others had responded in the same situation (consensus information). Numerous other studies have found evidence for the same tendency. In fact, the tendency to overattribute behavior to personal rather than situational causes is so pervasive that Ross (1977) has referred to it as the "fundamental attribution error."

Jones and Nisbett have proposed an intriguing qualification (1972) of this general tendency. They hypothesize that the bias towards overattributing behavior to dispositional causes is characteristic of observers, but not of the actor who performed the behavior. Specifically, Jones and Nisbett postulate that observers will tend to attribute an actor's behavior to her dispositional characteristics, but actors will tend to explain their own behavior in terms of situational causes. To cite one of Jones and Nisbett's examples, consider the case of a student who is doing poorly in a course. How is this behavior "explained" by the student and by his professor? The professor, noting the student's poor performance on tests, quizzes, and papers, would probably interpret this behavior as reflecting the student's modest level of ability and/or lack of motivation to achieve. Thus, another person's behavior is explained in terms of relatively stable dispositional characteristics. The student, on the other hand, would view his performance as a consequence of several situational factors with which he has had to contend—the fact that he has several difficult courses this term, his uncertainty regarding the choice of a major and his career goals, the emotional turmoil emanating from an uncertain romantic relationship, and so on. Who is right? This question is difficult, if not impossible, to answer. The important point is that both the professor and the student will believe their interpretations are correct, despite their widely divergent attributions.

The differing attributional tendencies of actors and observers was demonstrated in a study by Nisbett, Caputo, Legant, and Marecek (1973). These researchers had subjects make attributions about themselves and about several other persons (father, best friend, admired acquaintance, and Walter Cronkite) on a variety of trait characteristics. For each characteristic, subjects were to indicate which of three descriptions best described the stimulus person: a trait term (such as "dignified"), its polar opposite (such as "casual"), or the phrase "depends on the situation." The results showed that subjects made fewer trait attributions about themselves than about other people. That is, subjects consistently ascribed trait characteristics to others, but used the "depends on the situation" category more frequently in describing themselves.

Why do actors and observers have such divergent perceptions of the causes of behavior? Jones and Nisoett (1972) offer several suggestions. In several respects, actors and observers may have different kinds of information available to them. For example, an observer may be unaware of the actor's internal states at the time of the behavior. An unkind, sarcastic remark may be a result of stress which the actor is experiencing at the time. The observer may be unaware of this emotional component of the actor's behavior and be more inclined to construe the behavior as representative of the actor's nature. Similarly. the observer may not have access to the actor's intentions at a particular time. The sarcastic remark may be an uncontrolled outburst, or it may be an intentional act of hostility. If the observer infers intentions from observed behavior, she would be inclined to make dispositional attributions about the actor's personality. Additionally, the observer may not have access to the antecedent conditions which precipitated the observed behavior. If the observer has just arrived on the scene, she may not realize that the actor's sarcastic remark was a response to an insult just received from another person. Finally, the observer may have relatively little access to historical information of which the actor is quite aware. For example, the actor is familiar with his own personal history and may realize that he is rarely ever sarcastic. The observer, to the degree that she is unfamiliar with the actor's usual behavior, will not realize that his behavior is uncharacteristic and may assume that such behavior is typical. If so, she may be led to make a dispositional inference. In other words, the actor interprets his own behavior in the context of his knowledge of himself and his behavior over time and across many circumstances. In contrast, the observer interprets the actor's behavior in the context of her knowledge or expectations about how others would behave in the same circumstance. Each of these differences in the information available to actors and observers leads to the same consequence: The observer is more likely than the actor to view the behavior as representative of the actor's typical behavior patterns, and consequently will be more inclined to make dispositional attributions.

The most interesting hypothesis offered by Jones and Nisbett (1972), however, concerns differences not in *what* information is available, but in *how* actors and observers process this information. Actors and observers differ in their perceptual orientation when they view a behavioral act, so that different aspects of the stimulus field are salient to each group. And, Jones and Nisbett argue, information that is salient will influence the attributions made. This point has been succinctly stated by Nisbett et al. (1973):

> The actor's attention at the moment of action is focussed on the situational cues—the environmental attractions, repulsions, and constraints—with which his behavior is coordinated. It therefore appears to the actor that his behavior is a response to these cues, that is, caused by them. For the observer, however, it is not the situational cues that are salient but the behavior of the actor. In Gestalt terms, action is the figure against the ground of the situation. The observer is therefore more likely to perceive the actor's behavior as a manifestation of the actor and to perceive the cause of behavior to be a trait or quality inherent in the actor. (p. 154)

Nisbett et al.'s results (1973) demonstrated the differences in attributions made by actors and observers, but the process underlying their results is not clear. Most of the research stimulated by Jones and Nisbett's actor-observer hypothesis has focused on the second, or perspective, basis of these divergent attributions. A series of clever and interesting studies have given the hypothesis considerable support. In these experiments, the general strategy has been to alter the perspective, or perceptual orientation, of actors and/or observers, and to determine whether corresponding differences in attributions occur. In one study, Storms (1973) reversed the perspective of actors and observers by showing them videotapes presenting the other perspective. Thus, actors were shown a videotape of their own behavior, and observers were shown a videotape focusing on the situational cues to which the actor was responding. Under these conditions, actors attributed their behavior to dispositional causes more than did the observers.

In another study, Regan and Totten (1975) induced some of their observers to adopt the perspective of actors by instructing them to empathize with an actor whom they observed. Subjects in this experiment watched a videotape of a conversation between two persons who were presumably having a get-acquainted conversation. Half of the subjects were simply instructed to watch the videotape and were told that some questions would be asked about one of the participants at the end of the tape. The other half of the subjects were additionally instructed to empathize with one of the persons shown on the tape. The latter instructions told the subject to imagine how the target person feels and to think about her reactions during the conversation.

Regan and Totten hypothesized that if empathizing with another person involves "taking the role of the other" and adopting her phenomenological perspective, then observers given these instructions should be more attentive to the situational cues to which the target person is responding. If Jones and Nisbett's perspective hypothesis is correct, these subjects should attribute the target person's behavior more to situational factors and less to dispositional characteristics than should observers who were not given the empathy instructions. Regan and Totten's results supported this hypothesis.

In our discussion of attribution theories and some of the research stimulated by them, we have been concerned with the process of how people interpret and explain social behavior. From the evidence gathered it is clear that people arriving at such causal attributions do not engage in a thorough analysis of the various possible explanations for an event, and they often fail to consider aspects of the available information which are relevant to such judgments. Instead, people appear to search for a sufficient explanation, even though it may not be the best explanation. Evidence of this effect is seen in subjects' tendency to underuse information about how other people respond in the same situation as the actor (McArthur, 1972); in subjects' tendencies to overattribute the causes of a person's behavior to his dispositional characteristics, even when explanations in terms of powerful situational forces are readily available (Jones & Harris, 1967); and in the tendency for subjects' attributions to be heavily influenced by prominent aspects of the visual field (Taylor & Fiske, 1975). Although we began by noting that the perceiver and the psychologist have a common interest in explaining the causes of behavior, their similarity may not extend considerably beyond this shared goal. The perceiver has no obligation to search for the correct explanation, to go beyond what seems obvious, and to consider alternative possibilities. Indeed, in arriving at a sufficient explanation for behavior, the perceiver will often attribute causal influence to that aspect of the stimulus field which, for one reason or another, is most salient to her.

SUMMARY

The study of person perception is concerned with the way in which perceivers process and interpret information they acquire about others, how they form impressions and make judgments about others, and how they explain the behavior of others.

As perceivers, we have well-developed concepts and expectations about the nature of personality, and these cognitive structures influence the interpretation and meaning of the information we acquire about others. Perceivers have implicit personality theories which permit them to go beyond the actual information known about a person and to infer other characteristics that are likely to be true of the person also. Research has shown that these implicit personality theories can influence perceiver's judgments of others, and some evidence suggests that they may reflect the perceiver's own personalities and past experiences. More recently, research on schemas has shown that the perceiver's cognitive structures can influence the encoding, organization, interpretation, and retrieval of information acquired about another person.

The study of impression formation has been concerned with how the perceiver organizes and integrates information about another person into a coherent impression of that person. Much of this research has focused on how the perceiver combines that information in making judgments about the person. Studies have shown that not all information available will be regarded as equally important by the perceiver. Some items of information will be given more weight than others, including the first imformation learned about a person, negative information, unique information, and information whose content is highly relevant to the judgment being made.

Attribution theories assume that perceivers seek to understand the causes of behavior in order to be able to predict the behavior of others in the future. Consequently, research in this area has been concerned with variables influencing the perceiver's judgment regarding the causes of a person's behavior. An important distinction has been made between attributions to internal causes (in which a person's behavior is explained in terms of his dispositional characteristics) and attributions to external causes (in which the behavior is explained as being due to situational influences). Research evidence indicates that perceivers have a pervasive tendency to overattribute the behavior of others to internal causes and to make inferences about a person's dispositional characteristics. In contrast, in explaining their own behavior, persons tend to make situational attributions, viewing that behavior as responsive to external influences.

REFERENCES

Anderson, N. H. Information integration theory: A brief survey. In D. H. Krantz, R. C. Atkinson, R. D. Luce, & P. Suppes (Eds.), *Contemporary developments in mathematical psychology.* San Francisco: Freeman, 1974.

Asch, S. Forming impressions of personality. *Journal of Abnormal and Social Psychology,* 1946, **41,** 258–290.

Berscheid, E., & Walster, E. Physical attractiveness. In L. Berkowitz (Ed.), *Advances in experimental social psychology,* Vol. 7. New York: Academic Press, 1974.

Bower, G. "On injecting life into deadly prose": Studies in explanation-seeking. Paper presented at Western Psychological Association Convention, Seattle, Washington, 1977.

Bruner, J. S., & Tagiuri, R. Person perception. In G. Lindsey (Ed.), *Handbook of social psychology,* Vol. 2. Reading, Mass.: Addison-Wesley, 1954.

Cantor, N., & Mischel, W. Traits as prototypes: Effects on recognition memory. *Journal of Personality and Social Psychology,* 1977, **35,** 38–48.

Dornbusch, S. M., Hastorf, A. H., Richardson, S. A., Muzzy, R. E., & Vreeland, R. S. The perceiver and the perceived: Their relative influence on the categories of interpersonal cognition. *Journal of Personality and Social Psychology,* 1965, **1,** 434–440.

Duncan, B. L. Differential social perception and attribution of intergroup violence: Testing the lower limits of stereotyping of blacks. *Journal of Personality and Social Psychology,* 1976, **34,** 590–598.

Hamilton, D. L., Katz, L. B., & Leirer, V. O. Organizational processes in impression formation. In R. Hastie, T. M. Ostrom, E. B. Ebbesen, R. S. Wyer, D. L. Hamilton, & D. E. Carlston (Eds.), *Person memory: The cognitive basis of social perception.* Hillsdale, N.J.: Lawrence Erlbaum Associates, in press.

Heider, F. Social perception and phenomenal causality. *Psychological Review,* 1944, **51,** 358–374.

———. *The psychology of interpersonal relations.* New York: Wiley, 1958.

Jones, E. E., & Davis, K. E. A theory of correspondent inferences: From acts to dispositions. In L. Berkowitz (Ed.), *Advances in experimental social psychology,* Vol. 2. New York: Academic Press, 1965.

———, & Harris, V. A. The attribution of attitudes. *Journal of Experimental Social Psychology,* 1967, **3,** 1–24.

———, & Nisbett, R. E. The actor and the observer: Divergent perceptions of the causes of behavior. In E. E. Jones, D. E. Kanouse, H. H. Kelley, R. E. Nisbett, S. Valins, & B. Weiner (Eds.), *Attribution: Perceiving the causes of behavior.* Morristown, N.J.: General Learning Press, 1972.

Kelley, H. H. Attribution theory in social psychology. In D. Levine (Ed.), *Nebraska symposium on motivation.* Lincoln: University of Nebraska Press, 1967.

McArthur, L. A. The how and what of why: Some determinants and consequences of causal attribution. *Journal of Personality and Social Psychology,* 1972, **22,** 171–193.

Nisbett, R. E., Caputo, C., Legant, P., & Marecek, J. Behavior as seen by the actor and as seen by the observer. *Journal of Personality and Social Psychology,* 1973, **27,** 154–164.

Regan, D. T., & Totten, J. Empathy and attribution: Turning observers into actors. *Journal of Personality and Social Psychology,* 1975, **32,** 850–856.

Ross, L. The intuitive psychologist and his shortcomings: Distortions in the attribution process. In L. Berkowitz (Ed.), *Advances in experimental social psychology,* Vol. 10. New York: Academic Press, 1977.

Storms, M. D. Videotape and the attribution process:

Reversing actors' and observers' points of view. *Journal of Personality and Social Psychology,* 1973, **27,** 165–175.

Taylor, S. E., & Fiske, S. T. Point of view and perceptions of causality. *Journal of Personality and Social Psychology,* 1975, **32,** 439–445.

Wyer, R. S. Changes in meaning and halo effects in personality impression formation. *Journal of Personality and Social Psychology,* 1974, **29,** 829–835.

Zadney, J., & Gerard, H. B. Attributed intentions and informational selectivity. *Journal of Experimental Social Psychology,* 1974, **10,** 34–52.

Zanna, M. P., & Hamilton, D. L. Further evidence for meaning change in impression formation. *Journal of Experimental Social Psychology,* 1977, **13,** 224–238.

Reading 5

Enactment and Organizing

Karl E. Weick

The essence of enactment is found in these three exhibits:

1 "Experience is not what happens to a man. It is what a man does with what happens to him" (Huxley, cited in Auden and Kronenberger 1966, p. 54).

2 "Our so-called limitations, I believe,
Apply to faculties we don't apply.
We don't discover what we can't achieve
Until we make an effort not to try"
(Hein 1968, p. 33).

3 Imagine that you are playing a game of charades, and that you must act out the title of a movie. Imagine that you are given, as your title, the movie *Charade.* As the presenter, you probably would try somehow to get "outside" of the present game and point to it so that the observers would see that the answer is the very activity they are now engaged in. Alas, the observers are likely to miss this subtlety and instead to shout words like, "pointing," "finger," "excited," "all of this," and so forth.

One of the ironies in organizational analysis is that managers are described as "all business," "doers," "people of action," yet no one seems to understand much about the fine grain of their acting. "If we knew more about the normative theory of acting before you think, we could say more intelligent things about the function of management and leadership in organizations where organizations or societies do not know what they're doing" (March

and Olsen 1976, p. 79). This chapter is about acting that sets the stage for sense-making.

EXAMPLES OF ENACTMENT

The Enactment of Experience

There is no such thing as *experience* until the manager does something. Passive reception of a shower of inputs is not synonymous with having an experience (Simmel 1959). Experience is the consequence of activity. The manager literally wades into the swarm of "events" that surround him and actively tries to unrandomize them and impose some order. The manager acts physically in the environment, attends to some of it, ignores most of it, talks to other people about what they see and are doing (Brayorooke 1964). As a result the surroundings get sorted into variables and linkages and appear more orderly.

William James provides a vivid portrayal of what it takes to build an experience:

The world's contents are *given* to each of us in an order so foreign to our subjective interests that we can hardly by an effort of the imagination picture to ourselves what it is like. We have to break that order altogether, and by picking out from it the items that concern us, and connecting them with others far away, which we say "belong" with them, we are able to make out definite threads of sequence and tendency, to foresee particular liabilities and get ready for them, to enjoy simplicity and harmony in the place of what was chaos. . . . While I talk and the flies buzz, a seagull catches a fish at the mouth of the Amazon, a tree falls in the Adirondack wilderness, a man sneezes in Germany, a horse dies in Tartary, and twins are born in France. What does that mean? Does the contemporaneity of these events with each other and with a million more as disjointed as they form a rational bond between them, and unite them into anything that means for us a world? Yet just such a collateral contemporaneity, and nothing else, is the *real* order of the world. It is an order with which we have nothing to do but get away from it as fast as possible. As I said, we break it: we break it into histories, and we break it into arts, and we break it into sciences; and then we begin to feel at home. We make ten thousand separate serial orders of it. On any of these, we may react as if the rest did not exist. We discover among its parts relations that were never given to sense at all,— mathematical relations, tangents, squares, and roots and logarithmic functions,—and out of an infinite number of these we call certain ones essential and lawgiving, and ignore the rest. Essential these relations are, but only *for our purpose,* the other relations being just as real and present as they; and our purpose is to *conceive simply* and to *foresee* (James 1950, vol. 2, p. 635).

These statements summarize the nature of organizational sense-making. First of all, the chaos that is to be decomposed is both flowing and equivocal. People in organizations try to sort this chaos into items, events, and parts which are then connected, threaded into sequences, serially ordered, and related. The connections in which James is interested are those connections involving *sequence* and *tendency.* Sequence and tendency are the same sensible threads that occur in cause maps. Furthermore, the assertion that cause maps are inventions rather than discoveries is supported by James's point that when we create serial orders we often find relations that were never presented to the senses at all.

James also emphasizes that these sense-making efforts differ among people. This difference sets the stage for much activity that goes on in organizations: people spending time trying to make their views of the world more similar. What this means practically is that people negotiate over which nouns and verbs should be imposed on the flow and how those nouns and verbs are to be connected. Notice that if there is considerable difference among people's views of an organization, then the organization will be characterized by multiple realities and in all likelihood the resulting unit will appear to be loosely coupled since there is disagreement on what affects what.

James does not say how one knows whether an event is an antecedent or consequent, but this is not crucial because the labels *antecedent* and *consequent* are rather arbitrary distinctions, especially when variables exist in causal loops. Any variable can be either a cause or an effect, an antecedent or a consequent. It all depends on where you start and terminate a causal loop.

One of the nice things about James's remarks is that they are quite physical. Breaking an order, picking out items, connecting events all suggest sizable rearrangements of the displays that people face. If an individual breaks up chaos so that other forms of order can be created, then it stands to reason that what is eventually available for inspection is something very much of the individual's own making. And the act of breaking itself suggests isolating some portion of the flow of experience for closer attention, which is largely what enactment consists of.

The Enactment of Limitations

Perceptions of personal "limitations," in Piet Hein's view, turn out to be a failure *to act* rather than a failure *while acting.* Limitations are deceptive conclusions but, unfortunately, people don't realize this. What they don't realize is that limitations are based on presumptions rather than action. Knowledge of limitations is not based on tests of skills but rather on an *avoidance* of testing.

On the basis of avoided tests, people conclude that constraints exist in the environment and that limits exist in their repertoire of responses. Inaction is justified by the implantation, in fantasy, of constraints and barriers that make action "impossible." These constraints, barriers, prohibitions then become prominent "things" in the environment. They also become self-imposed restrictions on the options that managers consider and exercise when confronted with problems. Finally, these presumed constraints, when breached by someone who is more doubting, naive, or uninformed, often generate sizable advantages for the breacher.

As a laboratory exercise, Harold Garfinkel (1967) had some of his students go into a department store and offer a small fraction of the list price for some item. The students were apprehensive in advance about doing this, since an explicit rule presumed to exist in most American stores is that things must be bought for the list price. Much to their surprise, the students discovered that once they actually began to bargain for items, they were able to get rather substantial reductions in price. The interesting thing about the list price "rule" is that it seems to have force because everyone expects it to be followed and no one challenges it.

Even though organizations appear to be quite solid, in fact much of their substance may consist of spurious knowledge based on avoided tests. While Garfinkel does not formulate propositions about avoided tests, it *is* possible to speculate about the form such propositions would take. For example, implicit in his analysis is the suggestion that avoided tests may occur because people fear the experience of failure. Transformed into a proposition, it might be predicted that the greater the fear of failure, the greater the likelihood that a person's knowledge of the world is based on avoided tests.

Notice that if one were to fail while attempting a test, the results might or might not be reversible. In other words, a person might be able to undo the damage or might never be able to normalize the event. This suggests that the greater the difficulty of undoing an outcome, the more likely it is for a person to engage in avoided tests.

There appears to be a cognitive side to the avoidance of tests. So far it has been argued that immediate outcomes of pleasure or pain may control the choice to test or not. Notice, however, that there are subtleties in the interpretation of outcomes. If you go into a store, try to buy a 49-cent toothbrush for 40 cents, fail, and experience some embarrassment, you might interpret that outcome as one of those little stresses in life that "builds character." Thus, if individuals in organizations believe in such things as the cleansing power of suffering, the school of hard knocks, or the saneogenesis proposition that it is too little rather than too much stress that causes breakdown (Scher 1962), then those individuals will be more likely to attempt tests rather than to avoid them.

There is a parallel between avoided tests and the Ziergarnik Effect. An avoided test is like an unfinished task, especially if the person has wondered repeatedly whether a barrier is fictional or substantial. There is a distinct quality of unfinished business in avoided tests. This suggests that people should be more aware of their avoided tests than of their nonavoided tests.

Not very much is known about avoided tests, but it seems likely that they could be the basis for a substantial portion of the knowledge that organizations retain. The question of interest for organization epistemologists would be, "What precedes and is the occasion for an avoided versus an attempted test?"

A variation of the point that the ingenuous shall coopt the environment is the idea that people who seem backward historically are, in fact, privileged (Sahlins and Service 1960). Their privilege lies in the fact that they can benefit from the mistakes and oversights of pioneers. The "backward" group is able to leapfrog the pioneer and employ neglected actions to locate opportunities that prove beneficial. With both avoided tests and privileged backwardness it is inaction (a failure to enact) propped up by the fiction of constraints that erects trappings which, when treated irreverently, vanish abruptly.

Managers often know much less about their environments and organizations than they think. One reason for this imperfect knowing is that managers unwittingly collude among themselves to avoid tests. And they build elaborate explanations of why tests should be avoided, why one shouldn't/couldn't act within settings presumed to be dangerous. The disbeliever, the unindoctrinated, the newcomer, all wade in where avoiders fear to tread. Having waded in they find either that the avoider's fear is unfounded or that it is valid, in which case their demise provides vicarious learning for the avoiders.

The point is that the enormous amount of talk, socializing, consensus-building, and vicarious learning that goes on among managers often results in pluralistic ignorance (Shaw and Blum 1965) about the environment. Stunted enactment is the reason. Each person watches someone else avoid certain procedures, goals, activities, sentences, and pastimes and concludes that this avoidance is motivated by "real" noxiants in the environment. The observer profits from that "lesson" by himself then avoiding those acts and their presumed consequences. As this sequence of events continues to be repeated, managers conclude that they know more and more about something that none of them has actually experienced firsthand. This impression of knowing becomes strengthened because everyone seems to be seeing and avoiding the same things. And if everyone seems to agree on something, then it must exist and be true.

If people want to change their environment, they need to change themselves and their actions—not someone else. Repeated failures of organizations to solve their problems are partially explained by their failure to understand their own prominence in their own environments. Problems that never get solved, never get solved because managers keep tinkering with everything *but* what they do.

The Enactment of Charades

As the final example, Jencks and Silver (1973) provide a perfect description of charades when they call it an "acted out rebus." A rebus is a representation of original words or symbols by means of some other pictures or symbols that sound like the original. For example, ICURYY4me is a rebus for "I see you are too wise for me." Charades involve the same kind of representation. An object is symbolized by other objects that sound the same. According to Jencks and Silver, one of the all-time best (or worst?) solutions for a charade occurred when a person was given the name Salvador Dali and acted out the three words, "saliva," "tore," and "doily."

There are several interesting features of enactment in charades. The person doing the gesturing knows what he is perceived as enacting only after he hears the observers' guesses. That is, the actor produces a soliloquy, the punctuation of which is done by others. The actor produces an enacted environment as an output, but the observers are faced with a display that they can punctuate and connect in numerous ways. The actor imposes meanings on his environment that come back and organize his activities, except that the observers see these implanted meanings as puzzles rather than certainties. If the actor has enacted a puzzling or complicated or subtle environment, that enactment comes back and organizes him in the sense that he has to do enormous work to salvage, patch up, and redirect the observers' efforts to invent plausible constructions for his subtleties.

The image of a rebus is relevant for organizations because it captures the essence of enactment. People in organizations need to act to find out what they have done, and the person enacting a rebus needs to play out his version of the charade to see what he really is conveying to interested observers. The person acting out a charade enacts most of the environment for observers. And what we are arguing is that it isn't that much different in organizations. The environment that the organization worries over is put there by the organization.

Conclusion

The reciprocal linkage between ecological change and enactment in the organizing model is intended to depict the subjective origin of organizational realities (Israel 1972). People in organizations repeatedly impose that which they later claim imposes on them. Farmers with heavy tractors enact the packed earth (ecological change), which requires heavier tractors, more fuel, deeper plows, and/or wider tires to work. The presence of elaborate multitrack mixers in recording studios has compelled engineers to produce increasingly elaborate effects on recordings, which leads to demands for even more elaborate mixing equipment, and so on. Many listeners, however, have become fed up with this meddling and are now purchasing direct-to-disc music that bypasses the engineer, his busy hands, his passion for remixing, his elaborate technology, and his precious output (McDonough 1978). Nevertheless, engineers have enacted the environment of contrived music that now organizes and threatens to disorganize their jobs. Physicians, through nonsubtle diagnostic procedures ("hmmm, when did you start holding your head at that angle?"), often implant maladies that *weren't* there when the examination began. Their procedures consolidate numerous free-floating symptoms into the felt presence of a single, more specific, more serious problem. Physician-induced disease *(iatrogenics)* is a perfect example of people creating the environment that confronts them (Scheff 1965). Firemen on steam locomotives enacted the pattern of hot and cold spots within the boiler by their method of shoveling coal into it, which then constrained their subsequent attempts to preserve steam pressure (Withuhn 1975).

Examples like this are plentiful. The point is, much current work on the relationships between organizations and their environments tends to downplay the extent to which the boundaries between the two are blurred (Starbuck 1976, p. 1070) and the extent to which organizations produce their environments. In the remainder of this chapter we will try to remedy this imbalance.

CHARACTERISTICS OF ENACTMENT

Enactment as Bracketing

We have described enactment as a bracketing activity. To visualize what this means, imagine that the major input to be processed by employees is either a stock market tickertape with no spaces between symbols, or a teletype machine whose output contains no punctuation into sentences or paragraphs. In the unpunctuated output one does not know where one "story" leaves off and another story begins, or even whether a story is a reasonable unit of analysis. The same thing is true in the case of the unpunctuated stock market tickertape. In both cases there is a mass of data, without any hints concerning their importance. It's the job of the employee to tear off portions of the tickertape or teletype for further study. Those activities of tearing are crude kinds of enactments. Once something has been isolated, then that *is* the environment momentarily for the organization and that environment has been put into place by the very actions of the employees themselves.

To get a feeling for the phenomenon we're interested in, think back to times when you have read the verbatim protocol of some important speech. When these speeches are printed verbatim, the columns of type often continue uninterrupted without any indications of how the speech is structured. When a reader confronts this display of uninterrupted type he wonders such things as, "Where were the good parts?" "What was said that is new?" "What's different?" "What's surprising?" "What's the news?" As you read, these questions become frustrating because you basically have to decide for yourself what's new and different and good without any prompting from commentators. Confronted with an unpunctuated speech, you're in precisely the same position as an employee who confronts a flow of experience and has no one around to coach him on which are the good parts, the bad parts, the interesting parts, and the trivia. Those are all decisions involving bracketing.

When you pull out some portion of the text of the speech from its surrounding context, then the environment that you have bracketed for inspection is a different environment than the original one that contained intonations, facial expressions, and surrounding text. The reader of the extracted portion does see part of herself because her own interests influenced the process of extracting. And this is true whether those biases suggest that speeches are better at the end than at the beginning, or that paragraphs starting with personal pronouns are better than those that don't. The "chaos" of the speech transcript has been dealt with by breaking it into chunks, by ignoring portions of it, and by trying to figure out on the basis of the extracted chunk what kinds of decisions and situations on the part of the speaker would have generated those particular words (in other words, the bracketed portion is analyzed in terms of potential antecedents and consequences).

A suggestion of the way in which bracketing might operate is found in Neisser's (1976) recent discussion of the perceptual cycle. Neisser casts his discussion of perceptual cycles in terms of schemas used to aid interpretation. A schema is an abridged, generalized, corrigible organization of experience that serves as an initial frame of reference for action and perception. A schema is the belief in the phrase, "I'll see it when I believe it." Schemata constrain seeing and, therefore, serve to bracket portions of experience.

Neisser describes schemata as active, information-seeking structures that accept information and direct action. "The schema accepts information as it becomes available at sensory surfaces and is changed by that information; it directs movements and exploratory activities that make more information available, by which it is further modified" (Neisser 1976, p. 54). Neisser notes that schemata are analogous to things like formats in computer programing language, plans for finding out about objects and events, and genotypes that offer possibilities for development along certain general lines.

Examples of schemata in organizations are abundant. The most conspicuous example is the standard operating procedure (Allison 1971). A standard operating procedure is a schema that structures dealing with an environment. A standard operating procedure is a frame of reference that constrains exploration and often unfolds like a self-fulfilling prophecy (Martin 1977). The standard operating procedures direct attention toward restricted aspects of an object that, when sampled, seemingly justify routine application of the procedure.

Janis's (1972) description of groupthink has overtones of schema theory. The phenomenon of groupthink is important because it demonstrates some of the dysfunctional consequences when people are dominated by a single schema and this domination becomes self-reinforcing. Having become true believers of a specific schema, group members direct their attention toward an environment and sample it in such a way that the true belief becomes self-validating and the group becomes even more fervent in its attachment to the schema. What is underestimated is the degree to which the direction and sampling are becoming increasingly narrow under the influence of growing consensus and enthusiasm for the restricted set of beliefs. As Janis demonstrates, this spiral is frequently associated with serious misjudgments of situations.

Notice that any idea that restricts exploration and sampling will come to be seen as increasingly plausible by the very nature of that restriction. If a person has an idea and looks for "relevant" data, there's enough complexity and ambiguity in the world that relevance is usually found and the idea is usually judged more plausible.

Actors with bounded rationality presumably are more interested in confirming their schemata than in actively trying to disprove them. Even though people may build up schema anew each time they apply the schemata, they have to start this buildup with something. And it's that something, that assumption, that retrieved portion of the past, that can rather swiftly become elaborated into a schema that is like a previous schema and that has a controlling effect on what people perceive.

Enactment as Deviation Amplification

Minor disturbances, when they are embedded in a deviation-amplifying loop, can grow into major happenings with major consequences. When it is argued that organizations enact their environments, some readers may assume that these enactments have always been present on about the scale they now exhibit. That implication is not intended. The modest origins of consequential enactments are illustrated by efforts to desegregate the schools in San Francisco (Weiner 1976).

In trying to figure out how desegregation should be implemented in San Francisco, a Citizens Advisory Committee consisting of 67 citizens was appointed by the board of education. Over time this committee became increasingly influential in deciding how the desegregation order would be implement-

ed. The fascinating point for our analyses is the differential frequency with which these 67 people attended meetings.

The committee began its deliberations on February 16, 1971, and concluded them on June 2, 1971. During this time they held 70 meetings, or approximately one meeting every two days. This implies the obvious point that all members could not attend all meetings. This minor difference in participation rates soon became amplified:

> Deadlines led to a domination of the decision making process by middle and upper class white women, who had available time during the day because they were not employed and could arrange care for their children, and by other participants whose employers permitted them to devote daytime hours to the decision making process (Weiner 1976, pp. 234–35).

As a result, black members of the committee did not participate actively in developing the desegregation plan. But the issue here is not just one of time. There is the further issue of differential competence produced by differential attendance:

> As high participation rates continue the most active members become a relatively small group possessing a near monopoly position concerning the competencies required in decision making. The joint operation of these factors constitutes a positive feedback loop where activity causes greater competence and greater competence leads to increased activity. . . . Thus, one effect associated with the sharply increased participation rates by some participants in the choice is that the most active participants gain a much higher share of the competence and experience necessary to deal with the remaining problems. As they become substantially more competent it becomes more difficult for other potential participants to gain access to the decision making process (Weiner 1976, p. 247).

Weiner labels this phenomenon the *competence multiplier*. The participants who show up repeatedly produce an environment of sophisticated analyses that requires more participation from them, which makes them even more informed to deal with the issues that are presented. A vicious circle is created in which the regular participants of the advisory council enact the very sophisticated and subtle issues that their new-found competence enables them to deal with. People who attend less often feel less informed, increasingly unable to catch up, and more reluctant to enter the conversation at the level of sophistication voiced by the persistent participants. The relatively less informed people select themselves out of the decision-making process, and this elevates the level of desegregation planning to an even more detailed and complicated level where even fewer people can comprehend it. Over time the combination of high and low participation rates, a minor deviation in the beginning, changes the issues, plans, and environment that confronts the Citizens Advisory Committee.

The question of desegregation and how to implement it is not an external problem that is handed to the committee for its action. Instead, the issue that gets handed to them is an issue partly of their own making. The density of detail in the solution, the subtlety of the issues addressed, and the interests that are accommodated are all influenced by the patterns of participation at the meetings.

Once again we have a clear example of a deviation-amplifying loop. People with time to spend on a problem transformed that problem into something that only people with time to spend on the problem can manage. The resulting discussion is one from which infrequent attendees become more and more alienated because they understand fewer of its intricacies. Thus the mundane activity of simply showing up at meetings generates an environment that only those who show up at meetings are able to manage and control. Several iterations through the cycle are necessary for this consequence to occur, but again, its plausibility is evident and its relevance to enactment processes should be apparent.

Enactment as Self-fulfilling Prophecies

Enactment could be described as efferent sensemaking. The modifier *efferent* means centrifugal or conducted outward. The person's idea is extended outward, implanted, and then rediscovered as knowledge. The discovery, however, originated in a prior invention by the discoverer. In a crude but literal sense, one could talk about efferent sensemaking as thinking in circles.

A self-fulfilling prophecy involves

> behavior that brings about in others the reaction to which the behavior would be an appropriate reaction. For instance, a person who acts on the premise that "nobody likes me" will behave in a distrustful, stiff,

defensive, or aggressive manner to which others are likely to react unsympathetically, thus bearing out his original premise. What is typical about this sequence and makes it a problem of punctuation is that the individual concerned conceives of himself only as reacting to, but not as provoking, those attitudes (Watzlawick, Beavin, and Jackson 1967, pp. 98–99).

When managers confront equivocality and try to reduce it, they too often operate on the presumption of logic (Meyer, 1956). They assume that their views of and actions toward the world are valid, they assume that other people in the organization will see and do the same things, and it is rare for the managers to check these assumptions. Having presumed that the environment is orderly and sensible, managers make efforts to impose order, thereby enacting the orderliness that is "discovered." The presumption of nonequivocality provides the occasion for managers to see and do those things that transform the environment into something that is unequivocal.

A particularly good experimental example of self-fulfilling prophecies obtained under carefully controlled conditions is the study by Kelley and Stahelski (1970) of differences in the style of interaction between cooperative and competitive individuals. The striking finding of this study is that a competitive person's anticipations of how other people will behave tend to have a self-fulfilling aura that transforms those other individuals, regardless of their preference for cooperation, into competitors.

People were put into a standard prisoners' dilemma game that resembled the game of chicken. "Chicken" derives its name from the game occasionally played by young drivers who, on a dare, race toward each other on a highway both straddling the center line in order to see who will "chicken out" first and give way to one side. Chicken involves basically two moves: pulling off the road (response Y), or not pulling off the road (response W). Whoever pulls off the road (Y) loses, but if neither pulls off, the outcomes are poor (see Figure 5-1). Each person's best response depends on what the other one does.

Before they started to play chicken, subjects were asked what they wanted to achieve in the relationship with their partner. Their choices were between a cooperative goal ("I will try to cooperate with the

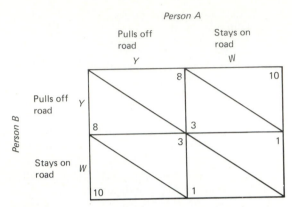

Figure 5-1

Expectations as to others orientations

	Cooperative			Competitive
Cooperative	X	X	X	X
		X	X	X
			X	X
Competitive				X

Figure 5-2 The triangle hypothesis. *(From Kelley and Stahelski, 1970, p. 77.)*

other player and will be concerned with my own score and the other player's score") or competitive ("I will work for myself against the other player and will be concerned only with my own score"). People were then paired off so that a cooperator was paired with a competitor, and the two people played for a series of trials. After several plays they were interrupted and asked to judge what the goals of their partner were. Errors in these judgments were rampant, and the most common error was the judgment by the competitor (the subject who chose the competitive goal) that his cooperative partner was also a competitor and had chosen a competitive goal. Essentially what happened during the game was that the competitor behaved in such a way that he shifted the cooperator's initial cooperative behavior toward his competitive style even though he didn't realize that *he* had caused his partner to do this.

On the basis of these studies it was suggested that competitive individuals tend to believe that other people are always competitive, whereas cooperative individuals believe that other people are heterogeneous and may be either cooperative or competitive. Kelley and Stahelski (1970) have represented this asymmetry in the form of a triangle hypothesis which is depicted in Figure 5-2.

The triangle hypothesis (Figure 5-2) simply summarizes the fact that cooperators and competitors develop different views of what other people are like. And in the case of competitors, their presumption that other individuals are universally competitive leads them to act in such a manner that they produce, in cooperative individuals, that competitiveness that they assume was there all along. The

competitive players simply don't see cooperative overtures in the beginning. Instead, they act in such a way that the cooperative players modify their efforts and become competitive, thereby fulfilling the original competitor's definition that all people are competitive.

The important point in this sequence of events is that there is a grain of truth to the competitor's sweeping assertion that everyone is competitive. What the competitor doesn't realize is that the grain of truth has been planted by personal actions, which produced the competitiveness in another individual who otherwise would have been cooperative. Thus, the competitor's claim that it's a dog-eat-dog world is a perfectly accurate reflection of what seems to have happened. But what the competitor underestimates is the extent to which he enacted that world.

The frequency with which self-fulfilling prophecies occur may be underestimated because of the inflated image implied by the phrase *self-fulfilling prophecy.* The image of a prophecy suggests something that is a major activity preceded by considerable fanfare and, consequently, rare. The more appropriate image would be that in everyday/anyday life people expect, anticipate, foresee, and make mundane predictions all the time. (For instance, I predict that when I turn the page there will be some print.)

Enactment as Social Construction of Reality

The concept of an *enacted environment* is not synonymous with the concept of a *perceived environment,* even though citations of the concept would suggest that it is. If a perceived environment were the essence of enactment then, as Lou Pondy suggested, the phenomenon would have been called enthinkment, not enactment.

We have purposely labeled the organizational equivalent of variation en*act*ment to emphasize that managers construct, rearrange, single out, and demolish many "objective" features of their surroundings. When people act they unrandomize variables, insert vestiges of orderliness, and literally create their own constraints. This holds true whether those constraints are created in fantasy to justify avoided tests or created in actuality to explain tangible bruises (Simmel 1959).

People have talked for some time about the fact that reality is constructed, stressing that reality is selectively perceived, rearranged cognitively, and negotiated interpersonally. In most cases it is assumed that something tangible is the target of these efforts and that what is required to locate this target is that one be clever enough to choose both a good partner and a good procedure to uncover this underlying order. Analyses of the social construction of reality emphasize that actors attain at least a partial consensus on the meaning of their behavior and that they look for patterns that underlie appearances, actions, events. These patterns are assumed to have an existence independent of the interpretation procedures (e.g., Goffman 1974, pp. 1–2; Gonos 1977).

A more extreme position is that the social order exists precariously and has no existence at all independent of the members' accounting and describing practices. The organizing model is based on the view that order is imposed rather than discovered, on the grounds that action defines cognition. The basic sense-making device used within organizations is assumed to be talking to discover thinking. How can I know what I think until I see what I say? In that sequence, the action of talking is the occasion for defining and articulating cognitions. When it is argued that organizational members spend much of their time uttering soliloquies, we are describing a crucial feature of enactment. The soliloquies are action soliloquies because it is action that leads and defines cognition. G. W. Bateson uses a similar image: "an explorer can never know what he is exploring until it has been explored" (1972, p. xvi).

The notion that reality is a product of social construction does have some connotation of action conveyed by the word *construction*. But this construction is usually thought to involve activities of negotiation between people as to what is out there. Less prominent in these analyses is the idea that people, often alone, actively *put* things out there

that they then perceive and negotiate about perceiving. It is that initial implanting of reality that is preserved by the word *enactment*.

Concepts such as the negotiated environment and the social construction of reality share a presumption that knowledge is acquired with the flow going from an object to a subject:

$$Object \longrightarrow Subject$$

The object is perceived, worked on cognitively, variously labeled, and coupled with various remote or distal events. Less attention is given to the possibility that understanding also moves in the opposite direction:

$$Object \longleftarrow Subject$$

The potential effect of the subject on the object signifies that knowledge is an activity in which the subject partly interacts with and constitutes the object (Gruber and Vonèche 1977). There is a reciprocal influence between subjects and objects, not a one-sided influence such as is implied by the idea that a stimulus triggers a response. This reciprocal influence is captured in the organizing model by the two-way influence between enactment and ecological change.

Another distinguishing feature of the enacted environment is that it is treated as an output of organizations, not as an input. Conventional treatments of the perceived environment argue that it is current personal definitions of the situation, not a material world, that influences the organization.

The enacted environment, being an output of organizing activities, is in some ways an anachronistic, dated, belated stimulus. The enacted environment is a sensible rendering of previous events stored in the form of causal assertions, and made binding on some current enactment and/or selection. There is a definite time lag and a definite tinge of retrospect to the definitions of the situation that are taken seriously within the organizing model.

CONCLUSION

The enactment perspective implies that people in organizations should be more self-conscious about and spend more time reflecting on the actual things they *do*. If people imagine that the environment is separate from the organization and lies out there to be scanned so that effective responses can be produced, then they will spend their resources outfitting themselves with the equivalents of high-powered binoculars to improve acuity. If people recognize that they create many of their own environments, then all of that effort to improve acuity is irrelevant. The organization concerned about its own enactment needs to discover ways to partial out the effects of its own interventions from effects that would have happened had the observer never obtruded in the situation in the first place. An organization that is sensitive to the fact that it produces enacted environments will be less concerned with issues of truth and falsity and more concerned with issues of reasonableness. If environments are enacted then there is no such thing as a representation that is true or false, there simply are versions that are more and less reasonable. Thus, endless discussion of questions about whether we see things the way they really are, whether we are right, or whether something is true will be replaced by discussions that focus on questions such as What did we do? What senses can we make of those actions? What didn't we do? What next step best preserves our options and does least damage to our repertoire? What do these bruises mean? How did we ruin that equipment?

REFERENCES

Allison, G. T. *Essence of decision: Explaining the Cuban missile crisis.* Boston: Little, Brown, 1971.

Auden, W. H., & Kronenberger, L. *The Viking book of aphorisms.* New York: Viking, 1966.

Bateson, G. W. *Steps to an ecology of mind.* New York: Ballantine, 1972.

Braybrooke, D. The mystery of executive success reexamined. *Administrative Science Quarterly,* 1964, **8,** 533–560.

Garfinkel, H. *Studies in ethnomethodology.* Englewood Cliffs, N.J.: Prentice-Hall, 1967.

Goffman, E. *Frame analysis.* New York: Harper & Row, 1974.

Gonos, G. "Situation" versus "frame": The "interactionist" and the "structuralist" analyses of everyday life. *American Sociological Review,* 1977, **42,** 854–867.

Gruber, H. E., & Voneche, J. J. (Eds.), *The essential Piaget.* New York: Basic Books, 1977.

Hein, P. *Grooks II.* Cambridge, Mass.: M.I.T. Press (Borgens Billigboger), 1968.

Israel, J. Stipulations and construction in the social sciences. In J. Israel and H. Tajfel (Eds.), *The context of social psychology.* New York: Academic, 1972.

James, W. *The principles of psychology,* Vols. 1 and 2. New York: Dover, 1950.

Janis, I. R. *Victims of groupthink.* Boston: Houghton Mifflin, 1972.

Jencks, C., & Silver, N. *Adhocism.* Garden City, N.Y.: Doubleday, Anchor Books, 1973.

Kelley, H. H., & Stahelski, A. J. Social interaction basis of cooperators' and competitors' beliefs about others. *Journal of Personality and Social Psychology,* 1970, **16,** 66–91.

McDonough, J. Review of The King James Version by Harry James. *Downbeat,* June 15, 1978, 28–29.

March, J. G., & Olsen, J. P. *Ambiguity and choice in organizations.* Bergen, Norway: Universitetsforlaget, 1976.

Martin, M. The philosophical importance of the Rosenthal effect. *Journal for the Theory of Social Behavior,* 1977, **7,** 81–97.

Meyer, L. B. *Emotion and meaning in music.* Chicago: University of Chicago Press, 1956.

Neisser, U. *Cognition and reality.* San Francisco: Freeman, 1976.

Sahlins, M. D., & Service, E. R. (Eds.), *Evolution and culture.* Ann Arbor: University of Michigan Press, 1960.

Scheff, T. J. Decision rules, types of error, and their consequences in medical diagnosis. In F. Massarik and P. Ratoosh (Eds.), *Mathematical explorations in behavioral science.* Homewood, Ill.: Dorsey, 1965.

Scher, J. M. Mind as participation. In J. M. Scher (Ed.), *Theories of the mind.* New York: Free Press, 1962.

Shaw, M. E., & Blum, J. M. Group performance as a function of task difficulty and the group's awareness of member satisfaction. *Journal of Applied Psychology,* 1965, **49,** 151–154.

Simmel, G. On the nature of philosophy. In K. H. Wolff (Ed.), *Essays on sociology, philosophy, and aesthetics.* New York: Harper, 1959.

Starbuck, W. H. Organizations and their environments. In M. D. Dunnette (Ed.), *Handbook of industrial and organizational psychology.* Chicago: Rand McNally, 1976.

Watzlawick, P., Beavin, J. H., & Jackson, D. D. *Pragmatics of human communication.* New York: Norton, 1967.

Weiner, S. S. Participation, deadlines, and choice. In J. G. March and J. P. Olsen (Eds.), *Ambiguity and choice in organizations.* Bergen, Norway: Universitetsforlaget, 1976.

Withuhn, B. A primer for coal shovelers. *Trainline,* Spring 1975, **6,** 5–6.

Reading 6

Motivation: A Diagnostic Approach

David A. Nadler
Edward E. Lawler III

What makes some people work hard while others do as little as possible?

How can I, as a manager, influence the performance of people who work for me?

Why do people turn over, show up late to work, and miss work entirely?

These important questions about employees' behavior can only be answered by managers who have a grasp of what motivates people. Specifically, a good understanding of motivation can serve as a valuable tool for *understanding* the causes of behavior in organizations, for *predicting* the effects of any managerial action, and for *directing* behavior so that organizational and individual goals can be achieved.

EXISTING APPROACHES

During the past twenty years, managers have been bombarded with a number of different approaches to motivation. The terms associated with these approaches are well known—"human relations," "scientific management," "job enrichment," "need hierarchy," "self-actualization," etc. Each of these approaches has something to offer. On the other hand, each of these different approaches also has its problems in both theory and practice. Running through almost all of the approaches with which managers are familiar are a series of implicit but clearly erroneous assumptions.

Assumption 1: All Employees Are Alike
Different theories present different ways of looking at people, but each of them assumes that all employees are basically similar in their makeup: Employees all want economic gains, or all want a pleasant climate, or all aspire to be self-actualizing, etc.

Assumption 2: All Situations Are Alike Most theories assume that all managerial situations are

alike, and that the managerial course of action for motivation (for example, participation, job enlargement, etc.) is applicable in all situations.

Assumption 3: One Best Way Out of the other two assumptions there emerges a basic principle that there is "one best way" to motivate employees.

When these "one best way" approaches are tried in the "correct" situation they will work. However, all of them are bound to fail in some situations. They are therefore not adequate managerial tools.

A NEW APPROACH

During the past ten years, a great deal of research has been done on a new approach to looking at motivation. This approach, frequently called "expectancy theory," still needs further testing, refining, and extending. However, enough is known that many behavioral scientists have concluded that it represents the most comprehensive, valid, and useful approach to understanding motivation. Further, it is apparent that it is a very useful tool for understanding motivation in organizations.

The theory is based on a number of specific assumptions about the causes of behavior in organizations.

Assumption 1: Behavior Is Determined by a Combination of Forces in the Individual and Forces in the Environment Neither the individual nor the environment alone determines behavior. Individuals come into organizations with certain "psychological baggage." They have past experiences and a developmental history which has given them unique sets of needs, ways of looking at the world, and expectations about how organizations will treat them. These all influence how individuals respond to their work environment. The work environment provides structures (such as a pay system or a supervisor) which influence the behavior of people. Different environments tend to produce different behavior in similar people just as dissimilar people tend to behave differently in similar environments.

Assumption 2: People Make Decisions about Their Own Behavior in Organizations While there are many constraints on the behavior of individuals in organizations, most of the behavior that is observed is the result of individuals' conscious decisions. These decisions usually fall into two categories. First, individuals make decisions about *membership behavior*—coming to work, staying at work, and in other ways being a member of the organization. Second, individuals make decisions about the amount of *effort* they will direct *towards performing their jobs*. This includes decisions about how hard to work, how much to produce, at what quality, etc.

Assumption 3: Different People Have Different Types of Needs, Desires and Goals Individuals differ on what kinds of outcomes (or rewards) they desire. These differences are not random; they can be examined systematically by an understanding of the differences in the strength of individuals' needs.

Assumption 4: People Make Decisions among Alternative Plans of Behavior Based on Their Perceptions (Expectancies) of the Degree to Which a Given Behavior will Lead to Desired Outcomes In simple terms, people tend to do those things which they see as leading to outcomes (which can also be called "rewards") they desire and avoid doing those things they see as leading to outcomes that are not desired.

In general, the approach used here views people as having their own needs and mental maps of what the world is like. They use these maps to make decisions about how they will behave, behaving in those ways which their mental maps indicate will lead to outcomes that will satisfy their needs. Therefore, they are inherently neither motivated nor unmotivated; motivation depends on the situation they are in, and how it fits their needs.

THE THEORY

Based on these general assumptions, expectancy theory states a number of propositions about the process by which people make decisions about their own behavior in organizational settings. While the

theory is complex at first view, it is in fact made of a series of fairly straightforward observations about behavior. (The theory is presented in more technical terms in Appendix A.) Three concepts serve as the key building blocks of the theory:

Performance-Outcome Expectancy Every behavior has associated with it, in an individual's mind, certain outcomes (rewards or punishments). In other words, the individual believes or expects that if he or she behaves in a certain way, he or she will get certain things.

Examples of expectancies can easily be described. An individual may have an expectancy that if he produces ten units he will receive his normal hourly rate while if he produces fifteen units he will receive his hourly pay rate plus a bonus. Similarly an individual may believe that certain levels of performance will lead to approval or disapproval from members of her work group or from her supervisor. Each performance can be seen as leading to a number of different kinds of outcomes and outcomes can differ in their types.

Valence Each outcome has a "valence" (value, worth, attractiveness) to a specific individual. Outcomes have different valences for different individuals. This comes about because valences result from individual needs and perceptions, which differ because they in turn reflect other factors in the individual's life.

For example, some individuals may value an opportunity for promotion or advancement because of their needs for achievement or power, while others may not want to be promoted and leave their current work group because of needs for affiliation with others. Similarly, a fringe benefit such as a pension plan may have great valence for an older worker but little valence for a young employee on his first job.

Effort-Performance Expectancy Each behavior also has associated with it in the individual's mind a certain expectancy or probability of success. This expectancy represents the individual's perception of how hard it will be to achieve such behavior and the probability of his or her successful achievement of that behavior.

For example, you may have a strong expectancy

that if you put forth the effort, you can produce ten units an hour, but that you have only a fifty-fifty chance of producing fifteen units an hour if you try.

Putting these concepts together, it is possible to make a basic statement about motivation. In general, the motivation to attempt to behave in a certain way is greatest when:

a The individual believes that the behavior will lead to outcomes (performance-outcome expectancy)
b The individual believes that these outcomes have positive value for him or her (valence)
c The individual believes that he or she is able to perform at the desired level (effort-performance expectancy)

Given a number of alternative levels of behavior (ten, fifteen, and twenty units of production per hour, for example) the individual will choose that level of performance which has the greatest motivational force associated with it, as indicated by the expectancies, outcomes, and valences.

In other words, when faced with choices about behavior, the individual goes through a process of considering questions such as, "Can I perform at that level if I try?" "If I perform at that level, what will happen?" "How do I feel about those things that will happen?" The individual then decides to behave in that way which seems to have the best chance of producing positive, desired outcomes.

A General Model

On the basis of these concepts, it is possible to construct a general model of behavior in organizational settings (see Figure 6-1). Working from left to right in the model, motivation is seen as the force on the individual to expend effort. Motivation leads to an observed level of effort by the individual. Effort, alone, however, is not enough. Performance results from a combination of the effort that an individual puts forth *and* the level of ability which he or she has (reflecting skills, training, information, etc.). Effort thus combines with ability to produce a given level of performance. As a result of performance, the individual attains certain outcomes. The model indicates this relationship in a dotted line, reflecting the fact that sometimes people perform but do not get desired outcomes. As this process of performance-reward occurs, time after time, the actual events serve to provide information which influences the individual's perceptions (particularly expectancies) and thus influences motivation in the future.

Outcomes, or rewards, fall into two major categories. First, the individual obtains outcomes from the environment. When an individual performs at a given level he or she can receive positive or negative outcomes from supervisors, co-workers, the organization's rewards systems, or other sources. These environmental rewards are thus one source of outcomes for the individual. A second source of outcomes is the individual. These include outcomes

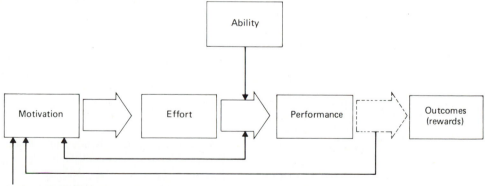

A person's motivation is a function of:

a. Effort-to-performance expectancies
b. Performance-to-outcome expectancies
c. Perceived valence of outcomes

Figure 6-1 The basic motivation-behavior sequence.

which occur purely from the performance of the task itself (feelings of accomplishment, personal worth, achievement, etc.). In a sense, the individual gives these rewards to himself or herself. The environment cannot give them or take them away directly; it can only make them possible.

Supporting Evidence

Over fifty studies have been done to test the validity of the expectancy-theory approach to predicting employee behavior.[1] Almost without exception, the studies have confirmed the predictions of the theory. As the theory predicts, the best performers in organizations tend to see a strong relationship between performing their jobs well and receiving rewards they value. In addition they have clear performance goals and feel they can perform well. Similarly, studies using the expectancy theory to predict how people choose jobs also show that individuals tend to interview for and actually take those jobs which they feel will provide the rewards they value. One study, for example, was able to correctly predict for 80 percent of the people studied which of several jobs they would take.[2] Finally, the theory correctly predicts that beliefs about the outcomes associated with performance (expectancies) will be better predictors of performance than will feelings of job satisfaction since expectancies are the critical causes of performance and satisfaction is not.

Questions about the Model

Although the results so far have been encouraging, they also indicate some problems with the model. These problems do not critically affect the managerial implications of the model, but they should be noted. The model is based on the assumption that individuals make very rational decisions after a thorough exploration of all the available alternatives and on weighing the possible outcomes of all these alternatives. When we talk or observe individuals, however, we find that their decision processes are frequently less thorough. People often stop considering alternative behavior plans when they find one that is at least moderately satisfying, even though more rewarding plans remain to be examined.

People are also limited in the amount of information they can handle at one time, and therefore the model may indicate a process that is much more complex than the one that actually takes place. On the other hand, the model does provide enough information and is consistent enough with reality to present some clear implications for managers who are concerned with the question of how to motivate the people who work for them.

Implications for Managers

The first set of implications is directed towards the individual manager who has a group of people working for him or her and is concerned with how to motivate good performance. Since behavior is a result of forces both in the person and in the environment, you as manager need to look at and diagnose both the person and the environment. Specifically, you need to do the following:

Figure Out What Outcomes Each Employee Values As a first step, it is important to determine what kinds of outcomes or rewards have valence for your employees. For each employee you need to determine "what turns him or her on." There are various ways of finding this out, including (a) finding out employees' desires through some structured method of data collection, such as a questionnaire, (b) observing the employees' reactions to different situations or rewards, or (c) the fairly simple act of asking them what kinds of rewards they want, what kind of career goals they have, or "what's in it for them." It is important to stress here that it is very difficult to change what people want, but fairly easy to find out what they want. Thus, the skillful manager emphasizes diagnosis of needs, not changing the individuals themselves.

Determine What Kinds of Behavior You Desire Managers frequently talk about "good performance" without really defining what good performance is. An important step in motivating is for you yourself to figure out what kinds of performances are required and what are adequate measures or indicators of performance (quantity, quality, etc.). There is also a need to be able to define those performances in fairly specific terms so that observ-

[1]For reviews of the expectancy theory research see Mitchell, T. R. Expectancy models of job satisfaction, occupational preference and effort: A theoretical methodological, and empirical appraisal. *Psychological Bulletin,* 1974, **81,** 1053–1077. For a more general discussion of expectancy theory and other approaches to motivation see Lawler, E. E. *Motivation in work organizations,* Belmont, Calif.: Brooks/Cole, 1973.

[2]Lawler, E. E., Kuleck, W. J., Rhode, J. G. & Sorenson, J. E. Job choice and post-decision dissonance. *Organizational Behavior and Human Performance,* 1975, **13,** 133–145.

able and measurable behavior can be defined and subordinates can understand what is desired of them (e.g., produce ten products of a certain quality standard—rather than only produce at a high rate).

Make Sure Desired Levels of Performance are Reachable The model states that motivation is determined not only by the performance-to-outcome expectancy, but also by the effort-to-performance expectancy. The implication of this is that the levels of performance which are set as the points at which individuals receive desired outcomes must be reachable or attainable by these individuals. If the employees feel that the level of performance required to get a reward is higher than they can reasonably achieve, then their motivation to perform well will be relatively low.

Link Desired Outcomes to Desired Performances The next step is to directly, clearly, and explicitly link those outcomes desired by employees to the specific performances desired by you. If your employee values external rewards, then the emphasis should be on the rewards systems concerned with promotion, pay, and approval. While the linking of these rewards can be initiated through your making statements to your employees, it is extremely important that employees see a clear example of the reward process working in a fairly short period of time if the motivating "expectancies" are to be created in the employees' minds. The linking must be done by some concrete public acts, in addition to statements of intent.

If your employee values internal rewards (e.g., achievement), then you should concentrate on changing the nature of the person's job, for he or she is likely to respond well to such things as increased autonomy, feedback, and challenge, because these things will lead to a situation where good job performance is inherently rewarding. The best way to check on the adequacy of the internal and external reward system is to ask people what their perceptions of the situation are. Remember it is the perceptions of people that determine their motivation, not reality. It doesn't matter for example whether you feel a subordinate's pay is related to his or her performance. Motivation will be present only if the subordinate sees the relationship. Many managers are misled about the behavior of their subordinates because they rely on their own perceptions of

the situation and forget to find out what their subordinates feel. There is only one way to do this: ask. Questionnaires can be used here, as can personal interviews. (See Appendix B for a short version of a motivation questionnaire.)

Analyze the Total Situation for Conflicting Expectancies Having set up positive expectancies for employees, you then need to look at the entire situation to see if other factors (informal work groups, other managers, the organization's reward systems) have set up conflicting expectancies in the minds of the employees. Motivation will only be high when people see a number of rewards associated with good performance and few negative outcomes. Again, you can often gather this kind of information by asking your subordinates. If there are major conflicts, you need to make adjustments, either in your own performance and reward structure, or in the other sources of rewards or punishments in the environment.

Make Sure Changes in Outcomes Are Large Enough In examining the motivational system, it is important to make sure that changes in outcomes or rewards are large enough to motivate significant behavior. Trivial rewards will result in trivial amounts of effort and thus trivial improvement in performance. Rewards must be large enough to motivate individuals to put forth the effort required to bring about significant changes in performance.

Check the System for Its Equity The model is based on the idea that individuals are different and therefore different rewards will need to be used to motivate different individuals. On the other hand, for a motivational system to work it must be a fair one—one that has equity (not equality). Good performers should see that they get more desired rewards than do poor performers, and others in the system should see that also. Equity should not be confused with a system of equality where all are rewarded equally, with no regard to their performance. A system of equality is guaranteed to produce low motivation.

Implications for Organizations

Expectancy theory has some clear messages for those who run large organizations. It suggests how organizational structures can be designed so that they increase rather than decrease levels of motivation of organization members. While there are many different implications, a few of the major ones are as follows:

Implication 1: The Design of Pay and Reward Systems Organizations usually get what they reward, not what they want. This can be seen in many situations, and pay systems are a good example.[3] Frequently, organizations reward people for membership (through pay tied to seniority, for example) rather than for performance. Little wonder that what the organization gets is behavior oriented towards "safe," secure employment rather than effort directed at performing well. In addition, even where organizations do pay for performance as a motivational device, they frequently negate the motivational value of the system by keeping pay secret, therefore preventing people from observing the pay-to-performance relationship that would serve to create positive, clear, and strong performance-to-reward expectancies. The implication is that organizations should put more effort into rewarding people (through pay, promotion, better job opportunities, etc.) for the performances which are desired, and that to keep these rewards secret is clearly self-defeating. In addition, it underscores the importance of the frequently ignored performance evaluation or appraisal process and the need to evaluate people based on how they perform clearly defined specific behaviors, rather than on how they score on ratings of general traits such as "honesty," "cleanliness," and other, similar terms which frequently appear as part of the performance appraisal form.

Implication 2: The Design of Tasks, Jobs, and Roles One source of desired outcomes is the work itself. The expectancy-theory model supports much of the job enrichment literature, in saying that by designing jobs which enable people to get their needs fulfilled, organizations can bring about higher levels of motivation.[4] The major difference between the traditional approaches to job enlargement or enrichment and the expectancy-theory approach is the recognition by the expectancy theory that different people have different needs and, therefore, some people may not want enlarged or enriched jobs. Thus, while the design of tasks that have more autonomy, variety, feedback, meaningfulness, etc., will lead to higher motivation in some, the organization needs to build in the opportunity for individuals to make choices about the kind of work they will do so that not everyone is forced to experience job enrichment.

Implication 3: The Importance of Group Structures Groups, both formal and informal, are powerful and potent sources of desired outcomes for individuals. Groups can provide or withhold acceptance, approval, affection, skill training, needed information, assistance, etc. They are a powerful force in the total motivational environment of individuals. Several implications emerge from the importance of groups. First, organizations should consider the structuring of at least a portion of rewards around group performance rather than individual performance. This is particularly important where group members have to cooperate with each other to produce a group product or service, and where the individual's contribution is often hard to determine. Second, the organization needs to train managers to be aware of how groups can influence individual behavior and to be sensitive to the kinds of expectancies which informal groups set up and their conflict or consistency with the expectancies that the organization attempts to create.

Implication 4: The Supervisor's Role The immediate supervisor has an important role in creating, monitoring, and maintaining the expectancies and reward structures which will lead to good performance. The supervisor's role in the motivation process becomes one of defining clear goals, setting clear reward expectancies, and providing the right rewards for different people (which could include both organizational rewards and personal rewards such as recognition, approval, or support from the supervisor). Thus, organizations need to provide supervisors with an awareness of the nature of motivation as well as the tools (control over organizational rewards, skill in administering those rewards) to create positive motivation.

[3]For a detailed discussion of the implications of expectancy theory for pay and reward systems, see Lawler, E. E. *Pay and organizational effectiveness: A psychological view.* New York: McGraw-Hill, 1971.

[4]A good discussion of job design with an expectancy theory perspective is in Hackman, J. R., Oldham, G. R., Janson, R., & Purdy, K. A new strategy for job enrichment. *California Management Review,* Summer, 1975, p. 57.

Implication 5: Measuring Motivation If things like expectancies, the nature of the job, supervisor-controlled outcomes, satisfaction, etc., are important in understanding how well people are being motivated, then organizations need to monitor employee perceptions along these lines. One relatively cheap and reliable method of doing this is through standardized employee questionnaires. A number of organizations already use such techniques, surveying employees' perceptions and attitudes at regular intervals (ranging from once a month to once every year-and-a-half) using either standardized surveys or surveys developed specifically for the organization. Such information is useful both to the individual manager and to top management in assessing the state of human resources and the effectiveness of the organization's motivational systems.[5] (Again, see Appendix B for excerpts from a standardized survey.)

Implication 6: Individualizing Organizations
Expectancy theory leads to a final general implication about a possible future direction for the design of organizations. Because different people have different needs and therefore have different valences, effective motivation must come through the recognition that not all employees are alike and that organizations need to be flexible in order to accommodate individual differences. This implies the "building in" of choice for employees in many areas, such as reward systems, fringe benefits, job assignments, etc., where employees previously have had little say. A successful example of the building in of such choice can be seen in the experiments of

TRW and the Educational Testing Service with "cafeteria fringe-benefits plans" which allow employees to choose the fringe benefits they want, rather than taking the expensive and often unwanted benefits which the company frequently provides to everyone.[6]

SUMMARY

Expectancy theory provides a more complex model of man for managers to work with. At the same time, it is a model which holds promise for the more effective motivation of individuals and the more effective design of organizational systems. It implies, however, the need for more exacting and thorough diagnosis by the manager to determine (a) the relevant forces in the individual, and (b) the relevant forces in the environment, both of which combine to motivate different kinds of behavior. Following diagnosis, the model implies a need to act—to develop a system of pay, promotion, job assignments, group structures, supervision, etc.—to bring about effective motivation by providing different outcomes for different individuals.

Performance of individuals is a critical issue in making organizations work effectively. If a manager is to influence work behavior and performance, he or she must have an understanding of motivation and the factors which influence an individual's motivation to come to work, to work hard, and to work well. While simple models offer easy answers, it is the more complex models which seem to offer more promise. Managers can use models (like expectancy theory) to understand the nature of behavior and build more effective organizations.

---

[5]The use of questionnaires for understanding and changing organizational behavior is discussed in Nadler, D. A. *Feedback and organizational development: Using data-based methods.* Reading, Mass.: Addison-Wesley, 1977.

[6]The whole issue of individualizing organizations is examined in Lawler, E. E. The individualized organization: Problems and promise. *California Management Review,* 1974, **17**(2), 31–39.

APPENDIX A: The Expectancy Theory Model in More Technical Terms

A person's motivation to exert effort towards a specific level of performance is based on his or her perceptions of associations between actions and outcomes. The critical perceptions which contribute

to motivation are graphically presented in Figure 6-2. These perceptions can be defined as follows:

a The effort-to-performance expectancy ($E{\rightarrow}P$):

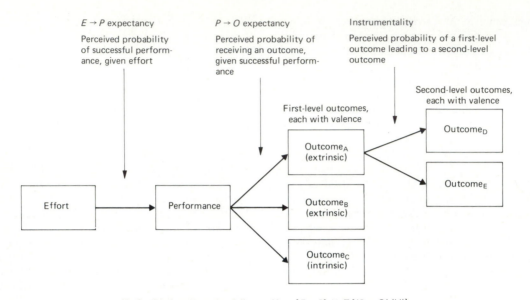

Motivation is expressed as follows: $M = [E \rightarrow P] \times \Sigma [(P \rightarrow O)(V)]$

Figure 6-2 Major terms in expectancy theory.

This refers to the person's subjective probability about the likelihood that he or she can perform at a given level, or that effort on his or her part will lead to successful performance. This term can be thought of as varying from 0 to 1. In general, the less likely a person feels that he or she can perform at a given level, the less likely he or she will be to try to perform at that level. A person's $E \rightarrow P$ probabilities are also strongly influenced by each situation and by previous experience in that and similar situations.

b The performance-to-outcomes expectancy ($P \rightarrow O$) and valence (V): This refers to a combination of a number of beliefs about what the outcomes of successful performance will be and the value or attractiveness of these outcomes to the individual. Valence is considered to vary from +1 (very desirable) to −1 (very undesirable) and the performance-to-outcomes probabilities vary from +1 (performance sure to lead to outcome) to 0 (performance not related to outcome). In general, the more likely a person feels that performance will lead to valent outcomes, the more likely he or she will be to try to perform at the required level.

c Instrumentality: As Figure 6-2 indicates, a single level of performance can be associated with a number of different outcomes, each having a certain degree of valence. Some outcomes are valent because they have direct value or attractiveness. Some

outcomes, however, have valence because they are seen as leading to (or being "instrumental" for) the attainment of other "second level" outcomes which have direct value or attractiveness.

d Intrinsic and extrinsic outcomes: Some outcomes are seen as occurring directly as a result of performing the task itself and are outcomes which the individual thus gives to himself (i.e., feelings of accomplishment, creativity, etc.). These are called "intrinsic" outcomes. Other outcomes that are associated with performance are provided or mediated by external factors (the organization, the supervisor, the work group, etc.). These outcomes are called "extrinsic" outcomes.

Along with the graphic representation of these terms presented in Figure 6-2, there is a simplified formula for combining these perceptions to arrive at a term expressing the relative level of motivation to exert effort towards performance at a given level. The formula expresses these relationships:

a The person's motivation to perform is determined by the $P \rightarrow O$ expectancy multiplied by the valence (V) of the outcome. The valence of the first order outcome subsumes the instrumentalities and valences of second order outcomes. The relationship is multiplicative since there is no motivation to perform if either of the terms is zero.

b Since a level of performance has multiple outcomes associated with it, the products of all probability-times-valence combinations are added together for all the outcomes that are seen as related to the specific performance.

c This term (the summed $P{\rightarrow}O$ expectancies times valences) is then multiplied by the $E{\rightarrow}P$ expectancy. Again the multiplicative relationship indicates that if either term is zero, motivation is zero.

d In summary, the strength of a person's motivation to perform effectively is influenced by (1) the person's belief that effort can be converted into performance, and (2) the net attractiveness of the events that are perceived to stem from good performance.

So far, all the terms have referred to the individual's perceptions which result in motivation and thus an intention to behave in a certain way. Figure 6-3 is a simplified representation of the total model, showing how these intentions get translated into actual behavior.[7] The model envisions the following sequence of events:

a First, the strength of a person's motivation to

[7]For a more detailed statement of the model see Lawler, E. E. Job attitudes and employee motivation: Theory, research and practice. *Personnel Psychology*, 1970, **23**, 223–237.

perform correctly is most directly reflected in his or her effort—how hard he or she works. This effort expenditure may or may not result in good performance, since at least two factors must be right if effort is to be converted into performance. First, the person must possess the necessary abilities in order to perform the job well. Unless both ability and effort are high, there cannot be good performance. A second factor is the person's perception of how his or her effort can best be converted into performance. It is assumed that this perception is learned by the individual on the basis of previous experience in similar situations. This "how to do it" perception can obviously vary widely in accuracy, and—where erroneous perceptions exist—performance is low even though effort or motivation may be high.

b Second, when performance occurs, certain amounts of outcomes are obtained by the individual. Intrinsic outcomes, not being mediated by outside forces, tend to occur regularly as a result of performance, while extrinsic outcomes may or may not accrue to the individual (indicated by the wavy line in the model).

c Third, as a result of the obtaining of outcomes and the perceptions of the relative value of the outcomes obtained, the individual has a positive or negative affective response (a level of satisfaction or dissatisfaction).

d Fourth, the model indicates that events which

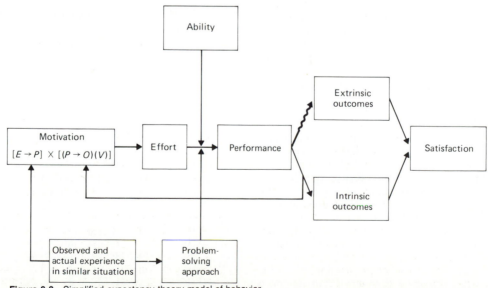

Figure 6-3 Simplified expectancy-theory model of behavior.

occur influence future behavior by altering the $E{\to}P$, $P{\to}O$, and V perceptions. This process is represented by the feedback loops running from actual behavior back to motivation.

APPENDIX B: Measuring Motivation Using Expectancy Theory

Expectancy theory suggests that it is useful to measure the attitudes individuals have in order to diagnose motivational problems. Such measurement helps the manager to understand why employees are motivated or not, what the strength of motivation is in different parts of the organization, and how effective different rewards are for motivating performance. A short version of a questionnaire used to measure motivation in organizations is included here.[8] Basically, three different questions need to be asked (see Tables 6-1, 6-2, and 6-3).

Using the Questionnaire Results

The results from this questionnaire can be used to calculate a *work-motivation score*. A score can be

[8]For a complete version of the questionnaire and supporting documentation see Nadler, D. A., Cammann, C., Jenkins, G. D., & Lawler, E. E. (Eds.) *The Michigan organizational assessment package* (Progress Report II). Ann Arbor: Survey Research Center, 1975.

calculated for each individual and scores can be combined for groups of individuals. The procedure for obtaining a work-motivation score is as follows:

a For each of the possible positive outcomes listed in questions 1 and 2, multiply the score for the outcome on question 1 ($P{\to}O$ expectancies) by the corresponding score on question 2 (valences of outcomes). Thus, score 1a would be multiplied by score 2a, score 1b by score 2b, etc.

b All of the 1 times 2 products should be added together to get a total of all expectancies times valences _____.

c The total should be divided by the number of pairs (in this case, eleven) to get an average expectancy-times-valence score _____.

d The scores from question 3 ($E{\to}P$ expectancies) should be added together and then divided by three to get an average effort-to-performance expectancy score _____.

Table 6-1 *Question 1:* Here are some things that could happen to people if they do their jobs *especially well*. How likely is it that each of these things would happen if you performed your job *especially well*?

		Not at all likely		Somewhat likely		Quite likely		Extremely likely
a	You will get a bonus or pay increase	(1)	(2)	(3)	(4)	(5)	(6)	(7)
b	You will feel better about yourself as a person	(1)	(2)	(3)	(4)	(5)	(6)	(7)
c	You will have an opportunity to develop your skills and abilities	(1)	(2)	(3)	(4)	(5)	(6)	(7)
d	You will have better job security	(1)	(2)	(3)	(4)	(5)	(6)	(7)
e	You will be given chances to learn new things	(1)	(2)	(3)	(4)	(5)	(6)	(7)
f	You will be promoted or get a better job	(1)	(2)	(3)	(4)	(5)	(6)	(7)
g	You will get a feeling that you've accomplished something worthwhile	(1)	(2)	(3)	(4)	(5)	(6)	(7)
h	You will have more freedom on your job	(1)	(2)	(3)	(4)	(5)	(6)	(7)
i	You will be respected by the people you work with	(1)	(2)	(3)	(4)	(5)	(6)	(7)
j	Your supervisor will praise you	(1)	(2)	(3)	(4)	(5)	(6)	(7)
k	The people you work with will be friendly with you	(1)	(2)	(3)	(4)	(5)	(6)	(7)

Table 6-2 *Question 2:* Different people want different things from their work. Here is a list of things a person could have on his or her job. How *important* is each of the following to you?

How Important Is . . . ?	Moderately important or less			Quite important			Extremely important
a The amount of pay you get	(1)	(2)	(3)	(4)	(5)	(6)	(7)
b The chances you have to do something that makes you feel good about yourself as a person	(1)	(2)	(3)	(4)	(5)	(6)	(7)
c The opportunity to develop your skills and abilities . .	(1)	(2)	(3)	(4)	(5)	(6)	(7)
d The amount of job security you have	(1)	(2)	(3)	(4)	(5)	(6)	(7)

How Important Is . . . ?							
e The chances you have to learn new things	(1)	(2)	(3)	(4)	(5)	(6)	(7)
f Your chances for getting a promotion or getting a better job	(1)	(2)	(3)	(4)	(5)	(6)	(7)
g The chances you have to accomplish something worthwhile.	(1)	(2)	(3)	(4)	(5)	(6)	(7)
h The amount of freedom you have on your job.	(1)	(2)	(3)	(4)	(5)	(6)	(7)

How Important Is . . . ?							
i The respect you receive from the people you work with	(1)	(2)	(3)	(4)	(5)	(6)	(7)
j The praise you get from your supervisor.	(1)	(2)	(3)	(4)	(5)	(6)	(7)
k The friendliness of the people you work with	(1)	(2)	(3)	(4)	(5)	(6)	(7)

e Multiply the score obtained in step c (the average expectancy times valence) by the score obtained in step d (the average $E{\rightarrow}P$ expectancy score) to obtain a total work-motivation score _____.

Additional Comments on the Work-Motivation Score

A number of important points should be kept in mind when using the questionnaire to get a work-motivation score. First, the questions presented here are just a short version of a larger and more comprehensive questionnaire. For more detail, the articles and publications referred to here and in the text should be consulted. Second, this is a general questionnaire. Since it is hard to anticipate in a general questionnaire what may be valent outcomes in each situation, the individual manager may want to add additional outcomes to questions 1 and 2. Third, it is important to remember that questionnaire results can be influenced by the feelings people have when they fill out the questionnaire. The use of the questionnaire as outlined above assumes a certain level of trust between manager and subordinates. People filling out questionnaires need to know what is going to be done with their answers and usually need to be assured of the confidentiality of their responses. Finally, the research indicates that, in many cases, the score obtained by simply averaging all the responses to question 1 (the $P{\rightarrow}O$ expectancies) will be as useful as the fully calculated work-motivation score. In each situation, the manager should experiment and find out whether the additional information in questions 2 and 3 aid in motivational diagnosis.

Table 6-3 *Question 3:* Below you will see a number of pairs of factors that look like this:

Warm weather→sweating   (1)   (2)   (3)   (4)   (5)   (6)   (7)

You are to indicate by checking the appropriate number to the right of each pair how often it is true for *you* personally that the first factor leads to the second on *your job*. Remember, for each pair, indicate how often it is true by checking the box under the response which seems most accurate.

		Never	Sometimes	Often	Almost always
a	Working hard → high productivity	(1) (2)	(3) (4)	(5) (6)	(7)
b	Workind hard → doing my job well	(1) (2)	(3) (4)	(5) (6)	(7)
c	Working hard → good job performance	(1) (2)	(3) (4)	(5) (6)	(7)

Reading 7

Satisfaction and Behavior

Edward E. Lawler III

Compared to what is known about motivation, relatively little is known about the determinants and consequences of satisfaction. Most of the psychological research on motivation simply has not been concerned with the kinds of affective reactions that people experience in association with or as a result of motivated behavior. No well-developed theories of satisfaction have appeared and little theoretically based research has been done on satisfaction. The influence of behaviorism on the field of psychology had a great deal to do with this lag in research. While psychology was under the influence of behaviorism, psychologists avoided doing research that depended on introspective self-reports. Behaviorists strongly felt that if psychology were to develop as a science, it had to study observable behavior. Since satisfaction is an internal subjective state that is best reported by the people experiencing it, satisfaction was not seen as a proper subject for study. Psychologists thought they should concentrate on those aspects of motivation that are observable (for exam-

ple, performance, hours of deprivation, strength of response, and so on).

Most of the research on the study of satisfaction has been done by psychologists interested in work organizations. This research dates back to the 1930s. Since that time, the term "job satisfaction" has been used to refer to affective attitudes or orientations on the part of individuals toward jobs. Hoppock published a famous monograph on job satisfaction in 1935, and in 1939 the results of the well-known Western Electric studies were published. The Western Electric studies (Roethlisberger & Dickson, 1939) emphasized the importance of studying the attitudes, feelings, and perceptions employees have about their jobs. Through interviews with over 20,000 workers, these studies graphically made the point that employees have strong affective reactions to what happens to them at work. The Western Electric studies also suggested that affective reactions cause certain kinds of behavior, such as strikes, absenteeism, and turnover. Although the studies

Excerpt from chap. 4 of E. E. Lawler III, *Motivation in work organizations*. Monterey, Calif.: Brooks/Cole, 1973.

failed to show any clear-cut relationship between satisfaction and job performance, the studies did succeed in stimulating a tremendous amount of research on job satisfaction. During the last 30 years, thousands of studies have been done on job satisfaction. Usually these studies have not been theoretically oriented; instead, researchers have simply looked at the relationship between job satisfaction and factors such as age, education, job level, absenteeism rate, productivity, and so on. Originally, much of the research seemed to be stimulated by a desire to show that job satisfaction is important because it influences productivity. Underlying the earlier articles on job satisfaction was a strong conviction that "happy workers are productive workers." Recently, however, this theme has been disappearing, and many organizational psychologists seem to be studying job satisfaction simply because they are interested in finding its causes. This approach to studying job satisfaction is congruent with the increased prominence of humanistic psychology, which emphasizes human affective experience.

The recent interest in job satisfaction also ties in directly with the rising concern in many countries about the quality of life. There is an increasing acceptance of the view that material possessions and economic growth do not necessarily produce a high quality of life. Recognition is now being given to the importance of the kinds of affective reactions that people experience and to the fact that these are not always tied to economic or material accomplishments. Through the Department of Labor and the Department of Health, Education, and Welfare, the United States government has recently become active in trying to improve the affective quality of work life. Job satisfaction is one measure of the quality of life in organizations and is worth understanding and increasing even if it doesn't relate to performance. This reason for studying satisfaction is likely to be an increasingly prominent one as we begin to worry more about the effects working in organizations has on people and as our humanitarian concern for the kind of psychological experiences people have during their lives increases. What happens to people during the work day has profound effects both on the individual employee's life and on the society as a whole, and thus these events cannot be ignored if the quality of life in a society is to be high. As John Gardner has said:

Of all the ways in which society serves the individual, few are more meaningful than to provide him with a decent job. . . . It isn't going to be a decent society for any of us until it is for all of us. If our sense of responsibility fails us, our sheer self-interest should come to the rescue [1968, p. 25].

As it turns out, satisfaction is related to absenteeism and turnover, both of which are very costly to organizations. Thus, there is a very "practical" economic reason for organizations to be concerned with job satisfaction, since it can influence organizational effectiveness. However, before any practical use can be made of the finding that job dissatisfaction causes absenteeism and turnover, we must understand what factors cause and influence job satisfaction. Organizations can influence job satisfaction and prevent absenteeism and turnover only if the organizations can pinpoint the factors causing and influencing these affective responses.

Despite the many studies, critics have legitimately complained that our understanding of the causes of job satisfaction has not substantially increased during the last 30 years (for example, see Locke, 1968, 1969) for two main reasons. The research on job satisfaction has typically been atheoretical and has not tested for causal relationships. Since the research has not been guided by theory, a vast array of unorganized, virtually uninterpretable facts have been unearthed. For example, a number of studies have found a positive relationship between productivity and job satisfaction, while other studies have found no evidence of this relationship. Undoubtedly, this disparity can be explained, but the explanation would have to be based on a theory of satisfaction, and at present no such theory exists. One thing the research on job satisfaction has done is to demonstrate the saying that "theory without data is fantasy; but data without theory is chaos!"

Due to the lack of a theory stating causal relationships, the research on job satisfaction has consistently looked simply for relationships among variables. A great deal is known about what factors are related to satisfaction, but very little is known about the causal basis for the relationships. This is a serious problem when one attempts to base change efforts on the research. This problem also increases the difficulty of developing and testing theories of satisfaction. Perhaps the best example of the resulting dilemma concerns the relationship between satisfaction and performance. If satisfaction causes performance, then organizations should try to see that their employees are satisfied; however, if performance causes satisfaction, then high satisfaction is not necessarily a goal but rather a by-product of an effective organization.

A MODEL OF FACET SATISFACTION

Figure 7-1 presents a model of the determinants of facet satisfaction. The model is intended to be applicable to understanding what determines a person's satisfaction with any facet of the job. The model assumes that the same psychological processes operate to determine satisfaction with job factors ranging from pay to supervision and satisfaction with the work itself. The model in Figure 4-1 is a discrepancy model in the sense that it shows satisfaction as the difference between *a,* what a person feels he should receive, and *b,* what he perceives that he actually receives. The model indicates that when the person's perception of what his outcome level is and his perception of what his outcome level should be are in agreement, the person will be satisfied. When a person perceives his outcome level as falling below what he feels it should be, he will be dissatisfied. However, when a person's perceived outcome level exceeds what he feels it should be, he will have feelings of guilt and

inequity and perhaps some discomfort (Adams, 1965). Thus, for any job factor, the assumption is that satisfaction with the factor will be determined by the difference between how much of the factor there is and how much of the factor the person feels there should be.

Present outcome level is shown to be the key influence on a person's perception of what rewards he receives, but his perception is also shown to be influenced by his perception of what his "referent others" receive. The higher the outcome levels of his referent others, the lower his outcome level will appear. Thus, a person's psychological view of how much of a factor he receives is said to be influenced by more than just the objective amount of the factor. Because of this psychological influence, the same amount of reward often can be seen quite differently by two people; to one person it can be a large amount, while to another person it can be a small amount.

The model in Figure 7-1 also shows that a person's perception of what his reward level should be is influenced by a number of factors. Perhaps the most important influence is perceived job inputs. These inputs include all of the skills, abilities, and training a person brings to the job as well as the behavior he exhibits on the job. The greater he perceives his inputs to be, the higher will be his perception of

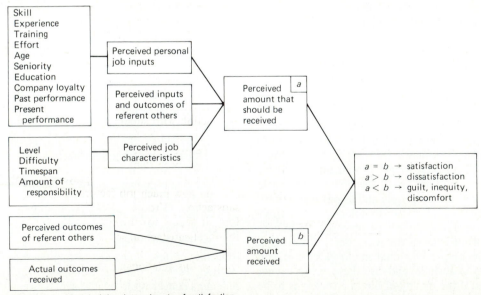

Figure 7-1   Model of the determinants of satisfaction.

what his outcomes should be. Because of this relationship, people with high job inputs must receive more rewards than people with low job inputs or they will be dissatisfied. The model also shows that a person's perception of what his outcomes should be is influenced by his perception of the job demands. The greater the demands made by the job, the more he will perceive he should receive. Job demands include such things as job difficulty, responsibilities, and organization level. If outcomes do not rise along with these factors, the clear prediction of the model is that the people who perceive they have the more difficult, higher level jobs will be the most dissatisfied.

The model shows that a person's perception of what his outcomes should be is influenced by what the person perceives his comparison-other's inputs and outcomes to be. This aspect of the model is taken directly from equity theory and is included to stress the fact that people look at the inputs and outcomes of others in order to determine what their own outcome level should be. If a person's comparison-other's inputs are the same as the person's inputs but the other's outcomes are much higher, the person will feel that he should be receiving more outcomes and will be dissatisfied as a result.

The model allows for the possibility that people will feel that their outcomes exceed what they should be. The feelings produced by this condition are quite different from those produced by under-reward. Because of this difference, it does not make sense to refer to a person who feels over-rewarded as being dissatisfied. There is considerable evidence that very few people feel over-rewarded, and this fact can be explained by the model. Even when people are highly rewarded, the social-comparison aspect of satisfaction means that people can avoid feeling over-rewarded by looking around and finding someone to compare with who is doing equally well. Also, a person tends to value his own inputs much higher than they are valued by others (Lawler, 1967). Because of this discrepancy, a person's perception of what his outcomes should be is often not shared by those administering his rewards, and is often above what he actually receives. Finally, the person can easily increase his perception of his inputs and thereby justify a high reward level.

As a way of summarizing some of the implications of the model, let us briefly make some statements

about who should be dissatisfied if the model is correct. Other things being equal:

1 People with high perceived inputs will be more dissatisfied with a given facet than people with low perceived inputs.
2 People who perceive their job to be demanding will be more dissatisfied with a given facet than people who perceive their jobs as undemanding.
3 People who perceive similar others as having a more favorable input-outcome balance will be more dissatisfied with a given facet than people who perceive their own balance as similar to or better than that of others.
4 People who receive a low outcome level will be more dissatisfied than those who receive a high outcome level.
5 The more outcomes a person perceives his comparison-other receives, the more dissatisifed he will be with his own outcomes. This should be particularly true when the comparison-other is seen to hold a job that demands the same or fewer inputs.

OVERALL JOB SATISFACTION

Most theories of job satisfaction argue that overall job satisfaction is determined by some combination of all facet-satisfaction feelings. This could be expressed in terms of the facet-satisfaction model in Figure 7-1 as a simple sum of, or average of, all $a - b$ discrepancies. Thus, overall job satisfaction is determined by the difference between all things a person feels he should receive from his job and all the things he actually does receive.

A strong theoretical argument can be made for weighting the facet-satisfaction scores according to their importance. Some factors do make larger contributions to overall satisfaction than others. Pay satisfaction, satisfaction with the work itself, and satisfaction with supervision seem to have particularly strong influences on overall satisfaction for most people. Also, employees tend to rate these factors as important. Thus, there is a connection between how important employees say job factors are and how much job factors influence overall job satisfaction (Vroom, 1964). Conceptually, therefore, it seems worthwhile to think of the various job-facet-satisfaction scores as influencing total satisfaction in terms of their importance. One way to express this relationship is by defining overall job satisfaction as being equal to Σ (facet satisfaction $\times$ facet importance). However, as stressed earlier, actually measuring importance and multiplying it by measured facet satisfaction often isn't necessary because the satisfaction scores themselves seem to take importance into account. (The most important items tend to be scored as either very satisfactory or very dissatisfactory; thus, these items have the most influence on any sum score.) Still, on a conceptual level, it is important to remember that facet-satisfaction scores do differentially contribute to the feeling of overall job satisfaction.

A number of studies have attempted to determine how many workers are actually satisfied with their jobs. Our model does not lead to any predictions in this area. The model simply gives the conditions that lead to people experiencing feelings of satisfaction or dissatisfaction. Not surprisingly, the studies that have been done do not agree on the percentage of dissatisfied workers. Some suggest figures as low as 13 percent, others give figures as high as 80 percent. The range generally reported is from 13 to 25 percent dissatisfied. Herzberg et al. (1957) summarized the findings of research studies conducted from 1946 through 1953. The figures in their report showed a yearly increase in the median percentage of job-satisfied persons (see Table 7-1). Figure 7-2 presents satisfaction-trend data for 1948 through 1971. These data also show an overall increase in the number of satisfied workers, which is interesting because of recent speculation that satisfaction is

decreasing. However, due to many measurement problems, it is impossible to conclude that a real decline in number of dissatisfied workers has taken place.

The difficulty in obtaining meaningful conclusions from the data stems from the fact that different questions yield very different results. For example, a number of studies, instead of directly asking workers "How satisfied are you?," have asked "If you had it to do over again, would you pick the same job?" The latter question produces much higher dissatisfaction scores than does the simply "how satisfied are you" question. One literature review showed that 54 percent of the workers tended to say that they were sufficiently dissatisfied with their jobs that they would not choose them again. On the other hand, the straight satisfaction question shows between 13 and 25 percent dissatisfied. However, even this figure is subject to wide variation depending on how the question is asked. When the question is asked in the simple form, "Are you satisfied, yes or no?," the number of satisfied responses is large. When the question is changed so that the employees can respond yes, no, or undecided—or satisfied, dissatisfied, or neutral—the number of satisfied responses drops.

Because of these methodological complexities, it is difficult to draw conclusions about the number of workers who are or are not satisfied with their jobs or with some facet of their jobs. This drawback does not mean, however, that meaningful research on satisfaction is impossible. On the contrary, interesting and important research has been and can be done on the determinants of job satisfaction. For example, the relationship between personal-input factors—such as education level, sex, and age and seniority—and job or facet satisfaction can be ascertained by simply comparing those people who report they are satisfied with those people who report they are dissatisfied and checking the results to see if the two groups differ in any systematic manner. The number of people reporting satisfaction is not crucial for this purpose. What is important is that we distinguish those people who tend to be more satisfied from those people who tend to be less satisfied. This distinction can be made with many of the better-known satisfaction-measuring instruments, such as the Job Description Index (Smith, Kendall, & Hulin, 1969) and Porter's (1961) need-satisfaction instrument.

Table 7-1 Median Percentage of Job-dissatisfied Persons Reported from 1946–1953
(From Herzberg et al., *Job Attitudes: Review of Research and Opinion.* Copyright 1957 by the Psychological Service of Pittsburgh. Reprinted by permission.)

Year	Median percentage of job dissatisfied
1953	13
1952	15
1951	18
1949	19
1948	19
1946–1947	21

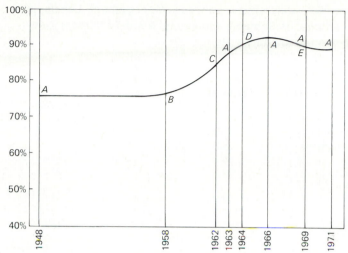

Figure 7-2 Percentage of "satisfied" workers, 1948–1971. *(From Quinn Staines, & McCollough, 1973.) Note:* "Don't know" and "uncertain" have been excluded from the base of the percentages. *Sources: A* = Gallup, or Gallup as reported by Roper; *B* = Survey Research Center (Michigan); *C* = NORC; *D* = Survey Research Center (Berkeley); *E* = 1969–1970 Survey of Working Conditions.

A number of studies have tried to determine the amount of employee dissatisfaction that is associated with different job facets. Although these studies have yielded interesting results, some serious methodological problems are involved in this work. As with overall job satisfaction, factors such as type of measurement scale used and manner of wording questions seriously affect the number of people who express dissatisfaction with a given facet. For example, a question about pay satisfaction can be asked in a way that will cause few people to express dissatisfaction, while a question about security satisfaction can be asked in a way that will cause many people to express dissatisfaction. In this situation, comparing the number of people expressing security satisfaction with the number of people expressing pay dissatisfaction might produce very misleading conclusions. This problem is always present no matter how carefully the various items are worded because it is impossible to balance the items so they are comparable for all factors.

Despite methodological problems, the data on relative satisfaction levels with different job factors are interesting. These data show that the factors mentioned earlier as being most important—that is, pay, promotion, security, leadership, and the work itself—appear in these studies as the major sources of dissatisfaction. Porter (1961) designed items using Maslow's needs as a measure of satisfaction. With these items, he collected data from various managers. The results of his study (see Table 7-2) show that more managers express higher order need dissatisfaction than express lower order need dissatisfaction. The results also show that a large number of managers are dissatisfied with their pay and with the communications in their organizations and that middle level managers tend to be better satisfied in all areas than lower level managers.

Porter's data also show that managers consider the areas of dissatisfaction to be the most important areas. It is not completely clear whether the dissatisfaction causes the importance or the importance causes the dissatisfaction. The research reviewed earlier suggests that the primary causal direction is from dissatisfaction to importance, although there undoubtedly is a two-way-influence process operating. The important thing to remember is that employees do report varying levels of satisfaction with different job factors, and the factors that have come out high on dissatisfaction have also been rated high in importance and have the strongest influence on overall job satisfaction.

A study by Grove and Kerr (1951) illustrates how strongly organizational conditions can affect factor satisfaction. Grove and Kerr measured employee satisfaction in two plants where normal work condi-

Table 4-2 Differences between Management Levels in Percentage of Subjects Indicating Need-Fulfillment Deficiencies (Adapted from Porter, 1961)

Questionnaire items	% Bottom management (N = 64)	% Middle management (N = 75)	% Difference
Security needs	42.2	26.7	15.5
Social needs	35.2	32.0	3.2
Esteem needs	55.2	35.6	19.6
Autonomy needs	60.2	47.7	12.5
Self-actualization needs	59.9	53.3	6.6
Pay	79.7	80.0	−0.3
Communications	78.1	61.3	16.8

tions prevailed and found that 88 percent of the workers were satisfied with their job security, which indicated that security was one of the least dissatisfying job factors for employees in these two plants. In another plant where layoffs had occurred, only 17 percent of the workers said they were satisfied with the job security, and job security was one of the most dissatisfying job factors for this plant's employees.

The research on the determinants of satisfaction has looked primarily at two relationships: (1) the relationship between satisfaction and the characteristics of the job, and (2) the relationship between satisfaction and the characteristics of the person. Not surprisingly, the research shows that satisfaction is a function of both the person and the environment. These results are consistent with our approach to thinking about satisfaction, since our model (shown in Figure 7-1) indicates that personal factors influence what people feel they should receive and that job conditions influence both what people perceive they actually receive and what people perceive they should receive.

The evidence on the effects of personal-input factors on satisfaction is voluminous and will be only briefly reviewed. The research clearly shows that personal factors do affect job satisfaction, basically because they influence perceptions of what outcomes should be. As predicted by the satisfaction model in Figure 7-1, the higher a person's perceived personal inputs—that is, the greater his education, skill, and performance—the more he feels he should receive. Thus, unless the high-input person receives

more outcomes, he will be dissatisfied with his job and the rewards his job offers. Such straightforward relationships between inputs and satisfaction appear to exist for all personal-input factors except age and seniority. Evidence from the study of age and seniority suggests a curvilinear relationship (that is, high satisfaction among young and old workers, low satisfaction among middle-age workers) or even a relationship of increasing satisfaction with old age and tenure. The tendency of satisfaction to be high among older, long-term employees seems to be produced by the effects of selective turnover and the development of realistic expectations about what the job has to offer.

CONSEQUENCES OF DISSATISFACTION

Originally, much of the interest in job satisfaction stemmed from the belief that job satisfaction influenced job performance. Specifically, psychologists thought that high job satisfaction led to high job performance. This view has now been discredited, and most psychologists feel that satisfaction influences absenteeism and turnover but not job performance. However, before looking at the relationship among satisfaction, absenteeism, and turnover, let's review the work on satisfaction and performance.

Job Performance

In the 1950s, two major literature reviews showed that in most studies only a slight relationship had been found between satisfaction and performance.

A later review by Vroom (1964) also showed that studies had not found a strong relationship between satisfaction and performance; in fact, most studies had found a very low positive relationship between the two. In other words, better performers did seem to be slightly more satisfied than poor performers. A considerable amount of recent work suggests that the slight existing relationship is probably due to better performance indirectly causing satisfaction rather than the reverse. Lawler and Porter (1967) explained this "performance causes satisfaction" viewpoint as follows:

> If we assume that rewards cause satisfaction, and that in some cases performance produces rewards, then it is possible that the relationship found between satisfaction and performance comes about through the action of a third variable—rewards. Briefly stated, good performance may lead to rewards, which in turn lead to satisfaction; this formulation then would say that satisfaction rather than causing performance, as was previously assumed, is caused by it.
>
> [Figure 7-3] shows that performance leads to rewards, and it distinguishes between two kinds of rewards and their connection to performance. A wavy line between performance and extrinsic rewards indicates that such rewards are likely to be imperfectly related to performance. By extrinsic rewards is meant such organizationally controlled rewards as pay, promotion, status, and security—rewards that are often referred to as satisfying mainly lower-level needs. The connection is relatively weak because of the difficulty of tying extrinsic rewards directly to performance. Even though an organization may have a policy of rewarding merit, performance is difficult to measure, and in dispensing rewards like pay, many other factors are frequently taken into consideration.

Quite the opposite is likely to be true for intrinsic rewards, however, since they are given to the individual by himself for good performance. Intrinsic or internally mediated rewards are subject to fewer disturbing influences and thus are likely to be more directly related to good performance. This connection is indicated in the model by a semi-wavy line. Probably the best example of an intrinsic reward is the feeling of having accomplished something worthwhile. For that matter any of the rewards that satisfy self-actualization needs or higher order growth needs are good examples of intrinsic rewards [p. 23-24].[1]

Figure 7-3 shows that intrinsic and extrinsic rewards are not directly related to job satisfaction, since the relationship is moderated by perceived equitable rewards (what people think they should receive). The model in Figure 7-3 is similar to the model in Figure 7-1, since both models show that satisfaction is a function of the amount of rewards a person receives and the amount of rewards he feels he should receive.

Because of the imperfect relationship between performance and rewards and the important effect of perceived equitable rewards, a low but positive relationship should exist between job satisfaction and job performance in most situations. However, in certain situations, a strong positive relationship may exist; while in other situations, a negative relationship may exist. A negative relationship would be expected where rewards are unrelated to performance or negatively related to performance.

[1]Lawler, E. E., and Porter, L. W. The effect of performance on job satisfaction. *Industrial Relations,* 1967, **7,** 20–28. Reprinted by permission of the publisher, Industrial Relations.

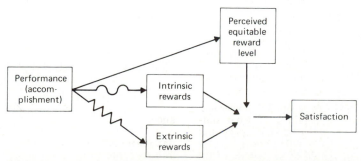

Figure 7-3 Model of the relationship of performance to satisfaction. *(From Lawler and Porter, The effect of performance on job satisfaction. Industrial Relations, 1967, 7, 20–28. Reprinted by permission of the publisher, Industrial Relations.)*

To have the same level of satisfaction for good performers and poor performers, the good performers must receive more rewards than the poor performers. The reason for this, as stressed earlier, is that performance level influences the amount of rewards a person feels he should receive. Thus, when rewards are not based on performance—when poor performers receive equal rewards or a larger amount of rewards than good performers—the best performers will be the least satisfied, and a negative satisfaction-performance relationship will exist. If, on the other hand, the better performers are given significantly more rewards, a positive satisfaction-performance relationship should exist. If it is assumed that most organizations are partially successful in relating rewards to performance, it follows that most studies should find a low but positive relationship between satisfaction and performance. Lawler and Porter's (1967) study was among those that found this relationship; their study also found that, as predicted, intrinsic-need satisfaction was more closely related to performance than was extrinsic-need satisfaction.

In retrospect, it is hard to understand why the belief that high satisfaction causes high performance was so widely accepted. There is nothing in the literature on motivation that suggests this causal relationship. In fact, such a relationship is opposite to the concepts developed by both drive theory and expectancy theory. If anything, these two theories would seem to predict that high satisfaction might reduce motivation because of a consequent reduction in the importance of various rewards that may have provided motivational force. Clearly, a more logical view is that performance is determined by people's efforts to obtain the goals and outcomes they desire, and satisfaction is determined by the outcomes people actually obtain. Yet, for some reason, many people believed—and some people still do believe—that the "satisfaction causes performance" view is best.

Turnover

The relationship between satisfaction and turnover has been studied often. In most studies, researchers have measured the job satisfaction among a number of employees and then waited to see which of the employees studied left during an ensuing time period (typically, a year). The satisfaction scores of the employees who left have then been compared with the remaining employees' scores. Although relationships between satisfaction scores and turnover have not always been very strong, the studies in this area have consistently shown that dissatisfied workers are more likely than satisfied workers to terminate employment; thus, satisfaction scores can predict turnover.

A study by Ross and Zander (1957) is a good example of the kind of research that has been done. Ross and Zander measured the job satisfaction of 2680 female workers in a large company. Four months later, these researchers found that 169 of these employees had resigned; those who left were significantly more dissatisfied with the amount of recognition they received on their jobs, with the amount of achievement they experienced, and with the amount of autonomy they had.

Probably the major reason that turnover and satisfaction are not more strongly related is that turnover is very much influenced by the availability of other positions. Even if a person is very dissatisfied with his job, he is not likely to leave unless more attractive alternatives are available. This observation would suggest that in times of economic prosperity, turnover should be high, and a strong relationship should exist between turnover and satisfaction; but in times of economic hardship, turnover should be low, and little relationship should exist between turnover and satisfaction. There is research evidence to support the argument that voluntary turnover is much lower in periods of economic hardship. However, no study has compared the relationship between satisfaction and turnover under different economic conditions to see if it is stronger under full employment.

Absenteeism

Like turnover, absenteeism has been found to be related to job satisfaction. If anything, the relationship between satisfaction and absenteeism seems to be stronger than the relationship between satisfaction and turnover. However, even in the case of absenteeism, the relationship is far from being isomorphic. Absenteeism is caused by a number of factors other than a person's voluntarily deciding not to come to work; illness, accidents, and so on can prevent someone who wants to come to work from actually coming to work. We would expect satisfaction to affect only voluntary absences; thus, satisfaction can never be strongly related to a measure of overall absence rate. Those studies that have separated voluntary absences from overall absences have, in fact, found that voluntary absence rates are much more closely related to satisfaction than are overall absence rates (Vroom, 1964). Of course, this outcome would be expected if satisfaction does influence people's willingness to come to work.

Organization Effectiveness

The research evidence clearly shows that employees' decisions about whether they will go to work on any given day and whether they will quit are affected by their feelings of job satisfaction. All the literature reviews on the subject have reached this conclusion. The fact that present satisfaction influences future absenteeism and turnover clearly indicates that the causal direction is from satisfaction to behavior. This conclusion is in marked contrast to our conclusion with respect to performance—that is, behavior causes satisfaction.

The research evidence on the determinants of satisfaction suggests that satisfaction is very much influenced by the actual rewards a person receives; of course, the organization has a considerable amount of control over these rewards. The research also shows that, although not all people will react to the same reward level in the same manner, reactions are predictable if something is known about how people perceive their inputs. The implication is that organizations can influence employees' satisfaction levels. Since it is possible to know how employees will react to different outcome levels, organizations can allocate outcomes in ways that will either cause job satisfaction or job dissatisfaction.

Absenteeism and turnover have a very direct influence on organizational effectiveness. Absenteeism is very costly because it interrupts scheduling, creates a need for overstaffing, increases fringe-benefit costs, and so on. Turnover is expensive because of the many costs incurred in recruiting and training replacement employees. For lower-level jobs, the cost of turnover is estimated at $2000 a person; at the managerial level, the cost is at least five to ten times the monthly salary of the job involved. Because satisfaction is manageable and influences absenteeism and turnover, organizations can control absenteeism and turnover. Generally,

by keeping satisfaction high and, specifically, by seeing that the best employees are the most satisfied, organizations can retain those employees they need the most. In effect, organizations can manage turnover so that, if it occurs, it will occur among employees the organization can most afford to lose. However, keeping the better performers more satisfied is not easy, since they must be rewarded very well.

REFERENCES

Adams, J. S. Injustice in social exchange. In L. Berkowitz (Ed.), *Advances in experimental social psychology,* Vol. 2. New York, Academic Press, 1965.

Gardner, J. W. *No easy victories.* New York, Harper & Row, 1968.

Grove, E. A., & Kerr, W. A. Specific evidence on origin of halo effect in measurement of employee morale. *Journal of Social Psychology,* 1951, **34,** 165–170.

Herzberg, F., Mausner, B., Peterson, R. O., & Capwell, D. I. *Job attitudes: Review of research and opinion.* Pittsburgh, Psychological Service of Pittsburgh, 1957.

Lawler, E. E. The multitrait multirater approach to measuring managerial job performance. *Journal of Applied Psychology,* 1967, **51,** 369–381.

Lawler, E. E., & Porter, L. W. The effect of performance on job satisfaction. *Industrial Relations,* 1967, **7,** 20–28.

Locke, E. A. What is job satisfaction? Paper presented at the APA Convention, San Francisco, September 1968.

Locke, E. A. What is job satisfaction? *Organizational Behavior and Human Performance,* 1969, **4,** 309–336.

Porter, L. W. A study of perceived need satisfactions in bottom and middle management jobs. *Journal of Applied Psychology,* 1961, **45,** 1–10.

Quinn, R. P., Staines, G., & McCullough, M. Job satisfaction in the 1970's. Recent history and a look to the future. *Manpower Monograph,* 1973.

Roethlisberger, F. I., & Dickson, W. I. *Management and the worker.* Cambridge, Mass., Harvard University Press, 1939.

Ross, I. E., & Zander, A. F. Need satisfaction and employee turnover. *Personnel Psychology,* 1957, **10,** 327–338.

Smith, P., Kendall, I., & Hulin, C. *The measurement of satisfaction in work and retirement.* Chicago, Rand McNally & Company, 1969.

Vroom, V. H. *Work and motivation.* New York, John Wiley & Sons, 1964.

Chapter 3

The Nature of Organizations

Any attempt to understand behavior in organizations cannot be complete unless one takes into account the nature of organizations as well as the nature of people. Over the past several decades, both practitioners and scholars have spent considerable effort in defining organizations and in analyzing their nature and structure. From these endeavors have emerged some identifiable approaches and some broad conclusions. However, as one reads through the selections in this chapter, it will be apparent that unanimity of opinion is lacking. Rather, what can be observed is that there are a variety of useful ways of looking at and thinking about organizations; and, perhaps most important, that each of these ways has both advantages and limitations. It will be one of the tasks of the reader to decide what is most important and useful among the various viewpoints and approaches described.

The first article, by Perrow, traces the history and development of organization theory. Perrow sets this history in a context that contrasts what he terms "the forces of light and the forces of darkness." In Perrow's view, and utilizing his metaphor, the forces of darkness have espoused the "mechanical school" of organizational theory, which emphasizes such

concepts and ideas (among others) as centralized authority, specialization and expertise, division of labor, and rules and regulations. The forces of light, on the other hand, have put more emphasis on the human component of organizations, drawing analogies more from biological than from engineering systems, and stressing such concepts as delegation of authority, trust and openness, and interpersonal dynamics.

In the article, Perrow begins his history with the scientific management, or so-called classical management, approach to organizations developed early in this century, followed by the "human relations" school, which emerged in response to the problems associated with a strict scientific management approach. These major ways of viewing and operating organizations were in turn followed by others that placed emphasis on a variety of variables, such as power, conflict, limited rationality in decision making, and technology. Overarching all of these approaches in recent years, as Perrow rightly points out, has been the "systems" view of organizations, which emphasizes the relationship of the organization to its environment and the interrelationships of parts within the organization. Perrow concludes by offering some interesting conclusions about what social scientists have learned about what works and, especially, what does *not* work in terms of prescriptions for those involved in managing organizations.

The next selection, taken from a book by Katz and Kahn, develops in detail a description of the systems view of organizations, which Perrow was able to cover only briefly in his historical overview. In the first part of this selection, Katz and Kahn define and identify organizations from a systems perspective, utilizing a model that focuses on the notions of inputs, transformation, and outputs, rather than on the classic view of organizations as a "social device for efficiently accomplishing through group means some stated purpose." The authors attempt to show why this latter definition is inadequate and why a systems approach provides greater understanding. They put particular emphasis on the feedback properties of systems (i.e., the fact that the "return from the output reactivates the system") and, particularly, the relation of the system to its environment. Hence, the emphasis is on "open" systems, i.e., systems that export to and import from the environment, in contrast to closed systems, which ignore the environment. As the authors acknowledge, the open-systems approach to organizations draws on a theory developed by a biologist, von Bertalanffy. In the latter part of this selection, the authors discuss several important consequences of viewing organizations as open systems. These include the necessity to avoid overconcentration on the internal functions of controls and coordination as ends in themselves, the need to recognize that there are more ways than one to produce a given outcome (the principle of equifinality), and the notion that variations in the environment are important to an organization and should be studied by it. They close with a note of caution, warning that "open is not a magic word, and pronouncing it is not enough to reveal what has been hidden in the organizational cave."

The article by Pfeffer and Salancik could have been included in Chapter 12 just as well as here. We place it here rather than later in the book because it does such a good job of summarizing a particular perspective about organizations: a coalitional model that explicitly focuses on the social composition of organizations. This model, as the authors stress, represents a clear alternative way of viewing organizations when compared to a "rational" or "bureaucratic" model (see the Perrow article). It is important for the reader to have this distinction clearly in mind, and this is the thrust of the first part of the Pfeffer and Salancik selection. This alternative approach to understanding organizations emphasizes a number of functions: limitations on information available to organizations, conflicting organizational goals, the relatively loose connection of organizations to their environments, and, especially, the existence of various competing coalitions or interest groups which strive to gain control of the activities and directions of the organization. The latter part of the article deals with a set of dilemmas involved in the design of organizations. The central theme is predicated on the assumption that "organizational design is . . . a process filled with contradictions and dilemmas." The article concludes with some imaginative ways of dealing with these design dilemmas (and, hence, the linkage with Chapter 12).

The final selection in this chapter, by Nadler and Tushman, shifts from broad theories of organizations to a proposed diagnostic model for understanding behavior in organizations. As this article is read, it will be important to recognize that the authors are particularly interested in the uility of this model from the *manager's* point of view. The model described in the article rests on a set of basic assumptions: (1) that organizations are dynamic, (2) that behavior in organizations exists at multiple levels (individual, group, and organizational), (3) that behavior in organizations occurs not in a vacuum but surrounded by a variety of technologies, and (4) that organizations have (as detailed in the Katz and Kahn selection) the characteristics of *open* social systems. In fact, the model makes explicit use of a "systems theory" perspective, in that it concentrates on analyzing inputs, transformation processes, and outputs. The authors stress a "problem-solving" orientation for managers to use in diagnosing organizations and the behavior of people in them, especially with respect to the necessity for continual evaluation of actions and their consequences. It will be interesting for the reader to assess this model and approach in the light of the various theories of organizations that are discussed in the first two readings in the chapter.

Reading 8

The Short and Glorious History of Organizational Theory
Charles Perrow

From the beginning, the forces of light and the forces of darkness have polarized the field of organizational analysis, and the struggle has been protracted and inconclusive. The forces of darkness have been represented by the mechanical school of organizational theory—those who treat the organization as a machine. This school characterizes organizations in terms of such things as:

- centralized authority
- clear lines of authority
- specialization and expertise
- marked division of labor
- rules and regulations
- clear separation of staff and line

The forces of light, which my mid-twentieth century came to be characterized as the human relations school, emphasizes people rather than machines, accommodations rather than machine-like precision, and draws its inspiration from biological systems rather than engineering systems. It has emphasized such things as:

- delegation of authority
- employee autonomy
- trust and openness
- concerns with the "whole person"
- interpersonal dynamics

THE RISE AND FALL OF SCIENTIFIC MANAGEMENT

The forces of darkness formulated their position first, starting in the early part of this century. They have been characterized as the scientific management or classical management school. This school started by parading simple-minded injunctions to plan ahead, keep records, write down policies, specialize, be decisive, and keep your span of control to about six people. These injunctions were needed as firms grew in size and complexity, since there were few models around beyond the railroads,

the military, and the Catholic Church to guide organizations. And their injunctions worked. Executives began to delegate, reduce their span of control, keep records, and specialize. Planning ahead still is difficult, it seems, and the modern equivalent is Management by Objectives.

- But many things intruded to make these simple-minded injunctions less relevant:

1 Labor became a more critical factor in the firm. As the technology increased in sophistication it took longer to train people, and more varied and specialized skills were needed. Thus, labor turnover cost more and recruitment became more selective. As a consequence, labor's power increased. Unions and strikes appeared. Management adjusted by beginning to speak of a cooperative system of capital, management, and labor. The machine model began to lose its relevancy.

2 The increasing complexity of markets, variability of products, increasing number of branch plants, and changes in technology all required more adaptive organization. The scientific management school was ill-equipped to deal with rapid change. It had presumed that once the proper structure was achieved the firm could run forever without much tampering. By the late 1930s, people began writing about adaptation and change in industry from an organizational point of view and had to abandon some of the principles of scientific management.

3 Political, social, and cultural changes meant new expectations regarding the proper way to treat people. The dark, satanic mills needed at the least a white-washing. Child labor and the brutality of supervision in many enterprises became no longer permissible. Even managers could not be expected to accept the authoritarian patterns of leadership that prevailed in the small firm run by the founding father.

4 As mergers and growth proceeded apace and the firm could no longer be viewed as the shadow of one man (the founding entrepreneur) a search for methods of selecting good leadership became a preoccupation. A good, clear, mechanical structure would no longer suffice. Instead, firms had to search

Reprinted, by permission of the publisher, from *Organizational Dynamics*, Summer 1973. Copyrighted © by AMACOM, a division of American Management Associations. All rights reserved.

for the qualities of leadership that could fill the large footsteps of the entrepreneur. They tacitly had to admit that something other than either "sound principles" or "dynamic leadership" was needed. The search for leadership traits implied that leaders were made, not just born, that the matter was complex, and that several skills were involved.

ENTER HUMAN RELATIONS

From the beginning, individual voices were raised against the implications of the scientific management school. "Bureaucracy" had always been a dirty word, and the job design efforts of Frederick Taylor were even the subject of a congressional investigation. But no effective counterforce developed until 1938, when a business executive with academic talents named Chester Barnard proposed the first new theory of organizations: Organizations are cooperative systems, not the products of mechanical engineering. He stressed natural groups within the organization, upward communication, authority from below rather than from above, and leaders who functioned as a cohesive force. With the spectre of labor unrest and the Great Depression upon him, Barnard's emphasis on the cooperative nature of organizations was well-timed. The year following the publication of his *Functions of the Executive* (1938) saw the publication of F. J. Roethlisberger and William Dickson's *Management and the Worker,* reporting on the first large-scale empirical investigation of productivity and social relations. The research, most of it conducted in the Hawthorne plant of the Western Electric Company during a period in which the workforce was reduced, highlighted the role of informal groups, work restriction norms, the value of decent, humane leadership, and the role of psychological manipulation of employees through the counseling system. World War II intervened, but after the war the human relations movement, building on the insights of Barnard and the Hawthorne studies, came into its own.

The first step was a search for the traits of good leadership. It went on furiously at university centers but at first failed to produce more than a list of Boy Scout maxims: A good leader was kind, courteous, loyal, courageous, etc. We suspected as much. However, the studies did turn up a distinction between "consideration," or employee-centered aspects of leadership, and job-centered, technical aspects labeled "initiating structure." Both were important, but the former received most of the attention and the latter went undeveloped. The former led directly to an examination of group process, an investigation that has culminated in T-group programs and is moving forward still with encounter groups. Meanwhile, in England, the Tavistock Institute sensed the importance of the influence of the kind of task a group had to perform on the social relations within the group. The first important study, conducted among coal miners, showed that job simplification and specialization did not work under conditions of uncertainty and nonroutine tasks.

As this work flourished and spread, more adventurous theorists began to extend it beyond work groups to organizations as a whole. We now knew that there were a number of things that were bad for the morale and loyalty of groups—routine tasks, submission to authority, specialization of task, segregation of task sequence, ignorance of the goals of the firm, centralized decision making, and so on. If these were bad for groups, they were likely to be bad for groups of groups—i.e., for organizations. So people like Warren Bennis began talking about innovative, rapidly changing organizations that were made up of temporary groups, temporary authority systems, temporary leadership and role assignments, and democratic access to the goals of the firm. If rapidly changing technologies and unstable, turbulent environments were to characterize industry, then the structure of firms should be temporary and decentralized. The forces of light, of freedom, autonomy, change, humanity, creativity, and democracy were winning. Scientific management survived only in outdated text books. If the evangelizing of some of the human relations school theorists was excessive, and if Likert's System 4 or MacGregor's Theory Y or Blake's 9 × 9 evaded us, at least there was a rationale for confusion, disorganization, scrambling, and stress: Systems should be temporary.

BUREAUCRACY'S COMEBACK

Meanwhile, in another part of the management forest, the mechanistic school was gathering its forces and preparing to outflank the forces of light. First came the numbers men—the linear programmers, the budget experts, and the financial analysts

—with their PERT systems and cost-benefit analyses. From another world, unburdened by most of the scientific management ideology and untouched by the human relations school, they began to parcel things out and give some meaning to those truisms, "plan ahead" and "keep records." Armed with emerging systems concepts, they carried the "mechanistic" analogy to its fullest—and it was very productive. Their work still goes on, largely untroubled by organizational theory; the theory, it seems clear, will have to adjust to them, rather than the other way around.

Then the works of Max Weber, first translated from the German in the 1940s—he wrote around 1910, incredibly—began to find their way into social science thought. At first, with his celebration of the efficiency of bureaucracy, he was received with only reluctant respect, and even with hostility. All writers were against bureaucracy. But it turned out, surprisingly, that managers were not. When asked, they acknowledged that they preferred clear lines of communication, clear specifications of authority and responsibility, and clear knowledge of whom they were responsible to. They were as wont to say "there ought to be a rule about this," as to say "there are too many rules around here," as wont to say "next week we've got to get organized," as to say "there is too much red t ape." Gradually, studies began to show that bureaucratic organizations could change faster than nonbureaucratic ones, and that morale could be higher where there was clear evidence of bureaucracy.

What was this thing, then? Weber had showed us, for example, that bureaucracy was the most effective way of ridding organizations of favoritism, arbitrary authority, discrimination, payola and kick-backs, and yes, even incompetence. His model stressed expertise, and the favorite or the boss' nephew or the guy who burned up· resources to make his performance look good was *not* the one with expertise. Rules could be changed; they could be dropped in exceptional circumstances; job security promoted more innovation. The sins of bureaucracy began to look like the sins of failing to follow its principles.

ENTER POWER, CONFLICT, AND DECISIONS

But another discipline began to intrude upon the confident work and increasingly elaborate models of the human relations theorists (largely social psychol-

ogists) and the uneasy toying with bureaucracy of the "structionalists" (largely sociologists). Both tended to study economic organizations. A few, like Philip Selznick, were noting conflict and differences in goals (perhaps because he was studying a public agency, the Tennessee Valley Authority), but most ignored conflict or treated it as a pathological manifestation of breakdowns in communication or the ego trips of unreconstructed managers.

But in the world of political parties, pressure groups, and legislative bodies, conflict was not only rampant, but to be expected—it was even functional. This was the domain of the political scientists. They kept talking about power, making it a legitimate concern for analysis. There was an open acknowledgement of "manipulation." These were political scientists who were "behaviorally" inclined —studying and recording behavior rather than constitutions and formal systems of government—and they came to a much more complex view of organized activity. It spilled over into the area of economic organizations, with the help of some economists like R. A. Gordon and some sociologists who were studying conflicting goals of treatment and custody in prisons and mental hospitals.

The presence of legitimately conflicting goals and techniques of preserving and using power did not, of course, sit well with a cooperative systems view of organizations. But it also puzzled the bureaucratic school (and what was left of the old scientific management school), for the impressive Weberian principles were designed to settle questions of power through organizational design and to keep conflict out through reliance on rational-legal authority and systems of careers, expertise, and hierarchy. But power was being overtly contested and exercised in covert ways, and conflict was bursting out all over, and even being creative.

Gradually, in the second half of the 1950s and in the next decade, the political science view infiltrated both schools. Conflict could be healthy, even in a cooperative system, said the human relationists; it was the mode of resolution that counted, rather than prevention. Power became reconceptualized as "influence," and the distribution was less important, said Arnold Tannenbaum, than the total amount. For the bureaucratic school—never a clearly defined group of people, and largely without any clear ideology—it was easier to just absorb the new data and theories as something else to be thrown into the pot. That is to say, they floundered, writing books that went from topic to topic, without a clear view of organizations, or better yet, producing "readers" and leaving students to sort it all out.

Buried in the political science viewpoint was a sleeper that only gradually began to undermine the dominant views. This was the idea, largely found in the work of Herbert Simon and James March, that because man was so limited—in intelligence, reasoning powers, information at his disposal, time available, and means of ordering his preferences clearly —he generally seized on the first acceptable alternative when deciding, rather than looking for the best; that he rarely changed things unless they really got bad, and even then he continued to try what had worked before; that he limited his search for solutions to well-worn paths and traditional sources of information and established ideas; that he was wont to remain preoccupied with routine, thus preventing innovation. They called these characteristics "cognitive limits on rationality" and spoke of "satisficing" rather than maximizing or optimizing. It is now called the "decision making" school, and is concerned with the basic question of how people make decisions.

This view had some rather unusual implications. It suggested that if managers were so limited, then they could be easily controlled. What was necessary was not to give direct orders (on the assumption that subordinates were idiots without expertise) or to leave them to their own devices (on the assumption that they were supermen who would somehow know what was best for the organization, how to coordinate with all the other supermen, how to anticipate market changes, etc.). It was necessary to control only the *premises* of their decisions. Left to themselves, with those premises set, they could be predicted to rely on precedent, keep things stable and smooth, and respond to signals that reinforce the behavior desired of them.

To control the premises of decision making, March and Simon outline a variety of devices, all of which are familiar to you, but some of which you may not have seen before in quite this light. For example, organizations develop vocabularies, and this means that certain kinds of information are highlighted and others are screened out—just as Eskimos (and skiers) distinguish many varieties of snow, while Londoners see only one. This is a form of attention directing. Another is the reward system.

Change the bonus for salesmen and you can shift them from volume selling to steady-account selling, or to selling quality products or new products. If you want to channel good people into a different function (because, for example, sales should no longer be the critical function as the market changes, but engineering applications should), you may have to promote mediocre people in the unrewarded function in order to signal to the good people in the rewarded one that the game has changed. You cannot expect most people to make such decision on their own because of the cognitive limits on their rationality, nor will you succeed by giving direct orders, because you yourself probably do not know whom to order where. You presume that once the signals are clear and the new sets of alternatives are manifest, they have enough ability to make the decision but you have had to change the premises for their decisions about their career lines.

It would take too long to go through the dozen or so devices, covering a range of decision areas (March and Simon are not that clear or systematic about them, themselves, so I have summarized them in my own book), but I think the message is clear.

It was becoming clear to the human relations school, and to the bureaucratic school. The human relationists had begun to speak of changing stimuli rather than changing personality. They had begun to see that the rewards that can change behavior can well be prestige, money, comfort, etc., rather than trust, openness, self-insight, and so on. The alternative to supportive relations need not be punishment, since behavior can best be changed by rewarding approved behavior rather than by punishing disapproved behavior. They were finding that although leadership may be centralized, it can function best through indirect and unobtrusive means such as changing the premises on which decisions are made, thus giving the impression that the subordinate is actually making a decision when he has only been switched to a different set of alternatives. The implications of this work were also beginning to filter into the human relations school through an emphasis on behavioral psychology (the modern version of the much maligned stimulus-response school) that was supplanting personality theory (Freudian in its roots, and drawing heavily, in the human relations school, on Maslow).

For the bureaucratic school, this new line of thought reduced the heavy weight placed upon the bony structure of bureaucracy by highlighting the muscle and flesh that make these bones move. A single chain of command, precise division of labor, and clear lines of communication are simply not enough in themselves. Control can be achieved by using alternative communication channels, depending on the situation; by increasing or decreasing the static or "noise" in the system; by creating organizational myths and organizational vocabularies that allow only selective bits of information to enter the system; and through monitoring performance through indirect means rather than direct surveillance. Weber was all right for a starter, but organizations had changed vastly, and the leaders needed many more means of control and more subtle means of manipulation than they did at the turn of the century.

THE TECHNOLOGICAL QUALIFICATION

By now the forces of darkness and forces of light had moved respectively from midnight and noon to about 4 A.M. and 8 A.M. But any convergence or resolution would have to be on yet new terms, for soon after the political science tradition had begun to infiltrate the established schools, another blow struck both of the major positions. Working quite independently of the Tavistock Group, with its emphasis on sociotechnical systems, and before the work of Burns and Stalker on mechanistic and organic firms, Joan Woodward was trying to see whether the classical scientific principles of organization made any sense in her survey of 100 firms in South Essex. She tripped and stumbled over a piece of gold in the process. She picked up the gold, labeled it "technology," and made sense out of her otherwise hopeless data. Job-shop firms, mass-production firms, and continuous-process firms all had quite different structures because the type of tasks, or the "technology," was different. Somewhat later, researchers in America were coming to very similar conclusions based on studies of hospitals, juvenile correctional institutions, and industrial firms. Bureaucracy appeared to be the best form of organization for routine operations; temporary work groups, decentralization, and emphasis on interpersonal processes appeared to work best for nonroutine operations. A raft of studies appeared and are still appearing, all trying to show how the

nature of the task affects the structure of the organization.

This severely complicated things for the human relations school, since it suggested that openness and trust, while good things in themselves, did not have much impact, or perhaps were not even possible in some kinds of work situations. The prescriptions that were being handed out would have to be drastically qualified. What might work for nonroutine, high-status, interesting, and challenging jobs performed by highly educated people might not be relevant or even beneficial for the vast majority of jobs and people.

It also forced the upholders of the revised bureaucratic theory to qualify their recommendations, since research and development units should obviously be run differently from mass-production units, and the difference between both of these and highly programmed and highly sophisticated continuous-process firms was obscure in terms of bureaucratic theory. But the bureaucratic school perhaps came out on top, because the forces of evil—authority, structure, division of labor, etc.—no longer looked evil, even if they were not applicable to a minority of industrial units.

The emphasis on technology raised other questions, however, A can company might be quite routine, and a plastics division nonroutine, but there were both routine and nonroutine units within each. How should they be integrated if the prescription were followed that, say, production should be bureaucratized and R&D not? James Thompson began spelling out different forms of interdependence among units in organizations, and Paul Lawrence and Jay Lorsch looked closely at the nature of integrating mechanisms. Lawrence and Lorsch found that firms performed best when the differences between units were *maximized* (in contrast to both the human relations and the bureaucratic school), as long as the integrating mechanisms stood half-way between the two—being neither strongly bureaucratic nor nonroutine. They also noted that attempts at participative management in routine situations were counterproductive, that the environments of some kinds of organizations were far from turbulent and customers did not want innovations and changes, that cost reduction, price, and efficiency were trivial considerations in some firms, and so on. The technological insight was demolishing our comfortable truths right and left. They were also being questioned from another quarter.

ENTER GOALS, ENVIRONMENTS, AND SYSTEMS

The final seam was being mined by the sociologists while all this went on. This was the concern with organizational goals and the environment. Borrowing from the political scientists to some extent, but pushing ahead on their own, this "institutional school" came to see that goals were not fixed; conflicting goals could be pursued simultaneously, if there were enough slack resources, or sequentially (growth for the next four years, then cost-cutting and profit-taking for the next four); that goals were up for grabs in organizations, and units fought over them. Goals were, of course, not what they seemed to be, the important ones were quite unofficial; history played a big role; and assuming profit as the pre-eminent goal explained almost nothing about a firm's behavior.

They also did case studies that linked the organization to the web of influence of the environment; that showed how unique organizations were in many respects (so that, once again, there was no one best way to do things for all organizations); how organizations were embedded in their own history, making change difficult, Most striking of all, perhaps, the case studies revealed that the stated goals usually were not the real ones; the official leaders usually were not the powerful ones; claims of effectiveness and efficiency were deceptive or even untrue; the public interest was not being served; political influences were pervasive; favoritism, discrimination, and sheer corruption were commonplace. The accumulation of these studies presented quite a pill for either the forces of light or darkness to swallow, since it was hard to see how training sessions or interpersonal skills were relevant to these problems, and it was also clear that the vaunted efficiency of bureaucracy was hardly in evidence. What could they make of this wad of case studies?

We are still sorting it out. In one sense, the Weberian model is upheld because organizations are not, *by nature,* cooperative systems; top managers must exercise a great deal of effort to control them. But if organizations are tools in the hands of leaders, they may be very recalcitrant ones. Like the broom in the story of the sorcerer's apprentice, they occa-

sionally get out of hand. If conflicting goals, bargaining, and unofficial leadership exists, where is the structure of Weberian bones and Simonian muscle? To what extent are organizations tools, and to what extent are they products of the varied interests and group strivings of their members? Does it vary by organization, in terms of some typological alchemy we have not discovered? We don't know. But at any rate, the bureaucratic model suffers again; it simply has not reckoned on the role of the environment. There are enormous sources of variations that the neat, though by now quite complex, neo-Weberian model could not account for.

The human relations model has also been badly shaken by the findings of the institutional school, for it was wont to assume that goals were given and unproblematical, and that anything that promoted harmony and efficiency for an organization also was good for society. Human relationists assumed that the problems created by organizations were largely limited to the psychological consequences of poor interpersonal relations within them, rather than their impact on the environment. Could the organization really promote the psychological health of its members when by necessity it had to define psychological health in terms of the goals of the organization itself? The neo-Weberian model at least called manipulation "manipulation" and was skeptical of claims about autonomy and self-realization.

But on one thing all the varied schools of organizational analysis now seemed to be agreed: organizations are systems—indeed, they are open systems. As the growth of the field has forced ever more variables into our consciousness, flat claims of predictive power are beginning to decrease and research has become bewilderingly complex. Even consulting groups need more than one or two tools in their kit-bag as the software multiplies.

The systems view is intuitively simple. Everything is related to everything else, though in uneven degrees of tension and reciprocity. Every unit, organization, department, or work group takes in resources, transforms them, and sends them out, and thus interacts with the larger system. The psychological, sociological, and cultural aspects of units interact. The systems view was explicit in the institutional work, since they tried to study whole organizations; it became explicit in the human relations school, because they were so concerned with the interactions of people. The political science and technology viewpoints also had to come to this realization, since they dealt with parts affecting each other (sales affecting production; technology affecting structure).

But as intuitively simple as it is, the systems view has been difficult to put into practical use. We still find ourselves ignoring the tenets of the open systems view, possibly because of the cognitive limits on our rationality. General systems theory itself has not lived up to its heady predictions; it remains rather nebulous. But at least there is a model for calling us to account and for stretching our minds, our research tools, and our troubled nostrums.

SOME CONCLUSIONS

Where does all this leave us? We might summarize the prescriptions and proscriptions for management very roughly as follows:

1 A great deal of the "variance" in a firm's behavior depends on the environment. We have become more realistic about the limited range of change that can be induced through internal efforts. The goals of organizations, including those of profit and efficiency, vary greatly among industries and vary systematically by industries. This suggests that the impact of better management by itself will be limited, since so much will depend on market forces, competition, legislation, nature of the work force, available technologies and innovations, and so on. Another source of variation is, obviously, the history of the firm and its industry and its traditions.

2 A fair amount of variation in both firms and industries is due to the type of work done in the organization—the technology. We are now fairly confident in recommending that if work is predictable and routine, the necessary arrangement for getting the work done can be highly structured, and one can use a good deal of bureaucratic theory in accomplishing this. If it is not predictable, if it is nonroutine and there is a good deal of uncertainty as to how to do a job, then one had better utilize the theories that emphasize autonomy, temporary groups, multiple lines of authority and communications, and so on. We also know that this distinction is important when organizing different parts of an organization.

We are also getting a grasp on the question of what is the most critical function in different types of organizations. For some organizations it is production; for others, marketing; for still others, development. Furthermore, firms go through phases whereby the initial development of a market or a product or manufacturing process or accounting scheme may require a non bureaucratic structure, but once it comes on stream, the structure should change to reflect the changed character of the work.

3 In keeping with this, management should be advised that the attempt to produce change in an organization through managerial grids, sensitivity training, and even job enrichment and job enlargement is likely to be fairly ineffective for all but a few organizations. The critical reviews of research in all these fields show that there is no scientific evidence to support the claims of the proponents of these various methods; that research has told us a great deal about social psychology, but little about how to apply the highly complex findings to actual situations. The key word is *selectivity:* We have no broad-spectrum antibiotics for interpersonal relations. Of course, managers should be sensitive, decent, kind, courteous, and courageous, but we have known that for some time now, and beyond a minimal threshold level, the payoff is hard to measure. The various attempts to make work and interpersonal relations more humane and stimulating should be applauded, but we should not confuse this with solving problems of structure, or as the equivalent of decentralization or participatory democracy.

4 The burning cry in all organizations is for "good leadership," but we have learned that beyond a threshold level of adequacy it is extremely difficult to know what good leadership is. The hundreds of scientific studies of this phenomenon come to one general conclusion: Leadership is highly variable or "contingent" upon a large variety of important variables such as nature of tasks, size of the group, length of time the group has existed, type of personnel within the group and their relationships with each other, and amount of pressure the group is under. It does not seem likely that we'll be able to devise a way to select the best leader for a particular situation. Even if we could, that situation would probably change in a short time and thus would require a somewhat different type of leader.

Furthermore, we are beginning to realize that leadership involves more than smoothing the paths of human interaction. What has rarely been studied in this area is the wisdom or even the technical adequacy of a leader's decision. A leader does more than lead people; he also makes decisions about the allocation of resources, type of technology to be used, the nature of the market, and so on. This aspect of leadership remains very obscure, but it is obviously crucial.

5 If we cannot solve our problems through good human relations or through good leadership, what are we then left with? The literature suggests that changing the structures of organizations might be the most effective and certainly the quickest and cheapest method. However, we are now sophisticated enough to know that changing the formal structure by itself is not likely to produce the desired changes. In addition, one must be aware of a large range of subtle, unobtrusive, and even covert processes and change devices that exist. If inspection procedures are not working, we are now unlikely to rush in with sensitivity training, nor would we send down authoritative communications telling people to do a better job. We are more likely to find out where the authority really lies, whether the degree of specialization is adequate, what the rules and regulations are, and so on, but even this very likely will not be enough.

According to the neo-Weberian bureaucratic model, as it has been influenced by work on decision making and behavioral psychology, we should find out how to manipulate the reward structure, change the premises of the decision makers through finer controls on the information received and the expectations generated, search for interdepartmental conflicts that prevent better inspection procedures from being followed, and after manipulating these variables, sit back and wait for two or three months for them to take hold. This is complicated and hardly as dramatic as many of the solutions currently being peddled, but I think the weight of organizational theory is in its favor.

We have probably learned more, over several decades of research and theory, about the things that do *not* work (even though some of them obviously *should* have worked), than we have about things that do work. On balance, this is an important gain and should not discourage us. As you know, organizations are extremely complicated. To have as much knowledge as we do have in a fledgling discipline that has had to borrow from the diverse tools and concepts of psychology, sociology, economics, engineering, biology, history, and even anthropology is not really so bad.

Reading 9
Organizations and the System Concept
Daniel Katz
Robert L. Kahn

THE DEFINITION AND IDENTIFICATION OF ORGANIZATIONS

The first problem in understanding an organization or a social system is its location and identification. How do we know that we are dealing with an organization? What are its boundaries? What behavior belongs to the organization and what behavior lies outside it? Who are the individuals whose actions are to be studied and what segments of their behavior are to be included?

The common-sense answer to such questions begins with the organizational name. The fact that popular names exist to label social organizations, however, is both a help and a hindrance. These labels represent socially accepted stereotypes about organizations and do not specify their role structure, their psychological nature, or their boundaries. On the other hand, these names help in locating the area of behavior in which we are interested. Moreover, the fact that people both within and without an organization accept stereotypes about its nature and functioning is one determinant of its character.

The second key characteristic of the common-sense approach to understanding an organization is to regard it simply as the epitome of the purposes of its designer, its leaders, or its key members.[1] The teleology of this approach is again both a help and a hindrance. Since human purpose is deliberately built into organizations and is specifically recorded in the

[1]See Chapter 15 for a further discussion of the problem of organizational goals.

Excerpted from Chapter 2 in D. Katz and R. L. Kahn, *The Social Psychology of Organizations* (2d ed.). © 1978 by John Wiley & Sons. Reprinted with permission.

social compact, the by-laws, or other formal protocol of the undertaking, it would be inefficient not to utilize these sources of information. In the early development of a group, many processes are generated that have little to do with its rational purpose, but over time there is a cumulative recognition of the devices for ordering group life and a deliberate use of these devices.

Apart from formal protocol, the primary mission of an organization as perceived by its leaders furnishes a highly informative set of clues for the researcher seeking to study organizational functioning. Nevertheless, the stated purposes of an organization as given by its by-laws or in the reports of its leaders can be misleading. Such statements of objectives may idealize, rationalize, distort, omit, or even conceal some essential aspects of the functioning of the organization. Nor is there always agreement about the mission of the organization among its leaders and members. The university president may describe the purpose of the institution as turning out national leaders; the academic dean sees it as imparting the cultural heritage of the past, the academic vice-president as enabling students to move toward self-actualization and development, the graduate dean as creating new knowledge, the dean of students as training young people in technical and professional skills which will enable them to earn their living, and the editor of the student newspaper as inculcating the conservative values that will preserve the status quo of an outmoded capitalistic society.

The fallacy here is equating the purposes or goals of organizations with the purposes and goals of individual members. The organization as a system has an output, a product or an outcome, but this is not necessarily identical with the individual purposes of group members. Though the founders of the organization and its key members do think in teleological terms about organizational objectives, we should not accept such practical thinking, useful as it may be, in place of a theoretical set of constructs for purposes of scientific analysis. Social science, too frequently in the past, has been misled by such shortcuts and has equated popular phenomenology with scientific explanation.

In fact, the classic body of theory and thinking about organizations has assumed a teleology of this sort as the easiest way of identifying organizational

structures and their functions. From this point of view an organization is a social device for efficiently accomplishing through group means some stated purpose; it is the equivalent of the blueprint for the design of a machine that is to be created for some practical objective. The essential difficulty with this purposive approach is that an organization characteristically includes more and less than is indicated by the design of its founder or the purpose of its leader. Some of the factors assumed in the design may be lacking or so distorted in operational practice as to be meaningless, while unforeseen embellishments dominate the organizational structure. Moreover, it is not always possible to ferret out the designers of the organization or to discover the intricacies of the design which they carried in their heads. The attempt by Merton (1957) to deal with the latent function of the organization in contrast with its manifest function is one way of dealing with this problem. The study of unanticipated consequences as well as anticipated consequences of organizational functioning is a similar way of handling the matter. Again, however, we are back to the purposes of the creators or leaders, dealing with unanticipated consequences on the assumption that we can discover the consequences anticipated by them and can lump all other outcomes together as a kind of error variance.

It would be much better theoretically, however, to start with concepts that do not call for identifying the purposes of the designers and then correcting for them when they do not seem to be fulfilled. The theoretical concepts should begin with the input, output, and functioning of the organization as a system and not with the rational purposes of its leaders. We may want to employ such purposive notions to lead us to sources of data or as subjects of special study, but not as our basic theoretical constructs for understanding organizations.

Our theoretical model for the understanding of organizations is that of an energic input-output system in which the energic return from the output reactivates the system. Social organizations are flagrantly open systems in that the input of energies and the conversion of output into further energic input consist of transactions between the organization and its environment.

All social systems, including organizations, consist of the patterned activities of a number of individuals. Moreover, these patterned activities are complementary or interdependent with respect to some common output or outcome; they are repeated, relatively enduring, and bounded in space and time. If the activity pattern occurs only once or at unpredictable intervals, we could not speak of an organization. The stability or recurrence of activities can be examined in relation to the *energic input* into the system, the *transformation of energies within the system,* and the *resulting product or energic output.* In a factory the raw materials and the human labor are the energic input, the patterned activities of production the transformation of energy, and the finished product the output. To maintain this patterned activity requires a continued renewal of the inflow of energy. This is guaranteed in social systems by the energic return from the product or outcome. Thus the outcome of the cycle of activities furnishes new energy for the initiation of a renewed cycle. The company that produces automobiles sells them and by doing so obtains the means of securing new raw materials, compensating its labor force, and continuing the activity pattern.

In many organizations outcomes are converted into money and new energy is furnished through this mechanism. Money is a convenient way of handling energy units both on the output and input sides, and buying and selling represent one set of social rules for regulating exchange. Indeed, these rules are so effective and so widespread that there is some danger of mistaking the business of buying and selling for the defining cycles of organization. It is a commonplace executive observation that businesses exist to make money, and the observation is usually allowed to go unchallenged. It is, however, a very limited statement about the purposes of business.

Some human organizations do not depend on the cycle of selling and buying to maintain themselves. Universities and public agencies depend rather on bequests and legislative appropriations, and in so-called voluntary organizations the output reenergizes the activity of organization members in a more direct fashion. Member activities and accomplishments are rewarding in themselves and tend therefore to be continued without the mediation of the outside environment. A society of bird watchers can wander into the hills and engage in the rewarding activities of identifying birds for their mutual edification and enjoyment. Organizations thus differ on

this important dimension of the source of energy renewal, with the great majority utilizing both intrinsic and extrinsic sources in varying degree. Most large-scale organizations are not as self-contained as small voluntary groups and are very dependent upon the social effects of their output for energy renewal.

Our two basic criteria for identifying social systems and determining their functions are (1) tracing the pattern of energy exchange or activity of people as it results in some output and (2) ascertaining how the output is translated into energy that reactivates the pattern. We shall refer to organizational functions or objectives not as the conscious purposes of group leaders or group members but as the outcomes that are the energic source for maintenance of the same type of output.

The problem of identifying the boundaries of an organization is solved by following the energic and informational transactions as they relate to the cycle of activities of input, throughput, and output. Behavior not tied to these functions lies outside the system. Many factors are related to the intake of materials into a structure but only those activities concerned with the actual importation of energy or information are part of that structure. Similarly, many processes are associated with the reception of outputs by the environment, but only those activities having to do with export of products are behavioral patterns of the organization. Obviously there is less difficulty in identifying the patterns of behavior responsible for the throughput of the system than for the boundary subsystems that deal with the environment. These subsystems do not always have clearly identifiable borders. Nor can the problem be handled by regarding any behavior of an organizational member as organizational behavior. A person in a boundary role may interact with members of another system as if he or she belonged to that system. Even the production worker's behavior, although physically taking place within the factory, at times may be social interaction with friends unrelated to the work role. In searching for criteria to define the boundaries of a system one looks for some qualitative break in the nature of the behavior pattern under scrutiny or some sudden quantitative change. These changes can be noted as the same people step out of their organizational roles and behave in radically different fashion or as we move to different people operating in different role systems.

This model of an energic input-output system is taken from the open system theory as promulgated by von Bertalanffy (1956). Theorists have pointed out the applicability of the system concepts of the natural sciences to the problems of social science. It is important, therefore, to examine in more detail the constructs of system theory and the characteristics of open systems.

System theory is basically concerned with problems of relationships, of structure, and of interdependence rather than with the constant attributes of objects. In general approach it resembles field theory except that its dynamics deal with temporal as well as spatial patterns. Older formulations of system constructs dealt with the closed systems of the physical sciences, in which relatively self-contained structures could be treated successfully as if they were independent of external forces. But living systems, whether biological organisms or social organizations, are acutely dependent on their external environment and so must be conceived of as open systems.

Before the advent of open system thinking, social scientists tended to take one of two approaches in dealing with social structures; they tended either (1) to regard them as closed systems to which the laws of physics applied or (2) to endow them with some vitalistic concept like entelechy. In the former case they ignored the environmental forces affecting the organization and in the latter case they fell back upon some magical purposiveness to account for organizational functioning. Biological theorists, however, have rescued us from this trap by pointing out that the concept of the open system means that we neither have to follow the laws of traditional physics, nor in deserting them do we have to abandon science. The laws of Newtonian physics are correct generalizations but they are limited to closed systems. They do not apply in the same fashion to open systems which maintain themselves through constant commerce with their environment, that is, a continuous inflow and outflow of energy through permeable boundaries.

The essential difference between closed and open systems can be seen in terms of the concept of entropy and the second law of thermodynamics. According to the second law of thermodynamics, a system moves toward equilibrium; it tends to run down, that is, its differentiated structures tend to move toward dissolution as the elements composing them become arranged in random disorder. For example, suppose that a bar of iron has been heated by the application of a blowtorch on one side. The arrangement of all the fast (heated) molecules on one side and all the slow molecules on the other is an unstable state, and over time the distribution of molecules becomes in effect random, with the resultant cooling of one side and heating of the other, so that all surfaces of the iron approach the same temperature. A similar process of heat exchange will also be going on between the iron bar and its environment, so that the bar will gradually approach the temperature of the room in which it is located, and in so doing will elevate somewhat the previous temperature of the room. More technically, entropy increases toward a maximum and equilibrium occurs as the physical system attains the state of the most probable distribution of its elements. In social systems, however, structures tend to become more elaborated rather than less differentiated. The rich may grow richer and the poor may grow poorer. The open system does not run down, because it can import energy from the world around it. Thus the operation of entropy is counteracted by the importation of energy and the living system is characterized by negative rather than positive entropy.

SOME CONSEQUENCES OF VIEWING ORGANIZATIONS AS OPEN SYSTEMS

Like most innovations in scientific theory, the open system approach was developed in order to deal with inadequacies in previous models. The inadequacies of closed system thinking about organizations became increasingly apparent during the mid-century decades of rapid societal changes. The limitations of empirical research based on closed system assumptions also pointed up the need for a more comprehensive theoretical approach. The consequences, or rather the potentialities, of dealing with organizations as open systems can best be seen in contrast to the limitations and misconceptions of closed system thinking. The most important of these misconceptions, almost by definition, is the failure to recognize fully the dependence of organizations on inputs from their environment. That inflow of materials and energy is neither constant nor assured, and when it is treated as a constant much of organizational behavior becomes unexplainable. The fact that organizations have developed protective devices to maintain stability and that they are notoriously difficult to change or reform should not be allowed to obscure their dynamic relationships with the social and natural environment. Changes in that environment lead to demands for change in the organization, and even the effort to resist those demands results in internal change.

It follows that the study of organizations should include the study of organization-environment relations. We must examine the ways in which an organization is tied to other structures, not only those that furnish economic inputs and support but also structures that can provide political influence and societal legitimation. The open system emphasis on such relationships implies an interest in properties of the environment itself. Its turbulence or placidity, for example, limits the kinds of relationships that an organization can form with systems in the environment and indicates also the kinds of relationships that an organization will require to assure its own survival.

The emphasis on openness is qualified, however. There is a duality to the concept of open system; the concept implies openness but it also implies system properties, stable patterns of relationships and behavior within boundaries. Complete openness to the environment means loss of those properties; the completely open organization would no longer be differentiated from its environment and would cease to exist as a distinct system. The organization lives only by being open to inputs, but selectively; its continuing existence requires both the property of openness and of selectivity.

The open system approach requires study of these selective processes, analysis of those elements in the environment that are actively sought, those disregarded, and those kept out or defended against. The basis of these choices, the means employed for their implementation, and the consequences for organizational effectiveness and survival becomes topics for research. In well-established organizations the internal arrangements for making and implementing such choices are highly developed, a fact that often allows such organizations to withstand environmental turbulence better than the reform or revolutionary movements that seek to displace them. Sustained supportive inputs are less predictable for groups attempting social change.

A second serious deficiency in closed system thinking, both theoretical and pragmatic, is overconcentration on principles of internal functioning. This could be viewed as merely another aspect of disregard for the environment, but it has consequences of its own. Internal moves are planned without regard for their effects on the environment and the consequent environmental response. The effects of such moves on the maintenance inputs of motivation and morale tend not to be adequately considered. Stability may be sought through tighter integration and coordination when flexibility may be the more important requirement. Coordination and control become ends in themselves, desirable states within a closed system rather than means of attaining an adjustment between the system and its environment. Attempts to introduce coordination in kind and degree not functionally required tend to produce new internal problems.

Two further errors derive from the characteristic closed system disregard of the environment and preoccupation with internal functions—the neglect of equifinality and the treatment of disruptive external events as error variance. The equifinality principle simply asserts that there are more ways than one of producing a given outcome. In a completely closed system, the same initial conditions must lead to the same final result; nothing has changed and therefore nothing changes. In open systems, however, the principle of equifinality applies; it holds true at the biological level, and it is more conspicuously true at the social level. Yet in practice most armies insist that there is one best way for all recruits to assemble their guns; most coaching staffs teach one best way for all baseball players to hurl the ball in from the outfield. And in industry the doctrine of scientific management as propounded by Taylor and his disciples begins with the assumption of the one best way: discover it, standardize it, teach it, and insist on it. It is true that under fixed and known conditions there is one best way, but in human organizations the conditions of life are neither fixed nor fully known. Such organizations are better served by the general principle, characteristic of all open systems, that there need not be a single method for achieving an objective.

The closed system view implies that irregularities in the functioning of a system due to environmental influences are error variances and should be treated accordingly. According to this conception, they should be controlled out of studies of organizations. From the organization's own operations they should be excluded as irrelevant and should be guarded against. The decisions of officers to omit a consideration of external factors or to guard against such influences in a defensive fashion, as if they would go away if ignored, is an instance of this type of thinking. So is the now outmoded "public be damned" attitude of business executives toward the clientele upon whose support they depend. Open system theory, on the other hand, would maintain that environmental influences are not sources of error variance but are integral to the functioning of a social system, and that we cannot understand a system without a constant study of the forces that impinge upon it.

Finally, thinking of organizations as closed systems result in failure to understand and develop the feedback or intelligence function, the means by which the organization acquires information about changes in the environment. It is remarkable how weak many industrial companies are in their market research departments when they are so dependent on the market. The prediction can be hazarded that organizations in our society will increasingly move toward the improvement of the facilities for research in assessing environmental forces. We are in the process of correcting our misconception of the organization as a closed system, but the process is slow.

Open system theory, we believe, has potentialities for overcoming these defects in organizational thinking and practice. Its potentialities, however, cannot be realized merely by acknowledging the fact of organizational openness; they must be developed. Open is not a magic word, and pronouncing it is not enough to reveal what has been hidden in the organizational cave.

Reading 10

Organization Design: The Case for a Coalitional Model of Organizations

Jeffrey Pfeffer
Gerald R. Salancik

Prescriptions for effective organization designs depend on one's view of organizations, how they operate, what their principal problems are, and how they are managed. One model of organizations is the rational model, which has formed the basis for most management theories as well as for the major sociological theories of organizations, such as the one proposed by Max Weber. Contingency approaches to organization design, advocated by those who would design organizations to match or fit the requirements of their technology, environment, or size, are logical extensions of the rational model of organizations.

In this article, we develop an alternative perspective on organizations and organization design. Since we call this model a coalitional model, the organization design problem posed becomes one of designing organizations that are at once effective and responsive to their own interests and to those of their constituents in the coalition. Our purpose is to provide further thinking about organization design using new metaphors, new perspectives, and new insights. We will first state the two perspectives on organizations and then examine their implications for the design of organizational structures.

THE RATIONAL MODEL

The rational model of organizations and organization design assumes that organizational effectiveness or performance criteria can be defined unambiguously; information about contingencies—size, technology, environmental uncertainty, and others—can be obtained; this information can be used in conjunction with some theoretical prescriptions to design organizational structures that, given the contingencies, will be seen as something rationally planned; and organizations are linked tightly

Reprinted, by permission of the publisher, from *Organizational Dynamics*, Autumn 1977. Copyrighted © by AMACOM, a division of American Management Associations. All rights reserved.

enough to their environments so that organizations with appropriate designs are more effective than organizations whose structures are less adequately matched to the various technological and environmental contingencies.

The rational model has been advanced both by those earlier theorists who sought a single best way of organizing or organizing principles that were universally applicable and by present-day theorists who believe that different organizational structures are appropriate for different circumstances. Both the universal and contingency approaches presume that designs are planned, that criteria exist by which good designs can be distinguished from bad designs in terms of how the structures operate, and that designs meeting these criteria contribute to organizational performance. The main difference between the advocates of universal principles and the advocates of a contingency approach is that the former require less information, since designs are not contingent on the kind of circumstances faced.

The assumptions embedded in what we have called the rational model are so reasonable, so much a part of the ideology of how management is practiced, that most people take them virtually for granted. If we examine them critically, however, we find that some of the assumptions are less than completely persuasive.

Consider the issue of criteria by which designs are evaluated. The problem of defining criteria that all the members of governmental or other nonprofit organizations can understand and accept is obvious; somewhat less obvious is the fact that a similar problem may exist in business as well. The global criterion of profit maximization begs the question of the time period over which the profit is to be maximized. Moreover, any given decision or set of policies may have unclear and tenuous connections to profits.

Organizational decisions are made by real managers interested in their own career advancement who operate with the blinders derived from their particular backgrounds, training, and organizational positions. Thus the fact that production executives frequently define problems as production problems and recommend solutions that benefit their department and their position in the organization is not merely evidence of self-aggrandizement at work. Instead, there is frequently enough uncertainty about the connections between actions and consequences,

enough ambiguity about the value of the decision outcome, to allow for disagreements among people who are all committed to the organization's long-run welfare. Profit maximization is fine for economic theory, but real managers in real organizations understand that there are many ramifications to any major decision, in part because such a decision is usually made under conditions of great uncertainty.

Information about various organizational contingencies can, indeed, be obtained. But such information is often open to a number of interpretations; moreover, information frequently is obtained to support the decision favored by those involved in the information collection process. This is why Peter Drucker has noted the importance of opinions and has argued that the search for "facts" may, in part, constitute a search for a mirage. An environment does not present itself to an organization neatly labeled as turbulent, uncertain, or placid. And judgments of the significance of a technology and the certainty or uncertainty of an environment are based on interpretations of events and information as construed by the managers in charge of the organization.

Although it is true that formal structures can be planned, major structural reorganization, or even structural planning, is a rare occurrence in most business organizations, occasioned only by the existence of severe operating problems and frequently only undertaken with the help of a consultant, to provide external legitimacy. Furthermore, structures almost never function as planned. The pattern of interactions, responsibilities, and communication flows invariably differs from the formally specified pattern. Structures, in the sense of the actual patterns of interactions, change as personnel and problems change and as organizational opportunities are redefined. Thus the formal structure of the organization is seldom planned, and the informal structure —the actual operating structure—is almost never planned.

The final assumption is also open to question. On close examination, the rational model of organization design looks much like rational economics and has the same underlying assumption—perfect environmental constraint. If organizations are not structured appropriately, diminished performance will result. Other than the fact that performance can be assessed in many ways, there is also the question of the extent to which organizations are tightly linked to their environments. Many organizations are public, receiving money through an incremental budgeting system that allocates resources with little regard to any consideration beyond the size of last year's budget and the power of the organization's constituency. In many industrial sectors, as well, the discipline imposed by competition is minor. Indeed, for firms such as IBM and General Motors that dominate important industrial sectors, the principal problem is how not to drive competitors out of business and thereby avoid raising the specter of antitrust action.

AN ALTERNATIVE MODEL

An alternative model can be called an external model, a political model, a coalitional model, a ceremonial model, or a loosely coupled model of organizations, depending upon which particular features are singled out for attention. Basically, this alternative perspective on organizations holds that information is limited and serves largely to justify decisions or positions already taken; goals, preferences, and effectiveness criteria are problematic and conflicting; organizations are loosely linked to their social environments; the rationality of various designs and decisions is inferred after the fact to make sense out of things that have already happened; organizations are coalitions of various interests; organization designs are frequently unplanned and are basically responses to contests among interest for control over the organization; and organization designs are in part ceremonial.

This alternative perspective attempts explicitly to recognize the social nature of organizations. All organizations exist embedded in a larger social system, dependent on that system for resources and because of the need to attract resources or a coalition of support sufficient to generate these resources. They are continually confronted with conflicting demands and constraints. For purposes of understanding organizations, the mistake made by microeconomic theory is not in assuming the goal is profit maximization rather than some other goal but in assuming a single or at least a consistent set of criteria by which decisions can be made.

As Richard Cyert and James March recognized years ago, organizations are coalitions of varying interests. Employees, shareholders, managers, customers, suppliers, and governmental agencies all impinge on the organization, and each has a distinct and different set of preferences for organizational action along with different criteria for evaluating organizational outcomes. Rather than viewing organizations as rational instruments, with the associated question of how the instrument can best be designed and employed to achieve some specified objective, this alternative conceptualization sees organizations as coalitional social systems. The important questions deal with whose interests are to be served, and who is to control and initiate organizational actions.

Not all participants in organizations are interested or even informed about all aspects of their operations. One of the important variables determining decision outcomes is who, precisely, becomes involved in the process of influencing the decision. The fact that participants are only partially included in the organization and partially involved in decisions, coupled with the imperfect distribution of information about organizational activities, means that organizations are relatively uncoupled both internally and externally. In other words, an action taken in one part of the organization, or a single organizational decision, may go unnoticed by other participants in the organization and can be inconsistent with other actions taken by the organization. As we will argue in more detail below, this decoupling of organizational actions and of subunits may be a reasonable way of simultaneously resolving conflicting demands and interests.

Organizations choose their environments by deciding what businesses they will be in. The decision to be in the oil pipeline business brings governmental regulation along with it. The decision to be in the metals mining and processing business brings with it environmental pressures from a variety of interested groups and organizations. Organizations also choose which groups to heed and what information to make public, at least within certain limits. In this sense we can say that organizations create or enact their environments.

Because organizations have resources and stores of energy and at the same time are the meeting places for a variety of interests and demands, we propose the analogy of organizations to economic markets. The difference is that in formal organizations it is influence and control—social power, if you will—that is being transacted. Certainly, no business executive who has witnessed the increasing intrusion of government, employee organizations, and various public interest groups in decision making that was formerly the prerogative of management can fail to see that much of what is called government-business, union-management, or business-social environmental relations is nothing more than a contest for control over various decisions and parts of the enterprise.

There are a number of solutions to the problem of maintaining control. One that has received less attention than it warrants is the possibility of ceremonial actions undertaken to provide symbolic recognition of a group's interest in the organization, while changing little that is fundamental about the organization. The possibility of formal structures serving ceremonial functions has been recognized explicitly by John Meyer in a study of public schools, and implicitly by Claes Fornell in a study of consumer affairs departments in American firms.

Meyer noted that, although the technology of education was imperfectly known, school organizations nevertheless developed elaborate formal structures. These structures were designed to coincide with environmental expectations rather than to solve any rationally defined technical problem. Social and environmental pressures dictated an emphasis on accounting procedures and certain forms of certification to the virtual exclusion of any evaluation of what was actually going on in the classroom. Similarly, Fornell found that in response to consumer activism, a number of firms set up consumer affairs departments. Such departments typically were only peripherally involved in decisions on product quality, pricing, or servicing. But the presence of such a department provided symbolic recognition of the rights of consumers and, more important, provided a buffer between the consumers and the rest of the organization, as well as a place where consumer action could be focused.

The alternative model recognizes that organizations are tied to their external environments by requirements for legitimacy and resources and at the same time are confronted with conflicting demands and preferences because such environments are multifaceted. Many interests attempt to initiate organizational actions for their own benefit, and one important issue becomes who controls the organization and its resources. Conflicting demands and the contest for control are never perfectly resolved once and for all. Thus organizational actions may appear at times to be inconsistent, unplanned, and loosely coupled. However, the reader should be cautioned that such characterizations are, in large measure, a reflection of the particular perspective and the criteria being employed.

ORGANIZATION DESIGN DILEMMAS

Because of conflicting demands, imperfect information, contests for control, and the loose coupling between organizations and environments, rational actions and rational designs are by definition virtually impossible. Imbedded in all definitions of rationality is the idea of goal attainment, but if there are multiple and conflicting goals, how can we define rationality? We want to suggest that organizational design is itself a process filled with contradictions and dilemmas. And we need to highlight some of these dilemmas before we consider design alternatives.

The principal dilemma involves the contradiction between learning what to do and executing decisions and policies. On the one hand, organizations can be portrayed as responding to external constraints and dependencies. From this perspective, the job of management is to be responsive. Responsiveness means being aware of the various demands and constraints and then molding organizational actions to take account of the most critical constraints and demands made by those on whom the organization is most dependent for its future survival. This view of organizations and their problems places the manager in a role similar to that of a politician—an assimilator and processor of demands. Descriptions of Mayor Richard Daley's way of governing Chicago or of Jerry Brown's current mode of operating in California illustrate this approach to management.

The problem is that the manager as a processor and assimilator of demands is not in an action mode. An organization designed to execute decisions requires more centralization of control, more unity of direction, more orderliness in decision processes, more hierarchy, more formal structure. These very attributes of structure, which make action possible, also limit the visibility of alternatives, minimize conflicting information, and prevent the intrusion of other perspectives.

One frequently attempted solution is to segment the two activities within organizations. Thus we see line management responsible for managing the day-to-day operations while various staff planning or environmental scanning groups do forecasting and gather information that will help to guide future actions. The problem is that such separation is usually so successful that staff reports and environmental scanning information are seldom translated into operating decisions. Whenever staff is used in reaching operating decisions, it is because organizational line management is involved in the planning process and the scanning and planning are done with a unity of objective and of orientation toward action. While making the results of staff effort easier to implement, however, this very rapprochement between line and staff may defeat the purpose of an independent staff, that is, to register alternatives and reflect environmental variety.

A second dilemma is posed by the need for organizations to be responsive to demands and constraints and at the same time to preserve the ability to adapt to changes in these constraints and interdependencies. The ability to adapt to changes requires the maintenance of discretion. In order to change with the demands of future contingencies, an organization must have some remaining latitude, some resource in reserve, some discretion in responding.

New York City presents a good illustration of the problems of administering a system that is too tightly constrained. In the past, various interests that together provided the support for the city administration were enlisted in the coalition through the provision of special favors: large pensions (and salaries) for municipal workers, rent-controlled apartments for the middle class, public housing for the poor, and so forth. When the cost of these various concessions became overwhelming, the city administration had no discretion left and no room within which to maneuver. As a consequence, for some period of time, control over basic budgetary decisions has been removed from the city government.

Thus organizations must, on the one hand, respond to demands and constraints and, on the other, retain flexibility and resources with which to deal with future contingencies. It is not enough to design organizations to be responsive or to preserve discretion; they must do both.

The final dilemma is that of the feasibility or desirability of organization design itself. On the one hand, there is demand for structural design, and if structures matter, which they clearly do, then there is a presumption that the design of structures should be planned. Such a perspective on the design process is itself part of a rational model of organizations. Just as one supposedly decides rationally to purchase some equipment or make some other investment decision, so one rationally determines the appropriate structure for the organization. But, we have argued, rationality is limited and sometimes retrospectively constructed, information is limited and often gathered after the decision is made for purposes of justification, goals and preferences are conflicting, and structures emerge in response to contests for control and environmental constraints.

Thus the alternative perspective suggests that organizations are not often planned, and, in fact, it may be impossible to design structures rationally. This idea is not new with us. Peter Vaill, dean of the business school at George Washington University, has suggested comparing actual patterns of interaction with intended designs. When the two do not correspond, instead of imposing additional controls to enforce conformity with the intended structure, Vaill argues that it might be more useful to change the intended structure, or design it, to bring it in line with the actual patterns of interaction. There is information available on how organizations actually operate and evolve. The idea of preplanned design presumes a foreknowledge of objectives, constraints, and possibilities. The idea of design as emergent assumes less about managerial prescience and extends the idea of a respondent model of managerial action.

ORGANIZATION DESIGN FOR AN EFFECTIVE MARKET

One conceptualization of organizations sees them as coalitions in which parties with various interests come together in partly cooperative, partly conflicting efforts. Furthermore, our model of organizations maintains that information is limited, planning is difficult, and an important function of management is to respond to external demands and constraints in ways that maintain adequate support for the organization. We have already used the analogy of organizations as markets for influence and control in which social power is transacted. Taking the analogy one step further, what are the design implications for making organizations more effective markets in which these social processes can operate?

If we borrow from the economists' definitions of perfect markets, we see two important considerations: one, information is available to all parties and, two, no single participant dominates the marketplace. We would translate these two conditions into the organizational requirements that information be widely distributed throughout the social system and that there be little opportunity for or realization of the institutionalization of control or power. If management is to respond to constraints and changing environmental contingencies, and if there are multiple and conflicting interests involved, then an effective organization design would prevent management from insulating itself from the environment or from the consequences of its own mistakes. To accomplish this, information would have to be widely shared and power less institutionalized.

The model we are using is quite straightforward. Environmental interdependence creates constraints and contingencies for the organization, and these, in turn, help determine the distribution of power and influence in the organization. The distribution of power and influence helps determine who holds the leadership positions and what actions and policies are adopted by the organization. As environmental interdependencies change, the organization should be able to register these changes and alter what it is doing. This process of adaptation is hindered, however, whenever control is institutionalized.

Control is institutionalized in many ways. When a firm introduces a resolution requiring, for example, a heavier percentage of affirmative votes for it to be acquired by another firm or taken over in a proxy fight, power has been institutionalized. Many firms have recently taken this action. When rules are changed to permit a manager to stay on past normal retirement, his or her normal term in office is lengthened and power has again been institutionalized. By the same token, rules that provide for automatic turnover and changes in control prevent the institutionalization of power.

It is almost inevitable that executives, once in power, act in ways that institutionalize control. The evidence is overwhelming that subordinates and staff members will be replaced by persons who share the executive's orientation and therefore are more likely to be loyal. Staff will probably be added to control and manage the operation better. Information systems will be expanded, and often centralized, providing further control. All these actions are taken because each executive honestly believes that he knows what is best for the organization and that what is needed is the mechanism to carry out decisions more effectively. The danger lies in personal fallibility. If a manager is firmly in control, when circumstances change and problems arise that require new skills and insights, the process of organizational change is more apt to be painful and involve major dislocations.

Proxy fights have been described as managerial revolutions. The analogy is a good one. Organizations must be structured so that changes do not require revolutions or severe organzational crises before a shift in control can take place.

One of the most important design considerations, in this connection, is the distribution of information. People cannot participate effectively in either economic or organizational markets without information. It is not surprising that secrecy is one of the practices used to institutionalize control, maintain power, and leave the organization with more discretion—at least on the surface. Confronted by groups with conflicting demands, managers may try to convince each one that the ability to respond to its demands is constrained by limited resources or by checks imposed by others. Such claims are more easily made when information on organizational resources and activities is secret. Claims of competence and assertions that interests are being satisfied are also facilitated by secrecy in operations. You are less likely to pay high legal fees willingly once it becomes apparent that the lawyer is using standardized forms from a book. Company claims of the impossibility or economic infeasibility of purchasing pollution-control equipment are more likely to appear credible when the company itself controls all the information needed to make such a determination.

Knowledge of organizational activities themselves may be kept secret. Some companies resisted making their equal employment data public, recognizing the potential these data had for inciting additional pressure from both the government and various civil rights groups. Similarly, it's easier to argue that consumer complaints are being handled fairly if no one has access to the data on the actual disposition of complaints. In many ways, secrecy helps to maintain organizational control. Power is easier to wield if few in the organization know exactly how it is exercised and if performance data or other indicators of problems are withheld. For these very reasons, widely shared information is important in designing organizations that are, in fact, responsive and adaptive to changing environmental conditions and resource interdependencies.

An effective organizational market requires open communication systems in which information on operations is widely distributed. The prescription for preventing the institutionalization of power and the suppression of information might include multiple chief executive positions; fixed, and relatively brief, terms of office; a system of multiple centers of power and control; and widespread dissemination of information about organization actions, outcomes, and alternatives.

The first recommendations fly in the face of the supposed need for single centers of final accountability and authority. This demand, in turn, arises because of the symbolic value of the single, visible leader. When things go wrong, it is important to have some one person who can be held responsible and fired, thus satisfying a demand for change. The problem is that this very lodging of responsibility and accountability in single positions provides the occupants of the positions with the power to institutionalize control and resist removal or change even if circumstances warrant their removal. Many American organizations have bought too much stability with solitary responsibility, at the cost of too much centralization and institutionalization of control. We could test this assertion empirically by considering how severe a crisis in performance has to be before the situation is changed. One classic instance is the turnaround at Memorex: The company found itself on the verge of bankruptcy before its principal creditor, the Bank of America, instituted the overthrow of the existing top management.

DESIGN FOR LEARNING

If organizations depend on external environments for resources, then valid information about those environments is required so that management can understand the constraints and contingencies with which it is confronted. Most organizations follow the easy path, relying upon available information—usually information generated by their accounting systems. Consequently, the information tends to be historical and to focus on internal operations, when what is needed is information that is oriented toward the future and about external conditions. It is small wonder that organizations frequently get into trouble.

Setting up environmental scanning units, such as long-range planning or social and economic forecasting units, may not solve the problem. Scanning units face two challenges: how to gather the needed information, and how to get the organization to act on that information. A scanning unit frequently deals with only one portion of the environment. Subunits established for a particular purpose typically hire specialists. A market research department, for example, may employ personnel with advanced degrees in market research, survey research, and statistics. Typically, these people will undertake consumer surveys. Thus the firm may have excellent information about alternative advertising media and a wealth of attitudinal data about the marketplace. What the firm probably will not have is information on where the product is stocked, what kind of shelf exposure or store promotion it is receiving, whether the sales force is doing a good job of promoting the product, and how well the product is performing. After all, the performance of the sales force is an issue for industrial psychologists interested in motivation, while shelf display is the business of specialists in marketing channels.

In other words, a scanning unit usually deals with only one dimension of a multidimensional world. The solution might be to establish multiple scanning units or units that contain personnel with a variety of backgrounds and expertise—interdisciplinary units. Although such a solution may overcome the problem of omitted data, it will probably only worsen the second problem—getting the assembled information used in organizational decision making.

There are several reasons why information is not utilized. One is that it is typically collected by staff departments composed of specialists with unique vocabularies, sophisticated methodologies, and, sometimes, little appreciation for the scope, content, and timing of operating decisions. The information must be used, of course, by line managers with decision-making responsibility. Communication may be difficult. Differences in perspective, vocabulary, and expertise, as well as separation in the organizational structure and physical distance, all hinder the dissemination and use of information collected about organizational environments.

An additional problem is that those who collect the information gather what they believe to be important. There is no assurance that operating managers share their judgments. This problem is not easily resolved since a person cannot always predict what information he would use if he had it. The usual response is to answer in terms of what has been used in the past or what has been available. Moreover, the manager himself may not be the best judge of what information is required since he operates on the basis of his previous actions. People develop patterns of decision making, and changing such styles may be difficult. Individuals accustomed to operating on the basis of certain information may see neither the need nor the desirability for additional data.

A third problem is the conflict in power and status between line and staff positions. To the extent that the manager relies on staff information, he loses discretion and admits the importance of the staff and his own dependence on them. One way of retaining power and control is to ignore staff information. The staff attempts to have its reports heeded at least in part to illustrate its power and importance in the organization. This contest for control and status, frequently exacerbated by differences in the backgrounds of the parties involved, hinders organizational learning.

To summarize our argument so far:

- The fact that organizations are interdependent with their environments supports the need for information about environments.
- Specialized scanning units may be ineffective in meeting that need.
- Specialized units collect specialized information that is limited, that may be perceived as irrelevant to actual decisions, and that may be perceived as a threat to the power and control of line managers.
- Scanning highlights and narrows the organization's attention, so the development of specialized scanning functions may, in reality, leave the organization more isolated and less informed than previously.

- The scanners, forecasters, and planners focus on routinized, quantitative data collection; prepare complex, difficult-to-understand reports; and then struggle with operating managers to have their efforts recognized.

We don't need specialized personnel to manage the organization's environmental interdependence. The necessary expertise and insight are already present within the organization—possessed by the operating managers themselves. Constantly in contact with the environment, they can scarcely be ignorant of what is going on. More probably, the press of day-to-day operating activities prevents them from considering the future, and their limited exposure to the total picture narrows their overall perspective. Thus a design that consciously engages operating personnel in planning and that facilitates this process of interaction with one another is called for so that insights and perspectives unique to each one can be shared with the others.

One strategy would be to bring together the various sources of expertise within the organization in a focused format. Techniques such as the Delphi and Nominal Group Technique, in which participants are systematically queried about forecasts, potential actions, and environmental information, provide distinct advantages over the use of specialized staff departments. The difficulty is that such exercises are often carried out on an infrequent, *ad hoc* basis.

(The Nominal Group Technique is a structured group meeting in which participants first generate ideas silently in writing; next record these ideas, discuss, and clarify them; and last vote on the merit of the ideas or proposals. The technique limits pressures to conform and the tendency to identify ideas with their source. In contrast, Delphi uses a structured questionnaire and feedback cycle in place of the group meeting. Each participant in the Delphi panel contributes ideas or opinions, and then the collected opinions are fed back to each panel member in an interactive process that often results in consensus or at least identifies the sources of differences of opinion.)

A potentially more satisfactory solution is to use an evaluation, reward, or incentive system that clearly defines planning and environmental scanning as part of the operating manager's job and an organizational structure and a physical layout that facilitate interaction among interdependent personnel—those who combine relevant environmental contacts with involvement in operating decisions that depend on such information. Task forces, or planning groups, composed of the operating managers who have responsibilities that require meeting on a periodic basis can be created. These groups will serve to institutionalize environmental scanning and forecasting in the operating part of the organization. We are familiar with some organizations that have adopted parts of this solution, but none that has duplicated the whole design.

DESIGN FOR MANAGING CONFLICTING DEMANDS

Because organizations represent accumulations of energy and resources, many groups will make demands or attempt to attain a measure of control over these organizations. The more useful the resources of an organization to others, the more demands it will face. Organizational efforts at diversification may link it with more diverse elements in the environment. Each of these may then seek something from the organization, subjecting it to even more competing demands. How can managers cope with the frequently conflicting interests of customers, suppliers, employees, owners, governmental agencies, and myriad other groups and organizations? One answer is differentiation and diversification.

Diversification, defined as developing new activities that make the organization dependent on new sources of supply and new markets, reduces the organization's dependence on any single environmental element. Thus diversification into new industries reduces a firm's dependence on a single labor union, or a single set of suppliers or customers, while diversification into adult education reduces a college's dependence on a single age group, in other words, those from 18 to 22 years of age. Dispersing dependency automatically reduces the impact of the organization's failure to respond to any particular demand. Thus the very diversity that confronts the organization with multiple and conflicting interests offers part of its own solution.

The second part of the answer lies in creating an internally differentiated, loosely coupled structure to confront the various interests. When the demands

themselves are not tightly interconnected, it is possible to satisfy conflicting claims on the organization by establishing subunits to cope with each interest. Consumers may demand better quality products and more control over product policies. In response, the organization can establish a consumer affairs department. Demands are registered and consumers, or organizations that represent them, are provided with both access to and a feeling of participation in the organization. At the same time, employees wanting more control can focus on the industrial relations department, while minorities can articulate their interests through affirmative action offices. This process of differentiation can proceed indefinitely subject only to the constraints imposed by limited resources, since all these subunits do require resources.

Differentiation to satisfy multiple constituencies simultaneously is a practice followed by many organizations. Universities, for example, establish research institutes to obtain money from diverse sources, academic departments to serve the interests of the various scholarly disciplines, and student and community service units to meet the expectations of these groups. A business firm may have a consumer affairs department, an affirmative action unit, a purchasing department, an industrial relations department, a shareholders' relations unit, and an environmental engineering group, each of which deals with a particular constituency.

Differentiation provides a solution to the problem of competing demands only when the subunits themselves are relatively independent. Each subunit must have the ability to take actions unconstrained by the actions of others. Independent or loosely coupled subunits assist organizations in coping with their environments by permitting new units to be created to absorb protests without requiring rationalization of the relationship among all other units. Thus small accommodations can be made to interest groups without redirecting the activities of the entire organization. A consumer affairs department can deal with complaints about a product with a letter and a free sample while the production and development departments remain unaffected.

A second benefit from establishing special departments is that each subsegment becomes partially co-opted. Because the subunit is its primary point of access to the organization, the survival of that subunit becomes important to the interest group. As a consequence, the external group may make less extreme demands or may accommodate itself in oҫer ways to the interests of the organization. For example, affirmative action units become important to groups seeking increased hiring of ethnic minorities or women. In other words, these groups develop a proprietary interest in the organizational subunits established to deal with them, thereby making such subunits more effective in managing conflicting interest-group demands.

A structural solution to conflicting demands, then, is a differentiated organization of loosely coupled subunits, each of which deals with specific environmental interests and each of which is only minimally interdependent with the rest of the organization. This solution depends on the availability of slack resources. Without slack, subunits could not be loosely connected and could not be created as easily. It is important to recognize that neither differentiation of the organization nor diversification reduces the organization's dependence on its environment. Rather, the nature of the interdependence is changed in ways that make it easier to manage. If numerous interests are making demands on the organization, the need to respond to any specific interest, which now comprises only a small part of the organization's activities, is reduced.

CONCLUSION

The reality of the design dilemmas posed earlier should now be clear. Designing diversified, differentiated, loosely coupled organizations makes it possible to absorb and co-opt protest and handle conflicting interdependencies and demands. At the same time, it makes control and rapid change in the entire organization very difficult to achieve. Information that is widely distributed and structures that help to ensure managerial succession prevent the institutionalization of power and increase the adaptability of the organization. At the same time, the ability to embark on long-range projects, the stability of control in the organization, and the accountability of a single person or a small group of persons are compromised. And the very act of design itself presumes that those who develop the structure know what the structure needs to accomplish. Yet, with conflicting interests, uncertainty about future changes, and the variety of possible effectiveness criteria, such certainty about the goals of structure is itself unlikely.

We have many more ideas about the problems that deserve consideration than we have pat answers. In fact, it is possible that only by expanding perspectives and approaches to the issue of structural design can we make real progress. Both the universal-principles and contingency approaches suffer severe inadequacies because both presume a unity of purpose, a managerial omniscience, and a rational decision-making framework that in truth contains more myth than fact. The issue posed in this article is both direct and difficult: How can structures be designed that incorporate a recognition of managerial fallibility and provide for the expression of alternative interests, preferences, and ideas and that at the same time provide enough order to facilitate action? The recommendations we propose tend to focus on the first problem rather than the second. This is based on our contention that most organizations have bought too much order and control at the expense of flexibility and the ability to respond to the external environment.

Reading 11

A General Diagnostic Model for Organizational Behavior: Applying a Congruence Perspective

David A. Nadler
Michael L. Tushman

Most of the job of management is the struggle to make organizations function effectively. The work of society gets done through organizations, and the function of management is to get those organizations to perform that work.

The task of getting organizations to function effectively is a difficult one, however. Understanding one individual's behavior is a challenging problem in and of itself. A group, made up of different individuals and multiple relationships among those individuals, is even more complex. Imagine, then, the mind-boggling complexity inherent in a large organization made up of thousands of individuals, hundreds of groups, and relationships among individuals and groups too numerous to count.

In the face of this overwhelming complexity, organizational behavior must be managed. Ultimately the work of organizations gets done through the behavior of people, individually or collectively, on their own or in collaboration with technology. Thus, central to the management task is the management of organizational behavior. To do this, there must be the capacity to *understand* the patterns of behavior at individual, group, and organizational levels, to *predict* what behavioral responses will be elicited by different managerial actions, and finally to use understanding and prediction to achieve *control*.

How can one achieve understanding, prediction, and control of organizational behavior? Given its inherent complexity and enigmatic nature, one needs tools to help unravel the mysteries, paradoxes, and apparent contradictions that present themselves in the everyday life of organizations. One kind of tool is the conceptual framework or model. A model is a theory which indicates which factors (in an organization, for example) are most critical or important. It also indicates how these factors are related, or which factors or combination of factors cause other factors to change. In a sense, then, a

model is a road map that can be used to make sense of the terrain of organizational behavior.

The models we use are critical because they guide our analysis and action. In any organizational situation, problem solving involves the collection of information about the problem, the interpretation of that information to determine specific problem types and causes, and the development of action plans. The models that individuals hold influence what data they collect and what data they ignore; models guide how people attempt to analyze or interpret the data they have; finally models aid people in choosing action plans.

Indeed, anyone who has been exposed to an organization already has some sort of implicit model. People develop these road maps over time, building on their own experiences. These implicit models (they usually are not explicitly written down or stated) guide behavior (Argyris & Schon, 1974). These models also vary in quality, validity, and sophistication depending on the nature and extent of the model builder's experience, as well as the model builder's perceptiveness, ability to conceptualize and generalize from experience, etc.

We are not solely dependent, however, on the implicit and experienced-based models that individuals develop. The last four decades have witnessed intense work including research and theory development related to organization behavior (see, for example, Dunnette. 1976). It is therefore possible to think about scientifically developed explicit models for the analysis of organizational behavior and for use in organizational problem solving.

This paper will present one particular research- and theory-based model. It is a general model of organizations. Rather than describe a specific phenomenon or aspect of organizational life (such as a model of motivation or a model of organizational design) it attempts to provide a framework for thinking about the organization as a total system. The major thrust of the model is that for organizations to be effective, their subparts or components must be consistently structured and managed—they must approach a state of congruence.

The paper will be organized into several sections. In the first section we will discuss the basic view of organizations which underlies the model—systems theory. In the second section, we will present and discuss the model itself. In the third section, we will present an approach to using the model for organizational problem analysis. Finally, we will discuss some of the implications of this model for thinking about organizations.

A BASIC VIEW OF ORGANIZATIONS

There are many different ways of thinking about organizations. Typically a manager who is asked to "draw a picture of an organization" will respond with some version of a pyramidal organizational chart. The model this rendition reflects is one which views the most critical factors as the stable formal relationships among the jobs and formal work units that make up the organization. While this clearly is one way to think about organizations, it is a very limited view. It excludes such factors as leader behavior, the impact of the environment, informal relations, power distribution, etc. Such a model can only capture a small part of what goes on in an organization. It is narrow and static in perspective.

Over the past twenty years there has been a growing consensus that a viable alternative to the static classical models of organizations is to think about organizations as social systems. This approach stems from the observation that social phenomena display many of the characteristics of natural or mechanical systems (Von Bertalanffy, 1968; Buckley, 1967). In particular it is argued that organizations can be better understood if they are considered as dynamic and open social systems (Katz & Kahn, 1966, 1978).

What is a system? In the simplest of terms, a system is a set of interrelated elements. These elements are related; thus change in one element may lead to changes in other elements. An *open system* is one that interacts with its environment. Thus it is more than just a set of interrelated elements. Rather, these elements make up a mechanism that takes input from the environment, subjects it to some form of transformation process, and produces output (Figure 11-1). At the most general

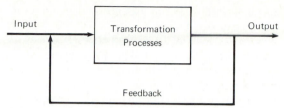

Figure 11-1 The basic systems model.

level, it should be easy to visualize organizations as systems. Let us consider a manufacturing plant, for example. It is made up of different related components (different departments, jobs, technologies, etc.). It receives input from the environment, including labor, raw materials, production orders, etc., and subjects those inputs to a transformation process to produce products.

Organizations as systems display a number of basic systems characteristics. Katz and Kahn (1966, 1978) discuss these in detail, but a few of the most critical characteristics will be mentioned here. First, organizations display degrees of internal *interdependence* (Thompson, 1967). Changes in one component or subpart of an organization frequently have repercussions for other parts—the pieces are interconnected. Returning to our manufacturing plant example, if changes are made in one element (for example, the skill levels of the people hired to do jobs), other elements will be affected (the productiveness of the equipment used, the speed or quality of production activities, the nature of supervision needed, etc.). Second, organizations have the capacity for *feedback* (see Figure 11-1). Feedback is information about the output of a system that can be used to control the system (Weiner, 1950). Organizations can correct errors and indeed change themselves because of this characteristic (Bauer, 1966). If, in our plant example, the plant management receives information about the declining quality of its product, it can use this information to identify factors in the system itself that contribute to this problem. It is important to note that unlike mechanized systems, feedback information does not always lead to correction. Organizations have the potential to use feedback and be self-correcting systems, but they do not always realize this potential.

A third characteristic of organizations as systems is *equilibrium*. Organizations develop energy to move toward states of balance. When an event occurs that puts the system out of balance, it reacts and moves toward a balanced state. If one work group in our plant example were suddenly to increase its performance dramatically, it would throw the system out of balance. This group would be making increasing demands on the groups that supply it with information or materials to give it what it needs. Similarly, groups that work with the output of the high-performing group would feel the pressure of work-in-process inventory piling up in front of them. Depending on the pay system used, other groups might feel inequity as this one group begins to earn more. We would predict that some actions would be taken to put the system back into balance. Either the rest of the plant would be changed to increase production and thus be back in balance with the single group or (more likely) actions would be taken to get this group to modify its behavior to be consistent with the levels of performance of the rest of the system (by removing workers, limiting supplies, etc.). The point is that somehow the system would develop energy to move back toward a state of equilibrium or balance.

Fourth, open systems display *equifinality*. In other words, different system configurations can lead to the same end or lead to the same type of input-output conversion. This means there is not a universal way, or "one best way," to organize. Finally, open systems need to display *adaptation*. For a system to survive, it must maintain a favorable balance of input and output transactions with the environment or it will run down. If our plant produces a product for which there are decreasing applications, it must adapt to the environmental changes and develop new products or ultimately the plant will simply have to close its doors. Any system, therefore, must adapt by changing as environmental conditions change. The consequences of not adapting to the environment can be seen in the demise of many once-prosperous organizations (such as the Eastern railroads) which did not alter in response to environmental changes.

Thus systems theory provides a different way of thinking about the organization, in more complex and dynamic terms. While systems theory is a valuable basic perspective on organizations, it is limited as a problem-solving tool. The reason is that as a model systems theory is too abstract to be used for day-to-day organizational behavior-problem analysis. Because of the level of abstraction of systems theory, we need to develop a more specific and pragmatic model based on the concepts of the open-systems paradigm.

A CONGRUENCE MODEL OF ORGANIZATIONAL BEHAVIOR

Given the level of abstraction of open-systems theory, our job is to develop a model which reflects the basic systems concepts and characteristics, but which will also be more specific and thus more usable as an analytic tool. In this section, we will describe a model which attempts to specify in more detail the critical inputs, the major outputs, and the transformation processes that characterize organizational functioning.

The model puts its greatest emphasis on the transformation process and in particular reflects the critical system property of interdependence. It views organizations as made up of components or parts which interact with each other. These components exist in states of relative balance, consistency, or "fit" with each other. The different parts of an organization can fit well together and thus function effectively, or fit poorly, thus leading to problems, dysfunctions, or performance below potential. Given the central nature of these "fits" among components in the model, we will talk about it as a *congruence model of organizational behavior,* since effectiveness is a function of the congruence among the various components.

The concept of congruence is not a new one. Homans (1952) in his pioneering work on social processes in organizations emphasized the interaction and consistency among key elements of organizational behavior. Leavitt (1965), for example, identified the four major components of organizations as people, tasks, technology, and structure. The model we will present here builds on these views and also draws from fit models developed and used by Seiler (1967), Lawrence and Lorsch (1969), and Lorsch & Sheldon (1972).

It is important to remember that we are concerned about modeling the *behavioral* system of the organization—the system of elements that ultimately produce patterns of behavior and thus performance of the organizations. In its simplest form we need to deal with the question of what inputs the system has to work with, what outputs it needs to and actually produces, and how the major components of the transformation process interact with each other.

Inputs

Inputs are those factors that are, at any one point in time, the "givens" that face the organization. They are the materials that the organization has to work with. There are several different types of inputs, each of which presents a different set of "givens" to the organization. (See Figure 11-2 for an overview of inputs.)

The first input is the *environment,* or all of those factors outside of the boundaries of the organization being examined. Every organization exists within the context of a larger environment which includes individuals, groups, other organizations, and even larger social forces, all of which have a potentially powerful impact on how the organization performs (Pfeffer & Salancik, 1978). Specifically, the environ-

ment includes markets (clients or customers), suppliers, governmental and regulatory bodies, labor unions, competitors, financial institutions, special-interest groups, etc. The environment is critical to organizational functioning (Aldrich & Pfeffer, 1976). In particular, for purposes of organizational analysis, the environment has three critical features. First, the environment makes demands on the organization. For example, it may require the provision of certain products or services, at certain levels of quality or quantity. Market pressures are particularly important here. Second, the environment may place constraints on organizational action. It may limit the types or kinds of activities in which an organization can engage. These constraints could range from limitations imposed by scarce capital all the way to governmental regulatory prohibitions. Third, the environment provides opportunities which the organization can explore. In total, then, the analysis of an organization needs to consider

Input	Environment	Resources	History	Strategy
DEFINITION	All factors, including institutions, groups, individuals, events, etc. outside of the boundaries of the organization being analyzed, but having a potential impact on that organization.	Various assets that organization has access to, including human resources, technology, capital, information, etc. as well as less tangible resources (recognition in the market, etc.).	The patterns of past behavior, activity, and effectiveness of the organization which may have an effect on current organizational functioning.	The stream of decisions made about how organizational resources will be configured against the demands, constraints and opportunities, within the context of history.
CRITICAL FEATURES OF THE INPUT FOR ANALYSIS	— What demands does the environment make on the organization? — environment puts constraints on organizational action.	— What is the relative quality of the different resources that the organization has access to? — To what extent are resources fixed, as opposed to flexible in their configuration?	— What have been the major stages or phases of development of the organization? — What is the current impact of historical factors such as — strategic decisions — acts of key leaders — crises — core values & norms	— How has the organization defined its core mission, including: — What markets it serves. — What products/services it provides to these markets. — On what basis does it compete? — What supporting strategies has the organization employed to achieve the core mission? — What specific objectives have been set for organizational output?

Figure 11-2 Key organizational inputs.

what factors are present in the environment of the organization and how those factors individually or in relation to each other create demands, constraints, or opportunities.

The *resources* of the organization are the second input. Any organization faces its environment with a range of different assets to which it has access and which it can employ. These include human beings, technology, capital, information, etc. Resources can also include certain less tangible assets, such as the perception of the organization in the marketplace or a positive organizational climate. A set of resources can be shaped, deployed, or configured in different ways by an organization. For analytic purposes, there are two features that are of primary interest. One aspect of resources concerns the relative quality of those resources, or the value they have in light of the nature of the environment. The second factor concerns the extent to which resources can be reconfigured, or how fixed or flexible different resources are.

The third input is the *history* of the organization. There is growing evidence that the contemporary functioning of many organizations is greatly influenced by events in the past (see Levinson, 1972, 1976). In particular, it is important to understand the major stages or phases of development of the organization over time (Galbraith & Nathanson, 1978) as well as the current impact of events that occurred in the past, such as key strategic decisions that were made, the acts or behavior of key leaders in the past, the nature of past crises and the organizational responses to them, and the evolution of core values and norms of the organization.

The final input is somewhat different than the others in that it in some ways reflects some of the factors in the environment, resources, and history of the organization. The fourth input is *strategy*. We will use this term in its most global and broad context (Hofer & Schendel, 1978) to describe the whole set of decisions that are made about how the organization will configure its resources against the demands, constraints, and opportunities of the environment within the context of its history. Strategy refers to the issue of matching the organization's resources to its environment, or making the fundamental decision of "what business are we in?" For analytic purposes, it is important to identify several aspects of strategy (Katz, 1970). First is the core mission of the organization, or what the organiza-

tion has defined as its basic purpose or function within the larger system or environment. The core mission includes decisions about what markets the organization will serve, what products or services it will provide to those markets, or what basis it will use to compete in those markets. Second, strategy includes the specific supporting strategies (or tactics) that the organization will employ or is employing to achieve its core mission. Third, the specific performance or output objectives that have been established.

Strategy is perhaps the most important single input for the organization (see the discussion in Nadler, Hackman, & Lawler, 1979). On one hand, strategic decisions implicitly determine the nature of the work that the organization should be doing or the tasks that it should perform. On the other hand, strategic decisions, and particularly decisions about objectives, serve as the oasis for determining what the outputs of the system should be. Based on strategy, one can determine what is the desired or intended output of the system.

In summary, there are three basic inputs, environment, resources, and history, and a fourth input, strategy, which reflects how the organization chooses to respond to or deal with those other inputs. Strategy is critical because it determines the work that the organization should be performing and it defines the nature of desired organizational outputs.

Outputs

Outputs describe what the organization produces, how it performs, or globally, how effective it is. There has been a lot of discussion about what makes for an effective organization (see Steers, 1978; Goodman & Pennings, 1978; Van de Ven & Ferry, 1980). For our purposes, however, it is possible to identify a number of key indicators of organizational output. First, we need to think about system output at different levels (see Figure 11-3). Obviously we can think about the output that the system itself produces, but we also need to think about the various other types of output that contribute to organizational performance, such as the functioning of groups or units within the organization as well as the functioning of individual organization members.

At the organizational level, it is important to keep three factors in mind in evaluating organizational performance. The first factor is goal attainment, or how well the organization meets its objectives (usu-

Organizational Functioning

— Goal attainment
— Resource utilization
— Adaptability

Group/Unit Functioning

Individual Functioning

— Behavior
— Affective reactions

Figure 11-3   Key organizational outputs.

ally determined by strategy). The second factor is resource utilization, or how well the organization makes use of resources that it has available to it. The question here is not just whether the organization meets its goals but whether it realizes all of the potential performance that is there and whether it achieves its goals by continuing to build resources or by "burning them up" in the process. The final factor is adaptability, or whether the organization continues to position itself in a favorable position vis-à-vis its environment—whether it is capable of changing and adapting to environmental changes.

Obviously, these organizational-level outputs are contributed to by the functioning of groups or units (departments, divisions, or other subunits within the organization). Organizational output also is influenced by individual behavior, and certain individual-level outputs (affective reactions, such as satisfaction, stress, or experienced quality of working life) may be desired outputs in and of themselves.

The Organization as a Transformation Process

So far, we have defined the nature of inputs and outputs for the organizational system. This approach leads us toward thinking about the transformation process. The question that any manager

faces, given an environment, a set of resources, and a history, is how to take a strategy and implement it to produce effective organizational, group/unit, and individual performances.

In our framework, the means for implementing strategies, or the transformation mechanism in the system, is the *organization*. We therefore think about the organization and its major component parts as the fundamental means for transforming energy and information from inputs into outputs (see Figure 11-4). The question, then, is to identify the key components of the organization and the critical dynamic which describes how those components interact with each other to perform the transformation function.

Organizational Components

There are many different ways of thinking about what makes up an organization. At this point in the development of a science of organizations, we probably do not know what is the one right or best way to describe the different components of an organization. The question, then, is to find approaches for describing organizations that are useful, help to simplify complex phenomena, and help to identify patterns in what may at first blush seem to be random sets of activities. The particular approach here views organizations as composed of four major components: (1) the task, (2) the individuals, (3) the formal organizational arrangements, and (4) the informal organization. We will discuss each one of these individually. (See Figure 11-5 for overviews of these components.)

The first component is the *task* of the organization. The task is defined as the basic or inherent work to be done by the organization and its subunits. The task (or tasks) is the activity the organization is engaged in, particularly in light of its strategy. The emphasis is on the specific work activities or

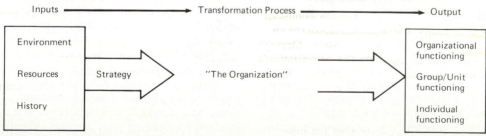

Figure 11-4   The organization as a transformation process.

Component	Task	Individual	Formal organizational arrangements	Informal organization
Definition	The basic and inherent work to be done by the organization and its parts.	The characteristics of individuals in the the organization.	The various structures processes, methods, etc. that are formally created to get individuals to perform tasks.	The emerging arrangements including structures, processes, relationships, etc.
Critical features of each component	— The types of skill and knowledge demands the work poses. — The types of rewards the work inherently can provide. — The degree of uncertainty associated with the work, including factors such as interdependence, routineness, etc. — The constraints on performance demands inherent in the work (given a strategy).	— Knowledge and skills individuals have. — Individual needs and preferences. — Perceptions and expectancies. — Background factors.	— Organization design, including grouping of functions, structure of subunits, and coordination and control mechanisms. — Job design — Work environment — Human resource management systems.	— Leader behavior. — Intragroup relations. — Intergroup relations. — Informal working arrangements. — Communication and influence patterns.

Figure 11-5 Key organizational components.

functions that need to be done and their inherent characteristics (as opposed to characteristics of the work created by how the work is organized or structured in this particular organization at this particular time). Analysis of the task would include a description of the basic work flows and functions, with attention to the characteristics of those work flows, such as the knowledge or skill demands made by the work, the kinds of rewards the work inherently provides to those who do it, the degree of uncertainty associated with the work, and the specific constraints inherent in the work (such as critical time demands, cost constraints, etc.). The task is the starting point for the analysis, since the assumption is that a primary (although not the only) reason for the organization's existence is to perform the task consistent with strategy. As we will see, the assessment of the adequacy of other components will be dependent to a large degree on an understanding of the nature of the tasks to be performed.

The second component of organizations concerns the *individuals* who perform organizational tasks.

The issue here is to identify the nature and characteristics of the individuals that the organization currently has as members. The most critical aspects to consider include the nature of individual knowledge and skills, the different needs or preferences that individuals have, the perceptions or expectancies that they develop, and other background factors (such as demographics) that may be potential influences on individual behavior.

The third component is the *formal organizational arrangements*. These include the range of structures, processes, methods, procedures, etc., that are explicitly and formally developed to get individuals to perform tasks consistent with organizational strategy. "Organizational arrangements" is a very broad term which includes a number of different specific factors. One factor of organizational arrangements is organization design—how jobs are grouped together into units, the internal structure of those units, and the various coordination and control mechanisms used to line the units together (see Galbraith, 1977; Nadler, Hackman, & Lawler,

1979). A second factor in organizational arrangements is how jobs are designed within the context of organizational designs (Hackman & Oldham, 1980). A third factor is the work environment, which includes a number of factors characterizing the immediate environment in which work is done, such as the physical working environment, the work resources made available to performers, etc. A final factor includes the various formal systems for attracting, placing, developing, and evaluating human resources in the organization.

Together, these factors combine to create the set of organizational arrangements. It is important to remember that these are the formal arrangements—formal in that they are explicitly designed and specified, usually in writing.

The final component is the *informal organization*. In any organization, while there is a set of formal organizational arrangements, over time another set of arrangements tends to develop or emerge. These arrangements are usually implicit and not written down anywhere, but they influence a good deal of behavior. For lack of a better term, these arrangements are frequently referred to as the "informal organization," and they include the different structures, processes, arrangements, etc., that emerge over time. These arrangements sometimes arise to complement the formal organizational arrangements by providing structures to aid work where none exist. In other situations they may arise in reaction to the formal structure, to protect individuals from it. They may, therefore, either aid or hinder organizational performance.

A number of aspects of the informal organization have a particularly critical effect on behavior and thus need to be considered. The behavior of leaders (as opposed to the formal creation of leader positions) is an important feature of the informal organization, as are the patterns of relationships that develop both within and between groups. In addition, there are different types of informal working arrangements (including rules, procedures, methods, etc.) that develop. Finally, there are the various communication and influence patterns that combine to create the informal organization design (Tushman, 1977).

Organizations can, therefore, be thought of as a set of components: the task, the individuals, the organizational arrangements, and the informal organization. In any system, however, the critical question is not what the components are, but rather the nature of their interaction. The question in this model is, then, What is the dynamic of the relationship among the components? To deal with this issue, we need to return to the concept of congruence or fit.

The Concept of Congruence

Between each pair of inputs, there exists in any organization a relative degree of congruence, consistency, or "fit." Specifically, the congruence between two components is defined as follows: "the degree to which the needs, demands, goals, objectives and/or structures of one component are consistent with the needs, demands, goals, objectives and/or structures of another component."

Congruence, therefore, is a measure of the goodness of fit between pairs of components. For example, consider two components, the task and the individual. At the simplest level, the task can be thought of as inherently presenting some demands to individuals who would perform it (i.e., skill/knowledge demands). At the same time, the set of individuals available to do the tasks have certain characteristics (i.e., levels of skill and knowledge). Obviously, when the individual's knowledge and skill match the knowledge and skill demanded by the task, performance will be more effective.

Obviously, even the individual-task congruence relationship encompasses more factors than just knowledge and skill. Similarly, each congruence relationship in the model has its own specific characteristics. At the same time, in each relationship, there also is research and theory which can guide the assessment of fit. An overview of the critical elements of each congruence relationship is provided in Figure 11-6.

The Congruence Hypothesis

Just as each pair of components has a high or low degree of congruence, so does the aggregate model, or whole organization, display a relatively high or low level of system congruence. The basic hypothesis of the model builds on this total state of congruence and is as follows: "Other things being equal, the greater the total degree of congruence or fit between the various components, the more effective will be the organization, effectiveness being defined as the degree to which actual organization outputs at individual, group, and organizational levels are simi-

Fit	The issues
Individual—organization	To what extent individual needs are met by the organization arrangements. To what extent individuals hold clear or distorted perceptions of organizational structures, the convergence of individual and organizational goals.
Individual—task	To what extent the needs of individuals are met by the tasks, to what extent individuals have skills and abilities to meet task demands.
Individual—informal organization	To what extent individual needs are met by the informal organization, to what extent does the informal organization make use of individual resources, consistent with informal goals.
Task—organization	Whether the organizational arrangements are adequate to meet the demands of the task, whether organization arrangements tend to motivate behavior consistent with task demands.
Task—informal organization	Whether the informal organization structure facilitates task performance or not, whether it hinders or promotes meeting the demands of the task.
Organization—informal organization	Whether the goals, rewards, and structures of the informal organization are consistent with those of the formal organization.

Figure 11-6 Definitions of "fits."

lar to expected outputs, as specified by strategy."

The basic dynamic of congruence thus views the organization as being more effective when its pieces fit together. If we also consider questions of strategy, the argument expands to include the fit between the organization and its larger environment. An organization will be most effective when its strategy is consistent with the larger environment (in light of organizational resources and history) and when the organizational components are congruent with the tasks to be done to implement that strategy.

One important implication of the congruence hypothesis is that organizational problem analysis (or diagnosis) involves description of the system, identification of problems, and analysis of fits to determine the causes of problems. The model also implies that different configurations of the key components can be used to gain outputs (consistent with the systems characteristic of equifinality). Therefore it is not a question of finding the "one best way" of managing, but of determining effective combinations of components that will lead to congruent fits among them.

The process of diagnosing fits and identifying combinations of components to produce congruence

is not necessarily intuitive. A number of situations which lead to congruence have been defined in the research literature. Thus, in many cases fit is something that can be defined, measured, and even quantified. There is, therefore, an empirical and theoretical basis for making an assessment of fit. In most cases, the theory provides considerable guidance about what leads to congruent relationships (although in some areas the research is more definitive and helpful than in others). The implication is that the manager who is attempting to diagnose behavior needs to become familiar with critical aspects of relevant organizational behavior models or theories in order to evaluate the nature of fits in a particular system.

The congruence model is thus a general organizing framework. The organizational analyst will need other, more specific "submodels" to define high and low congruence. Examples of such submodels that might be used in the context of this general diagnostic model would be (1) the Job Characteristics model (Hackman & Oldham, 1980) to assess and explain the fit between individuals and tasks as well as the fit between individuals and organizational arrangements (job design); (2) Expectancy Theory models of motivation (Vroom, 1964; Lawler, 1973) to explain the fit between individuals and the other three components; (3) the Information Processing model of organizational design (Galbraith, 1973; Tushman & Nadler, 1978) to explain the task–formal organization and task–informal organization fits; and (4) an organizational-climate model (Litwin & Stringer, 1968) to explain the fit between the informal organization and the other components. These models and theories are listed in illustrations of how more specific models can be used in the context of the general model. Obviously, those mentioned above are just a sampling of possible tools that could be used.

In summary, then, we have described a general model for the analysis of organizations (see Figure 11-7). The organization is seen as a system which takes inputs and transforms them into outputs. At the core of the model, the transformation process is the organization, seen as composed of four basic components. The critical dynamic is the fit or congruence among the components. We now turn our attention to the pragmatic question of how to use this model for analyzing organizational problems.

A PROCESS FOR ORGANIZATIONAL PROBLEM ANALYSIS

The conditions that face organizations are frequently changing, and as a consequence, managers are required to continually engage in problem identification and problem-solving activities (Schein, 1970).

To do this managers must be involved in gathering data on the performance of their organizations, comparing these data to desired performance levels, identifying the causes of problems, developing and choosing action plans, and finally implementing and evaluating these action plans. These phases can be viewed as a generic problem-solving process. For long-term organizational viability, some sort of problem-solving process needs to continually be in operation (Schein, 1970; Weick, 1969).

Experience with using the congruence model for organizations to do problem analysis in actual organizational settings has led to the development of an approach to using the model, based on the generic problem-solving processes described above (see Figure 11-8). In this section, we will "walk through" the process, describing the different steps and discussing how the model can be used at each stage. There are eight specific steps in the problem-analysis process, and each one will be described separately.

1 *Identify symptoms:* In any situation there is initial information that presents itself as an indication that problems may exist. We can think of this information as symptomatic data. These data tell us that a problem might exist, but they do not usually indicate what the problem is or what the causes are. It is important to note symptomatic data, however, since the symptoms or problems that present themselves may be important indicators of where to look for more complete data.

2 *Specify inputs:* Having noted the symptoms, the starting point for analysis is to identify the system

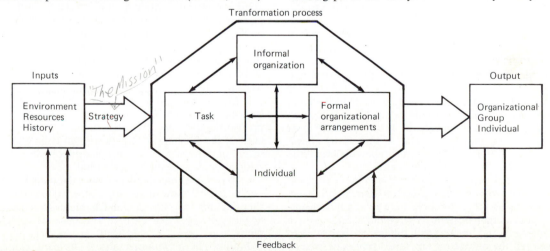

Figure 11-7 A congruence model for organizational analysis.

Step	Explanation
1. Identify symptoms	List data indicating possible existence of problems.
2. Specify inputs	Identify the system Determine nature of environment, resources, and history. Identify critical aspects of strategy
3. Identify outputs	Identify data that define the nature of outputs at various levels (individual, group/unit, organization) should include ' Desired outputs (from strategy) Actual outputs being obtained.
4. Identify problems	Identify areas where there are significant and meaningful differences between desired and actual outputs. To the extent possible, identify penalties, i.e., specific costs (actual and opportunity costs) associated with each problem.
5. Describe components of the organization	Describe basic nature of each of the four components with emphasis on their critical features.
6. Assessment of congruence (fit)	Do analysis to determine relative congruence among components (draw on submodels as needed)
7. Generate Identify causes	Analyze to associate fit with specific problems.
8. Identify action steps	Indicate what possible actions might deal with causes of problems.

Figure 11-8 Basic problem-analysis steps using the congruence model.

and the environment in which it functions. This means collecting data about the nature of the environment, the type of resources the organization has, and the critical aspects of its history. Input analysis also involves identifying the strategy of the organization, including its core mission, supporting strategies, and objectives.

3 *Identify outputs:* The third step is an analysis of the outputs of the organization at the individual, group, and organizational levels. Output analysis actually involves two elements. The first is to define the desired or planned output. This usually can be obtained from an analysis of strategy, which should explicitly or implicitly define what the organization is attempting to achieve in terms of output or performance indicators. The second is to collect data that would indicate what type of output the organization is actually achieving.

4 *Identify problems:* Symptoms indicate the possibility of problems. For our purposes, we will define problems as the differences between expected output and actual output. A problem exists when a significant and meaningful difference is observed between the output (at any level) that is desired or planned and the output that is actually being ob-

tained. Thus problems would be discrepancies (actual versus expected) in organizational performance, group functioning, and individual behavior or affective reactions. These data tell us that problems exist, but they do not specify what the causes are.

Where data are available, it is frequently useful to also identify the costs associated with the problems, or the *penalties* that the organization incurs by not fixing the problem. Penalties might be actual costs (increased expenses, etc.) or opportunity costs, such as revenue that could be realized if the problem were not there.

5 *Describe organizational components:* The next step begins analysis to determine the causes of problems. Data are collected about the nature of each of the four major organizational components, including information about the component and its critical features in this organization.

6 *Assess congruence (fits):* Using the data collected in step 5 as well as applicable submodels or theories, an assessment is made of the positive or negative fit between each of the pairs of components.

7 *Generate hypotheses about problem causes:* Having described the components and assessed congruence, the next step is to link the congruence analysis with the problem identification (step 4). Given the analysis, which poor fits seem to be associated with or account for the output problems that have been identified? The patterns of congruence and incongruence which appear to cause the patterns of problems are determined.

8 *Identify action steps:* The final step in problem analysis is to identify possible action steps. These steps might range from specific changes to dealing with relatively obvious problem causes to additional data collection to test the hypotheses developed concerning relatively more complex problems and causes.

In addition to these eight steps, some further steps need to be kept in mind. Once possible actions are identified, problem solving also involves making predictions about the consequences of those actions, choosing particular action steps, implementing the action steps, and evaluating the impact of those actions. In each case, it is, of course, important to have a general diagnostic framework to monitor the effects of actions.

The congruence model and this problem-analysis process outline are tools for structuring and dealing with the complex reality of organizations. Given the indeterminate nature of social systems, there is no one best way of handling a particular situation. The model and the process do, however, facilitate possible action. If these tools have merit, it is up to the manager to use them along with his or her intuitive sense (based on experience) to make the appropriate set of diagnostic, evaluative, and action decisions over time.

FUTURE DIRECTIONS

The model that we have presented here reflects a particular way of thinking about organizations. If that perspective has merit, then it may make sense to think about the possible extensions of the model as a tool for use in thinking about more complex problems or in structuring more complex situations. A number of directions for further thought, research, and theory development are as follows:

1 *Organizational change:* The issue of organizational change has received a good deal of attention from managers and academics alike. The question is how to implement organizational changes effective-ly. Much talk has centered on the lack of a general model of organizational change. In one sense, however, it is hard to think about a general model of organizational change in the absence of a general model of organizations. The congruence perspective outlined here may provide some guidance and direction toward the development of a more integrated perspective on the processes of organizational change. Initial work in that area (Nadler, 1981) is encouraging in terms of the applicability of the congruence model to the change issue.

2 *Organizational development over time:* There has been a growing realization that organizations grow and develop over time, that they face different types of crises, evolve through different stages, and develop along some predictable lines (see, for example, Greiner, 1972; Galbraith & Nathanson, 1978). A model of organizations such as the one presented here might be a tool for developing a typology of growth patterns by indicating the different configurations of task, individual, organizational arrangements, and informal organizations that might be most appropriate for organizations in different environments and at different stages of development.

3 *Organizational pathology:* Organizational problem solving ultimately requires some sense of what types of problems may be encountered and of the kinds or patterns of causes one might expect. It is reasonable to assume that most problems that organizations encounter are not wholly unique but, rather, are predictable and expectable. The often-heard view that "our problems are unique" reflects in part the fact that there is no framework of organizational pathology. The question is, Are there certain basic "illlnesses" which organizations suffer? Can a framework of organizational pathology, similar to the physician's framework of medical pathology, be developed? The lack of a pathology framework in turn reflects the lack of a basic functional model of organization. Again, development of a congruence perspective might be able to provide a common language to use for the identification of general pathological patterns of organizational functioning.

4 *Organizational solution types:* Closely linked to the problem of pathology is the problem of treatment, intervention, or solutions to organizational problems. Again, there is a lack of a general framework to consider the nature of organizational interventions. In this case too, the congruence model could have value as a means for conceptualizing and ultimately describing the different intervention options available in response to problems (see one attempt at this in Nadler & Tichy, 1980).

SUMMARY

This paper has presented a general approach for thinking about organizational functioning and a process for using a model to analyze organizational problems. This particular model is one way of thinking about organizations. It clearly is not the only model, nor can we claim definitively that it is the best model. It is one tool, however, that appears to be useful for structuring the complexity of organizational life and for helping managers in creating, maintaining, and developing effective organizations.

REFERENCES

Aldrich, H. E., & Pfeffer, J. Environments of organizations. *Annual Review of Sociology,* 1976, **2,** 79–105.

Argyris, C., & Schon, D. A. *Theory in practice.* San Francisco: Jossey-Bass, 1974.

Bauer, R. A. Detection and anticipation of impact: The nature of the task. In R. A. Bauer (Ed.), *Social indicators,* pp. 1–67. Boston: M.I.T. Press, 1966.

Buckley, W. *Sociology and modern systems theory.* Englewood Cliffs, N.J.: Prentice-Hall, 1967.

Dunnette, M. D. *Handbook of industrial and organizational psychology.* Chicago: Rand-McNally, 1976.

Galbraith, J. R. *Designing complex organizations.* Reading, Mass.: Addison-Wesley, 1973.

———. *Organization design.* Reading, Mass.: Addison-Wesley, 1977.

———, & Nathanson, D. A. *Strategy implementation: The role of structure and process.* St. Paul, Minn.: West, 1978.

Goodman, P. S., & Pennings, J. M. *New perspectives on organizational effectiveness.* San Francisco: Jossey-Bass, 1977.

Greiner, L. E. Evolution and revolution as organizations grow. *Harvard Business Review,* 1972.

Hackman, J. R., & Oldham, G. A. *Work redesign.* Reading, Mass.: Addison-Wesley, 1979.

Hofer, C. W., & Schendel, D. *Strategy formulation: Analytical concepts.* St. Paul, Minn.: West, 1978.

Homans, G. C. *The human group.* New York: Harcourt Brace Jovanovich, 1950.

Katz, D., & Kahn, R. L. *The social psychology of organizations,* New York: Wiley, 1966. 2d ed., 1978.

Katz, R. L. *Cases and concepts in corporate strategy.* Englewood Cliffs, N.J.: Prentice-Hall, 1970.

Lawler, E. E. *Motivation in work organizations.* Belmont, Calif.: Wadsworth, 1973.

Lawrence, P. R., & Lorsch, J. W. *Developing organizations: Diagnosis and action.* Reading, Mass.: Addison-Wesley, 1969.

Leavitt, H. J. Applied organization change in industry. In J. G. March (Ed.), *Handbook of organizations,* pp. 1144–1170. Chicago: Rand-McNally, 1965.

Levinson, H. *Organizational diagnosis.* Cambridge, Mass.: Harvard, 1972.

———. *Psychological man.* Cambridge, Mass.: Levinson Institute, 1976.

Litwin, G. H., & Stringer, R. A. *Motivation and organizational climate.* Boston: Harvard University Graduate School of Business Administration, 1968.

Lorsch, J. W., & Sheldon, A. The individual in the organization: A systems view. In J. W. Lorsch and P. R. Lawrence (Eds.), *Managing group and intergroup relations.* Homewood, Ill.: Irwin-Dorsey, 1972.

Nadler, D. A. An integrative theory of organizational change. *Journal of Applied Behavioral Science,* 1981 (in press).

———, & Tichy, N. M. The limitations of traditional intervention technology in health care organizations. In N. Margulies & J. A. Adams, *Organization development in health care organizations.* Reading, Mass.: Addison-Wesley, 1980.

———, Hackman, J. R., & Lawler, E. E. *Managing organizational behavior.* Boston: Little, Brown, 1979.

Salancik, G. R., & Pfeffer, J. *The external control of organizations.* New York: Wiley, 1978.

Schein, E. H. *Organizational psychology.* Englewood Cliffs, N.J.: Prentice-Hall, 1970.

Seiler, J. A. *Systems analysis in organizational behavior.* Homewood, Ill.: Irwin-Dorsey, 1967.

Steers, R. M. *Organizational effectiveness: A behavioral view.* Pacific Palisades, Calif.: Goodyear, 1977.

Thompson, J. D. *Organizations in action.* New York: McGraw-Hill, 1967.

Tushman, M. L. A political approach to organizations: A review and rationale. *Academy of Management Review,* 1977, **2,** 206–216.

Van de Ven, A., & Ferry, D. *Organizational assessment.* New York: Wiley Interscience, 1980.

von Bertalanffy, L. *General systems theory: Foundations, development applications* (Rev. ed.). New York: Braziller, 1968.

Vroom, V. H. *Work and motivation.* New York: Wiley, 1964.

Weick, K. E. *The social psychology of organizing.* Reading, Mass.: Addison-Wesley, 1969.

Wiener, N. *The human use of human beings: Cybernetics and society.* Boston: Houghton Mifflin, 1950.

Part Two

Development of Individual-Organization Relationships

Chapter 4

Choice Processes

The relationship between an individual and an organization begins with a process that requires two choices to be made. The individual must choose to join the organization and the organization must choose to admit the individual. Organizations differ substantially in the permeability of their boundaries. In some organizations, entry is easily accomplished and the selection process is of no consequence. However, in most work organizations the reverse is true. The boundaries are not permeable and the choice process both from the individual's and the organization's point of view is a major decision, since it involves the commitment of considerable time and money and may constitute the beginning of a lifetime relationship.

The article by Nadler, Hackman, and Lawler looks at both sides of the choice process, pointing out that conflicts are present in it and, as a result, that invalid information is often exchanged. The consequence of this may be that both the organization and the individual are harmed because a poor decision is made.

The article by Schein develops these ideas further. Schein particularly emphasizes the fact that if negative outcomes are to be avoided, both the individual and the organization must take steps to actively "manage" both the choice process and the entry stage. The individual, for example, faces a number of distinct tasks, such as making a preliminary occupational choice, developing a realistic self-concept, and developing realistic images of feasible occupations and organizations. If these tasks are neglected or handled inadequately, both the individual and the organization lose. A major problem for each side during this stage is to obtain accurate information about the other side. If this is not done, highly unrealistic expectations can be created which plant the seeds for later disappointments on the part of either or both parties. Schein suggests that each side must also be able to engage in mutual diagnosis *and* be able to look beyond the immediate short-range picture to what reality will be like for the match-up over the long run.

Because most past research has been directed toward helping organizations do a better job of choosing individuals, a great deal is known about how this decision should be made. For example, a considerable body of knowledge exists about the effectiveness of different selection approaches, and an extensive technology is available for assessing the effectiveness of these approaches. The reading by Zedeck and Blood reviews these findings and methods. It provides a good description of just what selection instruments can and cannot be expected to accomplish, and it provides an introduction to the basic methods used to assess the validity of different selection approaches.

The area of selection has become increasingly complex and controversial in the last ten years. Selection decisions involving women and members of minority groups have come under increasing scrutiny, and legislation now requires that organizations use only selection approaches that are demonstrably valid. Zedeck and Blood make this point in their discussion of "unfair discrimination." There also is a rising concern about the degree to which testing constitutes an unfair invasion of privacy. Because testing and selection have become so controversial, many organizations are reevaluating their selection procedures and are increasingly relying on instruments and approaches which have been developed and validated by professionals.

Compared with the amount of attention that has been given to how organizations can make better selection decisions, relatively little has been directed toward how individuals can make better decisions. however, there has been some interesting recent research on entering organizations from the individual's viewpoint. This research suggests that organizations may be able to help both themselves and the individual by providing applicants with better data upon which to base their decisions about employment. The article by Wanous summarizes this research, and makes some interesting points about both future research needs and changes in organizational employment practices that may be required in the years to come.

Reading 12

Staffing Organizations

David A. Nadler
J. Richard Hackman
Edward E. Lawler III

In 1972, when John D. deButts became the chief executive officer of the American Telephone and Telegraph Company, he took a job that by most standards is considered to be the largest managerial job in the world of business. The work force of AT&T numbers almost one million employees (it is larger than the U.S. Army), and it has $80 billion in assets. How does someone come to head a corporation the size of AT&T? Although it often looks like a haphazard process, in many cases it is the result of careful planning on the part of the individual and the organization. It took Mr. deButts thirty-six years and twenty-two jobs to reach the top. He joined AT&T straight out of college and quickly began to move up. He was transferred from one functional area to another so that he would become broadly familiar with the business. He eagerly sought out such transfers, realizing that the "only" way to get to the top was to have a broad range of knowledge. For its part, AT&T, which is committed to promotion from within, constantly assessed the performance of Mr. deButts and asked his bosses to report on his promotability.

Like many successful executives, deButts gained a considerable amount of visibility in his corporation, when he played a key role in helping AT&T successfully respond to a corporate crisis. In 1949, he wrote a carefully reasoned statement which argued that AT&T should remain highly integrated. The arguments in this paper were used by AT&T as the oasis for a successful defense in a Justice Department antitrust suit.

During most of his career at AT&T, the desire of Mr. deButts for an executive position and the needs of AT&T for well-trained top managers seemed to mesh well. Although no formal joint career planning took place between deButts and the members of top management, he developed several sponsors in top management who saw to it that he made the appropriate moves. However, one day in 1958, deButts got what he described as "the shock of my life." He was offered the position of general manager of New York Telephone's Westchester office. This represented a demotion, and he could not understand why he was being punished. He called a number of friends in top management to find out what was going on. He was told to take the job even though he did not want to. He did so, and years later learned that the move was brought about by the president of AT&T who wanted to test deButts's suitability for the top job. He passed this test with flying colors and years later the experience paid off with the presidency of the company.[1]

STAFFING DECISIONS IN ORGANIZATIONS

Staffing decisions are one of the most important types of decisions managers make. Some managers consider them the most important decisions because they so directly impact on how effectively work is done and often they represent an extremely large investment of organization resources that continues for years. It has been estimated that it often costs organizations the equivalent of one year's salary just to replace a middle-level manager.

Effective performance depends on finding and hiring individuals who have the capability and the motivation to perform effectively. The desired situation for most managers is easy to identify. Every job they supervise would be filled by an individual who has the skills to perform the job and who is motivated to perform it. In addition, capable replacements would be available should they lose anyone.

Organizations spend a great deal of effort on such things as training and selection programs in order to insure that jobs will be filled by people who are willing and able to perform them. Despite this, managers often find themselves having relatively

[1]Based on an article by A. M. Louis, *Fortune*, 94:6 (December 1976), pp. 122–136.

From Chapter 3 of *Managing Organizational Behavior* by D. A. Nadler, J. R. Hackman, and E. E. Lawler III, Copyright 1979. Reprinted by permission of the publisher, Little, Brown and Company.

untrained, poorly motivated individuals reporting to them, and as would be predicted by our model of individual performance, the result is poor performance.

Filling jobs with the right individuals is a dynamic process, extremely complex and difficult to manage. Although the individual manager can affect this process, his or her influence is limited because the process is also influenced by the personnel department, other managers, and labor market conditions, to mention just a few. Adequate staffing requires finding a good fit between two changing factors—the characteristics of jobs and the characteristics of employees. It would be hard enough to correctly staff organizations if people and jobs would just hold still; however, this is not the case. People's career aspirations and capabilities change as a result of things that happen to them at work and as a result of nonwork related events (for example, aging and family changes). The kinds of jobs that organizations need to have performed are also constantly changing as a result of a number of factors (such as the changing environment). Effective staffing, therefore, must deal with changes that create misfits in the way an organization is staffed. Some of these misfits are predictable because they result from planned events such as retirement, but many others are not, since they result from such unplanned events as accidents, sickness, and employee resignations.

The staffing problem can be brought into focus for the reader if he or she thinks of a football team or a symphony orchestra, since these are relatively small organizations with clearly identifiable roles. From the manager's point of view, our performance model indicates that the perfect situation would be one in which motivation was high and every position was filled by the best qualified player in the world. Somehow this never quite happens.

First, there is the problem of attracting the best players. Not all of them want to work for the same organization and, as a result, the pool of individuals applying for work in the organization is likely to be less than ideal. Secondly, there is the problem of selecting the applicants who will develop into the best players. Sometimes, the wrong decisions are made despite a careful analysis of the applicants. In football, for example, players who are not drafted or who are released by teams occasionally end up as stars (such as Johnny Unitas of the Baltimore Colts).

Finally, there is the problem of developing the individual players so that when a job opening appears (either because of personnel changes or because a new job has been created), someone will be available to fill it (such as John deButts at AT&T). All too often organizations simply do not have the individuals available to fill jobs when they open up. The reasons for this include their failure to develop individuals as well as the fact that individuals cannot be put on the shelf and stored until they are needed by the organization. People have their own personal goals and objectives, as the example of Mr. deButts illustrates.

Despite the fact that staffing is a difficult and complex area, clearly some things can be done to see that it is managed well. Three stages of the staffing task have been identified: attraction and selection, initial entry, and long-term career development. Each of these stages require different behavior on the part of managers if staffing is to be managed effectively. In the remainder of this chapter, we will consider each of these stages separately. Although the three stages of an individual's involvement will be looked at separately, it is important for the reader to remember that they are not independent stages. The early stages, which will be considered first, impact on what happens later in very important ways, because both people and organizations are affected by their past experiences.

MANAGING THE ATTRACTION AND SELECTION PROCESS

How the attraction-selection process is handled by a manager can have a large impact on whether the right people are hired. The key to making it go well is the open exchange of accurate information between the job candidate and the manager. Without accurate information, neither the individual nor the manager can make a good selection decision.

In many ways, the manager has the most options during the attraction-selection process, since he or she does not yet have commitments to the individuals involved. Most managers are aware of this and, as a result, spend a considerable amount of effort trying to attract good job applicants and to determine who should be hired. Unfortunately, the research evidence suggests that frequently managers do a poor job and end up with people who do not fit the jobs they are in (Schneider, 1976). The reasons for this are many and complex, but they stem from the stance that applicants and managers assume in such a situation. A brief review of these reasons is needed to clarify how the process should be managed and to explain why the open exchange of accurate information is difficult during this process.

Perspective of Individuals

Individuals seek a work setting where they can fulfill their needs and find satisfaction. They do this by gathering information about a number of organizations and then, as would be predicted by expectancy theory, attempting to join those that they perceive as offering the most desirable balance of outcomes. They gather information about organizations from a number of sources (such as advertisements and through friends) and usually end up with an incomplete and partially inaccurate picture of what particular organizations and jobs are like. As a consequence, they may or may not end up deciding to apply for the job that best fits them. Once they have decided which job or jobs to apply for, individuals then try to make themselves attractive to those organizations and, in most cases, they continue to try to gather information about the organization. In order to appear attractive, they may behave and dress in a certain way, or engage in any number of other activities that prevent the organization from getting accurate information.

The two goals that the individual is trying to accomplish in the selection situation—attracting the organization and evaluating the organization as a place to work—may at times come into conflict. The job applicant could do a number of things that might make him or her more attractive to the organization, but that would make it difficult to find out about what it would be like to work for the organization (for example, presenting his or her values as in line with those of the organization). Similarly, there are many things the individual might do that would provide valuable information about the organization but would decrease his or her attractiveness to it (for example, asking in an interview detailed questions concerning how much various managers are paid). Thus, the individual often finds the selection process a conflicting one.

Perspective of the Manager

From the manager's point of view, the attraction and selection process is a matter of both gathering the information that is needed for making selection decisions and attracting the kind of applicants who can and will do the job. Selection can never be very effective unless a relatively large pool of good applicants tries to obtain a job and those people who are offered jobs actually accept them. This often leads to the managerial strategy of presenting the job in the most favorable way. Many managers have their organizations spend large amounts of money on recruitment to attract the kind of people they want to hire. This attraction process is, of course, not independent of the selection process, since what goes on during selection influences the attractiveness of the organization. For example, there is evidence that the way in which the selection interview is conducted directly influences the probability that a person will take a job.

Because the selection process does influence the attractiveness of working for organizations, managers are faced with a difficult dilemma when considering which selection procedures to use. They need to design a system that attracts the right applicants and provides all the information that the organization needs to make intelligent selection decisions. Many approaches that are helpful in attracting people have questionable validity from a selection point of view, since they fail to distinguish the applicants who will perform the job effectively from those who will not (for example, wide-ranging, informal interviews). Further, some devices that produce good selection information can negatively affect the applicant's view of the organization. Certain kinds of psychological tests are good examples here. Sometimes they are valid, yet they often make the organization less attractive to the applicant.

Individual-Organization Conflicts

Because of the different objectives applicants and managers have in the attraction-selection situation, four separate processes are taking place: applicants attracting, applicants selecting, managers attracting, and managers selecting. The conflict arrow in Figure 12-1, between applicants attracting and applicants selecting, illustrates that the two objectives individuals often try to accomplish (that is, selection and attraction) are in conflict. The arrow between organizations selecting and attracting illustrates that the same is true for the objectives of managers. These are not the only conflicts that occur in the selection-attraction situation, however. In fact, they may be

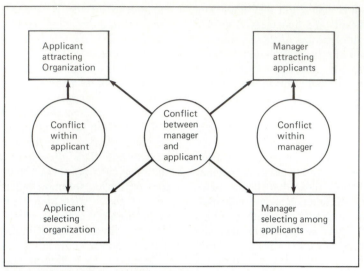

Figure 12-1 The attraction-selection situation.

less important than the two conflicts between the goals of the applicant and those of the manager.

As shown in Figure 12-1, the applicant's desire to attract the organization and the manager's desire to select among applicants are often in direct conflict. To make good selection decisions, managers need valid and complete information about applicants. This often comes into conflict with the desire of the applicants to make a favorable impression. How applicants and managers cope with this conflict strongly affects the selection process. The same point can be made about the conflict between an applicant's desire to choose the best job and a manager's desire to attract the best applicants. Applicants need complete, valid information about organizations and jobs in order to evaluate them; and managers feel that if they give out negative information about their organization, the jobs they need to fill may become less attractive to the applicants they would like to hire. Thus, whenever a manager attempts to attract an individual and the individual considers whether to join the organization, conflict may be present. This conflict may have a negative impact on the selection process because it will limit the open exchange of information.

Given the conflicts present in the attraction-selection process, is there anything managers can do to effectively manage the process? A considerable

body of research evidence suggests that there is (Wanous, 1977). Although some inherent conflicts occur in the process, the goals of the applicant and the manager are complementary in many ways. It is to everyone's advantage for employees to be effective in and satisfied with their jobs. Further, when managers correctly manage the attraction and selection processes, they can significantly increase their chances of obtaining employees who are effective and satisfied. Let us, therefore, turn to a consideration of what managers can do to make the attraction and selection process effective.

Attracting Individuals

The ideal organizational recruitment program draws in large numbers of qualified applicants who will take the job if offered it and will remain with the organization. At the same time, it does not attract those individuals who cannot do the job or will not be happy doing it. Attracting qualified individuals who become dissatisfied and leave the job is dysfunctional from the manager's point of view because this kind of turnover costs money, time, and resources. Attracting unqualified people is costly because they have to be processed and ultimately rejected, frequently resulting in their forming a negative impression of the organization.

Organizations do a number of things to attract job

applicants—advertise, visit schools, provide bonuses to current employees for recruiting applicants who are subsequently hired, and the like. Most of these approaches to recruiting are directed toward impressing on people the rewards associated with holding a particular job. There is little direct evidence that this approach is effective in attracting individuals, although it should be if it leads to the expectancy that valued rewards are associated with working for the organization. People do seem to apply for and choose those jobs that they feel offer the best mix of reward.

Evidence indicates that overemphasizing the positive aspects of prospective jobs to applicants can contribute to subsequent problems. It attracts the wrong individuals and creates unrealistic expectations on the part of those who take the jobs, thereby setting the stage for dissatisfaction and quick or early turnover. For example, when compared with job applicants who are given an unrealistic job preview, those who receive a realistic one show higher job satisfaction scores and lower turnover rates after they are on the job (Wanous, 1977). This suggests that attraction approaches which are based on creating an unrealistic set of expectations are functional for neither the individual nor the manager. What is needed is an attraction process based on the open exchange of accurate information between the applicant and the manager. The most important thing here is a realistic assessment of the job to be filled. Information needs to be provided to applicants on what capabilities the job requires as well as on what satisfactions and dissatisfactions the job provides, so the applicants have a realistic picture.

Information on what the manager expects of people and what kind of management style he or she uses can also be very helpful. One way of providing this information is through a combination of an interview with the manager and separate interviews with people who work for the manager (Gomersall and Myers, 1966). This approach may drive away a few applicants, but in the long run both the manager and the applicant should be better off.

How Organizations Select Individuals

A large number of instruments and approaches are used by organizations to help them decide whom to hire. The most commonly used devices are interviews, psychological tests, and application blanks.

Less commonly used are such devices as graphology and tests that simulate the job. The value of all these devices rests on their ability to predict job performance; that is, their validity. Considerable research has been done on just how valid these selection devices are (see Guion, 1965; Dunnette, 1966). The evidence shows that in most situations, no approach leads to highly accurate predictions (Ghiselli, 1966). One reason for this is that it is hard to assess in advance just how motivated individuals will be to perform the job once they take it. In addition, the available measures of capability are not perfect, and the requirements of jobs often change so that a previously valid measure may become invalid.

The interview is probably the most frequently used and misused selection device (Campbell et al., 1970). Almost every employee who is hired by an organization today is given some type of interview. The nature of these interviews varies widely, as does their validity. Psychologists have generally looked on the selection interview with considerable mistrust:

> The personnel interview continues to be the most widely used method for selecting employees, despite the fact that it is a costly, inefficient, and usually invalid procedure. (Dunnette and Bass, 1963)

Despite its problems, managers tend to have a great deal of faith in their ability to make decisions based on interview data. Managers should constantly be aware of the potential invalidity of the interview and, in most cases, use professionally validated approaches when they make selection decisions. This means working with the personnel department to determine what selection devices to use and relying on their expertise to a significant degree.

Unfortunately, there are no simple answers to questions concerning which devices should be used in a particular situation. Different sets of devices usually turn out to be valid in different instances. For example, a valid approach in selecting a salesperson might involve a psychological test, a structured interview with the sales manager, and an extensive written application blank, validated by reference checks. On the other hand, a skilled machinist often is best selected by a well-developed technical skills test. A number of highly technical problems are involved in determining just how valid a selection device is, and the help of a trained professional is needed when selection approaches are being designed. A manager's failure to obtain professional help in designing a selection approach can result in the use of invalid selection devices that are, at best, a waste of time and, at worst, discriminatory and illegal.

Summary: Attraction and Selection

Effective management of the selection process can contribute to increases in organizational effectiveness; however, the increases are not easy to obtain, since they require the exchange of valid information. The many conflicts present make it difficult to foster the exchange of accurate data. In many cases, the most effective things a particular manager can do is to be sure that the applicant has a realistic job preview and that the selection process has been validated by a professional.

ENTRY AND INITIAL SOCIALIZATION

Once the applicant has taken a job, the complex and often difficult initial adaptation period begins. The new employee and the manager must learn to adjust to each other. The nature of this relationship has been characterized as a sort of "psychological contract" (Levinson et al., 1962). This term means "a series of mutual expectations of which the parties to the relationship may not themselves be even dimly aware but which nonetheless govern their relationship to each other." In some instances the "marriage" settles down into an easy, comfortable relationship. In others, there is an abrupt separation that leaves scars with both parties. In between these two extremes are the majority of cases of individual-organization adaptation: flexible accommodations that result in a never-ending series of compromises —the individual never completely obtaining all he or she wants from the organization, and the manager never obtaining the performance wanted from the individual.

Available evidence is nearly unanimous in indicating that the very early employment period—the first year or even the first few months—is crucial to the development of a healthy individual-organizational relationship (Hall, 1976). One indication of the stressful nature of the early employment period is the relatively high rate (compared to later time periods) of avoidable employee turnover that occurs during it. Studies of college graduates have found that as many as half change jobs within three years of graduation, and that within five years over three-quarters do (Schein, 1978). This indicates that the individual-organization adaptation process breaks down in a relatively high percentage of cases, with consequent costs to both parties.

The key to understanding individual-organization adaptation and contracting lies in the recognition that it is two-way. The individual gives up a certain amount of freedom of action in joining an organization. As part of the psychological contract, he or she implicitly agrees that management will have some legitimate demands it can make (for example, requiring a certain number of work hours per week). The organization and its management actively aids and abets the shaping of the individual's behavior to its needs. This influence process is labeled *socialization*. It is as if the organization is "putting its fingerprints on people" (Schein, 1978). Simultaneously, however, a second process is occurring. The new employee is attempting to exert influence on the organization and his or her manager in order to create a work situation that will provide personal satisfaction. This personalization process can at times come into conflict with the socialization attempts of the organization.

How a manager handles the socialization experience of individuals can have a strong impact on the satisfaction of the relationships between the individual and the organization. A poorly managed process can lead to premature turnover or a psychological contract that involves doing only the minimal amount of work necessary. In the latter case, change can be particularly hard to produce because it involves unlearning an old contract as well as learning a new one. With this in mind, let us turn to a consideration of what methods can be used to promote effective socialization.

Methods of Promoting Socialization

All managers—whether they are in work organizations, religious orders, or prisons—have available a variety of possible means to promote the socialization of new and continuing members. Some methods (such as hazing) are not feasible for managers in most work organizations, but a number of socialization methods can be used. These include designing the selection process to acquaint the individual with the work environment, training experiences, initial job assignments, and the apprenticeship model in which new workers are assigned to older ones. All these approaches can contribute to a positive socialization experience, if they communicate realistic expectations and provide individuals with a positive work experience.

We have already discussed the key roles the selection process and managerial behavior during it can play. Now we will consider what a manager can do to create the right kind of immediate work environment during the early employment period. Three elements of this environment—the job content, the supervisor, and the work group—are critical (Feldman, 1976).

Job Content   Several studies have shown that it is very desirable for managers to give new employees challenging work assignments on which they can experience success (Hall, 1976). One study found that new employees who were fortunate enough to be given relatively demanding jobs in their early organizational careers seemed to be better prepared to perform with greater success on later job assignments. Apparently, an entering employee who is given initially challenging job duties tends to internalize high performance standards and positive expectancies about the rewards that performing effectively can bring. On the other hand, an entrant who is placed on a relatively easy first job does not have a chance to experience success (since he or she does not get much credit from anyone for doing such jobs well) and the motivation it produces.

Role of the Supervisor   In many ways, the supervisor *is* the organization to the new employee. If he or she does a good job of performing key tasks, the organization is usually viewed favorably. If a supervisor is ineffective in working with the newcomer, the organization itself is seen negatively. Supervisors need to do three primary tasks well (in addition to assigning the right kind of work) to be effective in dealing with new employees. First, they need to provide the employee with a clear description of the job to be done. Second, they need to be a source of technical information about how to perform the job. Finally, they need to provide the employee with feedback about how well that person is performing.

Selecting Supervisors for New Employees   One thing higher level managers can do to see that new members are well supervised is to carefully select the supervisors. In selecting supervisors, it is important to look for individuals who can perform the three primary tasks, but this is not enough. Supervisors must have a high degree of personal security so they will not feel threatened by either the failure or the marked success of new employees.

Often it is difficult to make desirable supervisory assignments for new employees because of other factors. Thus, many entrants are placed with supervisors not able to handle the newcomers' problems. In that case, management must rely on training to heighten the supervisors' awareness of the difficult problems they will face and to provide them with the interpersonal and technical skills they need. An interesting and novel approach to the training of supervisors who themselves are new to a particular job—and who have to deal with both new and experienced employees—was tried in one manufacturing company (Gomersall and Myers, 1966). In this case, the experienced operators trained the supervisors! This was accomplished by having pairs of operators instruct a new supervisor on such matters as the problems usually faced by the new supervisor and the way the job is viewed by the operators. This approach suggests that recently hired employees who have just gone through the critical entry period may be able to assist in training supervisors to handle new employees.

Work Group   The work group can play a very powerful role in the socialization of new employees. Acceptance by the work group is a key source of social need satisfaction, and groups have a powerful influence on the beliefs and attitudes of individuals about what the organization is like and how they should behave. Because the work group is so important, it is crucial that managers assign new employees to work groups that will have a positive impact.

Summary: Entry and Socialization

The initial experiences an individual has with an organization seem to be particularly important in shaping the long-term relationship between the individual and the organization. When the organization provides realistic information, challenging work, an effective supervisor, and a supportive work group, the result is a long-term, positive relationship between the individual and the organization. When they fail to provide them, the result is either turnover or a poor individual-organization relationship.

CAREERS IN ORGANIZATIONS

So far in this chapter, we have dealt with how the management of the selection and initial entry period affects organizational behavior. Now we would like to consider how the development of individuals can be managed in ways that will assure that an individual has a rewarding career in the organization and that the organization has the individuals it needs to function in the long term.

Staffing an organization adequately is not simply a matter of having all jobs filled by people who are capable of doing them competently and who are motivated to perform them effectively. The environment in which organizations exist is always changing, and as a result, the skills that are needed to carry out a job one day may not be the right skills another day. In addition, most organizations have life spans that exceed the career of any individual; thus, trained successors, like John deButts, must be available to fill in when jobholders retire, change organizations, or are promoted.

People can be developed through various kinds of training and other experiences. However, people are a unique resource and often prove difficult to develop, maintain, or utilize. They have their own career objectives, which may or may not fit the organization's short- and long-range plans. In the case of John deButts, it looked, at one point, as if a conflict between the organization's plans for him and his personal aspirations might cause him to resign. Finally, efforts to develop individuals may fail because the people are incapable of developing in a given way, the development is poorly planned or administered, or the people do not wish to develop in the way they are asked to.

What can a manager do to ensure that his or her organization's developmental efforts will be successful? Two things can help. First, they can be sure that efforts affecting their subordinates follow the research findings on what makes for a successful training program, and second, they can support the development of a formal career planning and development program in the organization.

Training Individuals

If training programs are to promote better performance, they must influence the employee's motivation or the employee's capability to perform the job. Influencing capability, and then performance, is a matter of identifying the changes that are needed and of picking the correct training experience for the individual who is to be trained. The first step requires determining what is to be taught. Managers need to spend considerable time before training starts, analyzing jobs and tasks and looking at behaviors that lead to successful performance of their subordinates' jobs. Unfortunately, this step is not taken by most managers; consequently, training programs often miss their mark (see Campbell et al., 1970).

Once it has been determined what kind of behavior is desired, managers are in a position to assess the individual who is to be trained. Important questions should be asked about the individual. First, is the training needed? To answer this question, managers must know whether the individual does in fact fail to behave in ways that he or she should if the job is to be performed effectively. There are a number of sources of information about this, including the results of formal performance appraisals.

If it is determined that the individual needs to learn a new behavior, a second issue arises: Does the individual have the necessary aptitude to learn the new behavior? Frequently, managers can get help in answering this question by checking with the personnel department, which often has ability tests on file for employees. If it doesn't, the personnel department is usually willing to give these tests.

Unless the individual who is to be trained and developed is motivated to learn the new behavior, it is not likely to be learned. This raises the third question that must be considered: Is the individual motivated to learn the behavior? One way to answer this question is by allowing the individual the chance to decide whether or not to go through the training experience. As we will discuss later, giving the individual a choice can be particularly effective if it is part of a systematic effort to involve individuals in planning their careers.

Next, the manager needs to consider how to teach the new behavior. Here again help from the personnel department is in order, since there are usually numerous ways to learn a new behavior or skill. Literally thousands of different management training programs are offered each year in the United States. Often, someone in the personnel department is familiar with the strengths and weaknesses of a number of training approaches and programs and can help identify a suitable one. Larger organizations frequently offer programs of their own, which are adequate for many training needs.

Once the training itself is completed, an important period begins, during which the trainee's supervisor plays a critical role. The supervisor must reward and support the behavior that was learned. If this does not happen, the learned behavior is likely to be quickly dropped (Campbell et al., 1970).

Career Planning

Career development is a function of a long series of job and training experiences. These experiences are cumulative and influence each other. Since each person has a unique set of background experiences, the same program is likely to impact on people in different ways. Furthermore, a person can make a number of moves in most organizations (John deButts held twenty-two different jobs), and receive many different kinds of training. However, people have only limited amounts of time in their work life; the number of moves they can make is limited as is the number of training programs they can attend.

The career of John deButts presents an interesting example of how an individual is prepared for top management by an organization. Like most managers who make it to the top, he had some powerful sponsors who "looked after him," and he was fortunate enough to have had some jobs that led to higher level managers noticing him. Careful career management is necessary if organizations are to develop individuals. Organizations must look at employees as individuals and systematically develop them in line with their needs for talent. Similarly, managers should consider their subordinates' personal goals and be constantly aware of their development. To help ensure that this happens, many organizations hold managers responsible for reporting each year on the development work they have done with their subordinates.

Organizations often see their development activities as a one-way process—as something they do to the person. This can result in organizations developing people for jobs that individuals do not see as congruent with their career goals. It also causes a great deal of miscommunication. It is not uncommon to find employees who have no idea why they are being transferred to a new job, while the organization views the move as a part of their development for top management. The opposite also occurs frequently. Moves that the organization sees as having no significance are seen by the individual as indicating that he or she has been picked for further advancement. Although, in the short run, this type of misconception may not be dysfunctional, in the long run it can be. The answer to these problems is for managers to make career planning a more open, two-way process in which the individual is actively involved in his or her own career development.

One specific thing that many organizations are doing to help career development be more public and participatory is to publicly post all job openings. This gives individuals the chance to demonstrate their desires for a different job. Some organizations also offer their employees the chance to go through assessment centers in which the employees are given feedback about their capabilities and chances to develop into effective managers.

Summary: Careers in Organizations

Individual development is a vital part of the staffing process in all organizations. Managers can do a number of things to ensure that it is effective. These include being sure that training sessions stress the correct behavior, are given to individuals who can profit from them, and are supported when the individual returns to work. In addition, managers can treat the development of individuals as a two-way communication exchange that is tied to the growth of individuals and is planned on a long-term basis.

SUMMARY: MANAGING STAFFING

What should managers do about staffing the jobs that report to them? Table 12-1 answers this question by summarizing the points made in this chapter. It shows some specific things that managers can do in order to see that the jobs which report to them are correctly staffed. When new employees are to be hired, they need to be sure that valid selection

Table 12-1 Critical Management Issues in Staffing

Attraction/selection	Initial entry	Career development

1. Assessment of job to be filled
2. Realistic information to applicant
3. With professional help, gather accurate data about the applicant
	1. Assign to a task that allows for challenge and success
	2. Feedback to employee to clarify role and performance expectations
	3. Assign to a work group that will be accepting and will communicate positive attitudes and beliefs
		1. Developing individuals
		  a. identify needed behaviors
		  b. evaluate individual
		  c. design training
		  d. support new behavior
		2. Career planning
		  a. develop systematic plans
		  b. make it an open two-way process

procedures are used. When new employees start work, managers must play a role in aiding the entry process and the initial socialization of new subordinates. Finally, managers should pay continued attention to the career development needs of their subordinates, to be sure that they are receiving the training and development they need and desire.

REFERENCES

Campbell, J. P., Dunnette, M. D., Lawler, E. E., & Weick, K. *Managerial behavior, performance, and effectiveness.* New York: McGraw-Hill, 1970.

Dunnette, M. D. *Personnel selection and placement.* Belmont, Calif.: Wadsworth, 1966.

———, & Bass, B. M. Behavioral scientists and personnel management. *Industrial Relations,* 1963, **2,** 115–130.

Feldman, D. C. A contingency theory of socialization. *Administrative Science Quarterly,* 1976, **21,** 433–452.

Ghiselli, E. E. *The validity of occupational aptitude tests.* New York: Wiley, 1966.

Gomersall, E. R., & Myers, M. S. Breakthrough in on-the-job training. *Harvard Business Review,* 1966, **44**(4), 62–72.

Guion, R. M. *Personnel testing.* New York: McGraw-Hill, 1965.

Hall, D. T. *Careers in organizations.* Pacific Palisades, Calif.: Goodyear, 1976.

Levinson, H., Price, C. R., Munden, H. J., & Solley, C. M. *Men, management and mental health.* Cambridge, Mass.: Harvard, 1962.

Porter, L. W., Lawler, E. E., III, & Hackman, J. R. *Behavior in organizations.* New York: McGraw-Hill, 1975.

Schein, E. H. *Career dynamics.* Reading, Mass.: Addison-Wesley, 1978.

Schneider, B. S. *Staffing organizations.* Pacific Palisades, Calif.: Goodyear, 1976.

Wanous, J. P. Organizational entry: Newcomers moving from outside to inside. *Psychological Bulletin,* 1977, **84,** 601–618.

Reading 13
Entry Into the Organizational Career
Edgar H. Schein

Every career transition can be viewed from two perspectives—the individual's and the organization's. What makes "career" a complicated concept is that one can view it from the perspective of the *individual* developing his or her own life pattern of work or as an *occupation, profession,* or *organization* creating a "path" for people to follow.

The same events will have a different meaning from the point of view of the manager in the organization who makes them happen (i.e., "putting someone through an initiation rite" or "teaching someone what the organization is ultimately all about") and from the point of view of the individual to whom they are happening (i.e., "getting a lot of mickeymouse work which isn't contributing anything" or "doing the organization's dirty work because no one else is willing to do it").

Entry into the organization is, from the individual's point of view, a process of breaking in and joining up, of learning the ropes, of figuring out how to get along and how to make it (Van Maanen, 1975). The same process from the point of view of the organization is one of induction, basic training, and socialization of the individual to the major norms and values of the organization and of testing new employees to make it possible to place them correctly in a job and career path (Schein, 1968). The two processes can be seen as a kind of negotiation between the "recruits" and the organizational members with whom they deal, leading to a viable *psychological contract*—a matching of what the individual will give with what the organization expects to receive, and what the organization will give relative to what the individual expects to receive (Schein, 1970).

This transition can be more clearly understood by classifying it into three stages and analyzing each stage in greater detail. The *first* stage, *"entry,"* includes the period of preparation and training on the part of the individual, the recruitment and selection process which occurs prior to accepting a job, and the actual hiring decision and initial job placement. The *second* stage is *"socialization"* and includes all of the early process of "learning the ropes," how to make it in the organization, how to get along, how to work, and so on (Van Maanen and Schein, 1977; Van Maanen, 1975). This is a period of mutual testing by the individual and the organization; some of the details of the psychological contract are worked out, the individual builds a picture of the organization and his or her future in it, and the organization develops a picture of its new employee and his or her future.

The *third* and final stage can be called *"mutual acceptance"* and includes the various processes of formally and informally granting full membership to the new employee through initiation rites, the conferring of special status or privileges, more challenging and important job assignments, and the working out of a viable psychological contract. At the end of this period the new employee is a fully accepted member of the organization, but is still in the early stages of the career and has not yet achieved "ten-

ure" or *permanent* membership. All that has been established is that there is enough of a match between what the individual needs and expects and what the organization needs and expects to continue the career in that organization. In fact, many midcareer problems stem from false hopes which are built up by both the organization and the individual in these early stages of the career.

These early career events can have one of two outcomes. The new employee either is successfully socialized into the organization or discovers that the degree of mismatch with the organization is so great that a job shift to another organization is necessary (initiated by either the employee or the employing organization). It is important to recognize that this transition involves a confrontation between two strong sets of forces: (1) the individual's talents, personality, prior attitudes, values, ambitions, and expectations formed by 20 or more years of childhood socialization and education; and (2) the organization's requirements and culture with its norms of what kind of work is valuable, how work should be done, what a good employee should be like, and so on.

In a period of economic affluence, in which job mobility is fairly easy, one might expect that neither the individual nor the organization will change its values where mismatches are discovered, thus leading inevitably to turnover. At the same time, it must be recognized that organizational culture is probably the more powerful force, which means that if persons for various reasons can *not* move to another organization, they will probably be subjected to strong pressures to conform to that culture and to change their own value system. The more they are constrained by various forces from leaving, the more likely it is that they will conform to the organizational culture and suppress their own creativity. As we look at the stages in greater detail, we must always bear in mind this inevitable confrontation between individual and organizational values and attempt to assess what kinds of resolution are optimal for both the individual and the employer.

TASKS OF THE ENTRY STAGE

The period of entry involves a number of developmental tasks for the individual.

Task 1 *The first task is to make some kind of*

preliminary occupational choice, which will de- termine what kind of education and training to pursue.

Task 2 *Next, one must develop a viable "dream" —an image of the occupation or organization which can serve as the outlet for one's talents, values, and ambitions.* One must be able to develop a self-concept as a "manager," "financial analyst," or "entrepreneur," for example, which is reasonably consistent with what is known about both the world of work and oneself.

One of the major problems of this period is how to develop reality tests, i.e., how to determine whether one's view of the occupation or of oneself is realistic when both the individual and the potential employer tend to collude to hide reality, to avoid the person's getting turned off and going into another occupation altogether. Every occupation has its unpleasant realities and its dirty work, a fact careful- ly concealed from outsiders to maintain the idealistic myths which the members of the occupation build and foster (Hughes, 1958). The kinds of realities concealed about management have to do with how boring and difficult much of the work is, how much personal values might have to be compromised to get the work done, and how much politics and other nonrational elements determine outcomes (Dalton, 1959).

In discussing the problem of early career develop- ment, senior executives in management programs sometimes blame the university for failing to pre- pare students for the "realities" of life in organiza- tions. They do not consider, however, that (1) those realities might turn too many high-talent students into cynics who might shift to other careers altogeth- er, and/or (2) students wouldn't believe much of the information anyway, because they cannot afford to give up a dream before it has even begun to be actualized. We all need to idealize the occupations we enter, and we are therefore highly resistant to data that life in that occupation might be stultifying or even involve value compromises we might not be prepared to make.

Task 3 *One must prepare oneself for the early career through "anticipatory socialization," in order to develop what one considers to be the attitudes and values necessary for succeeding in one's chosen occupation.* For a person entering business, such attitudes would include a commitment to the profit motive, a basic belief in the free-enterprise system

and economic competition, possibly a belief in the particular products or services produced by the business or industry being entered, and so on. These beliefs may or may not be "realistic" in the sense of being a requirement for entry, but they are a necessary part of the preparation of the individual for any given career.

Task 4 *As the period of education and training comes to a close, the individual is faced with "entry into the labor market," the realities of finding a first job.* Most schools support this process to some degree by making available the services of a place- ment office where recruiters from organizations and potential employees can come together or where information about jobs is available. There then ensues a complex interaction in which representa- tives of organizations and potential employees try to obtain valid information about each other. Through a few hours of mutual interviewing and possibly visiting the organization, the applicants are trying to determine whether to link an unknown number of years of their lives to a given employer and to assess whether their dreams and ambitions can be fulfilled there; the employer is trying to determine whether the candidate's talents, personality traits, attitudes, values, physical appearance, temperament, and en- ergy level "fit" with the organization's needs. Mis- takes can be costly on both sides, since each is investing time, energy, and money.

In a period of economic affluence, when plenty of jobs are available, individuals probably have less to lose if a mistake is made, since they will learn something valuable from their first year or so in *any* organization. For the organization, on the other hand, a recruiting/selection error is a no-return investment in human capital.

If jobs are scarce, however, individuals have more to lose from a bad choice, even though the pressures on them to take whatever is available are stronger. The danger in a tight labor market is that applicants will end up in an organization whose values are out of line with their own or whose opportunities are limited relative to their talents and that they will adapt to that organization by allowing themselves to be socialized to new values and by reducing their ambitions to the realities that are available. If that happens, both the individual and the organization are in a position of losing in the long run by under- or misutilizing the organization's most important resource—its human capital. Many midcareer problems can derive from an initial selection error combined with a failure on the part of the organization to manage such early mismatching. The employee overadapts, becomes complacent, and never achieves his or her full potential.

Problems in the Management of Entry Tasks

The recruitment/selection process creates several specific problems to which both the individual and the employing organization must be sensitive and with which they must cope.

1 *The problem of obtaining accurate information in a climate of mutual selling.* Since the organization is trying to attract the best possible candidates and the candidates are trying to find the best possible jobs, there are strong incentives for both sides to distort reality by overemphasizing positive features and hiding or minimizing negative ones. But each party knows that the other is distorting and is therefore in a game of trying to outguess the other.

2 *The problem of the organization and the individual unwittingly colluding in setting up unrealistic expectations about the early career.* Both are "future" oriented and are attempting to assess the *long-range* match between individual and organizational needs and resources, to the point where neither pays enough attention to the immediate *short-run events which will occur in the early part of the career.* This problem occurs especially with graduates of management schools, who are hired for their knowledge of and skill in *new* management technologies, e.g., the use of computers, mathematical techniques of analysis of financial and other problems, operations research, modeling, etc., but who are often brought into an organizational culture that will resist any of these techniques. Often the new recruit unwittingly becomes a change agent on behalf of one part of the organization that is trying to introduce new techniques into another, resisting part. For example, a graduate hired by a corporation specifically to introduce operations research techniques into a large plant was told within two weeks of arrival at his new assignment by the plant manager to "cool it." They were happy with how they were doing things, were hiding much of what they were doing from corporate headquarters, and were not about to let the new employee become either a spy or a boat rocker with his "fancy new techniques." He left the company roughly one year later, completely frustrated, and the plant continued to use its old methods of production.

3 *The recruitment process itself may build an incorrect image of the organization or socialize the individual to incorrect values.* For example, if the recruitment process creates a feeling in the recruits that they are a valuable resource being hired for their special talents, yet the first job turns out to be a period of indoctrination into company values, they may become very disillusioned about that company's commitment to using their talent. On the other hand, a tough period of recruitment and selection involving many tests can build a positive self-image and real commitment to the occupation in the recruit who passes the tough hurdles. As Van Maanen has shown in the recruitment of policemen, the very process of testing builds a commitment prior to selection. If recruits have invested heavily in getting into the organization, they will value their membership more (Van Maanen, 1973, 1974).

4 *The problems of deciding on a job without clear or reliable information about the future.* Assuming that one has a choice, one must make a decision which may commit one for an unknown length of time on the basis of very fragmentary and questionable information. Therefore, it is not surprising that there are nasty surprises ahead for both the individual and the organization. To minimize the negative consequences, it is important to provide many opportunities for mutual testing and validating in the early career. Ways must be found to make it possible for both the individual and the organization to communicate more fully and accurately their expectations, assumptions, and self-insights, even if some of this information is nonflattering. In the next section we will examine in some detail how this might be accomplished.

NEGATIVE OUTCOMES AND HOW TO AVOID THEM

In assessing outcomes, we must maintain three separate perspectives—that of the individual being recruited and attempting to launch his or her career, that of the organization trying to build up its human resources by hiring "good" people, and that of social institutions such as vocational or professional schools, counseling services, etc., whose function is to help society to maximize the utilization of its human resources by improving the process of matching individual talents with occupational and organizational needs for talent.

The Individual Perspective

From the point of view of the individual, the entry stage is a failure if it does not lead to a job in which there is the potential for talents to be utilized, needs to be met, and values to be actualized. Although individual talents, needs, and values vary, the goal of this stage must be for the individual to enter a work situation which is to some degree congruent with them. If the situation is either too challenging or too stultifying—lacking in opportunities for growth and development or demanding value compromises—one must either move to another organization or change some part of oneself. Adaptation is desirable only if one's self-image or needs were unrealistic; it is undesirable if one settles for less than one is capable of or compromises one's values and ambitions in the interest of the employing organization. Indeed, such compromise is undesirable in the long run for all parties concerned, since it represents wasted talent.

What can the *individual* do to prevent undesirable mismatching? *First,* it is obvious that as early as possible in their lives, people must develop a realistic appraisal of their talents, needs, and values and must attempt serious self-appraisals at important times throughout their lives. Without *self-insight* there can be no realistic assessment of either occupational opportunities or illusions that must be abandoned. Programs of counseling starting in high school and continuing through college and graduate school should be utilized as much as possible by people before they enter the labor market. Self-exposure to varied experiences in extracurricular activities is probably a good source of self-insight if one makes a conscious effort to learn about oneself from each experience. One can use the growing number of self-diagnostic books available to obtain a picture of at least one's interests, needs, and values (see bibliography). For self-assessment of *talent,* it may be desirable for the individual to go to assessment centers or vocational counseling centers, which emphasize testing the person across a wide range of intellectual and other activities. But such activities will not provide a completely accurate basis for self-assessment of ability to perform in actual job situations. Part-time work, summer work, volunteer work, co-op work-study programs, and any other vehicle for getting into real work situations are highly desirable supplements to any testing or counseling.

In addition to exposing oneself to situations which provide potential feedback, one has to train oneself to *assess* such feedback information. No matter how

sincere and dedicated the guidance counselor or vocational psychologist might be, his or her information cannot be taken at face value, because the predictive power of tests, interviews, and other diagnostics is depressingly low for complex occupations such as "management." People must learn how to interpret their own experience directly and to develop judgment criteria which tell them how they are doing. The earlier they learn to do this, the better, because feedback is always difficult to obtain, especially in organizational settings.

Second, people must learn how to *communicate* more accurately to others their own self-assessment of their talents, needs, and values. Self-insight is not enough; it must be accompanied by the ability to communicate one's insights to others so that the potential employer can assess more accurately the probability of a mismatch. Oral and written communication skills are critical for negotiating the interpersonal processes involved in any life transitions, whether they involve career, family, or self-development. Therefore, the earlier in life that people learn to communicate accurately about themselves, their feelings, and perceptions, the better off they will be in managing life tasks.

Communication skills of the kind I am referring to here apply to all kinds of personalities. I am *not* advocating that everyone learn to be more "open," because clearly individuals differ in ability to be open, and in many life situations openness is as much a handicap as an advantage. What I am advocating is that people develop ways of getting across to others their perceptions of themselves, particularly in transition situations such as those involving career choice. For example, a shy person is better off communicating this self-insight to a recruiter than ending up perpetually anxious or frustrated in a job situation which requires a high degree of extroversion. The more information the individual can get across to the recruiter, the better the match is likely to be, even if the recruiter is unable to reciprocate with good information about the organization. There is little to be gained in the long run by falsely selling oneself. The trick is to learn to be accurate—neither grandiose nor unnecessarily diffident or modest.

Third, people must learn to make *accurate diagnoses of potential job situations* from partial and often distorted information. In this area, especially, they can be helped by educational institutions' providing concepts and simulated experiences or cases to sharpen diagnostic skills. Whether or not the school provides such experiences, the individual must learn from interviews and visits how to assess an organization's culture in terms of both the short- and long-run job opportunities. The individual must also assess how realistic the recruiter is in assessing the individual's needs. Even though the job opportunity sounds glowing, is it safe to enter an organization without a clear feeling of being "understood" by that organization?

Student groups have been quite successful in improving their diagnostic skills by forming informal ad hoc seminars or discussion sessions during the job-search process. Such seminars can deal with the problem of how to draw inferences from the recruiters' behavior and what kinds of questions to ask which might reveal an aspect of the organization's culture. For example, one group developed the idea of asking recruiters about their own careers in some detail as a way of learning how the organization deals with people, but there is still much creativity needed in this area (Levinson, 1972).

To summarize, in order to avoid the negative outcomes of having to either move to a new job or change aspirations or values in an undesirable way, the individual must develop maximum self-insight, skills in communicating those insights accurately, and skills in diagnosing organizational settings from interview and observational data. Basically, one must develop one's own procedures for ensuring that each of these areas is optimally managed. An important by-product is that these skills are necessary for the management of any life situation and therefore represent an important area for people to invest in at all stages of their lives, not only during the early career.

The Organizational/Managerial Perspective

From the point of view of the organization, the preentry stage is a failure if any of the following occurs: (1) a high-potential recruit fails to accept a job offer; (2) a high-potential recruit joins the organization but soon leaves because of disappointment or disillusionment; (3) a high-potential recruit joins the organization but loses motivation and becomes a marginal performer; or (4) a seemingly high-potential recruit joins the organization but turns out to have low talent, low motivation, or values incompatible with those of the organization.

How can the organization manage the recruitment/selection process to avoid any of these negative outcomes? In a way, the solutions for the organization parallel those described above for the individual. *First,* the organization must have *self-insight;* i.e., those managers who initiate and manage the search for new employees must first have a very clear idea of what jobs need to be filled, what the characteristics of those jobs are both short- and long-run, how those jobs might change over time, and how someone who is successful in a job moves from that job to another part of the organization. In other words, the recruiting/selection system ought to be shaped in a manner consistent with how the parent organization works. If it is, then in screening interviews there is a greater possibility of accurately describing to recruits what they will be doing in both the short- and long-run.

For such information to be available, the organization must do both *strategic and human resource planning,* even though that planning may not result in clear-cut forecasts. It is better to communicate to a recruit that the best planning efforts still leave his or her future career with the company "uncertain" than to (1) come across as not knowing what the future might bring because no one has thought about it or (2) reveal that the managers who have thought about it have failed to communicate with those who are doing the recruiting. And it is certainly not reassuring to a reasonably intelligent recruit to hear glowing tales of challenge and opportunity which are on the face of it nothing more than a sales pitch. Many recruiters do not know how their own organizations work in terms of typical career moves, average length of time of a job, possible and impossible rotational assignments, long-range possibilities for managerial or technical growth, etc. Instead, they operate by "motherhood" statements, e.g., "Everyone with potential who performs will get ahead," or use their own stereotypes of what *they* believe happens as a basis for what they assert. The danger is that the high-potential recruit will cross-check the information, will ask a friend who works for that company, and in other ways will gather data which, if they conflict with what the recruiter said, make it more probable that he or she will seek employment elsewhere.

In the long run, it is probably a better strategy to say, "I don't know how our promotional system works in finance, but I'll try to find out," than to make up something or give vague generalities. The ultimate example of this "truth in recruiting" philosophy is probably the West Coast company that ran a full-page ad in a trade journal; at the bottom of an otherwise blank page was the message, "We don't know what to say in this ad but are looking for good people," and then gave the company's name and address. The firm reported receiving as many or more applicants as when it ran more detailed ads and was told by many applicants that they appreciated the candor of the advertisement.

In summary, a good principle for recruiting might be, "Know as much as possible about the job, the organization, and the career paths within it, and then tell the truth as much as possible; admit uncertainty and gray areas if they exist; don't over-sell, because a short-run success in getting bodies in the door does not solve the company's long-range human resource problems."

But what if the career development system of the organization is genuinely in flux and little accurate information can be provided to a recruit? I see nothing wrong with saying that point blank: "If you come to work for this company, we cannot guarantee what the situation will be like in one or two years or in which area of the company there will be opportunities for growth," if that is in fact the truth. It is indeed dangerous to set up false expectations by promising people promotions or new jobs on some kind of timetable, but there is nothing wrong with quoting historical facts that some people have moved up two levels in five years, others are still at the same level, and some have moved laterally. Whatever the facts are, they can be of value to the recruit without setting up false expectations, provided the recruiter quotes them simply as facts and not as part of a sales pitch.

Second, the recruitment/selection system must be able to *diagnose long-range growth potential in a person* as well as short-run performance potential. If the organization has done its homework and knows at some level what kind of people it needs for what kinds of work, it should then be possible to design interview, testing, and assessment procedures that are congruent with those requirements and with the organizational value system. I cannot in this book elaborate on the technology of diagnosing individual potential, which is a whole field in its own right (Schneider, 1976), but I do wish to make some comments about the necessity of making such assessment congruent with organizational values. Earlier in this chapter it was asserted that the recruitment/selection process is one of the primary bases on which potential new members form their image of their future employer. If the organization is seeking certain kinds of people, it must make sure that its own recruiting process does not turn those kinds of people off. For example, if a technical organization is seeking creative engineers, it might well be tempted to give psychological tests measuring creativity, but should resist the temptation until it has gathered data on what the impact would be on a potential creative recruit to be asked to take such a test. It might be that the *most* creative person would refuse to take the test or would refuse to work for an organization that would rely on such tests.

Finally, organizations must make more of an effort to *integrate the recruitment/selection activities with those of job placement and early supervision,* because lack of congruence at that interface runs the risk of producing early disillusionment and turnover (Schein, 1964). This integration can be accomplished in a variety of ways. Probably the most common technique used by organizations is to actively involve in the recruiting process those line managers who will supervise the new employee. If line managers are the actual recruiters or parts of the recruiting team, they can deal more authoritatively with questions that candidates may have about the nature of the work they will be doing and provide examples through their own physical presence of what work in the organization would be like. On the other hand, the line manager is often untrained in interviewing and assessing the candidate based on the interview. Working as a team with a trained recruiter is one way of overcoming this potential weakness.

If the number of people to be hired is too great to involve line management in recruiting, the next best method of integration is to have frequent contact between the recruiters and the line managers who will become the supervisors of the new hires. This contact can be provided by planning meetings, reviews of candidates, feedback meetings on how past hires have worked out, etc. But *someone,* either in personnel or in the line function, must be accountable for bringing the two groups together on a regular basis.

Just integrating the recruiting and selection function is not sufficient. Planning must be integrated as well. As I have argued throughout, equal attention must be given to planning for human resources, analyzing systematically what the jobs are like for which one is recruiting, and estimating how those jobs will change in the future. Furthermore, as human resources become more specialized and expensive, plans must be made for the continued career growth of all new recruits. Even though no specific commitments can be made and even though no clear paths can be defined, it is nevertheless necessary to consider options and lay the groundwork for future career moves, whether those involve promotion or simply new lateral assignments. It is suicidal to attempt to stockpile high-potential people without considering specifically what they will be doing and how they will be managed five, ten, and twenty years down the road.

To summarize, for organizations to avoid the negative outcomes of inability to hire desirable candidates, losing good people soon after hiring them, demotivating and underutilizing high-potential people, or mistakenly hiring someone of low potential, it is first of all necessary for management to have maximum insight into the organization's needs and how its own career system works. It is also necessary for those involved in recruiting to be able to communicate clearly and accurately what the organizational situation is, and it is necessary for them to diagnose accurately the potential of a given recruit to meet the set of short- and long-run organizational needs identified. Finally, I have argued that it is necessary for recruitment, selection, and placement to be integrated as much as possible and have proposed several ways of achieving such integration.

The Institutional Perspective

The transition from school to work is sufficiently difficult that it must be supported by various social institutions and/or by special occupations devoted to career transitions such as guidance counseling, vocational aptitude testing, etc. I will not review in detail all the things that such institutions or occupations can and should do, but can highlight one aspect.

Because it is so difficult to anticipate what work will really be like and get accurate information during the recruiting process itself, it would be highly desirable to improve the process of exposing students to real work situations before they have to make final commitments. Educational institutions can reinforce work/study programs, work with employers to develop summer apprenticeships or internships, bring members of the occupation onto the campus or into the high school to talk about life in that occupation, arrange for students to visit local factories, and in various other ways ensure greater familiarity early.

SUMMARY

This chapter has reviewed the major tasks of the entry stage, the problems likely to be encountered in the recruitment/selection process, the negative outcomes which may result from mismanagement of this process, and what the individual, the employer, and educational institutions can do to minimize those negative outcomes.

The entry stage ends with the decision to accept employment. Once the individual has made this decision and reports for work, he or she enters the next stage—"socialization."

REFERENCES

Dalton, M. *Men who manage.* New York: Wiley, 1959.

Hughes, E. C. *Men and their work.* Glencoe, Ill.: Free Press, 1958.

Levinson, H. *Organizational diagnosis.* Cambridge, Mass.: Harvard, 1972.

Schein, E. H. How to break in the college graduate. *Harvard Business Review,* 1964, **42,** 68–76.

————. Organizational socialization and the profession of management. *Industrial Management Review,* 1968, 1–15.

————. *Organizational psychology.* Englewood Cliffs, N.J.: Prentice-Hall, 1970.

Schneider, B. *Staffing organizations.* Pacific Palisades, Calif.: Goodyear, 1976.

Van Maanen, J. Observations on the making of policemen. *Human Organization,* 1973, **4,** 407–418.

————. Working the streets: A developmental view of police behavior. In H. Jacob (Ed.), *The potential for reform of criminal justice.* Beverly Hills, Calif.: Sage, 1974.

——. Breaking in: A consideration of organizational socialization. In R. Dubin (Ed.), *Handbook of work, organization, and society*. Chicago: Rand-McNally, 1975.

——, & Schein, E. H. Improving the quality of work life: Career development. In J. R. Hackman and J. L. Suttle (Eds.), *Improving life at work*. Los Angeles: Goodyear, 1977.

Reading 14

Selection and Placement

Sheldon Zedeck
Milton R. Blood

Selection involves accepting or rejecting applicants for membership in the organization, usually for a specific job. The usual form of the problem would be 26 applicants for 18 openings for machine operators. How do we decide which to accept? Occasionally, a selection process is used to promote current members of the organization. *Placement* is more complex because it requires the matching of several persons to several jobs. Placement decisions usually involve persons who have been accepted into the organization. We must decide what function each should fulfill. It is necessary, then, to specify clearly the goals of the placement decision—maximizing production, maximizing worker satisfaction, minimizing interpersonal conflict, and so on. Since the selection problem is more often encountered than the placement problem, we will consider selection in greater detail.

Before discussing some of the procedures for regulating selection and placement processes, one assumption of these procedures should be pointed out. The reader should consider carefully the implications and bear them in mind in any applied situation. Statistical procedures assume a measurable criterion which our selection decisions will maximize. Those persons will be chosen for each job who are predicted to perform best on the criterion for that job. The measure which is used as a criterion for the development of selection procedures can be [a] performance evaluation measure. . . . It can be whatever we would like to maximize. There will be jobs for which we would like to choose those who are predicted to have the greatest tenure. In other situations it may be appropriate to choose individuals on the basis of their trainability. Whatever we choose as our criterion measure, there is an assump-

tion in the statistical decision process that it is to be maximized.

DEVELOPMENT OF A GENERAL SELECTION SYSTEM

In the following sections we discuss the considerations necessary to developing a general selection system. We begin by identifying the personnel needs of the organization. Then we present the selection techniques. Finally, we discuss how to evaluate the usefulness of our selection procedures.

Manpower Planning

A complete program of new-member acquisition begins with a plan for manpower utilization which includes much more than the specifications of current openings in the organization. The first step in the program is the specification of expected short-term and long-term manpower needs. Using information about expansion or reduction plans and usual turnover rates for various jobs, reasonable forecasts can be made about future work force deficiencies and surpluses.

Once we estimate future manpower conditions, policy decisions can be made and the consequences of various selection and training schemes considered. These considerations should include the costs of training, the costs of recruiting, the costs of a selection system, the benefits of transferring workers from one job to another, the benefits of promoting within the organization, and so on. From careful deliberation on these points it is often possible to plan career ladders or progressive paths for members. Thus members are encouraged to stay in the organization without being locked into dead-end positions. A possible career ladder for ORG [a hypothetical organization that is to be staffed] may consist of hiring workers in a production unit with the intention of moving them up through the staff foreman position or into the salesman position.

Career ladders often imply that training will be carried out in the organization; that is, while at one step, members will be preparing for the next. A career-ladder strategy will mean that the most appropriate selection criterion will not necessarily be performance on the immediate task for which a person is hired. Selection procedures should instead consider how trainable the new members are and how readily they will adapt to later (probably more important) duties.

Though all forecasting is subject to error, intelligent planning can avoid shortages of persons with critical skills. Advance planning is the rule in administering production materials and facilities. The most important resource, manpower, should not be administered less thoughtfully.

Recruiting

The initial problem is to interest persons in becoming members. There are many ways to accomplish this—ads in newspapers and magazines, visits to college campuses, employment agencies, word of mouth, and so on. The technique should match the job available and the labor market. If an E.D.P. consultant is desired for ORG, an ad in a local newspaper will be less effective than a visit (or telephone call) to a college computer-science department. The methods of recruitment and publicity *do* influence the applicant population from which new members can be chosen. If one wishes, for example, to increase the number of applicants from minorities (or with high school degrees, sales experience, or money to invest), it is necessary to recruit in the locations and media which are most accessible to those special populations.

Recruitment costs should always be included in an assessment of the effectiveness of personnel policies. If qualified applicants regularly apply to the organization without solicitation, recruiting expenses are unnecessary. Because rare and valuable skills are more expensive to recruit, it is sometimes better to recruit and hire persons with lesser skills and to train them. There are few general rules for a ready-made recruiting policy, however, and policies usual-

ly should be tailored to the applicant population, the task, and the needs of the organization.

The characteristics of the applicant population are determined by the mode of recruitment, which in turn limits the appropriateness of the selection model and the information it provides for decision making in the specific situation. If the selection procedure is based on an applicant sample recruited in a specific manner, the results are appropriate only if succeeding applicants are recruited similarly.

Job Choice

Finally, before discussing the procedures of personnel selection, there is the matter of job choice. Job choice is personnel selection from the perspective of the potential employee rather than the organization. The selection problem is quite different from these two viewpoints. From the perspective of the organization, statistics can estimate the number (or percentage) of errors which will be made in the long run or over a large number of decisions ("How many of our 100 new production workers will perform at the minimum criterion level?"). For the individual, however, statistical methods estimate the risk involved in a single decision ("How likely is it that I will be successful if I take that job?").

Job choice has been discussed in terms of the developmental process of a personal career, the satisfaction of personal needs, and the grouping of persons with similar orientations in similar kinds of work (Crites, 1969; Holland, 1966; Roe, 1956; Super & Bohn, 1970). The two most popular instruments used in job counseling are the Kuder Preference Record (Kuder, 1960) and the Strong Vocational Interest Blank (Strong, 1966). It is not our intention to provide an introduction to the field of job choice; interested readers are encouraged to pursue the topic in the sources indicated above. All readers, however, are encouraged to recognize the difference in the individual and organizational approaches to selection problems and to understand that we deal here almost exclusively with the latter perspective. This does not imply that the individual perspective is less important, only that it is different.

VALIDITY

Since we are concerned with hiring employees who will be successful in ORG, it is necessary to establish a selection system. Stage 1 in the development of our selection system requires job analyses . . . and then determination of what we will consider as "success" in ORG and how it will be measured. . . .

Stage 2 requires formulating hypotheses which state the expected relationship between our criterion (criteria) and potential predictor(s). The results of hypotheses testing will be expressed by correlation coefficients. When correlation coefficients are used to show the relationship between predictors and criteria they are called validity coefficients. What information sources (tests, biographical information, and so on) can we use as possible predictors of the criteria? What information will reflect differences among the applicants? What information can be obtained from or about the applicant that is related to our criteria?

The initial formulation of these hypotheses is based on systematic job analyses, experience, information from other organizations with respect to the predictors they use, literature reviews, and "educated guesses." The latter are usually based on the *face validity* of the information source. That is, some sources, as judged from their items, questions, or content, "look as if" they are related to the criterion.

Our guesses, experience, and so on also may indicate that there are some abstract concepts related to the behavior we are trying to predict. If we have measures of these concepts, we can hypothesize that they will be potential predictors of the criterion behavior. For example, it has been assumed that general intelligence influences performance of many jobs. Before we can test the hypothesis that general intelligence is related to job performance, we must develop a measure of general intelligence. The ultimate assessment of whether, in fact, we have a measure of general intelligence is a judgmental decision inferred from research evidence that is accumulated over many studies. If our measure of general intelligence is related to concepts that we expect it to be related to *and* unrelated to concepts we expect it not to be related to, we may conclude that we have developed *construct validity* for our measure. . . .

Even though the choice of our potential predictor is based on construct validity, we must test the relationship between the construct and the criterion empirically, just as we would empirically test the relationship between any other potential predictor (picked on the basis of experience, face validity, and so on) and the criterion. Before we review the empirical validation, however, we should consider Stage 3 in our development of a selection system—possible information sources or predictors.

Information Sources

One of the most popular and frequently used sources of information is the *interview*. It is used primarily to obtain specific information about the applicant's character, personality, job knowledge, and attitude. If these aspects are assessed, weighted, or scored, the interview becomes a predictor which can and should be empirically validated. The interview also fulfills other functions. If it is the first step in the recruitment procedure (on the college campus, for example), it may serve a public relations function. The organization has an opportunity to "sell itself." Facts pertaining to the specific job, company policy, types of benefits, and so on can be presented to the interviewee. These facts should facilitate his decision as to whether he desires to pursue employment with the company. Initial interviews also serve a screening function. The organization can eliminate from further selection procedures applicants who have very little chance of being selected. If the interview is conducted after collecting other types of information, all predictor information may be combined to clarify and resolve any inconsistencies.

In some cases, the interviewer is required to examine all the data and make a decision to hire or reject. This decision making is based on the *clinical prediction* selection model in which the decision maker uses an intuitive strategy to combine and evaluate information. Evidence indicates that clinical prediction is not as good as systematic empirical prediction (Meehl, 1954). Because clinical prediction is an individual intuitive strategy, it is almost impossible to generalize from one decision maker to another or even to generalize from one situation to another for the same decision maker.

As a screening or decision-making device, the primary concern of the interview is negative information. Evidence indicates that interviews are particularly attentive to negative facts or information about the applicant, and this information contributes most to the interviewer's assessment (Mayfield, 1964).

In general, the interview, as a decision-making

device, is unreliable and not highly related to the criterion measure. The usefulness of the interview depends on its relative structure and the idiosyncracies of the interviewer. If the interview is relatively unstructured, reliable assessments are unlikely. If one applicant were interviewed twice, different questions might be asked each time and, consequently, different information given and different decisions made. On the other hand, if the interview were highly structured and interviewers asked the same questions, reliability would be increased. The totally structured interview, however, can be replaced with a questionnaire which saves time and money though diminishing the opportunity to pursue and develop responses. One strategy, thus, is the semistructured interview: ask a few prepared questions, but allow time to discuss and pursue points as they develop.

The problem of idiosyncracy cannot be alleviated by adjusting the format of the interview. Evidence indicates that interviewers' decisions are influenced by their stereotypes of good applicants, by biases formed early in the interview, by negative information, personal appearance, information already available to the interviewer (application blank or test scores), and even impressions of preceding applicants (Webster, 1964). Experienced interviewers can control how much the interviewee talks. The reactions of the interviewer—leaning forward or backward in the chair, sighing, frowning, or smiling—will influence the interviewee and are particularly important since they affect the interviewee's motivation (which he wants to maximize to present a favorable impression).

All these characteristics of the interview situation tend to restrict its reliability. Interviews do have value, however, as a public relations function and, with respect to selection, interviews are valuable as preliminary screening, when it is impossible to develop relatively good empirical procedures (the small company or small applicant sample), and when traits *can* be better assessed by the interview than other means. One special use of the interview is that it permits us to obtain and use as a predictor specific information about the job applicant's knowledge. Such interviews, *oral trade tests*, consist of questions which are phrased in the language of the worker and job.

Another information source which is a potential predictor is the *biographical information blank* (BIB) or *application blank*. Biographical information or application blanks contain personal, demographic, and situational information: age, sex, address, marital status, number of dependents, military status, past work experience, and so on. (See Glennon, Albright, & Owens, 1966, for a comprehensive catalog of potential items.) In addition, attitudes, preferences, and interests are frequently assessed. From this information one can obtain a systematic picture of the applicant which indirectly reflects his personal and motivational characteristics. One assumption underlying the use of questions pertaining to past work experience is that they may be the best predictor of future performance. In essence, BIBs are measures of those personal characteristics which are least susceptible to faking.

The essential point, however, is that the items comprising the BIB can and should be weighted and scored for use as a predictor. The easiest way to construct a predictor from a BIB is to select discriminatory items—that is, those which distinguish between successful and nonsuccessful workers on the performance criterion. For example, if 85 percent of our successful workers have two or more dependents whereas only 15 percent of those with zero or one dependent are successful, we obviously should prefer an applicant with two or more dependents. (Hypotheses pertaining to responsibility, mobility, and so on might explain this relationship.) The end result of an individual BIB is a sum of weighted scores on all items which is used as a predictor. (For a detailed discussion of weighting application blanks, see Guion, 1965.)

If items are used for decision making without evidence that they are related to the criterion, there may be evidence of unfair, illegal discrimination. Also, since many of the items can be more personal than a request for the applicant's age, the problem of invasion of privacy is very real. If the item does not help you to make a decision, why ask it?

References often are requested on application blanks. The information obtained often concerns the applicant's responsibility and motivation. Scoring reference information is difficult and requires a subjective evaluation or weighting.

Usually, previous employers and personal friends are listed as references. The lack of value to the employer of the latter source is obvious; it is not difficult to find a friend who will say a few good things in your behalf. References from a former boss are more difficult to evaluate. Does he really know enough about the applicant to write about him; can he evaluate the abilities that are necessary for the new job and the applicant's talent in relation to them? Then there are more cynical concerns. Some bosses will write a "great" letter so that the applicant will get the job and the present boss will be rid of him. Also, from the point of view of the new organization, "If he's so good, why don't you try to keep him?" Perhaps the best way to use a reference is as a screening device with emphasis on negative information.

The most obvious predictors are *tests*. Achievement tests measure how well an individual can presently perform; aptitude tests measure his potential. Tests can be differentiated into paper and pencil or performance; speed (how much you can do in a given time) or power (how much do you know); or verbal or nonverbal.

Tests of intellectual ability can measure general intelligence, verbal ability, numerical ability, convergent and divergent reasoning, creativity, and so on; psychomotor skill tests will measure dexterity, eye-hand or -finger coordination, and so on. Personality and motivation tests also can be used. The *job sample* is a specific test which requires the applicant to demonstrate that he possesses the necessary skills by actually doing the tasks. The job sample test is a simulation; it is representative of the work actually performed on the job and includes all of the important aspects of performance. If the job involves computations on an adding machine, the test would require the applicant to make similar computations. (For a general discussion of tests and testing see Cronbach, 1970. For a discussion of available tests see Buros, 1972.)

Basic Validation Procedures

Stage 4 in the selection process involves the examination of the relationship between one or more information sources (predictors) and the criterion or criteria. Because the purpose of a selection system is to facilitate selection of an applicant for a position, it is essential that we emphasize here, as we did when discussing manpower analysis, that the recruiting sample not only restricts the degree of generalization possible but, in effect, dictates the validation

model. Validity, generally speaking, is the degree to which one measure is related to another. In employment situations, validity reflects the degree to which a predictor or information source is related to performance on the job, the criterion.

One appropriate validation model involves *predictive validity*. The purpose of administering a predictor, or collecting information from an applicant, is to predict how that person will perform on the job. The process of examining the relationship between the predictor and subsequent performance, the criterion, is referred to as predictive validity or the follow-up method of validation.

An ideal predictive validity design would involve administration of a potential predictor (we will discuss multiple predictors below) to a group of applicants. Based on chance, lottery, or any other random procedure, but *not* on the basis of their predictor scores, these applicants would join the organization. Though this procedure would maximize the information from the predictive validity study only rarely is an organization willing to hire randomly. In actual practice, applicants are chosen on the basis of the existing selection system which the investigators hope to improve upon. The problem with this procedure is that the validation sample (the applicants who are *hired*) will not include persons who are rejected by the current system. Since we may not know the validity of the current system, some of the applicants may be rejected unfairly or potentially excellent workers may be rejected. We could never discover this if the current selection system is used as a screening device to determine who is hired into the validation sample.

In the ideal or actual case, if we are trying to validate a job knowledge test as a predictor, we would administer the test to the applicants and file the results without using the test scores for decision making. The results are filed because we have no justification for using them; at this point, we do not know if the test is valid in this application. After the applicants who were hired (the validation sample) have been on the job for a specified length of time, performance measures are obtained. The relationship between the scores on the potential predictor and the performance measure is examined and indicates the potential usefulness of the predictor.

Examine this procedure closely. It involves investing time and money in a predictor which may eventually prove to have no relationship to the criterion. The information necessary to determine the validity of the predictor may not be obtained until a year later, and then there is no guarantee that it will be valid. In addition to the cost and time, there is reluctance to hire anyone without using a "mystical" test score. In other words, the most appropriate validation model in its purest form is not that which most organizations would be willing to apply.

An alternative to the predictive validity model is *concurrent validity,* or present-employee validation. Concurrent validity involves the administration of the predictor to a group of incumbent workers, simultaneously obtaining criterion measures on them. Criterion measures can be obtained the day following predictor administration, the same day, or even a day before.

Now recall the purpose of validation and our discussion of recruitment. We are concerned with hiring new workers. What happens if we apply what we know about the relationship between the predictor and criterion for the incumbent workers to a group of applicants? First, the motivation level differs for the two groups. Our present workers will be told that the test scores "do not count," that they are being used for research. If the predictor is "valid," the new applicants will be told that test scores will be used to decide whether or not they are hired. The different instructions will affect motivation which in turn will affect results. Second, present workers have the advantage of experience when they provide potential predictor information. Their scores might be substantially different from those they would have obtained as applicants. Many applicants lack job experience. Consequently, the incumbent's experience will influence predictor results and affect any generalization to an applicant group. Furthermore, since those individuals who had performed poorly would no longer be on the job, the range of the criterion scores would be restricted. This would influence (lower) the predictor-criterion relationship. Concurrent validity is not appropriate for most situations. Unfortunately, however, many industries employ the model because it gives instant results! Concurrent validity, because of the problems mentioned above, and contrary to popular belief, is not an estimate (over or under) of predictive validity!

Concurrent validity may be appropriate for validating job sample tests, however. When we use job sample tests, we are concerned with whether the applicant can do the job *now,* today. That is, can the applicant type, operate the machine, and so on. Through a careful job analysis we would identify the important components of the job and how they are performed. We should attempt to validate a job sample test empirically. The concurrent validation model can be used to determine successful incumbents' performance level which, in turn, gives us a job sample standard for applicants. However, the predictive validation model again may be more appropriate. Because of organizational, situational, and personal characteristics, how someone *can* do the job may differ from how he *will* do the job.

Content validity is another alternative validation procedure, one which does not involve statistical relationships. Content validity is based on the judgment of the developer (a professional tester trained in the area of test construction) of the predictor measure. But it is important to distinguish between content and face validity. Content validity is established by a judgment that *the predictor is job-related.* Face validity means that *the predictor seems appropriate to the person being tested.* Though face validity may be useful in obtaining cooperation with the testing procedure or in convincing organization officials that the test is appropriate, it is not a sufficient (or necessary) condition for using a test as a predictor.

The judgment of content validity should be based on a careful and detailed analysis of the criterion which is to be predicted. This analysis will be either a total job analysis or, in the case of preparing predictors for part of a set of multiple criteria, an analysis of those job elements to be predicted. The developer of the predictor then constructs a test which will (in his judgment) representatively sample the skills, attitudes, or behaviors required by the job.

Content validity, therefore, is no better (or worse) than the trained judgment of the test builder. In some cases a predictive validity study may be appropriate for a predictor which has content validity. However, content validity frequently must be used if a predictive validity study is unfeasible: (1) there may be too few applicants to carry out the statistical analyses of predictive validity; (2) time constraints may prohibit waiting for the establishment of criteria performance levels; or (3) the job may be so critical or the consequences of poor performance so severe that one would not want to risk using the wide-range performance criteria required to establish predictive validity.

Results of Validation

We have mentioned *results of validation*. Whether predictive or concurrent validations, these results usually are correlation coefficients that are interpreted as *validity coefficients*. The validity coefficient r_{CP} ranges from -1.00 to $+1.00$, where the absolute value indicates the strength of relationship between the criterion *(C)* and the predictor *(P)*, and the sign indicates the direction of the relationship. The coefficient can be tested for statistical significance.

Several precautions must be observed when interpreting a validity coefficient. First, most correlation statistics are appropriate for linear relationships between the predictor and criterion. If a nonlinear relationship exists, the traditional Pearson correlation coefficient will provide an underestimation of validity.

Second, if we do not have the full range of possible scores on either the predictor or criterion, again we will get an underestimate of validity. This restriction of range might occur in concurrent validation with current workers, who are likely to be relatively successful, whereas those who were unsuccessful would no longer be with the organization. Consequently, we do not have the full range of possible scores on the criterion. Restriction of range on the potential predictor may occur in the predictive validation model if applicants are hired on a nonrandom basis. This may decrease the range of the potential predictor in the validation sample.

Third, reliability of both the predictor and criterion limit validity. If the predictor and/or criterion is unreliable and therefore inconsistent in assessing its own characteristic, we cannot expect one to measure the other. Thus, if we have poor reliabilities in the predictor and/or criterion we will get underestimates of validity. We can correct for this attenuation and obtain an estimate of validity that is based on the assumption of perfect reliabilities (see Guion, 1965, pp. 31–33). This estimate will indicate whether it is advantageous to improve upon the reliability of the predictor and/or criterion.

In addition to a validity coefficient, we also obtain a regression or prediction equation. The regression equation, in the form of $C' = a + bP$ (where P is the predictor score, a and b are statistical weights, and C' is a predicted criterion score), is that which we use to make predictions for individual applicants. This equation and the validity coefficient are computed on the data from our validity sample. The data are the predictor score and criterion score for each member of the validity sample. If we are satisfied with the strength of the validity coefficient and decide to use the predictor in selection, we administer the predictor to a new applicant. We can obtain the predicted criterion score, C', for the new applicant by substituting his score on the predictor in the regression equation. Suppose the regression equation developed on our validity sample is $C' = 10 + 2P$. If an applicant scores 40 on the predictor his predicted criterion or performance level would be 90 ($C' = 10 + 2(40)$). Another applicant with a predictor score of 33 would have a predicted criterion score of 76. We would use this information in selection decisions by hiring the applicants with the highest scores or by hiring all who score above a specified level. (See Ghiselli, 1964, for a detailed discussion of the statistics involved in validation and reliability.)

The results of validation also may be expressed in *expectancy charts* and *tables*. Expectancy charts express results in terms of probabilities. The *individual expectancy* chart (Figure 14-1) indicates the probabilities of applicant success on the criterion given their predictor score ranges. For example, if an applicant scores 18 on the predictor, he has a 63 percent chance of being successful on the criterion. The *institutional expectancy* chart (Figure 14-2) indi-

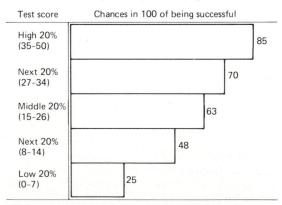

Figure 14-1 Individual expectancy chart.

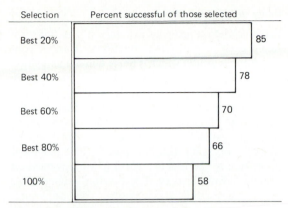

Selection	Percent successful of those selected
Best 20%	85
Best 40%	78
Best 60%	70
Best 80%	66
100%	58

Figure 14-2 Institutional expectancy chart.

cates to the organization the percentage of those selected who will be successful on the criterion, given that the organization selects certain percentages of the best "scores" on the predictor. For example, if the organization selects the top 40 percent scorers on the predictor, 78 percent of these will be successful on the criterion. (Procedures to construct these charts are described in Guion, 1965.)

Extension of the Basic Validation Procedure: Multiple Prediction and Multiple Cutoff

To this point, our discussion of validity has been restricted to the situation with one predictor and one criterion. However, as already indicated, there are several sources of predictor information. Using more than one type of predictor can increase our understanding and ability to predict the criterion.

With one predictor and one criterion, we are dealing with simple correlation (validity), r. If we decide to form a "test battery"—for example, use a BIB and an aptitude test as predictors—we can employ a model of validation which simultaneously uses more than one predictor. Multiple correlation, R, provides an estimate of the relationship between the criterion and the composite of, in this case, two predictor scores. If the aptitude test is correlated $+$ .30 with the criterion and the addition of BIB "scores" indicates a multiple correlation of $+$ .40, we may conclude that two predictors are better than one. The resulting prediction equation would be of the form $C' = a + b_1P_1 + b_2P_2$ (where a, b_1 and b_2 are weights, P_1 and P_2 are two predictors, and C' the predicted criterion value). Suppose the multiple

regression equation developed on our validity sample is $C' = 5 + 3P_1 + 1.5P_2$ (where P_1 and P_2 represent aptitude test scores and BIB scores, respectively). If an applicant scores 40 on the aptitude test and 6 on the BIB, his predicted criterion would be 134 ($C' = 5 + 3(40) + 1.5(6)$). Another applicant with an aptitude test score of 30 and a BIB score of 26 would also have a predicted criterion of 134.

The essential characteristic of multiple correlation is the composite of the two predictors; it is possible for one predictor to compensate for another. That is, a deficiency or low score by the second applicant on the aptitude test was overcome by his high score (favorable response) on the BIB. The combination of the two predictors and its relationship to the criterion is the essence of a *compensatory model of validation*.

An alternative to multiple correlation, or the compensatory model, is a *multiple cutoff* approach. Rather than permitting high scores on one predictor to compensate for low scores on another, the multiple cutoff model requires that a minimum score be obtained on *each* valid predictor. All predictor information is crucial; all characteristics, abilities, and so on are considered essential for successful performance. A decision to hire an applicant is made only if he scores at or above the cutoff on all predictors.

Two points should be made about multiple predictors. First, our examples have been restricted to two predictors. If three or more are used in either the compensatory or cutoff model, nothing changes conceptually (only more computer time is required); it is just an extension of the one or two predictor cases. Second, we have referred to the relationship between two predictors and one criterion. We do not mean to suggest that prediction of one criterion is an adequate basis for suitable selection systems. When more than one criterion is used, a battery or set of predictors is validated independently for each criterion.

Cross-Validation

In the discussion on validity, we have implied that if we have (for example) 100 applicants for a job, we administer a set of predictors to all applicants, hire all applicants, and finally evaluate their performance. We then compute a multiple correlation and prediction equation which is evaluated for statistical significance; if the significance is satisfactory, we subsequently use the predictors for selection decisions on new applicant samples.

This validation procedure is not complete. If we employ the procedure as described, there is the problem that the statistical results (prediction weights—*a*'s and *b*'s) may be biased or distorted due to capitalization on chance factors in that specific sample of 100. The regression equation may be unique to that specific validity sample and would not be useful in new but similar applicant samples. Consequently, it is necessary to *cross-validate,* or determine how effective the prediction equation is. We need to know whether the same equation would occur in similar samples.

Cross-validation usually involves splitting the *total initial sample* (100) into two subsamples (subsample sizes are arbitrary). The regression equation is computed for one subsample ($N = 67$) and then applied to the other subsample, the holdout group ($N = 33$). For this *first subsample,* we might obtain an equation such as $C' = 6 + 4P_1 + 3P_2$. If the predictor scores for the *holdout* group are substituted in this equation, we obtain a *predicted criterion score* for each member of the holdout group. However, we do know the *actual* criterion scores for the members of the holdout group. The correlation between the predicted and the actual scores for the holdout subsample is an indication of the *validity of the predictor battery*. If this coefficient is statistically significant, the prediction equation is potentially useful.

There is, however, a dilemma to cross-validation. By splitting the total sample into two subgroups we obtain an unbiased estimate of predictor validity for future samples. But the subsample regression equation itself is more likely to be in error than one based on a larger, total sample. Several researchers have investigated this dilemma (Campbell, 1967; Chandler, 1964; Gollob, 1967, 1968; Mosier, 1951; Normal, 1965), but there is no statistically satisfactory resolution.

We should emphasize that cross-validation is not independent of or in addition to the validity procedure previously described. Validation involves cross-validation; it is a simultaneous procedure. Validity results that do not include cross-validation should be regarded with caution.

Utility of Selection Systems

Cross-validation provides evidence of the *statistical* significance of prediction equations. Another consideration is utility, which is Stage 5 in our validation procedure. Does a valid selection system result in the hiring of a percentage of workers who will eventually be considered successful greater than the percentage of successful workers hired without the selection system? The basic parameter in a discussion of utility is the decision maker's value judgment in relation to the relative worth of various decision results, payoff matrices. These value judgments or statements are difficult to measure. The basic strategy is to maximize the average gain for the organization in obtaining satisfactory workers. The preferred selection strategy is that which provides the greatest gain or utility value. In evaluating the strategies, we consider the gain in hiring with a selection system as opposed to no selection system, one system as opposed to another, and cost and time of systematic selection. With respect to costs, we are concerned with recruiting, training, and material costs and costs due to incorrect decisions. If the company hires someone who turns out to be unsuccessful, the costs are obvious. However, we must consider the other possibility—the costs of rejecting someone who would have been successful. Not only does the organization lose, but the effects on the applicant may be severe. (See Cronbach & Gleser, 1965, for a discussion of utility in terms of decision theory.)

The simplest way to evaluate the utility of a selection system is to examine a scatterplot (Figure 14-3). The data used to form the scatterplot are obtained from the members of the validity sample.

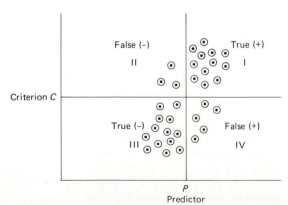

Figure 14-3   Scatterplot of criterion and predictor data.

Suppose Score C on the criterion is the point dividing successful and unsuccessful workers. Suppose, also, that score P on the predictor is the cut-off point that determines who is hired and rejected. This point can be determined so that the least number of errors is made—that is, the fewest number of unsuccessful workers would be hired and the fewest number of successful workers would be rejected. Unless the validity coefficient is one, there will be errors. Separating the group at P and C on the predictor and criterion respectively results in the division of the scatterplot into quadrants.

Quadrants I and III reveal the number of workers correctly identified, as either successful *(true positive)* or unsuccessful *(true negative)*. Quadrant II indicates the number of workers that the test indicates will do poorly (because they score below P) but who are evaluated eventually as successful (the *false negatives*). Quadrant IV indicates the number of workers who would be hired on the basis of their predictor score but who are subsequently evaluated as unsuccessful (the *false positives*).

To determine if the selection system is useful, the percentage of workers who would be considered successful if chosen on the basis of the selection system can be compared with the percentage considered successful and chosen without systematic predictor information. The latter percentage is the *base rate*. The base rate is determined by the ratio

$$\frac{I + II}{I + II + III + IV}$$

To determine the gain or percentage increase in successful workers if a new selection system is used, we can use the formula

$$\frac{I}{I + IV} - \frac{I + II}{I + II + III + IV}$$

The first part of the formula indicates the percentage of workers who are hired on the basis of the selection system and who are considered successful on the criterion. The second part of the formula is the base rate. The difference is the percentage improvement, or gain.

Taylor-Russell tables (1939) present the gain in using a selection system where a new predictor is added to existing selection procedures. The gain depends on validity coefficients, base rates, and selection ratios. The selection ratio is the number of people to be hired, divided by the number of applicants. If the validity coefficient and the base rate are held constant as the selection ratio is increased (the greater the percentage of people hired), the gain will decrease. If the validity coefficient and selection ratio are held constant, the greater the base rate, the less the gain. If the base rate and the selection ratio are held constant, as the validity coefficient increases so does the gain.

Reevaluation

Stage 6, the final stage in validation, requires that validity coefficients be reassessed periodically. Criteria and performance are dynamic. The job itself, the way tasks are performed, and the characteristics of the people performing the tasks change over time; thus, we also should expect validity coefficients to change. If we continuously use a predictor or set of predictors, we should regularly check the validity for any changes.

PLACEMENT

Placement problems arise after a decision has been made to hire an applicant. The basis for this initial decision may have been that the applicant possesses "general" abilities that the company likes to see in its workers, or that he is number one in his class, or that he is returning to the organization after a leave of absence and his previous job has been filled. Regardless of the reason, the organization has a member without a specific position in mind.

The objectives of placement are to place each applicant in a position in which he will do his best work, *or* in a position so that each position is filled by someone who meets at least minimum requirements, *or* in a position so that the organization will receive maximum performance from the group of applicants as a whole. If we are trying to accomplish the first objective, we need to predict how well the applicant will do in each of the available positions. To accomplish this objective we could use regression analysis to obtain a predicted criterion score for each of the positions for which he is considered. The decision then would be to place the applicant on the job for which he has the highest predicted criterion value. Or, with *pattern analysis* we use the predictor information of those workers who are presently considered successful. Pattern analysis requires comparison of the applicant's predictor scores with the average predictor score values of successful workers in each position. Similarity between these scores is the basis for the placement decisions. The similarity is assessed by profile statistics, profile coefficients, or "distance from the standard" scores (Nunnally, 1967). A simple example of a decision based on similarity is illustrated in Figures 14-4 and 14-5. The average predictor score values for successful production workers are shown by the bold line in Figure 14-4; the values for successful salesmen are shown in Figure 14-5. The predictor scores of a single applicant have been superimposed as a dotted line on each figure. From the figures it is clear that the applicant is more like successful salesmen than successful workers.

If we are trying to accomplish the second objective (filling each position with an applicant who meets minimum requirements), we need to set a cutoff for the predictors of each position and place applicants in any position for which they meet the multiple cutoff requirements.

To accomplish the third objective (the organization will receive maximum performance from the group of applicants as a whole), we can use a combination of the previous strategies. We can use regression and profile analysis to place each applicant in such a position that the total result of all placement decisions yields maximum performance for the organization. In other words, we may not place an applicant in the position for which he is predicted to do his best work if this meant that either another position would not be filled because there was no applicant or another applicant might be

without a suitable position. For example, if Allan Allaround is predicted to perform very successfully as a worker and adequately as a salesman, whereas Mike Minimal is predicted to perform adequately as a worker but poorly as a salesman, Allan is best placed as a salesman and Mike as a worker.

PREDICTION FOR PROMOTION AND TRANSFER DECISIONS

We mentioned previously that predictor information sources could be used when we want to promote or transfer current workers. If we were considering a worker in ORG who has applied for the position of salesman, we might administer the same predictor battery to him as we would to an applicant from outside ORG. There is nothing different about the validation procedures whether the predictors are being used for promotion or transfer decisions or for initial selection.

Some organizations have established career ladders for their workers. If the interval of time between someone's entry into one position and promotion to the next is relatively brief, initial gathering of information may include predictors for the second step position. Again, there is nothing different about validation in this situation.

Another approach to promotions which is currently receiving considerable emphasis is the use of *assessment centers* (Bray & Grant, 1966). Those employees being considered for promotion receive extensive examination with a variety of techniques. This usually involves one to three days of testing,

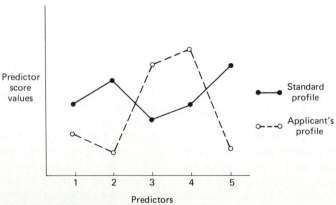

Figure 14-4 Pattern of predictor scores for workers.

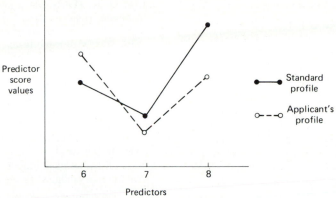

Figure 14-5 Pattern of predictor scores for salesmen.

interviewing, and participating in simulated job activities. All workers at managerial levels often participate in assessment centers regardless of their level of interest in promotions. The information obtained is used to identify candidates with promotion potential and to provide feedback to the participants about their strengths and weaknesses. If information from assessment center examinations is used for promotion decisions it should be validated as in any other situation.

UNFAIR DISCRIMINATION AND SELECTION SYSTEMS

Recent legislation (Civil Rights Act of 1964, Title VII), Supreme Court rulings (*Griggs vs. Duke Power,* March 1971), and guidelines (Equal Employment Opportunity Commission, 1970; Office of Federal Contract Compliance, 1971) have emphasized the problem of unfair discrimination towards minority groups and sexes with respect to selection and hiring. Unfair discrimination exists when applicants with equal probabilities of success on the job have unequal probabilities of being hired for the job (Guion, 1966).

One way to assess whether unfair discrimination exists is to divide the validity sample into groups on the basis of the variable of concern (race or sex) and compare the validity coefficients and the regression eq¢tions for each group. For example, Figure 14-6 illustrates the scatterplot for a case where two groups differ on average score on both the predictor and criterion, yet the regression equations are equal. In this case there is no unfair discrimination for there is equally good prediction for the two

groups; the group that has the higher predictor scores (Group 1) also is more successful on the criterion.

In contrast, the two groups in Figure 14-7 are equally successful on the criterion, but Group I scores higher on the predictor than Group II. Though the validity coefficients are equal, the regression equations are different. Consequently, if P_1 is chosen as the cutoff, there would be unfair discrimination against Group II. One solution would be to have two cutoffs—P_1 if the applicant is a member of Group I and P_{11} if the applicant is a member of Group II. Another solution would be to establish a separate regression equation for each group and to use the predicted criterion scores from the appropriate equation for each applicant. (An excellent article which illustrates interactions between predictor and criterion scores and their effect

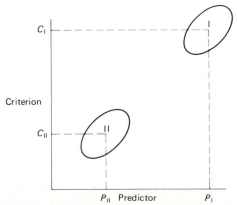

Figure 14-6 Comparison of two groups (I and II) that differ on average score on the predictor *(P)* and criterion *(C).*

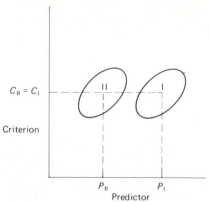

Figure 14-7 Comparison of two groups that differ in performance on the predictor, but perform similarly on the criterion.

on heterogeneous or socially mixed groups is presented by Bartlett and O'Leary, 1969).

With respect to whether discrimination exists, the burden of proof is on the employer. He must show that his predictor is related to performance and that the predictor is not differentially valid. To do this, the organization must conduct careful job analyses; develop reliable, relevant, and practical criterion measures; and perform appropriate and complete validity analyses.

REFERENCES

Job Choice

Crites, J. O. *Vocational psychology.* New York: McGraw-Hill, 1969.

Holland, J. L. *Psychology of vocational choice.* New York: Ginn, 1966.

Kuder, G. F. *Manual for the Kuder preference record—Vocational.* Chicago: Science Research Associates, 1960.

Roe, A. *Psychology of occupations.* New York: Wiley, 1956.

Strong, E. K., Jr. revised by D. P. Campbell. *Strong vocational interest blank: Manual.* Stanford, Calif.: Stanford University Press, 1966.

Super, D. E., & Bohn, M. J. *Occupational psychology.* Belmont, Calif.: Wadsworth, 1970.

Information Sources

Bray, D. W., & Grant, D. L. The assessment center in the measurement of potential for business management. *Psychological Monographs.* 1966, **80**(17, Whole No. 625).

Buros, O. K. (Ed.), *The seventh mental measurements yearbook.* Highland Park, N.J.: Gryphon, 1972.

Cronbach, L. J. *Essentials of psychological testing.* New York: Harper & Row, 1970.

Ghiselli, E. E. *The validity of occupational aptitude tests.* New York: Wiley, 1966.

Glennon, J. R., Albright, L. E., & Owens, W. A. *A catalog of life history items.* Reproduced by the Richardson Foundation, 1966.

Guion, R. M., & Gottier, R. F. Validity of personality measures in personnel selection. *Personnel Psychology,* 1965, **18,** 135–164.

Huck, J. R. Assessment centers: A review of the external and internal validities. *Personnel Psychology,* 1973, **26,** 191–212.

Mayfield, E. C. The selection interview—A reevaluation of published research. *Personnel Psychology,* 1964, **17,** 239–260.

Meehl, P. E. *Clinical vs. statistical prediction.* Minneapolis: University of Minnesota Press, 1954.

Webster, E. C. *Decision making in the employment interview.* Montreal: Industrial Relations Centre, McGill University, 1964.

Wernimont, P. R., & Campbell, J. P. Signs, samples and criteria. *Journal of Applied Psychology,* 1968, **52,** 372–376.

Validation

American Psychological Association. *Standards for educational and psychological tests and manuals.* Washington: 1966.

Campbell, J. P. Cross validation revisited. Paper presented at the meeting of the Midwestern Psychological Association, Chicago, 1967.

Chandler, R. E. Validity, reliability, baloney—and a little mustard. Paper presented at the meeting of the Midwestern Psychological Association, 1964.

Cronbach, L. J., & Gleser, G. C. *Psychological tests and personnel decisions.* Urbana, Ill., University of Illinois Press, 1965.

Dunnette, M. D. *Personnel selection and placement.* Belmont, Calif.: Wadsworth, 1966.

Ghiselli, E. E. *Theory of psychological measurement.* New York: McGraw-Hill, 1964.

Gollob, H. F. Cross-validation in fixed effects analysis of variance. Paper presented at the meeting of the American Psychological Association. San Francisco, 1968.

Gollob, H. F. Cross-validation using samples of size one. Paper presented at the meeting of the American Psychological Association, Washington, D.C., 1967.

Guion, R. M. *Personnel Testing.* New York: McGraw-Hill, 1965.

Mosier, C. I. Symposium. The need and means of cross-validation I. Problems and designs of cross-validation. *Educational and Psychological Measurement.* 1951, **11**, 5–11.

Naylor, J. C., & Shine, L. C. A table for determining the increase in mean criterion score obtained by using a selection device. *Journal of Industrial Psychology,* 1965, **3**, 33–42.

Norman, W. T. Double-split cross-validation. An extension of Mosier's design, two undesirable alternatives, and some enigmatic results. *Journal of Applied Psychology,* 1965, **49**, 348–357.

Nunnally, J. C. *Psychometric theory.* New York: McGraw-Hill, 1967.

Taylor, H. C., & Russell, J. T. The relationship of validity coefficients to the practical effectiveness of tests in selection: Discussion and tables. *Journal of Applied Psychology,* 1939, **23**, 565–578.

Zedeck, S. Problems with the use of "moderator" variables. *Psychological Bulletin,* 1971, **76**, 295–310.

Unfair Discrimination

Bartlett, C. J., & O'Leary, B. S. A differential prediction model to moderate the effects of heterogeneous groups in personnel selection and classification. *Personnel Psychology,* 1969, **22**, 1–17.

Equal Employment Opportunity Commission. Guidelines on employee selection procedures. *Federal Register,* 1970, **35**, 12333 (1–3).

Guion, R. M. Employment tests and discriminatory hiring. *Industrial Relations,* 1966, **5**, 20–37.

Office of Federal Contract Compliance Employee testing and other selection procedures. *Federal Register,* 1971, **36**, 19307–19310.

Reading 15

The Entry of Newcomers into Organizations

John P. Wanous

The entry of new personnel is an important event for both the individual and the organization, because an ineffective matching is costly to both. For example, a large Midwestern bank recently hired 600 tellers in one year just to maintain a steady teller workforce of 1,400. At a cost of about $2,000 per replacement, the bank spent close to $1,200,000 for teller turnover that year. Because the influx of newcomers can be viewed from either an individual or an organizational perspective, it is important that we examine the entry process from *both* these viewpoints.

The Matching Model shown in Figure 15-1 is a helpful way to organize and visualize the basic issues in organization entry (Wanous, 1980). It shows two ways in which individuals and organizations are matched. The "top" match between one's abilities and those required by the organization is, perhaps, the more familiar of the two since it has traditionally been of great concern in hiring new employees. The "bottom" match is also important, but for different reasons. Whereas job performance is the likely victim of a poor ability–job requirements match, low job satisfaction and organizational commitment are

Article prepared especially for this book.

the consequences of a poor human needs–organizational climates match.

The Matching Model shows only the most obvious relationships, not the less frequent ones. For example, it is possible for an ability mismatch to affect job satisfaction rather than performance when a person is *over*qualified for a job. Similarly, a poor match in terms of human needs sometimes can affect job performance as well as satisfaction. An employee whose human needs are frustrated in an organization is quite likely to withdraw almost all energy from work. The employee may even go so far as to commit sabotage as a way of "evening up the score" with the organization. While the Matching Model shows the most directly obvious effects of these two matchings, there *are* certain exceptions as indicated above.

The Matching Model is incomplete in another sense. It does not show all the forces that influence one's job performance. Specifically, work-motivation factors are excluded (see Reading 6 by Nadler and Lawler). This is because the Matching Model is concerned specifically with the entry of newcomers rather than other facets of employee behavior.

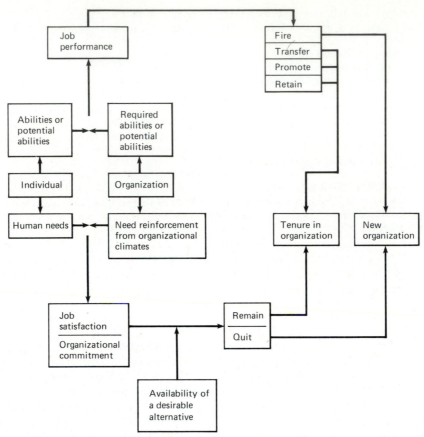

Figure 15-1 Matching individual and organization.

TOPICS IN ORGANIZATIONAL ENTRY

The entry of newcomers is a process, not a "one-shot," single event. The various components of the entry process are often hard to disentangle, but some arbitrary stages can be identified. Within each stage, the organizational entry process can be viewed from either the individual's or the organization's perspective.

1. How Do Individuals and Organizations Find Out About Each Other?

From the individual's viewpoint, the question of how individuals and organizations find out about each other can be split into: (a) how do job seekers learn about job openings? and (b) how do job seekers learn specific information about organizations? From the organization's perspective this question can be asked in terms of the sources used to obtain new employees.

Individuals learn about job openings either through formal sources (ads, governmental or private employment agencies) or through informal channels (friends or relatives). White-collar workers tend to use both formal and informal sources about equally, whereas blue-collar workers tend to rely more on informal word-of-mouth sources (Parnes, 1970). As will be seen shortly, the *source* of new employees is important to organizations. This is because there are significant differences in both job performance and turnover rates for employees from different sources.

As the Matching Model shows, individuals are concerned with how well a new organization's climate will be able to satisfy their various needs. In order to ascertain this, job candidates need information about organizations that is both accurate and complete. Do they get it? The accumulated research evidence shows that job candidates do *not* get accurate information (Wanous, 1980). Studies of newly entering AT&T managers, of "stayers" and "leavers" at the Ford Motor Company, of telephone operators, of new M.B.A. students, of Harvard Business School graduates, and of armed services personnel *all indicate that individuals who entered these organizations held unrealistically inflated expectations* (see Wanous, 1980, for details). The only time newcomers' expectations are accurate is when they concern factual, concrete factors, e.g., starting salary for employees or tuition costs for students. In virtually all other instances, expectations are inflated. This obviously presents serious problems for the effective matching of person and organization, because individuals cannot make informed choices about which organization to choose.

From the organization's viewpoint it does matter where new employees come from. A small number of research studies have related the job performance and turnover rates of newcomers to the source from which they came. The sources with the lowest turnover rates are referrals by present employees and reemployment of former personnel. Those with the highest rates of subsequent turnover tend to be newspaper ads and employment agencies. This difference may be explained by the greater amount and greater accuracy of information available to job candidates who previously worked at a company or who were referred by a present employee. Armed with this greater quantity and quality of organizational information, those people were able to make job choices that came closer to matching their own needs to organizational climates (Wanous, 1980).

2. What Happens When Individuals and Organizations Try to "Sell" Themselves to Each Other?

The organizational entry process is a bit like a courtship; i.e., each party tries to appear as attractive as possible to the other. Thus, individual job candidates emphasize their strengths and minimize (or try to conceal) their weaknesses. Similarly, organizations recruit new employees by stressing their most positive characteristics and minimizing negative information. As a result of this, both individuals and organizations present distorted images of themselves, making it difficult for each to make optimal choices of the other (Porter, Lawler, & Hackman, 1975).

Despite the fact that individuals and organizations

present only favorable images, the organization usually manages to learn more about the job candidate than the reverse. Through interviewing, testing, reference checks, and past employment history, the hiring organization is in a better position to uncover the faults and weaknesses of individuals. In contrast, it is much more difficult for the individual job candidate to thoroughly investigate an organization. One might be tempted to think that this problem for job candidates is typical for only lower-level employees. Actually, even executives who switch companies have similar problems. The most common misunderstandings at the executive level are about the actual scope of one's authority in the new organization.

In terms of the Matching Model, the primary concern of organizations has been to achieve sound matches in terms of abilities meeting job requirements. To a certain extent organizations also try to determine whether the newcomer will "fit" in the organization, as in the human-needs match with organizational climates. Methods for doing this latter matching are less well developed than techniques for matching abilities to job requirements. They include interviews, personality tests, personal essays about one's life/career goals, and even the use of "weighted" application blanks.

In contrast to the organization's prime concern with the ability match, job candidates are more concerned with whether their needs will be met in a new organization. Since organizations "sell" themselves to job candidates, individuals have a difficult time accurately choosing a job offer that matches their needs. Sometimes organizations attempt to do the human needs–organizational climates match for the job candidate. These attempts are doomed to failure, however, because job candidates can easily fake personality tests or be "on guard" during a job interview.

What can be done about this dilemma? The concept of the "realistic job preview" (RJP) (Wanous, 1975), or more simply "realistic recruitment" (Wanous, 1980), has been offered as one solution. In essence, the organization lets the job candidate decide whether the human needs–organizational climates matching is a good fit or not. The individual is able to do so because the organization provides accurate and fairly detailed information to job candidates during recruitment.

The RJP functions exactly like a medical vaccination; i.e., it can prevent a problem from occurring but cannot cure it once it has begun. The essence of a vaccination is to inject a person with a small dose of some germ so that his or her body can develop a natural resistance to that disease. So it is with the RJP. Job candidates are presented with a small dose of "organizational reality." This "vaccination" has been shown to have several beneficial effects for the entry process; e.g., more favorable attitudes and lower turnover among newcomers. Figure 15-2 shows a theory of how the RJP works.

To date, a total of thirteen experiments have been done to evaluate the specific effects of realistic recruitment (see Wanous, 1980, for details concerning these studies).

• Did the realistic information tend to "scare off" job candidates?

No. Five studies examined this specific possibility, and all five found no negative effects.

• Were the expectations of job candidates correctly "vaccinated"; i.e., lowered by the RJP?

Yes. All five studies which considered this particular question found lower expectations among those who were realistically recruited.

• Did the RJP affect candidate decisions to accept or reject a job offer?

No. In four of five studies the RJP was not potent enough to actually reverse a job candidate's initial organizational choice. This is not supportive of the theoretical model shown in Figure 15-2, which suggests that the RJP may have an effect on one's self-selection of organization.

• Were the job attitudes of realistically recruited newcomers more favorable than those recruited in a more traditional way?

Usually. In three of six studies which measured postentry job attitudes, they were more positive for those who received RJP's. In three others there were no differences. In no case were they worse for those realistically recruited.

• Was job performance affected by the RJP?

No. Of the eight studies which measured the job performance of newcomers, four found no differences between RJP recruits and other recruits, in one case performance was lower for the RJP recruits, and in three cases it was higher for the RJP recruits.

• Was turnover lowered using realistic recruitment?

Yes. In a statistical analysis done after my book was published, the turnover results were accumulated across all studies, totaling 4,372 persons. The turnover of RJP recruits was 16.5

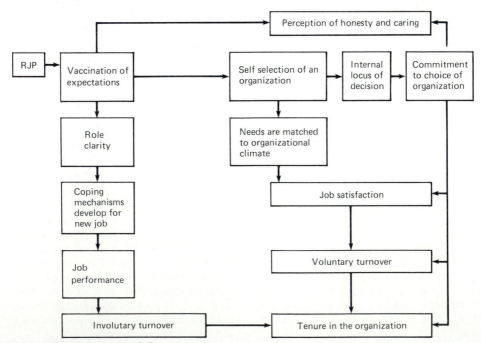

Figure 15-2 Psychological effects of the RJP.

percent, compared to 20.3 percent for those *not* realistically recruited (a statistically significant difference). The 3.8 percentage-point difference means that *turnover will be about 23 percent higher for an organization that does not use RJP's to recruit newcomers* (i.e., 3.8 ÷ 16.5 = 23%).

The *method* used to present realistic information may have an effect on whether turnover is reduced or not. For example, four of the thirteen studies used an oral presentation for the RJP, but not one of these found any significant lowering of turnover. Written booklets were used five times and significantly lowered turnover in four cases. Audiovisual methods were used three times, but only one lowered turnover significantly. Finally, a work sample test was used once and significantly lowered turnover.[1]

3. How Do Individuals Decide Which Organization to Enter?

Organizational entry is the result of a mutual choice. Individuals must seek out jobs, then be selected by an organization, and then must choose which organization to enter. Since the job-seeking individual initiates action at two points, it is important to understand how individuals choose organizations. First, individuals must make some effort to join an organization. Second, after the organization has made its selection decision, individuals must decide whether to accept or decline the offer of admission.

To understand how individuals make these two choices, we must consider what various psychologists have said. Unfortunately, those who have studied organizational choices are *not* in agreement on how they are made. There are, in fact, two rather different views about the organizational-choice process.

The first explanation of the individual's choice process is expectancy theory.[2] Basically, this view holds that people are fairly rational beings who seek out information about organizations and try to maximize their own satisfaction by choosing the

organization that will best meet their needs. This model of motivation, as applied to an organizational choice, can be represented as follows:

Total motivation (1) to join an organization	Expectancy of + being admitted to the organization	Attractiveness × of the organization

where,

Attractiveness (2) of an organization	Beliefs about = each outcome that will be obtained in the organization	Desirability × of each particular outcome to the job candidate

Equation (1) addresses the issue of what organizations people try to join. It clearly shows that individuals seek out jobs, schools, etc., that are not only desirable but also attainable. For example, a mediocre student may see Ivy League schools as highly desirable, but will not even apply to them since there is such a low chance of being accepted. Research concerning equation (1) has been rather infrequent. Two of the three studies conducted have supported equation (1), however (Wanous, 1980).

Equation (2) shows what makes an organization attractive to an individual. This is an important factor since it is the basis for a person's actual choice from among job offers. When an individual has offers of acceptance from several organizations, the "expectancy of being admitted" is irrelevant (it is then a 1.0 probability in expectancy-theory terms). Thus, one's choice of a job offer is based on comparing the perceived *attractiveness* of those organizations which extended job offers.

How accurate is expectancy theory when it comes to an individual's choice of a job offer? To answer this question, seven studies calculated organizational attractiveness based on questionnaire data. The researchers then checked to see how often the *actual* choice was also the organization regarded as the most attractive based on responses to a questionnaire. In other words, did job candidates do what they said they might do. The *average* "hit rate" was 73 percent, ranging from 54 percent to 87 percent (Wanous, 1980). Since questionnaires are imperfect measurement tools, this is a remarkably high level of agreement. It is strongly supportive of an expectancy-theory view of organizational choice.

---

[1]In a work-sample test, job candidates work on the actual apparatus used on the job. In this particular case the job was operating a sewing machine.

[2]See Reading 6. Nadler and Lawler use expectancy theory to explain how much effort a person expends on *work motivation*. In the present case it is effort directed toward *joining an organization*.

The alternative view of organizational choice is called "unprogrammed decision making." Individuals are viewed as far less systematic and rational than in expectancy-theory terms. One difference is that the unprogrammed view states that individuals consider only a small number of potential outcomes. In contrast, expectancy theorists believe individuals consider quite a few more. Another difference is that the outcomes considered are *not* "weighted" by their desirability to an individual as in equation (2). Instead, the unprogrammed view is that people consider outcomes as either crucial or practically irrelevant. The few outcomes that are considered are *all equally essential* to the choice. The third, and last, difference is that the unprogrammed model sees people as comparing organizations two at a time to assess which is the more attractive. In contrast, expectancy theory stipulates that an individual considers all the alternatives simultaneously. The unprogrammed view is more a sequential process of paired comparisons.

Both expectancy theory and unprogrammed decision making are similar in two respects. First, both suggest that job candidates are able to give fairly clear descriptions of what they are seeking in an organizational choice. Second, both agree that people will *say* they are being rational, even though they may act much less rationally according to the unprogrammed decision model.

Only three research studies have examined the unprogrammed model, and supporting data were found in only one case (Wanous, 1980). Nevertheless, it is an intriguing alternative to expectancy theory. It is also much harder to design a research study to give the unprogrammed model a fair test. It is likely that the "truth" probably lies somewhere in between the two views of how individuals choose organizations, but that is for future research to decide.

Regardless of *how* most people choose organizations, some researchers have suggested that people *should* be more rational. Whether or not people act in accordance with expectancy theory, Janis and Wheeler (1978) have described techniques to facilitate a systematic decision process much like expectancy theory. One of several techniques is the "balance sheet" approach, where individuals are assisted by a "decision counselor" to complete a written outline of the reasons for and against an

organizational choice. This involves getting people to articulate the "pushes and pulls" of various alternatives.

4. How Do Organizations Select Newcomers?

The important question of how organizations select newcomers has been the primary focus of industrial psychologists for many years. In a formal, scientific sense, personnel selection first got started in the United States as a consequence of World War I, when the nation had to mobilize human resources quickly.

In terms of the Matching Model (Figure 15-1), the traditional concern of selection has been to match abilities and job requirements. To achieve this matching, *many* types of psychological tests and other screening criteria (interviews and application blanks, for example) have been developed. Since this field is so vast, it is beyond our scope here to consider it in its entirety.

As an alternative, the selection of personnel will be considered from a more current perspective. Only those selection techniques that match both the abilities and the needs of newcomers to the organization will be considered.

Two selection procedures—realistic work-sample tests and assessment centers—focus on both matchups shown in Figure 15-1. The reason they are able to match job candidates both ways is that they also function much like the RJP, even though this is not their primary intent.

A *realistic work-sample test* is a simulation of the actual task one is being considered for. Thus, a simulation must be designed for *each* job. This is in contrast to psychological tests (e.g., I.Q. tests), which used to be applied across a wide variety of job situations (and without too much success either).

Realistic work-sample tests fall into two categories: verbal and manual. Group discussions and business games (for managers) and language interviews (for university applicants from foreign countries) are typical examples of verbal tests. Sewing machine tests for operators, rudder control tests for pilots, and road tests for a drivers license are examples of manual tests (see Asher and Sciarrino, 1974, for a summary of research on these).

The *assessment center* combines several different personnel selection methods into an intensive experience. Such "centers" have been used to select new personnel, to assess the strengths and weaknesses of current personnel for development purposes, and to identify management potential (see Moses and Byham, 1977; Reading 19 by Kraut).

Assessment center exercises include the use of in-baskets, management games, leaderless group discussions, oral presentations, role-playing, and paper-and-pencil tests. As individuals participate in these various exercises, they are observed by trained assessors who take careful notes. At the conclusion of the exercises the assessors meet as a group to discuss each candidate. It is at this time that judgments are made, but only *after* a thorough review of what the candidate *actually did*. For example, an assessor may indicate the fact that a candidate "spoke without the use of notes" but will *not* say that "the candidate seemed confident." The former is what actually happened, the latter is a conclusion. Conclusions are not drawn until the assessors have thoroughly discussed what each candidate did during the various exercises.

A *Wall Street Journal* reporter recently went through the Merrill Lynch assessment center for account executives and wrote of his experiences (Rout, 1979). His account nicely illustrates how this particular simulation provides both an RJP and a selection procedure. The job simulation was conducted after hours in the Merrill Lynch offices. Since it is much quieter then, a tape recording of office noise (telephones, tickertape, typing, voices, etc.) was played in the background. There was a very full in-basket that needed attention, sporadic telephone calls to interrupt one's train of thought, and an appointment calendar with time conflicts that needed resolution. An experienced employee also role-played a *very* angry customer who had just lost $97,000 of a $100,000 investment, based on *your* recommendation. You had to cope with his phone call.

Apparently this assessment center simulation has been successful in helping Merrill Lynch to hire competent people and also in providing job candidates with realistic information about the job duties and pressures of an account executive. It is not a thorough RJP, however, since information about the uniqueness of Merrill Lynch is not included. It is an RJP for the *job*, but not for the company. Nevertheless, it does seem to function as a procedure for both selection and realistic recruitment.

About twenty-five years ago AT&T was the assessment center pioneer in the business world. Even today AT&T continues to monitor the careers of those managers who were assessed and then hired during the 1956–60 period. The results of this AT&T "Management Progress Study" (Bray, Campbell, & Grant, 1974) are strong testimony for the effectiveness of assessment centers. These results also show that success on the job is influenced by the degree of job challenge in one's immediate working environment, as well as by how well one's abilities fit the job requirements.[3]

The accuracy of predictions about future promotions at AT&T based on the assessment center is rather high. For example, 64 percent of those individuals who were predicted to reach middle management in eight years actually did so. In contrast, only 32 percent of those *not* predicted to reach middle management actually did so (Wanous, 1980). It must be remembered that these predictions were based only on observations and conclusions derived during the time period of three and one-half days allotted to the assessment center. In terms of the Matching Model the assessors were aiming primarily at predicting accurate ability–job requirements match-ups. The assessors could not have known, nor could they have influenced, the type of environment into which these new hires were placed.

The degree of initial job challenge experienced on the job has been shown to have an influence on one's rate of promotion at AT&T (Berlew & Hall, 1966). When assessment center predictions about abilities and the effects of job challenge are considered together, an interesting picture emerges. Figure 15-3 shows one way to rearrange the data from the Management Progress Study (Bray et al. 1974).

5. What Happens When Individuals and Organizations Are Well Matched?

The Matching Model shows two types of matchings between people and organizations. Virtually all experts agree that it is desirable to match human abilities with job requirements. There is less agree-

---

[3]Job challenge was measured by two psychologists who evaluated tape recordings of annual interviews with managers. The overall measure of challenge was a composite of four factors: (1) the degree to which one's boss set a model for achievement, (2) the degree of job stimulation, (3) the extensiveness of supervisory responsibilities, and (4) the frequency of unstructured assignments.

Socialization	Selection prediction	
	Will be promoted	*Will not be promoted*
High job challenge	76% (25 ÷ 33)	61% (11 ÷ 18)
Medium or low job challenge	50% (14 ÷ 28)	20% (9 ÷ 44)

Figure 15-3 The interaction between selection predictions and newcomer socialization.

ment on the universal desirability of matching human needs to organizational climates, however. Some experts fear that conformity may be a by-product (see Reading 13 by Schein, or the earlier work by Argyris, 1958).

At the present time only four research studies have attempted to relate the degree of matching to various indicators of organizational success (e.g., job satisfaction, turnover, job performance). None of the four investigated possible effects on conformity. The four studies included nurses, students, machine operatives, and life insurance agents. In all four cases there were desirable outcomes resulting from matching human needs to organizational climates (Wanous, 1980). In one of the four, however, there was some indication that this type of matching is undesirable for *in*effective organizations, since it tends to perpetuate that ineffectiveness.

RECOMMENDATIONS FOR MANAGING THE ORGANIZATION ENTRY PROCESS

Based on this abbreviated review of research on organizational entry, several recommendations can be offered to both organizations and individuals. (See also Reading 53 by Kotter and Schlesinger.)

From the organization's perspective it would be wise to conduct research on the sources used to obtain newcomers. It is likely that informal sources will yield candidates less likely to quit. Organizations should also consider injecting more realistic information into the recruiting process. This should be done throughout the process, but it is most likely to have an impact when done at the initial contact with job candidates. Realistic recruitment can be integrated with accurate selection procedures by

using either work-sample tests or assessment centers. In both cases the key ingredient is the use of a realistic job simulation. Finally, new employees need to be placed in work environments high in job challenge.

The organizational-entry research suggests several guidelines for individuals seeking jobs. First of all, individuals must take the time and trouble to investigate organizations. This could include talking to both present and former employees. Printed material from organizations should be evaluated with a careful, cynical eye. If possible, meet the person who will be your immediate supervisor. Second, when actually making the job-choice decision, carefully outline *all* the forces and factors in that decision. At least try to behave in a systematically thorough way, similar to the expectancy-theory model or the decision counselor approach. Finally, be prepared to encounter a new environment that is likely to be much less attractive than you expected.

REFERENCES

Argyris, C. Some problems in conceptualizing organizational climate: A case study of a bank. *Administrative Science Quarterly,* 1958, **2,** 501–520.

Asher, J. J., & Sciarrino, J. A. Realistic work sample tests: A review. *Personnel Psychology,* 1974, **27,** 519–533.

Berlew, D. E., and Hall, D. T. The socialization of managers: Effects of expectations on performance. *Administrative Science Quarterly,* 1966, **11,** 207–233.

Bray, D. W., Campbell, R. J., & Grant, D. L. *Formative years in business.* New York: Wiley, 1974.

Janis, I. L., & Wheeler, D. Thinking clearly about career choices. *Psychology Today,* May 1978, 67 ff.

Moses, J. L., & Byham, W. C. (Eds.), *Applying the assessment center method.* Elmsford, N.Y.: Pergamon, 1977.

Parnes, H. S. Labor force and labor markets. In *A review of industrial relations research,* Vol. 1. Madison: University of Wisconsin, Industrial Relations Research Association, 1970.

Porter, L. W., Lawler, E. E., III, & Hackman, J. R. *Behavior in organizations.* New York: McGraw-Hill, 1975.

Rout, L. Going for broker: Our man takes part in a stock selling test. *Wall Street Journal,* April 4, 1979.

Wanous, J. P. Tell it like it is at realistic job previews. *Personnel,* 1975, **52**(4), 50–60.

———. Realistic job previews: Can a procedure to reduce turnover also influence the relationship between abilities and performance? *Personnel Psychology,* 1978, **31**, 249–258.

———. *Organizational entry: Recruitment, selection and socialization of newcomers.* Reading, Mass.: Addison-Wesley, 1980.

Chapter 5

Adaptation Processes

After individuals and organizations have chosen each other, the processes of adaptation and development begin. As in any type of social situation, the new member must learn about the group (in this case, the organization) he or she has joined, and the group (organization) will need to integrate the new member. These reciprocal processes start when the initial choices are made, but they never completely end. The member and the organization are continually influencing each other, both during the initial months of adaptation to each other and later. The organization is attempting to make the individual into as valuable a member as possible, and the individual, in turn, is attempting to utilize the organization for personal satisfaction in the work situation. Each party, as it were, helps to "develop" the other. When the processes work correctly, both gain in relation to what they started with at the time of the individual's entry into the organization.

The readings presented in this chapter provide conceptual views of these processes and examples of actual organizational practices in the development of human resources. In the first article, Feldman utilizes research findings from three studies to demonstrate how organizations can manage the socialization process more effectively for both their own benefit and that of their new employees. The article describes four elements of the overall socialization process: The development of work skills and abilities, the acquisition of appropriate role behaviors, the adjustment to the work group and its norms, and the learning of organizational values. For each of these subprocesses, Feldman maintains, active attention by the organization can facilitate the adjustment of the recently arrived member. As just one example, the author shows how the timing and equity of performance feedback can contribute to the *early* development of skills in the new work situation. Similarly, attempts to strengthen the credibility of information provided to recruits will aid in the learning of organizational values. Feldman goes on to summarize several common themes in the socialization process (e.g., "The socialization process is continuous") and then suggests several specific approaches to explicitly designing the process. Again, these suggestions are research-based and are useful in pointing out to organizations what they *should not* do as well as what they should be trying to implement effectively.

In the following article, Schein describes and

analyzes the "individual's movement through an organization"—in effect, the organizational career. The fundamental point in this article is that each career movement is an interaction of attributes of the person and of the organization. Given this, there is emphasis on the concepts of "socialization" (the influence of the organization on the individual) and "innovation" (the reciprocal process). Particularly crucial in this article is the way organizations are conceptualized. Schein puts forth a very useful way of thinking about them as "cones"—that is, structured vertically, horizontally, and circumferentially. This permits him to describe types of movements through the organization, the types of boundaries crossed, the attributes of boundaries, and the relation of boundary crossing to careers. The individual's adaptation and development in the organization is then logically viewed as a set of career steps or stages. Finally, the article puts forth several provocative hypotheses concerning career development. These hypotheses are useful not only in relation to this specific article, but also for the general issues they raise about organizational behavior.

In the last selection in this chapter the focus is on longer-term adaptation and development, namely, career management. The chief thesis of Hall and Hall (a husband-wife team of authors) is that organizations can better cope with problems created by no-growth situations if they give more attention, and adopt a more creative position, with respect to career planning for employees. The authors specifically address three types of problems found by many organizations: turnover among newly hired employees, the need for fast development of high-potential candidates for executive positions, and the need to increase promotional opportunities when the organization is stable or even contracting. The latter is a particularly sticky organizational problem, and Hall and Hall propose some innovative methods for dealing with it. They even bring up that almost "unmentionable" option: "downward transfers." As the authors point out, the common theme in their proposed approaches to dealing with the career development problem in slow-growth organizations is to "increase intraorganizational mobility." This is a laudable objective but often very difficult to achieve in practice. The article concludes with several helpful guidelines for improving the process of career management in organizations.

Reading 16

A Socialization Process That Helps New Recruits Succeed

Daniel C. Feldman

Management journals are replete with suggested strategies for coping with a variety of organizational problems: how to motivate employees, how to reward performance, how to evaluate employees, how to discipline. Yet many managers have a sneaking suspicion that learning more techniques to deal with these problems may be to miss the mark. Perhaps, some wonder, if only they had selected the right applicants, trained them correctly, and instilled in them the appropriate attitudes—in short, if they had socialized their employees correctly—they would have less need to deal with some of the problems that currently occupy their time.

This article gives a comprehensive picture of the multiple ways in which new organization members are socialized through the following distinct processes:

- The development of work skills and abilities.
- The acquisition of appropriate role behaviors.
- The adjustment to the work group and its norms.
- The learning of organizational values.

After tracing the common themes that run throughout the multiple socialization of organization members, the article sets forth implications on how to manage the socialization process to create conditions in which new employees can succeed.

This article is largely based on three major studies of organizational socialization that I've conducted. A recent longitudinal study focused on the socialization of graduate management students, and an earlier one looked at the differences in socialization experiences of professional, paraprofessional, and nonprofessional workers in hospitals. Both of these research projects involved intensive interviewing of participants as well as obtaining questionnaire data, archival information on selection criteria and demographic characteristics, and performance ratings in the organization. The third study involved a series of projects that Hugh Arnold, an assistant professor at the University of Toronto, and I conducted on how

people choose jobs and the relationship of job choice to socialization.

THE FOUR SOCIALIZATION PROCESSES

1. Socialization as the Development of Work Skills and Abilities

Three aspects of organizational entry significantly influence whether employee work skills and abilities will be developed in a new job: ability levels at time of selection, on-the-job training, and performance evaluation policies. Let's consider each of these in turn.

Ability Levels at Selection   As several industrial psychologists have pointed out, the ability levels of candidates at selection have a major impact on how new recruits will ultimately perform on the job. In fact, some present evidence pointing to a success spiral syndrome—that is, early career success leads both to opportunities to be more successful and to the desire to be more successful. So if new recruits enter an organization with appropriate skills and abilities, we could expect them to perform better initially and to seek out other tasks in which to excel later on in their organizational careers.

My research strongly supports this contention. In the study with graduate management students, both undergraduate grade point average and Graduate Management Aptitude Test scores predicted academic performance in school. Students entering the program with solid academic backgrounds or work experiences were less anxious than the other students about their ability to succeed and more willing to see faculty members outside of class, get involved in extracurricular activities, or take part-time jobs to open up more educational opportunities. On the other hand, those entering the program with poor backgrounds experienced a lot of debilitating anxiety about their ability to perform, and when they did more poorly in school, they had to spend more time studying and had less energy to get involved in other learning situations. Students who did poorly also changed majors and career choices more frequently than the students who were doing well.

In the hospital study, employees who felt that they were not well suited for their jobs initially were more likely to find their jobs less enjoyable and they often performed more poorly. This was borne out when labor shortages led to the hiring of some three-year diploma nurses (trained most heavily in floor administration and medications) onto geriatric wards requiring a lot of counseling of patients. These nurses found their jobs less satisfying and performed worse than did more appropriately skilled four-year degree nurses.

Jeff, a member of the hospital's engineering department, provides another case in point. When Jeff applied to the hospital to do mechanical work, there were no openings for mechanics, but the hospital was desperate for maintenance and renovation help. Jeff accepted the job as a maintenance worker, with both parties understanding that maintenance skills were not his primary abilities. Jeff worked hard to become proficient, but it took time. His performance evaluation reflected only a mediocre rating, leaving Jeff with the feeling that he had not been given credit for his effort.

It's important to note here that the biggest predictor of general satisfaction with a job is performance; employees who do perform well are more likely to appreciate the overall work situation. This makes the urgency of selecting employees with the appropriate skills even more salient. New recruits who are unprepared will be not only less competent, but also less satisfied.

On-the-Job Training A mass of evidence suggests that training can compensate for deficiencies in ability at entry. Indeed, in both the hospital and management studies, there were individuals who really excelled after participating in structured learning programs.

Training is sometimes so successful, in fact, that within just a few months, people forget how incompetent they felt upon entering the organization! Early in the socialization process, the graduate management students looked at prima facie indicators like undergraduate major and courses taken to judge how appropriate their skills were. Because of their strong quantitative backgrounds, for instance, engineering majors felt very' well prepared, while

humanities majors, often without much quantitative background or business knowledge, generally felt poorly equipped to excel. As the students began to experience success, they tried to infer from past history why they had been successful—but this time they employed different criteria to judge the appropriateness of their skill. For example, the successful humanities majors attributed their success to their analytic or verbal skills, while unsuccessful engineers, ironically, focused on not having social skills.

There are, however, some limits to the role of training programs in developing work skills and abilities.

1 Too many organizations have no needs assessment for designing training programs, or the needs assessment they have is inadequate.
2 At the higher organizational levels, much less emphasis is put on training than at lower levels. It is assumed—often incorrectly—that effective professional socialization reduces the need for socialization into organizations.
3 Those most in need of extra training are often those ones with the least time in which to take it, because they are already swamped with work.

Performance Evaluation Most managers recognize the importance of feedback in motivating employee behavior. Fewer recognize the relationship between giving feedback and the development of skills and abilities during socialization. Two attributes of the performance evaluation system in place have the greatest effect on the socialization process:

1 *Timing.* The probationary review not only provides feedback on work to date, but also signals the employee with the organization's initial "letting in" response to their "breaking in" efforts. When a full year goes by before the first feedback is given (as at the hospital), high performers are kept needlessly waiting for affirmation, and low performers—who often have assumed that no news is good news—wonder why they hadn't been notified of deficiencies earlier. On the other hand, when the first feedback is given very early (as early as two weeks in some groups), needless anxiety about performance potential is created. And no feedback at all is most frequently interpreted as disinterest or disappointment.
2 *Equity.* We know that when employees consider their performance ratings inequitable, they may begin to exert less effort because they don't see the

link between working hard and getting the rewards they want.

One reason that ratings may be seen as inequitable is that performance standards are often quite subjective and open to supervisory interpretation. At the hospital, for instance, the staff complained about being rated on dimensions like cooperation and initiative. With no behavioral anchors in rating employees, supervisors can really bias evaluations (and, indeed, ratings on these two dimensions were correlated over .90 with the overall supervisory rating). Several of the graduate management students complained about the "arbitrariness and capriciousness" of grading—yet they were not complaining about subjectivity or favoritism, but rather a lack of consistency among faculty members in setting cutoffs for grades. This of course echoes the lack of consistency among the hospital supervisors in applying standards.

2. Socialization as the Acquisition of Appropriate Role Behaviors

The job description of a position is generally couched in global terms. But employees have a way of injecting their own personalities into jobs— putting more emphasis on the tasks they particularly like to perform and less emphasis on those they like least or feel less competent to perform. Then, too, individual employees have to come to some implicit or explicit agreement with the work group on what tasks they are to perform, what the priorities among those tasks are to be, and how they are to allocate their time among them. Acquiring an appropriate role—the set of activities an employee repeatedly performs—is central to effective organizational socialization, since energy and attention focused on figuring out what to do detracts from energy and attention on actually *doing* the work.

There are three important components in acquiring an appropriate role: defining one's role in terms of one's own work group, in terms of other work groups in the organization, and in terms of people outside the organization. Let's look at each.

Role Definition in the Work Group   The aspect of socialization that most influences role definition within the work group is realistic expectations. When the students entered the graduate program

with realistic expectations, they quite often were more goal-directed in their studies and felt motivated and challenged to become successful. They knew exactly what they wanted to learn and had an easier time sorting out important classwork from busy work and relevant extracurricular activities from those with little educational or occupational value.

Those entering the program with unrealistic or no expectations had more difficulty in figuring out what to spend time on, in deciding what subject to major in, and in choosing what job to aim for. These students with poor ideas of what business school and management careers were like were less excited and motivated by the program, and "saw less point to the whole exercise." As one student remarked, "I feel like one of those confused baby squirrels running around outside College Hall—I'm scurrying about collecting acorns for winter, but I have no idea yet of what winter will be like."

There is also a relationship between the evaluation process and role definition. When supervisors in the hospital study felt particularly positive about employees, they gave workers more opportunities to learn new tasks and skills and were more willing to let them pass on unwanted chores to others.

Conflicting Role Demands at Work   It is not unusual for different organizational groups to put incompatible demands on an employee, or for the demands of one role to be incompatible with demands of another role occupied by the same individual. The nurses, for instance, frequently received conflicting demands from patients, doctors, and administration, while radiology technologists were continually torn between the demands of the several hospital groups (emergency room, operating room, outpatient clinic) that utilized their services.

Two characteristics of the socialization experience led to lessened confusion about role demands from other groups. The first is "protection," provided by a supervisor or mentor, from other groups. At least until employees had learned the ropes of their own position in their own work group, socialization ran more smoothly when their supervisors "ran interference" for them with other work groups.

The second is role modelling and coaching by the supervisor or mentor. New recruits are very sensitive to conflict in organizations and seek out clues on how best to deal with it. Those with supervisors who themselves dealt with conflict competently or who gave them specific suggestions had fewer problems defining their roles vis á vis other groups at work.

Resolution of Outside Life Conflicts Work and home can come into conflict over the employee's schedule (for example, number of hours worked and when they are scheduled, vacation time, days off), the demands on the employee's family (the need to entertain, join clubs, and so on), and the effect of the job on the quality of home life (amount of worry and preoccupation associated with work, demands on the family for emotional support, and so on). Employees who do not resolve these conflicts will feel pulled out of the organization, physically or psychically, at many points in their careers.

In the student study, being trusted and accepted personally by one's own work group made the biggest difference in resolving outside life conflicts. For the many younger students who were new to the area geographically, socializing with other students came naturally. Since they were often the same age and had similar interests, social life with other students was easier and more convenient than with nonstudents. For unpopular younger students, the experience could be like failing to be accepted into a one-caste society. "Natives" with existing social networks and older students who came back to school with spouses and children were less likely to get involved socially with other students and had more problems in maintaining a stable, separate outside life.

In the graduate school study, very few students in the sample were poor performers or became preoccupied with school problems. On the contrary, however, in the hospital study, where being a poor performer and having difficulty in getting good evaluations did create preoccupation and anxiety that spilled over outside the hospital. Employees reported wearing out their good graces with friends by constantly drawing on their support for work-related problems that their friends only remotely understood.

3. Socialization as Adjustment to the Group and Its Norms

A major part of the organizational socialization process is adjustment of the new recruit to the work group. A number of behavioral scientists have indi-cated that the work group can serve as a defense against oppressive forces in the organization, a source of possible solutions to work problems, and a normative referent for appropriate behavior. Several aspects of the socialization experience influence whether the new recruit adjusts to the work group:

Interpersonal/Intergroup Conflict When there is interpersonal and intergroup conflict in a work area, new employees are confused and hold back from making friends or being trusting until they can better understand the tension they sense. Moreover, where there is a low level of trust and friendship in a group, older recruits may withhold giving out information about supervisory personalities and preferences that is essential for new recruits to know to do their jobs well.

In the hospital study, for instance, employees in Nursing Service felt that some of the most important things to learn about their jobs were the moods and personalities of the doctors they worked with and their particular preferences about how medical and administrative procedures should be performed. On medical floors where there was a good deal of interpersonal conflict, new nurses had more difficulty both adjusting to the group and performing their jobs as the physicians wished.

Progress in Learning the Jobs Often, employees refrain from accepting new recruits personally until they have demonstrated some competence on the job. In the management school, for example, many classes demanded group work on projects, papers, or class presentations—and the students who were seen as competent were much more often sought out to work on group projects than were the slower students who were often avoided as "dead weight." The more frequently students worked in groups together, the more friends they made and the better integrated they became within the social system.

Initiation rites In some organizations, initiation rites or similarly symbolic acts certify a recruit's acceptance into the group. In the hospital study, this initiation took the form of being entrusted with confidential information by co-workers. Several workers reported other signs of acceptance: being included in an informal dining or sports group as a group initiation, being invited to workers' homes, or being shown a particular kindness in time of stress.

Although symbolic events may sometimes be helpful in increasing feelings of acceptance, however, they are not essential to producing them. It is more likely that feelings of acceptance emerge in two stages: (1) employees get over anxieties about feeling isolated from co-workers and (2) they then become comfortable with co-workers.

Individual versus Group Socialization When a recruit is the only new person to join a work group, there may be a longer delay in breaking in and feeling accepted by others. One problem is that the recruit lacks recourse to others with whom to check out initial perceptions and reactions. As one hospital billing clerk remarked, "Every time I look up from my desk I feel like they're all staring at me, and I wonder who's holding the black ball." An apprentice or mentor relationship with an incumbent group member can help mitigate such feelings.

A group that is socialized together quite often develops a collective consciousness and a group pride. This was very much the case with the graduate management students who were all assigned to the same classes. For one thing, they were able to share problems and attempted solutions with each other. Moreover, such a group is more able to resist attempts by older members of the organization to influence them. In subtle ways, a group of recruits can actually socialize the "socializers," especially when they outnumber them.

4. Socialization as the Learning of Organizational Values

Many managers depend on training, reward systems, and discipline to control behavior during socialization. Others depend more heavily on inculcating organizational values into new recruits, so that control will be exerted internally by the recruits themselves; this is particularly true in organizations that employ mainly professional staff. Certainly, as new recruits adopt the dominant values of the organization, their individual goals more closely approximate organizational goals and they are more likely to exhibit behaviors consistent with those values.

The learning of organizational values is dependent on three factors: (1) amount of exposure to information that supports organizational beliefs, (2) selective exposure to information that supports organizational values, and (3) credibility of the information communicated. Let's examine each of these factors in turn.

Amount of Exposure The more information supporting organizational values that is given recruits, the more likely the values are to be adopted. Most of the graduate students, for instance, reported becoming more conservative about starting new ventures or radically altering existing organizations. Exposure to many professors and speakers from a variety of disciplines bombards students with data on the high risks of entrepreneurial efforts and the formidable problems of implementing major organization changes. It is no surprise to see student images of fast and free-wheeling businesspeople melt away.

Selective Exposure Organizational groups filter out information that contradicts dominant organizational values so that values will be more readily accepted by recruits. For example, the set of values associated with public management—concern for security, less concern for money, more concern for causes, less desire for competition, and so on—differs from the set of values associated with commercial managers. Since students majoring in public management take all their courses together during their first school quarter, they are somewhat sheltered from dominant organizational values. Then, as the socialization process continues, public management students themselves seek out other people who share their values. By the end of the first year, they are spending most of their time with public management majors who share their values, both socially and in advanced courses. What selective exposure began, selective friendship completed.

Credibility of Information The more credible the information that is communicated about organizational values and attitudes, the more likely the recruit will be to adopt them. Recruits judge the credibility of information on the basis of the communicator's expertise and the similarity of the communicator to the recruit. For beliefs about how graduate school really operates and what it takes to be successful, senior graduate students are most credible; for beliefs about how programs and policies work in theory, faculty members are most credible; for beliefs about "what the real world is like," practitioners are the court of last resort. And when all these groups support the same value, the impact on new recruits is tremendous. Most students reported becoming much more negative about government regulation of industry, for instance—a belief widely shared and strongly espoused by all three groups.

It's important to note that a change in values is more a shifting of values to within a range of acceptability than it is conformity to a specific point of view. The socialization process works to cut off extreme values rather than to enforce compliance with well-articulated positions.

It's also important to note that when influence attempts are too strong, they defeat themselves. Students, for example, resist attempts to change values and attitudes that impinge upon their sense of self-control and self-determination. For example, some presentations by corporate recruiters in pushing a specific corporation or job were rejected because the influence attempts involved were perceived as too obvious, too self-serving, and too overbearing.

COMMON THEMES IN SOCIALIZATION

Although definitions of organizational socialization differ, several themes run throughout the multiple socialization of new organization members:

• *The socialization process is continuous.* Instead of occurring all at once, it is achieved rather slowly over time, although the early organizational learning period is particularly critical to the entire process. What's more, it usually starts *before* a person enters an organization, with such activities as occupational choice, attraction to organizations, and selection.

• *Organizational socialization involves change.* It can mean the relinquishing of certain attitudes, values, and behaviors, or the acquisition of new self-images, involvements, and accomplishments. One behavioral scientist, stressing the learning aspects of socialization, wrote that the new recruit must learn basic organizational goals, the means by which those goals should be attained, the basic responsibilities of the new role, the required behav-

ior patterns for effective performance, and a set of rules governing maintenance of the identity and integrity of the organization.

• *Socialization is a two-way process involving both individuals and organizations.* As another behavioral scientist has pointed out, the individual and the organization each have expectations of the other, and each changes those expectations and future behaviors as they observe each other's behaviors. In fact, some negotiation is possible and/or necessary in socialization—no matter how institutionalized the new recruit's role might be, and regardless of how aware either party may be that such negotiation is going on.

• *Socialization involves an increase in perceived personal control by recruits.* As socialization progresses, they realize that the responsibility for learning the job, getting performance feedback, and getting information about future roles is theirs—not that of the socialization agents. While new recruits may not necessarily see all aspects of the organization as capable of being controlled or predicted, they do perceive at least a reduction of randomness in the system; events that are not directly influenceable at least do not seem so arbitrary, capricious, or spontaneous.

A good example of this increase in personal control is seen in the changes students made in the way they evaluated feedback. Upon first entering management school, they saw themselves simply as the passive receivers of feedback, and thought they had to sit patiently (or impatiently) for exam grades or comments on papers. But as they progressed in the system, they discovered other ways of receiving feedback—by observing faculty reactions to them in class, by observing student reactions to their comments, by observing whether they were sought out by others to work on group projects. They received feedback from what has been called "reflective appraisal" and "comparative appraisal." In reflective appraisal, an individual obtains information about himself by observing and interpreting the actual behaviors of other individuals toward him; in comparative appraisal, the individual determines his relative standing vis à vis others simply by watching their performance to see if he is better or worse.

By the end of the first year, grades had become much less important to the students, and they were much more active about seeking out feedback when needed. Students began to take more personal responsibility for obtaining feedback and for interpreting it on an individual basis (my inputs/my outputs ratio) rather than in comparative terms. Moreover, students began to look at how they had allocated their time and energy among different classes and different activities to judge whether the feedback they were receiving was appropriate and justified.

• *Instead of producing conformity to a single standard, socialization decreases the extremes in behavior and attitudes.* In the hospital, there was more pressure *not* to produce extremely poorly than to produce at a specific level. In the graduate school study, there was more pressure *not* to hold extreme values or attitudes than to hold modal positions. Thus the socialization process works more efficiently to cut off the tails of the distribution curve than it does to produce total conformers. Most organizations can not invest the energy to obtain complete compliance, and most don't need uniformity to function smoothly. And, of course, if the influence attempts are too strong, they may be rejected totally.

• *During socialization, the concerns of new employees shift from the universal to the particular.* At the outset, new employees are concerned with the *general* management style, the *common* employee attitudes and values, and so on. But as socialization progresses, they become more concerned with their immediate environment: What are *my* co-workers like, what is *my* supervisor's management style, what are the norms of *my* work group? This shift reduces the amount of uncertainty that recruits have to deal with and focuses their attention on those aspects of the system that are most immediately relevant (and likely to be rewarded) in their jobs.

DESIGNING THE SOCIALIZATION PROCESS: SOME SUGGESTIONS

What can we conclude about designing socialization programs from this research? Consider the following:

1. *Many managers of organizational socialization programs have underestimated the role of ability and focused almost exclusively on orientation.* Clearly, the efficiency of the selection system in choosing recruits with appropriate skills largely determines how well organization members will perform. Moreover, additional opportunities to demonstrate competence and experience professional growth will open up to the more able recruits; able new recruits

not only perform better, but are in general more satisfied. The ability of organizations to provide rewarding socialization experiences for individuals who have inappropriate skills or who are poor performers is questionable. Organizations need to put more energy into analyzing which skills job incumbents need to succeed in their jobs, developing ways of measuring and predicting successful performance, and choosing new recruits on those criteria.

2 *The attraction and recruitment of new organization members has a wide-ranging impact on the organizational socialization process, an impact that should not be underestimated.* It has been found that realistic job expectations influence general satisfaction and turnover. This suggests that realistic expectations can also influence the likelihood that applicants will self-select themselves into the organization on relevant skills and abilities. Moreover, having realistic expectations influences internal work motivation by increasing the chance that new recruits will obtain jobs they find intrinsically interesting and goals they find challenging.

Although the benefits of realistic job previews have been identified by several researchers, many organizations are still hesitant to give recruits undistorted information—mainly because they fear placing themselves at a competitive disadvantage with organizations that do not give realistic job previews. Of course, many recruits give organizations misleading information about themselves; they, too, fear being at a competitive disadvantage —with candidates using a different game plan.

Even so, honest disclosure of skills, abilities, and training on the part of applicants and honest disclosure of job descriptions, rewards, and opportunities on the part of organizations are essential to getting the socialization process off on the right foot. The amount of time and energy that organizations have to spend in processing employees with inaccurate expectations is large indeed.

3. *Much of the training given to recruits during socialization is wasted because it is not relevant to their day-to-day activities.* So often, training programs are geared to such general matters that they provide little of the particular information new recruits want and need.

What many organizations need is not necessarily more training, but more focused training. Organizations need to put more thought into identifying job-relevant skills and providing training that will develop those skills. Packaged, or canned, training programs should not be purchased unless indicated by a good needs assessment effort.

The need for training, of course, doesn't stop at entry level. As recruits take on additional responsibilities or new jobs, additional training will very likely be needed. This is particularly true because organizations tend to promote employees on their technical competence even though the skills important in the current job may have no relationship to the demands of the next. Contrary to Dr. Peter's principle, perhaps people are not promoted to their level of incompetence; perhaps, instead, they are promoted to the level of their organization's incompetence in selection and training.

Furthermore, organizations tend to undervalue training for professional workers or for those at higher organizational levels. But as the management school study clearly shows, even professionally prepared recruits are going to need the specific organization they work for to fill in a lot of gaps in their knowledge. Failing to train these new organization members may prolong the time it takes for recruits to achieve at the high levels expected by the organization.

4. *The timing of feedback can either facilitate or retard organizational socialization.* Too many evaluation systems are geared to the calendar year rather than to what has been called the "time span of discretion"—the amount of time needed for (in)effective performance to show up. A well-timed probationary review can provide encouragement and affirmation for high performers and corrective coaching for poor performers.

The importance of identifying, at the time of selection, skills and abilities central to job performance carries over into the performance evaluation system. Without tangible criteria and objective performance measures, the organization leaves itself open to attack on charges of favoritism or bias. Without standardized evaluations across supervisors, organizations subtly encourage employees to request transfers to units supervised by "easier" evaluators. More important, however, an organization without good performance evaluation systems allows recruits to reject feedback—thus failing to learn from their experience—and to make short-run job changes that can adversely affect both their personal careers and the organization's workforce.

5. *The supervisor can make or break a newcomer's early career in an organization.* There is virtually no aspect of the socialization process that the supervisor cannot sabotage or smooth, depending on inclination and talent. There is even some general evidence that a "Pygmalion effect" operates: A supervisor who has positive expectations about how a subordinate can perform and communicates may actually facilitate the subordinate's performance. Yet because new recruits generally enter organizations only sporadically and often under conditions of low manpower, supervisors are sometimes unaware of the difficult problems the recruits face and they themselves receive no guidance in how to deal with those problems. In particular, immediate supervisors can best help new recruits in the following ways:

• Directly train new recruits in job specifics—or at least do a competent needs analysis so that training can be done elsewhere.
• Give new recruits challenging first assignments to motivate them to grow and stay with the organization.
• Use the opportunity to reallocate tasks or redesign work to create both more efficient and more satisfying work systems within the group.
• Conduct performance evaluations in a timely, constructive manner so that new recruits are neither overwhelmed by negative feedback nor "underwhelmed" by positive feedback.
• Buffer newcomers for a while from demands outside the work group so that they can more quickly and easily learn their jobs.
• Diagnose structural or interpersonal problems that generate conflicts on the job and provide positive role models and coaching in how to deal with conflict.

6. *Formal orientation programs are too often geared toward "selling the company" or creating organizational loyalty rather than toward dealing with the anxiety new recruits bring with them.* Some of these formal programs provide a slick, packaged indoctrination to a company; frequently considered "overkill," they are neither credible to, nor internalized by, newcomers. Such presentations more often overwhelm than relieve recruits, who hesitate even more to ask questions.

On the other hand, a more relaxed orientation that deals with the immediate feelings of new organization members can be successful. One such easy-going orientation program stressed making four points clear to the recruits:

- "Your opportunity to succeed is very good."
- "Disregard 'hall talk', 'hazing', and rumors."
- "Take the initiative in communication."
- "Get to know your supervisor" (with details about characteristics of specific supervisors provided).

The resulting communication was two-way, rather than one-way from management. The employees involved reached pre-established levels of competence a month earlier than expected, and their anxiety was reduced more quickly.

7. *Today, no organization can afford to leave the informal socialization of its new recruits to chance.* The pervasive impact of work group on newcomers makes it most important to monitor the informal socialization process and develop what has been called an effective method of "people processing." If the organization climate is positive, for instance, having new recruits socialized by former occupants of similar roles is logical: A sense of continuity and stability can be maintained, and job incumbents can help new members understand their new situation. On the other hand, of course, if the image that will be presented to new recruits is unpleasant, this "serial" socialization can exacerbate an already negative situation by reinforcing negative feelings. One study found that a key ingredient to successful orientation was the special selection of older workers to participate in the program. Since the internalization of values and beliefs depends so heavily on the selective filtering of information, its credibility, and the amount of exposure a new recruit has to the information, it makes sense to structure orientation so that incumbents with the most constructive approach get first crack at new recruits.

Reading 17

The Individual, the Organization, and the Career: A Conceptual Scheme
Edgar H. Schein

INTRODUCTION

The purpose of this paper is to present a conceptual scheme and a set of variables which make possible the description and analysis of an individual's movement through an organization. We usually think of this set of events in terms of the word "career," but we do not have readily available concepts for describing the multitude of separate experiences and adventures which the individual encounters during the life of his organizational career. We also need concepts which can articulate the relationship between (a) the career seen as a set of attributes and experiences of the *individual* who joins, moves through, and finally leaves an organization and (b) the career as defined by the *organization*—a set of expectations held by individuals inside the organization which guide their decisions about whom to move, when, how, and at what "speed." It is in the different perspectives which are held toward careers by those who act them out and those who make decisions about them that one may find some of the richest data for understanding the relationship between individuals and organizations.

The ensuing discussion will focus first on structural variables, those features of the organization, the individual, and the career which are the more or less stable elements. Then we will consider a number of "process" variables which will attempt to describe the dynamic interplay between parts of the organization and parts of the individual in the context of his ongoing career. Basically there are two kinds of processes to consider: (1) the influence of the organization on the individual, which can be thought of as a type of *acculturation* or *adult socialization,* and (2) the influence of the individual on the organization, which can be thought of as a process of

Reproduced by special permission from *Journal of Applied Behavioral Science,* 1971, **7**, 401–426. The ideas in this paper derive from research conducted from 1958 to 1964 with funds from the Office of Naval Research, Contract NONR 1841 (83), and subsequently with funds from the Sloan Research Fund, M.I.T.

innovation (Schein, 1968). Both socialization and innovation involve the relationship between the individual and the organization. They differ in that the former is initiated by the organization and reflects the relatively greater power of the social system to induce change in the individual, whereas the latter is initiated by the individual and reflects his power to change the social system. Ordinarily these two processes are discussed as if they were mutually exclusive of each other and as if they reflected *properties* of the organization or the individual. Thus certain organizations are alleged to produce conformity in virtually all of their members, while certain individuals are alleged to have personal strengths which make them innovators wherever they may find themselves. By using the concept of career as a process over time which embodies many different kinds of relationships between an organization and its members, I hope it can be shown that typically the same person is both influenced (socialized) and in turn influences (innovates), and that both processes coexist (though at different points in the life of a career) within any given organization.

THE STRUCTURE OF THE ORGANIZATION

Organizations such as industrial concerns, government agencies, schools, fraternities, hospitals, and military establishments which have a continuity beyond the individual careers of their members can be characterized structurally in many different ways. The particular conceptual model one chooses will depend on the purposes which the model is to fulfill. The structural model which I should like to propose for the analysis of careers is not intended to be a general organizational model; rather, it is designed to elucidate that side of the organization which involves the movement of people through it.

My basic proposition is that the organization should be conceived of as a three-dimensional space like a cone or cylinder in which the external vertical surface is essentially round and in which a core or inner center can be identified. What we traditionally draw as a pyramidal organization on organization charts should really be drawn as a cone in which the various boxes of the traditional chart would represent adjacent sectors of the cone but where movement would be possible within each sector toward or

away from the center axis of the cone. Figure 17-1 shows a redrawing of a typical organization chart according to the present formulation.

Movement within the organization can then occur along three conceptually distinguishable dimensions:

1 *Vertically*—corresponding roughly to the notion of increasing or decreasing one's *rank* or *level* in the organization;
2 *Radically*—corresponding roughly to the notion of increasing or decreasing one's *centrality* in the organization, one's degree of being more or less "on the inside";
3 *Circumferentially*—corresponding roughly to the notion of changing one's function or one's division of the organization.

Whether movement along one of these dimensions is ever independent of movement along another one is basically an empirical matter. For present purposes it is enough to establish that it would be, in principle, possible for an individual to move along any one of the dimensions without changing his position on either of the other ones, with one exception. Vertical movement usually produces some radical movement, i.e., increased rank increases centrality unless one posits a cylinder or some other *basic* shape.

Corresponding to the three types of movement one can identify three types of *boundaries* which characterize the internal structure of the organization:

1 *Hierarchical boundaries*—which separate the hierarchical levels from one another;
2 *Inclusion boundaries*—which separate individuals or groups who differ in the degree of their centrality;[1]
3 *Functional or departmental boundaries*—which separate departments, divisions, or different functional groupings from one another.

Boundaries can vary in (a) *number,* (b) *degree of permeability,* and (c) type of *filtering properties* which they possess. For example, in the military there are a great many functional boundaries sepa-

---

[1]The organization as a multilayered system corresponds to Lewin's (1948) concept of the personality as a multilayered system comparable to an onion.

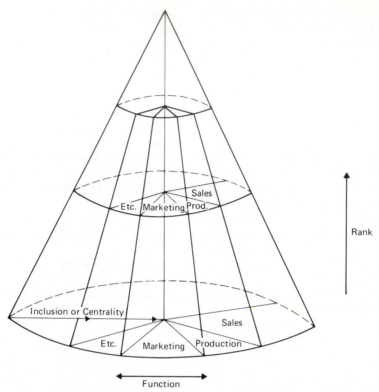

Figure 17-1   A three-dimensional model of an organization.

rating the different line and staff activities; but the overall policy of rotation and keeping all officers highly flexible makes these boundaries highly permeable in the sense that people move a great deal from function to function. On the other hand, a university would also have many functional boundaries corresponding to the different academic departments; but these would be highly impermeable in the sense that no one would seriously consider the movement of an English professor to a Chemistry department, or vice versa. A small family-run business, to take a third example, is an organization with very few functional boundaries in that any one manager may perform all of the various functions.

Similarly, with respect to hierarchical or inclusion boundaries one can find examples of organizations in which there are many or few levels, many or few degrees of "being in," with the boundaries separating the levels or inner regions being more or less permeable. The external inclusion boundary is, of course, of particular significance, in that its permea-

bility defines the ease or difficulty of initial entry into the organization. Those companies or schools which take in virtually anyone but keep only a small percentage of high performers can be described as having a highly permeable external inclusion boundary but a relatively impermeable inclusion boundary fairly close to the exterior. On the other hand, the company or school which uses elaborate selection procedures to take in only very few candidates, expects those taken in to succeed, and supports them accordingly can be described as having a relatively impermeable external inclusion boundary but no other impermeable boundaries close to the exterior.

Further refinement can be achieved in this model if one considers the particular types of filters which characterize different boundaries, i.e., which specify the process or set of rules by which one passes through the boundary. Thus, hierarchical boundaries filter individuals in terms of attributes such as seniority, merit, personal characteristics, types of attitudes held, who is sponsoring them, and so on. Functional boundaries filter much more in terms of the specific competencies of the individual or his "needs" for broader experience in some scheme of training and development (the latter would certainly not be considered in reference to hierarchical boundary). Inclusion boundaries are probably the most difficult to characterize in terms of their filtering characteristics in that the criteria may change as one gets closer to the inner core of the organization. Competence may be critical in permeating the external boundary, but factors such as personality, seniority, and willingness to play a certain kind of political game may be critical in becoming a member of the "inner circle."[2] Filter properties may be formally stated requirements for admission or may be highly informal norms shared by the group to be entered.

With reference to individual careers, organizations can be analyzed and described on the basis of (a) number of boundaries of each type, (b) the boundary permeability of the different boundaries, and (c) the filtering system which characterizes them. For example, most universities have two hierarchical boundaries (between the ranks of assistant, associate, and full professor), two inclusion boundaries (for initial entry and tenure), and as many functional boundaries as there are departments and schools. Filters for promotion and tenure may or may not be the same depending on the university but will generally involve some combination of scholarly or research publication, teaching ability, and "service" to the institution. Organizations like industrial ones which do not have a formal tenure system will be harder to diagnose as far as inclusion filters go, but the inclusion boundaries are just as much a part of their system. The variables identified thus far are basically intended as a set of categories in terms of which to describe and compare different types of organizations in respect to the career paths they generate.

A final variable which needs to be considered is the *shape* of the three-dimensional space which characterizes the organization. The traditional pyramidal organization would presumably become in this scheme a cone. An organization with very many levels could be thought of as a very steep cone, while one with few levels could be thought of as a flat cone. The drawing of the organization as a cone implies, however, that the person at the highest level is also the most central, which, of course, is not necessarily the case. If the top of the organization is a management team, one might think of a truncated cone; if there is a powerful board of directors who represent a higher level but a wider range of centrality, one might think of an inverted cone, the point of which touches the apex of the main cone and which sits on top of the main one. In universities where the number of full professors is as large as the number of assistant professors, one might think of the organization more as a cylinder with a small cone on top of its representing the administration.

I am not stating any requirements that the shape of the organization be symmetrical. If a certain department is very large but peripheral, it might best be thought of as a large bulge on an otherwise round shape. If one considers internal inclusion boundaries, one may have some departments which are in their entirety very central and thus reach the vertical axis (core), while other departments do not contain anyone who is very central in the organization and thus do not reach the core at all. The shape of the inner core is also highly variable. It may be an inverted cone, which would imply that the number of central people *increases* with rank. Or it might be a cylinder, which would imply that there are equal numbers of central people at all ranks. Or it might be some highly asymmetrical shape reflecting the reality that the number of central people varies with length of service, department, political connections with higher ranks, access to critical company information, and the like.[3]

Some Problems of Measuring Organizational Structure

The problem of measurement varies greatly as a function of the degree in which boundaries and their filtering characteristics are explicitly acknowledged by a given organization and by the wider society. Thus, hierarchical boundaries which separate levels

---

[2]One of the best descriptions of such filters in an organization can be founded in Dalton's (1959) discussion of career advancement in the companies studied.

[3]Dalton (1959) has identified what he calls "vertical cliques" which cover different ranks as well as departments of an industrial organization.

are a widely accepted fact of organizational life, and the rules for permeating them tend to be fairly explicit. To the extent that implicit informal factors do operate it becomes more difficult to measure the filtering properties of the hierarchical boundaries in any given organization.

Functional boundaries are generally the easiest to identify because our typical analysis of organizations emphasizes different functions and departments. Similarly, the rules of entry to a function or department tend to be fairly explicit.

The inclusion boundaries are the hardest to identify and measure because to a considerable extent their very existence usually remains implicit. While it may be clear to everyone in a company that there is an inner circle (which may cut across many rank levels), this fact may be denied when an outsider probes for the data. The filtering mechanism may be that more difficult to identify because even the willing informant, including members of the inner circle, may be unclear about the actual mechanisms by which people move toward the center. Even the *concept* of centrality is unclear in that it does not discriminate between (a) an individual person's *feeling* of being central or peripheral and (b) some *objective criterion* of his actual position in the organization's social structure.

In my discussion thus far, the term "centrality" denotes the person's objective position as measured by the degree to which company secrets are entrusted to him, by ratings of others of his position, and by his actual power. His subjective rating of himself might correlate highly with these other measures and thus might prove to be a simpler measuring device, but it does not basically define centrality because a person may misperceive his own position.

It may be argued that I have overstated the assumption that the organization is an integrated, unified entity. After all, it may be only a group of individual people or subgroups who are coordinating their activities in some degree but operating from quite different premises. Therefore, there are no "organizational" boundaries; there are only individual approaches to the movement and promotion of their subordinates.

There is ample evidence for the assertion that persons who associate with one another around a common task for any length of time *do* develop group boundaries of various sorts and a set of norms which define their permeability and filtering proper-

ties (e.g., Homans, 1950). But it is quite possible that several such groups coexist within a larger social system and that they develop different norms. In applying the concepts which I am outlining in this paper it is therefore necessary to identify as the "organization" a group which has interacted for a sufficient length of time to have developed some common norms. Later, in analyzing the progress of a career, it will of course be necessary to consider the difficulties which are created for the individual as he moves from a group with one set of norms about boundaries to another group with a different set of norms about boundaries, even though both groups are part of the same larger organization.

THE STRUCTURE OF THE INDIVIDUAL

Any given individual can be thought of as a more or less integrated set of social selves organized around a basic image or concept of self. His basic temperament, intellectual equipment, learned patterns of feeling expression, and psychological defenses underlie and partially determine this self-image and the kinds of social selves which the individual constructs for himself to deal with his environment. But our focus is on the "constructed" selves which make it possible for the individual to fulfill various role expectations in his environment, not on the more enduring underlying qualities or the basic self-image learned in childhood.

I am using the concept of a constructed social self in the sense of Mead (1934) and more recently Becker, Geer, Hughes, and Strauss (1961) and Goffman (1955, 1957, 1959), as the person's assumptions about, perceptions of, and claims on a given social situation in which role expectations may be more or less well defined. The basic rules of conduct and interaction in terms of which the person orients himself to any social situation are largely culturally determined, but these basic rules still leave each individual a wide latitude in how he will choose to present himself in any given situation (the "line" he will take) and how much social value or status he will claim for himself (his "face").

This conception of the individual places primary emphasis on those aspects of his total being which are the most immediate product of socialization, which most immediately engage other persons in daily life, and which are most dependent on the reinforcement or confirmation of others. For example, at a *basic* level, a person may be temperamentally easily frustrated, may have developed a character structure around the repression of strong aggressive impulses, and may rely heavily on denial and reaction-formation as defense mechanisms. These characteristics describe his basic underlying personality structure but they tell us little of how he presents himself to others, what his self-image is, how he behaves in occupational or social roles, how much value he places on himself, and what kind of interaction patterns he engages in with others.

Focusing on his constructed selves, on the other hand, might show us that this person presents himself to others as very even tempered and mild mannered, that in group situations he takes a role of harmonizing any incipient fights which develop between others, that he tries to appear as the logical voice of reason in discussions and is made uneasy by emotions, that he prefers to analyze problems and advise others rather than get into action situations (i.e., he prefers some kind of "staff" position), and that he does not get too close to people or depend too heavily upon them. None of the latter characteristics are inconsistent with the basic personality structure, but they could not have been specifically predicted from that structure. Persons with the same kind of underlying character structure might enter similar interactive situations quite differently. In other words, I am asserting that it is not sufficient to describe a person in terms of basic personality structure if we are to understand his relationship to organizations. Furthermore, I am claiming that it is possible to analyze the person's functioning at the social self level; and that this level of analysis is more likely to be productive for the understanding of career patterns and the reciprocal influence process between individual and organization.

Each of us learns to construct somewhat different selves for the different kinds of situations in which we are called on to perform and for the different kinds of roles we are expected to take. Thus, I am a somewhat different person at work than at home; I present myself somewhat differently to my superior than to my subordinate, to my wife than to my children, to my doctor than to a salesman, when I am at a party than when I am at work, and so on. The long and complex process of socialization teaches us the various norms, rules of conduct, values and attitudes, and desirable role behaviors through which one's obligations in situations and roles can be fulfilled. All of these patterns become part of us, so that to a large extent we are not conscious of the almost instantaneous "choices" we make among possible patterns as we "compose ourselves" for entry into a new social situation. Yet these patterns can be immediately brought to consciousness if the presented self chosen is one which does not fit the situation, that is, fails to get confirmation from others. Failure to get confirmation of a self which involves a certain claimed value is felt by the actor as a threat to his face; he finds himself in a situation in which he is about to lose face if he and the others do not take action to re-equilibrate the situation (Goffman, 1955).

The various selves which we bring to situations and among which we choose as we present ourselves to others overlap in varying degrees in that many of the attributes possessed by the person are relevant to several of his selves. Thus, emotional sensitivity may be just as relevant when a person is dealing with a customer in a sales relationship as it is with his wife and children in a family relationship. The person's attributes and underlying personality structure thus provide some of the common threads which run through the various social selves he constructs, and provide one basis for seeking order and consistency among them.

Another basis for such order and consistency is to be found in the role demands which the person faces. That is, with respect to each role which the person takes or to which he aspires, one can distinguish certain central expectations, certain essential attributes which the person must have, or certain behaviors he must be willing to engage in, in order to fulfill the role minimally (*pivotal* attributes or norms). Other attributes and behaviors are desirable and relevant though not necessary (*relevant* attributes or norms), while still another set can be identified as irrelevant with respect to the role under analysis although it includes various "latent" role capacities the person may have (*peripheral* attributes or norms).[4] The pivotal, relevant, and peripheral attributes of a role will define in some degree the filters which operate at the boundary guarding access to that role.

The changes which occur in a person during the course of his career as a result of adult socialization

---

[4]This analysis is based on the distinction made by Nadel (1957) and utilized in a study of out-patient nurses by Bennis (1959).

or acculturation are changes in the nature and integration of his social selves. It is highly unlikely that he will change substantially in his basic personality structure and his pattern of psychological defenses, but he may change drastically in his social selves in the sense of developing new attitudes and values, new competencies, new images of himself, and new ways of entering and conducting himself in social situations. As he faces new roles which bring new demands, it is from his repertoire of attributes and skills that he constructs or reconstructs himself to meet these demands.

A final point concerns the problem of locating what we ordinarily term as the person's beliefs, attitudes, and values at an appropriate level of his total personality. It has been adequately demonstrated (e.g., Adorno, Frenkel-Brunswick, Levinson, & Sanford, 1950; Smith, Bruner, & White, 1956; Katz, 1960) that beliefs, attitudes, and values are intimately related to basic personality structure and psychological defenses. But this relationship differs in different persons according to the functions which beliefs, attitudes, and values serve for them. Smith et al. (1956) distinguish three such functions: (1) *reality testing*—where beliefs and attitudes are used by the person to discover and test the basic reality around him; (2) *social adjustment*—where beliefs and attitudes are used by the person to enable him to relate confortably to others, express his membership in groups, and his social selves; and (3) *externalization*—where beliefs and attitudes are used to express personal conflicts, conscious and unconscious motives, and feelings.

The kind of function which beliefs and attitudes serve for the individual and the kind of flexibility he has in adapting available social selves to varying role demands will define for each individual some of his strengths and weaknesses with respect to organizational demands and the particular pattern of socialization and innovation which one might expect in his career.

For example, a given individual might well have a number of highly labile social selves in which his beliefs and attitudes serve only a social adjustment function. At the same time, he might have one or more other highly stable selves in which he shows great rigidity of belief and attitude. The process of socialization might then involve extensive adaptation and change on the part of the person in his "labile" social selves without touching other more

stable parts of him. He might show evidence of having been strongly influenced by the organization, but only in certain areas.[5] Whether this same person would be capable of innovating during his career would depend on whether his job would at any time call on his more stable social selves. The activation of such stable selves might occur only with promotion, the acquisition of increasing responsibility, or acceptance into a more central region of the organization.

When we think of organizations as infringing on the private lives of their members we think of a more extensive socialization process which involves changes in more stable beliefs and attitudes which are integrated into more stable social selves. Clearly, it is possible for such "deeper" influence to occur, but in assessing depth of influence in any given individual-organizational relationship we must be careful not to overlook adaptational patterns which *look* like deep influence but are only the activation of and changes in relatively more labile social selves.

Some Problems of Measuring Individual Structure

I do not know of any well-worked-out techniques for studying a person's repertoire of social selves, their availability, lability, and associated beliefs and attitudes. Something like rating behavior during role playing or sociodrama would be a possible method, but it is difficult to produce in full force the situational and role demands which elicit from us the social selves with which we "play for keeps." Assessment techniques which involve observing the person in actual ongoing situations are more promising but more expensive. It is possible that a well-motivated person would be able to provide accurate data through self-description, i.e., he might tell accurately how he behaves in situations that he typically faces.

If observation and interview both are impractical, it may be possible to obtain written self-descriptions or adjective checklist data (where the adjectives are specifically descriptive of interactional or social behavior) in response to hypothetical problem situations which are posed for the individual. The major difficulty with this technique stems from the likeli-

----

[5]For a relevant analysis of areas which the organization is perceived to be entitled to influence, *see* Schein and Ott (1962) and Schein and Lippitt (1966).

hood that much of the "taking" of a social self is an unconscious process which even a well-motivated subject could not reconstruct accurately. Hence his data would be limited to his conscious self-perceptions. Such conscious self-perceptions could, of course, be supplemented by similar descriptions of the subject made by others. Some recent research using a similar formulation has been reported by Hall (1968, 1971).

THE STRUCTURE OF THE CAREER

The career can be looked at from three points of view: (1) The individual moving through an organization builds certain perspectives having to do with advancement, personal success, nature of the work, and so on (Becker et al., 1961). (2) Those individuals who are in the organization as managers take the "organizational" point of view, build perspectives in terms of the development of human resources, allocation of the right people to the right slots, optimum rates of movement through departments and levels, and so on. (3) The outside observer of the whole process is struck by certain basic similarities between organizational careers and other transitional processes which occur in society such as socialization, education, the acculturation of immigrants, or initiation into groups. If one takes this observer perspective one can describe the structure and process of the career in terms of a set of basic *stages* which create transitional and terminal *statuses* or *positions* and involve certain psychological and organizational processes (*see* Table 17-1).

In the first column of the table, I have placed the basic stages as well as the key transitional events which characterize movement from one stage to another. The terminology chosen deliberately reflects events in organizations such as schools, religious orders, or fraternities where the stages are well articulated. These same stages and events are assumed to exist and operate in industrial, governmental, and other kinds of organizations even though they are not so clearly defined or labeled. Where a stage does not exist for a given organization, we can ask what the functional equivalent of that stage is. For example, the granting of tenure and the stage of permanent membership is not clearly identified in American business or industrial concerns, yet there are powerful norms operating in most such organizations to retain employees who

have reached a certain level and/or have had a certain number of years of service. These norms lead to personnel policies which on the average guarantee the employee a job and thus function as equivalents to a more formal tenure system.

It should be noted that the kinds of stages and terminology chosen also reflect the assumption that career movement is basically a process of learning or socialization (during which organizational influence is at a maximum), followed by a process of performance (during which individual influence on the organization is at a maximum), followed by a process of either becoming obsolete or learning new skills which lead to further movement. These are relatively broad categories which are not fully refined in the table. For example, in the case of becoming obsolete, a further set of alternative stages may be provided by the organizational structure—(a) retraining for new career; (b) lateral transfer and permanent leveling off with respect to rank, but not necessarily with respect to inclusion; (c) early forced exit ("early retirement"); or (d) retention in the given stage in spite of marginal performance (retaining "dead wood" in the organization).

In the second column of the table are found the kinds of terms which we use to characterize the statuses or positions which reflect the different stages of the career. In the third column I have tried to list the kinds of interactional processes which occur between the individual and the organization. These processes can be thought of as reflecting preparation of the incumbent for boundary transition; preparation of the group for his arrival; actual transition processes such as tests, rites of passage, and status-conferring ceremonies; and post-transition processes prior to preparation for new transitions.[6]

Boundary Passage

Basically the dynamics of the career can be thought of as a *sequence of boundary passages*. The person can move up, around, and in; and every career is some sequence of moves along these three paths. Thus it is possible to move primarily inward without moving upward or around as in the case of the janitor who has remained a janitor all of his career but, because of association with others who have risen in the hierarchy, enjoys their confidences and a

---

[6]*See* Strauss (1959) for an excellent description of some of these processes.

Table 17-1 Basic Stages, Positions, and Processes Involved in a Career

Basic stages and transitions	Statuses or positions	Psychological and organizational processes: Transactions between individual and organization
1. Pre-entry	Aspirant, applicant, rushee	Preparation, education, anticipatory socialization
Entry (transition)	Entrant, postulant, recruit	Recruitment, rushing, testing, screening, selection, acceptance ("hiring"); passage through external inclusion boundary; rites of entry; induction and orientation
2. Basic training, novitiate	Trainee, novice, pledge	Training, indoctrination, socialization, testing of the man by the organization, tentative acceptance into group
Initiation, first vows (transition)	Initiate, graduate	Passage through first inner inclusion boundary, acceptance as member and conferring of organizational status, rite of passage and acceptance
3. First regular assignment	New member	First testing by the man of his own capacity to function; granting of real responsibility (playing for keeps); passage through functional boundary with assignment to specific job or department
Substages 3a. Learning the job 3b. Maximum performance 3c. Becoming obsolete 3d. Learning new skills, et cetera		Indoctrination and testing of man by immediate workgroup leading to acceptance or rejection; if accepted, further education and socialization (learning the ropes); preparation for higher status through coaching, seeking visibility, finding sponsors
Promotion or leveling off (transition)		Preparation, testing, passage through hierarchical boundary, rite of passage; may involve passage through functional boundary as well (rotation)
4. Second assignment	Legitimate member (fully accepted)	Processes under no. 3 repeat
Substages 5. Granting of tenure	Permanent member	Passage through another inner inclusion boundary
Termination and exit (transition)	Old-timer, senior citizen	Preparation for exit, cooling the mark out, rites of exit (testimonial dinners, and so on)
6. Post-exit	Alumnus, emeritus, retired	Granting of peripheral status, consultant or senior advisor

certain amount of power through his opportunities to coach newcomers.

It is also possible to move primarily upward without moving very far inward or around, as in the case of the scarce and highly trained technical specialist who must be elevated in order to be held by the organization but who is given little administrative power or confidential information outside his immediate area. Such careers are frequently found in universities where certain scholars can become full professors without even taking the slightest interest in the university as an organization and where they are not seen as being very central to its functioning.

The problem of the professional scientist or engineer in industry hinges precisely on this issue, in that the scientist often feels excluded in spite of "parallel ladders," high salaries, frequent promotions, and fancy titles. Moving in or toward the center of an organization implies increase in power and access to information which enables the person to influence his own destiny. The "parallel ladder" provides rank but often deprives the professional in industry of the kind of power and sense of influence which is associated with centrality.

Finally, movement around without movement in or up is perhaps most clearly exemplified in the perpetual student, or the person who tries some new skill or work area as soon as he has reasonably mastered what he had been doing. Such circumferential or lateral movement is also a way in which organizations handle those whom they are unwilling to promote or get rid of. Thus they are transferred from one job to another, often with polite fiction that the transfers constitute promotions of a sort.

In most cases, the career will be some combination of movement in all three dimensions: the person will have been moved up, will have had experience in several departments, and will have moved into a more central position in the organization. Whether any given final position results from smooth or even movement or represents a zigzagging course is another aspect to consider. Because subcultures always tend to exist within a large organization, one may assume that any promotion or transfer results in some *temporary* loss of centrality, in that the person will not immediately be accepted by the new group into which he has been moved. In fact, one of the critical skills of getting

ahead may be the person's capacity to regain a central position in any new group into which he is placed.[7] In the military service, whether a person is ultimately accepted as a good leader or not may depend upon his capacity to take a known difficult assignment in which he temporarily loses acceptance and centrality, and in spite of this loss, to gain high productivity and allegiance from the men.

The attempt to describe the career in terms of sequential steps or stages introduces some possible distortions. For example, various of the stages may be collapsed in certain situations into a single major event. A young man may report for work and be given as his first assignment a highly responsible job, may be expected to learn as he actually performs, and is indoctrinated by his experiences at the same time that he is using them as a test of his self. The whole assignment may serve the function of an elaborate initiation rite during which the organization tests the man as well. The stages outlined in Table 17-1 all occur in one way or another, but they may occur simultaneously and thus be difficult to differentiate.

Another distortion is the implication in Table 17-1 that boundaries are crossed in certain set sequences. In reality it may be the case that the person enters a given department on a provisional basis before he has achieved any basic acceptance by the organization so that the functional boundary passage precedes inclusion boundary passage. On the other hand, it may be more appropriate to think of the person as being located in a kind of organizational limbo during his basic training, an image which certainly fits well those training programs which rotate the trainee through all of the departments of the organization without allowing him to do any real work in any of them.

A further complexity arises from the fact that each department, echelon, and power clique is a suborganization with a subculture which superimposes on the major career pattern a set of, in effect, subcareers within each of the suborganizations. The socialization which occurs in subunits creates difficulties or opportunities for the person in the degree that the subculture is well integrated with the larger

---

[7]In a fascinating experiment with children, Merei (1941) showed that a strong group could resist the impact of a strong leader child and force the leader child to conform to group norms; but that the skillful leader child first accepted the norms, gained acceptance and centrality, and then began to influence the group toward his own goals.

organizational culture. If conflicts exist, the person must make a complex analysis of the major organizational boundaries to attempt to discover whether subsequent passage through a hierarchical boundary (promotion) is more closely tied to acceptance or rejection of subcultural norms; i.e., does the filter operate more in terms of the person's capacity to show loyalty even in the face of frustration or in terms of disloyalty for the sake of larger organizational goals even though this entails larger personal risks?

IMPLICATIONS AND HYPOTHESES

Thus far I have tried to develop a set of concepts and a model of the organization, the individual, and the career. The kinds of concepts chosen were intended to be useful in identifying the interactions between the individual and the organization as he pursues his career within the organization. We need concepts of this sort to make it possible to compare organizations with respect to the kinds of career paths they generate, and to make it possible to describe the vicissitudes of the career itself. Perhaps the most important function of the concepts, however, is to provide an analytical frame of reference which will make it possible to generate some hypotheses about the crucial process of organizational influences on the individual (socialization) and individual influences on the organization (innovation). Using the concepts defined above, I would now like to try to state some hypotheses as a first step toward building a genuinely sociopsychological theory of career development.

Hypothesis 1

Organizational socialization will occur primarily in connection with the passage through hierarchical and inclusion boundaries; efforts at education *and* training *will occur primarily in connection with the passage through functional boundaries. In both instances, the amount of effort at socialization and/or training will be at a maximum just prior to boundary passage, but will continue for some time after boundary passage.*

The underlying assumption behind this hypothesis is that (a) the organization is most concerned about correct values and attitudes at the point where it is granting a member more authority and/or centrality,

and (b) the individual is most vulnerable to socialization pressures just before and after boundary passage. He is vulnerable before because of the likelihood that he is anxious to move up or in and is therefore motivated to learn organizational norms and values; he is vulnerable after boundary passage because of the new role demands and his needs to reciprocate with correct attitudes and values for having been passed. It is a commonly observed organizational fact that a griping employee often becomes a devoted, loyal follower once he has been promoted and acquired responsibility for the socialization of other employees.[8]

Hypothesis 2

Innovation, *or the individual's influence on the organization, will occur in the middle of a given stage of the career, at a maximum distance for past or future boundary passage.*

The person must be far enough from the earlier boundary passage to have learned the requirements of the new position and to have earned centrality in the new subculture, yet must be far enough from his next boundary passage to be fully involved in the present job without being concerned about preparing himself for the future. Also, his power to induce change is lower if he is perceived as about to leave (the "lame duck" phenomenon). Attempts to innovate closer to boundary passage either will meet resistance or will produce only temporary change.

Hypothesis 3

In general, the process of socialization will be more prevalent in the early stages of a career and the process of innovation late in the career, but both processes occur at all stages.

Figure 17-2 attempts to diagram the relationships discussed above. The boundaries that are most relevant to these influence processes are the hierarchical ones in that the power of the organization to socialize is most intimately tied to the status rewards it can offer. One cannot ignore, however, the crucial role which inclusion boundaries and centrality may play in affecting the amount of socialization or innovation. If it is a correct assumption that genuinely creative innovative behavior can occur only

---

[8]*See also* Lieberman (1956) for an excellent research study demonstrating attitude change after promotion.

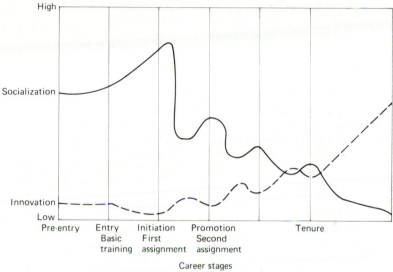

Figure 17-2 Socialization and innovation during the stages of a career.

when the person is reasonably secure in his position, this is tantamount to saying that he has to have a certain amount of acceptance and centrality to innovate. On the other hand, if the acceptance and centrality involve a subculture which is itself hostile to certain organizational goals, it becomes more difficult for the person to innovate (except in reference to subcultural norms). This is the case of the men in the production shop with fancy rigs and working routines which permit them to get the job done faster and more comfortably (thus innovating in the service of subgroup norms), yet which are guarded from management eyes and used only to make life easier for the men themselves. One thing which keeps these processes from being shared is the subgroup pressure on the individual and his knowledge that his acceptance by the subgroup hinges on his adherence to its norms. Innovation by individuals will always occur in some degree, but it does not necessarily lead to any new ideas or processes which are functional for the total organization.

Whether or not organizational innovation occurs, then, becomes more a function of the degree in which subgroup norms are integrated with the norms and goals of the total organization. In complex organizations there are many forces acting which tend to make groups defensive and competitive, thus increasing the likelihood of their develop-

ing conflicting norms (Schein, 1965). Where this happens the process of innovation can still be stimulated through something akin to the "heroic cycle" by which societies revitalize themselves. Campbell (1956) shows how the myth of the hero in many cultures is essentially similar. Some respected member of the total organization or society is sent away (freed from the subgroup norms) to find a magic gift which he must bring back to revitalize the organization. By temporarily stepping outside the organization the person can bring back new ideas and methods without directly violating subgroup norms and thus protect his own position as well as the face of the other group members.

Hypothesis 4

Socialization or influence will involve primarily the more labile social selves of the individual, while innovation will involve primarily the more stable social selves of the individual, provided the individual is not held captive in the organization.

I am assuming that if socialization forces encounter a stable part of the person which he is unable or unwilling to change, he will leave the organization if he can. On the other hand, if a given way of operating which flows from a stable portion of the individual is incompatible with other organizational procedures or norms, i.e., if innovation is impossible, the individual will also leave. The only condition under which neither of these statements would hold is the condition in which the individual is physically or psychologically unable to leave.

Hypothesis 5

A change in the more stable social selves as a result of socialization will occur only under conditions of coercive persuasion, i.e., where the individual cannot or does not psychologically feel free to leave the organization.

Conditions under which coercive persuasion (Schein, 1961) would operate can be produced by a variety of factors: a tight labor market in which movement to other organizations is constrained; an employment contract which involves a legal or moral obligation to remain with the organization; a reward system which subtly but firmly entraps the individual through stock options, pension plans, deferred compensation plans, and the like.

If conditions such as those mentioned above do operate to entrap the individual, and if he, in turn, begins to conform to organizational norms even in terms of the more stable parts of his self, he will indeed become unable to innovate. It is this pattern which has been identified by Robert K. Merton as operating in bueaucratic frameworks and which writers like W. H. Whyte have decried with the label of "organizational man." It should be noted, however, that this pattern occurs only under certain conditions; it should not be confused with normal processes of socialization, those involving the more labile parts of the person's self and the more pivotal role requirements or norms of the organization.

An important corollary of this hypothesis is that if organizations wish to ensure a high rate of innovation, they must also ensure highly permeable external boundaries; i.e., they must ensure that employees feel free to leave the organization. The less permeable the exit boundary, the greater the pressures for total conformity.

In conclusion, I have tried to show with this conceptual scheme and the hypotheses which can be derived from it that the concept of career and its attendant processes of socialization and innovation can be usefully employed as an analytical tool for exploring the complex relationship between the individual and the organization.

REFERENCES

Adorno, T. W., Frenkel-Brunswick, Else, Levinson, D. J., & Sanford, R. N. *The authoritarian personality.* New York: Harper, 1950.

Becker, H. S., Geer, Blanche, Hughes, E. C., & Strauss, A. S. *Boys in white.* Chicago, Ill.: Univer. of Chicago Press, 1961.

Bennis, W. G. The role of the nurse in the OPD. Boston Univer. Research Rep. No. 29, 1959.

Campbell, J. *The hero with a thousand faces.* New York: Meridian, 1956.

Dalton, M. *Men who manage.* New York: Wiley, 1959.

Goffman, E. On face work. *Psychiatry,* 1955, **18,** 213–231.

Goffman, E. Alienation from interaction. *Human Relat.,* 1957, **10,** 47–60.

Goffman, E. *The presentation of self in everyday life.* Garden City, N.J.: Doubleday Anchor, 1959.

Hall, D. T. Identity changes during an academic role transition. *School Rev.,* Dec. 1968, 445–469.

Hall, D. T. A theoretical model of career subidentity development in organizational settings. *Organization behavior and human performance,* 1971, **6,** 50–76.

Homans, G. C. *The human group.* New York: Harcourt, Brace, 1950.

Katz, D. (Ed.) Attitude change. *Pub. Opinion Q.,* 1960, **24,** 163–365.

Lewin, K. *Resolving social conflicts.* New York: Harper, 1948.

Lieberman, S. The effects of changes in roles on the attitudes of role occupants. *Human Relat.,* 1956, **9,** 385–402.

Mead, G. H. *Mind, self, and society.* Chicago, Ill.: Univer. of Chicago Press, 1934.

Merei, F. Group leadership and institutionalization. *Human Relat.,* 1941, **2,** 23–39.

Nadel, F. *The theory of social structure.* Glencoe, Ill.: Free Press, 1957.

Schein, E. H. *Coercive persuasion.* New York: Norton, 1961.

Schein, E. H. *Organizational psychology.* Englewood Cliffs. N.J.: Prentice-Hall, 1965.

Schein, E. H. Organizational socialization and the profession of management. *Indust. Mgmt. Rev.,* 1968, **9,** 1–15.

Schein, E. H., & Lippitt, G. L. Supervisory attitudes toward the legitimacy of influencing subordinates. *J. Appl. Behav. Sci.,* 1966, **2**(2), 199–209.

Schein. E. H., & Ott, J. S. The legitimacy of organizational influence. *Amer. J. Sociol.,* 1962, **6,** 682–689.

Smith, M. B., Bruner, J. S., & White, R. W. *Opinions and personality.* New York: Wiley, 1956.

Strauss, A. S. *Mirrors and masks.* Glencoe, Ill.: Free Press, 1959.

Reading 18

What's New in Career Management
Douglas T. Hall
Francine S. Hall

In many organizations, the largest item in the corporate budget consists of wages and salaries. For this
reason, financial problems that dictate cost reductions and increased efficiency usually boil down to
problems of personnel and human resource management. Therefore, more creative, flexible, and efficient utilization of human resources through better
corporate career planning can be a powerful means
of dealing with some of the current headaches of
managing a stable or shrinking organization in a
stagnant economy. In this article, we will review
some current (and probably all-too-familiar)
human-resource management problems and report
on how some organizations are coping with them
through creative techniques for career management.
We will also point out what is being neglected in the
area of career development. And we will conclude
with some general principles about how to make
corporate career planning more effective.

PROBLEM 1: HOW CAN WE REDUCE TURNOVER AMONG RECENTLY HIRED EMPLOYEES?

Students often graduate from college or business
school with unrealistically high expectations about
the amount of challenge and responsibility they will
find in their first job. Then they are put through a
job-rotation training program or into a fairly undemanding entry-level job, and they get turned off.
They experience "reality shock." The result is low
morale, low productivity, and high turnover. Some
companies lose as many as one-third or one-half of
their new recruits in the first year or two of employment. One company was hiring 130 people at one
time in order to have 30 at the end of the first year!

The cost of turnover is tremendous, especially
among professionals and management candidates.
Michael Alexander, of Touche, Ross & Co., calculated in 1973 that the total cost (including recruiting
expenses, training, reduced performance during orientation, and so on) of replacing a manager was
$25,000 to $30,000. After three years of inflation,

that figure might be closer to $40,000. Therefore, if
your company hires 100 new MBAs this year and
loses 25 of them in the first year, that first year of
"reality shock" may be adding $1,000,000 annually
to your operating expenses.

Obviously, then, you can save a lot of money by
managing the entry and first year of new employees
in a more satisfying way. As companies like AT&T
and General Electric have found, making initial jobs
more challenging and "stretching" not only decreases turnover, but also improves long-term career
performance. In one study of two AT&T operating
companies, David E. Berlew and Douglas T. Hall
(1966) found that management trainees who received the most challenging first-year jobs were the
most successful performers five to seven years later.

Select a Challenging First Job Granted, then,
that one answer to Problem One is to make the first
job more challenging. Just how do you go about it?
First, instead of simply putting the new employee
into any open job, give the matter more careful
thought. If more than one job assignment is available, purposely slot the new employee into the most
demanding one. "But," you ask, "how can I be sure
he or she can handle it?" Good question; obviously,
you can't be sure. However, our research shows that
managers are quite conservative on this issue and
usually err in the direction of making the first
assignment too easy. This may eliminate the possibility of failure, but it also prevents the employee
from achieving *psychological success,* the exhilarat-
ing sense of accomplishment that results only from
achieving a task that entailed a reasonable probability of failure. More likely than not, the new recruit
will perform well in a tough assignment—especially
if you are available to provide help and support
when needed.

Provide Job Enrichment A second way of enhancing the first job is to provide a measure of job
enrichment. How? Add more responsibility to the

job, give the new employee increased authority, and let the new person deal directly with clients and customers (not through you); if new employees are doing special projects and making recommendations to you, let them follow through and implement these ideas. AT&T is currently training supervisors of certain new employees in the skills of job enrichment as a way of making initial jobs more of a "stretching" experience.

Assign the New Recruit to Demanding Bosses   A third way of improving the first job is to give more care and thought to selecting the supervisor to whom you assign the new recruit. As J. Sterling Livingston has shown, there is a "Pygmalion effect" in the relationship between a new employee and his or her boss. The more the boss expects and the more confident and supportive the boss is of the new employee, the better the recruit will perform. So don't assign a new employee to a "dead wood," undemanding, or unsupportive supervisor. Choose high-performing supervisors who will set high standards for the new employee during the critical, formative first year.

Give Realistic Job Previews   If it's not possible to upgrade the first job experience, the opposite strategy is to provide the employee with realistic expectations during the recruiting process. Several organizations (Prudential Insurance Company, Texas Instruments, the Southern New England Telephone Company, and the U.S. Military Academy) have employed *realistic job previews* (RJPs) in the form of booklets, films, visits, or talks that convey not only the positive side of organizational life, but some of the problems and frustrations as well (example: the close supervision, lack of variety, limited socializing opportunities, and criticism experienced by telephone operators).

"But we'll never be able to hire anyone if we tell them the bad news about the job," you may be thinking. Research by John Wanous and others has shown, however, that these fears are unjustified. The recruitment rate is the same for people receiving RJPs as for those who get the more traditional one-sided information.

The big return comes later, after the person starts work: Among the recipients of RJPs, turnover and dissatisfaction are significantly lower than for people

on the receiving end of traditional job previews. So to retain more of your new recruits, as the (now somewhat dated) saying goes, "Tell it like it really is!"

A somewhat different form of the RJP has been experimentally introduced into management classrooms at the University of Wisconsin–Parkside in cooperation with the Goodyear Tire and Rubber Company's North Chicago Hose Plant. When a new recruit reacted to his first job with, "We never learned this in a classroom!" training manager Ernie LaBrecque gradually began to bring supervisors into Parkside's classes on a regular basis. The purpose is quite simple: to provide tomorrow's hires with firsthand knowledge of what to expect.

While the Parkside-Goodyear efforts have been limited, the model has significant potential for companies that recruit on a regular basis at particular universities. Not only are business leaders generally welcome in classes, but the opportunity to establish an ongoing relationship has obvious mutual benefits.

PROBLEM 2: HOW CAN WE QUICKLY DEVELOP HIGH-POTENTIAL CANDIDATES (ESPECIALLY WOMEN AND MINORITIES) FOR MANAGEMENT POSITIONS?

The problem of identifying and selecting high-potential management candidates has been well researched over the years and is pretty well understood. Job sampling and other ways of simulating management jobs, such as assessment centers, have been shown to be effective through expensive ways of identifying managerial talent. The real problems is how we can best *train and develop* these promising candidates once they are identified.

Assessment Centers for Development   Assessment centers were originally developed for selection purposes, to identify high-potential candidates for hiring or promotion. When used for selection purposes, the results of the assessment process are used by managers responsible for these personnel decisions and are often not fed back to the employee. More recently, however, assessment centers have also been used successfully for employee development. When they are used in this way, the emphasis is on feedback of results to the employee following the assessment experience. In a feedback session, a trained staff member points out the candidate's strong and weak points, illustrating them with examples of the candidate's behavior in the assessment activities. After the employee understands and accepts the feedback, the discussion turns to counseling and planning for future training experiences and developmental assignments that would lead to a particular target job in management.

Many companies, viewing the results of the assessment center experience as classified information, are reluctant to feed back this information to the employee. This secrecy represents a waste of extremely valuable developmental input, particularly in view of the high cost of putting the employee through the two- or three-day experience. Such secrecy also probably leads the candidate to develop unrealistically high expectations (as in the first job). If, on the other hand, assessment results are used for feedback and career counseling, several benefits are reaped: (1) The candidate's expectations are more realistic; (2) the candidate is helped in overcoming weaknesses; (3) the candidate has a specific career plan; and (4) the company is viewed as a partner rather than an adversary in career planning, something better calculated to result in career satisfaction.

Job Pathing The AT&T research cited earlier showed the impact the first job can have on the employee's development. A logical extension of this idea is that a *sequence of jobs* can have even greater effects on the person's career growth. In fact, we would argue that *carefully sequenced job assignments have greater impact on a person's development than any other kind of training experience.* Job requirements demand that a person learn certain job-related skills. Training programs, by contrast, by and large do not demand learning. Job activities and job-related learning are by definition integrated into the ongoing work environment, whereas off-the-job training programs are often hard to reconcile with the "back home" job environment.

The critical factors in using jobs for developmental purposes are to identify (1) the skills and experience a person needs to reach a certain target job and (2) which jobs, in what sequence, will provide these skills and experiences in small enough increments so the person will not be overwhelmed, but in large enough jumps so that the person is always being stretched—thus minimizing career time to reach the target job.

One large retailing organization, for example, is undertaking just such a job-pathing program in an attempt to reduce the amount of time it takes to "grow" a store manager. Conventional wisdom in the organization is that it takes around fifteen years, but initial experiences with careful job plotting indicate that it can probably be done in five. Another widely held belief in this organization is that there are one or two main paths to the store manager's position. Yet examination of several alternative paths, which are quite feasible but for some reason never used, indicates that the company has more flexibility in plotting career paths than it is currently using. Plotting paths through several different functions makes it possible to grow "broader" managers.

Talent Development Among Hourly Employees Several existing methods of developing managerial talent among hourly workers may need to be reexamined in light of the need to comply with legislation on equal employment opportunity. Companies are beginning to address the question: "How can we attract a substantial number of women and minorities into these presupervisory programs?" To answer this question, some have begun to assess employee *perceptions* of upward mobility opportunities, organizational barriers to or support mechanisms for upward mobility, and the self-perceptions and role perceptions held by women and minorities. When, for example, a plant manager in a brewing company queried a woman on the reasons she *resisted* the opportunity to move into management, she replied, "I thought a production supervisor had to be a 'Two-Ton Tony.'" Obviously, this woman's resistance stemmed at least in part from the discrepancy between her perception of the role requirements and her self-image.

Another approach has been the use of in-service training institutes conducted by professional or trade organizations. While these are common in manufacturing (the Midwest Manufacturing Association, for example, has sponsored numerous "certificate" programs), organizations such as the National Association of Banking Women are also seeking ways of developing their numbers. Frequently, women and minorities view the opportunity for training through these associations as being less competitive and more supportive than company-sponsored programs.

PROBLEM 3: HOW CAN WE INCREASE PROMOTION OPPORTUNITIES IN A STABLE OR CONTRACTING ORGANIZATION?

For many organizations, the current push for career development, especially for women and minority candidates, comes in an economic period when career growth is hardest to provide: a period of corporate slow-down or retrenchment. When many new management positions are opening up in an organization, career opportunities abound; when they dry up, career advancement requires more careful planning. How can we make the most of these declining opportunities?

Cross-Functional Moves One developmental method is the cross-functional or lateral transfer. Such rotational transfers may occur often at the beginning of a person's career. After a certain point, however, organizations tend to keep people in a particular functional area in which they can become highly trained and specialized and spend enough time to pay off the company's investment. In the long run, this policy leads to obsolescence; the person who is not forced to learn about new areas from time to time ends up stale, bored, and increasingly less creative and productive. Cross-functional transfers throughout the career keep a person fresh and open to new learning and give him or her a broader perspective on the company as a whole.

An example of this sort of transfer occurred at Union Carbide, where three executive vice-presidents traded jobs. The reason for the move was to give each one a better "big picture" view of the total organization and prepare them better for the presidency. One of the men, Warren M. Anderson, explained the value of the move in an article in *Business Week* (July 14, 1975, pp. 82, 84):

> We were a holding company until the mid-1950s, and you could count on your fingers the number of people who moved from division to division. You grow up in a division, and you get about four miles tall but not very broad. . . . Everybody had sneered at lateral transfers. Now, they can point to us. I feel this gives me a chance to see the whole business.

Job pathing enables us to identify jobs *at the same organizational level* that demand more skills in certain areas than do other jobs. Thus the great potential of lateral moves for development is more effectively tapped. After two people trade jobs, as one retailing organization found, it is possible for each to end up in a more demanding position!

A critical issue in any kind of lateral move is how the transfer decision is made. When personnel staff specialists make the decisions, the moves may make good, sound technical sense—but may be unacceptable to the bosses of the people to be moved. Also, this kind of decision-making process implies that career planning is purely a staff function, and not the manager's job.

Management-Personnel Committees One way of getting managers more involved in career planning is through the mechanism of management-personnel committees. In this structure, which is employed by the Southern New England Telephone Company (SNET), each personnel committee is made up of managers from all the functions at the same level of management. Each committee meets once every week or two to decide what transfers will be made between their departments among people who report to them. They also make recommendations on promotions. Employees are assessed in terms of their management potential, ranging from Category 1 (high-level potential) to Category 6 (not promotable even if the company is on the verge of going out of business).

According to Robert Neal, director of human resources development for SNET, this process results in a high quality of personnel decisions and in personnel actions that generally are well accepted by those affected—both the bosses and the transferred employees. The process does deal with tough issues of bargaining ("I'll take one from your Category 5, but let's agree in writing that you'll take him back in two years"). Actual contracts are written and signed, in much the way that "player swaps" are handled in professional sports. Another benefit of this system, according to Neal, is that a "Cat. 5" in one department—say, marketing—may blossom into a "Cat. 2" in traffic. Employees are periodically reassessed in light of *recent* performance, since these transfers enable an employee to demonstrate potential that might otherwise have been hidden forever if he or she had stayed in one function or department.

One disadvantage of this process, of course, is that like most committee structures, it takes a fair amount of time. However, the benefits seem to justify the time invested. Another management "plus" of this system is that the managers who serve on personnel committees develop a greater identification with the company as a whole. The decision process involved forces them to rise above their own department loyalties and look at decisions from a broader perspective. The rate of interfunctional movement has increased from 5 percent of all transfers in 1968 to 50 percent now.

Whenever we discuss developmental lateral moves with executives, the response is usually surprisingly strong, either pro or con. Some people see it as a radical, impractical idea because the need for retraining would be great, as would the organizational risk of having managers who are inexperienced in their new function or department. Lateral moves also buck a common norm in many organizations—namely, that the only good move is a promotion. Other managers report that they are beginning to experiment with cross-functional moves, and their experiences are generally favorable. Still others report they have never really thought about cross-functional moves, but they get very excited about this "creative new idea." There is nothing new or creative about lateral moves, however; the fact is that in many companies promotion policies are simply taken for granted, like "organization wallpaper," when they might quite easily and profitably be changed.

Fallback Positions   One risk of a cross-functional transfer or promotion, especially when it occurs at a senior level, is that the person may fail in the new job simply because it's too demanding. Because many organizations are reluctant to move people down a level, there is some risk that the cross-functional transferee may become stuck in a position beyond his or her level of competence—the Peter Principle in action.

A novel way of reducing this risk in a high-level job move is to identify a fallback position into which the person can move if he or she is not successful after promotion or transfer. The fallback position assures the person of a position equal in status and pay to his or her original job if things don't work out in the new one. Establishing a fallback position in advance lets everyone involved know that (1) there is some risk in the promotion or transfer, (2) the company is willing to accept some of the responsibility for it, and (3) moving into the fallback position does not constitute failure. As a result, the ratchet effect of upward-only movement is partially eliminated, and the organization's degree of freedom in manpower planning is substantially increased.

Consider this illustration of the fallback-position concept: In the Heublein organization, one management-information systems expert was moved to finance, and a human-resources specialist was transferred to a job in production management. Without the fallback position, neither person might have been willing to take the risk. With it, people who have become highly specialized (perhaps overspecialized) can be helped to work their way back into general management. Among the other companies that have employed fallback positions are Procter and Gamble, Continental Can, and Lehman Brothers (*Business Week*, September 28, 1974).

Downward Transfers   More dramatic than the establishment of fallback positions is the policy of legitimizing downward transfers (demotions). Being able to move people down as well as up introduces considerably more flexibility in manpower planning. As organizational growth decreases, and as more people elect to "stay put" in their present job (or are compelled to), the result could be corporate stagnation—with few people entering or leaving the organization. To maintain flexibility, therefore, new ways of creating internal mobility become critical. For every person moved downward, a shot at a promotion is created for numerous people below this level. Where there is a policy against moving people down, the only way a vacancy could open up would be through retirement or death (assuming no organizational growth or turnover).

The problem with downward transfers, obviously, is the strong norm in our society against moving down. Moving up is good, moving laterally is suspect, and moving down spells *failure*.

The upward-mobility norm is a tough one to buck, but it is being challenged on several fronts:

1 As concern over the quality of life increases,

more people are turning down promotions or accepting lower-level jobs in order to move to or to stay in such desirable geographical areas as San Diego, Minneapolis, Atlanta, and Seattle. When, for example, the department of psychology at San Diego State University advertised an opening for an assistant professor (a position generally filled by someone fresh out of graduate school), the department received many applications from full professors and department chairmen who were willing to move down in order to live in San Diego.

2 Realizing that growth opportunities are becoming more limited, people are willing to move down into a new area or company as a possible base from which to move up later on.

3 Given the option of being terminated or being demoted, people are often willing to accept a move down. As with many decisions in life, the attractiveness of a demotion often depends upon the nature of the alternatives. In recent cuts of technical personnel, companies such as General Electric and Chrysler first tried to place as many employees as possible in lower-level jobs rather than terminate them. Those who were moved down rather than out were viewed as being quite fortunate.

4 As the economy settles into a period of slower growth, expectations of rapid advancement may diminish and the upward-mobility norm may weaken. There is already evidence that the American success ethic is moving away from advancement and money as success symbols, toward self-fulfillment. As Daniel Yankelovich put it:

> Since World War II most Americans have shaped their ideas of success around money, occupational status, possessions, and the social mobility of their children. Now, ideas about success are beginning to revolve around various forms of self fulfillment. If the key motif of the past was "keeping up with the Joneses," today it is, "I have my own life to live, let Jones shift for himself."

As part of this quest for personal self-fulfillment (which does not necessarily have to occur on the job), people may be more likely to take a lower-level job that gives them more autonomy or challenge or simply more freedom to pursue fulfillment off the job.

Other organizations are using downward transfers to open up management training and mobility options that otherwise would not exist. One large Canadian oil company has been experimenting with downward transfers at senior executive levels. This company has learned certain principles that increase the success of downward transfers. First, the people who are chosen to be moved down should be people who are known (by themselves and other employees) to be outstanding performers. This helps dissociate downward movement from failure (and, it is to be hoped, may even associate it with success). Over time, if enough obviously competent people are moved down, the norm of promotion-as-a-sign-of-success may be placed with movement-as-a-sign-of-success. People to be moved down should be informed well in advance and told that they may be moved back to their present levels later.

Why are outstanding performers moved down? First, because even if a person is performing successfully at his or her job, there are still many equally promising people at the next level down, waiting for a higher-level challenge. Moving one person down temporarily gives many more people a good opportunity for development. The obviously successful person would be more secure and more effective in a downward move than would a less outstanding performer. Second, there may be "hot spots" at a lower level in the organization that call for the temporary trouble-shooting services of a successful higher-level person. Perhaps a tough marketing problem needs to be solved or maybe a department needs reorganizing. A key executive could come in on a one-year assignment, clean things up, and then move back to his previous level or to a new "hot spot."

A second principle is that important ground rules must be established: (1) No one will suffer a cut in pay as a result of a downward move, and (2) no one moved down will be terminated (to make it clear that the next move after moving down isn't out the door). People moved down thus received a sort of "tenure" that gave them more security than most other employees.

What are some of the preliminary results of the downward-transfer system in this firm? The most obvious is that intra-organizational mobility and flexibility have increased. More young people can move up into high-responsibility positions faster than before. They can also move back down and into other functional areas more easily.

What about the effects on the people moved down? According to the personnel director, the first few people (as one might anticipate) had mixed emotions about it. After several months, however, they began to appreciate the freedom from higher-level responsibilities and pressures. They appreciated having a bit more time to spend with their families, getting to know their grandchildren, and so on. They also enjoyed the stimulation of working with younger managers—learning new ideas and techniques from them and transmitting wisdom and experience to them.

An unintended consequence of these downward transfers has been an improvement in two-way communication, especially in the upward direction.

Corporate Tenure

Some of the career-management policies we have just discussed, such as cross-functional transfers and downward moves, are often difficult to implement because of the threats they may pose to the person's security in the organization. One way to increase employees' sense of security, and at the same time to establish tougher performance standards and feedback, is through a system of corporate tenure.

Such a novel system has been used in a medium-sized Pennsylvania manufacturing firm. The president of this firm, Robert Seidel, took a look at how various types of organizations develop personnel. He decided that universities, for all their problems, did have one promising feature: the tenure system. The tenure system forces the university to take a good hard look at a person's performance and to give him or her straight feedback: "up or out."

Seidel modified the tenure system in this way. When a new employee is hired, he or she is put on a short-term probation period, customary procedure in many organizations. At the end of the period, the employee's immediate superior and a personnel expert carefully appraise the person's performance. If it has been satisfactory, the employee is encouraged to stay on.

At this point, however, a novel twist occurs. The two evaluators make a second judgment: If there were to be an economic downturn and we had to make a 20 percent staff cut, would this person be in the 20 percent we would terminate? The answer to this question, which is fed back to the employee, gives him a realistic idea of where he stands with the company. People who are not in this 20 percent marginal group are thus granted a form of organiza-

tional tenure. Knowing that their jobs are secure, they feel freer to assume the risks of interdepartmental transfer, promotion, or demotion. Interestingly, this tenure does not result in "slacking off," perhaps because of clear standards of high performance in the organization.

What about the effect on the people in the 20 percent group? Often they elect to remain in the organization. In some cases, the feedback results in improved performance. One major advantage of this tenure system is that it forces the organization to appraise new employees all the time, not just on a "crash" basis when a personnel cut is necessary.

The Need for Internal Mobility

The common theme in all these methods of providing for better career development in a slower growth economy is increased intra-organizational mobility. If job changes are not going to be facilitated so much by the entrance or departure of people or by the opening up of new positions, we will have to find new ways to move people around within the organization.

We know from the work of Paul Lawrence and Jay Lorsch and others that organizations have to become more flexible if they are to adapt to changes and uncertainty in the external environment. The methods we have been discussing (downward transfers, cross-functional moves, and so on) are all specific ways in which the organization can increase its own flexibility and that of its human resources.

Executives are rethinking their norms about what kind of movement is appropriate. Both employees and the organization have to plan career moves more carefully and work harder at career development, because the economy is no longer doing the job for us. In an ironic twist, a slow growth economy is giving (or forcing upon) individuals and organizations more control over the way careers unfold.

WHAT IS NOT BEING DONE ABOUT CAREER DEVELOPMENT?

So much for the good news; now let's see where less progress is being made.

Integrating Career Development and Manpower Planning

Work on organizational careers has a schizophrenic aspect. On the other hand, there are attempts to facilitate the careers of individual employees through career counseling, goal setting, and so forth (the micro approach). At the other extreme, manpower planners chart the moves of large numbers of people through various positions in the organization —identifying future staffing gaps, "fast tracks," and the like (the macro approach). But these two types of career planning are rarely integrated.

Most organizations, in fact, use only one of these approaches—an unfortunate practice no matter which one they choose. The company that focuses on individuals, for example, may well do a good job of developing people—but if overall corporate manpower needs are ignored, these individuals may be "all developed with no place to go" or find themselves being routed into dead-end jobs.

On the other hand, the organization that develops corporate manpower plans without adequately developing and training people to move through various positions (or to move through a different sequence of positions) is not really managing and planning careers, but merely monitoring them. Even in the organization that is doing both micro and macro career planning, most of the potential of each approach is lost if (as is often the case) the micro and macro people don't talk to each other.

It seems almost trite to suggest that the micro and macro facets of career management be integrated because it seems so straightforward and reasonable. One wonders why this integration does not occur more often. One reason is that organizations large enough to need systematic career management generally have career counseling and manpower planning in different departments. Practitioners in each area often come out of different professional disciplines—counselors from psychology, and manpower planners from economic or systems analysis. And it is difficult to integrate the two—to undertake sound manpower forecasts and then to translate them into specific training and development activities.

Dealing with Second-Generation EEO Problems

Many organizations are now into what we might call Phase II of affirmative action. The main need in Phase I, which concerned recruitment and selection, was to get more women and minority employees to enter managerial and professional positions. Now that more women and minorities *are* entering these

positions, other problems arise—such as the need for training and development, meeting new needs of new kinds of employees, and coping with the reactions of white male employees.

The Problem of Providing Organizational Support A subtle pattern seems to be evolving, in which some executives subvert EEO goals while apparently implementing them. The equation for this process is "Equal opportunity + low support = discrimination." If a woman or minority employee is hired for a position traditionally occupied by white males, the new person will probably need some technical training as well as informal advice, coaching, and support. In fact, most of us need—and receive—all kinds of informal help and support in any new job. However, when female or minority employees are placed in a nontraditional position (that is, given equal employment opportunity), they are often socially isolated from peers and senior colleagues who could give them words of wisdom, feedback, prodding, encouragement, "Dutch uncle" talks, and the like; these new employees are simply left alone to do their job—and frequently to fail. One young woman, for example, was hired by a high-prestige (and high-pressure) university despite the concern some people felt about her lack of experience and confidence in dealing with the demanding students she would encounter. A senior faculty member assured the others that he would take her "under his wing" and help her cope with her environment. So she was hired—the first woman in her department—and all eyes were on her. And the senior professor left for a sabbatical as soon as she arrived! No one else was willing to act as a substitute sponsor in his absence. Without support or counsel, she floundered in the classroom. She spent so much time working on her teaching that she didn't spend much time on research—and no one "bugged" her to do any publishing. Now the reaction of her colleagues is, "Well, we tried giving a woman a chance; I guess we'd better not make *that* mistake again." Thus with equal opportunity and low support, low initial expectations for the person's success can create a vicious self-fulfilling prophecy.

The Problem of Meeting the Needs of the White Males Because of the slow economy, promotions are harder to come by these days—and those that *are* available are often used to advance women and minority employees. Consequently, the white male often feels frustrated and demotivated. It is no consolation to him to say that this reverse discrimination is a temporary corrective measure to make up for past generations of discrimination in favor of white males. After all, he wasn't responsible for what happened earlier, so why should he suffer now?

The group being hurt most is white males of average competence. Outstanding performers will always have corresponding career opportunities. And poor performers are likely always to have problems—but right now, EEO activity is giving them a handy scapegoat. It is the average white male who is most likely to lose out in competition with women and minorities who show equal performance and qualifications.

Most companies seem aware of this problem, but see little they can do about it. They often handle the issue by cloaking promotion data in great secrecy— perhaps in the hope that if white males aren't told they're not getting anywhere, maybe they won't notice it! The irony here is that in many companies white males tend to overestimate their relative disadvantage. More open information would probably show that white males are moving faster than their perceptions would suggest.

One way to deal with this issue is to be sure that white males receive at least as much career counseling and assistance in career planning as do women and minorities, because the former group may need to plan their career moves more carefully. The white male may have a greater need for occupational information inside and outside the company than do other, higher-priority groups. In fact, many companies started career-planning programs for women and minorities only and then opened them up to all employees. In these organizations, white males have more career-planning services now available than they ever would have had without EEO pressures.

Another strategy—a high-risk, but high-potential one—would be to hold career workshops in which male and female employees, black and white, meet to discuss their feelings about career opportunities and explore methods of aiding their career development. Such group sessions could meet employees' need for: (1) ventilating feelings, (2) being coun-

seled, (3) getting career information, (4) doing some self-assessment, and (5) solving career problems.

Managing Dual Careers

As more women embark upon full-time work careers, more dual-career families come into existence. When both husband and wife have full-time careers, their personal career flexibility decreases (if they want to live together), so career planning becomes more difficult and necessary. It is, of course more difficult to transfer a dual-career employee to a different city or, if the spouse is transferred by his or her firm, to attempt to make a similar move for the partner who works for you. You may find yourself losing good people because of a spouse's career. Alternatively, you might find it difficult to attract someone whose spouse could not find good career opportunities in your organization's geographical area.

The best way for organizations to deal with dual careers is not clear. Many executives do not yet see the problem as an important one. The first step, therefore, is to demonstrate to managers the ways in which dual careers can affect their organization. Our preliminary research indicates that the main problem caused by dual careers comes in making personnel transfers. Recruitment and hiring do not seem to be so strongly affected, although again managers may just be less aware of the dual-career people they lose in the hiring process than of the ones they hire and can't transfer.

Companies seem to be dealing with the transfer problem by adopting a more flexible attitude toward people who turn down transfers. An employee is now informally granted more transfer refusals without prejudice to future promotions than in the past. There also seems to be more effort to find developmental moves within the same geographic location. This is another reason why cross-functional moves may become more common.

Another corporate response to dual careers is an increasing awareness that the organization has some stake in the spouse's career, even if the spouse works elsewhere. Thus various supportive services, mainly informal, are being extended to unemployed spouses (for example, help in setting up job interviews with other organizations.) Neopotism rules are also being relaxed, making it easier for husband and wife to work for the same organization or even in the same department. (The emerging norm in many organization is that spouses can work in the same department as long as one is not supervising the other.) Flexible workhours are helpful, too.

Some organizations are finding that attracting dual-career people requires dual recruiting, or helping to find a job for the spouse as well as the primary candidate. This may require cooperative, interorganizational recruiting. Dealing with another organization's personnel executives, over whom you have no control, can be a real test of managerial and persuasive skills. The fact is, however, that the spouse's career opportunities have became a bargaining point in recruiting and retaining talented dual-career employees. This issue is just beginning to show up with younger, more junior people. In time, these will become key people and then the problem will be critical. The executive who responds that this is the couple's problem, not the organization's, will lose many good employees. The issue, we feel, is a real organizational "time bomb."

GENERAL PRINCIPLES OF EFFECTIVE CAREER PLANNING

So far, we've examined what novel ideas are being tried and what isn't being done. Let's conclude with a few general guidelines about what *should* be done in developing employee careers.

Utilize the Career-Growth Cycle

First, let's consider just how career growth occurs. This process, shown in Figure 18-1, is triggered by a job that provides challenging, stretching goals. The clearer and more challenging the goals, the more effort the person will exert—and the more effort exerted, the more likely it is that good performance will result. If the person does a good job and

receives positive feedback, he or she will feel successful (psychologically successful). Feelings of success increase a person's feelings of confidence, self-worth, or self-esteem. This internal gratification leads the person to become more involved in work, which in turn leads to the setting of future stretching goals. Let us consider more specifically how a company might use this growth cycle.

Plan and Utilize the Job Itself

Since the career-growth cycle is triggered by challenging work goals, the person's job should be made as challenging as possible (as we explained earlier). Too many companies see career development only as something done by "those people in personnel." Each job should represent a challenge, and the sequence of jobs should be planned to provide a systematic and continuing growth of career skills.

Goal Setting   In general, people tend not to set work goals for themselves. But when they do, the results can be dramatic. This doesn't mean that you need a formal MBO system—just mutual agreement between you, your boss, and your subordinate on a few specific objectives over the next few months that will help the employee focus his or her efforts.

Frequent Performance Review and Feedback   Although most organizations have formal policies regarding performance appraisals, few performance appraisals are actually handled properly for the benefit of employees. People need feedback to help assess how well they have performed and where changes should be made. Such feedback can be given informally, on a continuing basis, instead of in a stressful, formal, once-a-year ordeal. It is also easier to provide feedback if specific goals have been set; then you can talk not only about how well activities were carried out, but also about whether certain ones were carried out at all.

Counseling and support from the boss. When building the conditions for career success into the job, don't forget the boss. As a source of support (in translating goals into action) and counseling and planning (for translating involvement into future goals), supervisors can be far more influential than any personnel or career specialist. The supervisor is also the best person to provide goal-setting stimulation and performance feedback.

Figure 18-1   The career-growth cycle.

Train and Reward Supervisors for Career-Planning Skills

If the supervisor is to be expected to provide support, feedback, and counseling, don't think this will happen easily. One reason supervisors don't do more along these lines now is that they don't feel comfortable doing it. And they feel uncomfortable for a number of reasons. One is that they often lack the necessary skills. A second reason is that they often experience role conflict between being a "boss" and being a "helper." A two- or three-day training program would be an enormous aid for supervisors, enabling them to learn both how to conduct good performance appraisals and how to be good informal agents of career planning. This approach to career planning is already being taken in one of the major auto manufacturers, with good results.

Tying employee development specifically into the supervisor's own performance appraisal is another good way to reward these activities. This is a simple idea, but it is rarely practiced. General Electric has been successful in including managers' affirmative action progress in their performance appraisals. The result has been a great increase in EEO attainments. A large Canadian computer company requires each manager to pick and develop a successor before the manager will be considered for promotion. This is a very clear and powerful way of linking the career development of subordinates to the career progress of the manager.

Personnel Specialists as Monitors Tying career development into the everyday work environment of supervisors frees personnel specialists to act in an indirect, support role (which is what a staff function is intended to be, anyway). Personnel people can work in two ways: (1) They can train the supervisors in the career-developing skills just discussed, and (2) they can monitor the process to make sure the periodic goal setting, feedback, and career planning are discussed. The following application of these ideas gives more details.

An Illustrative Example: AT&T Several of these principles are illustrated in career programs being used at AT&T. Joel Moses, a personnel specialist, cites one early identification program—the Initial Management Development Program—for noncol-

lege employees being considered for management positions. The employees first go through a one-day assessment program. Then they are given feedback by a trained person (either in personnel or in the person's own department), who then continues to function as the employee's *career counselor*. Explicit career plans are made. Then the person and the boss jointly set work targets to help achieve the career plan. Although most of the planning is done within the employee's department, the personnel specialist functions as monitor of the process. The third-party career counselor is useful because of the high turnover in superior-subordinate relationships.

Another program is a successor to the Initial Management Development Program, but is more "user oriented" than IMDP. The stress is on *boss training* in the area of job design, joint target setting, and appraisal skills. At the end of the first year of employment, the person goes through a two-day assessment program. Following this is a meeting with the person's boss, a member of the assessment center, and a personnel coordinator. One of three decisions is made: Terminate, don't promote, or prepare for middle management. A feedback meeting is held with the employee to discuss the results of the assessment process. Then in the second year a career plan is drawn up—entailing a target job, the training needed, interim assignments, and a time frame. The three parties review this plan and the progress made every six months.

The following principles are reflected in these AT&T programs:

1 Emphasize the development of high-potential people. Don't try to change people who lack management potential.
2 Set specific development objectives. Identify specific job experiences and skills the person needs (for example, "ability to supervise a central office PBX group").
3 Train the supervisor to provide the day-to-day job experiences (for example, challenging goals and feedback) that facilitate career development.
4 Give personnel experts the responsibility for structuring and monitoring the development *process,* but reserve for the employee and the supervisor the responsibility for its actual content.

CONCLUSION

The more we use the job itself and the superior-subordinate relationship for career development and call upon the personnel department for outside resources and process monitors, the better use we are making of the respective resources of each.

We hope that the new process of career develop-ment will not be accepted or implemented without careful thought and planning, since it could become just another management fad. Rather, career development, the enhancement of human talent, should be viewed as a management function that has always been performed in effective organizations—yet one than can benefit from being conceptualized and practiced in new ways.

Chapter 6

Developmental Processes

A key element in the long-term relationship between an individual and an organization is the type of developmental experiences the individual has. The development of an individual in an organization is of keen interest to both the person and the organization. From the individual's point of view, development is required if the individual is to move upward in the organization and achieve his or her goals. From the organization's point of view, development of individuals is necessary because of the need for well-trained and highly skilled managers and technicians. People with the types of skills that are needed to manage and perform complicated technical processes and to occupy top-management positions do not appear by accident. It requires the careful identification of people who have the capability and a mutual process between the individual and the organization so that appropriate skills and career tracks are developed. When the process of development works correctly, both the individual and the organization gain. Unfortunately, often the process is not a smooth one, and individuals become disaffected with the type of development experiences they receive and/or the organization becomes disaffected with the type of development the individual is accomplishing.

The readings in this chapter examine three approaches to aiding the development process. The first, by Kraut, looks at the assessment center, an approach to aiding individual development that is increasingly coming into use. The article provides a description of how the assessment center can be utilized to assist organizations in determining the managerial capabilities of individuals. Assessment centers not only give organizations valuable and relevant information about their members, they also provide individuals with useful feedback concerning their own managerial skills and development needs. The article outlines in detail the assessment center methods and also discusses the usefulness of assessment centers in predicting future managerial success.

The second article, by Sorcher, examines management-training approaches, with particular emphasis on an approach called "behavior modeling." Sorcher reviews the traditional approaches to management development and points out why they so often fail. Then he explains the behavior-modeling approach, providing illustrations of how it proceeds. Existing data about the approach are supportive, and it also is more congruent with the principles of human learning than are many other training techniques. While it is not yet known how broadly applicable the approach is, initial results strongly suggest that it deserves—and is likely to get—widespread application as an approach to managerial training.

The final article, by London, is particularly interesting because it looks at promotion in a rather broad context. London points out that job changes can be important both as motivators and as development experiences. Indeed, it may be that promotions are too often used as rewards for past performance and not as development experiences. Success in a lower-level job may not predict performance in higher-level jobs, and as a result promotion based on performance can lead to poor staffing and missed development opportunities.

Reading 19

New Frontiers for Assessment Centers
Allen I. Kraut

The assessment center method has become one of the most powerful techniques available for identification of management potential. During the last six years, its use has spread to hundreds of business and government organizations, and there are many reasons for believing that this trend represents much more than just a passing fad. But, at the same time, serious concerns about the nature and validity of this technique have been raised by many interested parties, reflecting a need for a set of minimal professional standards for users of assessment centers.

Chaired by Dr. Joseph L. Moses of American Telephone and Telegraph Company, a group of professionals actively engaged in the assessment center method recently developed and issued a set of guidelines entitled "Standards and Ethical Considerations for Assessment Center Operations." These guidelines were endorsed in 1975 by the Third International Congress on the Assessment Center Method. More recently, they were admitted into evidence in the first court test of assessment center reliability, in which the city of Omaha was upheld in its use of the method (*Berry, Stokes, and Lant v. City of Omaha*).

WHAT IS AN ASSESSMENT CENTER?

An assessment center can be described as a multi-method, multitrait, and even multimedia technique (see Figure 19-1). Essentially, it is a series of individual and group exercises in which a number of candidates participate while being observed by several specially trained judges. The exercises are simulations of managerial tasks designed to test various managerial skills. They include written materials as well as behavioral simulations.

A typical example of an individual exercise is an "in-basket," which simulates the correspondence that managers may find on their desks after being away for a week or so. The items may be complex or simple, important or pedestrian, and candidates are assessed according to how well they handle them. For instance, do they set priorities? Do they delegate properly? Do they use good judgment in disposing of the items?

A "leaderless group discussion" is a typical example of a group exercise. In one popular version, a group of six participants is asked to boost a different candidate for promotion; at the same time, each is instructed to help the group as a whole arrive at a good decision. Thus managerial candidates can be judged on qualities such as oral communication and persuasiveness, sensitivity to others, interpersonal skills, and leadership in a group situation.

Most assessment centers have developed additional exercises and have tailored them to the needs of their own organizations. In addition, many programs use individual interviews and psychological tests. On the average, application of assessment procedures takes about two full days.

VARIETY OF USES

When one considers the variety of organizations in which assessment centers have been used and the variety of needs that this method can fulfill, it should not be surprising that it has been put to several different uses. Paramount among these has been the selection of people with greater ability for promotion to management. Similarly, it has been used to help identify people with management potential early in their careers.

In some organizations, however, assessment center results are not used simply for "go" or "no go" decisions but for the placement of individuals in positions that will use their talents and provide development essential for a meaningful, long-term career. In fact, some organizations use assessment programs exclusively for personal development in order to help people diagnose their competencies and to help improve them.

Figure 19-1 What an assessment center is and is not.

The Task Force on Development of Assessment Center Standards has recommended that a program be considered an assessment center only if it meets the following minimum requirements:

1 Multiple assessment techniques must be used. At least one of these techniques must be a simulation. (A *simulation* is an exercise or technique designed to elicit behaviors related to dimensions of performance on the job by requiring the participant to respond behaviorally to situational stimuli. The stimuli present in a simulation parallel or resemble stimuli in the work situation.)

2 Multiple assessors must be used. These assessors must receive training prior to participating in a center.

3 Judgments resulting in an outcome (that is, recommendation for promotion, specific training, or development) must be based on pooling information from assessors and techniques.

4 An overall evaluation of behavior must be made by assessors at a separate time from observation of behavior.

5 Simulation exercises are used. These exercises are developed to tap a variety of predetermined behaviors and have been pretested prior to use to ensure that the techniques provide reliable, objective, and relevant behavioral information for the organization in question.

6 The dimensions, attributes, characteristics, or qualities evaluated by the assessment center are determined by an analysis of relevant job behaviors.

7 The techniques used in the assessment center are designed to provide information that is used in evaluating the dimensions, attributes, or qualities previously determined.

The following activities *do not* constitute an assessment center:

1 Panel interviews or a series of sequential interviews as the sole technique.

2 Reliance on a specific technique (regardless of whether a simulation or not) as the sole basis for evaluation.

3 Using only a test battery composed of a number of pencil and paper measures, regardless of whether judgments are made by a statistical or judgmental pooling of scores.

4 Single assessor assessment (measurement by one individual using a variety of techniques such as pencil and paper tests, interviews, personality measures, or simulations).

5 Use of several simulations with more than one assessor where there is no pooling of data (that is, each assessor prepares a report on performance in an exercise, and individual, iunintegrated reports are used as the final product of the center).

6 A physical location labeled as an "assessment center" that does not conform to the requirements noted above.

IS THE METHOD VALID?

The validity of the assessment center method has been the subject of a large number of studies. Of these, the monumental "Management Progress Study" conducted by Douglas Bray and his associates at AT&T is perhaps the best known and best documented. They assessed several hundred first-line managers using non-company psychologists, locked up the data (which was never seen by AT&T officials), and ten years later checked the accuracy of their predictions about who would reach middle-management levels. Sixty-four percent of those predicted to achieve this level actually did so, compared with only 32 percent of those who were predicted not to reach this level.

In a study of several hundred sales representatives of office equipment who attended an operational assessment center program, I (with Grant Scott) found that high-rated participants were three times as likely as low-rated participants to be promoted to higher levels of management during the following few years. Even more dramatic, we found that low-rated individuals who went on to management jobs were more likely to be demoted. During the several years following the assessment center program, one-third of the people were promoted into the first level of management. Of these, only 4 percent of the high-rated people were later demoted, compared with 20 percent of the low-rated people.

Further, recent research by James Huck and Douglas Bray indicates that the assessment center method predicts job performance in an equally valid way for members of different minority groups. In fact, AT&T recently entered into a consent decree with the federal government to use assessment centers as a means of judging management potential of women to facilitate their upgrading. Thus, government officials seem to have tacitly approved the use of assessment centers as a tool for affirmative action. And the results at AT&T have been very promising; of more than 1,000 female supervisors assessed in this way, 42 percent have been judged to have the potential for middle-management positions.

HIGHLY REGARDED

The validity of the assessment center method should come as no surprise when its advantages over a traditional promotion system are considered. For example, in a typical assessment center program, multiple observers—chosen from managers two levels above the candidates being assessed—judge performance as opposed to a single, immediate superior. In addition, they assess candidates in a setting conducive to attentive observation, usually after receiving systematic training in what behaviors to observe in judging managerial potential. Further, assessment center observers judge candidates in similar situations and use common standards to measure their performance in simulations of potential management jobs, not in their current jobs.

A recent review by William Dodd of the reactions of participants and observers to assessment center experiences shows that both groups were very positive about assessment centers. Both cited their virtue of appearing to tap management abilities in useful ways and of helping to select individuals for promotion. What's more, even those assessees who knew they had done poorly in an assessment center program shared these positive sentiments.

THE COST/BENEFIT ISSUE

Despite some of the obvious advantages and successes of the assessment center method, a number of questions still remain. One key question often raised concerns the value added by assessment center programs to existing selection and placement systems, or, in other words, the issue of costs versus benefits.

A general estimate has been made by Huck of the contribution of the assessment center approach compared with more traditional methods. By combining a series of independent studies, he estimated

that the probability of selecting an above-average performer is 15 percent if individuals are chosen at random. Using traditional management-nomination techniques raises this probability to 35 percent. However, if a rating of "acceptable" in an assessment center program is combined with management recommendations, the probability of selecting an above-average performer increases to 76 percent, or over twice the probability using only traditional management-nomination techniques.

To some people, the cost of assessment center programs seems expensive. A figure commonly mentioned is about $500 per participant. Actually, most of this cost is made up of expenses for travel and room and board. Naturally, these costs can vary greatly, but in general, it's safe to say that the cost of an assessment center program is about the same as the cost of a management development program run under similar circumstances.

Costs are relative to the value of the information and the use to which such information is put. They must be weighed against the consequences of a poor decision. The information from an assessment center will be relatively more valuable when the performance of the person in a particular job really makes a big difference and when an ample number of candidates for such a job are available. As many executives recognize, merely picking the best salesman to be a sales manager may result simultaneously in the loss of a good salesman and the gain of a poor manager. And in some circumstances, where law or custom forbid, the removal of an inadequate manager may be very difficult and costly.

Still, it is highly desirable to get some hard figures on the amount of savings that can be achieved with the use of this method. One estimate, made by Logan Cheek in the selection of sales managers at Xerox, indicated that a net benefit of more than $4.9 million could be achieved for a cost of about $340,000. The exact cost/benefit ratio will, of course, vary with each situation.

IMPACT ON THE REST OF THE SYSTEM

An assessment center cannot be established in a vaccum. It becomes part of the organizational system for dealing with the identification and development of management talent. In planning and implementing an assessment center program, other parts of the system have to be considered.

Top management must be committed to the assessment center concept in order for it to succeed. Part of the plan for gaining an intelligent commitment should include an understanding of where a program will fit into and supplement the existing promotion system. Its impact on management-replacement-planning systems, existing appraisal programs, current methods of using promotion lists or promotion review boards, and related areas must be considered.

One of the key systems to consider is the motivational system of employees and existing managers. For example, if it is important for an organization to honor effective performance in the current job or to consider seniority, these requirements should be built into the minimum qualifications necessary to attend an assessment center. If it is important to maintain management responsibility in selecting and promoting individuals, the use of assessment center results should be monitored to ensure that these data are used in decision making merely as an additional input to managers' considerations of a subordinate's previous performance, experience, and education; qualifications of other candidates; and the needs of the particular opening.

The assessment center approach is not for all organizations. It may not be acceptable for philosophical reasons or for potential value. In some situations, such as conditions of rapid growth or geographical dispersion, assessment center data will be of greater value than in situations where these conditions are not present.

Minimum Training Requirements for Assessors[1]

Assessors should receive sufficient training to enable them to evaluate intelligently the behaviors measured in the center. "Sufficient training" will vary from organization to organization and is a function of many factors including:

● The length of time an individual serves as an assessor.
● The frequency of individual participation as an assessor.

[1]Recommended by the Task Force on Development of Assessment Center Standards. Copies of the standards are available from Dr. Joseph L. Moses, manager-personnel research, AT&T, 195 Broadway, New York, New York 10007.

● The amount of time devoted to assessor training.
● The qualifications and expertise of the assessment center trainer.
● The assessment experience of other staff members.
● The use of professionals (licensed or certified psychologists) as assessors.

Whatever the approach to assessor training, the essential goal is attaining accurate assessor judgments. A variety of training approaches can be used, as long as it can be demonstrated that accurate assessor judgments are obtained. The following minimum training is required:

● Knowledge of the assessment techniques used. This may include, for example, the kinds of behaviors elicited by each technique, relevant dimensions to be observed, expected or typical behaviors, and examples or samples of actual behaviors.
● Knowledge of the assessment dimensions. This may include, for example, definitions of dimensions, relationship to other dimensions, relationship to job performance, and examples of effective and ineffective performance.
● Knowledge of behavior observation and recording, including the forms used by the center.
● Knowledge of evaluation and rating procedures, including how data are integrated by the assessment center staff.
● Knowledge of assessment policies and practices of the organization, including restrictions on how assessment data are to be used.
● Knowledge of feedback procedures where appropriate.

SOME POTENTIAL PITFALLS

In all of the above applications, we must remember that the assessment center method represents a selection technique and, therefore, we should be concerned about its actual and demonstrated validity. Like other selection techniques, this one cannot be simply taken over and applied unthinkingly in another situation, with the hope that it will succeed as it has elsewhere. For this program to work, it is necessary to develop a clear understanding of the job requirements for the position to which we are predicting, to develop or adapt the exercises that will tap the required abilities, to ensure that we measure these qualities reliably through rigorous application of the technique, and to check the success of our predictions to determine the degree of validity the technique has in each particular situation.

It is equally important to check the reaction of participants and observers in each program and the various parts of the program. This can be done most simply by standardized questionnaires. In beginning programs, it may be more valuable to get this feedback through open-ended personal interviews.

A VALUABLE ADDITION

My experience in introducing the assessment center method in several countries outside the United States indicates that this technique can be used successfully in many other cultures. Nevertheless, an assessment center must be tailored to each culture, to each organization, and to each job family for which it is being used. This is necessary not only for providing face validity but also for improving the real accuracy of predictions.

The assessment center technique seems to have a number of advantages, logically and empirically, over other forms of evaluation such as paper and pencil tests and individual clinical evaluations. If it is combined with ongoing programs of recruitment, replacement, development, and coaching of job performance, it is likely to be a valuable addition to our techniques for identifying and selecting management potential. The increased use of this technique and the diversity of applications being developed are evidence that the assessment center technique is here to stay, and we should make the most of it.

Reading 20

Behavior Modeling and Motivational Skills
Melvin Sorcher

For decades psychologists and managers have searched for ways to help managers develop the interpersonal skills they need to effectively deal with and motivate their subordinates. Since having motivated and productive employees is very desirable, a great deal of money, time, and energy has been devoted to this pursuit. This chapter examines our search for an effective way to improve the motivational skills of managers.

TRADITIONAL TRAINING DOES NOT WORK

Some companies appoint managers and simply assume either that they possess or will easily acquire the skills to motivate their subordinates or that such skills are not very important. Most organizations, however, recognize the strong relationship between motivated employees and skilled supervisors, which explains why so many companies spend large sums of money and invest considerable time in supervisor training. They send supervisors and managers to training programs which run the range from traditional classroom lectures to motel marathons.

Most supervisory training programs, for both first-line and middle managers, consist of well-packaged and logically presented information which is designed to change attitudes. An underlying—and fallacious—assumption is that this attitude change will cause supervisors to change their behavior in interpersonal situations because they are logical individuals who respond to sound ideas. In fact, there is no reliable evidence that a supervisor's behavior can be changed as a result of traditional training programs. These programs typically focus on aspects of managing that are already well known to managers and supervisors, such as the need to give recognition, to motivate, and to appraise performance. What managers and supervisors need to learn is specifically *how* to recognize, motivate, and appraise performance, and so on. In short, they need to learn how to behave, they do not need to be told what the correct attitude is. In addition, it is very difficult to change behavior by first changing attitudes because attitudes are very resistant to change.

To illustrate the difficulty of the attitude-change process, imagine for a moment a neat pile of old cannon balls resting on the ground. The base of the pile is broad and narrows to a single ball perched on the top. Assume that this pile of cannon balls is a

Article prepared especially for this book.

depiction of an individual's personality, or belief system, since one definition of personality is that it is the sum total of our beliefs. Assume further that each cannon ball represents an attitude or belief. Next to this pile of cannon balls lies a single cannon ball. If you were asked to substitute the single ball on the ground for any one in the pile without changing the shape of the pile, you would, of course, choose the top ball. It is the easiest to replace. That top ball represents a peripheral and relatively unimportant belief, such as which airline provides better food. However, if you were asked to substitute the single ball for one which is deeper into the pile, you could not do it without changing the basic shape of the pile. Other balls would tumble down. These other cannon balls represent more deep-seated beliefs or attitudes and they provide actual support for still others. To remove one deep-seated ball requires, in effect, the removal of others, since some balls also exert pressure on other balls to remain in place.

Attitudes and beliefs exert similar pressure on each other, because if one of them is changed, others which are dependent on it must also be changed. Likewise, removing or changing certain attitudes or beliefs cannot be accomplished without changing the shape or nature of one's personality or effecting the apparent denial of one's experiences. This is a painful and difficult process for most people. Because the attitude-change approach to training requires changes in certain attitudes related to supervisor-employee relationships, this approach has not been effective. An example of this is the difficulty experienced by many organizations in obtaining attitude change toward minority and female employees despite the clarity of law, interminable logic, and mandate.

AN ALTERNATIVE APPROACH TO TRAINING: IMITATION, PRACTICE, REINFORCEMENT

Rather than following the traditional procedure of supervisory training programs (i.e., change attitudes to change behavior), consider a different format which is based upon some well-established principles of social learning. These principles are *imitation, practice,* and *reinforcement.* People do not learn social behavior by reading books or listening to lectures. Instead, we watch others (they *model* the behavior, we *imitate* it), we try out these new

behaviors (i.e., *practice* them), and we are rewarded or not (positive and negative *social reinforcement*). When we are rewarded positively for a behavior, we retain it in our repertoire. When we are not rewarded for a particular behavior, we drop it from our behavioral repertoire. Since other people serve as models for learning social behavior, the training technique based on this process is called "behavior modeling."

LEARNING TO SUPERVISE THROUGH BEHAVIOR MODELING

Behavior modeling is an approach to training which excludes theoretical explanations and minimizes rational appeals. It focuses entirely on the acquisition of specific behavior skills in supervisory situations. Further, it teaches these behavior skills in a way which maximizes transfer of training from the classroom to the job.

Imitation Behavior modeling can be, and has been, applied to interpersonal-skills training for supervisors in a number of organizations. First, "models" of effective supervisors are provided to enable imitation. While there are obvious practical constraints regarding live models, there are few constraints to using films or video-tapes of modeled behavior. Each modeling display (film or video-tape) depicts a supervisor interacting with an employee in a specific situation. The model demonstrates one effective way of handling an important or difficult interaction, but not necessarily the "ideal" way. The supervisor's behavior in a modeling display, therefore, is intended simply as a demonstration of an *effective* approach in a specific situation, not as the "only" approach.

While not a learning principle, supervisors learn why it is important not to threaten an employee's self-esteem and *how* to act in a way which supports it. They learn what to say when initiating a conversation with an employee whose performance has slipped: "John, I've got a few problems and I'm talking with the people who can give me the most help with them. In your area, for example, the quality-control charts show a drop of 10 percent last week. Have you got any ideas on the kinds of things that we ought to watch more carefully? I'd appreciate your ideas." This is very different than, "John, the quality-control charts show a drop of 10 percent in your area last week. What are you doing out there? You had better take care of this right away!" The supervisor showed little concern for the employee's self-esteem in the second instance, and the employee's reaction is predictable. In the first example, the supervisor focused on the problem. In the second problem, he focused on the person.

Learning how to be concerned about an employee's self-esteem is vital. The objective of most interactions can best be accomplished when the self-esteem of the employee is not threatened. When their self-esteem is threatened, people become defensive and have difficulty learning. For example, employees who are threatened will often blame their mistakes or inadequate performance on things beyond their control. They will blame equipment which needs repair, defective material, a conveyor which moves too fast, incorrect methods, or unclear instruction. When confronted by a supervisor with an accusation that their work is of poor quality, few employees will say, "Well, I guess I'm not as good at this as I thought I was." Instead, the response is more likely to be, "It's not my fault," a shrug, or a hostile comment. In any case, the response will be designed to protect the employee's self-esteem. On the other hand, when an employee produces work of low quality and the supervisor uses the approach of asking the employee for help in solving a work-quality problem because that employee, due to on-the-job knowledge, is the most qualified to assist with it, most employees will respond by improving the quality of their work to keep their performance in line with their self-esteem.

How do supervisors learn to carefully follow the behavior of a "model?" They can try to imitate as closely as possible, but this is difficult. Explicitly stated behavior guidelines, or *learning points,* can make all the difference in the world. Without learning points, trainees cannot critically observe or easily follow the model's behavior. The learning points must be concise behavioral guidelines. While they must help the supervisor protect the employee's self-esteem, they also must address the issue or problem at hand. For example, the learning points for improving poor performance are:

1 Focus on the problem, not the employee (don't personalize).
2 Ask for the employee's help and discuss the employee's ideas on how to solve the problem.

3 Come to agreement on steps to be taken by each of you.
4 Plan a specific follow-up date.

Following these points, a supervisor can handle a range of performance problems. Each of the points is a behavioral statement, not an attitudinal or cognitive one. They are designed for a "first-time" discussion and are easily adapted to specific situations and the supervisor's own personal style.

The modeling film or tape must be brief, about four to nine minutes long, so that certain key behaviors, or *behavioral learning points,* are not obscured. These learning points are clearly demonstrated by the model during the enacted situation. They guide the supervisor through the interaction. For example, the learning points to guide a supervisor through an interaction with a poor performer, or through a discussion of disciplinary action with an employee, or through a conversation in which an average employee is praised for dependability, are designed to apply to a wide range of employees.

Contrary to the first reactions of some participants, this kind of training does not "program" supervisors. Instead, it increases their flexibility by broadening their behavioral repertoire, since they learn other ways of handling situations while still following the learning points. Flexibility is very important for successful leadership in most situations, including supervisor-employee relationships, and the key behaviors (or learning points) serve as behavioral guides to which individual supervisors adapt their own personal "styles." The only requirement for improved supervisory effectiveness is guided practice during training.

Practice

Practice is the second element of the behavior-modeling approach to supervisor training. Participants in the training program must develop their skills in "imitating" the model. Practice takes the form of structured role-play which is actually behavior rehearsal, or skill practice. As the skill practice proceeds, participants provide additional models for each other and their skills are gradually shaped.

Skill practice is structured around the behavioral learning points. This is the sort of guided practice required by any work where skills must be developed. Most skills cannot be developed without practice. Professional musicians, for example, must practice systematically. Professional athletes must practice continually. Supervisors depend upon their skills for survival and should learn interpersonal skills in the same systematic manner. Structured practice offers this opportunity. The other advantage of practice is that it helps supervisors to become comfortable with behavior which initially may be awkward or even unfamiliar for them.

In behavior-modeling situations, supervisors in training take turns at the role of supervisor and employee in various situations. These role-plays (i.e., skill practice) are designed by the instructor to cover almost every imaginable interaction.

Practice in supervisory skills must be situationally specific. Building moon tents or role-playing a town hall meeting is not directly relevant to the situations which most supervisors experience. Training must impart skills which are directly transferable to the job. The more direct the transfer, the better the training. In effect, each skill practice is a simulation of an aspect of the job. The situations must include those which are encountered by supervisors and managers day-to-day. Examples of situations are: meeting a new employee, motivating a poor performer, dealing with excessive absenteeism or lateness, handling a disciplinary situation, giving recognition, giving a work assignment, conducting a performance appraisal, discussing a salary change, responding to a complaint from an employee, and so on. In each situation, the supervisor learns how to maintain the employee's self-esteem, why and how *not* to press for an immediate solution of "confession," how to behaviorally involve the employee in the situation, and how to use a follow-up meeting to ensure a good response from the employee or to provide the employee with recognition and personal appreciation.

Supervisors learn to follow the learning points closely in a specific situation, no matter whether the employee reacts defensively or aggressively. To illustrate with the learning points mentioned earlier, in a case where an employee complains of being picked on by a supervisor (because of personal dislike or perhaps because of age or race), the supervisor should not make a defensive statement such as, "But you are the only one who is missing a schedule." This statement violates the first point, which tells the supervisor not to personalize ("focus on the problem, not the person"). As soon as the supervi-

sor personalizes, the employee will become more defensive and there is little that can salvage their relationship in the future. On the other hand, the supervisor might react to the employee's accusation by saying, "Look, this is a problem and you probably know more about this kind of thing than anyone else around here. I need your help." A supervisor who learns to handle it this way, thereby protecting the employee's self-esteem, is far more likely to get a desirable response and improve their relationship, and, as well, will be better able to motivate the employee in the future. To do this, however, skill practice requires positive reinforcement or feedback from both the instructor and other peer-supervisors during the training sessions.

Reinforcement

Reinforcement for properly carrying out the key behaviors in each situation during training comes from the other participants in the program as well as the instructor. During skill practice, participants take turns in the role of supervisor and employee. Each skill practice is observed by the other participants and followed by a brief discussion on how well the "supervisor" handled the situation. The skill of the "supervisor" in following the key behaviors or learning points is discussed, and suggestions for improvement are made along with alternative ways of following a learning point. These discussions provide both positive and negative reinforcement. Participants observe successful behaviors as others practice their skills and will adopt the ones that work well. Behaviors which are not successful are dropped. Gradually, *behavioral shaping* takes place in specific interpersonal situations as supervisors acquire more skill.

Skill practice in a specific situation, such as how to motivate a poor performer or how to discuss salary change or how to delegate, usually requires a two-hour session. At the end of the session, the skills of participants in that interaction can be expected to be markedly improved.

TRANSFER OF TRAINING

To illustrate the processes of imitation, practice, and reinforcement with an analogy, most people have been to the seashore with a small child and have tried to encourage the child to play in the water.

Often, the child is afraid of the water which rushes back and forth over the sand. Swirling and bubbling water can be frightening to a small child. To encourage the child to enjoy the water, the parent does not usually spend much time sitting on the sand and trying to logically explain to the child what fun it is to play in the water. Instead, the parent typically takes the child by the hand, acting as a "model" to be *imitated,* and guides the child to the water with encouraging remarks. As the water comes in, the parent guides the child back and forth, thereby giving the child practice in playing in the surf. During the process, the parent makes encouraging remarks and signs to the child, i.e., *social reinforcement.* Before long the child is playing alone and happily in the water because there has been a *transfer of training* from the learning situation to the operational one.

After most supervisory training, participants find great difficulty applying what they have learned to job situations because there is no "bridge" available. With behavior-modeling training, guided practice structured about key behaviors *is* the bridge. Supervisors trained with this technique have little trouble transferring their learning recourse; like the child in the surf they have learned their new behaviors in the same types of situations in which they are expected to apply them.

CONTENT AND NUMBER OF SITUATIONS

A behavior-modeling program to teach interpersonal skills for supervisors should cover eight to twelve specific situations. As mentioned previously, the situations must be representative of those where a successful interaction is very important (e.g., motivating a poor performer, giving recognition to an average employee) or typical of situations which are uncomfortable for most supervisors (e.g., responding to a discrimination complaint, discussing inappropriate work habits with an employee). A survey of managers in an organization should provide information to identify situations where training can be most beneficial. Usually a core set of eight or ten situations is sufficiently generic for most organizations. In some cases, one or two of these situations are not appropriate and two or three others are developed to meet certain unique needs. In still other organizations, an entirely new set of situations

must be developed. In all cases, final selection of training modules, or situations, should be based on an analysis of what is needed in that organization.

A minimum of eight sessions is necessary for participants to learn how to be effective in a wider range of situations. For example, a modeling film on handling poor work-related habits may depict a supervisor discussing excessive absenteeism with an employee, but the learning points are appropriate for a wide variety of poor work habits, such as lateness, taking excessively long breaks or lunches, using offensive language, horseplay, and lining up early at a time clock. In fact, the instructor ensures that the skill practice which follows watching the film or video-tape includes a full range of issues which can be effectively handled with the learning points for that situation.

MODELING DISPLAYS

For the best results modeling displays (films and video-tapes) should be developed for the specific situations, contexts, and culture of an organization. For example, modeling films using actors with American accents and idioms should not be used in the United Kingdom, nor should films depicting factory workers with hard hats be used for training supervisors of office employees. For this reason, entirely new modeling displays were made by a major manufacturing company for supervisors in a Caribbean nation even though a set of films using American accents were already widely used within that company. Similarly, modeling displays depicting supervisor-employee interactions within a retail-store context were made for a large Canadian department-store chain even though the same generic situations were already available for manufacturing-plant situations. Models should be just that: models. They must facilitate identification for the participants. If the models on the displays inhibit participant identification, training is not likely to be as effective as it should be. Developing modeling displays is not a casual affair, as it may appear to an onlooker. Each display must be carefully designed so that the behaviorally specific learning points are clearly depicted. The learning points must be neither obscured nor diluted, and the entire display must provide motivational perspective for the participants.

To make a modeling film or tape, a script must be carefully prepared by a behavioral scientist or training specialist who is familiar with the research and literature on modeling and behavior modification *and* who is either equally experienced with the behavior-modeling process *or* prepared to experiment with it. Further, modeling displays made by "first timers" should not be used in actual training situations unless they are thoroughly pretested with representative sample groups. Finally, it is crucial that the modeling display show behavior which is known to be effective in the organization where the training will be done. Just as the situations used must be representative of the organization's situation, so must the content. All too often, managers are trained to perform behaviors that do not fit their organizations, simply because a training program is available or because some theory says it is the "best" way to manage. When this happens, the trained behavior is quickly put aside by the trainee.

NUMBER AND LENGTH OF SESSIONS

Ideally, only one situation should be covered in a single session. A session should last for two hours. This will enable each of about twelve participants to practice role-plays for that situation, following the learning points. During the role-plays, the participants take turns at the supervisor and employee roles. This continued observation and practice during a session quickly sharpens their skill. Taking both roles also provides them with a perspective not usually available in a supervisor training process. If there are ten situations to be covered in the program, a total of about twenty training hours is required.

The sessions should be spaced a week apart. This allows participants to try out or practice what they have learned in previous sessions. They are encouraged to practice in actual work situations and report the outcomes to their training class. Transfer of training is enhanced considerably by spacing sessions to enable on-the-job practice. While the ideal schedule is a weekly session to maximize transfer, the flexibility of the program facilitates arrangements to fit special work schedules or to overcome logistical problems.

Each session begins with a showing of the modeling film. This is followed by a brief discussion, led by the instructor, on how the modeled supervisor enacted the learning points. Next, the instructor leads the participants through skill-practice critiques until each participant has had an opportunity to practice the learning points.

EXAMPLES OF MORE AND LESS EFFECTIVE INTERACTIONS

The examples given below are transcripts of typical role-plays for participants in the "poor performance" session situation. The learning points on "How to Improve Poor Performance" should be reviewed:

- Focus on the problem, not the employee.
- Ask for the employee's help and discuss the employee's ideas on how to solve the problem.
- Come to an agreement on steps to be taken by each of you.
- Set a specific follow-up date.

These learning points are prominently displayed during the role-play. The "foreman" is instructed to follow the learning points and the "employee" is instructed to react as an employee might normally react.

Role-Play 1

A typical first role-play in a session is illustrated by the following transcript. The interaction is not successful, in spite of the learning points being prominently displayed as an aid to participants.

Foreman: How many times do I have to explain this job to you? If you recall when you came on the job a few weeks ago, my instructions were for you to perform this function and you're not doing it. It's a simple function and I just don't feel that I should keep coming back having to reinstruct you. What seems to be your problem?

Employee: I'm doing it the way you told me to do it. I don't know what the problem is.

Foreman: But you're not doing it the way I told you to do it. Your job here is to simply transfer these units from the end of the oven to this overhead conveyer. While you're doing it, you make a quick visual inspection to check whether or not there are plastic defects and you're not doing this.

Employee: I have been doing it. I've been doing it

just the way you told me to do it. What makes you think I haven't been doing it that way?

Foreman: I have just explained it to you again. I'm going to give you a brief period of time to do it. . . . like the remainder of the day. If at the end of the day you're still performing poorly, then I'm going to have to take some disciplinary action.

Employee: Well, you do what you have to, but I'm doing it the way you told me to do it, and if you don't think I'm doing it that way, then you can stand there and watch me.

Foreman: Do you understand how the job should be done in line with what I've just said?

Employee: Yes.

Foreman: Transferring units from the end of the oven.

Employee: That's what I've been doing. I've been doing it just the way you told me, and I don't see what the problem is.

Foreman: Are you're looking for obvious plastic defects?

Employee: Whatever I can see, I'm looking for those things. And if I can't see anything, well, I don't know what the hell you expect of me.

Foreman: Are you in trouble with your eyesight?

Employee: No.

Foreman: You can see all right?

Employee: Yes.

Foreman: It seems funny to me that you feel you've been doing the job properly and you've allowed units to go by with checks and scratches.

Employee: Well, there must be other people you can talk to about this. All I do is load them in there and if I don't see any problems, then there probably aren't any.

Foreman: Well, it's obvious that there are. And I don't want to tell you again.

Employee: That's what you say.

Foreman: You appear to be capable of doing it, and I think it's a matter of just not wanting to.

Employee: You know, it gets me mad when you say that, because I really want to. You think I want to stand here and not do the job right?

Foreman: I really don't know what you want to do. And your failure to do as I've instructed can result in disciplinary action and removal from the job.

Employee: This sure is a great place to work.

Foreman: If you feel it's so bad, maybe you should make arrangements to find a job elsewhere. You seem to be taking the attitude that you're just not going to do the job.

Employee: Oh, I've been trying to do the job. Why don't you just stand here and watch me?

Foreman: I'm not going to stand here and watch you do it. I've instructed you on how the job should be performed. However, I am going to come back at various intervals throughout the day to determine whether or not you've improved. If you feel you need any more instruction, you can either contact me or the machine attendant in the area.

Employee: All right.

Critique At the end of the situation, the supervisor who role-played the employee said that he found himself becoming very resentful of the foreman, yet afraid to express himself honestly because he was afraid that he (in his role as employee) would be punished for insubordination. All the participants agreed that the foreman ignored each of the learning points for this situation in addition to severely threatening the employee's self-esteem.

Role-Play 2

The next participant tries to build on the situation in his role as foreman.

Foreman: John, for the past few days, a great number of rejects have been passed by you as good units and you've done such a good job in the past I wonder if you have a problem in connection with work. Is there a problem?

Employee: I don't know what you're talking about, Carl. I don't see a problem here.

Foreman: Well, I notice the rejects over the past few days have been fairly obvious ones—bump checks, face plates and scratches—I realize there's been an increase in production schedule. You are handling a few more units than you've handled in the past, but in comparison to the standard you're familiar with, you're performing substantially below 100 percent effort.

Employee: Yes, I have been moving faster in the past three weeks since you've changed the line speed, but I have been watching out as best I could for rejects and defective units. I don't really think that I've been careless about this. The line is moving faster than before and it's pretty tough on us to watch this stuff. Every time we perform up to a level around here you guys change the line speed on us. It's not always easy to do the same thing as we've been doing all along and at the same time work faster. (Employee is being defensive in response to what he perceives as an attack by the foreman.)

Foreman: I can appreciate that. The change in line speed will create a problem. But this has gone on for about a week, and if there's something I can do in terms of your workplace layout, rearranging it in any way that may be helpful to you, I'll certainly do it, insofar as facilities will permit it.

Employee: Well, there's nothing you can do about workplace layout. I think as long as you're going to have us put out this many units an hour we can't possibly keep track of everything that we do when the line is moving slower. Have you talked to any of the other guys over there? How do you know these things are passing by me? Maybe they're not being picked up by Henry or the work station that comes after him. How do you know they're mine?

Foreman: Well, because the inspector is stationed just after your particular function and that's how I know that the rejects are occurring at your station. (Foreman personalizes.) Again, if there's anything I can do to be helpful to simplify what you're doing, I'll be glad to do it.

Employee: How about slowing down the line speed?

Foreman: We can't do that. We need the additional units.

Employee: Well, I can't do anything about that, Carl. I'm doing the very best job I can. Look, I've been working here for three years and you've never had trouble with me before. I'm surprised this is coming up now.

Foreman: Why don't we go over what you're required to do at this work station. Maybe you're doing something else. Something that isn't required.

Employee: What do you want?

Foreman: I'll reinstruct you at this point as to what I want in terms of identifying rejects. You may be spending more time than you should on the wrong things. Are you looking for screen holes?

Employee: Yes.

Foreman: Well, you don't have to do that here. Let's just go over that again. That's something you don't have to do.

Employee: O.K.

Foreman: We certainly appreciate your efforts in this respect, but it isn't required because it's done at

another point. (Foreman now reviews steps in production process.)

Employee: O.K.

Foreman: Do you think this reinstruction is going to help you? I've just pointed out some things you are not required to do.

Employee: Well, I'll try.

Foreman: O.K. We'll talk again in a day or so. I'm sure the problems will be eliminated by then.

Employee: O.K.

Critique The participants observed that the foreman focused on the employee, not on the problem, thus threatening the employee's self-esteem. He rejected the opportunity to involve the employee when he should have pursued it. In addition, by making all the suggestions, he did not give the employee the chance to correct the problem on his own. The foreman set a vague follow-up date and did not specify a time. Despite a more even tone than the first role-play, the foreman was not effective because he did not follow the key behavioral steps properly.

Role-Play 3

In this case, the foreman follows the learning points even though the employee is initially hostile. This results in the employee offering to solve the problem.

Foreman: Oh Jerry, thanks for stopping by. Could you sit down for a few minutes? I'd like to ask you a couple of questions please. Our weekly quality-control (QC) report has come out and they've identified several areas out on the line that have severe problems. They're seriously considering shutting down part of our line. One of those areas is yours. They've checked the operations prior to yours and after yours to see if it's anything there and so far they've come out pretty clean. We've got a problem and we really don't know what the cause is at this point in time.

Employee: Are you saying I'm doing a rotten job?

Foreman: I'm saying that there appear to be some problems in your area and we can't put our finger on them right now.

Employee: I don't know how you got that, Charlie. I've been on that job for four years now and I never had any problems before. I don't understand what's going on here.

Foreman: Don't take this as a personal attack on

you. Before we can get any kind of constructive job done, we have to first agree that there's a problem and QC has identified there is a problem. And it's a serious problem. Now in your work area, can you think of anything that would contribute to the cracking of that unit after it comes out?

Employee: It's that lousy timer they've got on that thing. I've been complaining about that for several months now and nobody's done anything about it. I think it must be the timer that's doing it because I've always run the job pretty well.

Foreman: All right. (Foreman writes down employee's suggestion.) We'll check that timer out tomorrow or, if we can, this afternoon. Is there anything else you think might be causing or contributing to the problem?

Employee: While you are checking into it, you might as well check out those engineers, because I don't think the product I've been getting in there the last couple of weeks is as good as it used to be. It just doesn't seem right to me, and maybe that's contributing to the problem.

Foreman: You think possibly the enamel itself has changed from what it was two or three months ago?

Employee: It seems so to me. Something's wrong.

Foreman: (Foreman writes down this second comment as well.) I'll check those two areas. I'll get back to you as soon as I know anything constructive —that should be by tomorrow morning—and I appreciate your ideas. This kind of thing is a common problem and the only way we're going to attack it is by using the experience that we both have. Thank you very much.

Employee: Thank you. If you check with those guys I'm sure we'll get things fixed up.

Critique This employee was fairly hostile at first, but the foreman was skillful in avoiding unnecessary conflict by not threatening his self-esteem. By writing them down, the foreman demonstrated that he valued the employee's suggestions.

Role-Play 4

This transcript illustrates an interaction successfully handled by the foreman.

Foreman: Hello, Max. How are you doing today?

Employee: Well.

Foreman: Come over here for a second. I've got a problem and I'd appreciate your help on this thing.

(Good approach by foreman, who asks for employee's help.)

Employee: All right.

Foreman: Max, you've been here for three years now and you've really been a good contributor to the operation. I know I can depend on you. I have in the past. I appreciate the work you've been doing, but we've got several problems with quality in this area. One of the problems is in the area of your work station. What's happening is that we've been getting units off the line with scratches along the tails. I wonder if you have any idea what might be causing this?

Employee: No, I don't.

Foreman: These scratches have been coming up in the past two days and the quality-control reports ended up on my desk about an hour ago and I thought I'd come down to this area since you know it better than anybody.

Employee: Are you saying you think the scratches are occurring at my work station or that I'm missing identifying scratches as they pass me?

Foreman: I don't know. I wanted to talk to you about it and get your thoughts on it. The scratches may be occurring at a work station prior to yours.

Employee: I follow the same handling procedures I always have, and I'm sure I'm not creating these scratches myself. As you know, they recently required us to work faster and increased the line speed, and it's conceivable that I haven't adapted to this speed yet and maybe I'm missing something.

Foreman: Is there anything you think I could do or you could do to see that this problem is taken care of? In other words, is there anything you can do specifically?

Employee: Yes. I could attempt to be more careful and take more time to look at these units as they go by. This may help. I would appreciate your doing one thing though.

Foreman: Sure.

Employee: Move the table on which the units are placed closer to the line. This would make a difference in walking time of about a couple of feet and might be helpful in solving the problem as far as my job is concerned.

Foreman: That's a very good suggestion, but we may not be able to do it because the carts may not be able to pass down the aisle. But let me check that out. (Foreman writes the suggestion down.) Is there anything else that I could be doing?

Employee: No, I don't think so. I'll do the best I can to identify these scratches, and if I see I can't keep up with it and can't do the job that should be done, I'll let you know.

Foreman: I really appreciate your help on this. And if you have any other ideas on what the cause might be or what the problems are with this, don't hesitate to let me know. In the meantime, I'll see about moving the table closer. Why don't you run another 200 units through? I'll check back with you about 3:30 and see what it looks like. (Foreman also writes down these comments and tells employee that he is simply noting what each of them will do as a follow-up.)

Employee: O.K.

Foreman: Great. I'll check back later at 3:30 and we'll see what's happened as a result. I really appreciate your helpful ideas on this, Max.

Employee: Any time, Phil.

Foreman: See you later.

Critique All the participants agreed that the foreman did a good job in this situation. He approached it as a joint problem-solving situation and was very supportive. Most important, he was specific about what each of them might do to solve the problem and he set a specific follow-up date.

SOME RESULTS OF BEHAVIOR-MODELING TRAINING

The first test of the behavior-modeling training approach in industry was in 1970 at three manufacturing plants of a major company (Sorcher, 1970). The project was carried out within an affirmative action context and its purpose was to reduce the turnover of new, young employees from disadvantaged backgrounds who were resigning at a rapid rate. Most were quitting their jobs after less than a month. The behavior-modeling program was initiated not only for the new employees but for their foremen as well. Employees were trained specifically on how to act when they were having difficulty learning their new tasks, how to act when their supervisor criticized their work, and how to act when other employees tried to persuade them to do as little as possible or to join them in resignation.

In parallel, but in different sessions, the foremen of new employees learned how to criticize, how to

dissuade a new employee from resigning, how to encourage or praise, and how to teach job skills to a new employee. In a real sense, both foremen and employees learned how to act toward each other in a manner designed to improve their relationship. A comparison of quit rates was made with similar groups where foremen and employees did not participate in a behavior-modeling program. The results revealed a 70 percent retention rate when foremen and employees participated in the behavior-modeling program versus only a 30 percent retention rate for the control group (Goldstein & Sorcher, 1974).

From among forty foremen in another manufacturing plant, ten foremen were randomly selected for behavior-modeling training and ten other foremen were identified as a control group. All foremen had previously participated in a more traditional training program. The criterion for this behavior-modeling training program was employee performance. Performance was measured in terms of actual productivity, which could be improved by increased employee effort or by spending less time in nonproductive activity.

Ten weeks after the program was completed, the performance of the employees reporting to both the trained and control-group foremen was compared. The results were very positive although not what was expected. Since foremen training was completed, the average performance for the employees reporting to trained foremen increased 3 percent while average performance for employees reporting to untrained foremen actually *declined* by over 17 percent. This interesting—and unexpected—finding was explained by the manager of manufacturing to be a consequence of generally bad business conditions resulted in an overall productivity decline, the trained foremen were able to manage their groups more effectively than the untrained supervisors (Goldstein & Sorcher, 1974).

In another large Midwestern appliance manufacturing plant, approximately 180 foremen were trained. One of the shop managers, who was trained as a behavior-modeling program instructor, measured the productivity of the employees reporting to eight of his foremen. He found an increase of 9 percent in units produced and an average decline in idle time of about 20 percent per week for each of the eight groups. Other groups in this plant reporting to foremen who had not yet been trained did not show any productivity improvement for the same three-month period (Goldstein & Sorcher, 1974).

An interesting evaluation of the behavior-modeling training approach was carried out in another company (Moses & Ritchie, 1976). Two groups of supervisors were chosen from two company locations. One group of ninety supervisors was exposed to the training program, while another group of ninety-three supervisors was not trained. Each of the supervisors was evaluated by a panel of judges on the ability to solve three problem situations. These problem situations included an employee with excessive absenteeism, a person with a complaint, and a third situation (alleged theft) which was not specifically dealt with during the training program to see how effectively the training concepts could be generalized. The success of each of the supervisors in both the trained and untrained groups in dealing with these problems was evaluated by the panel of judges. The results demonstrated the effectiveness of the behavior-modeling approach to training. Respectively, 84 percent of the trained supervisors were judged to perform exceptionally well or above average in how well they handled problem discussions with employees. Conversely, only 32 percent of the untrained supervisors were so rated. Further, 33 percent of the untrained supervisors were rated as below average or poor in handling problem discussions, while only 6 percent of the trained supervisors were rated below average or poor. The results are especially impressive since the trained and untrained groups were judged to be virtually identical prior to training.

Recently, the focus of a major research project was on the behavior and skills of 124 first- and second-level managers of administrative, technical, and professional employees. A dramatic improvement in interpersonal skills was found as a result of behavior-modeling training. In this study, ten training situations were identified during discussions with several groups of first- and second-level managers of technical people. Included among the ten situations in the managerial program were "How to Conduct a Performance Appraisal," "How to Discuss Salary Change," and "How to Discuss Career Planning with an Employee." These discussions to identify training needs focused on interpersonal situations which met these conditions:

1 Managers are frequently involved in them.
2 Managers often experience difficulty or discomfort in handling them.
3 Managers would like to have some guidance in these situations.
4 There are long-lasting and broad implications for subsequent employee performance and the manager-employee relationship.

This program was tested at major plants in six widely dispersed cities. To evaluate training effectiveness, trained managers were compared within one month after training with other managers at their location along four dimensions: (1) ability to maintain an employee's self-esteem, (2) ability to establish open and clear communication, (3) ability to maintain control of the situation, and (4) how well the objective of a given manager-employee interaction was accomplished.

Another group of randomly selected managers at both locations were identified as "judges" who would actually make the comparison. The judges had no knowledge of who was trained, the nature of the training, or the key behaviors.

After both the judge and the manager (either trained or control) were given brief statements describing the situations and conditions to be enacted, each judge took the employee role. The judges were instructed to react toward the manager as they thought an employee might react in that situation. Following the role-play, the judges rated the managers along the four dimensions. The evaluation procedures were especially designed to minimize rating bias. Three typical situations were selected for role-play evaluations: motivating a poor performer, recognizing an average employee, and giving a work assignment.

The trained managers were rated significantly higher in interpersonal effectiveness than the untrained managers. Further, the most dramatic aspect of this research occurred four months after the first evaluation. Judge ratings were again obtained to see whether change occurred over time, and the trained managers were rated as even *more* effective than previously. This is an especially important finding and it is consistent with the underlying rationale concerning transfer of training (Burnaska, 1976).

An evaluation of a behavior-modeling program was carried out with forty first-line supervisors

(Latham & Saari, 1979). The trained and control groups each consisted of twenty supervisors. The training program consisted of nine training modules (Sorcher, 1974) which included typical situations, such as recognition, motivating a poor performer, correcting poor work habits, and handling a complaint. Latham and Saari reported that the trained supervisors were significantly better than control-group supervisors on behavior simulations collected three months after training and on performance ratings collected one year after training. Superintendents who rated supervisors did not know who had been trained. Further, a learning test (comprising eighty-five situational questions) administered six months after training showed similar results.

An important point is that the superintendents of the control-group supervisors were instructed to praise them for engaging in the behaviors that the trained group was taught in the classroom. However, there was no change in the control group's behavior until *after* they had also been trained. After training the supervisors formerly in the control group, there was no significant difference between the initial trained group and the former control groups.

In a recent study Meyer and Raich (1980) evaluated the results of behavior-modeling training in a somewhat different situation. They designed an experiment to compare the sales results of salespersons trained with behavior modeling, with fifty-eight salespersons in the trained group and sixty-four salespersons in a control group. Sales records for the half-year preceding training were compared with sales records for the six months after training. Typical modules which were included in the training program included "Approaching a Customer" and "Closing the Sale."

The results of this study show that the average per-hour earnings for trained salespersons increased after training from $9.27 to $9.95. On the other hand, the average per-hour earnings of the control-group salespersons (not given behavior-modeling training) declined over the same period from $9.71 to $9.43. These figures contrast a 7 percent improvement with a 3 percent decline in average earnings.

OTHER APPLICATIONS OF BEHAVIOR MODELING

This training technique can be readily applied to a wide variety of situations where interpersonal skills

are important. For example, affirmative action programs are an excellent umbrella for a behavior-modeling approach. Within this context, some programs have already successfully taught young women supervisors to manage older male subordinates, other programs have taught supervisors how to respond to angry employee complaints of discrimination, and foremen and managers have been taught how to encourage minority employees to explore promotional opportunities.

Employees represent an interesting opportunity for training—why not teach employees how to be employees? They have roles, just as supervisors do, and their roles often involve considerable interpersonal contact. For example, in one program, a group of employees were taught how to obtain additional factual data from union organizers, while their foremen were taught how to respond to employee concerns about management-union issues. Employees can also be trained how to respond to constructive criticism, how to respond to a delegated assignment, and how to initiate a career discussion.

CONCLUSION

As with any new process or innovation, predictability of outcome is the sign of dependability. The results of the behavior-modeling process appear to be dependable in a variety of training situations and environments. Organizations and individuals who implement behavior modeling should, however, make special efforts to measure its effects. With evidence of a positive impact, the program and its proponents are likely to be even more effective. In addition a great deal of work is involved in setting up a behavior-modeling program, more than is involved in setting up most other training programs. This extra effort can only be justified if results are provided showing that it is effective. Based on the research done so far this should present no problem, since study after study has shown the superiority of the behavior-modeling approach.

REFERENCES

Burnaska, R. F. The effects of behavioral modeling training upon managers' behaviors and the employees' perceptions. *Personal Psychology,* 1976, **29,** 329–335.
Goldstein, A. P., & Sorcher, M. *Changing supervisor behavior.* New York: Pergamon, 1974.

Johnson, P. D., & Sorcher, M. Behavior modeling train-ing: Why, how, and what results. *Journal of European Training,* 1976, **5,** 62–69.

Kraut, A. I. Developing managerial skills via modeling techniques: Some positive research findings—a symposi-um. *Personnel Psychology,* 1976, **29,** 325–328.

Latham, G. P., & Saari, L. M. Application of social-learning theory to training supervisors through behavior modeling. *Journal of Applied Psychology,* 1979, **64,** 239–335.

Meyer, H. H., & Raich, M. S. An objective evaluation of a sales training program. Unpublished report, 1980.

Moses, J. L., & Ritchie, R. J. Supervisory relation-ships training: A behavioral evaluation of a behavior modeling program. *Personnel Psychology,* 1976, **29,** 337–343.

Sorcher, M. Behavior modeling for training supervisors. General Electric Personnel Research Report, 1970.

———. A behavior modification approach to supervisor training. *Professional Psychology,* 1971, **2,** 401.

———, & Goldstein, A. P. A behavior modeling approach in training. *Personnel Administration,* 1972, **35,** 35–41.

Spool, M. D. Training programs for observers of behavior: A review. *Personnel Psychology,* 1978, **31,** 853–888.

Reading 21

What Every Personnel Director Should Know About Management Promotion Decisions

Manuel London

Much of our knowledge of personnel selection deals with how professionals, such as interviewers, evalu-ate and choose candidates for entry-level positions. A great deal is also devoted to the technical aspects of selection, including test development and valida-tion. However, little attention has been devoted to how employees are selected for promotion.

Unlike hiring decisions, promotion decisions are generally not made by personnel experts. This is particularly true of management promotion deci-sions, which are usually made by individual manag-ers or groups of managers at any level or in any function. Nevertheless, the personnel staff may be asked to provide advice or establish formal proce-dures that guide the promotion process. Therefore, the personnel expert must be familiar with making promotion decisions and with the many factors that affect these decisions.

PROMOTION FROM WITHIN

Most large organizations have a formal or informal policy of promoting from within. In a survey of 33 industries that make special efforts to identify or enhance managerial talent, 96 percent were found to believe in promotion from within.[1] Only rapidly growing organizations that didn't have enough quali-fied personnel to fill higher positions selected indi-viduals from external sources. Other studies with larger samples have found similar results.[2]

Promotion from within occurs in several ways. One is to move an employee up a level within the same department. This is likely to happen when the vacant position requires a level of expertise that is not available elsewhere in the organization and qualified candidates are available in the unit. When the major qualifications of a vacant position involve general managerial skills, the search for qualified candidates can be organizationwide. In this case, an individual in one department may be promoted to the next organization level in another department. Of course, a vacancy can be filled by an employee at the same level who is willing to make a lateral transfer for a raise in pay, increase in status or a more interesting job. This could be viewed as a promotion within the same job level. Another type of promotion occurs when a valued employee re-ceives a change in title and salary as a reward, although there may be little change in job responsi-bilities.

Promotion from within has a number of advantag-es. Employees are likely to feel more secure and identify their long-term interests with an organiza-tion that guarantees them the first choice at job opportunities.[3] Another consideration is that many jobs above entry-level management require prior experience with the policies, procedures and products of the organization. Lower-level positions are then viewed as training ground for higher-level jobs. Training time would be considerably longer if individuals were hired from outside sources for higher jobs. In fact, in many organizations, particularly new industries, only inside sources provide adequate training. Expensive management development programs make companies who invest in these programs reluctant to look elsewhere for their top-level managers. Also, more information is available about current employees than would be available about external applicants. This decreases the risk in selecting an employee for a responsible position.

While a policy of promotion from within would seemingly lead to stagnation and foster the proverbial "Organization Man,"[4] there is evidence to indicate that this is not a problem. In their longitudinal study of managers in the Bell System, Bray, Campbell and Grant[5] reported that employees who were promoted into middle-management positions were not mirror images of one another. They were uniformly high on organizational identification, but they had varied job experiences and diverse life interests. Research on such standard devices as the assessment center has produced similar results.[6]

MANAGEMENT INVOLVEMENT IN PROMOTION DECISIONS

In many cases, the immediate supervisor must search for qualified candidates and make a choice when a vacancy arises. This process may be carried out in close consultation with one or more higher-level supervisors who ultimately have to approve the choice. On the other hand, the immediate supervisor may have almost total control over the decision.

The decision maker's individual characteristics may influence the process. For example, some managers seek all available candidates and investigate each one thoroughly. Other managers are less methodical or less compulsive in making promotion decisions. Politically sensitive decision makers may be influenced by higher-level managers who overtly or covertly exert pressure and might be swayed by what they judge to be politically wise for their own careers. The similarity of a candidate to the decision maker with respect to non-job-related characteristics may also bias the choice. In general, people are usually more attracted to individuals who seem similar to themselves.[7] A number of other characteristics and behavioral tendencies of the supervisor may influence the promotion process. These include the supervisor's competence, job experience, patience, willingness to take risks, and ability to integrate diverse information.[8]

The nature of the situation will influence the amount of discretion the supervisor has over a promotion decision. For example, let's say a new position is created in a unit as a result of an increased work load, a change in technology, or a different project assignment. The supervisor may be granted considerable discretion in designing the new position and determining the necessary qualifications that correspond to its specified duties and responsibilities. This situation may also allow the supervisor to write the job description with one individual in mind, thereby eliminating the need to search for other qualified candidates.

However, in many other cases, the immediate supervisor's latitude is severely curtailed. Here are three examples:

1 A position is left vacant when an employee transfers. A replacement must be found as soon as possible, and the immediate supervisor is not given enough time to conduct a thorough search and evaluation.

2 The personnel department requires that a minority or female employee be selected for a vacant middle-management position in order to meet an affirmative action objective, but a qualified white male has already been identified. Consequently, the decision maker either rejects the favored candidate and continues the search or delays the decision, hoping that a minority or female will be promoted into another position in the same job classification, thereby avoiding the need to consider affirmative action objectives in this decision.

3 The person who is selected for promotion will probably remain in the department longer than the immediate supervisor. As a result, the manager above the supervisor wants to have more say in identifying and evaluating candidates and making the final choice.

The effects of EEO on promotion decisions deserve special comment. Assuring equal employment opportunity is a major consideration in most organizations today. Like other personnel practices, such as hiring, transfers and layoffs, management promotion decisions are subject to EEO regulations.[9]

Discrimination barring women and minorities from higher level jobs is illegal, and the courts have not been lax in imposing remedies or obtaining stringent settlements.[10] Often, the first step in a promotion process is to determine whether affirmative action obligations will influence the choice of candidates.

IDENTIFYING CANDIDATES FOR PROMOTION

The source of candidates for promotion may be word of mouth, company personnel records or promotion lists based upon performance or managerial potential ratings. Many companies have formal programs for coordinating managers' careers and assessing advancement potential. Several examples of such programs are reviewed below.

A Human Resource Planning Program

Some companies have management development programs that assure the availability of sufficient numbers of candidates for projected job vacancies at all management levels. For example, Xerox has established a human resource planning program for zeroing in on the most valuable people and providing them with the development they will need for top-management positions.[11] All incumbent managers, as well as nonmanagement employees judged potentially promotable to the ranks of management within 24 months, complete a personal-history form. The form covers education, work experience, short and long-term career objectives and possibility of relocation. Employees and their supervisors discuss the realism of these objectives and agree on logical job moves to realize attainable career goals. They also decide upon an action plan for enhancing current job performance as well as for preparing for future assignments. The plan may require taking developmental courses, tackling special job assignments, or obtaining lateral transfers for training in other jobs. After higher-level management has approved the action plan, it is put into effect, and the information is entered in a human resource data base. When a vacancy occurs, the computer identifies candidates with appropriate work experience and educational background. The candidates are then evaluated on the basis of their performance strengths and weaknesses. Being on the human resource planning program does not guarantee promotion—it simply means that an employee's eligibility for promotion has been reviewed.

Management Potential Ratings

Ratings of potential for advancement can be used to formulate lists of promotable employees. For example, one department in a large company utilizes a procedure in which a manager's job performance and management potential are rated by the individual's supervisor once a year. The company recognizes that these two concepts are independent. That is, a person's job performance may be excellent, but his or her managerial skills may or may not be sufficient for future advancement. After the yearly rating, each group of supervisors at the same level confers with their supervisor about the performance and potential of their immediate subordinates. Together, they rank-order employees on the basis of their management potential. This list, which is kept highly confidential, is used to identify the top candidates for promotion when a vacancy arises.

Several companies in different industries have independently developed committee systems to assess the advancement potential of management employees and recommend managers for vacant positions. In one program, the potential of subordinates within the departments represented by each committee is evaluated approximately once every year. Committee meetings are then held to make promotion and transfer decisions as position vacancies arise. All such decisions are made in accordance with the company's affirmative action objectives. The committee responsible for making a decision identifies candidates from among employees rated as having high potential, while other committees are invited to submit the names of their most qualified candidates. The position is advertised in a company bulletin, and interested employees are encouraged to submit their own names. The immediate supervisor of the position is given an opportunity to respond to the committee's recommendation. If the supervisor can adequately justify disagreement with the decision, the committee then resumes the choice process. Final approval is obtained from a higher-level committee.

Other Identification Techniques

When management potential ratings or human resource programs are not available, informal methods are used to identify candidates for promotion. A department head trying to fill a vacancy can ask other department heads for suggestions. A notice of the vacancy may be circulated throughout the company. Supervisors searching for candidates may rely upon their own knowledge of qualified employees in the organization. The personnel department can usually supply names of eligible minorities or females. Sometimes a search is not necessary at all. This occurs when an obviously qualified individual is already employed in the department. If the person has been "groomed" for the position, the supervisor may assume that there are no other qualified employees in the organization. When several candidates are identified, an evaluation process is necessary to make the final selection. When there is only one candidate, the supervisor will probably be required to justify the selection of that individual.

EVALUATING CANDIDATES

There are a number of potential sources of information which can be used for evaluating and comparing candidates, many of which can also aid in identifying candidates. The most common types of information are tests, assessment centers, job experience in the organization, past participation in management training courses, seniority, performance appraisal forms, recommendations, interviews, and sponsors in top management.

Tests are used for promotion decisions to evaluate candidates' intellectual abilities and personalities. The selection and use of valid tests usually requires the services of a qualified psychologist. While large companies may have one or more psychologists on the staff, smaller ones usually engage outside consultants to evaluate candidates for particular positions. One procedure is to administer a battery of tests to assess mental ability, personality and/or interests. If tests are not administered when an employee is being considered for a promotion, test scores obtained at the time of hire may be reviewed. One study found that only about 40 percent of the companies they surveyed used tests as part of the assessment for promotion into management, but they concluded that "tests are ignored more often than not as decision making aids for internal promotions."[12] Tests may be given more consideration for the first movement into management. At higher levels, personal judgment seems to be the prime criterion.[13]

The most useful tests for measuring managerial ability are behavioral exercises. These include in-

baskets, group discussions and business games. Often these exercises are combined in *assessment centers* consisting of multiple simulations, interviews and psychological tests. This assessment procedure allows behavior to be observed and evaluated under controlled standardized conditions. Trained observers, usually higher-level managers in the organization, rate the participants in the assessment center on such dimensions as communication skill, resistance to stress, and ability to organize and plan. Pioneered by AT&T, assessment centers have been widely adopted by such major corporations as Standard Oil of Ohio, General Electric, Sears, Wickes and J. C. Penney, as well as several consulting firms specializing in their application.[14] Assessment centers are particularly useful since all participants are assessed on the same behaviors regardless of job history or prior opportunities to demonstrate their managerial skills.[15] Also, the behaviors observed are samples of what could be expected on the job, not signs or traits that may or may not be associated with specific behaviors.

Candidates for promotion can be also compared on the basis of their *job experience in the organization*. Promising employees are sometimes identified early in their careers and given special developmental experiences that prepare them for higher-level positions. Even when a formalized early identification program does not exist, promotion decisions are likely to be based on candidates' career experiences. Some jobs, especially key-line positions, may be viewed as requisites for higher level positions, and appropriate career planning is helpful for advancement.

Another basis for selecting candidates for promotion is their *past participation in management training courses*. Some organizations have specially designed training programs at universities or company schools. Other organizations send their personnel to short courses offered by local colleges or consulting firms.

Seniority can be a determinant of who receives a promotion. The longer a person has been employed by the organization, the more relevant experience the individual is assumed to have. Seniority is an objective criterion which can remove the burden of choice when a promotion decision must be made. However, the most qualified candidates are not always those with the most seniority.

Performance appraisal forms completed by current and previous supervisors can be helpful, particularly when the appraisals are recent and contain descriptions of the candidate's past behavior. Rating scales that limit the supervisor's responses to overall evaluations provide less information. Appraisals are usually more accurate when supervisors are trained to use the forms.[16]

Recommendations are another important source of information. The person giving the recommendation has a reputation to protect which supposedly would make him or her reluctant to give an inaccurate report. However, a supervisor who relishes the chance to lose a marginal performer may exaggerate the individual's strengths. Of course, some supervisors wouldn't want to spoil anyone's chances for advancement regardless of their performance record. Extremely glowing recommendations are usually questioned for these reasons. In general, the value of recommendations is subject to the ability of the person giving the recommendation to accurately express a viewpoint either in writing or orally.[17]

Interviews with candidates are not as widely used for promotion decisions as they are for selection of new-hires. The amount of information about current employees under consideration for promotion is usually far greater than is available for external applicants. Also, the decision maker is often personally acquainted with the candidates for promotion or knows people who are. Conducting interviews amounts to announcing that a search process is under way. Supervisors who wish to avoid raising candidates' expectations may be reluctant to interview anyone until the most qualified candidate has been identified by other means. At this time, an interview may ascertain whether the supervisor can work effectively with the candidate.

A "sponsor" in top management can sometimes guide an employee's path to higher levels in the hierarchy. For example, in a study of a giant conglomerate, Kanter[18] found that higher-level sponsors known as "godfathers" wangled promotions for their protégés despite claims to the contrary from top management and a rating system that tried to make advancement more open and equitable. "To get ahead, you need a manager strong enough to stand up for and fight for subordinates in places where they could not fight for themselves."[19] The powerful sponsor could highlight a person's strengths, distinguishing that individual from the crowd of potential competitors. However, this is not necessarily a bad system. If the organization trusts the judgment of its higher-level managers for other major decisions, why not for promotions? This may be a reasonable argument as long as the organization's EEO obligations are met.

THE FINAL CHOICE

Several decision-making strategies may be followed to make the final choice. The most difficult and time-consuming strategy is to evaluate all candidates as thoroughly as possible. When sufficient information has been collected regarding each person, a meaningful comparison can be made. However, this type of decision is complicated when different types of information are available about different candidates or when several people appear equally qualified. A somewhat simpler procedure is to screen all candidates quickly, and then thoroughly evaluate only the top ones. A less exact method is to evaluate each candidate one by one, stopping the evaluation process when a suitable individual is identified. While the best person for the job might not even be considered using this procedure, the person chosen is likely to be able to perform the job adequately.

Another decision strategy, mentioned earlier, occurs when a decision maker has one candidate in mind who seems to be highly qualified. The decision maker then searches for other candidates for comparison purposes. The author recalls the case of a supervisor who favored an acquaintance from a regional office for a promotion. To appear unbiased, the supervisor began a half-hearted search locally and discovered a candidate with equal if not superior qualifications. Recognizing that choosing the local candidate would be politically wiser, the supervisor rejected the initial front runner. This example indicates that the value of a thorough search and evaluation may not be evident before it is carried out.

The final step in the promotion process is usually to obtain approval at higher levels. A standard format used in some companies is to prepare a proposal which includes a brief job description and a list of potential candidates. The first name on the list is generally the preferred candidate. This procedure allows higher-level managers to exercise discretion in making the final choice. Finally, the recommendation to promote the top candidate often must be approved by the personnel department, which reviews the decision with respect to the company's affirmative action objectives.

Once the approval process is complete, the candidate is offered the job. Salary, starting dates, relocation procedures, if necessary, and other details are discussed at this time. Asking the employee to relocate is becoming increasingly difficult in these days of dual-career families and the preeminence of non-job-related activities in many peoples' lives.[20] Some individuals would rather decline a promotion than uproot their families, ask a spouse to change jobs, or relinquish community ties. Others would prefer to avoid the stress of increased responsibility that accompanies a promotion. If the top candidate rejects the offer, the decision maker must reevaluate the remaining candidates or reactivate the search process.

VALIDATING PROMOTION DECISIONS

Validating promotion decisions refers to determining the accuracy of the selection process. Was the right information utilized in a manner that resulted in an optimum choice? This question is difficult to answer for several reasons. First of all, the numbers of people promoted into similar positions are likely to be too small to make predictive validity feasible (i.e., statistically relating predictor scores to later performance). Second, the decisions are made on the basis of diverse information. For example, assessment center ratings may be the prime source of data for several candidates who are relatively new to the organization, while potential ratings may be the prime source for those with more tenure. This could seem like comparing apples and oranges to the person in charge of the decision. Certainly that individual must be able to synthesize diverse information and arrive at a final judgment. Third, the organization may want to predict on the basis of dimensions that are not important now but that may, however, be important to the position in the future. Furthermore, since certain jobs may be used as stepping stones for individuals who are expected to be of future value to the organization, a prime criterion could be future promotability. This requires predicting on the basis of dimensions that are

not important for the next-level job but that may be so for higher-level jobs. Such criteria may not be justifiable from the standpoint of equal employment opportunity if few people eventually reach those higher positions.[21] A fourth problem in assessing the accuracy of promotion decisions is the range of available candidates. Incompetent subordinates are usually terminated early or shunted aside into less valued positions. Therefore, the promotion process is not one of separating the chaff from the wheat, as is the selection of new hires, but one of identifying the cream of the crop. Consequently, the decision maker must be highly sensitive to subtle differences between candidates, differences that cannot be measured by several simple indices. Obviously, all of these considerations complicate the promotion choice process and mean that there can be no simple index of validity.

Despite these problems, several suggestions can be made for increasing the quality of an organization's promotion decisions. One is to develop a standardized, equitable promotion policy that specifies the procedures to be followed. This, of course, is easier said than done, since a policy must be accepted by the managers who are expected to use it and must be applicable in many different situations. In general, a clear policy that delineates criteria for promotion should be communicated to all employees so as to encourage the sort of behavior that is required for promotion.[22]

Another idea is to require that each promotion decision be justified to those at higher levels or to all interested employees. This may take the form of written answers to such questions as, "How were the candidates identified?" "Was the information used to evaluate candidates job related?" and "Were all the candidates given equal treatment?" While not a substitute for ascertaining the validity of specific selection devices, the answers could affect employee trust in the decision process and general acceptance of the decision.

An additional idea is to internally advertise position openings (job posting) and encourage employees to nominate themselves. Such a procedure would be valuable in assuring that all interested employees are given some consideration and in helping employees to direct their own careers.

In any case, the variety of methods discussed here demonstrates that no one procedure will be advantegous in all situations. Each organization must develop its own promotion process to assure that the most qualified employees are promoted and that the choices are in compliance with EEO regulations and goals.

REFERENCES

1 J. P. Campbell, M. D. Dunnette, E. E. Lawler III and K. E. Weick. *Managerial Behavior, Performance, and Effectiveness* (New York: McGraw-Hill, 1970), p. 23.

2 L. C. Megginson. "Management Selection, Development, and Motivation in the United States," *Management International*, 2 (1963): 97–106; Scientific American, *The Big Business Executive/1964* (New York: Scientific American, 1965).

3 Campbell, Dunnette, Lawler and Weick. *Managerial Behavior*, p. 443.

4 W. H. Whyte, Jr.. *The Organization Men* (Garden City, New York: Doubleday Anchor Books, 1956).

5 D. W. Bray, R. J. Campbell and D. L. Grant. *Formative Years in Business: A Long-Term AT&T Study of Managerial Lives* (New York: Wiley, 1973).

6 W. E. Dodd and A. I. Kraut. "Will Management Assessment Centers Insure Selection of the Same Old Types?" (Paper delivered at the American Psychological Association Convention, Miami Beach, Florida, 1970).

7 Campbell, Dunnette, Lawler and Weick. *Managerial Behavior*, p. 444.

8 K. R. MacCrimmon and R. N. Taylor. "Decision Making and Problem Solving," ed. M.D. Dunnette, *Handbook of Industrial and Organizational Psychology* (Chicago: Rand McNally, 1976), pp. 1397–1453.

9 Equal Employment Opportunity Commission, "Guide-lines on Employment Selection Procedures," Federal Register, 35 (1970): 12333–12335.

10 Bureau of National Affairs, Inc., "District Court Approves AT&T Agreement Granting $15 Million in Job Inequities," *Daily Labor Report,* January 19, 1973; W. E. Fulmer, "Supervisory Selection: The Acid Test of Affirmative Action," *Personnel,* 53 (1976): 40–46.

11 D. M. Reid. "Human Resource Planning: A Tool for People Development," *Personnel,* 54 (1977): 15–25.

12 Campbell, Dunnette, Lawler and Weick. *Managerial Behavior,* p. 28.

13 G. L. Freeman and E. K. Taylor. *How to Pick Leaders* (New York: Funk & Wagnalls, 1950).

14 R. B. Finkle. "Managerial Assessment Centers," ed. M.D. Dunnette, *Handbook of Industrial and Organizational Psychology, pp. 889–936.*

15 A. I. Kraut. "A Hard Look at Management Assessment Centers and Their Future," *Personnel Journal,* 51 (1972): 317–326.

16 G. P. Latham, K. N. Wexley and E. D. Pursell. "Training Managers to Minimize Errors in the Observation of Behavior," *Journal of Applied Psychology,* 60 (1975): 550–555.

17 R. M Guion. *Personnel Testing* (New York: McGraw-Hill, 1965), p. 14.

18 R. J. Kanter. "Power Games in the Corporation," *Psychology Today,* 11 (1977): 48–53.

19 Kanter, Ibid.

20 D. T. Hall and F. J. Hall. "What's New in Career Management?" *Organizational Dynamics,* 1976, pp. 17–33.

21 Equal Employment Opportunity Commission, "Guide-lines on Employment Selection Procedures," pp. 12333–12335.

22 G. Gemmill and D. DeSalvia. "The Promotion Beliefs of Managers As a Factor in Career Progress: An Exploratory Study," *Sloan Management Review,* Winter, 1977, pp. 75–81.

Part Three

Design of Work and Reward Systems

Chapter 7

Work Design

What constitutes a well-designed job? Until relatively recently, most guidelines for how work should be designed emphasized simple considerations of organizational efficiency: smooth workflow, minimal wasted effort, direct managerial control over the work, minimal training requirements, and so on. Industrial engineers conducted studies to determine the "best" job design (which often turned out to be the simplest possible job), time and motion analysts identified the most efficient way for the job to be performed, and management provided close supervision to ensure that the work was being done exactly as it was supposed to be done. Behavioral scientists had little to say about the design of work other than to be sure that jobs did not make demands on people that exceeded human capabilities, and to help in the selection of individuals who were qualified for the jobs.

In recent years, these guidelines have been undergoing change. In this country, the pioneering work of Frederick Herzberg and Louis Davis on the psychological and social aspects of job design has led to an increased awareness of the human part of person-job relationships. Numerous organizations have undertaken projects aimed at enriching jobs, and in many cases these experiments have improved both the quality of worklife for employees and organizational productivity. Overseas, even broader changes in jobs and work systems have been carried out, in the spirit of "industrial democracy."

The readings in this chapter were chosen to reflect current thought and practice of behavioral science about the design of work—including discussion of some of the problems that have appeared as increasing numbers of organizations have undertaken activities to redesign work. The chapter begins with one of the classics in the field: "One More Time: How Do You Motivate Employees?" by Herzberg. After exploring some common myths about employee motivation, Herzberg shows how his motivator-hygiene theory provides a way to build motivation directly into the work itself—that is, to "enrich" jobs. A case study is provided to illustrate the application of the principles, and to show the kinds of results that can be obtained when jobs are enriched.

The next reading, by Hackman, provides an alternative way of understanding why many employees respond positively to enriched work. Hackman explains how the characteristics of jobs can prompt employees to be internally motivated to do good work. He then draws on this model to provide some specific guidelines for proceeding with the redesign of work for individuals and for interacting teams of employees. Included is a discussion of ways to diagnose work systems prior to redesign, and some cautions about differences among people in their psychological readiness for enriched work.

In the third reading, Walton takes a broad look at ten years of work innovations in the United States. Walton finds that improving the design of work systems generally results in neither extreme successes nor extreme failures. He concludes that work innovations are not concrete solutions to specific problems, but instead represent a potentially valuable *approach* to looking at a variety of quality-of-worklife and productivity problems. He examines the lessons that have been learned in experiments to date, and concludes that work improvement efforts that stress *both* productivity and quality of worklife as goals are more likely to succeed than those that focus on one of these goals to the exclusion of the other.

The final reading in the chapter, by Fein, takes a skeptical look at work-redesign projects and their outcomes. Fein reviews the research literature on the topic and concludes that there are few, if any, genuine cases where job enrichment has been applied successfully to a large, heterogeneous workforce. He suggests that one reason for this is that the intrinsic nature of the job is of secondary importance to many blue-collar workers; instead, he argues, pay, job security, and work rules dominate the concerns of these workers. It is interesting to contrast the views and findings of the first three articles with those of this one—and to speculate about ways that they might be reconciled, if indeed a reconciliation is possible.

Reading 22

One More Time: How Do You Motivate Employees?

Frederick Herzberg

How many articles, books, speeches, and work-shops have pleaded plaintively, "How do you get an employee to do what I want him to do?"

The psychology of motivation is tremendously complex, and what has been unraveled with any degree of assurance is small indeed. But the dismal ratio of knowledge to speculation has not dampened the enthusiasm for new forms of snake oil that are constantly coming on the market, many of them with academic testimonials. Doubtless this article will have no depressing impact on the market for snake oil, but since the ideas expressed in it have been tested in many corporations and other organizations, it will help—I hope—to redress the imbalance in the aforementioned ratio.

"MOTIVATING" WITH KITA

In lectures to industry on the problem, I have found that the audiences are anxious for quick and practical answers, so I will begin with a straightforward, practical formula for moving people.

What is the simplest, surest, and most direct way of getting someone to do something? Ask him? But if he responds that he does not want to do it, then that calls for a psychological consultation to determine the reason for his obstinacy. Tell him? His response shows that he does not understand you, and now an expert in communication methods has to be brought in to show you how to get through to him. Give him a monetary incentive? I do not need to remind the reader of the complexity and difficulty involved in setting up and administering an incentive system. Show him? This means a costly training program. We need a simple way.

Every audience contains the "direct action" manager who shouts, "Kick him!" And this type of manager is right. The surest and least circumlocuted way of getting someone to do something is to kick him in the pants—give him what might be called the KITA.

Negative Physical KITA This is a literal application of the term and was frequently used in the past. It has, however, three major drawbacks: (1) it is inelegant; (2) it contradicts the precious image of benevolence that most organizations cherish; and (3) since it is a physical attack, it directly stimulates the autonomic nervous system, and this often results in negative feedback—the employee may just kick you in return. These factors give rise to certain taboos against negative physical KITA.

The psychologist has come to the rescue of those who are no longer permitted to use negative physical KITA. He has uncovered infinite sources of psychological vulnerabilities and the appropriate methods to play tunes on them. "He took my rug away"; "I wonder what he meant by that"; "The boss is always going around me"—These symptomatic expressions of ego sores that have been rubbed raw are the result of application of:

Negative Psychological KITA This has several advantages over negative physical KITA. First, the cruelty is not visible; the bleeding is internal and comes much later. Second, since it affects the higher cortical centers of the brain with its inhibitory powers, it reduces the possibility of physical backlash. Third, since the number of psychological pains that a person can feel is almost infinite, the direction and site possibilities of the KITA are increased many times. Fourth, the person administering the kick can manage to be above it all and let the system accomplish the dirty work. Fifth, those who practice it receive some ego satisfaction (one-upmanship), whereas they would find drawing blood abhorrent.

Reprinted, by permission of the *Harvard Business Review*. "One more time: How do you motivate employees?" by Frederick Herzberg (January–February 1968). Copyright © 1968 by the President & Fellows of Harvard College, all rights reserved.
Author's note: I should like to acknowledge the contributions that Robert Ford of the American Telephone and Telegraph Company has made to the ideas expressed in this paper, and in particular to the successful application of these ideas in improving work performance and the job satisfaction of employees.

Finally, if the employee does complain, he can always be accused of being paranoid, since there is no tangible evidence of an actual attack.

Now what does negative KITA accomplish? If I kick you in the rear (physically or psychologically), who is motivated? *I* am motivated; *you* move! Negative KITA does not lead to motivation, but to movement. So:

Positive KITA   Let us consider motivation. If I say to you, "Do this for me or the company, and in return I will give you a reward, an incentive, more status, a promotion, all the quid pro quos that exist in the industrial organization," am I motivating you? The overwhelming opinion I receive from management people is, "Yes, this is motivation."

I have a year-old Schnauzer. When it was a small puppy and I wanted it to move, I kicked it in the rear and it moved. Now that I have finished its obedience training, I hold up a dog biscuit when I want the Schnauzer to move. In this instance, who is motivated—I or the dog? The dog wants the biscuit, but it is I who want it to move. Again, I am the one who is motivated, and the dog is the one who moves. In this instance all I did was apply KITA frontally; I exerted a pull instead of a push. When industry wishes to use such positive KITAs, it has available an incredible number and variety of dog biscuits (jelly beans for humans) to wave in front of the employee to get him to jump.

Why is it that managerial audiences are quick to see that negative KITA is *not* motivation, while they are almost unanimous in their judgment that positive KITA *is* motivation? It is because negative KITA is rape, and positive KITA is seduction. But it is infinitely worse to be seduced than to be raped; the latter is an unfortunate occurrence, while the former signifies that you were a party to your own downfall. This is why positive KITA is so popular: it is a tradition; it is in the American way. The organization does not have to kick you; you kick yourself.

Myths about Motivation

Why is KITA not motivation? If I kick my dog (from the front or the back), he will move. And when I want him to move again, what must I do? I must kick him again. Similarly, I can charge a man's battery, and then recharge it, and recharge it again.

But it is only when he has his own generator that we can talk about motivation. He then needs no outside stimulation. He *wants* to do it.

With this in mind, we can review some positive KITA personnel practices that were developed as attempts to instill "motivation":

1. *Reducing time spent at work*—This represents a marvelous way of motivating people to work—getting them off the job! We have reduced (formally and informally) the time spent on the job over the last 50 or 60 years until we are finally on the way to the "6½-day weekend." An interest variant of this approach is the development of off-hour recreation programs. The philosophy here seems to be that those who play together, work together. The fact is that motivated people seek more hours of work, not fewer.

2. *Spiraling wages*—Have these motivated people? Yes, to seek the next wage increase. Some medievalists still can be heard to say that a good depression will get employees moving. They feel that if rising wages don't or won't do the job, perhaps reducing them will.

3. *Fringe benefits*—Industry has outdone the most welfare-minded of welfare states in dispensing cradle-to-the-grave succor. One company I know of had a informal "fringe benefit of the month club" going for a while. The cost of fringe benefits in this country has reached approximately 25% of the wage dollar, and we still cry for motivation.

People spend less time working for more money and more security than ever before, and the trend cannot be reversed. These benefits are no longer rewards; they are rights. A 6-day week is inhuman, a 10-hour day is exploitation, extended medical coverage is a basic decency, and stock options are the salvation of American initiative. Unless the ante is continuously raised, the psychological reaction of employees is that the company is turning back the clock.

When industry began to realize that both the economic nerve and the lazy nerve of their employees had insatiable appetites, it started to listen to the behavioral scientists who, more out of a humanist tradition than from scientific study, criticized management for not knowing how to deal with people. The next KITA easily followed.

4. *Human relations training*—Over 30 years of teaching and, in many instances, of practicing psychological approaches to handling people have resulted in costly human relations programs and, in the end, the same question: How do you motivate workers? Here too, escalations have taken place. Thirty years ago it was necessary to request, "Please don't spit on the floor." Today the same admonition requires three "please's" before the employee feels that his superior has demonstrated the psychologically proper attitudes toward him.

The failure of human relations training to produce motivation led to the conclusion that the supervisor or manager himself was not psychologically true to himself in his practice of interpersonal decency. So an advanced form of human relations KITA, sensitivity training, was unfolded.

5. *Sensitivity training*—Do you really, really understand yourself? Do you really, really, really trust the other man? Do you really, really, really, really cooperate? The failure of sensitivity training is now being explained, by those who have become opportunistic exploiters of the technique, as a failure to really (five times) conduct proper sensitivity training courses.

With the realization that there are only temporary gains from comfort and economic and interpersonal KITA, personnel managers concluded that the fault lay not in what they were doing, but in the employee's failure to appreciate what they were doing. This opened up the field of communications, a whole new area of "scientifically" sanctioned KITA.

6. *Communications*—The professor of communications was invited to join the faculty of management training programs and help in making employees understand what management was doing for them. House organs, briefing sessions, supervisory instruction on the importance of communication, and all sorts of propaganda have proliferated until today there is even an International Council of Industrial Editors. But no motivation resulted, and the obvious thought occurred that perhaps management was not hearing what the employees were saying. That led to the next KITA.

7. *Two-way communication*—Management ordered morale surveys, suggestion plans, and group participation programs. Then both employees and management were communicating and listening to each other more than ever, but without much improvement in motivation.

The behavioral scientists began to take another

look at their conceptions and their data, and they took human relations one step further. A glimmer of truth was beginning to show through in the writings of the so-called higher-order-need psychologists. People, so they said, want to actualize themselves. Unfortunately, the "actualizing" psychologists got mixed up with the human relations psychologists, and a new KITA emerged.

8. *Job participation*—Though it may not have been the theoretical intention, job participation often became a "give them the big picture" approach. For example, if a man is tightening 10,000 nuts a day on an assembly line with a torque wrench, tell him he is building a Chevrolet. Another approach had the goal of giving the employee a *feeling* that he is determining, in some measure, what he does on his job. The goal was to provide a *sense* of achievement rather than a substantive achievement in his task. Real achievement, of course, requires a task that makes it possible.

But still there was no motivation. This led to the inevitable conclusion that the employees must be sick, and therefore to the next KITA.

9. *Employee counseling*—The initial use of this form of KITA in a systematic fashion can be credited to the Hawthorne experiment of the Western Electric Company during the early 1930's. At that time, it was found that the employees harbored irrational feelings that were interfering with the rational operation of the factory. Counseling in this instance was a means of letting the employees unburden themselves by talking to someone about their problems. Although the counseling techniques were primitive, the program was large indeed.

The counseling approach suffered as a result of experiences during World War II, when the programs themselves were found to be interfering with the operation of the organizations; the counselors had forgotten their role of benevolent listeners and were attempting to do something about the problems that they heard about. Psychological counseling, however, has managed to survive the negative impact of World War II experiences and today is beginning to flourish with renewed sophistication. But, alas, many of these programs, like all the others, do not seem to have lessened the pressure of demands to find out how to motivate workers.

Since KITA results only in short-term movement, it is safe to predict that the cost of these programs will increase steadily and new varieties will be developed as old positive KITAs reach their satiation points.

HYGIENE VS. MOTIVATORS

Let me rephrase the perennial question this way: How do you install a generator in an employee? A brief review of my motivation-hygiene theory of job attitudes is required before theoretical and practical suggestions can be offered. The theory was first drawn from an examination of events in the lives of engineers and accountants. At least 16 other investigations, using a wide variety of populations (including some in the Communist countries), have since been completed making the original research one of the most replicated studies in the field of job attitudes.

The findings of these studies, along with corroboration from many other investigations using different procedures, suggest that the factors involved in producing job satisfaction (and motivation) are separate and distinct from the factors that lead to job dissatisfaction. Since separate factors need to be considered, depending on whether job satisfaction or job dissatisfaction is being examined, it follows that these two feelings are not opposites of each other. The opposite of job satisfaction is not job dissatisfaction but, rather, *no* job satisfaction; and, similarly, the opposite of job dissatisfaction is not job satisfaction, but *no* job dissatisfaction.

Stating the concept presents a problem in semantics, for we normally think of satisfaction and dissatisfaction as opposites—i.e., what is not satisfying must be dissatisfying, and vice versa. But when it comes to understanding the behavior of people in their jobs, more than a play on words is involved.

Two different needs of man are involved here. One set of needs can be thought of as stemming from his animal nature—the built-in drive to avoid pain from the environment, plus all the learned drives which become conditioned to the basic biological needs. For example, hunger, the basic biological drive, makes it necessary to earn money, and then money becomes a specific drive. The other set of needs relates to that unique human characteristic, the ability to achieve and, through achievement, to experience psychological growth. The stimuli for the growth needs are tasks that induce growth; in the

industrial setting, they are the *job content*. Contrariwise, the stimuli inducing pain-avoidance behavior are found in the *job environment*.

The growth or *motivator* factors that are intrinsic to the job are: achievement, recognition of achievement, the work itself, responsibility, and growth or advancement. The dissatisfaction-avoidance or *hygiene* (KITA) factors that are extrinsic to the job include: company policy and administration, supervision, interpersonal relationships, working conditions, salary, status, and security.

A composite of the factors that are involved in causing job satisfaction and job dissatisfaction, drawn from samples of 1,685 employees, is shown in *Exhibit 22-1*. The results indicate that motivators were the primary cause of satisfaction, and hygiene factors the primary cause of unhappiness on the job. The employees, studied in 12 different investigations, included lower-level supervisors, professional women, agricultural administrators, men about to retire from management positions, hospital maintenance personnel, manufacturing supervisors, nurses, food handlers, military officers, engineers, scientists, housekeepers, teachers, technicians, female assemblers, accountants, Finnish foremen, and Hungarian engineers.

They were asked what job events had occurred in their work that had led to extreme satisfaction or extreme dissatisfaction on their part. Their responses are broken down in the exhibit into percentages of total "positive" job events and of total "negative" job events. (The figures total more than 100% on both the "hygiene" and "motivators" sides because often at least two factors can be attributed to a single event; advancement, for instance, often accompanies assumption of responsibility.)

To illustrate, a typical response involving achievement that had a negative effect for the employee was, "I was unhappy because I didn't do the job successfully." A typical response in the small number of positive job events in the Company Policy and Administration grouping was, "I was happy because the company reorganized the section so that I didn't report any longer to the guy I didn't get along with."

As the lower right-hand part of the exhibit shows, of all the factors contributing to job satisfaction, 81% were motivators. And of all the factors contributing to the employees' dissatisfaction over their work, 69% involved hygiene elements.

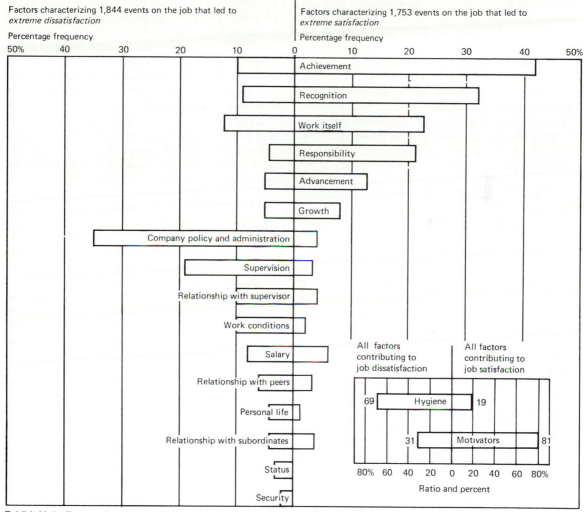

Factors characterizing 1,844 events on the job that led to *extreme dissatisfaction*

Factors characterizing 1,753 events on the job that led to *extreme satisfaction*

Exhibit 22-1 Factors affecting job attitudes, as reported in twelve investigations.

Eternal Triangle

There are three general philosophies of personnel management. The first is based on organizational theory, the second on industrial engineering, and the third on behavioral science.

The organizational theorist believes that human needs are either so irrational or so varied and adjustable to specific situations that the major function of personnel management is to be as pragmatic as the occasion demands. If jobs are organized in a proper manner, he reasons, the result will be the most efficient job structure, and the most favorable job attitudes will follow as a matter of course.

The industrial engineer holds that man is mechanistically oriented and economically motivated and his needs are best met by attuning the individual to the most efficient work process. The goal of personnel management therefore should be to concoct the most appropriate incentive system and to design the specific working conditions in a way that facilitates the most efficient use of the human machine. By structuring jobs in a manner that leads to the most efficient operation, the engineer believes that he can obtain the optimal organization of work and the proper work attitudes.

The behavioral scientist focuses on group sentiments, attitudes of individual employees, and the organization's social and psychological climate. According to his persuasion, he emphasizes one or more of the various hygiene and motivator needs. His approach to personnel management generally emphasizes some form of human relations education, in the hope of instilling healthy employee attitudes and an organizational climate which he considers to be felicitous to human values. He believes that proper attitudes will lead to efficient job and organizational structure.

There is always a lively debate as to the overall effectiveness of the approaches of the organizational theorist and the industrial engineer. Manifestly they have achieved much. But the nagging question for the behavioral scientist has been: What is the cost in human problems that eventually cause more expense to the organization—for instance, turnover, absenteeism, errors, violation of safety rules, strikes, restriction of output, higher wages, and greater fringe benefits? On the other hand, the behavioral scientist is hard put to document much manifest improvement in personnel management, using his approach.

The three philosophies can be depicted as a triangle, as is done in *Exhibit 22-2*, with each persuasion claiming the apex angle. The motivation-hygiene theory claims the same angle as industrial engineering, but for opposite goals. Rather than rationalizing the work to increase efficiency, the theory suggests that work be *enriched* to bring about effective utilization of personnel. Such a systematic

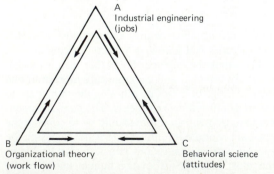

Exhibit 22-2 "Triangle" of philosophies of personnel management.

attempt to motivate employees by manipulating the motivator factors is just beginning.

The term *job enrichment* describes this embryonic movement. An older term, job enlargement, should be avoided because it is associated with past failures stemming from a misunderstanding of the problem. Job enrichment provides the opportunity for the employee's psychological growth, while job enlargement merely makes a job structurally bigger. Since scientific job enrichment is very new, this article only suggests the principles and practical steps that have recently emerged from several successful experiments in industry.

Job Loading

In attempting to enrich an employee's job, management often succeeds in reducing the man's personal contribution, rather than giving him an opportunity for growth in his accustomed job. Such an endeavor, which I shall call horizontal job loading (as opposed to vertical loading, or providing motivator factors), has been the problem of earlier job enlargement programs. This activity merely enlarges the meaninglessness of the job. Some examples of this approach, and their effect, are:

- Challenging the employee by increasing the amount of production expected of him. If he tightens 10,000 bolts a day, see if he can tighten 20,000 bolts a day. The arithmetic involved shows that multiplying zero by zero still equals zero.
- Adding another meaningless task to the existing one, usually some routine clerical activity. The arithmetic here is adding zero to zero.
- Rotating the assignments of a number of jobs that need to be enriched. This means washing dishes for a while, then washing silverware. The arithmetic is substituting one zero for another zero.
- Removing the most difficult parts of the assignment in order to free the worker to accomplish more of the less challenging assignments. This traditional industrial engineering approach amounts to substraction in the hope of accomplishing addition.

These are common forms of horizontal loading that frequently come up in preliminary brainstorming sessions on job enrichment. The principles of vertical loading have not all been worked out as yet, and they remain rather general, but I have furnished seven useful starting points for consideration in *Exhibit 22-3*.

Principle	Motivators involved
A. Removing some controls while retaining accountability	Responsibility and personal achievement
B. Increasing the accountability of individuals for own work	Responsibility and recognition
C. Giving a person a complete natural unit of work (module, division, area, and so on)	Responsibility, achievement, and recognition
D. Granting additional authority to an employee in his activity; job freedom	Responsibility, achievement, and recognition
E. Making periodic reports directly available to the worker himself rather than to the supervisor	Internal recognition
F. Introducing new and more difficult tasks not previously handled	Growth and learning
G. Assigning individuals specific or specialized tasks, enabling them to become experts	Responsibility, growth, and advancement

Exhibit 22-3 Principles of vertical job loading.

A Successful Application

An example from a highly successful job enrichment experiment can illustrate the distinction between horizontal and vertical loading of a job. The subjects of this study were the stockholder correspondents employed by a very large corporation. Seemingly, the task required of these carefully selected and highly trained correspondents was quite complex and challenging. But almost all indexes of performance and job attitudes were low, and exit interviewing confirmed that the challenge of the job existed merely as words.

A job enrichment project was initiated in the form of an experiment with one group, designated as an achieving unit, having its job enriched by the principles described in *Exhibit 22-3*. A control group continued to do its job in the traditional way. (There were also two "uncommitted" groups of correspondents formed to measure the so-called Hawthorne Effect—that is, to gauge whether productivity and attitudes toward the job changed artificially merely because employees sensed that the company was paying more attention to them in doing something different or novel. The results for these groups were substantially the same as for the control group, and for the sake of simplicity I do not deal with them in this summary.) No changes in hygiene were introduced for either group other than those that would have been made anyway, such as normal pay increases.

The changes for the achieving unit were introduced in the first two months, averaging one per week of the seven motivators listed in *Exhibit 22-3*. At the end of six months the members of the achieving unit were found to be outperforming their

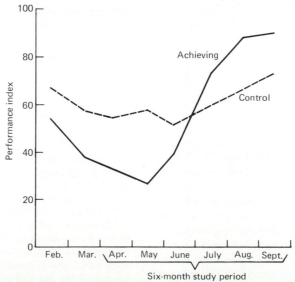

Exhibit 22-4 Shareholder service index in company experiment (three-month cumulative average).

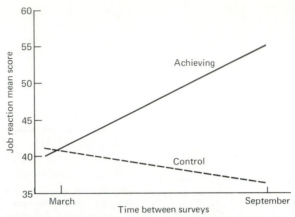

Exhibit 22-5 Changes in attitudes toward tasks in company experiment (changes in mean scores over six-month period).

counterparts in the control group, and in addition indicated a marked increase in their liking for their jobs. Other results showed that the achieving group had lower absenteeism and, subsequently, a much higher rate of promotion.

Exhibit 22-4 illustrates the changes in performance, measured in February and March, before the study period began, and at the end of each month of the study period. The shareholder service index represents quality of letters, including accuracy of information, and speed of response to stockholders' letters of inquiry. The index of a current month was averaged into the average of the two prior months, which means that improvement was harder to obtain if the indexes of the previous months were low. The "achievers" were performing less well before the six-month period started, and their performance service index continued to decline after the introduction of the motivators, evidently because of uncertainty over their newly granted responsibilities. In the third month, however, performance improved, and soon the members of this group had reached a high level of accomplishment.

Exhibit 22-5 shows the two groups' attitudes toward their job, measured at the end of March, just before the first motivator was introduced, and again at the end of September. The correspondents were asked 16 questions, all involving motivation. A typical one was, "As you see it, how many opportunities do you feel that you have in your job for making worthwhile contributions?" The answers were scaled from 1 to 5, with 80 as the maximum possible score. The achievers became much more positive about their job, while the attitude of the control unit remained about the same (the drop is not statistically significant).

How was the job of these correspondents restructured? *Exhibit 22-6* lists the suggestions made that were deemed to be horizontal loading, and the actual vertical loading changes that were incorporated in the job of the achieving unit. The capital letters under "Principle" after "Vertical loading" refer to the corresponding letters in *Exhibit 22-3*. The reader will note that the rejected forms of horizontal loading correspond closely to the list of common manifestations of the phenomenon on page 238, right column.

STEPS TO JOB ENRICHMENT

Now that the motivator idea has been described in practice, here are the steps that managers should take in instituting the principle with their employees:

1 Select those jobs in which (a) the investment in industrial engineering does not make changes too costly, (b) attitudes are poor, (c) hygiene is becoming very costly, and (d) motivation will make a difference in performance.

2 Approach these jobs with the conviction that they can be changed. Years of tradition have led managers to believe that the content of the jobs is sacrosanct and the only scope of action that they have is in the ways of stimulating people.

3 Brainstorm a list of changes that may enrich the jobs, without concern for their practicality.

Horizontal loading suggestions (rejected)	Vertical loading suggestions (adopted)	Principle
Firm quotas could be set for letters to be answered each day, using a rate which would be hard to reach.	Subject matter experts were appointed within each unit for other members of the unit to consult with before seeking supervisory help. (The supervisor had been answering all specialized and difficult questions.)	G
The women could type the letters themselves, as well as compose them, or take on any other clerical functions.	Correspondents signed their own names on letters. (The supervisor had been signing all letters.)	B
All difficult or complex inquiries could be channeled to a few women so that the remainder could achieve high rates of output. These jobs could be exchanged from time to time.	The work of the more experienced correspondents was proof-read less frequently by supervisors and was done at the correspondents' desks, dropping verification from 100% to 10%. (Previously, all correspondents' letters had been checked by the supervisor.)	A
The women could be rotated through units handling different customers, and then sent back to their own units.	Production was discussed, but only in terms such as "a full day's work is expected." As time went on, this was no longer mentioned. (Before, the group had been constantly reminded of the number of letters that needed to be answered.)	D
	Outgoing mail went directly to the mailroom without going over supervisors' desks. (The letters had always been routed through the supervisors.)	A
	Correspondents were encouraged to answer letters in a more personalized way. (Reliance on the form-letter approach had been standard practice.)	C
	Each correspondent was held personally responsible for the quality and accuracy of letters. (This responsibility had been the province of the supervisor and the verifier.)	B, E

Exhibit 22-6 Enlargement vs. enrichment of correspondents' tasks in company experiment.

4 Screen the list to eliminate suggestions that involve hygiene, rather than actual motivation.

5 Screen the list of generalities, such as "give them more responsibility," that are rarely followed in practice. This might seem obvious, but the motivator words have never left industry; the substance has just been rationalized and organized out. Words like "responsibility," "growth," "achievement," and "challenge," for example, have been elevated to the lyrics of the patriotic anthem for all organizations. It is the old problem typified by the pledge of allegiance to the flag being more important than contributions to the country—of following the form, rather than the substance.

6 Screen the list to eliminate any *horizontal* loading suggestions.

7 Avoid direct participation by the employees whose jobs are to be enriched. Ideas they have expressed previously certainly constitute a valuable source for recommended changes, but their direct involvement contaminates the process with human relations *hygiene* and, more specifically, gives them only a *sense* of making a contribution. The job is to be changed, and it is the content that will produce the motivation, not attitudes about being involved or the challenge inherent in setting up a job. That process will be over shortly, and it is what the employees will be doing from then on that will determine their motivation. A sense of participation will result only in short-term movement.

8 In the initial attempts at job enrichment, set up a controlled experiment. At least two equivalent groups should be chosen, one an experimental unit in which the motivators are systematically introduced over a period of time, and the other one a control group in which no changes are made. For both groups, hygiene should be allowed to follow its natural course for the duration of the experiment. Pre- and post-installation tests of performance and job attitudes are necessary to evaluate the effectiveness of the job enrichment program. The attitude test must be limited to motivator items in order to divorce the employee's view of the job he is given from all the surrounding hygiene feelings that he might have.

9 Be prepared for a drop in performance in the experimental group the first few weeks. The changeover to a new job may lead to a temporary reduction in efficiency.

10 Expect your first-line supervisors to experience some anxiety and hostility over the changes you are making. The anxiety comes from their fear that the changes will result in poorer performance for their unit. Hostility will arise when the employees start assuming what the supervisors regard as their own responsibility for performance. The supervisor without checking duties to perform may then be left with little to do.

After a successful experiment, however, the supervisor usually discovers the supervisory and managerial functions he has neglected, or which were never his because all his time was given over to checking the work of his subordinates. For example, in the R&D division of one large chemical company I know of, the supervisors of the laboratory assistants were theoretically responsible for their training and evaluation. These functions, however, had come to be performed in a routine, unsubstantial fashion. After the job enrichment program, during which the supervisors were not merely passive observers of the assistants' performance, the supervisors actually were devoting their time to reviewing performance and administering thorough training.

What has been called an employee-centered style of supervision will come about not through education of supervisors, but by changing the jobs that they do.

CONCLUDING NOTE

Job enrichment will not be a one-time proposition, but a continuous management function. The initial changes, however, should last for a very long period of time. There are a number of reasons for this:

- The changes should bring the job up to the level of challenge commensurate with the skill that was hired.
- Those who have still more ability eventually will be able to demonstrate it better and win promotion to higher-level jobs.
- The very nature of motivators, as opposed to hygiene factors, is that they have a much longer-term effect on employees' attitudes. Perhaps the job will have to be enriched again, but this will not occur as frequently as the need for hygiene.

Not all jobs can be enriched, nor do all jobs need to be enriched. If only a small percentage of the time and money that is now devoted to hygiene, however, were given to job enrichment efforts, the return in human satisfaction and economic gain would be one of the largest dividends that industry and society have ever reaped through their efforts at better personnel management.

The argument for job enrichment can be summed up quite simply: If you have someone on a job, use him. If you can't use him on the job, get rid of him, either via automation or by selecting someone with lesser ability. If you can't use him and you can't get rid of him, you will have a motivation problem.

Reading 23

Designing Work for Individuals and for Groups

J. Richard Hackman

As yet there are no simple or generally accepted criteria for a well-designed job, nor is a single technology acknowledged as the proper way to go about redesigning work. Moreover, it often is unclear in specific circumstances whether work should be structured to be performed by individual employees, or whether it should be designed to be carried out by a *group* of employees working together.

The first part of this selection reviews one model for work design that focuses on the individual performer. In the second part, discussion turns to a number of issues that must be dealt with when work is designed for interacting teams of employees.

DESIGNING WORK FOR INDIVIDUALS

A model specifying how job characteristics and individual differences interact to affect the satisfaction, motivation, and productivity of individuals at work has been proposed by Hackman and Oldham

Adapted from J. R. Hackman, "Work Design." In J. R. Hackman & J. L. Suttle (Eds.), *Improving Life at Work: Behavioral Science Approaches to Organizational Change*. Santa Monica: Calif. Goodyear, 1977; and from J. R. Hackman & G. R. Oldham, *Work Redesign*. Reading, Mass: Addison-Wesley, 1980. Portions of this material appeared originally in Hackman, Oldham, Janson, & Purdy (1975).

(1976, 1980). The model is intended specifically for use in planning and carrying out changes in the design of jobs. It is described below, and then is used as a guide for a discussion of diagnostic procedures and change principles that can be used in redesigning the jobs of individuals.

The Job Characteristics Model

The basic job characteristics model is shown in Figure 23-1. As illustrated in the figure, five core job dimensions are seen as creating three critical psychological states which, in turn, lead to a number of beneficial personal and work outcomes. The links among the job dimensions, the psychological states, and the outcomes are shown to be moderated by the strength of individuals' growth needs and by their task-relevant knowledge and skill. The major classes of variables in the model are reviewed briefly below.

Psychological States   The three following psychological states are postulated as critical in affecting a person's motivation and satisfaction on the job:

1 Experienced meaningfulness: The person must experience the work as generally important, valuable, and worthwhile.

2 Experienced responsibility: The individual must feel personally responsible and accountable for the results of the work he or she performs.

3 Knowledge of results: The individual must have understanding, on a fairly regular basis, of how effectively he or she is performing the job.

The more these three conditions are present, the more people will feel good about themselves when they perform well. Or, following Hackman and Lawler (1971), the model postulates that internal rewards are obtained by individuals when they *learn* (knowledge of results) that they *personally* (experienced responsibility) have performed well on a task that they *care about* (experienced meaningfulness). These internal rewards are reinforcing to the individual, and serve as incentives for continued efforts to perform well in the future. When the persons do not perform well, they do not experience a reinforcing state of affairs, and may elect to try harder in the future so as to regain the rewards that good performance brings. The net result is a self-perpetuating cycle of positive work motivation powered by self-generated rewards, that is predicted to continue until one or more of the three psychological states is no longer present—or until the individual no longer values the internal rewards that derive from good performance.

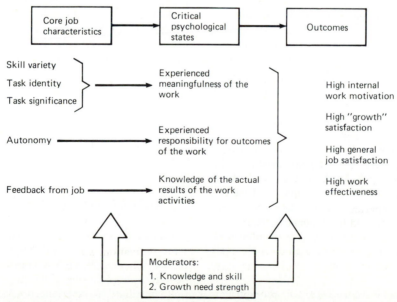

Figure 23-1   The job characteristics model of work motivation.

Job Dimensions   Of the five job characteristics shown in Figure 23-1 as fostering the emergence of the psychological states, three contribute to the experienced meaningfulness of the work, and one each contributes to experienced responsibility and to knowledge of results.

The three job dimensions that contribute to a job's *meaningfulness* are:

1 Skill variety   The degree to which a job requires a variety of different activities in carrying out the work, which involve the use of a number of different skills and talents of the person.

When a task requires a person to engage in activities that challenge or stretch his or her skills and abilities, that task almost invariably is experienced as meaningful by the individual. Many parlor games, puzzles, and recreational activities, for example, achieve much of their fascination because they tap and test the intellective or motor skills of the people who do them. When a job draws upon several skills of an employee, that individual may find the job to be of very high personal meaning—even if, in any absolute sense, it is not of great significance or importance.

2 Task identity   The degree to which the job requires completion of a "whole" and identifiable piece of work—that is, doing a job from beginning to end with a visible outcome.

If an employee assembles a complete product or provides a complete unit of service he or she should find the work more meaningful than if he or she were responsible for only a small part of the whole job—other things (such as skill variety) being equal.

3 Task significance   The degree to which the job has a substantial impact on the lives or work of other people—whether in the immediate organization or in the external environment.

When individuals understand that the results of their work may have a significant effect on the well-being of other people, the experienced meaningfulness of the work usually is enhanced. Employees who tighten nuts on aircraft brake assemblies, for example, are much more likely to perceive their work as meaningful than are workers who fill small boxes with paper clips—even though the skill levels involved may be comparable.

The job characteristic predicted to prompt feelings of personal *responsibility* for the work outcomes is autonomy. "Autonomy" is defined as the degree to which the job provides substantial freedom, independence, and discretion to the individual in scheduling the work and in determining the procedures to be used in carrying it out.

To the extent that autonomy is high, work outcomes will be viewed by workers as depending substantially on their *own* efforts, initiatives, and decisions, rather than on the adequacy of instructions from the boss or on a manual of job procedures. In such circumstances, individuals should feel a strong personal responsibility for the successes and failures that occur on the job.

The job characteristic that fosters *knowledge of results* is "feedback," which is defined as the degree to which carrying out the work activities required by the job results in the individual's obtaining direct and clear information about the effectiveness of his or her performance.

It can be useful to combine the scores of a job on the five dimensions described above into a single index reflecting the overall potential of the job to prompt self-generated work motivation on the part of job incumbents. Following the model diagramed in Figure 23-1, a job high in motivating potential must be high on at least one (and hopefully more) of the three dimensions that lead to experienced meaningfulness, *and* high on autonomy and feedback as well—thereby creating conditions for all three of the critical psychological states to be present. Arithmetically, scores of jobs on the five dimensions are combined as follows to meet this criterion:

$$\text{Motivating potential score (MPS)} = \left(\frac{\text{Skill Variety} + \text{Task Identity} + \text{Task Significance}}{3} \right)$$

$$\times \text{Autonomy} \times \text{Job Feedback}$$

As can be seen from the formula, a near-zero score of a job on either autonomy or feedback will reduce the overall MPS to near-zero; whereas a near-zero score on one of the three job dimensions that contribute to experienced meaningfulness cannot, by itself, do so.

Moderators   Some employees "take off" on jobs that are high in motivating potential; others are more likely to "turn off" when working on such jobs. Two characteristics of people seem particularly important in determining who will (and who will not) respond positively to high-MPS jobs: individual growth-need strength, and task-relevant knowledge and skill.

Growth-Need Strength   Some people have strong needs for personal accomplishment, for learning, and for developing themselves beyond where they are now. These people are said to have strong "growth needs," and they are predicted to develop high internal motivation when working on a complex, challenging job. Others have less strong needs for growth and may be less eager to exploit the opportunities for personal accomplishment that are provided by such a job. Indeed, individuals with low growth needs may not even recognize the existence of such opportunities—or may recognize them, but find themselves unable to respond because they are stretched too far by the psychological demands of the job.

Knowledge and Skill   People with sufficient knowledge and skill to perform well on jobs high in motivating potential should experience quite positive feelings about themselves as a result of their work activities. A high-MPS job "counts" for people, and doing such a job well can be an occasion for significant self-reward. But for precisely this reason, people who are *not* competent enough to perform well will experience a good deal of personal unhappiness and frustration when working on such jobs. The work is important to them too, but they do poorly at it. Withdrawal from the work setting (either psychologically, by convincing themselves that they do *not* care so much about the work, or behaviorally via high absence rates or resignation) is commonly observed in such circumstances.

Outcome Variables   Also shown in Figure 23-1 are several outcomes that are affected by the level of self-generated motivation experienced by people at work. Of special interest as an outcome variable is internal work motivation (Lawler & Hall, 1970; Hackman & Lawler, 1971), because it taps directly the contingency between effective performance and self-administered affective rewards. Typical questionnaire items measuring internal work motivation include: (1) I feel a great sense of personal satisfaction when I do this job well; (2) I feel bad and unhappy when I discover that I have performed poorly on this job; and (3) My own feelings are *not* affected much one way or the other by how well I do on this job (reversed scoring).

Other outcomes listed in Figure 23-1 include job satisfaction (particularly satisfaction with opportunities for personal growth and development on the job) and work effectiveness (particularly the *quality* of work performance). All of these outcomes are predicted to be affected positively by jobs that are high in motivating potential.

Validity of the Job Characteristics Model

Just how correct is the job characteristics model of work motivation? While there have been numerous studies of the Job Diagnostic Survey and other devices for *measuring* job characteristics, relatively few tests have been made of the *conceptual* proposition of the theory (see Hackman & Oldham, 1980, for references to these studies). In general, the model is probably more right than wrong, but it surely is inaccurate and incomplete in numerous specifics. Here are a number of concerns about the model that have surfaced in research on it.

1. Evidence about the proposed moderators is scattered and inconsistent. The moderating effects of knowledge and skill have not been systematically tested as yet. And while a large number of studies have assessed growth-need strength as a moderator, the results are mixed. That there are important differences among people in their motivational readiness for enriched work seems not at issue, but how best to construe and measure these differences remains very much an open question.

2. While existing evidence generally confirms that the job characteristics affect work outcomes *through* the psychological states as the model specifies, a number of anomalies have been found. Some of the job characteristics affect psychological states in addition to those the model says they are supposed to, and some of the psychological states are affected by other than model-specified job characteristics. So the links between the job characteristics and the psychological states are not as neat and clean as suggested in Figure 23-1.

3. The model treats the job characteristics as if they were independent (i.e., uncorrelated with one another), and this is not always true. Jobs high on one job characteristic often are high on some others (a job high in autonomy, for example, is likely to be high in skill variety as well). This nonindependence lessens the appropriateness of the multiplicative formula for MPS, and suggests that in many situations an estimate of the motivating potential of jobs that is obtained by simply summing the job characteristic scores will be as good (or better) than one involving the more complex MPS formula.

4. The concept of feedback in the model is flawed. Job incumbents, supervisors, and outside observers frequently disagree about how much feedback a given job actually provides. Moreover, the model does not address feedback from nonjob sources (such as supervisors or co-workers) that also affects one's knowledge of the results of the work. How a person reacts to feedback from the job itself may be altered by data about performance that come from nonjob sources such as these.

5. Finally, how objective properties of jobs relate to people's *perceptions* of those properties is not completely clear. People "redefine" their tasks cognitively to make them more consistent with their own needs, attitudes, and values—or in response to cues or direct influence from other people about the meaning of the work (Hackman, 1969; Weiss & Shaw, 1979). Yet the job characteristics model does not deal explicitly with the task redefinition process, and it is not yet known whether the motivational benefits of enriched work derive primarily from objective task characteristics or from employee perceptions of their jobs (which may, at times, diverge substantially from objective reality).

Diagnostic Use of the Model

The job characteristics model was designed so that each major class of variables (objective job characteristics, mediating psychological states, strength of the individual's need for growth, and work motivation and satisfaction) can be directly measured in actual work situations. Such measurements are obtained using the Job Diagnostic Survey (JDS), which is described in detail elsewhere (Hackman & Oldham, 1975, 1980). The major intended uses of the JDS are (1) to diagnose existing jobs before planned work redesign, and (2) to evaluate the effects of work redesign—for example, to determine which job dimensions did and did not change, to assess the impact of the changes on the motivation and satisfaction of employees, and to test for any possible alterations after the change in the need for growth of people whose jobs were redesigned.

In the paragraphs to follow, several steps are presented that might be followed by a change agent in carrying out a diagnosis using the JDS.

Step 1: Are Motivation and Satisfaction Really Problems? Sometimes organizations undertake job enrichment or work redesign to improve work motivation and satisfaction when in fact the real problem with work performance lies elsewhere—for example, in the equipment or technology of the job. It is important, therefore, to examine the level of employees' motivation and satisfaction at an early stage in a job diagnosis. If motivation and satisfaction are problems, and are accompanied by documented problems in work performance, absenteeism, or turnover as revealed by independent organizational indices, the change agent would continue to step 2. If not, the agent presumably would look to other aspects of the work situation (e.g., the technology, the workflow) to identify and understand the reasons for the problem which gave rise to the diagnostic activity.

Step 2: Is the Job Low in Motivating Potential? To answer this question, the change agent would examine the Motivating Potential Score of the target job, and compare it with the MPS scores of other jobs to determine whether or not the *job itself* is a probable cause of the motivational problems documented in step 1. If the job turns out to be low on MPS, he would continue to step 3; if it scores high, he would look for other reasons for the motivational difficulties (e.g., the pay plan, the nature of supervision, and so on).

Step 3: What Specific Aspects of the Job are Causing the Difficulty? This step involves examination of the job on each of the five core job dimensions, to pinpoint the specific strengths and weaknesses of the job as it currently exists. It is useful at this stage to construct a profile of the target job, to make visually apparent where improvements need to be made. An illustrative profile for two jobs (one "good" job and one job needing improvement) is shown in Figure 23-2.

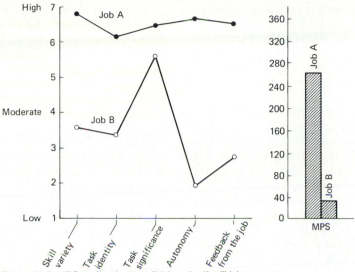

Figure 23-2 JDS profile of a "good" job and a "bad" job.

Job A is an engineering maintenance job, and is high on all of the core dimensions; the MPS of this job is very high: 260.[1] Job enrichment would not be recommended for this job; if employees working on the job are unproductive and unhappy, the reasons probably have little to do with the design of the work itself.

Job B, on the other hand, has many problems. This job involves the routine and repetitive processing of checks in a bank. The MPS of 30—which is quite low—would be even lower if it were not for the moderately high task significance of the job. (Task significance is moderately high because the people are handling large amounts of other people's money, and their efforts potentially have important consequences for the unseen clients.) The job provides the individuals with very little direct feedback about how effectively they are performing; the employees have little autonomy in how they go about doing the job; and the job is moderately low in both skill variety and task identity.

For Job B, then, there is plenty of room for improvement, and many avenues to consider in planning job changes. For still other jobs, the avenues for change may turn out to be considerably more specific: for example, feedback and autonomy may be reasonably high, but one or more of the core dimensions which contribute to the experienced

meaningfulness of the work (i.e., skill variety, task identity, and task significance) may be low. In such a case, attention would turn to ways to increase the standing of the job on these latter three dimensions.

Step 4: How Ready Are the Employees for Change? Once it has been documented that there is need for improvement in the focal job, and the particularly troublesome aspects of the job have been identified, then it is appropriate to begin planning the specific action steps which will be taken to enrich the job. An important factor in such planning is determining the strength of the employees' needs for growth, and whether or not they have sufficient knowledge and skill to perform a more complex and challenging job well.

The measure of need for growth provided by the JDS may be helpful in identifying which employees should be among the first to have their jobs changed (e.g., those whose needs for growth are strong), and how such changes should be introduced (e.g., perhaps with more caution for individuals whose growth-need strength is low). One should always obtain more than one measure of employees' psychological readiness for enriched work, because any single measure, including the one provided by the JDS, is inevitably flawed and incomplete. And it is important that some nonimpressionistic data be brought to bear on the question. To rely exclusively

---

[1]MPS scores can range from 1 to 343. The average is about 125.

on managerial assessments of employees' needs and wants is apt to be highly misleading.

The same is true for assessing employee knowledge and skill. Managerial judgments of the readiness of rank-and-file employees for more challenging work may significantly underestimate their true competence to do that work (either because the existing job does not allow that competence to be expressed or because employees are deliberately not showing in their work how much they know). Therefore, some relatively objective measures of task-relevant knowledge and skill should be brought to bear on the question of employee readiness whenever possible.

Step 5: What Special Problems and Opportunities Are Present in the Existing Work System? Before undertaking actual job changes, it is always advisable to search for any special roadblocks that may exist in the organizational unit as it currently exists, and for special opportunities that may be built upon in the change program.

Frequently of special importance in this regard is the level of *satisfaction* employees currently experience with various aspects of their organizational life. For example, the JDS provides measures of satisfaction with pay, job security, co-workers, and supervision. If the diagnosis reveals high dissatisfaction in one or more of these areas, then it may be very difficult to initiate and maintain a successful job redesign project (Oldham, 1976; Oldham, Hackman & Pearce, 1976). On the other hand, if satisfaction with supervision is especially high, then it might be wise to build an especially central role for supervisors in the initiation and management of the change process.

Of special importance is the amenability of existing organizational systems to the planned changes in job structure. Sometimes there are constraints in the work technology, in organizational control systems, or in personnel policies and practices that make it difficult or impossible to substantially enrich the work of rank-and-file employees (Hackman & Oldham, 1980, chap. 5). If these constraining systems cannot themselves be changed, it may be better not to proceed with work redesign than to introduce changes that are so negligible in degree that they cannot make much of a difference in work behavior.

Principles for Enriching Jobs

The core job dimensions specified in the job characteristics model are tied directly to a set of action principles for redesigning jobs (Hackman, Oldham, Janson & Purdy, 1975; Walters & Associates, 1975). As shown in Figure 23-3, these principles specify what types of changes in jobs are most likely to lead to improvements in each of the five core job dimensions, and thereby to an increase in the motivating potential of the job as a whole.

Principle 1: Forming Natural Work Units A critical step in the design of any job is the decision about how the work is to be distributed among the people who do it. Consider, for example, a typing pool—consisting of one supervisor and ten typists—that does all the typing for one division of an organization. Jobs are delivered in rough draft or dictated form to the supervisor, who distributes them as evenly as possible among the typists. In such circumstances the individual letters, reports, and other tasks performed by a given typist in one day or week are randomly assigned. There is no basis for identifying with the work or the person or department for whom it is performed, or for placing any personal value upon it.

By contrast, creating natural units of work increases employees' "ownership" of the work, and therefore improves the chances that employees will view it as meaningful and important rather than as irrelevant and boring. In creating natural units of

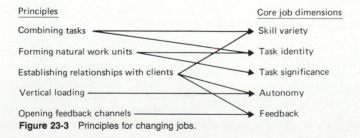

Figure 23-3 Principles for changing jobs.

work, one must first identify what the basic work items are. In the typing pool example, that might be "pages to be typed." Then these items are grouped into natural and meaningful categories. For example, each typist might be assigned continuing responsibility for all work requested by a single department or by several smaller departments. Instead of typing one section of a large report, the individual will type the entire piece of work, with knowledge of exactly what the total outcome of the work is. Furthermore, over a period of time the typist will develop a growing sense of how the work affects co-workers or customers who receive the completed product. Thus, as shown in Figure 23-3, forming natural units of work increases two of the core job dimensions that contribute to experienced meaningfulness—task identity and task significance.

It is still important that work be distributed so that the system as a whole operates efficiently, of course, and workloads must be arranged so that they are approximately equal among employees. The principle of natural work units simply requires that these traditional criteria be supplemented so that, insofar as possible, the tasks that arrive at an employee's work station form an identifiable and meaningful whole.

Principle 2: Combining Tasks The very existence of a pool made up entirely of persons whose sole function is typing reflects a fractionalization of jobs that sometimes can lead to such hidden costs as high absenteeism and turnover, extra supervisory time, and so on. The principle of combining tasks is based on the assumption that such costs often can be reduced by simply taking existing and fractionalized tasks and putting them back together again to form a new and larger module of work. At the Medfield, Massachusetts, plant of Corning Glass Works, for example, the job of assembling laboratory hotplates was redesigned by combining a number of previously separate tasks. After the change, each hotplate was assembled from start to finish by one operator, instead of going through several separate operations performed by different people.

Combining tasks (like forming natural work units) contributes in two ways to the experienced meaningfulness of the work. First, task identity is increased. The hotplate assembler, for example, can see and identify with a finished product ready for shipment —rather than a nearly invisible junction of solder.

Moreover, as more tasks are combined into a single worker's job, the individual must use a greater variety of skills in performing the job, further increasing the meaningfulness of the work.

Principle 3: Establishing Relationships with Clients By establishing direct relationships between workers and their clients, jobs often can be improved in three ways. First, feedback increases because additional opportunities are created for the employees to receive direct praise or criticism of their work outputs. Second, skill variety may increase, because of the need to develop and exercise one's interpersonal skills in managing and maintaining the relationship with the client. Finally, autonomy will increase to the degree that individuals are given real personal responsibility for deciding how to manage their relationships with the people who receive the outputs of their work.

Creating relationships with clients can be viewed as a three-step process: (1) identification of who the client actually is; (2) establishing the most direct contact possible between the worker and the client; and (3) establishing criteria and procedures so that the client can judge the quality of the product or service received and relay his judgments directly back to the worker. Especially important (and, in many cases, difficult to achieve) is identification of the specific criteria by which the work output is assessed by the client—and ensuring that both the worker and the client understand these criteria and agree with them.

Principle 4: Vertical Loading In vertical loading, the intent is to partially close the gap between the "doing" and the "controlling" aspects of the job. Thus, when a job is vertically loaded, responsibilities and controls that formerly were reserved for management are given to the employee as part of the job. Among ways this might be achieved are the following:

Giving job incumbents responsibility for deciding on work methods, and for advising or helping train less experienced workers.

Providing increased freedom in time management, including decisions about when to start and stop work, when to take a break, and how to assign work priorities.

Encouraging workers to do their own troubleshooting and manage work crises, rather than calling immediately for a supervisor.

Providing workers with increased knowledge of the financial aspects of the job and the organization, and increased control over budgetary matters that affect their own work.

When a job is vertically loaded, it inevitably increases in *autonomy*. And, as shown in Figure 23-1, this should lead to increased feelings of personal responsibility and accountability for the work outcomes.

Principle 5: Opening Feedback Channels In virtually all jobs there are ways to open channels of feedback to individuals to help them learn not only how well they are performing their jobs, but also whether their performance is improving, deteriorating, or remaining at a constant level. While there are various sources from which information about performance can come, it usually is advantageous for workers to learn about their performance *directly as they do the job*—rather than from management on an occasional basis.

Feedback provided by the job itself is more immediate and private than feedback provided by its supervisor, and can also increase workers' feelings of personal control over their work. Moreover, it avoids many of the potentially disruptive interpersonal problems which can develop when workers can find out how they are doing only by means of direct meassages or subtle cues from the boss.

Exactly what should be done to open channels for feedback from the job varies from job to job and organization to organization. In many cases, the changes involve simply removing existing blocks which isolate the individual from naturally occurring data about performance, rather than generating entirely new feedback mechanisms. For example:

Establishing direct relationships with clients (discussed above) often removes blocks between the worker and natural external sources of data about the work.

Quality control in many organizations often eliminates a natural source of feedback, because all quality checks are done by people other than the individuals responsible for the work. In such cases, feedback to the workers, if there is any, may be belated and diluted. By placing most quality-control functions in the hands of workers themselves, the quantity and quality of data available to them about their own performance will dramatically increase.

Tradition and established procedure in many organizations dictate that records about performance be kept by a supervisor and transmitted up (not down) the organizational hierarchy. Sometimes supervisors even check the work and correct any errors themselves. The worker who made the error never knows it occurred and is therefore denied the very information which can enhance both internal work motivation and the technical adequacy of his performance. In many cases, it is possible to provide standard summaries of performance records directly to the workers (and perhaps also to their superiors), thereby giving employees personally and regularly the data they need to improve their effectiveness.

Computers and other automated machines sometimes can be used to provide individuals with data now blocked from them. Many clerical operations, for example, are now performed on computer consoles. These consoles often can be programed to provide the clerk with immediate feedback in the form of a CRT display or a printout indicating that an error has been made. Some systems even have been programed to provide the operator with a positive feedback message when a period of error-free performance has been sustained.

Conclusion The principles for redesigning jobs reviewed above, while illustrative of the kinds of changes that can be made to improve the jobs of individuals in organizations, obviously are not exhaustive. They were selected for attention here because of the links (Figure 23-3) between the principles and the core job dimensions in the motivational model presented earlier. Other principles for enriching jobs (which, although often similar to those presented here, derive from alternative conceptual frameworks) are presented by Ford (1969), Glaser (1975), Herzberg (1974), and Katzell and Yankelovich (1975, chap. 6).

DESIGNING WORK FOR TEAMS

Sometimes work is designed to be performed by a *team* of employees rather than by individuals who work more or less independently. The objectives of the team design may be similar to those sought when individual jobs are enriched—that is, simultaneously to improve performance effectiveness and the quality of employee work experiences. The difference is that responsibility for managing work processes lies with the group as a whole rather than with individual employees. For this reason, such teams often are called "autonomous work teams" (Bucklow, 1972) or "self-regulating work groups" (Cummings, 1978).

When work is designed for a team, the task often can be larger, more challenging, and more meaningful than would be the case if it were broken up into segments to be performed by individuals. And opportunities are provided in the group for employees to develop close and socially satisfying work relationships with each other. This often is difficult to achieve for individual jobs in organizations, especially when work stations are so widely separated that meaningful interaction with others is all but precluded.

These benefits of a team design for work are important, but there also are some special difficulties in designing and managing work groups. It is not easy to set up a good team task, to provide work groups with appropriate organizational and managerial supports, or to help group members learn how to work together effectively.

One way of approaching the task of designing self-managing work groups is to identify the main hurdles that may impede the effectiveness of such groups—and then to see what might be done to help groups overcome those hurdles. Three performance hurdles faced by work groups can be readily identified. One is for group members to expend enough *effort* on the group task to get it accomplished well and on time. Another is for members to apply sufficient task-relevant *knowledge and skill* to their work on the task. And the third is for the group to devise and use *task-performance strategies* (i.e., ways of working together on the task) that are as

appropriate as possible for the task being performed.

If one could magically manipulate how a group deals with these three hurdles—i.e., adjust the effort group members expend, the expertise they bring to bear on the task work, and the performance strategies they use in carrying out that work—then one could powerfully affect the performance effectiveness of almost any task-oriented group. Since such magic is not available, we must suffice by attempting to *create conditions* in the group (and in the organization where it operates) that increase the chances that members themselves will be able to overcome the performance hurdles and go on to achieve both high work effectiveness and satisfying group experiences.

What are these conditions? They have to do with how the group is *designed* when it is created and given a job to do; with the *organizational supports* that are provided to the group; and with the kinds of *process aids* that are provided by organizational management (see Hackman & Oldham, 1980, chaps. 7–8).

Design of the Work Group

Three design features that are important in determining whether or not a group will overcome the performance hurdles are depicted in Figure 23-4 and discussed below. They are: (1) the structure of the group task, (2) the composition of the group, and (3) group norms about performance processes.

Structure of the Group Task   Following the ideas presented in the first part of this chapter, we would expect group members' motivation to work hard on

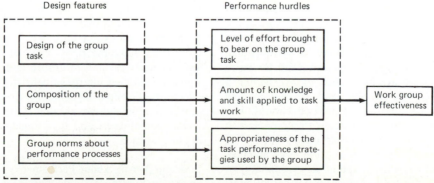

Figure 23-4 How the design of a work team relates to its performance effectiveness.

the group task to be high when the task is high in motivating potential. Thus, the group task should require the use of a variety of skills; it should be a whole and meaningful piece of work; it should "make a difference" to other people; it should provide autonomy for members to decide together how they will carry out the work; and it should provide members with regular and trustworthy feedback about how the group is performing.

To generate ideas for creating a group task high on these attributes, one can use the same "principles" for enriching jobs summarized in the previous section. It is important, however, to make sure that the focus of the design activities is on the overall task of the *group*, not on the tasks of individual group members, when these principles are applied.

Composition of the Group How a group is composed—that is, who is in the group—directly affects the amount of knowledge and skill that members can apply to their work on the group task. Four aspects of group composition have particularly strong influences on the amount of talent a group is actually able to *use* in its task work.

1. The group should include members who have high levels of task-relevant expertise. Far and away the most efficient means of increasing the knowledge and skill available for work on a group task is simply to put very talented people in the group. The skill requirements of the task can be assessed before the group is formed, and organizational selection and placement procedures can be used to make sure that the group does have among its members people who know how to do what needs to be done for the group to perform effectively.

2. The group should be large enough to do the work—but not much larger. Obviously there should be enough people in the group to get the work done, and those responsible for the design of work groups should be alert to the possibility of dysfunctional understaffing. Far more dangerous (and far more prevalent), however, is the risk of *overstaffing* a group: large work groups (and decision-making committees) are widely used in organizations. The reasons large groups are created often have less to do with considerations of group effectiveness than with emotional issues (such as using large numbers to share responsibility or spread accountability) or political considerations (like ensuring that all interested units are represented in the group so that they

will be more likely to accept its product). It usually is better to make groups and committees no larger than they absolutely must be to get the task accomplished, and to use alternative means for dealing with concerns about accountability and acceptance.

3. Group members should have at least a moderate level of interpersonal skill in addition to their task-relevant skills. As Argyris (1969) and others have shown, most individuals in organizations are not highly competent in managing complex and anxiety-arousing interpersonal situations. Yet if the group task is challenging and requires high member interdependence, then at least moderate interpersonal skills are required simply to bring the *task* skills of members effectively to bear on the work of the group. This is especially important when the group is demographically diverse (i.e., composed of people who differ in age, gender, or race).

4. Group composition should balance between excessive homogeneity and excessive heterogeneity of membership. If members are too much alike, some of the special advantages of having a team are lost (such as the chance for people to learn from one another, and the opportunity to bring special perspectives and unique expertise to bear on the task). Yet excessive heterogeneity also can impair group effectiveness, because there may be insufficient "common ground" among members for good communication or for needed interchangeability among members.

Composing a work team so that it meets the four criteria specified above is a complex undertaking. Standard job analysis and job selection procedures can be used to ensure that the group has members with sufficient task-relevant knowledge and skill, and a hard-nosed analysis of how many members are *actually* required to perform a task can lessen the risk that the group will be overstaffed. But it is a much more uncertain business to compose work groups that have the right "mix" of member skills and perspectives, and to ensure that members are sufficiently skilled interpersonally to work together effectively. Group composition deserves a good deal more attention and thought than it usually gets when teams, committees, and task forces are formed in organizations.

Group Norms About Performance Processes As shown in Figure 23-3, the norms of a group can affect the appropriateness of the performance strategies members use in carrying out work on the group task. Choices about performance strategy can be very important in determining how well a group performs. If, for example, successful completion of a certain task requires close coordination among members, with the contributions of each member made in a specific order at a specific time, then a group that has developed an explicit strategy for queuing and coordinating member inputs probably will perform better than a group that proceeds with the task using ad hoc or laissez faire procedures. What specific strategy will work best for a given group task, of course, depends heavily on the particular requirements of that task.

Performance strategies are generally under the control of group norms, in that members reach agreement early in their work on a task about how they will proceed to carry it out—and then routinely behave in accord with that decision. The way the group is working, or what it is attempting to achieve, may never again be addressed by members (even in those cases when the original performance strategy was agreed to implicitly rather than explicitly decided) (Hackman & Morris, 1975). And individuals who deviate from group expectations about how the work is to be done are likely to be brought quickly back into line by their fellow members.

The advantage of having clear norms about performance strategies is that the need to manage and coordinate group member behavior on a continuous basis is minimized, and more time thereby becomes available for actual productive work. The risk, of course, is that the performance strategies that are enforced may not be terribly appropriate for the task being performed. This is particularly a problem when task requirements or constraints change after questions of strategy have been settled—a not uncommon occurrence in organizational work.

The challenge in setting up a work group, then, is to help members develop norms that reinforce the use of strategies that are uniquely appropriate to the group task. This can be done by dictating performance strategies to the group (e.g., a manager diagnosing the requirements of the task and then telling members what they should do to perform it effectively). Reliance on an outsider, however, can significantly undermine the autonomy that group members experience in carrying out their work, and therefore can create motivational problems and/or relationship difficulties with the manager or consultant who tells them how they "should" behave.

An alternative (and often preferable) approach is to help group members learn how to develop and monitor their own norms about performance strategy. In effect, the persons responsible for creating the group help members develop a *general* norm that encourages open and self-conscious discussion of *specific* norms about how group members will work together on the task. While there is no guarantee that such discussions will actually generate innovative or uniquely task-appropriate performance strategies, at least *conditions have been created* such that questions of performance strategy—which are typically ignored or suppressed in work groups—are dealt with openly and explicitly.

The Organizational Context

There are numerous contextual factors that can affect work-group performance, ranging from mundane items, such as the ambience of the work place, to more significant features, such as the relationships between the work group and other groups with which it must deal. Three features of the organizational context deserve special attention here because they have direct relevance for group effort, knowledge and skill, and performance strategies. These contextual features can support and reinforce—or counteract and compromise—the impact of the design of the group itself. They are: (1) the reward system, (2) the educational system, and (3) the information system of the organization.

The Reward System The effectiveness of even a well-designed work group can be compromised if the organizational reward system is not congruent with how the work itself is structured. When the work is set up to be performed by a team, it often is advantageous for rewards to be made contingent on the performance of the group as a whole—or, when that is not feasible, on the performance of even larger organizational units, such as the department where the group is located (Lawler, 1977). A reward system that recognizes and reinforces excellent *group* performance can complement and amplify the motivational incentives that are built into the group task itself.

The same line of reasoning applies to *performance objectives* that are set for work groups. If specific, challenging objectives are set in collaboration with members of a well-designed work group, substantial motivational benefits often result.

On the other hand, problems may arise if the work is structured to be performed by an interacting team of employees, but individuals within the team are set off against one another in competing for scarce organizational rewards. When one decides to have a group perform work in an organization, one is accepting some constraints on the kind of reward system that is appropriate—a fact too often overlooked by managers who assign tasks to teams but pass out organizational rewards based on their perceptions of how well individual members are contributing to the team effort.

The Educational System   As we pointed out earlier, the talent a group has available for work on its task is most powerfully affected by how the group is composed in the first place. But good composition often is not enough: in addition, members may require education, training, and technical consultation as they proceed with their work—especially if the group task is particularly challenging or is unfamiliar to some group members.

Too often a work team is formed, given a large and complex task to perform, and then left to "work things out" on its own. If the knowledge and skill required for effective work on the task are not already available within the group, this can be both frustrating to group members and counterproductive.

In practice, it often is necessary to create new and direct organizational links between work teams and those staff groups that have special information, expertise, or training capabilities needed by those teams. Since such staff groups typically have dealt only with managers, it often is necessary for a line manager to help members of *both* the staff group and the work team learn that transactions between the two are not only appropriate but desirable. And sometimes training departments will have to add new "product lines" to their offerings (such as training in group problem-solving and decision-making skills) to meet the special educational needs of work groups.

Information System   Organizational information systems should provide work groups with clear information about performance requirements and constraints, and with whatever data about perform-ance processes and outcomes members need to monitor the adequacy of their task-performance strategies.

It was suggested earlier that a well-designed work group has a general norm that encourages active, inventive exploration of strategic alternatives for performing its task. The idea was that such a norm would improve the chances that a group would come up with an innovative or particularly task-effective way of proceeding. The success a group has in such an undertaking, however, also depends on how clearly members understand just what are (and are not) the outer-limit requirements and constraints under which the group must operate, and how well-informed they are about the likely consequences of various ways they might proceed with their work.

If task-relevant information is not available or is obscure, then group members will be handicapped in developing performance strategies that are task-appropriate. Indeed, they run the risk of developing and executing performance strategies that are nicely suited to a set of *incorrect* perceptions or assumptions about the nature of organizational reality. By ensuring that the work group has available to it clear and complete information about requirements, constraints, and the consequences of performance activities this risk is lessened—and the way is opened for members to develop strategies for proceeding with their work that are uniquely tailored to the idiosyncrasies of the task and the organizational unit where the work is being done.

Group Process Interventions

What about the interpersonal behaviors that take place within the work group itself? How do they affect the performance of the group, and how do they fit with the design of the group and the organizational context within which the group functions? Clearly, intermember relations in small work groups often leave much to be desired. Sometimes members fall too readily into competition and conflict among themselves, or provide too little support to one another in dealing with difficult and anxiety-arousing issues; other times groups may become so oriented toward sharing warmth, support, and good feelings that the task itself may be all but forgotten (Janis, 1972).

It would seem, therefore, that improving the quality of the interpersonal relations that develop among group members could help them improve their effectiveness. And a number of approaches to group consultation are based on this assumption (e.g., Argyris, 1962; Blake & Mouton, 1975). Such approaches often involve experiential sensitivity training or team building with intact groups, and they focus *directly* on the relations among members (more so than on the interface between the group and its task).

In general, research evidence suggests that such interventions can be powerful in changing what transpires in the training groups themselves and in altering member beliefs and attitudes about what behaviors are appropriate in a group setting. But the lessons learned seem not to transfer readily from the training to the work setting: the newly learned behaviors tend not to persist for very long in the absence of ongoing support and reinforcement; and the actual *task effectiveness* of groups receiving interpersonal training is rarely enhanced (and is sometimes impaired) (Kaplan, 1979). It therefore appears ill-advised to rely mainly on group process interventions for facilitating the performance of work teams in organizations. A more task-focused approach may be called for, one that gives special attention to those interpersonal issues that bear directly on how well a group is able to surmount the three performance "hurdles" we have been discussing (i.e., effort, knowledge and skill, and group performance strategies).

Effort   When effort is important in affecting how well a group performs, then process interventions that help members coordinate their activities in a way that minimizes the amount of effort that is wasted may improve the performance effectiveness of the group. There is always some slippage in the coordination of task-oriented efforts, which prevents groups from achieving their potential maximum productivity (Steiner, 1972). By helping a group identify the occasions when such slippage occurs and devise ways for minimizing it, a manager or consultant can increase the degree to which the potential of the group for hard and effective work is more fully realized.

Effort also is affected by how *committed* members are to the task, which suggests another opportunity for productivity-enhancing process interventions. Anything that can be done to increase the degree to which members value their membership, their

peers, and their work in the group should increase member commitment to the group and its work—and result in higher effort expended on the task.

Knowledge and Skill   The most troublesome process problem faced by groups working on tasks for which knowledge and skill are critical to performance effectiveness is the "weighting process" used to combine member contributions to the final group product. Too often the inputs of certain group members (e.g., those with high status) are given extra credence for reasons that have little to do with actual task-relevant knowledge or expertise. Interventions that help members improve the process by which they assess and weigh one another's contributions to the work of the group can be very helpful on tasks for which knowledge and skill are critical to team effectiveness.

Also useful are interventions that help members learn how to share with one another their own special task-relevant skills, and to work together to gain knowledge or generate skills that previously did not exist in the group at all. Members of newly formed work groups in traditional organizations often are not comfortable or competent in using one another as resources for individual and collective learning, and interventions that foster such learning activities can have significant long-term payoffs for the group and its members.

Performance Strategies   Managers or consultants can assist a work group in "reading" its task correctly, and in developing performance strategies that are well-tuned to task and organizational requirements and constraints. Such interventions can minimize the degree to which group members work at cross-purposes to task requirements or organizational objectives.

Interventionists also may be able to help group members learn how to invent performance strategies that foster "synergistic" effects in the process of the group. A group might, for example, become more experimental in thinking about how members could proceed with their work—e.g., trying one way of working together, assessing its effectiveness, and then either fine-tuning that approach or trying yet another way of proceeding. Experimentation and inventiveness are observed rarely in work teams. Interventions that help members learn *how* to experiment with their own performance strategies can, in some cases, set in motion an ongoing process of testing and exploration that results in more or less continuous improvement in how well members perform their work.

Summary

The model of work group effectiveness that has been developed in the preceding pages is summarized in Figure 23-5. To the extent that the model has validity (and it has not yet been subjected to systematic research testing), it suggests a five-step process for creating and managing work teams in organizations.

Step 1: Assessing Feasibility   Probably the single most significant choice that must be made when a work system is designed (or redesigned) is whether to use individuals or teams as the basic performing unit for carrying out the work. Sometimes there is not much choice: the work is such that it *must* be

done by an individual (e.g., conducting an orchestra) or by a team (e.g., playing a string quartet). Other times there is latitude, and those responsible for the design of the organization must decide one way or the other.

In most cases, however, one could go with *either* option. How should the choice be made? In an extended discussion of this question provided elsewhere (Hackman & Oldham, 1980), it is suggested that teams generally should be used only when they appear to offer substantial advantages over well-designed individual jobs. Why? For one thing, designing, implementing, and managing work teams requires a good deal of talent and sophistication on the part of organizational managers—qualities that may not be in abundant supply in many organizations where work traditionally has been structured exclusively for individual employees. Moreover, creating a *well-designed* team (i.e., one that meets the criteria specified in the preceding pages, not one

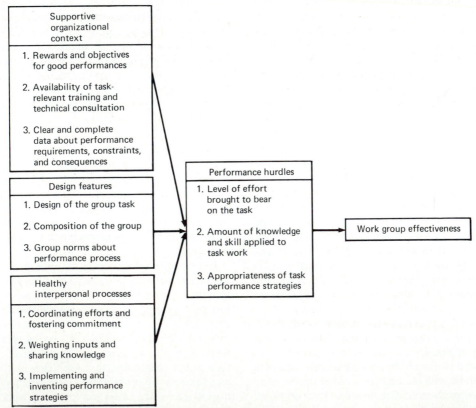

Figure 23-5   The effectiveness of self-managing work groups: a summary model.

formed merely by assembling a set of people and giving them a task to perform) typically requires more pronounced alterations of existing organizational practices and managerial styles than does the redesign of individual jobs.

Well-designed work groups *can* generate beneficial outcomes for the organization and for its employees that far exceed those of enriched individual jobs. But unless it is both feasible and clearly advantageous to design work for teams, it may be more prudent in traditional organizations to implement the less radical option of improving the design of the jobs of individual employees.

Step 2: Designing the Group   The next step is to invent a good design for the group, given organizational objectives and the imperatives of the work technology. Which of the three performance "hurdles" is most critical to team effectiveness for the work that is being done, and therefore deserving of the greatest attention when the group is designed? How can the group be set up so it has a good chance of surmounting the key performance hurdles? Can a highly motivating group task be structured? Can a reasonably *small* group be composed with a good mix of talented and socially skilled members? Can group norms be developed that foster open and inventive formulation of task-appropriate performance strategies?

Step 3: Forming the Group   It is not enough merely to bring the prospective members together, give them their task, and suggest that they get down to work. Instead, members will need some time, and perhaps some outside assistance, to develop their identity as a task-oriented social system and to assume responsibility for their own internal processes. In effect, responsibility for the process and performance of the group must be carefully and sensitively "handed off" from management to the group members.

Step 4: Providing Organizational Supports   Attention next turns to the organizational context in which the group will work. Can organizational policies and practices be put in place that support rather than impede the group in overcoming the performance hurdles? Can rewards and objectives be structured so that they encourage hard, effective work by group members? Can educational and consultative assistance be made readily available to the group if members need it (e.g., to hone their task skills or to deal with particularly challenging work problems)? Can organizational information systems be structured to provide groups with the data they need to manage their own work processes and to develop performance strategies that are uniquely suited to the group task?

Step 5: Fostering Good Interpersonal Processes   Finally, the interpersonal processes that develop among group members should be addressed. Do intermember behaviors and relationships foster or impede competent work on the group task? How well do members coordinate their task-oriented efforts? Is member commitment to the group and its work sufficiently high? How are the talents of different group members assessed, weighted, and brought to bear on the work? Are members sharing uniquely held knowledge and skills with one another and, even better, are they working together to enrich the overall pool of talent in the group? Are the performance strategies used by the group optimally appropriate for the task, or should members be encouraged to reconsider how they are proceeding with their work? Once strategies are selected, are members executing them well, or is there disagreement and confusion about how the group should operate?

Summary   The order of the five steps reviewed above is deliberate. Too often managers or consultants attempt to "fix" a group that has performance problems by going to work directly on obvious difficulties that exist in members' interpersonal processes. And, too often, these difficulties turn out not to be readily fixable because they are only symptoms of more basic flaws in the design of the group or in its organizational context. Process is indeed an important thing, but it is not the only thing.

REFERENCES

Argyris, C. *Interpersonal competence and organizational effectiveness.* Homewood, Ill.: Irwin-Dorsey, 1962.
———. The incompleteness of social psychological theory: Examples from small group, cognitive consistency, and attribution research. *American Psychologist*, 1969, **24**, 893–908.
Blake, R. R., & Mouton, J. S. Group and organizational team building: A theoretical model for intervening. In

C. L. Cooper (Ed.), *Theories of group processes*. New York: Wiley, 1975.

Bucklow, M. A new role for the work group. In L. E. Davis & J. C. Taylor (Eds.), *Design of jobs*. Middlesex, England: Penguin, 1972.

Ford, R. N. *Motivation through the work itself*. New York: American Management Association, 1969.

Glaser, E. M. *Improving the quality of worklife . . . And in the process, improving productivity*. Los Angeles: Human Interaction Research Institute, 1975.

Hackman, J. R. Toward understanding the role of tasks in behavioral research. *Acta Psychologica,* 1969, **31,** 97–128.

————, & Lawler, E. E. Employee reactions to job characteristics. *Journal of Applied Psychology Monograph,* 1971, **55,** 259–286.

————, & Oldham, G. R. Development of the Job Diagnostic Survey. *Journal of Applied Psychology,* 1975, **60,** 159–170.

————, & Oldham, G. R. Motivation through the design of work: Test of a theory. *Organizational Behavior and Human Performance,* 1976, **16,** 250–279.

————, & Oldham, G. R. *Work Redesign.* Reading, Mass.: Addison-Wesley, 1980.

————, Oldham, G. R. Janson, R., & Purdy, K. A new strategy for job enrichment. *California Management Review,* 1975, **17**(4), 57–71.

Herzberg, F. The wise old Turk. *Harvard Business Review,* 1974, **52,** 70–80.

Janis, I. L. *Victims of groupthink.* Boston: Houghton Mifflin, 1972.

Kaplan, R. E. The conspicuous absence of evidence that process intervention enhances performance. *Journal of Applied Behavioral Science,* 1979, **15,** 346–360.

Katzell, R. A., Yankelovich, D., et al. *Work, productivity and job satisfaction.* New York: The Psychological Corporation, 1975.

Lawler, E. E., III. Reward systems. In J. R. Hackman & J. L. Suttle (Eds.), *Improving life at work: Behavioral science approaches to organizational change.* Santa Monica, Calif.: Goodyear, 1977.

————, & Hall, D. T. The relationship of job characteristics to job involvement, satisfaction and intrinsic motivation. *Journal of Applied Psychology,* 1970, **54,** 305–312.

Oldham, G. R. Job characteristics and internal motivation: The moderating effect of interpersonal and individual variables. *Human Relations,* 1976, **29,** 559–569.

————, Hackman, J. R., & Pearce, J. L. Conditions under which employees respond postively to enriched work. *Journal of Applied Psychology,* 1976, **61,** 395–403.

Steiner, I. D. *Group process and productivity.* New York: Academic, 1972.

Walters, R. W., & Associates. *Job enrichment for results.* Reading, Mass.: Addison-Wesley, 1975.

Weiss, H. M., & Shaw, J. B. Social influences on judgments about tasks. *Organizational Behavior and Human Performance,* 1979, **24,** 126–140.

Reading 24

Work Innovations in the United States
Richard E. Walton

Americans tend to do things by trial and error, and in dealing with changes in the way they work, they are no different. Whereas changes in European workplaces tend to be guided by government intervention and ideological rationalizations and involve an explicit transfer of authority, innovations in American workplaces are voluntary and pragmatic and involve no such transfer.[1] Despite its random nature, however, much change that has been planned has occurred in American workplaces during the past ten years.

Observers differ about whether work improvement is a fad or a long-term transformation in the nature of work organizations. Scientists differ in their theoretical explanations of why it works or when the conditions are right for it. Managers invariably wonder whether it has application in their organizations, and some union officials are concerned about its implications for the union as an institution. These concerns imply varying concep-

[1]See Ted Mills, "Europe's Industrial Democracy: An American Response," *HBR* November–December 1978, p. 143.

Author's note: I wish to express my special thanks to Leonard Schlesinger, who has reviewed this manuscript at different stages of its development and made helpful suggestions for improving it.

tions of work innovaton and hence indicate the amount of confusion that exists about what work improvement is.

In this article, I want to look at what has actually changed in workplaces, find out what we can learn from these work improvement activities, and derive some principles from what is reflected in the most successful ones. First, though, let us clarify what "work improvement" means and how I will be using it in the remainder of this article.

WHAT WORK IMPROVEMENT IS

The planned changes called "work improvements" have appeared in workplaces in many guises—as "quality of work life," "humanization of work," "work reform," "work restructuring," "work design," and "sociotechnical systems."

Although some of these terms have special connotations for the professionals who employ them, in method and goals the actual activities pursued under the various labels are not very different. I find it useful to distinguish three separate aspects of a work improvement effort.

1. Design Techniques

The element of work improvement activities that is most apparent is the specific changes in the way work is organized and managed. For instance, the content of tasks changes when jobs are enriched, work teams affect the way tasks are organized and how they relate to each other, and consultative management gives workers the opportunity to influence decisions that affect them. The techniques may also affect the information provided workers as well as their compensation, security, physical environment, and access to due process.

The techniques employed and their possible combinations are many. For example, in changing assembly methods, auto plants have assigned related tasks to work teams, allowed them to decide how to allocate the work among themselves (provided they meet quality and quantity requirements), and created buffer inventories between adjacent work teams to increase latitude in the rhythm of their work. Also, management and unions in competitive manufacturing situations have designed plantwide schemes to share productivity increases and have

structured mechanisms to ensure the workers' ideas for improvement are considered.

2. Intended Results

Another aspect of work improvement is the results it is intended to produce. They can be either economic (for the benefit of the organization) or human (for the benefit of employees). The business benefits can take many forms—quality, delivery, materials, usage, machine capacity utilization, and labor efficiency. The human benefits can take form as real income, security, challenge, variety, advancement opportunity, dignity, equity, and sense of community. The relative importance of these depends on the needs and aspirations of the employees in question.

Most of the work improvement labels focus narrowly on either techniques or results. For example, "job enrichment" directs attention to the techniques level and only to one technique. The connotation of "job design" is only slightly broader. "Quality of work life" has the same limitations. It refers directly to an objective that can be served in innumerable ways. Moreover, as labels, "quality of work life" and its first cousin, "humanization of work," have serious drawbacks; they refer only to human gains, which in today's business environment need to be closely coupled with improved competitive performance.

In my experience, I have found that organizations can improve business results in a humane way and improve the quality of the human experience in a businesslike manner by identifying the work cultures that promote both improvements simultaneously. Such work cultures are the links between technique and results in my three-level conception of work improvements.

3. Work Culture: The Intermediate Effects

The combination of attitudes, relationships, developed capabilities, habits, and other behavioral patterns that characterize the dynamics of an organization is a work culture.

Some changes in the culture, such as high-cost consciousness, responsiveness to authority, and high activity norms, may promote performance but do little or nothing for people. Conversely, under some circumstances, high sensitivity to feelings and concern for the personal growth of the individual are cultural attributes that may be appreciated by the people affected but may not by themselves contribute to business performance.

In the most successful work improvement efforts, the culture simultaneously enhances business performance and the quality of human experience. In one food plant, for instance, management sought to promote employee identification with goals. Such positive identification increases not only workers' motivation to work but also their sense of belonging in the workplace and their pride in the plant's achievement. Similarly, a behavior pattern that influences both employee self-esteem and the soundness of business decisions is another desirable cultural attribute.

Identification and mutual influence are ideals common to many work improvement projects, but no single culture is ideal for all businesses or all people. What particular set of attitudes, capabilities, and relationships a company should emphasize will depend on its industry's strategic performance indexes and its employees' work life values. Whatever the work culture sought, it cannot be mandated by anyone. It can only be shaped over time by a combination of things—including the techniques by which work is organized and managed.

Let us review how these three aspects of work improvement activities relate to each other.

Techniques are the elements of the work organization that people can alter directly; intended results are the fundamental business and human criteria by which to judge effectiveness; and the work culture mediates the impact of the former on the latter. The techniques create the culture, which strongly influences business performance and the human experience at work.

According to this conception, one's choice of techniques is guided by continuously referring to the type of work culture that they promote, and in turn to projected business and human outcomes. For example, in a paper manufacturing plant, the business ends required that the manpower be flexible, and employees wanted the opportunity to acquire new skills. The plant adopted a design in which teams are responsible for a cluster of tasks and members are rewarded for acquiring the skills to perform all the team tasks. Such a design promotes both flexibility and opportunity. (The three-level conception of work improvement is shown in *Exhibit 24-1;* the arrows indicate influence.)

The exhibit illustrates how important it is to specify the proper business and work life outcomes for a particular company.

Applying this concept, one is also guided in the quality of choice one should make at each level. As one moves backward in the exhibit from intended results through work culture to design techniques, one's stance should become increasingly pragmatic. If the desired outcomes are clear and one's commitment to both business and human values is firm, then one can evaluate cultural attributes and in turn

Level I Design techniques	Level II Work culture ideals	Level III Intended results
Job design	High skill levels and flexibility in using them	*For business:*
Pay	Identification with product, process, and total business viewpoint	Low cost
Supervisor's role	Problem solving instead of finger pointing	Quick delivery
Training	Influence by information and expertise instead of by position	High-quality products
Performance feedback	Mutual influence	Low turnover
Goal setting	Openness	Low absenteeism
Communication	Responsiveness	Equipment utilization
Employment stability policies	Trust	*For quality of work life:*
Status symbols	Egalitarian climate	Self-esteem
Leadership oatterns	Equity	Economic well-being
		Security

Note: The design techniques, cultural ideals, and intended results listed above are presented as illustrative, not as comprehensive or even universally applicable. Also, the items in the three columns are not horizontally lined up to relate to each other. The arrows indicate influence.

Exhibit 24-1   Three-level conception of work improvement.

design techniques in terms of their efficacy in achieving the desired results.

INTEREST IN WORK INNOVATION

Over the past decade, media attention has gradually shifted from focusing on the symptoms of disaffection with work to possible solutions. The amount of work improvement activity in plants and offices throughout the United States has grown steadily, appearing to be on the path of a classical S growth curve, in which growth climbs slowly at first, accelerates, and then slows again. Today, the rate of growth in these experiments continues to increase annually, suggesting that we are approaching the steeper portion of the curve.

Extrapolating from available information, I estimate that an important minority of the *Fortune "500"* companies are attempting some significant work improvement projects. And, not surprisingly, the companies that have greater commitment to and experience with such projects are among the leaders in their respective industries: General Motors, Procter & Gamble, Exxon, General Foods, TRW, and Cummins Engine. Less prominent but similarly well-managed manufacturing companies such as Butler Manufacturing and Mars, Inc. have also become increasingly active in this area. Citibank is one company with major work improvement efforts in the office environment.[2] Prudential Insurance is another.

All of the manufacturing companies I have listed have regarded new plant start-ups as opportunities to introduce major new work structures. In recent years, major projects have begun in organizations of various sizes (from 100 to over 3,000), with varying technologies (from simple hand assembly to sophisticated continuous flow processes) and in different geographical locations (from upstate New York to the deep South and the West). As these companies extend their innovative work systems to other new plant sites, managers learn from the experience of the pioneers, and the systems cease to be regarded as experimental. Although the diffusion generally occurs slowly, the principles that underlie these new designs usually spread to companies' established

plants as well. Let us look at some of these work innovations in detail.

Individual Projects

HBR readers have been exposed to a number of accounts of individual efforts (e.g., the Topeka Pet Food Plant) and to the distinctive approaches of several U.S. companies (e.g., Donnelly Mirrors and Eaton Corporation).[3] Although not fully representative of the diverse practices that one can observe, these experiments do illustrate the growing work improvement activity in the United States.

To my knowledge, the activity of General Motors is the most extensive of any company in the United States and may be more extensive than that of Volvo, whose pioneering efforts have been well publicized internationally. GM's dozens of projects take a variety of forms. One long-term effort at GM began in the early 1970s in an assembly plant in Tarrytown, New York, What began as a "What-have-we-got-to-lose?" experiment in which workers and the union were involved in redesigning the hard- and soft-trim departments' facilities has blossomed into a plantwide quality of work life program involving over 3,500 people.

A different type of project at GM began in 1974 at a new battery plant in Fitzgerald, Georgia, where the pay system was set up to reward knowledge and skills acquisition. After four years, almost all workers there have become familiar with a wide range of jobs and have detailed knowledge of the production process. Initially, inspectors evaluated the workers' performance, out eventually the production teams themselves acquired the responsibility to ensure high-quality performance. Since 1977, work teams have prepared their own departmental budgets for materials and supplies. Managers provide workers with information such as cost data, which is traditionally now shown to them. The sparse and functional offices reveal the prevailing attitude about status symbols.

The pay system, self-supervision, and other design techniques have been combined at the Fitzger-

---

[2]See Richard J. Matteis, "The New Back Office Focuses on Customer Service," *HBR* March–April 1979, p. 146.

[3]See my article, "How to Counter Alienation in the Plant," *HBR* November–December 1972, p. 70; "Participative Management at Work," An Interview with John F. Donnelly, *HBR* January–February 1977, p. 117; and Donald N. Scobel, "Doing Away with the Factory Blues," *HBR* November–December 1975, p. 132.

ald plant to create a work culture characterized by flexibility, mutual trust, informality, equality, and commitment. Reportedly, the Fitzgerald plant's performance has been very favorable, compared both with other plants and with its own plan. Those familiar with the plant attribute much of its superior performance to the work structure and to the fact that workers take pride in establishing new levels of output and quality.

Another innovator in this field is as much a leader in nondurable consumer goods as GM is in durable goods but shuns publicity of any of its work improvements. It regards the knowledge it has developed about implementing innovative work systems as proprietary, similar to other types of know-how that give it a competitive edge.

In the late 1960s in one plant of a major division, this company introduced a new work system designed around the idea that workers would be paid according to their skill levels. Under this system, the company does not impose quotas to limit the number who could advance to higher levels. The work system promotes the development of relatively self-supervising work teams. The basic features of this system have been adapted to the six new plants built subsequently as well as to departments in the preexisting, unionized plants of the division.

Because successful work improvement approaches have not always spread to other plants within the same company, it is worth noting why transfer did occur in this case. The acceptance of change in the existing plants has been fueled by their need to remain competitive with the newer plants, which employ more productive work structures. The change has been facilitated by transferring managers with experience from the innovative plants to the established ones. Also, whenever a new technology or project has been launched or major physical renovations planned, work innovations have been introduced in the old plants.

I have observed many of the plants in this company. Without a doubt, their innovative work systems have contributed significantly to the impressive performance of these plants and to the fact that by a wide margin the plants are usually regarded as the best places to work in their respective communities.

Although GM and the manufacturer of nondurable goods are leaders in the field of work improvements, they are not typical. Most companies, such as

Butler Manufacturing, have only a few projects. In 1976, Butler introduced innovative work structures similar to the one at GM's Fitzgerald plant in two new plants. In one plant, the program is working exceptionally well; participants are enthusiastic about the work system and think it contributes strongly to their performance. According to pertinent internal criteria, this plant is 20% more productive and 35% more profitable than comparable plants in the same company.

The other new plant has experienced difficulties, and it is less clear that it has benefited from the work innovations.

The experience of a large paper company is also typical. With encouragement and support from the company's chairman, management launched two major facilitywide projects at the time of the plants' start-ups. When I last heard, the paper mill project was regarded as successful, but the other, in a converting plant, was not. Extenuating circumstances in the marketplace have contributed to the lack of profitability of the converting plant. Also, misjudgments in design reportedly have not been remedied, and optimism is declining.

Most companies experience both success and failure. One large company with four major plantwide projects has experienced almost the full spectrum. A plant that started up with a bold and imaginative work structure three and half years ago has been very disappointing in terms of economic performance and the work system itself. Local management and union officials judge a second plant to be only somewhat more effective than it would have been without the innovations. A third is solidly effective, and a fourth is a big success according to both human and economic criteria.

The examples I have discussed so far are plant projects, but comparably conceived work improvement efforts have been occurring in office settings as well. In 1972, the clerical work in the Group Policyholders' Service Department of the Guardian Life Insurance Company was fragmented. To process a case file required several steps, such performed by a different person at a different desk in assembly line fashion. Files were hard to find, and responses to client inquiries were delayed. No one person performed or had responsibility for a whole job. Consequently, there was little basis for meaningful recognition of achievement, and morale was low.

The work improvement effort created natural units of work by combining policyholder services and accounting functions for a particular geographic area. The new "account analyst" became identified with a limited and stable set of clients with whom he or she maintained contact and for whom he or she provided a number of services previously assigned to different desks. Control over individual aspects of the work was removed, and individual accountability for overall results was increased.

Although the new work system at Guardian required people to go through complex training, with the result that 6 out of 120 employees could not meet the demands of the redesigned jobs, management reports that the system was effective in producing cumulative increases in productivity of about 33% in four years.

Top Management Interest

Part of the evidence supporting my projection of a continued acceleration of the growth rate of new projects goes beyond concrete activities; it is found in the trend toward increased top management attention to work innovation. Whereas five years ago it was plant or division level managers who invariably sought educational or consultative assistance for potential projects, today it is equally likely that inquiries will come from top corporate managers who are interested in advancing their own understanding of the field, formulating appropriate policies, and promoting constructive corporate activity.

Also, whereas before managers would invite professors to meet with them and report on developments in the field, today it is equally likely that managers with direct experience in promoting work innovations will address these management groups. For example, the chairman of the board of a major packaging company recently assembled his top corporate and divisional executives to learn about the work innovations of a major automobile company by a firsthand report of the auto company's vice chairman.

A particularly striking example of the trend toward top management interest in work innovations and toward more manager-to-manager consultation on the subject is provided by a November 1977 conference sponsored by the American Center for the Quality of Working Life. Convened for the purpose of exchanging experiences and examining

from the "practical viewpoint of operating executives the principles underlying quality of work life efforts and their efficacy in society," the conference was attended by 40 senior executives from Xerox, General Motors, Nabisco, and Weyerhaeuser.

The "blue collar blues" may promote the adoption and diffusion of innovative work designs in a wide range of industries, from blue collar manufacturing work to white collar and service work and in both the private and the public sector, but a major reason companies are trying work improvement projects is competition. Another is the changing expectations of workers, whose consciousness of quality of work life issues continues to rise. Another is the implicit threat of legislation that might set new, more embracing quality of work environment standards or that might require workers to participate in the governance of private industry.

ASKING THE RIGHT QUESTIONS

Despite the many good reasons for attempting work improvement systems, their future depends on how managers approach some fundamental issues and whether they reject the myths surrounding these efforts. Some misconceptions yield easily to more valid assumptions; others appear to need more direct challenge.

Have Work Improvements Been Effective?

There has been a tendency for people to assume that work innovation projects are either spectacular successes or abject failures. At the expense of some widely held myths, however, people active in the field have become increasingly realistic, recognizing that, in fact, projects can and do fall at every point along a broad spectrum of effectiveness.

I have been deeply involved in 4 major projects and am familiar with aspects of another 30 or so. In terms of their effectiveness in achieving excellence in business and quality of work life outcomes, my impression is that these three dozen projects represent roughly a normal distribution around the mean, just as the effectiveness of more conventionally organized plants would be expected to form a normal distribution.

I believe that the average effectiveness of these innovative work systems is higher than the average of more conventionally organized but otherwise comparable plants. Certainly, however, the poorly managed innovative plants are less effective than the better managed conventional ones. I cannot offer proof that these assumptions are valid, but the mixed experiences of the companies I have discussed illustrate my observations.

Despite the evidence, the myths persist. I have visited a few innovative plants that were advertised as significantly successful, only to discover that they were at best marginally more effective than they would have been without the work innovations. And I have read reports of the "failures" of previously publicized projects, which, on investigation, I found were faulty. People had blown some difficulties encountered in the design or implementation of the projects way out of proportion.

Why these exaggerations? First, people view such efforts with emotion—some being deeply committed to work improvement activities, others being basically hostile to them. Second, where they are involved, the media deem dramatic successes and failures to be newsworthy. Third, because their expectations are high, people readily see any shortfall as a failure.

Even assuming that work innovations have merit, managers and researchers need to have the realistic expectation that their effectiveness will conform to some normal distribution.

What Are the Sponsors' Motives?

Myths have surrounded the motives of those promoting or undertaking work improvement activities. People see sponsors as narrowly interested in either productivity or the human condition, each at the expense of the other. During the early 1970s, when much interest in work improvement was stimulated by one of the two objectives, these beliefs had some basis in reality, but the situation has gradually changed.

In the successful innovations, managers behave as if both economic and human values count. I am familiar with several major innovative work systems that have taken a long time to become effective (and in one plant remain not very effective today) because management's choices were too heavily influenced by quality of work life considerations in the beginning.

In one case, for example, while stability of assignments and mastery of jobs was necessary to get the plant's new technology under control, employees were permitted to move among jobs and learn multiple skills that would advance their pay. Management later recognized that it had erred in not continuously keeping economic as well as human considerations in mind.

Conversely, I am aware of some abortive job redesign efforts in which management strictly viewed worker satisfaction either as a means to improve productivity or as an incidental by-product. Not surprisingly, management's orientation affected not only what changes were made but also workers' attitudes toward the changes. Many union officials believe it unwise to be publicly committed to productivity as well as to quality of work life goals lest the former be identified with speedups and other activities that achieve productivity at the workers' expense. Nevertheless, union officials often implicitly acknowledge the legitimacy of improved business results.

A commitment to dual outcomes is congruent with the values increasingly held by knowledgeable people, but also it has proved to be the most practical approach to making significant advances toward either end. Consider the point negatively. When changes in the work structure do not improve the work environment from a human perspective, they will not increase employees' contribution to the business; likewise, changes in work structure that require managers to relate differently to workers but do not also benefit the business are not as likely to sustained by those managers over time.

One should not confuse a dedication to achieving both results with the assumption that meeting one will guarantee the other; morale and productivity are not necessarily linked. Morale can be enhanced in any number of ways. Rather, a commitment to dual objectives sets in motion a search for the limited set of changes that will promote both human and economic ends.

Some issues will inevitably not yield to dual orientation. Planners and managers will have to make trade-off decisions in areas where achieving human goals can occur only at the expense of the business, and vice versa. Nevertheless, it is more important for those involved in work improvement to recognize that in most work structures there is an abundance of opportunities to make changes that will advance both objectives.

What Do Workers Really Want from Work?

Individuals and groups will always express broad differences in the types of work structure they prefer. Therefore, as the multiple-level framework indicates, the ideal culture and the design features of the work structure need to be responsive to the employee population at a given location. Even though researchers and managers are learning which questions about employees' needs and preferences will provide good guidelines to practice, they continue to ask a few either-or questions, which are more confusing than helpful.

Observers often ask variations of the following question: "Are people motivated more by intrinsic factors, such as tasks that use and develop their skills, or by extrinsic factors, such as variable pay for performance and the prospect of advancement?" Both kinds of factor are important, albeit one may be more important to any one group at any one time. The most significant question is how to integrate both extrinsic and intrinsic factors in a practical way.

My observation is that workers in innovative systems have not had to choose between more interesting work and more pay; and that where intrinsic satisfaction has increased, the pay has been improved, reflecting the workers' greater contribution. As Irving Bluestone of the UAW has said of the American worker, "While his rate of pay may dominate his relationship to his job, he can be responsive to the opportunity for playing an innovative, creative and imaginative role in the production process."[4]

A related question people often ask is: "Are people more interested in finding meaning in the workplace or in minimizing the time spent there?" While the answer to this question may add to our understanding of the sociology of work today, it is not a productive question for improving current practice. It is better to assume that the work force as a whole would like both in some measure.

But, even if some workers care more about time off than a meaningful work life, it may still pay to heed the lower priority issue because improving the meaning of the workplace may be much more feasible than reducing the workweek. Speculating

about workers' desires also leads to the related myths about regional differences and the need for selective hiring. Each myth is built on the assumption that a relatively small subset of the work force has attitudes and talents compatible with work restructuring. I have heard managers assert, "It may work in a plant located in a small town in the Midwest, but workers in the South (or the Northeast, California, big cities, and so on) are different."

If an innovative plant is located in an abundant labor market where supervisors screen, say, six times as many applicants as they actually hire, then their myth may be: "Only one in six is a high achiever who will be receptive to the new work structure. It is okay to redesign work if you can be selective but not if you are in a tight labor market."

What Economic Benefits Can One Expect?

Managers frequently ask: "How much productivity gain can one expect from work redesign?" Unfortunately, some advocates answer: "One should be able to achieve 15% to 20% improvement in productivity." The question itself is emphatically misdirected, and the response just cited is meaningless without knowing what index of productivity the questioner has in mind and whether it is appropriate. For example, the number of output units per man-hour may not be an important index when labor is a low fraction of total costs. Moreover, prior to analysis of the operations in question, one cannot assume a basis for the estimates.

An inquiry and response should focus on methods by which managers can answer the question for themselves. The form of potential gains will vary significantly according to the technology used. The magnitude of possible gains will depend on how well the unit is already performing and on whether the aspects of performance that can be improved are strongly influenced by employees' attitudes and skills. Finally, whether potential gains ever materialize depends on the quality of redesign ideas and their implementation.

The following examples illustrate how productivity indexes can take different forms:

• A facility that warehouses and supplies engine parts to dealers and dealer chains could gain new accounts by speeding up its delivery response; it could add very profitable business if it could promise

---

[4]See Irving Bluestone, "The Next Step Toward Industrial Democracy" (Detroit: UAW Paper 1972), p. 4.

certain large national chains 48 hours versus 72 hours for delivery.

- In a capital-intensive plant that machines casted parts, management determined that it was technically feasible to increase by 15% the maximum throughput of a $10 million segment of the technology manned by 10 employees. This rate has, however, been achieved only for brief periods of time because of the limitations of operating personnel. Running speeds and machine downtime play a similarly important role in other parts of this plant and strongly affect its competitiveness.

- In a relatively high labor-intensive business, management was experiencing a high rate of turnover. The particular tasks, mostly assembly line jobs, did not require great skill, but learning the idiosyncrasies of the company's many different products took a lot of time. While the new employees were learning to deal with these peculiarities, their higher scrap rates and lower labor efficiency significantly affected unit costs. As a result, the turnover costs were significant.

To assess the potential of work improvements in the foregoing operations, one should ask: "How much difference would it make if workers cared more and knew more about this work?" Let us examine the first example in light of this question to show how one can begin to analyze the situation.

First, one needs some facts: the replacement engine parts center employs about 100 hourly workers; the pay is good for this type of work in the area; turnover is relatively low; and labor relations are amicable. While workers do not especially identify with management and many are known to goof off whenever possible, they are not antagonistic.

After a preliminary analysis of the various ways in which performance is sensitive to employee motivation and knowledge, the management of the center estimated that:

1 Employees could reasonably handle a 10% additional volume, even allowing for increased time to be devoted to training and regular meetings. But the 10% savings would not create a net economic benefit because the wage increases reflecting greater job scope and skills would offset them.

2 The cost of errors (orders lost, wrong parts pulled, overages, underages, or damages in shipment due to carelessness) could be reduced by $100,000 per year.

3 The work system could reliably handle up to 25% of the facility's volume within a 48-hour response time, enabling the management to win over some additional accounts and increase the margins on some existing ones and thereby to add an estimated $200,000 more profit per year.

4 The potential benefits of $300,000 assumes a work force that cares more and knows more and that is amenable to flexibility in work assignments based on the needs of the business, the latter point being especially critical to reducing the center's response time.

The foregoing analysis illustrates good practice.

First, management identified particular points in the system where poor labor utilization, errors, and limitations in response time occurred. It did not rely on global hunches.

Second, by converting potential gains to annual dollar amounts, management could see the relative importance of error reduction and improved response time. Moreover, management could relate the benefits to other factors; for example, $300,000 would be a savings equal to 25% of the annual payroll.

Third, management understood these were potential benefits and not certain gains that would automatically flow from the adoption of some set of design techniques. Its ability to achieve any of these benefits depended on its ingenuity and skill. It always ran the risk that it would not be able to modify the work culture as intended.

Fourth, management knew that for any changes to be effective from a business standpoint, it would also have to improve the work from the workers' point of view.

Managers in the machining operation and assembly unit followed procedures similar to the one just outlined. However, their estimate of benefits took a different form. Because they could spread the large fixed interest and depreciated expenses, managers in the capital-intensive machining operation figured that increasing the output rate of finished parts by 15% would result in lower unit costs. The estimated annual savings represented 150% of the $140,000 payroll for the unit—that is, $210,000.

In the assembly line unit, the managers concluded that it was not feasible to reduce turnover significantly, that only modest improvements in scrap and labor efficiency were possible, and that costs associated with any changes contemplated would largely offset the estimated gains.

In cases such as those just described, management's analyses are limited by the same difficulties encountered in estimating the costs and benefits of untried technologies or management systems—that is, the estimates can prove to be incomplete, too optimistic, too conservative, and so on. Nevertheless, the analytic approach presented here illustrates the systematic and realistic efforts managers should make to assess the potential performance gains.

Which procedures a manager actually uses and the level of detail of the analysis is not the point. The important point is that planners have some systematic approach for assessing potential benefits that might accrue if the cultural ideals are actually realized. The methodology need not be elaborate.

SOME LESSONS FROM EXPERIENCE

For those who consider undertaking new initiatives and promoting the spread of successful innovations to other units in the organization, I offer the following guidelines. Though not comprehensive, they are nonetheless derived from observations of the contrasts between relatively effective work improvement efforts and less effective ones.

1. *Attempt work improvement because of its intrinsic positive values, not because it might be a way to avoid unionization.* Apart from the fact that I believe in the institution of collective bargaining, trying to avoid unionization has several drawbacks. One is that unions are more likely to join in efforts to adapt innovations to existing facilities if work patterns are not being used as an antiunion device in the new plants. Another is that, although most projects in the United States have been in non-unionized offices and plants, the amount of joint union-management cooperation is increasing. Such projects as Harman Industries, Weyerhaeuser, Tennessee Valley Authority, the Rushton Coal Mines, and Rockwell International attest to the benefit of cooperation.

As I stated earlier, GM and UAW have a very active program of work improvement. The approach, contractually agreed on by the parties, is oriented to quality of work life, but as the Tarrytown experience illustrates, management, union officials, and workers are all genuinely interested in the business results. Irving Bluestone, international vice president of the UAW, describes the joint GM-UAW program as follows:

"The objective of our quality of work life program

is to create a more participative and satisfying work environment. If, as a result of increased participation, unit costs are improved because turnover rates go down and product quality goes up, that is fine.

"But if a plant manager is thinking of a quality of work life project as a means for increasing productivity, we don't proceed. There are certain other constraints—people must not be compelled to work harder, changes must not result in workers getting laid off, and the local and national agreements remain inviolate. The projects must be from the ground up and participation voluntary on the part of workers. The first phase of all projects is to improve the climate of mutual respect between union and management; if this doesn't succeed, there is no basis to proceed on. Plant management and the local union must both be committed."[5]

During the past half dozen years, as work improvement activities have been growing in number, diversity, and visibility, both labor and management have encountered doubt within their own ranks. UAW officials have not found it easy to convince union members that the program is not a management gimmick to increase productivity and perhaps weaken the union.

At GM, managers at certain levels express concern that the program will result in a loss of authority and prestige. These fears are diminishing gradually but can flare up at any event that seems to support them. Still, the commitment at the top of both organizations has been extraordinary and is bolstered by a growing constituency of local managers and union officials who have had positive experiences.

According to Bluestone, very few projects have actually failed, but more time must pass before the majority of projects currently under way can be declared successes.

2. *Recognize the basic difference between opportunities in new facilities and opportunities in existing ones.* Once, most people assumed that the major innovations introduced in new plant start-ups could serve as inspirational and instructive examples for managements and union officials of established plants. I have concluded that providing examples of what was done in a new organization is not helpful in enabling managers of established units to visualize alternative futures for their units and is not an

[5]Irving Bluestone, in personal conversation with the author.

effective stimulus for developing a program for transforming them.

The reasons are severalfold and go beyond the fact that a particular work structure that is successful in a new plant may be inappropriate in an old one. More fundamentally, the processes of innovation (diagnosing, planning, inventing, and implementing) are significantly different for new and existing units. In established facilities, the level of aspiration for change and the time frame allotted for achieving it must be much more modest than in new facilities.

In selecting aspects of work structure that can be changed, planners need to be opportunistic—doing what they can when they can. Also, the main job of planners in old facilities is defrosting the old work culture and creating a sense of the potential for change. To do this, they need to give careful attention to the participative processes for deciding the direction and method of the change.

Fortunately, the literature is providing us with a growing number of instructive examples of productive change in established organizations. The Tarrytown plant is one such example.

3. *Avoid either-or conceptions of work organization.* An example of this faulty thinking relates to the sources and types of controls: "Traditional systems rely on hierarchical controls. The innovative system is the opposite; therefore, it must rely on individual or team self-management." Another example of this thinking is: "If we need to rely on self-discipline and peer group pressure to minimize counterproductive behavior, then there is no place for management-administered discipline."

Indeed, as managers in these work systems have sooner or later discovered, a selective emphasis and sensible mixture of management techniques are called for. A number of organizations have had to go through a period of permissiveness before management discovered the need to set and enforce certain boundaries on the behavior of members of the company.

Managers make a related mistake when they assume that an organization at start-up can be at an idealized, advanced state of development. Some plans for new plant organization neglect the important distinction between conceiving of the steady state design and designing the initial organization. These plants start up with workers and supervisors having roles and responsibilities that reflect the planners' idealized view of the mature organization. Workers lack the technical and human skills as well as the problem-solving capacities to perform effectively. Supervisors cannot merely "facilitate"—they must provide directive supervision.

Delegation is the cornerstone of new plant development. Such delegation must be rooted in careful diagnosis of the existing base of skills and capabilities in the work force and a realistic view of their ability to develop over time.

4. *Do not advocate one answer; spread a way of looking for answers.* Managers and planners need to inculcate their people with a way of thinking about the diagnosis and designing of innovative work structures, not the work structures themselves. This is a major implication of my three-level conception of work improvement activity. It is less appropriate (and sometimes counterproductive) to promote the spread of particular techniques—for example, enriched jobs, team concepts, productivity gain sharing—than it is to promote the diffusion of a diagnostic and innovative planning process.

Reading 25

Job Enrichment: A Reevaluation
Mitchell Fein

INTRODUCTION

The quality of working life, work humanization, job enrichment, restructure of work, and other such concerns are increasingly the subject of discussions and articles in the management literature and the press. A vocal school of social scientists is pressing government officials, legislators, and management to give serious attention to the signs of unrest in industry. Their proposals are summarized in *Work in America,* a study written for the Department of Health, Education, and Welfare.[1]

To a large extent this article disagrees with the findings of that study. In the first part of the article, the theory of job enrichment is examined in detail. It is suggested that job enrichment does not work as well as has been claimed. The second part of the article develops a more balanced framework for thinking about worker motivation and job enrichment.

THE THEORY BEHIND JOB ENRICHMENT

According to the study *Work in America,* the primary cause of the dissatisfaction of white and blue-collar workers is the nature of their work. ". . . significant numbers of American workers are dissatisfied with the quality of their working lives. Dull, repetitive, seemingly meaningless tasks, offering little challenge or autonomy, are causing discontent among workers at all occupational levels."[2] The study reports that the discontent of women, minorities, blue-collar workers, youth, and older adults would be considerably less if these Americans had an active voice in decisions at the work place that most directly affect their lives. "The redesign of jobs is the keystone of this report, . . ."; work must be made more meaningful to the workers.[3] The presumption is that blue-collar employees will work

harder if their jobs are enriched or expanded to give them greater control over the order of their work or its content, or to allow them more freedom from direct supervision. Far too many variations on the theme of job enrichment have appeared in the last ten years to attempt to describe even a small proportion of them. The following discussion therefore assumes that the reader is familiar with the basic ideas of job enrichment.

DO THE STUDIES SUPPORT THE THEORY?

Claims for the success and usefulness of job enrichment are based primarily on a number of job enrichment case histories and studies conducted over the past ten years. These studies attempt to prove that workers really want job enrichment. However, when they are examined closely, it is found that:

1 What actually occurred in the cases was often quite different from what was reported to have occurred.

2 Most of the cases were conducted with hand-picked employees, who were usually working in areas or plants isolated from the main operations and thus did not represent a cross section of the working population. Practically all experiments have been in nonunion plants.

3 Only a handful of job enrichment cases have been reported in the past ten years, despite the claims of gains obtained for employees and management through job changes.

4 In *all* instances the experiments were initiated by management, never by workers or unions.

A review of some of the more prominent studies illustrates these points.

Survey of Working Conditions[4]

This large scale study of workers' attitudes toward work and working conditions, conducted for the

---

[1]See *Work in America* [24].
[2]See *Work in America* [24], p. xv.
[3]See *Work in America* [24], p. xvii.

[4]See "Survey of Working Conditions" [26].

Department of Labor by the Survey Research Center at the University of Michigan, is cited in numerous articles and is a mainstay of the HEW study. When examined closely, however, several errors are revealed which cast serious doubt upon the validity of its conclusions.

In the study, the workers polled were asked to rank twenty-five aspects of work in order of importance to them. They ranked interesting work first; pay, fifth; and job security, seventh. The researchers neglected, however, to indicate that these rankings averaged together the survey results for all levels of workers, from managers and professionals to low skilled workers. The researchers created a composite image that they called a "worker." The study, however, was based on a cross section of the United States work force rather than just lower-level workers.

When separated into the basic occupational categories and analyzed separately, the data show that blue-collar workers rank pay and job security higher than interesting work. Interesting work was ranked so high in SRC's results because the responses of managers, professionals, and skilled people were averaged with the responses of lower-level workers.[5]

It seems reasonable to suspect that the attitudes of managers and professionals toward their jobs might be different from those of factory workers, and that there also might be differences between skilled and unskilled workers' attitudes within occupational groupings. When the data were compiled by SRC, each subject's occupation was identified, but the results presented in the final report were lumped together for all subjects.

The new data obtained by reanalyzing the SRC data by occupational categories is supported by a large scale study that was conducted abroad. In the first phase of a study covering 60,000 people in more than fifty countries (excluding the communist bloc), Sirota and Greenwood found that there was considerable similarity in the goals of employees around the world and that the largest and most striking differences are between jobs rather than between countries. Most interestingly, the security needs of people in lower-skilled jobs were found to be highest.[6] The final phase of the study is even more illuminating because the data include the full range

of occupations, from managers to unskilled workers, reported separately by seven occupational groups. Unskilled workers in manufacturing plants abroad ranked their needs in this order: physical conditions first, security second, earnings third, and benefits fourth. A factor labeled "interesting work" was not included, but there were several which in total encompass this factor. These were ranked far below the workers' top four needs.[7]

General Foods–Topeka

General Foods–Topeka has been widely cited to show how, when jobs are enriched according to organization development principals, productivity and employee satisfaction will rise. However, Walton's reporting of this case omits critical information which greatly affects the interpretation of what actually occurred and why.[8]

Walton attributes the success of the Topeka plant to the "...autonomous work groups... integrated support functions...challenging job assignments...job mobility and rewards for learning...facilitative leadership...managerial decision making for operations...self-government for the plant community...congruent physical and social context...learning and evolution..." which were established for the employees.[9] He does not mention that the sixty-three Topeka employees are a group of very special people who were carefully selected from 700 applicants in five screening interviews. The fourth screening was an hour long personal interview, and the fifth was an four-hour session that included a complex two-hour personality test.[10]

General Foods–Topeka is a controlled experiment in a small plant with conditions set up to achieve desired results. The employees are not a cross section of the larger employee population, or even of Topeka. The plant and its operations are not typical of those in industry today. The results obtained are valid only for this one plant. What are other managers to do? Should they screen out nine of ten possible candidates and hire only from the select group that remains? What happens to the other nine who were not selected?

If the investigators had shown how they converted

[5]See, for example, Fein [4].
[6]See Sirota and Greenwood [18].

[7]See Hofstede [9].
[8]See Walton [27].
[9]See Walton [28], p. 9.
[10]See King [12]. p. 9.

a plant bursting with labor problems into one where management and employees told glowingly of their accomplishments, the study would truly merit the praise it has received. Instead they turned their backs on the company's parent plant in Kankakee, which has many of the problems of big city plants. Even worse, they tantalize management with the prospect that, in building a new plant with equipment, carefully selected employees, and no union, productivity will be higher.

Many managers have dreamed of relocating their plants in the wheat fields or the hills to escape from the big city syndrome. Is this Walton's message to managers in his article, "How to Counter Alienation in the Plant?"[11]

Writers who extol the GF-Topeka case do not understand that what makes this plant so unique is not only the management style but the workers themselves, who were hand-picked. These are highly motivated workers who were isolated from the mainstream of workers and now are free to do their work in their own way. One wonders how these hand-picked workers would produce without any changes at all in management practices.

Procter & Gamble

Procter & Gamble is cited by Jenkins. "Without doubt the most radical organizational changes made on a practical, day-to-day basis in the United States have taken place at Procter & Gamble, one of America's largest companies, well known for its hardboiled, aggressive management practices."[12] What generally is not mentioned in any of the laudatory articles about P&G's organizational development practices is that P&G is an unusual company with a history of concern for its employees that is matched by few other firms in this country. In 1923 William C. Procter, then president of the company, recognized that the workers' problems were caused in large part by seasonal employment, and he established genuine job security. He guaranteed forty-eight weeks of employment a year. P&G has a long history of good wages and working conditions; they also have pioneered in old age pensions and profit sharing. Since P&G has a good reputation among workers, its plants attract some of the best workers in their areas. In seeking the reasons for P&G's success, one must not overlook their excellent bread and butter policies, among the best in the nation. Would their organizational development and job enrichment practices work without such policies?

Other Studies on Job Enrichment

Texas Instruments   The intensive job enrichment efforts of Texas Instruments management is unequalled in this country. Since 1952 the TI management has tried diligently to gain acceptance of its enrichment program by its workers. In 1968 the management announced that its goal was to involve 16 percent of its employees in job enrichment. Their data show that the actual involvement was 10.5 percent.[13] This is far from the huge success claimed in the numerous articles describing the program.

Polaroid Corporation   experiments involve only job rotation, not job enrichment. Foulkes reports that from 1959 to 1962, 114 employees out of 2000 were involved in changing their jobs.[14] Although management had guaranteed that employees could change their jobs and be assured of a return to their original jobs if they wished, less than 6 percent of the employees actually became involved. It does not appear that the employees favored the plan or that it was broadly successful.

Texas Instruments Cleaning and Janitorial Employees   The version of this report in *Work in America* states that when Texas Instruments took over the cleaning work formerly done by an outside contracting firm, the employees were ". . . given a voice in planning, problem solving, and goal setting for their own jobs . . . the team (had the) responsibility to act independently to devise its own strategies, plans, and schedules to meet the objective . . . the cleanliness level rating improved from 65 percent to 85 percent, personnel . . . dropped from 120 to 71, and quarterly turnover dropped from 100 percent to 9.8 percent . . . cost savings for the entire site averaged $103,000 per annum."[15]

What was not reported by the study was that the outside contractor's employees received only $1.40 per hour. When TI took over the program, the starting pay was raised to $1.94 per hour for the first

[11]See Walton [27].
[12]See Jenkins [10].

[13]See Fein [2].
[14]See Foulkes [7].
[15]See *Work in America* [24], p. 100.

shift, with $.10 extra added for the second shift and $.20 extra added for the third. The janitorial employees were given good insurance programs, profit sharing, paid vacations, sick leave, a good cafeteria, and working conditions similar to those of other employees at Texas Instruments. *Work in America* does not mention that in raising the pay by 46 percent and adding benefits worth one-third of their pay, TI was able to recruit better qualified employees. Yet the study insists on attributing the improved performance to job enrichment. The omission of this pay data is strange, since the data appear prominently in the report from which the HEW task force obtained the case material.[16]

American Telephone and Telegraph   Space does not permit a discussion of the various cases reported by Robert Ford.[17] To a large degree, he redesigned jobs at AT&T which had been ineffectively set up in the first place. To label such changes "job enrichment" is to render the phrase meaningless.

The Scandinavian Experience   *Work in America* suggests that worker initiative is inhibited by a lack of democracy at the work place. The study points to Europe and especially to the Scandinavian countries as examples of productivity gains through democracy in the plants.[18] The assumption is that European experience in industrial relations is directly transferable to this country. In fact, it may not be. Nat Goldfinger, Research Director of the AFL-CIO, believes ". . . that industrial democracy was not needed in America: 'The issue is irrelevant here. I would suspect that most of the issues that are bugging Europeans are taken care of here in collective bargaining.'"[19]

The study of worker participation councils covering fifty different countries cited earlier supports this position. It shows clearly that this movement is the European workers' way of institutionalizing union plant locals and of establishing collective bargaining on the plant floor. It is not a new form of worker democracy as described by the behaviorists.[20]

The examples discussed above are only a sampling of the job enrichment studies. Many more could be cited, but most of them are subject to criticisms already voiced. Only lack of space prevents a fuller discussion.

Job Enrichment or Common Sense?

Admittedly there are some cases where jobs have actually been productively enriched. Much more common, however, is the masquerading of common sense as job enrichment. Many studies have simply involved the elimination of an obviously bothersome problem, which hardly warrants the use of the term job enrichment. This paper is not directed toward the common sense applications of job enrichment. Rather this analysis is aimed at the broader claims of job enrichment success.

LIMITS TO JOB ENRICHMENT

One reason that job enrichment has not been widely implemented is that there are many factors operating within the work place to constrain its applicability. Several of these factors are discussed below.

Technology

The structure of jobs in American industry today is dictated largely by the technology employed in the production process. The size of the parts used, the equipment required for the operations, and the volume of production are all important determinants. When the blacksmith of a century ago shaped a piece of metal, his only capital equipment was a forge. He was the operator and the forge press. Today there are even large, specialized machines for parts which are viewed under a microscope. Much of the job redesign called for by proponents of job enrichment neglects the constraints imposed by technology.

There are few decisions on what to do in mass production. A piece is put into a press and hit. Two pieces or fifty are assembled in a given manner, simply because the pieces do not fit together in another way. In typing a letter or keypunching, the operators strike certain keys, not just any they wish. Even in the highly praised experimental Volvo plant where a small team assembles an engine, the workers have no choice in the selection of parts to be installed, and they must assemble the parts in a given sequence. While they may rotate their jobs

[16]See Rush [15], pp. 39–45.
[17]See Ford [5].
[18]See *Work in America* [24], pp. 103–105.
[19]See Jenkins [11], p. 315.
[20]See Roach [14].

within the group and thus obtain variety, this is not job enrichment or autonomy but job rotation.

In most instances it is impossible to add to jobs decision making of the kind that job enrichment theorists call for, simply because of the technology of the work. The job shops which produce only a small number of an item can provide true decision making for many of its employees, but these shops have not attracted the attention of job enrichers. They are worried about the mass production plants where work has been grossly simplified.

Another view of the technological constraints on job enrichment is offered by workers themselves. A full page article in a union newspaper recently denounced attempts by General Electric to combine the tasks of a thirty-two operator line producing steam irons into a single work station, with a headline: "Makes no difference how you slice it, it's still monotony and more speed up." Jim Matles, an officer of the United Electrical Workers, derides management's efforts, pointing out that, "As monotonous as that job was on that continuous assembly line, they were able to perform it practically without having to keep their minds on the job . . . they could talk to each other. On the new assembly line, however, the repetitiveness of the job was there just as much, but . . . they no longer could do it without being compelled to keep their minds on the job." Another Union leader in the plant said, "I've finally been able to show [management] that the more repetitive or rhythmic the job, the less unhappy the workers. On jobs where the rhythm is broken and unrepetitive, the employees are unhappy and must constantly fight these jobs [rather] than do them by natural reflex."[21]

It is not intended that technological constraints be thought of as structural barriers to job enrichment. In the long run technology can be changed. Workers and managers are by no means forever locked into the present means of production. At the very least, however, proponents of job enrichment have neglected badly the immediate problems posed by technology. At their worst they have intentionally ignored them. The purpose of this section is to restore a more balanced perspective to the relationship of technology to job enrichment.

Cost

Giving workers job rotation opportunities or combining jobs can increase costs. This occurred recently at the General Motors Corporation Truck and Coach Division. Early this year they initiated an experiment using teams of workers to assemble motor homes. *Business Week* reported that, "Six-member teams assembled the body while three-member teams put the chassis together. The move was an attempt to curb assembly line doldrums and motivate workers. Last month, the experiment was curtailed. The complexity of assembly proved too difficult for a team approach, which was too slow to meet GM's production standards."[22]

Increased costs from combining jobs and in job rotation also occurred in a case reported by Louis E. Davis, a prominent advocate of job redesign. He made studies to compare the levels of output obtained with a mechanically-paced conveyor line, a line with no pacing, and a line with individuals performing all of the jobs as a "one-man line." Using the average output of the nine-operator paced line as 100 percent, Davis found that the same non-paced line operated at 89 percent, and the "one-man line" operated at 94.0 percent. Translated into unit costs, the non-paced line cost 12.4 percent more and the individual line 6.4 percent more than the conventional paced line.[23] Suppose that the workers liked the non-pacing or the built up job better (although this did not happen to be true). Would the consumer be willing to pay the additional cost?

Relative Levels of Skill

The possibility of making enriching changes in jobs increases with the skill level of the jobs. However, relatively few jobs have a high skill content, and relatively few workers occupy these jobs. If widespread benefits are derived from job enrichment, these are most needed for workers in the low level jobs, where boredom presumably is highest. The work of skilled workers already has challenge and interest built into the jobs, requiring judgment, ingenuity and initiative. Adding job enrichment responsibilities in some cases may only be gilding the lily. What are managers to do with low-skilled

---

[21]See Matles [13].

[22]See "GM Zeroes in on Employee Discontent" [8], p. 140.
[23]See Davis and Canter [1], p. 279.

workers who make up the great majority of the work force? That is the essence of the problem confronting managers. When tested in the plant, enrichment programs do not operate as predicted. They usually can be applied only to the wrong people, to those who do not need them because their jobs potentially provide the necessary enrichment.

Work Group Norms

Studies from around the world, including the communist countries, demonstrate that the concepts of McGregor and Herzberg regarding workers' need to find fullfillment through work hold only for those workers who *choose* to find fulfillment through their work. Contrary to the more popular belief, the vast majority of workers seek fulfillment outside their work.[24] After almost twenty years of active research in job enrichment, it is clear that only a minority of workers is attracted to it. These workers are mostly in the skilled jobs or on their way up. However the social pressure in the plant from the workers who are not involved in job enrichment sets the plant climate, and they apparently oppose job changes. The effect of this opposition is minimal on the active minority, because they find their enrichment by moving up to the skilled jobs where they have greater freedom to exercise their initiative. Obviously, the isolation of small groups of workers is not possible in the real world industry. In the main plant, the pervasive social climate controls what goes on, and job enrichment may not be permitted to work.

Contrasting Employer and Employee Goals

Proponents of job enrichment often forget that management and workers are not motivated in the same direction; they have different goals, aspirations, and needs. The fact of life which workers see clearly, but which often is obscured to others, is that *if workers do anything to raise productivity, some of them will be penalized.*

Job enrichment predicts that increased job satisfaction will increase motivation and raise productivity. However workers know that if they increase production, reduce delays and waiting time, reduce crew sizes or cooperate in any way, less overtime will be available, some employees will be displaced, and the plant will require fewer employees. The

remaining workers will receive few financial benefits. What employee will voluntarily raise his production output, only to be penalized for his diligence?

This phenomenon does not occur with "exempt" employees, the executives, administrators, professionals, and salesmen. Have you ever heard of a manager who worked himself out of a job by superior performance? Have you ever heard of a salesman whose security was threatened because he sold too much or an engineer who caused the layoff of other engineers because he was too creative? These employees usually can anticipate rewards for their creativity and effectiveness.

When workers excel and raise productivity, the company benefits and management is pleased, but the workers usually do not benefit. On the contrary, in the short term their economic interests may be threatened; some suffer loss of income. When exempt employees are more effective, they cover themselves with glory; their economic security is enhanced not threatened. Ironically, the relationship between workers and management actually provides workers with the incentive not to cooperate in productivity improvement. Most companies offer their employees the opportunity to reduce their earnings and job security as they raise productivity. Management does not, of course, intend such results, but the system often operates that way in this country.

A recent study by the Harris organization, conducted for the National Commission on Productivity, provides support for this contention.

> Nearly 7 in 10 feel that stockholders and management would benefit a lot from increased productivity, compared with scarcely more than 1 in 3 who see the same gains for the country as a whole.
>
> The term "increased productivity" does not have a positive connotation for most people who work for a living.
>
> A majority believes the statement "companies benefit from increased productivity at the expense of workers." Hourly workers believe this by 80-14 percent.[25]

Is it any wonder that workers are alienated from their work? Would company executives improve the effectiveness of their work if they believed it would

---

[24]See, for example, Fein [2].

[25]See the Harris Survey published in *The Record* (Bergen, N.J.), 19 February 1973, p. A-3.

not benefit them, and more, that it would reduce their income and even cause their layoff?[26]

DO MANAGERS SUPPORT THE THEORY?

If job enrichment were the panacea it is so often claimed to be, then somewhere in this country some aggressive, farsighted manager should have been able, in the past ten years, to have made it operational on a large scale basis. The claims that large productivity gains will be made through job redesign should have spurred many companies to implement it. Yet there are few successful examples. Given this lack of acceptance, it is reasonable to assume that managers do not support job enrichment.

DO THE WORKERS SUPPORT THE THEORY?

Those advocating that work should be redesigned start with the premise that such changes are socially desirable and beneficial to workers. Curiously, however, these investigators are not supported in their claims by many workers or unions. There is a sharp difference of opinion between what workers say they want and what proponents of job enrichment say workers should want.[27]

Workers' opinions on the enrichment of jobs are expressed by William W. Winpisinger, Vice-President of the Machinists' Union.

In my years as a union representative and officer I've negotiated for a lot of membership demands. I've been instructed to negotiate on wages . . . noise . . . seniority clauses; fought for health and welfare plans, . . . and everything else you find in a modern labor-management contract. But never once have I carried into negotiations a membership mandate to seek job enrichment. In fact, quite to the contrary, working people want management to leave their jobs alone.[28]

The question of job enrichment and boredom on the job was discussed at last year's United Auto Workers convention and significantly was not made an issue in the following auto negotiations. Leonard Woodcock, President of the UAW, was sharply critical of the HEW report and a number of its suggestions. "Mr. Woodcock was very outspoken in his denunciation of government officials, academic writers and intellectuals who contend that boredom and monotony are the big problems among assembly workers. He said 'a lot of academic writers . . . are writing a lot of nonsense' . . . [he] expressed resentment over a recent government report on work as 'elitist' in its approach, describing assembly line workers as if they were 'subhumans'."[29]

A similar attitude on the part of European workers is reported by Basil Whiting of the Ford Foundation. He visited Europe to study their job enrichment efforts ". . . in terms of the experiments on job redesign: By and large all these experiments were initiated by management. We found no cases where they were initiated by unions and other forces in society."[30]

Despite the urgings for increased participation by workers, Strauss and Rosenstein also found that workers all over the world have failed to respond: "'Participation' is one of the most overworked words of the decade. Along with 'meaningful' and 'involvement' it appears in a variety of forms and context." "Participation in many cases has been introduced from the top down as symbolic solutions to ideological contradictions," especially in the countries with strong socialist parties.[31] "In general the impetus for participation has come more from intellectuals, propagandists and politicians (sometimes all three combined) than it has from the rank-and-file workers who were supposed to do the participating."[32] There is obviously a lack of worker interest in participation despite claims by intellectuals that the work place is dehumanizing.

A MORE BALANCED APPROACH TO WORKER MOTIVATION AND JOB ENRICHMENT

Studying satisfied and disatisfied workers, job enrichment theory contends that the intrinsic nature of the work performed is the main cause of the differ-

[26]A most ironic turn of events has occurred in plants with supplementary unemployment benefits (SUB). Unions are asking that layoffs occur in *inverse seniority,* with the highest seniority employees going first. By inverting seniority and giving the senior employees a choice, a layoff under SUB becomes a reward, not a penalty. For working diligently and working himself out of a job, a worker is rewarded by time off with pay.

[27]This divergence of opinion is explored in more detail by Fein [3].

[28]See Winpisinger [30].

[29]See "UAW Indicates It Will Seek to Minimize Local Plant Strikes in Talks Next Fall" [22].

[30]See his testimony before the Senate Subcommittee on Employment, Manpower, and Poverty [23].

[31]See Strauss and Rosenstein [21], pp. 197, 198.

[32]See Strauss and Rosenstein [21], p. 199.

ences between them. The job enrichment theorists propose to change the work of the dissatisfied workers to more closely resemble the work performed by the satisfied workers. There is, however, a large "if" to this approach. What if the nature of the work is not what primarily satisfies all satisfied workers? Restructuring the work and creating work involvement opportunities may ignite a small flame under some people, but to what extent is the nature of the work the determinant of a person's drive? *The simple truth is that there are no data which show that restructuring and enriching jobs will raise the will to work.*

The essential assumption of job enrichment theory is that the nature of the work performed determines to a large extent worker satisfaction or dissatisfaction. It is argued here that this is not always so. *The intrinsic nature of the work is only one factor among many that affect worker satisfaction.* Moreover, the available evidence suggests that its influence is very often subordinate to that of several other variables: pay, job security, and job rules. The inconclusive performance of job enrichment to date stems largely from those programs that have neglected to consider these factors.

A useful starting point in understanding how workers feel about their jobs is to look at how they choose their jobs. A "natural selection" model of job choice proves very fruitful in examining this process.

A "NATURAL SELECTION" MODEL OF JOB CHOICE

There is greater selection by workers of jobs than is supposed. The selection process in factories and offices often occurs without conscious direction by either workers or management. The data for white and blue-collar jobs show that there is tremendous turnover in the initial employment period, which drops sharply with time on the job. Apparently what happens is that a worker begins a new job, tries it out for several days or weeks, and decides whether the work suits his needs and desires. Impressions about a job are a composite of many factors: pay, proximity to home, the nature of the work, working conditions, the attitude of supervision, congeniality of fellow workers, past employment history of the company, job security, physical demands, oppor-

tunities for advancement, and many other related factors. A worker's choice of job is made in a combination of ways, through evaluating various trade-offs. Working conditions may be bad, but if pay and job security are high, the job may be tolerable. There are numerous combinations of factors which in total influence a worker's disposition to stay on the job or not.

There is dual screening which culls out those who will be dissatisfied with the work. The worker in the first instance decides whether to stay on the job, and management then has the opportunity to determine whether to keep him beyond the trial period. The combination of the worker's choice to remain and management's decision that the worker is acceptable initially screens out workers who might find the work dissatisfying.

INTRINSIC AND EXTRINSIC JOB CHARACTERISTICS

As a result of this selection process, workers are able to exert much control over the nature of the work which they finally accept. They can leave jobs that they do not like and only accept jobs which they find rewarding. The major constraint on the variety of work available to them is the intrinsic nature of the work itself. However, if there are no intrinsically rewarding jobs but a worker still must support his family, he will have to take an intrinsically unsatisfactory job.

Unlike the intrinsic nature of the work that he accepts, the worker has much less control over the extrinsic characteristics of his job. There may be many different kinds of jobs for which he is qualified, but most of them will pay about the same maximum salary or wage. Similarly, there will be few options regarding the different kinds of job security and work rule combinations which he can find. The suggested hypothesis is that the influence of extrinsic factors, particularly pay, job security, and work rules, on worker satisfaction has been obscured and neglected by job enrichment. Undoubtedly some workers are distressed by the highly routinized work that they may be performing, but to what extent is dissatisfaction caused by the intrinsic nature of their work? What proportion is caused by their insufficient pay? Would workers have a greater interest in the work if their living standards were raised and they could see their jobs as contributing to a good life?

Individual Differences in Job Preference

Work that one person views an interesting or satisfying may appear boring and dissatisfying to another. There are significant differences among workers, and their needs vary. Some workers prefer to work by rote without having to be bothered with decisions. Some workers prefer more complicated work. It is really a matter of individual preference.

There would undoubtedly be far greater dissatisfaction with work if those on the jobs were not free to make changes and selections in the work they do. Some prefer to remain in highly repetitive, low skill jobs even when they have an opportunity to advance to higher skill jobs through job bidding. A majority of workers strives to move into the skilled jobs such as machinists, maintenance mechanics, set-up men, group leaders, utility men, and other such positions where there is considerable autonomy in the work performed.

The continued evaluation of workers by management and the mobility available to workers to obtain jobs which suit them best refine the selection process. A year or two after entering a plant, most workers are on jobs or job progressions which suit them or which they find tolerable. Those who are no longer on the job have been "selected" out, either by themselves or by management. Given the distinction between intrinsic and extrinsic job characteristics and the greater degree of control which workers exert over the former, those who are left on the job after the selection process can be expected to be relatively more satisfied with the nature of their work than with their pay, job security, or work rules. In fact this prediction proves to be correct.

WORKERS' ATTITUDES TOWARD THEIR WORK

Work in America cites a Gallup Poll which found that 80 to 90 percent of American workers are satisfied with their jobs.[33] A more recent poll found that from 82 to 91 percent of blue and white-collar workers like their work. The workers were asked, "If there were one thing you could change about your job, what would it be?" Astonishingly, very few workers said that they would make their jobs " 'less boring' or 'more interesting'."[34]

In a recent study, David Sirota was surprised to find that the sewing operators in one plant found their work interesting. Since the work appeared to be highly repetitive, he had expected that they would say they were bored and their talents underutilized.[35] These workers' views are supported in a large scale study by Weintraub of 2535 female sewing machine operators in seventeen plants from Massachusetts to Texas. He found that "Most of the operators like the nature of their work. Of those who were staying (65%), 9 out of 10 feel that way. Even of those who would leave (35%), 7 out of 10 like their work."[36]

For the most part workers are satisfied with the nature of their work. What they find most discomforting is their pay, their job security, and many of the work rules with which they must cope. They can find their work engrossing and still express dissatisfaction because of other job related factors such as pay, working conditions, inability to advance, and so on. When a person says his work is satisfying, he inplies that his work utilizes his abilities to an extent *satisfactory to him.*

EXTRINSIC DETERMINANTS OF WORKER SATISFACTION

As the studies cited above indicate, most workers appear relatively more satisfied with the intrinsic nature of their jobs than with the extrinsic job factors. The major extrinsic factors are examined below.

Pay

Pay is very important in determining job satisfaction. This is hardly a novel observation, but it is one that is too often overlooked or forgotten in job

---

[33]See *Work in America* [24], p. 14.

[34]See Sorenson [20].
[35]Personal communication.
[36]See Weintraub [29], p. 349. The auto workers' jobs have been cited by many writers as the extreme of monotonous and dehumanizing work. However, a recent study of auto workers in the United States, Italy, Argentina, and India by W. H. Form found that "Most workers believe that their work integrates their lives . . . that their jobs are satisfying. Nowhere did assemblyline workers dwell upon monotony . . . Machine work does not make workers more unhappy at any industrial stage. Nor do workers heed the lament of the intellectuals that the monotony of the job drives them mad" (See Form [6], pp. 1, 15).

enrichment programs. Sheppard and Herrick, both of whom served on the *Work in America* task force, analyzed the SRC and other data and provided a cross section of feelings by workers about their jobs. The following quotations concerning pay are from their study.[37]

> It was found that dissatisfaction with work decreases steadily as pay rises. When earnings exceed $10,000 per year, dissatisfaction drops significantly.

If we knew why this occurs, we would probably have a major part of the answer to the question of why there is dissatisfaction at the work place. There is a cause and effect relationship involved in which it is difficult to evaluate how the various factors affect the employee. The higher the social value of the work performed, the higher is the pay. The higher the skill required of the employee, the higher is his opportunity for involvement in his work. As pay rises, to what extent does the pay level produce higher satisfaction with the affluence it brings? To what extent does the interesting content of the work cause higher satisfaction?

Construction workers are the highest paid of the blue-collar workers and have unexcelled benefits. Many professionals and managers earn less than construction workers. These workers are among the last of the craftsmen who still largely work with their hands and still may own their own tools. Their satisfaction may well come from their creative work, but to what extent does their high pay influence their attitudes?

> In the managerial, professional and technical occupations only 1 in 10 were dissatisfied.

Is it the attraction of their work or their pay which affords them their satisfaction?

> Slightly less than 1 in 4 manufacturing workers were dissatisfied. The data for workers in the service occupations and the wholesale-retail industry are about the same.

In 1971, Bureau of Labor Statistics data for blue-collar workers showed that 58.7 percent earned less than $150 per week, 24.6 percent earned from $150 to $199, and 16.8 percent earned over $200. In 1971, the BLS "lower level" budget for a family of four was $7214 per year.[38] The SRC data showed that 56.2 percent of the subjects reported having inadequate incomes. Considering the earnings statistics, it is a wonder that more workers are not dissatisfied.

Experience reveals that increasing the availability of interesting work will not compensate for a desire for increased pay, whereas increasing pay can go far to compensate for poor working conditions. This was vividly demonstrated by the workers who collect garbage in New York City. They perform their work in all kinds of weather. Their job is highly accident-ridden and is not held in high esteem by society. Ten years ago few people were interested in the job. Then the pay scale was raised to $10,500 per year with good benefits, and a long waiting line formed for the jobs. The nature of the work had not changed. It was the same dirty, heavy work, but now the pay was attractive.[39]

Job Security

A second critical component of the work environment is job security, the continuity of income. Pay must be not only sufficiently high but also fairly regular. No one can budget for a family if he is not reasonably sure of his income for some time into the future. Most people become distressed when faced with a layoff. Reduced employment affects the morale of everyone in the organization. When employment finally is stabilized and the threat of further reductions passes, fears and memories still linger.

Because it is such an important component of the work environment, *job security is an essential precondition to enhancing the will to work*. While the idea is not new that economic insecurity is a restraint on the will to work, its effect often is minimized by managers, behavioral scientists, and industrial engineers involved in productivity improvement. Job security is as vital to productivity improvement as advanced technical processes and new equipment.

What happens to feelings of identity and loyalty when employees see their increased productivity contributing to their layoff? It is hard to conceive of

---

[37]See Sheppard and Herrick [16].

[38]See *Handbook of Labor Statistics* [25].
[39]The average annual pay is now $12,886.

a manager who would cooperate in designing his own job out of existence, as might occur when several managerial jobs are combined and one person is no longer required. When managers consider their own job security, they quite expectedly have empathy for James F. Lincoln's truism: "No man will willingly work to throw himself out of his job, nor should he." Yet managers do not extend this obvious logic to their work force.

Managers must view job security not only in the social sense of how it affects workers' lives, but as absolutely essential to high levels of productivity. In the plants without job security, workers stretch out the work if they do not see sufficient work ahead of them.[40] They will not work themselves out of their jobs. When workers stretch out their jobs, though it is hidden from view, it is reflected in costs.

Managers historically have considered job security as a union demand to be bargained as are other issues. This has been a tragic error because whenever job security is lacking, labor productivity is restrained. Paradoxically, job security must be established as a demand of *management* if it hopes to increase productivity. What would happen in contract negotiations if management started off by demanding that the new contract include job protection for the employees? This radical act might encourage profound changes in employees' attitudes.

Unduly Restrictive Plant Rules

There are many other factors beside the work itself which affect workers' attitudes. In many companies workers still are considered "hands," hired by the hour with little consideration given to their needs and desires as "people." Some managers find it easier to lay workers off with four to eight hours notice than to plan production and avoid plant delays. In many plants, the plant rules, which management calls its prerogatives and guards jealously, are insulting to human sensibilities.

A worker's self-esteem is affected by how he is treated and how he rates with the others around him. Increasingly, workers want fair treatment for everyone. However, the "hands" concept still separates the white-collar from the blue-collar workers.

White-collar workers are generally paid a weekly salary and often do not punch a time clock. They have more leeway in lateness and often do not lose pay when absent. Most factory workers have few of these benefits. A white-collar worker often has a telephone available and can make personal calls during the day. Factory workers have great difficulty in making calls. Receiving calls usually is reserved for extreme emergencies. When a worker has a problem, he stays out.

The penned-in feeling of workers, which is stylishly called their blues, comes in large part from their inability to take care of these daily personal problems and needs. Any job enrichment program which hopes to succeed must effectively address the problems posed to workers by plant rules. Until now very few programs have acknowledged their importance.

WHAT SHOULD BE DONE?

Everyone will accept the idea that improvement of the quality of working life is a desirable social goal. However, how should this be done? David Sirota provides a concise statement of the problem. "I can't get it through some thick skulls that [many] people may want both—that they would like to finish a day's work and feel that they had accomplished something and still get paid for it."[41] A logical approach to formulating the problem must begin with a determination of who is now dissatisfied and why and with the recognition that people have individual needs and desires.

The *Work in America* task force believes that, ". . . pay . . . is important," it must support an 'adequate' standard of living, and be perceived as equitable—but high pay alone will not lead to job (or life) satisfaction.[42] They conclude that work must provide satisfaction and must be restructured to become the *raison d'etre* of people's lives. Their statement of the problem is correct, but their conclusion that work alone must provide satisfaction is wrong. Satisfaction can come from wherever people choose. It need not be only from their work.

The blues of many workers are due less to the nature of their work and more to what their work

---

[40]In a very fundamental way, work *does* expand to fill time (Parkinson's Law).

[41]Panel discussion between Louis E. Davis, Mitchell Fein, and David Sirota, Annual Convention of the American Institute of Industrial Engineers, 24 May 1973.
[42]See *Work in America* [24], p. 95.

will not bring them in their pay envelopes. Increasingly, workers also want freedom on their jobs. Some workers prefer enriched jobs with autonomy. Most workers want more freedom to act on personal things outside of their work place. Some may want the freedom to just "goof off" once in a while. In short, workers' blues are not formed solely around the work place. Blues are partly a work place reaction to non-work related problems.

Solving problems in the plants must start with the question why should workers want enriched jobs? It is readily apparent that management and the stockholders benefit from increased worker involvement which leads to reduced costs. For their part, if all the workers get is reduced hours or even layoffs, they must resist it. It is futile to expect that workers willingly will create more for management without simultaneously benefiting themselves. *The most effective productivity results will be obtained when management creates conditions which workers perceive as beneficial to them.* The changes must be genuine and substantial and in forms which eventually are turned into cash and continuity of income. Psychic rewards may look good on paper, but they are invisible in the pocketbook. If workers really want psychic job enrichment, management would have heard their demands loud and clear long ago.

Change must start with management taking the first steps, unilaterally and without *quid pro quo.* There must not be productivity bargaining at first. Management must provide the basic conditions which will motivate workers to raise productivity: job security, good working conditions, good pay and financial incentives. There must be a diminution of the win-lose relationship and the gradual establishment of conditions in which workers know that both they and management gain and lose together. Labor, management, and government leaders are very concerned that rising wages and costs are making goods produced in this country less competitive in the world markets. Increasingly all three parties are engaging in meaningful dialogue to address these problems[43]

There are unquestionably enormous potentials for increased productivity which workers can unleash—

if they want to. The error of job enrichment is that it tries to talk workers into involvement and concern for the nature of their work when their memories and experiences have taught them that increased productivity only results in layoffs. Only management can now create conditions which will nullify the past.

Companies which are experimenting with new work methods probably will increase their efforts. As viable methods and approaches are developed, more companies will be tempted to innovate approaches suited to their own plants. The greatest progress will come in companies where workers see that management protects their welfare and where productivity gains are shared with the employees.

In the ideal approach, management should leave to workers the final choice regarding what work they find satisfying. In real life, this is what occurs anyway. Workers eschew work that they find dissatisfying or they find ways of saying loudly and clearly how they feel about such work. We should learn to trust workers' expressions of their wants. Workers will readily signal when they are ready for changes.

REFERENCES

[1] Davis, L. E. and Canter, R. R. "Job Design Research." *The Journal of Industrial Engineering 7* (1956): 275–282.
[2] Fein, M. "Motivation for Work." In *Handbook of Work, Organization and Society,* edited by R. Dubin. Chicago: Rand McNally, 1973.
[3] ———. "The Myth of Job Enrichment." *The Humanist,* September–October 1973, pp. 30–32.
[4] ———. "The Real Needs of Blue Collar Workers." *The Conference Board Record,* February 1973, pp. 26–33.
[5] Ford, R. N. *Motivation Through Work Itself.* New York: American Management Association, 1969.
[6] Form, W. H. "Auto Workers and Their Machines: A Study of Work, Factory, and Job Satisfaction in Four Countries." *Social Forces* 52 (1973): 1–15.
[7] Foulkes, F. K. *Creating More Meaningful Work.* New York: American Management Association, 1969.
[8] "GM Zeroes in on Employee Discontent." *Business Week,* 12 May 1973, pp. 140–144.
[9] Hofstede, G. H. "The Colors of Collars." *Columbia Journal of World Business,* September–October 1972, pp. 72–80.
[10] Jenkins, D. "Democracy in the Factory." *The Atlantic,* April 1973, pp. 78–83.
[11] ———. *Job Power: Blue and White Collar Democracy.* New York: Doubleday, 1973.

[43]See, for example, the articles on the experimental negotiating agreement in the basic steel industry by I. W. Abel and R. Heath Larry, in this issue.

[12]King, D. C. "Selecting Personnel for a Systems 4 Organization." Paper read at NTL Institute for Applied Behavioral Science Conference, 8–9 October 1971.

[13]Matles, J. "Humanize the Assembly Line?" *UE News,* 13 November 1972, p. 5.

[14]Roach, J. M. "Worker Participation: New Voices in Management." The Conference Board, Report 594, 1973.

[15]Rush, H. M. F. *Job Design for Motivation.* New York: The Conference Board, 1971.

[16]Sheppard, H. L., and Herrick, N. Q. *Where Have All The Robots Gone?* New York: New Press, 1972.

[17]Sirota, D. "Job Enrichment—Another Management Fad?" *The Conference Board Record,* April 1973, pp. 40–45.

[18]Sirota, D., and Greenwood, J. M. "Understand Your Overseas Work Force." *Harvard Business Review,* January–February 1971, pp. 53–60.

[19]Sorcher, M. "Motivating the Factory Workers." In *The Failure of Success,* edited by A. J. Morrow. New York: American Management Association, 1972.

[20]Sorenson, T. C. "Do Americans Like Their Jobs?" *Parade,* 3 June 1973, pp. 15–16.

[21]Strauss, G., and Rosenstein, E. "Workers Participation: A Critical View." *Industrial Relations* 9 (1970): 197–214.

[22]"UAW Indicates It Will Seek to Minimize Local Plant Strikes in Talks Next Fall." *Wall Street Journal,* 20 February 1973, p. 5.

[23]U.S., Congress, Senate, Subcommittee on Employment, Manpower, and Poverty, Labor and Public Welfare Committee, *Worker Alienation, 1972,* 92nd Cong., 2d sess., S. 3916, July 25 and 26, 1972.

[24]U.S., Department of Health, Education, and Welfare. *Work in America.* Report of a Special Task Force to the Secretary of Health, Education, and Welfare. Prepared under the Auspices of the W.E. Upjohn Institute for Employment Research. Cambridge: MIT Press, 1973.

[25]U.S., Department of Labor. *Handbook of Labor Statistics 1972.* Bulletin 1735, Bureau of Labor Statistics. Washington, D.C.: Government Printing Office, 1972.

[26]———. "Survey of Working Conditions, November 1970." Prepared by the Survey Research Center of the University of Michigan. Washington, D.C.: Government Printing Office, 1971.

[27]Walton, R. E. "How to Counter Alienation in the Plant." *Harvard Business Review,* November–December 1972, pp. 70–81.

[28]———. "Work Place Alienation and the Need for Major Innovation." Paper prepared for a Special Task Force to the Secretary of Health, Education, and Welfare (for *Work in America*), May 1972. Unpublished.

[29]Weintraub, E. "Has Job Enrichment Been Oversold?" Address to the 25th Convention of the American Institute of Industrial Engineers, May 1973. Reprinted in the technical papers of the convention.

[30]Winpisinger, W. P. Paper presented to University Labor Education Association, 5 April 1973, at Black Lake, Michigan.

Chapter 8

Evaluating and Rewarding Work Effectiveness

The measurement of performance and the giving of rewards are very visible and important features of almost every organization. They also are among the most controversial. The literature is full of debates about how performance should be appraised and how pay should be administered. "New" approaches are constantly being suggested, but the basic issues remain the same. In the area of performance appraisal, they concern how performance can best be measured; in the area of rewards, they concern how rewards (such as pay) should be related to performance and how rewards can be distributed equitably.

Performance appraisal is intended to serve a number of important functions in most organizations; it is supposed to provide feedback to employees about their performance, increase motivation, identify employees' development needs, form the basis for the giving of rewards, identify promotable employees, and aid in planning and control. The debates about which approach to performance appraisal is the best have been many and long.

The article by Meyer points to some of the reasons why it is difficult to do performance apprais-

al and then suggests some possible solutions. At present, there is no one approach that is unanimously acclaimed as the best. However, it does seem that there is agreement that approaches which rely solely on ratings (e.g., "How friendly is the person?" [low] 1 2 3 4 5 [high]) are inferior to systems that rely on agreed-to objectives and that are clearly based on work behavior. There also is general agreement that it is difficult simultaneously to appraise performance for the purposes of giving rewards and for exploring the developmental needs of employees. The article by Kerr points out that there are problems with an objectives-based system, even though it seems to be preferable to many others. Kerr also provides a number of useful suggestions about how to make objectives-based systems more effective. As the next article (by Latham and Locke) points out, one element of any discussion about performance is goal-setting. When this is done well, it can have a very positive effect on motivation.

Although there is a great deal of debate about how pay can best be related to performance and distributed equitably, there is little disagreement about the desirability of these aspirations. Most agree that when pay and other rewards are related to performance, motivation is increased, and that when pay is equitably distributed, turnover and absenteeism tend to be low. However, this is where the agreement ends. As the reading by Lawler points out, it is one thing to get agreement on the principle, but it is another to successfully operationalize the principle. Lawler notes that organizations frequently end up administering pay in ways that prevent pay from being an important motivator —despite the avowed intention to have it function as a motivator. He goes on to suggest some approaches which organizations need to use more frequently if they are going to use pay as a motivator.

The last few years have seen an increased interest in the application of Skinnerian behavior-modification techniques to organizations. The reading by Hamner and Hamner is illustrative of the recent writing in this area. It contends that a potential improvement in organizational effectiveness can be gained by the application of behavior-modification techniques. And it shows that when rewards are tied to performance, behavior change does occur.

Reading 26

The Annual Performance Review Discussion—Making It Constructive

Herbert H. Meyer

The personnel program in any production or service organization which employs more than a few hundred people would not be considered as completely respectable if it did not include a systematic performance appraisal program. Under such a program the performance of each employee is appraised and carefully documented at least annually. Moreover such appraisal programs almost always require that the supervisor who appraises must discuss the individual appraisals with the respective employees.

Typically, such programs have two primary objectives: (1) To provide an *inventory* of human resources talent in the organization, and (2) to *motivate* employees. Motivation is accomplished in two ways. First, the performance appraisal is usually tied into the salary administration program. That is, a "merit pay" philosophy is endorsed under which an individual's pay should coincide with demonstrated performance excellence. Secondly, the feedback discussion of the appraisal should provide an effective source of motivation. Each employee is counseled on how performance may be improved.

In theory, the performance appraisal program appears to be indisputably sound and logical. Yet the program has proved to be an enigma to both personnel experts and line managers. Both the rating process itself and the feedback interview have presented almost insolvable problems in most appraisal programs. There has already been much discussion of various methods to produce more reliable and valid ratings, particularly when tied to a merit pay program.

Even more problematic in an appraisal program is the feedback discussion. Objective evidence has shown that appraisal interviews seldom have the positive effect attributed to them. Some research actually indicates that such discussions often do more harm than good.[1]

These findings lead us to reexamine the theory on which appraisal interviews are based. As a result, I have come to the conclusion that the annual apprais-al interview is *not* a psychologically sound procedure. For one thing, the feedback to the individual is poorly timed. In most appraisal programs this intensive, comprehensive feedback comes but once a year. It is certainly a well-established psychological fact that feedback associated immediately with an act is much more effective than delayed feedback.

An even more serious problem with the appraisal feedback discussion is the fact that it often has a negative side effect on an employee's occupational self-esteem. Our research[2] found that employees were more likely to react defensively than constructively to suggestions for improving performance.

Social psychologists have researched the issue of how people handle threats to their self-esteem and found that a number of unconstructive reactions are typically used to cope with such threats.[3] First, the individual may question the measurement criteria used or he may minimize the importance of the activity. Another undesirable response to threats to self-esteem is the tendency to demean the source.

The potential negative effects of threats to self-esteem in appraisal interviews are minimized by the fact that, typically, managers make few discriminations in their ratings. Almost everyone receives an above-average rating.

A BETTER WAY

Despite all of the problems with appraisal interviews cited here, it does seem that an annual review discussion between supervisor and employee could serve some constructive purposes. Employees do want to know how they are regarded and what the future might hold for them in the organization. The problem is to design a format for accomplishing this which the average manager can use without a great deal of training, and which is not demeaning to the person being assessed. We think we have found the solution to this problem.

We started by formulating some specifications for

a constructive annual discussion between manager and employees. The first of these, and perhaps the most important, was to minimize the authoritarian character of the interaction. The usual appraisal feedback procedure, where the manager discusses *his* or *her* ratings of a subordinate, is a highly authoritarian process. There is no doubt about who is the dominant person. Submissive behavior is appropriate for the subordinate. For this reason, the appraisal interview procedure is becoming more and more anachronistic in today's culture. Young people, especially, are likely to reject authoritarianism. As a solution to this problem, we felt that the discussion must be structured in such a way that the two parties participate more as equals.

Secondly, we felt that if the two parties were to participate as equals, both should prepare for the discussion. The employee, as well as the manager, should think through in advance, and possibly even make notes, about concerns or issues that he or she would like to discuss with the manager in this interview.

A third specification, which follows from the first two, is that the interview format or process should be structured in such a way as to insure *two-way* communication.

A fourth objective for the new procedure was that threats to the individual's self-esteem should be minimized. If an individual is to be effective on the job, he or she must have high occupational self-esteem. This does not mean that needed changes in behavior or performance should not be discussed. However, it does mean that discussions of such issues should be problem oriented and not personalized. Unless an individual really is a misfit in the job, it is important that he or she really thinks that his or her performance is good.

A fifth specification for a constructive annual discussion is that it should not incorporate a "report card" type of rating form. Grades on a form of this kind are not only likely to be threatening to the subordinate, but also to have a demeaning effect. The report card emphasizes the subordinate's dependent status.

A final specification for the procedure is that the manager should not try to cover all issues or aspects of the job in a single interview. A constructive outcome of a discussion of this kind is more likely to result if the manager focuses on just one or two issues or problems. To attempt to cover all aspects of the job, with suggestions for performance improvement or behavior change in a number of areas, is an unrealistic goal for a single interview.

THE DISCUSSION FORMAT

Based on the above specifications, we designed a format for an annual discussion which we thought might be more constructive than the usual appraisal interview. As indicated in the specifications, the first step in the process is to notify the employee that a discussion is scheduled. The employee is invited to prepare by thinking about his or her role in the organization, how individual contribution could be enhanced, and what kinds of plans or aspirations he or she has for the future.

In the discussion itself, the manager will usually start by again reviewing the purpose of the discussion. However, it is important that following this opening statement, the actual discussion of issues be started by giving the initiative to the interviewee. Specifically, the manager might start this discussion by asking, "How do you feel things are going on the job? What kinds of concerns do you have?"

We have found that this is the only way to insure that there will be genuine two-way communication. If the manager starts by expressing his or her own point of view about the employee's performance of their working relationship, the interview almost invariably develops in a predominately one-way communication pattern.

It is only after they have discussed the employee's topics, concerns and suggestions that the manager's viewpoint should be presented. This might include a general impression of performance. For example, the manager might say "I've been very pleased . . . ," or "I've been somewhat disappointed in the way things have been working out. . . . " Certainly a manager should take this opportunity to commend the employee for significant accomplishments, and especially for improvements, and especially for improvements that might have been made on the basis of previous discussions or coaching.

The manager can then introduce the discussion of opportunities for growth or improvement in job performance. Many times the most effective way to accomplish this is to ask the employee to take the initiative here. It is much easier to react to, and perhaps to expand on, plans that someone has for changing performance or behavior than it is to make such suggestion directly. The odds of the individual's self-esteem being threatened are certainly much less if this approach is used. In either case, the manager should try to maintain a problem-solving, rather than a blame-placing approach. The focus should be on future opportunities and plans rather than on past failures.

A natural closing topic of discussion will be what the future might hold for the individual. However, in many organizations this may not be a relevant topic for many people. In a very stable organization, for example, there may be little chance of advancement for many employees. To bring up the topic each year would probably be more threatening than constructive for such employees. On the other hand, for the high-performing employee with obvious potential to advance, a discussion of possible future opportunities and self development plans might be very important to the motivation and retention of that individual.

Figure 26-1 presents an outline which we prepared for the supervisor to be used as a guide to both preparing for and conducting the discussion. The supervisor will find it helpful to make notes in advance relating not only to the topics or issues to be discussed, but also regarding the strategy to be used in introducing each of these topics or issues. Note that the form does not require scaled ratings of any kind.

The primary purpose of an annual discussion along these lines is not performance feedback and coaching. Performance feedback and coaching must be a day-to-day activity. Effective coaching must be associated immediately and directly with the performance at issue. This annual discussion is designed to open communication channels and to develop a better working relationship between the two parties involved. It is especially valuable in providing a formalized method of insuring *upward* communication. The manager can learn how employees view the work situation and what their concerns are.

A TEST OF THE PROCEDURE

This approach to the performance review discussion has been used successfully in several organizations with a variety of employees, from assembly line workers to engineers and managers. Invariably, both the managers and employees like the proce-

---

Employee's name _____

Date of discussion _____

Introduction

Put employee at ease.
Purpose: mutual discussion of how things are going.

Employee's view

How does he/she view job and working climate?
Any problems?
Suggestions for changes, improvement?

Supervisor's view of employee's performance

Summary statement only.
Avoid comparisons to others.

Behaviors desirable to continue

Mention one or two items only.

Opportunities for improvement

No more than one or two items.
Do not present as "shortcomings."
Keep it work-related.

Performance improvement plans

Plan should be employee's plan.
Supervisor merely tries to help and counsel.

Future opportunities

Advancement possibilities?
Future pay increase possibilities?
Warning for poor performer.

Questions

Any general concerns?
Close on constructive, encouraging note.

Figure 26-1 Performance-review discussion.

dure much better than the more traditional rating-form approach to appraisal.

An ideal opportunity for a more objective test of this discussion procedure arose at a new plant. The personnel staff at the plant had planned to introduce a new appraisal program for hourly employees. Their program conformed to the traditional format —that is, ratings in critical dimensions of the job. Since the plant was composed of two large buildings where similar manufacturing operations were performed, it seemed like an ideal situation for an experiment. Therefore, we decided to introduce the traditional program in one building and the new approach, described here, in the other building. An attempt was made in each case to provide the training supervisors would need to carry out the respective programs effectively.

After the two programs had been in effect long enough for all employees to have been appraised, a survey was carried out to measure their reactions to the appraisal programs. This survey showed that reactions of employees who experienced the new approach were significantly more favorable than the reactions of employees in the building where the more traditional appraisal program was used. For example, employees in the building where the new approach to appraisal was used were more likely to say that:

1 Their supervisor recognized and appreciated their work;
2 they got answers to their own questions;
3 they had an opportunity to participate in the discussion;
4 they had received help in performing their job better;
5 judgments the supervisor made about their work were accurate; and
6 the discussion increased their feeling of pride in their work.

Supervisors who used this recommended approach to the performance review discussion also reported, in almost every case, that they like the procedure better than rating programs they had used in the past. Many said that they especially liked the fact that they did not have to assign and discuss numerical grades in various aspects of job performance.

PROVIDING FOR ADMINISTRATIVE NEEDS

Many personnel administrators insist that numerical grades of some kind must be assigned to each of the employees in the organization. They maintain that such grades provide a systematic basis for administrative decisions which need to be made relating to the status or treatment of individuals.

The most common administrative purpose of performance ratings is to implement a merit pay plan. Most organizations use a pay plan at least for professional and managerial personnel which pro-

vides for differential increases to individuals depending on their performance ratings. However, there is no reason to believe that a merit pay program could not be administered without necessarily assigning numbers or grades to the performance of individuals. As a matter of fact, in almost any organization there are factors which influence the size of salary increases granted to individuals other than just performance level achieved in the previous year. Decisions regarding amount of salary increase to be granted, and reasons for the size of increase involved, can certainly be communicated to an employee without necessarily attaching a specific number or grade to the employee's performance level. This decision might be communicated in the annual review discussion recommended here, or in a separate discussion, depending on the timing of the increase, the manager's preference, or similar considerations.

Another administrative need for which appraisal information is likely to be generated is to facilitate manpower planning. Here, again, qualitative information rather than qualified grades or classifications can be recorded for this purpose and discussed with the individuals involved. As a matter of fact, experience of personnel specialists has shown that qualitative information in the form of written out performance or behavioral descriptions on appraisal forms usually proves to be of greater value for manpower planning purposes than the grades or ratings assigned to employees.

In most organizations, promotions to higher-level positions are rarely based on the performance appraisals which managers record as a part of the annual rating program. In almost every case, more comprehensive information is obtained on the qualifications of candidates relating to the specifications for the open position. The opinions of many people in the organization, other than the individual's immediate manager, are likely to be sought. Moreover, in many organizations today "assessment center" type of programs are used to provide more detailed and objective data for making promotional decisions than is typically revealed in the documented annual appraisals.

When we consider an even more critical personnel decision, the decision to demote or terminate an employee, many personnel administrators have insisted that we need systematically recorded annual appraisals to protect the organization against discrimination suits. However, it is very doubtful that a subjective judgment of the supervisor or manager, regardless of how precisely this judgment is categorized, will be accepted in court if the manager is accused of bias. In fact, experience to date has shown that such ratings are not accepted as unbiased in discrimination cases.[4]

To be accepted in a court of law, decisions to demote or terminate an individual will undoubtedly have to be backed up by objective performance evidence. This kind of evidence will also have to be recorded, and should be communicated to the respective individual at the time of occurrence—not on the occasion of the employee's anniversary date when his or her performance review is scheduled. Whether the supervisor judges performance to warrant a "2" or a "4" or "poor" or whatever, will be immaterial in court in most situations. On the other hand, specific descriptions of performance failures, preferably backed by objective data are much more likely to be accepted. This kind of documentation will be necessary to substantiate critical decisions like terminations, whether or not the organization has a formal program for annual performance review.

Many of the problems that we have had with appraisal programs appear to stem from the fact that we try to achieve too many objectives with a single program. Some of those objectives are incompatible. For example, we may expect the same program to provide the kind of detailed and candid data needed to make hard administrative decisions, and at the same time expect the manager to use such data in a supportive manner to stimulate improved performance. This often proves to be an impossible task: either the data get distorted so that the message is palatable, or the feedback is so threatening to the individual that the results are more negative than constructive.

Appraisal to be effective must be an *ad hoc* procedure. We must use different approaches to satisfy different objectives.

With the approach described here, we have concluded that an annual review discussion can be constructive if we set relatively modest, although important, objectives for it. Admittedly it does not provide for all appraisal needs. It does appear, however, to serve one important need very well—that of opening communication channels between manager and employee. This is likely to be much more than is accomplished with programs that are designed to serve a much broader range of needs.

REFERENCES

1 See, for example, H.H. Meyer, E. Day and J.R.P. French, Jr. "Split Roles in Performance Appraisal," *Harvard Business Review* Jan–Feb. 1965.
2 Ibid.
3 See, for example, Sander, Alvin "Research on Self-Esteem, Feedback and Threats to Self-Esteem," in Zander, A. (Ed.) *Performance Appraisals: Effects on Employees and Their Performance.* Ann Arbor, Mich.: The Foundation for Research in Human Behavior, 1963.
4 See, for example, Layer, Robert I. "The 'Discrimination' Danger in Performance Appraisal," *The Conference Board Record.* March, 1976.

Reading 27
Making MbO Effective
Steven Kerr

"Management by Objectives" (MbO) is a term employed by numerous authors and practitioners to describe a wide variety of procedures and programs. Typically, MbO is characterized by joint goal-setting between members of two consecutive levels of management; expression of objectives, whenever possible, in quantifiable terms, such as dollars, units, and percentages; and periodic measurement and comparison of actual performance with agreed-upon objectives (Filley et al., 1976).

Despite tremendous interest in MbO, and its extensive use in industry as a developmental tool,

Tosi and Bigoness pointed out in 1974 that "research examining the planning, implementation and evaluation of MbO systems has been surprisingly scarce" (p. 44). This state of affairs remains true today. Little is known about the dysfunctions that often plague MbO introductions and implementations.

There are two major problems with trying to evaluate MbO. One, as already mentioned, is that "Management by Objectives" is a catchall title for several different, if related, approaches. The other is that, when introduced as a total management system, MbO constitutes a simultaneous assault upon an organization's authority, reward, communications, and control systems, changing so many variables at once that careful study is all but impossible.

I am not prepared to claim that Management by Objectives is or is not working in organizations today. Based on a review of the MbO literature and on related research, however, and aided by personal contact with MbO in four organizations (twice as an employee, twice as a consultant), I am prepared to suggest that most MbO efforts are accompanied by a number of dysfunctions serious enough in many cases to keep the system from performing efficiently.

MbO is often sold as a total managerial system. I hope to show that MbO is *not* likely to be effective when employed as a total system, because the typical MbO process contains logical inconsistencies and makes implicit assumptions which are contrary to things we know about organizations and about people.

Some of the explicit claims and implicit assumptions that have been made on behalf of MbO are as follows:

Assumption 1: "Joint" Goal-setting Among Hierarchical Unequals Is Possible This premise lies at the heart of MbO philosophy, and presumes that a superior can comfortably go from the "boss-judge" role to one of "friend-helper" (and, presumably, back again). It is claimed of one participative system, for example, that evaluation meetings between a boss and subordinates can be "strictly man to man in character. . . . In listening to the subordinate's review of performance, problems, and failings, the manager is automatically cast in the role of *counselor*. This role for the manager, in turn, results naturally in a problem-solving discussion" (Meyer et al., 1969).

The assumption that such schizoid behavior can be induced on any kind of regular basis is naive. The research literature (Blau & Scott, 1962) provides abundant evidence that hierarchical status differences produce some very predictable effects upon interaction patterns, subordinate defensiveness, and quantity and quality of communications, and these effects stack the deck against joint goal-setting by unequals. Bennis (1960) has summarized some of the difficulties:

Two factors seem to be involved. . . . The superior as a helper, trainer, consultant, and co-ordinator, and the superior as an instrument and arm of reality, a man with power over the subordinate. . . . For each actor in the relationship, a *double* reference is needed. . . . The double reference approach requires a degree of maturity, more precisely a commitment to maturity, on the part of both the superior and the subordinate that exceeds that of any other organizational approach. . . . It is suggestive that psychiatric patients find it most difficult to see the psychiatrist both as a human being and helper and an individual with certain perceived powers. The same difficulty exists in the superior-subordinate relationship.

Assumption 2: MbO Can Be Effective at the Lowest Managerial Levels Proponents have contended that successful implementation will enable MbO to permeate the entire organization and to be effective even at the lowest level of management. However, several studies have concluded that this filtering-down process very often fails to occur, and that the lower the manager's hierarchical status, the less the manager is likely to be a genuine participant in the goal-setting process (Ivancevich, 1972). In part this reflects the inherent problem of attempting joint goal-setting among hierarchical unequals.

Another reason for the failure of MbO to be effective at the lower managerial levels is an illogicality in the process itself. Even if we assume truly democratic, participative goal-setting at the very top of the firm (say, between the president and the divisional vice-president), the meeting must still ultimately produce firm, hard goals for the months ahead. The most collegial atmosphere in the world cannot keep these goals, once agreed upon, from being perceived as commitments by the parties concerned. These commitments must then serve as lower limits—as "monkeys on the back" of any vice-president who then seeks to establish democratic, participative goal-setting with his or her own subordinates. Having agreed with the president that 12 percent growth in sales is a fair goal for the coming year, the marketing vice-president is unlikely to accept the sales manager's carefully worded argument that 9 percent is better. While lower-level managers may enjoy the fiction of participation, they will probably soon realize that most of their objectives have already been locked in by meetings held at higher levels. They of course retain the freedom to set objectives even more challenging than those agreed upon higher up; they will seldom be able to set objectives less challenging.

Varying the goal-setting sequence can serve to alter this chain of events but will seldom improve upon it. For example, some MbO proponents claim that simultaneous goal-setting at all managerial levels produces genuine participation. However, the ensuing problems of coordination and communications border on the unreal. The marketing vice-president might under these conditions meet with the president and agree "tentatively" that 12 percent sales growth sounds pretty good for the next year. After meeting with the sales manager, who prefers 9 percent, the vice-president again meets with the president to renegotiate. If 10 percent is now agreed on the vice-president once more meets with the sales manager, to democratically explain why 9 percent is too low. Meanwhile, however, the sales manager has held meetings with the district managers and perhaps become convinced that 9 percent is too high. At this point the marketing vice-president presumably returns to the presidential "friend-helper" for another round of "joint" goal-setting.

The only way to ensure that low-level managers have influence is for them to initiate the process, by communicating to their superior the goals they wish to pursue during the coming period. Their superior would then set objectives based on their objectives, and so on up the line. This gain in low-level influence may be costly, however, since a firm's goals are essentially being set by those at the bottom of the hierarchy, who (usually) are less educated, trained, and experienced, and who may possess inadequate information. Technical drawbacks aside, this alternative is likely to be politically unacceptable to managers at the top. It is therefore no surprise that

many studies have shown MbO to be increasingly ineffective at successively lower levels.

Assumption 3: MbO Is an Aid in Evaluating and Rewarding Performance Management by Objectives is often used in conjunction with management-appraisal programs. Some writers recommend linking it directly to the compensation program, under the assumption that MbO provides "a means of measuring the true contribution of managerial and professional personnel" (Odiorne, 1963, p. 55). However, this assumption calls to mind some impossible-to-answer questions and very often leads to information suppression and risk-avoidance behavior, particularly in highly uncertain and rapidly changing organizational units.

The impossible-to-answer questions include:

1. How do you tell whether the goals whose accomplishment you are rewarding are challenging?

Padding by subordinates of the time it will take or the money it will cost may be detectable when the superior has technical expertise in the area for which the objective is being set, and when the task depends on technology which is stable and predictable. There are numerous instances, however, in engineering, marketing, product development, and other areas, when even the most astute superior will be unable to determine whether target dates have a built-in safety factor.

2. How do you ensure that all your subordinates have goals which are of equal difficulty?

If MbO is to be useful as an evaluation-compensation tool, subordinates must perceive that they have a fair chance to obtain organizational rewards. Yet it is virtually impossible to devise any system which will provide for goals which are equally challenging to all subordinates.

3. What do you do when conditions change?

Suppose that a new competitor or a new credit rating comes along, and what formerly were challenging goals suddenly become easy goals, or impossible goals. In a truly stable environment this may not be a daily concern, but in our age of continuous "future shock," stable environments are becoming unusual. Even a modest technological development or a small change in company policy can eliminate the challenge from objectives previously set. Do we now reward for goal attainment when a ten-year-old could also have been successful? Do we punish nonattainment of objectives which have become herculean in difficulty? Or do we spend the better part of every afternoon negotiating?

The practical dilemma posed by these last two questions is poignantly revealed in an interview by Ford (1979, pp. 53–54) of a plant manager, who remarked:

It's pretty hard to tell a guy who has been told that his pay raise is going to be evaluated on the basis of his objective-achievement to forget such-and-such an objective because we're going to reverse direction or something new is going to take priority because of changes in our situation. You can imagine his attitude when he sees one of his peers rolling along smoothly toward achieving his objectives. The time involved in making these adjustments and holding everyone's hand is fearsome. I have little time for anything else and it hurts.

4. Is exceeding the objective good?

Even aside from the fact that conditions continually change, this question is more difficult than it may seem. In one firm I am familiar with, the completion of a task in seven weeks when it was forecasted to take ten weeks brings mild *disapproval* rather than praise. The rationale is creditable enough—it is that others with whom the goal-setter interacts are not expecting the guidebook, product, software package, or whatever to be ready and so cannot take advantage of the fact that it is ready. This organization takes the position that deviations from standard in *either direction* are usually undesirable. While this may or may not be the best approach, the point is that it is seldom possible to determine whether early completion of a task is an indication of good performance or of bad planning. That the individual worked like the dickens is seldom sufficient to resolve this dilemma.

5. How do you "objectively" reward performance under MbO?

Proponents of Management by Objectives take special pains to avoid this question, since it is obviously one for which there is no answer. Odiorne, for example, asserts that MbO "determines who should get the pay increases. . . . The increases are allocated on the basis of results achieved against agreed upon goals at the beginning of the period" (Odiorne, 1963, p. 66). The problem with this, however, is that no formula for comparing "results achieved against agreed-upon goals" exists. Researchers have correctly cautioned that "evaluations

should rarely be based on whether or not the objective is accomplished or on the sheer number accomplished," and have listed other factors that must be taken into account, including:

- proper allocations of time to given objectives
- type and difficulty of objectives
- creativity in overcoming obstacles
- efficient use of resources
- use of good management practices in accomplishing objectives (cost reduction, delegation, good planning, etc.)
- avoidance of conflict-inducing or unethical practices (Carroll & Tosi, 1973, p. 83)

Certainly it is necessary to consider these and other factors; otherwise subordinates could better themselves by taking shortcuts which negatively affect total organizational effectiveness. But take another look at the above list of "other factors" to be considered. Have you ever seen a list which calls for greater *subjectivity*? Could you possibly establish *objective* measures of whether "proper" time was allocated to given objectives, whether "creativity" was used to overcome obstacles, or whether "good" management practices were used? In short, MbO leaves you as dependent on subjectivity as you were before, only with the additional problem that expectations of "fair" and "objective" evaluation and reward systems have been created, making employee dissatisfaction more likely.

If the added objectivity promised by Management by Objectives typically turns out to be illusory, the information suppression and risk-avoidance behavior often brought on by linking MbO to rewards is certainly no illusion. Common sense suggests that many employees will build margins for error into their cost estimates and target dates, and in this case common sense is supported by research (Carroll & Tosi, 1970). Even workers high in need for achievement will often create safety cushions, privately setting moderate-risk objectives against which they can compete. I have seen or heard of many cases where employees set objectives on projects which were virtually or actually completed. You may be quick to brand such actions unethical; can you as quickly deny that they are rational responses to a system which requests of employees that they voluntarily set challenging, risky goals, only to face smaller paychecks and possibly damaged careers if these goals are not accomplished?

Assumption 4: Objectives Should Be as Specific as Possible   Although in recent years there has been a shift away from rigid formulas and toward great flexibility (McConkie, 1979), many MbO approaches continue to encourage quantitative goal-setting, with intermediate and final results all expressed in dollars, dates, or percentages. While such quantification is often possible and desirable, MbO encourages it to such an extent that goal displacement and inefficiency sometimes result. Studies indicate that the MbO process can cause employees to overconcentrate their efforts in areas for which objectives have been written, to the virtual exclusion of other activities (Raia, 1966). Since it is seldom possible to write quantifiable objectives about innovation, creativity, and interpersonal relations, employees under MbO are seldom evaluated in these areas and may consequently worry little about coming up with new ideas or improving relations with other organizational units.

Even in areas for which objectives do exist, excessive emphasis on quantifiable objectives encourages (and, when linked to compensation, rewards) performance in accordance with the *letter,* not the *spirit,* of the objective. Attempting to measure and reward accuracy in paying surgical claims, for example, one insurance firm requires that managers set objectives about the number of returned checks and letters of complaint received from policyholders. However, underpayments are likely to provoke cries of outrage from the insured, while overpayments are often accepted in courteous silence. Since it is often impossible to tell from the physician's statement which of two surgical procedures, with different allowable benefits, was performed, and since writing for clarification will interfere with other objectives concerning "percentage of claims paid within two days of receipt," the new hire in more than one claims section is soon acquainted with the informal norm: "When in doubt, pay it out!" (Kerr, 1975). The managers of these sections regularly meet or exceed their objectives in the areas of both quality (accuracy) and quantity. But at what cost to the organization?

Assumption 5: MbO Is Useful in a Dynamic Changing Environment   Certainly, the dynamic environment is where new systems of planning, evaluation, and communications are most needed. We already know quite a bit about managing the stable, highly certain segments of business, and a variety of techniques such as PERT are available to use and work particularly well when parameters are known. MbO, however, is less useful when conditions are changing and the future is uncertain. We have already suggested that risk-avoidance by subordinates will most often occur under conditions of uncertainty, and we have also pointed out that under such circumstances goal difficulty is so likely to change that systematic reward and punishment under MbO is impossible.

One reviewer of the MbO literature found that "the most striking result is the emphasis on the need for goal clarity (low role conflict and ambiguity) if Management by Objectives is to be an effective planning procedure" (Miner, 1973). Low role conflict and ambiguity can be fairly well established by job descriptions in the stable, highly certain parts of most firms; they are nearly impossible to come by in uncertain areas. MbO, after all, attempts to produce a mutually acceptable job description, and "no matter how detailed the job description it is essentially static—that is, a series of statements. . . . The more complex the task and the more flexible the man must be in it, the less any fixed statement of job elements will fit what he does. . . . " (Levinson, 1970, p. 126).

I have to this point tried to demonstrate that Management by Objectives is a sometimes overrated, flawed system which may introduce more problems than it solves. Rather than join those who attribute its failures to "errors in implementation," "not enough time," or "lack of top-management support," I believe its difficulties stem from the fact that it depends upon assumptions which are contrary to what we know about organizations and about people.

Of course, if you are *not* knee-deep in pseudo-participation caution-crazy subordinates, and make-believe objectivity, don't let me convince you that you're sick when you're not. In this age of situational theories it is no more possible to state that something will not work than to claim it always will. However, if you *are* having problems of the kind I have described, and if you buy my argument that MbO is at least partially responsible, you may still feel that sunk cost and political realities argue against trying to quit cold turkey. The remainder of this article is aimed, therefore, at separating those parts of MbO worth keeping from those which ought to be discarded.

FEATURES WORTH KEEPING

1. Conscious Emphasis on Goal-Setting Considerable research suggests that systematic, periodic goal-setting positively affects performance and can alter an organization's activities-oriented approach in favor of one that is more results-oriented (see, for example, Quick, 1979; Latham & Locke, 1979, Reading 28).

2. Frequent Interaction and Feedback Between Superior and Subordinates These have been found to be related to "higher goal success, improvement in relationships with the boss, goal clarity, a feeling of supportiveness and interest from one's superior, a feeling that one can participate in matters affecting him, and satisfaction with the superior" (Carroll & Tosi, 1969). Feedback frequently is particularly important "to managers low in self-assurance, cautious in decision making, and with jobs involving frequent change" (Tosi & Bigoness, 1974, p. 46).

3. Opportunities for Participation The dimensions and consequences of the participation of subordinates in goal-setting, decision making, and evaluation have been explored in recent works by Greller (1978), and Dachler and Wilpert (1978). Although it is erroneous to assume that hierarchically unequal individuals can comfortably engage in joint goal-setting this does not mean that all forms of participation under MbO are impossible. Even chances to give advice about matters which will ultimately be decided higher up often have favorable effects upon subordinate attitudes. While not all workers respond positively to participation, studies indicate that performance will seldom suffer merely because of such opportunities.

One way to increase participation under MbO is for the peer group to develop their objectives as a group and subsequently appraise performance as a group (Howell, 1967; Levinson, 1976; French & Hollmann, 1975). Status differences are likely to be less important, freeing individuals from the need to be cautious and deferential (Howell, 1967). Peer group goal-setting should serve to minimize duplica-

tion of objectives and reduce paperwork. Successful negotiation with the boss should be easier, since group support would tend to offset the boss's higher rank. Communications should be facilitated, and the present tendency of MbO to reward for *individual* performance at the expense of overall harmony or efficiency should be reduced.

Another way to improve participation under MbO is for the organization to provide training to all subordinates, and especially to all managers, who will be required to operate under the system. The skills and attitudes necessary for MbO to be effective are neither intuitive nor "natural" to individuals brought up in traditionally bureaucratic organizations. Both book learning and simulated experiences will probably be necessary before those who will be living with the system become competent even to try it. This point should be so obvious as to be unworthy of mention, yet comparatively few MbO change-agents include systematic skills and attitude training as part of their programs.

FEATURES TO DISCARD

1. Linking MbO to the Compensation System
The only areas where tying MbO to reward will not tend to induce risk-avoidance and goal-displacement are those where conditions are so predictable that no deceit is possible. In these areas, however, incentive plans and piecework, commission, and bonus systems are already available.

2. Using MbO as an "Objective" Way to Measure Performance While requesting that managers in their feedback sessions with subordinates totally suppress consideration of whether agreed-upon objectives have been met is probably futile, formal comparisons of goals accomplished against goals set should definitely be avoided. Such comparisons *will not* enable performance reviews to be carried out on a more objective basis, but *will* cause the risk-avoidance and goal-displacement behavior described above.

3. Focusing Attention upon Only Those Objectives Which Can Easily Be Quantified Objectives should be written "in every area where performance and results directly and vitally affect the survival and prosperity of the business" (Drucker, 1954). This is true *whether or not* quantification is possible! Numerous instances could be cited where performance suffered either because nonquantifiable objectives were ignored altogether or because some simpleminded number (e.g., patents as *the* measure of creativity) was substituted for them (Kerr, 1975). Conversely, performance may be improved by keeping in mind that "although in many areas the qualitative aspects of output may have to be assessed largely in terms of value judgments, the discipline of prescribing standards of performance and of testing results against them can improve the control process" (Hancock, 1974).

4. Making the Personnel Division Responsible for Maintenance   Once it is decided that MbO will not be used as an instrument of evaluation and reward, the rationale for active involvement by the personnel division largely vanishes. Such involvement will serve mainly to increase both the volume of required paperwork and the degree of threat perceived by lower-level participants.

5. Forms, Forms, and More Forms   The problem of excessive paperwork has been found to be a major impediment to the effective use of MbO (Raia, 1974). Once the notion of using MbO for evaluation and control is abandoned, surprisingly few forms are really necessary.

6. Prepackaged Programs and Costly Consultants
Although these may or may not be necessary for successful introduction and maintenance of the change-everything-at-once-and-see-what-happens king-sized version of MbO, they are probably unnecessary for the "mini-MbO" that will remain once the preceding five "features to discard" are discarded.

CONCLUSIONS

In sum:

1. Management by Objectives is at present a high-cost long-run package whose success is by no means guaranteed. It generates many side effects impossible to predict or control. Two competent researchers speak of MbO as a "complex organizational change process which may be painful and time-consuming" (Tosi & Carroll, 1969), and another points out that "it will take four to five years to achieve a fully effective Management by Objectives system" (Howell, 1970).

2. Management by Objectives is yet another technique that requires friendly, helpful superiors, honest and mature subordinates, and a climate of mutual trust. Carvalho has cautioned that "successful implementation of MbO requires, even demands, that all managers have a fundamental results-oriented attitude," as well as "an attitude which accepts collaboration, cooperation, and joint sharing of responsibilities as the norm rather than the exception." He goes on to state that such attitudes are hardly commonplace in most organizations today, and that to develop them a "mini-cultural revolution" will probably be needed (Carvalho, 1972). And we have already taken note of Bennis's opinion that the double-reference approach necessary for MbO to work "requires a degree of maturity, more precisely a commitment to maturity, on the part of both the superior and the subordinate that exceeds that of any other organizational approach" (Bennis, 1960, p. 286). In short, *MbO often works best for those individuals who need it least.*

3. Management by Objectives is best suited to those static environments in which we already have sufficient technology to manage competently. Rapidly changing conditions and high role conflict and ambiguity seriously impair its usefulness. In short, *MbO often works best in those situations where we need it least.*

4. We must stop pretending that MbO adds much to our ability to reward and evaluate. It is unlikely to be effective when employed as a "total" management system. Its strength lies in its emphasis on goal-setting, its provisions for feedback and interaction, and its opportunities for participation. These features can and should be maintained, but not at the cost of jolting the organization with massive and simultaneous changes. A good illustration of this point is given by Lasagna (1971), who described the problems which afflicted his organization as a result of attempting to use MbO for too many purposes. He reports that they had much better success when they substituted a mini-MbO which was not tied to evaluation and compensation.

The advantages that would accrue to users of a

"mini-system" of MbO are due to the fact that such an approach would introduce fewer new variables, require less time to take effect, cost far less, and minimize unpredictable side effects. It would be particularly effective in combating the increase in employee anxiety and defensiveness which so often accompanies MbO introduction. Furthermore, a mini-MbO would be less likely to cause management to forget that the system is in no sense a cure-all, but is rather just another tool in the managerial kit. Finally, a "mini-system" of MbO would for the first time enable scientific study of costs and benefits to be conducted, so that we may at last discover whether or not Management by Objectives is worth its cost.

REFERENCES

Bennis, Warren G. Leadership theory and administrative behavior: The problem of Authority. *Administrative Science Quarterly,* 1960, 285–287.

Blau, Peter M., & W. Richard Scott. *Formal Organizations,* 121–124 and 242–244. (San Francisco: Chandler, 1962).

Carroll, Stephen J., & Henry L. Tosi. The relation of characteristics of the review process as moderated by personality and situational factors to the success of the "Management by Objectives" approach. *Academy of Management Proceedings,* 1969, 141.

———, & Henry L. Tosi, Jr. Goal characteristics and personality factors in a Management by Objectives program. *Administration Science Quarterly,* 1970, 295–303.

Carvalho, G. F. Installing MbO: A new perspective on Organizational change. *Human Resources Management,* Spring 1972, 23–30.

Dachler, H. Peter, & Bernhard Wilpert. Conceptual dimensions and boundaries of participation in organizations: A critical evaluation. *Administrative Science Quarterly,* 1978, **23,** 1–39.

Drucker, Peter F. *The Practice of Management.* New York: Harper & Row, 1954.

Filley, Alan C., Robert J. House, & Steven Kerr. *Managerial process and organizational behavior.* (2d ed.) Glenview, Ill.: Scott, Foresman., 1976.

Ford, Charles H. MbO: An idea whose time has gone? *Business Horizons,* December 1979, 48–55.

French, Wendell I., & Robert W. Hollmann. Management by Objectives: The team approach. *California Management Review,* 1975, **17,** 13–22.

Greller, Martin M. The nature of subordinate participation in the appraisal interview. *Academy of Management Journal,* 1978, **21,** 646–658.

Hancock, C. J. MbO raises management effectiveness in government service. *Management by Objectives,* 1974, **3**(4), 12.

Howell, Robert A. A fresh look at Management by Objectives. *Business Horizons,* 1967, 55.

———, Managing by Objectives—A three stage system. *Business Horizons,* February 1970, 43.

Ivancevich, John M. A longitudinal assessment of Management by Objectives. *Administrative Science Quarterly,* 1972, 126–138.

Kerr, Stephen. On the folly of rewarding A, while hoping for B. *Academy of Management Journal,* 1975, **18**(4), 769–783.

Lasagna, John B. Make your MbO pragmatic. *Harvard Business Review,* November–December 1971, 64–69.

Latham, Gary P., & Edwin A. Locke. Goal-setting: A motivational technique that works. *Organizational Dynamics,* Autumn 1979, **8,** 68–80.

Levinson, Harry. Appraisal of what performance? *Harvard Business Review,* July–August 1976, 30–48.

———. Management by whose objectives. *Harvard Business Review,* July–August 1970.

McConkie, Mark L. A clarification of the goal-setting and appraisal processes in MbO. *Academy of Management Review,* 1979, **4,** 29–40.

Meyer, Herbert H., Emanuel Kay, & John R. P. French, Jr. Split roles in performance appraisal. *Harvard Business Review,* January–February 1965, 129.

Miner, John B. *The management process: Theory, research, and practice.* New York: Macmillan, 1973.

Odiorne, George S. *Management by Objectives: A system of managerial leadership.* New York: Pitman, 1963.

Quick, James C. Dyadic goal setting within organizations: Role-making and motivational considerations. *Academy of Management Review,* 1979, **4,** 369–380.

Raia, Anthony P. A second look at management goals and controls. *California Management Review,* 1966, 49–53.

———. *Managing by Objectives.* Glenview, Ill: Scott, Foresman, 1974.

Tosi, Henry L., & Stephen J. Carroll. Some structural factors related to goal influence in the Management by Objectives process. *Business Topics,* Spring 1969, 50.

———, and William J. Bigoness. MbO and Personality: A search for comparability. *Management by Objectives,* 1974, **3**(4).

Reading 28

Goal Setting—A Motivational Technique That Works

Gary P. Latham
Edwin A. Locke

The problem of how to motivate employees has puzzled and frustrated managers for generations. One reason the problem has seemed difficult, if not mysterious, is that motivation ultimately comes from within the individual and therefore cannot be observed directly. Moreover, most managers are not in a position to change an employee's basic personality structure. The best they can do is try to use incentives to direct the energies of their employees toward organizational objectives.

Money is obviously the primary incentive, since without it few if any employees would come to work. But money alone is not always enough to motivate high performance. Other incentives, such as participation in decision making, job enrichment, behavior modification, and organizational development, have been tried with varying degrees of success. A large number of research studies have shown, however, that one very straightforward technique—goal setting—is probably not only more effective than alternative methods, but may be the major mechanism by which these other incentives affect motivation. For example, a recent experiment on job enrichment demonstrated that unless employees in enriched jobs set higher, more specific goals than do those with unenriched jobs, job enrichment has absolutely no effect on productivity. Even money has been found most effective as a motivator when the bonuses offered are made contingent on attaining specific objectives.

THE GOAL-SETTING CONCEPT

The idea of assigning employees a specific amount of work to be accomplished—a specific task, a quota, a performance standard, an objective, or a deadline—is not new. The task concept, along with time and motion study and incentive pay, was the cornerstone of scientific management, founded by Frederick W. Taylor more than 70 years ago. He used his system to increase the productivity of blue collar workers.

About 20 years ago the idea of goal setting reappeared under a new name, management by objectives, but this technique was designed for managers.

In a 14-year program of research, we have found that goal setting does not necessarily have to be part of a wider management system to motivate performance effectively. It can be used as a technique in its own right.

Laboratory and Field Research

Our research program began in the laboratory. In a series of experiments, individuals were assigned different types of goals on a variety of simple tasks—addition, brainstorming, assembling toys. Repeatedly it was found that those assigned hard goals performed better than did people assigned moderately difficult or easy goals. Furthermore, individuals who had specific, challenging goals outperformed those who were given such vague goals as to "do your best." Finally, we observed that pay and performance feedback led to improved performance only when these incentives led the individual to set higher goals.

While results were quite consistent in the laboratory, there was no proof that they could be applied to actual work settings. Fortunately, just as Locke published a summary of the laboratory studies in 1968, Latham began a separate series of experiments in the wood products industry that demonstrated the practical significance of these findings. The field studies did not start out as a validity test of a laboratory theory, but rather as a response to a practical problem.

In 1968, six sponsors of the American Pulpwood Association became concerned about increasing the productivity of independent loggers in the South. These loggers were entrepreneurs on whom the multimillion-dollar companies are largely dependent for their raw material. The problem was twofold. First, these entrepreneurs did not work for a single company; they worked for themselves. Thus they were free to (and often did) work two days one week, four days a second week, five half-days a third week, or whatever schedule they preferred. In short, these workers could be classified as marginal from the standpoint of their productivity and attendance, which were considered highly unsatisfactory by conventional company standards. Second, the major approach taken to alleviate this problem had been to develop equipment that would make the industry less dependent on this type of worker. A limitation of this approach was that many of the logging supervisors were unable to obtain the financing necessary to purchase a small tractor, let alone a rubber-tired skidder.

Consequently, we designed a survey that would help managers determine "what makes these people tick." The survey was conducted orally in the field with 292 logging supervisors. Complex statistical analyses of the data identified three basic types of supervisor. One type stayed on the job with their men, gave them instructions and explanations, provided them with training, read the trade magazines, and had little difficulty financing the equipment they needed. Still, the productivity of their units was at best mediocre.

The operation of the second group of supervisors was slightly less mechanized. These supervisors provided little training for their workforce. They simply drove their employees to the woods, gave them a specific production goal to attain for the day or week, left them alone in the woods unsupervised, and returned at night to take them home. Labor turnover was high and productivity was again average.

The operation of the third group of supervisors was relatively unmechanized. These leaders stayed on the job with their men, provided training, gave instructions and explanations, and in addition, set a specific production goal for the day or week. Not only was the crew's productivity high, but their injury rate was well below average.

Two conclusions were discussed with the managers of the companies sponsoring this study. First, mechanization alone will not increase the productivity of logging crews. Just as the average tax payer would probably commit more mathematical errors if he were to try to use a computer to complete his income tax return, the average logger misuses, and frequently abuses, the equipment he purchases (for example, drives a skidder with two flat tires, doesn't change the oil filter). This increases not only the logger's downtime, but also his costs which, in turn, can force him out of business. The second conclusion of the survey was that setting a specific production goal combined with supervisory presence to ensure goal commitment will bring about a significant increase in productivity.

These conclusions were greeted with the standard, but valid, cliché, "Statistics don't prove causation." And our comments regarding the value of machinery were especially irritating to these managers, many of whom had received degrees in engineering. So one of the companies decided to replicate the survey in order to check our findings.

The company's study placed each of 892 independent logging supervisors who sold wood to the company into one of three categories of supervisory styles our survey had identified—namely, (1) stays on the job but does not set specific production goals; (2) sets specific production goals but does not stay on the job; and (3) stays on the job and sets specific production goals. Once again, goal setting, in combination with the on-site presence of a supervisor, was shown to be the key to improved productivity.

TESTING FOR THE HAWTHORNE EFFECT

Management may have been unfamilar with different theories of motivation, but it was fully aware of one label—the Hawthorne effect. Managers in these wood products companies remained unconvinced that anything so simple as staying on the job with the men and setting a specific production goal could have an appreciable effect on productivity. They pointed out that the results simply reflected the positive effects any supervisor would have on the work unit after giving his crew attention. And they were unimpressed by the laboratory experiments we cited—experiments showing that individuals who have a specific goal solve more arithmetic problems or assemble more tinker toys than do people who are told to "do your best." Skepticism prevailed.

But the country's economic picture made it critical to continue the study of inexpensive techniques to improve employee motivation and productivity. We were granted permission to run one more project to test the effectiveness of goal setting.

Twenty independent logging crews who were all

but identical in size, mechanization level, terrain on which they worked, productivity, and attendance were located. The logging supervisors of these crews were in the habit of staying on the job with their men, but they did not set production goals. Half the crews were randomly selected to receive training in goal setting; the remaining crews served as a control group.

The logging supervisors who were to set goals were told that we had found a way to increase productivity at no financial expense to anyone. We gave the ten supervisors in the training group production tables developed through time-and-motion studies by the company's engineers. These tables made it possible to determine how much wood should be harvested in a given number of manhours. They were asked to use these tables as a guide in determining a specific production goal to assign their employees. In addition, each sawhand was given a tallymeter (counter) that he could wear on his belt. The sawhand was asked to punch the counter each time he felled a tree. Finally, permission was requested to measure the crew's performance on a weekly basis.

The ten supervisors in the control group—those who were not asked to set production goals—were told that the researchers were interested in learning the extent to which productivity is affected by absenteeism and injuries. They were urged to "do your best" to maximize the crew's productivity and attendance and to minimize injuries. It was explained that the data might be useful in finding ways to increase productivity at little or no cost to the wood harvester.

To control for the Hawthorne effect, we made an equal number of visits to the control group and the training group. Performance was measured for 12 weeks. During this time, the productivity of the goal-setting group was significantly higher than that of the control group. Moreover, absenteeism was significantly lower in the groups that set goals than in the groups who were simply urged to do their best. Injury and turnover rates were low in both groups.

Why should anything so simple and inexpensive as goal setting influence the work of these employees so significantly? Anecdotal evidence from conversations with both the loggers and the company foresters who visited them suggested several reasons.

Harvesting timber can be a monotonous, tiring job with little or no meaning for most workers. Introducing a goal that is difficult, but attainable, increases the challenge of the job. In addition, a specific goal makes it clear to the worker what it is he is expected to do. Goal feedback via the tallymeter and weekly recordkeeping provide the worker with a sense of achievement, recognition, and accomplishment. He can see how well he is doing now as against his past performance and, in some cases, how well he is doing in comparison with others. Thus the worker not only may expend greater effort, but may also devise better or more creative tactics for attaining the goal than those he previously used.

NEW APPLICATIONS

Management was finally convinced that goal setting was an effective motivational technique for increasing the productivity of the independent woods worker in the South. The issue now raised by the management of another wood products company was whether the procedure could be used in the West with company logging operations in which the employees were unionized and paid by the hour. The previous study had involved employees on a piece-rate system, which was the practice in the South.

The immediate problem confronting this company involved the loading of logging trucks. If the trucks were unloaded, the company lost money. If the trucks were overloaded, however, the driver could be fined by the Highway Department and could ultimately lose his job. The drivers opted for underloading the trucks.

For three months management tried to solve this problem by urging the drivers to try harder to fill the truck to its legal net weight, and by developing weighing scales that could be attached to the truck. But this approach did not prove cost effective, because the scales continually broke down when subjected to the rough terrain on which the trucks traveled. Consequently, the drivers reverted to their former practice of underloading. For the three months in which the problem was under study the trucks were seldom loaded in excess of 58 to 63 percent of capacity.

At the end of the three-month period, the results of the previous goal-setting experiments were explained to the union. They were told three things—that the company would like to set a specific net weight goal for the drivers, that no monetary reward or fringe benefits other than verbal praise could be expected for improved performance, and that no one would be criticized for failing to attain the goal. Once again, the idea that simply setting a specific goal would solve a production problem seemed too incredible to be taken seriously by the union. However, they reached an agreement that a difficult, but attainable, goal of 94 percent of the truck's legal net weight would be assigned to the drivers, provided that no one could be reprimanded for failing to attain the goal. This latter point was emphasized to the company foremen in particular.

Within the first month, performance increased to 80 percent of the truck's net weight. After the second month, however, performance decreased to 70 percent. Interviews with the drivers indicated that they were testing management's statement that no punitive steps would be taken against them if their performance suddenly dropped. Fortunately for all concerned, no such steps were taken by the foremen, and performance exceeded 90 percent of the truck's capacity after the third month. Their performance has remained at this level to this day, seven years later.

The results over the nine-month period during which this study was conducted saved the company $250,000. This figure, determined by the company's accountants, is based on the cost of additional trucks that would have been required to deliver the same quantity of logs to the mill if goal setting had not been implemented. The dollars-saved figure is even higher when you factor in the cost of the additional diesel fuel that would have been consumed and the expenses incurred in recruiting and hiring the additional truck drivers.

Why could this procedure work without the union's demanding an increase in hourly wages? First, the drivers did not feel that they were really doing anything differently. This, of course, was not true. As a result of goal setting, the men began to record their truck weight in a pocket notebook, and they found themselves bragging about their accomplishments to their peers. Second, they viewed goal setting as a challenging game: "It was great to beat the other guy."

Competition was a crucial factor in bringing about goal acceptance and commitment in this study. However, we can reject the hypothesis that improved performance resulted solely from competition, because no special prizes or formal recognition programs were provided for those who came closest to, or exceeded, the goal. No effort was made by the company to single out one "winner." More important, the opportunity for competition among drivers had existed before goal setting was instituted; after all, each driver knew his own truck's weight, and the truck weight of each of the 36 other drivers every time he hauled wood into the yard. In short, competition affected productivity only in the sense that it led to the acceptance of, and commitment to, the goal. It was the setting of the goal itself and the working toward it that brought about increased performance and decreased costs.

PARTICIPATIVE GOAL SETTING

The inevitable question always raised by management was raised here: "We know goal setting works. How can we make it work better?" Was there one best method for setting goals? Evidence for a "one best way" approach was cited by several managers, but it was finally concluded that different approaches would work best under different circumstances.

It was hypothesized that the woods workers in the South, who had little or no education, would work better with assigned goals, while the educated workers in the West would achieve higher productivity if they were allowed to help set the goals themselves. Why the focus on education? Many of the uneducated workers in the South could be classified as culturally disadvantaged. Such persons often lack self-confidence, have a poor sense of time, and are not very competitive. The cycle of skill mastery, which in turn guarantees skill levels high enough to prevent discouragement, doesn't apply to these employees. If, for example, these people were allowed to participate in goal setting, the goals might be too difficult or they might be too easy. On the other hand, participation for the educated worker was considered critical in effecting maximum goal acceptance. Since these conclusions appeared logical, management initially decided that no research was necessary. This decision led to hours of further discussion.

The same questions were raised again and again

by the researchers. What if the logic were wrong? Can we afford to implement these decisions without evaluating them systematically? Would we implement decisions regarding a new approach to tree planting without first testing it? Do we care more about trees than we do about people? Finally, permission was granted to conduct an experiment.

Logging crews were randomly appointed to either participative goal setting, assigned (nonparticipative) goal setting, or a do-your-best condition. The results were startling. The uneducated crews, consisting primarily of black employees who participated in goal setting, set significantly higher goals and attained them more often than did those whose goals were assigned by the supervisor. Not surprisingly, their performance was higher. Crews with assigned goals performed no better than did those who were urged to do their best to improve their productivity. The performance of white, educationally advantaged workers was higher with assigned rather than participatively set goals, although the difference was not statistically significant. These results were precisely the opposite of what had been predicted.

Another study comparing participative and assigned goals was conducted with typists. The results supported findings obtained by researchers at General Electric years before. It did not matter so much *how* the goal was set. What mattered was *that* a goal was set. The study demonstrated that both assigned and participatively set goals led to substantial improvements in typing speed. The process by which these gains occurred, however, differed in the two groups.

In the participative group, employees insisted on setting very high goals regardless of whether they had attained their goal the previous week. Nevertheless, their productivity improved—an outcome consistent with the theory that high goals lead to high performance.

In the assigned-goal group, supervisors were highly supportive of employees. No criticism was given for failure to attain the goals. Instead, the supervisor lowered the goal after failure so that the employee would be certain to attain it. The goal was then raised gradually each week until the supervisor felt the employee was achieving his or her potential. The result? Feelings of accomplishment and achievement on the part of the worker and improved productivity for the company.

These basic findings were replicated in a subsequent study of engineers and scientists. Participative goal setting was superior to assigned goal setting only to the degree that it led to the setting of higher goals. Both participative and assigned-goal groups outperformed groups that were simply told to "do your best."

An additional experiment was conducted to validate the conclusion that participation in goal setting may be important only to the extent that it leads to the setting of difficult goals. It was performed in a laboratory setting in which the task was to brainstorm uses for wood. One group was asked to "do your best" to think of as many ideas as possible. A second group took part in deciding, with the experimenter, the specific number of ideas each person would generate. These goals were, in turn, assigned to individuals in a third group. In this way, goal difficulty was held constant between the assigned-goal and participative groups. Again, it was found that specific, difficult goals—whether assigned or set through participation—led to higher performance than did an abstract or generalized goal such as "do your best." And, when goal difficulty was held constant, there was no significant difference in the performance of those with assigned as compared with participatively set goals.

These results demonstrate that goal setting in industry works just as it does in the laboratory. Specific, challenging goals lead to better performance than do easy or vague goals, and feedback motivates higher performance only when it leads to the setting of higher goals.

It is important to note that participation is not only a motivational tool. When a manager has competent subordinates, participation is also a useful device for increasing the manager's knowledge and thereby improving decision quality. It can lead to better decisions through input from subordinates.

A representative sample of the results of field studies of goal setting conducted by Latham and others is shown in Figure 28-1. Each of these ten studies compared the performance of employees given specific challenging goals with those given "do best" or no goals. Note that goal setting has been successful across a wide variety of jobs and industries. The effects of goal setting have been recorded for as long as seven years after the onset of the program, although the results of most studies have been followed up for only a few weeks or months.

Researcher(s)	Task	Duration of study or of significant effects	Percent of change in performance[a]
Blumenfeld & Leidy	Servicing soft drink coolers	Unspecified	+27
Dockstader	Keypunching	3 mos.	+27
Ivancevich	Skilled technical jobs	9 mos.	+15
Ivancevich	Sales	9 mos.	+24
Kim and Hamner	5 telephone service jobs	3 mos.	+13
Latham and Baldes	Loading trucks	9 mos.[b]	+26
Latham and Yukl	Logging	2 mos.	+18
Latham and Yukl	Typing	5 weeks	+11
Migliore	Mass production	2 years	+16
Umstot, Bell, and Mitchell	Coding land parcels	1-2 days[c]	+16

[a]Percentage changes were obtained by subtracting pre-goal-setting performance from post-goal-setting performance and dividing by pre-goal-setting performance. Different experimental groups were combined where appropriate. If a control group was available, the percentage figure represents the difference of the percentage changes between the experimental and control groups. If multiple performance measures were used, the median improvement on all measures was used. The authors would like to thank Dena Feren and Vicki McCaleb for performing these calculations.

[b]Performance remained high for seven years.

[c]Simulated organization.

Figure 28-1 Representative field studies of goal-setting.

The median improvement in performance in the ten studies shown in Figure 28-1 was 17 percent.

A CRITICAL INCIDENTS SURVEY

To explore further the importance of goal setting in the work setting. Dr. Frank White conducted another study in two plants of a high-technology, multinational corporation on the East Coast. Seventy-one engineers, 50 managers, and 31 clerks were asked to describe a specific instance when they were especially productive and a specific instance when they were especially unproductive on their present jobs. Responses were classified according to a reliable coding scheme. Of primary interest here are the external events perceived by employees as being responsible for the high-productivity and low-productivity incidents. The results are shown in Figure 28-2.

The first set of events—pursuing a specific goal, having a large amount of work, working under a deadline, or having an uninterrupted routine—accounted for more than half the high-productivity events. Similarly, the converse of these—goal blockage, having a small amount of work, lacking a deadline, and suffering work interruptions—accounted for nearly 60 percent of the low-productivity events. Note that the first set of four categories all are relevant to goal setting and the second set to a lack of goals or goal blockage. The

goal category itself—that of pursuing an attainable goal or goal blockage—was the one most frequently used to describe high- and low-productivity incidents.

The next four categories, which are more pertinent to Frederick Herzberg's motivator-hygiene theory—task interest, responsibility, promotion, and recognition—are less important, accounting for 36.8 percent of the high-productivity incidents (the opposite of these four categories accounted for 19.1 percent for the lows). The remaining categories were even less important.

Employees were also asked to identify the responsible agent behind the events that had led to high and low productivity. In both cases, the employees themselves, their immediate supervisors, and the organization were the agents most frequently mentioned.

The concept of goal setting is a very simple one. Interestingly, however, we have gotten two contradictory types of reaction when the idea was introduced to managers. Some claimed it was so simple and self-evident that everyone, including themselves, already used it. This, we have found, is not true. Time after time we have gotten the following response from subordinates after goal setting was introduced: "This is the first time I knew what my supervisor expected of me on this job." Conversely, other managers have argued that the idea would not work, precisely *because* it is so simple (implying that

Event	Percent of Times Event Caused	
	High Productivity	Low Productivity
Goal pursuit/Goal blockage	17.1	23.0
Large amount of work/Small amount of work	12.5	19.0
Deadline or schedule/No deadline	15.1	3.3
Smooth work routine/Interrupted routine	5.9	14.5
Intrinsic/Extrinsic factors	50.6	59.8
Interesting task/Uninteresting task	17.1	11.2
Increased responsibility/Decreased responsibility	13.8	4.6
Anticipated promotion/Promotion denied	1.3	0.7
Verbal recognition/Criticism	4.6	2.6
People/Company conditions	36.8	19.1
Pleasant personal relationships/Unpleasant personal relationships	10.5	9.9
Anticipated pay increase/Pay increase denied	1.3	1.3
Pleasant working conditions/Unpleasant working conditions	0.7	0.7
Other (Miscellaneous)	——	9.3

N = 152 in this study by Frank White.

Figure 28-2 Events perceived as causing high and low productivity.

something more radical and complex was needed). Again, results proved them wrong.

But these successes should not mislead managers into thinking that goal setting can be used without careful planning and forethought. Research and experience suggest that the best results are obtained when the following steps are followed:

Setting the Goal The goal set should have two main characteristics. First, it should be specific rather than vague: "Increase sales by 10 percent" rather than "Try to improve sales." Whenever possible, there should be a time limit for goal accomplishment: "Cut costs by 3 percent in the next six months."

Second, the goal should be challenging yet reachable. If accepted, difficult goals lead to better performance than do easy goals. In contrast, if the goals are perceived as unreachable, employees will not accept them. Nor will employees get a sense of achievement from pursuing goals that are never attained. Employees with low self-confidence or ability should be given more easily attainable goals than those with high self-confidence and ability.

There are at least five possible sources of input, aside from the individual's self-confidence and ability, that can be used to determine the particular goal to set for a given individual.

The scientific management approach pioneered by Frederick W. Taylor uses time and motion study to determine a fair day's work. This is probably the most objective technique available, but it can be used only where the task is reasonably repetitive and standardized. Another drawback is that this method often leads to employee resistance, especially in cases where the new standard is substantially higher than previous performance and where rate changes are made frequently.

More readily accepted, although less scientific than time and motion study, are standards based on the average past performance of employees. This method was used successfully in some of our field studies. Most employees consider this approach fair but, naturally, in cases where past performance is far below capacity, beating that standard will be extremely easy.

Since goal setting is sometimes simply a matter of judgment, another technique we have used is to allow the goal to be set jointly by supervisor and subordinate. The participative approach may be less scientific than time and motion study, but it does lead to ready acceptance by both employee and immediate superior in addition to promoting role clarity.

External constraints often affect goal setting, especially among managers. For example, the goal to produce an item at a certain price may be dictated by the actions of competitors, and deadlines may be imposed externally in line with contract agreements. Legal regulations, such as attaining a certain reduction in pollution levels by a ceratin date, may affect goal setting as well. In these cases, setting the goal is not so much the problem as is figuring out a method of reaching it.

Finally, organizational goals set by the board of directors or upper management will influence the goals set by employees at lower levels. This is the essence of the MbO process.

Another issue that needs to be considered when setting goals is whether they should be designed for individuals or for groups. Rensis Likert and a number of other human relations experts argue for group goal setting on grounds that it promotes cooperation and team spirit. But one could argue that individual goals better promote individual responsibility and make it easier to appraise individual performance. The degree of task interdependence involved would also be a factor to consider.

Obtaining Goal Commitment If goal setting is to work, then the manager must ensure that subordinates will accept and remain committed to the goals. Simple instruction backed by positive support and an absence of threats or intimidation were enough to ensure goal acceptance in most of our studies. Subordinates must perceive the goals as fair and reasonable and they must trust management, for if they perceive the goals as no more than a means of exploitation, they will be likely to reject the goals.

It may seem surprising that goal acceptance was achieved so readily in the field studies. Remember, however, that in all cases the employees were receiving wages or a salary (although these were not necessarily directly contingent on goal attainment). Pay in combination with the supervisor's benevolent authority and supportiveness were sufficient to bring about goal acceptance. Recent research indicates that whether goals are assigned or set participatively, supportiveness on the part of the immediate superior is critical. A supportive manager or supervisor does not use goals to threaten subordinates, but rather to clarify what is expected of them. His or her role is that of a helper and goal facilitator.

As noted earlier, the employee gets a feeling of pride and satisfaction from the experience of reaching a challenging but fair performance goal. Success in reaching a goal also tends to reinforce acceptance of future goals. Once goal setting is introduced, informal competition frequently arises among the employees. This further reinforces commitment and may lead employees to raise the goals spontaneously. A word of caution here, however: We do not recommend setting up formal competition, as this may lead employees to place individual goals ahead of company goals. The emphasis should be on accomplishing the task, getting the job done, not "beating" the other person.

When employees resist assigned goals, they generally do so for one of two reasons. First, they may think they are incapable of reaching the goal because they lack confidence, ability, knowledge, and the like. Second, they may not see any personal benefit—either in terms of personal pride or in terms of external rewards like money, promotion, recognition—in reaching assigned goals.

There are various methods of overcoming employee resistance to goals. One possibility is more training designed to raise the employee's level of skill and self-confidence. Allowing the subordinate to participate in setting the goal—deciding on the goal level—is another method. This was found most effective among uneducated and minority group employees, perhaps because it gave them a feeling of control over their fate. Offering monetary bonuses or other rewards (recognition, time off) for reaching goals may also help.

The last two methods may be especially useful where there is a history of labor-management conflict and where employees have become accustomed to a lower level of effort than currently considered acceptable. Group incentives may also encourage goal acceptance, especially where there is a group goal, or when considerable cooperation is required.

Providing Support Elements A third step to take when introducing goal setting is to ensure the availability of necessary support elements. That is, the employee must be given adequate resources—money, equipment, time, help—as well as the freedom to utilize them in attaining goals, and company policies must not work to block goal attainment.

Before turning an employee loose with these resources, however, it's wise to do a quick check on whether conditions are optimum for reaching the goal set. First, the supervisor must make sure that the employee has sufficient ability and knowledge to

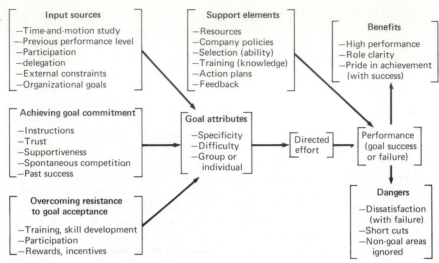

Figure 28-3 Goal-setting model.

be able to reach the goal. Motivation without knowledge is useless. This, of course, puts a premium on proper selection and training and requires that the supervisor know the capabilities of subordinates when goals are assigned. Asking an employee to formulate an action plan for reaching the goal, as in MbO, is very useful, as it will indicate any knowledge deficiencies.

Second, the supervisor must ensure that the employee is provided with precise feedback so that he will know to what degree he's reaching or falling short of his goal and can thereupon adjust his level of effort or strategy accordingly. Recent research indicates that, while feedback is not a sufficient condition for improved performance, it is a necessary condition. A useful way to present periodic feedback is through the use of charts or graphs that plot performance over time.

Elements involved in taking the three steps described are shown in Figure 28-3, which illustrates in outline form our model of goal setting.

CONCLUSION

We believe that goal setting is a simple, straightforward, and highly effective technique for motivating employee performance. It is a basic technique, a method on which most other methods depend for their motivational effectiveness. The currently popular technique of behavior modification, for example, is mainly goal setting plus feedback, dressed up in academic terminology.

However, goal setting is no panacea. It will not compensate for underpayment of employees or for poor management. Used incorrectly, goal setting may cause rather than solve problems, If, for example, the goals set are unfair, arbitrary, or unreachable, dissatisfaction and poor performance may result. If difficult goals are set without proper quality controls, quantity may be achieved at the expense of quality. If pressure for immediate results is exerted without regard to how they are attained, short-term improvement may occur at the expense of long-run profits. That is, such pressure often triggers the use of expedient and ultimately costly methods—such as dishonesty, high-pressure tactics, postponing of maintenance expenses, and so on—to attain immediate results. Furthermore, performance goals are more easily set in some areas than in others. It's all too easy, for example, to concentrate on setting readily measured production goals and ignore employee development goals. Like any other management tool, goal setting works only when combined with good managerial judgment.

Reading 29

Merit Pay: An Obsolete Policy?
Edward E. Lawler III

The idea of merit pay, or pay for performance, is so widely accepted that almost every organization says that it has a merit pay system. Even the United States government calls its system a merit pay system, and recently legislation (the Civil Service Reform Act) was passed that calls for the system to be more dependent on merit. The major reason for the popularity of merit pay is the belief that it can motivate job performance and increase organizational effectiveness. The research evidence clearly supports this view. It shows that pay can be a motivator of effective performance when it has two fundamental properties. First, it has to be important to people; second, it has to be tied to their performance in ways that are visible, creditable, and perceived by them to be direct (see Lawler, 1971). For most people, pay is important, so typically this is not a problem in using pay as a motivator. The critical issue is whether a perceived relationship exists between pay and performance.

Despite the existence of widespread support for the policy of merit pay, there is considerable evidence that in most organizations merit pay systems fail to create a perceived relationship between pay and performance. As a result of this failure, they also fail to produce the positive effects which are expected of them. In addition, there are some reasons to believe that in the future, it is going to be harder to have effective merit pay programs. But before we consider what the future holds, a brief review of the reasons why merit pay systems often do not produce the perception that pay and performance are related will serve to highlight the problems in using pay as motivator of performance.

PROBLEMS WITH MERIT PAY SYSTEMS

Poor Performance Measures

Fundamental to any effective merit pay system are objective, comprehensive measures of performance. Without these, it is impossible to relate pay to performance. There is a great deal of evidence that in most organizations, performance appraisal is not

Article prepared especially for this book.

done well, and that as a result, no good measures of individual performance exist (see, e.g., Meyer, Reading 26, and Kerr, Reading 27). Sometimes good measures of plant or group performance exist, but often even these are not adequate, because they do not measure all aspects of performance. In the absence of good objective measures of performance, most organizations rely on the judgments of managers. These judgments are often seen by subordinates as invalid, unfair, and discriminatory. Because the performance measures are not trusted when pay is based on them, little is done to create the perception that pay is based on performance (Meyer et al., 1965; Lawler, 1981). Indeed, in the eyes of many employees, merit pay is a fiction, a myth that managers try to perpetuate.

Poor Communication

The salaries of many individuals in organizations have traditionally been kept secret. In addition, some organizations keep many of their pay practices secret. For example, it is common for organizations to keep secret such things as how much was given out in salary increases or bonuses and what the highest and lowest raises were. Thus, the typical employee is often in the position of being asked to accept as an article of faith that pay and performance are related. Given secrecy, it is simply impossible to determine whether they are.

In situations of high trust, employees may accept the organization's statement that merit pay exists. However, trust depends on the open exchange of information, and thus with secrecy it is not surprising that many individuals are mistrustful. In a significant number of organizations, the communication situation is worsened because the organizations do not expend the time or energy needed to explain the system. They also communicate in ways that lead people to question the creditability of the system. For example, organizations often state that all pay increases are based on merit, even though virtually everyone gets an increase because of inflation and changes in the labor market. Given this, it is hardly surprising that individuals often question how much merit had to do with their "merit increase."

Poor Delivery Systems

The actual policies and procedures which make up a merit pay system often lead to actions which do little to actually relate pay to performance. In addition, the policies and procedures often are so complex that they do more to mystify and obfuscate than to clarify the relationship between pay and performance. The typical merit salary increase is particularly poor at actually relating pay and performance, because it allows only small changes in total pay to occur in one year. It further compounds the problem by making past "merit payments" part of the individual's base salary. This means that an individual can be a poor performer for several years, after having been a good performer, and still be highly paid. Bonus plans typically are better at relating pay to performance, but they are sometimes flawed by policies which fund them at such low levels as to be insignificant and by procedures which lead everyone to get the same bonus.

Poor Managerial Behavior

Managers do a number of things that negatively affect the perceived connection between pay and performance. Perhaps the most serious is the failure to recommend widely different pay increases or bonuses for their subordinates when large performance differences exist. Some managers are unwilling to recommend very large and very small pay actions, even when they are warranted. One reason for this seems to be the unpleasant task it leads to of explaining why someone got a low raise or bonus.

The difficulty of explaining low raises or bonuses often leads to a second very destructive behavior on the part of managers: disowning the pay decision. Despite the fact that they may have made a recommendation for a small raise and believe it is appropriately given, supervisors sometime deny or discount their role in determining their subordinates' pay. They may, for example, say that they fought hard for the subordinate to get a "good" raise but lost out. This clearly communicates to the subordinate that pay increases are beyond their control and thus not based on performance.

Conclusion

The existence in most corporations of one of the common problems which plague the administration of merit pay programs is usually enough to destroy the belief that pay is related to performance in the eyes of most employees. In reality the merit pay systems of most organizations typically suffer from all or most of these problems. As a result, the policy of merit pay at best fails to achieve its intended objectives and at worst becomes an embarrassment which undermines management's credibility.

FORCES ACTING FOR AND AGAINST MERIT PAY

Given the rather questionable history of merit pay, is there any reason to believe that things can or will get better? Putting aside for the moment the issue of whether they can get better, let us first look at the forces and trends that are operating in the environment which threaten merit pay and those which favor it.

The list of trends and forces acting against paying for performance is long. Taken together, they make a rather impressive and depressing list for those who believe that pay and performance should be related. Let me briefly review them:

1 Inflation More and more organizations seem to be falling into the practice of simply giving across-the-board increases in order to keep everybody "whole" in periods of high inflation. This, of course, serves to keep people from losing real income, but it fails to relate pay and performance. The problem can be compounded by government wage-control programs. With the limited amount of money available because of controls, many organizations seem to feel obliged to give it out equally— because there is such a limited budget, and inflation is affecting everyone so negatively.

2 Organization Size In large organizations, it is often particularly difficult to tie pay to performance. Size can mean that many jobs are created in organizations that do not have a direct interface with the external environment, and therefore do not have clear performance goals and measures. Needless to say, as performance becomes more difficult to measure, so does tying pay to it.

3 Production and Service Organizations There is a clear tendency for more and more jobs to fall into the service sector and into organizations with a process technology (e.g., chemicals, oil, food). This represents a serious problem for tying pay to performance because, usually, it is more difficult to measure performance in service and process production organizations. Just as was true with the impact of organization size, as performance becomes more difficult to measure, it is less likely to be done, and pay is less likely to be related to it.

4 New Forms of Organizations During the last decade, we have seen as increasing growth of new organizational forms. Probably, the leading one is the matrix structure. There are a number of advantages to matrix structures, but one of them is not in the area of tying pay to performance. The matrix structure tends to make it more difficult to measure individual performance and, as a result, to tie pay to it. The problem with measuring performance in matrix structures is one of clarifying who is to do it and what criteria are to be used.

5 Benefits Growth The strong push for benefits by unions has had, and promises to continue to have, a negative impact on the cash available for merit pay. Most organizations have a tendency to pass on whatever benefits they give to their unionized employees. As a result, compensation dollars which could be spent on merit pay end up getting spent on fringe benefits, many of which some people do not even want. The impact of this, of course, is to reduce further the tie between pay and performance, because the cash simply is not available to distinguish between the better and worse performers. Interestingly enough, this problem occurs even in nonunionized companies. The tendency there is to give everybody union-type benefits in order to prevent union organizing drives from succeeding.

6 Due Process/Employee Rights Consciousness There is clear evidence that employee expectations concerning due process and public accountability in decision making are increasing. Further, there is evidence that individuals, when they feel unfairly treated and denied due process in the area of salary decisions, are willing to go to court. One answer to this is to move toward open decisions, public accountability, and appeal processes, but the more this occurs, the more some managers seem to back off from making tough decisions that will reward performance. Another way of saying this is that the more managers are held accountable for their pay decisions, the more they tend to fall into the homogeneous treatment of individuals in order to avoid the discomfort of defending differential treatment. In the past, of course, this discomfort might only have been interpersonal discomfort in confronting an unhappy subordinate. Today, it may involve court appearances, financial losses for the organization, and considerable loss of face for the manager. The result is that more and more managers seem to be thinking two or three times before they withhold a pay increase.

7 Performance Appraisal The more we study performance appraisal, the more we seem to be able to identify all the problems and difficulties it entails. Unfortunately, we do not seem to be able to improve the state of the art proportionately. The result is that many people who work with performance appraisal systems are rather depressed about the ability of performance appraisals to result in valid measures of performance. Given this, it is difficult to argue strongly for using subjective appraisals of performance as a basis for establishing a pay-performance link. This, of course, is not a problem where objective measures are available, but in many situations, objective measures of performance simply are not available.

8 Mistrust of Large Organizations Recent survey data have shown that more and more people mistrust managers and mistrust the reward systems in the society. Stated another way, they are less likely to feel that good performance will lead to rewards and that the managers of organizations are doing a good job and can be trusted. Given this, it is likely to be more difficult in the future to convince people that in their particular work situation, pay and performance are related. They may have to see much more dramatic evidence than in the past, when the prevailing belief was that in the American Society, hard work paid off.

Overall, the future of merit pay looks pretty bleak—indeed, worse than in the past. At this point, you might expect a conclusion that we should forget about the whole idea of merit pay and concentrate on keeping pay rates equitable in order to attract and retain the best employees. In some situations this may be the best approach, but the situation for merit pay is not all negative—there are some positive trends that need to be mentioned.

1 Need for Performance Motivation More than ever, organizations need the performance motivation that can be generated when pay is successfully tied to performance. Many organizations face tough international competition, and they have to deal with a workforce that is new and different in a number of important ways (e.g., values, education, demographics). Clearly, paying for performance cannot solve all the motivation problems associated with the new workforce and strong international competition. However, it can be an important part of a total management system which is designed to create a highly motivating work environment, and the realization of this fact makes continuing efforts to develop effective merit pay systems both likely and important.

2 Inflation Inflation does not have to be a negative force as far as tying pay to performance is concerned. It can be a strong, positive force because it generates a larger pool of money for pay increases. Because a larger pool is present, the possibility exists of substantially differentiating people in the amount of increase that they get. For organizations that have not paid for performance in the past, it can represent a unique opportunity to get total compensation levels more in line with performance. In some respects, it is harder to make these differentiations when the failure to get an increase means a loss in real income for the individual, but for an organization that is strongly committed to paying for performance, inflation can provide an opportunity to tie pay more closely to performance.

3 Values There is a continuing belief on the part of the American workforce that pay *should be* related to performance. Despite the fact that there is a growing mistrust of the way rewards are distributed in society, there is no evidence that the historically strong belief that pay and performance should be related is going away. Indeed, in my surveys, employees at all levels in organizations still state that they think people should be paid for their performance and that pay for performance is a valid principle for salary administration (see, e.g., Lawler, 1981). Employees typically also see a large gap between the degree to which pay and performance are related and the degree to which they feel they should be.

4 Information Systems The growing sophistication of many management information systems can be a positive force in relating pay to performance. It can help make up for many of the inadequacies of today's performance appraisal systems and, as such, increase the validity of pay-for-performance systems. For this to happen, management information systems must be developed that will allow individual and/or group performance to be measured in a way that allows pay and performance to be related. What is needed is a set of comprehensive, objective measures that can account for the variances in performance that are under the control of the individual or group. Systems which measure things that cannot be controlled are not particularly helpful in this respect.

5 Decentralization and Diversification The tendency of many large organizations to decentralize and to diversify can provide a real basis for improving the relationship between pay and performance. Both decentralization and diversification have the effect of breaking up the organization into a number of mini-enterprises. This allows for better measurement of group, unit, and sometimes individual performance, and this, in turn, makes it more feasible to relate pay to performance, because it improves the organization's ability to measure performance in objective and valid ways.

6 Openness/Participation Some organizations have combined more openness and employee participation with better-pay-for-performance systems (Lawler, 1981). This is not a necessary or inevitable consequence of openness and participation, but it is a possible one when the openness and participative process are handled effectively. In some organizations, in fact, peer groups measure performance and determine rewards in an open discussion. Interestingly enough, in cases where this has been tried, it has often proved to be more effective in relating pay to performance than the typical one-on-one superior-subordinate pay-administration decision process. Peers have better information, and when they are motivated to do a good appraisal, they can often do a better appraisal and make better judgments than the supervisor can alone.

7 Importance of Pay Finally, it is worth noting that there is survey research evidence that pay is becoming more important to people in the American society (see, e.g., Quinn & Staines, 1979). This means that efforts which *do* successfully tie pay to performance are likely to pay off in the area of motivation, since the more important pay becomes, the more motivational potential it has. There is no convincing evidence as to why pay is becoming more important, but it is not hard to guess. With inflation eroding incomes, people are becoming more dissatisfied with their pay, and there is considerable evidence that when people become more dissatisfied with their pay, it becomes more important to them (Lawler, 1971).

MERIT PAY IN THE FUTURE

What should organizations do in the future with respect to merit pay? One clear implication of the discussion so far is that they should not automatically say that they have a merit pay policy. It seems clear that a number of organizations have "bought" the concept of merit pay without being aware of what is needed to make a merit system work. Full exploration of whether a merit system fits should lead a number of organizations to conclude that it does not fit all or part of their operations. For them, it is obsolete and should be abandoned, a step which could have some very positive results. At the very least, it should increase the credibility of management. It may also serve to eliminate unneeded superior-subordinate conflicts and to save administrative time. For those organizations that decide to have merit pay, the following points warrant serious consideration.

1 The possibility of using a bonus system or systems should be examined. As delivery systems, they have a number of advantages, and there is increasing evidence that bonus plans of a number of different types can be effective. There has been a recent increase in the use of bonus systems at the top-management level and at the plant level, but they still seem to be underutilized. Particularly underutilized are group- and plant-level gain-sharing systems like the Scanlon plan, the Rucker

plan, and the Lincoln Electric plan. All too often, organizations have tried piece-rate pay plans, have found them to be unacceptable for a number of reasons, and have abandoned the idea of tying pay to performance through bonus-type plans. Group plans and plant-level plans are entirely different from individual piece-rate plans, and as a result they can work when piece-rate plans cannot. Indeed, going back to the problems in tying pay to performance that were mentioned earlier, many of them are not problems in group- and plant-level plans—primarily because larger aggregations of people (e.g., a total) often allow for better performance measurements. Recognizing this, a number of large companies have installed multiple gain-sharing plans (e.g., General Electric, Midland Ross, Dana, and TRW).

2 Attention needs to be paid to the process involved in merit pay issues. A good delivery system is important in any merit pay plan. but so are good communication policies and proper decision processes. Without these, the best merit pay system will fail, because employees will not see the relationship between pay and performance. This point is particularly pertinent in light of the changing nature of the workforce. It is quite possible that in the future, due process and open communication will be necessary if merit pay systems are to operate at all. The evidence on participation in pay decisions suggests that the use of participation can make decisions more creditable (see Lawler, 1981). In any case, considerable attention needs to be devoted to a description of the system and to correctly identifying what is and is not a merit salary action.

3 Performance appraisals must be taken seriously. In order for appraisals to be effective, people need to be trained, systems developed, and time spent by both the appraiser and the person appraised. Having an untrained appraiser spend a few minutes reviewing the performance of a subordinate and then making a pay recommendation is simply not acceptable. Performance measures need to be mutually agreed to, results jointly reviewed, and pay action discussed. If these practices are not acceptable or possible, then merit pay should not be based on performance appraisal results.

4 Attention needs to be focused on key organizational factors which affect the pay system. Often a poor merit pay system is a symptom of other problems and cannot be improved until they are solved. It is impossible to have an effective merit pay system, for example, if jobs are poorly designed and an organization is poorly designed. With these conditions it is simply too difficult to measure performance and assign responsibility for it. Similarly, without a good information system in place, it is often impossible to validly measure individual performance.

SUMMARY AND CONCLUSION

To summarize, it is going to be more difficult to administer merit pay systems in the future. Organizations are becoming more complex, society is more complex, and the workforce is more demanding. But it is also more important than ever that appropriate pay should be tied to performance. Finally, there is reason to believe that calling a pay plan a "merit pay plan" and then not delivering will become less and less acceptable. Taken together, this

suggests that some organizations need to partially or completely abandon their merit pay plans, while others need to invest heavily in making theirs more effective.

REFERENCES

Lawler, E. E. *Pay and organizational effectiveness.* New York: McGraw-Hill, 1971.

————. *Pay and organization development.* Reading, Mass.: Addison-Wesley, 1981.

Meyer, H. H., Kay, E., & French, J. R. R. Split roles in performance appraisal. *Harvard Business Review,* 1965, **43**(1), 123–129.

Quinn, R. P., & Staines, G. L. *The 1977 quality of employment survey.* Ann Arbor, Mich.: Institute for Social Research, 1979.

Reading 30

Behavior Modification on the Bottom Line

W. Clay Hamner
Ellen P. Hamner

It may be easy to say *what* a manager does. Telling *how* he influences the behavior of the employee in the direction of task accomplishment is far more difficult to comprehend and describe. The purpose of this article is to describe and spell out the determinants of employee productivity or performance from a reinforcement theory point of view, and to show how managing the contingencies of positive reinforcement in organizational settings leads to successful management. We hope these descriptions will enable the manager to understand how his or her behavior affects the behavior of subordinates and to see that, in many cases, a worker's failure to perform a task properly is a direct outcome of the manager's own behavior. The employee has failed to perform because the manager has failed to motivate.

MANAGING THE CONTINGENCIES OF REINFORCEMENT

The interrelationship among three components—work environment, task performance, and consequences of reinforcements—are known as the contingencies of reinforcement. The reward that is

contingent upon good performance in a given work situation (environment) acts as a motivator for future performance. The manager controls the *work environment* (Where am I going? What are the goals? Is the leader supportive? Is this a pleasant place to work?), the *task assignment* (How will I get there? What behavior is desired? What is considered appropriate performance?), and the *consequences* of job performance (How will I know when I've reached the desired goal? Is the feedback relevant and timely? Is my pay based upon my performance?). By shaping these three components of behavior so that all are positive, the manager can go a long way toward creating a work climate that supports high productivity.

ARRANGING THE CONTINGENCIES OF REINFORCEMENT

Someone who expects to influence behavior must be able to manipulate the consequences of behavior. Whether managers realize it or not, they constantly shape the behavior of their subordinates by the way they utilize the rewards at their disposal. Employers intuitively use rewards all the time—but their efforts often produce limited results because the methods are used improperly, inconsistently, or inefficiently. In many instances employees are given rewards that are not conditional or contingent on the behavior the manager wishes to promote. Even when they are, long delays often intervene between the occurrence of the desired behavior and its intended consequences. Special privileges, activities, and rewards are often furnished according to length of service rather than performance requirements. In many cases, positive reinforcers are inadvertently made contingent upon the wrong kind of behavior. In short, intuition provides a poor guide to motivation.

A primary reason managers fail to "motivate" workers to perform in the desired manner is their failure to understand the power of the contingencies of reinforcement over the employee. The laws or principles for arranging the contingencies to condition behavior are not hard to understand; if properly applied, they constitute powerful managerial tools that can be used for increasing supervisory effectiveness.

Conditioning is the process by which behavior is modified through manipulation of the contingencies of behavior. To understand how this works, we will first look at various kinds of arrangements of the contingencies: *positive reinforcement* conditioning, *escape* conditioning, *extinction* conditioning, and *punishment* conditioning. The differences among these kinds of contingencies depend on the consequences that result from the behavioral act. Positive reinforcement and avoidance learning are methods of strengthening desired behavior, while extinction and punishment are methods of weakening undesired behavior.

Positive Reinforcement According to B. F. Skinner, a positive reinforcer or reward is a stimulus that, when added to a situation, strengthens the probability of the response in that situation. Behavior that appears to lead to a positive consequence tends to be repeated, while behavior that appears to lead to a negative consequence tends not be repeated.

Once it has been determined that a specific consequence has reward value to a work group, we can use it to increase that group's performance. Thus the first step in the successful application of reinforce-

ment procedures is to select reinforcers that are sufficiently powerful and durable to establish and strengthen desired behavior. These could include such things as an interesting work assignment, the chance to use one's mind, seeing the results of one's work, good pay, recognition for a job well done, promotion, freedom to decide how to do a job, and so on.

The second step is to design the contingencies in such a way that the reinforcing events are made contingent on the desired level of performance. This is the rule of reinforcement most often violated. Rewards *must* result from performance—and the better an employee's performance is, the greater his or her rewards should be.

Unless a manager is willing to discriminate among employees on the basis of their performance levels, the effectiveness of his or her power over the employee is nil. For example, Edward E. Lawler III, a leading researcher on pay and performance, has noted that one of the major reasons managers are unhappy with their salary system is that they do not perceive the relationship between how hard they work (productivity) and how much they earn. In a survey of 600 managers, Lawler found virtually no relationship between their pay and their rated level of performance.

The third step is to design the contingencies in such a way that a reliable procedure for eliciting or inducing the desired response patterns is established; when desired responses rarely occur, there are few opportunities to influence behavior through contingency management. Training programs, goal-setting programs and similar efforts should be undertaken to let workers know what is expected of them. If the criterion for reinforcement is unclear, unspecified or set too high, most—if not all—of the worker's responses go unrewarded; eventually his or her efforts will be extinguished.

Escape Conditioning The second kind of contingency arrangement available to the manager is called escape or avoidance conditioning. Just as with positive reinforcement, this is a method of strengthening desired behavior. A contingency arrangement in which an individual's performance can terminate a noxious environment is called escape learning. When behavior can prevent the onset of a noxious stimulus, the procedure is called avoidance learning.

An employee is given an unpleasant task assignment, for example, with the promise that when he completes it, he can move on (escape) to a more pleasant job. Or a manager is such an unpleasant person to be around that the employees work when he is present in order to "avoid" him.

Let's note the distinction between strengthening behavior through positive reinforcement techniques and doing so through avoidance learning techniques. In one case, the individual works hard to gain the consequences from the environment (provided by the manager in most cases) that result from good work, and in the second case, the individual works hard to avoid the negative aspects of the environment itself (again, the manager is the source). In both cases the same behavior is strengthened over the short run. In escape learning, however, the manager is more process-oriented; he or she must be present in order to elicit the desired level of performance. Under positive reinforcement, however, the manager is outcome-oriented and does not have to be physically present at all times in order to maintain the desired level of performance.

Extinction   When positive reinforcement for a learned or previously conditioned response is withheld, individuals will still continue to exhibit that behavior for an extended period of time. With repeated nonreinforcement, however, the behavior decreases and eventually disappears. This decline in response rate as a result of nonrewarded repetition of a task is defined as *extinction*.

This method, when combined with a positive reinforcement method, is the procedure of behavior modification recommended by Skinner. It leads to the fewest negative side effects. Using the two methods together allows employees to get the rewards they desire and allows the organization to eliminate the undesired behavior.

Punishment   Punishment is the most controversial method of behavior modification. Punishment is defined as presenting an aversive or noxious consequence contingent upon a response, or removing a positive consequence contingent upon a response. The Law of Effect operates here, too: As rewards strengthen behavior, punishment weakens it. Notice carefully the difference between withholding rewards in the punishment process and withholding rewards in the extinction process. In the extinction

process, we withhold rewards for behavior that has previously been rewarded because the behavior was previously desired. In punishment, we withhold a reward because the behavior is undesired, has never been associated with the reward before, and is plainly an undesirable consequence.

RULES FOR USING OPERANT CONDITIONING TECHNIQUES

Rule 1. Don't Give the Same Level of Reward to All   Differentiate rewards based on performance in relation to defined objectives or standards. We know that people compare their performance with the performance of their peers to determine how well they are doing and that they compare their rewards with peer rewards to determine how to evaluate theirs. Some managers may think that the fairest compensation system is one in which everyone in the same job classification gets the same pay, but employees want differentiation as evidence of how important their services are to the organization. Managers who reward all people at the same level are simply encouraging, at most, only average performance. Behavior leading to high performance is being extinguished (ignored), while average and poor performance are being strengthened by means of positive reinforcement.

Rule 2. Failure to Respond to Behavior Has Reinforcing Consequences   Managers who find the job of differentiating between workers so unpleasant or so difficult that they fail to respond to their behavior must recognize that failure to respond is itself a form of response that, in turn, modifies behavior. Superiors are bound to shape the behavior of their subordinates by the way in which they utilize the rewards at their disposal. Therefore, managers must be careful that they examine the consequences on performance of their nonactions as well as their actions.

Rule 3. Tell a Person What Behavior Gets Reinforced   By making clear to a worker the contingencies of reinforcement, a manager may actually be increasing his individual freedom. The employee who has a standard against which to measure his job will have a built-in feedback system that allows him or her to make judgments about his or her own level of performance. The awarding of reinforcements in an organization where workers' goals are specified will be associated with worker performance, not supervisory bias. The assumption is, of course, that the supervisor rates the employee accurately and then reinforces the employee according to his ratings. If the supervisor fails to rate accurately or administer rewards based on performance, then the worker will be forced to search for the "true" contingencies—that is, what behavior he or she should display in order to get rewarded (ingratiation? loyalty? positive attitude?).

Rule 4. Tell a Person What He or She Is Doing Wrong As a general rule, very few people find failure rewarding. One assumption of behavior conditioning therefore is that a worker wants to be rewarded for positive accomplishments. A supervisor should never use extinction or punishment as the sole method for modifying behavior—but if one of these is used judiciously in conjunction with positive reinforcement techniques, such combined procedures can hasten the change process. If the supervisor fails to specify why a reward is being withheld, the employee may associate the withholding of the reward with past desired behavior instead of the behavior that the supervisor is trying to extinguish. Thus the supervisor extinguishes good performance while having no effect on the undesired behavior.

Rule 5. Don't Punish in Front of Others The reason for this rule is quite simple. The punishment (for example, a reprimand) should be enough to extinguish the undesired behavior. By administering the punishment in front of the work group, the worker is doubly punished; he also "loses face." This additional punishment may lead to negative side-effects in three ways. First, the worker whose self-image is damaged may feel that he must retaliate in order to protect himself. Therefore, the supervisor has actually increased undesired responses. Second, the work group may associate the punishment with another behavior of the worker and, through "avoidance learning" techniques, may modify their own behavior in ways not intended by the supervisor. Third, the work group is also being punished—in the sense that observing a member of their team being reprimanded is unpleasant to most people. This may result in lowered performance of the total work group.

Rule 6. Make the Consequences Equal to the Behavior In other words, don't cheat the worker out of his just rewards. If he is a good worker, tell him. Many supervisors find it very difficult to praise an employee. Others find it very difficult to counsel an employee about what he is doing wrong. When a manager fails to use these reinforcement tools, he is actually reducing his effectiveness. Overrewarding a worker may make him feel guilty and certainly reinforces his current performance level. If the performance level is lower than that of others who get the same reward, he has no reason to increase his output. When a worker is underrewarded, he becomes angry with the system. His behavior is being extinguished and the company may be forcing the good employee (underrewarded) to seek employment elsewhere while encouraging the poor employee (overrewarded) to stay on.

SETTING UP A POSITIVE REINFORCEMENT PROGRAM IN INDUSTRY

Many organizations are setting up formal motivational programs in an attempt to use the principles of positive reinforcement to increase employee productivity.

A positive reinforcement approach to management differs from traditional motivational theories in two basic ways. First, as noted above, a positive reinforcement program calls for the maximum use of reinforcement and the minimum use of punishment. Punishment tends to leave the individual feeling controlled and coerced. Second, a positive reinforcement program avoids psychological probing into the worker's attitudes as a possible cause of behavior. Instead, the work situation itself is analyzed, with the focus on the reward contingencies that cause a worker to act the way in which he does.

A positive reinforcement program, therefore, is results-oriented rather than process-oriented. Geary A. Rummler, president of Praxis Corporation, a management consultant firm, claims that the motivational theories of such behavioral scientists as Herzberg and Maslow, which stress worker's psychological needs, are impractical. "They can't be made operative. While they help classify a problem, a positive reinforcement program leads to solutions."

Stages in Program Development Positive reinforcement programs currently used in industry generally involve at least four stages. The *first stage,* according to Edward J. Feeney, formerly vice-president, systems, of Emery Air Freight Corporation, is to define the behavioral aspects of performance and do a performance audit. This step is potentially one of the most difficult, since some companies do not have a formal performance evaluation program, especially for nonmanagerial employees, and those that do have a program often rate the employee's behavior on nonjob related measures (such as friendliness, loyalty, cooperation, overall attitude, and so on). But once these behavioral aspects are defined, the task of convincing managers that improvement is needed and of persuading them to cooperate with such a program is simplified. Feeney asserts, "Most managers genuinely think that operations in their bailiwick are doing well; a performance audit that proves they're not comes as a real and unpleasant surprise."

The *second stage* in developing a working positive reinforcement program is to develop and set specific goals for each worker. Failure to specify concrete behavioral goals is a major reason many programs do not work. Goals should be expressed in such terms as "decreased employee turnover" or "schedules met" rather than only in terms of "better identification with the company" or "increased job satisfaction." The goals set, therefore, should be in the same terms as those defined in the performance audit, goals that specifically relate to the task at hand. Goals should be reasonable—that is, set somewhere between "where you are" (as spelled out in the performance audit) and some ideal.

While it is important for the manager to set goals, it is also important for the employee to accept them. An approach that tends to build in goal acceptance is to allow employees to work with management in setting work goals. According to John C. Emery, president of Emery Air Freight Corporation, the use of a participatory management technique to enlist the ideas of those performing the job not only results in their acceptance of goals, but also stimulates them to come up with goals.

The *third stage* in a positive reinforcement program is to allow the employee to keep a record of his or her own work. This process of self-feedback maintains a continuous schedule of reinforcement for the worker and helps him obtain intrinsic rein-

forcement from the task itself. Where employees can total their own results, they can see whether they are meeting their goals and whether they are improving over their previous performance level (as measured in the performance audit stage). In other words, the worker has two chances of being successful—either by beating his previous record or by beating both his previous record and his established goal. E. D. Grady, general manager—operator services for Michigan Bell, maintains that the manager should set up the work environment in such a way that people have a chance to succeed. One way to do this, he says, is to "shorten the success interval." Grady says, "If you're looking for success, keep shortening the interval of measurement so you can get a greater chance of success which you can latch on to for positive reinforcements." Instead of setting monthly or quarterly goals, for example, set weekly or daily goals.

The *fourth stage*—the most important step in a positive reinforcement program—is one that separates it from all other motivation plans. The supervisor looks at the self-feedback report of the employee and/or other indications of performance (sales records, for example) and then praises the positive aspects of the employee's performance (as determined by the performance audit and subsequent goal setting). This extrinsic reinforcement should strengthen the desired performance, while the withholding of praise for substandard performance should give the employee incentive to improve that performance level. Since the worker already knows the areas of his or her deficiencies, there is no reason for the supervisor to criticize the employee. In other words, negative feedback is self-induced, whereas positive feedback comes from both internal and external sources.

As noted previously, this approach to feedback follows the teachings of B. F. Skinner, who believes that use of positive reinforcement leads to a greater feeling of self-control, while the avoidance of negative reinforcement keeps the individual from feeling controlled or coerced. Skinner says, "You can get the same effect if the supervisor simply discovers things being done right and says something like 'Good, I see you're doing it the way that works best.'"

While the feedback initially used in step four of the positive reinforcement program is praise, it is important to note that other forms of reinforcement can have the same effect. M. W. Warren, the director of organization and management development at the Questor Corporation, says that the five "reinforcers" he finds most effective are (1) money (but only when it is a consequence of a specific performance and when the relation to the performance is known); (2) praise or recognition; (3) freedom to choose one's own activity; (4) opportunity to see oneself become better, more important, or more useful; and (5) power to influence both co-workers and management. Warren states, "By building these reinforcers into programs at various facilities, Questor is getting results." The need for using more than praise after the positive reinforcement program has proved effective is discussed by Skinner.

> It does not cost the company anything to use praise rather than blame, but if the company then makes a great deal more money that way, the worker may seem to be getting gypped. However, the welfare of the worker depends on the welfare of the company, and if the company is smart enough to distribute some of the fruits of positive reinforcement in the form of higher wages and better fringe benefits, everybody gains from the supervisor's use of positive reinforcements. (*Organizational Dynamics,* Winter, 1973, p. 35.)

EARLY RESULTS OF POSITIVE REINFORCEMENT PROGRAMS IN ORGANIZATIONS, 1969–1973

Companies that claimed to be implementing and using positive reinforcement programs such as the one described above include Emery Air Freight, Michigan Bell Telephone, Questor Corporation, Cole National Company in Cleveland, Ford Motor Company, American Can, Upjohn, United Air Lines, Warner-Lambert, Addressograph-Multigraph, Allis-Chalmers, Bethlehem Steel, Chase Manhattan Bank, IBM, IT&T, Procter and Gamble, PPG Industries, Standard Oil of Ohio, Westinghouse, and Wheeling-Pittsburgh Steel Corporation (see *Business Week,* December 18, 1971 and December 2, 1972). Because such programs are relatively new in industrial settings (most have begun since 1968), few statements of their relative effectiveness have been reported. In the Winter 1973 issue of *Organizational Dynamics* (p. 49), it was stated that "there's little objective evidence available, and what evidence there is abounds in caveats—the technique will work under the proper circumstances, the parameters of which are usually not easily apparent."

In the area of employee training, Northern Systems Company, General Electric Corporation, and Emery Air Freight claim that positive reinforcement has improved the speed and efficiency of their training program. In their programmed learning program, the Northern Systems Company structures the feedback system in such a way that the trainee receives positive feedback only when he demonstrates correct performance at the tool station. The absence of feedback is experienced by the trainee when he fails to perform correctly. Therefore, through positive reinforcements, he quickly perceives that correct behaviors obtain for him the satisfaction of his needs, and that incorrect behaviors do not. Emery has designed a similar program for sales trainees. *Business Week* reported the success of the program by saying:

> It is a carefully engineered, step-by-step program, with frequent feedback questions and answers to let the saleman know how he is doing. The course contrasts with movies and lectures in which, Feeney says, the salesman is unable to gauge what he has learned. The aim is to get the customer on each sales call to take some kind of action indicating that he will use Emery services. Significantly, in 1968, the first full year after the new course was launched, sales jumped from $62.4 million to $79.8 million, a gain of 27.8 percent compared with an 11.3 percent rise the year before.

Since 1969, Emery has instituted a positive reinforcement program for all of its employees and credits the program with direct savings of the company of over $3 million in the first three years and indirectly with pushing 1973 sales over the $160 million mark. While Emery Air Freight is and remains the biggest success story for a positive reinforcement program to date, other companies also claim improvements as a result of initiating similar programs. At Michigan Bell's Detroit office, 2,000 employees in 1973 participated in a positive reinforcement program. Michigan Bell credits the program with reducing absenteeism from 11 percent to 6.5 percent in one group, from 7.5 percent to 4.5 percent in another group, and from 3.3 percent to 2.6 percent for all employees. In addition, the program has resulted in the correct completion of reports on time 90 percent of the time as compared with 20 percent of the time before the program's implementation. The Wheeling-Pittsburgh Steel

Corporation credits its feedback program with saving $200,000 a month in scrap costs.

In an attempt to reduce the number of employees who constantly violated plant rules, General Motors implemented a plan in one plant that gave employees opportunities to improve or clear their records by going through varying periods of time without committing further shop violations. They credit this positive reinforcement plan with reducing the number of punitive actions for shop-rule infractions by two-thirds from 1969 to 1972 and the number of production-standard grievances by 70 percent during the same period.

While there was a great deal of interest in applying behavior modification in industrial settings after the success of Emery Air Freight and others who followed suit were made known in 1971, the critics of this approach to worker motivation predicted that it would be short-lived. Any success would owe more to a "Hawthorne Effect" (the positive consequences of paying special attention to employees) than to any real long-term increase in productivity and/or worker satisfaction. The critics pointed out— quite legitimately, we might add—that most of the claims were testimonial in nature and that the length of experience between 1969–1973 was too short to allow enough data to accumulate to determine the true successes of positive reinforcement in improving morale and productivity. With this in mind, we surveyed ten organizations, all of which currently use a behavior modification approach, to see if the "fad" created by Emery Air Freight had died or had persisted and extended its gains.

Specifically, we were interested in knowing (1) how many employees were covered; (2) the kinds of employees covered: (3) specific goals (stages 1 & 2); (4) frequency of self-feedback (stage 3); (5) the kinds of reinforcers used (stage 4); and (6) results of the program. A summary of companies surveyed and the information gained are shown in Figure 1.

CURRENT RESULTS OF POSITIVE REINFORCEMENT PROGRAMS IN ORGANIZATIONS

The ten organizations surveyed included Emery Air Freight, Michigan Bell—Operator Services, Michigan Bell—Maintenance Services, Connecticut General Life Insurance Company, General Electric, Standard Oil of Ohio, Weyerhaeuser, City of De-

troit, B. F. Goodrich Chemical Company, and ACDC Electronics. In our interviews with each of the managers, we tried to determine both the successes and the failures they attributed to the use of behavior modification or positive reinforcement techniques. We were also interested in whether the managers saw this as a fad or as a legitimate management technique for improving the productivity and quality of work life among employees.

Emery Air Freight   Figure 30-1 shows Emery Air Freight still using positive reinforcement as a motivational tool. John C. Emery commented: "Positive reinforcement, always linked to feedback systems, plays a central role in performance improvement at Emery Air Freight. *All* managers and supervisors are being trained via self-instructional, programmed instruction texts—one on reinforcement and one on feedback. No formal off-the-job training is needed. Once he has studied the texts, the supervisor is encouraged immediately to apply the learning to the performance area for which he is responsible."

Paul F. Hammond, Emery's manager of system performance and the person currently in charge of the positive reinforcement program, said that there are a considerable number of company areas in which quantifiable success has been attained over the last six or seven years. Apart from the well-publicized container savings illustration (results of which stood at $600,000 gross savings in 1970 and over $2,000,000 in 1975), several other recent success stories were noted by Emery and Hammond. They include:

• Standards for customer service on the telephone had been set up and service was running 60 to 70 percent of standard. A program very heavily involved with feedback and reinforcement was introduced a few years ago and increased performance to 90 percent of objectives within three months—a level that has been maintained ever since.
• Several offices have installed a program in which specified planned reinforcements are provided when targeted levels of shipment volume are requested by Emery customers. All offices have increased revenue substantially; one office doubled the number of export shipments handled, and another averages an additional $60,000 of revenue per month.
• A program of measuring dimensions of certain

Organization and person surveyed	Length of program	Number of employees covered/ total employees	Type of employees	Specific Goals	Frequency of feedback	Reinforcers used	Results
General Electric[1] Melvin Sorcher, Ph. D., formerly Director of Personnel Research Now Director of Management Development, Richardson-Merrell, Inc.	1973–1976	1000	Employees at all levels	(a) Meet EEO objectives (b) Decrease absenteeism & turnover (c) Improve training (d) Increase productivity	Immediate—uses modeling & role playing at training tools to teach interpersonal exchanges & behavior requirements	Social reinforcers (Praise, rewards, & constructive feedback)	(a) Cost savings can be directly attributed to the program (b) Productivity has increased (c) Worked extremely well in training minority groups and raising their self-esteem (d) Direct labor cost decreased
Standard Oil of Ohio T. E. Standings, Ph. D., Manager of Psychological Services	1974	28	Supervisors	Increase supervisor competence	Weekly over 5 weeks (25-hour) training	Feedback	(a) Improved supervisory ability to give feedback judiciously (b) Discontinued because of lack of overall success
Weyerhaeuser Company Gary P. Latham, Ph. D., Manager of Human Resource Research	1974–1976	500/40,000	Clerical, production (tree planters) & middle-level management & scientists	(a) To teach managers to minimize criticism & to maximize praise (b) To teach managers to make rewards contingent on specified performance levels & (c) To use optimal schedule to increase productivity	Immediate—daily & quarterly	(a) Pay (b) Praise & recognition	(a) Using money, obtained 33% increase in productivity with one group of workers, an 18% increase with a second group, and an 8% decrease in a third group (b) Currently experimenting with goal setting & praise and/or money at various levels in organization (c) With a lottery-type bonus, the cultural & religious values of workers must be taken into account

Figure 30-1 Results of positive reinforcement and similar behavior-modification programs in organizations in 1976.

Organization and person surveyed	Length of program	Number of employees covered/ total employees	Type of employees	Specific goals	Frequency of feedback	Reinforcers used	Results
Emery Air Freight John C. Emery, Jr., *President* Paul F. Hammond, *Manager—Systems Performance*	1969–1976	500/2800	Entire workforce	(a) Increase productivity (b) Improve quality of service	Immediate to monthly, depending on task	Previously only praise and recognition; others now being introduced	Cost savings can be directly attributed to the program
Michigan Bell— Operator Services E. D. Grady, *General Manager— Operator Services*	1972–1976	2000/5500	Employees at all levels in operator services	(a) Decrease turnover & absenteeism (b) Increase productivity (c) Improve union-management relations	(a) Lower level— weekly & daily (b) Higher level— monthly & quarterly	(a) Praise & recognition (b) Opportunity to see oneself become better	(a) Attendance performance has improved by 50% (b) Productivity and efficiency has continued to be above standard in areas where positive reinforcement (PR) is used
Michigan Bell— Maintenance Services Donald E. Burwell, *Division Superintendent, Maintenance & Services* Dr. W. Clay Hammer, *Consultant*	1974–1976	220/5500	Maintenance workers, mechanics, & first- & second-level supervisors	Improve (a) productivity (b) quality (c) safety (d) customer employee relations	Daily, weekly, and quarterly	(a) Self-feedback (b) Supervisory feedback	(a) Cost efficiency increase (b) Safety improved (c) Service improved (d) No change in absenteeism (e) Satisfaction with superior & co-workers improved (f) Satisfaction with pay decreased
Connecticut General Life Insurance Co. Donal D. Illig, *Director of Personnel Administration*	1941–1976	3000/13,500	Clerical employees & first-line supervisors	(a) Decrease absenteeism (b) Decrease lateness	Immediate	(a) Self-feedback (b) System-feedback (c) Earned time off	(a) Chronic absenteeism & lateness has been drastically reduced (b) Some division refuse to use PR because it is "outdated"

Figure 30-1 Continued

Organization and person surveyed	Length of program	Number of employees covered/ total employees	Type of employees	Specific Goals	Frequency of feedback	Reinforcers used	Results
City of Detroit Garbage Collectors[2]	1973-1975	1122/1930	Garbage collectors	(a) Reduction in paid man-hour per ton (b) Reduction on overtime (c) 90% of routes completed by standard (d) Effectiveness (quality)	Daily & quarterly based on formula negotiated by city & sanitation union	Bonus (profit sharing) & praise	(a) Citizen complaints declined significantly (b) City saved $1,654,000 first year after bonus paid (c) Worker bonus = $307,000 first year or $350 annually per man (d) Union somewhat dissatisfied with productivity measure and is pushing for more bonus to employee (e) 1975 results not yet available
B. F. Goodrich Chemical Co. Donald J. Barnicki, *Production Manager*	1972-1976	100/420	Manufacturing employees at all levels	(a) Better meeting of schedules (b) Increase productivity	Weekly	Praise & recognition; freedom to choose one's own activity	Production has increased over 300%
ACDC Electronics Division of Emerson Electronics Edward J. Feeney, *Consultant*	1974-1976	350/350	All levels	(a) 96% attendance (b) 90% engineering specifications met (c) Daily production objectives met 95% of time (d) Cost reduced by 10%	Daily & weekly feedback from foreman to company president	Positive feedback	(a) Profit up 25% over forecast (b) $550,000 cost reduction on $10 M sales (c) Return of 1900% on investment including consultant fees (d) Turnaround time on repairs went from 30 to 10 days (e) Attendance is now 98.2% (from 93.5%)

[1]Similar programs are now being implemented at Richardson-Merrell under the direction of Dr. Sorcher and at At&T under the direction of Douglas W. Bray, Ph.D., director of management selection and development, along with several other smaller organizations (see A. P. Goldstein, Ph.D. & Melvin Sorcher, Ph.D., *Changing Supervisor Behavior*, Pergamon Press, 1974).

[2]From *Improving Municipal Productivity: The Detroit Refuse Incentive Plan*, The National Commission on Productivity, April, 1974.

Figure 30-1 Continued

lightweight shipments to rate them by volume rather than weight uses reinforcement and feedback extensively. All measures have increased dramatically since its inception five years ago, not the least of which is an increase in revenue from $400,000 per year to well over $2,000,000 per year.

While this latest information indicates that positive reinforcement is more than a fad at Emery Air Freight, Emery pointed out that a major flaw in the program had to be overcome. He said, "Inasmuch as praise is the most readily available no-cost reinforcer, it tends to be the reinforcer used most frequently. However, the result has been to *dull* its effect as a reinforcer through its sheer repetition, even to risk making praise an *irritant* to the receiver." To counter this potential difficulty, Emery managers and supervisors have been taught and encouraged to expand their reinforcers beyond praise. Among the recommended reinforcers have been formal recognition such as a public letter or a letter home, being given a more enjoyable task after completing a less enjoyable one, invitations to business luncheons or meetings, delegating responsibility and decision making, and tying such requests as special time off or any other deviation from normal procedure to performance. Thus it seems that Skinner's prediction made in 1973 about the need for using more than praise after the reinforcement program has been around for a while has been vindicated at Emery Air Freight.

Michigan Bell—Operator Service The operator services division is still actively using positive reinforcement feedback as a motivational tool. E. D. Grady, general manager for Operator Services said, "We have found through experience that when standards and feedback are not provided, workers generally feel their performance is at about the 95 percent level. When the performance is then compared with clearly defined standards, it is usually found to meet only the 50 percentile in performance. It has been our experience, over the past ten years, that when standards are set and feedback provided in a positive manner, performance will reach very high levels—perhaps in the upper 90th percentile in a very short period of time. . . . We have also found that when positive reinforcement is discontinued, performance returns to levels that existed prior to the establishment of feedback."

Grady said that while he was not able at this point to put a specific dollar appraisal on the cost savings from using a positive reinforcement program, the savings were continuing to increase and the program was being expanded.

In one recent experiment, Michigan Bell found that when goal setting and positive reinforcement were used in a low-productivity inner-city operator group, service promptness (time to answer call) went from 94 to 99 percent of standard, average work time per call (time taken to give information) decreased from 60 units of work time to 43 units of work time, the percentage of work time completed within ideal limits went from 50 to 93 percent of ideal time (standard was 80 percent of ideal), and the percentage of time operators made proper use of references went from 80 to 94 percent. This led to an overall productivity index score for these operators that was significantly higher than that found in the control group where positive reinforcement was not being used, even though the control group of operators had previously (six months earlier) been one of the highest producing units.

Michigan Bell—Maintenance Services Donald E. Burwell, Division Superintendent of Maintenance and Services at Michigan Bell established a goal-setting and positive reinforcement program in early 1974. He said, "After assignment to my present area of responsibility in January, I found that my new department of 220 employees (maintenance, mechanics, and janitorial services), including managers, possessed generally good morale. However, I soon became aware that 1973 performances were generally lower than the 1973 objectives. In some cases objectives were either ambiguous or nonexistent."

With the help of a consultant, Burwell overcame the problem by establishing a four-step positive reinforcement program similar to the one described earlier in this article. As a result, the 1974 year-end results showed significant improvements over the 1973 base-year averages in all areas, including safety (from 75.6 to 89.0), service (from 76.4 to 83.0), cost performance/hour (from 27.9 to 21.2, indexed), attendance (from 4.7 to 4.0) and worker satisfaction and cooperation (3.01 to 3.51 on a scale of 5), and worker satisfaction with the supervisors (2.88 to 3.70, also on a scale of five). 1975 figures reflect continuing success.

While Burwell is extremely pleased with the results of this program to date, he adds a word of caution to other managers thinking of implementing such a program: "I would advise against accepting any one method, including positive reinforcement, as a panacea for all the negative performance trends that confront managers. On the other hand, positive reinforcement has aided substantially in performance improvement for marketing, production, and service operators. Nevertheless, the manager needs to know when the positive effects of the reinforcement program have begun to plateau and what steps he should consider taking to maintain his positive performance trends."

Connecticut General Life Insurance Company
The Director of Personnel Administration at Connecticut General Life Insurance Company, Donald D. Illig, stated that Connecticut General has been using positive reinforcement in the form of an attendance bonus system for 25 years with over 3,200 clerical employees. Employees receive one extra day off for each ten weeks of perfect attendance. The results have been outstanding. Chronic absenteeism and lateness have been drastically reduced, and the employees are very happy with the system. Illig noted, however, that, "Our property and casualty company, with less than half the number of clerical employees countrywide, has not had an attendance-bonus system . . . and wants no part of it. At the crux of the problem is an anti-Skinnerian feeling, which looks at positive reinforcement—and thus an attendance-bonus system—as being overly manipulative and old-fashioned in light of current theories of motivation."

General Electric A unique program of behavior modification has been introduced quite successfully at General Electric as well as several other organizations by Melvin Sorcher, formerly director of personnel research at G.E. The behavior modification program used at G.E. involves using positive reinforcement and feedback in training employees. While the first program centered primarily on teaching male supervisors how to interact and communicate with minority and female employees and on teaching minority and female employees how to become successful by improving their self-images, subsequent programs focused on the relationship between supervisors and employees in general. By using a reinforcement technique known as behavior modeling, Sorcher goes beyond the traditional positive reinforcement ("PR") program. The employee is shown a videotape of a model (someone with his own characteristics—that is, male or female, black or white, subordinate or superior) who is performing in a correct or desired manner. Then, through the process of role playing, the employee is encouraged to act in the successful or desired manner shown on the film (that is, he is asked to model the behavior). Positive reinforcement is given when the goal of successful display of this behavior is made in the role-playing session.

Sorcher notes that this method has been successfully used with over 1,000 G.E. supervisors. As a result, productivity has increased, the self-esteem of hard-core employees has increased, and EEO objectives are being met. He says, "The positive results have been the gratifying changes or improvements that have occurred, especially improvements that increase over time as opposed to the usual erosion of effort after most training programs have passed their peak. . . . On the negative side, some people and organizations are calling their training 'behavior modeling' when it does not fit the criteria originally defined for such a program. For example, some programs not only neglect self-esteem as a component, but show little evidence of how to shape new behaviors. . . . Regarding the more general area of behavior modification and positive reinforcement, there is still a need for better research. There's not a lot taking place at present, which is unfortunate because on the surface these processes seem to have a lot of validity."

Standard Oil of Ohio T. E. Standings, manager of psychological services at SOHIO, tried a training program similar to the one used by Sorcher at General Electric. After 28 supervisors had completed five weeks of training, Standings disbanded the program even though there were some short-term successes. He said, "My feelings at this point are that reinforcement cannot be taught at a conceptual level in a brief period of time. (Of course, the same comments can no doubt be made about Theory Y, MBO, and TA.) I see two alternatives: (1) Identify common problem situations, structure an appropriate reinforcement response for the supervisor, and teach the response through the behavioral model, or (2) alter reinforcement contingencies affecting defined behaviors through direct alternatives in procedural and/or informational systems without going through the supervisor directly."

Weyerhaeuser Company Whereas Emery Air Freight has the longest history with applied reinforcement theory, Weyerhaeuser probably has the most experience with controlled experiments using goal setting and PR techniques. The Human Resource Research Center at Weyerhaeuser, under the direction of G. P. Latham, is actively seeking ways to improve the productivity of all levels of employees using the goal-setting, PR feedback technique.

According to Dr. Latham, "The purpose of our positive reinforcement program is threefold: (1) To teach managers to embrace the philosophy that 'the glass is half-full rather than half-empty.' In other words, our objective is to teach managers to minimize criticism (which is often self-defeating since it can fixate the employee's attention on ineffective job behavior and thus reinforce it) and to maximize praise and hence fixate both their and the employee's attention on effective job behavior. (2) To teach managers that praise by itself may increase job satisfaction, but that it will have little or no effect on productivity unless it is made contingent upon specified job behaviors. Telling an employee that he is doing a good job in no way conveys to him what he is doing correctly. Such blanket praise can inadvertently reinforce the very things that the employee is doing in a mediocre way. (3) To teach managers to determine the optimum schedule for administrating a reinforcer—be it praise, a smile, or money in the employee's pocket."

Weyerhaeuser has found that by using money as a reinforcer (that is, as a bonus over and above the worker's hourly rate), they obtained a 33 percent increase in productivity with one group of workers, an 18 percent increase in productivity with a second group of workers, and an 8 percent decrease in productivity with a third group of workers. Latham says, "These findings point out the need to measure and document the effectiveness of any human resource program. The results obtained in one industrial setting cannot necessarily be expected in another setting."

Latham notes that because of its current success with PR, Weyerhaeuser is currently applying reinforcement principles with tree planters in the rural South as well as with engineers and scientists at their corporate headquarters. In the latter case, they are comparing different forms of goal setting (assigned, participative, and a generalized goal of "do your best") with three different forms of reinforcement (praise or private recognition from a supervisor, public recognition in terms of a citation for excellence, and a monetary reward). Latham adds, "The purpose of the program is to motivate scientists to attain excellence. Excellence is defined in terms of the frequency with which an individual displays specific behaviors that have been identified by the engineers/scientists themselves as making the difference between success and failure in fulfilling the requirements of their job."

City of Detroit, Garbage Collectors In December 1972, the City of Detroit instituted a unique productivity bonus system for sanitation workers engaged in refuse collection. The plan, which provides for sharing the savings for productivity improvement efforts, was designed to save money for the city while rewarding workers for increased efficiency. The city's Labor Relations Bureau negotiated the productivity contract with the two unions concerned with refuse collection: The American Federation of State, County and Municipal Employees (AFSCME), representing sanitation laborers (loaders), and the Teamsters Union, representing drivers. The two agreements took effect on July 1, 1973.

The bonus system was based on savings gained in productivity (reductions in paid man-hours per ton of refuse collected, reduction in the total hours of overtime, percentage of routes completed on schedule, and effectiveness or cleanliness). A bonus pool was established and the sanitation laborers share 50-50 in the pool with the city—each worker's portion being determined by the number of hours worked under the productivity bonus pool, exclusive of overtime.

By any measure, this program was a success. Citizen complaints decreased dramatically. During 1974, the city saved $1,654,000 after the bonus of $307,000 ($350 per man) was paid. The bonus system is still in effect, but the unions are currently disputing with the city the question of what constitutes a fair day's work. Both unions involved have expressed doubts about the accuracy of the data used to compute the productivity index or, to be more precise, how the data are gathered and the index and bonus computed. Given this expected prenegotiation tactic by the unions, the city and the customers both agree that the plan has worked.

B. F. Goodrich Chemical Company   In 1972, one of the production sections in the B.F. Goodrich Chemical plant in Avon Lake, Ohio, as measured by standard accounting procedures, was failing. At that time, Donald J. Barnicki, the production manager, introduced a positive reinforcement program that included goal setting and feedback about scheduling, targets, costs, and problem areas. This program gave the information directly to the foreman on a once-a-week basis. In addition, daily meetings were held to discuss problems and describe how each group was doing. For the first time the foreman and their employees were told about costs that were incurred by their group. Charts were published that showed area achievements in terms of sales, cost, and productivity as compared with targets. Films were made that showed top management what the employees were doing, and these films were shown to the workers so they would know what management was being told.

According to Barnicki, this program of positive reinforcement turned the plant around. "Our productivity has increased 300 percent over the past five years. Costs are down. We had our best startup time in 1976 and passed our daily production level from last year the second day after we returned from the holidays."

ACDC Electronics   Edward J. Feeney, of Emery Air Freight fame, now heads a consulting firm that works with such firms as General Electric, Xerox, Braniff Airways, and General Atomic in the area of positive reinforcement programs. One of Mr. Feeney's current clients is the ACDC Electronics Company (a division of Emerson Electronics). After establishing a program that incorporated the four-step approach outlined earlier in this article, the ACDC Company experienced a profit increase of 25 percent over the forecast; a $550,000 cost reduction or $10 million in sales; a return of 1,900 percent on investment, including consultant fees; a reduction in turnaround time on repairs from 30 to 10 days; and a significant increase in attendance.

According to Ken Kilpatrick, ACDC President, "The results were as dramatic as those that Feeney had described. We found our output increased 30–40 percent almost immediately and has stayed at that high level for well over a year." The results were not accomplished, however, without initial problems, according to Feeney. "With some managers there were problems of inertia, disbelief, lack of time to implement, interest, difficulty in defining output for hard-to-measure areas, setting standards, measuring past performance, estimating economic payoffs, and failure to apply all feedback or reinforcement principles." Nevertheless, after positive results began to surface and initial problems were overcome, the ACDC management became enthused about the program.

CONCLUSION

This article has attempted to explain how reinforcement theory can be applied in organizational settings. We have argued that the arrangement of the contingencies of reinforcement is crucial in influencing behavior. Different ways of arranging these contingencies were explained, followed by a recommendation that the use of positive reinforcement combined with oral explanations of incorrect behaviors, when applied correctly, is an underestimated and powerful tool of management. The correct application includes three conditions: *First,* reinforcers must be selected that are sufficiently powerful and durable to establish and strengthen behavior; *second,* the manager must design the contingencies in such a way that the reinforcing events are made contingent on the desired level of performance; *third,* the program must be designed in such a way that it is possible to establish a reliable training procedure for inducing the desired response patterns.

To meet these three conditions for effective contingency management, many firms have set up a formal positive reinforcement motivational program. These include firms such as Emery Air Freight, Michigan Bell, Standard Oil of Ohio, General Electric, and B. F. Goodrich, among others. Typically, these firms employ a four-stage approach in designing their programs: (1) A performance audit is conducted in order to determine what performance patterns are desired and to measure the current levels of that performance; (2) specific and reasonable goals are set for each worker; (3) each employee is generally instructed to keep a record of his or her own work; and (4) positive aspects of the employee's performance are positively reinforced by the supervisor. Under this four-stage program, the employee has two chances of being successful—he can beat his previous level of performance or he can beat that plus his own goal. Also under this system, negative feedback routinely comes only from the employee (since he knows when he failed to meet the objective), whereas positive feedback comes from both the employee and his supervisor.

While we noted that many firms have credited this approach with improving morale and increasing profits, several points of concern and potential shortcomings of this approach should also be cited. Many people claim that you cannot teach reinforcement principles to lower-level managers very easily and unless you get managers to understand the principles, you certainly risk misusing these tools. Poorly designed reward systems can interfere with the development of spontaneity and creativity. Reinforcement systems that are deceptive and manipulative are an insult to employees.

One way in which a positive reinforcement program based solely on praise can be deceptive and manipulative occurs when productivity continues to increase month after month and year after year, and the company's profits increase as well, but employee salaries do not reflect their contributions. This seems obviously unethical and contradictory. It is unethical because the workers are being exploited and praise by itself will not have any long-term effect on performance. Emery Air Freight, for example, has begun to experience this backlash effect. It is contradictory because the manager is saying he believes in the principle of making intangible rewards contingent on performance but at the same time refuses to make the tangible monetary reward contingent on performance. Often the excuse given is that "our employees are unionized." Well, this is not always the case. Many firms that are without unions, such as Emery, refuse to pay on performance. Many other firms with unions have a contingent bonus plan. Skinner in 1969 warned managers that a poorly designed monetary reward system may actually reduce performance. The employee should be a willing party to the influence attempt, with both parties benefitting from the relationship.

Peter Drucker's concern is different. He worries that perhaps positive reinforcers may be misused by management to the detriment of the economy. He says, "The carrot of material rewards has not, like the stick of fear, lost its potency. On the contrary, it has become so potent that it threatens to destroy the earth's finite resources if it does not first destroy more economies through inflation that reflects rising expectations." In other words, positive reinforcement can be too effective as used by firms concerned solely with their own personal gains.

Skinner in an interview in *Organizational Dynamics* stated that a feedback system alone may not be enough. He recommended that the organization should design feedback and incentive systems in such a way that the dual objective of getting things done and making work enjoyable is met. He says what must be accomplished, and what he believes is currently lacking, is an effective training program for managers. "In the not-too-distant future, however, a new breed of industrial managers may be able to apply the principles of operant conditioning effectively."

We have evidence in at least a few organizational settings that Skinner's hopes are on the way to realization, that a new breed of industrial managers are indeed applying the principles of operant conditioning effectively.

Part Four

Interpersonal and Group Processes

Chapter 9

Interpersonal Processes in Organizations

Many factors combine to determine what happens in an organization: the characteristics of organization members, the structure and technology of the organization itself, various organizational policies and practices, and so on. The other chapters of this book provide abundant testimony about the importance of such factors in affecting behavior in organizations. Yet because organizations involve people working collectively toward some shared goals, *relationships among people* always serve as one of the basic vehicles for carrying out the work, and for carrying on the organization.

In this chapter, we look at these relationships—the forms they can take, how they develop, and their consequences for people and for the organization. The chapter opens with a classic report by Roy on his participation in a group of employees performing monotonous, repetitive factory work. Roy shows how the relationships among the workers provided a means for dealing with the tedium of the work itself. The devices they employed included creating structured "times" (such as "banana time") that broke up the day, and enacting various "themes" in their interaction (such as the "poom poom" theme) that provided both fun and continuity for the group from day to day. Relationships, in this case, clearly provided a way for group members to salvage some interest and meaning out of a work system that inherently provided few built-in rewards.

Relationships are not, of course, always helpful to people, nor do they necessarily have a positive influence on organizational goal attainment. In the next article, Argyris points out how interpersonal relationships can serve as barriers to effective organizational decision making. He describes a research project that examined the characteristics of interpersonal behavior in managerial decision-making situations. The results showed that such behaviors as interpersonal risk-taking, mutual helping, and authentic expressions of trust and feelings occur rarely —despite the fact that group members expressed a strong desire for such behaviors. Argyris offers some explanations for the discrepancy he found between word and deed, and then suggests ways that people can learn *how* to behave in ways that are more consistent with their expressed values and with the requirements for good organizational decision making.

One strategy for improving relationships in organizations is explored in depth in the next article, by

Harrison. This approach is called "role negotiation," and it is especially useful in situations where relationships are plagued by excessively high levels of interpersonal conflict. In role negotiation, the focus is on the actual behavior of participants, and they are encouraged to bargain explicitly about the concessions one person is willing to make in exchange for altered behavior by another person. Feelings are viewed as secondary to behavior and get little explicit attention; the use of power and sanctions, on the other hand, is accepted as a reasonable way to back up and enforce negotiated agreements among the parties. This approach, which Harrison characterizes as "tough-minded," provides an interesting alternative to the "human-relations" orientation that has characterized much previous work on the resolution of interpersonal conflict. Indeed, it is interesting to speculate about the similarities and differences between the kinds of interpersonal interventions proposed by Argyris in the preceding article and the one proposed by Harrison here.

In the final reading in the chapter, Porter, Allen, and Angle look at yet another aspect of interpersonal relationships in organizations: political behaviors intended to influence someone who is higher than the actor in the formal organizational hierarchy. Heretofore, there has been little systematic research on the political dimension of relationships in organizations, and Porter, Allen, and Angle lay out a framework for studying and dealing with these important phenomena. How do organization members learn about political norms in the organization? What factors heighten or lessen the amount of political activity that takes place? Who is (and who is not) likely to engage in political behaviors? Who, on the other hand, is viewed as an especially good "target" for a political influence attempt? And what methods do people use to achieve political influence in different circumstances? The authors provide the beginnings of answers to these questions and, in the process, help legitimize an important topic that too often has been considered "taboo" for discussion by both managers and organizational researchers.

Reading 31

"Banana Time":
Job Satisfaction and Informal Interaction
Donald F. Roy

My account of how one group of machine operators kept from "going nuts" in a situation of monotonous work activity attempts to lay bare the tissues of interaction which made up the content of their adjustment. The talking, fun, and fooling which provided a solution to the elemental problem of "psychological survival" will be described according to their embodiment in intra-group relations. In addition, an unusual opportunity for close observation of behavior involved in the maintenance of group equilibrium was afforded by the fortuitous introduction of a "natural experiment." My unwitting injection of explosive materials into the stream of interaction resulted in sudden, but temporary, loss of group interaction.

My fellow operatives and I spent our long days of simple, repetitive work in relative isolation from other employees of the factory. Our line of machines was sealed off from other work areas of the plant by the four walls of the clicking room. The one door of this room was usually closed. Even when it was kept open, during periods of hot weather, the consequences were not social; it opened on an uninhabited storage room of the shipping department. Not even the sounds of work activity going on elsewhere in the factory carried to this isolated work place. There were occasional contacts with "outside" employees, usually on matters connected with the work; but, with the exception of the daily calls of one fellow who came to pick up finished materials for the next step in processing, such visits were sporadic and infrequent.

Moreover, face-to-face contact with members of the managerial hierarchy were few and far between. No one bearing the title of foreman ever came around. The only company official who showed himself more than once during the two-month observation period was the plant superintendent. Evidently overloaded with supervisory duties and production problems which kept him busy elsewhere, he managed to pay his respects every week or two.

His visits were in the nature of short, businesslike, but friendly exchanges. Otherwise he confined his observable communications with the group to occasional utilization of a public address system. During the two-month period, the company president and the chief chemist paid one friendly call apiece. One man, who may or may not have been of managerial status, was seen on various occasions lurking about in a manner which excited suspicion. Although no observable consequences accrued from the peculiar visitations of this silent fellow, it was assumed that he was some sort of efficiency expert, and he was referred to as "The Snooper."

As far as our work group was concerned, this was truly a situation of laissez-faire management. There was no interference from staff experts, no hounding by time-study engineers or personnel men hot on the scent of efficiency or good human relations. Nor were there any signs of industrial democracy in the form of safety, recreational, or production committees. There was an international union, and there was a highly publicized union-management cooperation program; but actual interactional processes of cooperation were carried on somewhere beyond my range of observation and without participation of members of my work group. Furthermore, these union-management get-togethers had no determinable connection with the problem of "toughing out" a twelve-hour day at monotonous work.

Our work group was thus not only abandoned to its own resources for creating job satisfaction, but left without that basic reservoir of ill-will toward management which can sometimes be counted on to stimulate the development of interesting activities to occupy hand and brain. Lacking was the challenge of intergroup conflict, that perennial source of creative experience to fill the otherwise empty hours of meaningless work routine.[1]

[1] Donald F. Roy, "Work Satisfaction and Social Reward in Quota Achievement: An Analysis of Piecework Incentive," *American Sociological Review,* XVIII (October, 1953), 507–514.

Excerpted from D. F. Roy, " 'Banana Time': Job Satisfaction and Informal Interaction." Reproduced by permission of the Society for Applied Anthropology. From *Human Organization* **18**(4):158–168, 1960.

The clicking machines were housed in a room approximately thirty by twenty-four feet. They were four in number, set in a row, and so arranged along one wall that the busy operator could, merely by raising his head from his work, freshen his reveries with a glance through one of three large barred windows. To the rear of one of the end machines sat a long cutting table; here the operators cut up rolls of plastic materials into small sheets manageable for further processing at the clickers. Behind the machine at the opposite end of the line sat another table which was intermittently the work station of a female employee who performed sundry scissors operations of a more intricate nature on raincoat parts. Boxed in on all sides by shelves and stocks of materials, this latter locus of work appeared a cell within a cell.

The clickers were of the genus punching machines; of mechanical construction similar to that of the better-known punch presses, their leading features were hammer and block. The hammer, or punching head, was approximately eight inches by twelve inches at its flat striking surface. The descent upon the block was initially forced by the operator, who exerted pressure on a handle attached to the side of the hammer head. A few inches of travel downward established electrical connection for a sharp, power-driven blow. The hammer also traveled, by manual guidance, in a horizontal plane to and from, and in an arc around, the central column of the machine. Thus the operator, up to the point of establishing electrical connections for the sudden and irrevocable downward thrust, had flexibility in maneuvering his instrument over the larger surface of the block. The latter, approximately twenty-four inches wide, eighteen inches deep, and ten inches thick, was made, like a butcher's block, of inlaid hardwood; it was set in the machine at a convenient waist height. On it the operator placed his materials, one sheet at a time if leather, stacks of sheets if plastic, to be cut with steel dies of assorted sizes and shapes. The particular die in use would be moved, by hand, from spot to spot over the materials each time a cut was made; less frequently materials would be shifted on the block as the operator saw need for such adjustment.

Introduction to the new job, with its relatively simple machine skills and work routines, was accomplished with what proved to be, in my experience, an all-time minimum of job training. The clicking machine assigned to me was situated at one end of the row. Here the superintendent and one of the operators gave a few brief demonstrations, accompanied by bits of advice which included a warning to keep hands clear of the descending hammer. After a short practice period, at the end of which the superintendent expressed satisfaction with progress and potentialities, I was left to develop my learning curve with no other supervision than that afforded by members of the work group. Further advice and assistance did come, from time to time, from my fellow operatives, sometimes upon request, sometimes unsolicited.

THE WORK GROUP

Absorbed at first in three related goals of improving my clicking skill, increasing my rate of output, and keeping my left hand unclicked, I paid little attention to my fellow operatives save to observe that they were friendly, middle-aged, foreign-born, full of advice, and very talkative. Their names, according to the way they addressed each other, were George, Ike, and Sammy.[2] George, a stocky fellow in his late fifties, operated the machine at the opposite end of the line; he, I later discovered, had emigrated in early youth from a country in Southeastern Europe. Ike, stationed at George's left, was tall, slender, in his early fifties, and Jewish: he had come from Eastern Europe in his youth. Sammy, number three man in the line, and my neighbor, was heavy set, in his late fifties, and Jewish; he had escaped from a country in Eastern Europe just before Hitler's legions had moved in. All three men had been downwardly mobile as to occupation in recent years. George and Sammy had been proprietors of small businesses; the former had been "wiped out" when his uninsured establishment burned down; the latter had been entrepreneuring on a small scale before he left all behind him to flee the Germans. According to his account, Ike had left a highly skilled trade which he had practiced for years in Chicago.

I discovered also that the clicker line represented a ranking system in descending order from George to myself. George not only had top seniority for the group, but functioned as a sort of leadman. His superior status was marked in the fact that he

2All names used are fictitious.

received five cents more per hour than the other clickermen, put in the longest workday, made daily contact, outside the workroom, with the superintendent on work matters which concerned the entire line, and communicated to the rest of us the directives which he received. The narrow margin of superordination was seen in the fact that directives were always relayed in the superintendent's name; they were on the order of, "You'd better let that go now, and get on the green. Joe says they're running low on the fifth floor," or, "Joe says he wants two boxes of the 3-die today." The narrow margin was also seen in the fact that the superintendent would communicate directly with his operatives over the public address system; and, on occasion, Ike or Sammy would leave the workroom to confer with him for decisions or advice in regard to work orders.

Ike was next to George in seniority, then Sammy. I was, of course, low man on the totem pole. Other indices to status differentiation lay in informal interaction, to be described later.

With one exception, job status tended to be matched by length of workday. George worked a thirteen-hour day, from 7 A.M. to 8:30 P.M. Ike worked eleven hours, from 7 A.M. to 6:30 P.M.; occasionally he worked until 7 or 7:30 for an eleven and a half- or a twelve-hour day. Sammy put in a nine-hour day, from 8 A.M. to 5:30 P.M. My twelve hours spanned from 8 A.M. to 8:30 P.M. We had a half hour for lunch, from 12 to 12:30.

The female who worked at the secluded table behind George's machine put in a regular plant-wide eight-hour shift from 8 to 4:30. Two women held this job during the period of my employment; Mable was succeeded by Baby. Both were Negroes, and in their late twenties.

A fifth clicker operator, an Arabian *emigré* called Boo, worked a night shift by himself. He usually arrived about 7 P.M. to take over Ike's machine.

THE WORK

It was evident to me, before my first workday drew to a weary close, that my clicking career was going to be a grim process of fighting the clock, the particular timepiece in this situation being an old-fashioned alarm clock which ticked away on a shelf near George's machine. I had struggled through many dreary rounds with the minutes and hours during the various phases of my industrial experi-

ence, but never had I been confronted with such a dismal combination of working conditions as the extra-long workday, the infinitesimal cerebral excitation, and the extreme limitation of physical movement. The contrast with a recent stint in the California oil fields was striking. This was no eight-hour day of racing hither and yon over desert and foothills with a rollicking crew of "routabouts" on a variety of repair missions at oil wells, pipe lines, and storage tanks. Here there were no afternoon dallyings to search the sands for horned toads, tarantulas, and rattlesnakes, or to climb old wooden derricks for raven's nests, with an eye out, of course, for the telltale streak of dust in the distance which gave ample warning of the approach of the boss. This was standing all day in one spot beside three old codgers in a dingy room looking out through barred windows at the bare walls of a brick warehouse, leg movements largely restricted to the shifting of body weight from one foot to the other, hand and arm movements confined, for the most part, to a simple repetitive sequence of place the die,____ punch the clicker,____ place the die,____ punch the clicker, and intellectual activity reduced to computing the hours to quitting time. It is true that from time to time a fresh stack of sheets would have to be substituted for the clicked-out old one; but the stack would have been prepared by someone else, and the exchange would be only a minute or two in the making. Now and then a box of finished work would have to be moved back out of the way, and an empty box brought up; but the moving back and the bringing up involved only a step or two. And there was the half hour for lunch, and occasional trips to the lavatory or the drinking fountain to break up the day into digestible parts. But after each momentary respite, hammer and die were moving again: click, ____ move die,____ click,____ move die.

Before the end of the first day, Monotony was joined by his twin brother, Fatigue. I got tired. My legs ached, and my feet hurt. Early in the afternoon I discovered a tall stool and moved it up to my machine to "take the load off my feet." But the superintendent dropped in to see how I was "doing" and promptly informed me that "we don't sit down on this job." My reverie toyed with the idea of quitting the job and looking for other work.

The next day was the same: the monotony of the work, the tired legs and sore feet and thoughts of quitting.

INFORMAL SOCIAL ACTIVITY OF THE WORK GROUP: TIMES AND THEMES

The change came about when I began to take serious note of the social activity going on around me; my attentiveness to this activity came with growing involvement in it. What I heard at first, before I started to listen, was a stream of disconnected bits of communication which did not make much sense. Foreign accents were strong and referents were not joined to coherent contexts of meaning. It was just "jabbering." What I saw at first, before I began to observe, was occasional flurries of horseplay so simply and unvarying in pattern and so childish in quality that they made no strong bid for attention. For example, Ike would regularly switch off the power at Sammy's machine whenever Sammy made a trip to the lavatory or the drinking fountain. Correlatively, Sammy invariably fell victim to the plot by making an attempt to operate his clicking hammer after returning to the shop. And, as the simple pattern went, this blind stumbling into the trap was always followed by indignation and reproach from Sammy, smirking satisfaction from Ike, and mild paternal scolding from George. My interest in this procedure was at first confined to wondering when Ike would weary of his tedious joke or when Sammy would learn to check his power switch before trying the hammer.

But, as I began to pay close attention, as I began to develop familiarity with the communication system, the disconnected became connected, the nonsense made sense, the obscure became clear, and the silly actually funny. And, as the content of the interaction took on more and more meaning, the interaction began to reveal structure. There were "times" and "themes," and roles to serve their enaction. The interaction had subtleties, and I began to savor and appreciate them. I started to record what hitherto had seemed unimportant.

Times

This emerging awareness of structure and meaning included recognition that the long day's grind was broken by interruptions of a kind other than the formally instituted or idiosyncratically developed disjunctions in work routine previously described. These additional interruptions appeared in daily repetition in an ordered series of informal interac-

tions. They were, in part, but only in part and in very rough comparison, similar to those common fractures of the production process known as the coffee break, the coke break, and the cigarette break. Their distinction lay in frequency of occurrence and in brevity. As phases of the daily series, they occurred almost hourly, and so short were they in duration that they disrupted work activity only slightly. Their significance lay not so much in their function as rest pauses, although it cannot be denied that physical refreshment was involved. Nor did their chief importance lie in the accentuation of progress points in the passage of time, although they could perform that function far more strikingly than the hour hand on the dull face of George's alarm clock. If the daily series of interruptions be likened to a clock, then the comparison might best be made with a special kind of cuckoo clock, one with a cuckoo which can provide variation in its announcements and can create such an interest in them that the intervening minutes become filled with intellectual content. The major significance of the interactional interruptions lay in such a carryover of interest. The physical interplay which momentarily halted work activity would initiate verbal exchanges and thought processes to occupy group members until the next interruption. The group interactions thus not only marked off the time; they gave it content and hurried it along.

Most of the breaks in the daily series were designated as "times" in the parlance of the clicker operators, and they featured the consumption of food or drink of one sort or another. There was coffee time, peach time, banana time, fish time, coke time, and, of course, lunch time. Other interruptions, which formed part of the series but were not verbally recognized as times, were window time, pickup time, and the staggered quitting times of Sammy and Ike. These latter unnamed times did not involve the partaking of refreshments.

My attention was first drawn to this times business during my first week of employment when I was encouraged to join in the sharing of two peaches. It was Sammy who provided the peaches; he drew them from his lunch box after making the announcement, "Peach time!" On this first occasion I refused the proffered fruit, but thereafter regularly consumed my half peach. Sammy continued to provide the peaches and to make the "Peach time!" announcement, although there were days when Ike would remind him that it was peach time, urging him to hurry up with the mid-morning snack. Ike invariably complained about the quality of the fruit, and his complaints fed the fires of continued banter between peach donor and critical recipient. I did find the fruit a bit on the scrubby side but felt, before I achieved insight into the function of peach time, that Ike was showing poor manners by looking a gift horse in the mouth. I wondered why Sammy continued to share his peaches with such an ingrate.

Banana time followed peach time by approximately an hour. Sammy again provided the refreshments, namely, one banana. There was, however, no four-way sharing of Sammy's banana. Ike would gulp it down by himself after surreptitiously extracting it from Sammy's lunch box, kept on a shelf behind Sammy's work station. Each morning, after making the snatch, Ike would call out, "Banana time!" and proceed to down his prize while Sammy made futile protests and denunciations. George would join in with mild remonstrances, sometimes scolding Sammy for making so much fuss. The banana was one which Sammy brought for his own consumption at lunch time; he never did get to eat his banana, but kept bringing one for his lunch. At first this daily theft startled and amazed me. Then I grew to look forward to the daily seizure and the verbal interaction which followed.

Window time came next. It followed banana time as a regular consequence of Ike's castigation by the indignant Sammy. After "taking" repeated references to himself as a person badly lacking in morality and character, Ike would "finally" retaliate by opening the window which faced Sammy's machine, to let the "cold air" blow in on Sammy. The slandering which would, in its echolalic repetition, wear down Ike's patience and forbearance usually took the form of the invidious comparison: "George is a good daddy! Ike is a bad man! A very bad man!" Opening the window would take a little time to accomplish and would involve a great deal of verbal interplay between Ike and Sammy, both before and after the event. Ike would threaten, make feints toward the window, then finally open it. Sammy would protest, argue, and make claims that the air blowing in on him would give him a cold; he would eventually have to leave his machine to close the window. Sometimes the weather was slightly chilly,

and the draft from the window unpleasant; but cool or hot, windy or still, window time arrived each day. (I assume that it was originally a cold season development.) George's part in this interplay, in spite of the "good daddy" laudations, was to encourage Ike in his window work. He would stress the tonic values of fresh air and chide Sammy for his unappreciativeness.

Following window time came lunch time, a formally designated half-hour for the midday repast and rest break. At this time, informal interaction would feature exchanges between Ike and George. The former would start eating his lunch a few minutes before noon, and the latter, in his role as straw boss, would censure him for malobservance of the rules. Ike's off-beat luncheon usually involved a previous tampering with George's alarm clock. Ike would set the clock ahead a few minutes in order to maintain his eating schedule without detection, and George would discover these small daylight saving changes.

The first "time" interruption of the day I did not share. It occurred soon after I arrived on the job, at eight o'clock. George and Ike would share a small pot of coffee brewed on George's hot plate.

Pickup time, fish time, and coke time came in the afternoon. I name it pickup time to represent the official visit of the man who made daily calls to cart away boxes of clicked materials. The arrival of the pickup man, a Negro, was always a noisy one, like the arrival of a daily passenger train in an isolated small town. Interaction attained a quick peak of intensity to crowd into a few minutes all communications, necessary and otherwise. Exchanges invariably included loud depreciations by the pickup man of the amount of work accomplished in the clicking department during the preceding twenty-four hours. Such scoffing would be on the order of "Is that all you've got done? What do you boys do all day?" These devaluations would be countered with allusions to the "soft job" enjoyed by the pickup man. During the course of the exchanges news items would be dropped, some of serious import, such as reports of accomplished or impending layoffs in the various plants of the company, or of gains or losses in orders for company products. Most of the news items, however, involved bits of information on plant employees told in a light vein. Information relayed by the clicker operators was usually told about each other, mainly in the form of summaries of the most recent kidding sequences. Some of this material was repetitive, carried over from day to day. Sammy would be the butt of most of this newscasting, although he would make occasional counter-reports on Ike and George. An invariable part of the interactional content of pickup time was Ike's introduction of the pickup man to George. "Meet Mr. Papeatis!" Ike would say in mock solemnity and dignity. Each day the pickup man "met" Mr. Papeatis, to the obvious irritation of the latter. Another pickup time invariably would bring Baby (or Mable) into the interaction. George would always issue the loud warning to the pickup man: "Now I want you to stay away from Baby! She's Henry's girl!" Henry was a burly Negro with a booming bass voice who made infrequent trips to the clicking room with lift-truck loads of materials. He was reputedly quite a ladies' man among the colored population of the factory. George's warning to "Stay away from Baby!" was issued to every Negro who entered the shop. Baby's only part in this was to laugh at the horseplay.

About mid-afternoon came fish time. George and Ike would stop work for a few minutes to consume some sort of pickled fish which Ike provided. Neither Sammy nor I partook of this nourishment, nor were we invited. For this omission I was grateful; the fish, brought in a newspaper and with head and tail intact, produced a reverse effect on my appetite. George and Ike seemed to share a great liking for fish. Each Friday night, as a regular ritual, they would enjoy a fish dinner together at a nearby restaurant. On these nights Ike would work until 8:30 and leave the plant with George.

Coke time came late in the afternoon, and was an occasion for total participation. The four of us took turns in buying the drinks and in making the trip for them to a fourth floor vending machine. Through George's manipulation of the situation, it eventually became my daily chore to go after the cokes; the straw boss had noted that I made a much faster trip to the fourth floor and back than Sammy or Ike.

Sammy left the plant at 5:30, and Ike ordinarily retired from the scene an hour and a half later. These quitting times were not marked by any distinctive interaction save the one regular exchange between Sammy and George over the former's "early washup." Sammy's tendency was to crowd his washing up toward five o'clock, and it was George's concern to keep it from further creeping advance. After Ike's departure came Boo's arrival. Boo's was a striking personality productive of a change in topics of conversation to fill in the last hour of the long workday.

Themes

To put flesh, so to speak, on this interactional frame of "times," my work group had developed various "themes" of verbal interplay which had become standardized in their repetition. These topics of conversation ranged in quality from an extreme of nonsensical chatter to another extreme of serious discourse. Unlike the times, these themes flowed one into the other in no particular sequence of predictability. Serious conversation could suddenly melt into horseplay, and vice versa. In the middle of a serious discussion on the high cost of living, Ike might drop a weight behind the easily startled Sammy, or hit him over the head with a dusty paper sack. Interaction would immediately drop to a low comedy exchange of slaps, threats, guffaws, and disapprobations which would invariably include a ten-minute echolalia of "Ike is a bad man, a very bad man! George is a good daddy, a very fine man!" Or, on the other hand, a stream of such invidious comparisons as followed a surreptitious switching-off of Sammy's machine by the playful Ike might merge suddenly into a discussion of the pros and cons of saving for one's funeral.

"Kidding themes" were usually started by George or Ike, and Sammy was usually the butt of the joke. Sometimes Ike would have to "take it," seldom George. One favorite kidding theme involved Sammy's alleged receipt of $100 a month from his son. The points stressed were that Sammy did not have to work long hours, or did not have to work at all, because he had a son to support him. George would always point out that he sent money to his daughter; she did not send money to him. Sammy received occasional calls from his wife, and his claim that these calls were requests to shop for groceries on the way home were greeted with feigned disbelief. Sammy was ribbed for being closely watched, bossed, and henpecked by his wife, and the expression, "Are you man or mouse?" became an echolalic utterance, used both in and out of the original context.

Ike, who shared his machine and the work scheduled for it with Boo, the night operator, came in for constant invidious comparison on the subject of output. The socially isolated Boo, who chose work rather than sleep on his lonely night shift, kept up a high level of performance, and George never tired of pointing this out to Ike. It so happened that Boo, an Arabian Moslem from Palestine, had no use for Jews in general; and Ike, who was Jewish, had no use for Boo in particular. Whenever George would extol Boo's previous night's production, Ike would try to turn the conversation into a general discussion on the need for educating the Arabs. George, never permitting the development of serious discussion on this topic, would repeat a smirking warning, "You watch out for Boo! He's got a long knife!"

The "poom poom" theme was one that caused no sting. It would come up several times a day to be enjoyed as unbarbed fun by the three older clicker operators. Ike was usually the one to raise the question, "How many times you go poom poom last night?" The person questioned usually replied with claims of being "too old for poom poom." If this theme did develop a goat, it was I. When it was pointed out that I was a younger man, this provided further grist for the poom poom mill. I soon grew weary of this poom poom business, so dear to the hearts of the three old satyrs, and, knowing where the conversation would inevitably lead, winced whenever Ike brought up the subject.

I grew almost as sick of a kidding theme which developed from some personal information contributed during a serious conversation on property ownership and high taxes. I dropped a few remarks about two acres of land which I owned in one of the western states, and from then on I had to listen to questions, advice, and general nonsensical comment in regard to "Danelly's farm."[3] This "farm" soon became stocked with horses, cows, pigs, chickens, ducks, and the various and sundry domesticated beasts so tunefully listed in "Old McDonald Had a Farm." George was a persistent offender with this theme. Where the others seemed to be mainly interested in statistics on livestock, crops, etc., George's teasing centered on a generous offering to help with the household chores while I worked in

the fields. He would drone on, *ad nauseam,* "when I come to visit you, you will never have to worry about the housework, Danelly. I'll stay around the house when you go out to dig the potatoes and milk the cows, I'll stay in and peel potatoes and help your wife do the dishes." Danelly always found it difficult to change the subject on George, once the latter started to bear down on the farm theme.

Another kidding theme which developed out of serious discussion could be labelled "helping Danelly find a cheaper apartment." It became known to the group that Danelly had a pending housing problem, that he would need new quarters for his family when the permanent resident of his temporary summer dwelling returned from a vacation. This information engendered at first a great deal of sympathetic concern and, of course, advice on apartment hunting. Development into a kidding theme was immediately related to previous exchanges between Ike and George on the quality of their respective dwelling areas. Ike lived in "Lawndale," and George dwelt in the "Woodlawn" area. The new pattern featured the reading aloud of bogus "apartment for rent" ads in newspapers which were brought into the shop. Studying his paper at lunchtime, George would call out, "Here's an apartment for you, Danelly! Five rooms, stove heat, $20 a month, Lawndale Avenue!" Later, Ike would read from his paper, "Here's one! Six rooms, stove heat, dirt floor. $18.50 a month! At 55th and Woodlawn." Bantering would then go on in regard to the quality of housing or population in the two areas. The search for an apartment for Danelly was not successful.

Serious themes included the relating of major misfortunes suffered in the past by group members. George referred again and again to the loss, by fire, of his business establishment. Ike's chief complaints centered around a chronically ill wife who had undergone various operations and periods of hospital care. Ike spoke with discouragement of the expenses attendant upon hiring a housekeeper for himself and his children; he referred with disappointment and disgust to a teen-age son, an inept lad who "couldn't even fix his own lunch. He couldn't even make himself a sandwich!" Sammy's reminiscences centered on the loss of a flourishing business when he had to flee Europe ahead of Nazi invasion.

But all serious topics were not tales of woe. One

---

[3]This spelling is the closest I can come to the appellation given me in George's broken English and adopted by other members of the group.

favorite serious theme which was optimistic in tone could be called either "Danelly's future" or "getting Danelly a better job." It was known that I had been attending "college," the magic door to opportunity, although my specific course of study remained somewhat obscure. Suggestions poured forth on good lines of work to get into, and these suggestions were backed with accounts of friends, and friends of friends, who had made good via the academic route. My answer to the expected question, "Why are you working here?" always stressed the "lots of overtime" feature, and this explanation seemed to suffice for short-range goals.

There was one theme of especially solemn import, the "professor theme." This theme might also be termed "George's daughter's marriage theme"; for the recent marriage of George's only child was inextricably bound up with George's connection with higher learning. The daughter had married the son of a professor who instructed in one of the local colleges. This professor theme was not in the strictest sense a conversation piece; when the subject came up, George did all the talking. The two Jewish operatives remained silent as they listened with deep respect, if not actual awe, to George's accounts of the Big Wedding which, including the wedding pictures, entailed an expense of $1,000. It was monologue, but there was listening, there was communication, the sacred communication of a temple, when George told of going for Sunday afternoon walks on the Midway with the professor, or of joining the professor for a Sunday dinner. Whenever he spoke of the professor, his daughter, the wedding, or even of the new son-in-law, who remained for the most part in the background, a sort of incidental like the wedding cake, George was complete master of the interaction. His manner, in speaking to the rank-and-file of clicker operators, was indeed that of master deigning to notice his underlings. I came to the conclusion that it was the professor connection, not the straw-boss-ship or the extra nickel an hour, which provided the fount of George's superior status in the group.

If the professor theme may be regarded as the cream of verbal interaction, the "chatter themes" should be classed as the dregs. The chatter themes were hardly themes at all; perhaps they should be labelled "verbal states," or "oral autisms." Some were of doubtful status as communication; they were like the howl or cry of an animal responding to its own physiological state. They were exclamations, ejaculations, snatches of song or doggerel, talkings-to-oneself, mutterings. Their classification as themes would rest on their repetitive character. They were echolalic utterances, repeated over and over. An already mentioned example would be Sammy's repetition of "George is a good daddy, a very fine man! Ike is a bad man, a very bad man!" Also, Sammy's repetition of "Don't bother me! Can't you see I'm busy? I'm a very busy man!" for ten minutes after Ike had dropped a weight behind him would fit the classification. Ike would shout "Mamariba!" at intervals between repetition of bits of verse, such as:

Mama on the bed,
Papa on the floor,
Baby in the crib
Says giver some more!

Sometimes the three operators would pick up one of these simple chatterings in a sort of chorus. "Are you man or mouse? I ask you, are you man or mouse?" was a favorite of this type.

So initial discouragement with the meagerness of social interaction I now recognized as due to lack of observation. The interaction was there, in constant flow. It captured attention and held interest to make the long day pass. The twelve hours of "click, move die, click, move die" became as easy to endure as eight hours of varied activity in the oil fields or eight hours of playing the piecework game in a machine shop. The "beast of boredom" was gentled to the harmlessness of a kitten.

Reading 32

Interpersonal Barriers to Decision Making

Chris Argyris

The actual behavior of top executives during decision-making meetings often does not jibe with their attitudes and prescriptions about effective executive action. The gap that often exists between what executives say and how they behave helps create barriers to openness and trust, to the effective search for alternatives, to innovation, and to flexibility in the organization. These barriers are more destructive in important decision-making meetings than in routine meetings, and they upset effective managers more than ineffective ones.

The barriers cannot be broken down simply by intellectual exercises. Rather, executives need feedback concerning their behavior and opportunities to develop self-awareness in action. To this end, certain kinds of questioning are valuable; playing back and analyzing tape recordings of meetings has proved to be a helpful step; and laboratory education programs are valuable.

These are a few of the major findings of a study of executive decision making in six representative companies. The findings have vital implications for management groups everywhere; for while some organizations are less subject to the weaknesses described than are others, *all* groups have them in some degree. In this article I shall discuss the findings in detail and examine the implications for executives up and down the line. (For information on the company sample and research methods used in the study, see Figure 32-1.)

WORDS VERSUS ACTIONS

According to top management, the effectiveness of decision-making activities depends on the degree of innovation, risk taking, flexibility, and trust in the executive system. (Risk taking is defined here as any act where the executive risks his self-esteem. This could be a moment, for example, when he goes against the group view; when he tells someone, especially the person with the highest power, some-

thing negative about his impact on the organization; or when he seeks to put millions of dollars in a new investment.)

Nearly 95 percent of the executives in our study emphasize that an organization is only as good as its top people. They constantly repeat the importance of their responsibility to help themselves and others to develop their abilities. Almost as often they report that the qualities just mentioned—motivation, risk taking, and so on—are key characteristics of any successful executive system. "People problems" head the list as the most difficult, perplexing, and crucial.

In short, the executives vote overwhelmingly for executive systems where the contributions of each executive can be maximized and where innovation, risk taking, flexibilty, and trust reign supreme. Nevertheless, the *behavior* of these same executives tends to create decision-making processes that are *not* very effective. Their behavior can be fitted into two basic patterns:

Pattern A—thoughtful, rational, and mildly competitive. This is the behavior most frequently observed during the decision-making meetings. Executives following this pattern own up to their ideas in a style that emphasizes a serious concern for ideas. As they constantly battle for scarce resources and "sell" their views, their openness to others' ideas is relatively high, not because of a sincere interest in learning about the point of view of others, but so they can engage in a form of "one-upmanship"—that is, gain information about the others' points of view in order to politely discredit them.

Pattern B—competitive first, thoughtful and rational second. In this pattern, conformity to ideas replaces concern for ideas as the strongest norm. Also, antagonism to ideas is higher—in many cases higher than openness to ideas. The relatively high antagonism scores usually indicate, in addition to high competitiveness, a high degree of conflict and pent-up feelings.

The six companies studied include: (1) an electronics firm with 40,000 employees, (2) a manufacturer and marketer of a new innovative product with 4,000 employees, (3) a large research and development company with 3,000 employees, (4) a small research and development organization with 150 employees, (5) a consulting-research firm with 400 employees, and (6) a producer of heavy equipment with 4,000 employees.

The main focus of the investigation reported here was on the behavior of 165 top executives in these companies. The executives were board members, executive committee members, upper-level managers, and (in a few cases) middle-level managers.

Approximately 265 decision-making meetings were studied and nearly 10,000 units of behaviaor analyzed. The topics of the meetings ranged widely, covering investment decisions, new products, manufacturing problems, marketing strategies, new pricing policies, administrative changes, and personnel issues. An observer took notes during all but 10 of the meetings; for research purposes, these 10 were analyzed "blind" from tapes (i.e., without ever meeting the executives). All other meetings were taped also, but analyzed at a later time.

The major device for analyzing the tapes was a new system of categories for scoring decision-making meetings.[1] Briefly, the executives' behavior was scored according to how often they—owned up to and accepted responsibility for their ideas or feelings; opened up to receive others' ideas or feelings; experimented and took risks with ideas or feelings; helped others to own up, be open, and take risks; did not own up; were not open; did not take risks; and did not help others in any of these activities.

A second scoring system was developed to produce a quantitative index of the *norms* of the executive culture. There were both positive and negative norms. The positive norms were:

1. *Individuality*, especially rewarding behavior that focused on and valued the uniqueness of each individual's ideas and feelings.
2. *Concern* for others' ideas and feelings.
3. *Trust* in others' ideas and feelings.

The negative norms were:

1. *Conformity* to others' ideas and feelings.
2. *Antagonism* toward these ideas and feelings.
3. *Mistrust* of these ideas and feelings.

In addition to our observations of the men at work, at least one semistructured interview was conducted with each executive. All of these interviews were likewise taped, and the typewritten protocols served as the basis for further analysis.

[1]For a detailed discussion of the system of categories and other aspects of methodology, see my book, *Organization and Innovation* (Homewood, Illinois, Richard D. Irwin, Inc., 1965).

Figure 32-1 Nature of the study.

Exhibit 32-1 summarizes data for four illustrative groups of managers—two groups with Pattern A characteristics and two with Pattern B characteristics.

Practical Consequences

In both patterns executives are rarely observed:

Taking risks or experimenting with new ideas or feelings;
Helping others to own up, be open, and take risks;
Using a style of behavior that supports the norm of individuality and trust as well as mistrust;
Expressing feelings, positive or negative.

These results should not be interpreted as implying that the executives do not have feelings. We know from the interviews that many of the executives have strong feelings indeed. However, the overwhelming majority (84%) feel that it is a sign of immaturity to express feelings openly *during decision-making meetings*. Nor should the results be interpreted to mean that the executives do not enjoy risk taking. The data permit us to conclude only that few risk-taking actions were *observed* during the meetings. (Also, we have to keep in mind that the executives were always observed in groups; it may be that their behavior in groups varies significantly from their behavior as individuals.)

Before I attempt to give my views about the

| | Pattern A | | | | Pattern B | | | |
| | Group 1: 198 units* | | Group 2: 143 units* | | Group 3: 201 units* | | Group 4: 131 units* | |
Units characterized by:	Number	Percent	Number	Percent	Number	Percent	Number	Percent
Owning up to own ideas and feelings	146	74	105	74	156	78	102	78
Concern for others' ideas and feelings	122	62	89	62	52	26	56	43
Conformity to others' ideas and feelings	54	27	38	26	87	43	62	47
Openness to others' ideas and feelings	46	23	34	24	31	15	8	19
Individuality.	4	2	12	8	30	15	8	6
Antagonism to others' ideas and feelings	18	9	4	3	32	16	5	4
Unwillingness to help others own up to their ideas	5	2	3	2	14	7	4	3

*A unit is an instance of a manager speaking on a topic. If during the course of speaking he changes to a new topic, another unit is created.

Exhibit 32-1   Management groups with Pattern A and Pattern B characteristics.

reasons for the discrepancy between executives' words and actions, I should like to point out that these results are not unique to business organizations. I have obtained similar behavior patterns from leaders in education, research, the ministry, trade unions, and government. Indeed, one of the fascinating questions for me is why so many different people in so many different kinds of organizations tend to manifest similar problems.

WHY THE DISCREPANCY?

The more I observe such problems in different organizations possessing different technologies and varying greatly in size, the more I become impressed with the importance of the role played by the values or assumptions top people hold on the nature of effective human relationships and the best ways to run an organization.

Basic Values

In the studies so far I have isolated three basic values that seem to be very important:

1. *The significant human relationships are the ones which have to do with achieving the organization's objective.* My studies of over 265 different types and sizes of meetings indicate that executives almost always tend to focus their behavior on "getting the job done." In literally thousands of units of behavior, almost none are observed where the men spend some time in analyzing and maintaining their group's effectiveness. This is true even though in many meetings the group's effectiveness "bogged down" and the objectives were not being reached because of interpersonal factors. When the execu-

tives are interviewed and asked why they did not spend some time in examining the group operations or processes, they reply that they were there to get a job done. They add: "If the group isn't effective, it is up to the leader to get it back on the track by directing it."

2. *Cognitive rationality is to be emphasized; feelings and emotions are to be played down.* This value influences executives to see cognitive, intellectual discussions as "relevant," "good," "work," and so on. Emotional and interpersonal discussions tend to be viewed as "irrelevant," "immature," "not work," and so on.

As a result, when emotions and interpersonal variables become blocks to group effectiveness, all the executives report feeling that they should *not* deal with them. For example, in the event of an emotional disagreement, they would tell the members to "get back to facts" or "keep personalities out of this."

3. *Human relationships are most effectively influenced through unilateral direction, coercion, and control, as well as by rewards and penalties that sanction all three values.* This third value of direction and control is implicit in the chain of command and also in the elaborate managerial controls that have been developed within organizations.

Influence on Operations

The impact of these values can be considerable. For example, to the extent that individuals dedicate themselves to the value of intellectual rationality and "getting the job done," they will tend to be aware of and emphasize the intellectual aspects of issues in an organization and (consciously or unconsciously) to suppress the interpersonal and emotional aspects, especially those which do not seem relevant to achieving the task.

As the interpersonal and emotional aspects of behavior become suppressed, organizational norms that coerce individuals to hide their feelings or to disguise them and bring them up as technical, intellectual problems will tend to arise.

Under these conditions the individual may tend to find it very difficult to develop competence in dealing with feelings and interpersonal relationships. Also, in a world where the expression of feelings is not valued, individuals may build personal and organizational defenses to help them suppress their own feelings or inhibit others in such expression. Or they may refuse to consider ideas which, if explored, could expose suppressed feelings.

Such a defensive reaction in an organization could eventually inhibit creativity and innovation during decision making. The participants might learn to limit themselves to those ideas and values that were not threatening. They might also decrease their openness to new ideas and values. And as the degree of openness decreased, the capacity to experiment would also decrease, and fear of taking risks would increase. This would reduce the *probability* of experimentation, thus decreasing openness to new ideas still further and constricting risk taking even more than formerly. We would thereby have a closed circuit which could become an important cause of loss of vitality in an organization.

SOME CONSEQUENCES

Aside from the impact of values on vitality, what are some other consequences of the executive behavior patterns earlier described on top management decision making and on the effective functioning of the organization? For the sake of brevity, I shall include only examples of those consequences that were found to exist in one form or another in all organizations studied.

Restricted Commitment

One of the most frequent findings is that in major decisions that are introduced by the president, there tends to be less than open discussions of the issues, and the commitment of the officers tends to be less than complete (although they may assure the president to the contrary). For instance, consider what happened in one organization where a major administrative decision made during the period of the research was the establishment of several top management committees to explore basic long-range problems:

As is customary with major decisions, the president discussed it in advance at a meeting of the executive committee. He began the meeting by circulating, as a basis for discussion, a draft of the announcement of the committees. Most of the members' discussion was concerned with raising questions about the wording of the proposal:

"Is the word *action* too strong?"
"I recommend that we change 'steps can be taken' to 'recommendations can be made.'"
"We'd better change the word 'lead' to 'maintain.'"

As the discussion seemed to come to an end, one executive said he was worried that the announcement of the committees might be interpreted by the people below as an implication "that the executive committee believes the organization is in trouble. Let's get the idea in that all is well."

There was spontaneous agreement by all executives: "Hear, hear!"

A brief silence was broken by another executive who apparently was not satisfied with the concept of the committees. He raised a series of questions. The manner in which it was done was interesting. As he raised each issue, he kept assuring the president and the group that he was not against the concept. He just wanted to be certain that the executive committee was clear on what it was doing. For example, he assured them:

"I'm not clear. Just asking."
"I'm trying to get a better picture."
"I'm just trying to get clarification."
"Just so that we understand what the words mean."

The president nodded in agreement, but he seemed to become slightly impatient. He remarked that many of these problems would not arise if the members of these new committees took an overall company point of view. An executive commented (laughingly), "Oh, I'm for motherhood too!"

The proposal was tabled in order for the written statement to be revised and discussed further during the next meeting. It appeared that the proposal was the president's personal "baby," and the executive committee members would naturally go along with it. The most responsibility some felt was that they should raise questions so the president would be clear about *his* (not *their*) decision.

At the next meeting the decision-making process was the same as at the first. The president circulated copies of the revised proposal. During this session a smaller number of executives asked questions. Two pushed (with appropriate care) the notion that the duties of one of the committees were defined too broadly.

The president began to defend his proposal by citing an extremely long list of examples, indicating that in his mind "reasonable" people should find the duties clear. This comment and the long list of examples may have communicated to others a feeling that the president was becoming impatient. When he finished, there was a lengthy silence. The president then turned to one of the executives and asked directly, "Why are you worried about this?" The executive explained, then quickly added that as far as he could see the differences were not major ones and his point of view could be integrated with the president's by "changing some words."

The president agreed to the changes, looked up, and asked, "I take it now there is common agreement?" All executives replied "yes" or nodded their heads affirmatively.

As I listened, I had begun to wonder about the commitment of the executive committee members to the idea. In subsequent interviews I asked each about his view of the proposal. Half felt that it was a good proposal. The other half had reservation ranging from moderate to serious. However, being loyal members, they would certainly do their best to make it work, they said.

Subordinate Gamesmanship

I can best illustrate the second consequence by citing from a study of the effectiveness of product planning and program review activities in another of the organizations studied:

It was company policy that peers at any given level should make the decisions. Whenever they could not agree or whenever a decision went beyond their authority, the problem was supposed to be sent to the next higher level. The buck passing stopped at the highest level. A meeting with the president became a great event. Beforehand a group would "dry run" its presentation until all were satisfied that they could present their view effectively.

Few difficulties were observed when the meeting was held to present a recommendation agreed to by all at the lower levels. The difficulties arose when "negative" information had to be fed upward. For example, a major error in the program, a major delay, or a major disagreement among the members was likely to cause such trouble.

The dynamics of these meetings was very interesting. In one case the problem to present was a major delay in a development project. In the dry run the subordinates planned to begin the session with information that "updated" the president. The information was usually presented in such a way that slowly and carefully the president was alerted to the fact that a major problem was about to be announced. One could hear such key phrases as:

"We are a bit later than expected."
"We're not on plan."
"We have had greater difficulties than expected."
"It is now clear that no one should have promised what we did."

These phases were usually followed by some reassuring statement such as:

"However, we're on top of this."
"Things are really looking better now."
"Although we are late, we have advanced the state of the art."
"If you give us another three months, we are certain that we can solve this problem."

To the observer's eyes, it is difficult to see how the president could deny the request. Apparently he felt the same way because he granted it. However, he took nearly 20 minutes to say that this shocked him; he was wondering if everyone was *really* doing everything they could; this was a serious program; this was not the way he wanted to see things run; he was sure they would agree with him; and he wanted their assurances that this would be the final delay.

A careful listening to the tape after the meeting brought out the fact that no subordinate gave such assurances. They simply kept saying that they were doing their best; they had poured a lot into this; or they had the best technical know-how working on it.

Another interesting observation is that most subordinates in this company, especially in presentations to the president, tended to go along with certain unwritten rules:

1 Before you give any bad news, give good news. Especially emphasize the capacity of the department to work hard and to rebound from a failure.

2 Play down the impact of a failure by emphasizing how close you came to achieving the target or how soon the target can be reached. If neither seems reasonable, emphasize how difficult it is to define such targets, and point out that because the state of the art is so primitive, the original commitment was not a wise one.

3 In a meeting with the president it is unfair to take advantage of another department that is in trouble, even if it is a "natural enemy." The sporting thing to do is say something nice about the other department and offer to help it in any way possible. (The offer is usually not made in concrete form, nor does the department in difficulty respond with the famous phrase, "What do you have in mind?")

The subordinates also were in agreement that too much time was spent in long presentations in order to make the president happy. The president, however, confided to the researcher that he did not enjoy listening to long and, at times, dry presentations (especially when he had seen most of the key data anyway). However, he felt that it was important to go through this because it might give the subordinates a greater sense of commitment to the problem!

Lack of Awareness

One of our most common observations in company studies is that executives lack awareness of their own behavioral patterns as well as of the negative impact of their behavior on others. This is not to imply that they are completely unaware; each individual usually senses some aspects of a problem. However, we rarely find an individual or group of individuals who is aware of enough of the scope and depth of a problem so that the need for effective action can be fully understood.

For example, during the study of the decision-making processes of the president and the vice presidents of a firm with nearly 3,000 employees, I concluded that the members unknowingly behaved in such a way as *not* to encourage risk taking, openness, expression of feelings, and cohesive, trusting relationships. But subsequent interviews with the 10 top executives showed that they held a completely different point of view from mine. They admitted that negative feelings were not expressed, but said the reason was that "we trust each other and respect each other." According to 6 of the men, individuality was high and conformity low; where conformity was agreed to be high, the reason given was the necessity of agreeing with the man who is boss. According to eight of the men, "We help each other all the time." Issues loaded with conflict were not handled during meetings, it was reported, for these reasons:

"We should not discuss emotional disagreements before the executive committee because, when people are emotional, they are not rational."

"We should not air our dirty linen in front of the people who may come in to make a presentation."

"Why take up people's time with subjective debates?"

"Most members are not acquainted with all the details. Under our system the person who presents the issues has really thought them through."

"Prediscussion of issues helps to prevent anyone from sandbagging the executive committee."

"Rarely emotional; when it does happen, you can pardon it."

The executive committee climate or emotional tone was characterized by such words as:

"Friendly."
"Not critical of each other."
"Not tense."
"Frank and no tensions because we've known each other for years."

How was I to fit the executives' views with mine? I went back and listened to all the interviews again. As I analyzed the tapes, I began to realize that an interesting set of contradictions arose during many of the interviews. In the early stages of the interviews the executives tended to say things that they contradicted later; Exhibit 32-2 contains examples of contradictions repeated by six or more of the ten top executives.

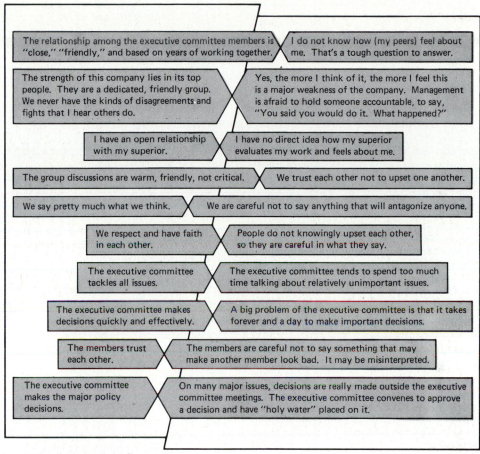

The relationship among the executive committee members is "close," "friendly," and based on years of working together.

I do not know how (my peers) feel about me. That's a tough question to answer.

The strength of this company lies in its top people. They are a dedicated, friendly group. We never have the kinds of disagreements and fights that I hear others do.

Yes, the more I think of it, the more I feel this is a major weakness of the company. Management is afraid to hold someone accountable, to say, "You said you would do it. What happened?"

I have an open relationship with my superior.

I have no direct idea how my superior evaluates my work and feels about me.

The group discussions are warm, friendly, not critical.

We trust each other not to upset one another.

We say pretty much what we think.

We are careful not to say anything that will antagonize anyone.

We respect and have faith in each other.

People do not knowingly upset each other, so they are careful in what they say.

The executive committee tackles all issues.

The executive committee tends to spend too much time talking about relatively unimportant issues.

The executive committee makes decisions quickly and effectively.

A big problem of the executive committee is that it takes forever and a day to make important decisions.

The members trust each other.

The members are careful not to say something that may make another member look bad. It may be misinterpreted.

The executive committee makes the major policy decisions.

On many major issues, decisions are really made outside the executive committee meetings. The executive committee convenes to approve a decision and have "holy water" placed on it.

Exhibit 32-2 Contradictory statements.

What accounts for these contradictions? My explanation is that over time the executives had come to mirror, in their behavior, the values of their culture (e.g., be rational, nonemotional, diplomatically open, and so on). They had created a culture that reinforced their own leadership styles. If an executive wanted to behave differently, he probably ran the risk of being considered a deviant. In most of the cases the executives decided to forgo this risk, and they behaved like the majority. These men, in order to live with themselves, probably had to develop various defenses and blinders about their acquiescence to an executive culture that may not have been the one they personally preferred and valued.

Incidentally, in this group there were two men who had decided to take the other route. Both men were viewed by the others as "a bit rough at the edges" or "a little too aggressive."

To check the validity of some of the findings reported, we interviewed the top 25 executives below the executive committee. If our analysis was correct, we knew, then they should tend to report that the members of the executive committee were low in openness to uncomfortable information, risk taking, trust, and capacity to deal with conflicts openly, and high in conformity. The results were as predicted (see Exhibit 32-3).

Blind Spots

Another result found in all organizations studied is the tendency for executives to be unaware of the negative feelings that their subordinates have about them. This finding is not startling in view of the fact

	Low	Moderate	High
Characteristic rated:			
Openness to uncomfortable information*	12	6	4
Risk taking	20	4	1
Trust	14	9	2
Conformity	0	2	23
Ability to deal with conflict	19	6	0

*Three executives gave a "don't know" response.

Exhibit 32-3 How the executive committee was rated by twenty-five executives below it.

that the executive problem-solving processes do not tend to reward the upward communication of information about interpersonal issues that is emotionally laden and risky to communicate. To illustrate:

In one organization, all but one of the top executive committee members reported that their relationships with their subordinates were "relatively good to excellent." When asked how they judged their relationships, most of the executives responded with such statements as: "They do everything that I ask for willingly," and "We talk together frequently and openly."

The picture from the middle management men who were the immediate subordinates was different. Apparently, top management was unaware that:

• 71% of the middle managers did not know where they stood with their superiors; they considered their relationships as ambiguous, and they were not aware of such important facts as how they were being evaluated.
• 65% of the middle managers did not know what qualities led to success in their organizations.
• 87% felt that conflicts were very seldom coped with; and that when they were, the attempts tended to be inadequate.
• 65% thought that the most important unsolved problem of the organization was that the top management was unable to help them overcome the intergroup rivalries, lack of cooperation, and poor communications; 53% said that if they could alter one aspect of their superior's behavior, it would be to help him see the "dog eat dog" communication problems that existed in middle management.
• 59% evaluated top management effectiveness as not too good or about average; and 62% reported that the development of a cohesive management team was the second most important unsolved problem.
• 82% of the middle managers wished that the status of their function and job could be increased

but doubted if they could communicate this openly to the top management.

Interestingly, in all the cases that I have observed where the president asked for a discussion of any problems that the top and middle management men present thought important, the problems mentioned above were never raised.

Rather, the most frequently mentioned problem (74% of the cases) was the overload problem. The executives and managers reported that they were overloaded and that the situation was getting worse. The president's usual reply was that he appreciated their predicament, but "that is life." The few times he asked if the men had any suggestions, he received such replies as "more help," "fewer meetings," "fewer reports," "delay of schedules," and so on. As we will see, few of these suggestions made sense, since the men were asking either for increases in costs or for a decrease in the very controls that the top management used to administer the organization.

Distrust and Antagonism

Another result of the behavior patterns earlier described is that management tends to keep promotions semisecret and most of the actual reasons for executive changes completely secret. Here is an example from an organization whose board we studied in some detail over a period of two years:

The executives complained of three practices of the board about which the board members were apparently unaware: (1) the constant alteration of organizational positions and charts, and keeping the most up-to-date versions semiconfidential; (2) shifting top executives without adequate discussion with all executives involved and without clearly communicating the real reasons for the move; and (3) developing new departments with product goals that overlapped and competed with the goals of already existing departments.

The board members admitted these practices but tended not to see them as being incompatible with the interests of the organization. For example, to take the first complaint, they defended their practice with such statements as: "If you tell them everything, all they do is worry, and we get a flood of rumors"; "The changes do not *really* affect them"; and, "It will only cut in on their busy schedule and interrupt their productivity."

The void of clear-cut information from the board was, however, filled in by the executives. Their explanations ranged from such statements as "They must be changing things because they are not happy with the way things are going" to "The unhappiness is so strong they do not tell us." Even the executives who profited from some of these moves reported some concern and bewilderment. For example, three reported instances where they had been promoted over some "old-timers." In all cases they were told to "soft-pedal the promotion aspect" until the old-timers were diplomatically informed. Unfortunately, it took months to inform the latter men, and in some cases it was never done.

There was another practice of the board that produced difficulties in the organization:

Department heads cited the board's increasing intervention into the detailed administration of a department when its profit picture looked shaky. This practice was, from these subordinates' view, in violation of the stated philosophy of decentralization.

When asked, board members tended to explain this practice by saying that it was done only when they had doubts about the department head's competence, and then it was always in the interests of efficiency. When they were alerted about a department that was not doing well, they believed that the best reaction was to tighten controls, "take a closer and more frequent look," and "make sure the department head is on top of things." They quickly added that they did not tell the man in question they were beginning to doubt his competence for fear of upsetting him. Thus, again we see how the values of deemphasizing the expression of negative feelings and the emphasizing of controls influenced the board's behavior.

The department heads, on the other hand, reported different reactions. "Why are they bothered with details? Don't they trust me? If not, why don't they say so?" Such reactions tended to produce more conformity, antagonism, mistrust, and fear of experimenting.

Still another board practice was the "diplomatic" rejection of an executive's idea that was, in the eyes of the board, offbeat, a bit too wild, or not in keeping with the corporate mission. The reasons given by the board for not being open about the evaluation again reflected adherence to the pyramidal values. For example, a board member would say, "We do not want to embarrass them," or "If you really tell them, you might restrict creativity."

This practice tended to have precisely the impact that the superiors wished to *avoid*. The subordinates reacted by asking, "Why don't they give me an opportunity to explain it?" or "What do they mean when they suggest that the 'timing is not right' or 'funds are not currently available'?"

Processes Damaged

It is significant that defensive activities like those described are rarely observed during group meetings dealing with minor or relatively routine decisions. These activities become most noticeable when the decision is an important one in terms of dollars or in terms of the impact on the various departments in the organization. *The forces toward ineffectiveness operate most strongly during the important decision-making meetings.* The group and organizational defenses operate most frequently when they can do the most harm to decision-making effectiveness.

Another interesting finding is that the more effective and more committed executives tend to be upset about these facts, whereas the less effective, less committed people tend simply to lament them. They also tend to take on an "I told them so" attitude—one of resignation and noninvolvement in correcting the situation. In short, it is the better executives who are negatively affected.

WHAT CAN BE DONE?

What can the executive do to change this situation?

I wish that I could answer this question as fully as I should like to. Unfortunately, I cannot. Nevertheless, there are some suggestions I can make.

Blind Alleys

First, let me state what I believe will *not* work.

Learning about these problems by listening to lectures, reading about them, exploring them through cases is not adequate; an article or book can pose some issues and get thinking started, but—in this area, at least—it cannot change behavior. Thus, in one study with 60 top executives:

Lectures were given and cases discussed on this subject for nearly a week. A test at the end of the week showed that the executives rated the lecturers very high, liked the cases, and accepted the diagnoses. Yet when they attempted to apply their new-found knowledge outside the learning situation, most were unable to do so. The major problem was that they had not learned how to make these new ideas come to life in their behavior.

As one executive stated, pointing to his head: "I know up here what I should do, but when it comes to a real meeting, I behave in the same old way. It sure is frustrating."[1]

Learning about these problems through a detailed diagnosis of executives' behavior is also not enough. For example:

I studied a top management group for nearly four months through interviews and tape recordings of their decision-making meetings. Eventually, I fed back the analysis. The executives agreed with the diagnosis as well as with the statement by one executive that he found it depressing. Another executive, however, said he now felt that he had a clearer and more coherent picture of some of the causes of their problems, and he was going to change his behavior. I predicted that he would probably find that he would be unable to change his behavior—and even if he did change, his subordinates, peers, and superiors might resist dealing with him in the new way.

The executive asked, "How can you be so sure that we can't change?" I responded that I knew of no case where managers were able to alter successfully their behavior, their group dynamics, and so forth by simply realizing intellectually that such a change was necessary. The key to success was for them to be able to show these new strategies in their behavior. To my knowledge, behavior of this type, groups with these dynamics, and organizational cultures endowed with these characteristics were very difficult to change. What kind of thin-skinned individuals would they be, how brittle would their groups and their organizations be if they could be altered that easily?

Three of the executives decided that they were going to prove the prediction to be incorrect. They took my report and studied it carefully. In one case the executive asked his subordinates to do the same. Then they tried

to alter their behavior. According to their own accounts, they were unable to do so. The only changes they reported were (1) a softening of the selling activities, (2) a reduction of their aggressive persuasion, and (3) a genuine increase in their asking for the subordinates' views.

My subsequent observations and interviews uncovered the fact that the first two changes were mistrusted by the subordinates, who had by now adapted to the old behavior of their superiors. They tended to play it carefully and to be guarded. This hesitation aggravated the executives, who felt that their subordinates were not responding to their new behavior with the enthusiasm that they (the superiors) had expected.

However, *the executives did not deal with this issue openly*. They kept working at trying to be rational, patient, and rewarding. The more irritated they became and the more they showed this irritation in their behavior, the more the subordinates felt that the superiors' "new" behavior was a gimmick.

Eventually, the process of influencing subordinates slowed down so much that the senior men returned to their more controlling styles. The irony was that in most cases the top executives interpreted the subordinates' behavior as proof that they needed to be needled and pushed, while the subordinates interpreted the top managers' behavior as proof that they did not trust their assistants and would never change.

The reason I doubt that these approaches will provide anything but temporary cures is that they do not go far enough. If changes are going to be made in the behavior of an executive, if trust is to be developed, if risk taking is to flourish, he must be placed in a different situation. He should be helped to (a) expose his leadership style so that he and others can take a look at its true impact; (b) deepen his awareness of himself and the dynamics of effective leadership; and (c) strive for these goals under conditions where he is in control of the amount, pace, and depth of learning.

These conditions for learning are difficult to achieve. Ideally, they require the help of a professional consultant. Also, it would be important to get away from the organization—its interruptions, pressures, and daily administrative tensions.

Value of Questions

The executive can strive to be aware that he is probably programmed with a set of values which cause him to behave in ways that are not always

---

[1]See my article, "Explorations in Interpersonal Competence II," *Applied Behavioral Science*, Vol. 1, No. 3, 1965, p. 255.

helpful to others and which his subordinates will not discuss frankly even when they believe he is not being helpful. He can also strive to find time to uncover, through careful questioning, his impact on others. Once in a while a session that is focused on the "How am I doing?" question can enlighten the executive and make his colleagues more flexible in dealing with him.

One simple question I have heard several presidents ask their vice presidents with success is: "Tell me what, if anything, I do that tends to prevent (or help) your being the kind of vice president you wish to be?" These presidents are careful to ask these questions during a time when they seem natural (e.g., performance review sessions), or they work hard ahead of time to create a climate so that such a discussion will not take the subordinate by surprise.

Some presidents feel uncomfortable in raising these questions, and others point out that the vice presidents are also uncomfortable. I can see how both would have such feelings. A chief executive officer may feel that he is showing weakness by asking his subordinates about his impact. The subordinate may or may not feel this way, but he may sense that his chief does, and that is enough to make him uncomfortable.

Yet in two companies I have studied where such questions were asked, superiors and subordinates soon learned that authority which gained strength by a lack of openness was weak and brittle, whereas authority resting on open feedback from below was truly strong and viable.

Working with the Group

Another step that an executive can take is to vow not to accept group ineffectiveness as part of life. Often I have heard people say, "Groups are no damned good; strong leadership is what is necessary." I agree that many groups are ineffective. I doubt, however, if either of the two leadership patterns described earlier will help the situation. As we have seen, both patterns tend to make the executive group increasingly less effective.

If my data are valid, the search process in executive decision making has become so complicated that group participation is essential. No one man seems to be able to have all the knowledge necessary to make an effective decision. If individual contributions are necessary in group meetings, it is important that a climate be created that does not discourage innovation, risk taking, and honest leveling between managers in their conversations with one another. The value of a group is to maximize individual contributions.

Interestingly, the chief executive officers in these studies are rarely observed making policy decisions in the classic sense, viz., critical selections from several alternatives and determination of future directions to be taken. This does not mean that they shy away from taking responsibility. Quite the contrary. Many report that they enjoy making decisions by themselves. Their big frustration comes from realizing that most of the major decisions they face are extremely complex and require the coordinated, honest inputs of many different executives. They are impatient at the slowness of meetings, the increasingly quantitative nature of the inputs, and, in many cases, their ignorance of what the staff groups did to the decision inputs long before they received them.

The more management deals with complexity by the use of computers and quantitative approaches, the more it will be forced to work with inputs of many different people, and the more important will be the group dynamics of decision-making meetings. If anyone doubts this, let him observe the dry runs subordinates go through to get a presentation ready for the top. He will observe, I believe, that much data are included and excluded by subordinates on the basis of what they believe those at the top can hear.

In short, *one of the main tasks of the chief executive is to build and maintain an effective decision-making network.* I doubt that he has much choice *except* to spend time in exploring how well his group functions.

Such explorations could occur during the regular workday. For example:

In one organization the president began by periodically asking members of his top group, immediately after a decision was made, to think back during the meeting and describe when they felt that the group was not being as effective as they wished. How could these conditions be altered?

As trust and openness increased, the members began to level with each other as to when they were inhibited, irritated, suppressed, confused, and withholding information. The president tried to be as encouraging as he could, and he especially rewarded people who truly leveled. Soon the executives began to think of mechanisms they could build into their group functioning so they would be alerted to these group problems and correct them early. As one man said, "We have not eliminated all our problems, but we are building a competence in our group to deal with them effectively if and when they arise."

Utilizing Feedback

Another useful exercise is for the superior and his group members to tape-record a decision-making meeting, especially one which is expected to be difficult. At a later date, the group members can gather and listen to the tape. I believe it is safe to say that simply listening to the tape is an education in itself. If one can draw from skilled company or outside help, then useful analyses can be made of group or individual behavior.

Recently, I experimented with this procedure with an "inside" board of directors of a company. The directors met once a month and listened to tape recordings of their monthly board meetings. With my help they analyzed their behavior, trying to find how they could improve their individual and group effectiveness. Listening to tapes became a very involving experience for them. They spent nearly four hours in the first meeting discussing less than ten minutes of the tape.

"Binds" Created   One of the major gains of these sessions was that the board members became aware of the "binds" they were creating for each other and of the impact they each had on the group's functioning. Thus:

Executive A was frequently heard antagonizing Executive B by saying something that B perceived as "needling." For example, A might seem to be questioning B's competence. "Look here," he would say, "anyone who can do simple arithmetic should realize that. . . ."

Executive B responded by fighting. B's way of fighting back was to utilize his extremely high capacity to verbalize and intellectualize. B's favorite tactic was to show A where he missed five important points and where his logic was faulty.

Executive A became increasingly upset as the "barrage of logic" found its mark. He tended to counteract by (a) remaining silent but manifesting a sense of being flustered and becoming redfaced; and/or (b) insisting

that his logic *was* sound even though he did not express it in "highfalutin language" as did B.

Executive B pushed harder (presumably to make A admit he was wrong) by continuing his "barrage of logic" or implying that A could not see his errors because he was upset.

Executive A would respond to this by insisting that he was not upset. "The point you are making is so simple, why, anyone can see it. Why should I be upset?"

Executive B responded by pushing harder and doing more intellectualizing. When Executive A eventually reached his breaking point, he too began to shout and fight.

At this point, Executives C, D, and E could be observed withdrawing until A and B wore each other out.

Progress Achieved   As a result of the meetings, the executives reported in interviews, board members experienced fewer binds, less hostility, less frustration, and more constructive work. One member wondered if the group had lost some of its "zip," but the others disagreed. Here is an excerpt from the transcript of one discussion on this point:

Executive A: My feeling is, as I have said, that we have just opened this thing up, and I for one feel that we have benefited a great deal from it. I think I have improved; maybe I am merely reflecting the fact that you [Executive B] have improved. But at least I think there has been improvement in our relationship. I also see signs of not as good a relationship in other places as there might be.

I think on the whole we are much better off today than we were a year ago. I think there is a whole lot less friction today than there was a year ago, but there's still enough of it.

Now we have a much clearer organization setup; if we were to sit down here and name the people, we would probably all name exactly the same people. I don't think there is much question about who should be included and who should not be included; we've got a pretty clean organization.

Executive B: You're talking now about asking the consultant about going on with this week's session?

Executive A: It would be very nice to have the consultant if he can do it; then we should see how we can do it without him, but it'd be better with him.

Executive B: But that's the step, as I understand it, that should be taken at this stage. Is that right?

Executive A: Well, I would certainly favor doing

something; I don't know what. I'm not making a specific recommendation; I just don't like to let go of it.

Executive C: What do you think?

Executive D: I'm not as optimistic as A. I wonder if anybody here agrees with me that maybe we haven't made as much progress as we think. I've personally enjoyed these experiences, and I'd like to see them continued.

Executive A: Would you like to venture to say why I think we have made progress and why I might be fooled?

Executive D: Well, I think maybe you are in the worst position to evaluate progress because if the worst possible thing that can happen is for people to no longer fight and struggle, but to say, "yes, sir," you might call that progress. That might be the worst thing that could happen, and I sort of sense some degree of resignation—I don't think it's progress. I don't know. I might be all alone in this. What do you think?

Executive C: On one level it is progress. Whether it is institutional progress and whether it produces commensurate institutional benefits is a debatable question. It may in fact do so. I think it's very clear that there is in our meetings and in individual contact less heat, less overt friction, petulance, tension, than certainly was consistently the case. Do you agree?

Executive D: Yes, I think so.

Executive C: It has made us a great deal more aware of the extent and nature of the friction and clearly has made all of us intent on fighting less. There's some benefit to it; but there are some drawbacks.

Executive A: Well, if you and D are right, I would say for that reason we need more of the program.

Laboratory Training

Another possibility is for the executive to attend a program designed to help increase competence in this area, such as laboratory education and its various offshoots ("T-groups," the "managerial grid," "conflict management labs," and so on[2]). These learning experiences are available at various university and National Training Laboratory executive programs. They can also be tailor-made for the individual organization.

I believe outside programs offer the better way of becoming acquainted with this type of learning. Bear in mind, though, that since typically only one or two executives attend from the same organization, the biggest payoff is for the individual. The inside program provides greater possibilities for payoff to the organization.

At the same time, however, it should also be kept in mind that in-house programs *can* be dangerous to the organization. I would recommend that a thorough study be made ahead of time to ascertain whether or not a laboratory educational experience would be helpful to company executives individually and to the organization.

Open Discussion

I have never observed a group whose members wanted it to decay. I have never studied a group or an organization that was decaying where there were not some members who were aware that decay was occurring. Accordingly, one key to group and organizational effectiveness is to get this knowledge out into the open and to discuss it thoroughly. The human "motors" of the group and the organization have to be checked periodically, just as does the motor of an automobile. Without proper maintenance, all will fail.

[2]For detailed discussions of such variations see my article, "T-Groups for Organizational Effectiveness," *Harvard Business Review* March–April 1964, p. 60; R. R. Blake, J. S. Mouton, L. B. Barnes, and L. E. Greiner, "Breakthrough in Organization Development," *Harvard Business Review* November–December 1964, p. 135; and Edgar Schein and Warren Bennis, *Personal and Organizational Change Through Laboratory Methods* (New York, Wiley, 1965).

Reading 33

Role Negotiation: A Tough-Minded Approach to Team Development

Roger Harrison

The development of psychological mindedness among business executives has been associated with a philosophical trend in behavioral science which is concerned primarily with human relations. It tends to be egalitarian rather than elitist, oriented toward the development of persons rather than task efficiency, and concerned with feelings, attitudes and interpersonal relationships rather than with power and authority or knowledge and competence. In its application to human relations in work, practitioners in this tradition tend to work for the development in the organization of openness of communication, collaborative relationships based on mutual trust, and democratic decision making in small groups. The assumption underlying such approaches is that people will function effectively in work settings if they can be taught to treat one another with trust, openness, acceptance and understanding. McGregor's Theory Y and Argyris's Interpersonal Competence are representative of the human relations tradition in behavioral theory and the T group exemplifies its application to managerial education and organization development.

A competing behavioral philosophy which has enjoyed considerable influence in some quarters may be termed achievement oriented. It is oriented towards production and achievement, finding interest and challenge in work using one's skills and knowledge. Practitioners work to develop the individual's abilities and creativity and his willingness to accept and exercise personal responsibility for decisions, productivity and quality. Herzberg's and McClelland's theories of the motivation to work are representative of this school of thought. Management by Objectives, Achievement Motivation Training and Job Enrichment are typical interventions flowing from these theories, as is the conscious attempt to push responsibility and decision making down to lower levels in the organization.

The underlying assumption here is that men work effectively when they are given opportunities to achieve, create, learn, accept responsibility. Human relations tend to be ignored or relegated to a lesser status (e.g., Herzberg's "hygiene factors").

Both of these dominant approaches may be termed tender minded, in that they tend to assume that people at work will be collaborative and productive if only the barriers to their doing so are removed. Competition, conflict and the struggle for power tend to be explained away. They may be seen as the result of frustration of basic needs for achievement, growth and relatedness. They may be explained as deriving from misperception of basically collaborative situations (seeing the situation as "win-lose" rather than as "win-win"), or as forced by roles in organizations which require people to compete. Competition, conflict and the struggle for power thus are seen as derivative, symptomatic *effects*, rather than as basic, ubiquitous *causes*. The problem of organizational change is seen as one of *releasing* human potential for collaboration and productivity, rather than as one of controlling or checking greed, competitiveness and exploitation.

I have worked in and from time to time contributed to the tender minded approaches of behavioral science to the problems of management and organization. My hopes and values are still with these optimistic and growth oriented views of the nature of man, but my experience increasingly convinces me that these approaches are incomplete and to some extent naive in that they fail to deal realistically or effectively with power and coercion. I increasingly see these latter processes as highly significant forces for both change and stability in organizations, and it begins to seem strange to me that behavioral scientists have so little that is constructive to say to managers about these forces. Most of what we have to say is negative: For example, we point out the restrictive effect of power differences on upward communication in the organization. But we are strangely silent when it comes to the *use* of power and coercion, as though power corrupts not only those who have it, but also those who study its use and function. Often we seem to be trying to convince managers not only that the use of their power is immoral, but that it is ineffective as well. We also imply to managers that their view of organizational reality is faulty. We tell them that what is most *real* is not the competitiveness, exploitation, coercion and control which they experience, but rather the drives toward openness, collaboration, productivity and responsibility which we see lying hidden and untapped in the humans who make up the organization. In some managerial education of which the T group is an example, we may encourage the manager to act in the organization as though our reality was actual and his was not. The results of the manager's acting on this teaching have been reported by my clients as painful and dangerous.

My growing conviction is that my clients have a more accurate and reality based map of the forces affecting them in their organizational lives than do my academic colleagues. Among other things, their map usually charts power and influence, and whether people are on their side or against them. Clearly marked are indications as to whom one can be open and honest with, and who will use the information you give against you. My clients do not chart an organizational world which is safe for openness, collaboration, creativity and personal growth.

I do not mean to imply that the more optimistic behavioral science approaches to business are so naive as to claim the world is quite safe for the processes they try to promote. What I am concerned about is the failure to work with the forces which *are* in ascendance. In this paper I shall present a modest program for working with human problems in organizations which does work directly with issues of power, competitiveness and coercion. The use of this method also involves an attempt to work from the clients' views of their problems and situations without making initial assumptions about what their "real" needs are, either for interpersonal relationships or for challenging and stimulating work.

This program which is called Role Negotiation makes one basic assumption: that most people in organizations prefer a fair negotiated settlement to a state of unresolved conflict. To operate the program a modest but significant risk is called for from the participants: They must be specific about what changes in behavior, authority, responsibility, etc., they wish to obtain from others in the situation. If the participants take the risk asked of them and do specify quite concretely the changes desired on the part of others, then significant changes in work group effectiveness can usually be obtained. I shall outline the rather simple series of steps in this program and then discuss why I think it represents a useful alternative to more tender minded approaches. For the sake of illustration we shall assume that a consultant is working with a natural work group of five to seven people which includes a boss and his subordinates, two levels in the formal organization.

PHASE 1: WARM UP

As in any team development work, some low threat activities are needed to reduce the mistrust of the consultant, establish his credibility and areas of competence and bring the group to talk more easily about work problems with the consultant. This phase may last a few minutes or several months, depending upon how sophisticated and confident the group is in the use of behavioral science resources. With one group this may take the form of long lunch and dinner meetings in which the consultant is probed and tested for soundness on a wide range of topics which may seem to have little to do with team development. The group appears to be trying indirectly to find out whether the consultant is "enough like us" to be trusted. Another group may wish to hear the consultant lecture on behavioral science topics and may then critically challenge and argue with him on the points which he raises. Another may wish to discuss problems which they have with other groups and levels in the organization before they deal with their internal difficulties. With other, more ready groups this phase may be dispensed with almost immediately in favor of the actual team development work. But I seldom work with any group which does not have some need to test me as a person and as a professional before serious work can begin. When I try to hurry this stage too much it usually results in ineffective work in the next phases.

PHASE 2: CONTRACT SETTING

This phase merges naturally with the previous one, and there is often no clear dividing line between them. Its purpose is to get clear between the group and the consultant what each may expect from the other. This is a critical step in the change process. It controls and channels everything which happens afterwards. I work toward a contract with the following provisions which it is helpful to get written down as a first practice step in the rather formal way of working which I try to establish.

1 It is not legitimate for the consultant to press or probe anyone's *feelings*. We are concerned about work: who does what, how and with whom. How people feel about their work or about others in the group is their own business, to be introduced or not according to their own judgment and desire. The expression or nonexpression of feelings is not part of the contract. The consultant agrees to adopt a laissez faire role with respect to expression of feelings.

2 Openness and honesty about *behavior* are expected and essential for the achievement of results. This means
   a   that the consultant will ask for full disclosure about *what* work people do, *how* they do it, and *with whom* they do it; and
   b   that the consultant will probe for people to be specific and concrete in expressing their expectations and demands for the *behavior* of others. Each team member is expected to be open and specific about what he wants others to do *more* or *do better* or *do less* or maintain unchanged.

3 No expectation or demand is adequately communicated until it has been *written down* and is clearly understood by both sender and receiver, or will any change process be engaged in until this has been done.

4 The full sharing of expectations and demands does not constitute a completed change process. It is only the precondition for change to be agreed through negotiation. It is unreasonable for anyone in the group, boss or subordinate, to expect that any change will take place merely as a result of communicating a demand or expectation. Unless a team member is willing to change his own behavior in order to get what he wants from the other(s), he is likely to waste his and the group's time talking about the issue. When a member makes a request or demand for changed behavior on the part of another, the consultant will always ask what quid pro quo (something for something) he is willing to give in order to get what he wants. This goes for the boss as well as for the subordinates. If the boss can get what he wants simply by issuing orders or clarifying expectations from his position of authority, he probably does not need a consultant or a change process.

5 The change process is essentially one of bargaining and negotiation in which two or more members each agree to change behavior in exchange for some desired change on the part of the other. This process is not complete until the agreement can be *written down* in terms which include the agreed changes in behavior and make clear what each party is expected to give in return.

6 Threats and pressures are neither illegitimate nor excluded from the negotiation process. However, group members should realise that overreliance on the negative quid pro quo usually results in defensiveness, concealment, decreased communication and retaliation, and may lead to breakdown of the negotiation. The consultant will do his best to help members to accomplish their aims with positive incentives wherever possible.

During the discussion of the contract, I try to help participants see that each member has power and influence in the group, both positively to reward and collaborate with others, and negatively to resist, block or punish. Each uses his power and influence to create a desirable and satisfying work situation for himself. When this process takes place covertly and/or only partly consciously, people often use much time and energy in it unproductively. It is unproductive because people are often unsure about others' desires and intentions. This makes it difficult to judge how a particular pressure or proffered reward will be responded to. We often judge others' wants and needs as though they were as our own. We "do unto others as we would have them do unto us," and because they are not in all respects like us, our ignorance results in ineffectiveness. We make guesses about how others will respond to our attempts to influence their behavior, and when the guesses are wrong we have no option other than to continue the laborious process of trial and error, slowly building up our knowledge of what is and is not effective with each other person through a clumsy and not very systematic experimentation.

In stable, slowly changing organizational situations, this trial and error process may be satisfactory, because people do learn how to influence one another given a sufficient period of contact. When situations and personnel change more rapidly (over periods of months rather than years), then this most primitive learning process does not do the job fast enough. The more fluid the system, the more important it is to develop information rapidly which will permit people to influence one another effectively. I try to get my clients to see that if information about desires and intentions is equally shared, then they will all increase the effectiveness of their influence attempts. Further, when others try to influence them the proffered quid pro quo will be more likely to be one which they really want and need. Following the terms of the contract will then not only have the effect of resolving current problems but also of increasing knowledge within the group of how effectively to influence one another. The intended effect is that the *total amount of influence of group members on one another should increase*. There is no intention that the amount of influence one member exerts relative to that of another should change or stay the same. This is left free to vary, but the consultant so conducts himself that opportunities to increase one's influence within the system are as nearly equal as possible.

PHASE 3: DIAGNOSIS

The next stage in the Role Negotiation process is for the group and the consultant to develop a shared understanding of how work actually gets done in the group. In diagnosis, I focus on decision making and communication, as these are the vehicles by which power and influence are exercised in the organization. Any of the following activities may be helpful in clarifying work processes.

1 Find out and list what are the major *kinds* of decisions which are made by members of the group.

2 For each type of decision, list *who* is involved, in order of the influence which each has on the final outcome.

3 Draw an organization chart in which the vertical dimension indicates the number and importance of decisions in which the individual plays a key role.

4 Connect members on the chart by "communication lines" as follows:

    a _____ frequent communication on important matters

    b _____ regular communication on important matters

    c _____ occasional communication on important matters

5 Add arrows to the above lines, indicating who generally initiates the communication.

6 Discuss the organization chart, raising questions about how the work of the group is conducted and decisions made (e.g., how many layers are involved in decisions? why? why are some people involved or left out of some decisions? is this the kind of organization the group members feel is most effective? if not, how should it be different?)

These diagnostic activities are useful for the consultant if he does not know the group's operations and relationships very well, and they serve as a second warm up activity for the group. They are somewhat less personal and threatening than the more confronting diagnostic activities to which we turn next.

7 Ask each person by himself to consider the organization charts and the lists of decisions and to reflect on his satisfactions and dissatisfactions with the way business is conducted within the group. What things would he change if he could? What things would he particularly like to keep as they are? Who and what would have to change in order to improve things?

Each member is asked to take a paper, one piece for each other member of the group, and to consider and list for each person things which influence the writer's work effectiveness. For each person he makes three lists.

    a   Those things which the other person should do *more* or do *better*.

    b   Those things which the other should do *less*.

    c   Those things the other does which facilitate the writer's effectiveness and should not be changed.

These lists are exchanged so that each person has all the lists which pertain to his work behavior. Each member makes a master list for himself on a large piece of (flip chart) paper on which he shows the behavior which each other person desires him to do *more* or *better, less,* or *continue* unchanged. These are posted so that the entire group can peruse and refer to each list. Each member is allowed to question the others who have sent messages about his behavior, querying the what? why? and how? of their requests, but no one is allowed a rebuttal, defence or even a yes or no reply to the messages he has received. The consultant intervenes in the discussion to make sure that only clarification is taking place and that argument, discussion and decision making about issues is not engaged in at this stage.

The purpose of this rather rigid and formal control on communication by the consultant is to make sure that the group does not have a negative problem solving experience and that members do not get polarized on issues or take up extreme positions which they will feel impelled to defend in order to save face. Communication is controlled in order to prevent escalation of actual or potential conflicts. The strategy is to channel the energy which has been generated or released by the sharing of demands and expectations into successful problem solving and mutual influence. The consultant intervenes to inhibit hostile and destructive expression at this point and later to facilitate constructive bargaining and negotiation of mutually beneficial agreements. This initial sharing of desires and change goals leads to a point at which the team development process is most vulnerable, because if sufficient anger and defensiveness are generated by the problem sharing, the consultant will not be able to hold the negative processes in check long enough for the development of the positive problem solving spiral on which the process depends for its effectiveness. However, my guess is that groups in which the latent anger is too great will usually avoid the team development activity altogether; at any rate, such an uncontrollable breakthrough of hostility has not yet occurred in my experience with the method. My concern over the negative possibilities is in part responsible for the slow, deliberate and rather formal development of the confrontation of issues within the group.

PHASE 4: NEGOTIATION

After each member has had an opportunity to clarify the messages he has received, the group proceeds to the selection of issues for negotiation. The consultant begins this phase by reemphasizing that unless a quid pro quo can be offered in return for a desired behavior change, there is little point in having a discussion about it: *unless behavior changes on both sides the most likely prediction is that the status quo will continue.* (It can be argued that this is an extremely conservative point of view and that behavior does in fact change between men of good will simply as a result of an exchange of views. While I do not deny that this occurs, I do not assume it in my practice and I allow myself to be pleasantly surprised when it happens!).

Each participant is asked to indicate two or more issues on which he particularly wants to get some change on the part of another. He is also asked to select one or more issues on which he feels it may be possible for him to move in the direction desired by others. He does this by marking his own flip chart and those of the other members. In effect, each person is indicating the issues upon which he most wants to exert influence and those on which he is most willing to accept influence. With the help of the consultant the group then goes through the lists to select the "most negotiable issues," those where there is a combination of a high desire for change on the part of an initiator and a willingness to negotiate on the part of the person whose behavior is the target of the change attempt. The consultant asks for a group of two or more persons who are involved in one such issue to volunteer for a negotiation demonstration before the rest of the group.

The negotiation process consists of the parties making contingent offers to one another of the form, "if you do X, I will do Y." The negotiation ends when all parties are satisfied that they will receive a reasonable return for whatever they are agreeing to give. The consultant asks that the agreement be formalized in writing which states specifically and concretely what each party is going to give and receive in the bargain. He also asks the participants to discuss openly what sanctions can be applied in the case of nonfulfillment of the bargain by one or another party. Often this involves no more than reversion to the status quo, but it may involve the application of pressures and penalties as well.

After the negotiation demonstration the members are asked to select other issues they wish to work on. A number of negotiations may go on simultaneously, the consultant being involved at the request of any party to any negotiation. All agreements are published to the entire group, however, and questioned by the consultant and the other members to test the good faith and reality orientation of the parties in making them. Where agreement proves impossible, the consultant and other group members try to help the parties find further incentives (positive or, less desirably, coercive) which they may bring to bear to encourage agreement.

This process is, of course, not so simple as the bare bones outlined here. All kinds of difficulties can occur, from bargaining in bad faith, to refusal to bargain at all, to dangerous escalation of conflict. In my experience, however, group members tend to be rather wise about the issues they can and cannot deal with, and I refrain from pushing them to negotiate issues they feel are unresolvable. My aim is to create a beginning to team development with a successful experience which group members will see as a fruitful way of improving their effectiveness and satisfaction. I try to go no further than the members feel is reasonable.

PHASE 5: FOLLOW UP

At the conclusion of a team development cycle as outlined above, I suggest that the group test the firmness of the agreements they have negotiated by living with them awhile before trying to go further. We can then get together later to review the agreement, renegotiate ones which have not held or which are no longer viable, and continue the team development process by dealing with new issues. Hopefully, the group will eventually take over the conduct of the Role Negotiation activity and the consultant's role will whither away. This can occur when the group has developed sufficient control over the dangers, avoidances and threats involved in the negotiation process that they no longer need third party protection or encouragement. However, I do not claim any greater success than my tender minded colleagues in freeing clients from dependence on my services. What I do find is that there is less backsliding between visits in teams I have

worked with using this method than when I have applied more interpersonally oriented change interventions. The agreements obtained through Role Negotiation seem to have more "teeth" in them than those which rely on the softer processes of interpersonal trust and openness. This is not a description of the world as I wish it to be; it is how I find it.

THE DYNAMICS OF ROLE NEGOTIATION

Role Negotiation intervenes directly into the relationships of power, authority and influence within the group. The change effort is directed at the work relationships among members. It encourages members to attempt to change their roles vis-à-vis one another, hence the name, Role Negotiation. Role Negotiation avoids probing into the likes and dislikes of members for one another and their personal feelings about one another. In this it is more consonant with the task oriented organizational norms of impersonality than are more interpersonal interventions. I have found that groups with whom I have had difficulty working when I focused on interpersonal issues dropped their resistance and returned willingly to problem solving when I shifted my approach to Role Negotiation. Clients seem more at home with problems of power and influence than they do with interpersonal issues. They feel more competent and less dependent upon the skill and trustworthiness of the consultant in dealing with these issues, and so they are ready to work sooner and harder. I also find my own skill not so central to the change process as it is when I am dealing with interpersonal issues. Because clients are less dependent upon the consultant, I suspect that the amount of skill and professional training which is required to conduct Role Negotiation is less than for more sensitive approaches.

This is not to say that Role Negotiation poses no threat to organization members. The consultant asks participants to be open about matters which are often covert in normal life. The effect of a thorough Role Negotiation is to expose the *real* power and influence of organization members, and this may be either more or less than they would wish to have known. Both those who bluff and those who operate behind the scenes may feel their positions threatened by the open discussion of influence processes which is the stuff of Role Negotiation. Persons who rely upon their formal authority and status for personal security may be discomfited by the revelation that some others in the group pay only lip service to the formal authority and are more concerned about what they can get away with than about the rules and regulations. Conversely, these latter may feel it is to their advantage to conceal their true assessment of the realities of power and influence behind an appearance of loyal compliance. The processes of diagnosis and negotiation run counter to the political practices of concealment and deception. Resistance to negotiation develops when openness about needs, intentions and goals is felt to show weakness or expose one to manipulation or exploitation. For this reason it is likely that groups which are engaged in really serious internal political or power struggles will find it quite difficult to engage effectively in Role Negotiation.

I have, however, had success in working with groups in which more minor forms of politicking were going on. As mentioned above, members tend to limit the issues dealt with to those which they feel are safe. These provide a foothold for an opening up of communication and constructive problem solving. As members become more confident and adept with the process, they can bring more touchy issues into the arena. The method does not require that members proceed to expose issues more rapidly than they feel is to their advantage. Nor does the consultant try to establish a norm (or myth) of trust and good will. Rather he encourages members to deal with those issues they can tackle and to be aware of the limitations placed on this process by competition for personal advantage. The hope is that members will find gradually that they can achieve more for themselves by open negotiation than they can by private competition and that the more constructive process will in time replace the more restrictive and limiting one. This is a hope, not a promise. However, my experience convinces me that Role Negotiation is less sensitive and vulnerable to mistrust and seeking for personal advantage than approaches to team development which deal directly with interpersonal ano emotional issues.

Role Negotiation is vulnerable, however, in two ways. One is the failure of rewards and sanctions to motivate the agreed upon behavior. This may occur when the bargaining was conducted at a rather

superficial level or in bad faith (where there is a partly or wholly conscious intention to subvert the agreement). In such a case the incentives are simply not strong enough. Or it may happen that one party to the agreement continues to keep his part of the bargain even though the other defaults on his. This happens when the injured party is unwilling to precipitate open conflict. These are the kinds of issues we can expect to encounter in follow up sessions to the original Role Negotiation.

Another vulnerability is to external interventions which upset the balance of give and take achieved during a successful negotiation. Others, outside or inside the organization, may change so as to reward or punish behavior which was the subject of negotiation, making it less attractive to adhere to the original agreement. This may eventually make it necessary to widen the scope of the team development effort beyond the boundaries of the original team. A model for Intergroup Role Negotiation is, of course, practical. Indeed, the processes described in this paper have been applied to intergroup conflict resolution for much longer than they have been used for team development. An outcome of Role Negotiation as a team development approach is the development of skill in the processes of issue definition and negotiation which are useful in dealing with intergroup conflict. In this, Role Negotiation has an advantage over team development approaches based on openness, trust and caring. These latter tend to be ineffective in the initial stages of intergroup problem solving, when the groups are often oriented almost exclusively toward competition.

THE ECONOMICS OF ROLE NEGOTIATION

One disadvantage of interpersonal approaches to team development is that the level of skill and experience demanded of the consultant is very high indeed. Managers are not confident in dealing with these issues. Because they feel at risk they reasonably want to have as much safety and skill as money can buy. The great demand for skilled consultants on interpersonal and group processes has created an extreme shortage and a meteoric rise in consulting fees. It seems unlikely that the supply will soon catch up with the demand.

The shortage of highly skilled workers in team development argues for deskilling the requirements for effective consultant performance. Examples of deskilled approaches to team development are Robert Blake's Managerial Grid and Ralph Coverdale's training programs in group effectiveness, both of which steer away from deeper emotional issues with the team. I see Role Negotiation as another way of reducing the skill requirements for the consultant in team development. I hope and believe that Role Negotiation can be practiced by management development specialists with substantial experience in group work, a fair degree of personal sensitivity, and familiarity with behavioral science concepts. I do not think it demands professional training in the behavioral sciences or the ability to conduct T groups.

A SUMMARY COMPARISON OF ROLE NEGOTIATION WITH HUMAN RELATIONS ORIENTED APPROACHES

The following comparison highlights the differences between the Role Negotiation approach and the tender minded interpersonal approaches which I feel are direct competitors with it. The differences have been highlighted rather than the similarities to define more sharply the Role Negotiation approach.

Human Relations Approach

Assumes people collaborate naturally if we remove the barriers of suspicion, mistrust and stereotyped perception. At bottom, people's interests are similar and compatible. They will tend to be trustworthy, mutually supportive, and helpful if they are given a chance.

The effective alternative to competition is trust, openness and voluntary collaboration.

Diagnosis of difficulties focuses on the perceptions, needs, attitudes and feelings of persons toward one another's personal style.

Resolution of interpersonal difficulties is approached by working toward understanding and acceptance of one another's needs, attitudes and feelings.

The targets of change are interpersonal relationships: trust, confidence, openness, acceptance and understanding among persons.

The forces maintaining changes come from the desire of persons to maintain satisfying relationships of openness, caring and trust.

Changes are vulnerable to
1 erosion of trust and openness when persons follow organizational norms and requirements for impersonal behavior toward one another;
2 role requirements which are incompatible with trust, collaboration and caring;
3 competition between commitment to tasks and commitment to persons when these compete for scarce time and personal resources.

Role Negotiation

Assumes people have truly different and sometimes opposed interests. Conflict and competition are normal, natural states of affairs. People will try to maximize what they perceive to be their own interests. If it is to their advantage, they can be expected to be exploitative, untrustworthy and competitive.

The effective alternative to competition and mistrust is a negotiated agreement based on enforceable guarantees of mutual observance.

Diagnosis of difficulties focuses on the rights, powers, privileges, demands and requirements which incumbents of roles have with respect to one another.

Resolution of differences is approached by working toward negotiated settlement of differences based on a quid pro quo.

The targets of change are working relationships: duties, responsibilities, authority, and accountability of persons in roles.

The forces maintaining changes come from the ability and willingness of parties to an agreement to administer and withhold rewards and sanctions for others' compliance with or violation of negotiated agreements.

Changes are vulnerable to
1 failure of the original agreement to be based on sufficiently potent rewards and sanctions;
2 unwillingness or inability of either party to apply rewards or sanctions to enforce agreements;
3 imbalance of rewards and sanctions caused by third party intervention from parties outside the agreement.

TOWARD AN INTEGRATION OF THE HUMAN RELATIONS AND ROLE NEGOTIATION APPROACHES

I have in this paper contrasted the human relations and Role Negotiation approaches. In doing so I have emphasized the differences between them in order to highlight the unique characteristics of the Role Negotiation methods and give them a promising and attractive image. Yet it seems to me that the two approaches may bear an organic and developmental relationship to each other, in which the Role Negotiation methods lay the groundwork for effective and lasting work at the interpersonal and emotional levels. I believe that the process of getting responsibility, authority, accountability and competition for rewards under control and subject to agreement forms the necessary basis for resolution of interpersonal problems. If we try to skip this more mundane step, the harder, tougher issues pose a continual threat to resolutions based on tender minded assumptions. I think that if we can achieve stable, viable resolutions of the hard issues they may then form a realistic basis for the trust and openness without which interpersonal problem solving is impossible.

Role Negotiation may now facilitate the transition towards a greater depth and interpersonal confrontation. For example, I have used it in this way in a T group where the managers (strangers to each other) were uneasy about dealing directly with interpersonal issues. The Role Negotiation focused on behavior changes which members wanted from one another. The structural support and the emphasis on behavior rather than upon feelings reduced the threat of dealing with interpersonal issues. The emphasis on the quid pro quo as a basis for negotiated change legitimized resistance to change and provided individuals with protection against group conformity pressures. I and the participants felt the method provided a safe and effective way of moving into interpersonal issues. As the T group members developed more confidence, they found they could do without the structure and the extra safety. It had served its purpose.

This experience did not take place in an ongoing work group. The members did not have ambitions and goals as competitive as those I commonly find in client groups. It would be pleasant to think that a stable resolution of differences based on Role Negotiation could indeed pave the way for members to deal openly and understandingly with one another as persons. At present this is only a hope on my part. A tough minded approach continues to form the basis for effective work with the problems presented by my clients.

Reading 34

The Politics of Upward Influence in Organizations

Lyman W. Porter
Robert W. Allen
Harold L. Angle

The existence of political processes in organizations has been well recognized in the "popular" management press, yet a mid-1970s survey of more than seventy textbooks in industrial-organizational psychology, management, and organizational behavior revealed only seventy pages in which the topic of organizational politics was addressed—about two-tenths of one percent of the textbook content! A review of eight of the most appropriate academic journals revealed less than a dozen articles on the topic, out of a total of more than 1,700 articles over a sixteen-year period (Porter, 1976). In light of this scarcity of serious attention to the topic, it is our contention that a joint examination of organizational politics and upward influence may help point the way toward some important issues in analyzing behavior processes in organizations.

It is worth noting that the two topics are not unrelated. It appears reasonable to say that while not all (or even most) upward influence involves

Adapted from a chapter by the authors in B. Staw and L. Cummings (Eds.), *Research in Organizational Behavior.* (Vol. 3) Copyright © 1981 by JAI Press, Inc. Reprinted with permission.

political behavior, most political behavior (in organizations) does involve upward influence. Taking the first part of this statement, much of upward influence involves, of course, the normal routine reporting relationships that exist in all organizations. We would contend, however, that there is a substantial segment of upward influence that involves what can be labeled as "political behavior" (to be defined later). The other part of the statement about the realtionship between the two topics—that most political behavior in organizations involves upward influence—is based on the assumption that the typical object of influence will be someone or some group possessing more formal, legitimate power than the would-be political actor. While it is possible to cite clear exceptions to this proposition, we would, nevertheless, contend that the vast majority of *political* attempts at influence are in the upward direction.

In this paper, we intend to maintain a focus on political influence as an individual phenomenon. This is not because we consider coalitional political processes in organizations either uninteresting or unimportant. On the contrary, the many-on-one (or many-on-several) influence event is a fairly common fact of organizational life. However, we believe that the one-on-one political-influence situation is a particularly prevalent, albeit little-understood, organizational reality. In the ensuing analysis, therefore, the focus will be on gaining a better understanding of the decision logic of the individual "politician."

Before proceeding further, two definitional matters must be dealt with: (1) "upward influence," and (2) "political behavior." The first is simple, the second complex. For our purposes, we will define "upward influence" as an attempt or attempts to influence someone higher in the *formal hierarchy* of authority in the organization. The fact that the person attempting to exercise influence cannot rely on formal authority results in a situation that is distinctly different from that of downward influence.

"Political behavior in organizations," or "organizational politics," is not an easy term to define. Despite this, a number of authors have recently offered definitions (e.g., Frost & Hayes, 1977; Mayes & Allen, 1977; Robbins, 1976), and our definitional framework will be consistent generally with the thrust of these definitions. However, any one of them may not include all four of the elements contained in our definition. For the purposes of the present paper, "organizational political behavior" is defined as: social influence attempts that are (1) discretionary (i.e., outside the behavioral zones prescribed or prohibited by the formal organization), (2) intended (designed) to promote or protect the self-interests of individuals and groups (units), and (3) threaten the self-interests of others (individuals, units).

A few brief comments seem in order about each of the components of the definition. First, we take it as a given that regardless of what else it is, political behavior is behavior aimed at influencing others; behavior carried out in such a way that there are no intended direct effects on others would fall into the category of nonpolitical behavior. Second, any behavior that the organization ordinarily requires and expects is nonpolitical; e.g., coming to work every day and carrying out the assignments and expectations of the formal role. Likewise, behavior forbidden by formal rules or commonly accepted standards of behavior (e.g., fighting, stealing, etc.) would be excluded. That leaves discretionary behavior relating to the work situation (and meeting the other definitional requirements) as that which would be labeled "political." Third, we believe that the intention of promoting or protecting self-interests is a necessary (though not sufficient) element of political behavior. Of course, attributions of intention often vary widely between those who are the source of the behavior and those who are observing or labeling the behavior. It is our contention that if the behavior is *seen* by organizational participants as intended to promote or protect self-interests, then (meeting the other criteria) the label "political" is appropriate. Finally, we believe that unless the behavior threatens the self-interests of others, it is nonpolitical. This puts political behavior squarely in the camp of competitive as opposed to collaborative behavior, and focuses on the zero-sum aspect of organizational resource allocation. In the words of Frost and Hayes (1977), this last part of the definition emphasizes that political behavior is "nonconsensus" behavior.

KEY CONSIDERATIONS

Certain considerations emerge as particularly salient when one considers the present state of knowledge (or gaps in our knowledge) of political influence in organizations. What (if any) political norms exist in organizations, and how do organizational members learn about them? What situational factors influence the prevalence of political activity? Further, what kinds of individuals are prone to engage in organizational politics? Finally, what factors lead to the selection of particular organizational members as political-influence targets, and what methods are available, and preferred, for political influence?

Political Norms

Our definition of organizational politics has incorporated the notion that organizationally political behaviors fall outside the range of behaviors either prescribed or prohibited by the organization. At first blush, the implication would seem to be that "political" behaviors in organizations take place outside the normative framework. No such conclusion, however, is intended. It is very likely that strong norms do exist in organizations, relative to "political" activity. However, the basis for these norms will not be found in official prescriptions originated by the formal organization. Rather, the signals by which the organization member pieces together a picture of "political reality" originate from the informal organization, and are apt to be sent in disguised format and against a noisy background.

Two basic issues appear salient with respect to the micropolitical norms of upward influence. First, what norms exist? Do norms ever permit or prescribe upward political-influence attempts, or are all such attempts acts of deviance? What are the contingent factors? Do political norms differ in different parts of the organization? How does the goal or purpose behind an influence attempt bear upon its acceptability? Do norms prescribe or proscribe particular influence tactics?

A second general issue relates to the way political norms are learned in organizations. How clear are the "norm messages" regarding upward political influence? Are they transmitted "in the clear," or are they buried in subtlety and innuendo? This raises the parallel issue of norm consensus. Is there sufficient exchange of unambiguous norm information to permit consensual validation? How accurate are individual perceptions of the extent to which upward influence is attempted and the purpose or intent of the actor when such attempts are perceived?

Political Norm Structure

There is ample reason to believe that informal "political" norms abound in organizations. Schein (1977) asserted that political processes "may be as endemic to organizational life as planning, organizing, directing and controlling" (p. 64). It is unlikely, however, that these political norms are invariant, either across all situations or in all parts of the organization.

Political behavior that clearly would be considered "deviant" at certain times may be seen as less so at other times. For instance, it has been suggested that the process of allocating scarce organizational resources typically has two phases. In the earlier phase, conflict is clearly institutionalized. Interested parties are expected to maneuver and bargain, in order to clarify the organization's values, goals, and priorities (Frost & Hayes, 1977). Later on, after values, goals, and priorities have been defined, *consensus* rather than conflict becomes institutionalized. "Political" behaviors that may have been tolerated earlier are now considered clearly inappropriate.

Not only will political norms vary over time, they may also differ with location in the organization. One study, for example, found that more than 90 percent of managers interviewed reported that organizational politics occurred more frequently at upper and middle levels of management than at lower managerial levels (Madison et al., 1980). A related study (Allen et al., 1979b) found that lower-level managers describe the traits of political actors in more pejorative terms than do upper-level managers, indicating perhaps that political activity is more often considered counter-normative at lower hierarchical levels. In addition, managers in the Madison et al. study reported political activity as more prevalent in staff as opposed to line positions. Departments in which organizational politics were seen as most prevalent were marketing and sales, while accounting/finance and production were seen as lowest in political activity.

It appears, then, that the "politically active" functional areas are those in which uncertainty is most prevalent. Organizational members in such roles may need to rely on political skill to deal with the conflicting demands of intra- and extra-organizational associates. Thus, norms that favor political influence as a means of conducting the day's business may arise out of necessity in such subunits.

In summary, searching for the political norms of the organization as a whole might be far too simplistic a pursuit. We should, instead, be prepared to discover a mosaic of political-norm subsystems embedded in organizations.

Learning the Norms of Upward Political Influence

The period of organizational entry is always especially stressful. The initiate is faced with an intrinsically ambiguous yet crucial task—that of "learning the ropes." We believe that the learning of *political* norms will pose special difficulties. Unlike many organizational norms, these are exclusively the purview of the informal organization. Since the formal organization neither prescribes nor forbids political behaviors, such norms cannot be transmitted in the form of explicit organizational policy. Moreover, there are constraints on feasible modes of communication, even by the "informal" organization. Unlike the cues provided for other types of norms, political-norm cues frequently will be implicit, requiring considerable sensitivity on the part of the receiver. In this respect, messages regarding norms that *condone* political behaviors may be more vague than those that *condemn* such behaviors.

A key aspect of our definition of organizational politics is the idea that "political" behavior is self-serving but at the same time is not intended to serve others (or is intended, in fact, to misserve others). Such behavior, then, will be resisted *if recognized* by others (Frost & Hayes, 1977). The implication is that the actor often will take pains to conceal attempts at political influence, adding to the ambiguity encountered by observers.

In discussing the acquisition of organizational power, a pursuit closely related to political influence, Moberg (1977) asserted that societal norms require unobtrusiveness. "Politicians" must take care to avoid having others attribute their behavior to a self-serving intent. Creation of the impression that such behavior is legitimate (or nonexistent) may be accomplished by acting in ways that make reliable attributions difficult. Some of the "smokescreen" tactics aimed at manipulating observers' attributions might include making certain that there is a reasonably credible organizational rationale for one's actions, acting so enigmatically that observers lose confidence in their attributions, or publicly advocating a "version" or interpretation of organizational goals that actually serves personal objectives.

Such tactics can seriously undermine "political" social learning. One's ability to behave appropriately in a social situation is determined in part by the accuracy with which one perceives the existing system norms. It is commonly assumed that members of a social system both share and are aware of each other's norms for the behavior of all members (Biddle, 1964). However, when either communication or behavior observation is restricted, a state of "pluralistic ignorance" can exist. In effect, members of a social group might come to share a wholly mistaken view of the group's norms. Furthermore, the false consensus concerning these norms may become self-perpetuating. In view of the particular problems that surround the learning of political norms, it would appear the political-influence norms in organizations constitute a prime candidate for "pluralistic ignorance."

Thus, a misleading consensus may come to exist with respect to which "political" behaviors are condemned by the informal organization and which are condoned. This, in turn, may lead political actors to overestimate the extent of their own deviancy, resulting in their taking great pains to disguise their behavior. The vicious circle thus created can perpetuate a situation in which discovery of the "real" political norms in an organization may pose serious problems for researchers and organization members alike.

As we have seen, informal political norms are a critical contextual factor in the politics of upward influence. There are also other contextual considerations surrounding any potential political act. The following section discusses several such situational factors.

Situational Factors

There is some evidence that certain organizational situations tend to be intrinsically "political." Madison et al. (1980) reported that managers saw certain situations as characterized by relatively high levels of political activity. Examples of such situations included reorganization changes, personnel changes, and budget allocation. On the other hand, such organizational situations as rule and procedure changes, establishment of individual performance standards, and the purchase of major items were characterized as relatively low in prevalence of political activity. These differences were discussed by Madison et al. in terms of three variables: (1)

uncertainty, (2) importance of the activity to the larger organization, and (3) salience of the issue to the individual.

The situations in which political activity may be most prevalent seem to combine situational ambiguity with sufficient personal stake to activate the individual to consider actions that fall outside the boundaries of the formal organizational-norm system. While lack of structure or situational ambiguity may provide recognition of *opportunity* to engage in upward political influence, it is personal stake that may provide the *incentive* to engage in political behavior per se.

Another situational factor which appears particularly relevant to organizational politics is resource scarcity. The essence of the political process is the struggle over the allocation of scarce resources; i.e., who gets what, where and when (Lasswell, 1951). The relative abundance of resources represented by various organizational issues may have a great deal of influence regarding the extent to which "political" means become employed in their resolution.

While the preceding discussion of norms and of situational factors has described some aspects of what potential political actors *find* in the way of contextual factors—factors that may influence their "political" activity in the organization—it is also necessary to consider what the individual *brings* to the situation. These actor characteristics will now be considered.

Actor Characteristics

Each potential agent of upward political influence brings to the scene a rich array of personal characteristics. Such individual factors could easily lead two different organizational members either to perceive an identical situation differently or, even if they share identical perceptions, to behave characteristically in different ways. This now leads us to consider some particular classes of individual differences that might help predict organizational members' relative propensities to engage in upward political influence.

Beliefs about Action-Outcome Relationships   The truism that "organizational behavior is a function of its perceived consequences" is certainly as applicable in the arena of organizational politics as it is in other spheres of organizational life. It is a basic psychological tenet that behavior that has been rewarded in the past becomes more probable in the future.

From the perspective of expectancy theory (Vroom, 1964), it is believed that organization members behave in a manner that maximizes their net outcomes. This, in turn, suggests that organization members undertake a series of subjective cost-benefit analyses, using salient available information. Some of the more explicit information available is the political actor's knowledge of the results of past attempts at social influence. Thus, the individual's "expectancy set" regarding the efficacy of engaging in upward political influence will be at least in part determined by what has gone before.

Manifest Needs   Most substantive or content theories of human motivation are based on the premise that individuals harbor a relatively stable set of needs, and that these needs incite action directed toward need satisfaction. While the assumption base underlying the need-satisfaction paradigm has not gone unchallenged, the concept of manifest needs, stemming from Murray's (1938) pioneering work, continues to influence research.

Although Murray's taxonomy included as many as twenty needs, the focus in recent studies, particularly those conducted in organizational settings, seems to have settled on the need for achievement (nAch) and the need for power (nPow) (Atkinson & Feather, 1966; McClelland, 1965; McClelland & Burnham, 1976). In particular, nPow appears to be a likely candidate for investigation as a correlate of political activity in organizations.

Researchers have found nPow to be widely distributed, particularly among successful managers, in organizations (McClelland & Burnham, 1976). While power motivation, according to McClelland, can often be "socialized" (i.e., oriented toward organizational rather than personal objectives), nPow can also center on the desire to further one's own goals. Shostrom (1967) characterized man as a manipulator and set forth the view that for many people, control of others can become its own reward apart from any extrinsic accomplishment that might be the ostensible object of the maneuver. Among the individual differences that might influence the accuracy of Shostrom's characterization, it would seem that nPow would be rather important.

Locus of Control The theory (Rotter, 1954, 1966) that highlights this variable holds that people differ systematically in their beliefs as to whether their personal successes and failures are the result of uncontrollable external forces or of their own actions. "Internals" tend to view their outcomes as the result of ability or effort, while "externals" regard personal consequences as the result of innate task difficulty or of luck (Weiner, 1974). Thus, when faced with a problem in which upward political influence might be within the feasible set of coping strategies, it might seem reasonable that an "internal" would arrive at a different expectancy computation than an "external." For the average outcome, an "internal" will probably assume a higher expectancy of effort leading to attainment. This might, in turn, lead "internals" to favor political activism, while "externals" might be more prone toward political apathy.

Risk-Seeking Propensity Decision makers differ in their psychological reaction to risk. While some exhibit a conservative bias, avoiding risk when possible, others appear to place a positive value on risk per se. In the language of decision theory, the former are termed "risk averters" while the latter are called "risk seekers" (Keeney & Raiffa, 1976). (There are also many people, of course, who are essentially "risk neutral.") To the extent that an organization member is a risk seeker, it might be reasonable to expect that he or she would be tempted to engage in a political-influence attempt (which can indeed be dangerous) that might be shunned by a risk averter.

Next, we turn to consideration of the other participant in the dyadic process of upward political influence—the influence target.

Target Selection

Importance of Power Engaging in organizational politics necessitates the selection of a target(s) of influence. An essential ingredient that a chosen target must possess is the control of scarce resources or the ability to influence scarce-resource controllers. This is basically a question of who has either the *power* to allocate desired resources or the ability to *influence* other desired-resource powerholders. Power is considered to be the capacity to influence, while influence is viewed as a process of producing behavioral or psychological (e.g., values, beliefs, attitudes) effects in a target person. The political actor is concerned with identifying and selecting as a target an individual(s) who possesses an appropriate base, or bases, of power that, as indicated earlier, is sufficiently high to do or get done what the political actor desires. This point was recognized by Teoeschi, Schlenker, and Lindskold (1972), when they indicated that individuals possessing relatively greater expertise, status, or prestige than the source will be prime candidates as targets of influence.

Costs of Approaching Target It seems clear that the potential risks or costs to the political actor are also an important consideration in choosing among various powerholders in the organization as potential targets of political influence. The target must possess sufficient power to accomplish the outcome desired by the source *and* at a minimal, or acceptable, cost to the political actor. By "costs to the agent" we are referring to possible negative outcomes that may be experienced by the agent as a result of the influence attempt. These negative outcomes range from the agent's failure to promote or protect self-interests in the specific situation at hand to loss of the ability to promote or protect self-interests in future situations. Indeed, the ultimate cost could be loss of position within the organization.

Therefore, while especially powerful individuals may be able to do what the agent desires, these are the same individuals who can impose the greatest adverse effects (costs) upon the agent. The power that makes a person attractive as a target could be used, were the target so to choose, against the source. Tedeschi et al. (1972) clearly recognized this point when they proposed that the most probable influence target would be the weakest person who possesses sufficient power to enable the influencer to realize the desired goal. It was suggested, with respect to target selection in organizations, that "people have a 'natural' tendency to go through the channels of authority" (p. 314); i.e., the most likely target of influence would be the immediate superior. Allen, Angle, and Porter (1979a) found that the immediate superior is, in fact, the most frequent target of attempted influence. About two-thirds of their respondents (143) selected their immediate superior as a fitst-choice target of influence.

Agent-Target Relationship An important consideration concerning the potential costs in selecting a target from among various powerholders in the organization may be the concept of interpersonal attraction between the agent and the potential target(s). Ideally, the selected target will possess sufficient power to provide the outcomes desired by the political actor *and* sufficiently high interpersonal attraction to be willing to do so at minimal or acceptable costs to the agent.

In upward influence, the political actor does not enjoy a given target or even a "natural" set of targets. The appropriateness of a particular individual as an influence target is situationally determined; i.e., the target will vary according to the outcomes desired by the source. The common denominator of potential political targets is the possession of sufficient power to provide, or assist in providing, outcomes desired by the political actor. It is the political actor's task to identify, select, and induce these organizational influentials to comply, willingly or unwittingly, with the intent of the political actor.

Methods of Upward Influence

The one inescapable fact about upward influence—that the agent of influence possesses less formal authority than the target of influence—colors any examination of the selection of methods of upward political influence. The fact that the political actor cannot rely on formal authority, and most likely has considerably less power (compared to a downward situation) to wield positive and negative sanctions, means that the search for an effective method or methods of upward influence will be different from the search that takes place in downward attempts.

Before discussing a classification of possible methods of upward political influence and the factors that will affect the choice of methods, it is important to keep in mind another aspect of the situation—the methods can be utilized (as Allen et al., 1979b, have pointed out) either to promote self-interests (usually in a proactive manner) or to protect those interests (usually in a reactive manner). The former use refers to upward-influence attempts designed to advance self-interests and move the agent from a current position (in terms of access to organizational resources and rewards) to a better position. Such upward-influence attempts typically require *initiation* by the agent. In the latter mode, ordinarily

requiring a *response* by the agent, attempts are made to reduce or minimize potential damage to self-interests that would tend to move the agent from a current position to a less desirable position. It is clear that political attempts at upward influence can be exercised in either of these modes.

Classification of Methods A categorization scheme that may be useful for the purposes of analyzing upward political influence is shown in Table 34-1. As can be seen, influence methods have been classified into two major categories: sanctions and informational. In turn, sanctions have been divided into the familiar sets, "positive" and "negative," while informational methods have been divided into three types: "persuasion" (both the actor's objective and the influence attempt are open); "manipulative persuasion" (the objective is concealed but the attempt is open); and "manipulation" (both the objective and the attempt are concealed).

Each of the five methods listed in Table 34-1 can be considered for possible use by individual political actors. As will be discussed below, and as shown in Table 34-1, we have indicated what we think is the relative frequency of use: namely, positive and negative sanctions are not likely, persuasion is low to medium in likelihood, and manipulative persuasion and manipulation are (relatively) highly likely.

Considering each of the five methods in turn:

Positive sanctions In upward-political-influence situations, it is unlikely (though certainly by no means impossible) that individuals will very widely utilize the method of positive sanctions, i.e., rewards and promises of rewards. The apparent reason is that individuals vis-à-vis their upward targets are unlikely to control a wide range of rewards. To put it simply, while the upward target can do a lot for the would-be political actor in the way of provid-

Table 34-1 Classification of Methods of Upward Political Influence

	Types of methods	Predicted relative frequency of use
I. Sanctions	A. Positive	Low
	B. Negative	Low
II. Informational	A. Persuasion	Low to Medium
	B. Manipulative Persuasion	High
	C. Manipulation	High

ing rewards, the would-be actor is relatively limited in the rewards that can be administered upward to the target. The sources do have their own performance that can serve as a reward—for example, helping make the boss look good—but since relatively good performance is such an expected part of normal organizational behavior, it is not likely to serve as a frequent reward in an upward direction unless it is truly exceptional performance. Other types of rewards (e.g., favors) can be promised by the lower-level individual attempting upward influence, but on balance they are likely to be of limited and circumscribed impact.

Negative sanctions As Mechanic (1962) noted, "secretaries . . . accountants . . . attendants in mental hospitals, and even . . . inmates in prisons" (p. 350) can individually, if they wish, "gum up the works" by various tactics. Whether this is a very prevalent method, however, is a function of the possible costs or penalties for doing so. In particular, when influence is being attempted hierarchically upward, there are normative restrictions on the use of negative sanctions. While both the superior and the subordinate may fully understand that the subordinate is in a threatening posture, face-saving norms (Goffman, 1955) may require that neither party openly acknowledge the subordinate's threat. Were the threat to become overt, the superior would likely be compelled to retaliate. Thus, upward threats seldom will be explicit; rather, to the extent that they exist at all, upward negative sanctions will tend to take the form of what Berne (1964) termed "covert transactions." In general, it is our view that negative sanctions will not be selected often as a viable upward-influence method.

Persuasion The term "persuasion" is usually substituted as a shorthand term for open informational methods. It seems obvious that persuasion, or the open utilization of an informational base, is a frequent and common method of *non*political upward influence on the part of the individual agent. However, when the aim of such persuasion is the promotion or protection of the self-interests of the influence agent, and where the self-interests of others are threatened, its use becomes far more problematical. Since the intentions of the influence agent are open as well as the method (i.e., a direct attempt to convince), the response will be based directly on the target's evaluation of the message

and the source of the message. The "costs," therefore, may be greatly increased because of the possibility of a negative reaction on the part of the target—as opposed, perhaps, to mere indifference in nonpolitical situations. For this reason, we would argue that the likelihood of persuasion being utilized in upward-political-influence situations would be low to moderate.

It should be noted that the nature of the arguments in persuasion can take many forms, including pointing out probable consequences to the target for complying or failing to comply with the agent's wishes. Tedeschi et al. (1972) refer to this type of argument as the use of "warnings and mendations" (as contrasted with such direct sanctions as threats, punishments, and promises of rewards). "The important distinction between a threat and a warning is that the source controls the punishment in the first instance but not in the second" (p. 292).

Manipulative persuasion The essence of this method of upward influence involves the agent's deliberately attempting to conceal or disguise the true objectives *even though* remaining *open* about the fact that an influence attempt is taking place—it is the objective, not the influence attempt, that is concealed. This is illustrated by the well-known "hidden agenda" phenomenon.

We contend that manipulative persuasion is a frequently utilized approach to upward influence of a political sort. The reason, of course, is the influence agent's belief that if the (higher-level) target knew what the source was trying to accomplish, the target would reject or ignore the message and thus avoid being influenced, or might even penalize the source. In this method, agents openly attempt to influence but simultaneously attempt to disguise their intentions. The effectiveness of the influence method, therefore, depends on the effectiveness of the disguising of objectives. There is probably no message so *in*effective as one that is labeled by the target: "He/she is only trying to get me to do that because it will advance his/her own self-interests."

Manipulation This form of influence involves the concealment of *both* the intent of the political actor *and* the fact that an influence attempt is taking place. This obviously involves greater effort on the part of the influence agent, as both intentions and the attempt must be disguised. Despite the potential difficulties, this is a common method of upward political influence. For example, in a study of managerial perceptions of the utilization of political tactics, Allen et al. (1979b) found that "the instrumental use of information" was one of the three most commonly observed tactics mentioned by the managerial respondents from thirty small- to medium-sized industrial firms. As these authors pointed out, this category of tactics involved withholding or distorting information (short of outright lying) or overwhelming the target with too much information. The other two tactics most frequently cited by the respondents in the Allen et al. study could also be interpreted as the utilization of pure manipulation: namely, "attacking or blaming others" and "image building/impression management." Obviously, the success of these and similar tactics, including ingratiation, would appear to depend largely on how effectively the influence agent's intentions and the attempt at influence are concealed. Attacking others, for example, is likely to be dismissed if it is regarded as being only, or primarily, in the service of the attacker's self-interests and/or as an influence attempt.

Factors in the Choice of Method   If we assume that an individual or a group in an organization has made a decision to attempt upward influence for the purpose of promoting or protecting self-interests, then that person or group faces the choice of what method to use. Since we are focusing on *upward* influence, the choice will be greatly affected by the knowledge that the target has more formal authority than the agent. A choice that might be effective in downward influence might not, as noted earlier, be equally effective in the upward direction.

The choice of method is likely to be affected by the agent's instrumental motivation—the attempt to obtain particular outcomes (with satisfaction deriving from the attainment of the outcomes rather than from the process of attaining them). Agents are presumed to have some notion of what values they place on certain outcomes, and some idea of the probability that a given action will lead to various outcomes. It is this latter factor, the calculation of the probability that a particular method will lead to valued outcomes, that would seem to be the key ingredient in the choice of methods of influence. Alternatively, this could be thought of as a calculation of cost-benefit ratios for various possible methods. Those methods would be chosen which would bring the greatest benefits at the lowest cost.

Such calculations can be presumed to be dependent on the agent's assessment of: (1) agent (self-) characteristics; (2) target characteristics; (3) situational characteristics; and (4) method characteristics. Agent characteristics would include the various resources the agent possesses vis-à-vis the target: e.g., degree of expertise, potential to provide the target with positive or negative outcomes, possession of exclusive information, ability to disguise true intentions, general persuasive ability, risk-taking propensity, and the like. Target characteristics would include such variables as perceived susceptibility to persuasion, likelihood of attributing self-interest motivation to the agent, power to provide the desired outcome, and so forth. Finally, some assessment would be made of the characteristics (costs and benefits) of the method itself. For example, in deciding whether to use some form of manipulation, such as withholding information or attempting ingratiation, the *perceived* costs involved in detection may or may not be viewed as greater than the potential gains of straightforward persuasion. It would appear, then, that the choice of methods of influence, particularly in an upward situation, is a complex process.

CONCLUDING OBSERVATIONS

Some years ago, Leavitt (1964) observed: "People perceive what they think will help satisfy needs; ignore what is disturbing; and again perceive disturbances that persist and increase" (p. 33). It is interesting to apply the selective-perception framework to the relative prominence given by the field of organizational behavior to downward- and lateral-influence processes, on the one hand, compared to the lack of attention given to upward-influence processes and organizational politics, on the other. We believe there has been an overfocus on the former, and that the field needs to redress the imbalance by giving increased emphasis to the latter.

One can speculate as to why this imbalance has occurred. In part, at least, it has come about because those who run organizations traditionally have been interested in improving the performance of those being led or managed. Hence, they have pressed social and behavioral scientists to learn more about leadership and motivation. This has created a ready market for knowledge directed toward influencing subordinates to perform in a desired manner. Another factor shaping research, particularly with respect to both downward- and lateral-influence processes, has been the small-group tradition in social psychology. When only small groups, as opposed to (large) formal organizations, are the object of study, it is likely that the focus will be strongly downward, or perhaps lateral —as in the case of group dynamics. Chains of authority exist only in organizations of some size, and thus if groups only are being researched, it is difficult to investigate the intricacies of upward-influence linkages—except for the limited case of the group's impact on the immediate leader (and it should be stressed that even this circumscribed type of upward influence has only recently begun to be examined by organizational-behavior researchers). Our point is not that upward influence is more important than lateral or downward influence, only that it should be studied as much as the other two types. And when one gets into the topic of upward influence in organizations, one is *inevitably* drawn into the realm of organizational politics. This, in turn, is a subject that has long been regarded as somewhat "taboo" by both organizations and researchers because of its mildly disturbing negative connotations—clandestine, self-serving, dysfunctional, etc.

Finally, we feel that a broadened influence perspective—one that incorporates the concept of organizational politics—can contribute significantly to an understanding of many facets of organizational behavior, such as decision making, organizational design, communication, motivation, and organizational development.

REFERENCES

Allen, R. W., H. L. Angle, & L. W. Porter. A study of upward influence in political situations in organizations. Unpublished manuscript, University of California, Irvine, 1979a.

———, D. L. Madison, L. W. Porter, P. A. Renwick, & B. T. Mayes. Organization politics: Tactics and personal characteristics of political actors. *California Management Review*, 1979b, 22(4), 77–83.

Atkinson, J. W., & N. T. Feather (Eds.), *A theory of achievement motivation*. New York: Wiley, 1966.

Berne, E. *Games people play*. New York: Grove Press, 1964.

Biddle, B. J. Roles, goals, and value structures in organizations. In W. W. Cooper, H. J. Leavitt, & M. W. Shelly II (Eds.), *New perspectives in organization research*. New York: Wiley, 1964.

Frost, P. J., & D. C. Hayes. An exploration in two cultures of political behavior in organizations. Paper presented at the Conference on Cross-Cultural Studies of Organizational Functioning. Honolulu: University of Hawaii, September 1977.

Goffman, E. On facework. *Psychiatry*, 1955, 18, 213–231.

Keeney, R. L., & H. Raiffa. *Decisions and multiple objectives: Preferences and value tradeoffs*. New York: Wiley, 1976.

Lasswell, H. D. Who gets what, when, how. In the *Political Writings of Harold D. Lasswell*. Glencoe, Ill.: Free Press, 1951.

Leavitt, H. J. *Managerial psychology*, Rev. Ed. Chicago: University of Chicago Press, 1964.

McClelland, D. C. Toward a theory of motive acquisition. *American Psychologist*, 1965, 20, 321–333.

———, & D. H. Burnham. Power is the great motivator. *Harvard Business Review*, 1976, 54(2), 100–110.

Madison, D. L., R. W. Allen, L. W. Porter, P. A. Renwick, & B. T. Mayes. Organizational politics: An exploration of managers' perceptions. *Human Relations*, 1980, 33, 79–100.

Mayes, B. T., & R. W. Allen. Toward a definition of organizational politics. *Academy of Management Review*, 1977, 2, 672–678.

Mechanic, D. Sources of power of lower participants in complex organizations. *Administrative Science Quarterly*, 1962, 7, 349–364.

Moberg, D. J. Organizational politics: Perspectives from attribution theory. Paper presented to the 1977 Meeting of the American Institute for Decision Sciences, Chicago, Ill.

Murray, H. A. *Explorations in personality*. New York: Oxford, 1938.

Porter, L. W. Organizations as political animals. Presidential Address, Division of Industrial-Organizational Psychology, 84th Annual Meeting of the American Psychological Association, Washington, D.C., 1976.

Robbins, S. P. *The administrative process: Integrating theory and practice*. Englewood Cliffs, N.J.: Prentice-Hall, 1976.

Rotter, J. B. *Social learning and clinical psychology*. Englewood Cliffs, N.J.: Prentice-Hall, 1954.

Rotter, J. B. Generalized expectancies for internal versus external locus of control. *Psychological Monographs*, 1966, 80, 1–28.

Schein, V. Individual power and political behaviors in organizations: An inadequately explored reality. *Academy of Management Review,* 1977, **2,** 64–72.

Shostrom, E. L. *Man, the manipulator,* Nashville, Tenn.: Abingdon, 1967.

Tedeschi, J. T., B. R. Schlenker, & S. Lindskold. The exercise of power and influence: The source of influ-ence. In J. T. Tedeschi (Ed.), *The social influence process.* Chicago: Aldine-Atherton, 1972.

Vroom, V. H. *Work and motivation.* New York: Wiley, 1964.

Weiner, B. An attributional interpretation of expectancy-value theory. In B. Weiner (Ed.), *Cognitive views of human motivation.* New York: Academic, 1974.

Chapter 10

Group Processes in Organizations

There are many kinds of groups in organizations. At one extreme, a group can be a collection of workers in a shop, each carrying out his or her own tasks, aware of one another but not interacting with each other for any work-related purpose. Or a group can be several individuals working together temporarily to solve a problem, make a decision, or carry out a specific task. Or a group can be a set of people who work together intensively, day in and day out, with substantial and continuing responsibility for some aspect of the overall organizational task.

In recent years, groups have become increasingly popular as a way of getting things done in organizations. The idea of "quality circles," originating in Japan, has gained great currency in this country. And the notion of the "autonomous work group," popular first in Europe and Scandinavia, has become a standard organizational-design device in many U.S. corporations. Health care teams, teaching teams, and project teams all have become more widespread in this country in recent years. Indeed, some organizations have even established an "office of the president" in which the top management of the organization as a whole is handled by a team.

In the first reading in this chapter, Leavitt explores what might happen if we *really* took groups seriously in organizations—that is, if we used groups rather than individuals as the basic building blocks of organizations. He points out the many advantages groups have for individuals (such as satisfying social needs and providing social support) and for organizations (such as promoting innovation, providing for informal but direct control of individual behavior, and buffering the effect of large organizational size). Leavitt then offers some ideas about how groups might be more widely used in organizations, and suggests some of the changes that might be needed in other aspects of organizations if groups were the basic performing units.

The next article, by Janis, provides a counterpoint to the optimism about groups expressed by Leavitt. Janis describes and explores a phenomenon he calls "groupthink," in which highly cohesive groups composed of talented members develop and implement plans of action that turn out to be grossly inappropriate and ineffective. Janis identifies some of the causes and indicators of groupthink, illustrates the phenomenon by reviewing cases of policy-making fiascoes executed by groups of high-level governmental officials, and concludes by offering some guidelines for avoiding the groupthink trap.

The last article in the chapter, by Maier, provides a balanced view of the assets and liabilities that groups have for solving problems. While groups do have many advantages over individual problem-solvers (such as greater and more diverse resources), they also have some built-in liabilities which, if not carefully monitored, can more than overcome the assets. Maier views the role of the leader as critical in group problem solving, and proposes a metaphor of the leader as the central nervous system of the group—gathering and disseminating information, facilitating communication, and integrating member responses so that a single unified group response to the problem occurs. If this integrating function is not performed, Maier argues, the inherent liabilities of the group may dominate—and poor problem solving may be the result.

Reading 35

Suppose We Took Groups Seriously . . .

Harold J. Leavitt

INTRODUCTION

This chapter is mostly a fantasy, but not a utopian fantasy. As the title suggests, it tries to spin out some of the things that might happen if we really took small groups seriously; if, that is, we really used groups, rather than individuals, as the basic building blocks for an organization.

This seems an appropriate forum for such a fantasy. It was fifty years ago, at Hawthorne, that the informal face-to-face work group was discovered. Since then groups have been studied inside and out; they have been experimented with, observed, built, and taken apart. Small groups have become the major tool of the applied behavioral scientist. Organizational Development methods are group methods. Almost all of what is called participative management is essentially based on group techniques.

So the idea of using groups as organizational mechanisms is by no means new or fantastic. The fantasy comes in proposing to start with groups, not add them in; to design organizations from scratch around small groups, rather than around individuals.

But right from the start, talk like that appears to violate a deep and important value, individualism. But this fantasy will not really turn out to be anti-individualistic in the end.

The rest of this chapter will briefly address the following questions: (1) Is it fair to say that groups have not been taken very seriously in organizational design? (2) Why are groups even worth thinking about as organizational building materials? What are the characteristics of groups that might make them interesting enough to be worth serious attention? (3) What would it mean "to take groups seriously?" Just what kinds of things would have to be done differently? (4) What compensatory changes would probably be needed in other aspects of the organization, to have groups as the basic unit? And

finally, (5) is the idea of designing the organization around small face-to-face groups a very radical idea, or is it just an extension of a direction in which we are already going?

Haven't Groups Been Taken Seriously Enough Already?

The argument that groups have not been taken "seriously" doesn't seem a hard one to make. The contemporary ideas about groups didn't really come along until the 30's and 40's. By that time a logical, rationalistic tradition for the construction of organizations already existed. That tradition was very heavily based on the notion that the individual was the construction unit. The logic moved from the projected task backward. Determine the task, the goal, then find an appropriate structure and technology, and last of all fit individual human beings into predefined man-sized pieces of the action. That was, for instance, what industrial psychology was all about during its development between the two world wars. It was concerned almost entirely with individual differences and worked in the service of structuralists, fitting square human pegs to predesigned square holes. The role of the psychologist was thus ancillary to the role of the designers of the whole organization. It was a back up, supportive role that followed more than it led design.

It was not just the logic of classical organizational theory that concentrated on the individual. The whole entrepreneurial tradition of American society supported it. Individuals, at least male individuals, were taught achievement motivation. They were taught to seek individual evaluation, to compete, to see the world, organizational or otherwise, as a place in which to strive for individual accomplishment and satisfaction.

In those respects the classical design of organizations was consonant with the then existent cultural landscape. Individualized organizational structures blended with the environment of individualism. All the accessories fell into place: individual incentive schemes for hourly workers, individual merit rating and assessment schemes, tests for selection of individuals.

The unique characteristic of the organization was that it was not simply a race track within which individuals could compete, but a system in which somehow the competitive behavior of individuals could be coordinated, harnessed and controlled in the interest of the common tasks. Of course one residual of all that was a continuing tension between individual and organization, with the organization seeking to control and coordinate the individual's activities at the same time that it tried to motivate him; while the competitive individual insisted on reaching well beyond the constraints imposed upon him by the organization. One product of this tension became the informal organization discovered here at Western; typically an informal coalition designed to fight the system.

Then it was discovered that groups could be exploited for what management saw as positive purposes, *toward* productivity instead of away from it. There followed the era of experimentation with small face-to-face groups. We learned to patch them on to existing organizations as bandaids to relieve tensions between individual and organization. We promoted coordination through group methods. We learned that groups were useful to discipline and control recalcitrant individuals.

Groups were fitted onto organizations. The group skills of individual members improved so that they could coordinate their efforts more effectively, control deviants more effectively and gain more commitment from subordinate individuals. But groups were seen primarily as tools to be tacked on and utilized in the pre-existing individualized organizational system. With a few notable exceptions, like Rensis Likert (1961), most did not design organizations around groups. On the contrary, as some of the ideas about small groups began to be tacked onto existing organizational models, they generated new tensions and conflicts of their own. Managers complained not only that groups were slow, but that they diffused responsibility, vitiated the power of the hierarchy because they were too "democratic" and created small in-group empires which were very hard for others to penetrate. There was the period, for example, of the great gap between T-group

training (which had to be conducted on "cultural islands") and the organization back home. The T-groupers therefore talked a lot about the "reentry problem," which meant in part the problem of movement from a new culture (the T-group culture) designed around groups back into the organizational culture designed around individuals.

But of course groups didn't die despite their difficulties. How could they die? They had always been there, though not always in the service of the organization. They turned out to be useful, indeed necessary, though often unrecognized tools. For organizations were growing, and professionalizing, and the need for better coordination grew even as the humanistic expectations of individuals also grew. So "acknowledged" groups (as distinct from "natural," informal groups) became fairly firmly attached even to conservative organizations, but largely as compensating addenda very often reluctantly backed into by organizational managers.

Groups have never been given a chance. It is as though someone had insisted that automobiles be designed to fit the existing terrain rather than build roads to adapt to automobiles.

Are Groups Worth Considering as Fundamental Building Blocks?

Why would groups be more interesting than individuals as basic design units around which to build organizations? What are the prominent characteristics of small groups? Why are they interesting? Here are several answers:

First, small groups seem to be good for people. They can satisfy important membership needs. They can provide a moderately wide range of activities for individual members. They can provide support in times of stress and crisis. They are settings in which people can learn not only cognitively but empirically to be reasonably trusting and helpful to one another. Second, groups seem to be good problem finding tools. They seem to be useful in promoting innovation and creativity. Third, in a wide variety of decision situations, they make better decisions than individuals do. Fourth, they are great tools for implementation. They gain commitment from their members so that group decisions are likely to be willingly carried out. Fifth, they can control and discipline individual members in ways that are often extremely difficult through more impersonal quasi-legal disciplinary systems. Sixth, as organizations grow large, small groups appear to be useful mechanisms for fending off many of the negative effects of large size. They help to prevent communication lines from growing too long, the hierarchy from growing too steep, and the individual from getting lost in the crowd.

There is a seventh, but altogether different kind of argument for taking groups seriously. Thus far the designer of organizations seemed to have a choice. He could build an individualized *or* a groupy organization. A groupy organization will, de facto, have to deal with individuals; but what was learned here so long ago is that individualized organizations, must de facto, deal with groups. Groups are natural phenomena, and facts of organizational life. They can be created but their spontaneous development cannot be prevented. The problem is not shall groups exist or not, but shall groups be planned or not? If not, the individualized organizational garden will sprout groupy weeds all over the place. By defining them as weeds instead of flowers, they shall continue, as in earlier days, to be treated as pests, forever fouling up the beauty of rationally designed individualized organizations, forever forming informally (and irrationally) to harass and outgame the planners.

It is likely that the reverse could also be true, that if groups are defined as the flowers and individuals as the weeds, new problems will crop up. Surely they will, but that discussion can be delayed for at least a little while.

Who Uses Groups Best?

So groups look like interesting organizational building blocks. But before going on to consider the implications of designing organizations around groups, one useful heuristic might be to look around the existing world at those places in which groups seem to have been treated somewhat more seriously.

One place groups have become big is in Japanese organizations (Johnson & Ouchi, 1974). The Japanese seem to be very groupy, and much less concerned than Americans about issues like individual accountability. Japanese organizations, of course, are thus consonant with Japanese culture, where notions of individual aggressiveness and competitiveness are de-emphasized in favor of self-

effacement and group loyalty. But Japanese organizations seem to get a lot done, despite the relative suppression of the individual in favor of the group. It also appears that the advantages of the groupy Japanese style have really come to the fore in large technologically complex organizations.

Another place to look is at American conglomerates. They go to the opposite extreme, dealing with very large units. They buy large organizational units and sell units. They evaluate units. In effect they promote units by offering them extra resources as rewards for good performance. In that sense conglomerates, one might argue, are designed around groups, but the groups in question are often themselves large organizational chunks.

Groups in an Individualistic Culture

An architect can design a beautiful building which either blends smoothly with its environment or contrasts starkly with it. But organization designers may not have the same choice. If we design an organization which is structurally dissonant with its environment, it is conceivable that the environment will change to adjust to the organization. It seems much more likely, however, that the environment will reject the organization. If designing organizations around groups represents a sharp counterpoint to environmental trends maybe we should abort the idea.

Our environment, one can argue, is certainly highly individualized. But one can also make a less solid argument in the other direction; an argument that American society is going groupy rather than individual this year. Or at least that it is going groupy as well as individual. The evidence is sloppy at best. One can reinterpret the student revolution and the growth of anti-establishment feelings at least in part as a reaction to the decline of those institutions that most satisfied social membership needs. One can argue that the decline of the Church, of the village and of the extended family is leaving behind a vacuum of unsatisfied membership and belongingness motives. Certainly popular critics of American society have laid a great deal of emphasis on the loneliness and anomie that seem to have resulted not only from materialism but from the emphasis on individualism. It seems possible to argue that, insofar as there has been any significant change in the work ethic in America, the change has been toward a desire for work which is socially as well as egoistically fulfilling, and which satisfies human needs for belongingness and affiliation as well as needs for achievement.

In effect, the usual interpretation of Abraham Maslow's need hierarchy may be wrong. Usually the esteem and self-actualization levels of motivation are emphasized. Perhaps the level that is becoming operant most rapidly is neither of those, but the social-love-membership level.

The rising role of women in American society also has implications for the groupiness of organizations. There is a moderate amount of evidence that American women have been socialized more strongly into affiliative and relational sorts of attitudes than men. They probably can, in general, more comfortably work in direct achievement roles in group settings, where there are strong relational bonds among members, than in competitive, individualistic settings. Moreover it is reasonable to assume that as women take a more important place in American society, some of their values and attitudes will spill over to the male side.

Although the notion of designing organizations around groups in America in 1974 may be a little premature, it is consonant with cultural trends that may make the idea much more appropriate ten years from now.

But groups are becoming more relevant for organizational as well as cultural reasons. Groups seem to be particularly useful as coordinating and integrating mechanisms for dealing with complex tasks that require the inputs of many kinds of specialized knowledge. In fact the development of matrix-type organizations in high technology industry is perhaps one effort to modify individually designed organizations toward a more groupy direction; not for humanistic reasons but as a consequence of tremendous increases in the informational complexity of the jobs that need to be done.

What Might a Seriously Groupy Organization Look Like?

Just what does it mean to design organizations around groups? Operationally how is that different from designing organizations around individuals? One approach to an answer is simply to take the things organizations do with individuals and try them out with groups. The idea is to raise the level

from the atom to the molecule, and *select* groups rather than individuals, *train* groups rather than individuals, *pay* groups rather than individuals, *promote* groups rather than individuals, *design jobs* for groups rather than for individuals, *fire* groups rather than individuals, and so on down the list of activities which organizations have traditionally carried on in order to use human beings in their organizations.

Some of the items on that list seem easy to handle at the group level. For example, it doesn't seem terribly hard to design jobs for groups. In effect that is what top management already does for itself to a great extent. It gives specific jobs to committees, and often runs itself as a group. The problem seems to be a manageable one: designing job sets which are both big enough to require a small number of persons and also small enough to require only a small number of persons. Big enough in this context means not only jobs that would occupy the hands of group members but that would provide opportunities for learning and expansion.

Ideas like evaluating, promoting, and paying groups raise many more difficult but interesting problems. Maybe the best that can be said for such ideas is that they provide opportunities for thinking creatively about pay and evaluation. Suppose, for example, that as a reward for good work the group gets a larger salary budget than it got last year. Suppose the allocation for increases within the group is left to the group members. Certainly one can think up all sorts of difficulties that might arise. But are the potential problems necessarily any more difficult than those now generated by individual merit raises? Is there any company in America that is satisfied with its existing individual performance appraisal and salary allocation schemes? At least the issues of distributive justice within small groups would presumably be open to internal discussion and debate. One might even permit the group to allocate payments to individuals differentially at different times, in accordance with some criteria of current contribution that they might establish.

As far as performance evaluation is concerned, it is probably easier for people up the hierarchy to assess the performance of total groups than it is to assess the performance of individual members well down the hierarchy. Top managers of decentralized organizations do it all the time, except that they usually reward the formal leader of the decentralized unit rather than the whole unit.

The notion of promoting groups raises another variety of difficulties. One thinks of physically transferring a whole group, for example, and of the costs associated with training a whole group to do a new job, especially if there are no bridging individuals. But there may be large advantages too. If a group moves, its members already know how to work with one another. Families may be less disrupted by movement if several move at the same time.

There is the problem of selection. Does it make sense to select groups? Initially, why not? Can't means be found for selecting not only for appropriate knowledge and skill but also for potential ability to work together? There is plenty of groundwork in the literature already.

After the initial phase, there will of course be problems of adding or subtracting individuals from existing groups. We already know a good deal about how to help new members get integrated into old groups. Incidentally, I was told recently by a plant manager in the midwest about an oddity he had encountered; the phenomenon of groups applying for work. Groups of three or four people have been coming to his plant seeking employment together. They wanted to work together and stay together.

Costs and Danger Points

To play this game of designing organizations around groups, what might be some important danger points? In general, a group-type organization is somewhat more like a free market than present organizations. More decisions would have to be worked out ad hoc, in a continually changing way. So one would need to schedule more negotiation time both within and between groups.

One would encounter more issues of justice, for the individual vis-à-vis the group and for groups vis-à-vis one another. More and better arbitration mechanisms would probably be needed along with highly flexible and rapidly adaptive record keeping. But modern record keeping technology is, potentially, both highly flexible and rapidly adaptive.

Another specific issue is the provision of escape hatches for individuals. Groups have been known to be cruel and unjust to their deviant members. One existing escape route for the individual would of course continue to exist: departure from the organization. Another might be easy means of transfer to another group.

Another related danger of a strong group emphasis might be a tendency to drive away highly individualistic, nongroup people. But the tight organizational constraints now imposed do the same thing. Indeed might not groups protect their individuals better than the impersonal rules of present day large organizations?

Another obvious problem: If groups are emphasized by rewarding them, paying them, promoting them, and so on, groups may begin to perceive themselves as power centers, in competitive conflict with other groups. Intergroup hostilities are likely to be exacerbated unless we can design some new coping mechanisms into the organization. Likert's proposal for solving that sort of problem (and others) is the linking pin concept. The notion is that individuals serve as members of more than one group, both up and down the hierarchy and horizontally. But Likert's scheme seems to me to assume fundamentally individualized organizations in the sense that it is still individuals who get paid, promoted and so on. In a more groupy organization, the linking pin concept has to be modified so that an individual might be a part-time member of more than one group, but still a real member. That is, for example, a portion of an individual's pay might come from each group in accordance with that group's perception of his contribution.

Certainly much more talk, both within and between groups, would be a necessary accompaniment of group emphasis; though we might argue about whether more talk should be classified as a cost or a benefit. In any case careful design of escape hatches for individuals and connections among groups would be as important in this kind of organization as would stairways between floors in the design of a private home.

There is also a danger of over-designing groups. All groups in the organization need not look alike. Quite to the contrary. Task and technology should have significant effects on the shapes and sizes of different subgroups within the large organization. Just as individuals end up adjusting the edges of their jobs to themselves and themselves to their jobs, we should expect flexibility within groups, allowing them to adapt and modify themselves to whatever the task and technology demand.

Another initially scary problem associated with groups is the potential loss of clear formal individual leadership. Without formal leaders how will we motivate people? Without leaders how will we control and discipline people? Without leaders how will we pinpoint responsibility? Even as I write those questions I cannot help but feel that they are archaic. They are questions which are themselves a product of the basic individual building block design of old organizations. The problem is not leaders so much as the performance of leadership functions. Surely groups will find leaders, but they will emerge from the bottom up. Given a fairly clear job description, some groups, in some settings, will set up more or less permanent leadership roles. Others may let leadership vary as the situation demands, or as a function of the power that individuals within any group may possess relative to the group's needs at that time. A reasonable amount of process time can be built in to enable groups to work on the leadership problem, but the problem will have to be resolved within each group. On the advantage side of the ledger, this may even get rid of a few hierarchical levels. There should be far less need for individuals who are chiefly supervisors of other individuals' work. Groups can serve as hierarchical leaders of other groups.

Two other potential costs: With an organization of groups, there may be a great deal of infighting, and power and conflict issues will come even more to the fore than they do now. Organizations of groups may become highly political, with coalitions lining up against one another on various issues. If so, the rest of the organizational system will have to take those political problems into account, both by setting up sensible systems of intercommunications among groups, and by allocating larger amounts of time and expertise to problems of conflict resolution.

But this is not a new problem unique to groupy organizations. Conflict among groups is prevalent in large organizations which are political systems now. But because these issues have not often been foreseen and planned for, the mechanisms for dealing with them are largely ad hoc. As a result, conflict is often dealt with in extremely irrational ways.

But there is another kind of intergroup power problem that may become extremely important and difficult in groupy organizations. There is a real danger that relatively autonomous and cohesive groups may be closed, not only to other groups but more importantly to staff advice or to new technological inputs.

These problems exist at present, of course, but they may be exacerbated by group structure. I cannot see any perfect way to handle those problems. One possibility may be to make individual members of staff groups part time members of line groups. Another is to work harder to educate line groups to potential staff contributions. Of course the reward system, the old market system, will probably be the strongest force for keeping groups from staying old-fashioned in a world of new technologies and ideas.

But the nature and degree of many of the second order spinoff effects are not fully knowable at the design stage. We need to build more complete working models and pilot plants. In any case it does not seem obvious that slowdowns, either at the work face or in decision-making processes, would necessarily accompany group based organizational designs.

Some Possible Advantages to the Organization

Finally, from an organizational perspective, what are the potential advantages to be gained from a group based organization? The first might be a sharp reduction in the number of units that need to be controlled. Control would not have to be carried all the way down to the individual level. If the average group size is five, the number of blocks that management has to worry about is cut to 20% of what it was. Such a design would also probably cut the number of operational levels in the organization. In effect, levels which are now primarily supervisory would be incorporated into the groups that they supervise.

By this means many of the advantages of the small individualized organization could be brought back. These advantages would occur within groups simply because there would be a small number of blocks, albeit larger blocks, with which to build and rebuild the organization.

But most of all, and this is still uncertain, despite the extent to which we behavioral scientists have been enamoured of groups, there would be increased human advantages of cohesiveness, motivation, and commitment, and via that route, both increased productivity, stronger social glue within the organization, and a wider interaction between organization and environment.

SUMMARY

Far and away the most powerful and beloved tool of applied behavioral scientists is the small face-to-face group. Since the Western Electric researches, behavioral scientists have been learning to understand, exploit and love groups. Groups attracted interest initially as devices for improving the implementation of decisions and to increase human commitment and motivation. They are now loved because they are also creative and innovative, they often make better quality decisions than individuals, and because they make organizational life more livable for people. One can't hire an applied behavioral scientist into an organization who within ten minutes will not want to call a group meeting and talk things over. The group meeting is his primary technology, his primary tool.

But groups in organizations are not an invention of behavioral types. They are a natural phenomenon of organizations. Organizations develop informal groups, like it or not. It is both possible and sensible to describe most large organizations as collections of groups in interaction with one another; bargaining with one another, forming coalitions with one another, cooperating and competing with one another. It is possible and sensible too to treat the decisions that emerge from large organizations as a resultant of the interplay of forces among groups within the organization, and not just the resultant of rational analysis.

On the down side, small face-to-face groups are great tools for disciplining and controlling their members. Contemporary China, for example, has just a fraction of the number of lawyers in the United States. Partially this is a result of the lesser complexity of Chinese society and lower levels of education. But a large part of it, surprisingly enough, seems to derive from the fact that modern China is designed around small groups. Since small groups take responsibility for the discipline and control of their members many deviant acts which would be considered illegal in the United States never enter the formal legal system in China. The law controls individual deviation less, the group controls it more (Li, 1971).

Control of individual behavior is also a major problem of large complex western organizations. This problem has driven many organizations into elaborate bureaucratic quasi-legal sets of rules, ranging from job evaluation schemes to performance evaluations to incentive systems; all individually based, all terribly complex, all creating problems of distributive justice. Any organizational design that might eliminate much of that legalistic superstructure therefore begins to look highly desirable.

Management should consider building organizations using a material now understood very well and with properties that look very promising, the small group. Until recently, at least, the human group has primarily been used for patching and mending organizations that were originally built of other materials.

The major unanswered questions in my mind are not in the understanding of groups, nor in the potential utility of the group as a building block. The more difficult answered question is whether or not the approaching era is one in which Americans would willingly work in such apparently contra-individualistic units. I think we are.

REFERENCES

Johnson, Richard T. and William G. Ouchi. Made in America (under Japanese management). *Harvard Business Review,* September–October 1974.

Li, Victor. The Development of the Chinese Legal System, in John Lindbeck (ed.), *China: The Management of a Revolutionary Society.* Seattle: University of Washington Press, 1971.

Likert, Rensis. *New Patterns of Management.* New York: McGraw-Hill, 1961.

Reading 36

Groupthink

Irving L. Janis

"How could we have been so stupid?" President John F. Kennedy asked after he and a close group of advisers had blundered into the Bay of Pigs invasion. For the last two years I have been studying that question, as it applies not only to the Bay of Pigs decision-makers but also to those who led the United States into such other major fiascos as the failure to be prepared for the attack on Pearl Harbor, the Korean War stalemate and the escalation of the Vietnam War.

Stupidity certainly is not the explanation. The men who participated in making the Bay of Pigs decision, for instance, comprised one of the greatest arrays of intellectual talent in the history of American government—Dean Rusk, Robert McNamara, Douglas Dillon, Robert Kennedy, McGeorge Bundy, Arthur Schlesinger Jr., Allen Dulles and others.

It also seemed to me that explanations were incomplete if they concentrated only on disturbances in the behavior of each individual within a decision-making body: temporary emotional states of elation, fear, or anger that reduce a man's mental efficiency, for example, or chronic blind spots arising from a man's social prejudices or idiosyncratic biases.

I preferred to broaden the picture by looking at the fiascos from the standpoint of group dynamics as it has been explored over the past three decades, first by the great social psychologist Kurt Lewin and later in many experimental situations by myself and other behavioral scientists. My conclusion after poring over hundreds of relevant documents—historical reports about formal group meetings and informal conversations among the members—is that the groups that committed the fiascos were victims of what I call "groupthink."

"Groupy"

In each case study, I was surprised to discover the extent to which each group displayed the typical phenomena of social conformity that are regularly encountered in studies of group dynamics among ordinary citizens. For example, some of the phenomena appear to be completely in line with findings from social-psychological experiments showing that powerful social pressures are brought to bear by the members of a cohesive group whenever a dissident begins to voice his objections to a group consensus. Other phenomena are reminiscent of the shared illusions observed in encounter groups and friendship cliques when the members simultaneously reach a peak of "groupy" feelings.

Above all, there are numerous indications pointing to the development of group norms that bolster morale at the expense of critical thinking. One of the most common norms appears to be that of remaining loyal to the group by sticking with the policies to which the group has already committed itself, even when those policies are obviously working out badly and have unintended consequences that disturb the conscience of each member. This is one of the key characteristics of groupthink.

1984

I use the term groupthink as a quick and easy way to refer to the mode of thinking that persons engage in when *concurrence-seeking* becomes so dominant in a cohesive ingroup that it tends to override realistic appraisal of alternative courses of action. Groupthink is a term of the same order as the words in the newspeak vocabulary George Orwell used in his dismaying world of *1984*. In that context, groupthink takes on an invidious connotation. Exactly such a connotation is intended, since the term refers to a deterioration in mental efficiency, reality testing and moral judgments as a result of group pressures.

The symptoms of groupthink arise when the members of decision-making groups become motivated to avoid being too harsh in their judgments of their leaders' or their colleagues' ideas. They adopt a soft line of criticism, even in their own thinking. At their meetings, all the members are amiable and seek complete concurrence on every important issue, with no bickering or conflict to spoil the cozy, "we-feeling" atmosphere.

Kill

Paradoxically, soft-headed groups are often hard-hearted when it comes to dealing with outgroups or enemies. They find it relatively easy to resort to dehumanizing solutions—they will readily authorize bombing attacks that kill large numbers of civilians in the name of the noble cause of persuading an unfriendly government to negotiate at the peace table. They are unlikely to pursue the more difficult and controversial issues that arise when alternatives to a harsh military solution come up for discussion. Nor are they inclined to raise ethical issues that carry the implication that *this fine group of ours, with its humanitarianism and its high-minded principles, might be capable of adopting a course of action that is inhumane and immoral.*

Norms

There is evidence from a number of social-psychological studies that as the members of a group feel more accepted by the others, which is a central feature of increased group cohesiveness, they display less overt conformity to group norms. Thus we would expect that the more cohesive a group becomes, the less the members will feel constrained to censor what they say out of fear of being socially punished for antagonizing the leader or any of their fellow members.

In contrast, the groupthink type of conformity tends to increase as group cohesiveness increases. Groupthink involves nondeliberate suppression of critical thoughts as a result of internalization of the group's norms, which is quite different from deliberate suppression on the basis of external threats of social punishment. The more cohesive the group, the greater the inner compulsion on the part of each member to avoid creating disunity, which inclines him to believe in the soundness of whatever proposals are promoted by the leader or by a majority of the group's members.

In a cohesive group, the danger is not so much that each individual will fail to reveal his objections to what the others propose but that he will think the proposal is a good one, without attempting to carry out a careful, critical scrutiny of the pros and cons of the alternatives. When groupthink becomes domi-

nant, there also is considerable suppression of deviant thoughts, but it takes the form of each person's deciding that his misgivings are not relevant and should be set aside, that the benefit of the doubt regarding any lingering uncertainties should be given to the group consensus.

Stress

I do not mean to imply that all cohesive groups necessarily suffer from groupthink. All ingroups may have a mild tendency toward groupthink, displaying one or another of the symptoms from time to time, but it need not be so dominant as to influence the quality of the group's final decision. Neither do I mean to imply that there is anything necessarily inefficient or harmful about group decisions in general. On the contrary, a group whose members have properly defined roles, with traditions concerning the procedures to follow in pursuing a critical inquiry, probably is capable of making better decisions than any individual group member working alone.

The problem is that the advantages of having decisions made by groups are often lost because of powerful psychological pressures that arise when the members work closely together, share the same set of values and, above all, face a crisis situation that puts everyone under intense stress.

The main principle of groupthink, which I offer in the spirit of Parkinson's Law, is this:

> The more amiability and esprit de corps there is among the members of a policy-making ingroup, the greater the danger that independent critical thinking will be replaced by groupthink, which is likely to result in irrational and dehumanizing actions directed against outgroups.

Symptoms

In my studies of high-level governmental decision-makers, both civilian and military, I have found eight main symptoms of groupthink.

1 Invulnerability   Most or all of the members of the ingroup share an *illusion* of invulnerability that provides for them some degree of reassurance about obvious dangers and leads them to become overoptimistic and willing to take extraordinary risks. It also causes them to fail to respond to clear warnings of danger.

The Kennedy ingroup, which uncritically accepted the Central Intelligence Agency's disastrous Bay of Pigs plan, operated on the false assumption that they could keep secret the fact that the United States was responsible for the invasion of Cuba. Even after news of the plan began to leak out, their belief remained unshaken. They failed even to consider the danger that awaited them: a worldwide revulsion against the U.S.

A similar attitude appeared among the members of President Lyndon B. Johnson's ingroup, the "Tuesday Cabinet," which kept escalating the Vietnam War despite repeated setbacks and failures. "There was a belief," Bill Moyers commented after he resigned, "that if we indicated a willingness to use our power, they [the North Vietnamese] would get the message and back away from an all-out confrontation. . . . There was a confidence—it was never bragged about, it was just there—that when the chips were really down, the other people would fold."

A most poignant example of an illustion of invulnerability involves the ingroup around Admiral H. E. Kimmel, which failed to prepare for the possibility of a Japanese attack on Pearl Harbor despite repeated warnings. Informed by his intelligence chief that radio contact with Japanese aircraft carriers had been lost, Kimmel joked about it: "What, you don't know where the carriers are? Do you mean to say that they could be rounding Diamond Head (at Honolulu) and you wouldn't know it?" The carriers were in fact moving full-steam toward Kimmel's command post at the time. Laughing together about a danger signal, which labels it as a purely laughing matter, is a characteristic manifestation of groupthink.

2 Rationale   As we see, victims of groupthink ignore warnings; they also collectively construct rationalizations in order to discount warnings and other forms of negative feedback that, taken seriously, might lead the group members to reconsider their assumptions each time they recommit themselves to past decisions. Why did the Johnson ingroup avoid reconsidering its escalation policy when time and again the expectations on which they based their decisions turned out to be wrong? James C. Thompson, Jr., a Harvard historian who spent five years as an observing participant in both the State Department and the White House, tells us that the policymakers avoided critical discussion of their prior decisions and continually invented new rationalizations so that they could sincerely recommit themselves to defeating the North Vietnamese.

In the fall of 1964, before the bombing of North Vietnam began, some of the policymakers predicted that six weeks of air strikes would induce the North Vietnamese to seek peace talks. When someone asked, "What if they don't?" the answer was that another four weeks certainly would do the trick.

Later, after each setback, the ingroup agreed that by investing just a bit more effort (by stepping up the bomb tonnage a bit, for instance), their course of action would prove to be right. *The Pentagon Papers* bear out these observations.

In *The Limits of Intervention,* Townsend Hoopes, who was acting Secretary of the Air Force under Johnson, says that Walt W. Rostow in particular showed a remarkable capacity for what has been called "instant rationalization." According to Hoopes, Rostow buttressed the group's optimism about being on the road to victory by culling selected scraps of evidence from news reports or, if necessary, by inventing "plausible" forecasts that had no basis in evidence at all.

Admiral Kimmel's group rationalized away their warnings, too. Right up to December 7, 1941, they convinced themselves that the Japanese would never dare attempt a full-scale surprise assault against Hawaii because Japan's leaders would realize that it would precipitate an all-out war which the United States would surely win. They made no attempt to look at the situation through the eyes of the Japanese leaders—another manifestation of groupthink.

3 Morality   Victims of groupthink believe unquestioningly in the inherent morality of their ingroup; this belief inclines the members to ignore the ethical or moral consequences of their decisions.

Evidence that this symptom is at work usually is of a negative kind—the things that are left unsaid in group meetings. At least two influential persons had doubts about the morality of the Bay of Pigs adventure. One of them, Arthur Schlesinger Jr., presented his strong objections in a memorandum to President Kennedy and Secretary of State Rusk but suppressed them when he attended meetings of the Kennedy team. The other, Senator J. William Fullbright, was not a member of the group, but the President invited him to express his misgivings in a speech to the policymakers. However, when Fullbright finished speaking the President moved on to other agenda items without asking for reactions of the group.

David Kraslow and Stuart H. Loory, in *The Secret Search for Peace in Vietnam,* report that during 1966 President Johnson's ingroup was concerned primarily with selecting bomb targets in North Vietnam. They based their selection on four factors—the military advantage, the risk to American aircraft and pilots, the danger of forcing other countries into the fighting, and the danger of heavy civilian casualties. At their regular Tuesday luncheons, they weighed these factors the way school teachers grade examination papers, averaging them out. Though evidence on this point is scant, I suspect that the group's ritualistic adherence to a standardized procedure induced the members to feel morally justified in their destructive way of dealing with the Vietnamese people—after all, the danger of heavy civilian casualties from U.S. air strikes was taken into account on their checklists.

4 Stereotypes   Victims of groupthink hold stereotyped views of the leaders of enemy groups: they are so evil that genuine attempts at negotiating differences with them are unwarranted, or they are too weak or too stupid to deal effectively with whatever attempts the ingroup makes to defeat their purposes, no matter how risky the attempts are.

Kennedy's groupthinkers believed that Premier Fidel Castro's air force was so ineffectual that obsolete B-26s could knock it out completely in a surprise attack before the invasion began. They also believed that Castro's army was so weak that a small Cuban-exile brigade could establish a well-protected beachhead at the Bay of Pigs. In addition, they believed that Castro was not smart enough to put down any possible internal uprisings in support of the exiles. They were wrong on all three assumptions. Though much of the blame was attributable to faulty intelligence, the point is that none of Kennedy's advisers even questioned the CIA planners about these assumptions.

The Johnson advisers' sloganistic thinking about "the Communist apparatus" that was "working all around the world" (as Dean Rusk put it) led them to overlook the powerful nationalistic strivings of the North Vietnamese government and its efforts to ward off Chinese domination. The crudest of all stereotypes used by Johnson's inner circle to justify their policies was the domino theory ("If we don't stop the Reds in South Vietnam, tomorrow they will be in Hawaii and next week they will be in San Francisco," Johnson once said). The group so firmly accepted this stereotype that it became almost impossible for any adviser to introduce a more sophisticated viewpoint.

In the documents on Pearl Harbor, it is clear to see that the Navy commanders stationed in Hawaii had a naive image of Japan as a midget that would not dare to strike a blow against a powerful giant.

5 Pressure   Victims of groupthink apply direct pressure to any individual who momentarily expresses doubts about any of the group's shared illusions or who questions the validity of the arguments supporting a policy alternative favored by the majority. This gambit reinforces the concurrence-seeking norm that loyal members are expected to maintain.

President Kennedy probably was more active than anyone else in raising skeptical questions during the Bay of Pigs meetings, and yet he seems to have encouraged the group's docile, uncritical acceptance of defective arguments in favor of the CIA's plan. At every meeting, he allowed the CIA representatives to dominate the discussion. He permitted them to give their immediate refutations in response to each tentative doubt that one of the others expressed, instead of asking whether anyone shared the doubt or wanted to pursue the implications of the new worrisome issue that had just been raised. And at the most crucial meeting, when he was calling on each member to give his vote for or against the plan, he did not call on Arthur Schlesinger, the one man there who was known by the President to have serious misgivings.

Historian Thomson informs us that whenever a member of Johnson's ingroup began to express doubts, the group used subtle social pressures to "domesticate" him. To start with, the dissenter was made to feel at home, provided that he lived up to two restrictions: 1) that he did not voice his doubts to outsiders, which would play into the hands of the opposition; and 2) that he kept his criticisms within the bounds of acceptable deviation, which meant not challenging any of the fundamental assumptions that went into the group's prior commitments. One such "domesticated dissenter" was Bill Moyers. When Moyers arrived at a meeting, Thomson tells us, the President greeted him with, "Well, here comes Mr. Stop-the-Bombing."

6 Self-censorship Victims of groupthink avoid deviating from what appears to be group consensus; they keep silent about their misgivings and even minimize to themselves the importance of their doubts.

As we have seen, Schlesinger was not at all hesitant about presenting his strong objections to the Bay of Pigs plan in a memorandum to the President and the Secretary of State. But he became keenly aware of his tendency to suppress objections at the White House meetings. "In the months after the Bay of Pigs I bitterly reproached myself for having kept so silent during those crucial discussions in the cabinet room," Schlesinger writes in *A Thousand Days*. "I can only explain my failure to do more than raise a few timid questions by reporting that one's impulse to blow the whistle on this nonsense was simply undone by the circumstances of the discussion."

7 Unanimity Victims of groupthink share an *illusion* of unanimity within the group concerning almost all judgments expressed by members who speak in favor of the majority view. This symptom results partly from the preceding one, whose effects are augmented by the false assumption that any individual who remains silent during any part of the discussion is in full accord with what the others are saying.

When a group of persons who respect each other's opinions arrives at a unanimous view, each member is likely to feel that the belief must be true. This reliance on consensual validation within the group tends to replace individual critical thinking and reality testing, unless there are clear-cut disagreements among the members. In contemplating a course of action such as the invasion of Cuba, it is painful for the members to confront disagreements within their group, particularly if it becomes apparent that there are widely divergent views about whether the preferred course of action is too risky to

undertake at all. Such disagreements are likely to arouse anxieties about making a serious error. Once the sense of unanimity is shattered, the members no longer can feel complacently confident about the decision they are inclined to make. Each man must then face the annoying realization that there are troublesome uncertainties and he must diligently seek out the best information he can get in order to decide for himself exactly how serious the risks might be. This is one of the unpleasant consequences of being in a group of hardheaded, critical thinkers.

To avoid such an unpleasant state, the members often become inclined, without quite realizing it, to prevent latent disagreements from surfacing when they are about to initiate a risky course of action. The group leader and the members support each other in playing up the areas of convergence in their thinking, at the expense of fully exploring divergencies that might reveal unsettled issues.

"Our meetings took place in a curious atmosphere of assumed consensus," Schlesinger writes. His additional comments clearly show that, curiously, the consensus was an illusion—an illusion that could be maintained only because the major participants did not reveal their own reasoning or discuss their idiosyncratic assumptions and vague reservations. Evidence from several sources makes it clear that even the three principals—President Kennedy, Rusk and McNamara—had widely differing assumptions about the invasion plan.

8 Mindguards Victims of groupthink sometimes appoint themselves as mindguards to protect the leader and fellow members from adverse information that might break the complacency they shared about the effectiveness and morality of past decisions. At a large birthday party for his wife, Attorney General Robert F. Kennedy, who had been constantly informed about the Cuban invasion plan, took Schlesinger aside and asked him why he was opposed. Kennedy listened coldly and said, "You may be right or you may be wrong, but the President has made his mind up. Don't push it any further. Now is the time for everyone to help him all they can."

Rusk also functioned as a highly effective mindguard by failing to transmit to the group the strong objections of three "outsiders" who had learned of the invasion plan—Undersecretary of State Chester Bowles, USIA Director Edward R. Murrow, and Rusk's intelligence chief, Roger Hilsman. Had Rusk done so, their warnings might have reinforced Schlesinger's memorandum and jolted some of Kennedy's ingroup, if not the President himself, into reconsidering the decision.

Products

When a group of executives frequently displays most or all of these interrelated symptoms, a detailed study of their deliberations is likely to reveal a number of immediate consequences. These consequences are, in effect, products of poor decision-making practices because they lead to inadequate solutions to the problems being dealt with.

First, the group limits its discussions to a few alternative courses of action (often only two) without an initial survey of all the alternatives that might be worthy of consideration.

Second, the group fails to reexamine the course of action initially preferred by the majority after they learn of risks and drawbacks they had not considered originally.

Third, the members spend little or no time discussing whether there are nonobvious gains they may have overlooked or ways of reducing the seemingly prohibitive costs that made rejected alternatives appear undesirable to them.

Fourth, members make little or no attempt to obtain information from experts within their own organizations who might be able to supply more precise estimates of potential losses and gains.

Fifth, members show positive interest in facts and opinions that support their preferred policy; they tend to ignore facts and opinions that do not.

Sixth, members spend little time deliberating about how the chosen policy might be hindered by bureaucratic inertia, sabotaged by political opponents, or temporarily derailed by common accidents. Consequently, they fail to work out contingency plans to cope with foreseeable setbacks that could endanger the overall success of their chosen course.

Support

The search for an explanation of why groupthink occurs has led me through a quagmire of complicated theoretical issues in the murky area of human motivation. My belief, based on recent social psychological research, is that we can best understand the various symptoms of groupthink as a mutual effort among the group members to maintain self-esteem and emotional equanimity by providing social support to each other, especially at times when they share responsibility for making vital decisions.

Even when no important decision is pending, the typical administrator will begin to doubt the wisdom and morality of his past decisions each time he receives information about setbacks, particularly if the information is accompanied by negative feedback from prominent men who originally had been his supporters. It should not be surprising, therefore, to find that individual members strive to develop unanimity and esprit de corps that will help bolster each other's morale, to create an optimistic outlook about the success of pending decisions, and to reaffirm the positive value of past policies to which all of them are committed.

Pride

Shared illusions of invulnerability, for example, can reduce anxiety about taking risks. Rationalizations help members believe that the risks are really not so bad after all. The assumption of inherent morality helps the members to avoid feelings of shame or guilt. Negative stereotypes function as stress-reducing devices to enhance a sense of moral righteousness as well as pride in a lofty mission.

The mutual enhancement of self-esteem and morale may have functional value in enabling the members to maintain their capacity to take action, but it has maladaptive consequences insofar as concurrence-seeking tendencies interfere with critical, rational capacities and lead to serious errors of judgment.

While I have limited my study to decision-making bodies in Government, groupthink symptoms appear in business, industry and any other field where small, cohesive groups make the decisions. It is vital, then, for all sorts of people—and especially group leaders—to know what steps they can take to prevent groupthink.

Remedies

To counterpoint my case studies of the major fiascos, I have also investigated two highly successful group enterprises, the formulation of the Marshall

Plan in the Truman Administration and the handling of the Cuban missile crisis by President Kennedy and his advisers. I have found it instructive to examine the steps Kennedy took to change his group's decision-making processes. These changes ensured that the mistakes made by his Bay of Pigs ingroup were not repeated by the missile-crisis ingroup, even though the membership of both groups was essentially the same.

The following recommendations for preventing groupthink incorporate many of the good practices I discovered to be characteristic of the Marshall Plan and missile-crisis groups:

1 The leader of a policy-forming group should assign the role of critical evaluator to each member, encouraging the group to give high priority to open airing of objections and doubts. This practice needs to be reinforced by the leader's acceptance of criticism of his own judgments in order to discourage members from soft-pedaling their disagreements and from allowing their striving for concurrence to inhibit criticism.

2 When the key members of a hierarchy assign a policy-planning mission to any group within their organization, they should adopt an impartial stance instead of stating preferences and expectations at the beginning. This will encourage open inquiry and impartial probing of a wide range of policy alternatives.

3 The organization routinely should set up several outside policy-planning and evaluation groups to work on the same policy question, each deliberating under a different leader. This can prevent the insulation of an ingroup.

4 At intervals before the group reaches a final consensus, the leader should require each member to discuss the group's deliberations with associates in his own unit of the organization—assuming that those associates can be trusted to adhere to the same security regulations that govern the policy-makers—and then to report back their reactions to the group.

5 The group should invite one or more outside experts to each meeting on a staggered basis and encourage the experts to challenge the views of the core members.

6 At every general meeting of the group, whenever the agenda calls for an evaluation of policy alternatives, at least one member should play devil's advocate, functioning as a good lawyer in challenging the testimony of those who advocate the majority position.

7 Whenever the policy issue involves relations with a rival nation or organization, the group should devote a sizable block of time, perhaps an entire session, to a survey of all warning signals from the rivals and should write alternative scenarios on the rivals' intentions.

8 When the group is surveying policy alternatives for feasibility and effectiveness, it should from time to time divide into two or more subgroups to meet separately, under different chairmen, and then come back together to hammer out differences.

9 After reaching a preliminary consensus about what seems to be the best policy, the group should hold a "second-chance" meeting at which every member expresses as vividly as he can all his residual doubts, and rethinks the entire issue before making a definitive choice.

How

These recommendations have their disadvantages. To encourage the open airing of objections, for instance, might lead to prolonged and costly debates when a rapidly growing crisis requires immediate solution. It also could cause rejection, depression and anger. A leader's failure to set a norm might create cleavage between leader and members that could develop into a disruptive power struggle if the leader looks on the emerging consensus as anathema. Setting up outside evaluation groups might increase the risk of security leakage. Still, inventive executives who know their way around the organizational maze probably can figure out how to apply one or another of the prescriptions successfully, without harmful side effects.

They also could benefit from the advice of outside experts in the administrative and behavioral sciences. Though these experts have much to offer, they have had few chances to work on policy-making machinery within large organizations. As matters now stand, executives innovate only when they need new procedures to avoid repeating serious errors that have deflated their self-images.

In this era of atomic warheads, urban disorganization and ecocatastrophes, it seems to me that policy-makers should collaborate with behavioral scientists and give top priority to preventing groupthink and its attendant fiascos.

Reading 37

Assets and Liabilities in Group Problem Solving: The Need for an Integrative Function

Norman R. R. Maier

A number of investigations have raised the question of whether group problem solving is superior, inferior, or equal to individual problem solving. Evidence can be cited in support of each position so that the answer to this question remains ambiguous. Rather than pursue this generalized approach to the question, it seems more fruitful to explore the forces that influence problem solving under the two conditions (see reviews by Hoffman, 1965; Kelley and Thibaut, 1954). It is hoped that a better recognition of these forces will permit clarification of the varied dimensions of the problem-solving process, especially in groups.

The forces operating in such groups include some that are assets, some that are liabilities, and some that can be either assets or liabilities, depending upon the skills of the members, especially those of the discussion leader. Let us examine these three sets of forces.

GROUP ASSETS

Greater Sum Total of Knowledge and Information

There is more information in a group than in any of its members. Thus problems that require the utilization of knowledge should give groups an advantage over individuals. Even if one member of the group (e.g., the leader) knows much more than anyone else, the limited unique knowledge of lesser-informed individuals could serve to fill in some gaps in knowledge. For example, a skilled machinist might contribute to an engineer's problem solving and an ordinary workman might supply information on how a new machine might be received by workers.

Greater Number of Approaches to a Problem

It has been shown that individuals get into ruts in their thinking (Duncker, 1945; Maier, 1930; Wertheimer, 1959). Many obstacles stand in the way of achieving a goal, and a solution must circumvent these. The individual is handicapped in that he tends to persist in his approach and thus fails to find another approach that might solve the problem in a simpler manner. Individuals in a group have the same failing, but the approaches in which they are persisting may be different. For example, one researcher may try to prevent the spread of a disease by making man immune to the germ, another by finding and destroying the carrier of the germ, and still another by altering the environment so as to kill the germ before it reaches man. There is no way of determining which approach will best achieve the desired goal, but undue persistence in any one will stifle new discoveries. Since group members do not have identical approaches, each can contribute by knocking others out of ruts in thinking.

Participation in Proolem Solving Increases Acceptance

Many problems require solutions that depend upon the support of others to be effective. Insofar as group problem solving permits participation and influence, it follows that more individuals accept solutions when a group solves the problem than when one person solves it. When one individual solves a problem, he still has the task of persuading others. It follows, therefore, that when groups solve such problems, a greater number of persons accept and feel responsible for making the solution work. A low-quality solution that has good acceptance can be more effective than a higher-quality solution that lacks acceptance.

Better Comprehension of the Decision

Decisions made by an individual, which are to be carried out by others, must be communicated from the decision maker to the decision executors. Thus individual problem solving often requires an additional stage—that of relaying the decision reached. Failures in this communication process detract from the merits of the decision and can even cause its failure or create a problem of greater magnitude than the initial problem that was solved. Many organizational problems can be traced to inadequate communication of decisions made by superiors and transmitted to subordinates, who have the task of implementing the decision.

The chances for communication failures are greatly reduced when the individuals who must work together in executing the decision have participated in making it. They not only understand the solution because they saw it develop, but they are also aware of the several other alternatives that were considered and the reasons why they were discarded. The common assumption that decisions supplied by superiors are arbitrarily reached therefore disappears. A full knowledge of goals, obstacles, alternatives, and factual information is essential to communication, and this communication is maximized when the total problem-solving process is shared.

GROUP LIABILITIES

Social Pressure

Social pressure is a major force making for conformity. The desire to be a good group member and to be accepted tends to silence disagreement and favors consensus. Majority opinions tend to be accepted regardless of whether or not their objective quality is logically and scientifically sound. Problems requiring solutions based upon facts, regardless of feelings and wishes, can suffer in group problem-solving situations.

It has been shown (Maier and Solem, 1962) that minority opinions in leaderless groups have little influence on the solution reached, even when these opinions are the correct ones. Reaching agreement in a group often is confused with finding the right answer, and it is for this reason that the dimensions of a decision's acceptance and its objective quality must be distinguished (Maier, 1963).

Valence of Solutions

When leaderless groups (made up of three or four persons) engage in problem solving, they propose a variety of solutions. Each solution may receive both critical and supportive comments, as well as descriptive and explorative comments from other partici-

pants. If the number of negative and positive comments for each solution are algebraically summed, each may be given a *valence index* (Hoffman and Maier, 1964). The first solution that receives a positive valence value of 15 tends to be adopted to the satisfaction of all participants about 85 percent of the time, regardless of its quality. Higher quality solutions introduced after the critical value for one of the solutions has been reached have little chance of achieving real consideration. Once some degree of consensus is reached, the jelling process seems to proceed rather rapidly.

The critical valence value of 15 appears not to be greatly altered by the nature of the problem or the exact size of the group. Rather, it seems to designate a turning point between the idea-getting process and the decision-making process (idea evaluation). A solution's valence index is not a measure of the number of persons supporting the solution, since a vocal minority can build up a solution's valence by actively pushing it. In this sense, valence becomes an influence in addition to social pressure in determining an outcome.

Since a solution's valence is independent of its objective quality, this group factor becomes an important liability in group problem solving, even when the value of a decision depends upon objective criteria (facts and logic). It becomes a means whereby skilled manipulators can have more influence over the group process than their proportion of membership deserves.

Individual Domination

In most leaderless groups a dominant individual emerges and captures more than his share of influence on the outcome. He can achieve this end through a greater degree of participation (valence), persuasive ability, or stubborn persistence (fatiguing the opposition). None of these factors is related to problem-solving ability, so that the best problem solver in the group may not have the influence to upgrade the quality of the group's solution (which he would have had if left to solve the problem by himself).

Hoffman and Maier (1967) found that the mere fact of appointing a leader causes this person to dominate a discussion. Thus, regardless of his problem-solving ability a leader tends to exert a major influence on the outcome of a discussion.

Conflicting Secondary Goal: Winning the Argument

When groups are confronted with a problem, the initial goal is to obtain a solution. However, the appearance of several alternatives causes individuals to have preferences and once these emerge the desire to support a position is created. Converting those with neutral viewpoints and refuting those with opposed viewpoints now enters into the problem-solving process. More and more the goal becomes that of winning the decision rather than finding the best solution. This new goal is unrelated to the quality of the problem's solution and therefore can result in lowering the quality of the decision (Hoffman and Maier, 1966).

FACTORS THAT SERVE AS ASSETS OR LIABILITIES, DEPENDING LARGELY UPON THE SKILL OF THE DISCUSSION LEADER

Disagreement

The fact that discussion may lead to disagreement can serve either to create hard feelings among members or lead to a resolution of conflict and hence to an innovative solution (Hoffman, 1961; Hoffman, Harburg, and Maier, 1962; Hoffman and Maier, 1961; Maier, 1958, 1963; Maier and Hoffman, 1965). The first of these outcomes of disagreement is a liability, especially with regard to the acceptance of solutions; while the second is an asset, particularly where innovation is desired. A leader can treat disagreement as undesirable and thereby reduce the probability of both hard feelings and innovation, or he can maximize disagreement and risk hard feelings in his attempts to achieve innovation. The skill of a leader requires his ability to create a climate for disagreement which will permit innovation without risking hard feelings. The leader's perception of disagreement is one of the critical factors in this skill area (Maier and Hoffman, 1965). Others involve permissiveness (Maier, 1953), delaying the reaching of a solution (Maier and Hoffman, 1960b; Maier and Solem, 1962), techniques for processing information and opinions (Maier, 1963; Maier and Hoffman, 1960a; Maier and Maier, 1957), and techniques for separating idea-getting from idea-evaluation (Maier, 1960, 1963; Osborn, 1953).

Conflicting Interests versus Mutual Interests

Disagreement in discussion may take many forms. Often participants disagree with one another with regard to solutions, but when issues are explored one finds that these conflicting solutions are designed to solve different problems. Before one can rightly expect agreement on a solution, there should be agreement on the nature of the problem. Even before this, there should be agreement on the goal, as well as on the various obstacles that prevent the goal from being reached. Once distinctions are made between goals, obstacles, and solutions (which represent ways of overcoming obstacles), one finds increased opportunities for cooperative problem solving and less conflict (Hoffman and Maier, 1959; Maier, 1960, 1963; Maier and Solem, 1962; Solem, 1965).

Often there is also disagreement regarding whether the objective of a solution is to achieve quality or acceptance (Maier and Hoffman, 1964b), and frequently a stated problem reveals a complex of separate problems, each having separate solutions so that a search for a single solution is impossible (Maier, 1963). Communications often are inadequate because the discussion is not synchronized and each person is engaged in discussing a different aspect. Organizing discussion to synchronize the exploration of different aspects of the problem and to follow a systematic procedure increases solution quality (Maier and Hoffman, 1960a; Maier and Maier, 1957). The leadership function of influencing discussion procedure is quite distinct from the function of evaluating or contributing ideas (Maier, 1950, 1953).

When the discussion leader aids in the separation of the several aspects of the problem-solving process and delays the solution-mindedness of the group (Maier, 1958, 1963; Maier and Solem, 1962), both solution quality and acceptance improve; when he hinders or fails to facilitate the isolation of these varied processes, he risks a deterioration in the group process (Solem, 1965). His skill thus determines whether a discussion drifts toward conflicting interests or whether mutual interests are located. Cooperative problem solving can only occur after the mutual interests have been established, and it is surprising how often they can be found when the discussion leader makes this his task (Maier, 1952, 1963; Maier and Hayes, 1962).

Risk Taking

Groups are more willing than individuals to reach decisions involving risks (Wallach and Kogan, 1965; Wallach, Kogan, and Bem, 1962). Taking risks is a factor in acceptance of change, but change may either represent a gain or a loss. The best guard against the latter outcome seems to be primarily a matter of a decision's quality. In a group situation this depends upon the leader's skill in utilizing the factors that represent group assets and avoiding those that make for liabilities.

Time Requirements

In general, more time is required for a group to reach a decision than for a single individual to reach one. Insofar as some problems require quick decisions, individual decisions are favored. In other situations acceptance and quality are requirements, but excessive time without sufficient returns also represents a loss. On the other hand, discussion can resolve conflicts, whereas reaching consensus has limited value (Wallach and Kogan, 1965). The practice of hastening a meeting can prevent full discussion, but failure to move a discussion forward can lead to boredom and fatigue-type solutions, in which members agree merely to get out of the meeting. The effective utilization of discussion time (a delicate balance between permissiveness and control on the part of the leader), therefore, is needed to make the time factor an asset rather than a liability. Unskilled leaders tend to be too concerned with reaching a solution and therefore terminate a discussion before the group potential is achieved (Maier and Hoffman, 1960b).

Who Changes

In reaching consensus or agreement, some members of a group must change. Persuasive forces do not operate in individual problem solving in the same way they operate in a group situation; hence, the changing of someone's mind is not an issue. In group situations, however, who changes can be an asset or a liability. If persons with the most constructive views are induced to change, the end-product suffers; whereas if persons with the least constructive points of view change, the end-product is upgraded. The leader can upgrade the quality of a decision because his position permits him to protect the person with a minority view and increase his opportunity to influence the majority position. This protection is a constructive factor because a minority viewpoint influences only when facts favor it (Maier, 1950, 1952; Maier and Solem, 1952).

The leader also plays a constructive role insofar as he can facilitate communications and thereby reduce misunderstandings (Maier, 1952; Solem, 1965). The leader has an adverse effect on the end-product when he suppresses minority views by holding a contrary position and when he uses his office to promote his own views (Maier and Hoffman, 1960b, 1962; Maier and Solem, 1952). In many problem-solving discussions the untrained leader plays a dominant role in influencing the outcome, and when he is more resistant to changing his views than are the other participants, the quality of the outcome tends to be lowered. This negative leader-influence was demonstrated by experiments in which untrained leaders were asked to obtain a second solution to a problem after they had obtained their first one (Maier and Hoffman, 1960a). It was found that the second solution tended to be superior to the first. Since the dominant individual had influenced the first solution, he had won his point and therefore ceased to dominate the subsequent discussion which led to the second solution. Acceptance of a solution also increases as the leader sees disagreement as idea-producing rather than as a source of difficulty or trouble (Maier and Hoffman, 1965). Leaders who see some of their participants as troublemakers obtain fewer innovative solutions and gain less acceptance of decisions made than leaders who see disagreeing members as persons with ideas.

THE LEADER'S ROLE FOR INTEGRATED GROUPS

Two Differing Types of Group Process

In observing group problem solving under various conditions, it is rather easy to distinguish between cooperative problem-solving activity and persuasion or selling approaches. Problem-solving activity includes searching, trying out ideas on one another, listening to understand rather than to refute, making relatively short speeches, and reacting to differences in opinion as stimulating. The general pattern is one of rather complete participation, involvement, and interest. Persuasion activity includes the selling of opinions already formed, defending a position held, either not listening at all or listening in order to be able to refute, talking dominated by a few members, unfavorable reactions to disagreement, and a lack of involvement of some members. During problem solving the behavior observed seems to be that of members interacting as segments of a group. The interaction pattern is not between certain individual members, but with the group as a whole. Sometimes it is difficult to determine who should be credited with an idea. "It just developed," is a response often used to describe the solution reached. In contrast, discussions involving selling or persuasive behavior seem to consist of a series of interpersonal interactions with each individual retaining his identity. Such groups do not function as integrated units but as separate individuals, each with an agenda. In one situation the solution is unknown and is sought; in the other, several solutions exist and conflict occurs because commitments have been made.

The Starfish Analogy

The analysis of these two group processes suggests an analogy with the behavior of the rays of a starfish under two conditions; one with the nerve ring intact, the other with the nerve ring sectioned (Hamilton, 1922; Moore, 1924; Moore and Doudoroff, 1939; Schneirla and Maier, 1940). In the intact condition, locomotion and righting behavior reveal that the behavior of each ray is not merely a function of local stimulation. Locomotion and righting behavior reveal a degree of coordination and interdependence that is centrally controlled. However, when the nerve ring is sectioned, the behavior of one ray still can influence others, but internal coordination is lacking. For example, if one ray is stimulated, it may step forward, thereby exerting pressure on the sides of the other four rays. In response to these external pressures (tactile stimulation), these rays show stepping responses on the stimulated side so that locomotion successfully occurs without the aid of neural coordination. Thus integrated behavior can occur on the basis of external control. If, however, stimulation is applied to opposite rays, the specimen may be "locked" for a time, and in some species the conflicting locomotions may divide the animal, thus destroying it (Crozier, 1920; Moore and Doudoroff, 1939).

Each of the rays of the starfish can show stepping responses even when sectioned and removed from the animal. Thus each may be regarded as an individual. In a starfish with a sectioned nerve ring the five rays become members of a group. They can successfully work together for locomotion purposes by being controlled by the dominant ray. Thus if uniformity of action is desired, the group of five rays can sometimes be more effective than the individual ray in moving the group toward a source of stimulation. However, if "locking" or the division of the organism occurs, the group action becomes less effective than individual action. External control, through the influence of a dominant ray, therefore can lead to adaptive behavior for the starfish as a whole, but it can also result in a conflict that destroys the organism. Something more than external influence is needed.

In the animal with an intact nerve ring, the function of the rays is coordinated by the nerve ring. With this type of internal organization the group is always superior to that of the individual actions. When the rays function as a part of an organized unit, rather than as a group that is physically together, they become a higher type of organization—a single intact organism. This is accomplished by the nerve ring, which in itself does not do the behaving. Rather, it receives and processes the data which the rays relay to it. Through this central organization, the responses of the rays become part of a larger pattern so that together they constitute a single coordinated total response rather than a group of individual responses.

The Leader as the Group's Central Nervous System

If we now examine what goes on in a discussion group, we find that members can problem-solve as individuals, they can influence others by external pushes and pulls, or they can function as a group with varying degrees of unity. In order for the latter function to be maximized, however, something must be introduced to serve the function of the nerve ring. In our conceptualization of group problem solving and group decision (Maier, 1963), we see this as the function of the leader. Thus the leader does not serve as a dominant ray and produce the solution. Rather, his function is to receive information, facilitate communications between the individuals, relay messages, and integrate the incoming responses so that a single unified response occurs.

Solutions that are the product of good group discussions often come as surprises to discussion leaders. One of these is unexpected generosity. If there is a weak member, this member is given less to do, in much the same way as an organism adapts to an injured limb and alters the function of other limbs to keep locomotion on course. Experimental evidence supports the point that group decisions award special consideration to needy members of groups (Hoffman and Maier, 1959). Group decisions in industrial groups often give smaller assignments to the less gifted (Maier, 1952). A leader could not effectually impose such differential treatment on group members without being charged with discriminatory practices.

Another unique aspect of group discussion is the way fairness is resolved. In a simulated problem situation involving the problem of how to introduce a new truck into a group of drivers, the typical group solution involves a trading of trucks so that several or all members stand to profit. If the leader makes the decision, the number of persons who profit is often confined to one (Maier and Hoffman, 1962; Maier and Zerfoss, 1952). In industrial practice, supervisors assign a new truck to an individual member of a crew after careful evaluation of needs. This practice results in dissatisfaction, with the charge of *unfair* being leveled at him. Despite these repeated attempts to do justice, supervisors in the telephone industry never hit upon the notion of a general reallocation of trucks, a solution that crews invariably reach when the decision is theirs to make.

In experiments involving the introduction of change, the use of group discussion tends to lead to decisions that resolve differences (Maier, 1952, 1953; Maier and Hoffman, 1961, 1964a, 1964b). Such decisions tend to be different from decisions reached by individuals because of the very fact that disagreement is common in group problem solving and rare in individual problem solving. The process of resolving difference in a constructive setting causes the exploration of additional areas and leads to solutions that are integrative rather than compromises.

Finally, group solutions tend to be tailored to fit the interests and personalities of the participants; thus group solutions to problems involving fairness, fears, face-saving, etc., tend to vary from one group to another. An outsider cannot process these variables because they are not subject to logical treatment.

If we think of the leader as serving a function in the group different from that of its membership, we might be able to create a group that can function as an intact organism. For a leader, such functions as rejecting or promoting ideas according to his personal needs are out of bounds. He must be receptive to information contributed, accept contributions without evaluating them (posting contributions on a chalk board to keep them alive), summarize information to facilitate integration, stimulate exploratory behavior, create awareness of problems of one member by others, and detect when the group is ready to resolve differences and agree to a unified solution.

Since higher organisms have more than a nerve ring and can store information, a leader might appropriately supply information, but according to our model of a leader's role, he must clearly distinguish between supplying information and promoting a solution. If his knowledge indicates the desirability of a particular solution, sharing this knowledge might lead the group to find this solution, but the solution should be the group's discovery. A leader's contributions do not receive the same treatment as those of a member of the group. Whether he likes it or not, his position is different. According to our conception of the leader's contribution to discussion, his role not only differs in influence, but gives him an entirely different function. He is to serve much as the nerve ring in the starfish and further to refine this function so as to make it a higher type of nerve ring.

This model of a leader's role in group process has served as a guide for many of our studies in group problem solving. It is not our claim that this will lead to the best possible group function under all conditions. In sharing it, we hope to indicate the nature of our guidelines in exploring group leadership as a function quite different and apart from group membership. Thus the model serves as a stimulant for research problems and as a guide for our analyses of leadership skills and principles.

CONCLUSIONS

On the basis of our analysis, it follows that the comparison of the merits of group versus individual problem solving depends on the nature of the problem, the goal to be achieved (high quality solution, highly accepted solution, effective communication and understanding of the solution, innovation, a quickly reached solution, or satisfaction), and the skill of the discussion leader. If liabilities inherent in groups are avoided, assets capitalized upon, and conditions that can serve either favorable or unfavorable outcomes are effectively used, it follows that groups have a potential which in many instances can exceed that of a superior individual functioning alone, even with respect to creativity.

This goal was nicely stated by Thibaut and Kelley (1961) when they

> wonder whether it may not be possible for a rather small, intimate group to establish a problem-solving process that capitalizes upon the total pool of information and provides for great interstimulation of ideas without any loss of innovative creativity due to social restraints [p. 268].

In order to accomplish this high level of achievement, however, a leader is needed who plays a role quite different from that of the members. His role is analogous to that of the nerve ring in the starfish which permits the rays to execute a unified response. If the leader can contribute the integrative requirement, group problem solving may emerge as a unique type of group function. This type of approach to group processes places the leader in a particular role in which he must cease to contribute, avoid evaluation, and refrain from thinking about solutions or group *products*. Instead he must concentrate on the group *process*, listen in order to understand rather than to appraise or refute, assume responsibility for accurate communication between members, be sensitive to unexpressed feelings, protect minority points of view, keep the discussion moving, and develop skills in summarizing.

REFERENCES

Crozier, W. J. Notes on some problems of adaptation. *Biological Bulletin,* 1920, **39:** 116–29.

Duncker, K. On problem solving. *Psychological Monographs,* 1945, **58**(5, whole no. 270).

Hamilton, W. F. Coordination in the starfish. III. The righting reaction as a phase of locomotion (righting and locomotion). *Journal of Comparative Psychology,* 1922, **2:**81–94.

Hoffman, L. R. Conditions for creative problem solving. *Journal of Psychology,* 1961, **52:**429–44.

Hoffman, L. R. Group problem solving. In L. Berkowitz (ed.), *Advances in experimental social psychology,* Volume 2. New York: Academic Press, 1965, pp. 99–132.

Hoffman, L. R., Harburg, E., and Maier, N. R. F. Differences and disagreement as factors in creative group problem solving. *Journal of Abnormal and Social Psychology,* 1962, **64:**206–14.

Hoffman, L. R., and Maier, N. R. F. The use of group desicion to resolve a problem of fairness. *Personnel Psychology,* 1959, **12:**545–59.

Hoffman, L. R.. and Maier, N. R. F. Quality and acceptance of problem solutions by members of homogeneous and heterogeneous groups. *Journal of Abnormal and Social Psychology,* 1961, **62:**401–407.

Hoffman, L. R., and Maier, N. R. F. Valence in the adoption of solutions by problem-solving groups: Concept, method, and results. *Journal of Abnormal and Social Psychology,* 1964, **69:**264–71.

Hoffman, L. R., and Maier, N. R. F. Valence in the adoption of solutions by problem-solving groups: II. Quality and acceptance as goals of leaders and members. Unpublished manuscript, 1967. (Mimeo).

Kelley, H. H., and Thibaut, J. W. Experimental studies of group problem solving and process. In G. Lindzey (ed.), *Handbook of social psychology.* Cambridge, Mass.: Addison Wesley, 1954, pp. 735–85.

Maier, N. R. F. Reasoning in humans. I. On direction. *Journal of Comparative Psychology,* 1930, **10:**115–43.

Maier, N. R. F. The quality of group decisions as influenced by the discussion leader. *Human Relations,* 1950, **3:**155–74.

Maier, N. R. F. *Principles of human relations.* New York: Wiley, 1952.

Maier, N. R. F. An experimental test of the effect of training on discussion leadership. *Human Relations,* 1953, **6:**161–73.

Maier, N. R. F. *The appraisal interview.* New York: Wiley, 1958.

Maier, N. R. F. Screening solutions to upgrade quality: A new approach to problem solving under conditions of uncertainty. *Journal of Psychology,* 1960, **49:**217–31.

Maier, N. R. F. *Problem solving discussions and conferences: Leadership methods and skills.* New York: McGraw-Hill, 1963.

Maier, N. R. F., and Hayes, J. J. *Creative management.* New York: Wiley, 1962.

Maier, N. R. F., and Hoffman, L. R. Using trained "developmental" discussion leaders to improve further the quality of group decisions. *Journal of Applied Psychology,* 1960, **44:**247–51. (a)

Maier, N. R. F., and Hoffman, L. R. Quality of first and

second solutions in group problem solving. *Journal of Applied Psychology,* 1960, **44:**278–83. (b)

Maier, N. R. F., and Hoffman, L. R. Organization and creative problem solving. *Journal of Applied Psychology,* 1961, **45:**277–80.

Maier, N. R. F., and Hoffman, L. R. Group decision in England and the United States. *Personnel Psychology,* 1962, **15:**75–87.

Maier, N. R. F., and Hoffman, L. R. Financial incentives and group decision in motivating change. *Journal of Social Psychology,* 1964, **64:**369–78. (a)

Maier, N. R. F., and Hoffman, L. R. Types of problems confronting managers. *Personnel Psychology,* 1964, **17:** 261–69. (b)

Maier, N. R. F., and Hoffman, L. R. Acceptance and quality of solutions as related to leaders' attitudes toward disagreement in group problem solving. *Journal of Applied Behavioral Science,* 1965, **1:**373–86.

Maier, N. R. F., and Maier, R. A. An experimental test of the effects of "developmental" versus "free" discussions on the quality of group decisions. *Journal of Applied Psychology,* 1957, **41:**320–23.

Maier, N. R. F., and Solem, A. R. The contribution of a discussion leader to the quality of group thinking: The effective use of minority opinions. *Human Relations,* 1952, **5:**277–88.

Maier, N. R. F., and Solem, A. R. Improving solutions by turning choice situations into problems. *Personnel Psychology,* 1962, **15:**151–57.

Maier, N. R. F., and Zerfoss, L. F. MRP: A technique for training large groups of supervisors and its potential use in social research. *Human Relations,* 1952, **5:** 177–86.

Moore, A. R. The nervous mechanism of coordination in the crinoid *Antedon rosaceus. Journal of Genetic Psychology,* 1924, **6:**281–88.

Moore, A. R., and Doudoroff, M. Injury, recovery and function in an aganglionic central nervous system. *Journal of Comparative Psychology,* 1939, **28:**313–28.

Osborn, A. F. *Applied imagination.* New York: Scribner's, 1953.

Schneirla, T. C., and Maier, N. R. F. Concerning the status of the starfish. *Journal of Comparative Psychology,* 1940, **30:**103–10.

Solem, A. R. 1965: Almost anything I can do, we can do better. *Personnel Administration,* 1965, **28:**6–16.

Thibaut, J. W., and Kelley, H. H. *The social psychology of groups.* New York: Wiley, 1961.

Wallach, M. A., and Kogan, N. The roles of information, discussion and concensus in group risk taking. *Journal of Experimental and Social Psychology,* 1965, **1:**1–19.

Wallach, M. A., Kogan, N., and Bem, D. J. Group influence on individual risk taking. *Journal of Abnormal ano Social Psychology,* 1962, **65:**75–86.

Wertheimer, M. *Productive thinking.* New York: Harper, 1959.

Part Five

Intergroup and Structural Factors

Chapter 11

Intergroup Processes in Organizations

In the previous two chapters we have examined, in turn, interpersonal relations and group processes in organizations. Now we move up a level of generality and review what is known about the relations that exist *between* groups in organizations.

Traditionally, researchers have looked at intergroup relations primarily in terms of the conflicts that sometimes develop between groups that have to deal with one another but that do not get along well. Examples include staff-line conflicts, conflicts between production and marketing departments, conflicts between groups that are regulated and the groups that do the regulating, and so on. Moreover, intergroup theory has been useful in understanding conflicts between people of different races and between nations.

In selecting readings for this chapter, we have tried to take a somewhat broader perspective, to include material on intergroup relations that extends beyond the fact that groups sometimes come into conflict with one another. Our goal is to illustrate the pervasiveness as well as the potency of intergroup phenomena in organizational life.

The first article, by Smith, suggests that what happens *between* groups may be as important as what takes place *within* them in understanding many aspects of organizational life. He considers, in particular, how people perceive organizational "reality," who becomes a group leader under what circumstances, and how the personal "identity" of group members changes and evolves over time. Smith illustrates intergroup influences on these phenomena with case materials drawn from a school system, from an experiential "power laboratory," and from a group of survivors of an aircraft crash. By examining the nature of intergroup dynamics, he concludes, one can gain significantly greater understanding of group and interpersonal processes than can be obtained by looking only at the properties of individual group members, or at things that happen within the group itself.

In the second reading, Alderfer develops the beginnings of a general theory of intergroup behavior. He reviews the many different kinds of groups that exist in organizations (such as identity groups, gender groups, generational groups, task groups, hierarchical groups, and so on), and shows how powerful these groups can be in affecting behavior and attitudes at work. He points out that people are always members of many different groups (and different kinds of groups) at the same time—a fact that both complicates and enriches organizational life. Indeed, in its strongest form, intergroup theory implies that people can *never* be understood apart from their group memberships, and that no one is ever really free of significant group forces. In the closing section of his reading, Alderfer suggests some implications of these views for personal and organizational change.

The last article in the section, by Salancik and Pfeffer, is about power: who gets it, and how they hold on to it. While at first glance this topic might seem out of place in a chapter on intergroup relations, it turns out that intergroup issues are among the most important of all in understanding and managing power dynamics in organizations. The model of power advanced in the article is called "strategic-contingency" theory, a view that sees power as something that accrues to organizational units that have a unique contribution to make to solving critical organizational problems. In this model, one's own power depends on other people and groups in at least two ways. First, if others can provide an equivalent contribution to organizational needs, then one's power is lessened. One's power also is diminished if others are able to define as not very critical to the real needs of the organization precisely those problems that one is most ready and able to solve. These factors plant the seeds for interesting relationships among groups in organizations, since groups are likely to be prominent in defining what problems are and are not critical to the organization, and in deciding which group's activities are most useful in dealing with those problems. Thus, when managers argue about what is "really critical" to the organization, or who is "really on top of" some problem, they, *as group representatives,* often are in fact fine-tuning the balance of power that exists in the social system.

Reading 38

An Intergroup Perspective on Individual Behavior
Ken K. Smith

The history of psychology has been filled with attempts to understand the behavior of people either in terms of their personality, or as an interaction of individual and environmental characteristics (Lewin, 1947). In the latter case, the environment has been conceptualized at many levels, ranging from global influences of the culture at large to specific properties of the groups of which individuals are members. Although a great deal of attention has been given to group influences on individuals' beliefs, values, perceptions, and behaviors (Hackman, 1976), to date the impact on individuals of forces generated by relationships *between* groups has been largely unexplored.

Since there now exists an expanding body of knowledge about intergroup processes (Sherif, 1962; Rice, 1969; Levine & Campbell, 1972; Lorsch & Lawrence, 1972; Smith, 1974; Alderfer, 1977; Alderfer, Brown, Kaplan, & Smith, in press), our concept of individual behavior can be significantly augmented by including this aspect of the social environment as a determinant of how people behave.

In this paper I explore the proposition that, when intergroup situations exist, *behavior can be viewed primarily as an enactment of the forces those intergroup processes generate.* This is not to claim that individual or group interpretations of the same behaviors have no validity. Rather, it is simply an assertion that if an analysis is made at an intergroup level, a substantial proportion of the variation in individual behavior is explainable in terms of the intergroup dynamics. I propose that intergroup processes: (1) color profoundly our perceptions of the world, and may play a critical role in determining how we construct our personal sense of reality; (2) help define our individual identities; and (3) contribute significantly to the emergence of behavior patterns that we traditionally label as leadership. Each of these assertions will be explored and

illustrated by examining salient data from three very different social systems: (1) the experiences of a high school principal, and the way his personal sense of reality has been influenced by the various intergroup forces in his school system; (2) the development of the individual identity of a "village lunatic" in an experiential laboratory; and (3) the repeated changes of leadership behaviors in a group of survivors from an aircraft crash.

THE INTERGROUP AS A DETERMINER OF AN INDIVIDUAL'S PERCEPTIONS OF REALITY

It has long been recognized that people in different groups often perceive and understand the same event in radically different ways, particularly when there is an "ingroup" and an "outgroup." In such cases, one group usually will perceive an event in highly favorable terms, while the other sees the same event in an entirely derogatory manner. This phenomenon, referred to as "ethnocentrism" by Levine and Campbell (1972), is so powerful that group members may be unable to develop a view of reality that is independent of the group they belong to. The phenomenon becomes additionally potent when a person is caught in the context of multiple intergroups that involve interlocking sequences of events across time, and when the groups exist in a hierarchy of power relationships. Under these circumstances, the way one constructs his or her sense of reality may be almost completely determined by the interplay of intergroup processes.

Smith (1974) illustrates such a situation in his description of how Lewis Brook, principal of the high school in Ashgrove (New England), constructed his sense of what was taking place within the school system. Brook's perspectives changed dramatically from moment to moment, and these changes often were related directly to changes in his

I wish to gratefully acknowledge the critiques offered by J. L. Suttle, E. J. Woodhouse and C. P. Alderfer on an earlier version of this paper. Copyrighted by Ken K. Smith. Used with permission.

relative position in the power hierarchy of inter-group relationships.

For example, on one occasion Principal Brook was vociferously berating the superintendent, his superior, for something the superintendent had recently "done to" him. Lewis's recounting of the episode was cut short by a teacher who entered his office. Whereupon Lewis, without a moment's pause, responded to the teacher exactly as the superintendent had interacted with him. When confronted with this resounding obviousness, Lewis refused (or was unable) to see the similarity. When the two sets of events were dissected so that Lewis was caught by the brutal certitude of the similarities, he responded, "But it's different! I have reasons for treating the teacher that way." And when it was suggested that perhaps the superintendent had reasons for his treatment of the principal, Lewis, with more than a hint of impatience in his voice, retorted, "But mine were reasons; the superintendent's were merely rationalizations!"

This observation led me to formulate a theory of hierarchical intergroup relations in which the behavior of a person can be examined from the relative positions of upper, middle, and lower in the organizational structures in which he or she is embedded. Lewis Brook, as principal of the Ashgrove high school, had three assistant principals and a staff of one hundred teachers who served the educational needs of some 1,400 children in the ninth to twelfth grades. Relative to these two groups, the teachers and the students, Lewis was in an *upper* position. Superimposed on the school was an administrative and political hierarchy of a superintendent and an elected Board of Education. In relation to these two groups, Lewis was in a *lower* position. Finally, Lewis was in a *middle* position in the constellation of relationships between his subordinates (the teachers and students) and his superiors (the superintendent's office). Brook's life as principal can be examined from each of these three relative positions in the hierarchical structure, as shown in Figure 38-1. In particular, it is possible to see how his perceptions of events were influenced by the position he happened to occupy at the time they took place.

Lewis as a Lower

When in a lower position, Brook regularly demonstrated a high degree of suspicion and excessive personal sensitivity. For example, on the day follow-

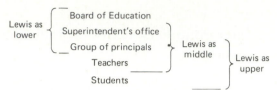

Figure 38-1 Constellation of intergroup relations with Lewis Brook in each of the three positions.

ing each Board of Education meeting, Lewis would sit for long, anxious hours waiting for a call from the superintendent advising him of Board discussions that might be relevant to the life of his school. Usually no such call would come, and Lewis complained regularly and bitterly about how he was so faithfully ignored. But his protestation never triggered anything more than a retort from the superintendent that if anything relevant to his high school was discussed, he would be contacted within hours.

From the Board of Education's upper perspective, it was simple to conclude that if Lewis heard nothing it simply meant that the Board had not been debating anything relevant to his school's life. But from Lewis's lower perspective, hearing nothing did *not* mean that nothing was happening. Rather it meant "all hell is about to break loose," an inference that activated his "lower paranoia." Because Lewis assumed there was a conspiracy of silence, he would fantasize with meticulous dedication about all the possible things that could be "done to him," and would search for cues that might validate his worst suspicions. His failure to uncover a "plot" designed to undo him as principal was never interpreted by Lewis to mean that no such plot existed. Instead, he would conclude that his detection devices simply lacked the finesse required to detect what was happening in the "closed" ranks of the uppers.

Ironically, while Lewis was overcome with all this suspicion, reality for the Board of Education was that they were doing "nothing to anybody." In fact, they felt so paralyzed by their own stagnant inactivity that they would have been simultaneously dismayed and pleased to discover that someone, in his wildest imagination, was perceiving them as being in a state other than immobility. Ignorant of this alternative view, Lewis continued to construct a picture of the world about him that hung on trivial contingencies, but which for him was the pillar of his personal reality.

Brook's suspiciousness and oversensitivity when

in a lower position can be seen as being a direct consequence of how people who feel powerless respond in intergroup exchanges with more powerful groups. Lower groups often develop strong protective devices and high cohesion to lessen their feelings of vulnerability. And one result of this response is that a lower group comes to define its essence in terms of this very cohesion and unity. In order to feed this sense of unity, members feel the need for the external threat to be continued. This creates a double bind: if the uppers cease to present a threat, that situation may be experienced by lowers as equally threatening, for it lessens the demand for their cohesion. This, in turn, recreates the sense of vulnerability of the lower group, because the *lack* of overt attack is a challenge to the very basis of unity on which group life is predicated. Either way it becomes imperative for members of the lower group to treat the uppers with suspicion. The bind reads as follows: "If they're getting at us, we've got to watch out. If they're not getting at us we've also got to watch out because they'll probably be getting at us in the long run by taking our unity away from us now by lessening the threat we feel." It is this process that ensures a lower group's paranoia and which, in my opinion, stirred Lewis Brook's intense feelings of sensitivity and suspiciousness when relating to his superiors.

Lewis as an Upper

Despite the disdain Lewis felt about his superiors' failure to consult him on matters in which he believed he had a basic right to participate, he reacted toward his own subordinate teachers and students with an equally elitist air. When in his upper position, Lewis always had a myriad of reasons why it was impossible to let the teachers participate fully in decisions that influenced their lives. The teachers felt these reasons were without substance, and they were perpetually distressed by the lack of confidence shown toward them by their principal, who demanded that approval be obtained for even the most trivial and routine of tasks.

When Lewis was in an upper position, he acted out the tendency of superior groups to see the behavior of subordinates in pessimistic terms—the very behaviors that he reacted to so negatively when he was a lower. As a member of the upper group, Lewis, like other uppers, tended to delegate responsibilities very willingly, but not the authority re-

quired to carry through on those responsibilities. This behavior of superiors guarantees that the actions of subordinate groups will not fulfill satisfactorily the expectations implied when the responsibilities are delegated. Although such shortcomings are caused largely by the uppers' withholding of necessary authority, they also are used by the superiors as justification for their original unwillingness to delegate authority. This phenomenon ensures a self-reinforcing and self-repeating set of perceptions, in that it heightens the likelihood that the subordinate groups will be seen as less competent than is desirable.

An insidious dimension of this phenomenon is that it enables upper groups to avoid taking full responsibility for their own behavior. In taking for themselves the role of designing organizational policy—but then delegating the implementation of that policy to the middle group—the uppers are able to build for themselves the perfect defense against failure. They can always conclude that their own policy was good but that the middles simply failed to implement it satisfactorily. Negative feedback can then be viewed merely as an indicator that subordinate groups are not as competent as is necessary. And, at the same time, the superiors can continue to avoid confronting their own expertise (or lack thereof) as uppers. Such a process locks upper groups into a way of viewing the world that ensures they will see the behavior of subordinates in increasingly depreciating terms.

Lewis Brook, as a member of an upper group, was caught by this intergroup dynamic as strongly as he was by the double binds of suspiciousness when he was located in a lower position.

Lewis as a Middle

When Brook was in a middle position, he was always espousing the need for "better communication" within the system. Despite this, he became caught in the trap of wanting to restrict information flow by making sure upper and lower groups communicated with each other only through him and his middle group. This situation is illustrated by the event described below.

Lewis was regularly embarrassed by learning about what was happening in his school for the first time from superiors who had been "leaked" information from below. Since he was an upper within the confines of the school itself, he often was unheeding to things teachers were trying to say to him. Therefore, they regularly felt the need to circumvent him in order to have their concerns attended to by the superintendent or the Board of Education. When teachers made attempts to contact the superintendent directly, Lewis became highly threatened and eventually decreed that no one could have access to the superintendent without first obtaining permission from one of the principals. By this action, Lewis clearly was working to preserve the centrality of his middle group's role as moderator of information flow.

Not to be daunted by this restriction on their liberties, the teachers found informal ways to gain access to the superintendent. The most frequently used device was to apply for study leave, even when not qualified for it. Such an application automatically led to an interview with the superintendent, which Lewis Brook allowed to occur without questioning his teachers. When ritualistically informed by the superintendent that they had not met the prerequisite conditions for study leave, the teachers willingly withdrew their applications and then confided the real reasons why they had sought an audience with him.

Lewis Brook never became aware of this practice, but he always felt distressed by the amount of information about his school of which the superintendent was aware. This distress only reinforced his dedication to make sure that teachers used his office alone as the means of communicating with the upper echelons of the system—an aspiration that he never realized.

To legitimize their own place in the system, middle groups need the uppers and lowers to be operating in a relatively polarized and noncommunicating fashion. Indeed, one of the ways for middle groups to be "confirmed" in the system is for them to become the central communication channel between the two extreme groups. This is possible primarily because both upper and lower groups use the withholding of information as a major strategy for dealing with each other. Upper groups limit information flow by using labels (such as "secret" or "in confidence") that designate who has legitimate access to what. For lowers, ground rules specifying what constitutes loyalty to the group determines what can be said to whom and under what circumstances, with the major concern being to minimize the vulnerability of the group.

If it were not for the rigid polarization of uppers and lowers, and their refusal to allow information to flow freely in the system, the middles might not be needed. But once the middle's role has become established as the communication link between upper and lower groups, the middles become very anxious to keep those polarized groups from talking frankly and openly. The middles become most threatened when the other two groups pass information to each other directly, or through any channel other than those the middles feel they have legitimized for the system. For this reason, the middles invest an inordinate amount of energy in defending the principle that all communication must pass through them. The net result of this dynamic is that middles will be constantly talking about the need to improve system-wide communication—while at the same time playing a vigorous role in restricting direct communication between other groups.

Summary

From the above account it is possible to recognize that intergroup processes cause groups at each of the three levels to become locked into a particular set of binds, and to create unique views of reality that are characteristic of those specific levels of the system. If these intergroup phenomena are conceded, it is predictable that an individual in a lower position will be supersensitive and suspicious of the activities of others. In an upper position, he or she will view the behavior of subordinates in a pessimistic light, and accordingly will delegate responsibility without the necessary authority. When in a middle position, the individual will espouse the need for greater communication, while acting to keep many communications restricted.

All these behaviors were exhibited by Lewis Brook in his role as Ashgrove's high school principal. It is easy to attribute these behaviors to Brook's unique personality. Yet, when viewed in the context of the intergroups operating in Brook's school system, it also becomes possible to understand how powerfully his own behavior and sense of reality were influenced by intergroup phenomena.

THE INTERGROUP AS A DETERMINANT OF INDIVIDUAL IDENTITY

Smith (1976) describes how intergroup interactions in a five-day power laboratory led to the creation of an identity for one individual that other members of the social system came to symbolize as "the village lunatic."

A power laboratory is an experiential, social, and psychological simulation designed for people interested in experiencing and learning about the dynamics of power and powerlessness. The laboratory is structured to create three classes of people: (1) the powerful "elite," who have access to and control over all the basic resources of the society, such as food, housing, money, and so forth; (2) the "ins," who have minimal control over some resources, at the discretion of the elites; and (3) the powerless "outs" who are totally deprived and have no control over any community resources. All conditions of living, such as standards of housing, quality of food, and so on, are differentiated to heighten "class" differences. For example, the outs live in a ghetto-like life style, while the elites live in comparatively leisurely luxury. On arrival at the laboratory all members are "born into" one of these three classes, without individual choice.

In the power laboratory described by Smith, the elite group of seven arrived half a day before the middles, and produced a plan which would enable them to keep their eliteness hidden. They decided to act as if they were regular, nonelite participants, while they actually would be quietly and powerfully pulling the strings of the social system like backstage puppeteers.

The plan ran into trouble, however, within hours of the arrival of the nine middles. The "birth" trauma of the middles was quite extreme: at induction, they had all their belongings (save one change of underwear) taken from them, an event that stirred their anger and their determination to discern "who did this to us." Anthony, one of the middles, had brought with him a tape recorder that he wanted to use for his learning and post-laboratory reflections. He was not allowed to keep the recorder, however, and his resentment about this heightened his sensitivity as to who was powerful and who was powerless in the system. It took him very little time to differentiate the elites from the nonelites—simply by observing the interactions that took place among various participants. In response to his awareness, Anthony tried to initiate a public debate intended to flush out the elite group. He was generally unsuccessful in this, partly because others lacked his acumen in discerning what was taking place, and partly because of the skill of the elite group in keeping their identity hidden.

After half a day all but two members of the elite group had tired of the charade and had made public their real status. This made the middle group angry, and Anthony became even more determined to end the elites' game of phantomness. But this did not occur. The most influential member of the upper group—Richard, a tall, strong, bearded, black man —did not identify himself as an elite and remained with the middles, continuing to manipulate them to do exactly as the elites ordained.

The successful smoking out of most of the elite group fanned Anthony's fires. He became consumed with his fixation to force all the elites to become visible, Richard included. That was not to be, because Richard was blessed with a resolve equal to Anthony's and the two became bitterly pitted against each other. Anthony's energies were focused entirely on Richard's eviction from the middle group, while Richard, with a simple indifference to these pressures, worked at massaging the middles into accepting obediently their role as servants of the elites.

Whenever Richard attempted to make an initiative, Anthony immediately attempted to frustrate it by accurately, though boringly, accusing him of being an elite spy, and arguing that the middles should no nothing until such time as all the elites had been ousted. Eventually Richard became symbolized as a force for *activity* while Anthony came to be seen as someone reinforcing *stagnation*. Richard skillfully presented himself as the champion of the middles' cause, and successfully led negotiations with the elites for return of some of their personal belongings. This success elevated Richard to the sole leadership role in the bourgeoise and he accordingly dealt with Anthony's accusations by simply dismissing them as part of a personal vendetta against him as the middles' leader.

The middle group did very little in the first day and a half other than debate the spy issue, and this inactivity produced such intense frustration that some reached the point of being willing to do anything, including being led down any path by Richard, simply to escape the paralysis of their inertia. Whether or not he was a spy ceased to matter much.

Anthony recognized that his group had adopted the spirit of going along with anything that produced activity, yet he could not reconcile himself to the fact that almost everything Richard proposed served to make the middles into the elite's lackeys. Soon Anthony's fight was being stifled by others in his group who would audibly groan their protest over his persistent regurgitation of a theme they all wanted to ignore. To buffer himself against this visible hostility, Anthony began to preface his remarks with a statement designed to lessen his vulnerability. He could have said, "I know I'm the only person who is concerned about this issue," but that's not the way he phrased his protective remarks. Instead he would say, "I know you think this is just my problem, but . . ."

By articulating this "buffer" statement in this way, Anthony provided other middles with the opportunity they had been looking for. By simply agreeing, "Yes, Anthony, that's just *your* problem," they could quickly close him down and avoid the agony of further monotonous reiteration of the spy theme.

The symbolization processes began to develop at a fast pace, and very soon the middle group had made "Anthony's problem" the receptacle for all of their frustrations. (Of course, the middles would have experienced frustration having to do with their need to keep their relationships with both elites and outs functional, independent of Anthony's role. As middles, they found that whenever they acted in the possible interest of the elites, the outs would abuse them for having been co-opted. And whenever they responded to pressures from the outs, the elites would treat them punitively and leave them feeling alienated and alone. The reality was that no matter what they did—even if they did nothing—the middles would end up feeling uncomfortable.)

Since the middles had begun to believe that the cause of their discomfort was "Anthony's problem," they came to view that "problem" in more extreme form as their sense of impotence heightened. Eventually they settled on the belief that "he really must be crazy." To make matters worse, Anthony had been successful enough to convince many of the middles that the spy issue was critical, but this only reverberated back on him: given the way the group's "problem" had become symbolized and projected into Anthony, it made more sense to many members of the middle group to suspect that Anthony was the real spy rather than Richard.

When this possibility was raised in the group, Anthony recognized that his battle was lost. By then he was so much on the periphery of the group that he knew there was little chance of his finding a comfortable place in the middle group. He therefore began to search for an alternative role in the system. The alternatives were, of course, very limited. The doors of the elites clearly were closed to him. That left only the outs—who in fact welcomed him with open arms. For them, the possibility of someone becoming *downwardly* mobile had real strategic value in this particular society, and they quickly grasped at the opportunity Anthony's plight presented. In addition, the outs had developed a strong emotional support system. They sensed Anthony's pain, and willingly reached out to provide him a haven.

Anthony became so overwhelmed by the level of acceptance and warmth accorded him by the outs that he quickly concluded that this was where he wanted to see out his days in the society. Here he ran into a new problem. It had been their common pain, their collective fears and uncertainties, and their desperate need for each other in psychological survival tasks that had forged the group of outs into its particular shape. Nothing in Anthony's middle experience paralleled those forces, and there was no way to revise the "out history" to allow Anthony to be made a full partner in the "real" life of the group. At best, he could become only an adopted son.

Anthony needed acceptance by the outs so badly that he was willing to comply uncritically to any of the group's wishes. And here, Anthony's "way of being" changed dramatically. The overly perceptive characteristics he displayed in his bourgeois period now became clouded by an obsessional overconforming to the norms of the out group—a response which attempted to compensate for his sense of historical exclusion from the outs' world, and to pay an adequate price for his acceptance by them.

Another event added appreciably to the complexity of everyone's perceptions of Anthony's behavior. At the time of Anthony's migration to the outs, Richard (keen to keep tranquility disjointed) returned to the relative comfort of the elite group. However, still wishing to maximize deception, the elites continued the charade by refusing to acknowledge that Richard had been one of them all along. Instead they described his move as "upward mobility," provided to Richard because of his good leadership behavior and his service to the society.

The impact of the dual departures of Richard and Anthony from the middles left a powerful vacuum. The remaining middles started to experiment with new behaviors. Collectively (though only temporarily) they gained a new sense of vitality. This caused them to lay, even more vehemently than previously, total responsibility for their earlier stagnation at Anthony's feet. They attributed none of it to Richard. For his departure they grieved. For Anthony's, they celebrated.

The remaining history of this laboratory was filled with examples of how tension in the system—the byproduct of unhandled intergroup conflict—became attributed to Anthony's "craziness." No matter what discomforting event occurred, it was symbolized as being Anthony's fault.

Why?

My basic thesis is that once the society had created for Anthony alone a totally unique experience within the society, and once a chance was provided for his behavior to be seen as "crazy," the system gave him an identity that powerfully served the needs of the intergroup exchanges. The "village lunatic" identity provided a receptacle for the craziness of the whole system—the deceit, the multiple and conflicting senses of reality, the myriad of covert, unarticulable processes, and so forth—which enabled the society at large to avoid having to confront its own pathology. In short, the social system had a vested interest in having Anthony become and remain crazy because it served admirably the continuation of the essential intergroup exchanges of the society at large.

And what became of Anthony himself?[1] Initially he was convinced his own perceptions were accurate. But across time, as others failed to see what was so obvious to him, he began to doubt his own sense of reality (even when he actually was perceiving correctly) and to wonder whether he was going mad. This eventually forced him to experience such discomfort that all of his energy became directed toward uncritically finding a place where he could feel support and acceptance. When the society

transformed him into the "village lunatic," it created a form of madness aptly described by the poet Roethke, as mere "nobility of soul, at odds with circumstance."

One further question remains. What was it about Anthony as a person that caused him to become the lunatic? In my view, it was virtually accidental. The fact that he came originally with a tape recorder (and with a very high investment in being able to use it for his personal learning) meant that Anthony felt even more deprived than the others at induction time. This additional sense of deprivation heightened his activity to find out who the elites were much earlier than his fellow middles. Because he saw things differently than did the others, he started to become separated from the dominant sense of "reality" in the system. From there, the processes already described took off.

If Anthony had not come to this laboratory, would someone else have been made into a "lunatic" for the society's purposes? I suspect not. The forces which ended up focussing on him might well have been acted out in some other way—perhaps by creating another special identity for one individual, or by generating conditions of war between the groups, or even by the collapse of the society at large. The intergroup dynamics had to find *some* way to be acted out; the particular circumstances surrounding Anthony and his induction into the system were such that he became a convenient and useful vehicle for meeting that need.

The learning of overwhelming importance from this account is that often the personages or identities we take on may have very little to do with our own desires for ourselves, with our particular upbringings, or with our own values. Instead, they may, in fact, be mostly defined for us and forced upon us by external processes similar to those experienced by Anthony in the power laboratory.

THE INTERGROUP AS A DETERMINANT OF BEHAVIORS CHARACTERIZED AS LEADERSHIP

Perhaps one of the most gripping, passionate, and socially educative experiences ever recorded is the story of sixteen Uruguayan football players and their friends who not only survived an aircraft crash in the completely inaccessible heights of the Chilean Andes, but then existed for ten weeks in icy and

---

[1]Anthony left the laboratory in good emotional health. During the critique phase of the experience, the staff of the laboratory spent a great deal of time with Anthony and others exploring how this "village lunatic" phenomenon had occurred.

desolate conditions with only the wrecked fuselage of the aircraft as their shelter and home (Read, 1974).

Of the original forty-three people on board, sixteen were killed in the crash or died in the next few days from injuries. Seventeen days later the surviving twenty-seven were further reduced to a group of nineteen by an avalanche of snow that buried alive almost the whole group, eight of whom could not be dug out before they froze to death. After the avalanche, the group of survivors (reduced later by another three deaths) kept alive for fifty more days before two of their number, under unbelievable conditions, climbed a cliff-faced mountain of ice to a height of 13,500 feet, and eventually stumbled across civilization and help.

The story is a deeply touching account of human relationships under the most extreme survival conditions. In order to stay alive, it was necessary for group members, despite the repugnancy of the idea, to eat the raw flesh of the dead. Much of the early life and struggles of these survivors revolved around the agonies of acknowledging and accepting this imperative. As dreams of rescue faded, and as the struggle together under intense conditions heightened, the earlier revulsions became translated into a very mystical and religious experience—to the extent that several of the boys, when they realized that their own deaths were imminent, asked their comrades to feel free to eat their bodies.

In the discussion that follows, I will explore the social system composed of the survivors, and show how behaviors that traditionally would be described as personal "leadership" can be understood in terms of the relationships between various groups that emerged within that system. Specifically, I will propose that who becomes focal in leadership activities (and what leadership behaviors are seen as appropriate) changes radically from situation to situation—largely as a function of changing intergroup dynamics.

Immediately after the crash, many of the survivors were bleeding and in desperate need of medical care. In this initial phase, during which group life was defined by the visibility of wounded bodies, the key survival task was seen as caring for the bleeding. Accordingly, two of the group, who had been medical students in the earliest phases of their training, were automatically elevated to dominant status. An intergroup structure emerged which delineated all survivors into one of three classes—the wounded, the potential workers, and the doctors. The medical students were given tremendous power, despite the fact that their skills and competence in the setting were minimal, especially given that they had not facilities or medical supplies. Others willingly subjected themselves to directives the students issued around appropriate work or treatment programs. The need for medical help was so intense that the differential status of the survivors enabled limited skill to become symbolized as expert competence, which, in turn, gave the "doctors" inordinate power to influence everyone else's behavior.

Within a day or so, new demands appeared. The acquisition of food and water, and the preservation of hygiene in the fuselage—which constituted the only shelter from sub-zero temperatures, blizzards, and thoroughly treacherous conditions—became critical. These demands required a group structure that was radically different from the one that had developed in the period immediately after the crash. In particular, it became important for someone to play an overall "social maintenance" role to give coherence to the whole system. The captain of the football team, who had been overshadowed in the first day by the medical students, was reelevated to his former position. Beneath him were two groups of approximately equal status: (1) the medical team of two "doctors" and a couple of helpers, and (2) a group that searched battered luggage for tidbits of food, and who made water by melting snow on metal sheets and bottling it in old soda bottles. At a still lower level, was a group of the younger boys who served as a clean-up crew to maintain livable conditions in the cabin. The football captain himself became the general coordinator, and at noon each day he distributed the carefully rationed food to each person. In this role he clearly brought with him the ethos of his earlier influence as captain on the sports field.

The hierarchies of social influence changed during this period. The medical group now were granted authority related only to their specialist function, and they lost virtually all of their influence over nonmedical domains of the social system. For several days the football captain remained the key figure, mediating potential clashes over the food, and dealing with conflicts between the medical and work teams. Much of his power was predicated on his effusive optimism that they would all be rescued within a few days. He used this hope, which he constantly rekindled, as the major substance for social cohesion. But as time passed, and it became clear that rescue was not imminent, the hopes he had fostered began to sour and the captain's social maintenance skills slowly became devalued.

A new plight confronted the survivors several days after the crash. The food supplies were nearly exhausted. It was clear that if survival were to be sustained, the group maintenance orientation of the captain would no longer suffice. Parrado, who previously had played no significant role, moved to prominence. During the past few days he had been coping with the loss of both his mother and his sister, who had died from crash injuries. In the process, he had developed an unbelievable desire to survive. Parrado became the articulator of two new and key dimensions in the life of the group: (1) the suggestion that the only hope of rescue was for a group of expeditionaries to walk out of the mountains, and (2) the idea that life depended on consumption of the flesh of the dead, which was being preserved by the freezing cold. The force of these suggestions provided new energy for the group, and started the process of delineating new internal social structures within the mountain-top society.

At the same time, the role of the "doctors" was further diminished. With virtually no medical supplies, their "special expertise" had been exhausted. The worst cases had died, and it was now clear to everyone that there was very little more that could be offered in the medical domain. The collapse of the medical team's function added to the power vacuum and increased the uncertainty about social relationships among group members.

Eventually another new social structure did emerge. It was defined primarily by each person's willingness or reluctance to eat human flesh. Those who did so early, and with a reasonable degree of spontaneity, were the ones who maintained the physical energy to persevere—and thereby to provide vitality for the endurance of the social system itself. Those who could not bring themselves to overcome their natural abhorrence to the idea became weak, and eventually degenerated into a new "poorer class." A third group struggled with the tensions of survival on the one hand, and their natural revulsion to the consumption of human flesh on the other. In so doing, members of this group came to formulate a new way of symbolizing the activity. They developed a very mystical and spiritual interpretation of their group experience, reinterpreting the eating of the flesh of the dead as being parallel to a religious communion in which they would consume the body and blood of Christ. This resymbolization of experience facilitated survival by helping everyone respond to the imperative that they eat the flesh of the dead, no matter how strongly the idea initially had repelled them.

During this period, the football captain moved further from his earlier position of prominence. This was, in part, because of his unwillingness to take the lead in eating human flesh. But, in addition, the captain lost credibility because his repeated assurances that rescue was imminent came increasingly to sound hollow.

When the survivors eventually heard on a transistor radio that all rescue operations had been called off, the energy in the system changed dramatically. Despair and outrage hit members like clenched fists, and produced radically different responses in different people. Parrado was ready to leave on an expedition immediately, while others were ready to resign themselves to the inevitability of death. Despair was heightened further a couple of days later when an avalanche of snow caused the death of eight more persons, including the football captain. Reluctantly, it was concluded that an expedition now offered the only hope for survival. And the internal social structure of the system went through yet another readjustment in response to this imperative.

Any social system can become subjected to crisis conditions which produce extreme pressures from the outside, or from within. When this happens, members of the system must respond to these pressures or else risk long-term internal chaos. One common response is for clusters of people to form which eventually evolve into critical groups for the system. Moreover, the pressures that emerge from crisis experiences invariably demand that groups within the system relate to each other more intensely than had previously been the case. Even the composition of these groups will need to change. In the present case, the medical group was dominant initially, with others subservient to them. This structure was altered by the emergence of the football captain as the major mediator between several specialized work groups, and eventually by the emergence of an entirely new social structure defined in terms of members' willingness to consume human flesh.

When these changes are taking place in response to extreme pressures, it often is most unclear what should happen to produce a new form of stability in which both directionality and internal coherence are present. What an individual might do personally to provide leadership is unclear and speculative. Instead, each new set of stresses causes changes in group memberships or behaviors which, in turn, move the system toward some new equilibrium. As this happens, power, authority, critical resources, and ability to influence events become distributed differently than before. Only when the directionality and coherence of the system achieve a reasonable degree of stability is it possible to determine which behaviors actually moved the system in productive directions, or served to keep the various parts of the system integrated. Acts of leadership, then, are merely responses to the forces that emerge from the exchanges among groups within the system, and it would *not* be valid to construe them as reflecting a conscious intent to lead. If, in hindsight, an act appears to have been one of effective leadership, it may have been virtually accidental at the time it happened—and identifiable as leadership only in retrospect. This phenomenon is especially visible in the next phase of the survivors' experiences.

As preparations for the expedition went forward, all energies were dedicated to that task. Medical duties had slipped from any prominence, and the doctors simply took their place in the mainstream of the social structure. Four identifiable groups emerged as planning for the expedition proceeded. They were: (1) a collection of ten individuals who were designated as too weak to undertake any significant walking; (2) three first choices for the expedition, including one of the ex-doctors and Parrado, whose robust constitution and steely resolve to escape had helped buoy the energy of the fainthearted; (3) three cousins who were not fit for the expedition and who previously had not played significant roles in the system—but who had coalesced as a critical subgroup because of their strong support for each other in a common struggle (theirs,

a blood relationship, was the only precrash grouping of friends that had not been fragmented by the ordeal); and (4) a trio of younger fellows who were potential expeditionaries—but who first had to be tested to prove their fitness.

Eventually a group of four was selected as the key expeditionaries. Once chosen, they became virtually a "warrior class" with extra rights and privileges. They were allowed to do anything that could be construed as bettering their physical condition. The whole group coddled them, both physically and psychologically, and everyone made sure that the only conversations within their earshot were optimistic in tone.

Read (1974) reports that the expeditionaries were *not* the leaders of the society. They were basically a class apart, linked to the rest of the system by the group of cousins, whose cohesion was the only force available to balance the unbelievable power that had been given to the expeditionaries. Because the cousins were the only ones able to keep the "warriors" in check (and thereby keep the system in equilibrium) they became the major locus of power within the remainder of the system. They virtually ruled from then on. The cousins controlled food allocation, determined who should do what work, and mediated when the "workers" (those who cut meat, prepared water, attended to hygiene, and so forth) felt that some of the sick were merely "malingering" and therefore should not be fed unless they also worked.

Beneath the cousins, a second echelon of three emerged. These individuals took roles equivalent to noncommissioned officers, receiving orders from above and giving them to those below. One of this trio, the second of the two doctors, became the "detective" in this phase of the society. He took upon himself the task of investigating misdemeanors and norm violations, and he flattered those more senior to him while bullying those more subservient.

It was several weeks before the expeditionaries departed. There were some valid reasons for the delay, but eventually everyone began to suspect that the ex-doctor was stalling and that he was using his expectant expeditionary status as a way of accruing privileges and minimizing work. At that point, his privileges were terminated. When one of the cousins volunteered to go in his place, the ex-doctor stirred himself and prepared for what proved to be a successful expedition: after a grueling ten-day trek, help was located and the remaining survivors were rescued.

One would have imagined that the ordeal was now over, but the system still had to face another extremely difficult event. Within a short time after the rescue, news leaked that the survivors had sustained themselves by consuming the flesh of the dead. This produced a strong reaction, especially among members of the press, who were poised to give world-wide publicity to this remarkable story. Religious figures, parents, and close friends were basically supportive during this period of new threat. But it soon became obvious that, if the survivors were ever to return to normal lives, it would be necessary for them to confront this issue together. So they called a press conference to tell their story.

The group debated at length as to who should explain the eating of human flesh. Several individuals felt they would be too emotional. It was eventually agreed that Delgado, who had been almost completely insignificant on the mountain top, should describe this aspect of their experience. His public presence and his eloquence—which of course had been of no value during the seventy-day ordeal—now came into its own, and he mediated brilliantly between the survivors, and the press, relatives, and other interested parties. His statement was a moving, passionate, religious, and emotional event, and through it he provided a way for everyone to resymbolize the meaning of the survival experience, thereby quelling criticism and laying to rest concerns over the consumption of the dead.

In this setting, Delgado's behavior, which to date had influenced nothing, was now seen by others as outstanding leadership. But did he lead? Or was it simply that his particular response to the tensions which intersected in his personhood in that situation touched the nerve fibers of the new sets of intergroup interactions, thereby triggering a new directionality and a wholesome coherence for the system?

CONCLUSION

The literature of organizational behavior is filled with concepts that help us understand the behavior of people in terms of their personal characteristics, or as a response to what takes place in the groups of which they are members. The material presented in this paper offers an alternative view: namely, that it is imperative to move beyond explanations that lie within people and within groups—and to include perspectives that derive from more global and systemic forces, including forces that derive from the dynamics of intergroups.

If, for example, the tools of personality theorists alone were applied to Lewis Brook in Ashgrove or to Anthony's identity struggle, we would obtain only a limited understanding of what affected their perceptions and their behaviors. Likewise, if we restricted our explorations of leadership among the aircraft survivors to traditional concepts that imply specific intentionality on the part of individuals (i.e., using notions such as participation, initiation of structure, socioemotional behavior, and so on), much of the essence of the leadership phenomena that developed on the mountain top would have been lost.

But how much relevance do the principles extracted from the materials presented in this paper have for understanding everyday experiences in everyday organizations? I submit, a great deal—and more than we usually realize or are comfortable acknowledging.

REFERENCES

Alderfer, C. P. Group and intergroup relations. In J. R. Hackman and J. L. Suttle (Eds.), *Improving life at work: Behavioral science approaches to organizational change.* Pacific Palisades, Calif.: Goodyear, 1977.

Alderfer, C. P., Brown, L. D., Kaplan, R. E., & Smith, K. K. *Group relations and organizational diagnosis.* London: Wiley, in press.

Hackman, J. R. Group influences on individuals in organizations. In M. D. Dunnette (Ed.), *Handbook of industrial and organizational psychology.* Chicago: Rand-McNally, 1976.

Levine, R. A., & Campbell, D. T. *Ethnocentrism.* New York: Wiley, 1972.

Lewin, K. Frontiers in group dynamics. *Human Relations,* 1947, **1,** 5–41.

Likert, R. *New patterns of management.* New York: McGraw-Hill, 1964.

Lorsch, J. W., & Lawrence, P. R. *Managing group and intergroup relations.* Homewood, Ill.: Irwin, 1972.

Read, P. P. *Alive.* London: Pan Books, 1974.

Rice, A. K. Individual, group and intergroup processes. *Human Relations,* 1969, **22,** 565–585.

Sherif, M. (Ed.), *Intergroup relations and leadership.* New York: Wiley, 1962.

Smith, K. K. *Behavioral consequences of hierarchical*

structures. Unpublished doctoral dissertation, Yale University, 1974.

Smith, K. K. The village lunatic. Unpublished manuscript, University of Melbourne, 1976.

Reading 39

Intergroup Relations and Organizations

Clayton P. Alderfer

INTRODUCTION

This article is taken from a longer analysis of diagnosing group and intergroup relations in organizations.[1] The purpose of the selection is to present the major concepts and key propositions for understanding organizations from an intergroup perspective. Intergroup theory, as it is presented here, offers the possibility of explaining behavior from the vantage points of several "levels" of analysis. Intrapsychic, interpersonal, intragroup, intergroup, and intraorganizational events can all be examined through the use of intergroup concepts. The theory thus offers a robust set of concepts for dealing with much of the complexity of organizational behavior. The major strength of such a point of view is the holistic orientation it takes toward human behavior. Its primary weakness is that no theory, including this one, accounts for all phenomena. For some readers the theory may also violate their sense of individualism. It suggests that we are all much more creatures of our groups and their relations to one another than much of contemporary American ideology proposes.

PROPERTIES OF GROUP AND INTERGROUP RELATIONS

Behavioral scientists have shown a variety of ambivalent reactions to groups and the relationship of groups to individuals and organizations. On

the positive side, the earliest studies of behavior in organizations uncovered potent group effects (e.g., Roethlisberger & Dickson, 1939), and more recent reviews summarize extensive evidence about the effects of groups on individuals (e.g., Hackman, 1976) and of the consequences of taking groups seriously (Leavitt, 1975). On the negative side, however, despite the now extensive list of empirical studies demonstrating the effects of intergroup conflicts in organizations (e.g., Sayles & Strauss, 1953; Sayles, 1958; Dalton, 1959; Crozier, 1964; Blake, Shepard, & Mouton, 1964), with the exception of Rice (1969), investigators have not attempted to formulate an intergroup theory of organizations. The reluctance to utilize intergroup concepts has also been maintained despite the evidence from methodological analyses that intergroup effects not only may account for what happens to organization members but also may explain some of the major difficulties encountered by researchers who study organizations (e.g., Kahn & Mann, 1952; Adams & Preiss, 1960; Becker, 1967; Merton, 1972). Nevertheless, a major new stimulus for developing and using intergroup theory has arisen from the variety of successful and unsuccessful efforts by behavioral scientists to change organizations (Lewicki & Alderfer, 1973; Alderfer & Brown, 1975; Berg, 1977; Nadler, 1978; Alderfer, Alderfer, Tucker, & Tucker, 1980). The present perspective draws on each of these traditions and offers an intergroup theory for both understanding and changing organizational behavior.

The key terms include a definition of groups in organizations and a series of propositions for explaining intergroup dynamics in social systems.

---

[1]*Group Relations and Organizational Diagnosis,* by C. P. Alderfer, L. D. Brown, R. E. Kaplan, & K. K. Smith (New York: Wiley, in press). © by John Wiley & Sons, in press. Reprinted with permission.

Definition of Groups in Organizations

Within the social psychology literature there is no shortage of definitions of groups, but there is also no clear consensus among those who propose definitions (Cartwright & Zander, 1968). Because much of the work leading to these definitions has been done by social psychologists studying internal properties of groups in laboratories, the resulting concepts have been comparatively limited in recognizing the external properties of groups. Looking at *groups in organizations,* however, produces a definition that gives more balanced attention to both internal and external properties (Alderfer, 1977a).

A human group is a collection of individuals (1) who have significantly interdependent relations with each other, (2) who perceive themselves as a group, reliably distinguishing members from nonmembers, (3) whose group identity is recognized by nonmembers, (4) who, as group members acting alone or in concert, have significantly interdependent relations with other groups, and (5) whose roles in the group are therefore a function of expectations from themselves, from other group members, and from non–group members.

This idea of a group begins with individuals who are interdependent, moves to the sense of the group as a significant social object whose boundaries are confirmed from inside and outside, recognizes that the group-as-a-whole is an interacting unit through representatives or by collective action, and returns to the individual members whose thoughts, feelings, and actions are determined by forces within the individual and from both group members and non–group members. This conceptualization of a group makes every *individual* member into a *group* representative wherever he or she deals with members of other groups and treats transactions among individuals as at least in part intergroup events (Rice, 1969; Smith, 1977).

Properties of Intergroup Relations

Research on intergroup relations has identified a number of properties characteristic of intergroup relations, regardless of the particular groups or the specific setting where the relationship occurs (Sumner, 1906; Coser, 1956; Sherif & Sherif, 1969; van den Bergh, 1972; Levine & Campbell, 1972; Billig, 1976; Alderfer, 1980). These phenomena include:

a Group boundaries. Group boundaries, both physical and psychological, determine who is a group member and regulate transactions among groups by variations in their permeability (Alderfer, 1977b). Boundary permeability refers to the ease with which boundaries can be crossed.

b Power differences. Groups differ in the types of resources they can obtain and use (Lasswell & Kaplan, 1950). The variety of dimensions on which there are power differences and the degree of discrepancy among groups on these dimensions influence the degree of boundary permeability among groups.

c Affective patterns. The permeability of group boundaries varies with the polarization of feeling among the groups; that is, to the degree that group members split their feelings so that mainly positive feelings are associated with their own group and mainly negative feelings are projected onto other groups (Sumner, 1906; Coser, 1956; Levine & Campbell, 1972).

d Cognitive formations, including "distortions." As a function of power differences and affective patterns, groups tend to develop their own language (or elements of language, including social categories), condition their members' perceptions of objective and subjective phenomena, and transmit sets of propositions—including theories and ideologies—to explain the nature of experiences encountered by members and to influence relations with other groups (Sherif & Sherif, 1969; Blake, Shepard, & Mouton, 1964; Tajfel, 1971; Billig, 1976).

e Leadership behavior. The behavior of group leaders and of members representing a group reflects the boundary permeability, power differences, affective patterns, and cognitive formations of their group in relation to other groups. The behavior of group representatives, including formally designated leaders, is both cause and effect of the total pattern of intergroup behavior in a particular situation.

GROUP RELATIONS IN ORGANIZATIONS

Every organization consists of a large number of groups, and every organization member represents a number of these groups in dealing with other people in the organization. The full set of groups in an organization can be divided into two broad classes: identity groups and organizational groups. An *identity group* may be thought of as a group whose members share some common biological characteristic (such as sex), have participated in equivalent historical experiences (such as migration), currently are subjected to certain social forces (such as unemployment), and as a result have similar worldviews. As people enter organizations they carry with them their ongoing membership in identity groups based on variables such as their ethnicity, sex, age, and family. An *organizational group* may be conceived of as one whose members share (approximately) common organizational positions, participate in equivalent work experiences, and, as a consequence, have similar organizational views. Organizations assign their members to organizational groups based on division of labor and hierarchy of authority. One critical factor in understanding intergroups in organizations is that identity-group membership and organizational-group membership are frequently highly related. Depending on the nature of the organization and the culture in which it is embedded, certain organizational groups tend to be populated by members of particular identity groups. In the United States, for example, upper-management positions tend to be held by older white males, and certain departments and ranks tend to be more accepting of females and minorities than others (Loring & Wells, 1972; Purcell & Cavanagh, 1972).

Considering the definition of a human group given above, we can observe how both identity groups and organizational groups fit the five major criteria. First, identity group members have significant interdependencies because of their common historical experiences, and organizational groups because of their equivalent work or organizational experiences. Second, organization-group and identity-group members can reliably distinguish themselves as members from nonmembers on the basis of either ethnicity, sex, etc., or of location in the organization. However, the precision of this identification process can vary depending on both the permeability of group boundaries and the fact that many groups overlap significantly, with individuals having multiple group memberships. A similar point applies to the third definitional characteristic, the ability of nonmembers to recognize members; this again will vary depending on the permeability of the group's boundaries. The less permeable the boundaries, the more easily recognizable are members. The fourth and fifth aspects of the definition are highly linked when applied to identity and organiza-

tional groups. For example, members may be more or less aware of the extent to which they are acting, or being seen, as group representatives when relating to individuals from other groups. Every person has a number of identity- and organizational-group memberships. At any given moment an individual may be simultaneously a member of a large number, if not all, of these groups. However, what group will be focal at the moment will depend on who else representing which other groups is present and what identity-group and organizational-group issues are critical in the current intergroup exchanges. A white person in a predominantly black organization, for example, can rarely escape representing "white people" at some level, regardless of performance. But the same white person placed in a predominantly white organization will not be seen as representing "white people," but rather some other group, such as a particular hierarchical level. Rarely are individuals "just people" when they act in organizations. When there are no other group representatives present, individuals may experience themselves as "just people" in the context of their own group membership, but this subjective experience will quickly disappear when the individual is placed in a multiple-group setting. How group members relate to each other within their group, and the expectations placed upon them by others, is highly dependent on the nature of both the intragroup and intergroup forces active at that time.

The concepts of identity groups and organizational groups do not permit an exhaustive listing of the elements in either set. In any particular setting, the relevant identity groups and organizational groups can be determined only by detailed study using intergroup methods. But it is possible to specify the more frequently observed identity groups and organizational groups and to note major issues around which those intergroup relations develop.[2]

Identity Groups

The essential characteristic of identity groups is that individuals join them at birth. While there is little

[2]The treatment given to each of these in the following paragraph is inevitably incomplete. A more extended analysis of ethnicity, gender, and age as they relate to organizations and organizational groups may be found in Alderfer (1977a), which also includes an extended bibliography. Guzzo and Epstein (1979) provide an analogous bibliography on family businesses, and Paolino and McCrady (1978) present a most useful collection of essays on families.

choice about physical membership in identity groups, there is some degree of "negotiation" about psychological membership. A person may behave, think, and feel more or less as if a member of an identity group. Identity-group membership precedes organizational-group membership. The identity groups to which we give attention are gender, ethnicity, family, and age.

Gender differences between men and women in organizations reflect the effects of unequal influence, stereotypical perceptions, and sexuality. Although we are living in an era of significant social change, the historical and contemporary relationships between men and women in the United States are unequal. In general, women tend to have less access to a variety of resources (e.g., income, position, and information) than men. There are views held by many men about the fitness of women for certain kinds of responsibilities, and there are increasingly successful efforts on the part of women and men to identify and change the consequences of these perceptions both for themselves and for the total culture. Research on female-male dynamics in organizations has documented structural, interpersonal, and personal effects of the power and perception inequities between men and women (cf. Kanter, 1977; Filene, 1974).

Male-female dynamics in organizations are also determined by sexual dynamics, an area in which there has been less research, for understandable reasons. There are cultural taboos against discussing sexual behavior, except under relatively narrowly defined circumstances (e.g., with one's sex partner, in a therapy setting, or as part of legal proceedings to determine whether sexual harassment has occurred). But these prohibitions and inhibitions do not keep sexual feelings from arising and influencing the behavior and perceptions of men and women in organizations.

Ethnic differences are closely tied to the historical relationships between the most numerous ethnic groups in a region (van den Berghe, 1972; Te Selle, 1973; Glazer & Moynihan, 1975). Specific kinds of work and organizational roles tend to be available only to members of particular ethnic groups. A struggle among ethnic groups for control of material, positional, and informational resources is more visible at some times (e.g., when violence breaks out or when nonviolent demonstrations occur) than at others (e.g., when surface appearances suggest

peace). The potential for serious conflict among ethnic groups is present as long as access to resources is understood to be inequitably distributed and group members believe that their ethnic identity is the basis for their losing or not receiving access to resources. In the United States the most severe ethnic conflicts have been between blacks and whites (Kerner & Lindsay, 1968).

As a result of cultural traditions and contemporary experiences, ethnic groups develop different ways of explaining what happens to themselves and to others: they have different "theories" to explain the world. Dominant groups tend to assume that their theories are correct. They either define other groups' views as wrong or they remain largely unaware that alternative theories exist. Less-dominant groups tend to be aware of both majority and minority theories, and they expect their theories to be ignored or devalued by dominant groups (Billig, 1976).

Family groups play an especially prominent role in business enterprises that were built around the contributions of family members (cf. Sofer, 1961; Miller & Rice, 1967). Family groups become a significant force shaping intergroup relations after the business grows to the point where non-family people are necessary to maintain or enhance the human capacities of the organization. When a substantial proportion of non–family members become organization members, the intergroup relationship between family and non–family people takes on the dynamics of an overbounded system (i.e., the family) dealing with an underbounded system (i.e., the nonfamily).[3] Family members face questions about whether they wish to share or give up control of the enterprise to non–family members. Non–family members struggle with whether they wish to remain psychologically outside the family or strive to earn the status of adopted daughters or sons, thereby enhancing their influence as individuals while maintaining the dominance of the founding family.

The pattern of relations between family members and non–family members is also related to generational intergroup dynamics. Non–family members often must compete with daughters and sons of the entrepreneur for positions of influence in the enter-

---

[3]Clearly not all families are overbounded systems. But it seems unlikely that members of a family who work in the same family-owned business can escape being overbounded as a result of their internal dynamics and their relations with non–family members.

prise. Children of the entrepreneur, depending on the nature of their family relationships, must struggle more or less with their parents about whether they stay in or leave the business and with the implications of that decision for their standing in the family and in the business.

Generational groups, unlike the other identity groups, have the property that everyone who lives long enough will inevitably belong to several. As a result, members of older groups have the potential for developing empathy for members of younger groups because they inevitably have had some of the same experiences. But members of younger groups, because of their more limited experience, have far less potential for understanding the experiences of members of older groups. Levinson et al. (1978), for example, have noted the rather profound ways that individuals do not understand the significance of life events until they have passed through identifiable life phases.

The patterns of dominance and subordination characteristic of generational groups are also unique in relation to other identity groups. In the culture of the United States, members of the middle-aged group (roughly late thirties to late fifties) tend to dominate both younger and older groups. But the younger people contend with their subordination knowing that at least some of their members will reach more influential positions, while the older people face the reality that their influence is determined to decrease with the passage of time. Generational groups tend to be bound together by their members sharing a common historical experience that in some material and symbolic way resulted in their members sharing some common deprivation (Feurer, 1969). The loosely defined ideology that evolves from the generational experience provides the rationale both for one generational group rebelling or resisting another and for one group dominating the others.

Organizational Groups

The essential characteristic of organizational groups is that individuals belong to them as a function of negotiated exchange between the person and the organization. Often the exchange is voluntary, as when a person decides to work to earn a living or volunteers to work for a community agency. But the exchange may also be involuntary, as when children must attend school, draftees must join the military,

and convicted criminals must enter a prison. Regardless of whether the exchange about entry is mainly voluntary or involuntary, becoming an organization member assigns a person to membership in both a task group and a hierarchical group. A person who stops being an organization member, for whatever reason, also gives up membership in the task and hierarchical groups. In this way task-group and hierarchical-group memberships differ from identity-group affiliations.

Task-group membership arises because of the activities (or, in some unusual cases, such as prisons or hospitals, the *in*activities) members are assigned to perform. The activities typically have a set of objectives, role relationships, and other features that shape the task-group members' experiences. As a result people develop a perspective on their own group, other groups, and the organization-as-a-whole, which in turn shapes their behavior and attitudes.

Membership in task groups also tends to be transferable from one organization to another because people can carry the knowledge and skill necessary to perform particular tasks with them if they leave one system and attempt to join another. As a function of developing and maintaining certain knowledge and skills, people may belong to known professional or semiprofessional organizations outside their employing (or confining) organizations. Support from these "outside interest groups" may help people achieve more power within the system where they are working, and it may make it more possible for them to leave the one system and join another.

Hierarchical-group membership is assigned by those in the system with the authority to determine rank in the system. The determination of a member's hierarchical position in an organization is typically a carefully controlled, and often highly secret, process. One's place in the hierarchy determines one's legitimate authority, decision-making autonomy, and scope of responsibility. Group effects of the hierarchy arise from the nature of the work required of people who occupy the different levels, from the various personal attributes that the work calls for from incumbents, and from the relations that develop between people who occupy different positions in the hierarchy (Smith, 1974; Oshry, 1977).

People at the *top* of the hierarchy carry the

burden of responsibility for large segments of the institution (or for the whole organization). They have access to more resources than lower-ranking members, including relatively more autonomy in determining how to define and conduct their assignments. They also tend to maintain a larger network of relationships with key people outside the institution than lower-ranking members.

By the very nature of the hierarchy people at or near the top have more potential power than lower-ranking people. However great their actual power, higher-ranking people tend to be seen by lower-ranking members as possessing more power than they experience themselves as being able to use effectively. The world faced by higher-ranking people is typically very complex, and the untoward effects of misusing their power is often much clearer to them than to lower-ranking people, who typically face less complex environments.

The positional attributes of higher-ranking people affect communication with people below them in the system. Because there are hazards to bearing bad news, lower-ranking people tend to censor information flowing upward so that it has a positive flavor. Because of the complexity of their work and the public visibility of controversial events, higher-ranking people naturally prefer good news. Thus, an unwitting collusion develops between higher- and lower-ranking people, which tends to keep higher-ranking people better informed about good news than about bad.

People in the *middle* of the organization have the task of holding together an easy alliance between the highest- and lowest-ranking members. They are truly people in the middle. They are more in touch with the concrete day-to-day events than those above them, and they have more power, authority, and autonomy than those below them. They are aware of the tensions and pressures faced by those at the top, and they can be conscious of the deprivations and struggles faced by those below them. They must exercise some control over those below them in the system, and they must satisfy those above them if they are to retain their positions.

The middle holds the system together by dispensing rewards and punishment downward, and by exchanging information upward. They send information upward on the basis of judgments of what serves the joint needs of upper and middle people. The exercise of control is a balancing process: too

much restriction foments rebellion, and too little permits chaos. The balance of rewards and punishments depends on the quality of interaction between middle and lower people. The more the affective balance is positive, the more rewards are used to influence behavior (and conversely). The more the affective balance is negative, the more punishments are used to shape behavior (and conversely).

People at the *bottom* of the system execute the concrete work for which the system was created. In terms of material needs and formal influence, they are the most deprived (Argyris, 1957). They have fewer material resources, and, as individuals working alone, wield less power than any other class of individuals in the system. There is a sense of anonymity about being at the bottom of large systems—a consequence that encourages people to lose their individuality in groups and not to feel responsible for their actions.

The people at the bottom of the system cope with their relative deprivation and alienation by both passive and aggressive means. When times are "calm" they withhold some of their potential involvement in objectives set for them by middles in order to retain a modicum of control over their lives. They may also covertly undermine vulnerable parts of the larger system. When times are "turbulent" they organize and openly resist initiatives and structures set out by the middles (Brown, 1978). A portion of the lower group also identifies with the middle and upper groups; they are most susceptible to the rewards and punishments offered by the middle, and they often share and support the control of their "peers" by the middle group (Bettelheim, 1960).

No one who belongs to an organization escapes the effects of hierarchy. Finer differentiations than the three offered here (e.g., upper upper, lower middle, etc.) can be made, but the most prominent effects of hierarchy can be observed using the three level distinction. The effects of hierarchy are "system" characteristics; anyone occupying a particular position in the hierarchy will tend to show the traits associated with that level.

EMBEDDED INTERGROUP RELATIONS

Any intergroup relationship occurs within an environment shaped by the characteristics of the suprasystem in which it is embedded. In observing an intergroup relationship one has several perspectives:

1 The effects on *individuals* who represent the groups in relation to one another
2 The consequences for *subgroups* within groups as the groups deal with one another
3 The outcomes for *groups-as-a-whole* when they relate to significant other groups
4 The impact of *suprasystem* forces on the intergroup relationship in question

Regardless of which level one observes, the phenomenon of "interpenetration" among levels will be operating. Individuals carry images of their own and other groups as they serve in representational roles. Subgroup splits within face-to-face groups reflect differing degrees of identification and involvement with the group itself, which are in turn shaped by the group-as-a-whole's relationship to other groups. Then the group-as-a-whole develops a sense—which may be more or less unconscious—of how its interests are cared for or abused by the suprasystem. The concept of embedded intergroup relations applies to both identity and task groups (Alderfer & Smith, 1981).

Figure 39-1 provides a diagram to illustrate how to think about embedded-intergroup relations from a system's perspective.[4] The picture shows how to construct an embedded-intergroup analysis from an understanding of a particular group's place in a given social system. As group members look toward the suprasystem, they make assessments as to whether their own or another group is in control of distributing scarce resources. When one's own group is in charge or has significant influence, the situation is less hazardous than when the other group dominates. The effects of one's own group occupying a favorable position in a system may be muted by its being at a relative disadvantage in the suprasystem (Alderfer & Smith, 1981).

In the particular example shown in Figure 39-1 the

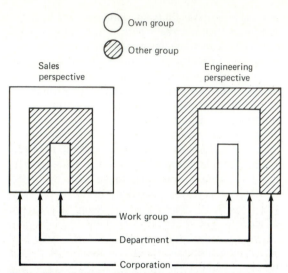

Figure 39-1 Analysis of embedded intergroup relations. *Example:* The relationship between sales and engineering work groups in a department dominated by engineers, which in turn is in a corporation dominated by sales.

relationship is between two task groups, sales and engineering. Both groups do work that is essential for their corporation and, since they are "functional" groups, might be conventionally viewed as having about equal standing in the corporation. But closer examination would probably reveal a pattern of differences, perhaps like that shown in the diagram. Any understanding of the relationship between the groups would be limited if it did not take account of different patterns of embeddedness for the group.

IMPLICATIONS

Intergroup theory provides a way to understand events inside and outside organizations. It suggests that the behavior, cognition, and feeling of people are powerfully shaped by the relations between their own groups and other significant groups with whom they interact. In its strongest form intergroup theory implies that people cannot be understood apart from their memberships.

People who wish to use intergroup theory to enhance their self-awareness face a formidable task. From inside, the process begins by learning to understand the many messages that one's own groups send. It includes examining one's role in key groups and how that role shapes one's responses to

[4]The embedded-intergroups perspective complements and contrasts with much of the intergroup analysis most often found in social psychology (cf. especially Sherif & Sherif, 1969; Blake, Shepard, & Mouton, 1964). This social psychology perspective tends to treat groups and their representatives as equal in most important respects and generally overlooks suprasystem effects. Thus it does not take account of either the hierarchical or the embedded phenomena that tend to be present in natural settings (cf. van den Bergh, 1972; and Billig, 1976, for sociological and social psychological alternatives).

the messages sent by one's own group members. From outside, the analysis includes understanding how one's own group is affected by the actions of other groups and how as a person one is treated by others as a group representative. The problem of self-development as seen from an intergroup perspective is in part the question of which groups in what kind of relations with other groups one wishes to join. Simply stating the issue in this form underlines the complexity and difficulty of intergroup dynamics. Only a small number of the groups that one might wish to enter are open to new membership, and it is usually unlikely that one person can significantly alter the relations among groups without at least partial inclusion.

Intergroup theory may also be used to suggest ways to change the behavior of organizations and the groups within them. The theory indicates that one's membership in identity and organization groups will strongly influence how one's actions and words are perceived by the members of one's own group and by members of other groups. Cooperative efforts to effect change, therefore, depend on forming new units of people who represent the relevant groups in the system. Efforts to harm or destroy groups in political warfare establish common experiences for group members and have consequences for the relations among groups far beyond the period when the conflict occurs. An awareness of one's own group memberships and the ways those memberships are likely to shape one's actions and perceptions provides the opportunity of being less a creature of intergroup dynamics. This may happen because of separating from one's groups or (more likely) because of being able to establish mutually beneficial relations with people who represent other groups.

Intergroup theory proposes that no one is ever free of significant group forces. Objectivity and independence are therefore largely impossible for individuals to achieve. A more realistic goal is to establish mechanisms that respect group differences and permit negotiations among parties who do not attempt to deny or destroy each other's understanding of organizational reality.

REFERENCES

Adams, R. N., & Preiss, J. J. (Eds.). *Human organization research.* Homewood, Ill.: Dorsey, 1960.

Alderfer, C. P. Group and intergroup relations. In J. R. Hackman & J. L. Suttle (Eds.), *Improving life at work.* Santa Monica, Calif.: 1977a.

————. Improving organizational communication through long-term intergroup intervention. *Journal of Applied Behavioral Science,* 1977b, **13,** 193–210.

————, Alderfer, C., Tucker, L., & Tucker, R. Diagnosing race relations in management. *Journal of Applied Behavioral Science,* 1980, **16,** 135–166.

————, & Brown, L. D. *Learning from changing: Organizational diagnosis and development.* Beverly Hills, Calif.: Sage, 1975.

————, & Smith, K. K. Studying intergroup relations embedded in organizations, 1981, under review.

Argyris, C. *Personality and organization.* New York: Harper, 1957.

Becker, H. S. Whose side are we on? In W. J. Filstead (Ed.), *Qualitative methodology.* Chicago: Markham, 1967.

Berg, D. N. Failure at entry. In P. H. Mirvis and D. N. Berg (Eds.), *Failures in organization development and change.* New York: Wiley, 1977.

Bettelheim, B. *The informed heart.* New York: Free Press, 1960.

Billig, M. *Social psychology and intergroup relations.* London: Academic Press, 1976.

Blake, R. R., Shepard, H. A., & Mouton, J. S. *Managing intergroup conflict in industry.* Houston: Gulf, 1964.

Brown, L. D. Toward a theory of power and intergroup relations. In C. L. Cooper & C. P. Alderfer (Eds.), *Advances in experiential social processes,* Vol. 1. London: Wiley, 1978.

Cartwright, D., & Zander, A. *Group dynamics.* 3d ed. Evanston: Row-Peterson, 1968.

Coser, L. A. *The functions of social conflict.* Glencoe: Free Press, 1956.

Crozier, M. *The bureaucratic phenomenon.* Chicago: University of Chicago Press, 1964.

Dalton, M. *Men who manage.* New York: Wiley, 1959.

Feurer, L. S. *The conflict of the generations.* New York: Basic Books, 1969.

Filene, P. G. *Him, Her, Self.* New York: Harcourt, Brace, Jovanovich, 1974.

Glazer, N., & Moynihan, D. P. *Ethnicity: Theory and experience.* Cambridge, Mass.: Harvard, 1975.

Guzzo, R. A., & Epstein, G. *Behavioral issues in family businesses: An annotated bibliography.* Montreal: School of Management, McGill University, 1979.

Hackman, J. R. Group influences on individuals. In M. D. Dunnette (Ed.), *Handbook of industrial and organizational psychology.* Chicago: Rand-McNally, 1976.

Homans, G. *The human group.* New York: Harcourt, Brace, & World, 1950.

Kahn, R. L., & Mann, F. C. Developing research partnerships. *Journal of Social Issues,* 1952, **8,** 4–10.

Kanter, R. *Men and women of the corporation.* New York: Basic Books, 1977.

Kerner, O., & Lindsay, J. *Report of the National Advisory Commission on Civil Disorders.* New York: Dutton, 1968.

Lasswell, H. D., & Kaplan, A. *Power and society.* New Haven: Yale, 1950.

Leavitt, H. J. Suppose we took groups seriously . . . . In E. L. Cass & F. G. Zimmer (Eds.), *Man and work in society.* New York: Van Nostrand Reinhold, 1975.

Levine, R. A., & Campbell, D. T. *Ethnocentrism.* New York: Wiley, 1972.

Levinson, D. J. Role, personality, and social structure in the organizational setting. *Journal of Abnormal and Social Psychology,* 1959, **58,** 170–180.

———, Darrow, C. N., Klein, E. B., Levinson, M. B., & McKee, B. *The seasons of a man's life.* New York: Knopf, 1978.

Lewicki, R. J., & Alderfer, C. P. The tensions between research and intervention in intergroup conflict. *Journal of Applied Behavioral Science,* 1973, **9,** 424–449.

Likert, R. *New patterns of management.* New York: McGraw-Hill, 1961.

Loring, R., & Wells, T. *Breakthrough: Women into management.* New York: Van Nostrand Reinhold, 1972.

Merton, R. K. Insiders and outsiders. *American Journal of Sociology,* 1972, **78,** 9–47.

Miller, E. J., & Rice, A. K. *Systems of organization.* London: Tavistock, 1967.

Miller, J. G. *Living systems.* New York: McGraw-Hill, 1978.

Nadler, D. N. Consulting with labor and management: Some learnings from quality of work life projects. In W. W. Burke (Ed.), *The cutting edge: Current theory and practice in organization development.* LaJolla, Calif.: University Associates, 1978.

Oshry, B. *Power and position.* Boston: Power & Systems Training, 1977.

Paolino, T. J., & McCrady, B. S. *Marriage and marital therapy.* New York: Brunner/Mazel, 1978.

Purcell, T. V., & Cavanagh, G. F. *Blacks in the industrial world.* New York: Free Press, 1972.

Rice, A. K. Individual, group, and intergroup processes. *Human Relations,* 1969, **22,** 565–584.

Roethlisberger, F. J., & Dickson, W. J. *Management and the worker.* New York: Wiley, 1939.

Sayles, L. R. *Behavior of industrial work groups.* New York: Wiley, 1958.

———, & Strauss, G. *The local union: Its place in the industrial plant.* New York: Harper, 1953.

Sherif, M., & Sherif, C. *Social psychology.* New York: Harper & Row, 1969.

Smith, K. K. Behavioral consequences of hierarchical structures. Unpublished doctoral dissertation, Yale University, 1974.

———. An intergroup perspective on individual behavior. In J. R. Hackman, E. E. Lawler, & L. W. Porter (Eds.), *Perspectives on behavior in organizations.* New York: McGraw-Hill, 1977.

Sofer, C. *The organization from within.* London: Tavistock, 1961.

Strauss, G. Tactics of lateral relationships: The purchasing agent. *Administrative Science Quarterly,* 1962, **7,** 161–187.

———. Workflow frictions, interfunctional rivalry, and professionalism: A case study of purchasing agents. *Human Organization,* 1964, **23,** 137–149.

Sumner, W. G. *Folkways.* New York: Ginn, 1906.

Tajfel, H. Experiments in intergroup discrimination. *Scientific American,* 1970, **223,** 96–102.

Te Selle, S. (Ed.), *The rediscovery of ethnicity.* New York: Harper, 1973.

Van Den Berge, P. (Ed.), *Intergroup relations.* New York: Basic Books, 1972.

Wells, L., Jr. The group-as-a-whole. In C. P. Alderfer and C. L. Cooper (Eds.), *Advances in experiential social processes,* Vol. 2. London: Wiley, 1980.

Reading 40

Who Gets Power—And How They Hold on to It:
A Strategic-Contingency Model of Power

Gerald R. Salancik
Jeffrey Pfeffer

Power is held by many people to be a dirty word or, as Warren Bennis has said, "It is the organization's last dirty secret."

This article will argue that traditional "political" power, far from being a dirty business, is, in its most naked form, one of the few mechanisms available for aligning an organization with its own reality. However, institutionalized forms of power—what we prefer to call the cleaner forms of power: authority, legitimization, centralized control, regulations, and the more modern "management information systems"—tend to buffer the organization from reality and obscure the demands of its environment. Most great states and institutions declined, not because they played politics, but because they failed to accommodate to the political realities they faced. Political processes, rather than being mechanisms for unfair and unjust allocations and appointments, tend toward the realistic resolution of conflicts among interests. And power, while it eludes definition, is easy enough to recognize by its consequences —the ability of those who possess power to bring about the outcomes they desire.

The model of power we advance is an elaboration of what has been called strategic-contingency theory, a view that sees power as something that accrues to organizational subunits (individuals, departments) that cope with critical organizational problems. Power is used by subunits, indeed, used by all who have it, to enhance their own survival through control of scarce critical resources, through the placement of allies in key positions, and through the definition of organizational problems and policies. Because of the processes by which power develops and is used, organizations become both more aligned and more misaligned with their environments. This contradiction is the most interesting aspect of organizational power, and one that makes administration one of the most precarious of occupations.

WHAT IS ORGANIZATIONAL POWER?

You can walk into most organizations and ask without fear of being misunderstood, "Which are the powerful groups or people in this organization?" Although may organizational informants may be *unwilling* to tell you, it is unlikely they will be *unable* to tell you. Most people do not require explicit definitions to know what power is.

Power is simply the ability to get things done the way one wants them to be done. For a manager who wants an increased budget to launch a project that he thinks is important, his power is measured by his ability to get that budget. For an executive vice-president who wants to be chairman, his power is evidenced by his advancement toward his goal.

People in organizations not only know what you are talking about when you ask who is influential but they are likely to agree with one another to an amazing extent. Recently, we had a chance to observe this in a regional office of an insurance company. The office had 21 department managers; we asked ten of these managers to rank all 21 according to the influence each one had in the organization. Despite the fact that ranking 21 things is a difficult task, the managers sat down and began arranging the names of their colleagues and themselves in a column. Only one person bothered to ask, "What do you mean by influence?" When told "power," he responded, "Oh," and went on. We compared the rankings of all ten managers and found virtually no disagreement among them in the managers ranked among the top five or the bottom five. Differences in the rankings came from department heads claiming more influence for themselves than their colleagues attributed to them.

Such agreement on those who have influence, and those who do not, was not unique to this insurance company. So far we have studied over 20 very different organizations—universities, research firms, factories, banks, retailers, to name a few. In each one we found individuals able to rate themselves and their peers on a scale of influence or power. We have done this both for specific decisions and for general impact on organizational policies. Their agreement was unusually high, which suggests that distributions of influence exist well enough in everyone's mind to be referred to with ease—and we assume with accuracy.

WHERE DOES ORGANIZATIONAL POWER COME FROM?

Earlier we stated that power helps organizations become aligned with their realities. This hopeful prospect follows from what we have dubbed the strategic-contingencies theory of organizational power. Briefly, those subunits most able to cope with the organization's critical problems and uncertainties acquire power. In its simplest form, the strategic-contingencies theory implies that when an organization faces a number of lawsuits that threaten its existence, the legal department will gain power and influence over organizational decisions. Somehow other organizational interest groups will recognize its critical importance and confer upon it a status and power never before enjoyed. This influence may extend beyond handling legal matters and into decisions about product design, advertising production, and so on. Such extensions undoubtedly would be accompanied by appropriate, or acceptable, verbal justifications. In time, the head of the legal department may become the head of the corporation, just as in times past the vice-president for marketing had become the president when market shares were a worrisome problem and, before him, the chief engineer, who had made the production line run as smooth as silk.

Stated in this way, the strategic-contingencies theory of power paints an appealing picture of power. To the extent that power is determined by the critical uncertainties and problems facing the organization and, in turn, influences decisions in the organization, the organization is aligned with the realities it faces. In short, power facilitates the organization's adaptation to its environment—or its problems.

We can cite many illustrations of how influence derives from a subunit's ability to deal with critical contingencies. Michael Crozier described a French cigarette factory in which the maintenance engineers had a considerable say in the plantwide operation. After some probing he discovered that the group possessed the solution to one of the major problems faced by the company, that of troubleshooting the elaborate, expensive, and irrascible automated machines that kept breaking down and dumbfounding everyone else. It was the one problem that the plant manager could in no way control.

The production workers, while troublesome from time to time, created no insurmountable problems; the manager could reasonably predict their absenteeism or replace them when necessary. Production scheduling was something he could deal with since, by watching inventories and sales, the demand for cigarettes was known long in advance. Changes in demand could be accommodated by slowing down or speeding up the line. Supplies of tobacco and paper were also easily dealt with through stockpiles and advance orders.

The one thing that management could neither control nor accommodate to, however, was the seemingly happenstance breakdowns. And the foremen couldn't instruct the workers what to do when emergencies developed since the maintenance department kept its records of problems and solutions locked up in a cabinet or in its members' heads. The breakdowns were, in truth, a critical source of uncertainty for the organization, and the maintenance engineers were the only ones who could cope with the problem.

The engineers' strategic role in coping with breakdowns afforded them a considerable say on plant decisions. Schedules and production quotas were set in consultation with them. And the plant manager, while formally their boss, accepted their decisions about personnel in their operation. His submission was to his credit, for without their cooperation he would have had an even more difficult time in running the plant.

Ignoring Critical Consequences

In this cigarette factory, sharing influence with the maintenance workers reflected the plant manager's awareness of the critical contingencies. However, when organizational members are not aware of the critical contingencies they face, and do not share influence accordingly, the failure to do so can create havoc. In one case, an insurance company's regional office was having problems with the performance of one of its departments, the coding department. From the outside, the department looked like a disaster area. The clerks who worked in it were somewhat dissatisfied; their supervisor paid little attention to them, and they resented the hard work. Several other departments were critical of this manager, claiming that she was inconsistent in meeting deadlines. The person most critical was the claims manager. He resented having to wait for work that was handled by her department, claiming that it held up his claims adjusters. Having heard the rumors about dissatisfaction among her subordinates, he attributed the situation to poor supervision. He was second in command in the office and therefore took up the issue with her immediate boss, the head of administrative services. They consulted with the personnel manager and the three of them concluded that the manager needed leadership training to improve her relations with her subordinates. The coding manager objected, saying it was a waste of time, but agreed to go along with the training and also agreed to give more priority to the claims department's work. Within a week after the training, the results showed that her workers were happier but that the performance of her department had decreased, save for the people serving the claims department.

About this time, we began, quite independently, a study of influence in this organization. We asked the administrative services director to draw up flow charts of how the work of one department moved onto the next department. In the course of the interview, we noticed that the coding department began or interceded in the work flow of most of the other departments and casually mentioned to him, "The coding manager must be very influential." He said "No, not really. Why would you think so?" Before we could reply he recounted the story of her leadership training and the fact that things were worse. We then told him that it seemed obvious that the coding department would be influential from the fact that all the other departments depended on it. It was also clear why productivity had fallen. The coding manager took the training seriously and began spending more time raising her workers' spirits than she did worrying about the problems of all the departments that depended on her. Giving

priority to the claims area only exaggerated the problem, for their work was getting done at the expense of the work of the other departments. Eventually the company hired a few more clerks to relieve the pressure in the coding department and performance returned to a more satisfactory level.

Originally we got involved with this insurance company to examine how the influence of each manager evolved from his or her department's handling of critical organizational contingencies. We reasoned that one of the most important contingencies faced by all profit-making organizations was that of generating income. Thus we expected managers would be influential to the extent to which they contributed to this function. Such was the case. The underwriting managers, who wrote the policies that committed the premiums, were the most influential; the claims managers, who kept a lid on the funds flowing out, were a close second. Least influential were the managers of functions unrelated to revenue, such as mailroom and payroll managers. And contrary to what the administrative services manager believed, the third most powerful department head (out of 21) was the woman in charge of the coding function, which consisted of rating, recording, and keeping track of the codes of all policy applications and contracts. Her peers attributed more influence to her than could have been inferred from her place on the organization chart. And it was not surprising, since they all depended on her department. The coding department's records, their accuracy and the speed with which they could be retrieved, affected virtually every other operating department in the insurance office. The underwriters depended on them in getting the contracts straight; the typing department depended on them in preparing the formal contract document; the claims department depended on them in adjusting claims; and accounting depended on them for billing. Unfortunately, the "bosses" were not aware of these dependences, for unlike the cigarette factory, there were no massive breakdowns that made them obvious, while the coding manager, who was a hard-working but quiet person, did little to announce her importance.

The cases of this plant and office illustrate nicely a basic point about the source of power in organizations. The basis for power in an organization derives from the ability of a person or subunit to take or not take actions that are desired by others. The coding manager was seen as influential by those who depended on her department, but not by the people at the top. The engineers were influential because of their role in keeping the plant operating. The two cases differ in these respects: The coding supervisor's source of power was not as widely recognized as that of the maintenance engineers, and she did not use her source of power to influence decisions; the maintenance engineers did. Whether power is used to influence anything is a separate issue. We should not confuse this issue with the fact that power derives from a social situation in which one person has a capacity to do something and another person does not, but wants it done.

POWER SHARING IN ORGANIZATIONS

Power is shared in organizations; and it is shared out of necessity more than out of concern for principles of organizational development or participatory democracy. Power is shared because no one person controls all the desired activities in the organization. While the factory owner may hire people to operate his noisy machines, once hired they have some control over the use of the machinery. And thus they have power over him in the same way he has power over them. Who has more power over whom is a mooter point than that of recognizing the inherent nature of organizing as a sharing of power.

Let's expand on the concept that power derives from the activities desired in an organization. A major way of managing influence in organizations is through the designation of activities. In a bank we studied, we saw this principle in action. This bank was planning to install a computer system for routine credit evaluation. The bank, rather progressive-minded, was concerned that the change would have adverse effects on employees and therefore surveyed their attitudes.

The principal opposition to the new system came, interestingly, not from the employees who performed the routine credit checks, some of whom would be relocated because of the change, but from the manager of the credit department. His reason was quite simple. The manager's primary function was to give official approval to the applications, catch any employee mistakes before giving approval, and arbitrate any difficulties the clerks had in deciding what to do. As a consequence of his role, others in the organization, including his superiors, subordinates, and colleagues, attributed considerable importance to him. He, in turn, for example, could point to the low proportion of credit approvals, compared with other financial institutions, that resulted in bad debts. Now, to his mind, a wretched machine threatened to transfer his role to a computer programmer, a man who knew nothing of finance and who, in addition, had ten years less seniority. The credit manager eventually quit for a position at a smaller firm with lower pay, but one in which he would have more influence than his redefined job would have left him with.

Because power derives from activities rather than individuals, an individual's or subgroup's power is never absolute and derives ultimately from the context of the situation. The amount of power an individual has at any one time depends, not only on the activities he or she controls, but also on the existence of other persons or means by which the activities can be achieved and on those who determine what ends are desired and, hence, on what activities are desired and critical for the organization. One's own power always depends on other people for these two reasons. Other people, or groups or organizations, can determine the definition of what is a critical contingency for the organization and can also undercut the uniqueness of the individual's personal contribution to the critical contingencies of the organization.

Perhaps one can best appreciate how situationally dependent power is by examining how it is distributed. In most societies, power organizes around scarce and critical resources. Rarely does power organize around abundant resources. In the United States, a person doesn't become powerful because he or she can drive a car. There are simply too many others who can drive with equal facility. In certain villages in Mexico, on the other hand, a person with a car is accredited with enormous social status and plays a key role in the community. In addition to scarcity, power is also limited by the need for one's capacities in a social system. While a racer's ability to drive a car around a 90° turn at 80 mph may be sparsely distributed in a society, it is not likely to lend the driver much power in the society. The ability simply does not play a central role in the activities of the society.

The fact that power revolves around scarce and critical activities, of course, makes the control and organization of those activities a major battleground in struggles for power. Even relatively abundant or trivial resources can become the bases for power if one can organize and control their allocation and the definition of what is critical. Many occupational and professional groups attempt to do just this in modern economies. Lawyers organize themselves into associations, regulate the entrance requirements for novitiates, and then get laws passed specifying situations that require the services of an attorney. Workers had little power in the conduct of industrial affairs until they organized themselves into closed and controlled systems. In recent years, women and blacks have tried to define themselves as important and critical to the social system, using law to reify their status.

In organizations there are obviously opportunities for defining certain activities as more critical than others. Indeed, the growth of managerial thinking to include defining organizational objectives and goals has done much to foster these opportunities. One sure way to liquidate the power of groups in the organization is to define the need for their services out of existence. David Halberstam presents a description of how just such a thing happened to the group of correspondents that evolved around Edward R. Murrow, the brilliant journalist, interviewer, and war correspondent of CBS News. A close friend of CBS chairman and controlling stockholder William S. Paley, Murrow, and the news department he directed, were endowed with freedom to do what they felt was right. He used it to create some of the best documentaries and commentaries ever seen on television. Unfortunately, television became too large, too powerful, and too suspect in the eyes of the federal government that licensed it. It thus became, or at least the top executives believed it had become, too dangerous to have in-depth, probing commentary on the news. Crisp, dry, uneditorializing headlines were considered safer. Murrow was out and Walker Cronkite was in.

The power to define what is critical in an organization is no small power. Moreover, it is the key to understanding why organizations are either aligned with their environments or misaligned. If an organization defines certain activities as critical when in fact they are not critical, given the flow of resources

coming into the organization, it is not likely to survive, at least in its present form.

Most organizations manage to evolve a distribution of power and influence that is aligned with the critical realities they face in the environment. The environment, in turn, includes both the internal environment, the shifting situational contexts in which particular decisions get made, and the external environment that it can hope to influence but is unlikely to control.

THE CRITICAL CONTINGENCIES

The critical contingencies facing most organizations derive from the environmental context within which they operate. This determines the available needed resources and thus determines the problems to be dealt with. That power organizes around handling these problems suggests an important mechanism by which organizations keep in tune with their external environments. The strategic-contingencies model implies that subunits that contribute to the critical resources of the organization will gain influence in the organization. Their influence presumably is then used to bend the organization's activities to the contingencies that determine its resources. This idea may strike one as obvious. But its obviousness in no way diminishes its importance. Indeed, despite its obviousness, it escapes the notice of many organizational analysts and managers, who all too frequently think of the organization in terms of a descending pyramid, in which all the departments in one tier hold equal power and status. This presumption denies the reality that departments differ in the contributions they are believed to make to the overall organization's resources, as well as to the fact that some are more equal than others.

Because of the importance of this idea to organizational effectiveness, we decided to examine it carefully in a large midwestern university. A university offers an excellent site for studying power. It is composed of departments with nominally equal power and is administered by a central executive structure much like other bureaucracies. However, at the same time it is a situation in which the departments have clearly defined identities and face diverse external environments. Each department has its own bodies of knowledge, its own institutions, its own sources of prestige and resources.

Because the departments operate in different external environments, they are likely to contribute differentially to the resources of the overall organization. Thus a physics department with close ties to NASA may contribute substantially to the funds of the university; and a history department with a renowned historian in residence may contribute to the intellectual credibility or prestige of the whole university. Such variations permit one to examine how these various contributions lead to obtaining power within the university.

We analyzed the influence of 29 university departments throughout an 18-month period in their history. Our chief interest was to determine whether departments that brought more critical resources to the university would be more powerful than departments that contributed fewer or less critical resources.

To identify the critical resources each department contributed, the heads of all departments were interviewed about the importance of seven different resources to the university's success. The seven included undergraduate students (the factor determining size of the state allocations by the university), national prestige, administrative expertise, and so on. The most critical resource was found to be contract and grant monies received by a department's faculty for research or consulting services. At this university, contract and grants contributed somewhat less than 50 percent of the overall budget, with the remainder primarily coming from state appropriations. The importance attributed to contract and grant monies, and the rather minor importance of undergraduate students, was not surprising for this particular university. The university was a major center for graduate education: many of its departments ranked in the top ten of their respective fields. Grant and contract monies were the primary source of discretionary funding available for maintaining these programs of graduate education, and hence for maintaining the university's prestige. The prestige of the university itself was critical both in recruiting able students and attracting top-notch faculty.

From university records it was determined what relative contributions each of the 29 departments made to the various needs of the university (national prestige, outside grants, teaching). Thus, for instance, one department may have contributed to the university by teaching 7 percent of the instructional units, bringing in 2 percent of the outside contracts and grants, and having a national ranking of 20. Another department, on the other hand, may have taught one percent of the instructional units, contributed 12 percent to the grants, and be ranked the third best department in its field within the country.

The question was: Do these different contributions determine the relative power of the departments within the university? Power was measured in several ways; but regardless of how measured, the answer was "Yes." Those three resources together accounted for about 70 percent of the variance in subunit power in the university.

But the most important predictor of departmental power was the department's contribution to the contracts and grants of the university. Sixty percent of the variance in power was due to this one factor, suggesting that the power of departments derived primarily from the dollars they provided for graduate education, the activity believed to be the most important for the organization.

THE IMPACT OF ORGANIZATIONAL POWER ON DECISION MAKING

The measure of power we used in studying this university was an analysis of the responses of the department heads we interviewed. While such perceptions of power might be of interest in their own right, they contribute little to our understanding of how the distribution of power might serve to align an organization with its critical realities. For this we must look to how power actually influences the decisions and policies of organizations.

While it is perhaps not absolutely valid, we can generally gauge the relative importance of a department of an organization by the size of the budget allocated to it relative to other departments. Clearly it is of importance to the administrators of those departments whether they get squeezed in a budget crunch or are given more funds to strike out after new opportunities. And it should also be clear that when those decisions are made and one department can go ahead and try new approaches while another must cut back on the old, then the deployment of the resources of the organization in meeting its problems is most directly affected.

Thus our study of the university led us to ask the

following question: Does power lead to influence in the organization? To answer this question, we found it useful first to ask another one, namely: Why should department heads try to influence organizational decisions to favor their own departments to the exclusion of other departments? While this second question may seem a bit naive to anyone who has witnessed the political realities of organizations, we posed it in a context of research on organizations that sees power as an illegitimate threat to the neater rational authority of modern bureaucracies. In this context, decisions are not believed to be made because of the dirty business of politics but because of the overall goals and purposes of the organization. In a university, one reasonable basis for decision making is the teaching workload of departments and the demands that follow from that workload. We would expect, therefore, that departments with heavy student demands for courses would be able to obtain funds for teaching. Another reasonable basis for decision making is quality. We would expect, for that reason, that departments with esteemed reputations would be able to obtain funds both because their quality suggests they might use such funds effectively and because such funds would allow them to maintain their quality. A rational model of bureaucracy intimates, then, that the organizational decisions taken would favor those who perform the stated purposes of the organization —teaching undergraduates and training professional and scientific talent—well.

The problem with rational models of decision making, however, is that what is rational to one person may strike another as irrational. For most departments, resources are a question of survival. While teaching undergraduates may seem to be a major goal for some members of the university, developing knowledge may seem so to others; and to still others, advising governments and other institutions about policies may seem to be the crucial business. Everyone has his own idea of the proper priorities in a just world. Thus goals rather than being clearly defined and universally agreed upon are blurred and contested throughout the organization. If such is the case, then the decisions taken on behalf of the organization as a whole are likely to reflect the goals of those who prevail in political contests, namely, those with power in the organization.

Will organizational decisions always reflect the distribution of power in the organization? Probably not. Using power for influence requires a certain expenditure of effort, time, and resources. Prudent and judicious persons are not likely to use their power needlessly or wastefully. And it is likely that power will be used to influence organizational decisions primarily under circumstances that both require and favor its use. We have examined three conditions that are likely to affect the use of power in organizations: scarcity, criticality, and uncertainty. The first suggests that subunits will try to exert influence when the resources of the organization are scarce. If there is an abundance of resources, then a particular department or a particular individual has little need to attempt influence. With little effort, he can get all he wants anyway.

The second condition, criticality, suggests that a subunit will attempt to influence decisions to obtain resources that are critical to its own survival and activities. Criticality implies that one would not waste effort, or risk being labeled obstinate, by fighting over trivial decisions affecting one's operations.

An office manager would probably balk less about a threatened cutback in copying machine usage than about a reduction in typing staff. An advertising department head would probably worry less about losing his lettering artist than his illustrator. Criticality is difficult to define because what is critical depends on people's beliefs about what is critical. Such beliefs may or may not be based on experience and knowledge and may or may not be agreed upon by all. Scarcity, for instance, may itself affect conceptions of criticality. When slack resources drop off, cutbacks have to be made—those "hard decisions," as congressmen and resplendent administrators like to call them. Managers then find themselves scrapping projects they once held dear.

The third condition that we believe affects the use of power is uncertainty: When individuals do not agree about what the organization should do or how to do it, power and other social processes will affect decisions. The reason for this is simply that, if there are no clear-cut criteria available for resolving conflicts of interest, then the only means for resolution is some form of social process, including power, status, social ties, or some arbitrary process like flipping a coin or drawing straws. Under conditions of uncertainty, the powerful manager can argue his case on any grounds and usually win it. Since there is no real consensus, other contestants are not likely to develop counter arguments or amass sufficient opposition. Moreover, because of his power and their need for access to the resources he controls, they are more likely to defer to his arguments.

Although the evidence is slight, we have found that power will influence the allocations of scarce and critical resources. In the analysis of power in the university, for instance, one of the most critical resources needed by departments is the general budget. First granted by the state legislature, the general budget is later allocated to individual departments by the university administration in response to requests from the department heads. Our analysis of the factors that contribute to a department getting more or less of this budget indicated that subunit power was the major predictor, overriding such factors as student demand for courses, national reputations of departments, or even the size of a department's faculty. Moreover, other research has shown that when the general budget has been cut back or held below previous uninflated levels, leading to monies becoming more scarce, budget allocations mirror departmental powers even more closely.

Student enrollment and faculty size, of course, do themselves relate to budget allocations, as we would expect since they determine a department's need for resources, or at least offer visible testimony of needs. But departments are not always able to get what they need by the mere fact of needing them. In one analysis it was found that high-power departments were able to obtain budget without regard to their teaching loads and, in some cases, actually in inverse relation to their teaching loads. In contrast, low-power departments could get increases in budget only when they could justify the increases by a recent growth in teaching load, and then only when it was far in excess of norms for other departments.

General budget is only one form of resource that is allocated to departments. There are others such as special grants for student fellowships or faculty research. These are critical to departments because they affect the ability to attract other resources, such as outstanding faculty or students. We examined how power influenced the allocations of four resources department heads had described as critical and scarce.

When the four resources were arrayed from the most to the least critical and scarce, we found that departmental power best predicted the allocations of the most critical and scarce resources. In other words, the analysis of how power influences organizational allocations leads to this conclusion: Those subunits most likely to survive in times of strife are those that are more critical to the organization. Their importance to the organization gives them power to influence resource allocations that enhance their own survival.

HOW EXTERNAL ENVIRONMENT IMPACTS EXECUTIVE SELECTION

Power not only influences the survival of key groups in an organization, it also influences the selection of individuals to key leadership positions, and by such a process further aligns the organization with its environmental context.

We can illustrate this with a recent study of the selection and tenure of chief administrators in 57 hospitals in Illinois. We assumed that since the critical problems facing the organization would enhance the power of certain groups at the expense of others, then the leaders to emerge should be those most relevant to the context of the hospitals. To assess this we asked each chief administrator about his professional background and how long he had been in office. The replies were then related to the hospitals' funding, ownership, and competitive conditions for patients and staff.

One aspect of a hospital's context is the source of its budget. Some hospitals, for instance, are run much like other businesses. They sell bed space, patient care, and treatment services. They charge fees sufficient both to cover their costs and to provide capital for expansion. The main source of both their operating and capital funds is patient billings. Increasingly, patient billings are paid for, not by patients, but by private insurance companies. Insurers like Blue Cross dominate and represent a potent interest group outside a hospital's control but critical to its income. The insurance companies, in order to limit their own costs, attempt to hold down the fees allowable to hospitals, which they do effectively from their positions on state rate boards. The squeeze on hospitals that results from fees increasing slowly while costs climb rapidly more and more demands the talents of cost accountants or people trained in the technical expertise of hospital administration.

By contrast, other hospitals operate more like social service institutions, either as government healthcare units (Bellevue Hospital in New York City and Cook County Hospital in Chicago, for example) or as charitable institutions. These hospitals obtain a large proportion of their operating and capital funds, not from privately insured patients, but from government subsidies or private donations. Such institutions rather than requiring the talents of a technically efficient administrator are likely to require the savvy of someone who is well integrated into the social and political power structure of the community.

Not surprisingly, the characteristics of administrators predictably reflect the funding context of the hospitals with which they are associated. Those hospitals with larger proportions of their budget obtained from private insurance companies were most likely to have administrators with backgrounds in accounting and least likely to have administrators whose professions were business or medicine. In contrast, those hospitals with larger proportions of their budget derived from private donations and local governments were most likely to have administrators with business or professional backgrounds and least likely to have accountants. The same held for formal training in hospital management. Professional hospital administrators could easily be found in hospitals drawing their incomes from private insurance and rarely in hospitals dependent on donations or legislative appropriations.

As with the selection of administrators, the context of organizations has also been found to affect the removal of executives. The environment, as a source of organizational problems, can make it more or less difficult for executives to demonstrate their value to the organization. In the hospitals we studied, long-term administrators came from hospitals with few problems. They enjoyed amicable and stable relations with their local business and social communities and suffered little competition for funding and staff. The small city hospital director who attended civic and Elks meetings while running the only hospital within a 100-mile radius, for example, had little difficulty holding on to his job. Turnover was highest in hospitals with the most problems, a phenomenon similar to that observed in a study of industrial organizations in which turnover

was highest among executives in industries with competitive environments and unstable market conditions. The interesting thing is that instability characterized the industries rather than the individual firms in them. The troublesome conditions in the individual firms were attributed, or rather misattributed, to the executives themselves.

It takes more than problems, however, to terminate a manager's leadership. The problems themselves must be relevant and critical. This is clear from the way in which an administrator's tenure is affected by the status of the hospital's operating budget. Naively we might assume that all administrators would need to show a surplus. Not necessarily so. Again, we must distinguish between those hospitals that depend on private donations for funds and those that do not. Whether an endowed budget shows a surplus or deficit is less important than the hospital's relations with the benefactors. On the other hand, with a budget dependent on patient billing, a surplus is almost essential; monies for new equipment or expansion must be drawn from it, and without them quality care becomes more difficult and patients scarcer. An administrator's tenure reflected just these considerations. For those hospitals dependent upon private donations, the length of an administrator's term depended not at all on the status of the operating budget but was fairly predictable from the hospital's relations with the business community. On the other hand, in hospitals dependent on the operating budget for capital financing, the greater the deficit the shorter was the tenure of the hospital's principal administrators.

CHANGING CONTINGENCIES AND ERODING POWER BASES

The critical contingencies facing the organization may change. When they do, it is reasonable to expect that the power of individuals and subgroups will change in turn. At times the shift can be swift and shattering, as it was recently for powerholders in New York City. A few years ago it was believed that David Rockefeller was one of the ten most powerful people in the city, as tallied by *New York* magazine, which annually sniffs out power for the delectation of its readers. But that was before it was revealed that the city was in financial trouble, before Rockefeller's Chase Manhattan Bank lost some of its own financial luster, and before brother Nelson lost some of his political influence in Washington. Obviously David Rockefeller was no longer as well positioned to help bail the city out. Another loser was an attorney with considerable personal connections to the political and religious leaders of the city. His talents were no longer in much demand. The persons with more influence were the bankers and union pension fund executors who fed money to the city; community leaders who represent blacks and Spanish-Americans, in contrast, witnessed the erosion of their power bases.

One implication of the idea that power shifts with changes in organizational environments is that the dominant coalition will tend to be that group that is most appropriate for the organization's environment, as also will the leaders of an organization. One can observe this historically in the top executives of industrial firms in the United States. Up until the early 1950s, many top corporations were headed by former production line managers or engineers who gained prominence because of their abilities to cope with the problems of production. Their success, however, only spelled their demise. As production became routinized and mechanized, the problem of most firms became one of selling all those goods they so efficiently produced. Marketing executives were more frequently found in corporate boardrooms. Success outdid itself again, for keeping markets and production steady and stable requires the kind of control that can only come from acquiring competitors and suppliers or the invention of more and more appealing products—ventures that typically require enormous amounts of capital. During the 1960s, financial executives assumed the seats of power. And they, too, will give way to others. Edging over the horizon are legal experts, as regulation and antitrust suits are becoming more and more frequent in the 1970s, suits that had their beginnings in the success of the expansion generated by prior executives. The more distant future, which is likely to be dominated by multinational corporations, may see former secretaries of state and their minions increasingly serving as corporate figureheads.

THE NONADAPTIVE CONSEQUENCES OF ADAPTATION

From what we have said thus far about power aligning the organization with its own realities, an intelligent person might react with a resounding ho-hum, for it all seems too obvious: Those with the ability to get the job done are given the job to do.

However, there are two aspects of power that make it more useful for understanding organizations and their effectiveness. First, the "job" to be done has a way of expanding itself until it becomes less and less clear what the job is. Napoleon began by doing a job for France in the war with Austria and ended up Emperor, convincing many that only he could keep the peace. Hitler began by promising an end to Germany's troubling postwar depression and ended up convincing more people than is comfortable to remember that he was destined to be the savior of the world. In short, power is a capacity for influence that extends far beyond the original bases that created it. Second, power tends to take on institutionalized forms that enable it to endure well beyond its usefulness to an organization.

There is an important contradiction in what we have observed about organizational power. On the one hand we have said that power derives from the contingencies facing an organization and that when those contingencies change so do the bases for power. On the other hand we have asserted that subunits will tend to use their power to influence organizational decisions in their own favor, particularly when their own survival is threatened by the scarcity of critical resources. The first statement implies that an organization will tend to be aligned with its environment since power will tend to bring to key positions those with capabilities relevant to the context. The second implies that those in power will not give up their positions so easily; they will pursue policies that guarantee their continued domination. In short, change and stability operate through the same mechanism, and, as a result, the organization will never be completely in phase with its environment or its needs.

The study of hospital administrators illustrates how leadership can be out of phase with reality. We argued that privately funded hospitals needed trained technical administrators more so than did hospitals funded by donations. The need as we perceived it was matched in most hospitals, but by no means in all. Some organizations did not conform with our predictions. These deviations imply that some administrators were able to maintain their positions independent of their suitability for those positions. By dividing administrators into those with long and short terms of office, one finds that the characteristics of longer-termed administrators were virtually unrelated to the hospital's context. The shorter-termed chiefs on the other hand had characteristics more appropriate for the hospital's problems. For a hospital to have a recently appointed head implies that the previous administrator had been unable to endure by institutionalizing himself.

One obvious feature of hospitals that allowed some administrators to enjoy a long tenure was a hospital's ownership. Administrators were less entrenched when their hospitals were affiliated with and dependent upon larger organizations, such as governments or churches. Private hospitals offered more secure positions for administrators. Like private corporations, they tend to have more diffused ownership, leaving the administrator unopposed as he institutionalizes his reign. Thus he endures, sometimes at the expense of the performance of the organization. Other research has demonstrated that corporations with diffuse ownership have poorer earnings than those in which the control of the manager is checked by a dominant shareholder. Firms that overload their boardrooms with more insiders than are appropriate for their context have also been found to be less profitable.

A word of caution is required about our judgment of "appropriateness." When we argue some capabilities are more appropriate for one context than another, we do so from the perspective of an outsider and on the basis of reasonable assumptions as to the problems the organization will face and the capabilities they will need. The fact that we have been able to predict the distribution of influence and the characteristics of leaders suggests that our reasoning is not incorrect. However, we do not think that all organizations follow the same pattern. The fact that we have not been able to predict outcomes with 100 percent accuracy indicates they do not.

MISTAKING CRITICAL CONTINGENCIES

One thing that allows subunits to retain their power is their ability to name their functions as critical to the organization when they may not be. Consider again our discussion of power in the university. One might wonder why the most critical tasks were defined as graduate education and scholarly re-

search, the effect of which was to lend power to those who brought in grants and contracts. Why not something else? The reason is that the more powerful departments argued for those criteria and won their case, partly because they were more powerful.

In another analysis of this university, we found that all departments advocate self-serving criteria for budget allocation. Thus a department with large undergraduate enrollments argued that enrollments should determine budget allocations, a department with a strong national reputation saw prestige as the most reasonable basis for distributing funds, and so on. We further found that advocating such self-serving criteria actually benefited a department's budget allotments but, also, it paid off more for departments that were already powerful.

Organizational needs are consistent with a current distribution of power also because of a human tendency to categorize problems in familiar ways. An accountant sees problems with organizational performance as cost accountancy problems or inventory flow problems. A sales manager sees them as problems with markets, promotional strategies, or just unaggressive salespeople. But what is the truth? Since it does not automatically announce itself, it is likely that those with prior credibility, or those with power, will be favored as the enlightened. This bias, while not intentionally self-serving, further concentrates power among those who already possess it, independent of changes in the organization's context.

INSTITUTIONALIZING POWER

A third reason for expecting organizational contingencies to be defined in familiar ways is that the current holders of power can structure the organization in ways that institutionalize themselves. By institutionalization we mean the establishment of relatively permanent structures and policies that favor the influence of a particular subunit. While in power, a dominant coalition has the ability to institute constitutions, rules, procedures, and information systems that limit the potential power of others while continuing their own.

The key to institutionalizing power always is to create a device that legitimates one's own authority and diminishes the legitimacy of others. When the "Divine Right of Kings" was envisioned centuries ago it was to provide an unquestionable foundation for the supremacy of royal authority. There is generally a need to root the exercise of authority in some higher power. Modern leaders are no less affected by this need. Richard Nixon, with the aid of John Dean, reified the concept of executive privilege, which meant in effect that what the President wished not to be discussed need not be discussed.

In its simpler form, institutionalization is achieved by designating positions or roles for organizational activities. The creation of a new post legitimizes a function and forces organization members to orient to it. By designating how this new post relates to older, more established posts, moreover, one can structure an organization to enhance the importance of the function in the organization. Equally, one can diminish the importance of traditional functions. This is what happened in the end with the insurance company we mentioned that was having trouble with its coding department. As the situation unfolded, the claims director continued to feel dissatisfied about the dependency of his functions on the coding manager. Thus he instituted a reorganization that resulted in two coding departments. In so doing, of course, he placed activities that affected his department under his direct control, presumably to make the operation more effective. Similarly, consumer-product firms enhance the power of marketing by setting up a coordinating role to interface production and marketing functions and then appoint a marketing manager to fill the role.

The structures created by dominant powers sooner or later become fixed and unquestioned features of the organization. Eventually, this can be devastating. It is said that the battle of Jena in 1806 was lost by Frederick the Great, who died in 1786. Though the great Prussian leader had no direct hand in the disaster, his imprint on the army was so thorough, so embedded in its skeletal underpinnings, that the organization was inappropriate for others to lead in different times.

Another important source of institutionalized power lies in the ability to structure information systems. Setting up committees to investigate particular organizational issues and having them report only to particular individuals or groups, facilitates their awareness of problems by members of those groups while limiting the awareness of problems by the members of other groups. Obviously, those who

have information are in a better position to interpret the problems of an organization, regardless of how realistically they may, in fact, do so.

Still another way to institutionalize power is to distribute rewards and resources. The dominant group may quiet competing interest groups with small favors and rewards. The credit for this artful form of co-optation belongs to Louis XIV. To avoid usurpation of his power by the nobles of France and the Fronde that had so troubled his father's reign, he built the palace at Versailles to occupy them with hunting and gossip. Awed, the courtiers basked in the reflected glories of the "Sun King" and the overwhelming setting he had created for his court.

At this point, we have not systematically studied the institutionalization of power. But we suspect it is an important condition that mediates between the environment of the organization and the capabilities of the organization for dealing with that environment. The more institutionalized power is within an organization, the more likely an organization will be out of phase with the realities it faces. President Richard Nixon's structuring of his White House is one of the better documented illustrations. If we go back to newspaper and magazine descriptions of how he organized his office from the beginning in 1968, most of what occurred subsequently follows almost as an afterthought. Decisions flowed through virtually only the small White House staff; rewards, small presidential favors of recognition, and perquisites were distributed by this staff to the loyal; and information from the outside world—the press, Congress, the people on the streets—was filtered by the staff and passed along only if initialed "bh." Thus it was not surprising that when Nixon met war protestors in the early dawn, the only thing he could think to talk about was the latest football game, so insulated had he become from their grief and anger.

One of the more interesting implications of institutionalized power is that executive turnover among the executives who have structured the organization is likely to be a rare event that occurs only under the most pressing crisis. If a dominant coalition is able to structure the organization and interpret the meaning of ambiguous events like declining sales and profits or lawsuits, then the "real" problems to emerge will easily be incorporated into traditional molds of thinking and acting. If opposition is designed out of the organization, the interpretations will go unquestioned. Conditions will remain stable until a crisis develops, so overwhelming and visible that even the most adroit rhetorician would be silenced.

IMPLICATIONS FOR THE MANAGEMENT OF POWER IN ORGANIZATIONS

While we could derive numerous implications from this discussion of power, our selection would have to depend largely on whether one wanted to increase one's power, decrease the power of others, or merely maintain one's position. More important, the real implications depend on the particulars of an organizational situation. To understand power in an organization one must begin by looking outside it—into the environment—for those groups that mediate the organization's outcomes but are not themselves within its control.

Instead of ending with homilies, we will end with a reversal of where we began. Power, rather than being the dirty business it is often made out to be, is probably one of the few mechanisms for reality testing in organizations. And the cleaner forms of power, the institutional forms, rather than having the virtues they are often credited with, can lead the organization to become out of touch. The real trick to managing power in organizations is to ensure somehow that leaders cannot be unaware of the realities of their environments and cannot avoid changing to deal with those realities. That, however, would be like designing the "self-liquidating organization," an unlikely event since anyone capable of designing such an instrument would be obviously in control of the liquidations.

Management would do well to devote more attention to determining the critical contingencies of their environments. For if you conclude, as we do, that the environment sets most of the structure influencing organizational outcomes and problems, and that power derives from the organization's activities that deal with those contingencies, then it is the environment that needs managing, not power. The first step is to construct an accurate model of the environment, a process that is quite difficult for most organizations. We have recently started a project to aid administrators in systematically understanding their environments. From this experience, we have learned that the most critical blockage to perceiving an organization's reality accurately is a failure to incorporate those with the relevant expertise into the process. Most organizations have the requisite experts on hand but they are positioned so that they can be comfortably ignored.

One conclusion you can, and probably should, derive from our discussion is that power—because of the way it develops and the way it is used—will always result in the organization suboptimizing its performance. However, to this grim absolute, we add a comforting caveat: If any criteria other than power were the basis for determining an organization's decisions, the results would be even worse.

Chapter 12

Organizational Structure and Design

All of us, at one time or another, have participated in a variety of types of organizations—schools, companies, government agencies, the armed forces, hospitals, and so forth. Such experiences should have served to demonstrate—perhaps dramatically so in some instances—that the way organizations are designed and structured influences the behavior of their members. The same individual may behave quite differently in two organizations that serve the same function in society but are designed and structured differently (e.g., two business firms or two city governments). The issue that has to be kept in mind, however, is not just that design and structure have an impact on behavior; rather, the issue is: *in what ways* do structural factors influence the behavior of members? An equally important issue is the following: Can management alter and change the design of organizations in ways that benefit both members and the organizations? To what extent is such change feasible, even if desirable? These are some of the kinds of issues that are dealt with in this chapter.

The opening article, by Galbraith, presents a particular perspective on organizational design: namely, an information-processing viewpoint. In this selection the emphasis is on how the organiza-tion can deal with uncertainties in its task environ-ment. Obviously, the more turbulent and dynamic the environment, the greater the necessity for the organization to design strategies for coping with uncertainty. As Galbraith points out, organizations can try to preplan, they can attempt to "increase their flexibility to adapt to their inability to pre-plan," or they can try to decrease the level of performance required for continued existence. In design terms, four options are listed by Galbraith for dealing with uncertainty: (1) creation of slack re-sources, (2) creation of self-contained tasks. (3) investment in vertical information systems, and (4) creation of lateral relationships. Each option, of course, has its associated set of benefits and costs. The important goal, for Galbraith, is the matching of information requirements and the capacity of the organization to process information. If the organiza-tion does not make conscious attempts to get the best match possible, it will "receive" a match in the form of severe organizational problems.

"Like an architect planning a house" is the analo-gy that emerges in Lorsch's article dealing with organizational design. In this selection the author draws on considerable research carried out by himself and his colleagues that resulted in focusing the attention of organizational scholars on two concepts of organizational design: differentiation (of the parts of the organization) and integration (of the parts). The view that Lorsch espouses throughout the second article in this chapter is that of a "situational perspective," the idea that the appropriateness of behavior patterns in organizations depends on the type of environment faced by the organization and on the personalities of its members. In a word, the design of the organization must mesh with the environment and the members' personalities in a *compatible* manner. What may be the "right" design for Organization A may be exactly the "wrong" design for Organization B. In achieving this compatability, all organizations face the design question of how much the parts should be differentiated. The tasks faced by the organization in dealing with its environment will supply the answer, but regardless of the degree of differentiation the organization also must spend considerable effort simultaneously to achieve integration. One without the other leads to an ill-designed house, so to speak.

In the third article, by Duncan, the issue of how to select the "correct" structure for an organization is answered through the description and elaboration of a "decision-tree" analysis. Developing this decision-tree approach, the author first focuses on what he terms the two major objectives of organizational structure: to facilitate the flow of information within the organization and to achieve effective coordination (or what Lorsch labels "integration"). To attain these objectives several steps are necessary: to identify or define the organization's environment, to understand what state it (the environment) currently is in, and to select an appropriate structure. Step 2, diagnosing the current state of the environment, is especially important and involves analyses of two key dimensions: whether it is simple or complex, and whether it is static or dynamic. Once these determinations have been made, the basis is laid for following a decision-tree in making judgments about what type of structure to try to bring about. In general, the author advocates functional organizations where the environment is both simple and static, and structures that emphasize *lateral* relations where the environment tends toward high complexity and high degree of change. Mixed environments require mixed designs, often of a decentralized nature.

The final article in this chapter, by Greiner, presents an interesting proposition that organizations proceed through at least five developmental phases of growth. Each phase consists of a period of evolution followed by a revolution that serves as a transition to the next evolutionary phase. Just as other articles in this chapter have argued that a structure that is appropriate for one type of environment may be quite inappropriate for a different set of circumstances, Greiner contends that organizational structure can strongly influence management strategy and that strategy can in turn determine how well the organization can move to the next phase. As he points out, structure and management practices appropriate for an earlier time, *if not abandoned* when conditions change, may cause organizations to cease to grow or even to fail. In Greiner's words, "the critical task for management in each revolutionary period is to find a new set of organization practices that will be the basis of managing the next period of evolutionary growth." In the latter part of the article the author draws three very important conclusions that managers need to consider in actively designing their organizations: recognize which developmental phase the organization is in, be aware of the limited range of solutions for that phase, and, most crucially, "realize that solutions breed new problems."

Reading 41

Organization Design: An Information Processing View
Jay R. Galbraith

THE INFORMATION PROCESSING MODEL

A basic proposition is that the greater the uncertainty of the task, the greater the amount of information that has to be processed between decision makers during the execution of the task. If the task is well understood prior to performing it, much of the activity can be preplanned. If it is not understood, then during the actual task execution more knowledge is acquired which leads to changes in resource allocations, schedules, and priorities. All these changes require information processing *during* task performance. Therefore *the greater the task uncertainty, the greater the amount of information that must be processed among decision makers during task execution in order to achieve a given level of performance.* The basic effect of uncertainty is to limit the ability of the organization to preplan or to make decisions about activities in advance of their execution. Therefore it is hypothesized that the observed variations in organizational forms are variations in the strategies of organizations to 1) increase their ability to preplan, 2) increase their flexibility to adapt to their inability to preplan, or, 3) to decrease the level of performance required for continued viability. Which strategy is chosen depends on the relative costs of the strategies. The function of the framework is to identify these strategies and their costs.

THE MECHANISTIC MODEL

This framework is best developed by keeping in mind a hypothetical organization. Assume it is large and employs a number of specialist groups and resources in providing the output. After the task has been divided into specialist subtasks, the problem is to integrate the subtasks around the completion of the global task. This is the problem of organization design. The behaviors that occur in one subtask cannot be judged as good or bad *per se*. The

behaviors are more effective or ineffective depending upon the behaviors of the other subtask performers. There is a design problem because the executors of the behaviors cannot communicate with all the roles with whom they are interdependent. Therefore the design problem is to create mechanisms that permit coordinated action across large numbers of interdependent roles. Each of these mechanisms, however, has a limited range over which it is effective at handling the information requirements necessary to coordinate the interdependent roles. As the amount of uncertainty increases, and therefore information processing increases, the organization must adopt integrating mechanisms which increase its information processing capabilities.

1 Coordination by Rules or Programs

For routine predictable tasks March and Simon have identified the use of rules or programs to coordinate behavior between interdependent subtasks [March and Simon, 1958, Chap. 6]. To the extent that job related situations can be predicted for these situations, programs allow an interdependent set of activities to be performed without the need for interunit communication. Each role occupant simply executes the behavior which is appropriate for the task related situation with which he is faced.

2 Hierarchy

As the organization faces greater uncertainty its participants face situations for which they have no rules. At this point the hierarchy is employed on an exception basis. The recurring job situations are programmed with rules while infrequent situations are referred to that level in the hierarchy where a global perspective exists for all affected subunits. However, the hierarchy also has a limited range. As uncertainty increases the number of exceptions increases until the hierarchy becomes overloaded.

Reprinted from "Organizational Design: An Information Processing View," by Jay R. Galbraith. *Interfaces*, vol. 4, no. 3, May 1974, pp. 28–36, published by the Institute of Management Sciences.

3 Coordination by Targets or Goals

As the uncertainty of the organization's task increases, coordination increasingly takes place by specifying outputs, goals or targets [March and Simon, 1958, p. 145]. Instead of specifying specific behaviors to be enacted, the organization undertakes processes to set goals to be achieved and the employees select the behaviors which lead to goal accomplishment. Planning reduces the amount of information processing in the hierarchy by increasing the amount of discretion exercised at lower levels. Like the use of rules, planning achieves integrated action and also eliminates the need for continuous communication among interdependent subunits as long as task performance stays within the planned task specifications, budget limits and within targeted completion dates. If it does not, the hierarchy is again employed on an exception basis.

The ability of an organization to coordinate interdependent tasks depends on its ability to compute meaningful subgoals to guide subunit action. When uncertainty increases because of introducing new products, entering new markets, or employing new technologies these subgoals are incorrect. The result is more exceptions, more information processing, and an overloaded hierarchy.

DESIGN STRATEGIES

The ability of an organization to successfully utilize coordination by goal setting, hierarchy, and rules depends on the combination of the frequency of exceptions and the capacity of the hierarchy to handle them. As the task uncertainty increases the organization must again take organization design action. It can proceed in either of two general ways. First, it can act in two ways to reduce the amount of information that is processed. And second, the organization can act in two ways to increase its capacity to handle more information. The two methods for reducing the need for information and the two methods for increasing processing capacity are shown schematically in Figure 41-1. The effect of all these actions is to reduce the number of exceptional cases referred upward into the organization through hierarchical channels. The assumption is that the critical limiting factor of an organizational form is its ability to handle the non-routine, consequential events that cannot be anticipated and planned for in advance. The non-programmed events place the greatest communication load on the organization.

1 Creation of Slack Resources

As the number of exceptions begin to overload the hierarchy, one response is to increase the planning targets so that fewer exceptions occur. For example, completion dates can be extended until the number of exceptions that occur are within the existing information processing capacity of the organization. This has been the practice in solving job shop scheduling problems [Pounds, 1963]. Job shops quote delivery times that are long enough to keep the scheduling problem within the computational and information processing limits of the organization. Since every job shop has the same problem standard lead times evolve in the industry. Similarly budget targets could be raised, buffer inventories employed, etc. The greater the uncertainty, the greater the magnitude of the inventory, lead time or budget needed to reduce an overload.

All of these examples have a similar effect. They represent the use of slack resources to reduce the amount of interdependence between subunits [March and Simon, 1958, Cyert and March, 1963].

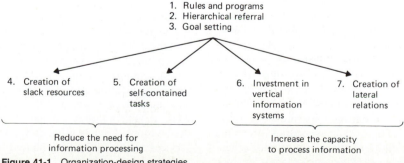

Figure 41-1 Organization-design strategies.

This keeps the required amount of information within the capacity of the organization to process it. Information processing is reduced because an exception is less likely to occur and reduced interdependence means that fewer factors need to be considered simultaneously when an exception does occur.

The strategy of using slack resources has its costs. Relaxing budget targets has the obvious cost of requiring more budget. Increasing the time to completion date has the effect of delaying the customer. Inventories require the investment of capital funds which could be used elsewhere. Reduction of design optimization reduces the performance of the article being designed. Whether slack resources are used to reduce information or not depends on the relative cost of the other alternatives.

The design choices are: (1) among which factors to change (lead time, overtime, machine utilization, etc.) to create the slack, and (2) by what amount should the factor be changed. Many operations research models are useful in choosing factors and amounts. The time-cost trade off problem in project networks is a good example.

2 Creation of Self-Contained Tasks

The second method of reducing the amount of information processed is to change the subtask groupings from resource (input) based to output based categories and give each group the resources it needs to supply the output. For example, the functional organization could be changed to product groups. Each group would have its own product engineers, process engineers, fabricating and assembly operations, and marketing activities. In other situations, groups can be created around product lines, geographical areas, projects, client groups, markets, etc., each of which would contain the input resources necessary for creation of the output.

The strategy of self-containment shifts the basis of the authority structure from one based on input, resource, skill, or occupational categories to one based on output or geographical categories. The shift reduces the amount of information processing through several mechanisms. First, it reduces the amount of output diversity faced by a single collection of resources. For example, a professional organization with multiple skill specialties providing service to three different client groups must schedule the use of these specialties across three demands

for their services and determine priorities when conflicts occur. But, if the organization changed to three groups, one for each client category, each with its own full complement of specialties, the schedule conflicts across client groups disappear and there is no need to process information to determine priorities.

The second source of information reduction occurs through a reduced division of labor. The functional or resource specialized structure pools the demand for skills across all output categories. In the example above each client generates approximately one-third of the demand for each skill. Since the division of labor is limited by the extent of the market, the division of labor must decrease as the demand decreases. In the professional organization, each client group may have generated a need for one-third of a computer programmer. The functional organization would have hired one programmer and shared him across the groups. In the self-contained structure there is insufficient demand in each group for a programmer so the professionals must do their own programming. Specialization is reduced but there is no problem of scheduling the programmer's time across the three possible uses for it.

The cost of the self-containment strategy is the loss of resource specialization. In the example, the organization foregoes the benefit of a specialist in computer programming. If there is physical equipment, there is a loss of economies of scale. The professional organization would require three machines in the self-contained form but only a large time-shared machine in the functional form. But those resources which have large economies of scale or for which specialization is necessary may remain centralized. Thus, it is the degree of self-containment that is the variable. The greater the degree of uncertainty, other things equal, the greater the degree of self-containment.

The design choices are the basis for the self-contained structure and the number of resources to be contained in the groups. No groups are completely self-contained or they would not be part of the same organization. But one product divisionalized firm may have eight of fifteen functions in the division while another may have twelve of fifteen in the divisions. Usually accounting, finance, and legal services are centralized and shared. Those functions which have economies of scale, require specialization or are necessary for control remain centralized and not part of the self-contained group.

The first two strategies reduced the amount of information by lower performance standards and creating small autonomous groups to provide the output. Information is reduced because an exception is less likely to occur and fewer factors need to be considered when an exception does occur. The next two strategies accept the performance standards and division of labor as given and adapt the organization so as to process the new information which is created during task performance.

3 Investment in Vertical Information Systems

The organization can invest in mechanisms which allow it to process information acquired during task performance without overloading the hierarchical communication channels. The investment occurs according to the following logic. After the organization has created its plan or set of targets for inventories, labor utilization, budgets, and schedules, unanticipated events occur which generate exceptions requiring adjustments to the original plan. At some point when the number of exceptions becomes substantial, it is preferable to generate a new plan rather than make incremental changes with each exception. The issue is then how frequently should plans be revised—yearly, quarterly, or monthly? The greater the frequency of replanning the greater the resources, such as clerks, computer time, input-output devices, etc., required to process information about relevant factors.

The cost of information processing resources can be minimized if the language is formalized. Formalization of a decision-making language simply means that more information is transmitted with the same number of symbols. It is assumed that information processing resources are consumed in proportion to the number of symbols transmitted. The accounting system is an example of a formalized language.

Providing more information, more often, may simply overload the decision maker. Investment may be required to increase the capacity of the decision maker by employing computers, various man-machine combinations, assistants-to, etc. The cost of this strategy is the cost of the information processing resources consumed in transmitting and processing the data.

The design variables of this strategy are the decision frequency, the degree of formalization of language, and the type of decision mechanism which will make the choice. This strategy is usually operationalized by creating redundant information channels which transmit data from the point of origination upward in the hierarchy where the point of decision rests. If data is formalized and quantifiable, this strategy is effective. If the relevant data are qualitative and ambiguous, then it may prove easier to bring the decisions down to where the information exists.

4 Creation of Lateral Relationships

The last strategy is to employ selectively joint decision processes which cut across lines of authority. This strategy moves the level of decision making down in the organization to where the information exists but does so without reorganizing around self-contained groups. There are several types of lateral decision processes. Some processes are usually referred to as the informal organization. However, these informal processes do not always arise spontaneously out of the needs of the task. This is particularly true in multi-national organizations in which participants are separated by physical barriers, language differences, and cultural differences. Under these circumstances lateral processes need to be designed. The lateral processes evolve as follows with increases in uncertainty.

4.1 Direct Contact between managers who share a problem. If a problem arises on the shop floor, the foreman can simply call the design engineer, and they can jointly agree upon a solution. From an information processing view, the joint decision prevents an upward referral and unloads the hierarchy.

4.2 Liaison Roles When the volume of contacts between any two departments grows, it becomes economical to set up a specialized role to handle this communication. Liaison men are typical examples of specialized roles designed to facilitate communication between two interdependent departments and to by-pass the long lines of communication involved in upward referral. Liaison roles arise at lower and middle levels of management.

4.3 Task Forces Direct contact and liaison roles, like the integration mechanisms before them, have a limited range of usefulness. They work when two managers or functions are involved. When problems arise involving seven or eight departments, the decision making capacity of direct contacts is exceeded. Then these problems must be referred upward. For uncertain, interdependent tasks such situations arise frequently. Task forces are a form of horizontal contact which is designed for problems of multiple departments.

The task force is made up of representatives from each of the affected departments. Some are full-time members, others may be part-time. The task force is a temporary group. It exists only as long as the problem remains. When a solution is reached, each participant returns to his normal tasks.

To the extent that they are successful, task forces remove problems from higher levels of the hierarchy. The decisions are made at lower levels in the organization. In order to guarantee integration, a group problem solving approach is taken. Each affected subunit contributes a member and therefore provides the information necessary to judge the impact on all units.

4.4 Teams The next extension is to incorporate the group decision process into the permanent decision processes. That is, as certain decisions consistently arise, the task forces become permanent. These groups are labeled teams. There are many design issues concerned in team decision making such as at what level do they operate, who participates, etc. [Galbraith, 1973, Chapters 6 and 7]. One design decision is particularly critical. This is the choice of leadership. Sometimes a problem exists largely in one department so that the department manager is the leader. Sometimes the leadership passes from one manager to another. As a new product moves to the marketplace, the leader of the new product team is first the technical manager followed by the production and then the marketing manager. The result is that if the team cannot reach a consensus decision and the leader decides, the goals of the leader are consistent with the goals of organization for the decision in question. But quite often obvious leaders cannot be found. Another mechanism must be introduced.

4.5 Integrating Roles The leadership issue is solved by creating a new role—an integrating role [Lawrence and Lorsch, 1967, Chapter 3]. These roles carry the labels of product managers, program managers, project managers, unit managers (hospitals), materials managers, etc. After the role is created, the design problem is to create enough power in the role to influence the decision process. These roles have power even when no one reports directly to them. They have some power because they report to the general manager. But if they are selected so as to be unbiased with respect to the groups they integrate and to have technical competence, they have expert power. They collect information and equalize power differences due to preferential access to knowledge and information. The power equalization increases trust and the quality of the joint decision process. But power equalization occurs only if the integrating role is staffed with someone who can exercise expert power in the form of persuasion and informal influences rather than exert the power of rank or authority.

4.6 Managerial Linking Roles As tasks become more uncertain, it is more difficult to exercise expert power. The role must get more power of the formal authority type in order to be effective at coordinating the joint decisions which occur at lower levels of the organization. This position power changes the nature of the role which for lack of a better name is labeled a managerial linking role. It is not like the integrating role because it possesses formal position power but is different from line managerial roles in that participants do not report to the linking manager. The power is added by the following successive changes:

a The integrator receives approval power of budgets formulated in the departments to be integrated.
b The planning and budgeting process starts with the integrator making his initiation in budgeting legitimate.
c Linking manager receives the budget for the area of responsibility and buys resources from the specialist groups.

These mechanisms permit the manager to exercise influence even though no one works directly for him. The role is concerned with integration but exercises power through the formal power of the position. If this power is insufficient to integrate the subtasks and creation of self-contained groups is not feasible, there is one last step.

4.7 Matrix Organization The last step is to create the dual authority relationship and the matrix organization [Galbraith, 1971]. At some point in the organization some roles have two superiors. The design issue is to select the locus of these roles. The result is a balance of power between the managerial linking roles and the normal line organization roles. Figure 41-2 depicts the pure matrix design.

The work of Lawrence and Lorsch is highly consistent with the assertions concerning lateral relations [Lawrence and Lorsch, 1967, Lorsch and Lawrence, 1968]. They compared the types of lateral relations undertaken by the most successful firm in three different industries. Their data are summarized in Table 16-1. The plastics firm has the greatest rate of new product introduction (uncertainty) and the greatest utilization of lateral processes. The container firm was also very successful but utilized only standard practices because its information processing task is much less formidable. Thus, the greater the uncertainty the lower the level of decision making and the integration is maintained by lateral relations.

Table 41-1 points out the cost of using lateral relations. The plastics firm has 22% of its managers in integration roles. Thus, the greater the use of lateral relations the greater the managerial intensity. This cost must be balanced against the cost of slack resources, self-contained groups and information systems.

CHOICE OF STRATEGY

Each of the four strategies has been briefly presented. The organization can follow one or some combination of several if it chooses. It will choose that strategy which has the least cost in its environmental context. [For an example, see Galbraith, 1970.] However, what may be lost in all of the explanations is that the four strategies are hypothesized to be an exhaustive set of alternatives. That is, if the organization is faced with greater uncertainty due to technological change, higher performance standards due to increased competition, or diversifies its product line to reduce dependence, the amount of information processing is increased. *The organization must adopt at least one of the four strategies when faced with greater uncertainty.* If it does not consciously choose one of the four, then the first, reduced performance standards, will happen automatically. The task information requirements and the capacity of the organization to process information are always matched. If the organization does not consciously match them, reduced performance through budget and schedule overruns will occur in order to bring about equality.

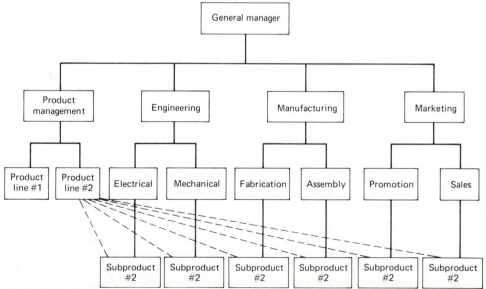

Figure 41-2 A pure matrix organization.

Table 41-1

	Plastics	Food	Container
% new products in last ten years	35%	20%	0%
Integrating Devices	Rules	Rules	Rules
	Hierarchy	Hierarchy	Hierarchy
	Planning	Planning	Planning
	Direct Contact	Direct Contact	Direct Contact
	Teams at 3 levels	Task forces	
	Integrating Dept.	Integrators	
% Integrators/Managers	22%	17%	0%

[Adopted from Lawrence and Lorsch, 1967, pp. 86–138 and Lorsch and Lawrence, 1968].

Thus the organization should be planned and designed simultaneously with the planning of the strategy and resource allocations. But if the strategy involves introducing new products, entering new markets, etc., then some provision for increased information must be made. Not to decide is to decide, and it is to decide upon slack resources as the strategy to remove hierarchical overload.

There is probably a fifth strategy which is not articulated here. Instead of changing the organization in response to task uncertainty, the organization can operate on its environment to reduce uncertainty. The organization through strategic decisions, long term contracts, coalitions, etc., can control its environment. But these maneuvers have costs also. They should be compared with costs of the four design strategies presented above.

SUMMARY

The purpose of this paper has been to explain why task uncertainty is related to organizational form. In so doing the cognitive limits theory of Herbert Simon was the guiding influence. As the consequences of cognitive limits were traced through the framework, various organization design strategies were articulated. The framework provides a basis for integrating organizational interventions, such as information systems and group problem solving, which have been treated separately before.

BIBLIOGRAPHY

Cyert, Richard, and March, James, *The Behavioral Theory of the Firm,* Prentice-Hall, Englewood Cliffs, N.J., 1963.

Galbraith, Jay, "Environmental and Technological Determinants of Organization Design: A Case Study" in Lawrence and Lorsch (ed.) *Studies in Organization Design,* Richard D. Irwin Inc., Homewood, Ill., 1970.

Galbraith, Jay, "Designing Matrix Organizations," *Business Horizons,* (Feb. 1971), pp. 29–40.

Galbraith, Jay, *Organization Design,* Addison-Wesley Pub. Co., Reading, Mass., 1973.

Lawrence, Paul, and Lorsch, Jay, *Organization and Environment,* Division of Research, Harvard Business School, Boston, Mass., 1967.

Lorsch, Jay, and Lawrence, Paul, "Environmental Factors and Organization Integration," Paper read at the Annual Meeting of the American Sociological Association, August 27, 1968, Boston, Mass.

March, James, and Simon, Herbert, *Organizations,* John Wiley & Sons, New York, N.Y., 1958.

Pounds, William, "The Scheduling Environment" in Muth and Thompson (eds.) *Industrial Scheduling,* Prentice-Hall Inc., Englewood Cliffs, N.J., 1963.

Simon, Herbert, *Models of Man,* John Wiley & Sons, New York, N.Y., 1957.

Reading 42

Organization Design: A Situational Perspective

Jay W. Lorsch

The approach to organization design I am going to advance is based upon a situational theory, not a theory that explains cause-and-effect relationships. It will not, for example, tell us that if we design a particular structural form it will cause a particular behavior. The state of existing knowledge, given the complexity of organizational phenomena, does not justify such theories. Rather, it is an explanatory theory or a conceptual framework intended to help us understand the complex interrelationship among variables that affect the way people behave in an organization.

DEFINITIONS

The phrases "organization design" and "situational" require definition. The term "situational" means that what are appropriate behavior patterns in an organization depend on the environment that confronts the organization and on the personalities of the members of the organization. Because organization design is an *important* means of influencing the pattern of behavior in an organization, it follows that what is an appropriate organization design also depends upon the nature of the organization's environment and the personality of its members.

"Organization design," like many managerial terms, has taken on several different meanings, and we want to be explicit here. An organization design is management's formal and explicit attempt(s) to indicate to organization members what is expected of them. It includes the following elements:

- *Organization structure.* The definition of individual jobs and their expected relationship to each other as depicted on organization charts and in job descriptions. In essence, this is management's attempt to draw a map of whom they want to do what.
- *Planning, measurement, and evaluation schemes.* The procedures established to define the organization's goals and the methods for achieving them, and the methods used to measure progress

against these plans and to provide feedback about performance.

- *Rewards.* The explicit rewards given by management in return for the individual's work. These include money, career opportunities, and other rewards. Of concern here is not only the "size" of such rewards but also how they relate to what results.
- *Selection criteria.* The guidelines used to select incumbents for various positions. These obviously affect the personalities, experience, and skills of organization members. They, in turn, can affect how these individuals respond to the signals conveyed by other design elements.
- *Training.* The formally established educational programs, both on and off the job, that not only impart knowledge and skill but also provide another means for management to indicate how it expects organization members to behave on the job.

While my focus will be on these organization design elements, they are not the only ways managers communicate their expectations. Clearly, they do this through their own personal actions and contacts. The traditions or culture of an organization also consist of implicit messages about how members should behave. These, in turn, have a major impact on how people think and act. My focus on organization design stems from the fact that we now have available a theory and some experience that can help managers to understand better the substance and process of organization design decisions.

SOURCES OF IDEAS

Shortly, I shall elaborate more on situational theory and how it illuminates issues of organizational design. First, it is important to emphasize that the question of how to design organizations is one that traditionally concerned writers about management. The so-called classical writers on organizations had developed many principles from their own experience in a particular industry—for example, James

Mooney in the automotive industry and Henri Fayol in mining. From them came ideas such as authority must equal responsibility, spans of control should be from six to nine people, and the staff advises, the line decides.

Managers also have always looked at the experience of other institutions for ideas about how best to organize their own companies. The Catholic Church and the military, for example, were early models for the way managers in private enterprise might think about organization design. Similarly, the early large companies, like the transcontinental railroads, became the source of organization design ideas for other firms. The same can be said for Du Pont and General Motors. How many company managements have borrowed the ideas of Pierre Du Pont and Alfred P. Sloan? And, of course, managers constantly look at the contemporary experiences of other firms, competitors and those in other industries, as models for their own thinking.

Another source of ideas for most managers is, of course, their own prior experience. The manager who has had a successful career at one company is tempted to apply the ideas he learned there with his new employer—sometimes with unfortunate results.

There is nothing inherently wrong with any of these ideas for designing organizations. Together, they provide a rich array of ideas about how to structure an organization, how to reward managers, how to evaluate their performance, and so on. The problem arises because managers have no systematic way of discriminating among the many ideas available and deciding which are relevant to their particular situation. The classical writers were interested in providing principles of organization that applied to most companies. The problem with ideas gleaned from one's own experience or the observation of other company practices is that they do not come with warning lights, whistles, or bells that assert that they work in this situation but not in that one or that this idea about structure will not work unless it is tied to that concept about measurement.

Variations in markets, in processing technology, in the state of scientific knowledge, and so on, all impose different requirements on organizational arrangements. So do the varying sizes of companies. Small companies, for example, can be managed with less formality and more emphasis on personal leadership than larger companies. Similarly, cultures in different countries provide different imperatives about how people expect to be rewarded, about how much they expect to be involved in decisions, and about other expectations.

During the last decade, academics have agreed on a set of ideas that together provide a theory for understanding the situational factors that affect organization design choices. The contributors I have in mind range from James March and Herbert Simon at Carnegie-Mellon to Jay Galbraith at Wharton. Two of the early contributors died prematurely (James Thompson, 1967, from Vanderbilt, and Joan Woodward, 1970, of Imperial College in London). These authors were concerned primarily with examining issues of organization theory. Edward Lawler III and his colleagues have been developing ideas about reward schemes that throw light on the situational factors related to this element of organization design. Other contributors have been my co-authors, Paul Lawrence, Stephen Allen, and John Morse, and me.

SITUATIONAL THEORY

Situational theory, as I suggested above, provides managers with a way to think about organization design issues in relation to the environmental and human characteristics of their situation. Even more important, perhaps, the theory enables managers to understand the complex causes of the organizational problems they face and can help them use their own creativity to invent new designs uniquely suited to their situation.

Since situational theory is a relatively new development, it has many of the problems of any young body of knowledge. It is not well integrated. There are still disputes about the relevant variables and the meaning of certain terminology. It is also a relatively complex set of ideas. So what follows is my own personal version of these ideas. It is based on the ideas gained in systematic research and in over ten years of applying these ideas to consulting problems. If the reader wants a different or more thorough perspective on these theories, the books listed at the end of this article can provide it.

At the outset, we need to define four terms:

1 The *environment* refers to the forces and institutions outside the firm with which its members must

deal to achieve the organization's purposes. These include competitors' actions, customer requirements, financial constraints, scientific and technological knowledge, and so on. A common denominator is that all these elements provide information that is used to make and implement decisions inside the organization.

2 The organization's *strategy* is a statement of the environment(s) or business(es) relevant to the organization, the purposes of the organization within that context, and the distinctive means by which these goals will be achieved. In this sense, the strategy defines the environment in which an organization operates. A strategy may be explicitly stated or it may simply exist as an implicit idea based on the actions of the organization's managers over time.

3 A *task* is the actions members must take to implement the organization's strategy in a particular environment. The term *task* generally refers to the activities of a particular set of individuals in dealing with the environment; for example, the task of a sales department or the task of division general managers.

4 *Psychological characteristics of members* are the enduring factors in an individual's personality that lead him or her to behave in a consistent fashion over time. It is not necessary to debate here about whether these should be labeled needs, values, interests, expectations, or all of these. The important point is that individuals do have qualities that vary greatly from those of other people, and organization design decisions must take these differences into account.

THE FIT BETWEEN TASK, PEOPLE, AND ORGANIZATION

With these definitions in mind, let us examine the first of several relationships that are important to understand in making organization design decisions—that between the individual member, his or her task, and the organization. Basically, research indicates that if there is a fit between the individuals' psychological makeup, the nature of their task, and the organization, two things are accomplished: first, the individuals gain a sense of competence, which is an important psychological reward, and, second, as they gain this sense of competence, they perform their work effectively and the organization achieves its goal. As the two-headed arrows in Figure 42-1 illustrate, this is not a simple cause-and-effect chain. Rather, as all the ideas I shall discuss indicate,

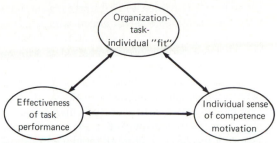

Figure 42-1   The concept of fit.

organizations are complex social systems in which many variables interact to cause behavior.

Several points about these relationships are important to emphasize:

- An individual's sense of competence is a self-reinforcing reward. As an individual performs a job successfully, feelings of competence encourage continued effort to do the job well.
- Different tasks seem to be attractive to persons with different psychological makeups. For example, research scientists who work on uncertain, complex, and long-range tasks prefer to work alone, with freedom from supervision, and enjoy highly ambiguous and complex tasks. In contrast, factory managers, whose jobs are more certain, predictable, and short range, prefer more directive leadership, closer relationships with colleagues, and less ambiguity.
- When I refer to the organization, I mean all the factors that influence an individual's behavior—leadership style, culture, *and* organization design. But the implication for organization design choices is clear. Design structure, measurement, and reward practices should fit the nature of the task to be done and the psychological makeup of the individuals selected to do the work. If they do, the probability is that the individuals will achieve the psychological rewards of feeling competent and will work effectively. This implies a management approach that acknowledges and appreciates differences in people. By recognizing different personality patterns, managers endow each individual with a sense of competence at work and highlight the dignity and worth of every man and woman in the organization.

DIFFERENTIATION OF UNITS

A second important relationship follows from the concept of fit. This is the fact that the performance of a functional unit (for example, sales, manufacturing, or R&D) is related to that unit's organization fitting the part of the environment with which it carries out transactions. As suggested above, a research laboratory whose members deal with an uncertain environment that provides feedback about results only after long intervals requires an organization design with low formality and infrequent but general measures of performance. On the other hand, a manufacturing plant in the same organization is faced with more rapid feedback and more certain information about its environment and requires more formality and more specific and frequent measures of performance. Figure 42-2 illustrates this contrast.

A research laboratory or manufacturing plant that does not provide the appropriate design is in for serious trouble. For example, take the comment of a researcher in a not very successful drug laboratory that required written progress reports every two weeks:

> We're required to write a report on the progress of our work every two weeks. Sometimes there's not much new to talk about. We don't necessarily work on projects that you can make a breakthrough on every two weeks. But we know that we're being evaluated on our reports, so informal guidelines have developed. One guideline, for example, is that the less that's happened since the last report, the longer the current report is. It gets so you wrack your brain trying to write a report that makes you look good every two weeks rather than wracking your brain to crack open the research problem.

Any organization design has to permit differences between subunits. These differences in design are necessary, our research indicates, because they encourage the behavior that is required for the members of each unit to deal effectively with the specific nature of their part of the environment. The members of each unit must develop differential patterns of behavior and ways of thinking consistent with who they are and what tasks they must perform in dealing with their particular part of the environment. Although the above examples of R&D and manufacturing managers illustrate the point, I use such functional units as examples for two reasons. First, much of the research was conducted in such settings. Second, such functional units are the basic building blocks of even small business organizations, and they are also the basic units around which product divisions are structured in larger firms. However, the need for differentiation is also present among product divisions in multibusiness companies. Each product division must have an organization design, leadership style, and culture that fit its particular business environment.

Before concluding this discussion, it is important to emphasize that the amount of differentiation that is necessary will vary from one business environment to another. Three examples will illustrate the point:

1. As an example of minimal differentiation required across functions, take a firm in the business of producing corrugated containers—boxes and car-

Design dimension	R & D Lab	Manufacturing plant
Structure		
Spans of control	Wide	Narrow
Number of levels in hierarchy	Many	Few
Job definitions	General and broad	Specific and detailed
Measurement	General and less frequent (for example, quarterly)	Specific and frequent (for example, daily or even hourly)
Planning	General and as related to goals	Specific, with detailed methods
Rewards	Money, professional recognition, scientific careers	Money, management careers
Selection	Qualified technically Interest in industrial research	Leadership ability Process knowledge Cost analysis Scheduling and so on
Training	Professional conferences	Human skills Quantitative skills Technology

Figure 42-2 Contrasting organization designs.

tons. This firm has only two major functions—selling and manufacturing—and they have different goals. The sales personnel focus on prompt customer delivery and high quality as well as competitive pricing; the manufacturing managers are concerned with low cost and want to avoid quality and delivery requirements that affect costs adversely. Beyond these different goals there are few differences between the two functions. Both are focused on short-term results and are involved in relatively predictable tasks. Thus a more formal organization design and more directive leadership make sense to both production and sales personnel.

2. A company in the cosmetics industry requires more differentiation. It has four major functions—marketing, sales, manufacturing, and technical research. Each has a defined set of goals. Marketing personnel are concerned with advertising, sales promotion, and pricing policies that will lead to an expanding market share. Field sales personnel are, of course, concerned with market share, but their views on how to influence it focus on maintaining shelf space in retail outlets, keeping the channels of distribution well supplied, and so on. Manufacturing personnel are concerned with an efficient operation and the maintenance of product quality. The research personnel are aiming at new products. With the marketing personnel, they share a concern for intermediate and long-term results. Of course, the marketing personnel also share a concern for immediate results with the manufacturing and sales functions.

In addition to these differences, differences in management style and organization design across these functions will be important for the success of each function. In such a situation, management must act so that each of these units develops structures, measurement schemes, and reward practices that encourage their members to focus on the appropriate set of activities and issues.

3. Last, we can look at a business requiring even greater differentiation—a basic plastic materials business (for example, polystyrene or polyvinylchloride). Here we find the functions of sales, manufacturing, research, and technical services. The manufacturing personnel, like those in the previous examples, will be primarily concerned with near-term results in the areas of cost and quality. But since they are operating a much more capital-intensive technology, they may be much less flexible about interrupting product flows or making process changes than their counterparts in other businesses. The sales personnel will be concerned with customer relations and competitive pricing. Again, their focus will be largely on the near term, but they will also devote some attention to the future and to new products. The technical services group will focus on providing technical services to the customer in support of the sales force, and thus will be primarily concerned with immediate results. At the same time, however, they are responsible for applied research aimed at developing new and improved products and processes and therefore must also focus some attention on the long term. Finally, the research unit will be involved in more basic research—understanding the structure of materials and using this understanding to develop entirely new products and processes as well as to improve existing ones. Their time horizon may be several years out. Each of these units needs to have an organization design and management style that will allow it to match its highly differentiated task and members.

While these models are drawn from manufacturing enterprises, similar examples can be found in retailing (merchants versus store operations personnel), insurance (sales versus underwriters), and banks (loan officers versus operations). These examples are also oversimplified in that, for instance, they have omitted the financial function, which has its own distinct point of view. Although these cases are drawn from single business organizations, varying degrees of differentiation also exist among the product divisions of multibusiness firms, depending on how diversified the businesses are. For example, companies like Textron, Litton, and TRW require a high degree of differentiation among their various businesses. A company like General Foods needs less differentiation among the product divisions, because it is basically in the consumer food business.

Let us assume that an effective R&D laboratory and an effective manufacturing plant are in the same organization. We would expect the points of differentiation to be diverse. Leadership styles would differ: R&D managers would lead by encouraging participation in decision making; by contrast, the plant managers, although not completely autocratic, would take a more directive approach to supervision and coordination. Units would also differ, not only in the formality of organization practices and in members, goals, time, and interpersonal relations, but also in the goals and time dimensions implicit in formal practices. Members would also tend to different predispositions, including different cognitive styles, different levels of tolerance for ambiguity—stronger among the R&D managers—and different attitude toward authority and toward people in general.

DIFFERENTIATION AND INTEGRATION

There is a cost connected with differentiation. This becomes clear in examining the relationship between differentiation and integration.

Differentiation, as previously described, means that members of each unit will see problems that involve them with other units primarily from their own point of view. It is not surprising, therefore, that differentiation produces conflict. The sales manager wants to move up scheduling an order from a big customer. The plant manager is opposed because such an interruption will lead to higher manufacturing costs. Resolving such conflicts is the stuff of which management is made.

The more differentiation, the more varied the viewpoints of the units involved in decisions and, therefore, the more difficult it is to achieve integration. (By integration we mean simply the quality of the necessary relationships among the units of the organization if the organization's overall goals are to be achieved.) Stated more formally, the more differentiated the units are, the more difficult it is to achieve integration among them—that is, the more difficult it is to coordinate their efforts to achieve higher-level goals. Research findings show that a high quality of integration is related to goal achievement for an organization.

The difficulty in achieving integration is also affected by several other factors (see Figure 42-3). First and most obvious is the number of units whose activities must be integrated. The more units that are involved, the more difficult collaboration becomes. Second is the pattern of interdependence. As Figure 42-4 suggests, we can identify three patterns.

1 *Pooled.* Subsidiary units are each interdependent with a central unit. The best example of this is the relationship between the corporate headquarters and product divisions in a diversified company in which no attempt is made at interdivisional integration.

2 *Sequential.* As the term implies, each unit is interdependent with the unit ahead of it in the flow. An example is production departments in a manufacturing plant.

3 *Reciprocal.* This is the final pattern and, as the diagram indicates, it is one of mutual interdependence among all the units. An example is the relationship among marketing, R&D, and manufacturing in product innovation.

James Thompson reported that it is increasingly difficult to achieve integration as one moves from pooled to sequential to reciprocal interdependence because of the growing number and complexity of the relationships involved.

A third factor is the frequency of interaction required among units. Other things being equal, the more frequently contact is necessary, the harder it is to achieve integration. Thus it is probably relatively easier to achieve integration around issues of production scheduling between sales and manufacturing

Factor	Difficulty of achieving integration		
	Low		High
Degree of differentiation	Small		Large
Number of units requiring integration	Few		Many
Pattern of integration	Pooled		Reciprocal
Frequency of integration required	Infrequent contact		Frequent contact-daily or more often
Importance of integration to organization's strategy	Marginal		Critical
Complexity and uncertainty of information	Simple and highly certain		Highly complex and uncertain

Figure 42-3 Factors affecting the difficulty of achieving integration.

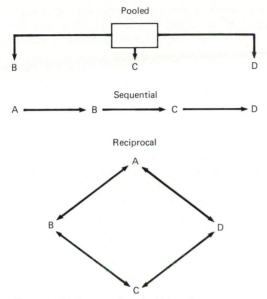

Figure 42-4 Patterns of required integration.

if such schedules can be set on a quarterly basis. If the environment calls for more frequent—say, monthly—schedule adjustments, the problems of integration will increase.

The importance of integration in the organization's strategy is another factor that bears on the difficulty of achieving it. If the issues are central to the firm's strategic goals, it may be necessary to expend more effort to integrate than would be desirable if only peripheral issues were involved.

Last, the complexity and uncertainty of the information involved have an effect on the problems of integrating. The more uncertain or complex the information, the more time and effort must be expended to sort out, understand, and resolve conflicting points of view.

ACHIEVING INTEGRATION

Two sets of factors determine how well an organization achieves integration, given the difficulties imposed by its environment and strategy. First are the design elements intended to foster integration. These can cover a wide range. At one extreme are integrating departments, which may be labeled product management or program management. Such departments are separate units under their own managers created to facilitate cross-unit integration.

Integrative roles can also be established. These differ from integrative departments in that the role players, whatever their titles, report directly to the general manager in charge of the total organization. Both devices move the organization into a matrix structure in which one dimension is responsible for cross-unit integration while the other is responsible for the management of the differentiated units.

Cross-unit teams or committees are another structural device for achieving integration. They can be used in lieu of or in addition to integrating roles and departments. The planning and measurement scheme, as well as financial rewards and recognition, also can be designed to encourage personnel to make a collaborative effort. The best-known example of such attempts are the profit or investment-center measurement and reward schemes used in most multibusiness firms. In essence, they motivate the managers in a particular business, whatever their functional allegiance, to work collaboratively toward the superordinate goal of that business.

Which and how many of the devices should be designed into a particular organization depends first on how difficult the integrative task is. But this decision also depends upon which of the factors shown in Figure 3 are present. For example, integration may require sales and manufacturing to decide production schedules and inventory levels on a quarterly basis. A planning scheme and an occasional meeting between representatives of the two units may be all that's needed.

On the other hand, in a high-technology business, integration around new product development needs may involve completely different requirements. Probably sales, manufacturing, and research and development engineering will take part. There will be a great deal of uncertainty and complexity in the information. Integrative devices that encourage face-to-face contact among representatives of the units involved will have to be used on a continuing basis.

Since these units are apt to be highly differentiated, it may also be necessary to assign a specific person to an integrative role. Such a person should be someone who commands the respect of those whose efforts he is integrating and should have some familiarity with the problems and points of view of the various units with which he is working. In this way, the integrator will have a relatively balanced viewpoint about the issues involved and, equally important, is apt to be perceived as neutral and objective by the others. Finally, such a person should have the interpersonal skills necessary to help resolve the conflicts that emerge from the different points of view.

Resolving Interunit Conflicts

The second set of factors related to an organization's effectiveness in achieving integration is how its managers go about resolving interunit conflicts. Many factors are involved, but two seem most important. The first is the pattern of behavior used to resolve conflict. If the managers work in a problem-solving mode to get the various viewpoints out on the table and work through to the best overall solution, our evidence indicates they will be most effective at achieving integration. If, on the other hand, they smooth over or avoid conflict or let a party with greater power force a solution on others, their efforts at achieving integration will be less effective.

Similarly, conflict resolution is more effective when the distribution of real influence in the organization is consistent with the knowledge and ability to contribute to decisions. For example, if one unit's members have much to contribute to decisions but are not allowed to make this contribution, conflict will not be resolved in a manner that leads to effective integration.

When I speak of "real influence," I mean influence as it is actually deployed in the company, not just as it is reflected in an organization chart or position description. Of course, the latter can have an impact on the distribution of influence. But so do the culture of the organization, the nature of the business, and other organization design elements. For example, in many consumer product firms, marketing personnel have an inordinate amount of influence compared with their peers in research and development. Their influence is based on the key role they must play in formulating strategy in this environment and is exacerbated by the fact that top management is often recruited from marketing personnel. All this leads to a culture in which marketing is expected to be king, adding further to its influence.

If management desires to improve conflict resolu-

tion practices, one design element that can be effective is training and education programs. Through such programs, managers can be educated to the need for changes in the way conflict is resolved and can develop skill in more effective practices. Of course, the way rewards are distributed and jobs are defined can also affect the balance of influence, if this is a desired goal. However, in my experience, bringing about a desired change in conflict resolution practices is very difficult because, as was pointed out above, they are so intertwined with the culture and leadership style in the organization.

PROBLEMS OF APPLICATION

In applying these ideas, the organization designer must deal with certain issues. First, he must assess the environmental requirements faced by his organization. Some instruments have been developed to do this, but in my experience, the best data can be obtained from careful interviews with knowledgeable executives. How certain are the various units about their part of the environment? What is the time frame within which results can be assessed? What are their goals? What units require integration around which issues? How frequently?

A similar set of issues presents itself in assessing individual needs. Again, instruments are available for this purpose, but knowledgeable managers make their own assessments. They only need to step back and think about what the personnel in different units prefer in terms of their relations with supervisors and peers, what the rapidity of feedback is, and how much tolerance they have for ambiguity.

We shouldn't forget to take account of both the culture of the organization and the leadership style of top management. While there has been little systematic research into the relationship between these factors and organization design, it seems clear that decisions about organization design must be consistent with top management's style of leadership. It is doubtful that an organization design can be implemented effectively if top management finds it at odds with its own preferences.

The question of culture and organization design is more complicated. The first problem is understanding what the culture is. What is the traditional pecking order among units? What are the norms for interpersonal interaction, conflict resolution, behavior that will be rewarded, and so on? When they can answer these questions, those involved in designing the organization must then ask themselves if they want to support the existing culture or move the culture in some new direction. The answer, of course, will determine how closely the organization design conforms to the existing culture.

A final issue is the necessity of arranging the various elements in the organization design to make them consistent with each other. Too often, for example, the personnel function designs a reward scheme and the controller's staff designs a measurement scheme, and the two schemes present contradictory signals to line management. If the underlying premise of the situational approach is followed, the organization design must fit both the environment and the individual member's needs. All the elements of an organization's management processes should fit together to produce the desired result—an effective organization.

In sum, the organization designer must create a structure, rewards and measurements, and other elements compatible with the external environment, strategy, tasks, organization members, top-management style, and existing culture. This may

seem like an impossible task, but it really resembles an architect planning a house. The architect starts with the character and shape of the land and the requirements of the occupants and then considers costs, building codes, and other relevant factors. To pursue this analogy, the requirements based on the character of the land and the occupants are like the environmental, strategic, task, and individual requirements facing the organization designer. Once he understands what the ideal organization to meet these conditions would be, the designer can begin to consider alternatives and trade-offs that are more suitable to the style of top management. Similarly, he can make judgments about the extent to which the design is compatible with the existing culture and which changes in the design should be used to shift the culture.

Perhaps the architectural analogy is not a perfect one, but it does emphasize once again that the ideas we have described are only tools. Managers, like architects, must be skilled in using their tools and must enjoy the process of creative problem solving. Without these ingredients in their makeup, they will be unable to take advantage of the tools available to them.

Reading 43

What Is the Right Organization Structure? Decision Tree Analysis Provides the Answer

Robert Duncan

Organization design is a central problem for managers. What is the "best" structure for the organization? What are the criteria for selecting the "best" structure? What signals indicate that the organization's existing structure may not be appropriate to its tasks and its environment? This article discusses the purposes of organization structure and presents a decision tree analysis approach to help managers pick the right organization structure.

THE OBJECTIVES OF ORGANIZATIONAL DESIGN

What is organization structure and what is it supposed to accomplish? Organization structure is

more than boxes on a chart; it is a pattern of interactions and coordination that links the technology, tasks, and human components of the organization to ensure that the organization accomplishes its purpose.

An organization's structure has essentially two objectives: First, it facilitates the flow of information within the organization in order to reduce the uncertainty in decision making. The design of the organization should facilitate the collection of the information managers need for decision making. When managers experience a high degree of uncertainty—that is, when their information needs are great—the structure of the organization should not be so rigid as to inhibit managers from seeking new sources of information or developing new procedures or methods for doing their jobs. For example, in developing a new product, a manufacturing department may need to seek direct feedback from customers on how the new product is being accepted; the need to react quickly to customer response makes waiting for this information to come through normal marketing and sales channels unacceptable.

The second objective of organization design is to achieve effective coordination–integration. The structure of the organization should integrate organizational behavior across the parts of the organization so it is coordinated. This is particularly important when the units in the organization are interdependent. As James Thompson had indicated, the level of interdependence can vary. In *pooled interdependence* the parts of the organization are independent and are linked together only in contributing something to the same overall organization. In many conglomerates, the divisions are really separate organizations linked only in that they contribute profits to the overall organization. Simple rules—procedures—can be developed to specify what the various units have to do. In *sequential interdependence,* however, there is an ordering of activities, that is, one organizational unit has to perform its function before the next unit can perform its. For example, in an automobile plant manufacturing has to produce the automobiles before quality control can inspect them. Now such organizations have to develop plans to coordinate activities; quality control needs to know when and how many cars to expect for inspection.

Reciprocal interdependence is the most complex type of organizational interdependence. Reciprocal interdependence is present when the output of Unit A become the inputs of Unit B and the outputs of B cycle back to become the inputs of Unit A. The relationship between the operations and maintenance in an airline is a good example of this type of interdependence. Operations produces "sick" airplanes that need repair by maintenance. Maintenance repairs these planes and the repaired planes become inputs to the operations division to be reassigned to routes. When reciprocal interdependence between organization units is present, a more complex type of coordination is required. This is coordination by feedback. Airline operations and

maintenance must communicate with one another so each one will know when the planes will be coming to them so they can carry out their respective functions.

Organizational design, then, is the allocation of resources and people to a specified mission or purpose and the structuring of these resources to achieve the mission. Ideally, the organization is designed to fit its environment and to provide the information and coordination needed.

It is useful to think of organization structure from an information-processing view. The key characteristic of organizational structure is that it links the elements of the organization by providing the channels of communication through which information flows. My research has indicated that when organizational structure is formalized and centralized, information flows are restricted and, as a consequence, the organization is not able to gather and process the information it needs when faced with uncertainty. For example, when an organization's structure is highly centralized, decisions are made at the top and information tends to be filtered as it moves up the chain of command. When a decision involves a great deal of uncertainty, it is unlikely therefore that the few individuals at the top of the organization will have the information they require to make the best decision. So decentralization, that is, having more subordinates participate in the decision-making process, may generate the information needed to help reduce the uncertainty and thereby facilitate a better decision.

ALTERNATIVE ORGANIZATIONAL DESIGNS

The key question for the manager concerned with organization design is what are the different structures available to choose from. Contingency theories of organization have shown that there is no one best structure. However, organization theorists have been less clear in elaborating the decision process managers can follow in deciding which structure to implement.

In discussing organization design, organization theorists describe structure differently from the way managers responsible for organization design do. Organizational theorists describe structure as more or less formalized, centralized, specialized, or hierarchical. However, managers tend to think of organizational structure in terms of two general types, the *functional* and the *decentralized*. Most organizations today are either functional or decentralized or some modification or combination of these two general types. Therefore, if we are to develop a heuristic for helping managers make decisions about organization structure, we need to think of structures as functional or decentralized and not in terms of the more abstract dimensions of formalization, centralization, and so on, that organizational theorists tend to use.

ORGANIZATIONAL ENVIRONMENT AND DESIGN: A CRITICAL INTERACTION

In deciding on what kind of organization structure to use, managers need to first understand the characteristics of the environment they are in and the demands this environment makes on the organization in terms of information and coordination. Once the environment is understood, the manager can proceed with the design process.

The first step in designing an organization structure, therefore, is to identify the organization's environment. The task environment constitutes that part of the environment defined by managers as relevant or potentially relevant for organizational decision making. Figure 43-1 presents a list of environmental components managers might encounter. Clearly, no one organization would encounter all these components in decision making, but this is the master list from which organizational decision makers would identify the appropriate task environments. For example, a manager in a manufacturing division could "define an environment consisting of certain personnel, certain staff units and suppliers, and perhaps certain technological components. The usefulness of the list in Figure 43-1 is that it provides a guide for decision makers, alerting them to the elements the environment they might consider in decision making.

Once managers have defined the task environment, the next step is to understand the state of that environment. What are its key characteristics? In describing organizational environments, we emphasize two dimensions: simple-complex and static-dynamic.

The simple-complex dimension of the environment focuses on whether the factors in the environment considered for decision making are few in number and similar or many in number and different. An example of a *simple* unit would be a

Internal environment	External environment
Organizational personnel component —Educational and technological background and skills —Previous technological and managerial skill —Individual member's involvement and commitment to attaining system's goals —Interpersonal behavior styles —Availability of manpower for utilization within the system Organizational functional and staff units component —Technological characteristics of organizational units —Interdependence of organizational units in carrying out their objectives —Intraunit conflict among organizational functional and staff units —Intraunit conflict among organizational functional and staff units Organizational level component —Organizational objectives and goals —Integrative process integrating individuals and groups into contributing maximally to attaining organizational goals —Nature of the organization's product service	Customer component —Distributors of product or service —Actual users of product of service Suppliers component —New materials suppliers —Equipment suppliers —Product parts suppliers —Labor supply Competitor component —Competitors for suppliers —Competitors for customers Sociopolitical component —Government regulatory control over the industry —Public political attitude toward industry and its particular product —Relationship with trade unions with jurisdiction in the organization Technological component —Meeting new technological requirements of own industry and related industries in production of product or service —Improving and developing new products by implementing new technological advances in the industry

Figure 43-1 Environmental components list.

lower-level production unit whose decisions are affected only by the parts department and materials department, on which it is dependent for supplies, and the marketing department, on which it is dependent for output. An example of a *complex* environment would be a programming and planning department. This group must consider a wide variety of environmental factors when making a decision. It may focus on the marketing and materials department, on customers, on suppliers, and so on. Thus this organizational unit has a much more heterogeneous group of environmental factors to deal with in decision making—its environment is more complex than that of the production unit.

The static-dynamic dimension of the environment is concerned with whether the factors of the environment remain the same over time or change. A *static* environment, for example, might be a production unit that has to deal with a marketing department whose requests for output remain the same and a materials department that is able to supply a steady rate of inputs to the production unit. However, if the marketing department were continually changing its requests and the materials department were inconsistent in its ability to supply parts, the production unit would be operating in a more *dynamic* environment.

Figure 43-2 provides a four-way classification of organizational environments and some examples of organizations in each of these environments. Complex-dynamic (Cell +) environments are probably the most characteristic type today. These environments involve rapid change and create high uncertainty for managers. The proper organizational structure is critical in such environments if managers are to have the information necessary for decision making. Also, as organizations move into this turbulent environment, it may be necessary for them to modify their structures. For example, AT&T has moved from a functional organization to a decentralized structure organized around different markets to enable it to cope with more competition in the telephone market and in communications. This change in structure was in response to the need for more information and for a quicker response time to competitive moves.

STRATEGIES FOR ORGANIZATIONAL DESIGN

Once the organization's environment has been diagnosed, what type of structure the organization should have becomes the key question.

Simple Design Strategy

When the organization's environment is relatively simple, that is, there are not many factors to consider in decision making, and stable, that is, neither the make-up of the environment nor the demands made

	Simple		Complex	
Static	*Low perceived uncertainty* Small number of factors and components in the environment Factors and components are somewhat similar to one another Factors and components remain basically the same and are not changing *Example:* Soft drink industry 1		2 *Moderately low perceived uncertainty* Large number of factors and components in the environment Factors and components are not similar to one another Factors and components remain basically the same *Example:* Food products	
Dynamic	*Moderately high perceived uncertainty* 3 Small number of factors and components in the environment Factors and components are somewhat similar to one another Factors and components of the environment are in continual process of change *Example:* Fast food industry		4 *High perceived uncertainty* Large number of factors and components in the environment Factors and components are not similar to one another Factors and components of environment are in a continual process of change *Examples:* Commercial airline industry Telephone communications (AT&T)	

Figure 43-2 Classification of organizational environments.

by environmental components are changing, the information and coordination needs for the organization are low. In such circumstances, a *functional organization structure* is most appropriate.

A key characteristic of the functional organization is specialization by functional areas. Figure 43-3 presents a summary of this structure's strengths and weaknesses. The key strengths of the functional organization are that it supports in-depth skill development and a simple decision-communication network. However, when disputes or uncertainty arises among managers about a decision, they get pushed up the hierarchy to be resolved. A primary weakness of the functional organization, therefore, is that when the organization's environment becomes more dynamic and uncertainty tends to increase, many decisions move to the top of the organization. Lower-level managers do not have the information required for decision making so they push decisions upward. Top-level managers become overloaded and are thus slow to respond to the environment.

Organizational Design Dilemma

The organizational designer faces a dilemma in such situations. Designs can be instituted that *reduce* the amount of information required for decision making. Decentralization is the principal strategy indicated. Or organizations can develop more lateral relations to *increase* the amount of information available for decision making.

A decentralized organization is possible whenever an organization's tasks are self-contained. Decentralized organizations are typically designed around products, projects, or markets. The decentralized

healthcare organization in Figure 43-4 is organized around product areas (Medical and Dental) and market area (International). Each division has all the resources needed to perform its particular task. For example, Medical Products (Figure 43-4) has its own functional organization consisting of production, marketing, and R&D to carry out its mission. The information needed by Medical Products Division's managers is reduced because they have organized around a set of common medical products, and they don't have to worry about dental, pharmaceutical, or hospital support services or products.

In the decentralized organization, managers only have to worry about their own products or services; they have the resources to carry out these activities, and they don't have to compete for shared resources or schedule shared resources. There is also a full-time commitment to a particular product line. The decentralized structure is particularly effective when the organization's environment is very complex, that is, there are a large number of factors to be considered in decision making, and the environment can be segmented or broken down into product or market areas around which the organization can structure itself. For example, the health products organization (Figure 43-4) probably started out as a functional organization. However, as its product line increased, it undoubtedly became more difficult for one manufacturing unit to have the expertise to produce such a wide range of products efficiently and to handle the diversity of information needed to do it. It would also be difficult for one marketing unit to market such a diverse group of products; different kinds of information and skills would be

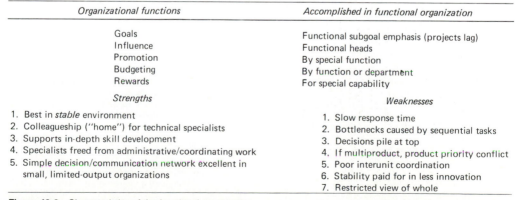

Organizational functions	Accomplished in functional organization
Goals	Functional subgoal emphasis (projects lag)
Influence	Functional heads
Promotion	By special function
Budgeting	By function or department
Rewards	For special capability

Strengths	Weaknesses
1. Best in *stable* environment	1. Slow response time
2. Colleagueship ("home") for technical specialists	2. Bottlenecks caused by sequential tasks
3. Supports in-depth skill development	3. Decisions pile at top
4. Specialists freed from administrative/coordinating work	4. If multiproduct, product priority conflict
5. Simple decision/communication network excellent in small, limited-output organizations	5. Poor interunit coordination
	6. Stability paid for in less innovation
	7. Restricted view of whole

Figure 43-3 Characteristics of the functional organization.

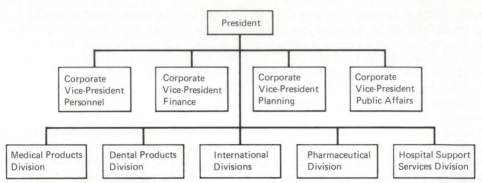

Figure 43-4 Decentralized organization.

required to sell the different products. Segmenting this complex environment into product areas facilitates increased specialization. As a result, divisional managers need less information than if they had to deal with all the products and services of the corporation.

Figure 43-5 summarizes the characteristics and the strengths and weaknesses of the decentralized organization. Decentralized organizations face several problems. For example, it is sometimes difficult to decide what resources are to be pooled in a corporate staff to be used to service the entire organization. If the divisions are very different from one another in terms of products, customers, technology, and so on, however, it becomes very difficult to staff a corporate services unit with the diverse knowledge needed to be able to help the divisions.

A restricted approach to innovation is another problem decentralized organizations may encounter. Because each division is organized around a particular product or geographic area, each manager's attention is focused on his or her special area. As a result, their innovations focus on their particular specialties. Managers don't have the diverse information needed to produce radical innovations.

One major liability of decentralized organizations is their relative inability to provide integration–coordination among the divisions, even when their interdependence increases. When divisions are relatively autonomous and have only pooled interdependence, there is not much need for coordination. However, when uncertainty increases and the divisions have to work together because of increased either sequential or reciprocal interdependence be-

Organizational functions	Accomplished in decentralized organization
Goals	Special product emphasis (technologies lag)
Influence	Product, project heads
Promotion	By product management
Budgeting	By product, project, program
Rewards	For integrative capability

Strengths	Weaknesses
1. Suited to fast change	1. Innovation/growth restricted to existing project areas
2. High product, project, or program visibility	2. Tough to allocate pooled resources (i.e., computer, lab)
3. Full-time task orientation (i.e., dollars, schedules, profits)	3. Shared functions hard to coordinate (i.e., purchasing)
4. Task responsibility, contact points clear to customers or clients	4. Deterioration of in-depth competence —hard to attract technical specialists
5. Processes multiple tasks in parallel, easy to cross functional lines	5. Possible internal task conflicts, priority conflicts
	6. May neglect high level of integration required in organization

Figure 43-5 Characteristics of the decentralized organization.

tween the units, decentralized organizations have no formal mechanisms to coordinate and resolve the increased needs for information.

Since today's organizational environments are becoming more complex and interdependent, large decentralized corporations are finding that the need to integrate has increased for at least five reasons:

1. The increased level of regulation organizations face requires more and more coordination across divisions to be sure that all regulatory requirements are being met. For example, crackdowns by the SEC on illegal foreign payments and the increased liabilities of boards of directors have required organizations to have better control systems and information sources to enable their headquarters staff groups to know what's going on in the divisions. Affirmative action requirements have required that divisions share information on how they are doing and where possible pools of affirmative action candidates may be found.

2. Organizational environments are changing, and this can lead to a requirement of more coordination across divisions. New customer demands may require what were previously autonomous divisions to coordinate their activities. For example, if the International Group in the health products company mentioned earlier faces a demand to develop some new products for overseas, it may be necessary to provide a means by which the Medical Products and Pharmaceutical Divisions can work in a coordinated and integrated way with International to develop these new products.

3. Technological changes are placing more emphasis on increased interaction among divisions. More and more, computer systems and R&D services are being shared, thus compelling the divisions to interact more with one another.

4. The cost of making "wrong" strategic decisions is increasing in terms of both sunk costs and losses because of failure to get market share. Since such "wrong" decisions sometimes result from a lack of contact between divisions, it emphasizes the need to have more coordination across divisions and more sharing of information. For example, AT&T has just recently begun to market telephone and support equipment to counter the competition of other suppliers of this equipment that have entered the market. To do this AT&T has organized around markets. It has also increased the opportunities for

interaction among these market managers so they can share information, build on one another's expertise and competence, and ensure required coordination.

5. Scarce resources—for example, capital and raw materials—will require more interaction among divisions to set overall priorities. Is a university, for example, going to emphasize its undergraduate arts program or its professional schools? By setting up task forces of the deans of the schools, the university might be able to identify opportunities for new innovative programs that could benefit the entire organization. New programs in management of the arts—museums, orchestras, and so on—could draw on the expertise of the arts department and the business school and would not require a lot of new venture capital.

For a number of reasons, then, there is a need for increased coordination among divisions in decentralized organizations. Given the decentralized organization's weakness, organizational designers need to implement the second general design strategy, increasing the information flow to reduce uncertainty and facilitate coordination.

Lateral Relations: Increasing Information Available for Decision Making

Lateral relations is really a process that is overlaid on an existing functional or decentralized structure. Lateral relations as a process moves decision making down to where the problem is in the organization. It differs from decentralization in that no self-contained tasks are created.

Jay Galbraith has identified various types of lateral relations. *Direct contact,* for example, can be used by managers of diverse groups as a mechanism to coordinate their different activities. With direct contact, managers can meet informally to discuss their common problems. *Liaison roles* are a formal communication link between two units. Engineering liaison with the manufacturing department is an excellent example of the liaison role. The engineer serving in the liaison role may be located in the production organization as a way of coordinating engineering and production activities.

When coordination between units becomes more complex, an *integrator role* may be established. Paul Lawrence and Jay Lorsch have indicated that the integrator role is particularly useful when organizational units that must be coordinated are differentiated from one another in terms of their structure, subgoals, time, orientation, and so on. In such situations, there is the possibility of conflict between the various units. For example, production, marketing, and R&D units in an organization may be highly differentiated from one another. Marketing, for example, is primarily concerned with having products to sell that are responsive to customer needs. R&D, on the other hand, may be concerned with developing innovative products that shape customer needs. Production, for its part, may want products to remain unchanged so that manufacturing set-ups don't have to be modified. Obviously there are differences among the three units in terms of their subgoals. The integrator role is instituted to coordinate and moderate such diverse orientations. The integrator could be a materials manager or a group executive whose additional function would be to coordinate and integrate the diverse units in ways that meet the organization's common objectives.

To be effective as an *integrator,* a manager needs to have certain characteristics. First, he needs wide contacts in the organization so that he possesses the relevant information about the different units he is attempting to integrate. Second, the integrator needs to understand and share, at least to a degree, the goals and orientations of the different groups. He cannot be seen as being a partisan of one particular group's perspective. Third, the integrator has to be rather broadly trained technically, so that he can talk the language of the different groups. By being able to demonstrate that he has some expertise in each area, he will be viewed as more credible by each group and will also be better able to facilitate information exchange between the units. The integrator can in effect become an interpreter of each group's position to the others. Fourth, the groups that the integrator is working with must trust him. Again, the integrator is trying to facilitate information flow and cooperation between the groups and thus the groups must believe that he is working toward a solution acceptable to all the groups. Fifth, the integrator needs to exert influence on the basis of his expertise rather than through formal power. The integrator can provide information and identify alternative courses of action for the different units as they attempt to coordinate their activities. The more he can get them to agree on solutions and courses of action rather than having to

use his formal power, the more committed they will be to implementing the solution. Last, the integrator's conflict resolution skills are important. Because differentiation between the units exists, conflict and disagreement are inevitable. It is important, therefore, that confrontation is used as the conflict resolution style. By confrontation we mean that parties to the conflict identify the causes of conflict and are committed to adopting a problem-solving approach to finding a mutually acceptable solution to the conflict. The parties must also be committed, of course, to work to implement that solution.

When coordination involves working with six or seven different units, then task forces or teams can be established. Task forces involve a group of managers working together on the coordination problems of their diverse groups. For example, in a manufacturing organization, the marketing, production, R&D, finance, and engineering managers may meet twice a week (or more often when required) to discuss problems of coordination that they may be having that require their cooperation to solve. In this use a task force is a problem-solving group formed to facilitate coordination.

The matrix type of structure is the most complex form of lateral relations. The matrix is typically a formal structure in the organization; it is not a structure that is often added temporarily to an existing functional or decentralized structure. As Lawrence, Kolodny, and Davis have indicated in their article "The Human Side of the Matrix" (*Organizational Dynamics,* Summer 1977), there are certain key characteristics of a matrix structure. The most salient is that there is dual authority, that is, both the heads of the functions and the matrix manager have authority over those working in the matrix unit.

The matrix was initially developed in the aerospace industry where the organization had to be responsive to products/markets as well as technology. Because the matrix focuses on a specific product or market, it can generate the information and concentrate the resources needed to respond to changes in that product or market rapidly. The matrix is now being used in a variety of business, public, and health organizations. Figure 43-6 provides a summary of the characteristics and strengths and weaknesses of the matrix form of organization.

The matrix structure is particularly useful when an organization wants to focus resources on produc-

Organizational functions	Accomplished in matrix organization
Goals	Emphasis on product/market
Influence	Matrix manager and functional heads
Promotion	By function or into matrix manager job
Budgeting	By matrix organization project
Rewards	By special functional skills and performance in matrix

Strengths	Weaknesses
1. Full-time focus of personnel on project of matrix	1. Costly to maintain personnel pool to staff matrix
2. Matrix manager is coordinator of functions for single project	2. Participants experience dual authority of matrix manager and functional area managers
3. Reduces information requirements as focus is on single product/market	3. Little interchange with functional groups outside the matrix so there may be duplication of effort, "reinvention of the wheel"
4. Masses specialized technical skills to the product/market	4. Participants in matrix need to have good interpersonal skills in order for it to work.

Figure 43-6 Characteristics of the matrix organization.

ing a particular product or service. The use of the matrix in the aerospace industry, for example, allowed these organizations to build manufacturing units to product particular airplanes, thus allowing in-depth attention and specialization of skills.

Matrix organizations, however, are complicated to manage. Because both project managers and traditional functional area managers are involved in matrix organizations, personnel in the matrix have two bosses, and there is an inherent potential for conflict under such circumstances. As a result, the matrix form of lateral relations should only be used in those situations where an organization faces a unique problem in a particular market area or in the technological requirements of a product. When the information and technological requirements are such that a full-time focus on the market or product is needed, a matrix organization can be helpful. Citibank, for example, has used a matrix structure in its international activity to concentrate on geographic areas. Boeing Commercial Airplane has used the matrix to focus resources on a particular product.

Lateral relations require a certain organizational design and special interpersonal skills if this process for reducing uncertainty by increasing the information available for improving coordination is going to be effective. From a design perspective, four factors are required:

1 The organization's reward structure must support and reward cooperative problem solving that leads to coordination and integration. Will a manager's performance appraisal, for example, reflect his or her participation in efforts to achieve coordination and integration? If the organization's reward system does not recognize joint problem-solving efforts, then lateral relations will not be effective.

2 In assigning managers to participate in some form of lateral relations, it is important that they have responsibility for implementation. Line managers should be involved since they understand the problems more intimately than staff personnel and, more importantly, they are concerned about implementation. Staff members can be used, but line managers should be dominant since this will lead to more commitment on their part to implementing solutions that come out of lateral relations problem-solving efforts.

3 Participants must have the authority to commit their units to action. Managers who are participating in an effort to resolve problems of coordination must be able to indicate what particular action their units might take in trying to improve coordination. For example, in the manufacturing company task force example mentioned earlier, the marketing manager should be able to commit his group to increasing the lead time for providing information to production on deadlines for delivering new products to customers.

4 Lateral processes must be integrated into the vertical information flow. In the concern for increasing information exchange *across* the units in the organization there must be no loss of concern for vertical information exchange so that the top levels in the organization are aware of coordination efforts.

Certain skills are also required on the part of participants for lateral relations to work:

1 Individuals must deal with conflict effectively, in the sense of identifying the sources of conflict and t¢n engaging in problem solving to reach a mutually acceptable solution to the conflict situation.

2 Participants need good interpersonal skills. They must be able to communicate effectively with one another and avoid making other participants defensive. The more they can learn to communicate with others in a descriptive, nonevaluative manner, the more open the communication process will be.

3 Participants in lateral relations need to understand that influence and power should be based on expertise rather than formal power. Because of the problem-solving nature of lateral relations, an individual's power and influence will change based on the particular problem at hand and the individual's ability to provide key information to solve the problem. At various times different members will have more influence because of their particular expertise.

Lateral relations, then, is a process that is overlaid onto the existing functional or decentralized organi-

zation structure. Lateral relations requires various skills, so it is imperative that an organization never adopts this approach without training the people involved. Before implementing lateral relations, team building might be used to develop the interpersonal skills of the participating managers. These managers might spend time learning how to operate more effectively in groups, how to improve communication skills, and how to deal with conflict in a positive way so that it does not become disruptive to the organization.

The Organizational Design Decision Tree

We have discussed the different kinds of organization structure that managers can implement. We are now prepared to identify the decision-making process the manager can use in selecting the appropriate structure to "fit" the demands of the environment. Figure 43-7 presents a decision tree analysis for selecting either the functional or decentralized organization structure. This decision analysis also indicates when the existing functional or decentralized organization structure should be supplemented with some form of lateral relations in the form of a task force or team or a matrix. In general, an organization should use one of the simpler forms of lateral reactions rather than the more complex and expensive matrix. In using this decision tree, there are a number of questions that the designer needs to ask.

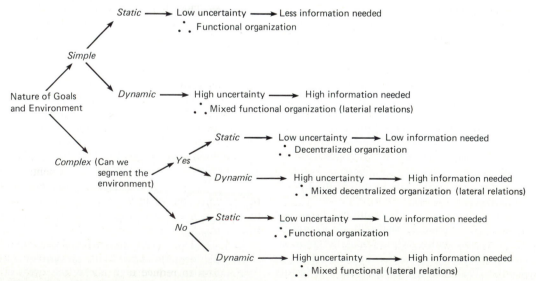

Figure 43-7 Organizational-design decision-tree heuristic.

The first question is whether the organization's environment is *simple,* that is, there are few factors to consider in the environment, or *complex,* that is, there are a number of different environmental factors to be considered in decision making. If the environment is defined as *simple,* the next question focuses on whether the environmental factors are *static,* that is, remain the same over time, or are *dynamic,* that is, change over time. If we define the environment as static, there is likely to be little uncertainty associated with decision making. In turn, information requirements for decision making are low. In this simple–static environment, the functional organization is most efficient. It can most quickly gather and process the information required to deal with this type of environment.

At this point the question might be raised, are there any organizational environments that are in fact both simple and static or is this a misperception on the part of the managers that oversimplifies the environment? There may be environments like this, but the key is that these environments may change, that is, they may become more dynamic as the marketplace changes, as resources become scarce, or the organization's domain is challenged. For example, the motor home/recreational vehicle industry was very successful in the early 1970s. Its market was relatively homogeneous (simple) and there was a constantly high demand (static) for its products. Then the oil embargo of 1973 hit, and the environment suddenly became dynamic. The industry had a very difficult time changing because it had done no contingency planning about "what would happen if" demand shifted, resources became scarce, and so on. The important point is that an organization's environment may be simple and static today but change tomorrow. Managers should continually scan the environment and be sensitive to the fact that things can change and contingency planning may be useful.

If this simple environment is defined as dynamic, with some components in the environment changing, some uncertainty may be experienced by decision makers. Thus information needs will be greater than when the environment was static. Therefore, in this simple–dynamic environment the mixed functional organization with lateral relations is likely to be the most effective in gathering and processing the information required for decision making. Because the organization's environment is simple, the cre-

ation of self-contained units would not be efficient. It is more economical to have central functional areas responsible for all products and markets as these products and markets are relatively similar to one another. However, when uncertainty arises and there is need for more information, some form of lateral relations can be added, to the existing functional organization.

Figure 43-8 shows the functional organization of a manufacturing organization. The organization suddenly may face a problem with its principal product. Competitors may have developed an attractive replacement. As a result of this unique problem, the president of the firm may set up a task force chaired by the vice-president of sales to develop new products. The task force consists of members from manufacturing, sales, research, and engineering services. Its function, obviously, will be to develop and evaluate suggestions for new products.

If the organization's environment is defined by the managers as complex, that is, there are a large number of factors and components that need to be considered in decision making, the next question to ask is, can the organization *segment* its environment into geographic areas, market, or product areas? If the environment is defined as segmentable, then the next question focuses on whether the environment is static or dynamic. If the environment is defined as static, there is going to be low uncertainty, and thus information needs for decision making are not going to be high. Thus, in the complex–segmentable–static environment, the decentralized organization is most appropriate, and the health products organization discussed earlier is a good example of this. The organization can break the environment apart in the sense that it can organize around products or markets, for example, and thus information, resources, and so forth, are only required to produce and market these more homogeneous outputs of the organization.

In the complex–segmentable–dynamic environment there is a change in the components of the environment and the demands they are making on the organization, or in fact the organization has to now consider different factors in the environment that it had not previously considered in decision making. Uncertainty and coordination needs may be higher. The result is that decision makers need more information to reduce uncertainty and provide information to facilitate coordination. The mixed de-

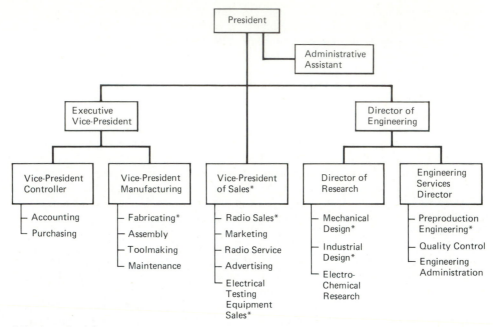

* Members of task force

Figure 43-8 Functional organization with task force.

centralized organization with lateral relations is the appropriate structure here.

Figure 43-9 presents the design of a multidivision decentralized health products organization. Some form of lateral relations may be added to this structure to help generate more information. For example, the International Division may be attempting to develop new products but may be encountering problems, with the result that the entire organization, stimulated by the president's concern, may be experiencing uncertainty about how to proceed. In such a situation, a task force of the manager of the International Group and the Dental Group and the Pharmaceutical Group might work together in developing ideas for new products in the International Division. The lateral relations mechanism of the task force facilitates information exchange *across* the organization to reduce uncertainty and increase coordination of the efforts of the divisions that should be mutually supportive. By working together, in the task force, the division managers will be exchanging information and will be gaining a better understanding of their common problems and how they need to work and coordinate with one another in order to solve these problems.

If the organization's complex environment is de-

fined by managers as nonsegmentable, the functional organization will be appropriate because it is not possible to break the environment up into geographic or product/service areas.

In effect, there simply might be too much interdependence among environmental components, or the technology of the organization may be so interlinked, that it is not possible to create self-contained units organized around components of the environment.

A hospital is a good example of this organization type. The environment is clearly complex. There are numerous and diverse environmental components that have to be considered in decision making (for example, patients, regulatory groups, medical societies, third-party payers, and suppliers). In the complex–nonsegmentable–static environment, environmental components are rather constant in their demands. Thus here the functional organization is most appropriate.

However, the functional organization, through its very specific rules, procedures, and channels of communication, will likely be too slow in generating the required information. Therefore, some form of lateral relations may be added to the functional organization. Figure 43-10 presents an example of

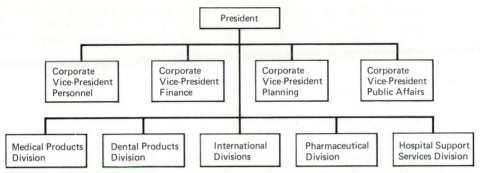

Figure 43-9 Decentralized organization with lateral relations.

an aerospace functional organization that uses a matrix structure for its airplane and missile products divisions. The matrix structure provides in-depth concentration of personnel and resources on these different product areas, each of which has its own very unique information and technological requirements.

SYMPTOMS OF INAPPROPRIATE ORGANIZATIONAL STRUCTURE

The key question at this point is "So what?" What are the costs to an organization if it is using the wrong structure, given its product/service and the environment in which it operates? In order to be effective, an organization needs to attain its goals and objectives, it needs to adapt to the environment, and last, it should be designed in such a way

that its managers experience low role conflict and ambiguity.

Therefore, there are certain kinds of information the manager responsible for organizational design should be sensitive to in monitoring whether the appropriate structure is being used. While using the appropriate structure may have some direct impact on the organization's ability to attain its goals, its biggest impact will probably be on the adaptability of the organization and the role behavior of its managers.

Certain kinds of symptoms regarding ineffective adaptability may occur. For example:

• Organizational decision makers may not be able to anticipate problems before they occur. There may be a tendency in the organization to wait until problems occur and then react to them because the

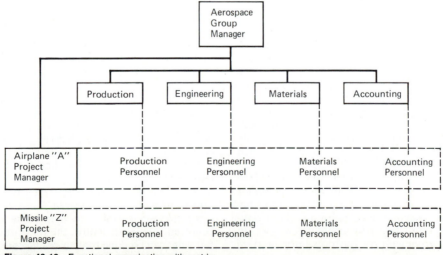

Figure 43-10 Functional organization with matrix.

organization simply does not have enough information to develop contingency plans.

• Decision makers may err in trying to predict trends in their decision environment. Without proper coordination across divisions, the organization may lose control over the relationships between its internal functioning and its environment.

• The organization may not be able to get key information for decision making to the right place for effective decision making. For example, division managers from different product groups may have information that quality and liability standards on their respective products are unrealistically high. However, because of decentralization and lack of effective coordination through some form of lateral relations, this information may not get to the staff groups in the organization that are responsible for setting corporate policy in this area.

• The organization, having identified a problem via-à-vis its environment, may simply not be able to take corrective action quickly enough.

Symptoms of poor fit between structure and environment may also show at the level of the individual in terms of some increase in either role conflict or role ambiguity. It is important, therefore, that the organization monitor the level of role conflict and role ambiguity among its managers and the resulting stress they experience so the system has a baseline for comparison. If there is a significant increase from this baseline in conflict and ambiguity and stress, then the organization may consider that the increase is a symptom of an organizational design problem. For example:

• Individuals may be experiencing increased role conflict. This may occur when the organization is implementing a functional organization in a dynamic environment. The environment may be changing and the individuals may be required to make quick responses to this changing environment. Having to wait for new policy changes to come down the hierarchy may delay the organization from responding appropriately. Decision makers at the top of the organization will also suffer from role conflict when the environment is changing rapidly. In the functional organization, when new situations occur they are referred to higher levels of the organization for decision and action. The result is that top-level decision makers become overloaded and the organization's response to the environment slows down. In a dynamic environment, the functional organization

constrains the decision-making adaptation process.

• Individuals in the organization also may experience increased role ambiguity—they may be unclear as to what is expected of them in their roles. For example, role ambiguity is likely to occur when the decentralized organization is implemented without some effective use of lateral relations. Individuals may feel they don't have the information needed for decision making. Divisional managers may not know what the corporate staff's policy is on various issues, and corporate staff may have lost touch with the divisions.

These are the kinds of information managers should be aware of as indicators of dysfunctional organization design. These data can be collected in organizational diagnosis surveys that we have developed so that a more systemic monitoring of structure exists just as we monitor organizational climate. As fine tuning the organization's design to its environment becomes more critical, organizations will begin to monitor their organizational design more systematically.

SUMMARY

What are the advantages to managers in using the design decision tree? There appear to be several:

1 It provides a *broad framework* for identifying the key factors a manager should think about in considering an organizational design. For example: What is our environment? What different structural options do we have?

2 It forces the manager to *diagnose* the decision environment. What is our environment like? How stable is it? How complex is it? Is it possible to reduce complexity by segmenting the environment into product or geographical subgroups?

3 It causes managers to think about *how much interdependence* there is among segments of the organization. How dependent on one another are different parts of the organization in terms of technology, services, support, help in getting their tasks completed? The decision points in the heuristic forces managers to question themselves about what other parts of the organization they need to coordinate their activities with, and then to think about how to do it.

4 Once the organization is in either a functional or decentralized structure, the decision tree points out what can be done to meet *the increased needs for* *information* through the use of lateral relations. Lateral relations provide a mechanism for supplementing the existing structure to facilitate dealing with the organization's increased needs for information and coordination.

Managers in a variety of organizations have commented that the decision tree gives them ". . . a handle for thinking about organizational design so we can tinker with it, fine tune it, and make it work better. We don't have to be concerned by structure. We now have a better feel for when certain structures should be used and for the specific steps we can take to make a given structure work."

Reading 44

Evolution and Revolution as Organizations Grow
Larry E. Greiner

A small research company chooses too complicated and formalized an organization structure for its young age and limited size. It flounders in rigidity and bureaucracy for several years and is finally acquired by a larger company.

Key executives of a retail store chain hold on to an organization structure long after it has served its purpose, because their power is derived from this structure. The company eventually goes into bankruptcy.

A large bank disciplines a "rebellious" manager who is blamed for current control problems, when the underlying cause is centralized procedures that are holding back expansion into new markets. Many younger managers subsequently leave the bank, competition moves in, and profits are still declining. The problems of these companies, like those of many others, are rooted more in past decisions than in present events or outside market dynamics. Historical forces do indeed shape the future growth of organizations. Yet management, in its haste to grow, often overlooks such critical developmental questions as: Where has our organization been? Where is it now? And what do the answers to these questions mean for where we are going? Instead, its gaze is fixed outward toward the environment and the future—as if more precise market projections will provide a new organizational identity.

Companies fail to see that many clues to their future success lie within their own organizations and their evolving states of development. Moreover, the inability of management to understand its organization development problems can result in a company becoming "frozen" in its present stage of evolution or, ultimately, in failure, regardless of market opportunities.

My position in this article is that the future of an organization may be less determined by outside forces than it is by the organization's history. In stressing the force of history on an organization, I have drawn from the legacies of European psychologists (their thesis being that individual behavior is determined primarily by previous events and experiences, not by what lies ahead). Extending this analogy of individual development to the problems of organization development, I shall discuss a series of developmental phases through which growing companies tend to pass. But, first, let me provide two definitions:

1 The term *evolution* is used to describe prolonged periods of growth where no major upheaval occurs in organization practices.

2 The term *revolution* is used to describe those periods of substantial turmoil in organization life.

As a company progresses through developmental phases, each evolutionary period creates its own revolution. For instance, centralized practices eventually lead to demands for decentralization. Moreover, the nature of management's solution to each revolutionary period determines whether a company will move forward into its next stage of evolutionary growth. As I shall show later, there are at least five phases of organization development, each characterized by both an evolution and a revolution.

KEY FORCES IN DEVELOPMENT

During the past few years a small amount of research knowledge about the phases of organization development has been building. Some of this research is very quantitative, such as time-series analyses that reveal patterns of economic performance over time.[1] The majority of studies, however, are case-oriented and use company records and interviews to reconstruct a rich picture of corporate development.[2] Yet both types of research tend to be heavily empirical without attempting more generalized statements about the overall process of development.

A notable exception is the historical work of Alfred D. Chandler, Jr., in his book *Strategy and Structure.*[3] This study depicts four very broad and general phases in the lives of four large U.S. companies. It proposes that outside market opportunities determine a company's strategy, which in turn determines the company's organization structure. This thesis has a valid ring for the four companies examined by Chandler, largely because they developed in a time of explosive markets and technological advances. But more recent evidence suggests that organization structure may be less malleable than Chandler assumed; in fact, structure can play a critical role in influencing corporate strategy. It is this reverse emphasis on how organization structure affects future growth which is highlighted in the model presented in this article.

From an analysis of recent studies,[4] five key

[1]See, for example, William H. Starbuck, "Organizational Metamorphosis," in *Promising Research Directions*, edited by R. W. Millman and M. P. Hottenstein (Tempe, Arizona, Academy of Management, 1968), p. 113.

[2]See, for example, the *Grangesberg* case series, prepared by C. Roland Christensen and Bruce R. Scott, Case Clearing House, Harvard Business School.

[3]*Strategy and Structure: Chapters in the History of the American Industrial Enterprise* (Cambridge, Massachusetts, The M.I.T. Press, 1962).

[4]I have drawn on many sources for evidence: (a) numerous cases collected at the Harvard Business School; (b) *Organization Growth and Development*, edited by William H. Starbuck (Middlesex, England, Penguin Books, Ltd., 1971), where several studies are cited; and (c) articles published in journals, such as Lawrence E. Fouraker and John M. Stopford, "Organization Structure and the Multinational Strategy," *Administrative Science Quarterly*, Vol. 13, No. 1, 1968, p. 47; and Malcolm S. Salter, "Management Appraisal and Reward Systems," *Journal of Business Policy*, Vol. 1, No. 4, 1971.

dimensions emerge as essential for building a model of organizational development:

1 Age of the organization.
2 Size of the organization.
3 Stages of evolution.
4 Stages of revolution.
5 Growth rate of the industry.

I shall describe each of these elements separately, but first note their combined effect as illustrated in *Exhibit 44-1*. Note especially how each dimension influences the other over time; when all five elements begin to interact, a more complete and dynamic picture of organizational growth emerges.

After describing these dimensions and their interconnections, I shall discuss each evolutionary revolutionary phase of development and show (a) how each stage of evolution breeds its own revolution, and (b) how management solutions to each revolution determine the next stage of evolution.

Age of the Organization

The most obvious and essential dimension for any model of development is the life span of an organization (represented as the horizontal axis in *Exhibit 44-1*). All historical studies gather data from various points in time and then make comparisons. From these observations, it is evident that the same organization practices are not maintained throughout a long time span. This makes a most basic point: management problems and principles are rooted in time. The concept of decentralization, for example, can have meaning for describing corporate practices at one time period but loses its descriptive power at another.

The passage of time also contributes to the institutionalization of managerial attitudes. As a result, employee behavior becomes not only more predictable but also more difficult to change when attitudes are outdated.

Size of the Organization

This dimension is depicted as the vertical axis in *Exhibit 44-1*. A company's problems and solutions tend to change markedly as the number of employees and sales volume increase. Thus, time is not the only determinant of structure; in fact, organizations that do not grow in size can retain many of the same management issues and practices over lengthy peri-

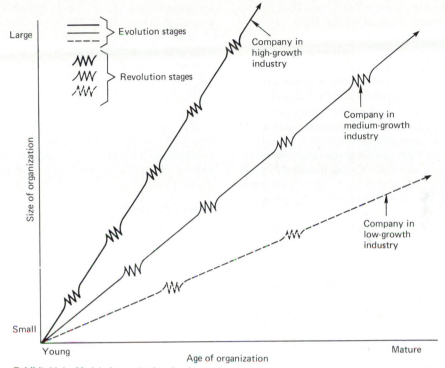

Exhibit 44-1   Model of organization development.

ods. In addition to increased size, however, problems of coordination and communication magnify, new functions emerge, levels in the management hierarchy multiply, and jobs become more interrelated.

Stages of Evolution

As both age and size increase, another phenomenon becomes evident: the prolonged growth that I have termed the evolutionary period. Most growing organizations do not expand for two years and then retreat for one year; rather, those that survive a crisis usually enjoy four to eight years of continuous growth without a major economic setback or severe internal disruption. The term evolution seems appropriate for describing these quieter periods because only modest adjustments appear necessary for maintaining growth under the same overall pattern of management.

Stages of Revolution

Smooth evolution is not inevitable; it cannot be assumed that organization growth is linear.

Fortune's "500" list, for example, has had significant turnover during the last 50 years. Thus we find evidence from numerous case histories which reveals periods of substantial turbulence spaced between smoother periods of evolution.

I have termed these turbulent times the periods of revolution because they typically exhibit a serious upheaval of management practices. Traditional management practices, which were appropriate for a smaller size and earlier time, are brought under scrutiny by frustrated top managers and disillusioned lower-level managers. During such periods of crisis, a number of companies fail—those unable to abandon past practices and effect major organization changes are likely either to fold or to level off in their growth rates.

The critical task for management in each revolutionary period is to find a new set of organization practices that will become the basis for managing the next period of evolutionary growth. Interestingly enough, these new practices eventually sow their own seeds of decay and lead to another period of revolution. Companies therefore experience the irony of seeing a major solution in one time period become a major problem at a later date.

Growth Rate of the Industry

The speed at which an organization experiences phases of evolution and revolution is closely related to the market environment of its industry. For example, a company in a rapidly expanding market will have to add employees rapidly; hence, the need for new organization structures to accommodate large staff increases is accelerated. While evolutionary periods tend to be relatively short in fast-growing industries, much longer evolutionary periods occur in mature or slowly growing industries.

Evolution can also be prolonged, and revolutions delayed, when profits come easily. For instance, companies that make grievous errors in a rewarding industry can still look good on their profit and loss statements; thus they can avoid a change in management practices for a longer period. The aerospace industry in its infancy is an example. Yet revolutionary periods still occur, as one did in aerospace when profit opportunities began to dry up. Revolutions seem to be much more severe and difficult to resolve when the market environment is poor.

PHASES OF GROWTH

With the foregoing framework in mind, let us now examine in depth the five specific phases of evolution and revolution. As shown in *Exhibit 44-2,* each evolutionary period is characterized by the dominant *management style* used to achieve growth, while each revolutionary period is characterized by the dominant *management problem* that must be solved before growth can continue. The patterns presented in *Exhibit 44-2* seem to be typical for companies in industries with moderate growth over a long time period; companies in faster growing industries tend to experience all five phases more rapidly, while those in slower growing industries encounter only two to three phases over many years.

It is important to note that *each phase is both an effect of the previous phase and a cause for the next phase.* For example, the evolutionary management style in Phase 3 of the exhibit is "delegation," which grows out of, and becomes the solution to, demands

for greater "autonomy" in the preceding Phase 2 revolution. The style of delegation used in Phase 3, however, eventually provokes a major revolutionary crisis that is characterized by attempts to regain control over the diversity created through increased delegation.

The principal implication of each phase is that management actions are narrowly prescribed if growth is to occur. For example, a company experiencing an autonomy crisis in Phase 2 cannot return to directive management for a solution—it must adopt a new style of delegation in order to move ahead.

Phase 1: Creativity . . .

In the birth stage of an organization, the emphasis in on creating both a product and a market. Here are the characteristics of the period of creative evolution:

- The company's founders are usually technically or entrepreneurially oriented, and they disdain management activities; their physical and mental energies are absorbed entirely in making and selling a new product.
- Communication among employees is frequent and informal.
- Long hours of work are rewarded by modest salaries and the promise of ownership benefits.
- Control of activities comes from immediate marketplace feedback; the management acts as the customers react.

. . . the Leadership Crisis   All of the foregoing individualistic and creative activities are essential for the company to get off the ground. But therein lies the problem. As the company grows, larger production runs require knowledge about the efficiencies of manufacturing. Increased numbers of employees cannot be managed exclusively through informal communication; new employees are not motivated by an intense dedication to the product or organization. Additional capital must be secured, and new accounting procedures are needed for financial control.

Thus the founders find themselves burdened with unwanted management responsibilities. So they long for the "good old days," still trying to act as they did in the past. And conflicts between the harried leaders grow more intense.

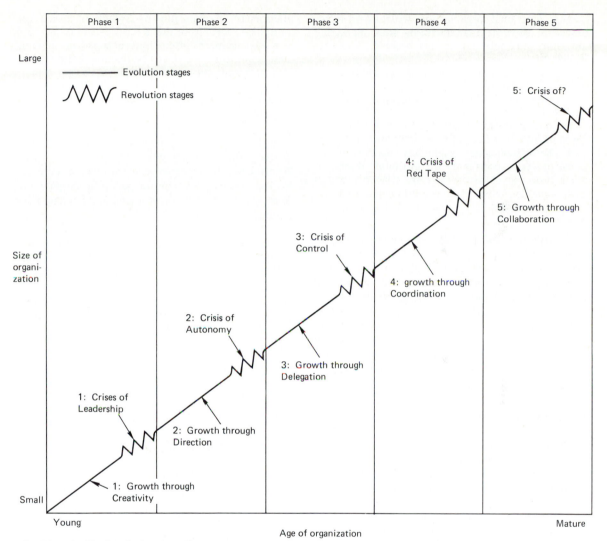

Exhibit 44-2   The five phases of growth.

At this point a crisis of leadership occurs, which is the onset of the first revolution. Who is to lead the company out of confusion and solve the managerial problems confronting it? Quite obviously, a strong manager is needed who has the necessary knowledge and skill to introduce new business techniques. But this is easier said than done. The founders often hate to step aside even though they are probably temperamentally unsuited to be managers. So here is the first critical developmental choice—to locate and install a strong business manager who is acceptable to the founders and who can pull the organization together.

Phase 2: Direction . . .

Those companies that survive the first phase by installing a capable business manager usually embark on a period of sustained growth under able and directive leadership. Here are the characteristics of this evolutionary period:

• A functional organization structure is introduced to separate manufacturing from marketing activities, and job assignments become more specialized.

• Accounting systems for inventory and purchasing are introduced.

• Incentives, budgets, and work standards are adopted.

• Communication becomes more formal and impersonal as a hierarchy of titles and positions builds.

• The new manager and his key supervisors take most of the responsibility for instituting direction, while lower-level supervisors are treated more as functional specialists than as autonomous decision-making managers.

. . . the Autonomy Crisis   Although the new directive techniques channel employee energy more efficiently into growth, they eventually become inappropriate for controlling a larger, more diverse and complex organization. Lower-level employees find themselves restricted by a cumbersome and centralized hierarchy. They have come to possess more direct knowledge about markets and machinery than do the leaders at the top: consequently, they feel torn between following procedures and taking initiative on their own.

Thus the second revolution is imminent as a crisis develops from demands for greater autonomy on the part of lower-level managers. The solution adopted by most companies is to move toward greater delegation. Yet it is difficult for top managers who were previously successful at being directive to give up responsibility. Moreover, lower-level managers are not accustomed to making decisions for themselves. As a result, numerous companies flounder during this revolutionary period, adhering to centralized methods while lower-level employees grow more disenchanted and leave the organization.

Phase 3: Delegation . . .

The next era of growth evolves from the successful application of a decentralized organization structure. It exhibits these characteristics:

• Much greater responsibility is given to the managers of plants and market territories.

• Profit centers and bonuses are used to stimulate motivation.

• The top executives at headquarters restrain themselves to managing by exception, based on periodic reports from the field.

• Management often concentrates on making new acquisitions which can be lined up beside other decentralized units.

• Communication from the top is infrequent, usually by correspondence, telephone, or brief visits to field locations.

The delegation stage proves useful for gaining expansion through heightened motivation at lower levels. Decentralized managers with greater authority and incentive are able to penetrate larger markets, respond faster to customers, and develop new products.

. . . the Control Crisis   A serious problem eventually evolves, however, as top executives sense that they are losing control over a highly diversified field operation. Autonomous field managers prefer to run their own shows without coordinating plans, money, technology, and manpower with the rest of the organization. Freedom breeds a parochial attitude.

Hence, the Phase 3 revolution is under way when top management seeks to regain control over the total company. Some top managements attempt to return to centralized management, which usually fails because of the vast scope of operations. Those companies that move ahead find a new solution in the use of special coordination techniques.

Phase 4: Coordination . . .

During this phase, the evolutionary period is characterized by the use of formal systems for achieving greater coordination and by top executives taking responsibility for the initiation and administration of these new systems. For example:

• Decentralized units are merged into product groups.

• Formal planning procedures are established and intensively reviewed.

• Numerous staff personnel are hired and located at headquarters to initiate companywide programs of control and review for line managers.

• Capital expenditures are carefully weighed and parceled out across the organization.

• Each product group is treated as an investment center where return on invested capital is an important criterion used in allocating funds.

- Certain technical functions, such as data processing, are centralized at headquarters, while daily operating decisions remain decentralized.
- Stock options and companywide profit sharing are used to encourage identity with the firm as a whole.

All of these new coordination systems prove useful for achieving growth through more efficient allocation of a company's limited resources. They prompt field managers to look beyond the needs of their local units. While these managers still have much decision-making responsibility, they learn to justify their actions more carefully to a "watchdog" audience at headquarters.

. . . the Red-Tape Crisis But a lack of confidence gradually builds between line and staff, and between headquarters and the field. The proliferation of systems and programs begins to exceed its utility; a red-tape crisis is created. Line managers, for example, increasingly resent heavy staff direction from those who are not familiar with local conditions. Staff people, on the other hand, complain about uncooperative and uninformed line managers. Together both groups criticize the bureaucratic paper system that has evolved. Procedures take precedence over problem solving, and innovation is dampened. In short, the organization has become too large and complex to be managed through formal programs and rigid systems. The Phase 4 revolution is under way.

Phase 5: Collaboration . . .

The last observable phase in previous studies emphasizes strong interpersonal collaboration in an attempt to overcome the red-tape crisis. Where Phase 4 was managed more through formal systems and procedures, Phase 5 emphasizes greater spontaneity in management action through teams and the skillful confrontation of interpersonal differences. Social control and self-discipline take over from formal control. This transition is especially difficult for those experts who created the old systems as well as for those line managers who relied on formal methods for answers.

The Phase 5 evolution, then, builds around a more flexible and behavioral approach to management. Here are its characteristics:

- The focus is on solving problems quickly through team action.
- Teams are combined across functions for task-group activity.
- Headquarters staff experts are reduced in number, reassigned, and combined in interdisciplinary teams to consult with, not to direct, field units.
- A matrix-type structure is frequently used to assemble the right teams for the appropriate problems.
- Previous formal systems are simplified and combined into single multipurpose systems.
- Conferences of key managers are held frequently to focus on major problem issues.
- Educational programs are utilized to train managers in behavioral skills for achieving better teamwork and conflict resolution.
- Real-time information systems are integrated into daily decision making.
- Economic rewards are geared more to team performance than to individual achievement.
- Experiments in new practices are encouraged throughout the organization.

. . . the ? Crisis What will be the revolution in response to this stage of evolution? Many large U.S. companies are now in the Phase 5 evolutionary stage, so the answers are critical. While there is little clear evidence, I imagine the revolution will center around the "psychological saturation" of employees who grow emotionally and physically exhausted by the intensity of teamwork and the heavy pressure for innovative solutions.

My hunch is that the Phase 5 revolution will be solved through new structures and programs that allow employees to periodically rest, reflect, and revitalize themselves. We may even see companies with dual organization structures: a "habit" structure for getting the daily work done, and a "reflective" structure for stimulating perspective and personal enrichment. Employees could then move back and forth between the two structures as their energies are dissipated and refueled.

One European organization has implemented just such a structure. Five reflective groups have been established outside the regular structure for the purpose of continuously evaluating five task activities basic to the organization. They report directly to the managing director, although their reports are made public throughout the organization. Membership in each group includes all levels and functions, and employees are rotated through these groups on a six-month basis.

Other concrete examples now in practice include providing sabbaticals for employees, moving managers in and out of "hot spot" jobs, establishing a four-day workweek, assuring job security, building physical facilities for relaxation *during* the working day, making jobs more interchangeable, creating an extra team on the assembly line so that one team is always off for reeducation, and switching to longer vacations and more flexible working hours.

The Chinese practice of requiring executives to spend time periodically on lower-level jobs may also be worth a nonideological evaluation. For too long U.S. management has assumed that career progress should be equated with an upward path toward title, salary, and power. Could it be that some vice presidents of marketing might just long for, and even benefit from, temporary duty in the field sales organization?

IMPLICATIONS OF HISTORY

Let me now summarize some important implications for practicing managers. First, the main features of this discussion are depicted in *Exhibit 44-3,* which shows the specific management actions that characterize each growth phase. These actions are also the solutions which ended each preceding revolutionary period.

In one sense, I hope that many readers will react to my model by calling it obvious and natural for depicting the growth of an organization. To me this type of reaction is a useful test of the model's validity.

But at a more reflective level I imagine some of these reactions are more hindsight than foresight. Those experienced managers who have been through a developmental sequence can empathize with it now, but how did they react when in the middle of a stage of evolution or revolution? They can probably recall the limits of their own developmental understanding at that time. Perhaps they resisted desirable changes or were even swept emotionally into a revolution without being able to propose constructive solutions. So let me offer some explicit guidelines for managers of growing organizations to keep in mind.

Know Where You Are in the Developmental Sequence

Every organization and its component parts are at different stages of development. The task of top management is to be aware of these stages; otherwise, it may not recognize when the time for change has come, or it may act to impose the wrong solution.

Top leaders should be ready to work with the flow of the tide rather than against it; yet they should be cautious, since it is tempting to skip phases out of impatience. Each phase results in certain strengths and learning experiences in the organization that will be essential for success in subsequent phases. A child prodigy, for example, may be able to read like a teenager, but he cannot behave like one until he ages through a sequence of experiences.

Category	Phase 1	Phase 2	Phase 3	Phase 4	Phase 5
Management focus	Make and sell	Efficiency of options	Expansion of market	Consolidation or organization	Problem solving and innovation
Organization structure	Informal	Centralized and functional	Decentralized and geograohical	Line-staff and product groups	Matrix of teams
Top management style	Individualistic and entrepreneurial	Directive	Delegative	Watchdog	Participative
Control system	Market results	Standards and cost centers	Reports and profit centers	Plans and investment centers	Mutual goal setting
Management reward emphasis	Ownership	Salary and merit increases	Individual bonus	Profit sharing and stock options	Team bonus

Exhibit 44-3 Organization practices during evolution in the five phases of growth.

I also doubt that managers can or should act to avoid revolutions. Rather, those periods of tension provide the pressure, ideas, and awareness that afford a platform for change and the introduction of new practices.

Recognize the Limited Range of Solutions

In each revolutionary stage it becomes evident that this stage can be ended only by certain specific solutions; moreover, these solutions are different from those which were applied to the problems of the preceding revolution. Too often it is tempting to choose solutions that were tried before, which makes it impossible for a new phase of growth to evolve.

Management must be prepared to dismantle current structures before the revolutionary stage becomes too turbulent. Top managers, realizing that their own managerial styles are no longer appropriate, may even have to take themselves out of leadership positions. A good Phase 2 manager facing Phase 3 might be wise to find another Phase 2 organization that better fits his talents, either outside the company or with one of its newer subsidiaries.

Finally, evolution is not an automatic affair; it is a contest for survival. To move ahead, companies must consciously introduce planned structures that not only are solutions to a current crisis but also are fitted to the *next* phase of growth. This requires considerable self-awareness on the part of top management, as well as great interpersonal skill in persuading other managers that change is needed.

Realize That Solutions Breed New Problems

Managers often fail to realize that organizational solutions create problems for the future (i.e., a decision to delegate eventually causes a problem of control). Historical actions are very much determinants of what happens to the company at a much later date.

An awareness of this effect should help managers to evaluate company problems with greater historical understanding instead of "pinning the blame" on a current development. Better yet, managers should be in a position to *predict* future problems, and thereby to prepare solutions and coping strategies before a revolution gets out of hand.

A management that is aware of the problems ahead could well decide *not* to grow. Top managers may, for instance, prefer to retain the informal practices of a small company, knowing that this way of life is inherent in the organization's limited size, not in their congenial personalities. If they choose to grow, they may do themselves out of a job and a way of life they enjoy.

And what about the managements of very large organizations? Can they find new solutions for continued phases of evolution? Or are they reaching a stage where the government will act to break them up because they are too large.

CONCLUDING NOTE

Clearly, there is still much to learn about processes of development in organizations. The phases outlined here are only five in number and are still only approximations. Researchers are just beginning to study the specific developmental problems of structure, control, rewards, and management style in different industries and in a variety of cultures.

One should not, however, wait for conclusive evidence before educating managers to think and act from a developmental perspective. The critical dimension of time has been missing for too long from our management theories and practices. The intriguing paradox is that by learning more about history we may do a better job in the future.

Part Six

Leadership and Organizational Change

Chapter 13

Managerial Leadership

Leadership is a crucial topic for anyone interested in behavior in organizations. We all have been affected by the actions of leaders, and, at one time or another, most of us have assumed leadership positions. Leadership can be thought of as a special case of social influence. Just as groups can influence individual members, so can particular individuals—those we label "leaders" in given situations—influence other individuals. As one goes through the articles in this chapter, it will be especially useful to keep the notion of social influence to the forefront. Unfortunately, however, attempts to unravel the processes by which certain individuals at certain times—leaders in specific situations—exert this influence have proved to be somewhat difficult for behavioral scientists. Part of the problem is definitional: how does one unambiguously distinguish leadership from all other kinds of influence behavior? Also, though, research has produced relatively little in the way of strongly consistent and reliable findings. Progress has been made, but it has been slower than might be expected given the generally accepted importance attached to the concept of leadership. It seems likely, nevertheless, that the next decade may bring about some substantial ad-

vances in our understanding of the topic. Some of the bases of knowledge for making these advances are illustrated in the articles in this chapter.

The opening article, by McCall, provides an overview of issues important to understanding leadership. In this reading, McCall faces the issue of why the popular literature on leadership seems so much more exciting than the scientific literature. After reviewing problems in defining "leadership," McCall outlines the major theoretical and empirical developments in the area. As the reader will see, great emphasis is placed on the necessity of focusing on the "demands of the leadership role" and analyzing the kinds of activities engaged in by leaders. From this material, McCall generates some thoughts about the training of leaders and proposes some new ways of looking at leadership processes.

The *symbolic* nature of leadership serves as the cornerstone for the article by Pfeffer. He focuses on the fact that "leadership is attributed by observers," and thus exists in the eye of the beholder at least as much as in "objective" reality. As the author states, "*whether or not* leader behavior actually influences performance or effectiveness, it is important because people believe it does." It is people's beliefs about causality, their attributions, that result in so much attention being paid to leadership. Pfeffer precedes this attribution analysis by highlighting three types of problems with the concept of leadership: the ambiguity involved in its definition, the question of whether leadership has demonstrable effects on organizational results, and problems in the leadership selection processes that often result in the application of irrelevant criteria of selection. Particularly interesting in the author's analysis is the issue of whether leaders have major impacts on organizational outcomes. Several persuasive arguments are advanced as to why such effects may be relatively small. In any event, as we have noted above, to Pfeffer an important consideration is what sense the observers of "leaders" are trying to make of events.

One of the most important theories of recent years relating to the phenomenon of leadership is the so-called path-goal theory. While a number of scholars had a part in developing this approach in the early 1970s, perhaps one of the clearest explications of it is contained in the article by House and Mitchell. The basis for the path-goal conceptualization is a theory of motivation called "expectancy theory." This latter theory emphasizes what people want to obtain in a situation and what they see as the probabilities (expectancies) that a certain level or type of behavior on their part will lead to these desired outcomes. Building on this basic motivational foundation, the path-goal theory of leadership focuses on what the leader can do to provide valued rewards and, especially, how the leader can help to clarify the *paths* to these goals so that they can be more readily obtained. The emphasis here is on the contingent nature of rewards: the leader must make sure (from the leader's perspective) that the rewards subordinates want depend on (or follow from) the kind of behavior (i.e., high performance) the leader wants to induce. In addition to setting up contingent reward situations, the leader must also help to make clear just what these contingencies (paths) are. In addition, the leader has a definite role, according to the theory, in assisting subordinates in achieving high performance so that they, in turn, can obtain their goals. The theory is rich in generating testable propositions relating to the effects of leader behavior.

Vroom, in the fourth article in this chapter, places

great importance on the idea that individuals can *learn* how to lead effectively. He stresses the decision-making aspect of leadership and then illustrates his approach with an analysis of how the leader should go about ascertaining whether or not to utilize a subordinate's participation in particular situations. The decision-making model Vroom presents is explicitly normative, in that it prescribes a "correct" style of leadership for various specific situational circumstances. It will be seen that he believes strongly that training can help leaders "enlarge their repertoire" of leadership styles.

The article by Mitchell and Green deals with one of the most important tasks faced by those in leadership positions: how to respond to poor performance on the part of subordinates. This article, like the one by Pfeffer, utilizes an attributional-analysis framework. As the authors point out, attribution theory focuses on the issues of perceived *intentions* and perceived personal and environmental causes of behavior. The critical perceptions are whether the causes of behavior (as inferred by the observer) are internal (to the person) or external (outside the person). As further discussed in the article, it is necessary to realize that two types of bias can creep into the inference process: one is the actor/observer distinction, in which the behavior of other people is attributed to internal causes, but one's own behavior is due to external factors ("circumstances"). The other type of bias is labeled "defensive attributions": people attribute their own successes to internal factors and their failures to external factors, but make exactly the opposite attribution with respect to someone else's success or failure. Mitchell and Green then proceed in the article to put this line of argument (based on research) into the leadership setting. If the subordinate's performance is poor, certain attributions are made, depending on the leader's relation to the subordinate, the likelihood that the poor performance will reflect on the leader, and the like. Most importantly, this "information processing" by the leader will in turn lead to a particular set of leader actions depending on the attributions of cause that are made. The authors conclude the article by drawing some significant implications for understanding why leaders react to poor subordinate performance in the way they do.

In the concluding article in this chapter, Kerr

draws our attention to an often-neglected point: In organizational settings there are a number of (potential) substitutes for hierarchical leadership: e.g., high levels of subordinate ability, unambiguous tasks, cohesive work groups, "professional orientation," and the like. One of the main implications of this fundamental idea is that organizations could benefit from more explicit attention to "building in" these substitutes and thus lessening the need for traditional hierarchical leadership. This attention to leadership substitutes, Kerr argues, has generally been missing in the past, on the part of both organizations and those researchers who study leadership. In effect, Kerr is suggesting that both organizations and leadership researchers should change their frame of reference regarding what constitutes "leadership" and look at the leadership possibilities in organizations in a much broader light than has been the case in the past. By so doing, the author contends, greater understanding of how to improve organizational effectiveness should be possible.

Reading 45

Leaders and Leadership: Of Substance and Shadow
Morgan W. McCall, Jr.

There are at least two ways to approach the topic of leadership. The first is from the emotional, experiential frame of reference which captures the colorful and dramatic flavor of myth and legend—of the fate of nations and the course of history. The second is an empirical approach based on research about this nebulous topic. If the former is bright orange, the latter is decidedly slate gray.

The bright orange side of leadership emerges when people are asked to name highly effective leaders. The most frequently mentioned—Hitler, Churchill, Kennedy, Roosevelt, Eisenhower, Gandhi—all played a significant part in world history. The characteristics attributed to such effective leaders—charisma, intelligence, persuasiveness, dynamism, energy—also reflect the almost mystical power of central figures in world events.

The essence of the powerful leader's impact has been captured in song, poem, and novel. One example is Tolstoy's description of Napoleon:

> Napoleon was standing a little in front of his marshals, on a little grey horse, wearing the same blue overcoat he had worn throughout the Italian campaign. He was looking intently and silently at the hills, which stood up out of the sea of mist, and the Russian troops moving across them in the distance, and he listened to the sounds of firing in the valley. His face—still thin in those days—did not stir a single muscle: his gleaming eyes were fixed intently on one spot. . . .
>
> When the sun had completely emerged from the fog, and was glittering and dazzling brilliance over the fields and the mist (as though he had been waiting for that to begin the battle), he took his glove off his handsome white hand, made a signal with it to his marshals, and gave orders for the battle to begin. (From *War and Peace*)

Given the emotional power of leadership, it is no surprise that social scientists have devoted massive amounts of time and resources to studying it. Researchers have looked at leadership in almost every conceivable setting, from army squads to executives; they have examined personality traits, leadership styles, situational contingencies, and a multitude of other topics pertinent to leadership. With leadership studies appearing at a rate of more than 170 a year,[1] it seems reasonable to ask what we know about this elusive topic.

SKIPPING THROUGH A MINEFIELD

At a recent conference on the "frontiers" of leadership research, the concluding speaker made the following comment:

> The heresy I propose is that the concept of leadership itself has outlived its usefulness. Thus I suggest we abandon it in favor of some other more fruitful way of cutting up the theoretical pie. (Miner, 1975, p. 5)

After over forty years of empirical investigation, leadership remains an enigma. In 1959, Warren Bennis suggested reasons for this state of affairs, and over twenty years later his points still seem valid.

First, the term "leadership" has never been clearly defined. Ralph Stogdill, in a mammoth review of the leadership research, pointed out that "there are almost as many different definitions of leadership as there are persons who have attempted to define the concept" (1974, p. 7). Perhaps the closest thing to a consensus on a definition for leadership is that it is a social-influence process. Since most interactions involve social influence, such categorizations of leadership have not helped much.

The lack of a generally agreed upon definition of the central concept has led to a proliferation of terms to deal with leadership phenomena. The last fifteen years have seen the appearance of at least four different "contingency" models, as well as path-goal and open system models, not to mention transactional and vertical dyad approaches, normative and integrative models, four-factor and behavioral theories, and attribution explanations.

Second, the "growing mountain" of research data

---

[1]Based on a search of *Psychological Abstracts*.

A version of this paper was presented at the annual meeting of the British Psychological Society, Occupational Psychology Section, Keefe, Staffordshire, England, January 1976. Copyrighted by Morsau W. McCall, Jr. Used with permission.

has produced an impressive mass of contradictions. The dimensions of the mountain were suggested by Stogdill's (1974) review of the leadership literature which covered over 3,000 studies. While numerous models, theories, and approaches exist, the accumulated research has not yet produced a unified and generally accepted paradigm for research on the topic, much less a clear understanding of the phenomenon. In fact, Warren Bennis's summary is even more accurate today:

> Of all the hazy and confounding areas in social psychology, leadership theory undoubtedly contends for top nomination. And, ironically, probably more has been written and less known about leadership than about any other topic in the behavioral sciences. (1959)

Naturally enough, much of the early work on leadership attempted to isolate the characteristics of people, distinguishing leaders from nonleaders, or successful from unsuccessful leaders. Almost every conceivable trait and characteristic, from activity to weight, have been examined, but the results have been equivocal. The initial hope that leaders shared common characteristics across situations has not been borne out, and it now appears that personal characteristics are related to leadership outcomes only in the context of specific situations (Gibb, 1969; Campbell, Dunnette, Lawler, & Weick, 1970). Unfortunately, it is not yet clear which aspects of the situation are most critical.

Another major approach to leadership involves the "style" a leader uses in dealing with subordinates. Many different labels have been generated to describe essentially two styles of leadership (the number of "styles" ranges from two to five): (1) task oriented and (2) person (consideration) oriented. While initially intended to reflect the *behavior* of leaders, styles are most commonly measured by one of several paper-and-pencil questionnaires; thus, they represent self- or others' reported perceptions rather than actual behavior.

The human-relations school at first contended that leaders should emphasize considerate, participative styles. Consideration of employees' feelings and allowing employees' participation in decision making would result in increased satisfaction which, it was thought, would improve performance. While considerate behavior by leaders did generally lead to increased satisfaction, satisfaction did not necessarily lead to improved performance. Equivocal and sometimes negative results (Stogdill, 1974) indicated that this normative approach was not the answer in all situations.

Other researchers (e.g., Blake & Mouton, 1964) argued that an effective leader must be high on structuring *and* high on consideration. Again, the data did not clearly conform to the normative prescriptions (e.g., Larson, Hunt, & Osborn, 1975). Further refinements aimed at isolating the specific situations in which certain styles are effective (e.g., Vroom & Yetton, 1973) have replaced the earlier, simpler models, but as yet no adequate taxonomy of situational components exists. In fact, recent theorizing suggests that leader style says more about follower attributions than it does about leaders (Calder, 1977; Pfeffer, 1978).

Data do exist, however, which indicate that leaders change their behavior in response to situational conditions (Hill & Hughes, 1974) and to subordinates' behaviors (Lowin & Craig, 1968; Farris & Lim, 1969; Greene, 1975). Leaders are not perceived by subordinates as having "one style" (Hill, 1973), nor do they treat all subordinates the same way (Graen & Cashman, 1975). Thus, the search for invariant truth—the one-best-way approach—may not hold answers, even when the model includes situational moderators. Leaders may have numerous behaviors to choose from (not two or three) and may face a wide variety of different situations. A number of leadership behaviors may be equally effective in the same situation. As researchers include task structures, power, hierarchical level, subordinate expectations, and other organizational characteristics in their models, predictive power and model complexity increase. But only one thing is clear—no one leadership style is effective in all situations.

Thus early work made an important contribution to understanding leadership. It showed that neither personal characteristics nor styles of leadership behavior could predict leadership effectiveness across situations. More importantly, these findings steered researchers toward identifying the characteristics of situations which might interact with personality or style dimensions to generate positive outcomes.

Most of the current theories have retained the basic ingredients of the earlier models while adding situational contingencies. Although the specific variables included vary, the basic contingency approach is illustrated in Table 45-1.

The relationships studied in contingency frameworks still reflect leadership's research origins in individual and group psychology. The focal unit is the leader and a group of followers. The outcomes (dependent variable) generally represent an index of the performance or satisfaction of the follower group, and the independent variables are still characteristics or "behaviors" of the leader. The relationships between the leader and group outcomes are contingent on some aspect of the situation.

Fiedler's (1967) contingency theory has been a focus for many current researchers and provides a good example of the contingency approach. Fiedler postulated that the effectiveness of a group depends on the leader's motivational orientation (person versus task) and on the nature of the situation (determined by the structuredness of the task, the position of power of the leader, and the quality of leader-member relations). The elaborate model contains a continuum of situational favorableness (from highly favorable to highly unfavorable) and postulates that task-motivated leaders are effective in both highly favorable and unfavorable situations, while person-motivated leaders are effective in the moderate situations.

The path-goal model (Evans, 1970; House, 1971) provides another example of the contingency approach. Built on an expectancy-theory framework, the path-goal model argues that a leader's style (task or person orientation) is effective when it clarifies linkages between subordinate effort and valued outcomes. Thus, leaders' behavior has contingent effects on group outcomes depending upon the presence or absence of performance-outcome linkages.

In spite of their logical appeal, the contingency models have still yielded contradictory research results. As Korman (1974) has pointed out, the contingency approach "has been a great leap forward in the complexity and sophistication of theoretical formulations and the range of variables which have come under consideration," but he adds, "There has also been a neglect of some basic considerations." Included in such considerations are issues of measurement, the continued focus on personality constructs, a static rather than dynamic view of leadership processes, and a failure to extend situational factors beyond those relevant to the immediate work group.

In the long run, the test of leadership theory is its utility for those individuals who find themselves in leadership roles. The bulk of current research has made some contribution by sensitizing practitioners to the differences among leadership styles and, in general, to the complexity of the leadership process. But researchers are still a long way from an integrated understanding of leadership processes, and equally far from providing organizational leaders with integrated and validated models of leadership.

Relative to the bulk of research on styles, characteristics, and contingencies, a small number of studies have examined what organizational leaders actually do (McCall, Morrison, & Hannan, 1978). Many researchers dismiss the results of such studies because, it is argued, leadership and management (or headship) are different things. Unfortunately, the lack of consensus about the meaning of "leadership" makes it difficult to find leaders and follow them around. People who occupy leadership roles in organizations (foremen, managers, executives), however, can be identified and studied. The results of such efforts have produced some thought-provoking approaches which might clarify some of the confusion in the more traditional leadership literature.

Table 45-1 The Basic Model for Contingency Approaches to Leadership

Characteristic of leader (e.g., style, personality)	Characteristic of situation (e.g., group task, members' expectations)	Relationship with group outcome (e.g., performance or satisfaction)
A	X	Positive
A	Y	Negative or unrelated
B	X	Negative or unrelated
B	Y	Positive

DEMANDS OF THE LEADERSHIP ROLE

No es lo mismo hablar de toros, que estar en el redondel.[2]

[2]This is an old Spanish proverb which means, "It is not the same to talk of bulls as to be in the bullring."

Data on the day-to-day activities of those who occupy leadership roles shed some light on (a) the pace of management work, (b) the degree to which the work group itself is a focus of managerial interaction, (c) the kinds of media central to managerial activity, and (d) a global picture of what life is like in the leadership bullring. These, in turn, challenge several assumptions which seemingly underlie leadership theories based on the leader-group paradigm.

The Pace of Managerial Work

Many models of leadership, particularly those advocating participative management or situational determination of an appropriate leadership style, seem to assume that leaders have (a) a relatively small number of events about which style decisions must be made, and (b) enough time to analyze the situation and choose a style.

Two studies of foremen provide an interesting insight into these assumptions. In one study, foremen engaged in an average of 583 activities in a day (Guest, 1955–56); and in another, foremen averaged between 200 and 270 activities per eight-hour day. Other studies of higher level managers confirm the unrelenting pace of managerial work. One study of a Swedish top executive found that he was undisturbed for twenty-three minutes or more only twelve times in thirty-five days (Carlson, 1951). Mintzberg (1973), in a study of five top executives, found that half of their activities lasted nine minutes or less, and only a tenth lasted more than one hour. Mintzberg's observations led him to conclude that a manager's activities are "characterized by brevity, variety, and fragmentation" (1973, p. 31).

The hectic pace of managerial work is exacerbated by the manager's relative lack of control over it. Mintzberg (1975) found, for example, that the managers in his study initiated only 32 percent of their contacts and that 93 percent of the contacts were arranged on an "ad hoc" basis.

The pace of the work has implications for training, research, and practice. Because there are so many activities in a day and because there is so little uninterrupted time, the occupant of a formal leadership role must be, as Mintzberg (1973) calls it, "proficient at superficiality." Training models which advocate "rational" decision strategies (e.g., analyzing each situation to determine the appropriate decision style) make sense, but they are extremely

difficult for a manager to implement. Research approaches which ignore the day-to-day process of leading are missing what may be critical dimensions —the crunch of the pace and the breadth of the activities. Finally, managers themselves can be easily overwhelmed. The work is demanding and largely reactive. Activities that require little time and are relatively routine may postpone other activities that are ambiguous and have no routine solution. Thus, larger decisions may be made by default.

Time with the Work Group

The fact that almost all current models of leadership focus on the leader and the immediate work group suggests that the relationship between leader and led is the most important aspect of the leadership process. Translated into what managers do, one might expect that almost all of a manager's time is spent with members of the group.

Dubin's (1962) review indicates that foremen spend between 34 and 60 percent of their *interaction* time with subordinates. Mintzberg's (1973) executives spent only 48 percent of their *contact time* with subordinates, even though the subordinate groups contained most of their respective organizational memberships. Managers, then, spend about a third of their total time and roughly half their contact time with subordinates. About an equal amount of interaction is with nonsubordinates—a group including superiors, peers, professional colleagues, members of other departments and units, and outsiders. Dubin concluded in his review:

> It cannot be too strongly emphasized that horizontal relations among peers in management and the nonformal behavior systems through which such interactions are carried out constitute a dimension of organizational behavior long neglected and probably as important as authority relations. (1962, p. 15)

Surprisingly, managers spend relatively little of their interaction time with their superiors (Brewer & Tomlinson, 1963–64); seldom more than one fifth and usually closer to one tenth (according to Mintzberg, 1973).

The mosaic of available data shows that there is considerable variability in the amount of time a manager spends in contact with subordinates. While it is generally true that interactions with subordinates consume the largest single block of a manager's time, it should not be concluded that leader-subordinate relationships are the only—or even the most important—aspect of the leadership process. In one study of sixty managers, group members accounted for an average of only 23.4 percent of the total number of information sources listed by the leader (McCall, 1974).

More research on leadership needs to focus on the leader-system relationship and how the organizational leader fits into the interaction matrix. Sayles (1964, 1979) and Mintzberg (1973), among others, have emphasized the major importance and complexity of the managers' information network. Unfortunately, empirical investigation of the impact of nonsubordinates' interactions on leadership effectiveness is sorely lacking.

Many leadership development programs also suffer because of narrow leader-follower paradigms. Since there are few data on the impact and nature of other relationships, it is not surprising that few training programs deal with them. One cannot help wondering, though, if we are creating a generation of managers who believe that their style with their immediate subordinates is the only matter of concern.

Managers and Media

Studies of what managers do consistently find that their work is primarily oral. Dubin and Spray (1964), Mintzberg (1973), Brewer and Tomlinson (1963–64), Kurke & Aldrich (1979), and Dubin (1962) all cite evidence emphasizing the high percentage of managerial time spent talking. Much of this talk is directed at exchanging information (Mintzberg, 1973; Horne & Lupton, 1965), and very little of it is spent giving orders or issuing instructions (Horne & Lupton, 1965).

With between 60 and 80 percent of their time spent in oral exchanges, formal leaders cannot spend too much time with written communications (Dubin, 1962). A successful leader, therefore, must have the ability to selectively "hear," retain, and transmit vast quantities of oral information and, perhaps even more difficult, selectively utilize a vast volume of written information provided routinely by the organization.[3] In communicating with others,

the manager would do well to remember that other managers, too, are focusing on the spoken word—things in writing just do not get the time, in general, that is available for an oral communication.

What Leaders Do: An Integration

For formal leaders in organizations, the data indicate that the world consists of many activities (most of them of short duration), frequent interruptions, a large network of contacts extending far beyond the immediate work group, and a preponderance of oral interaction. How do these characteristics fit in with the mythology and empirical work on leadership?

First, notice that these dimensions of leadership represent the day-to-day processes that go on between the leader's "moments of glory." It is easy to latch onto the "Ich bin ein Berliner" and "I have nothing to offer but blood, toil, tears and sweat," thereby ignoring what Kennedy or Churchill did in the daily conduct of their leadership roles. To the extent that we do know what these leaders were like, we owe that knowledge to journalists and not to the empirical leadership literature.[4] Most of the leaders with whom we have direct contact—our bosses, politicians, community figures, and gang leaders—have less grandiose moments of glory, but they too engage in the process of leading. What observational studies have shown us is that the leadership we react to—the inspiration, or lack of it, the autocratic behavior—is only a part of the larger and more complex set of phenomena comprising the role of leader.

Second, leadership models which emphasize the "style" of a leader vis-à-vis the follower group have limited utility, even when they introduce situational contingencies. They have no explanatory power when it comes to nonsubordinate interactions, and it is difficult to understand the relationship between some global measure of a leader's style and the literally hundreds of activities that are part of the daily life of a manager. The concentration on leadership style that pervades all of the mainstream leadership research reminds one of what Omar Bradley once said in a different context: "This strategy would involve us in the wrong war, at the wrong place, at the wrong time, and with the wrong enemy."

Third, the results of observational studies suggest

---

[3]Ackoff (1967) has discussed the problems managers face with one type of written information—that provided by managerial information systems. One of his conclusions is that managers have too much, rather than too little, information.

[4]Vaill (1978) made this point by arguing that the *New Yorker* is the best social science journal.

a host of different variables and questions that might direct future leadership research and which pose challenges for leadership development. The presence of nonauthority relationships and the emphasis on oral communication, coupled with the nonrational way decisions get made (e.g., Cyert & March, 1963; March & Simon, 1958; Katz & Kahn, 1966; Pettigrew, 1973), suggest that a major element of the leadership process is political. While social scientists have advocated the inclusion of political activity in studies of leadership (e.g., Lundberg, 1978, has talked about coalitions, lieutenants, and shadows), little empirical work *in leadership* has confronted these issues directly.

Another approach involves looking systematically at the impact of oral communication on leadership processes and outcomes. Skill in oral communication is measured routinely in some assessment center operations (Bray, Campbell, & Grant, 1974), but it has not received adequate attention as a variable in leadership (except in some small group studies where total talk time has been related to the group's nomination of a leader, e.g., Jaffee & Lucas, 1969). Related to the communication dimension are the cognitive processes wherein individuals in leadership roles somehow retain the information transmitted in oral interactions. Unlike the written word, which automatically creates a record for future reference, the spoken word is easily lost.

More intriguing yet is Mintzberg's notion of proficient superficiality. Plagued by interruptions and activities of short duration, how do leaders synthesize, integrate, and understand the larger picture? Direct observation of behavior can produce a catalog of activities, but it cannot shed much light on the actor's mediation of events. How do all those activities fit together for the leader? One interpretation of the huge number of activities in the manager's day is that each activity represents a different situation. Most current leadership theories would imply that the manager should apply the correct style in each situation and thereby achieve the greatest effectiveness. Another way of looking at the problem is to say that leaders face a near-infinite set of situations and engage in a near-infinite set of behaviors. Many different combinations of behaviors may be effective in a given situation, so there may not be any one best way of responding. If so, the search for invariant truth is an academic exercise and any real understanding of leadership will involve a more holistic approach—one that looks beyond superficial behaviors and simplified taxonomies of situations.

TRAINING AND LEADERSHIP

If our understanding of leadership is less than adequate, then we might predict that training based on that knowledge would produce equivocal research results. Campbell reviewed the empirical literature on training and development and concluded, "In sum, we know a few things but not very much" (1971, p. 593). Stogdill also reviewed the leadership training literature and reached a similar concise conclusion: "It must be concluded that the research on leadership training is generally inadequate in both design and execution. It has failed to address itself to the most crucial problems of leadership" (1974, p. 199).

Most leadership training based on the behavioral-science approach to leadership repeats the mistakes of leadership research: (a) It tends to focus quite narrowly on the relationship between the leader and the group, and specifically on the issue of leadership style. (b) It fails to take into account the nature of managerial work—many activities, fragmentation, variety, nonhierarchical relationships, etc. (c) When situational considerations are including in training, they tend to be limited to the situation of the immediate work group (e.g., the task of the group or the nature of the immediate problem).

It may be useful for leaders to develop a knowledge of leadership styles and a sensitivity to their contingent application, but applying such learning on the job is a different matter. Instead of teaching content, leadership training courses might better focus on creating situations reflecting the daily demands of the leadership role, and, through the use of extensive feedback, allow the trainees to study their performances and their impact. While the value of simulations for research and training purposes has been articulated for some time (e.g., Weick, 1965), few *organizational* simulations have been designed and utilized.[5]

One result of the hectic pace of managerial work is that managers seldom have time to reflect on their behavior. On-the-job feedback is likely to be fragmented, badly timed, vague, or even entirely lack-

---

[5]One review of the literature turned up only two organizational simulations used for leadership assessment (Omstead et al., 1973).

ing. One valuable outcome of a training experience is that it can provide the time for reflection on the process of being a leader. To maximize this potential, the training must generate behaviors approximating those of the organizational role and must provide valid feedback on what the behaviors were and what their impact was. T-groups are high in generating feedback, but they create a situation with few parallels in the organizational setting. Thus, transfer of learning from the training situation to the job is difficult (Campbell & Dunnette, 1968). Simulations, too, can only be approximations of reality, but we do know enough about the context of managerial work to create reasonable approximations.

TAKING PROCESS SERIOUSLY

In 1970, Campbell et al. depicted the leadership process as a function of the person, the behavior, the outcomes of behavior, environmental influences, and feedback. Advocacy of a "systems" perspective on organizations and the leadership process within them is not new (e.g., Katz & Kahn, 1966; Weick, 1969; Rosen, 1970; Rubin & Goldman, 1968), and the current abundance of contingency models of leadership is a sign that researchers are moving more in that direction. Still, a number of current trends in leadership research seem to be holding back progress: (1) attempting to categorize a wide range of leadership behaviors into a few simple categories (e.g., structure and consideration), (b) defining the situation as a few simple categories focused on only the immediate situation (e.g., the task of the group) and the interpersonal relations between leader and led, (c) measuring leadership outcomes solely on the basis of group effectiveness, and (d) emphasizing static rather than dynamic components of the organizational context (i.e., assuming that the situation stays the same over time).

While it is relatively easy to be critical of social science, it is more challenging to offer alternative approaches. Fortunately, there are alternatives for looking at leadership.

First, Mintzberg (1973) has shown that the classification of leaders' behaviors can be extended beyond the two basic styles of structure and consideration. Drawing on his observations of managerial work, he generated ten basic roles which he argued are typical of most managerial jobs. Only one, what he calls "leader," focuses exclusively on the leader-subordinate interaction, while the other nine encompass such activities as monitoring and disseminating information, acting as a figurehead, negotiating, handling disturbances, etc. Mintzberg's work is only a beginning, but breaking the set of leadership styles—and moving toward a more representative sampling of the behaviors involved in leadership—heralds a productive advance in research and training.

Second, the introduction of environmental (as opposed to situational) variables into the leadership context has yielded some interesting results. Pfeffer (1978), for example, has argued that leadership doesn't matter as much as we think it does. Reviewing a number of studies which examined the impact of such things as budgets, economic conditions, changes in top executive positions, and role-set expectations, he found that these and similar factors frequently override the effects of leadership on organizational outcomes.

To date, most leadership theories make the implicit assumption that the leader has a great deal of unilateral control: if the leader only used the appropriate style, the group would be more productive; if the leader understood group processes, the group would be more cohesive, creative, and effective. Understanding how nonleader variables influence such outcomes would help both researchers and leaders by providing a more realistic perspective on just what the leader can and cannot hope to achieve.

Third, the measure of a leader's effectiveness is not and cannot be a simple index of group productivity or satisfaction. While group-level variables are important, there are too many factors mitigating the effects of the leader's behavior on work-group outcomes; and there are many leadership roles for which the "work group" cannot be identified precisely (for example, the role of senator) or for which group output is heavily determined by some factor such as technology (for example, on the assembly line). At a minimum, both researchers and practitioners must realize that leadership effectiveness involves a number of areas of functioning—including how well the leader deals with nonsubordinate relationships, how structures are designed and modified, development of human resources in the organization, utilization and dissemination of knowledge, creating and coping with change, and actual task performance by the leader. The point is that simplified criteria are misleading, and breaking the rut of current leadership research will require increasing emphasis on the development of realistic performance measures.

Fourth, in most leadership research (and training) the situation is treated as a given. The technology is this, the climate is that, the task is something else. In reality, these and other components of a system are constantly changing. New machinery, new policies, new people are always entering systems (though the rate of change may vary), and the degree to which organizational components are interdependent is itself a variable (Weick, 1974). Leaders, then, do not simply face a number of different situations, but the situations themselves are changing. Part of the leadership process is clearly the leader's attempt to map the organizational dynamics which influence his or her functioning in the leadership role. Another component is how leaders influence the dynamics of their organizational environments by using, modifying, and implementing structure.

SOME CONCLUDING REMARKS

When managers are told that their work is characterized by brevity, variety, fragmentation, a lot of activities, and oral communication, they frequently respond, "You didn't have to tell us that." But these characteristics of managerial work, coupled with the organizational and environmental context within which the work takes place, suggest some new ways of focusing on leadership processes.

First, it is a mistake for leaders or researchers to assume that "the situation" is composed of a small number of fixed parts. The organization, and its environment, are dynamic. An act of Congress, a new invention, or a new corporate president may change all existing cause and effect relationships overnight. Effective leadership behavior must involve flexibility in thinking about the givens of organizational life. Fire-fighting is the bane of many a manager's existence, but the ability of a leader to negotiate successfully through a constant barrage of changes and incongruities is an important component of the leadership process.

Second, it is a mistake to assume that a leadership

role, even with its trappings of authority, implies unilateral control by the leader. Organizational rewards and structures, as well as external forces, limit both the leader's and the group's flexibility. Another important component of leadership, then, is how the role occupants create, modify, work around, or ignore the structures imposed on them and their followers. Kerr (1975) has provided numerous examples of how organizations (and the leaders in them) hope for one behavior and get another by inadvertently rewarding the wrong things. DeVries (1978) has shown that relatively simple structures used by a teacher can facilitate classroom learning. These two examples indicate that leaders can succeed not just because of personal charisma or social influence, but because of a sensitivity to, and awareness of, organizational structures and reward systems.

Third, much of human learning is dependent on the receipt of valid and timely feedback on the results of behavior. With all its variety and fragmentation, managerial work provides inadequate feedback—and sometimes none at all. Occupants of leadership roles carry a double burden because they must not only assure themselves of adequate feedback, but also must facilitate feedback to their subordinates (and to other units or individuals working with the unit). Since much of managerial communication is oral, the job of obtaining and transmitting feedback requires substantial effort. No individual in a leadership role can hope to take full responsibility for providing feedback for all who need it. While the personal element cannot be ignored, the leader's use of structural (e.g., designing tasks to provide feedback or *using* an appraisal system to generate valid data) and reward (e.g., basing part of promotion or salary on feedback generation) systems may be a critical component.

Fourth, political activity—in the sense of developing and maintaining a network of contacts throughout the organization and its environment (Mintzberg, 1973)—is a real part of managerial work. Research has not revealed much about how these networks are created and used, but most people in leadership roles know how important contacts can be. Many of the contacts are in nonauthority relationships with the leader, and this may be the arena where the critical social and political influence aspects of leadership are played out (Pettigrew, 1973).

Certainly, leadership research and theory should begin including this dimension, and practitioners might look at some of their problems in "getting things done" in light of their own interconnectedness with key people in the organization.

The four areas outlined above by no means cover all of the possibilities for expanding thinking about leadership processes. They do reflect some areas which have received insufficient attention in leadership research and training. In sum, the focus on leader-group interactions has yielded some useful information, but much remains to be learned about the leadership processes going on outside of the immediate work setting. By learning more about what leaders actually do, researchers can expose themselves to numerous activities not considered by most traditional approaches to the topic. It is in the day-to-day activities of leaders that the situational-organizational context of leadership is sharply reflected.

Peter Vaill, (1978), has defined an art as "the attempt to wrest more coherence and meaning out of more reality than we ordinarily try to deal with." In this context, he has described management as a performing art (1974). The analogy of leaders as artists is potent because effective leaders orchestrate a complex series of processes, events, and systems. Understanding bits and pieces—using a stop-frame on Nureyev—can never capture the whole. Perhaps neither researchers nor practitioners will ever understand the particular magic that makes the legends of leadership. To the extent that constant practice makes the artist more than he or she might have been, expanding our knowledge of the complex processes involved in leadership may, one day, provide part of that magic formula for success.

REFERENCES

Ackoff, R. L. Management misinformation systems. *Management Science,* 1967, **14,** B147–B156.

Bennis, W. G. Leadership theory and administrative behavior: The problem of authority. *Administrative Science Quarterly,* 1959, **4,** 259–301.

Blake, R. R., & Mouton, J. S. *The managerial grid.* Houston: Gulf, 1964.

Bray, D. W., Campbell, R. J., & Grant, D. L. *Formative years in business.* New York: Wiley, 1974.

Brewer, E., & Tomlinson, J. W. C. The manager's work-

ing day. *Journal of Industrial Economics,* 1963–64, **12,** 191–197.

Calder, B. J. An attribution theory of leadership. In B. M. Staw & G. R. Salancik (Eds.), *New directions in organizational behavior.* Chicago: St. Clair Press, 1977.

Campbell, J. P. Personnel training and development. In P. Mussen & M. Rosenzweig (Eds.), *Annual Review of Psychology,* 1971, **22,** 565–602.

———, & Dunnette, M. D. Effectiveness of T-group experiences in managerial training and development. *Psychological Bulletin,* 1968, **70,** 73–104.

———, Dunnette, M. D., Lawler, E. E., III, & Weick, K. E., Jr. *Managerial behavior, performance, and effectiveness.* New York: McGraw-Hill, 1970.

Carlson, S. *Executive behaviour.* Stockholm: Strombergs, 1951.

Cyert, R. M., & March, J. G. *A behavioral theory of the firm.* Englewood Cliffs, N.J.: Prentice-Hall, 1963.

De Vries, D. L., & Slavin, R. E. Teams-Games-Tournaments (TGT): Review of ten classroom experiments. *Journal of Research and Development in Education,* 1978, **12,** 28–38.

Dubin, R. Business behavior behaviorally viewed. In G. B. Strother (Ed.), *Social science approaches to business behavior.* Homewood, Ill.: Dorsey, 1962.

———, & Spray, S. L. Executive behavior and interaction. *Industrial Relations,* 1964, **3**(2), 99–108.

Evans, M. The effects of supervisory behavior on the path-goal relationship. *Organizational Behavior and Human Performance,* 1970, **5,** 277–298.

Farris, G. F., & Lim, F., Jr. Effects of performance on leadership, cohesiveness, influence, satisfaction, and subsequent performance. *Journal of Applied Psychology,* 1969, **53,** 490–497.

Fiedler, F. E. *A theory of leadership effectiveness.* New York: McGraw-Hill, 1967.

Gibb, C. A. Leadership. In G. Lindzey & E. Aronson (Eds.), *The handbook of social psychology,* 2d ed., Vol. 4. Reading, Mass.: Addison-Wesley, 1969.

Graen, G., & Cashman, J. F. A role-making model of leadership in formal organizations: A developmental approach. In J. G. Hunt & L. L. Larson (Eds.), *Leadership frontiers.* Kent, Ohio: Kent State University Press, Comparative Administration Research Institute, 1976.

Greene, C. N. The reciprocal nature of influence between leader and subordinate. *Journal of Applied Psychology,* 1975, **60,** 187–193.

Guest, R. H. Of time and the foreman. *Personnel,* 1955–56, **32,** 478–486.

Hill, W. Leadership style: Rigid or flexible. *Organizational Behavior and Human Performance,* 1973, **9,** 35–47.

———, & Hughes, D. Variations in leader behavior as a

function of task type. *Organizational Behavior and Human Performance,* 1974, **11,** 83–86.

Horne, J. H., & Lupton, T. The work activities of "middle" managers—an exploratory study. *Journal of Management Studies,* 1965, **2**(1), 14–33.

House, R. J. A path goal theory of leader effectiveness. *Administrative Science Quarterly,* 1971, **16,** 321–338.

Jaffee, C. L., & Lucas, R. L. Effects of rates of talking and correctness of decisions on leader choice in small groups. *Journal of Social Psychology,* 1969, **79,** 247–254.

Katz, D., & Kahn, R. L. *The social psychology of organizations.* New York: Wiley, 1966.

Kerr, S. On the folly of rewarding A, while hoping for B. *Academy of Management Journal,* 1975, **18,** 769–783.

Korman, A. K. Contingency approaches to leadership: An overview. In J. G. Hunt & L. L. Larson (Eds.), *Contingency approaches to leadership.* Carbondale: Southern Illinois University Press, 1974.

Kurke, L. B., & Aldrich, H. E. Mintzberg was right: A replication and extension of *The Nature of Managerial Work.* In R. Osborn (Chair), *Managerial roles in formal organizations.* Symposium presented at the meeting of the Academy of Management, Atlanta, August 1979.

Larson, L. L., Hunt, J. G., & Osborn, R. N. The great hi-hi leader behavior myth: A lesson from Occam's razor. In A. G. Bedeian et al. (Eds.), *Proceedings of the 35th Annual Meeting of the Academy of Management,* 1975, 170–172.

Lowin, A., & Craig, J. R. The influence of level of performance on managerial style: An experimental object-lesson in the ambiguity of correlational data. *Organizational Behavior and Human Performance,* 1968, **3,** 440–458.

Lundberg, C. The unreported research of Dr. Hypothetical: Six variables in need of recognition. In M. W. McCall, Jr., & M. M. Lombardo (Eds.), *Leadership: Where else can we go?* Durham, N.C.: Duke University Press, 1978.

McCall, M. W., Jr. The perceived cognitive role requirements of formal leaders. In N. A. Rosen (Chair), *Some neglected aspects of research on leadership in formal organizations.* Symposium presented at the meeting of the American Psychological Association, New Orleans, August 1974.

———, Morrison, A. M., & Hannan, R. L. *Studies of managerial work: Results and methods* (Tech. Rep. No. 9). Greensboro, N.C.: Center for Creative Leadership, 1978.

March, J. G., & Simon, H. A. *Organizations.* New York: Wiley 1958.

Miner, J. B. *The uncertain future of the leadership concept: An overview.* Paper presented at the Southern Illinois Leadership Conference, Carbondale, Ill., 1975.

Mintzberg, H. *The nature of managerial work.* New York: Harper & Row, 1973.

———. The manager's job: Folklore and fact. *Harvard Business Review,* 1975, **53**(4), 49–61.

Omstead, J. A., et al. *Development of leadership assessment simulations* (HumRRO Tech. Rep. 73–21). Arlington, Va.: Human Resources Research Organization, September 1973.

Pettigrew, A. M. *The politics of organizational decision-making.* London: Tavistock, 1973.

Pfeffer, J. The ambiguity of leadership. In M. W. McCall, Jr., & M. M. Lombardo (Eds.), *Leadership: Where else can we go?* Durham, N.C.: Duke University Press, 1978.

Rosen, N. A. *Leadership change and work-group dynamics.* London: Staples Press, 1970.

Rubin, I. M., & Goldman, M. An open system model of leadership performance. *Organizational Behavior and Human Performance,* 1968, **3,** 143–156.

Sayles, L. *Managerial behavior: Administration in complex organizations.* New York: McGraw-Hill, 1964.

———. *Leadership: What effective managers really do . . . and how they do it.* New York: McGraw-Hill, 1979.

Stogdill, R. M. *Handbook of leadership.* New York: Free Press, 1974.

Vaill, P. B. *On the general theory of management.* Paper presented at the Washington, D.C., chapter of the Society for Humanistic Management, November 19, 1974.

———. Towards a behavioral description of high-performing systems. In M. W. McCall, Jr., & M. M. Lombardo (Eds.), *Leadership: Where else can we go?* Durham, N.C.: Duke University Press, 1978.

Vroom, V. H., & Yetton, P. W. *Leadership and decision making.* Pittsburgh: University of Pittsburgh Press, 1973.

Weick, K. E. Laboratory experimentation with organizations. In J. G. March (Ed.), *Handbook of organizations.* Chicago: Rand McNally, 1965.

———. *The social psychology of organizing.* Reading, Mass.: Addison-Wesley, 1969.

———. Middle range theories of social systems. *Behavioral Science,* 1974, **19,** 357–367.

Reading 46

The Ambiguity of Leadership

Jeffrey Pfeffer

Leadership has for some time been a major topic in social and organizational psychology. Underlying much of this research has been the assumption that leadership is causally related to organizational performance. Through an analysis of leadership styles, behaviors, or characteristics (depending on the theoretical perspective chosen), the argument has been made that more effective leaders can be selected or trained or, alternatively, the situation can be configured to provide for enhanced leader and organizational effectiveness.

Three problems with emphasis on leadership as a concept can be posed: (a) ambiguity in definition and measurement of the concept itself; (b) the question of whether leadership has discernible effects on organizational outcomes; and (c) the selection process in succession to leadership positions, which frequently uses organizationally irrelevant criteria and which has implications for normative theories of leadership. The argument here is that leadership is of interest primarily as a phenomenological construct. Leaders serve as symbols for representing personal causation of social events. How and why are such attributions of personal effects made? Instead of focusing on leadership and its effects, how do people make inferences about and react to phenomena labelled as leadership (5)?

THE AMBIGUITY OF THE CONCEPT

While there have been many studies of leadership, the dimensions and definition of the concept remain unclear. To treat leadership as a separate concept, it must be distinguished from other social influence phenomena. Hollander and Julian (24) and Bavelas (2) did not draw distinctions between leadership and other processes of social influence. A major point of the Hollander and Julian review was that leadership research might develop more rapidly if more general theories of social influence were incorporated. Calder (5) also argued that there is no unique content to the construct of leadership that is not subsumed under other, more general models of behavior.

Kochan, Schmidt, and DeCotiis (33) attempted to distinguish leadership from related concepts of authority and social power. In leadership, influence rights are voluntarily conferred. Power does not require goal compatability—merely dependence—but leadership implies some congruence between the objectives of the leader and the led. These distinctions depend on the ability to distinguish voluntary from involuntary compliance and to assess goal compatibility. Goal statements may be retrospective inferences from action (46, 53) and problems of distinguishing voluntary from involuntary compliance also exist (32). Apparently there are few meaningful distinctions between leadership and other concepts of social influence. Thus, an understanding of the phenomena subsumed under the rubric of leadership may not require the construct of leadership (5).

While there is some agreement that leadership is related to social influence, more disagreement concerns the basic dimensions of leader behavior. Some have argued that there are two tasks to be accomplished in groups—maintenance of the group and performance of some task or activity—and thus leader behavior might be described along these two dimensions (1, 6, 8, 25). The dimensions emerging from the Ohio State leadership studies—consideration and initiating structure—may be seen as similar to the two components of group maintenance and task accomplishment (18).

Other dimensions of leadership behavior have also been proposed (4). Day and Hamblin (10) analyzed leadership in terms of the closeness and punitiveness of the supervision. Several authors have conceptualized leadership behavior in terms of the authority and discretion subordinates are permitted (23, 36, 51). Fiedler (14) analyzed leadership in terms of the least-preferred-co-worker scale (LPC), but the meaning and behavioral attributes of

Author's note: An earlier version of this paper was presented at the conference, Leadership: Where Else Can We Go?, Center for Creative Leadership, Greensboro, North Carolina, June 30–July 1, 1975.

this dimension of leadership behavior remain controversial.

The proliferation of dimensions is partly a function of research strategies frequently employed. Factor analysis on a large number of items describing behavior has frequently been used. This procedure tends to produce as many factors as the analyst decides to find, and permits the development of a large number of possible factor structures. The resultant factors must be named and further imprecision is introduced. Deciding on a summative concept to represent a factor is inevitably a partly subjective process.

Literature assessing the effects of leadership tends to be equivocal. Sales (45) summarized leadership literature employing the authoritarian-democratic typology and concluded that effects on performance were small and inconsistent. Reviewing the literature on consideration and initiating structure dimensions, Korman (34) reported relatively small and inconsistent results, and Kerr and Schriesheim (30) reported more consistent effects of the two dimensions. Better results apparently emerge when moderating factors are taken into account, including subordinate personalities (50), and situational characteristics (23, 51). Kerr, et al. (31) list many moderating effects grouped under the headings of subordinate considerations, supervisor considerations, and task considerations. Even if each set of considerations consisted of only one factor (which it does not), an attempt to account for the effects of leader behavior would necessitate considering four-way interactions. While social reality is complex and contingent, it seems desirable to attempt to find more parsimonious explanations for the phenomena under study.

THE EFFECTS OF LEADERS

Hall asked a basic question about leadership: is there any evidence on the magnitude of the effects of leadership (17, p. 248)? Surprisingly, he could find little evidence. Given the resources that have been spent studying, selecting, and training leaders, one might expect that the question of whether or not leaders matter would have been addressed earlier (12).

There are at least three reasons why it might be argued that the observed effects of leaders on organizational outcomes would be small. First, those obtaining leadership positions are selected, and perhaps only certain, limited styles of behavior may be chosen. Second, once in the leadership position, the discretion and behavior of the leader are constrained. And third, leaders can typically affect only a few of the variables that may impact organizational performance.

Homogeneity of Leaders

Persons are selected to leadership positions. As a consequence of this selection process, the range of behaviors or characteristics exhibited by leaders is reduced, making it more problematic to empirically discover an effect of leadership. There are many types of constraints on the selection process. The attraction literature suggests that there is a tendency for persons to like those they perceive as similar (3). In critical decisions such as the selections of persons for leadership positions, compatible styles of behavior probably will be chosen.

Selection of persons is also constrained by the internal system of influence in the organization. As Zald (56) noted, succession is a critical decision, affected by political influence and by environmental contingencies faced by the organization. As Thompson (49) noted, leaders may be selected for their capacity to deal with various organizational contingencies. In a study of characteristics of hospital administrators, Pfeffer and Salancik (42) found a relationship between the hospital's context and the characteristics and tenure of the administrators. To the extent that the contingencies and power distribution within the organization remain stable, the abilities and behaviors of those selected into leadership positions will also remain stable.

Finally, the selection of persons to leadership positions is affected by a self-selection process. Organizations and roles have images, providing information about their character. Persons are likely to select themselves into organizations and roles based upon their preferences for the dimensions of the organizational and role characteristics as perceived through these images. The self-selection of persons would tend to work along with organizational selection to limit the range of abilities and behaviors in a given organizational role.

Such selection processes would tend to increase homogeneity more within a single organization than across organizations. Yet many studies of leadership effect at the work group level have compared groups within a single organization. If there comes to be a widely shared, socially constructed definition of leadership behaviors or characteristics which guides the selection process, then leadership activity may come to be defined similarly in various organizations, leading to the selection of only those who match the constructed image of a leader.

Constraints on Leader Behavior

Analyses of leadership have frequently presumed that leadership style or leader behavior was an independent variable that could be selected or trained at will to conform to what research would find to be optimal. Even theorists who took a more contingent view of appropriate leadership behavior generally assumed that with proper training, appropriate behavior could be produced (51). Fiedler (13), noting how hard it was to change behavior, suggested changing the situational characteristics rather than the person, but this was an unusual suggestion in the context of prevailing literature which suggested that leadership style was something to be strategically selected according to the variables of the particular leadership theory.

But the leader is embedded in a social system, which constrains behavior. The leader has a role set (27), in which members have expectations for appropriate behavior and persons make efforts to modify the leader's behavior. Pressures to conform to the expectations of peers, subordinates, and superiors are all relevant in determining actual behavior.

Leaders, even in high-level positions, have unilateral control over fewer resources and fewer policies than might be expected. Investment decisions may require approval of others, while hiring and promotion decisions may be accomplished by committees. Leader behavior is constrained by both the demands of others in the role set and by organizationally prescribed limitations on the sphere of activity and influence.

External Factors

Many factors that may affect organizational performance are outside a leader's control, even if he or she were to have complete discretion over major areas of organizational decisions. For example, consider the executive in a construction firm. Costs are largely determined by operation of commodities and labor markets; and demand is largely affected by interest rates, availability of mortgage money, and economic conditions which are affected by governmental policies over which the executive has little control. School superintendents have little control over birth rates and community economic development, both of which profoundly affect school system budgets. While the leader may react to contingencies as they arise, or may be a better or worse forecaster, in accounting for variation in organizational outcomes, he or she may account for relatively little compared to external factors.

Second, the leader's success or failure may be partly due to circumstances unique to the organization but still outside his or her control. Leader positions in organizations vary in terms of the strength and position of the organization. The choice of a new executive does not fundamentally alter a market and financial position that has developed over years and affects the leader's ability to make strategic changes and the likelihood that the organization will do well or poorly. Organizations have relatively enduring strengths and weaknesses. The choice of a particular leader for a particular position has limited impact on these capabilities.

Empirical Evidence

Two studies have assessed the effects of leadership changes in major positions in organizations. Lieberson and O'Connor (35) examined 167 business firms in 13 industries over a 20 year period, allocating variance in sales, profits, and profit margins to one of four sources: year (general economic conditions), industry, company effects, and effects of changes in the top executive position. They concluded that compared to other factors, administration had a limited effect on organizational outcomes.

Using a similar analytical procedure, Salancik and Pfeffer (44) examined the effects of mayors on city budgets for 30 U.S. cities. Data on expenditures by budget category were collected for 1951–1968. Variance in amount and proportion of expenditures was apportioned to the year, the city, or the mayor. The mayoral effect was relatively small, with the city accounting for most of the variance, although the mayor effect was larger for expenditure categories that were not as directly connected to important interest groups. Salancik and Pfeffer argued that the effects of the mayor were limited both by absence of power to control many of the expenditures and tax sources, and by construction of policies in response to demands from interests in the environment.

If leadership is defined as a strictly interpersonal phenomenon, the relevance of these two studies for the issue of leadership effects becomes problematic. But such a conceptualization seems unduly restrictive, and is certainly inconsistent with Selznick's (47) conceptualization of leadership as strategic management and decision making. If one cannot observe differences when leaders change, then what does it matter who occupies the positions or how they behave?

Pfeffer and Salancik (41) investigated the extent to which behaviors selected by first-line supervisors were constrained by expectations of others in their role set. Variance in task and social behaviors could be accounted for by role-set expectations, with adherence to various demands made by role-set participants a function of similarity and relative power. Lowin and Craig (37) experimentally demonstrated that leader behavior was determined by the subordinate's own behavior. Both studies illustrate that leader behaviors are responses to the demands of the social context.

The effect of leadership may vary depending upon level in the organizational hierarchy, while the appropriate activities and behaviors may also vary with organizational level (26, 40). For the most part, empirical studies of leadership have dealt with first-line supervisors or leaders with relatively low organizational status (17). If leadership has any impact, it should be more evident at higher organizational levels or where there is more discretion in decisions and activities.

THE PROCESS OF SELECTING LEADERS

Along with the suggestion that leadership may not account for much variance in organizational outcomes, it can be argued that merit or ability may not account for much variation in hiring and advancement of organizational personnel. These two ideas are related. If competence is hard to judge, or if leadership competence does not greatly affect organizational outcomes, then other, person-dependent criteria may be sufficient. Effective leadership styles may not predict career success when other variables such as social background are controlled.

Belief in the importance of leadership is frequently accompanied by belief that persons occupying leadership positions are selected and trained according to how well they can enhance the organization's performance. Belief in a leadership effect leads to development of a set of activities oriented toward enhancing leadership effectiveness. Simultaneously, persons managing their own careers are likely to place emphasis on activities and developing behaviors that will enhance their own leadership skills, assuming that such a strategy will facilitate advancement.

Research on the bases for hiring and promotion has been concentrated on examination of academic positions (e.g., 7, 19, 20). This is possibly the result of availability of relatively precise and unambiguous measures of performance, such as number of publications or citations. Evidence on criteria used in selecting and advancing personnel in industry is more indirect.

Studies have attempted to predict either the compensation or the attainment of general management positions of MBA students, using personality and other background information (21, 22, 54). There is some evidence that managerial success can be predicted by indicators of ability and motivation such as test scores and grades, but the amount of variance explained is typically quite small.

A second line of research has investigated characteristics and backgrounds of persons attaining leadership positions in major organizations in society. Domhoff (11), Mills (38), and Warner and Abbeglin (52) found a strong preponderance of persons with upper-class backgrounds occupying leadership positions. The implication of these findings is that studies of graduate success, including the success of MBA's, would explain more variance if the family background of the person were included.

A third line of inquiry uses a tracking model. The dynamic model developed is one in which access to elite universities is affected by social status (28) and, in turn, social status and attendance at elite universities affect later career outcomes (9, 43, 48, 55).

Unless one is willing to make the argument that attendance at elite universities or coming from an upper-class background is perfectly correlated with merit, the evidence suggests that succession to leadership positions is not strictly based on meritocratic criteria. Such a conclusion is consistent with the inability of studies attempting to predict the success of MBA graduates to account for much variance, even when a variety of personality and ability factors are used.

Beliefs about the bases for social mobility are important for social stability. As long as persons believe that positions are allocated on meritocratic grounds, they are more likely to be satisfied with the social order and with their position in it. This satisfaction derives from the belief that occupational position results from application of fair and reasonable criteria, and that the opportunity exists for mobility if the person improves skills and performance.

If succession to leadership positions is determined by person-based criteria such as social origins or social connections (16), then efforts to enhance managerial effectiveness with the expectation that this will lead to career success divert attention from the processes of stratification actually operating within organizations. Leadership literature has been implicitly aimed at two audiences. Organizations were told how to become more effective, and persons were told what behaviors to acquire in order to become effective, and hence, advance in their careers. The possibility that neither organizational outcomes nor career success are related to leadership behaviors leaves leadership research facing issues of relevance and importance.

THE ATTRIBUTION OF LEADERSHIP

Kelley conceptualized the layman as:

> an applied scientist, that is, as a person concerned about applying his knowledge of causal relationships in order to *exercise control* of his world (29, p. 2).

Reviewing a series of studies dealing with the attributional process, he concluded that persons were not only interested in understanding their world correctly, but also in controlling it.

> The view here proposed is that attribution processes are to be understood not only as a means of providing the individual with a veridical view of his world, but as a means of encouraging and maintaining his effective exercise of control in that world (29, p. 22).

Controllable factors will have high salience as candidates for causal explanation, while a bias toward the more important causes may shift the attributional emphasis toward causes that are not controllable (29, p. 23). The study of attribution is a study of naive psychology—an examination of how persons make sense out of the events taking place around them.

If Kelley is correct that individuals will tend to develop attributions that give them a feeling of control, then emphasis on leadership may derive partially from a desire to believe in the effectiveness and importance of individual action, since individual action is more controllable than contextual variables. Lieberson and O'Connor (35) made essentially the same point in introducing their paper on the effects of top management changes on organizational performance. Given the desire for control and a feeling of personal effectiveness, organizational outcomes are more likely to be attributed to individual actions, regardless of their actual causes.

Leadership is attributed by observers. Social action has meaning only through a phenomenological process (46). The identification of certain organizational roles as leadership positions guides the construction of meaning in the direction of attributing effects to the actions of those positions. While Bavelas (2) argued that the functions of leadership, such as task accomplishment and group maintenance, are shared throughout the group, this fact provides no simply and potentially controllable focus for attributing causality. Rather, the identification of leadership positions provides a simpler and more readily changeable model of reality. When causality is lodged in one or a few persons rather than being a function of a complex set of interactions among all group members, changes can be made by replacing or influencing the occupant of the leadership position. Causes of organizational actions are readily identified in this simple causal structure.

Even if, empirically, leadership has little effect, and even if succession to leadership positions is not predicated on ability or performance, the belief in leadership effects and meritocratic succession provides a simple causal framework and a justification for the structure of the social collectivity. More importantly, the beliefs interpret social actions in terms that indicate potential for effective individual intervention or control. The personification of social causality serves too many uses to be easily overcome. Whether or not leader behavior actually influences performance or effectiveness, it is important because people believe it does.

One consequence of the attribution of causality to leaders and leadership is that leaders come to be symbols. Mintzberg (39), in his discussion of the roles of managers, wrote of the symbolic role, but more in terms of attendance at formal events and formally representing the organization. The symbolic role of leadership is more important than implied in such a description. The leader as a symbol provides a target for action when difficulties occur, serving as a scapegoat when things go wrong. Gamson and Scotch (15) noted that in baseball, the firing of the manager served a scapegoating purpose. One cannot fire the whole team, yet when performance is poor, something must be done. The firing of the manager conveys to the world and to the actors involved that success is the result of personal actions, and that steps can and will be taken to enhance organizational performance.

The attribution of causality to leadership may be reinforced by organizational actions, such as the inauguration process, the choice process, and providing the leader with symbols and ceremony. If leaders are chosen by using a random number table, persons are less likely to believe in their effects than if there is an elaborate search or selection process followed by an elaborate ceremony signifying the changing of control, and if the leader then has a variety of perquisites and symbols that distinguish him or her from the rest of the organization. Construction of the importance of leadership in a given social context is the outcome of various social processes, which can be empirically examined.

Since belief in the leadership effect provides a feeling of personal control, one might argue that efforts to increase the attribution of causality to leaders would occur more when it is more necessary and more problematic to attribute causality to controllable factors. Such an argument would lead to the hypothesis that the more the *context* actually effects organizational outcomes, the more efforts will be made to ensure attribution to *leadership*. When leaders really do have effects, it is less necessary to engage in rituals indicating their effects. Such rituals are more likely when there is uncertainty and unpredictability associated with the organization's operations. This results both from the desire to feel control in uncertain situations and from the fact that in ambiguous contexts, it is easier to attribute consequences to leadership without facing possible disconfirmation.

The leader is, in part, an actor. Through statements and actions, the leader attempts to reinforce the operation of an attribution process which tends to vest causality in that position in the social structure. Successful leaders, as perceived by members of the social system, are those who can separate themselves from organizational failures and associate themselves with organizational successes. Since the meaning of action is socially constructed, this involves manipulation of symbols to reinforce the desired process of attribution. For instance, if a manager knows that business in his or her division is about to improve because of the economic cycle, the leader may, nevertheless, write recommendations and undertake actions and changes that are highly visible and that will tend to identify his or her behavior closely with the division. A manager who perceives impending failure will attempt to associate the division and its policies and decisions with others, particularly persons in higher organizational positions, and to disassociate himself or herself from the division's performance, occasionally even transferring or moving to another organization.

CONCLUSION

The theme of this article has been that analysis of leadership and leadership processes must be contingent on the intent of the researcher. If the interest is in understanding the causality of social phenomena as reliably and accurately as possible, then the concept of leadership may be a poor place to begin. The issue of the effects of leadership is open to question. But examination of situational variables that accompany more or less leadership effect is a worthwhile task.

The more phenomenological analysis of leadership directs attention to the process by which social causality is attributed, and focuses on the distinction between causality as perceived by group members and causality as assessed by an outside observer. Leadership is associated with a set of myths reinforcing a social construction of meaning which legitimates leadership role occupants, provides belief in potential mobility for those not in leadership roles, and attributes social causality to leadership roles, thereby providing a belief in the effectiveness of individual control. In analyzing leadership, this mythology and the process by which such mythology is created and supported should be separated from analysis of leadership as a social influence process, operating within constraints.

REFERENCES

1 Bales, R. F. *Interaction Process Analysis: A Method for the Study of Small Groups* (Reading, Mass.: Addison-Wesley, 1950).

2 Bavelas, Alex. "Leadership: Man and Function," *Administrative Science Quarterly,* Vol. 4 (1960), 491–498.

3 Berscheid, Ellen, and Elaine Walster. *Interpersonal Attraction* (Reading, Mass.: Addison-Wesley, 1969).

4 Bowers, David G., and Stanley E. Seashore. "Predicting Organizational Effectiveness with a Four-Factor Theory of Leadership." *Administrative Science Quarterly,* Vol. 11 (1966), 238–263.

5 Calder, Bobby J. "An Attribution Theory of Leadership," in B. Staw and G. Salancik (Eds.), *New Directions in Organizational Behavior* (Chicago: St. Clair Press, 1976), in press.

6 Cartwright, Dorwin C., and Alvin Zander. *Group Dynamics: Research and Theory,* 3rd ed. (Evanston, Ill.: Row, Peterson, 1960).

7 Cole, Jonathan R., and Stephen Cole. *Social Stratification in Science* (Chicago: University of Chicago Press, 1973).

8 Collins, Barry E., and Harold Guetzkow. *A Social Psychology of Group Processes for Decision-Making* (New York: Wiley, 1964).

9 Collins, Randall. "Functional and Conflict Theories of Stratification," *American Sociological Review,* Vol. 36 (1971), 1002–1019.

10 Day, R. C., and R. L. Hamblin. "Some Effects of Close and Punitive Styles of Supervision," *American Journal of Sociology,* Vol. 69 (1964), 499–510.

11 Domhoff, G. William. *Who Rules America?* (Englewood Cliffs, N.J.: Prentice-Hall, 1967).

12 Dubin, Robert. "Supervision and Productivity: Empirical Findings and Theoretical Considerations," in R. Dubin, G. C. Homans, F. C. Mann, and D. C. Miller (Eds.), *Leadership and Productivity* (San Francisco: Chandler Publishing Co., 1965), pp. 1–50.

13 Fiedler, Fred E. "Engineering the Job to Fit the Manager," *Harvard Business Review,* Vol. 43 (1965), 115–122.

14 Fiedler, Fred E. *A Theory of Leadership Effectiveness* (New York: McGraw-Hill, 1967).

15 Gamson, William A., and Norman A Scotch. "Scapegoating in Baseball," *American Journal of Sociology,* Vol. 70 (1964), 69–72.

16 Granovetter, Mark. *Getting a Job* (Cambridge, Mass.: Harvard University Press, 1974).

17 Hall, Richard H. *Organizations: Structure and Process* (Englewood Cliffs, N.J.: Prentice-Hall, 1972).

18 Halpin, A. W., and J. Winer. "A Factorial Study of the Leader Behavior Description Questionnaire," in R. M. Stogdill and A. E. Coons (Eds.), *Leader Behavior: Its Description and Measurement* (Columbus, Ohio: Bureau of Business Research, Ohio State University, 1957), pp. 39–51.

19 Hargens, L. L. "Patterns of Mobility of New Ph.D.'s Among American Academic Institutions," *Sociology of Education,* Vol. 42 (1969), 18–37.

20 Hargens, L. L., and W. O. Hagstrom. "Sponsored and Contest Mobility of American Academic Scientists," *Sociology of Education,* Vol. 40 (1967), 24–38.

21 Harrell, Thomas W. "High Earning MBA's," *Personnel Psychology,* Vol. 25 (1972), 523–530.

22 Harrell, Thomas W., and Margaret S. Harrell. "Predictors of Management Success." *Stanford University Graduate School of Business, Technical Report No. 3 to the Office of Naval Research.*

23 Heller, Frank, and Gary Yukl. "Participation, Managerial Decision-Making, and Situational Variables," *Organizational Behavior and Human Performance,* Vol. 4 (1969), 227–241.

24 Hollander, Edwin P., and James W. Julian. "Contemporary Trends in the Analysis of Leadership Processes," *Psychological Bulletin,* Vol. 71 (1969), 387–397.

25 House, Robert J. "A Path Goal Theory of Leader Effectiveness," *Administrative Science Quarterly,* Vol. 16 (1971), 321–338.

26 Hunt, J. G. "Leadership Style Effects at Two Managerial Levels in a Simulated Organization," *Administrative Science Quarterly,* Vol. 16 (1971), 476–485.

27 Kahn, R. L., D. M. Wolfe, R. P. Quinn, and J. D. Snoek. *Organizational Stress: Studies in Role Conflict and Ambiguity* (New York: Wiley, 1964).

28 Karabel, J., and A. W. Astin. "Social Class, Academic Ability, and College 'Quality'," *Social Forces,* Vol. 53 (1975), 381–398.

29 Kelley, Harold H. *Attribution in Social Interaction* (Morristown, N.J.: General Learning Press, 1971).

30 Kerr, Steven, and Chester Schriesheim. "Consideration, Initiating Structure and Organizational Criteria—An Update of Korman's 1966 Review," *Personnel Psychology,* Vol. 27 (1974), 555–568.

31 Kerr, S., C. Schriesheim, C. J. Murphy, and R. M. Stogdill, "Toward A Contingency Theory of Leadership Based Upon the Consideration and Initiating Structure Literature," *Organizational Behavior and Human Performance,* Vol. 12 (1974), 62–82.

32 Kiesler, C., and S. Kiesler. *Conformity* (Reading, Mass.: Addison-Wesley, 1969).

33 Kochan, T. A., S. M. Schmidt, and T. A. DeCotiis. "Superior-Subordinate Relations: Leadership and Headship," *Human Relations,* Vol. 28 (1975), 279–294.

34 Korman, A. K. "Consideration, Initiating Structure, and Organizational Criteria—A Review," *Personnel Psychology,* Vol. 19 (1966), 349–362.

35 Lieberson, Stanley, and James F. O'Connor. "Leadership and Organizational Performance: A Study of Large Corporations," *American Sociological Review,* Vol. 37 (1972), 117–130.

36 Lippitt, Ronald. "An Experimental Study of the Effect of Democratic and Authoritarian Group Atmospheres," *University of Iowa Studies in Child Welfare,* Vol. 16 (1940), 43–195.

37 Lowin, A., and J. R. Craig. "The Influence of Level of Performance on Managerial Style: An Experimental Object-Lesson in the Ambiguity of Correlational Data," *Organizational Behavior and Human Performance,* Vol. 3 (1968), 440–458.

38 Mills, C. Wright. "The American Business Elite: A Collective Portrait," in C. W. Mills, *Power, Politics, and People* (New York: Oxford University Press, 1963), pp. 110–139.

39 Mintzberg, Henry. *The Nature of Managerial Work* (New York: Harper and Row, 1973).

40 Nealey, Stanley M., and Milton R. Blood. "Leadership Performance of Nursing Supervisors at Two Organizational Levels," *Journal of Applied Psychology,* Vol. 52 (1968), 414–442.

41 Pfeffer, Jeffrey, and Gerald R. Salancik. "Determinants of Supervisory Behavior: A Role Set Analysis," *Human Relations,* Vol. 28 (1975), 139–154.

42 Pfeffer, Jeffrey, and Gerald R. Salancik. "Organizational Context and the Characteristics and Tenure of Hospital Administrators," *Academy of Management Journal,* Vol. 20 (1977), in press.

43 Reed, R. H., and H. P. Miller. "Some Determinants of the Variation in Earnings for College Men," *Journal of Human Resources,* Vol. 5 (1970), 117–190.

44 Salancik, Gerald R., and Jeffrey Pfeffer. "Constraints on Administrator Discretion: The Limited Influence of Mayors on City Budgets," *Urban Affairs Quarterly,* in press.

45 Sales, Stephen M. "Supervisory Style and Productivity: Review and Theory," *Personnel Psychology,* Vol. 19 (1966), 275–286.

46 Schutz, Alfred. *The Phenomenology of the Social World* (Evanston, Ill.: Northwestern University Press, 1967).

47 Selznick, P. *Leadership in Administration* (Evanston, Ill.: Row, Peterson, 1957).

48 Spaeth, J. L., and A. M. Greeley. *Recent Alumni and Higher Education* (New York: McGraw-Hill, 1970).

49 Thompson, James D. *Organizations in Action* (New York: McGraw-Hill, 1967).

50 Vroom, Victor H. "Some Personality Determinants of the Effects of Participation," *Journal of Abnormal and Social Psychology,* Vol. 59 (1959), 322–327.

51 Vroom, Victor H., and Philip W. Yetton. *Leadership and Decision-Making* (Pittsburgh: University of Pittsburgh Press, 1973).

52 Warner, W. L., and J. C. Abbeglin. *Big Business Leaders in America* (New York: Harper and Brothers, 1955).

53 Weick, Karl E. *The Social Psychology of Organizing* (Reading, Mass.: Addison-Wesley, 1969).

54 Weinstein, Alan G., and V. Srinivasan. "Predicting Managerial Success of Master of Business Administration (MBA) Graduates," *Journal of Applied Psychology,* Vol. 59 (1974), 207–212.

55 Wolfle, Dael. *The Uses of Talent* (Princeton: Princeton University Press, 1971).

56 Zald, Mayer N. "Who Shall Rule? A Political Analysis of Succession in a Large Welfare Organization," *Pacific Sociological Review,* Vol. 8 (1965), 52–60.

Reading 47

Path-Goal Theory of Leadership

Robert J. House
Terence R. Mitchell

An integrated body of conjecture by students of leadership, referred to as the "Path-Goal Theory of Leadership," is currently emerging. According to this theory, leaders are effective because of their impact on subordinates' motivation, ability to perform effectively and satisfactions. The theory is called Path-Goal because its major concern is how the leader influences the subordinates' perceptions of their work goals, personal goals and paths to goal attainment. The theory suggests that a leader's behavior is motivating or satisfying to the degree that the behavior increases subordinate goal attainment and clarifies the paths to these goals.

From *Journal of Contemporary Business,* Autumn 1974, 81–97. Reprinted with permission.

HISTORICAL FOUNDATIONS

The path-goal approach has its roots in a more general motivational theory called expectancy theory, (Mitchell, 1974a). Briefly, expectancy theory states that an individual's attitudes (e.g., satisfaction with supervision or job satisfaction) or behavior (e.g., leader behavior or job effort) can be predicted from: (1) the degree to which the job, or behavior, is seen as leading to various outcomes called (expectancy) and (2) the evaluation of these outcomes called (valences). Thus, people are satisfied with their job if they think it leads to things that are highly valued, and they work hard if they believe that effort leads to things that are highly valued. This type of theoretical rationale can be used to predict a variety of phenomena related to leadership, such as why leaders behave the way they do (Nebeker and Mitchell, 1974) or it can help us to understand how leader behavior influences subordinate motivation.

This latter approach is the primary concern of this article. The implication for leadership is that subordinates are motivated by leader behavior to the extent that this behavior influences expectancies, e.g., goal paths and valences, e.g., goal attractiveness.

Several writers have advanced specific hypotheses concerning how the leader affects the paths and the goals of subordinates (Evans, 1970; Hammer and Dachler, 1973; Dansereau et al, 1973; House, 1971; Mitchell, 1973; Graen et al, 1972; House and Dessler, 1974). These writers focused on two issues: (1) how the leader affects subordinates' expectations that effort will lead to effective performance and valued rewards, and (2) how this expectation affects motivation to work hard and perform well.

While the state of theorizing about leadership in terms of subordinates' paths and goals is in its infancy, we believe it is promising for two reasons. First, it suggests effects of leader behavior that have not yet been investigated but which appear to be fruitful areas of inquiry. And, second, it suggests with some precision the situational factors on which the effects of leader behavior are contingent.

The initial theoretical work by Evans (1970, 1974) asserts that leaders will be effective by making rewards available to subordinates and by making these rewards contingent on the subordinates accomplishment of specific goals. Evans argued that one of the strategic functions of the leader is to clarify for subordinates the kind of behavior that leads to goal accomplishment and valued rewards. This function might be referred to as path clarification. Evans also argued that the leader increases the rewards available to subordinates by being supportive toward subordinates, i.e., by being concerned about their status, welfare and comfort. Leader supportiveness is in itself a reward that the leader has at his or her disposal, and the judicious use of this reward increases the motivation of subordinates.

Evans studied the relationship between the behavior of leaders and the subordinates' expectations that effort leads to rewards and also studied the resulting impact on ratings of the subordinates' performance. He found that when subordinates viewed leaders as being supportive (considerate of their needs) and when these superiors provided directions and guidance to the subordinates, there was a positive relationship between leadership behavior and subordinates' performance ratings.

However, leader behavior was only related to subordinates' performance when the leader's behavior also was related to the subordinates' expectations that their effort would result in desired rewards. Thus, Evans' findings suggest that the major impact of a leader on the performance of subordinates is clarifying the path to desired rewards and making such rewards contingent on effective performance.

Stimulated by this line of reasoning House (1971) and House and Dessler (1974) advanced a more complex theory of the effects of leader behavior on the motivation of subordinates. The theory intends to explain the effects of four specific kinds of leader behavior on the following three subordinate attitudes or expectations: (1) the satisfaction of subordinates, (2) the subordinates' acceptance of the leader and (3) the expectations of subordinates that effort will result in effective performance and that effective performance is the path to rewards. The four kinds of leader behavior included in the theory are: (1) directive leadership, (2) supportive leadership, (3) participative leadership, and (4) achievement-oriented leadership. Directive leadership is characterized by a leader who lets subordinates know what is expected of them, gives specific guidance as to what should be done and how it should be done, makes his or her part in the group understood, schedules work to be done, maintains definite standards of performance and asks that group members follow standard rules and regulations. Supportive leadership is characterized by a friendly and approachable leader who shows concern for the status, well-being and needs of subordinates. Such a leader does little things to make the work more pleasant, treats members as equals and is friendly and approachable. Participative leadership is characterized by a leader who consults with his subordinates, solicits their suggestions and takes these suggestions seriously into consideration before making a decision. An achievement-oriented leader sets challenging goals, expects subordinates to perform at their highest level, continuously seeks improvement in performance *and* shows a high degree of confidence that the subordinates will assume responsibility, put forth effort and accomplish challenging goals. This kind of leader constantly emphasizes excellence in performance and simultaneously displays confidence that subordinates will meet high standards of excellence.

A number of studies suggest that these different leadership styles can be shown by the same leader in various situations (House and Dessler, 1974; Stogdill, 1965; House, Velancy and Van der Krabben, unpublished). For example, a leader may show directiveness toward subordinates in some instances and be participative or supportive in other instances (Hill, 1974). Thus, the traditional method of characterizing a leader as either highly participative and supportive *or* highly directive is invalid; rather, it can be concluded that leaders vary in the particular fashion employed for supervising their subordinates. Also, the theory, in its present stage, is a tentative explanation of the effects of leader behavior—it is incomplete because it does not explain other kinds of leader behavior and does not explain the effects of the leader on factors other than subordinate acceptance, satisfaction and expectations. However, the theory is stated so that additional variables may be included in it as new knowledge is made available.

PATH-GOAL THEORY
General Propositions

The first proposition of path-goal theory is that leader behavior is acceptable and satisfying to subordinates to the extent that the subordinates see such behavior as either an immediate source of satisfaction or as instrumental to future satisfaction.

The second proposition of this theory is that the leader's behavior will be motivational i.e., increase effort, to the extent that (1) such behavior makes satisfaction of subordinates' needs contingent on effective performance and (2) such behavior complements the environment of subordinates by providing the coaching, guidance, support and rewards necessary for effective performance.

These two propositions suggest that the leader's strategic functions are to enhance subordinates' motivation to perform, satisfaction with the job and acceptance of the leader. From previous research on expectancy theory of motivation (House, Shapiro, and Wahba, 1974) it can be inferred that the strategic functions of the leader consist of: (1) recognizing and/or arousing subordinates' needs for outcomes over which the leader has some control, (2) increasing personal payoffs to subordinates for work-goal attainment, (3) making the path to those payoffs easier to travel by coaching and direction, (4) helping subordinates clarify expectancies, (5) reducing frustrating barriers and (6) increasing the opportunities for personal satisfaction contingent on effective performance.

Stated less formally, the motivational functions of the leader consist of increasing the number and kinds of personal payoffs to subordinates for work-goal attainment, and making paths to these payoffs easier to travel by clarifying the paths, reducing road blocks and pitfalls and increasing the opportunities for personal satisfaction en route.

Contingency Factors

Two classes of situational variables are asserted to be contingency factors. A contingency factor is a variable which moderates the relationship between two other variables such as leader behavior and subordinate satisfaction. For example, we might suggest that the degree of structure in the task moderates the relationship between the leaders' directive behavior and subordinates' job satisfaction. Figure 47-1 shows how such a relationship might look. Thus, subordinates are satisfied with directive behavior in an unstructured task and are satisfied with nondirective behavior in a structured task. Therefore, we say that the relationship between leader directiveness and subordinate satisfaction is contingent upon the structure of the task.

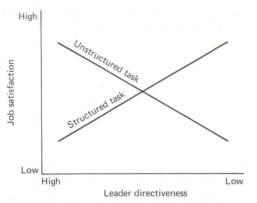

Figure 47-1 Hypothetical relationship between directive leadership and subordinate satisfaction with task structure as a contingency factor.

The two contingency variables are (a) personal characteristics of the subordinates and (b) the environmental pressures and demands with which the subordinates must cope in order to accomplish the work goals and to satisfy their needs. While other situational factors also may operate to determine the effects of leader behavior, they are not presently known.

With respect to the first class of contingency factors, the characteristics of subordinates, path-goal theory asserts that leader behavior will be acceptable to subordinates to the extent that the subordinates see such behavior as either an immediate source of satisfaction or as instrumental to future satisfaction. Subordinates' characteristics are hypothesized to partially determine this perception. For example, Runyon (1973) and Mitchell (1974b) show that the subordinate's score on a measure called Locus of Control moderates the relationship between participative leadership style and subordinate satisfaction. The Locus-of-Control measure reflects the degree to which an individual sees the environment as systematically responding to his or her behavior. People who believe that what happens to them occurs because of their behavior are called internals; people who believe that what happens to them occurs because of luck or chance are called externals. Mitchell's (1974) findings suggest that internals are more satisfied with a participative leadership style and externals are more satisfied with a directive style.

A second characteristic of subordinates on which

the effects of leader behavior are contingent is subordinates' perception of their own ability with respect to their assigned tasks. The higher the degree of perceived ability relative to task demands, the less the subordinate will view leader directiveness and coaching behavior as acceptable. Where the subordinate's perceived ability is high, such behavior is likely to have little positive effect on the motivation of the subordinate and to be perceived as excessively close control. Thus, the acceptability of the leader's behavior is determined in part by the characteristics of the subordinates.

The second aspect of the situation, the environment of the subordinate, consists of those factors that are not within the control of the subordinate but which are important to need satisfaction or to ability to perform effectively. The theory asserts that effects of the leader's behavior on the psychological states of subordinates are contingent on other parts of the subordinates' environment that are relevant to subordinate motivation. Three broad classifications of contingency factors in the environment are:

- The subordinates' tasks
- The formal authority system of the organization
- The primary work group

Assessment of the environmental conditions makes it possible to predict the kind and amount of influence that specific leader behaviors will have on the motivation of subordinates. Any of the three environmental factors could act upon the subordinate in any of three ways: first, to serve as stimuli that motivate and direct the subordinate to perform necessary task operations; second, to constrain variability in behavior. Constraints may help the subordinate by clarifying expectancies that effort leads to rewards or by preventing the subordinate from experiencing conflict and confusion. Constraints also may be counterproductive to the extent that they restrict initiative or prevent increases in effort from being associated positively with rewards. Third, environmental factors may serve as rewards for achieving desired performance, e.g., it is possible for the subordinate to receive the necessary cues to do the job and the needed rewards for satisfaction from sources other than the leader, e.g., coworkers in the primary work group. Thus, the effect of the leader on subordinates' motivation will be a function of how deficient the environment is with respect to motivational stimuli, constraints or rewards.

With respect to the environment, path-goal theory asserts that when goals and paths to desired goals are apparent because of the routine nature of the task, clear group norms or objective controls of the formal authority systems, attempts by the leader to clarify paths and goals will be both redundant and seen by subordinates as imposing unnecessary, close control. Although such control may increase performance by preventing soldiering or malingering, it also will result in decreased satisfaction (see Figure 47-1). Also with respect to the work environment, the theory asserts that the more dissatisfying the task the more the subordinates will resent leader behavior directed at increasing productivity or enforcing compliance to organizational rules and procedures.

Finally, with respect to environmental variables the theory states that leader behavior will be motivational to the extent that it helps subordinates cope with environmental uncertainties, threats from others or sources of frustration. Such leader behavior is predicted to increase subordinates' satisfaction with the job context and to be motivational to the extent that it increases the subordinates' expectations that their effort will lead to valued rewards.

These propositions and specification of situational contingencies provide a heuristic framework on which to base future research. Hopefully, this will lead to a more fully developed, explicitly formal theory of leadership.

Figure 47-2 presents a summary of the theory. It is hoped that these propositions, while admittedly tentative, will provide managers with some insights concerning the effects of their own leader behavior and that of others.

EMPIRICAL SUPPORT

The theory has been tested in a limited number of studies which have generated considerable empirical support for our ideas and also suggest areas in which the theory requires revision. A brief review of these studies follows.

Leader Directiveness

Leader directiveness has a positive correlation with satisfaction and expectancies of subordinates who are engaged in ambiguous tasks and has a negative correlation with satisfaction and expectancies of subordinates engaged in clear tasks. These findings were predicted by the theory and have been replicated in seven organizations (House, 1971; House and Dessler, 1974; Sims and Szilagyi, 1974; Dermer, 1974; Smetana, 1974). They suggest that when task demands are ambiguous or when the organization procedures, rules and policies are not clear, a leader behaving in a directive manner complements the tasks and the organization by providing the necessary guidance and psychological structure for subordinates. However, when task demands are clear to subordinates, leader directiveness is seen more as a hindrance.

However, other studies have failed to confirm these findings (Weed, Mitchell, and Smyser, 1974; Dermer and Siegel, 1973; Schuler, 1973; Downey et al., 1974; Stinson and Johnson, 1974). A study by

Leader behavior	Contingency and factors	Cause	Subordinate attitudes and behavior
1 Directive	1 Subordinate characteristics Authoritarianism	Personal	1 Job satisfaction Job → rewards
2 Supportive	Locus of control Ability	Influence > perceptions	
			2 Acceptance of leader Leader → rewards
3 Achievement oriented	2 Environmental factors The task	Influence > Motivational Stimuli	
	Formal authority system	Constraints	3 Motivational behavior Effort → performance
4 Participative	Primary work group		Performance → rewards

Figure 47-2 Summary of path-goal relationships.

Dessler (1973) suggests a resolution to these conflicting findings—he found that for subordinates at the lower organizational levels of a manufacturing firm who were doing routine, repetitive, unambiguous tasks, directive leadership was preferred by closed-minded, dogmatic, authoritarian subordinates and nondirective leadership was preferred by nonauthoritarian, open-minded subordinates. However, for subordinates at higher organizational levels doing nonroutine, ambiguous tasks, directive leadership was preferred for both authoritarian and nonauthoritarian subordinates. Thus, Dessler found that two contingency factors appear to operate · simultaneously: subordinate task ambiguity and degree of subordinate authoritarianism. When measured in combination, the findings are as predicted by the theory; however, when the subordinate's personality is not taken into account, task ambiguity does not always operate as a contingency variable as predicted by the theory. House, Burill and Dessler (unpublished) recently found a similar interaction between subordinate authoritarianism and task ambiguity in a second manufacturing firm, thus adding confidence in Dessler's original findings.

Supportive Leadership

The theory hypothesizes that supportive leadership will have its most positive effect on subordinate satisfaction for subordinates who work on stressful, frustrating, or dissatisfying tasks. This hypothesis has been tested in 10 samples of employees (House, 1971; House and Dessler, 1974; Sims and Szalagyi, 1974; Stinson and Johnson, 1974; Schuler, 1973; Downey et al, 1974; Weed et al., 1974) and in only one of these studies was the hypothesis disconfirmed (Sims and Szalagyi, 1974). Despite some inconsistency in research on supportive leadership the evidence is sufficiently positive to suggest that managers should be alert to the critical need for supportive leadership under conditions where tasks are dissatisfying, frustrating or stressful to subordinates.

Achievement-oriented Leadership

The theory hypothesizes that achievement-oriented leadership will cause subordinates to strive for higher standards of performance and to have more confidence in the ability to meet challenging goals. A recent study by House, Valency and Van der Krabben provides a partial test of this hypothesis

among white collar employees in service organizations. For subordinates performing ambiguous, nonrepetitive tasks, they found a positive relationship between the amount of achievement orientation of the leader and subordinates' expectancy that their effort would result in effective performance. Stated less technically, for subordinates performing ambiguous, nonrepetitive tasks, the higher the achievement orientation of the leader, the more the subordinates were confident that their efforts would pay off in effective performance. For subordinates performing moderately unambiguous, repetitive tasks, there was no significant relationship between achievement-oriented leadership and subordinate expectancies that their effort would lead to effective performance. This finding held in four separate organizations.

Two plausible interpretations may be used to explain these data. First, people who select ambiguous, nonrepetitive tasks may be different in personality from those who select a repetitive job and may, therefore, be more responsive to an achievement-oriented leader. A second explanation is that achievement orientation only affects expectancies in ambiguous situations because there is more flexibility and autonomy in such tasks. Therefore, subordinates in such tasks are more likely to be able to change in response to such leadership style. Neither of the above interpretations have been tested to date; however, additional research is currently under way to investigate these relationships.

Participative Leadership

In theorizing about the effects of participative leadership it is necessary to ask about the specific characteristics of both the subordinates and their situation that would cause participative leadership to be viewed as satisfying and instrumental to effective performance.

Mitchell (1973) recently described at least four ways in which a participative leadership style would impact on subordinate attitudes and behavior as predicted by expectancy theory. First, a participative climate should increase the clarity of organizational contingencies. Through participation in decision making, subordinates should learn what leads to what. From a path-goal viewpoint participation would lead to greater clarity of the paths to various goals. A second impact of participation would be that subordinates, hopefully, should select goals they highly value. If one participates in decisions about various goals, it makes sense that this individual would select goals he or she wants. Thus, participation would increase the correspondence between organization and subordinate goals. Third, we can see how participation would increase the control the individual has over what happens on the job. If our motivation is higher (based on the preceding two points), then having greater autonomy and ability to carry out our intentions should lead to increased effort and performance. Finally, under a participative system, pressure towards high performance should come from sources other than the leader or the organization. More specifically, when people participate in the decision process they become more ego-involved; the decisions made are in some part their own. Also, their peers know what is expected and the social pressure has a greater impact. Thus, motivation to perform well stems from internal and social factors as well as formal external ones.

A number of investigations prior to the above formulation supported the idea that participation appears to be helpful (Tosi, 1970; Sadler, 1970; Wexley et al., 1973), and Mitchell (1973) presents a number of recent studies that support the above four points. However, it is also true that we would expect the relationship between a participative style and subordinate behavior to be moderated by both the personality characteristics of the subordinate and the situational demands. Studies by Tannenbaum and Alport (1966) and Vroom (1959) have shown that subordinates who prefer autonomy and self-control respond more positively to participative leadership in terms of both satisfaction and performance than subordinates who do not have such preferences. Also, the studies mentioned earlier by Runyon (1973) and Mitchell (1974b) showed that subordinates who were external in orientation were less satisfied with a participative style of leadership than were internal subordinates.

House (1974) has also reviewed these studies in an attempt to explain the ways in which the situation or environment moderates the relationship between participation and subordinate attitudes and behavior. His analysis suggests that where participative leadership is positively related to satisfaction, regardless of the predispositions of subordinates, the tasks of the subjects appear to be ambiguous and ego-involving. In the studies in which the subjects' personalities or predispositions moderate the effect of participative leadership, the tasks of the subjects are inferred to be highly routine, and/or nonego-involving tasks.

House reasoned from this analysis that the task may have an overriding effect on the relationship between leader participation and subordinate responses, and that individual predispositions or personality characteristics of subordinates may have an effect only under some tasks. It was assumed that when task demands are ambiguous, subordinates will have a need to reduce the ambiguity. Further, it was assumed that when task demands are ambiguous, participative problem solving between the leader and the subordinate will result in more effective decisions than when the task demands are unambiguous. Finally, it was assumed that when the subordinates are ego-involved in their tasks they are more likely to want to have a say in the decisions that affect them. Given these assumptions, the following hypotheses were formulated to account for the conflicting findings reviewed above:

• When subjects are highly ego-involved in a decision or a task and the decision or task demands are ambiguous, participative leadership will have a positive effect on the satisfaction and motivation of the subordinate, *regardless* of the subordinate's predisposition toward self-control, authoritarianism or need for independence.
• When subordinates are not ego-involved in their tasks and the task demands are clear, subordinates who are not authoritarian and who have high needs for independence and self-control will respond favorably to leader participation and their opposite personality types will respond less favorably.

These hypotheses were derived on the basis of path-goal theorizing, i.e., the rationale guiding the analysis of prior studies was that both task characteristics and characteristics of subordinates interact to determine the effect of a specific kind of leader behavior on the satisfaction, expectancies and performance of subordinates. To date, one major investigation (Schuler, 1974) has supported some of these predictions in which personality variables, amount of participative leadership, task ambiguity and job satisfaction were assessed for 324 employees of an industrial manufacturing organization. As expected, in nonrepetitive, ego-involving tasks, employees (regardless of their personality) were more satisfied under a participative style than a nonparticipative style. However, in repetitive tasks which were less ego-involving the amount of authoritarianism of subordinates moderated the relationship between leadership style and satisfaction. Specifically, low authoritarian subordinates were *more satisfied* under a participative style. These findings are exactly as the theory would predict, thus it has promise in reconciling a set of confusing and contradictory findings with respect to participative leadership.

SUMMARY AND CONCLUSIONS

We have attempted to describe what we believe is a useful theoretical framework for understanding the effect of leadership behavior on subordinate satisfaction and motivation. Most theorists today have moved away from the simplistic notions that all effective leaders have a certain set of personality traits or that the situation completely determines performance. Some researchers have presented rather complex attempts at matching certain types of leaders with certain types of situations, e.g., the articles written by Vroom and Fiedler in this issue. But, we believe that a path-goal approach goes one step further. It not only suggests what type of style may be most effective in a given situation—it also attempts to explain *why* it is most effective.

We are optimistic about the future outlook of leadership research. With the guidance of path-goal theorizing, future research is expected to unravel many confusing puzzles about the reasons for and the effects of leader behavior that have, heretofore, not been solved. However, we add a word of caution: the theory, and the research on it, are relatively new to the literature of organizational behavior. Consequently, path-goal theory is offered more as a tool for directing research and stimulating insight than as a proven guide for managerial action.

REFERENCES

Atkinson, J. W. and Raynor, J. O. Motivation and achievement, V. H. Winston and Sons, Washington, D.C., 1974.

Dansereau, F., Jr., Cashman, J. and Graen, C. Instrumentality theory and equity theory as complementary approaches in predicting the relationship of leadership and turnover among managers. *Organizational Behavior and Human Performance,* **10,** 184–200, 1973.

Dermer, J. D. and Siegel, J. P. A test of path goal theory: disconfirming evidence and a critique. Unpublished mimeography, Faculty of Management Studies, University of Toronto, 1973.

Dermer, J. D. Supervisory behavior and budget motivation. Unpublished manuscript, Working Paper W. P. Sloan School of Management, Massachusetts Institute of Technology, Cambridge, Massachusetts, 1974.

Dessler, G. An investigation of the path goal theory of leadership. Unpublished doctoral dissertation, Bernard M. Baruch College, City University of New York, 1973.

Downey, H. K., Sheridan, J. E. and Slocum, J. W., Jr. Analysis of relationships among leader behavior, subordinate job performance and satisfaction: a path goal approach. Unpublished mimeograph, 1974.

Evans, M. G. The effects of supervisory behavior on the path goal relationship. *Organization Behavior and Human Performance,* 1970, **55,** 277–298.

Evans, M. G. Extensions of a path goal theory of motivation. *Journal of Applied Psychology,* 1974, **59,** 172–178.

Graen, G., Dansereau, F., J. and Minami, T. Disfunctional leadership styles. *Organization Behavior and Human Performance,* **7,** 216–236, 1972(a).

Graen, G., Dansereau, F., Jr. and Minami, T. An empirical test of the man-in-the-middle hypothesis among executives in a hierarchical organization employing a unit analysis, *Organization Behavior and Human Performance,* **8,** 161–285, 1972(b).

Hammer, T. H. and Dachler, H. P. The process of supervision in the context of motivation theory, Research Report No. 3, Dept. of Psychology, University of Maryland, 1973.

Haythorn, W., Couch, A., Haefner, D., Langham, P. and Carter, L. The effects of varying combinations of authoritarian and equalitarian leaders and followers, *Journal of Abnormal Social Psychology, 1956,* **53,** 210–219.

Hill, W. A., and Ruhe, J. A. Attitudes and behavior of black and white supervisors in problem solving groups, *Organization Behavior and Human Performance,* (in press).

House, R. J. A path-goal theory of leader effectiveness, *Administrative Science Quarterly,* **16,** 3, September, 1971, 321–338.

House, R. J. and Dessler, G. The path-goal theory of leadership: some post hoc and a priori tests. To appear in Hunt, J. G. (Ed.), *Contingency Approaches to Leadership.* Carbondale, Illinois: Southern Illinois University Press, 1974.

House, R. J., Shapiro, H. J. and Wahba, M. A. Expectancy theory as a predictor of work behavior and attitude, a re-evaluation of empirical evidence. *Decision Sciences,* (in press).

House, R. J., Valency, A. and Van der Krabben, R. Some tests and extensions of the path goal theory of leadership, in preparation.

Mitchell, T. R. Expectancy model of job satisfaction, occupational preference and effort: A theoretical, methodological and empirical appraisal. *Psychological Bulletin,* (in press), 1974a.

Mitchell, T. R., Smyser, C. R., and Weed, S. E. Locus of control: supervision and work satisfaction, unpublished. Technical Report No. 74–56, University of Washington, (1974b)

Mitchell, T. R. Motivation and participation: an integration, *Academy of Management Journal,* 1973, **16,** (4) 160–679.

Nebeker, D. M. and Mitchell, T. R. Leader behavior: An expectancy theory approach. *Organizational Behavior and Human Performance,* 1974.

Runyon, K. E. Some interactions between personality variables and management styles, *Journal of Applied Psychology,* 1973, **57,** (3), 288–294.

Sadler, J. Leadership style, confidence in management and job satisfaction, *Journal of Applied Behavioral Sciences,* 1970, **6,** 3–19.

Schuler, R. S. A path goal theory of leadership: an empirical investigation. Doctoral dissertation, Michigan State University, East Lansing, Michigan, 1973.

Schuler, R. S. Leader participation, task structure and subordinate authoritarianism, unpublished mimeograph, Cleveland State University, 1974.

Stinson, J. E. and Johnson, T. W. The path goal theory of leadership: a partial test and suggested refinement, *Proceedings,* 7th Annual Conference of the Mid-West, Division of the Academy of Management, Kent, Ohio, April, 1974, 18–36.

Stogdill, R. M. *Managers, employees, organization.* Bureau of Business Research, Division of Research, College of Commerce and Administration. The Ohio State University, 1965.

Szalagyi, A. D. and Sims, H. P. An exploration of the path goal theory of leadership in a health care environment. *Academy of Management Journal,* (in press).

Tannebaum, A. S. and Allport, F. H. Personality structure and group structure: an interpretive study of their relationship through an event-structure hypothesis. *Journal of Abnormal and Social Psychology,* 1956, **53,** 272–280.

Tosi, H. A re-examination of personality as a determinant of the effects of participation. *Personnel Psychology,* 1970, **23,** 91–99.

Vroom, V. H. Some personality determinants of the effects of participation, *Journal of Abnormal Social Psychology,* 1959, **59,** 322–327.

Weed, S. E., Mitchell, T. R. and Smyser, C. R. A test of House's path goal theory of leadership in an organizational setting. Paper presented at Western Psychological Association, 1974.

Wexley, K. N., Singh, J. P. and Yukl, J. A. Subordinate personality as a moderator of the effects of participation in three types of appraisal interviews, *Journal of Applied Psychology,* 1973, **83,** (1), 54–59.

Reading 48

Can Leaders Learn to Lead?

Victor H. Vroom

Like my fellow authors, I start with certain preconceptions. These preconceptions—some may call them biases—influence the way in which I view issues of leadership, particularly leadership in training. I have tried to depict these preconceptions in Figure 48-1.

The central variable in this figure is the behavior of the leader, which I believe is determined by two classes of variables, attributes of the leader himself and attributes of the situation he encounters. Furthermore, I assume that many of the differences in the behavior of leaders can be explained only by examining their joint effects, including interactions between these two classes of variables.

The left-hand portion of the diagram is the descriptive side of the leader behavior equation. Much of my research has focused on these relationships in an attempt to understand the ways in which managers actually respond to situations that vary in a number of dimensions. If you examine the right-

Reprinted from *Organizational Dynamics,* Winter 1976, 17–28, with permission of the publisher. Copyright © 1976 by AMACOM, a division of American Management Associations.

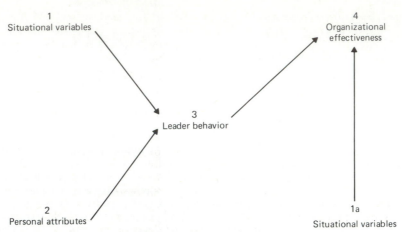

Figure 48-1 Schematic representation of variables used in leadership research.

hand side of Figure 48-1, however, you encounter issues that are potentially normative or prescriptive in character. They deal with the consequences of leader behavior for the organization and here I share with Fiedler (and probably disagree with Argyris) a conviction that a contingency model is required. I do not see any form of leader behavior as optimal for all situations. The contribution of a leader's actions to the effectiveness of his organization cannot be determined without considering the nature of the situation in which that behavior is displayed.

WORKING WITH THE CONTINGENCY MODEL

I am going to assume that most of you are familiar with the model that Phil Yetton and I developed and have described in detail in our recent book. As a normative model, it deals with the right-hand side of Figure 48-1, but it is a limited model because it deals with only one facet of leadership behavior—the extent to which the leader shares his decision-making power with his subordinates.

Figure 48-2 shows the latest version of our model. For purposes of simplicity, the presentation here is restricted to the model for group problems, that is, problems or decisions that affect all or a substantial portion of the manager's subordinates. At the top of the figure are problem attributes—that is, situational variables that ought to influence the decision process used by the leader—specifically, the amount

of opportunity that the leader gives his subordinates to participate in the making of a decision. To use the model, one first selects an organization problem to be solved or decision to be made. Starting at the left-hand side of the diagram, one asks oneself the question pertaining to each attribute that is encountered, follows the path developed, and finally determines the problem type (numbered 1 through 12). This problem type specifies one or more decision processes that are deemed appropriate to that problem. These decision processes are called the "feasible set" and represent the methods that remain after a set of seven rules has been applied. The first three of these rules eliminate methods that threaten the quality of the decisions, while the last four rules eliminate methods that are likely to jeopardize acceptance of the decision by subordinates.

For those who are unfamiliar with the Vroom-Yetton model, let me point out that the decision processes are described here in a kind of code. AI and AII are variants of an autocratic process. In AI the manager solves the problem by himself using whatever information is available to him at that time; in AII he obtains any necessary information of a specific nature from his subordinates before making the decision himself. CI and CII are variants of a consultative process. In CI he shares the problem with relevant subordinates individually, getting their ideas and suggestions before making the decision; CII is similar, but the consultation takes place within the context of a group meeting. Finally, GII corre-

A. Does the problem possess a quality requirement?
B. Do I have sufficient information to make a high-quality decision?
C. Is the problem structured?
D. Is acceptance of the decision by subordinates important for effective implementation?
E. If I were to make the decision by myself, am I reasonably certain that it would be accepted by
    my subordinates?
F. Do subordinates share the organizational goals to be attained in solving this problem?
G. Is conflict among subordinates likely in preferred solutions?

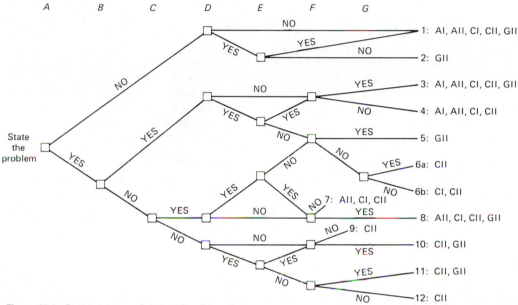

Figure 48-2 Decision-process flowchart (feasible set).

sponds with Norman Maier's concept of group decision in which the manager's role is that of chairperson of a group meeting aimed at reaching consensus on the action to be taken.

The part of the model described so far specifies how decisions should *not* be made, not how they should be made. For most problem types, there exist more than one decision process consistent with the rules and therefore contained in the feasible set. We have also been concerned with the consequences of various ways of choosing from these alternatives. There is considerable evidence that the time required to make the decision (defined either as the elapsed time or the number of man-hours needed to make the decision) increases with the intensity of involvement or participation of subordinates. Thus a time-efficient model (which we term Model A) would select the most autocratic alternative within the feasible set, a choice that would be clearly

indicated in crisis or emergency situations and in situations in which one seeks to minimize the number of man-hours that enter into making the decision.

Of course, time is not the only dimension to include in deciding the degree to which the leader should encourage the participation of his subordinates in decision making. In addition to the possibilities that participation may increase decision quality or its acceptance (considerations that are incorporated into the rules referred to previously), there are also grounds for believing that participation contributes to individual and team development and is likely to result in more informed and responsible behavior by subordinates in the future. Hence Model B, which could be thought of as a time-investment or developmental model, dictates the choice of the most participative process within the feasible set. It is important to note that Models A and B are consistent with the same rules (to protect decision quality and acceptance) but represent extremely different ways of operating within these rules. Model A maximized a short-run value—time; Model B maximizes a long-run value—development.

What is the image of the effective leader portrayed by this normative model? He is neither universally automatic nor universally participative but utilizes either approach in response to the demands of a situation *as he perceives them.* Above all, he is a flexible leader who has thought through his values and who has a repertoire of skills necessary to execute effectively each of the decision processes.

VALIDATING THE MODEL

When Philip Yetton and I wrote our book, we had no evidence validating the model other than the consistency of our rules with existing empirical evidence concerning the consequences of alternative approaches. During the past six months, Art Jago and I have been working to remedy this deficiency. We have asked managers, all of whom were unfamiliar with the model, to select two decisions that they had made—one that proved to be successful and one that proved to be unsuccessful. Each manager wrote up each decision situation as a case and specified the decision process he used in solving the problem. Later these managers were trained in the problem attributes and went back over each of these two cases, coding each in a manner that would permit the researcher to determine the problem type and the feasible set of methods for that problem type.

The data for this study are still coming in. To date, we have written accounts of 46 successful decisions and of 42 unsuccessful ones. (It seems that some managers have difficulty in recalling the decisions they made that did not turn out too well!) Figure 48-3 shows the results available so far. These results clearly support the validity of the model. If the manager's method of dealing with the case corresponded with the model, the probability of the decision's being deemed successful was 65 percent; if the method disagreed with the model, the probability of it's being deemed successful was only 29 percent.

It is important to note, however, that behavior

	Percent suc- cessful	Percent unsuc- cessful	Total
Method used agrees with feasible set	65	35	100%
Method used disagrees with feasible set	29	71	100%

Figure 48-3 Relationship between model agreement and decision outcome.

that corresponds with the model is no guarantee that the decision will ultimately turn out to be successful —nor is behavior outside the feasible set inevitably associated with an unsuccessful decision.

To create a model of decision processes that completely predicts decision outcomes (that is, which generates 100 percent observations in upper left and lower right cells) is an impossibility. Any fantasies that we may have entertained about having created a model of process that would completely determine decision outcomes have been permanently dashed against the rocks of reality! Insofar as organizations are open systems and decisions within them are made under conditions of risk and uncertainty, it will be impossible to generate complete predictability for a model such as ours. To be sure, we may be able to use the data from the study I have described to improve the "batting average" of the model, but the limit of success must be less than perfection.

IMPLICATIONS FOR TRAINING

I would now like to turn to the central issue of this symposium, the use of the model in leadership training. Over the past few years, several thousand managers have received training in the concepts underlying the model. The workshops have ranged from two to over five days in length, and the participants have included admirals, corporation presidents, school superintendents, and senior government officials. I have been personally involved in enough of this training to have learned some important things about what to do and what not to do. And because I believe that there are substantial but understandable misconceptions about how training based on the Vroom and Yetton model works, I would like to describe the things I have learned.

It would have been possible to build a training program around the model that was completely cognitive and mechanistic. Participants would be sold on the model and then trained in its use through intensive practice—first on standardized cases and later on real problems drawn from their own experiences. Such an approach would represent a new domain for Taylorism and could even be accomplished through Skinnerian programmed learning. I believe that, at best, this behavioral approach would influence what Agyris calls espoused theories and would not have any long-lasting behavioral effects.

Our methods have been much more influenced by Carl Rogers than by B. F. Skinner. We have assumed that behavioral changes require a process of self-discovery and insight by each individual manager.

One method of stimulating this process is to provide the participant with a picture of his own leadership style. This picture includes a comparison of his style with that of others, the situational factors that influence his willingness to share his power with others, and similarities and differences between his own "model" and the normative models.

In advance of the training program, each participant sits down with a set of cases, each of which depicts a leader confronted with an actual organizational problem. We call these cases "problem sets," and the number of cases in different problem sets ranges from 30 to 54. The common feature in each of the eight or nine problem sets that have been developed is that the cases vary along each of the situational dimensions used in the construction of the normative model. The set is designed such that the variation is systematic and that the effects of each situational attribute on a given manager's choice of decision process can be readily determined. This feature permits the assessment of each of the problem attributes in the decision processes used by a given manager.

The manager's task is to select the decision process that comes closest to depicting what he would do in each situation. His responses are recorded on a standardized form and processed by computer along with other participants' responses in the same program.

Rather than talk about the information contained on a printout, I thought it might be more efficient to let you see what it looks like. The next figure reproduces three of the seven pages of feedback that a manager recently received. Examine the first page of the printout shown in Figure 48-4. Consider A first in that figure. The first row opposite "your frequency" shows the proportion of cases in which the manager indicated he would use each of the five decision processes. The next row (opposite "peer frequency") shows the average use of these processes by the 41 managers constituting his training group. A comparison of these two rows indicates the methods he used more and less frequently than average.

The third row shows the distribution of decision processes that would be used by a manager using Model A, the time-efficient model in the 30 cases. The final row shows a distribution for Model B, the developmental or time-investment model.

To obtain an overall picture of how participative this manager's responses are in relation to other members of his training group and to Models A and B, it is necessary to assign scale values to each of the five decision processes. The actual numbers used for this purpose are based on research on the relative amounts of participation perceived to result from each process. AI is given a value of 0; AII a value of 1; CI a value of 5; CII a value of 8; and GII a value of 10.

With the aid of these scale values a mean score can be computed for the manager, his peers, and both models. These are obtained by multiplying the percentage of times each process is used by its scale value and dividing by 100. These mean scores are shown in B along with the standard deviation (SD), a measure of dispersion around the mean—that is, an indicator of how much behavior is varied over situations.

These mean scores are shown graphically in the figure at the bottom. Each asterisk is the mean score of one of the group members. The symbol X is printed underneath this manager's mean score, the symbol P under the group average, and the symbols A and B show the location on the scale of Models A and B respectively.

D through F in Figure 48-4 show the second page of the printout. As we have previously mentioned, the normative model identifies 12 problem types corresponding to the terminal nodes of the decision tree shown in Figure 48-2. There is at least one case within the set of 30 problems that has been designated by the authors and most managers as representative of each type. The problem types and corresponding problem numbers are shown in the two left-hand columns of D. In the third and fourth columns, the prescriptions of Models A and B are given, and the fifth column shows the feasible set for that problem type. The last column, marked "your behavior," indicates the manager's responses to each of the cases of the indicated problem type. If there is more than one case of that type, the methods used are shown in the same order as the· problem numbers at the left-hand side.

E reports the frequency with which the manager's behavior agreed with the feasible set, with Model A, and with Model B. For comparison purposes, the average rates of agreement for members of the manager's training group are also presented.

Each time our manager chose a decision process that was outside the feasible set, he violated at least one of the seven rules underlying the model. F in Figure 48-4 reports the frequencies with which each rule was violated both by this manager and by his peer group. The right-hand column shows the specific cases in which the rule violations occurred. It

should be noted that each manager understands the seven rules by the time he receives the feedback, and it is possible for him to reexamine the problems with the appropriate rule in mind.

We have previously noted that the cases included in a problem set are selected in accordance with a multifactorial experimental design. Each of the problem attributes is varied in a manner that will permit the manager to examine its role in his leadership style. Figure 48-4 (page 3 of printout) depicts these results. Consider problem attribute A—the importance of the quality of the final solution. The problem set contains cases that have a high quality requirement and those without a quality requirement (the identifying numbers of these cases are shown at the right-hand side of this table).

The mean scores for the manager's behavior on these two sets of cases are specified at the left-hand side of each row and are designated by the symbol X. They are also designated by the symbol X on each of the scales, and the slope of the line made by connecting the two letters (X) provides a visual representation of that difference.

If the score opposite "high" is greater (that is,

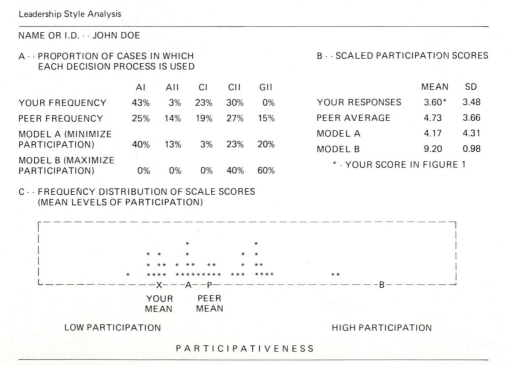

Leadership Style Analysis

NAME OR I.D. - - JOHN DOE

A - - PROPORTION OF CASES IN WHICH EACH DECISION PROCESS IS USED

	AI	AII	CI	CII	GII
YOUR FREQUENCY	43%	3%	23%	30%	0%
PEER FREQUENCY	25%	14%	19%	27%	15%
MODEL A (MINIMIZE PARTICIPATION)	40%	13%	3%	23%	20%
MODEL B (MAXIMIZE PARTICIPATION)	0%	0%	0%	40%	60%

B - - SCALED PARTICIPATION SCORES

	MEAN	SD
YOUR RESPONSES	3.60*	3.48
PEER AVERAGE	4.73	3.66
MODEL A	4.17	4.31
MODEL B	9.20	0.98

* - YOUR SCORE IN FIGURE 1

C - - FREQUEŃCY DISTRIBUTION OF SCALE SCORES (MEAN LEVELS OF PARTICIPATION)

YOUR MEAN   PEER MEAN

LOW PARTICIPATION   HIGH PARTICIPATION

P A R T I C I P A T I V E N E S S

Figure 48-4   Page 1 of printout.

Leadership Style Analysis

D ---- BEHAVIOR BY PROBLEM TYPE

E ---- FREQUENCY OF AGREEMENT WITH THE NORMATIVE MODEL

PROBLEM TYPE	PROBLEM NUMBERS	MODEL "A"	"B"	FEASIBLE SET		YOUR BEHAVIOR		
1	14,15,17,28	AI	GII	AI,AII,CI,CII,GII	AI	AI	AI	AI
2	3,5,	GII	GII	GII		CII	AI	
3	2,22,27,30	AI	GII	AI,AII,CI,CII,GII	AI	AI	AI	CII
4	12,25,26,29	AI	CII	AI,AII,CI,CII	AI	CI	CI	AI
5	7,8,20	GII	GII	GII	CII	CII	CI	
6A	1,10	CII	CII	CII		CI	CI	
6B	11	CI	CII	CI,CII		CII		
7	21,24	AII	CII	AII,CI,CII		CII	AI	
8	19,23	AII	GII	AII,CI,CII,GII		AI	AII	
9	4,16	CII	CII	CII		CII	CI	
10	6,9	CII	GII	CII,GII		AI	CI	
11	13	GII	GII	GII		CII		
12	18	CII	CII	CII		CII		

	YOUR MEAN	PEER AVERAGE
AGREEMENT WITH FEASIBLE SET	17 (57%)	20.8 (69%)
AGREEMENT MODEL A (MINIMUM PARTICIPATION)	12 (40%)	12.1 (40%)
AGREEMENT WITH MODEL B (MAXIMUM PARTICIPATION)	4 (13%)	6.3 (21%)

F ---- FREQUENCY OF RULE VIOLATIONS

	RULE	RESPONSES IN VIOLATION	YOUR FREQUENCY	PEER AVERAGE	PROBLEM NUMBERS
1	LEADER INFORMATION RULE	AI	3.0 (25%)*	0.7 (6%)	6 19 24
2	GOAL CONGRUENCE RULE	GII	0.0 (0%)	1.3 (10%)	0
3	UNSTRUCTURED PROBLEM RULE	AI,AII,CI	3.0 (50%)	2.8 (47%)	6 9 16
4	ACCEPTANCE RULE	AI,AII	1.0 (10%)	1.3 (13%)	5
5	CONFLICT RULE	AI,AII,CI	3.0 (60%)	1.9 (39%)	1 5 10
6	FAIRNESS RULE	AI,AII,CI,CII	2.0 (100%)	1.3 (63%)	3 5
7	ACCEPTANCE PRIORITY RULE	AI,AII,CI,CII	4.0 (100%)	2.9 (72%)	7 8 13 20

*---PROBABILITY OF RULE VIOLATION (THAT IS, FREQUENCY OF VIOLATION EXPRESSED AS A PERCENTAGE OF RULE APPLICABILITY)

Figure 48-4(Continued) Page 2 of printout.

more toward the right-hand side of the scale), it means that the manager encourages more participation from his subordinates on important decisions than on so-called "trivial" ones. However, if the score opposite "high" is lower, it means that the manager is willing to use more participative methods on problems for which the course of action adopted makes little difference and is more autocratic on "important" decisions.

The letter P shown on both scales designates the average effects of this attribute on the manager's peer group, and the letters A and B designate the effects on Models A and B respectively.

A similar logic can be used in interpreting the effects of each of the other attributes in the model. At the bottom of the page, the computer prints out the three attributes that have the greatest effect on the manager's behavior—magnitude of effect referring to the amount of difference the attribute makes in his willingness to share his decision-making power with subordinates.

The results shown in Figure 48-4 pertain to only

one manager and to his peer group. Similar data have been obtained from several thousand managers, a sufficient number to provide the basis for some tentative generalizations about leadership patterns. One of our conclusions is that differences among managers in what might be termed a general trait of participativeness or authoritarianism are small in comparison with differences within managers. On the standardized cases in the problem sets, no manager has indicated that he would use the same decision process on all problems or decisions—and most use all methods under some circumstances.

It is clear that no one score computed for a manager and displayed on his printout adequately represents his leadership style. To begin to understand his style, the entire printout must be considered. For example, two managers may appear to be equally participative or autocratic on the surface, but a close look at the third page of the printout (Figure 48-4) may reveal crucial differences. One manager may limit participation by his subordinates

Leadership Style Analysis

G ---- MAIN EFFECTS OF PROBLEM ATTRIBUTES

		YOUR MEAN = X	MODEL A MEAN = A
		PEER MEAN = P	MODEL B MEAN = B

PARTICIPATIVENESS ON PROBLEMS WITH ATTRIBUTE

PROBLEM ATTRIBUTES		< LOW PARTICIPATION HIGH PARTICIPATION >	PROBLEMS WITH ATTRIBUTE
IMPORTANCE OF THE QUALITY OF THE FINAL SOLUTION (ATTRIBUTE A)	HIGH X=4.17	P=4.97 A=4.38 ·······XA····P·······················B·········	(1,2,4,6,7,8,9,10,11,12,13, 16,18,19,20,21,22,23,24,25, 26,27,29,30)
	LOW X=1.33	P=3.75 A=3.33 ·······X·······A··P··························B	(3,5,14,15,17,28)
ADEQUACY OF MANAGER'S INFORMATION AND EXPERTISE (ATTRIBUTE B)	HIGH X=3.67	P=4.24 A=2.75 ·········A····X····P···············B·········	(1,2,8,11,12,20,22,25,26, 27,29,30)
	LOW X=4.67	P=5.71 A=6.00 ···················X····P A···········B·········	(4,6,7,9,10,13,16,18,19, 21,23,24)
DEGREE OF STRUCTURE IN PROBLEM (ATTRIBUTE C)	HIGH X=3.67	P=4.97 A=3.67 ···············X·····P···············B·········	(7,10,19,21,23,24)
	LOW X=5.67	P=6.46 A=8.33 ·······························X···P········A··B·········	(4,6,9,13,16,18)
IMPORTANCE OF SUBORDINATE ACCEPTANCE (ATTRIBUTE D)	HIGH X=3.80	P=5.30 A=5.35 ·····················X·····P···············B·········	(1,3,5,6,7,8,10,11,12,13,14, 15,16,18,19,20,22,24,29,30)
	LOW X=3.20	P=3.59 A=1.80 ·············A·······X··P··················B·········	(2,4,9,17,21,23,25,26,27,28)
PROBABILITY OF LEADER'S SELLING HIS OWN SOLUTION (ATTRIBUTE E)	HIGH X=1.30	P=3.68 A=1.80 ·······X··A········P···················B·········	(6,12,14,15,16,19,22,24,29,30)
	LOW X=6.30	P=6.91 A=8.90 ···························X···P·········A··B·········	(1,3,5,7,8,10,11,13,18,20)
DEGREE TO WHICH SUBORDINATES SHARE GOALS (ATTRIBUTE F)	HIGH X=3.58	P=5.45 A=4.83 ·············X········A·····P···············B	(2,6,7,8,9,13,19,20,22, 23,27,30)
	LOW X=4.75	P=4.49 A=3.92 ··················A··P···X·············B·········	(1,4,10,11,12,16,18,21,24, 25,26,29)
PROBABILITY OF CONFLICT AMONG SUBORDINATES (ATTRIBUTE G)	HIGH X=3.27	P=3.99 A=4.27 ·············X··P·A···················B·········	(1,2,5,8,9,10,13,15,16,19, 21,22,26,28,29)
	LOW X=3.93	P·5.47 A=4.07 ···················X·······P·············B·········	(3,4,6,7,11,12,14,17,18, 20,23,24,25,27,30)

* * * * * *   NOTE: THE THREE ATTRIBUTES WITH THE GREATEST EFFECT ON YOUR RESPONSES ARE A, C, AND E.   * * * * * *

Figure 48-4(Continued)   Page 3 of printout.

to decisions where the quality element is unimportant, such as the time and place of the company picnic, while the other manager may limit participation by his subordinates to those decisions with a demonstrable impact on important organizational goals.

In about two-thirds of the cases we have examined —both those used in the problem sets and those reported to us by managers from their experiences— the manager's behavior was consistent with the feasible set of methods given by the model. Rules that helped ensure the acceptance of or commitment to a decision tend to be violated much more frequently than rules that protect the quality of the decision. Our findings suggest strongly that decisions made by typical managers are more likely to prove ineffective because of deficiencies in acceptance by subordinates rather than deficiencies in decision quality.

Let me now turn to another thing that we have learned in the design of this training—the usefulness of the small, informal group as a vehicle in the change process. The first four or five hours in the training process are spent in creating six- to eight-person teams operating under conditions of openness and trust. Each participant spends more than 50 percent of the training time with his small group before receiving feedback. Group activities include discussing cases in the problem set and trying to reach agreement on their mode of resolution, practicing participative leadership styles within their own groups, analyzing videotapes of group problem-solving activities; then group members give one another feedback on the basis of predictions of one another's leadership styles.

After feedback, group members compare results with one another and with their prior predictions and share with one another what they have learned as well as their plans to change. The use of small, autonomous groups greatly decreases the dependence of participants on the instructor for their learning and increases the number of people who can undergo the training at the same time. I have personally worked with as many as 140 managers at the same time (22 groups), and 40 to 50 is commonplace.

One criticism that has been correctly leveled at the Vroom and Yetton work stems from the fact that the data on which the feedback is based are, at best, reports of intended actions rather than observations of actual behavior. While we have evidence that most managers honestly try to portray what they think they would do in a particular situation rather than what they think they should do, I am persuaded by Argyris's evidence that many people are unaware of discrepancies between their espoused theories and their actions. Small groups can be helpful in pointing out these discrepancies. I have seen managers who were universally predicted by other group members to have a highly autocratic style, who were provided with very specific evidence of the ground for this assumption by other group members, but who later received a printout reflecting a much more participative style. I am less concerned about the relative validity of these discrepant pieces of data than I am about the fact that they are frequently confronted and discussed in the course of the training experience.

In fact, we have begun using a different source of potential inconsistencies, and it is logical to assume that this source will have more information about a manager's behavior than do the other members of his small group. I am referring to the manager's subordinates. In a recent variant of the training program described, they were asked to predict their managers' behavior on each of the cases in the problem set. These predictions were made individually and processed by computer, which generated for each manager a detailed comparison of his perceptions of his leadership style with the mean perception of his subordinates. Not surprisingly, these two sources of information are not always in perfect agreement. Most managers, as seen by their subordinates, are substantially more autocratic (about one point on the 10-point scale) and in substantially less agreement with the model. Once again, I am less concerned with which is the correct description of the leader's behavior than I am with the fact that discrepancies generate a dialogue between the manager and his subordinates that can be the source of mutual learning.

We are still experimenting with methods of using the Vroom-Yetton model in leadership training and, I believe, still learning from the results of this experimentation. How effective is the training in its present form? Does it produce long-lasting behavioral changes? I must confess that I do not know. Art Jago and I are in the first stages of designing an extensive follow-up study of almost 200 managers in 20 different countries who have been through a four or five-day version of the training within the past two and one-half years. If we can solve the incredible logistical and methodological problems in a study of this kind, we should have results within a year.

On the basis of the evidence, I am optimistic on two counts: first, as to the leader's potential to vary his style to meet the requirements of a situation; second, as to the leader's ability, through training and development, to enlarge the repertoire of his styles. In short, like Argyris and unlike Fiedler, I believe that managers can learn to become more effective leaders. But like Fiedler (and unlike Argyris), I believe that such effectiveness requires a matching of one's leadership style to the demands of the situation. I also am confident that 50 years from now both contingency models will be found wanting in detail if not in substance. If we are remembered at that time, it will be for the kinds of questions we posed rather than the specific answers we provided.

Reading 49

Leadership and Poor Performance: An Attributional Analysis

Terence R. Mitchell
Stephen G. Green

Dealing with poor performance is a crucial problem in today's organizations. Tardiness, absenteeism, turnover, sabotage, and lack of effort cause losses in the billions of dollars each year. In addition to this global analysis, poor performance has detrimental effects for the individual leader and employee. An inordinate amount of any manager's time is spent thinking about and dealing with the poor performer. It is an unpleasant part of any leader's job, and it is hard on the employee as well.

Unfortunately, we know very little about leaders' responses to a subordinate's poor performance, or how this response affects future performance. Numerous research studies have focused on the development of better performance measures. But these measures are designed simply to tell us when poor performance has occurred. What we need now is information about (a) how leaders diagnose poor performance, and (b) what they do about it. The following paper investigates these two questions.

We are constantly involved in the evaluation of other people's behavior. It occurs in all of our interpersonal interactions. However, in the organizational setting the importance of this evaluation increases. It is the responsibility of leaders not only to evaluate performance but to do something about it. There is the clear charge that poor performance should be corrected and result in increased effectiveness. The important questions for the leader are, "Why did this poor performance occur?" and "What is my most appropriate response?" Thus, the inference about the cause of the poor performance (e.g., laziness, lack of information) and the choice of an appropriate response (e.g., training, a reprimand) are the focus of this paper.

ATTRIBUTION THEORY

In the last twenty years, a body of psychological knowledge has developed under the label of "attribution theory" (Shaver, 1975). Attribution theory attempts to explain (a) how people make inferences about the causes of their own and other people's behavior, and (b) how they act upon those inferences. Since these questions parallel the questions about a leader's reaction to poor performance, attribution theory serves as the foundation for our analysis.

The initial ideas for attribution theory can be traced to the work of Fritz Heider (1944, 1958), who argued that all of us strive to understand the world around us, especially the behavior of others. An understanding of interpersonal behavior helps us to reduce uncertainty and increases the predictability, and hence our control, of other people's behavior. To do this, Heider argued, we develop and use rather naive theories of the causes of behavior.

Central to the theory developed by Heider were the questions of *intention* and of the personal and environmental *causes* of behavior. That is, the observer attempts to determine whether the actor's behavior was intentional and whether the intended action was caused by internal personal factors, such as personality characteristics and abilities, or external environmental factors, such as social pressure or the demands of the task.

Out of this and subsequent work by people like Kelley (1971, 1973) and Jones and Davis (1965) came a number of interesting conclusions. There was general agreement that a systematic attributional process did indeed occur. People initially (a) observe action, (b) infer intentionality, (c) make attributions about the internal or external causes of the action, and (d) respond to the action in light of the attribution.

The Internal/External Issue

An important issue pertaining to a leader's evaluation of poor performance focuses upon whether the cause of the poor performance is seen as internal or external. If a leader believes that a subordinate has, for example, failed to meet a deadline and that the failure is due to lack of effort (an internal attribution), he is more likely to reprimand the subordinate

Paper presented at the 86th Annual Convention of the American Psychological Association, Toronto, 1978.

than if he believes the failure was due to a computer breakdown (an external attribution). Internal attributions should result in the leader trying to change the behavior of the subordinate. External attributions should result in the leader trying to change the task or the surrounding environment.

Kelley's work (1971, 1973) is particularly useful in describing the information that is necessary for making internal or external attributions. He argues that the observer uses three kinds of information: distinctiveness, consistency, and consensus. *Distinctiveness* refers to a comparison between the subordinate's performance in this particular task and in other tasks; the more distinctive, the more likely an external attribution. That is, when a subordinate fails on one task but does well on many others, the supervisor is likely to attribute the poor performance to external causes.

Consistency concerns how well the subordinate does on the same task over time. If the subordinate continues to fail at the task, the observer is more likely to make an internal attribution. Finally, there is consensus: How do other people do? Does everyone fail at this task? The more consensus, the more likely an external attribution.

Research by Weiner et al. (1971) argues that there is a further distinction within the internal/external categories that is important. They suggest that there are stable and unstable factors within each of these categories. Their position is that the attributor goes one step further than just an internal/external distinction. The attributor also tries to determine whether the cause was stable or unstable. In the case of internal attributions, the cause of poor performance may be lack of effort or lack of ability. Effort is seen as unstable—that is, it changes from time to time and task to task—while ability is seen as an enduring characteristic. In the case of external attributions, the cause may be a task that is too difficult or factors beyond anyone's control (e.g., bad luck, a computer failure). Bad luck is an unstable factor, while a difficult task would be a stable one. This analysis, together with what has been presented thus far, leads to Figure 49-1.

Observational Bias

Besides increasing our understanding of the inference process, the attributional research also revealed another important point: People make systematic errors in their inferences about the causes of behavior. While numerous examples are available, two biases seem most relevant here. First, there is an actor/observer distinction (Jones & Nisbett, 1971). When making attributions about other people's behavior, one tends to utilize internal causes. In contrast, when accounting for one's own behavior, one tends to attribute actions to external demands. When one is an actor, the environment is the central focus, but when one is an observer, the focus is upon the behavior of the other person and the underlying, internal, causes of that behavior. This difference in focus leads us to believe that the environment is the cause of our own behavior while the behavior of others is caused by their personal characteristics. This inference is often incorrect.

A second bias which is closely related to the actor/observer distinction is called "defensive attributions" (Shaver, 1970). This bias suggests that one is likely to attribute one's successes to personal factors and one's failures to environmental factors. People see their successes as caused by their abilities and their failures as caused by factors over which

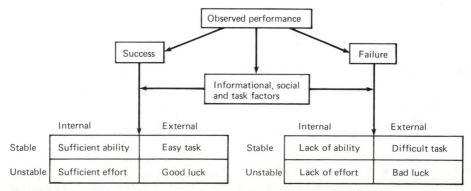

	Internal	External			Internal	External
Stable	Sufficient ability	Easy task		Stable	Lack of ability	Difficult task
Unstable	Sufficient effort	Good luck		Unstable	Lack of effort	Bad luck

Figure 49-1

they have no control. However, when judging others observers are relatively more likely to attribute failures to internal personal causes and successes to external environmental causes. These biases are partly explained by the fact that the observer does not have access to the actor's perception and understanding of the environment. All the observer sees is the behavior and its effects. Nevertheless, these findings suggest that leaders frequently will make errors in their attributions and that these errors may influence their actions.

A PROPOSED ATTRIBUTIONAL MODEL OF LEADERSHIP

Given all of this background, we have developed an *initial* model of the evaluation process in the leadership context. This model is presented in Figure 49-2.

The process begins when the leader observes an example of what he or she judges to be poor performance. This may be a missed deadline, a failure to follow instructions, absenteeism, or low output. In some cases, either the organization or the supervisor may have a preestablished policy for handling the problem. Perhaps one unexcused absence a month goes unmentioned, two require a reprimand, and three result in a reduction in pay. Under circumstances in which such a policy already exists, little, if any, attributional work will go on.

When policies do not exist, attributions about the

causes of the poor performance are made and this process is labeled "link #1" in the model. At this point, we see three sets of variables influencing the attribution that is made: informational factors, social factors, and biases.

The informational factors include the content characteristics suggested by Kelley: distinctiveness, consistency, and consensus. We have already discussed the impact of these variables on the attributional process.

Some social factors also appear to be important. That is, some dimensions of the leader-subordinate *relationship* affect the attribution. For example, the more similar the leader is to the subordinate, the more likely the leader is to attribute the causes of poor performance to external factors, just as would be the case if the leader were evaluating his or her own poor performance (Jones & Nisbett, 1971). Similar results can be expected when the leader has had a great deal of experience with the subordinate's job. In both cases, the leader's experience or empathy will increase the chance of the leader's seeing the situation from the subordinate's perspective and therefore inferring an external cause.

On the other hand, when the subordinate's poor performance reflects upon the leader, the leader is likely to attribute the poor performance to internal causes. The same should be true with increasing power for the leader. What we are suggesting is that if the subordinate's poor performance were seen as

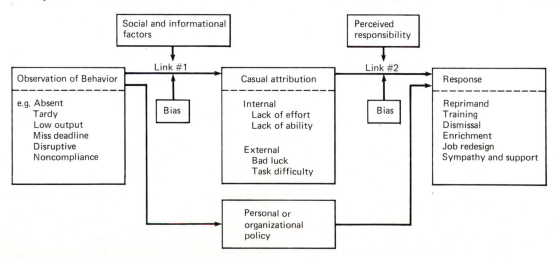

Figure 49-2 An attributional model of a leader's response to a subordinate's poor performance.

caused by external factors (e.g., supervision), it might place blame on the supervisor. Therefore, it is more likely that the supervisor will attribute the poor performance to internal characteristics of the subordinate than to external environmental factors. Thus, involvement in the relationship will affect the leader's attributions.

Aspects of the task also are important. Any factor that increases the judgment that effort is high will lead to an ability attribution when poor performance occurs. For example, when social pressure is intense, supervision is close, or the financial rewards are high, we would expect someone to try to do well. If failure ensues, we are likely to attribute it to a lack of ability (keeping in mind the observer's general bias to infer internal causes for another person's poor performance).

The more general actor/observer and defensive attributional biases also influence this link. They make it much more likely that a subordinate's poor performance will be attributed to a lack of effort or ability than to external events. Thus, informational, social, and task factors will all contribute to the attribution that is made.

Once the attribution is made, the next step is to analyze what the leader does about it. This process appears as "link #2" in Figure 49-2. In general, we believe that the internal/external and stable/unstable distinctions will be important for understanding the course of action and the severity of the action taken by the leader. If lack of effort is seen as the cause, then a reprimand or some other motivational strategy is likely to be used. If ability is the perceived cause, then training or transfers might occur. If the task is perceived as the problem, then perhaps job redesign or enrichment might be tried, and if bad luck is the attribution then perhaps sympathy and support will be in order. So, it appears to us that particular attributions will correspond fairly directly to particular actions on the part of the supervisor.

Some factors probably moderate this relationship. First, the leader's perception of the degree to which the subordinate is intentionally or personally responsible for the action will probably affect the extremity of the supervisor's corrective action. For example, a subordinate might fail to exert effort because of (a) illness (low responsibility) or (b) not caring (high responsibility). Similar distinctions can be made for ability. Somehow a subordinate is seen

as responsible for some personal trait such as being too assertive but not responsible for lack of intellectual skill. It is likely that more extreme steps will follow actions for which the leader believes the subordinate is responsible.

Finally, we suspect that there are biases in this second link as well. We merely "suspect" this because there is less literature available to substantiate our arguments than there is for the actor/observer and defensive attributional biases. One bias that is readily apparent is that observers have difficulty separating an actor's behavior from its effects. For example, a supervisor is more likely to utilize extreme corrective action if a subordinate's failure to meet a deadline results in a million-dollar contract loss rather than a one-hundred-dollar loss. Thus, the result of the behavior is likely to bias the extremity of the response even though the behavior and the attribution are the same. It is not yet clear to us whether judgments about (a) the responsibility for the action and (b) the effects of behavior have their effects upon attributional uncertainty and thus on the zeal with which the supervisor takes corrective action or merely upon the extremity of the corrective action itself. This will be a point for research.

A second suspected bias is that leaders see some things as easier to change than others. In general, people's behavior is seen as more changeable than the environment. And, within the internal category, effort is seen as more easily changed than traits or abilities. The reason for this bias is twofold. First, just about all of us see ourselves as experts on human behavior. On the surface, understanding and changing behavior seems rather simple: just tell the person how to behave. On the other hand, the environment is seen as less flexible, and until recently (e.g., the work of Hackman & Oldham, 1976) we have had little research on ways to design and enrich organizational tasks.

All of this leads us to the final conclusions: Leaders are likely to attribute the causes of subordinate failure to internal motivational causes. They are therefore likely to use reprimands and dismissals as the responses to poor performance. Our analyses, if correct, would suggest that these inferences and responses are frequently in error. It is our contention that leaders can correct their errors and increase the appropriateness of their responses by a better understanding of the attributional process.

DISCUSSION

We feel that the proposed model can be a valuable addition to our understanding of the leadership process in two main ways. First, information-processing explanations of behavior in general, and attributional analyses in particular, are dominating the field of social psychology. Many researchers feel that this type of approach has dramatically increased our understanding of the causes of behavior.

However, little of this research has been generalized to the area of organizational behavior. The most recent review of organizational behavior in the *Annual Review of Psychology* (Mitchell, in press) discusses the areas in which attributional ideas have been applied and points out their positive utility. Thus, the use of an attributional analysis of leadership is likely to increase our understanding of the evaluation process and the effectiveness with which this process is conducted.

A second area of relevant research is the literature on leadership itself. The major emphasis of the research over the past twenty years has been on the effects of leader behavior, not on its causes. Only recently has a shift in this focus been apparent (Mitchell, in press). The research by Graen (1976), Hollander (1978), and Hunt and Osborn (1978) best represents this shift. An examination of why leaders respond the way they do to poor performance seems long overdue.

And the model has relevance for practice as well. First, dealing with poor performance is an unpleasant part of any supervisor's job. Few people enjoy giving reprimands, negative feedback, and being generally seen as the "heavy." Besides, most people want to be liked by their subordinates, and giving negative feedback may be seen as a hindrance to the development of such relationships. It would appear logical that helping people to understand the attribution and response process would decrease their negative feelings about the activity, and perhaps more attention would be directed toward doing it well.

But a second and more important point going beyond the fact that people do not like dealing with poor performance, is that most supervisors do not do it very well. Lots of biases enter in, and their awareness of these biases is limited at best. Based on our model, supervisors will tend to err by overusing internal attributions and personal negative sanc-

tions. The inaccuracies of the attributions and the responses tend to perpetuate the negative feelings surrounding the task and also tend to be ineffective in improving subordinate performance.

Therefore, it seems to us that a thorough understanding of the attributional process and its effects on behavior will be helpful for leaders on both a personal and a professional level. They will find the task of responding to poor performance less onerous, and they will do better at it.

REFERENCES

Graen, G. Role making processes within complex organizations. In M. D. Dunnette (Ed.), *The handbook of industrial and organizational psychology.* Chicago: Rand McNally, 1976.

Hackman, J. R., & Oldham, G. R. Motivation through the design of work: Test of a theory. *Organizational Behavior and Human Performance,* 1976, **16,** 259–279.

Heider, F. Social perception and phenomenal causality. *Psychological Review,* 1944, **51,** 358–374.

———. *The psychology of interpersonal relations.* New York: Wiley, 1958.

Hollander, E. P. *Leadership dynamics: A practical guide to effective relationship.* New York: Free Press, 1978.

Hunt, J. G., & Osborn, R. N. A multiple approach to leadership for managers. In J. Stinson & P. Hersey (Eds.), *Leadership for practitioners.* Athens: Center for Leadership Studies, Ohio University, 1978.

Jones, E. E., & Davis, K. E. From acts to dispositions: The attribution process in person perception. In L. Berkowitz (Ed.), *Advances in experimental social psychology,* Vol. 2. New York: Academic Press, 1965.

———, & Nisbett, R. E. *The actor and the observer: Divergent perceptions of the causes of behavior.* Morristown, N.J.: General Learning Press, 1971.

Kelley, H. H. *Attribution in social interaction.* Morristown, N.J.: General Learning Press, 1971.

———. The processes of causal attribution. *American Psychologist,* 1973, **28,** 107–128.

Mitchell, T. R. Organizational behavior. *Annual Review of Psychology,* in press.

Shaver, K. G. Defensive attribution: Effects of severity and relevance on the responsibility assigned for an accident. *Journal of Personality and Social Psychology,* 1970, **14,** 101–113.

Shaver, K. G. *An introduction to attribution processes.* Cambridge, Mass.: Winthrop, 1975.

Weiner, B., Frieze, I., Kukla, A., Reed, L., Rest, S., & Rosenbaum, R. M. *Perceiving the causes of success and failure.* Morristown, N.J.: General Learning Press, 1971.

Reading 50

Substitutes for Leadership: Some Implications for Organizational Design

Steven Kerr

The design of tasks, jobs, and organizations—which began so long ago with Durkheim, Smith, Weber, and Taylor (or was it with Cyrus in 400 B.C.?)—has now come full circle. The early concern was with tasks which *all men* could perform in the "one best way" and with organizational forms which might protect us from our own vices and limitations. Consistent with the engineering and mass-production manufacturing backgrounds of so many of its apostles, classical management considered individual worker differences primarily as something to be overcome. It was hoped that, with careful attention to detail, impersonality could be achieved, and our organizations made to operate efficiently. During this phase selection techniques were emphasized, although training was conducted to accomplish standardization.

Soon afterward we heard from the humanists, who were not at all reluctant to acquaint us with *their* orientations and value systems. We were informed that our methods were inhuman and our results dehumanizing, and that we ought to be more concerned with worker health and morale, and less obsessed with efficiency. Even those in the movement who were of good business background sought to persuade us that it was not only nice to be nice, but profitable as well, that we could (in Tom Lehrer's words) "do well by doing good." The emphasis then was not on job but on people design, i.e., training, the object of which was not to eliminate but to accentuate people's differences. Now we would develop people's potentialities, help them to "find" themselves, and prepare them for the psychological as well as physiological demands of the workplace.

In the most recent phase, now in vogue, if the worker cannot be so prepared, the workplace simply must adjust to him. Some small part of this adjustment has taken the form of job enrichment programs for low-level workers; however, the primary thrust has been the rearrangement of ground-rules, tasks, and reporting relationships so as to provide managerial-level employees the challenge, freedom, recognition, and responsibility required for self-actualization. Many job enrichment programs are of this nature, for example, and so are most approaches to management by objectives. Once again the emphasis is on task, job, and organizational design, but now the value orientation of the engineer has been replaced by that of the behavioral scientist.

The phases described above are pertinent to organization theory in general but have their counterpart in leadership theory and practice. Research on leadership was guided mainly by trait theories until the late 1940s and was accompanied by great interest in selection techniques. Behavioral leadership theories came into prominence in the 1950s and generated considerable interest in training methods since leader behaviors, unlike traits, are amenable to change through training. Currently the emphasis is on situational (contingency) approaches to leadership, which are attractive to the practicing manager because they increase his options. Certainly he may still attempt selection or training, and all presently popular situational theories permit him to do so. In addition, however, he may elect to change the situation—that is, in Fiedler's terms the job may be engineered to fit the hierarchical superior. When we consider the lackluster records compiled by most available selection and training techniques, this is no small incremental benefit.

The problem though, is that current approaches to leadership and organizational design are as enmeshed in their promoters' beliefs and value systems, and are as influenced by the selective perceptions of those who espouse them, as were the earlier ones. The internal consistency which is an attractive feature of many (though by no means all) of our theories and models is often achieved at the expense of external validity, and many prescriptions and principles which permeate the organizational design and leadership literature may, therefore, be said to contradict a considerable body of existing data.

This paper seeks to identify and re-evaluate some of these principles in the light of existing research

From *Organization and Administrative Sciences*, **8**, 135–146.

evidence and to make recommendations for organizational design consistent with leadership research, and with what is generally known about organizations and about people. The framework within which this re-evaluation is attempted can best be understood in terms of the concept of "substitutes for leadership."

HIERARCHICAL LEADERSHIP

A number of theories and models of leadership presently exist, each seeking to most clearly identify and best explain the supposedly powerful effects of hierarchical leadership upon the satisfaction, morale, and performance of subordinates. While failing to agree in many important respects, almost all modern leadership theories and models assume that no leadership trait or behavioral style exists strong enough to be effective in all situations. The focus of present-day theory and research is, therefore, primarily upon identification and analysis of *situational contingencies* under which different leader characteristics contribute toward improved subordinate performance and satisfaction. For example:

> Path-goal theory asserts that leader behavior will be acceptable to subordinates to the extent that subordinates see such behavior as either an immediate source of satisfaction or as instrumental to future satisfaction. . . . A second characteristic of subordinates on which the effects of leader behavior are contingent is subordinates' perception of their own ability with respect to their assigned tasks. The higher the degree of perceived

ability relative to task demands, the less the subordinate will view leader directiveness and coaching behavior as acceptable. . . . The theory [also] asserts that effects of the leader's behavior on the psychological states of subordinates are contingent on other parts of the subordinates' environment . . . (House and Mitchell, 1974).

Based upon a comprehensive review, Kerr et al. (1974), summarized the voluminous literature on leader consideration (leader-subordinate relations which feature mutual trust and respect for subordinates' ideas and feelings) and initiating structure (structuring by the leader of his or her own role and subordinates' roles toward goal attainment—Fleishman and Peters, 1962). Kerr et al. also put forth ten propositions which were consistent with, and in many cases similar to, hypotheses described in House's (1971) path-goal theory. These propositions are summarized in Table 50-1.

SUBSTITUTES FOR HIERARCHICAL LEADERSHIP

Present-day theories and models of leadership share another important assumption—that hierarchical leadership is always important. Even those models most concerned with situational contingencies assume that while the style of leadership most likely to be effective will vary with the situation, *some* leadership style will be effective regardless of the situation. Of course, the extent to which this assumption is explicated varies greatly: for example, the vertical dyad linkage model developed by Graen and his associates (cf. Graen et al., 1972) is fairly explicit in

---

Table 50-1   Situational Propositions From the Consideration—Initiating Structure Literature

1. The greater the pressure, the greater will be subordinate tolerance of leader initiating structure, and the greater will be the positive relationships between structure and satisfaction and performance criteria.
2. The greater the intrinsic satisfaction from the task, the less positive will be relationships between consideration and satisfaction and performance criteria, the less negative will be relationships between structure and subordinate satisfaction, and the less positive will be relationships between structure and performance.
3. The smaller the informational needs of subordinates, the lower will be their tolerance for leader initiating structure, and the less positive will be relationships between structure and satisfaction criteria.
4. The greater the task certainty, the greater will be the positive relationships between leader consideration and subordinate satisfaction.
5. The less the agreement between subordinate expectations of leader consideration and structure and their observations of these behaviors, the lower will be the levels of subordinate satisfaction and performance.
6. The less higher management is perceived by subordinates to exhibit consideration, the lower will be the positive relationships between lower-level supervisors' consideration and subordinate satisfaction.
7. The greater the perceived organizational independence of subordinates, the greater will be the positive relationships between leader behavior and subordinate satisfaction and performance criteria.
8. The greater the perceived upward influence of the leader, the greater will be the positive relationships between consideration and subordinate satisfaction.

Note: adapted from Kerr, et al., 1974:73–74.

its attribution of importance to hierarchical leadership without concern for the situation, while House's path-goal theory is considerably less so. Path-goal theory does, however, predict that even unnecessary and redundant leader behaviors will affect subordinate satisfaction, morale, motivation, performance, and acceptance of the leader (House and Mitchell, 1974; House and Dessler, 1974). While leader attempts to clarify paths and goals are therefore recognized by path-goal theory to be unnecessary and redundant in certain situations, in no situation are they explicitly hypothesized by path-goal (or any other leadership theory) to be irrelevant.

This lack of recognition is unfortunate. As has been pointed out by Woodward (1973:66):

> In the earliest and simplest kinds of work organization and control, the subordinate has tasks allocated to him by his superior, is accountable to him for end results, and refers back to him problems which he cannot solve. The spheres of influence and authority and the size of the area of discretion become larger as the individual moves up the hierarchical pyramid. This concept of a pyramid of authority and influence is so much a part of both management ideology and sociological conceptualization, that it is almost impossible to think about management control in any other way. . . . This picture of control, however, is an over-simplified one.

As Woodward suggests, we must abandon the over-simplified picture that control is exercised almost exclusively through the personal hierarchy of the organization's structure. Once we do, we are forced to recognize that many individual, task, and organizational characteristics have the capacity to act as "substitutes for hierarchical leadership," in that they often serve to neutralize or substitute for the formal leader's ability to influence work group satisfaction and performance for either better or worse. Such substitutes for leadership are apparently prominent in a wide variety of modern organizational settings and may help to account for the fact that data from many studies suggest that in some situations hierarchical leadership per se does not seem to matter.

What is clearly needed is a taxonomy of situations where we should probably not be studying "leadership" (in the formal sense) at all. Development of such a taxonomy is still at an early stage, but Woodward (1973) and Miner (1975) have laid important groundwork by providing classifications of systems of control, and some research into the effects of nonleader sources of clarity has been conducted by Hunt (1975) and Hunt and Osborne (1975). In addition, the previously cited reviews of the leadership literature by House and Mitchell (1974) and Kerr et al. (1974) suggest that characteristics such as those in Table 50-2 will help to determine whether or not hierarchical leadership is likely to make an important difference.

The leadership substitutes construct has potential importance not only for the study of leadership, but also for organizational design and development. If the existence of substitutes for hierarchical leader-

Table 50-2   Potential Substitutes for Hierarchical Leadership

Subordinate	Task	Organization
Ability	Repetitiveness and unambiguity	Formalization
Experience	Methodological invariance	Inflexibility
Training	Intrinsic satisfaction	Highly-specified, active advisory and staff functions
Knowledge	Task-provided feedback concerning accomplishment	
"Professional" orientation		Closely-knit, cohesive work groups
Need for independence		Rewards not within the leader's control
Indifference toward organizational rewards		Spatial distance between leader and subordinates

ship is ignored, then efforts at leadership training, organizational development, and task design may well result in ineffectiveness for the organization and frustration for its members, as they come to realize that inflexible policies, invariant work methodologies, or other barriers mentioned in Table 50-2 are interfering with intended changes and preventing desired benefits.

LEADER BEHAVIORS AS CAUSE AND EFFECT

It is now evident from a variety of field and laboratory studies (e.g., Lowin and Craig, 1968; Lowin et al., 1969; Greene, 1973) that leader behavior may result from as well as cause subordinate attitudes and performance. In some studies reciprocal causality has been found to exist to such an extent that determination of any primary thrust was impossible. Other investigations have concluded that causation was primarily in one direction (in some studies from leader behaviors to subordinate outcomes, in other the reverse). Even in these instances, however, chain reactions were apparently formed which affected both predictors and criteria in subsequent time periods.

In retrospect, it is not surprising that leader behaviors and subordinate attitudes and activities have been found to exert reciprocal influence. What is surprising is that so many prescriptions, both for leadership and for organizational design, continue to be founded upon outmoded and over-simplified notions of one-way causation. Numerous design and developmental efforts have been undertaken as though we knew for a fact that broad delegation of authority, task design (e.g., MBO and job enrichment), and supervisory training in PERT-CPM (structure) and human relations (consideration) logically precede and consistently result in high member satisfaction and work group performance. It has also often been assumed that this would be the case regardless of the situation, i.e., irrespective of whether substitutes for leadership exist.

However unsubstantiated, this assumption underlies many currently popular approaches to training and organizational design. When initiated without adequate attention being paid to the probable direction of causation, such approaches may prove costly and irrelevant. For example, it is well established that a strong positive relationship exists between leader consideration egalitarianism and subordinate

satisfaction. It might, therefore, seem logical to undertake job design or management training such that low-level subordinates are provided greater opportunities to participate in the planning process, thereby enhancing their satisfaction. Let us assume, however, that important substitutes for leadership exist, in the form of highly formalized policies and objectives and highly invariant work methodologies. As has already been mentioned, the effect of such factors should be to reduce sharply the extent to which the (newly) egalitarian leader can implement his changed behaviors or attitudes. On the other hand, there seems no reason why leadership substitutes should prevent changes in leader behaviors and attitudes which *result* from different levels of subordinate satisfaction. Under such circumstances it is most likely that either no important changes at all would result, or that subordinate satisfaction might change due to circumstances unrelated to the design or training program, and leader egalitarianism might then change in the same direction.

EGALITARIANISM AMONG HIERARCHICAL UNEQUALS

Many leadership training programs, and several major approaches to job redesign (for example, management by objectives), depend for their internal consistency upon the assumption that egalitarianism is possible among employees who are at different levels of the organizational hierarchy. It is claimed of one participative system, for example, that even that most sensitive of interactions, the formal appraisal interview between superior and subordinate, can be "strictly man-to-man in character. . . . In listening to the subordinate's review of performance, problems, and failings, the manager is automatically cast in the role of counselor. This role for the manager, in turn, results naturally in a problem-solving discussion" (Meyer et al., 1965:129).

There are probably many situations where substitutes for leadership are strong or numerous enough to neutralize the usual inequality of superior-subordinate authority. It is possible, for example, that where subordinates possess unique and critical job knowledge, or are indifferent toward rewards within the leader's control, the kind of relationship described by Meyer et al. may be attained. In general, however, the research literature (cf., Blau and Scott, 1962) clearly suggests that hierarchical inequalities produce very predictable effects upon interaction patterns, subordinate anxiety and defensiveness, and quality and quantity of communications, and that these effects seriously interfere with "joint" goal-setting, problem-solving, etc., by unequals. Bennis has succinctly summarized some of these difficulties:

> Two factors seem to be involved. . . . The superior as a helper, trainer, consultant, and coordinator, and the superior as an instrument and arm of reality, a man with power over the subordinate. . . . For each actor in the relationship, a *double reference* is needed. . . . The double reference approach requires a degree of maturity, more precisely a commitment to maturity, on the part of both the superior and subordinate that exceeds that of any other organizational approach. . . . It is suggestive that psychiatric patients find it most difficult to see the psychiatrist both as a human being and helper and an individual with certain perceived powers. The same difficulty exists in the superior-subordinate relationship (1960:285–287).

As a general rule, then, it may be said that leader training and organizational design programs which depend for their success upon democracy and egalitarianism among hierarchical unequals are unlikely to be successful. This will tend to be true unless such programs are able simultaneously to increase the strength and number of available substitutes for leadership and by so doing minimize the leader's dominant position. One method for accomplishing this is to increase the work group's ability to serve as a substitute and formalize its function in that regard. For example, it has been recommended by several MNO theorists that subordinates meet and set objectives with their superior *as a group*, since "status differentials are likely to be less important, freeing individuals of the need to be cautious and deferential. . . . Successful negotiation with the boss should be easier, since group support would tend to offset the boss's higher rank" (Kerr, 1976:17).

STABILITY OF LEADER BEHAVIORS

As already mentioned, the emphasis today in leadership theory and research is upon situational approaches, which supposedly increase the alternatives available to the practicing manager by encouraging adjustments to job content, reporting requirements, task structure, etc., so as to provide a better fit between the leader's behavioral style and his work situation. Fiedler (1967), Chemers and Rice (1974), and others have suggested situational change as a workable alternative to traditional selection and training techniques.

This approach to leader effectiveness and job design depends, however, upon the assumption that while task demands and the working environments of leaders are amenable to conscious and systematic manipulation, such manipulation will not simultaneously alter their behavioral patterns and leadership styles. This approach further assumes that the leader's behavioral style will not change easily by itself, i.e., without conscious and systematic manipulation. Only by accepting such assumptions can we remain untroubled by Chemers and Rice's reminder that the Fiedler Contingency Model "makes its predictions on the basis of a static LPC store" (1974:114) and acquiescent toward Fiedler's (1973) argument that leadership training and experience will typically change the leader's situation, but not his LPC score.

Such assumptions and arguments are inconsistent, however, with a growing and increasingly-convincing body of research which shows leader behavior and personality measures to be quite unstable over time and across situations. Leader LPC scores, for example, have often been found to change dramatically over relatively short periods of time, whether or not accompanied by planned change (cf., Stinson and Tracy, 1973; Farris, 1975). Similar changes in leader behavior patterns after training (as evidenced by test-retest correlations of .54 and .49 for LOQ consideration and structure, and .27 and .22 for SBDQ consideration and structure) have also been observed (Fleishman et al., 1955; Harris and Fleishman, 1955, respectively).

Only by disregarding such accumulating evidence are proponents of situational engineering able to seriously recommend the redesign of jobs and work environments so as to better "fit" the manager. More careful attention to existing data would probably lead to the less decisive but more accurate conclusion that planned change may under different conditions affect leader behavior, the working environment, both, or neither. Certainly there will be instances where training will result in an altered work situation, while leaving unchanged the leader's personality and behavioral style. On other occasions, however, particularly when strong substitutes for leadership exist, leadership training or experience may succeed in changing the leader but not the situation, as characteristics of the organization, tasks, or subordinates prevent the "changed" leader from influencing his or her environment.

While organizational and task design may, therefore, be highly appropriate in some cases to improve the fit between the leader and his or her work situation, such efforts should not be undertaken in situations where the leader's attitudes and behaviors are themselves subject to subsequent change, lest continual redesign be necessary. The accumulating research evidence suggests that Fiedler's (1965) recommendation that we "engineer the job to fit the manager" may be impractical in all but a few special cases.

EFFECTS OF "PROFESSIONAL" NORMS AND STANDARDS

There are several reasons why the working environment of professionals employed in organizations presents special opportunities for leadership substitutes to flourish and hierarchical leadership to be consequently less important. The professional's expertise, normally acquired as a result of specialized training in a body of abstract knowledge, often serves to reduce the need for structuring information; furthermore, a belief in peer review and collegial maintenance of standards often causes the professional to look to fellow professionals rather than to the hierarchical leader for what informational needs remain. Even concerning performance feedback, which was described earlier as typically transmitted from formal superior to subordinates, substitutes for leadership may exist:

First, professionals may deny that their hierarchical superiors have the skills to determine whether performance standards are being met. From the professional's viewpoint, only fellow professionals know enough about their work to evaluate it competently. Second, professionals may deny that their superior's performance standards are even relevant. Such attributes as knowledge of the specialty, originality of approach, and impact upon the professional community may seem reasonable criteria for performance evaluation to the professional, but may not even be a part of the organiza-

tion's formal evaluation procedure (Filley et al., 1976:385).

Clearly, many of the substitutes for hierarchical leadership mentioned in Table 50-2 (e.g., knowledge, training, group cohesiveness) are pertinent to professionals in organizations. Yet despite the frequent tendency for such substitutes to exist and exert influence in professional settings, leadership research has seldom taken systematic cognizance of this influence. One consequence is that data obtained from professionals in hospitals, R&D laboratories, and other settings often diverge from patterns of data obtained in non-professional work sites.

Perhaps the most important deficiency of research conducted in settings where hierarchical supervision was found to be inconsequential has been the failure of researchers to investigate the kinds, strength, and effects of those substitutes for leadership which exist. In the same vein, designers of tasks and jobs in professional organizations have inadequately attended to matters pertaining to the creation, maintenance, and institutionalization of professional norms and standards. Certainly it is true that such norms and standards are generally derived from formal academic training prior to employment; nonetheless, they tend to be maintained subsequent to employment, if necessary through informal means in organizations which do not provide for them formally. It is, therefore, likely that important advantages would accrue to organizations the tasks, reporting arrangements, and evaluation procedures of which were designed to be supportive of, not antagonistic toward, professional norms and standards.

For example, despite professionals' interest in collegial maintenance of standards, and although research has shown peer ratings to be attractive in many situations as a supplement (even an alternative) to traditional leader-rating systems, very few organizations have designed and made use of peer evaluation processes. This is even the case in professionally oriented settings where substitutes for leadership flourish. Nor are professionals organized so that they are encouraged or required to develop goals and work objectives as a group. This is true despite some evidence that such collegial activities can facilitate communications and help to reduce inequities of power and status.

As noted above, collegial activities and lateral relationships will manifest themselves to some extent in any organization where professionals are employed. If necessary these processes will occur informally, even in opposition to the formal structure. However, "their use can be substantially improved by designing them into the formal organization. At the very least, organizations can be designed so as not to prevent these processes from arising spontaneously, and reward systems can be designed to encourage such processes" (Galbraith, 1973:47; see also Farris, 1971).

SUMMARY

I have suggested that a number of individual, task, and organizational characteristics often act as substitutes for hierarchical leadership, impairing the leader's ability to influence the attitudes and performance of his work group for either better or worse. I have also argued here that the leadership substitutes construct, though important, has been underattended by both leadership theorists and organizational designers, and this lack of attention has been to the detriment of organization theory, research, and practice.

It follows that greater attention needs to be paid to the identification of substitutes for hierarchical leadership, and to the design of authority, control, evaluation, and reward systems which are explicitly cognizant of their existence. Such an approach will require greater imagination and creativity than has been evident in the past and will require us to abandon naive assumptions which have served us poorly (for example, those concerning stable personality measures and one-way causation) in favor of what research evidence is available.

It also follows that we should begin to think seriously about not only the identification, but the systematic *creation*, of substitutes for hierarchical leadership. In particular, to the extent that we value and wish to promote egalitarianism and subordinate participation in organizational planning, control, and goal-setting activities, it may be absolutely essential that we build group MBO, task provided feedback, peer evaluation systems, and other potential substitutes for leadership into our typically autocratic organizations, so as to permit communications among hierarchical unequals to flow more freely and collegial norms to flourish.

REFERENCES

Bennis, Warren G. "Leadership Theory and Administrative Behavior: The Problem of Authority." *Administrative Science Quarterly*, 1960, **4:**259–301.

Blau, Peter M., and W. Richard Scott. *Formal Organizations.* San Francisco, Ca.: Chandler, 1962.

Chemers, Martin M., and Robert W. Rice. "A Theoretical and Empirical Examination of Fiedler's Contingency Model of Leadership Effectiveness." In James G. Hunt and Lars L. Larson (eds.), *Contingency Approaches to Leadership.* Carbondale, Ill.: Southern Illinois University Press, 1974.

Farris, George F. "Organizing Your Informal Organization," *Innovation,* 1971.

———. "Does Performance Affect LPC?" unpublished manuscript, 1975.

Fiedler, Fred E. "Engineer the Job to Fit the Manager." *Harvard Business Review,* 1965, **43:**115–122.

———. *A Theory of Leadership Effectiveness.* New York: McGraw-Hill, 1967.

———. "Predicting the Effects of Leadership Training and Experience From the Contingency Model: A Clarification." *Journal of Applied Psychology,* 1973, **57:**110–13.

Filley, Alan C., Robert J. House, and Steven Kerr. *Managerial Process and Organizational Behavior* (2nd. ed.). Glenview, Ill.: Scott, Foresman, 1976.

Fleishman, Edwin A., E. F. Harris, and Harold E. Burtt. *Leadership and Supervision in Industry.* Columbus: Bureau of Educational Research, The Ohio State University, 1955.

Fleishman, Edwin A., and D. R. Peters. "Interpersonal Values, Leadership Attitudes and Managerial Success." *Personnel Psychology,* 1962, **5:**127–43.

Galbraith, Jay. *Designing Complex Organizations.* Reading, Mass.: Addison-Wesley, 1973.

Graen, George, Fred Dansereau, Jr., and Takao Minami. "Dysfunctional Leadership Styles." *Organizational Behavior and Human Performance,* 1972, **7:**216–36.

Greene, Charles N. "A Longitudinal Analysis of Relationships Among Leader Behavior and Subordinate Performance and Satisfaction." *Academy of Management Proceedings,* 1973, 433–40.

Harris, E. G., and Edwin A. Fleishman. "Human Relations Training and the Stability of Leadership Patterns." *Journal of Applied Psychology,* 1955, **39:**20–25.

House, Robert J. "A Path-Goal Theory of Leader Effectiveness." *Administrative Science Quarterly,* 1971, **16:**321–38.

House, Robert J., and Gary Dessler. "The Path-Goal Theory of Leadership: Some Post Hoc and A Priori Tests." In James G. Hunt and Lars L. Larson (eds.), *Contingency Approaches to Leadership.* Carbondale: Southern Illinois University Press, 1974.

House, Robert J., and Terence R. Mitchell. "Path-Goal

Theory of Leadership." *Journal of Contemporary Business,* 1974, **3:**81–97.

Hunt, James G. "Different Nonleader Clarity Sources as Alternatives to Leadership." *Proceedings of the Twelfth Annual Conference.* Eastern Academy of Management, State College, Pennsylvania, 1975.

Hunt, James G., and Richard N. Osborne. "An Adaptive-Reactive Theory of Leadership." In James G. Hunt and Lars L. Larson (eds.), *Leadership Frontiers.* Carbondale, Ill.: Southern Illinois University Press, 1975.

Kerr, Steven. "Overcoming the Dysfunctions of MBO." *Management by Objectives,* 1976, **5:**13–19.

Kerr, Steven, Chester Schriesheim, Charles Murphy, and Ralph M. Stogdill. "Toward a Contingency Theory of Leadership Based Upon the Consideration and Initiating Structure Literature." *Organizational Behavior and Human Performance,* 1974, **12:**62–82.

Lowin, Aaron, and J. R. Craig. "The Influence of Level of Performance on Managerial Style: An Experimental Object-Lesson in the Ambiguity of Correlational Data." *Organizational Behavior and Human Performance,* 1968, **3:**440–58.

Lowin, Aaron, W. J. Hrapchak, and Michael J. Kavanagh. "Consideration and Initiating Structure: An Experimental Investigation of Leadership Traits." *Administrative Science Quarterly,* 1969, **14:**238–53.

Meyer, Herbert H., Emanual Kay, and J. R. p. French. "Split Roles in Performance Appraisal." *Harvard Business Review,* 1965, **43:**21–29.

Miner, John B. "The Uncertain Future of the Leadership Concept: An Overview." In James G. Hunt and Lars L. Larson (eds.), *Leadership Frontiers.* Kent, Oh.: Comparative Administration Research Institute, 1975.

Stinson, John E., and Lane Tracy. "The Stability and Interpretation of the LPC Score." *Academy of Management Proceedings.* (32nd annual meeting) Minneapolis, Minnesota, 1973, 182–184.

Woodward, Joan. "Technology, Material Control, and Organizational Behavior." In Anant R. Negandhi (ed.), *Modern Organizational Theory.* Kent, Oh.: Kent State University Press, 1973.

Chapter 14

Approaches to Organizational Change

How does one go about changing an organization? Can planned change efforts which are designed to utilize existing research knowledge about organizational design and management succeed? Or do the forces that most influence what happens in organizations lie beyond the domain of management research and theory—deriving instead from technological developments, from changes in the national economy and the labor market, and from government legislation and regulatory practices? This chapter explores these issues and also considers how change can best be introduced and managed.

There certainly is no dearth of techniques for improving organizational effectiveness through planned change. Some techniques take a strongly psychological approach, aspiring to achieve organizational change by improving selection and placement practices, by improving the training organization members receive, or by increasing employees' motivation and commitment. Other approaches have an interpersonal focus, attempting to improve the quality of communication that takes place within and between groups in organizations, to reduce dysfunctional conflict, and to improve the quality of managerial leadership processes. Still other change approaches involve structural alterations, including changes in the organizational structure itself and the redesigning of the roles and jobs of organization members.

There are a number of examples of success using planned approaches to change. The article by Walton looks at some of them and deals with a second issue, the dissemination of these changes. As he points out, success in one organizational location does not assure dissemination to another. Dissemination must be planned for and managed. The second article, by Greiner, looks in more detail at the kinds of problems which often prevent organizational development programs from succeeding. It points out that many of the problems can be overcome if the right strategic approach is taken.

The last two articles in the chapter address broad questions and assumptions having to do with managing change. Rather than exploring in depth particular techniques or strategies for change, these readings attempt to identify what the key issues are in managing *any* planned change. As the articles point out, managers are constantly involved in change and if they do not manage it they are likely to be victims of it. The article by Kotter and Schlesinger and the article by Nadler provide a number of helpful perspectives for the manager who wants to develop a workable planned-change program—a skill that is likely to become increasingly important as organizations face even more turbulent environments.

Reading 51

Successful Strategies for Diffusing Work Innovations
Richard E. Walton

In a previous article, the analysis presented showed that in seven of eight companies studied, the success of work restructuring in a single plant was *not* accompanied by wide diffusion of the innovation to other plants in the firm, even though, in most cases, there was a stated company policy favoring diffusion.[1]

Since completion in 1974 of the studies on which the earlier article was based, the size of the sample of innovating companies has grown substantially. Each year practitioners in the field of work restructuring are learning more about how to diffuse these complex social innovations. As of 1977, there were a number of diffusion programs that were successful or very promising.

This paper will analyze in detail three such programs which are particularly instructive. The three cases include the most successful diffusion firm in the earlier sample, Volvo, whose program has continued to expand. The other cases are TRW, Inc., which has a promising diffusion record to date in a program started in 1974; and a company we shall call "ABC" which has the longest and most impressive record in this field. Both TRW and ABC are United States firms.

The "work restructuring" approach pursued in some cases over the years has the dual goal of improving productivity and improving the quality of work life. It embraces many aspects of work, including the content of the job, compensation schemes, social structure, status hierarchy, scope of worker responsibility for supervision and decision making. The design of each element is intended to contribute to an internally consistent work culture—typically one that enlarges workers' scope of influence, enhances their mastery of new skills, strengthens their sense of association with co-workers, increases their identification with the product and promotes their sense of dignity and self-worth.

In gross terms, the present rate of work restructuring in the United States seems satisfactory. Given the current state of the art of tailoring work structures to particular technologies, work forces and economic frameworks, and given our present capacity to implement them, a much faster growth of restructuring activity throughout U.S. industry might inhibit the longer-run diffusion of the innovations. In the process, we would be exposed to too many abortive innovations—ones that either are ill-conceived or poorly implemented.

Hence, at this time, it is more interesting to describe diffusion within a firm than in the spread of work restructuring throughout industry. Diffusion within a firm has advantages. The expertise gained in earlier projects can be applied more readily to subsequent ones. Moreover, the spread of innovation within a system is almost essential for the long-term thriving of the initial innovation, which otherwise tends to become isolated and then threatened.

By "diffusion of work restructuring with a firm," we do not necessarily mean that a particular work design is adopted by other plants in the system, although this could be the firm in which diffusion takes place. Rather, here it means that at least the same general approach used initially in one or several plants also is utilized in other plants. In the latter case, the similarity across projects may be confined to the fact that diagnoses and changes are made within the same philosophical framework.

ABC DIVISION

The Diffusion Record

Here we present analysis of diffusion within ABC, a relatively autonomous division of a large firm. The division has a dozen plants today. In 1977, roughly a decade after the first major effort was launched in one new plant, the division had seven more new plants that had incorporated the innovations

*I wish to acknowledge the assistance of two colleagues: Mr. Sheldon Davis, with whom I share an intellectual and practical interest in this subject, and Mr. Max Hall, who offered criticism of an earlier draft of this paper. Research support was provided by the Division of Research, Harvard Graduate School of Business Administration.

From *Journal of Contemporary Business*, Spring 1977, 1–22. Reprinted with permission.

throughout all their operations. Three of the older plants, all unionized, had adopted work innovations in one or more departments. Only one plant had no significant work innovations. The twelve plants have a range of from several hundred to more than a thousand employees. These plants are characterized by a very high average capital investment per employee. No other manufacturing system of this size has utilized innovative work structures as effectively and as systematically as ABC division. Without question, the innovations have contributed significantly to the performance of the division and have made these plants unusually attractive work places within their communities.

The division has not been without its abortive efforts, but those efforts are a small minority of the projects undertaken. Only one of the eight plants in which innovation was introduced at start-up has not realized its potential, generally, and its innovative work system has not been particularly successful. In the older plants where innovations have taken place on a departmental basis, the "batting average" is not as high, but it is still impressive.

The innovations in all of the start-up plants incorporated a central principle of compensation, that is, a skill-based pay scheme. Management's elements of the work structure were important too, for example, formation of work teams; integration of set-up, maintenance and inspection into the duties of operating teams; mechanisms for worker involvement in addressing plant-wide issues; symbols of a more egalitarian community, for instance, common cafeteria and parking privileges; and major investments in training. Some of the new plants, particularly the third and fourth, were more ambitious than others in their goals for developing and utilizing the capacities of workers. Still, the pattern of these innovations is remarkably uniform throughout the system. Even in the existing plants in which the innovations tend to be less comprehensive at the start, they still fall into the same conceptual pattern.

How do we explain the widespread use of work innovations throughout this multiplant system in ABC?

Situational Factors, Strategies and Tactics

The first major factor is the division's growth pattern. A decade ago the division had four plants in two locations. Success in the marketplace has required the addition of geographically dispersed facilities at a rate of one new plant about every 1½ years.

After the first new plant featured an innovative work structure that was deemed successful, management incorporated it into the design of the next new plant, with modifications based on the experience. This process has repeated itself as each new plant has started.

The rate of addition of new plants created an excellent opportunity for diffusion, but other management choices ensured that the opportunity was used. After the first new plant, the management of each new plant included many people with positive experiences in one of the earlier innovative plants. Thus they came to a new plant determined both to incorporate the best of the innovations in which they had been involved and to improve on them. One plant manager, in particular, played an instrumental role in several new plants, carrying his personal experience from one start-up situation to the next.

The division's ability to develop a sufficient pool of experienced managers to staff an additional new plant every 1½ years requires explanation. The division used first-line supervisory positions as the gateway to assimilate and develop large numbers of college graduates each year. The growth rate, in turn, made this initial assignment, which included working rotating shifts with the work teams they supervised, acceptable to the college graduates. The growing demand for managers assured them that after a couple of years they would be promoted from shift work. This supervisory assignment policy ensured that those who were hired into one of the innovative plants would have first-hand understanding of the innovations as they moved to higher management positions.

The rate of growth of the division and the promotion-from-within policy did more than enable management to field good plant start-up teams; it brought to the top of the division the managers who had direct experience, often first-line, with the plant-level innovations. Thus, by 1976 one could observe a high degree of consensus within management about the type of organizational culture that is desirable and the work structures that tend to create that work culture.

An interesting question arises here: Why didn't the ABC's initial project experience the same tendency toward "self-encapsulation" which existed in many of the pilot projects studied earlier? Ironically, the very success of the pilot projects in these other cases had created organization dynamics that discouraged rather than encouraged diffusion. There was a "star-envy" phenomenon, whereby the attention given pilot units "turned off" managers of peer units and made them disinclined to follow the example. Also the more impressive the pioneer's results, the less favorable were the career payoffs for success and the greater the risks for failure for those managers who followed suit. In addition, the extraordinary esprit de corps and sense of being special that tended to develop in the pilot unit made the work innovations appear less generalizable to other plant managers. ABC neatly by-passed all of these organization dynamics when they used a core group of managers who had major roles in the first innovative plant to design and start up the second new plant organization.

Thus, several growth-related policies combined to drive and support the diffusion process: the rate of growth; the fact that growth took the form of constructing new plants rather than acquiring them; the start-up of new plants by managers experienced with work innovations; the promotion-from-within policy; and the use of the first-line role as the entry position.

The second major factor affecting diffusion is the nature of the division's products and manufacturing processes. The division's technologies, although diverse in appearance and in the skills and knowledge they require, all tended to be continuous and capital-intensive in nature. In these and other respects, the work situation was such that there was significant economic leverage if employees had positive attitudes and if they developed more than customary operational knowledge and skills. In turn, the work situation had the potential to be relatively satisfying.

As stated earlier, the new plants were added to meet growth in demand for existing product lines. Hence, though not all plants were identical in output and technologies, almost all products were produced at several plants. The resulting similarity among plants had certain consequences for diffusion. There was a presumption that an effective work innovation developed at one plant deserved serious consideration at other plants. Also, because each plant made products which also were produced at other plants in the system, division management was able to com-

pare and rank the cost, delivery and quality performance among those plants producing any particular line.

The growth-related policies discussed earlier were especially relevant to the diffusion via the *new* plants added to the system, but they were less relevant to introducing change in *existing* plants, which is a much more difficult task. It is more difficult because attitudes, behavior and relationships already are established there, whereas a brand-new unit has no history and, thus, individuals' expectations can be influenced readily as they enter into the organization. Moreover, a less obvious but important difference between introducing work innovations into the design of a new plant and the redesign of an existing plant is the presence of a natural deadline in the new plant and the absence of the deadline in the old one. A plant management team of an established plant may be genuinely interested in work innovations and may see significant potential, but because the payoff from this activity tends to be longer run, management may tend to procrastinate.

Nevertheless, the innovations pioneered in the new ABC plants gradually are being adapted and utilized in the three established, unionized plants mentioned earlier. The need to compete with directly comparable operations in the newer, higher-performing plants has been an important stimulus to innovation in the older plants. This stimulus has been aided by the transfer of some managers from new plants to the established plants and by the support given by division management for the innovations.

Also facilitating innovation in existing plants have been the constructive labor relations that management has developed over the years. This made it natural for the managers to consult with the union on the particular innovations they wanted to introduce.

In addition, plant managers have been astute in choosing the time and place for introducing innovations into existing plant organizations—for example, to coincide with an important change in product or processes; with the establishment of a new department required by a new product; or with major renovations of physical plant. Such changes in existing plants provide a measure of the same advantages offered by a new plant, because there are firm deadlines established for planning and implementing the social innovation. Physical changes can help unfreeze an established culture.

Another strategic dimension of the ABC diffusion was its pragmatic orientation. In many work innovation programs studied earlier, diffusion was inhibited by the use of concepts which, although inspiring, were unrealistic, such as using "autonomous groups" as a term for work teams to which some self-supervisory responsibilities were delegated. A second inhibiting tendency was for advocates of the new work structures to develop a missionary zeal, which often caused others to take the innovations less seriously. Unrealistic concepts and missionary zeal were absent from almost all ABC projects; they were moderately present in only two of them.

ABC's innovative plants were given little or no external publicity, which further increased the tendency for the managers involved to view them as a way of doing business rather than as social experiments.

Within this pragmatic framework, ABC made excellent use of specialists in organization change. The division has a good record, not only in being well managed but also in using methods of organization development in a balanced and tailored way. Management often had made effective use of external consultants and had reduced its reliance upon them by developing internal consulting expertise as a particular methodology of organization development matured.

An example of the strategic contribution of ABC's consulting staff is a methodology for designing new plants, which includes an intensive 2-week meeting of the nucleus of the new plant management to examine alternative organization designs, to formulate performance goals and to gain cohesion and common commitment. This methodology was utilized designing the third new plant and all subsequent new plants.

VOLVO

The Diffusion Record

Volvo's earliest diffusion efforts began about 1970. Two pioneering projects previously had occurred more or less spontaneously in the auto assembly plant at Torslanda and at a neighboring truck assembly plant.

By 1975, work improvements had been undertaken in at least eight different locations.[2] Common to each of the following was the development of mechanisms for enabling large numbers of workers to participate in the consideration of a range of issues on which they previously had not been consulted. The following descriptions identify particularly the variety of other work improvements that distinguish the projects.

At the Torslanda auto plant which employed 8,000 workers, changes have been occurring incrementally since the earlier experiments. However, except for a few relatively small departments which have employed a more comprehensive approach to restructuring, the program has been characterized by a variety of modest changes made on the margin. These include: (1) physical renovation in the body shop to control noise and to improve ventilation and the plant's color scheme, (2) job enlargement in the assembly plant and (3) delegation of responsibility for quality in the paint shop.

At factories in Oofström and Konga, which employ 5,000 workers and produce auto body components and some of Volvo's own manufacturing machinery, changes have occurred in many departments. The changes have centered on the actual design of work activity, including enlargement of individual jobs, rotation among jobs, formation of work groups and the delegation of supervisory tasks and responsibilities to the work groups. These changes have been accompanied by major training investments to upgrade the participative skills of supervisors and to increase the job-design knowledge of industrial engineers. Engineering efforts have resulted in mechanizations of monotonous work stations; they have also resulted in the insertion of buffer inventories that reduce the rigidity of the tie between workers and production speed.

At Bergslag, where 4,000 workers are employed in the production of transmission components, much of the work improvement has taken the form of mechanization. The plant has made imaginative use of industrial robots, inventing a mechanical hand to do work that is dirty, heavy or monotonous.

At the Arvika foundry, which employs 500 workers, the physical environment for certain work stations has been upgraded significantly.

At Kalmar, Volvo designed a truly revolutionary plant, which began production in the Spring of 1974. Assembly work at Kalmar is performed by about twenty-five groups, each typically composed of about fifteen workers. A group has responsibility for a complete component of the car, such as the electrical system, instrumentation or wheels and brakes. Employees can develop professional pride as they acquire expertise in an entire subsystem of the automobile. The members of the team can influence the working procedures, the internal distribution of jobs and variation in the rate of work. The team is responsible for supplies of materials and plays an active part in quality inspection. The foreman can devote more time to long-range planning and coordination among areas.

The building has been designed to create a small workshop atmosphere. Each group has at its disposal a floor area screened from the view of the other teams, and each has a separate place for relaxation. Instead of moving on a conveyor line, car bodies are transported on battery-driven trolleys, carefully designed to provide more flexibility in the work organization. Buffer areas that hold two trolleys separate groups, providing each group with a measure of independence from the larger system and permit it to vary its pace without affecting downstream operations. The trolleys permit two different work arrangements within an assembly group: straight assembly, in which each worker can specialize in tasks with 5-minute cycle times, and dock assembly, in which each worker performs work with a 20- to 30-minute cycle time as a member of a 3-man team that performs all the work for which the 15-person group is responsible.

At the large engine complex in Skövde, similarly comprehensive innovations have occurred in a new unit put in operation in late 1974. The unit eventually will employ about 900 workers. Most of the work structure principles which characterize the Kalmar plant also were incorporated in the design of both the machinery and assembly areas of this unit.

Volvo has planned a final assembly plant to help serve the U.S. market in Chesapeake, Virginia. The intention there is to build upon the Kalmar work innovations.

How impressive is the record just outlined? The author's judgment is that, on the one hand, when compared with ABC a smaller proportion of Volvo workers is affected, the work experience of those who are involved is affected less dramatically, their mental capacities are less fully utilized in the regular

work activities and the economic payoff to the firm (for example, savings as a percentage of payroll costs) is probably much less. On the other hand, there can be no question that Volvo's achievements are extraordinary. The production technologies of the auto industry lend themselves much less naturally to the type of restructuring employed by ABC in all its plants. Moreover, Volvo's diffusion program is of more recent origin. Perhaps the best appraisal is that the work innovations at Volvo were as attuned to the concerns of its work force in Sweden as ABC's were to its work force in America.

How do we explain Volvo's diffusion record? At least seven explanatory factors can be identified.

Situational Factors, Strategies and Tactics

First, the particular impetus to action was by its nature, a relatively effective one. In the late 1960's turnover in Volvo's plants was very high and rising. One could state dramatically, as Volvo's president did, that unless auto work was made more hospitable to Swedish workers, auto makers could not continue to operate in Sweden. Thus, turnover became the primary target for work innovations and their diffusion.

The turnover target had several characteristics that were conducive to an action-oriented work improvement program. It is a direct symptom of the quality of work life and yet also is linked readily to a variety of business costs. The objective to reduce turnover is neutral ideologically and absolutely uncontroversial—and turnover rate is one of the more readily measured symptoms in the work place.

The turnover focus had other advantages. Turnover was a symptom common to all plants. No plant management could argue that their turnover need not or could not be reduced. Turnover also was a type of target that could be attacked in many ways—from spending large sums on the physical environment to the imaginative reconception of work organization. Thus, improving work to reduce turnover was a game in which everyone had to play—and one in which everyone could play.

Second, the characteristics of some of the particular work improvements which emerged help explain why so many plants could participate in the program within a short period of time. Some work improvements, such as those made in the Arvika Foundry, were relatively straightforward changes in work procedures and physical environment that required no new social or technical skills for implementation. They are simpler to diffuse than the complex and innovative work organizations in Skövde and Kalmar. Other work improvements involved robots, buffers and maneuverable trolleys in lieu of conveyors. The strictly technical aspects of these improvements can be diffused without simultaneously implementing significant social changes, but once installed these devices permit, indeed invite, the development of different organizational forms. Moreover, there is operating in a company like Volvo a technological imperative, such that, once developed, technologies like the engine trolley for Skövde and the larger car trolley for Kalmar undoubtedly will be diffused to all new facilities and progressively introduced in the renovation of existing ones. In many respects the diffusion of these technical innovations will spearhead the diffusion of more advanced work organizations with which they are compatible.

Third, a cooperative union-management framework was a major enabling factor. Union officials supported the projects described above, in part because they could emphasize the worker consultation dimension of these projects as a step toward the union's own objective of creating industrial democracy, and in part because of the care which management took to involve the union at each stage of a project.

Fourth, one cannot explain the diffusion at Volvo without acknowledging the positive leadership provided by the firm's president, Mr. Pehr Gyllenhammar, who articulated in a dramatic way the turnover threat to the Swedish auto industry. Gyllenhammar has been in the forefront among businessmen in western countries in calling for humanization of work, both for the benefit of the human beings themselves and for businesses that employ them. Moreover, he has played a direct role in insisting that the project teams associated with Kalmar and Skövde think boldly and that they not confine themselves to making changes on the margin. Thus Mr. Gyllenhammar deserves some personal credit for the technical innovations which enabled Volvo to break out of the constraints of the conventional conveyor-belt assembly line. He also has backed his rhetoric by approving substantial funds for the work projects.

Such public statements have served as a model for subordinates; equally important, they have publicly committed the firm to a leadership position in addressing the issue. Once established, this public image increased the cost of not following through—to the firm in terms of public relations and to Mr. Gyllenhammar in terms of personal credibility.

Fifth, some features of the Swedish society seem to help explain the amount of diffusion in Volvo. During 1970–76, there was more general interest and support for work innovations in Sweden than in the United States. Also, Sweden has institutional processes for translating general concern into action. There is a pattern in Sweden of responding to guidance from central authorities. At the national level, this has given the Swedish Employers' Federation more leverage over Swedish employers in fostering work innovations throughout Swedish industry than we can ever imagine happening in U.S. industry. At the firm level, the fact that top leadership in Volvo made it company policy to humanize work had more leverage over plant management than it would have in the United States.

Sixth, the organizational mechanisms for pursuing work improvement were apparently effective ones. In existing plants, special working groups were formed to gather data, consult with others and define problems or opportunities. In planning for the new facilities, project organizations were formed to involve managers, union officials, workers and specialists from various industries and academic disciplines. After providing initial impetus and perhaps early guidance, these special units typically were dissolved and their functions absorbed in the line organization.

The communication efforts designed to aid diffusion have included circulation of working papers on technical and other ideas, exchange visits between plants and a conference in 1974 to compare project experiences.

Note that several of the existing plants began their exploration of work improvement in 1970 and 1971 and that both of the new plants at Skövde and Kalmar were being planned in the same time period, that is, during 1972–73. The more dramatic innovations in new plants occurred *after*—and built upon—the experiments previously conducted in existing plants. These patterns avoided the pilot-project syndrome.

Seventh, special note must be made of the importance to Volvo's diffusion (present and potential) of the reorienting and educating of industrial engineers and then making an important part of their task the humanization of work and the physical environment. Swedish engineering ingenuity has led Swedish industry in other respects. Volvo's channeling of this ingenuity into the work improvement program was an important facet of its diffusion program.

TRW, INC.

Though ABC, Volvo and TRW are all treated here as positive examples of diffusion, their records are not comparable. The innovations at ABC and Volvo have proven viable over an extended period of time. TRW appears to be on a relatively impressive path of diffusion, but the projects started are generally too young to be termed viable.

The Diffusion Record

Early in 1974, the Vice President and Direction of Organization Development and Vice President and Director of Industrial Relations, with the active support of their common superior who heads the corporate personnel function in TRW, launched a work restructuring effort.[3] They were assisted initially by a team of several internal professionals and a few external consultants with experience in the field.

In the background at the time the program began was a work restructuring experiment in a small department of one TRW plant, although it did not appear to serve as a pilot project for the program. The program consultants were more oriented to plant-wide projects and to tapping the experience of other firms with projects on that scale. Thus, a general approach to innovation rather than a specific innovation was to be tried initially and improved upon as it was diffused more widely.

By early 1977 the following initiatives had occurred. In eighteen separate locations, one or more exploratory sessions had occurred between a top plant team (or comparable unit[4] of knowledgeable workers) and members of the consulting team. Typically these sessions were intended to clarify the philosophy of the TRW program, to familiarize members of the plant team with the many forms that work restructuring can take, to illustrate how the ideas might be applied to the plant in question and, finally, to leave the plant team with an approach for

determining the feasibility and desirability of undertaking a project there. The following quote is illustrative of the message left with a plant team:

Your answers to the following questions are relevant not only to whether a project is feasible, but also to how the work organization should be designed or redesigned. Preliminary answers to these questions are required in the feasibility phase. More thorough answers are needed in developing and refining a tentative design.

First, are the productivity and quality of work life objectives understood and shared within the team considering work restructuring?

Second, are work restructuring ideas applicable to the technology and work force in question? How?

Third, are there significant potential economic benefits? How much? And how are they estimated?

Fourth, are there significant potential benefits to the employees affected? In what form?

Fifth, can management become committed? Does it have or can it acquire requisite attitudes and skills?

Sixth, can the union, as well as employees, be expected to support the project?

In fourteen out of eighteen cases, the initial visit was followed up by serious exploration on the part of the plant team and by additional consulting visits. Of these fourteen cases, twelve remained active after an initial test of feasibility. One of the two dropouts resulted when the union membership failed to vote a sufficient majority for establishing a plant-wide productivity bonus, which had been conceived as the most appropriate initial step in the work restructuring plan. The second dropout occurred after a plant study team had investigated two different approaches; these investigations came to a halt when an economic recession began to preoccupy plant management. These two plants may yet resume their exploration of work restructuring.

Of the twelve projects which remained active after an initial testing phase, there were actual steps to restructure work in nine. However, one of the nine projects essentially was nullified when the plant's business dropped off sharply. The other three projects were still in the study stage early in 1977.

Thus in the spring of 1977 it was appropriate to count eight work-restructuring projects which were being facilitated by the corporate-level program.

Four of the projects involved new plants; two other projects were in established manufacturing plants with unions; and, finally, two of the "plants" had major departments which employed professionals. Each of those plants employing professionals involved less than fifty people. The other 6 projects ranged from slightly less than 100 people to just under 1,000.

The nature of these innovations varied widely. The work structures in the four new plants have similar features, conceptually; that is, skill-based pay schemes, work teams, support activities integrated into the line and lean supervisory arrangements. However, the translation of these concepts into operational systems with actual procedures and roles has created a variation in design considerably greater than in the case of the new plants in the ABC Division.

One of the projects in an established unionized plant started with a plant-wide productivity bonus. By 1977 this step not only had achieved gains in productivity and quality of work life, but also had created a favorable climate in which other work restructuring steps could be considered, for example, formation of work teams that can assume more self-supervisory responsibility.

The other project in a unionized plant had as its initial focus the development of trust and problem-solving between union and management officials. This was followed by an open process of eliciting ideas for quality of work life and productivity improvement from the shop floor and then by the negotiation of an agreement to allow work restructuring experiments to occur on a departmental basis.

Without describing the two other projects which involved professionals, it is important to note that they take forms different from any of the above. This adds further to the diversity of forms which work restructuring has taken in the TRW program.

As indicated earlier, most of the innovations in these eight projects were not yet well established, and a few projects took only one or two steps toward comprehensive work restructuring. Nonetheless, most and maybe all of the eight reasonably may be counted as instances of diffusion. Failure, if it occurs, probably will be due to deficiencies in design and implementation or bad luck rather than to the fact that diffusion did not take place.

A 3-day "Plant Managers' Workshop" held in February 1977, attended by teams from seven of the projects where work restructuring was underway, confirmed for all participants as well as for other observers that the TRW work restructuring program was well launched and that it was entering a new stage.

How do we explain this diffusion within TRW? First it is important to understand how the strategy relates to background factors; then it is relevant to consider the elements of the diffusion strategy and the functions they are intended to perform. However, any assessments offered about the actual effects of particular elements of the diffusion strategy or related background factors are hypotheses and are offered in advance of systematic evidence.[5]

Situational Factors, Strategies and Tactics

The TRW firm is a large manufacturing plant which is highly diversified. Its growth pattern historically had been by acquisitions as well as by internal growth.

Each of the factors had implications for diffusion. First, because there were more than 100 plants, even if only a small fraction of the firm's plants were ready to explore innovations, it still would be possible to achieve a critical mass of effort to create a corporate program with momentum. Also if the initial innovations proved effective, the large number of remaining plants would provide a correspondingly large opportunity to achieve a return on the initial effort and risk.

Second, the fact that it was a manufacturing-based firm means that innovations that promised advantage in the manufacturing arm of the business could, and perhaps would need to, receive top management attention.

Third, because the manufacturing system was highly diversified, the learning in one plant was not necessarily directly applicable to other plants. TRW, Inc. businesses included electronics and computer-based services; car and truck production and replacement parts; spacecraft and propulsion products; fasteners, tools and bearings; and energy products and services. Some plants were capital-intensive, others were labor-intensive. Some were characterized by assembly or batch processes, others by continuous-process technology. Some were marginal plants that produced for a commodity market, while others were highly profitable plants that served a unique niche in the marketplace. For some plants cost was the basic competitive factor; for others delivery and quality were strategic. Some plants were characterized by mature technologies; others were distinguishable by relatively rapid rates of technological change. Thus in contrast to the ABC situation, the economic payoffs and improved quality of work life that derived from innovations in one plant could not be assumed to be available in the next plant in the same order of magnitude.

This meant that there was greater need for a methodology for assessing the size of the dollar stakes and psychological stakes associated with a particular project and also for an educational effort to ensure that project-by-project assessments would be made.

Moreover, again in contrast to ABC, the work structure that proved effective in one plant (for example, team composition, compensation scheme, training investment, supervisory roles) was not necessarily appropriate in the next plant. The learning transferred from one plant to the next had to occur at a higher level of abstraction (principles of design rather than designs themselves).

Fourth, to the extent that growth had been achieved through acquisition rather than from within, TRW was a mosaic of management subcultures, in contrast to the more or less uniform management cultures found in Volvo. The varied management philosophies meant that different management groups in TRW would approach the question of plant floor innovations very differently, thus requiring a diffusion strategy that recognized "market segments"—to borrow an important principle from marketing science.

The first two background factors, size and the manufacturing dominance, had positive implications for the diffusion effort. On the other hand, diversification and the acquisitions history complicated the diffusion task in TRW (relative to that faced by ABC and Volvo) and required a more deliberate program for promoting diffusion.

When the program was launched in 1974, it included an objective to initiate several projects more or less simultaneously. One rationale for this was to avoid the self-encapsulation tendency of a single pilot project. By the same logic, the aim was to have a project in each of four major business groups; the company wished to overcome a proclivity to concentrate resources in groups which were

characterized by management philosophies most receptive to the innovations.

Additional considerations argued for initiating on several fronts at once. Because of the size of the firm, in order for a program to be taken seriously as a corporate program, it had to quickly achieve a level of activity and results that would be associated with a portfolio of plant projects rather than a pilot project. Also, because of the diversity of the large TRW plant system which constituted the eventual market for work innovations, to achieve diversity became the goal in the initial wave of projects along as many of the following dimensions as possible: new and established plants; unionized and nonunionized plants; white-collar and blue-collar work forces; and assembly, batch and continuous-process technology.

The fact that this corporate-wide program was launched in 1974 after there was some credible experience outside TRW and at least one instructive grass-roots experiment in one location within TRW was important because it enabled those who conceived of a corporate-wide program to be bold and ambitious.

The objective of launching a number of projects in a relatively short period of time was achieved. This relatively rapid development of momentum had important consequences beyond those reported above as part of the rationale. The momentum had a very favorable impact on the commitment of several types of groups associated with the program—the participating plants which were reassured by the fact that there are other innovating plants; the internal and external consultants whose efforts were reinforced by the evidence of progress; and the top corporate supporters of the program who could better justify the attention and priority being given it.

The parallel progress of several projects provided both an advantage and a disadvantage for the process of cross-project learning. The advantage was that what was learned in one innovating plant could be considered quickly in another plant. The disadvantage was that sometimes the things learned in one plant occurred too late to prevent another plant from making the same mistake.

The above discussion had addressed the overall diversity of TRW's plant system, but within any one of the firm's twelve operating divisions, there often were several plants producing the same product or similar products. Hence, within a division one aspect of the strategy used at ABC could be employed, namely, after a new plant pioneers the innovation and demonstrates its effectiveness, the established plants begin to take more interest in the innovation. By early 1977 this process already had worked in one division and had potential in several others.

Another strategic dimension of the diffusion program was its pragmatic versus romantic orientation. The pragmatic formulation of the TRW program was reflected in the fact that initially projects were called "productivity projects," although it was understood from the outset that they were designed to promote both productivity and quality of work life. Later the rhetoric referring to the goals of the program became more balanced.

From the beginning, it was understood by all concerned that to be successful, projects must be owned by line management. Plant managers, for example, must see the work innovations as an integral component of how they manage their business, not as a personnel policy or practice that could be designed or implemented by others.

The pragmatic orientation was reflected in a growing recognition of several "realities." First, different projects would and should take quite different forms. Second, comprehensive change in existing

plants might often require a period of several years and might involve several steps, each more or less "digested" before the next is undertaken. Third, highly positive work cultures, characterized by self-management capabilities, cannot be created overnight but must be instituted progressively, hand-in-hand with the development of the work culture which it contemplates.

Although pragmatic, the program was based on two articles-of-faith assumptions which formed the basis of all activities of the program. The first idea was that in a large fraction of work organizations today there exists a significant potential for improving business results and quality of work life by modifying the work organization. The magnitude of this potential must be assessed on a case-by-case basis. The second idea was that all elements of the work system need to reinforce one another.

The program structure and its activities were designed to fit the background factors and strategic objectives of the program described above. The activities and the functions they were intended to perform are presented in Figure 51-1.

The diagram is to some degree self-explanatory. Many of the activities and their functions already have been referred to above. Four structural elements of the program, however, deserve comment: first is the cochairmanship of the program by the top

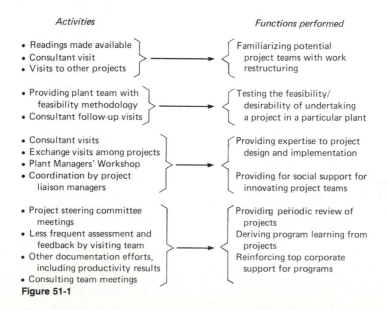

Figure 51-1

organizational development executive and the top industrial relations executive, who clearly communicated their joint commitment to the program. This joint commitment was especially important in the case of diffusion to unionized plants. Second is the project liaison manager, for example, the person on the program consulting team who was responsible for providing lead consultation to the project, monitoring and reporting developments in the project and coordinating all outside assistance provided to the project. Third a structural element that has been used in some projects is a "project steering committee," comprised of members of plant and division management, one or more consultants and perhaps others. The idea is to provide for a periodic review of the progress of a project, to provide a sounding board for the project team and to ensure that the team is getting the outside support it required from the division and consultants. More frequent meetings were especially useful during the late design stage and during approximately the first year of implementation. A fourth important and unique structural element of the program is a "consulting team" which had held 2-day meetings, twice a year since mid-1974. The consulting team included (1) the cochairmen of the program and their superior; (2) the several internal consultants who report to them and who spend full-time on the project activities; (3) corporate-level staff specialists on compensation, communication, finance and manufacturing; (4) a number of division and group-level personnel managers; and (5) a few outside consultants. All are considered program "consultants" who may be deployed to contribute to a particular project or to contribute to the development of a methodology which can be used across many projects, for example, the assessment methodology referred to above.

Of course, as intended, the consulting team has helped ensure that project-level learnings are shared, that consulting resources are deployed strategically and that the need for new program methodologies are identified and then met.

An additional effect of creating this forum of interdisciplinary specialists and personnel generalists from various business groups in TRW has been to create a broad base of ownership for the program. That they have been used as consultants has reinforced a basic tenet of the program, which is that "consultants" should be referred to with a small

"c"—that is, they are where you find them, which is not always represented by a shingle or a business card.

CONCLUSIONS

What can we learn from these three cases of diffusion? At the first level, these cases demonstrate that it *is* possible to diffuse work innovations systematically and effectively throughout a multiplant system.

At the second level, we can learn something about a number of issues that must be considered in formulating a diffusion strategy. Perhaps the three cases can shed light on each of seven issues framed below as questions:

1. *In what types of firms can ambitious work restructuring programs be undertaken?* The most striking similarity of these firms is that all three are well managed and their managements are relatively attuned to the human dimension. Perhaps those are two prerequisites. The dissimilarities among the three systems in other respects are equally interesting, indicating the variety of firms that can undertake work restructuring on an ambitious scale. Their competitive orientations vary—ABC is marketing-oriented, Volvo is engineering-oriented and TRW is manufacturing-oriented—although their business orientations do not necessarily cover a broad spectrum. The fact that impressive diffusion occurred in multiplant systems with three types of interdependence among plants is also significant: ABC plants comprised a series of parallel production capacities not linked by product flow but often "competitively" producing the same product for the market; Volvo was a highly integrated system with the products of one plant flowing to another; the plants within one of TRW's more than twenty divisions or groups typically were interdependent in one of the above ways, but these divisions and groups themselves were generally unrelated, making the system, as a whole, rate low on interdependence among its parts.

2. *Toward what goals should the work restructuring program be directed?* At one level of abstraction the goals were the same in all three cases—namely, the innovations should serve the business needs of the organization and the human needs of the members of the organization. In none of the cases was there any attempt to blur the fact that the managers associated with the program saw the innovations as good business. The pragmatic orientation was essential for the diffusion achieved.

At a more concrete level the three cases had different foci: increasing "productivity" was the by-word in TRW; "turnover" was the frequently cited target in Volvo; and something like "system performance," including high utilization of a very expensive technology, was always in the minds of ABC innovators. As argued in the case of Volvo, the selection of concrete goals can be an important tactical choice in implementing a diffusion program.

3. *Where should program leadership emanate from?* Although top leadership seemed critically important in Volvo, the absence of any comparable public commitment by the top executives in ABC and TRW was not disabling. Leadership for the innovations in ABC resided for a long period in managers of innovative plants. Eventually the innovations merely became a pervasive part of the total division culture and leadership equally diffused. Leadership in TRW at the program level was provided by the corporate personnel function, and at the project level, it was provided by plant managers.

Significantly all three firms took an inclusive, constructive stance toward the unions when innovations were contemplated in unionized plants.

4. *How concretely versus abstractly should one characterize the innovative approach one wants to diffuse?* In the ABC case in which the plants were very similar to each other, the innovations were transferred from one plant to the next with relatively little variation. Thus, the characterization of the innovations being diffused could be and were at a relatively concrete level. TRW offered a contrasting case. The system was highly diversified and the forms which work restructuring took were highly varied. Therefore, the innovations needed to be characterized at a higher level of generality. Concreteness in the case of TRW had to be achieved by pointing to several specific alternatives.

As a general proposition it may be desirable not to go to a higher level of abstraction than necessary, but that level itself depends on the diversity of the system.

5. *Which is better—a single pilot project or several projects initiated simultaneously?* ABC avoided the self-encapsulating tendency of a single pilot project by drawing managers for the second project from the pool of managers involved in the first project. Both Volvo and TRW avoided this by initiating multiple projects. The latter strategy is more available today because more design knowledge and experience are available to draw on.

6. *Is it better to start with existing plants or to wait for a new plant startup?* Volvo was able to make marginal innovations in large departments and more comprehensive experiments in small departments in existing plants during 1970–73 before its more radical innovations in two near facilities which began operations in 1974. ABC began with a new plant, and only after several new plants had adopted the new work structure did some innovations begin to spread to the older plants. TRW, in effect, started with both. Thus, it appears that either way can work well. It would appear that one can afford to be opportunistic on this dimension.

7. *What should be the core methodology for transmitting innovations?* The vehicles for diffusion varied across the three cases, each a natural fit to the situation.

ABC illustrates the powerful effect of moving managers who have direct experience with work innovations into other units of the organization. Volvo illustrates the potential effect of developing technological innovations that are interrelated with work arrangements. The channels and roles within a firm that normally ensure the diffusion of technical innovations are added to those which one otherwise might have used to promote the social innovation by itself.

TRW illustrates the potential in certain circumstances for using a plant-wide productivity bonus as the leading edge for change in existing plants in a way analogous to Volvo's use of a technological device like trolleys, buffers or robots. TRW's plant-wide productivity bonus has its own effect, but even more importantly it enabled other restructuring steps to happen—as does Volvo's technological devices.

TRW also best illustrates the development of explicit structures, roles and activities that may be used to implement a diffusion strategy; indeed, that are required if diffusion is to occur at a reasonable rate throughout a system comprised of highly diversified parts—diversified in terms of technologies, business strategies and management cultures.

Assistance from a central group was more pronounced in TRW than in either ABC or Volvo.

The answers to many of the seven questions strike a theme—that is, "it depends." This theme signals a third level of learning about diffusion programs.

ABC management achieved an impressive record of diffusion by certain conscious steps, in particular, interplant transfers of personnel and interplant comparisons. Why these steps were effective only could be understood in reference to the division's growth pattern and the nature of its products.

The Volvo and TRW situations differed in important respects, requiring that the diffusion strategy be formulated differently. Their strategies appear to be as well suited to their respective situations as the ABC strategy was to its own.

The general lesson that emerges is that although a corporate program may usefully borrow elements from the successful programs of other firms, the overall strategy must be developed on the basis of a thorough understanding of the firm, for example, the larger social context, the firm's patterns, prod-

ucts, technologies, management culture and prior experience in organization development.

NOTES

1 Richard E. Walton, "The Diffusion of New Work Structures' Explaining Why Success Didn't Take," *Organizational Dynamics* (Winter 1975).
2 Rolf Lindholm and Jan-Peder Norstedt, *The Volvo Report* (Stockholm: Swedish Employers' Confederation, 1975).
3 The purpose and approval of the TRW effort is outlined in "Employee Productivity Projects," a working paper drafted in 1974 by Mr. Sheldon A. Davis and Mr. Robert Hauserman and periodically revised on the basis of experience and input from members of the consulting team.
4 For easy reference we refer to all of the TRW units as "plants."
5 A more systematic assessment of the extent and determinants of TRW's diffusion of work restructuring as well as of two other organization development methodologies, namely "team building" and "organization sensing," is being conducted by Ove Myrseth, a doctoral student at the Harvard Business School.

Reading 52

Red Flags in Organization Development
Larry E. Greiner

Many organizations have embarked in recent years on ambitious programs of large-scale change labeled with the high-sounding title of "organization development" (or OD, as it has come to be called by its devotees.) A very special meaning has become attached to OD, usually referring to the widespread application of an intensive educational program within an organization for the twin purposes of changing managerial behavior and improving the total performance of the organization.

A basic proposition underlying these OD programs centers around the notion that if an educational program can cause a large number of individual managers to alter their behavioral styles in working with others, then the organization as a whole will be transformed—and so will its over-all effectiveness.

Although some of these programs have been uniquely designed for a particular organization, a great majority are prepacked by outside consultants. Such packaged programs include the managerial grid, versions of sensitivity training, synectics, and a host of lesser known programs designed by small consulting companies and academics who have moved forward to meet the demand.

Despite the differences between one OD program and the next, there are some common features that apply to all of them. Basically, they center around an educational training program attended by, preferably, a large number of managers and even nonmanagerial employees from a single organization. These training laboratories concentrate on presenting a new role model or behavioral style for managers and employees to emulate back on the job when solving problems in interpersonal settings. The role model tends to be universally prescribed for all who attend the laboratory sessions—that is, if you change your individual styles to this one "best" approach, then you and the organization will perform better.

This learning experience is intensive and intended to be long range; the learning message is not imparted in a one-day session, but begins with a one- to two-week educational laboratory conducted away from the job. It is usually followed by numerous on-the-job learning activities after the initial training session in order to make the reeducation "stick."

NEED FOR PERSPECTIVE

For the last few years, two colleagues of mine, Louis Barnes of Harvard and Paul Leitch, formerly of Harvard, have joined me in studying and learning about the application of various approaches to OD. Out of these efforts has come an increasing concern with some disturbing trends recurring in the design and conduct of many organization development programs.

My purpose in this article is to build on this experience by taking a critical look at these trends and offering some additional perspective on them. To date, this perspective seems to be lacking. Too many organizations have embarked on OD for a number of ill-founded reasons—because it is the "thing to do," or because "change is the watchword of the day," or because "I went to one of their laboratory training sessions; it was good for me, and it will be good for my managers."

To an extent this new initiative has been healthy. A growing number of consultants and companies have at least taken the leap to utilize nontraditional approaches for improving behavioral conditions within their firms. No longer can the behavioral scientist be condemned for sitting in his ivory tower conducting meaningless experiments on his students. Nor can the manager be criticized for forgetting about the human aspects of his organization while drumming away on production at all costs.

But there is also much to be concerned about when examining such an enthusiastic rush into organization development. Numerous methods used in these programs are relatively untested; their deficiencies have not been weeded out through long experience or research.

Moreover, disturbing symptoms of the failure of current brands of OD have been appearing frequently in research studies, in anecdotal comments by managers, and in the literature of organizations. Some skeptics contend that OD is a luxury afforded only by affluent organizations, but which is usually discarded when a major crisis arises. One study has shown that a major OD effort in a government agency failed to make any impact on the climate of the organization, although it did produce small increments in behavioral change.[1] In this case, one wonders how long the individual changes will last.

A thoughtful review of many studies of OD by Dunnette and Campbell has concluded:

. . . none of the studies yields any evidence that the changes in job behavior have any favorable effect on actual performance effectiveness. Thus, there is little to support a claim that T-group or laboratory education effects any substantial behavior change back on the job for any large proportion of trainees. Whatever change does occur seems quite limited in scope and may not contribute in any important way to changes in overall job effectiveness.[2]

Of considerable concern, in the absence of more convincing research, has been the tendency for consultants and organizations to "freeze" prematurely on particular approaches, indicating that they have already found the one "best" approach. Vested interests no doubt help to explain this absence of self-critique; if I as a consultant design a program, I have a strong commitment and personal interest in its success. Therefore, while I may make small refinements in my methodology, I am not likely to alter its basic approach. Similarly, if I as a manager have committed funds and support to a particular program, I am not likely to treat it as an academic experiment where the chips fall as they may. Rather, I want it to succeed just as I do with any program implemented within my organization.

It is this unhealthy trend toward premature commitment that should be questioned, especially in

[1]Larry Greiner, D. Paul Leitch, Louis B. Barnes, "The Simple Complexity of Organizational Climate in a Government Agency," in R. Tagiuri and George Litwin, eds., *Organizational Change: Explorations of a Concept* (Boston: Division of Research, Harvard Business School, 1968).

[2]Marvin D. Dunnette and John P. Campbell, "Laboratory Education: Impact on People and Organizations," in Gene Dalton and others, eds., *Organization Change and Development* (Homewood, Ill.: Richard D. Irwin, 1970).

terms of what has been working and not working. Such a reexamination seems essential if we are to benefit from our experience instead of slipping back into the pitfall of making the same mistakes again.

SIX RED FLAGS

I wish to raise red flags by questioning six trends that may be preventing the very changes that are being sought. For each warning signal, I will suggest an alternative way of thinking that might open up other directions for future OD programs.

Flag #1—Individual Before the Organization

Many OD programs are characterized by a seemingly logical sequence of learning and behavior change, beginning typically with an exclusive focus on the individual employee and his style of behavior. Next, attention is given to the small group in which the employee works, assuming that if the individual is to change his behavior, there must be support in his immediate work surroundings. Third, once many individuals and small groups are changing, emphasis shifts to intergroup issues, such as resolving conflicts between R&D and production. Finally, after these basic subunits of the organization have been reeducated, consideration is given to issues affecting the entire organization, such as its corporate strategy.[3]

There are two principal reasons why I wish to question this gradually expanding sequence from individual to organization. First, the problems of a particular organization may not fit this exact sequence. It could well be that issues of over-all company strategy are dominant in the beginning and that, until these are more clearly resolved, there can be little clarity of direction for specific changes within basis subunits. A second concern with the "individual first" logic is that spontaneity of problem solving can easily be stifled. I have seen organizations in which certain managers have discovered a serious interdepartmental problem early in their OD program, only to be told by higher management to "cool it" and work on their own team first, since this was the prescribed stage of OD at that time.

To replace the individual-to-organization sequence, I would suggest a more situational and issue-centered approach. That is, if the management of the organization is not using OD to attack major problems affecting a majority of employees, then employees are likely to turn off quite rapidly on OD. For example, if problems center more around formal organization structure, it makes little sense for OD to begin with the behavioral styles of individual managers. Why not change the structure instead of beating around the bush?

Another important guideline is to work simultaneously on both the individual and his surroundings. We know from research on the dynamics of learning and psychotherapy that individuals do not make changes in their behavior entirely on their own initiative. They require strong support from all levels of their environment. Thus, employees in organizations need reinforcement from not only their immediate work groups, but also from the climate of their departments and the formal organization itself. For instance, if a centralized structure is being adjusted to be more decentralized, individual managers will usually have to be assisted in learning through reeducation new behavior skills for acting more autonomously.

Flag #2—Informal Before Formal Organization

A strong assumption among many OD advocates is that informal organization takes precedence over formal organization. Therefore, they concentrate their educational efforts primarily on the teaching of new "values" or social norms which, if accepted by many colleagues, create social pressure for conformity to new behavior patterns.

Clearly, the informal culture of an organization is a strong determinant of how individuals behave; therefore, it must be addressed in organization change efforts. Yet any manager can tell you that the formal aspects of his organization are also quite important. An OD program may teach the value of participative behavior, but it will not make much headway if managers in this same organization are working under a very rigid and autocratic budget-setting method.

A major reason why formal organization is omitted from many OD efforts is that a taboo frequently exists among OD proponents which says that formal organization is bad or unimportant. This is largely a hangover from the old human relations days when humanistic behavioral scientists preferred to believe

[3]A clear statement of this sequence is described in Robert R. Blake and Jane S. Mouton, *The Managerial Grid* (Houston: Gulf Publishing Co., 1964).

that formal organization was only something written on paper or that it was a tool of scientific management to produce mass conformity among employees.

Now we know a great deal more about formal organization, and it is not necessarily as bad as the humanists have contended. Several researchers have shown that formal organization can, indeed, significantly affect the behavior of employees, and that much of this behavior cannot be described as oppressive. For example, Lawrence and Lorsch have shown that formal project teams with considerable delegated formal responsibility can operate in a participative and creative manner. Or advocates of management by objectives have shown how informal participation can be incorporated into formal goal-setting methods.[4]

Therefore, we need to design OD efforts that incorporate a closer connection between formal and informal organization. During the educational phases of OD, managers need to be taught more about formal organization and how it can be used to complement and reinforce changes in their behavior. Many alternative forms of structure are available to managers, not just pyramids with limits on span of control: there are also product, project, and matrix forms of organization. Assumptions that there is one best type of formal organization are as parochial as the mentality that believes in one best type of organization development.

Flag #3—Behavior Before Diagnosis

Most OD programs stress a new behavioral model in reeducating managers. Whether the program be based on sensitivity training, the managerial grid, or management by objectives, the learning content of these programs is based on the assimilation of a new form of work behavior that will supposedly be more effective in decision making.

In other words, they are teaching managers to *act* differently—to be more "participative," "open," "confronting," or "authentic," depending upon the value orientation of the program.

What concerns me about this behavioral emphasis

is that the thinking side of managers is frequently overlooked. Where their outward behavior is considered by OD, their conceptual thought process are neglected in terms of how they analyze problems or think about their organizations. This oversight can result in some interesting dilemmas once managers begin to behave differently.

One organization with which I am acquainted began an OD effort that stressed team problem solving and the open confrontation of troublesome issues. This was a big step forward for the organization, whose key managers had previously avoided discussions of important problems because of vested interests among them. However, once these managers took the step and placed the issues on the table, they were not particularly adept at making a thorough intellectual analysis of their problems, which were extremely complicated, interwoven with both emotional and technical aspects.

OD programs need to stress the cognitive along with the behavioral and emotional dimensions of more effective problem solving. For example, at the Harvard Business School, we work very hard in the classroom to teach two important aspects of managerial thinking. First, the student must learn to conceive of an organization as an open system and to think in terms of the important conceptual variables that are relevant to a systemic way of thinking about behavior in organizations.

Second, we see a need to practice over and over again a systematic diagnosis of numerous case situations so that these future managers can more quickly ferret out the problems of a situation and design unique solutions. Sharp and objective intellectual insights into management problems seldom come through brilliant lectures or interesting books on problem solving.

Flag #4—Process Before Task

A large majority of OD programs place primary emphasis on improving the behavioral processes of decision making while deemphasizing or ignoring the content and task aspects of operating issues facing the organization. Thus, for example, it is assumed that if a manager can learn to participate more skillfully in team meetings, the content of team decisions will be dealt with more effectively.

While attention to behavioral processes is indeed a worthy focal point, there is a danger that managers

---

[4]Paul Lawrence and Jay Lorsch, *Organization and Environment* (Cambridge: Harvard Business School, 1967); Joan Woodward, *Management and Technology* (London: Her Majesty's Stationery Office, 1958); John Humble, *Management by Objectives in Action* (New York: McGraw-Hill Book Company, 1970).

will become preoccupied with, and even oversensitive to, their own behavior. As a consequence, meetings will be called to discuss the most trivial of issues in order to avoid affronting people; at the opposite extreme, personal issues will be put on the agenda for team discussion when they might better be discussed privately between two individuals.

This new norm of openness, as taught in many OD programs, is frequently abused in a carte blanche manner without thoughtful attention being paid to questions of whom to be open with, about what, and where and when. In order to make these decisions, one must also keep in mind the task aspects of the job. It makes little sense to call a meeting when knowledge for making a decision rests outside the group or when little content preparation has been done ahead of time to shed light on difficult problem issues.

It is no wonder that some managers are frequently turned off by OD programs that place exclusive stress on behavioral processes. These same managers are often dismissed by the consultants as being afraid or insensitive. Yet another plausible explanation is that these managers are understandably concerned about making progress toward solving difficult operating problems. They want to get on with the work, not just sit around contemplating their navels. Of course, this work-oriented preoccupation can be an obstacle too, since these same managers may ignore the importance of building behavioral commitment to decisions they wish to make.

My suggestion to the OD advocates is for them to strive for a better understanding of how task demands influence the behavioral process, not just the other way around. I have seen great OD progress made in one company when a group of conflicting functional managers were brought together for one day to discuss a single operating problem. Prior to this meeting, they had argued mainly over the telephone or behind the backs of other managers about the problem.

In this situation, the OD advocate with a process orientation might have focused the meeting on the question of "Why are you in conflict?" Yet the consultant involved here made no explicit reference to interpersonal conflicts. Instead, he focused the group's attention on analyzing the particular operating problem and reaching a consensus solution by the end of the day. And this is just what the group did, although it took a great deal of argument and soul searching.

What is fascinating about the outcome of this meeting is that a lot of individual stereotypes about other people were changed, as each manager's preconceived opinions began to break down under a more constructive arrangement for problem solving. In other words, behavioral processes were facilitated by a productive task discussion, even when behavioral problems were not the explicit agenda.

Flag #5—Experts Before the Manager

Since the technology of OD is often elaborate, wordy, and known only to outside consultants (or staff personnel responsible for OD), these professionals are tempted to presume more than they know and to "talk down" to practicing managers. It is a reflection of the old dichotomy of we (the consultants or staff) are the experts and you (the Managers) are the doers. Therefore, we, the "knowledge guys," are here to tell you, the "practitioners," how to improve your organization.

There are understandable reasons for this point of view. The experts will often argue convincingly that OD is such powerful stuff that, if directed by untrained people, it can result in very naive applications that can hurt rather than help an organization. And managers will often subscribe to this argument too, preferring to believe that the experts know more about their concepts and methods than they do; therefore, we, the managers, who know more about action taking, will confine ourselves to carrying out their recommendations.

Several pitfalls are hidden in this rather arbitrary role division. First, there is the possibility that managers will become overdependent on the experts. As a result, dependent managers do not question or argue with the professionals; they just keep looking to them for direction. Second, the experts seldom know the particular organization as well as the managers themselves. Therefore, the outsiders often end up recommending general methods and techniques that have been useful in prior situations, but which may or may not be relevant to the problems at hand. Third, the experts are removed from responsibility for daily operating decisions, thereby making it difficult for them to respond continuously to the important issues that come up daily while OD is in progress. Finally, and perhaps most serious, the experts usually feel more responsibility for and have more commitment to what they are doing than the managers. The OD program, in essence, becomes the experts' program rather than the organization's.

One way out of this dilemma is to share and develop more expertise and commitment between experts and managers. Organizations which have recognized this need have sought to train not only their own internal staff people but also their line managers for assuming a more active role in the conduct of organization development.

Early in the planning of OD, there is a special need to involve key managers in the diagnosis and planning of the direction and methods for implementing the program. Here the managers must exercise sufficient independence to tell the experts that they are "all wet" when foreign ideas seem irrelevant. To do this requires more knowledge than managers typically have about organization development; hence, their own background should contain an exposure to various methods for introducing OD. This does not mean that they should become OD experts, but that they should have sufficient exposure to see through the jargon that so often pervades the OD field.

In addition, managers should be prepared to make known what they are most familiar with—the specific characteristics of the operation they manage and what they perceive to be the main developmental needs. Here is where the experts would be advised to sit still and listen carefully.

Flag #6—The Package Before the Situation

Underlying much of what has been said so far is the deductive fallacy of imposing a program of organization development that has been designed by outsiders who do not know the organization. As a result, there is an insensitive application of a nicely packaged program, based on general theories or misleading past experiences. The organization is asked to fit itself to the package, not vice versa.

This deductive approach is not unknown in the consulting world. Consulting firms, like any other business organization, develop a product to sell. Moreover, they find that the more specific and tangible their product, the more the customer will be attracted to it. Only a few large management consulting firms, such as McKinsey and Booz, Allen & Hamilton, have been able to develop multiple services that can be applied flexibly, though even here each of these firms is frequently identified as being keen on certain solutions which they have grown accustomed to over the years.

I would suggest a more tailor-made approach to the design of OD programs. Here the program is fitted to the situation. This does not mean that a completely new package has to be designed for each customer. Rather, the OD expert must have a larger number of tools in his kit so that he can apply a wrench, not a hammer, when only bolts need tightening. Another guideline, as urged earlier, is to encourage managers from within the organization to provide more data and suggestions on what needs to be done. They may have a much more intimate knowledge of company problems than do the outsiders. Their handicap is that they are seldom mobilized to put their heads together, due largely to barriers in communication processes within the organization.

A nice combination of an outsider-insider approach is reflected in the work of Beckhard.[5] He provides a learning structure for managers to get together but does not define their problems and solutions for them. Rather the managers, by being asked to meet in small groups to confront and identify major issues facing the organization, are the ones who give substance to their organization development efforts. In such cases, Beckhard uses his position as an outside expert to convene the meeting and arrange a focus for productive discussion, but he does not presume to have the answers.

FUTURE ACTIONS

New directions in organization development depend upon a critical assessment of where we are today. I have pointed to six questionable trends that give rise for concern. These include tendencies for OD to begin with the individual before the organization, stress informal values over formal organization, prescribe behavioral actions without diagnostic skills, focus more on behavioral relationships than task accomplishment, adhere to standardized pro-

[5]Richard Beckhard, "The Confrontation Meeting," *Harvard Business Review* (May-June, 1967).

grams over situational needs, and place the expert ahead of the manager. Failure to take account of these other realities of organization life has, I believe, seriously limited the promised impact of organization development. So where do we go from here?

It would be a serious mistake to swing over completely to the other end of the themes; this would only raise six more flags. In doing so, we would prevent the use of the very real expertise that currently resides with experts in the field of organizational development. Instead, I have suggested alternative actions that attempt to build on the strengths from both extremes, since each points to a piece of reality that should be considered in organization development.

First, begin OD with specific and major problem issues founded in the developmental needs facing the organization and many of its employees. These needs may lie in the individual domain with the styles of managers or they may lie in the strategy of the firm. Whichever the case, we know that at some point in any organization change the units of individual, group, intergroup, and organization will have to be addressed, but we should not prescribe the exact sequence ahead of time.

Second, be ready to achieve a more complementary relationship between formal and informal organization during organization development. New informal values will not be accepted for long unless they are reinforced by parallel changes in formal prescriptions. Nor will changes in formal structure be sufficient unless the informal culture is adjusted to accept and encourage the directions implied by new formal designs.

Third, stress a closer integration of diagnostic and action-oriented role models so that we "look while we leap," and we keep on looking as we continue to act. If an educational program is called for, then do not simply stress a single action model, one that, for example, relies exclusively on team problem solving. Instead, sharpen a manager's intellectual insights so that he may choose his actions more appropriately and flexibly.

Yet his action skills should not be neglected, since bright insights are not always equivalent to skillful behavior. Let him know, for instance, that participative behavior can produce certain beneficial results, but also inform him that, under certain conditions, participation can be inappropriate.

Fourth, place more emphasis on the task concerns of managers while educating them in behavioral processes. We cannot ignore the reality of work and the continuing pressure upon managers to deal with the immediate task issues facing them. They may show greater appreciation for the behavioral dynamics in decision making if they can more directly experience task accomplishment at the same time.

Fifth, achieve a more collaborative planning and problem-solving relationship between experts and managers in designing OD programs. Avoid the arbitrary role division of expert as planner and manager as doer. Managers have much to contribute in diagnosing their own ills while experts can provide new tools and fresh perspectives for enlivening managerial insight—without going so far as to recommend one "best" solution.

Sixth, improve the integration of packaged OD materials with the unique demands of each organizational situation. OD tools are just that—handy to have available but applied only when needed. A greater variety of tools must be developed so that they can deal with all points on the continua described in the six flag dimensions. These tools must not be overdesigned, however, since their more important function may be to spade up the data in each situation, not mold the organization or its members in a predetermined fashion.

A little more emphasis on development for OD could head us in a more promising direction.

Reading 53

Choosing Strategies for Change

John P. Kotter
Leonard A. Schlesinger

*It must be considered that there is nothing more difficult to carry out,
nor more doubtful of success, nor more dangerous to handle,
than to initiate a new order of things.*[1]

In 1973, The Conference Board asked 13 eminent authorities to speculate what significant management issues and problems would develop over the next 20 years. One of the strongest themes that runs through their subsequent reports is a concern for the ability of organizations to respond to environmental change. As one person wrote: "It follows that an acceleration in the rate of change will result in an increasing need for reorganization. Reorganization is usually feared, because it means disturbance of the status quo, a threat to people's vested interests in their jobs, and an upset to established ways of doing things. For these reasons, needed reorganization is often deferred, with a resulting loss in effectiveness and an increase in costs."[2]

Subsequent events have confirmed the importance of this concern about organizational change. Today, more and more managers must deal with new government regulations, new products, growth, increased competition, technological developments, and a changing work force. In response, most companies or divisions of major corporations find that they must undertake moderate organizational changes at least once a year and major changes every four or five.[3]

Few organizational change efforts tend to be complete failures, but few tend to be entirely successful either. Most efforts encounter problems; they often take longer than expected and desired, they sometimes kill morale, and they often cost a great deal in terms of managerial time or emotional upheaval. More than a few organizations have not even tried to initiate needed changes because the managers involved were afraid that they were simply incapable of successfully implementing them.

In this article, we first describe various causes for resistance to change and then outline a systematic way to select a strategy and set of specific approaches for implementing an organizational change effort. The methods described are based on our analyses of dozens of successful and unsuccessful organizational changes.

DIAGNOSING RESISTANCE

Organizational change efforts often run into some form of human resistance. Although experienced managers are generally all too aware of this fact, surprisingly few take time before an organizational change to assess systematically who might resist the change initiative and for what reasons. Instead, using past experiences as guidelines, managers all too often apply a simple set of beliefs—such as "engineers will probably resist the change because they are independent and suspicious of top management." This limited approach can create serious problems. Because of the many different ways in which individuals and groups can react to change, correct assessments are often not intuitively obvious and require careful thought.

Of course, all people who are affected by change experience some emotional turmoil. Even changes that appear to be "positive" or "rational" involve loss and uncertainty.[4] Nevertheless, for a number of different reasons, individuals or groups can react very differently to change—from passively resisting it, to aggressively trying to undermine it, to sincerely embracing it.

To predict what form their resistance might take, managers need to be aware of the four most common reasons people resist change. These include: a desire not to lose something of value, a misunderstanding of the change and its implications, a belief

Author's note: This article is adapted from a chapter in a forthcoming Dow Jones–Irwin book. We wish to thank Vijay Sathe for his help in preparing the article.

that the change does not make sense for the organization, and a low tolerance for change.

Parochial Self-Interest

One major reason people resist organization change is that they think they will lose something of value as a result. In these cases, because people focus on their own best interests and not on those of the total organization, resistance often results in "politics" or "political behavior."[5] Consider these two examples:

□After a number of years of rapid growth, the president of an organization decided that its size demanded the creation of a new staff function—New Product Planning and Development—to be headed by a vice president. Operationally, this change eliminated most of the decision-making power that the vice presidents of marketing, engineering, and production had over new products. Inasmuch as new products were very important in this organization, the change also reduced the vice presidents' status which, together with power, was very important to them.

During the two months after the president announced his idea for a new product vice president, the existing vice presidents each came up with six or seven reasons the new arrangement might not work. Their objection grew louder and louder until the president shelved the idea.

□A manufacturing company had traditionally employed a large group of personnel people as counselors and "father confessors" to its production employees. This group of counselors tended to exhibit high morale because of the professional satisfaction they received from the "helping relationships" they had with employees. When a new performance appraisal system was installed, every six months the counselors were required to provide each employee's supervisor with a written evaluation of the employee's "emotional maturity," "promotional potential," and so forth.

As some of the personnel people immediately recognized, the change would alter their relationships from a peer and helper to more of a boss and evaluator with most of the employees. Predictably, the personnel counselors resisted the change. While publicly arguing that the new system was not as good for the company as the old one, they privately put as much pressure as possible on the personnel vice president until he significantly altered the new system.

Political behavior sometimes emerges before and during organizational change efforts when what is in the best interests of one individual or group is not in the best interests of the total organization or of other individuals and groups.

While political behavior sometimes takes the form of two or more armed camps publicly fighting things out, it usually is much more subtle. In many cases, it occurs completely under the surface of public dialogue. Although scheming and ruthless individuals sometimes initiate power struggles, more often than not those who do are people who view their potential loss from change as an unfair violation of their implicit, or psychological, contract with the organization.[6]

Misunderstanding and Lack of Trust

People also resist change when they do not understand its implications and perceive that it might cost them much more than they will gain. Such situations often occur when trust is lacking between the person initiating the change and the employees.[7] Here is an example:

□When the president of a small midwestern company announced to his managers that the company would implement a flexible working schedule for all employees, it never occurred to him that he might run into resistance. He had been introduced to the concept at a management seminar and decided to use it to make working conditions at his company more attractive, particularly to clerical and plant personnel.

Shortly after the announcement, numerous rumors began to circulate among plant employees—none of whom really knew what flexible working hours meant and many of whom were distrustful of the manufacturing vice president. One rumor, for instance, suggested that flexible hours meant that most people would have to work whenever their supervisors asked them to—including evenings and weekends. The employee association, a local union, held a quick meeting and then presented the management with a nonnegotiable demand that the flexible hours concept be dropped. The president, caught completely by surprise, complied.

Few organizations can be characterized as having a high level of trust between employees and managers; consequently, it is easy for misunderstandings to develop when change is introduced. Unless managers surface misunderstandings and clarify them rapidly, they can lead to resistance. And that resistance can easily catch change initiators by surprise, especially if they assume that people only resist change when it is not in their best interest.

Different Assessments

Another common reason people resist organizational change is that they assess the situation differently from their managers or those initiating the change and see more costs than benefits resulting from the change, not only for themselves but for their company as well. For example:

☐The president of one moderate-size bank was shocked by his staff's analysis of the bank's real estate investment trust (REIT) loans. This complicated analysis suggested that the bank could easily lose up to $10 million, and that the possible losses were increasing each month by 20%. Within a week, the president drew up a plan to reorganize the part of the bank that managed REITs. Because of his concern for the bank's stock price, however, he chose not to release the staff report to anyone except the new REIT section manager.

The reorganization immediately ran into massive resistance from the people involved. The group sentiment, as articulated by one person, was: "Has he gone mad? Why in God's name is he tearing apart this section of the bank? His actions have already cost us three very good people [who quit], and have crippled a new program we were implementing [which the president was unaware of] to reduce our loan losses."

Managers who initiate change often assume both that they have all the relevant information required to conduct an adequate organization analysis and that those who will be affected by the change have the same facts, when neither assumption is correct. In either case, the difference in information that groups work with often leads to differences in analyses, which in turn can lead to resistance. Moreover, if the analysis made by those not initiating the change is more accurate than that derived by the initiators, resistance is obviously "good" for the organization. But this likelihood is not obvious to some managers who assume that resistance is always bad and therefore always fight it.[8]

Low Tolerance for Change

People also resist change because they fear they will not be able to develop the new skills and behavior

that will be required of them. All human beings are limited in their ability to change, with some people much more limited than others.[9] Organizational change can inadvertently require people to change too much, too quickly.

Peter F. Drucker has argued that the major obstacle to organizational growth is managers' inability to change their attitudes and behavior as rapidly as their organizations require.[10] Even when managers intellectually understand the need for changes in the way they operate, they sometimes are emotionally unable to make the transition.

It is because of people's limited tolerance for change that individuals will sometimes resist a change even when they realize it is a good one. For example, a person who receives a significantly more important job as a result of an organizational change will probably be very happy. But it is just as possible for such a person to also feel uneasy and to resist giving up certain aspects of the current situation. A new and very different job will require new and different behavior, new and different relationships, as well as the loss of some satisfactory current activities and relationships. If the changes are significant and the individual's tolerance for change is low, he might begin actively to resist the change for reasons even he does not consciously understand.

People also sometimes resist organizational change to save face; to go along with the change would be, they think, an admission that some of their previous decisions or beliefs were wrong. Or they might resist because of peer group pressure or because of a supervisor's attitude. Indeed, there are probably an endless number of reasons why people resist change.

Assessing which of the many possibilities might apply to those who will be affected by a change is important because it can help a manager select an appropriate way to overcome resistance. Without an accurate diagnosis of possibilities of resistance, a manager can easily get bogged down during the change process with very costly problems.

DEALING WITH RESISTANCE

Many managers underestimate not only the variety of ways people can react to organizational change, but also the ways they can positively influence specific individuals and groups during a change. And, again because of past experiences, managers sometimes do not have an accurate understanding of the advantages and disadvantages of the methods with which they *are* familiar.

Education and Communication

One of the most common ways to overcome resistance to change is to educate people about it beforehand. Communication of ideas helps people see the need for and the logic of a change. The education process can involve one-on-one discussions, presentations to groups, or memos and reports. For example:

☐As a part of an effort to make changes in a division's structure and in measurement and reward systems, a division manager put together a one-hour audiovisual presentation that explained the changes and the reasons for them. Over a four-month period, he made this presentation no less than a dozen times to groups of 20 or 30 corporate and division managers.

An education and communication program can be ideal when resistance is based on inadequate or inaccurate information and analysis, especially if the initiators need the resistors' help in implementing the change. But some managers overlook the fact that a program of this sort requires a good relationship between initiators and resistors or that the latter may not believe what they hear. It also requires time and effort, particularly if a lot of people are involved.

Participation and Involvement

If the initiators involve the potential resistors in some aspect of the design and implementation of the change, they can often forestall resistance. With a participative change effort, the initiators listen to the people the change involves and use their advice. To illustrate:

☐The head of a small financial services company once created a task force to help design and implement changes in his company's reward system. The task force was composed of eight second- and third-level managers from different parts of the company. The president's specific charter to them was that they recommend changes in the company's benefit package. They were given six months and asked to file a brief progress report with the president once a month. After they had made their recommendations, which the president largely accepted, they were asked to help the company's personnel director implement them.

We have found that many managers have quite strong feelings about participation—sometimes positive and sometimes negative. That is, some managers feel that there should always be participation during change efforts, while others feel this is virtually always a mistake. Both attitudes can create problems for a manager, because neither is very realistic.

When change initiators believe they do not have all the information they need to design and implement a change, or when they need the wholehearted commitment of others to do so, involving others makes very good sense. Considerable research has demonstrated that, in general, participation leads to commitment, not merely compliance.[12] In some instances, commitment is needed for the change to be a success. Nevertheless, the participation process does have its drawbacks. Not only can it lead to a poor solution if the process is not carefully managed, but also it can be enormously time consuming. When the change must be made immediately, it can take simply too long to involve others.

Facilitation and Support

Another way that managers can deal with potential resistance to change is by being supportive. This process might include providing training in new skills, or giving employees time off after a demanding period, or simply listening and providing emotional support. For example:

☐Management in one rapidly growing electronics company devised a way to help people adjust to frequent organizational changes. First, management staffed its human resource department with four counselors who spent most of their time talking to people who were feeling "burnt out" or who were having difficulty adjusting to new jobs. Second, on a selective basis, management offered people four-week minisabbaticals that involved some reflective or educational activity away from work. And, finally, it spent a great deal of money on in-house education and training programs.

Facilitation and support are most helpful when fear and anxiety lie at the heart of resistance. Seasoned, tough managers often overlook or ignore this kind of resistance, as well as the efficacy of facilitative ways of dealing with it. The basic drawback of this approach is that it can be time consuming and expensive and still fail.[13] If time, money, and patience just are not available, then using supportive methods is not very practical.

Negotiation and Agreement

Another way to deal with resistance is to offer incentives to active or potential resistors. For instance, management could give a union a higher wage rate in return for a work rule change; it could increase an individual's pension benefits in return for an early retirement. Here is an example of negotiated agreements:

☐In a large manufacturing company, the divisions were very interdependent. One division manager wanted to make some major changes in his organization. Yet, because of the interdependence, he recognized that he would be forcing some inconvenience and change on other divisions as well. To prevent top managers in other divisions from undermining his efforts, the division manager negotiated a written agreement with each. The agreement specified the outcomes the other division managers would receive and when, as well as the kinds of cooperation that he would receive from them in return during the change process. Later, whenever the division managers complained about his changes or the change process itself, he could point to the negotiated agreements.

Negotiation is particularly appropriate when it is clear that someone is going to lose out as a result of a change and yet his or her power to resist is significant. Negotiated agreements can be a relatively easy way to avoid major resistance, though, like some other processes, they may become expensive. And once a manager makes it clear that he will negotiate to avoid major resistance, he opens himself up to the possibility of blackmail.[14]

Manipulation and Co-optation

In some situations, managers also resort to covert attempts to influence others. Manipulation, in this context, normally involves the very selective use of information and the conscious structuring of events.

One common form of manipulation is co-optation. Co-opting an individual usually involves giving him or her a desirable role in the design or implementation of the change. Co-opting a group involves giving one of its leaders, or someone it respects, a key role in the design or implementation of a change. This is not a form of participation, however, because the initiators do not want the advice of the co-opted, merely his or her endorsement. For example:

☐One division manager in a large multibusiness corporation invited the corporate human relations vice president, a close friend of the president, to help him and his key staff diagnose some problems the division was having. Because of his busy schedule, the corporate vice president was not able to do much of the actual information gathering or analysis himself, thus limiting his own influence on the diagnoses. But his presence at key meetings helped commit him to the diagnoses as well as the solutions the group designed. The commitment was subsequently very important because the president, at least initially, did not like some of the proposed changes. Nevertheless, after discussion with his human relations vice president, he did not try to block them.

Under certain circumstances co-optation can be a relatively inexpensive and easy way to gain an individual's or a group's support (cheaper, for example, than negotiation and quicker than participation). Nevertheless, it has its drawbacks. If people feel they are being tricked into not resisting, are not being treated equally, or are being lied to, they may respond very negatively. More than one manager has found that, by his effort to give some subordinate a sense of participation through co-optation, he created more resistance than if he had done nothing. In addition, co-optation can create a different kind of problem if those co-opted use their ability to influence the design and implementation of changes in ways that are not in the best interests of the organization.

Other forms of manipulation have drawbacks also, sometimes to an even greater degree. Most people are likely to greet what they perceive as covert treatment and/or lies with a negative response. Furthermore, if a manager develops a reputation as a manipulator, it can undermine his ability to use needed approaches such as education/communication and participation/involvement. At the extreme, it can even ruin his career.

Nevertheless, people do manipulate others successfully—particularly when all other tactics are not feasible or have failed.[15] Having no other alternative, and not enough time to educate, involve, or support people, and without the power or other resources to negotiate, coerce, or co-opt them, managers have resorted to manipulating information channels in order to scare people into thinking there is a crisis coming which they can avoid only by changing.

Explicit and Implicit Coercion

Finally, managers often deal with resistance coercively. Here they essentially force people to accept a change by explicitly or implicitly threatening them (with the loss of jobs, promotion possibilities, and so forth) or by actually firing or transferring them. As with manipulation, using coercion is a risky process because inevitably people strongly resent forced change. But in situations where speed is essential and where the changes will not be popular, regardless of how they are introduced, coercion may be the manager's only option.

Successful organizational change efforts are always characterized by the skillful application of a number of these approaches, often in very different combinations. However, successful efforts share two characteristics: managers employ the approaches with a sensitivity to their strengths and limitations (see *Exhibit 53-1*) and appraise the situation realistically.

The most common mistake managers make is to use only one approach or a limited set of them *regardless of the situation*. A surprisingly large number of managers have this problem. This would include the hard-boiled boss who often coerces people, the people-oriented manager who constantly tries to involve and support his people, the cynical boss who always manipulates and co-opts others, the intellectual manager who relies heavily on education and communication, and the lawyerlike manager who usually tries to negotiate.[16]

A second common mistake that managers make is to approach change in a disjointed and incremental way that is not a part of a clearly considered strategy.

CHOICE OF STRATEGY

In approaching an organizational change situation, managers explicitly or implicitly make strategic choices regarding the speed of the effort, the amount of preplanning, the involvement of others, and the relative emphasis they will give to different approaches. Successful change efforts seem to be those where these choices both are internally consistent and fit some key situational variables.

The strategic options available to managers can be usefully thought of as existing on a continuum (see *Exhibit 53-2*).[17] At one end of the continuum, the change strategy calls for a very rapid implementation, a clear plan of action, and little involvement of others. This type of strategy mows over any resist-

Approach	Commoly used in situations	Advantages	Drawbacks
Education + communication	Where there is a lack of information or inaccurate information and analysis.	Once persuaded, people will often help with the implementation of the change.	Can be very time-consuming if lots of people are involved.
Participation + involvement	Where the initiators do not have all the information they need to design the change, and where others have considerable power to resist.	People who participate will be committed to implementing change, and any relevant information they have will be integrated into the change plan.	Can be very time-consuming if participators design an inappropriate change.
Facilitation + support	Where people are resisting because of adjustment problems.	No other approach works as well with adjustment problems.	Can be time-consuming, expensive, and still fail.
Negotiation + agreement	Where someone or some group will clearly lose out in a change, and where that group has considerable power to resist.	Sometimes it is a relatively easy way to avoid major resistance.	Can be too expensive in many cases if it alerts others to negotiate for compliance.
Manipulation + co-optation	Where other tactics will not work, or are too expensive.	It can be a relatively quick and inexpensive solution to resistance problems.	Can lead to future problems if people feel manipulated.
Explicit + implicit coercion	Where speed is essential, and the change initiators possess considerable power.	It is speedy, and can overcome any kind of resistance.	Can be risky if it leaves people mad at the initiators.

Figure 53-1 Methods for dealing with resistance to change.

Fast	Slower
Clearly planned.	Not clearly planned at the beginning.
Little involvement of others.	Lots of involvement of others.
Attempt to overcome any resistance.	Attempt to minimize any resistance.
Key situational variables	
The amount and type of resistance that is anticipated.	
The position of the intiators vis-a-vis the resistors (in terms of power, trust, and so forth).	
The locus of relevant data for designing the change, and of needed energy for implementing it.	
The stakes involved (e.g., the presence or lack of presence of a crisis, the consequences of resistance and lack of change).	

Figure 53-2   Strategic continuum.

ance and, at the extreme, would result in a fait accompli. At the other end of the continuum, the strategy would call for a much slower change process, a less clear plan, and involvement on the part of many people other than the change initiators. This type of strategy is designed to reduce resistance to a minimum.[18]

The further to the left one operates on the continuum in *Exhibit 53-2,* the more one tends to be coercive and the less one tends to use the other approaches—especially participation; the converse also holds.

Organizational change efforts that are based on inconsistent strategies tend to run into predictable problems. For example, efforts that are not clearly planned in advance and yet are implemented quickly tend to become bogged down owing to unanticipated problems. Efforts that involve a large number of people, but are implemented quickly, usually become either stalled or less participative.

Situational Factors

Exactly where a change effort should be strategically positioned on the continuum in *Exhibit 53-2* depends on four factors:

1 The amount and kind of resistance that is anticipated. All other factors being equal, the greater the anticipated resistance, the more difficult it will be simply to overwhelm it, and the more a manager will need to move toward the right on the continuum to find ways to reduce some of it.[19]

2 The position of the initiator vis-à-vis the resistors, especially with regard to power. The less power the initiator has with respect to others, the more the initiating manager *must* move to the left on the continuum.[20] Conversely, the stronger the initiator's position, the more he or she can move to the right.

3 The person who has the relevant data for designing the change and the energy for implementing it. The more the initiators anticipate that they will need information and commitment from others to help design and implement the change, the more they must move to the right.[21] Gaining useful information and commitment requires time and the involvement of others.

The stakes involved. The greater the short-run potential for risks to organizational performance and survival if the present situation is not changed, the more one must move to the left.

Organizational change efforts that ignore these factors inevitably run into problems. A common mistake some managers make, for example, is to move too quickly and involve too few people despite the fact that they do not have all the information they really need to design the change correctly.

Insofar as these factors still leave a manager with some choice of where to operate on the continuum, it is probably best to select a point as far to the right as possible for both economic and social reasons. Forcing change on people can have just too many negative side effects over both the short and the long term. Change efforts using the strategies on the right of the continuum can often help develop an organization and its people in useful ways.[22]

In some cases, however, knowing the four factors may not give a manager a comfortable and obvious choice. Consider a situation where a manager has a weak position vis-à-vis the people whom he thinks need a change and yet is faced with serious consequences if the change is not implemented immediately. Such a manager is clearly in a bind. If he somehow is not able to increase his power in the situation, he will be forced to choose some compromise strategy and to live through difficult times.

Implications for Managers

A manager can improve his chance of success in an organizational change effort by:

1 Conducting an organizational analysis that identifies the current situation, problems, and the forces that are possible causes of those problems. The analysis should specify the actual importance of the problems, the speed with which the problems must be addressed if additional problems are to be avoided, and the kinds of changes that are generally needed.

2 Conducting an analysis of factors relevant to producing the needed changes. This analysis should focus on questions of who might resist the change, why, and how much; who has information that is needed to design the change, and whose cooperation is essential in implementing it; and what is the position of the initiator vis-à-vis other relevant parties in terms of power, trust, normal modes of interaction, and so forth.

3 Selecting a change strategy, based on the previous analysis, that specifies the speed of change, the amount of preplanning, and the degree of involvement of others; that selects specific tactics for use with various individuals and groups; and that is internally consistent.

4 Monitoring the implementation process. No matter how good a job one does of initially selecting a change strategy and tactics, something unexpected will eventually occur during implementation. Only by carefully monitoring the process can one identify the unexpected in a timely fashion and react to it intelligently.

Interpersonal skills, of course, are the key to using this analysis. But even the most outstanding interpersonal skills will not make up for a poor choice of strategy and tactics. And in a business world that continues to become more and more dynamic, the consequences of poor implementation choices will become increasingly severe.

REFERENCES

1 Niccolò Machiavelli, *The Prince*.

2 Marvin Bower and C. Lee Walton, Jr., "Gearing a Business to the Future," in *Challenge to Leadership* (New York: The Conference Board, 1973), p. 126.

3 For recent evidence on the frequency of changes, see Stephen A. Allen, "Organizational Choice and General Influence Networks for Diversified Companies," *Academy of Management Journal,* September 1978, p. 341.

4 For example, see Robert A. Luke, Jr., "A Structural Approach to Organizational Change," *Journal of Applied Behavioral Science,* September-October 1973, p. 611.

5 For a discussion of power and politics in corporations, see Abraham Zaleznik and Manfred F. R. Kets de Vries, *Power and the Corporate Mind* (Boston: Houghton Mifflin, 1975), Chapter 6; and Robert H. Miles, *Macro Organizational Behavior* (Pacific Palisades, Calif.: Goodyear, 1978), Chapter 4.

6 See Edgar H. Schein, *Organizational Psychology* (Englewood Cliffs, N.J.: Prentice-Hall, 1965), p. 44.

7 See Chris Argyris, *Intervention Theory and Method* (Reading, Mass.: Addison-Wesley, 1970), p. 70.

8 See Paul R. Lawrence, "How to Deal with Resistance to Change," HBR May–June 1954, p. 49; reprinted as HBR Classic, January–February 1969, p. 4.

9 For a discussion of resistance that is personality based, see Goodwin Watson, "Resistance to Change," in *The Planning of Change,* eds. Warren G. Bennis, Kenneth F. Benne, and Robert Chin (New York: Holt, Rinehart, and Winston, 1969), p. 489.

10 Peter F. Drucker, *The Practice of Management* (New York: Harper and Row, 1954).

11 For a general discussion of resistance and reasons for it, see Chapter 3 in Gerald Zaltman and Robert Duncan, *Strategies for Planned Change* (New York: John Wiley, 1977).

12 See, for example, Alfred J. Marrow, David F. Bowers, and Stanley E. Seashore, *Management by Participation* (New York: Harper and Row, 1967).

13 Zaltman and Duncan, *Strategies for Planned Changes,* Chapter 4.

14 For an excellent discussion of negotiation, see Gerald J. Nierenberg, *The Art of Negotiating* (Birmingham, Ala.: Cornerstone, 1968).

15 See John P. Kotter, "Power, Dependence, and Effective Management," HBR July-August 1977, p. 125.

16 Ibid., p. 135.

17 See Larry F. Greiner, "Patterns of Organization Change," HBR May–June 1967, p. 119; and Larry E. Greiner and Louis B. Barnes, "Organization Change and Development," in *Organizational Change and Development,* eds. Gene W. Dalton and Paul R. Lawrence (Homewood, Ill.: Irwin, 1970), p. 3.

18 For a good discussion of an approach that attempts to minimize resistance, see Renato Tagiuri, "Notes on the Management of Change: Implication of Postulating a Need for Competence," in John P. Kotter, Vijay Sathe, and Leonard A. Schlesinger, *Organization* (Homewood, Ill.: Irwin, to be published in 1979).

19 Jay W. Lorsch, "Managing Change," in *Organizational Behavior and Administration,* eds. Paul R. Lawrence, Louis B. Barnes, and Jay W. Lorsch (Homewood, Ill.: Irwin, 1976), p. 676.

20 Ibid.

21 Ibid.

22 Michael Beer, *Organization Change and Development: A Systems View* (Pacific Palisades, Calif., Goodyear, to be published in 1979).

Reading 54

Concepts for the Management of Organizational Change

David A. Nadler

INTRODUCTION

Bringing about major change in a large and complex organization is a difficult task. Policies, procedures, and structures need to be altered. Individuals and groups have to be motivated to continue to perform in the face of major turbulence. People are presented with the fact that the "old ways," which include familiar tasks, jobs, procedures, and structures, are no longer applicable. Political behavior frequently becomes more active and more intense. It is not surprising, therefore, that the process of effectively implementing organizational change has long been a topic that both managers and researchers have pondered. While there is still much that is not understood about change in complex organizations, the experiences and research of recent years do provide some guidance to those concerned with implementing major changes in organizations.

This paper is designed to provide some useful concepts to aid in understanding the dynamics of change and to help in the planning and managing of major organizational changes. The paper is organized into several sections. We will start with a brief discussion of a model of organizational behavior. This discussion is necessary since it is difficult to think about changing organizations without some notion of why they work the way they do in the first place. Second, we will define what we mean by organizational change and identify criteria for effective management of change. Third, we will discuss some of the basic problems of implementing change. In the last section, we will list some specific methods and tools for effective implementation of organizational changes.

A VIEW OF ORGANIZATION

There are many different ways of thinking about organizations and the patterns of behavior that occur within them. During the past two decades, however, there has been an emerging view of organizations as complex open social systems (Katz & Kahn, 1966). Organizations are seen as mechanisms which take input from the larger environment and subject that input to various transformation processes which result in output.

As systems, organizations are seen as composed of interdependent parts. Change in one element of the system will result in changes in other parts of the system. Similarly, organizations have the property of equilibrium; the system will generate energy to move toward a state of balance. Finally, as open systems, organizations need to maintain favorable transactions of input and output with the environment in order to survive over time.

While the systems perspective is useful, systems theory by itself may be too abstract a concept to be a

Article prepared especially for this book.

usable tool for managers. Thus, a number of organizational theorists have attempted to develop more pragmatic theories or models based on the system paradigm. There are a number of such models currently in use. One of these will be employed here.

The particular approach, called a "Congruence Model of Organizational Behavior" (Nadler & Tushman, 1979, 1982) is based on the general systems model. The model uses input, transformation process, and output perspective. In this framework, the major inputs to the system of organizational behavior are the *environment*, which provides constraints, demands, and opportunities, the *resources* available to the organization, and the *history* of the organization. A fourth input, and perhaps the most crucial, is the organization's *strategy*. Strategy is the set of key decisions about the match of the organization's resources to the opportunities, constraints, and demands in the environment within the context of history.

The output of the system is in general the effectiveness of the organization in performing consistently with the goals of strategy. Specifically, the output includes *organizational performance*, as well as *group performance* and *individual behavior and affect*, which, of course, contribute to organizational performance.

The basic framework thus views the organization as being the mechanism that takes inputs (strategy and resources in the context of history and environment) and transforms them into outputs (patterns of individual, group, and organizational behavior). This view is portrayed in Figure 54-1.

The major focus of organizational analysis is therefore this transformation process. The model conceives of the organization as being composed of four major components. The first component is the *task* of the organization, or the work to be done and its critical characteristics. The second component is composed of the *individuals* who are to perform organizational tasks. The third component includes all of the *formal organizational arrangements,* including various structures, processes, systems, etc., which are designed to motivate and facilitate individuals in the performance of organizational tasks. Finally, there is a set of *informal organizational arrangements*, which are usually neither planned nor written, but which tend to emerge over time. These include patterns of communication, power and influence, values and norms, etc., which characterize how an organization actually functions.

How do these four components (task, individuals, organizational arrangements, and the information organization) relate to one another? The relationship among components is the basic dynamic of the model. Each component can be thought of as having a relationship with each of the other components. Between each pair, then, we can think of a relative degree of consistency, congruence, or "fit." For example, if we look at the type of work to be done (task) and the nature of the people available to do the work (individuals) we could make a statement about the congruence between the two by seeing whether the demands of the work are consistent with the skills and abilities of the individuals. At the same time we would compare the rewards that the work provides with the needs and desires of the

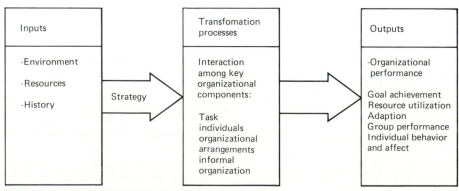

Figure 54-1   The systems model applied to organizational behavior.

individuals. By looking at these factors, we would be able to assess how congruent the nature of the task was with the nature of the individuals in the system.

In fact, we could look at the question of congruence between all the components, or in terms of all six of the possible relationships among them (see Figure 54-2). The basic hypothesis of the model is, therefore, that *organizations will be most effective when their major components are congruent with each other.* To the extent that organizations face problems of effectiveness due to management and organizational factors, these problems will stem from poor fit, or lack of congruence, among organizational components.

This approach to organizations is thus a contingency approach. There is not one best organization design, or style of management or method of working. Rather, different patterns of organization and management will be most appropriate in different situations. The model recognizes the fact that individuals, tasks, strategies, and environments may differ greatly from organization to organization.

THE TASK OF IMPLEMENTING CHANGE

Having briefly presented some concepts that underlie our thinking about organizations, the question of change can now be addressed. Managers are frequently concerned about implementing organizational changes. Often changes in the environment

necessitate organizational change. For example, factors related to competition, technology, or regulation shift and thus necessitate changes in organizational strategy. If a new strategy is to be executed, the organization and its various subunits (departments, groups, divisions, etc.) must perform tasks that may be different than those previously performed. Building on the organizational model presented above, this means that there may be a need for modifications in organizational arrangements, individuals, and the informal organization.

Typically, implementing a change involves moving an organization to some desired future state. As illustrated in Figure 54-3, we can think of changes in terms of transitions (Beckhard & Harris, 1977). At any point in time, the organization exists in a current state (A). The current state describes how the organization functions now. The future state (B), on the other hand, is how the organization should be functioning in the future. It is the desired state that would ideally exist after the change. The period between A and B can be thought of as the transition state (C). In its most general terms, then, the effective management of change involves developing an understanding of the current state (A), developing an image of a desired future state (B), and moving the organization from A through a transition period to B (Beckhard & Harris, 1977).

Major transitions usually occur in response to changes in the nature of organizational inputs or

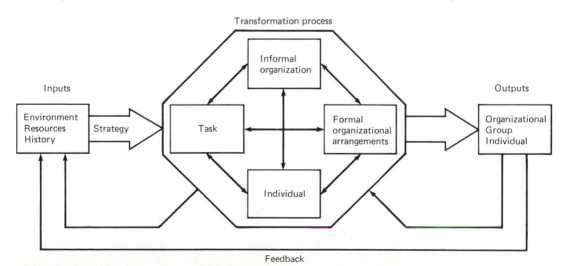

Figure 54-2 A congruence model of organizational behavior.

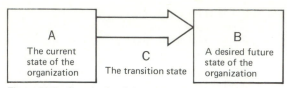

Figure 54-3 Organizational change as a transition state.

outputs. Most significant changes are in response to or in anticipation of environmental or strategic shifts, or problems of performance. In terms of the congruence model, then, a change occurs when managers determine that the configuration of the components in the current state is not effective and the organization must be reshaped. Often this means a rethinking and redefining of the organization's task followed by changes in other components to support that new task (see Figure 54-4).

What constitutes effective management of change? Several criteria can be thought of. Building on the transition framework presented above, organizational change is effectively managed when:

1 The organization is moved from the current state to the future state.
2 The functioning of the organization in the future state meets expectations: i.e., it works as planned.
3 The transition is accomplished without undue cost to the organization.
4 The transition is accomplished without undue cost to individual organizational members.

Of course, not every organizational change can be expected to meet these criteria, but such standards provide a target for planning change. The question is how to manage the way in which the change is implemented so as to maximize the chances that the change will be effective. Experience has shown that the process of how a change is implemented can influence the effectiveness of the transition as much as the content of what the change is.

PROBLEMS IN IMPLEMENTING CHANGE

Experience and research have shown that the process of creating change is more difficult than it might seem. It is seductive to think of an organization as a large machine whose parts can be replaced at will. On the contrary, the task of changing the behavior of organizations, groups, and individuals has turned out to be a difficult and often frustrating endeavor.

Using the organizational model presented above, we can envision how organizations, as systems, are resistant to change. The forces of equilibrium tend to work to cancel out many changes. Changing one component of an organization may reduce its congruence with other components. As this happens, energy develops in the organization to limit, encapsulate, or revise the change.

The first issue in many changes is to diagnose the current system to identify the source of problems (or opportunities for improvement). In a large organization, this frequently leads to a rethinking of strategy and a redefinition of the organization's task or work. For example, an AT&T examines the environment and determines that it needs to change the primary orientation of its strategy and thus its task from service toward marketing.

The analysis of strategy and redefinition of task is an important step in changing an organization. On the other hand, many of the most troublesome problems of changing organizations occur not in the strategic/task shift but in the implementation of the organizational transition to support the change in the nature of the strategy and the work. More specifically, any major organizational change presents three major problems which must be dealt with.

First is the problem of *resistance* to change (Watson, 1969: Zaltman & Duncan, 1977). Individuals faced with a change in the organization in which they work may be resistant for a variety of different reasons. People have needs for a certain degree of stability or security. Change presents unknowns which cause anxiety. In addition, changes that are imposed on individuals reduce their sense of autonomy or self-control. Furthermore, people typically develop patterns for coping with or managing the current structure and situation. Change means that they will have to find new ways of managing their own environments—ways that might not be as successful as those currently used. In addition, people who have power in the current situation may resist change because it threatens that power. They have a vested interest in the status quo. Finally, individuals may resist change for ideological reasons; they truly believe that the way things are currently done is better than the proposed change. Whatever the source, individual resistance to change must be overcome for successful implementation.

Second is the problem of organizational *control*.

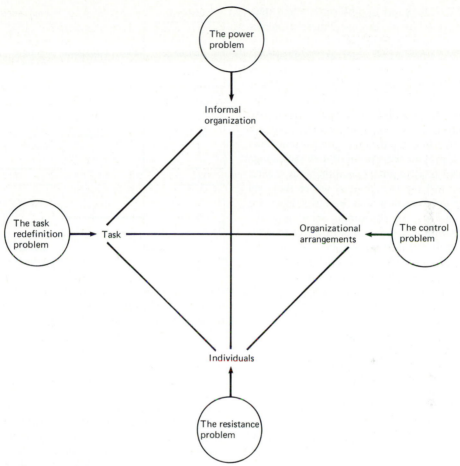

Figure 54-4   Problems of change in relation to the components of the organizational model.

Change disrupts the normal course of events within an organization.· It thus disrupts and undermines existing systems of management control, particularly those developed as part of the formal organizational arrangements. Change may make those systems irrelevant and/or inappropriate. As a result, during a change, it may become easy to lose control of the organization. As goal structures and people shift, it becomes difficult to monitor performance and make corrections as in normal control processes.

A related problem is that more formal organizational arrangements are designed for stable states, not transition states. Managers become fixated with the future state (B) and assume that all that is needed is to design the most effective organizational arrangements for the future. They think of change from A to B as simply a mechanical or procedural detail. The problems created by the lack of concern for the transition state are compounded by its inherent uniqueness. In most situations, the management systems and structures developed to manage A or B are simply not appropriate or adequate for the management of C. They are steady-state management systems, designed to run organizations already in place rather than transitional management systems.

The third problem is *power*. Any organization is a political system made up of different individuals, groups, and coalitions competing for power (Tushman, 1977; Salancik & Pfeffer, 1977). Political behavior is thus a natural and expected feature of organizations. This occurs in both state A and state B. In state C (transition), however, these dynamics become even more intense as the old order is dismantled and a new order emerges. This happens because any significant change poses the possibility of upsetting or modifying the balance of power among groups. The uncertainty created by change creates ambiguity, which in turn tends to increase the probability of political activity (Thompson & Tuden, 1959). Individuals and groups may take action based on their perception of how the change will affect their relative power position in the organization. They will try to influence where they will "sit" in the organization that emerges from the transition, and will be concerned about how the conflict of the transition period will affect the balance of power in the future state. Finally, individuals and groups may engage in political action because of their ideological position on the change—it may be inconsistent with their shared values or image of the organization (Pettigrew, 1972).

In some sense, each of these problems relates primarily to one of the components of the organization (see Figure 54-4). Resistance relates to the individual component, getting people to change their behavior. Control concerns the design of appropriate organizational arrangements for the transition period. Power relates to the reactions of the informal organization to change. The implication is that if a change is to be effective, all three problems —resistance, control, and power—must be addressed.

GUIDELINES FOR IMPLEMENTING CHANGE

The three basic problems that are inherent in change each lead to a general implication for the management of change (see Figure 54-5).

The implication of the resistance problem is the need to *motivate* changes in behavior by individuals. This involves overcoming the natural resistance to change that emerges and getting individuals to behave in ways consistent with both the short-run goals of change and the long-run organizational strategy.

The implication of the control problem is the need to *manage the transition* period. Organizational arrangements need to be designed and used to ensure that control is maintained during and after the

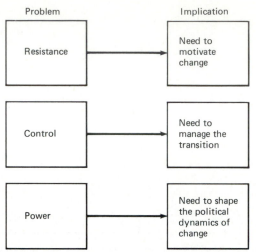

Figure 54-5 Problems of change and implications for change management.

transition. These devices and approaches need to be ones specifically appropriate to the transition period rather than the current or future state.

Finally, the implication of the power issue is the need to *shape the political dynamics of change* so that power centers develop that support the change rather than block it (Pettigrew, 1975).

Each of these general implications suggests specific actions that can be taken to improve the probabilities of achieving an effective change. A number of these action steps can be identified for each of the three implications.

Action Steps to Motivate Change

The first action step is to *identify and surface dissatisfaction with the current state*. As long as people are satisfied with the current state, they will not be motivated to change; people need to be "unfrozen" out of their inertia in order to be receptive to change (Lewin, 1947; Bennis et al., 1973). The greater the pain and dissatisfaction with the current state, then, the greater the motivation to change and the less the resistance to change. As a consequence, the management of change may require the creation of pain and dissatisfaction with the status quo. Dissatisfaction most commonly results from information concerning some aspect of organizational performance which is different than either desired or expected performance. Discrepancies can therefore be used to create dissatisfaction.

As a result, data can be an important tool to initiate a process of change (Nadler, 1977).

The second action step is to build in *participation* in the change. One of the most consistent findings in the research on change is that participation in the change tends to reduce resistance, build "owner-ships" of the change, and thus motivate people to make the change work (Coch & French, 1948; Vroom, 1964; Kotter & Schlesinger, 1979). Participation also facilitates the communication of information about what the change will be and why it has come about. Participation may also lead to obtaining new information from those participating, information that may enhance the effectiveness of the change or the future state.

On the other hand, participation has costs since it involves relinquishing control, takes time, and may create conflict. For each situation, different degrees of participation may be most effective (Vroom & Yetton, 1973). Participation may involve work on diagnosing the present situation, in planning change, in implementing change, or in combinations of the above. Participation may also vary in the specific devices that are used, ranging from large-scale data collection to sensing groups, to questionnaires, to cross-unit committees, etc.

A third action step is to build in *rewards* for the behavior that is desired both during the transition state and in the future state. Our understanding of motivation and behavior in organizations suggests that people will tend to be motivated to behave in ways that they perceive as leading to desired outcomes (Vroom, 1964; Lawler, 1973). The implication of this is that both formal and informal rewards need to be identified and tied to the behavior that is needed, both for the transition and for the future state. The most frequent problem is that organizations expect individuals to behave in certain ways (particularly in a transition) while rewarding them for other conflicting behaviors (Kerr, 1975). In particular, rewards such as bonuses, pay systems, promotion, recognition, job assignment, and status symbols all need to be carefully examined during major organizational changes and restructured to support the direction of the transition.

Finally, people need to be provided with the *time and opportunity to disengage from the present state.* Change frequently creates feelings of loss, not unlike a death. People have needs to mourn for the old system or familiar way of doing things. This frequently is manifested in the emergence of stories or myths about the "good old days," even when those days weren't so good. The process of dealing with a loss and going through mourning takes time, and those managing change need to take this into account. This factor underscores the need to provide information about the problems of the status quo and also to plan for enough time in advance of a change to allow people to deal with the loss and prepare for it.

Action Steps to Manage the Transition

One of the first and most critical steps for managing the transition state is to *develop and communicate a clear image of the future* (Beckhard & Harris, 1977). Resistance and confusion frequently develop during an organizational change because people are unclear about what the future state will look like. Thus the goals and purposes of the change become blurred, and individual expectancies frequently take form on the basis of information that is erroneous. In the absence of a clear image of the future, rumors develop; people design their own fantasies and act on them. The implication is that as clear an image as possible of the future state needs to be developed to serve as a guideline, target, or goal. In particular, a written statement or description of the future state may be of value in clarifying the image. Similarly, it is important to communicate information to those involved in the change, including what the future state will look like, how the transition will come about, why the change is being implemented, and how individuals will be affected by the change. This communication can be accomplished in a variety of ways, ranging from written communications to small-group meetings, large briefing sessions, videotaped presentations, etc.

A second action step for managing the transition involves the use of *multiple and consistent leverage points.* If, building on the model presented above, an organization is made up of components which are interdependent, then the successful alteration of organizational behavior patterns needs to involve the use of multiple leverage points. Structural change, task change, change in the social environment, as well as changes in individuals themselves, are all needed to bring about significant and lasting changes in the patterns of organizational behavior.

Changes that are targeted at individuals and social relations (such as training, group interventions, etc.) tend to fade out quickly with few lasting effects when done in isolation (Porter, Lawler, & Hackman, 1975). On the other hand, task and structural changes alone, while powerful and enduring, frequently produce unintended and dysfunctional consequences (see, for example, the literature on control systems; e.g., Lawler & Rhode, 1976). Change which is in the direction intended and which is lasting, therefore, requires the use of multiple leverage points, or modifications in the larger set of components which shape the behavior of the organization and the people in it (Nadler & Tichy, 1980). Similarly, the changes have to be structured so that they are consistent; the training of individuals, for example, should dovetail with new job descriptions, reward systems, or reporting relationships. In the absence of consistency, changes run the risk of creating new "poor fits" between organizational components. The result is either an abortive change or decreases in organizational performance.

The third action step involves a number of different activities. The implication is that *organizational arrangements for the transition* need to be explicitly considered, designed, and used. As mentioned earlier, the organizational arrangements that function in either the present or the future state are typically steady-state designs rather than designs for use in managing the transition state. The whole issue of developing structures to manage the transition has been discussed in depth elsewhere (see Beckhard & Harris, 1977), but a number of the most important elements should be mentioned here. In particular, the following organizational arrangements are important for managing the change:

a. A Transition Manager Someone needs to be designated as the manager of the organization for the transition state. This person may be a member of management, a chief executive, or someone else, but frequently it is difficult for one person to manage the current state, prepare to manage the future state, and simultaneously manage the transition. This person should have the power and authority needed to make the transition happen, and should be appropriately linked to the steady-state managers, particularly the future-state manager.

b. Resources for the Transition Major transitions involve potentially large risks for organizations. Given this, they are worth doing well and it is worth providing the needed resources to make them happen effectively. Resources such as personnel, dollars, training expertise, consultative expertise, etc., need to be provided for the transition manager.

c. Transition Plan A transition is a movement from one state to another. To have that occur effectively, and to measure and control performance, a plan is needed with benchmarks, standards of performance, and similar features. Implicit in such a plan is a specification of the responsibilities of key individuals and groups.

d. Transition Management Structures Frequently it is difficult for a hierarchy to manage the process of changing itself. As a result, it may be necessary to develop other structures or use other devices outside of the regular organizational structure during the transition management period. Special task forces, pilot projects, experimental units, etc., need to be designed and employed for this period (see again Beckhard & Harris, 1977, for a discussion of these different devices).

The final action implication for transition management involves developing *feedback mechanisms* to provide transition managers with information on the effectiveness of the transition and provide data on areas which require additional attention or action. There is a huge amount of anecdotal data about senior managers ordering changes and assuming those changes were made, only to find out to their horror that the change never occurred. Such a situation develops because managers lack feedback devices to tell them whether actions have been effective or not. During stable periods, effective managers tend to develop various ways of eliciting feedback. During the transition state, however, these mechanisms often break down due to the turbulence of the change or because of the natural inclination not to provide "bad news." Thus it becomes important for transition managers to develop multiple, redundant, and sensitive mechanisms for generating feedback about the transition. Devices such as surveys, sensing groups, consultant interviews, etc., as well as informal communication channels need to be developed and used during this period.

Action Steps for Shaping the Political Dynamics of Change

If an organization is a political system composed of different groups, each competing for power, then the most obvious action step involves *assuring or developing the support of key power groups*. For a change to occur successfully, then, a critical mass of power groups needs to be assembled and mobilized in support of the change. Those groups that oppose the change have to be compensated in some way or have their effects neutralized. Not all power groups have to be intimately involved in the change. Some may support the change on ideological grounds, while others may support the change because it enhances their own power position. Still other groups have to be included in the planning of the change so that their participation will motivate them or co-opt them (Selznick, 1949). Yet others may have to be dealt with by bargaining or negotiations. The key point is that the key groups that may be affected by the change need to be identified, and strategies for building support among a necessary portion of those groups need to be developed and carried out (Sayles, 1979).

A major factor affecting the political terrain of an organization is the behavior of key and powerful leaders. Thus a second major action step involves *using leader behavior to generate energy in support of the change*. Leaders can mobilize groups, generate energy, provide models, manipulate major rewards, and do many other things which can affect the dynamics of the informal organization. Sets of leaders working in a coordinated manner can have a tremendously powerful impact on the informal organization. Thus leaders need to think about using their own behavior to generate energy (see House, 1976, on charismatic leadership) as well as building on the support and behavior of other leaders (both formal and informal) within the organization.

The third action implication in this area is related to the question of leadership. Energy also gets created by the use of *symbols and language* (Peters, 1978; Pfeffer, 1980). By providing a language to describe the change and symbols that have emotional impact, it is possible to create new power centers or to bring together power centers under a common banner. Language is also important in defining an ambiguous reality. If a change, for example, is declared a success, then it may become a success in the perceptions of others.

Finally, there is the need to *build in stability*. Organizations and individuals can only stand so much uncertainty and turbulence. An overload of uncertainty may create dysfunctional effects, and people may begin to panic, engage in extreme defensive behavior, and become irrationally resistant to any new change proposed. Thus the increase of anxiety created by constant change has its costs. One way of dealing with this is to provide some sources of stability (structures, people, physical locations, etc., that stay the same) to serve as "anchors" for people to hold onto and provide a means for definition of the self in the midst of turbulence. While too many anchors can encourage resistance, it is important to provide some stability. More importantly, it is important to communicate the stability. People may not take comfort from something that is stable if they are unsure of its stability. Thus those aspects of the organization that will not change during a transition period need to be identified and communicated to organization members.

SUMMARY

This paper has attempted to identify some of the problems and issues in bringing about changes in complex organizations. At the same time, a number of general and specific action steps have been suggested. To understand how to change organizational behavior, we need a tool to understand how it occurs in the first place. The model used here (Nadler & Tushman, 1979, 1982) suggests that any change will encounter three general problems: resistance, control, and power. The general implication is the need to motivate change, manage the transition, and shape the political dynamics of change. For each of these three general implications, a number of specific action steps have been identified (see Figure 54-6).

Obviously, each of these action steps will be more or less critical (and more or less feasible) in different situations. Thus both students of organization and managers need to be diagnostic in their approach to the problems of managing change. Each situation,

Implication	Action steps
Need to motivate change	1. Surface dissatisfaction with the present state
	2. Participation in change
	3. Rewards for behavior in support of change
	4. Time and opportunity to disengage from the present state
	5. Develop and communicate a clear image of the future
Need to manage the transition	6. Use multiple and consistent leverage points
	7. Develop organizational arrangements for the transition
	8. Build in feedback mechanisms
Need to shape the political dynamics of change	9. Assure the support of key power groups
	10. Use leader behavior to generate energy in support of change
	11. Use symbols and language
	12. Build in stability

Figure 54-6 Implications for change management and related action steps.

while reflecting general patterns, has its own unique characteristics, based on its own differences of individuals, history, and situation. Thus specific variants of the action steps need to be developed for specific situations. To do this, managers need diagnostic models to understand problems, as well as guidelines for implementing changes, as presented here. Together, however, these two types of tools can be powerful aids in building and maintaining effective organizations.

REFERENCES

Beckhard, R. & Harris, R. *Organizational transitions.* Reading, Mass.: Addison-Wesley, 1977.

Bennis, W. G., Berlew, D. E., Schein, E. H., & Steele, F. I. *Interpersonal dynamics: Essays and readings on human interaction.* Homewood, Ill.: Dorsey, 1973.

Coch, L. & French, J. R. P., Jr. Overcoming resistance to change. *Human Relations,* 1948, **11,** 512–532.

House, Robert J. A 1976 theory of charismatic leadership. Mimeo. Faculty of Management Studies, University of Toronto, 1976.

Katz, D., & Kah, R. L. *The social psychology of organizations.* New York: Wiley, 1966.

Kerr, S. On the folly of rewarding A while hoping for B. *Academy of Management Journal,* December 1975, 769–783.

Kotter, J. P., & Schlesinger, L. A. Choosing strategies for change. *Harvard Business Review,* March–April 1979, 106–114.

Lawler, E. E. *Motivation in work organizations.* Belmont, Calif.: Wadsworth, 1973.

———, & Rhode, J. G. *Information and control in organizations.* Santa Monica, Calif.: Goodyear, 1976.

Lewin, K. Frontiers in group dynamics. *Human Relations,* 1947, **1,** 5–41.

Nadler, D. A. *Feedback and organization development: Using data based methods.* Reading, Mass.: Addison-Wesley, 1977.

———, & Tichy, N. M. The limitations of traditional intervention technology in health care organizations. In N. Margulies & J. Adams (Eds.), *Organization development in health care organizations.* Reading, Mass.: Addison-Wesley, 1980.

———, & Tushman, M. L. A congruence model for diagnosing organizational behavior. In D. Kolb, I. Rubin, & J. McIntyre. *Organizational psychology: A book of readings.* 3d ed. Englewood Cliffs, N.J.: Prentice-Hall, 1979.

———, & Tushman, M. L. A model for diagnosing organizational behavior: Applying a congruence perspective. In D. A. Nadler, M. L. Tushman, & N. G. Hatvany (Eds.), *Approaches to managing organizations: Readings and cases.* Boston: Little, Brown, 1982.

Peters, T. J. Symbols, patterns, and settings: An optimistic case for getting things done. *Organizational Dynamics,* Autumn 1978, 3–23.

Pettigrew, A. *The politics of organizational decision-making.* London: Tavistock, 1972.

———. Towards a political theory of organizational intervention. *Human Relations,* 1978, **28,** 191–208.

Pfeffer, J. Management as symbolic action: The creation and maintenance of organizational paradigms. In L. L. Cummings & B. M. Staw (Eds.), *Research in organizational behavior,* Vol. 3. Greenwich, Conn.: JAI Press, 1980.

Porter, L. W., Lawler, E. E., & Hackman, J. R. *Behavior in organizations.* New York: McGraw-Hill, 1975.

Salancik, G. R., & Pfeffer, J. Who gets power—And how they hold on to it: A strategic-contingency model of power. *Organizational Dynamics,* Winter 1977, 3–21.

Sayles, L. R. *Leadership: What effective managers really do and how they do it.* New York: McGraw-Hill, 1979.

Selznick, P. *TVA and the Grass Roots*. Berkeley: University of California Press, 1949.

Thompson, J. D., & Tuden, A. Strategies, structures and processes of organizational decision. In J. D. Thompson et al. (Eds.), *Comparative studies in administration*. Pittsburgh: University of Pittsburgh Press, 1959.

Tushman, M. L. A political approach to organizations: A review and rationale. *Academy of Management Review,* 1977, **2,** 206–216.

Vroom, V. H. *Work and motivation*. New York: Wiley, 1964.

———, & Yetton, P. W. *Leadership and decision making*. Pittsburgh: University of Pittsburgh Press, 1973.

Watson, G. Resistance to change. In W. G. Bennis, K. F. Benne, & R. Chin (Eds.), *The planning of change*. New York: Holt, Rinehart, & Winston, 1969.

Zaltman, G., & Duncan, R. *Strategies for planned change*. New York: Wiley, 1977.

Chapter 15

Normative Views of Organizational Change

How should organizations be managed in the future? What is likely to happen to them in the years to come? These questions are addressed by the three articles presented in this chapter. All of them present normative views of how organizations should be managed in the future. Although they approach the question from different perspectives, they all offer rather clear-cut and similar views as to how organizations *should* evolve. They are, however, less clear in their predictions about the likely future of work organizations. Indeed, although they all offer tantalizing possibilities with respect to how effective and humane organizations might become, they leave the key question—what will organizations be like in the future?—largely unanswered.

All three articles describe images and ideal states that can be important influences on the way organizations are managed in the future. Thus, these three readings should be looked upon as offering possible models that can inspire, direct, and potentially influence the way organizations are managed. They also offer conceptual models that can be useful in testing specific practices and policies to see whether they are consistent or congruent with approaches to management which are likely to be effective in the future.

The first article, by Ouchi and Price, provides a historical overview of normative or prescriptive approaches to organization design. They review the writings of such influential thinkers as Likert, Argyris, and McGregor, all of whom have made substantial contributions to organization theory. Ouchi and Price point to the limitations of these theories and help explain why they have not been universally adopted by managers as the "correct" way to manage work organizations. The article does not stop with simply critiquing past theories, but talks about the elements that Ouchi and Price feel are necessary for an organization to be effective. In many respects this may be the article's most important contribution, since it points the way to greater organizational effectiveness. An additional interesting feature of this article is its discussion of Japanese management and what makes it effective. The authors suggest that some of the things that make Japanese management effective also could improve the effectiveness of work organizations in the United States.

The article by Lawler focuses on what we can learn about managing work organizations from the experimentation that has been going on with new plant design in the United States. He presents in some detail the features that seem to be associated with the success of new high-involvement work organizations. He argues that in many respects these features might be equally effective in traditional organizations, and concludes by proposing that new high-involvement organizations offer a normative model toward which many organizations should aspire. There is considerable overlap between the kinds of normative prescriptions made by Ouchi and Price and by Lawler. Key among them is the fact that a total-organization perspective is needed in thinking about normative models of organization, and that a very strong emphasis on an overall organizational philosophy is crucial.

In the final article, Hackman and Oldham raise what is perhaps the key question for this section. That is, which type of organizational model will be dominant in the future? They point out that the choice is a relatively clear one. Organizations can go with the type of thinking represented by such normative management theorists as Ouchi, Price, and Lawler, or they can continue with more traditional models which are based on economics and engineering. Hackman and Oldham are not optimistic that the more humanistic models will dominate, because implementation of these models is so difficult. Nevertheless, their discussion helps place these new models in societal and technological perspective and it leaves us with an air of realism about the future.

Reading 55

Hierarchies, Clans, and Theory Z: A New Perspective on Organization Development

William G. Ouchi
Raymond L. Price

Bureaucratic hierarchy is not as indispensable to industrialized settings as is commonly assumed. Another quite different form of organization, the hierarchical clan (or Type Z), also appears to succeed in such settings. In fact, these industrialized clans share many of the properties of the organizations described by Elton Mayo, Chris Argyris, Douglas McGregor, and Rensis Likert, the founding fathers of humanistic organizational development. Indeed, we may regard the Type Z organization as a description, in sociological terms, of the same organizations described by these authors in more psychological terms. The addition of the sociological perspective to our understanding of humanistic organization has a number of implications for organizational development.

One major implication of this new perspective should be a better understanding of why current approaches to OD have not been more successful, as well as a broader understanding of effective approaches to organizational change. Many who have attempted large-scale OD efforts have faced a familiar dilemma: On the one hand, the evidence seems to indicate that group-based change fails more often than it succeeds; on the other hand, there are no alternatives to group-based change.

This limited choice may be, we argue, the result of widespread acceptance of the model of humanistic organization in which industrialization inevitably results in a hierarchy because of the properties of managerial control inherent in hierarchies. At the same time, hierarchy is inevitably harmful to the psychological success of individuals. Successful organizations have been shown to contain unusually large numbers of cohesive small working teams; therefore, the alternative to hierarchy is group-based change. But there may be errors in this model. In particular, perhaps hierarchy is not the only efficient means of organizing in an industrial setting, and perhaps small groups are the results, rather than the cause, of organizational success.

AN OVERVIEW OF ORGANIZATIONAL DEVELOPMENT

Although many excellent reviews of the field already exist, perhaps the most complete was recently presented by Porras and Berg (1978), who considered 160 published studies and classified 35 of them as representing one or another approach to OD. Porras and Berg defined five categories of change interventions, based on people and organizational processes:

1 Laboratory training with a process emphasis.
2 Laboratory training with a task emphasis.
3 Managerial Grid® or Grid OD.
4 Survey feedback.
5 Complementary techniques, such as process consultation and counseling.

On the basis of their analysis of these studies they conclude that OD programs rely overwhelmingly on various small-group techniques, especially the T-group and team building:

> To many, OD and T-group intervention approaches are synonymous . . . although T-groups account for a relatively large percentage of the dominant intervention approaches (23 percent), by far the most frequent approach to change has been the team building/team development technique.

As a matter of contemporary practice, we can regard OD as a people- and process-oriented approach to change that relies on small-group techniques and whose objectives are the improvement of both organizational effectiveness and individual psychological success. Of greater interest, however, is the finding by Porras and Berg that the successes of current OD attempts are not reliable:

Author's note: We are greatly indebted to our colleague Joanne Martin for questioning many of our ideas, although we retain the responsibility for what appears here. Robert Bies and Anne Peters also offered helpful comments on an earlier draft.

The data support the belief that OD does not have an important impact on overall organizational processes but instead impacts primarily on the individual. . . . The findings were also consistent with the view that OD intervention activities such as T-groups, encounter groups, and sensitivity training groups do not have a strong impact on the processes and outcomes of organizations. This class of intervention techniques resulted in the lowest percentage of reported change.

These findings are consistent with other evaluations of the success of OD techniques. Richard Walton (1973) has observed that even a successful change effort in a plant rarely diffuses to other parts of the same company. George Strauss (1973) has argued that current approaches to OD are not more successful because they limit themselves to group-based change techniques.

That is not to say that OD never succeeds. Indeed, there are notable successes. However, there seems to be no reliable approach to ensure successful OD. Moreover, it appears that group-based change techniques, which are the dominant form, are rarely successful in producing changes in processes or outcomes.

This is the starting point in our argument. Apparently, small-group-based OD does not work. On the other hand, as we shall see, many humanistic scholars have clearly demonstrated that organizations successful on the humanistic level are characterized by having a rich network of effective, cohesive working teams. These organizations have overcome many of the negative effects of hierarchy. Indeed, it appears that the current approach to OD is based on the belief that, because humanistically successful organizations are demonstrably rich in cohesive small groups, a less healthy organization can be improved by creating effective small groups. As we have suggested, this basic belief underlies contemporary OD and may represent an error in causal attribution. Perhaps cohesive teams are mostly a result rather than a cause of organizational success. Perhaps healthy organizations provide the kind of environment in which teamwork naturally develops. And perhaps teams do not develop unless the organizational environment is right.

In order to answer this question, it will be helpful to consider the basic theoretical ideas underlying contemporary OD. These seminal ideas can be found in the work of four scholars who have been among the most influential contributors to the theory and practice of organizational development: Elton Mayo, Christ Argyris, Douglas McGregor, and Rensis Likert.

THE FOUNDATIONS OF ORGANIZATIONAL DEVELOPMENT

Mayo, Argyris, McGregor, and Likert all focused their attention on one underlying theme: how to mitigate the negative effects of hierarchy. Each of them concentrated on understanding different facets of the problem, and each came to a unique conclusion. A close review of their basic work reveals that they did not all agree that group-based approaches are the answer to hierarchical constraints. While they all observed that humanistically successful organizations tend to have many cohesive working groups in them, they were cautious about concluding that organizational success can be achieved through group development.

Elton Mayo: The Social Problems of an Industrial Civilization

We can consider the work of Elton Mayo (1945) to be the intellectual starting point of the humanistic view of organizations. It was Mayo who initiated the line of research at Harvard that produced the Hawthorne studies at Western Electric Company. Mayo related his interests to the work of two Frenchmen, Durkheim and Le Play. Summarizing what he believed to be the critical issue raised by Le Play, Mayo wrote:

> . . . in simple communities . . . there is a stability of the social order that has ceased to characterize highly developed industrial centers. In these simpler communities every individual understands the various economic activities and social functions, and, in greater or less degree, participates in them. . . . The situation is not simply that the society exercises a powerful compulsion on the individual; on the contrary, the social code and the desires of the individual are, for all practical purposes, identical. Every member participates in social activities because it is his chief desire to do so.

Mayo's central concern was that the natural attitude of cooperation brought on by a complete merging of individual and societal interests is absent in industrialized societies. In a stable, traditional society, the relationships between technology, work, family, and society work as a harmonious whole. When any of the elements changes rapidly, however, harmony between the elements does not occur naturally. Thus, Mayo observes: "The problem of cooperation, to which I shall address myself in all that follows, is far more difficult of solution with us than in a simple or primitive community."

Having defined the problem, Mayo next searched for a social mechanism that would achieve the necessary social integration. Left alone, he believed that industrialized societies would fail to develop the necessary integration and would then fall into a state of chaos. Indeed, Mayo feared that American industry in 1944 was inherently in this state and was held together only by a universal commitment to the war effort. In his search, Mayo considered and rejected contemporary sociology, psychology, political science, and economics. He finally discovered his solution by again looking at traditional societies. He noted that, in traditional societies, the fundamental social order is maintained not by a direct tie between each individual and the state but, rather, by the relationship of each individual to a clan; a smaller, primary group; all clans were then related to the larger government of the state. Mayo seized upon this observation and concluded that the natural state of social relations is for all individuals to be members of stable primary or face-to-face groups. He believed this to be as natural to modern industry as to traditional societies:

> Management, in any continuously successful plant, is not related to single workers but always to working groups. In every department that continues to operate, the workers have—whether aware of it or not—formed themselves into a group with appropriate customs, duties, routines, even rituals. . . . This, for example, occurred in the relay assembly test room at Hawthorne.

From this reasoning, Mayo concluded that the fundamental objective of a management must be to aid the creation and the maintenance of stable, effective working groups within the enterprise. In order to complete his thesis, he also developed the assumption that participation in small groups is a fundamental desire of all people:

> Man's desire to be continuously associated in work with his fellows is a strong, if not the strongest, human characteristic. Any disregard of it by management or

any ill-advised attempt to defeat this human impulse leads instantly to some form of defeat for management itself.

Thus Mayo provided a powerful, broad, conceptual justification for developing cohesive small groups in industrial settings. Fundamentally, all contemporary efforts at organizational development can be said to conform to his basic principle. While Mayo advocated the formation of natural groups, he did not consider the relationship of groups to hierarchy. He carefully considered the disruptive effects of industrialization on social cooperation, but he did not recognize hierarchy as the principal organizational tool of industrialization.

Chris Argyris: Integrating the Individual and the Organization

Whereas Mayo was a student of industrial history, Chris Argyris drew upon contemporary social science to bolster his arguments (1957, 1964). What we find in Argyris's work is a thoroughly developed understanding of the individual psychology of humanistic organizations. Although the scope of Argyris's work is broad, encompassing organizational structure and organization-environment relationships, his focus is on the psychology of the individual. And in contrast to Mayo's concentration on developing a rationale to explain why cooperation will not occur naturally in industrial nations, Argyris considered that issue briefly and accepted the proposition that a complete merging of individual and organizational interests is impossible. However, he did view this inherent conflict of interests as a positive feature of modern life:

> It is our hypothesis that the incongruence between the individual and the organization can provide the basis for a continued challenge which, as it is fulfilled, will tend to help man to enhance his own growth and to develop organizations that will tend to be viable and effective.

When he returned to this issue later on, Argyris argued that the efficiency of industrial organizations demands specialization of jobs to the point where the organizations become psychologically stultifying. Although these effects can be mitigated, he asserted that lower-level employees will inevitably be subjected to at least somewhat alienating work. His objective became to understand more fully the reasons for the negative impact of job alienation on psychological health in order to concentrate on redesigning the most damaging features of industrial organizations.

Psychological health (or success) consists of a high level of self-esteem and an active attempt to self-actualize. The exact components of psychological success are shaped by the larger culture in which the individual has developed. There are two principal conditions for psychological success, according to Argyris:

> The individuals must value themselves and aspire to experience an increasing sense of competence. . . . The second requirement is an organization that provides opportunities for work in which the individual is able to define his immediate goals, define his own paths to these goals, relate these to the goals of the organization, evaluate his own effectiveness, and constantly increase the degree of challenge at work.

The key characteristic of a humanistic organization, in this view, is that it minimizes the dependence of subordinates on superiors and maximizes the autonomy of the employee, which in turn is subject to the coordinative needs of the organization. An important characteristic of such an organization is a climate in which superiors trust subordinates:

> Under a climate of trust, the individuals may increase their opportunities for psychological success. With trust, the management may tend to feel less of a need to develop tight control mechanisms, thereby creating greater opportunity for psychological success.

Argyris next observed that the conditions necessary for the development of trust and of psychological success are rarely met in industrial organizations, because of the inherent conflict between the productive goals of the organization on the one hand and the psychological needs of the employee on the other:

> The formal organization . . . and the administrative control system typically used in complex formal organizations . . . is based on such "Principles" of administration as specialization of work, chain of command, unity of direction, and span of control. The strategy creates a complex of organizational demands that tend to require individuals to experience dependence and submissiveness and to utilize few of their relatively peripheral abilities.

The properties of this pyramidal structure are convincingly demonstrated to have negative impacts both on effectiveness and on psychological success as well as on emotional health at the lower, middle, and upper levels of organizations. Indeed, the review of research presented by Argyris leaves little question that an overwhelming percentage of complex organizations produce predictably negative consequences.

Argyris next argued, from a somewhat abstract theoretical position, that organizations that share power among their participants and link their different pieces together create the conditions for effectiveness. He noted that the designs offered by Burns and Stalker, Likert, Bennis, Shepard, McGregor, and Barnes all contain features consistent with his effective organization: trust, a lack of dependency, and shared decision making, power, and responsibility. Here we have the clearest attack on the pyramidal structure as the source of dependency, invalid information, lack of trust, and ineffectiveness. Argyris recognized that the pyramidal structure has certain properties that make it essential to industry, but he sought to mitigate its negative effects, insofar as possible.

Argyris made two points of critical interest to us. First, he argued that hierarchy in organizations is inevitably hostile to the development of personal autonomy, which is in turn necessary for psychological success. Second, he provided a model through which we can explicitly understand the process by which the organizational setting influences the basic personality of the individual.

The work of Argyris emphasized job enrichment—creating more autonomy, less specialization, and more control over the methods of getting the job done to decrease feelings of meaninglessness and powerlessness on the job. In addition, he more recently advocated an organizational system that will generate valid information, create free and informed choice, and produce internal commitment. To achieve these organizational characteristics, he proposed methods of decreasing the discrepancy between individuals' theories-in-use and espoused theories. However, his major contribution provided a theoretical understanding that can be used in a variety of practical applications. Certainly, Argyris did not conclude that building cohesive small groups should be the major practical implication of his ideas.

Douglas McGregor: The Human Side of Enterprise

The practical implications of the theories expressed by Mayo and by Argyris emerged in the work of McGregor. McGregor accepted the notion that the attainment of cooperation is more difficult in an industrialized society than in a traditional one. He also accepted the idea that the development of social skills is a critical need for contemporary managers. McGregor also took from Argyris the fundamental belief that dependence produces psychological discomfort. He recognized that, given a division of labor in society and in firms, interdependence is inevitable:

> No individual in society is completely independent. Interdependence is a central characteristic of the modern, complex society. . . . Growing up and learning to live in this complex of interdependent relationships is not without its emotional conflicts . . . we remain sensitive when we are placed in a situation which resembles, even remotely, the dependence of infancy. To be a subordinate in an organization is to be placed in a dependent relationship which has enough of the elements of the earlier one to be sensitive and, under certain conditions, explosive.

In order to moderate the effects of dependent relationships in organizations, McGregor emphasized the need for the development of a philosophy of assumptions about people in which the climate reflects basic trust, or Theory Y. In describing the implications of Theory Y for job design, compensation plans, and decision making, McGregor followed closely the principles of psychological success laid out by Argyris. However, McGregor emphasized throughout the critical importance of the point that these are only tools that must reflect an underlying positive culture or philosophy:

> The climate is more significant than the type of leadership or the personal 'style' of the superior. . . . Formal policies, programs, and procedures will be administered, and in turn perceived in the light of the managerial climate. Its importance is primary—the 'machinery' of administration is secondary.

Thus McGregor, like Argyris, emphasized the importance of the cultural setting of the organization. McGregor also believed that a forceful manager is the essential ingredient for initiating the development of a healthy climate or culture in an organization.

Like Mayo and Argyris, McGregor stressed the importance of developing social skills or interpersonal competence. The interdependencies of organizational life are so great that in order to avoid frustration and a subsequent increase in the use of psychologically harmful hierarchical power, a high level of social skill is called for. McGregor explicitly advocated the use of the sensitivity training group, or T-group, as a medium in which these skills can effectively be learned. He also emphasized the advances made in group dynamics, especially by Kurt Lewin and his associates. These advances, he argued, should be put to use in industry in order to improve the effectiveness of the teamwork that is an inevitable accompaniment to interdependence.

Fundamentally, McGregor seems to have accepted the notion that hierarchy is inimical to psychological growth and that hierarchy is, nonetheless, necessary to industrial organization. Therefore, his objective was to discover ways of ameliorating the dependent aspects of hierarchy. He suggested three basic means, which include the development of:

1 A climate or philosophy that leads to the humanistic utilization of a hierarchy.
2 Interpersonal skills through the use of T-groups.
3 The improved effectiveness of small working groups (the inevitable basic links between interdependent individuals in organizations).

Rensis Likert: The Human Organization

We turn last to the work of Rensis Likert. Possibly the most distinctive feature of Likert's contribution to the study of humanistic organizations was his definition of the properties of such an organization, for which he systematically collected and tested the data to refine his definition. From this empirical base, he was able to understand both the theoretical and the practical implications of organization. The survey research technology used by Likert was focused on interpersonal relationships. Such a technique is inappropriate for studying the societal basis of organization, as Mayo did, and it is also relatively ineffective for studying the psychological structure of personality, as Argyris did. Its great strength, however, is in how it reveals the patterns of interaction between individuals in humanistically successful organizations versus those that are unsuccessful.

Likert accepted the notion that the division of labor in a complex modern organization inevitably gives rise to problems of cooperation. He did not delve into the societal basis of this phenomenon, nor did he dwell on its consequences for the basic psychological organization of the self. Rather, he concentrated on empirically discovering those forms of organization that most successfully overcome the problems of cooperation plus the low motivation that attends industrial organization.

While it is not possible to summarize the wealth of empirical findings reported by Likert in this analysis, his results appear to demonstrate repeatedly that successful organizations consist of cohesive work groups knitted together through common participation in an organizational culture. He stated that: "A unit with a high degree of group loyalty will strive hard to achieve the goal it has set for itself" and "all managers in the offices in Set V (high performance) use group methods of supervision; none does in Set I (low performing)." He then went on to say:

> A highly productive organization is much more than a conglomeration of strangers. If a firm were to consist of individuals each of whom had excellent aptitude and training for his particular job but knew absolutely nothing about any other member, the productivity and performance of such an organization would be poor. Highly productive organizations . . . are tightly knit social systems.

Likert emphasized, as did McGregor, that the overall climate (which Likert referred to as the "system") must be consistent. He maintained it is the consistency with which the parts mesh together that is more important than the character of any of the specific techniques of management or organization:

> The communication processes of System 1 are incompatible with any aspect of System 3 or System 4. The same is true of the decision-making processes and the compensation plans. The management system of an organization must have compatible component parts if it is to function effectively.

Likert also asserted that the natural tendency in hierarchies is to resort to mechanisms of control, such as coercion and economic reward, which in turn intensify the conflicts between individuals and groups that arise naturally through the division of labor in the organization. He emphasized that, only through a commitment to group decision making and training in interpersonal skills, can these natural conflicts be kept under control. He then gave a more complete development to this emphasis on group decision making, which Mayo and McGregor also emphasized; he also argued that group decision making is consistent with the idea of individual responsibility, a concept to which most managers are deeply committed.

Likert explicitly recognized that the creation of effective groups does not solve the problem of cooperation. Indeed, the creation of internally cohesive groups may serve only to move the organization from conflict between individuals to conflict between groups. In order to avoid this possibility, Likert emphasized the importance of a common culture. For the promotion of the creation of a common culture, he suggested the rotation of managers between functions and the use of multiple-overlapping group memberships. These would constitute the structural tools whose function is stimulation of the development of a companywide culture rather than a merely local one.

Last, Likert designed a matrix organization. As Davis and Lawrence recently observed after a thorough study of matrix organizations (1977), the matrix provides a high level of effective communication between highly differentiated subunits. But this can be accomplished only if the managers in the matrix have a high level of interpersonal skill and share a common culture that supports this collective approach to problem solving and decision making.

THE HUMANISTIC VIEW IN PERSPECTIVE

The work of these four scholars is highly individual. Any attempt to summarize their conclusions must necessarily fall short of completeness. It is possible, however, to identify a few of the central ideas that appeared consistently in their work and which have formed the basis of much contemporary organizational development.

In the work of Argyris, McGregor, and Likert, we

find a consistent assertion that hierarchical organizations are naturally and inevitably hostile to the growth needs of individuals. In the first place, they argued that hierarchy enables the more powerful to impose commands and restrictions on the less powerful, thereby fostering a state of dependence that restricts psychological success. Second, they believed that hierarchical organizations create a level of specialization that leaves lower-level participants in psychologically unsatisfying jobs. Third, they contended that narrow, economic measurements of managerial performance in hierarchies lead to interpersonal difficulties, competition, and frustration among the higher-level participants. These analyses led them to seek the limitation of the power differences in hierarchies and the amelioration of the negative impact of hierarchy on people.

In the work of Mayo, McGregor, and Likert, we find consistent assertions that the development of internally cohesive small groups that are linked to each other leads to organizational success. This assertion seems to be derived from a comparison, either through formal research or through life experience, between successful and unsuccessful organizations. They have observed that successful organizations are characterized by having many cohesive working groups that are linked together, while unsuccessful organizations frustrate the development of such groups. McGregor did not hypothecate that group cohesiveness may be the result of organizational success. Rather, he stated that it *is* a major cause of such successes, so he advocated the active creation of cohesive work groups in all organizations in order to assure organizational success.

The work of all four scholars advocates the development of interpersonal skill. All of them concluded that complex organizations present managers with tensions and conflicts that too often are resolved through an arbitrary use of power, leading to poor performance and psychological failure. They therefore advocated the development of interpersonal skill to enable managers to cope with the inevitable emotional strains that accompany problem solving under conflict-ridden conditions. The results, they claimed, are better creative problem solving, less arbitrary use of power, and higher performance with the concomitant benefit of psychological success.

But a question arises here. Though the negative properties of hierarchy were amply recorded (and

are clear), and the positive properties of cohesive groups were likewise well documented (and are also clear), it is *not* clear in any of the foregoing why the creation of cohesive groups in organizations can solve the problems brought on by hierarchy. Indeed, Argyris very carefully reasoned out the negative effects of hierarchical dependence on both performance and psychological growth. But he never advocated the use of multiple overlapping small groups nor of small cohesive groups of any sort as a resolution. He dealt with the problem at an abstract level but apparently did not feel that teamwork at the group level can solve the problems of organizational hierarchy.

More importantly, in this review we find a lack of clarity in the relationships among industrialization, hierarchy, alienation, and small group formation. None of the authors dealt in detail with all of these underlying critical issues in organization development. Mayo argued that industrialization produces alienation, and the others argued that hierarchy produces alienation. All suggested that membership in groups is an antidote to alienation. But we find no explanation for why hierarchy seems to be the inevitable response to industrialization. This omission may be critical. If hierarchy as a mode of organizing work is uniquely suited to modern industry, then it must be that hierarchy fulfills certain essential functions of managerial control. If we can isolate these essential properties of hierarchy, then we can begin to see why the hierarchical form is so persistent. And we can also see why it is hostile to the formation of both individual autonomy and small groups.

SOCIAL ORGANIZATION MECHANISM

Hierarchy is a means of organizing cooperative effort among an aggregation of individuals. It is not the only means for doing so; therefore, it is not inevitable in the ultimate sense. However, it may well be that hierarchy is the most efficient means of organizing effort in industrial settings, ergo, it may be quite inevitable in contemporary times. In order to see why this may be, let us consider a general framework within which we can understand the role played by hierarchy in the organization of work.

It has recently been suggested (Ouchi, 1978) that organized effort can be managed through one of three basic social mechanisms, markets, bureaucracies (hierarchies), and clans. Each mechanism is capable of providing the two ingredients to any continuing work relationship: the motivation to pursue acceptable goals and the information necessary to execute goal achievement effectively.

Markets

In a market, one basic mechanism of control is price. If prices are properly set, each individual simply seeks to maximize personal wealth (thus relying on selfish motives). The result is coordinated decisions or acts that simultaneously satisfy both the individual and the organization. For example, a company that treats each division purely as a profit or investment center relies on the desire of division managers to maximize their divisions' profits and thus their personal advancement. If intracompany transfer prices have been perfectly set, then the individual division managers will then be led to simultaneously maximize their own welfare as well as that of the company as a whole. Of course, prices cannot be set perfectly if there is a great deal of ambiguity about who contributes what or about the value of a unique product or service. The result is that few, if any, companies rely entirely on a price mechanism to control their divisions.

Ordinarily, the price mechanism is supplemented by the use of a bureaucratic hierarchy. In a bureaucratic hierarchy, the fundamental mechanism of control is the specification and monitoring of rules—either rules about how to act, or rules about how much output or how much quality to produce. Because a rule is a rather crude informational device (more so than a price), a rule can be used in most organizational settings, even when ambiguity concerning the value or source of output is severe. For example, a company may employ output-oriented rules, such as production cost standards and acceptable variances; it may also employ behavior rules, such as specifying which workers will do which tasks on what schedules. The exact value of these activities may be unknown, precluding the setting of prices, but the rules themselves can be specified and monitored.

Bureaucratic Hierarchies

A bureaucratic hierarchy also rests critically on the use of legitimate authority. It must have employees who willingly grant to their superiors the right to tell them (within some zone of indifference) what to do. The employees must also willingly allow their superiors to closely monitor their activities and outputs. The first right is a critical one because no organization can specify, in advance, a rule for every possible future event; superiors must be able, in effect, to make up rules as needed. The second right is critical because, unlike the market situation, the employee does not have a selfish interest in doing that which the organization would like him to do; superiors must thus be able to check up on them. Note that, in a pure market, there are no superiors and there is no monitoring, because all are expected simply to behave in their own self-interest.

In order to facilitate the operation of the hierarchical mechanism, the bureaucracy also typically engages in a high level of job specialization. This has the effect of breaking jobs down into simple pieces that can be learned quickly and easily and which can be monitored effectively. A complex task (such as that of a surveyor) is far more difficult to monitor than a simple task (that of a keypunch operator).

The great advantage a bureaucratic hierarchy has over a market is that it can tolerate more ambiguity. On the other hand, a bureaucratic hierarchy imposes a dependent relationship on employees; subordinates must be dependent upon superiors to direct and evaluate their work. Chaos would result if subordinates were left to specify and evaluate their own work (as autonomous work groups attempt to do), with neither the motivation to serve the company nor information as to how best to serve it. If subordinates were given that much freedom and also had both the motivation and the information to simultaneously serve their personal interests as well as those of the company, then we would have not a bureaucratic hierarchy but rather a market.

Clans

A clan is a culturally homogeneous organization, one in which most members share a common set of values or objectives plus beliefs about how to coordinate effort in order to reach common objectives. The clan functions by socializing each member completely so that each merges individual goals with the organizational ones, thus providing them with the motivation to serve the organization. The merged goals socialize the individuals completely and provide them with information on the best way to get things done, thus making this decision-making process almost instinctual. However, this socialization is possible only when new members already share values quite similar to those of the organizational culture, which makes radical resocialization unnecessary. This is all possible only when membership turnover is low, thus giving members a greater vested interest in integrating themselves personally and completely into the organization. For example, in the U.S. Foreign Service or an investment bank, each job is unique, making performance comparisons difficult. As a result, neither price nor bureaucratic surveillance mechanisms are capable of providing control. In such cases, the only new employees selected are those who have been largely presocialized by having had similar family and educational backgrounds, which have socialized them so extensively that they will espouse the appropriate organizational values and beliefs. Thus, although effective evaluation of individual performance is impossible, the acculturation is nearly complete and the organization can, in such instances, be reasonably sure that each employee is striving to accomplish the organization's goals in an effective manner.

As Mayo noted, a clan, like a market, has few problems of employee alienation. However, while a market achieves integration by having a price mechanism that allows everyone to behave selfishly and still serve organizational objectives, the clan achieves this end through socialization. If socialization is total (a pure but probably unrealistic state), then selfish behavior is in the organization's interest, since the employee has been socialized into desiring that which serves the organization. A strong form of this complete socialization is seen in such total institutions as the Marine Corps and some monasteries. But it probably exists in a weaker form in all organizations.

Hierarchy is thus only one among the three mechanisms of social control over collective tasks. However, while markets require highly sophisticated price information for their operation and clans require extreme homogeneity and stability, bureaucratic hierarchies can operate with only partially committed, largely unsocialized employees, working under conditions of extreme ambiguity. If we pursue Mayo's reasoning, we may conclude that industrialization produces a level of mobility that is destructive

of clans and produces levels of technological change and interdependence that frustrate market mechanisms. Perhaps hierarchical bureaucracy is inevitable under these conditions. If a bureaucracy is the only social control mechanism that can withstand the conditions accompanying industrialization, then we must agree with Mayo, Argyris, McGregor, and Likert that bureaucratic hierarchy is here to stay.

THE HUMANISTIC HIERARCHY

It now becomes difficult to understand how the formation of cohesive work groups can mitigate the effects of hierarchy without also diminishing the effectiveness of the organization. If small groups protect employees against either hierarchical evaluation or hierarchical direction, the employees can threaten the efficiency of the firm by promoting job rotation or other devices that reduce specialization, thereby frustrating the control apparatus and decreasing organizational effectiveness. Indeed, it seems that small groups can appear to mitigate the negative effects of hierarchy only if those effects are accompanied by the increase of either the market or the clan mechanisms, which in turn replace some of the intended deemphasis on hierarchical control. A stronger form of this argument would assert that only if the clan form significantly (but not necessarily entirely) replaces the bureaucratic hierarchy, will the effects (and therefore the negative effects) of hierarchy diminish. Cohesive small groups may flourish in such a setting.

This line of argument seems to be consistent with the work of the humanistic proponents reviewed earlier. They argued, as we have, that the negative effects of hierarchy are due largely to its creation of dependency and extreme task specialization. They felt, as we do, that hierarchy dominates other forms of organization due to its unique suitability to modern industrialism. However, they did not have a conceptual framework that enabled them to compare hierarchy to other forms of organizing work relationships, such as the market and the clan. Thus they did not isolate the basic, essential managerial control functions fulfilled by hierarchies. Lacking this point of view, derived from the sociology rather than the psychology of organizations, they were unable to assess that humanistic change techniques were more or less capable of replacing basic control functions of hierarchy. McGregor argued for the development of small groups as a mechanism for mitigating the negative effects of hierarchy without assessing the capacity of group formation to replace the organization control properties of hierarchy. He did not see that, unless essential control properties are replaced, hierarchy cannot be replaced. Furthermore, it seems reasonable to expect that hierarchy cannot even coexist with any humanistic technique whose success depends on its ability to dampen hierarchical effects without replacing them with either market or clan mechanisms.

It would be a vast overstatement, however, to contend that the humanists were unaware of these issues. Indeed, the explicit attention given by them to the importance of climate, atmosphere, and philosophy seems to be consistent with the notion of building a cultural or clan form of control. It would be reasonable to suggest that their work can be interpreted as advocating the development of industrial clans. What we intend to do here is bring out more clearly the sociological implications of the humanistic approach to organizations, because we believe them to be critical to the understanding of organizational development. If we suppose that Mayo, Argyris, McGregor, or Likert had studied a successful humanistic organization from a sociological rather than a psychological frame of reference, what might they have observed? Let us attempt to gain at least partial insight into an answer to this question by reviewing some recent research that takes a more sociological view of a successful humanistic organization. Through this exercise, we may be able to flesh out more completely some of the basic characteristics that such an organization would have.

CONTEMPORARY INDUSTRIAL CLANS: TYPE Z ORGANIZATIONS

Some large, modern organizations appear to have successfully maintained many elements of clan forms of control. They also appear to rely somewhat less on bureaucratic hierarchy, therefore suffering fewer of its negative consequences. However, no organization can be expected to achieve any of the three control types (market, bureaucratic hierarchy, clan) in its pure form. Each industrial clan, however, seems to have found a way to combine market,

bureaucratic, and clan mechanisms in a way that is at least interesting and perhaps provides a model for future organizational development. Let us briefly consider a general type of industrial clan and then a specific example.

Probably the most striking examples of industrial clans are to be found in Japan (Johnson and Ouchi, 1974). Many authors have described the relatively complete socialization process and the initially homogeneous workforce that permits Japanese organizations to achieve strikingly high rates of productivity and employee loyalty. Japanese organizations, both governmental and private, employ many bureaucratic and market mechanisms; but they rely to a great extent on common socialization into and acceptance of the values and beliefs of a homogeneous culture (see Rohlen, 1974). Japanese industry is reported to show average absentee rates below 2 percent and has achieved productivity increases two to three times over the U.S. rate of the past three decades. Japan has alcoholism rates one-fourth those of the United States. National surveys in Japan reveal that up to 85 percent of that population would willingly give up a seat on a crowded bus to a superior from their company! More interesting, however, is the observation that Japanese organizations operate in a highly industrialized setting, yet they have developed a mechanism of control that relies far less on bureaucratic hierarchy than do Western organizations. This suggests that bureaucratic hierarchy is not nearly as inevitable in industrial societies as we have thought.

The Type Z Organization

Recently, a research group at the Graduate School of Business at Stanford University identified a purely American form of organization that appears to have many of the Japanese characteristics. We referred to this American organization as the Type Z organization (out of deference to McGregor). Through an extended series of interviews with managers from many companies, we identified a set of companies that is widely believed to exhibit Type Z characteristics: Kodak, Procter & Gamble, Hewlett-Packard, IBM, Cummins Engine Company, and a few others. Through a survey study (Ouchi and Johnson, 1978) of companies in the electronics industry (including the 22 largest such firms in the United States), we found that perceived corporate prestige, managerial ability, and reported corporate earnings are all strongly positively correlated with the Z-ness of the organization. This result suggested to us that the Type Z organization may combine the economic and psychological success sought by humanistic scholars.

We proceeded to select from the electronics industry the purest example of Type Z organization and the purest example of the opposite, referred to as a Type A organization. Our interest was in identifying their basic control properties from a sociological point of view, as summarized in Figure 55-1.

Basically, the Type Z organization closely resembles the Japanese form, depending critically as it does on stable, long-term employment. This permits relatively complete socialization into the organizational culture. The practice of moderate career specialization by rotating people through different functions aids the integration of internal parts. The slow process of evaluation and promotion ensures that no one is advanced into a position of responsibility until complete socialization has taken place. This leads to natural consensual decision making. The combination of collective decision making with a commonly shared culture reduces the need for explicit supervision, coordination, and evaluation. Because relationships are long term, they become quite broad, with the result that superiors develop a relatively wholistic concern for subordinates.

Type Z organizations have managed to stop the rapid movement and turnover that apparently characterizes many other industrial organizations. Exactly how they achieve this stability is not completely clear, but they do appear to consciously stay out of highly volatile markets, to sub-contract out necessary but unstable tasks, and to reduce voluntary turnover by offering attractive working conditions.

(It should be noted, however, that at all levels the Type Z company pays wages that are at the industry average.) Their extremely high stability permits Type Z organizations to develop philosophies and cultures that approximate the features of clans in more traditional settings. Of course, Type Z organizations exist within a highly industrialized setting, and they are not able to achieve the levels of stability experienced by true clans; thus they must supplement the mechanisms of control by using some bureaucratic and market mechanisms.

The Type Z organization we studied, for example, calculated the profitability of each of its divisions, but it did not operate a strict profit center or other marketlike mechanism. Rather, decisions were frequently made by division managers who were guided by broader corporate concerns, even though their own divisional earnings may have suffered as a result. This occurred because each division manager had long tenure with the firm, anticipated a lifelong career with the firm, and had both the information and the motivation to make decisions in the broader corporate interest.

The Type Z organization, like any clan, on the other hand, has some outstanding weaknesses. Because it is so homogeneous with respect to values and beliefs, it is hostile to deviant views, including those that may be important for future adaptation and survival. Employees who are culturally dissimilar, such as women, and minorities, are regularly excluded from the mainstream; they experience relatively great alienation and psychological failure.

By and large, the Type Z organization is integrated into the values of the larger society. Therefore, it presents its members with few conflicts between their personal goals (which are derived from those of the larger society) and the organization's goals (which are also consonant with those of the larger

Type A	Type Z
Short-term employment	Long-term employment
Rapid evaluation and promotion	Slow evaluation and promotion
Highly specialized careers	Moderately specialized careers
Individual decision making	Consensual decision making
Individual responsibility	Individual responsibility
Explicit, formal control	Implicit, informal control (but with explicit measures)
Segmented concern	Wholistic concern

Figure 55-1 Two organizational types.

society). Indeed, the Type Z organization is frequently criticized by experts in economics and finance as having slack—operating inefficiently because it pays social costs it does not have to. However, this responsiveness to broader social concerns, such as community responsibility and employee welfare, seems to be essential to the maintenance of a corporate culture into which members of the society can be acculturated. Put another way, because the Type Z organization is itself well integrated into the society, it can relatively effortlessly take people from this society and integrate them into itself. Thus alienation and dependence are minimized, socialization and commitment are maximized, and organizational cooperation is secured without recourse to the more extreme forms of explicit, hierarchical control.

The Type Z organization partially replaces the control properties of a hierarchy with those of a clan and is therefore able to reduce hierarchical dependence and extreme task specialization for all ranks. Employees in all ranks of the Type Z organization display unusually high rates of psychological success and of emotional well-being, with the organization maintaining rates of growth and of profitability well above the industry average. The culture of this type of organization is not developed after it becomes economically successful. An analysis of historical records shows that, since the founding of these companies, consistency has usually existed in their managerial philosophies and internal cultures.

Although the Type Z organization is characterized by many cohesive, overlapping work groups, it does not differ greatly from the Type A organization in this respect. Indeed, much of the group activity in the company seems to be expressive in nature. Employees frequently do things in groups simply because they enjoy working together and enjoy demonstrating to themselves and others their skill at managing complex collective relationships. Moreover, the use of clan mechanisms of control permits the formation of cohesive work groups without threatening the basis of organizational efficiency.

In summary, as one of the authors has written "the ideal Type Z organization combines a basic cultural commitment to individual values with a highly collective nonindividual pattern of interaction. It simultaneously satisfies old norms of independence and present needs for affiliation. Employ-

ment is effectively (although not officially) for a lifetime; and turnover is low. Decision making is consensual, and there is often a self-conscious attempt to preserve the consensual mode."

DEVELOPING AN ORGANIZATIONAL PHILOSOPHY

New or deviant points of view in an established field are generally nothing more than something previously overlooked or undervalued in classic works. This is our claim. We offer the observation that successful humanistic organizations did not become that way due to an organization development program. This applies to Japanese organizations, to those studied by Mayo, Argyris, McGregor, and Likert, and to the Type Z organization. There is little apparent basis for the current emphasis on group-based approaches to OD being considered a very recent or new development.

By reexamining the evidence, we can interpret some of the early basic work on humanistic organization as supporting the idea that clan forms of organization, rather than small-group development, are the proper focus for developmental efforts. Perhaps the more sociology-minded and organizationally oriented theories of the humanistic authors were previously overlooked because they had not been stated crisply and concretely. More importantly, the small-group aspects of their work may have been pursued because the technology of group development had only recently been developed and looked to be amenable to industrial application.

The implications of this new perspective for the theory and practice of organizational development are not yet clear. However, it is possible to focus on one critical element of the Type Z organization with relatively clear implications for OD: the development of an organizational philosophy. The clarity and the widespread acceptance of an organizational philosophy most clearly separates the Type Z from the Type A organization in our study. It is also striking that most large Japanese organizations have a similarly developed philosophy and that many chief executives of major Japanese firms have written books describing their philosophies of management.

What is the function of a philosophy? An organizational philosophy is primarily a mechanism for integrating an individual into an organization. By providing a clear understanding of the organization's goals, objectives, and methods for accomplishing those goals, a philosophy permits individuals to link their own individual goals with those of the company.

An organizational philosophy is also a mechanism for integrating an organization into the society. All societies value the emotional well-being of people, but (as Likert has observed) the price mechanism governing private organizations does not take human assets into account. Thus a firm which exclusively seeks to maximize profits will "use up" and discard its human assets and in the process will become alienated from the society. The firm that abuses its employees will suffer some loss of efficiency, but it does not bear the full social cost of alienated employees who have developed a diminished sense of self-worth. An extremely alienating work experience, according to Argyris, will depress the general life activity and satisfaction of individuals, but these costs are external to the firm, just as the social costs of polluted air and water until recently were external. If such abuses become widespread, we can expect the society to impose legal restrictions on firms that force them to protect human welfare, as has occurred recently in many European countries. However, although human assets cannot be measured and incorporated into a price mechanism, they can be taken into account if the organization has a consistent and concrete philosophy that managers apply in their decision making. A philosophy of management can provide a consistent guide to decision making that will supplement profit considerations.

An organizational philosophy may also be regarded as an elegant informational device. What might otherwise be a diffuse and ambiguous set of values gains sufficient concreteness through actions and the recounting of actual events to serve as a guide to decision making and to action. Thus a philosophy of management provides a form of control at once all pervasive and effective because it consists of a basic theory of how the firm should be managed. Any manager who grasps this essential theory can deduce from it the appropriate response to any novel situation.

For example, during one of the author's visits to a Japanese bank in California, both the Japanese president and the American vice-president accused the other of being unable to formulate objectives. The Americans meant that the Japanese president could not or would not give them explicit, quantified targets to attain over the next three to six months, while the Japanese meant that the Americans could not see that once they understood the company's philosophy, they would be able to deduce for themselves the proper objectives for any conceivable situation.

A second example came from a young product manager who was trying to make some important decisions concerning the development of a new product. When he approached his manager for an answer, he was told to reread the corporate objectives and to deduce for himself what the correct answer would be. The objectives that dealt with product quality and customer satisfaction eliminated the problem he faced. The question facing the young product manager was whether to set the price at a figure that would not yield a profit for eight months, but would leave the company way ahead when sales reached the projected volume. The company's objectives stated that its goal was to produce products of value to its customers and that profits were its reward for so doing. The decision was clear: The product should be priced from the beginning at a figure that yielded a profit.

In another instance in the same organization, two market studies concurred that the potential market for a projected new product was very small and the anticipated profits marginal. Yet the product would constitute a very real service to a very limited number of customers. The company in keeping with its philosophy of service, went ahead with the project. And in this case, much to the surprise of everyone involved in the decision, the market studies were in error; sales were much greater than anticipated, and the profits were proportionately higher.

If organizational philosophies have so many advantages, why don't all organizations develop explicit philosophies? The question is complex, but at least two major explanations are apparent. In the first place, philosophies that will integrate organizations into the society do not develop because organizations have little incentive to be integrated into the society. Just as the price mechanism does not take into account the value of clean air or water, it does not take into account the value of psychological success. Just as firms polluted the air and water until laws were passed that laid down standards and imposed penalties, they can be expected to abuse employee welfare until regulations are imposed. In traditional societies, firms were small and managers had intimate ties to church, neighbors, and local clubs, which imposed on them an inescapable sense of social responsibility. In industrialized nations, those traditional social control mechanisms are largely destroyed, with the result that managers and firms are driven to maximize short-term profits without any countervailing force that impels them toward community responsibility. The ultimate solution may be regulation by government; a preferable solution would be the development of socially integrated organizational philosophies.

In the second place, most managers do not have the luxury of starting their own company and infusing it with a philosophy from the beginning. Most managers work in large organizations where a new plant may develop a philosophy but even that is difficult to maintain let alone spread to the rest of the company. So how can a philosophy be developed?

An organizational philosophy can be the creation of a single charismatic leader or of a group of managers. It must be developed at the top of an organizational unit that is autonomous enough to establish and maintain its own style. For example, General Motors Corporation has a corporatewide organizational philosophy that was first developed largely by Alfred P. Sloan, whereas Hewlett-Packard's philosophy is the joint product of its co-founders. Philosophies or cultures unique to one part of the corporation are widely believed to exist within the finance function of the Ford Motor Company, and we have worked for the past three years with a group of managers who together developed and implemented their philosophy within one division of a multi-billion-dollar company.

Implementation of a philosophy may take many forms. At first, those who have created it must work through at least some of its practical implications to see whether it really fits their goals. Then, a process of teaching and learning will ensue, during which the philosophy is explained to others and is modified by the new issues that they will inevitably raise. If the philosophy truly integrates organizational goals with broad societal goals, then most employees will readily accept it, and no one will have to be "brainwashed." More traditional forms of OD, including group training, will be helpful during implementation to give people practice in working through the practical implications of an organizational philosophy.

Last, a philosophy should deal with fundamental, long-range goals and values. Although operating procedures will be deduced from a philosophy, they will change from month to month and should not be perceived by employees as part of the philosophy. In this manner, an organizational philosophy can maintain its ability to provide stable direction over the years while also being flexible enough to adapt to short-run changing conditions.

There really is no trick to developing an organizational culture or an organizational philosophy. It simply means recognizing the plain fact that measurable, quantifiable techniques of control are helpful but incomplete, and that, if the equally important but more subtle goals of the organization are not expressed openly through a philosophy, then numbers will rule, to the detriment of the organization. It is to be hoped that the concerns of scientific management will be counterbalanced with the concerns of cultural management.

Reading 56

Creating High-Involvement Work Organizations

Edward E. Lawler III

The 1970s saw the successful construction, start-up, and operation of a significant number of new plants that are different from traditional plants in some important ways. These plants are different in how they are designed and managed, and in the high level of involvement that seems to characterize their workforces. The list of companies with these new plants reads like an excerpt from *Fortune's* 500. They include General Foods, PPG Industries, Procter & Gamble, Sherwin-Williams, TRW, Rockwell, General Motors, Mead Corporation, and Cummins Engine. Many of these organizations have started not one high-involvement plant, but two, three, four, or more. At this point no one knows precisely how many organizations have initiated new high-involvement plants, or how many of them exist. A good guess would be that more than twenty large organizations have at least one, and that, overall, more than a hundred are currently in operation.

It is possible that these high-involvement plants are merely an intriguing novelty which, although successful, can teach us little about how to create more effective work organizations. On the other hand, it is possible that they represent a broadly applicable approach to management that can teach us a great deal about how we can create more effective organizations and that, as such, they are a very important social invention which warrants careful study. Before we can determine just how applicable this approach is, we need to briefly review the characteristics of these plants and then to consider what has been learned about their effectiveness.

CHARACTERISTICS OF THE PLANTS

One of the most interesting aspects of the plants is the number of innovations common to all or almost all of them. These innovations are most interesting because of their potential for diffusion to other organizations. A review of the innovations will indicate how specific areas of management are handled in the high-involvement plants and how they differ from traditional plants.

Employee Selection

The traditional approach to employee selection has largely gone by the board. Instead of the personnel departments carefully screening, testing, and selecting among applicants, a process is used that includes helping the job applicant make a valid decision about taking the job and getting production employees more involved in the selection decision.

The selection process places a great deal of emphasis on acquainting applicants with the nature of the jobs they are expected to fill and the nature of the managerial style that will be used in the plant. They can then decide whether the particular job situation is right for them. Before start-up, a group interview is held by the managers and workers who will interact with new employees so they can decide together whether the job applicants will fit the management approach that will be used in the organization. After the plant becomes operational this approach to selection continues and work-team members are given the responsibility for selecting new members of their teams. In some cases, the personnel department does some initial screening of applicants and, where appropriate, administers tests and checks references.

Design of the Plant and Physical Layout

Many of the plants make an effort to have at least a few members of the workforce on board early enough to participate in decisions about the layout of machinery, equipment, and the recreational and personal areas of the plant. Often employees from existing plants—many of whom will be reassigned to the new plant—are asked to participate in the design. The idea is to capture the employees' ideas and implement them to improve the design of the plant. In some cases, experts in sociotechnical system design are also called in to make certain that the

Adapted from Lawler, Edward E. "The New Plant Revolution," *Organizational Dynamics*, Winter 1978, 3–12. © Edward E. Lawler III, 1980. Used with permission.

physical layout is congruent with the desired social system.

Frequently a strong egalitarian approach is taken to how the work and nonwork areas in the new plants are laid out. Rather than having separate areas in which managers eat and spend their non-work time, everyone uses the same eating, rest-room, and recreational facilities. In many plants the entrances and parking areas are common to all employees. In other words, employees all receive a clear message that at least in terms of the physical facilities and typical perquisites of office, a relatively egalitarian system exists at the plant level.

Security

Most plants are publicly committed to no-lay-off policies. So far, all of them I am aware of have been able to live up to their policies by using part-time employees during busy periods and by doing mainte-nance and other nonproductive work during slow periods. This policy is important because it assures people that they will not produce themselves out of a job and it shows that the company is willing to make a commitment to all employees.

Job Design

In all the plants, an attempt is made to see that employees have jobs that are challenging, motivat-ing, and satisfying. In some cases this is done through individually based job-enrichment ap-proaches that emphasize personal responsibility for a whole piece of meaningful work. In most cases, however, it is accomplished through the creation of autonomous work groups or teams (see, e.g., Poza & Markus, 1980).

Typically, teams are given the responsibility for the production of a whole product or a significant part of one. They are self-managing in the sense that they make decisions about who performs which tasks on a given day, they set their own production goals, and they are often also responsible for quality control, purchasing, and discipline. Most teams emphasize the desirability of job rotation for their members, and team members are expected to learn all the jobs that fall within the purview of the team.

In some plants an effort has even been made to mix interesting tasks with routine jobs. For example, one plant made the maintenance jobs part of the same team as warehousing so that no one would spend all of his or her time on the relatively boring warehousing tasks. The end result of the use of work teams usually is that the people participating feel responsible for a large work area, experience a sense of control, and develop an understanding of a large segment of the production process.

Pay System

Most plants have taken a different approach to establishing base pay levels for employees. Instead of using a traditional job-evaluation approach which scores jobs on their characteristics in order to deter-mine the pay rates for every job in the plant, they evaluate the skills of each individual. Typically, everyone starts at the same salary. As employees learn new skills, their salaries go up. When this system is combined with job rotation, workers doing relatively low-level jobs may be quite highly paid because they are capable of performing a large number of other, more skilled tasks (see Lawler, 1981).

This approach has two main advantages: It tends to create a flexible, highly trained workforce that can adapt to most changes in product demand and staffing since ready replacements are available. It also promotes the development of the work team because it gives employees a broader knowledge of how the plant operates. This is important because it enables individuals to participate in more decisions and it aids identification with the goals of the plant.

In about half the new plants with which I am familiar, decisions about whether or not an individu-al has mastered a new job well enough to deserve a salary increase are left to the members of his or her team. This approach to pay decisions reinforces the participative management style that is very impor-tant to the way high-involvement plants are man-aged.

A few (but not most) of the plants have moved toward one of two approaches to tying pay to performance. Some have introduced a merit-salary-increase component into their skill-based pay sys-tems. A few others have introduced plantwide profit-sharing or gain-sharing plans after they have operated long enough to develop a stable perform-ance history. It is possible that as more of them mature and establish stable base periods for the measurement of productivity gains, more of them will adopt these plans. This seems likely, since organizationwide sharing of productivity gains is congruent with the team concept of management and the general participative, egalitarian principles that underlie the design of these plants.

Organizational Structure

One of the really striking features of these plants is their structural hierarchy. All the plants have located the plant manager only a few levels above the production workers. In some cases, the foreman's role has been eliminated completely. In others, the foremen report directly to the plant manager, and such traditional intermediate levels as general foreman and superintendent have been eliminated.

Where there are no foremen, several teams usually report to a single supervisor, and the teams are envisaged as being self-managed. Most of the time they elect a team leader who is then responsible for communicating with the rest of the organization. This person undertakes the kinds of lateral relations with other functional and line departments that that consume so much of the time and constitute such an important responsibility for the typical first-line supervisor (see Walton & Schlesinger, 1979).

High-involvement plants also deemphasize functional-area responsibility. Rather than being organized on a functional basis (maintenance, production, and so on), they tend to be organized on a product or an area basis. Thus individuals have the responsibility for the production of something rather than for general maintenance or engineering. This system provides more meaningful job structures and creates a feeling of commitment to the product rather than to a function.

Because of the way they are structured, most plants have fewer staff and indirect-labor people assigned to them. Since many of the typical staff functions are handled by the work teams, not as many support people are needed. For example, since some scheduling is done by the teams, fewer people are needed in this support group.

Approach to Training

All the new plants place a heavy emphasis on training, career planning, and the personal growth and development of employees. This is usually backed up with extensive in-plant training programs and strong encouragement for employees to take off-the-job training, usually paid for by the organization.

There have been some interesting innovations in in-company training. For example, in some plants employees may take courses in the economics of the plant's business and are rewarded with higher pay when they complete such courses. On-the-job training by other employees is also very common and is necessary to implement the concept of multi-skilled employees. Regular career-planning sessions are also scheduled. In some plants, employees present a personal career-development plan to their team members; in others, the process is handled by someone in management. As a result of the strong emphasis on training, workers develop the feeling that personal development and growth are desirable goals.

Management Style

Most of the practices I have cited are an integral part of what it means to practice participative management. Operationally, this translates into pushing decisions as far down in the organization as possible. As we have seen, in high-involvement plants, production-line employees make purchasing decisions and even personnel-selection decisions. When decisions cannot be pushed down, it is typical for inputs to be gathered from everyone in the organization before the final decision is made. For example, a number of plants have delayed establishing personnel policies until the workforce has been hired and everyone has had the chance to have a say on what these policies should be.

Summary and Conclusions

Overall, these new plants are clearly different from traditional plants in a number of important ways. Almost no aspect of the organization has been left untouched. The reward systems, the structure, the physical layout, the personnel-management system, and the nature of the jobs have all been changed—and in significant ways. Because so many particulars have been altered, in aggregate they amount to a new kind of organization.

I must stress, however, that most plants are still regarded by both employees and management as being in an evolutionary stage. They are being modified and altered continually on the basis of experience and changes in local conditions. Thus, although it is clear that a common set of practices is being tried by these organizations, every plant and organization that adopts them is simultaneously adapting them in ways that make the management system and overall design of each unique.

It is instructive to compare these high-involvement plants to the approach to management that is commonly used in Japan (see Reading 55). In many respects they are similar. For example, both use groups and emphasize job security. But it would be wrong to consider them to be essentially equivalent. The high-involvement plants differ in some important ways. Two of the most important are in their pay systems and their management style. Japanese organizations do not use skill-based pay and gain sharing. In addition, their management style seems to be best described as a mixture of paternalism and consultation. They simply are not as participative as the high-involvement plants. For example, they use quality-control circles but assign them a recommendations role, not a decision-making role, and they do not expect them to deal with pay decisions, hiring decisions, and normal operating decisions.

EFFECTIVENESS OF THE PLANTS

There are almost no hard data on how effective most of the new-design plants are. In a few cases, the plants have been measured by outsiders, who report positive results. For example, the Topeka plant of General Foods has been studied by Richard Walton and by Douglas Jenkins and myself. Both studies reported low absenteeism, low turnover, low production costs, and high employee satisfaction. I have had the chance to study five other plants in considerable detail. I would rate four of these as highly successful since they have negligible turnover and absenteeism and their financial performance is from 10 percent to 40 percent better than comparable plants. Finally, survey data clearly show that these plants do have highly involved and highly motivated employees.

Unfortunately, the plants which have been studied are the exception as far as public data on organizational effectiveness are concerned. Comparable data simply are not available on most plants. There is, however, a good deal of circumstantial evidence that most, if not all, are highly successful in

terms of productivity, costs, and the quality of worklife. Although this is not hard proof of success, it is known that Procter & Gamble has closed its plants to researchers and others because it believes that it now enjoys a competitive advantage and does not want to share it.

It is also significant that most corporations that have tried one plant have gone on to try others (for example, Procter & Gamble, TRW, and General Motors). It would seem that they must be meeting with favorable results. Finally, it is interesting that the demand from other companies to visit high-involvement plants is great. Some of those that allow visitors even charge for tours and still report waiting lists. Apparently the word has gotten around that these plants have obtained impressive results, and people want to see for themselves. Overall, it is too early to make a valid analysis of the long-term success of most plants. Although a few have been around for some time (seven years), most were set up only in the past two or three years. It is not too early, however, to identify some of the problems that characterize these plants.

Unrealistic Expectations

The innovative employee-selection process used in many of the plants has often combined with the initial enthusiasm of the managers involved to create very high expectations on the part of the workforce. Because of the stress that the selection interviews place on challenging work and autonomy, employees not unreasonably conclude that things will be totally different from the way they are in a typical plant. They expect their work to be interesting all the time, and they expect to be in total control of their worklives. When these expectations are not met, it has created problems. Typically, workers have either quit or stayed on and complained about the inconsistency between what they were told the work would be like and what it turned out to be like.

The irony is that even where this is a problem, the work situations have, in fact, offered more autonomy and interesting work than usual. Unfortunately, this has been offset by the failure to fulfill the employees' high expectations. The solution seems to be to counsel employees to have more realistic expectations and to listen sympathetically to all problems. Realistic expectations are not easy to achieve in a new plant. Often management itself does not really know what will evolve and there is no existing work model for future employees to look at in order to ground their expectations in reality.

Individual Differences

People differ in their needs, skills, abilities, values, and preferences. A great deal of research has shown that not everyone responds positively to the kinds of innovations that are being tried in these plants (see Lawler, 1974). Some simply prefer the more traditional ways of doing things. In most plants the selection process screens out many of the people who do not fit the new-design approach, but some always manage to slip through. There are applicants who are not even aware of their strong orientation toward more traditional approaches, and the group-interview method may fail to identify this preference. The failure of the group approach is not surprising; group interviews are not known for their validity. The result of this mismatch in most plants has been a limited amount of turnover and the need to work with some individuals in a more traditional manner.

In some ways the problem of finding workers who fit the management style of the organization is probably less severe in the case of high-involvement plants than it is in traditional ones. Compared with the available opportunities, a large number of workers seem to want to work in this kind of situation. Plants that have advertised for employees who want to work in a participative environment have found themselves swamped with applicants.

Role of First-Level Supervision

Probably the most frequent and most difficult problem involves the role of the first-level supervisor (see Walton and Schlesinger, 1979). In some plants, relatively traditional foremen are in place; in others, there is no first-level supervisor present in work groups, the assumption being that these groups will be self-managing or that they will elect a leader or straw boss. In still other situations, individuals have been put in as acting first-level supervisors and told to work themselves out of a job within a year or a year and a half of the start-up.

In almost all instances, first-level supervisors and elected leaders have complained about a lack of role clarity and confusion about what decisions they could and could not make. Typically, they are uncomfortable with ordering and directing people, because they feel things should get done on a participative basis. But in many cases they do not know how to function as participative managers. Often they lack the skills to help the group become a functioning team, make decisions, and work through issues. They also have a great deal of difficulty in deciding which decisions should be made on a participative basis and which should not. Foremen have ended up asking for participation on issues when they already had all the information and technical expertise that were needed to make the decision. Conversely, and perhaps more frequently, because many supervisors come from a traditional background, they make decisions unilaterally when they should involve the work team.

Perhaps the best way to delineate the problem is to point out that there is no clear-cut description of the correct behavior for a first-level supervisor in these plants. Therefore, there is no adequate training program or selection method to fit a person to this position. Training is on a hit-or-miss basis, and the failure rate for those chosen is often high. Several organizations are trying to solve this problem by developing appropriate training programs, but to the best of my knowledge, no adequate program exists. The best approach seems to be extensive on-the-job training in which a clear job definition is developed and a good deal of one-on-one counseling is provided.

Permissiveness versus Participation

One of the hardest issues that managers in new plants confront is differentiating between permissiveness and participation. In most plants, workers have raised issues that seemed to the managers concerned to go "too far." For example, in one case employees wanted to install a color television set in a work area. The managers considered this undesirable but had a great deal of difficulty dealing with the issue. They felt that if they said no they would be violating the participative spirit of the plant. They finally did refuse, because they felt that it would harm productivity and that it represented an example of permissiveness rather than participative management.

The difficulty this group of managers had is typical of the problems experienced in other plants when workers have requested unusual personnel rules and work procedures. Unfortunately, the difference between what constitutes a reasonable request for the abandonment of a rule or policy and what constitutes an unreasonable request is often unclear. There probably is no way to deal with this kind of issue in advance, but it is clear that when such issues arise, how they are dealt with can greatly influence the future of the plant. Arbitrary turndowns of such requests can destroy the participative spirit of the plant, just as quick acceptance of every suggestion for eliminating rules, regulations, and discipline can.

Finally, it is crucial that management not abdicate its responsibility for what occurs in the plant. Regardless of how the decision is made, management is accountable in the eyes of people outside the plant. This means that it has the responsibility for seeing that the process for making the decisions is a good one and that the tough issues are dealt with (e.g., favoritism in allocating raises, discipline). Sometimes this means that members of management must actually intervene in order to assure that decisions are being made appropriately. It also means that when participation is not appropriate, management must make the decision.

Office Personnel

Most new plants have had a great deal of difficulty coming up with innovative ways to treat their office and clerical employees. As a result, these employees often feel relatively unappreciated and deprived when they look at what is happening in the production areas. They often do exactly the same jobs they would do in a more traditional plant. Although they may be supervised in a more participative manner, their life simply is not that different, even though they are often told they are in a "new type of organization." What is needed, of course, are innovative approaches to organizing, training, and paying people in offfice situations. Some attempts have been made to improve matters—for example, by rotating employees between shipping and office jobs (an effort which was abandoned). The best solution at the moment seems to be to treat these employees as a team with all this implies.

Personnel Function

The personnel function is usually much more important in new plants than in traditional ones, and indeed, it is often the one staff function that is more heavily staffed than in a traditional plant. It tends to become a real stress point and requires a very different set of skills from those possessed by the traditional personnel manager. Since many of the typical personnel tasks are assigned to the work teams (for example, selection and pay administration), they are subtracted from the duties of the personnel manager. However, the personnel manager cannot simply ignore these areas, but instead must work with the line organization to facilitate the accomplishment of these tasks. The personnel manager must have good interpersonal skills and must function as a key resource on how the new practices should be implemented.

The personnel manager needs to be an expert in job design, pay systems, training, and so on, so that other employees will have someone to consult when they need advice. In many cases, the personnel manager ends up with a difficult and frustrating job. The skill demands are much different and often much greater than those required in a typical plant. The personnel manager may be asked to solve problems that have never been tackled before and that have no established solutions.

Establishing Standards

Adequate standards in such areas as production and performance are difficult to establish in any organization, and particularly difficult to establish in new organizations, because they lack a track record. Thus it is not surprising that high-involvement plants seem to have trouble developing criteria upon which to base such things as pay raises and promotions. The normal problems that are part of any start-up operation are compounded for them because in these plants employees are typically asked to set the standards for their peers. Unless these employees receive a great deal of help, they find it hard to develop objective, challenging yardsticks for measuring their co-workers, particularly when such matters as compensation are involved. This is hardly surprising, since they usually have little prior experience and it is easier to be a good guy and set relatively low standards. Some plants deal with this problem by having employees develop written tests of job knowledge and set minimum time periods that must elapse before raise applications will be considered.

Regression Under Pressure

At some point in the history of most plant start-ups, whether high-involvement or not, intense pressure for production develops. The pressure stems from the need to get the plant on-line in accordance with a predetermined production schedule. This period has proved to be particularly crucial in the life of most plants. Managers tend to revert to traditional management practices in times of crisis. They jump in and try to take charge.

Needless to say, such an act can be very damaging to the successful start-up of a high-involvement plant. It communicates to everyone that the new principles of management apply only when things are going well. Not all plants get through this period with their commitment to participative management intact. In one instance, at least, start-up problems led the plant manager to declare that the participative-management program was officially abandoned. The problems in this plant stemmed from the fact that no preparation had been made to deal with the necessity for making some decisions, particularly technical ones, in a nonparticipative way. The plant also suffered from a severe learning-overload problem. People were trying to learn a new approach to management as well as a complex new production process. It was simply too much to learn in a very short period of time. What is needed, of course, is either a realistic learning schedule or a workforce that has a good background in either the technology or the management system.

Timing of Start-Up Decisions

At present, no clear timetable exists of when various activities should begin in the start-up of a new-design plant (see Lawler & Olsen, 1977). Thus every organization that has launched such a plant has wrestled with issues like: When should the pay system be developed? When are personnel policies to be set? When should the first employees be hired? When should autonomous work groups be established?

Factors such as the type of technology and the skills of the employees need to be taken into account in drawing up an implementation schedule. Where the technology will change during the growth of the plant, it may be best to think in terms of an intermediate organization design, something to be abandoned once the technology has stabilized.

Some projects have gotten into trouble because they tried to proceed immediately to the final organization-design stage, despite the fact that it was not appropriate to do so during the start-up period. For example, efforts have been made to set up autonomous work groups as soon as production began even though the nature of the technology did not permit stable group membership at that time.

Interface with the Rest of the Organization

In one sense, high-involvement plants are foreign bodies inside larger organizations. They differ in a number of important ways from the organizations that created them and to which they are responsible. For every new plant—successful or not—this has created a number of interface problems. The most public attention has been devoted to the case of a Topeka dog food plant, but problems are by no means restricted to that situation (Walton, 1975). High-involvement plants are living demonstrations of a different way to operate, and as such they automatically raise the question of whether the rest of the organization needs to change.

Various vested interests inevitably feel threatened and challenged by this question. Managers on the corporate staff, for example, may feel threatened because many issues for which they have stock answers are dealt with in an individualized manner at the plant level. Such an approach can jeopardize their job security by fostering demands for change from other parts of the organization.

Some managers may feel threatened because the plants operate without managers in the same or similar positions. In addition, managers in other plants may be concerned that they will have to change their whole approach to management if the new plants succeed. Finally, other managers may feel that their upward mobility in the organization will be hindered if the managers in the new plants do well and their operations are highly profitable.

At this time, no organization has solved the interface issue, but some are trying intriguing approaches; the most successful seem to revolve around an emphasis on decentralization and communications (Walton, 1977, Reading 51). On the one hand, companies using this approach stress that it is okay to be different. On the other hand, they are dealing with the communications issue by a number of devices, including seminars, task forces to study and design new plants, and frequent visits by managers from other locations to the high-involvement plants.

DIFFUSION OF NEW APPROACHES

Despite their visibility and importance, at this point only a minute fraction of the population of the United States works in high-involvement plants. What does the future hold? It seems clear that more new plants like the ones mentioned in this article will be started in the next few years. Diffusion of these practices to many new plants seems almost certain because of the success of the existing ones and because knowledge about how to do it is rapidly growing.

But what about older plants? Many of the practices mentioned here are also being tried in established locations, although few have tried the kind of total-system approach that is characteristic of the new plants. This is a crucial difference. Can the total approach be applied successfully to existing plants? Can it provide a much-needed model for how organizations can be made more effective? The jury is still out on this one, but there is reason to believe that it has tremendous potential.

The high-involvement model is a seemingly successful total-system approach to the management of plants. It translates vague terms like "participative management" and "concern for human resources" into actual policies and practices. Thus, there is something substantial to disseminate. Many organizations' new plants are being used for training people who can apply their concepts elsewhere. Interestingly, all the managers I have interviewed in new plants have said that they did not want to go back to a more traditional approach. Finally, in a number of cases, pressure for dissemination is building up because of the success of the new plants. After all, it is hard to ignore plants which are more effective.

Perhaps the most difficult problem in applying the high-involvement model to existing plants stems from the fact that it is successful precisely because it is an internally consistent total approach to management. It is impossible in most existing organizations to install all the practices which are characteristic of the high-involvement model in a short period of time. This means that a transition period is needed during which new practices are being installed and costs are being incurred but no results are seen because enough new practices are not in place. In many respects installation would be a great deal easier if a few changes could be made and positive results shown, but this seems unlikely since people respond to their total environment, and with a few changes they are not likely to experience a significantly different management system. The challenge at this point, therefore, is one of devising effective implementation strategies for a system of management which seems to have great potential. If this can be done I have no doubt that we will see many older plants slowly but successfully convert to the high-involvement model.

REFERENCES

Lawler, E. E. The individualized organization: Problems and promise. *California Management Review,* 1974, **17**(2).

———. *Pay and organization development.* Reading, Mass.: Addison-Wesley, 1981.

———, & Olsen, R. N. Designing reward systems for new organizations. *Personnel,* 1977, **54**(5), 48–60.

Poza, E. J., & Markus, M. L. Success story: The team approach to work restructuring. *Organizational Dynamics,* Winter 1980, 3–25.

Walton, R. E. The diffusion of new work structures: Explaining why success didn't take. *Organizational Dynamics,* Winter 1975, 3–22.

———. Successful strategies for diffusing work innovations. *Journal of Contemporary Business,* Spring 1977, 1–22.

——— & Schlesinger, L. A. Do supervisors thrive in participative work systems? *Organizational Dynamics,* Winter 1979, 25–38.

Reading 57

Work Redesign in Organizational and Societal Context

J. Richard Hackman
Greg R. Oldham

How useful are innovations in work structure as points of departure for initiating broad-scale organizational changes? Given present trends in society, what will be the shape of organizational life in the future? And to what extent are future directions amenable to influence by those who favor a more "humanistic" than "scientific" approach to the design and management of productive organizations?

WORK REDESIGN AS A TECHNIQUE OF PLANNED ORGANIZATIONAL CHANGE

There are reasons both for optimism and pessimism about the use of work redesign as a device for organizational change. When meaningful improvements in jobs can actually be made and supported over time, their effects can be powerful. Yet significant restructuring of work is very difficult to accomplish, especially under "normal" circumstances when organizational systems are operating relatively smoothly. Just how feasible is it to use work redesign as a point of leverage for planned change in organizations?

An Optimistic View

Work redesign has some special advantages in dealing with three key change problems. The first is simply *getting behavior to change*. Many change attempts are based on the hope that if people's attitudes change, or if they learn better what they are supposed to do and how to do it, or if they are helped to understand better the nonobvious causes of their and others' behavior in organizations, then behavioral changes will "naturally" follow.

Research evidence forces us to be skeptical about such hopes. People do not always behave consistently with their attitudes or with what they cognitively "know" they should do. People who have high job satisfaction do not always work hard and effectively. And, in most organizations, vast amounts of task-relevant knowledge and skill are untapped either because people choose not to use their talents in

organizational work or because they do not have the opportunity to.

On the other hand, people *do* perform the tasks they have accepted. How well they perform them depends on many factors, including how the tasks are designed. But people perform them. Redesigning jobs, then, is almost certain to result in changes in the overt behavior of the people who hold those jobs. If the changes require people to know more than they now know, then they may become motivated to increase their on-the-job skills. And if the changes turn out to prompt hard, task-oriented work, the people may, over time, develop beliefs and attitudes that support these new work behaviors.

Work redesign, then, does not rely on getting beliefs or attitudes or skills changed first (such as by inducing a worker to "care more" about work outcomes, as in zero defects programs) and hoping that such changes will generalize to work behavior. Instead, the thrust of the change is to alter behavior itself. Attitudes, beliefs, knowledge, and skills will follow these behaviors and gradually become consistent with them.

The second problem of planned change is *getting behavior to stay changed*. After jobs are changed it is difficult for jobholders to slip back into old ways of behaving. The old ways are just not appropriate for the new tasks. Moreover, the requirements and reinforcements built into the new tasks support the new ways of behaving. So one need not worry too much about the kind of "backsliding" that occurs so often after training or attitude change activities, especially those that take place away from the job itself. The stimuli that direct and constrain the person's behavior are experienced right on the job, day after day. And once those stimuli have been changed, they are likely to stay that way until the job is once again redesigned.

The third organizational change problem is *getting the changes to spread* to other organizational systems and practices. What happens in an organization is complexly and redundantly determined. A change in any single organizational system or practice, no matter how competently carried out, cannot be expected to result in a basic reorientation of how an organization operates. If overall organizational change is desired, then eventually the initial changes must spread to and affect other structures, systems, and practices.

Changes in jobs invariably place strains on other aspects of the organization—ranging from personnel practices and reward systems to the style of organizational management. These pressures, if followed up with vigor and competence, can serve as points of entry for broad-scale organizational improvements. Even organizational practices that previously may have defied all attempts at planned change (such as compensation arrangements or control systems) may now become amenable to change because everyone agrees that they *need* to be changed to fit with the new ways the work is being done. And behavioral science professionals may find themselves freed from the old difficulty of selling their wares to skeptical managers who are not really sure anything is wrong—or, if there is, that they want to hear about it.

Much is required for competent organizational change and for following up and diffusing changes that are made. There are many more "change problems" than the three listed above. But for initiating far-reaching changes, these three—getting behavior to change, getting it to stay changed, and getting the changes to spread—are critical. And for these problems work redesign has some special advantages in comparison to other organization development approaches.

A Pessimistic View

Work redesign has now been available as a device for organizational change for many years. If it is such a good point of leverage for broad-scale organizational change, why do we not see more organizations that have been "turned around" through the redesign of work? There are, we believe, at least three reasons for the limited impact of work redesign. Taken together, they call into question the efficacy and permanence of planned organizational change that begins with the redesign of tasks and jobs.

First, managers often anticipate negative effects of job changes on other organizational systems as plans for work redesign are being made. This can prompt numerous small compromises from the ideal design for work in that setting to minimize the anticipated disruptiveness and cost of the planned changes. The result is what we call the "small change" effect, in which the job changes that actually get made are much less pronounced than those originally contemplated and not substantial enough to generate meaningful alterations in employee behavior, let alone set in motion forces for improving other organizational systems.

Second, if substantial changes in work design actually are made, then the resultant stresses and strains on other organizational systems may be viewed simply as "unfortunate problems" that must be corrected. (This is, perhaps, a more likely view than the alternative suggested earlier—namely, that such stresses provide special opportunities for initiating developmental changes in the affected systems.) In many cases, the result is that the innovations in work design are slowly chipped away and rendered impotent. This we call the "vanishing effects" phenomenon: work design comes up against established organizational systems and managerial practices—and loses.

The third reason for pessimism about work redesign as a strategy for far-reaching organizational change has more to do with how the redesign process takes place than with the content or consequences of the changes themselves. Managers are familiar with, and practiced in dealing with, various kinds of prepackaged programs that can be adopted to "fix" defined problems or accomplish specific objectives. Many technological solutions to production problems are of this type, as are certain kinds of marketing and sales programs. There is a tendency for work redesign to be dealt with in the same general way, for changes to be made using essentially a mechanistic installation process.

The problem, of course, is that behavioral science changes such as job redesign tend not to work if they are treated as something that can be simply plugged in and turned on. Thus, if managers view work redesign as yet another program that can be bought, installed, and then left to generate all manner of beneficial effects, those effects are most unlikely to appear. In fact, the redesign of work is much more a *way of managing* than it is a prepackaged "fix" for problems of employee motivation and satisfaction. Unless managers understand this, and are prepared to alter how they run their organizations after the work itself is changed, then the prospects for broad-scale improvements in organizational functioning are quite dim.

Mechanistic use of work redesign, while often observed in practice, at least does not run much risk of covert manipulation of the work motivation and attitudes of employees. It is hard to conjecture how giving a person (or a group) meaningful work, autonomous responsibility for the work outcomes, and task-based knowledge of results would be very effective as a manipulative tactic. If, in fact, these conditions are created, then the manager who created them is much more at the mercy of the employee (who may or may not choose to work hard and well) than vice versa. The work situation becomes one that allows and encourages *pro*action rather than requires *re*action. So it is more likely, when a manager carries out work redesign mechanistically, that he or she simply will fail to create the appropriate conditions for internal work motivation. And the result will be yet another "failure of work redesign" rather than a success in using the device to covertly manipulate the people whose jobs were changed.

The Case for Caution

How do the optimistic and pessimistic views summarized above balance out? That is a question readers will have to address on their own. Our view is a fairly conservative one. While we find the advantages of work redesign as an "organization development" technique to be real and important, the conditions required to secure and retain these advantages in relatively stable, ongoing organizations appear to be present only occasionally.

To redesign work halfheartedly or to use flawed change processes is, in most cases, to assure failure. And it is *hard* to do work redesign well. It requires highly skilled managers and change agents to carry out diagnostic and implementation processes competently and to avoid the "mechanistic installation" problem. It requires a good deal of vision, commitment, and risk taking on the part of those responsible for the changes to ensure that the "small change" effect does not so compromise what is done that nobody notices that anything is different afterwards. And it requires that existing organizational structures, systems, and practices be supportive of the changes (or, alternatively, themselves be amena-

ble to redesign to make them more supportive) to avoid the "vanishing effects" phenomenon.

It appears that only organizations that are already relatively well designed and well managed are likely to meet the conditions required for successful use of work redesign as a strategy for planned change of intact and relatively stable organizational systems. What we may have, then, is yet another case in organizational life where the rich get richer, and the poor—if they try to make the leap—are likely to fail.

We must emphasize, however, that what we have been discussing here is relatively radical and far-reaching change of existing organizations, with work redesign used as an organization development technique to get things under way. As will be seen below, this is far from the only appropriate use of the principles of work redesign.

ALTERNATIVE USES OF WORK REDESIGN

Our suggestion that work redesign can only occasionally be used to "turn around" intact work systems could be taken as an occasion for great pessimism. Indeed, one conclusion could be that we should give up on job redesign as a change strategy, that the cause is hopeless. We disagree. For one thing, organizational circumstances sometimes are such that it *is* possible to successfully introduce substantial changes in work systems. When this is the case, we endorse such applications with enthusiasm. Moreover, how work is structured does affect, powerfully, both organizational productivity and the lives of organization members. These effects, in our view, are far too consequential for the principles of work redesign to be blithely abandoned merely because they cannot be used routinely for radical change of intact work systems.

What, then, are the alternatives to using work redesign as an "organization development" technique? Three possibilities are reviewed below.

Designing New Organizational Units

As noted above, our conservatism about the use of work redesign as an organization development technique stems primarily from the difficulty of getting changes in jobs to take root and prosper in relatively stable, ongoing organizational units. The changes often just do not have a good enough chance against the "big guys"—the interdependent operating systems, organizational structures, and management practices that give the organization its stability.

When, however, new organizations are designed (or when there is a *major* reorganization of an existing unit), it is possible to design organizational systems, structures, and practices from the ground up, and to design them in a way that supports rather than undermines nontraditional work structures. The result can be substantial innovations in the design of work that have powerful and beneficial effects (Lawler, 1978).

Yet even when new organizations are designed (or old ones are redesigned top to bottom) questions of priority and precedence emerge. Consider, for example, how decisions are made about the structure of an organization. By structure, we mean those arrangements often expressed by boxes and lines on organizational charts that divide up and coordinate authority, responsiblity, and information in an organization. Decisions about structure include choices about how centralized authority will be, whether the organization will be arranged along functional or product lines, how staff and line relationships will be structured and coordinated, and so on.

At minimum, an organizational structure provides the following:

• Means for managing organization-environment relations, including responses to environmental changes (in the labor market, the competitive environment, or regulatory context).
• Means for coordinating organizational units and assuring an appropriate flow of information and influence—both up and down the organizational hierarchy and laterally across different functional and substantive areas.
• Means for supporting and managing the work activities of organization members—providing direction, information, supplies, technical assistance, and so on, to those who are actually generating the goods or services that the organization exists to produce.

Traditional wisdom about organizational design suggests that the structure of an organization should be responsive to (1) the imperatives of the core technology of the organization, (2) the demands and opportunities in the environment (including how stable and predictable the environment is), and (3) the strategic directions for the organization that have been selected by top management. Thus, the shape of an organization that produces inexpensive furniture for a stable mass market using production line technology would be quite different from that of an organization that produces hand-crafted custom furniture in response to special customer orders.

Decisions about the design of work usually are made within the limits imposed by these presumably more basic decisions about how the organization as a whole is structured. The problem is that after all structural decisions are made there may be few realistic options remaining for how the work can be designed. This can be true even in new organizational units if decision making about the design of work comes only after most other questions of organizational design have been settled.

An alternative approach to the design of organizations would give design of work considerations greater priority, even placing them ahead of decisions about the shape and structure of the organization itself. How this might be done in setting up a new organization is illustrated in the following four-step process.[1]

First, the strategy of the organization would be determined by top management. Based on the properties of the organizational environment, the position of the organization in its market, and the goals and values of management, the major aspirations and performance objectives of the organization as a whole would be specified.

Second, designers would identify those special resources and constraints in the organization and its environment that bear on the accomplishment of these strategic objectives. These might include the availability of special work technologies, regulatory constraints, the supply of capital, the character of the labor market, the level of managerial talent available, and so on.

Third, explicit consideration would be given to how the *work* should be arranged to contribute most directly to the accomplishment of strategic objectives given any special resources of the organization (such as a readily available pool of skilled workers) and any constraints within which it must operate (that only a single type of technology is viable for the kind of work that is to be done, for example).

Finally, attention would turn to alternative struc-

---

[1]The steps below are written as if the organization in question were an industrial firm. The same logic, albeit with different words, can be applied to other types of organizations, including those in the public and nonprofit sectors.

tures for supporting and managing key work activities, for coordinating and controlling organizational units, and for managing organization-environment relationships. Decisions about these matters would follow from, and be responsive to, the three issues highlighted above: the strategy of the organization, special resources and constraints, and the design of core work activities.

This approach obviously gives greater precedence to design of work considerations than they usually receive when organizations are designed. And it is close to what actually has been done in many successful "new plant" experiments involving innovations in work structures (such as at the Topeka plant of General Foods, discussed by Walton, 1977, Reading 51). Indeed, at the Kalmar plant of Volvo, even the core technology of the organization (which usually is considered an immutable given) was redesigned to make possible a design for work that would be consistent with the organization's strategic objectives about its product and its use of human resources (Gyllenhammer, 1977).

In sum, the design of a new organization (or the major reorganization of an old one) offers many opportunities for use of the principles of work redesign that we have been discussing in this book. However, even in these relatively benign circumstances one must be careful not to put design decisions having to do with the work itself last, among those issues that are dealt with when all of the "important" organizational design questions have been settled. For to do so risks exactly the same kinds of "small change" and "vanishing effects" problems that often compromise attempts to redesign work within intact, ongoing organizational units.

Seizing Opportunities

The chance to wholly redesign an organization comes only rarely. Yet there are many other occasions when the principles of work redesign can be used appropriately and with considerable impact, particularly when those "stable" organizational systems that make planned change so difficult become temporarily *unstable*. During such periods of turbulence, the defenses of an organization against change are down. And therefore it may be possible both to introduce meaningfully large changes in jobs and to work out an appropriate fit between those

innovations and the surrounding organizational systems before things settle down again.

This is precisely the strategy used by a middle manager in a large bank who more than once had tried, and failed, to get certain jobs redesigned in her department. On this occasion, virtually all organizational systems were thrown into disarray as plans were laid for introducing new data processing equipment into the department and, as a byproduct, reducing staff size by almost one-third. The manager had responsibility for figuring out how to set up the workflow using the new equipment, and she took that opportunity to create a set of jobs that were quite well designed from a motivational point of view.

She began by conducting a diagnosis of the existing jobs to identify motivational strengths and weaknesses in how the work presently was designed. She then convened her staff to generate ideas for how the new jobs might þe structured so they would be higher in motivating potential. The new ideas that the managers came up with were then tried out with some of the people who would fill the redesigned jobs and were further revised based on their reactions and suggestions. Finally, when the basic workflow and set of job descriptions were almost ready, she examined each of the operating systems of the unit and made changes where necessary to make sure that those systems would support the work and the employees as fully as possible. When, eventually, members of top management came around to see how the new data-processing system was operating, they discovered that more than they had anticipated had been changed. But it was all working quite nicely, and they were pleased.

The "opening" for work redesign in this case was provided by a technological change. Because new work technologies invariably require some adjustment of jobs and workflows, they can provide excellent opportunities for reviewing and revising the motivational structure of the work and for improving the design of organizational systems and practices that support the work. And line managers sometimes can have a good deal of influence over how work is restructured in response to technological innovations.

The increasing use of microprocessing technologies in secretarial and clerical functions is a good case in point. Consider, for example, word processing. State-of-the-art word-processing equipment offers the chance for great increases in the efficiency and quality of secretarial work. But the technology itself is relatively neutral about how jobs and organizations are designed to take advantage of these opportunities. So managers who tilt toward a scientific management view of organizations have capitalized on word-processing technology to create secretarial jobs that are highly simplified, specialized, and routinized. A pool of data entry personnel is often formed, whose members do nothing but enter into the machinery materials supplied by word-processing users. Other staff members serve reception and telephone functions for a large group of users, and still others specialize in travel arrangements and administrative chores. Nobody has a motivationally well-designed job, and users of the word-processing service often feel that they have lost their secretaries in the bargain.

Alternatively, the same technology can be used to create secretarial jobs that are both efficient and well designed motivationally. By providing secretaries with remote word-processing terminals, it remains possible for them to have their desks near those of their clients and to maintain special relationships with them. At the same time, the variety of tasks that are performed using the terminals increases, the amount of routine retyping is reduced, and the net effect can be both greater productivity *and* a motivationally improved secretarial job.

For word processing, then, there is a good deal of discretion about how work will be designed to take advantage of a technological advance. In other cases, however, it will be nearly impossible to create well-designed jobs within the limitations imposed by a new technology. Sometimes, for example, line managers are presented with an intact, highly efficient and motivationally disastrous package of equipment and work procedures that is the product of literally years of careful work by engineers and systems analysts. There will be nothing the managers can do but plug in the technology and then attempt to deal with the resulting motivational and organizational problems however they can. (Work design consultants are sometimes called in for advice about the emergent "people problems" in such circumstances, but they are not likely to be of much help: the problems are rooted in the technology, and the technology cannot be changed.)

The forward-looking manager, then, will keep in close contact with those groups who are developing equipment and procedures for future use in the manager's organization. This will usually be difficult, since research and development, systems, and engineering groups are often both functionally and geographically remote from the line manager. But unless influence can be wielded at the time work technologies are designed and developed, line managers may later find themselves with serious motivational problems on their hands—problems for which no immediate remedies are apparent.

We have focused above on the "openings" provided by technological changes in work organizations. There are numerous other kinds of changes and instabilities that also can be used by watchful managers and consultants as occasions for revising the way jobs and work systems are structured. Such opportunities include a change of senior managers (which may provide a "honeymoon" period during which significant changes can be made relatively easily), the introduction of a new product or service, changes in the economy or the labor market, revisions of the legislative or regulatory context in which the organization operates, and significant fluctuations in the market for the goods or services provided by the firm.

In sum, organizations regularly move back and forth between periods of relative stability and periods of transition and instability. Rather than use work redesign to try to change an organization when things are relatively stable (for example, by sending human resource staff members around the organization to sell their wares to whatever management groups will provide an audience), it may be better for human resource professionals to lie in wait for those times when the organization is (for whatever reasons) particularly receptive to the possibility of change in how work is structured. The wait rarely will be long.

Local Changes

When planned, developmental changes in organizations using work redesign are infeasible, and when there are not naturally occurring "openings" for change, must work redesign simply be set aside until more favorable conditions prevail? No, there is yet another option. Individual managers often can proceed on their own initiative to make enriching changes in the work of the people they supervise. Managers can release some of their own decision-making responsibilities to subordinates; they can place subordinates in direct contact with the "clients" of their work; they can encourage sharing and rotation of responsibilities on an informal basis; they can combine fragmented tasks into more meaningful jobs; and so on (Oldham, 1976).

No complex diagnosis of the work system is involved in such undertakings, no planning groups sit down to "greenlight" possible changes, and there is no outside evaluation of how the jobs were changed and with what effects. The manager simply decides that he or she is going to do everything that can be done to create conditions for high internal motivation and personal growth at work within his or her own domain. Sometimes there is quite a lot that can be done (for example, in decentralized, low-technology units where the manager has considerable discretion); other times the manager has less latitude. But there almost always are *some* changes that can be made, in the work or in the manager's own behavior, to improve the motivational properties of subordinates' jobs.

As we noted earlier, work redesign is really more a way of managing than it is a formal intervention technique, and the potential payoffs to people and to organizations from "local" changes in how jobs are designed should not be underestimated. Indeed, there is probably more job enrichment going on at local initiative today than there are "seized opportunities" and planned change programs combined.

Summary

In this section we have reviewed three alternatives to the use of work redesign as a device for planned, developmental change of intact organizational systems. Each of these—designing new organizational units, seizing serendipitous opportunities for change, and informal change at the initiative of local management—offers the chance to bring the principles of work redesign to bear on the life and work of people in organizations.

Yet whether any or all of these approaches will be used to good effect depends heavily on what managers *want* to do and on what they are *able* to do. What does the future portend for work redesign in U.S. organizations? Will we decide that we want to create jobs high in complexity, challenge, and autonomy?

And, if so, will we become more competent than we are at the moment in designing such jobs and managing people who work on them? As will be seen in the section to follow, we may be very near the point at which such questions will be decided.

THE DESIGN OF WORK IN THE FUTURE

In the preceding pages we have provided an assessment of where organizational change through the redesign of work stands at present. While we could not be terribly optimistic about using work redesign to reorient entire organizations, we did see many useful alternative applications of the approach.

What of the future? How is work likely to be arranged in the decade to come? Will the idea of enriched, internally motivating work catch on and become dominant in how organizations are managed? Or do we have here a passing fad that, like so many other behavioral science interventions, soon will be laid to rest in favor of the next new idea to come along?

Here are two possible scenarios for the future, two routes that could be followed in designing work for the 1980s. The first route involves fitting jobs to people and is consistent with enriched work and personal growth. The second emphasizes fitting people to jobs and attempts to maximize technological and engineering efficiency. As will be seen below, what work will look like in organizations in the next decade greatly depends on which route is chosen.

Route One: Fitting Jobs to People

The basic notion of Route One is that by designing work so that people can be *internally* motivated to perform well, gains will be realized both in the productive effectiveness of organizations and in the personal well-being of the work force.

Under Route One, work would sometimes be designed to be done by individuals working more or less autonomously, and other times it would be set up to be performed by self-managing work groups. But in either case the aspiration would be to arrange things so that employees (1) experience the work as inherently meaningful, (2) feel personal (or collective) responsibility for the outcomes of the work, and (3) receive, on a regular basis, trustworthy knowledge about the results of the work activities.

Assuming we follow Route One, and do so competently and successfully, here are some speculations about how work might be designed and managed by the late 1980s.

1. Responsibility for work will be clearly pegged at the organizational level where the work is done. No longer will employees experience themselves as people who merely execute activities that "belong" to someone else (such as a line manager). Instead, they will feel, legitimately, that they are both responsible and accountable for the outcomes of their work. Moreover, the resources and the information needed to carry out the work (including feedback about how well the work is getting done) will be provided directly to employees without being filtered first through line and staff managers. As a result, we will see an increase in the personal motivation of employees to perform well and a concomitant increase in the quality of the work that is done.

2. Questions of employee motivation and satisfaction will be considered explicitly when new technologies and work practices are invented and engineered (just as intellectual and motor capabilities are presently considered). No longer will work systems be designed solely to optimize technological or engineering efficiency, with motivational problems left for managers to deal with after the systems are installed. Moreover, there will be no single "right answer" about how best to design work and work systems. In many cases work will be "individualized" to improve the fit between the characteristics of an employee and the tasks that he or she performs. Standard managerial practices that apply equally well to all individuals in a work unit will no longer be appropriate. Instead, managers will have to become as adept at adjusting jobs to people as they now are at adjusting people to fit the demands and requirements of fixed jobs.

3. Organizations will be viewed as places where people grow and learn new things. Organizations will support and nurture employees' aspirations for personal development, and will provide a buffet of means for these aspirations to be pursued. As a result, people will tend more to see themselves as having personal control of their careers (rather than as pawns moved about by their employers), and most will find work a fulfilling part of their lives. This kind of fulfillment, it should be noted, goes far beyond simple "job satisfaction." People can be made "satisfied" at work simply by paying them adequately, keeping bosses off their backs, putting them in pleasant work spaces with pleasant people, and arranging things so that the days pass without undue stress and strain. The kind of satisfaction we will see in the late 1980s is different: it is a satisfaction that develops when people are stretching and growing as human beings and increasing their feelings of self-worth as productive organization members.

4. Organizations will be leaner, with fewer hierarchical levels and fewer managerial and staff personnel whose jobs are primarily documentation, supervision, and inspection of work done by others. This will require new ways of managing people at work, and will give rise to new kinds of managerial problems. For example, to the extent that significant motivational gains are realized by enriched work in individualized organizations, managers will no longer have the problem of "how to get these lazy incompetents to put in a decent day's work." Instead, the more pressing problem may be what to do *next* to keep people challenged and interested in their work. For as people become accustomed to personal growth and learning on the job, what was once a challenge may eventually become routine, and ever more challenge may be required to keep frustration and boredom from setting in. How to manage an organization so that growth opportunities are continuously available may become a difficult managerial challenge, especially if, as predicted, there is shrinkage in the number of managerial slots into which employees can be promoted.

5. Finally, if the previous predictions are correct, there eventually will be a good deal of pressure on the broader political and economic system to find ways to use effectively human resources that no longer are needed to populate the bowels of work organizations. Imagine that organizations eventually do become leaner and more effective and, at the same time, the rate of growth of society as a whole is reduced to near zero. Under such circumstances, there will be large numbers of people who are "free" for meaningful employment outside traditional private and public sector work organizations. To expand welfare services and compensate such individuals for not working (or for working only a small portion of the time they have available for

594   LEADERSHIP AND ORGANIZATIONAL CHANGE

productive activities) would be inconsistent with the overall thrust of Route One. What, then, is to be done with such individuals? Can we imagine groups of public philosophers, artists, and poets compensated by society for contributing to the creation of an enriched intellectual and aesthetic environment for the populace? An interesting possibility, surely, but one that would require radical rethinking of public decision making about the goals of society and the way shared resources are to be allocated toward the achievement of those goals.

Route Two: Fitting People to Jobs

If we take Route Two, the idea is to design and engineer work for maximum economic and technological efficiency, and then do whatever must be done to help people adapt in personally acceptable ways to their work experiences. No great flight of imagination is required to guess what work will be like in the late 1980s if we follow Route Two, as the sprouts of this approach are visible at present. Work is designed and managed in a way that clearly subordinates the needs and goals of people to the demands and requirements of fixed jobs. External controls are employed to ensure that individuals do in fact behave appropriately on the job. These include close and directive supervision, financial incentives for correct performance, tasks that are engineered to minimize the possibility of human mistakes, and information and control systems that allow management to monitor the performance of work systems as closely and continuously as possible. And, throughout, productivity and efficiency tend to dominate quality and service as the primary criteria for assessing organizational performance.

If we continue down Route Two, what might be predicted about the design and management of work in the late 1980s? Here are our guesses.

1. Technological and engineering considerations will dominate decision making about how jobs are designed. Technology is becoming increasingly central to many work activities, and that trend will accelerate. Also, major advances will be achieved in techniques for engineering work systems to make them ever more efficient. Together, these developments will greatly boost the productivity of individual workers and, in many cases, result in jobs that are nearly "people proof" (that is, work that is arranged to virtually eliminate the possibility of error due to

faulty judgment, lapses of attention, or misdirected motivation). Large numbers of relatively mindless tasks, including many kinds of inspection operations, will be automated out of existence.

Simultaneous with these technological advances will be a further increase in the capability of industrial psychologists to analyze and specify in advance the knowledge and skills required for a person to perform satisfactorily almost any task that can be designed. Sophisticated employee assessment and placement procedures will be used to select people and assign them to tasks, and only rarely will individuals be placed on jobs for which they are not fully qualified.

The result of all of these developments will be a quantum improvement in the efficiency of most work systems, especially those that process physical materials or paper. And while employees will receive more pay for less work than they presently do, they will also experience substantially less discretion and challenge in their work activities.

2. Work performance and organizational productivity will be closely monitored and controlled by managers using highly sophisticated information systems. Integrated circuit microprocessors will provide the hardware needed to gather and summarize performance data for work processes that presently defy cost-efficient measurement. Software will be developed to provide managers with data about work performance and costs that are far more reliable, more valid, and more current than is possible with existing information systems. Managers increasingly will come to depend on these data for decision making and will use them to control production processes vigorously and continuously.

Because managerial control of work will increase substantially, responsibility for work outcomes will lie squarely in the laps of managers, and the gap between those who do the work and those who control it will grow. There will be accelerated movement toward a two-class society of people who work in organizations, with the challenge and intrinsic interest of key managerial and professional jobs increasing even as the work of rank-and-file employees becomes more controlled and less involving.

3. Desired on-the-job behavior will be elicited and maintained by extensive and sophisticated use of extrinsic rewards. Since (if our first prediction is correct) work in the late 1980s will be engineered for clarity and simplicity, there will be little question about what each employee should (and should not) do on the job. Moreover (if our second prediction is correct), management will have data readily at hand to monitor the results of the employee's work on a more or less continuous basis. All that is required, then, are devices to ensure that the person *actually* does what he or she is *supposed* to do. Because many jobs will be routinized, standardized, and closely controlled by management, it is doubtful that employee motivation to perform appropriately can be created and maintained using intrinsic rewards (people working hard and effectively because they enjoy the tasks or because they obtain internal rewards from doing them well). So it will be necessary for management to use extrinsic rewards (such as pay or supervisory praise) to motivate employees by providing such rewards contingent on behavior that agrees with the wishes of management. The most sophisticated strategy for accomplishing this, and one that is wholly consistent with increased management control of organizational behavior is "behavior modification." If Route Two is followed, we predict that behavior modification programs will be among the standard motivational techniques used in work organizations by the late 1980s.

4. Most organizations will sponsor programs to help people adapt to life at work, including sophisticated procedures for assisting employees and their families in dealing with alcohol and drug abuse problems. Such problems will become much more widely offered (and needed) than they are at present because of unintended spin-offs of the movement toward the productive efficiencies promised at the end of Route Two.

Consider, for example, a man currently working on an undemanding, repetitive, and routine job. It might be someone who matches checks and invoices, and then clips them together to be processed by another employee. The job is low in motivating potential, and the outcomes from hard work probably have more to do with headaches and feelings of robothood than with any sense of meaningful personal accomplishment from high on-the-job effort. Clearly, there is a lack of any positive, internal motivation to work hard and effectively.

Now let us transport that employee via time machine to the mid-1980s, and place him on a very similar job under full-fledged Route Two conditions.

The work is just as routine and undemanding as it was before. But now there is greater management control over hour-by-hour operations, and valued external rewards are available, but only when the employee behaves according to explicit management specifications. How will our hypothetical employee react to that state of affairs?

At first, he is likely to feel even more like a small cog in a large wheel than before. Whereas prior to the introduction of the new management controls he could get away with some personal games and fantasies on the job, that is now much harder to do. Moreover, the problem is exacerbated, not relieved, by the addition of the performance-contingent rewards. The negative intrinsic outcomes that were contingent on the hard work before are still felt, but they have been supplemented (not replaced) by a set of new and positive *extrinsic* outcomes. So the employee is faced with contingencies that specify, "The harder I work, the more negative I feel about myself and what I'm doing, the more likely I am to get tired and headachy on the job, *and* the more likely I am to get praise from my supervisor and significant financial bonuses." This state of affairs—having strong positive and strong negative outcomes contingent on the same behavior—prompts some people to engage in maladaptive behaviors such as drug usage and alcoholism, and to exhibit signs of "craziness."

So if we move vigorously down Route Two, we should expect an increase in behavioral problems among employees. However, only a small proportion of the work force will show signs of serious "sickness," even under full-fledged Route Two conditions. The reason is that people have a good deal of resilience and usually can adapt to almost any work situation if given plenty of time and a little support. So although we can predict that numerous individuals will feel tension and stress in adjusting to work in the 1980s, and that their aspirations for personal growth and development at work may be significantly dampened, major overt problems will be observed infrequently.

Yet because *any* "crazy" employee behavior is an anathema to management (and clearly dysfunctional for organizational effectiveness), managers will attempt to head off such behaviors before they occur. When they do occur, management will deal with them as promptly and as helpfully as possible. So we should see in the late 1980s a substantial elaboration of organizational programs to help people adapt in healthy ways to their work situations. All will applaud such programs because they will benefit both individual human beings and their employing organizations. Few will understand that the need for such programs came about, in large part, as a result of designing work and managing organizations according to the technological and motivational "efficiencies" of Route Two.

At the Fork in the Road

Which will it be in the 1980s—Route One, or Route Two? Actually, there will be no occasion for making an explicit choice between the two. Instead, the choice will be enacted as seemingly insignificant decisions are made about immediate questions such as how to design the next generation of a certain technology, how to motivate employees and increase their commitment to their present jobs, or how best to use the sophisticated information technologies that are becoming available.

Our view, based on the choices that we now see being made, is that we are moving with some vigor down Route Two. That direction, moreover, seems unlikely to change in the foreseeable future for at least two reasons.

What Is Known We know *how* to operate according to Route Two rules, while we tend to fumble when we try to redesign work according to Route One. The issue is not that we are lacking theories about what makes a good job or a good work group. The problem, instead, is that our knowledge about how to *use* those theories is still rather primitive, particularly regarding the process by which changes in jobs and work systems are installed, and strategies for supporting them once they are in place. Present knowledge allows little more than specification of some choices that must be made when work systems are redesigned. That is not enough for either a theory of organizational intervention through work redesign or for the development of guidelines that specify how best to proceed to change jobs under various organizational circumstances.

Moreover, scholars are only just beginning to develop procedures for carrying out robust evaluations of the economic costs and benefits of innovative work designs (see, for example, Macy and Mirvis, 1976) and for reconciling the dual criteria of efficiency and quality of worklife in designing work systems (Lupton, 1975). These are particularly important tasks, given the understandable propensity of managers to ask about the "bottom line" in considering whether and how to redesign work systems. The challenge is considerable. It is now generally agreed that simple measures of job satisfaction are not adequate for assessing work redesign activities. Neither do simple measures of productivity do the trick (that is, quantity of production as a function of labor cost). Yet other outcomes, including many that are perhaps among those most appropriate for assessing the results of work redesign activities, are currently extremely difficult to measure. What is the cost of poor quality work? Of "extra" supervisory time? Of redundant inspections? Of absenteeism, soldiering, and sabotage? Until we are able to measure the effects of work redesign on such outcomes, it will continue to be nearly impossible to determine unambiguously whether job changes "pay off" for organizations or to specify with certainty what kinds of benefits should and should not be anticipated from this change strategy.

Finally, we currently know very little about the conditions that are required for innovations in work design to persist across time and to diffuse across organizational units. Even when clearly successful changes in jobs have been made they often fail to diffuse throughout the larger organization where they were developed—let alone to different organizations where the same kind of work is done (Walton, 1975).

What Is Valued Even if we did know more about how to design, manage, and diffuse work structured according to Route One, our guess is that most organizations would decide not to use that knowledge very extensively. There are many reasons why. For one, Route One is heavily dependent on behavioral science knowledge and techniques, whereas Route Two depends more on "hard" engineering technology and traditional economic models of organizational efficiency. If behavioral science has ever won out over an amalgam of engineering and economics, the case has not come to our attention. Moreover, Route One solutions, if they are to prosper, require major changes in how organizations themselves are designed and managed; Route Two solutions, on the other hand, fit nicely with traditional hierarchical organizational models and controlling managerial practices. Again, it seems not to be much of a contest.

But perhaps most telling is the fact that Route Two is more consistent with the behavioral styles and values of both employees and managers in contemporary organizations. Experienced employees know how to adapt and survive on relatively routine, unchallenging jobs. Would individuals who are comfortable and secure in their worklives, leap at a chance for a wholly different kind of work experience in an organization designed according to the principles of Route One? Some would, to be sure, especially among the younger and more adventurous members of the work force, but many would not. Learning how to function within a Route One organization could be a long and not terribly pleasant process, and it is unclear how many would be willing to tolerate the upset and the anxiety of the change process long enough to gain a sense of what work in a Route One organization might have to offer.

Managers, too, have good reasons to be skeptical about Route One and its implications. The whole idea flies in the face of beliefs and values about people and organizations that have become well learned and well accepted by managers of traditional organizations (for example, that organizations are supposed to be run from the top down, not from the bottom up; that many employees have neither the competence nor the commitment to take real responsibility for carrying out the work of the organization on their own; that organizational effectiveness should be measured primarily, if not exclusively, in terms of the economic efficiency of the enterprise; that more management control of employee behavior is better management).

Reversing Directions

Are we being too pessimistic? Perhaps. There are documented instances where employees and managers alike have responded with enthusiasm to work redesign activities that had many of the trappings of Route One.

Yet if one suspects that current trends in management tend to favor Route Two (which we do), and

doesn't like that idea (which we don't), what is to be done about it? For one thing, better understanding of organizational changes that involve redesigning work is needed. As noted above, there is a pressing need to know more about (1) the process of carrying out planned change of work systems, (2) strategies for conducting informative evaluations of work redesign activities that account for the multiplicity of their effects, and (3) factors that affect the persistence and diffusion of innovations in the design of work.

Such knowledge, however, would merely improve our capability to begin moving down Route One. It would not make us *want* to go that direction. Providing the social "push" for a reversal of direction, we believe, will require some combination of the following.

1. Organized labor decides to make improvements in the quality of life at work a high-priority item. At present, some union leaders find their members to be uninterested in job enrichment or quality of worklife issues; other labor spokespersons argue that such issues ought to be high on the list of objectives of the labor movement, and are providing leadership in bringing these matters to the attention of their members. Which set of views will dominate in the years to come? What, indeed, are the rewards and risks for unions and for union leaders if they take the lead on this issue?

2. Significant numbers of managers in major corporations, or in large public bureaucracies, decide that work redesign pays off in coin they value. Managers, generally, are adept at identifying indicators of organizational performance that "count" in the eyes of significant others (such as stockholders, members of congress, or high-level managers) and then managing their organizational units so that the performance indicators are favorable. What kinds of data would it take to convince results-oriented managers that their own objectives would be well served by introducing and supporting innovative designs for work? Or are fundamental changes in organizational control systems and accounting practices required before this can happen? Are such changes likely? Who might initiate them?

3. Government decides to require or encourage organizations to improve the quality of worklife of their employees. Some commentators (e.g., Lawler, 1982) have argued that government might wish to legislate improvements in the quality of worklife, even to the extent of fining organizations that persist in providing a poor quality of worklife for their employees. Others (e.g., Locke, 1976) find government regulation in this area a perfectly awful idea. Would such an approach be politically feasible? Would it work? Are there other ways the government could encourage innovation in work design? How about financial encouragement of organizational experimentation with new ways of designing work? Or, perhaps most significantly, could the present economic incentives that favor capital utilization (through the investment tax credit, which encourages the purchase of technology that often eliminates or routinizes jobs) and that discourage labor utilization (through social security and unemployment taxation) be tilted somewhat more in favor of effective use of human resources?

4. The cultural climate changes to support the idea that work experiences should be more fulfilling and growth enhancing. Will the large numbers of people whose jobs are currently far beneath their qualifications begin to speak with a common voice and demand more personally meaningful work? Will the continued exposure of successful organizational innovations in the media gradually engender a positive cultural value for enriched and challenging work? Will people start to *care* more about the quality of their own and others' experiences on the job?

5. The national economy collapses or enters a period of significant crisis. While not a change strategy that many would wish to actively pursue, in fact an economic crisis might provide a once-in-a-lifetime opportunity to significantly alter how work is designed and how organizations are run. If those who favor Route One solutions were ready with an attractive vision and a road map for making that vision reality when the present system quits working, then *real* change just might be achieved.

All five of these possible forces for change have one thing in common: they involve changes in what people want or what they need. They deal with the reward contingencies that others have created for us or that we have created for ourselves. For that reason, they deal with power—and, as always is the case for power, they ultimately deal with values.

To the extent that as managers, as consultants, or as scholars we have a bit of power to change how work is designed, how do we want to use it? *What kind of life do we want to create for the people who do the productive work of our society—and how much are we willing to pay for it?* The answer to that question, far more than the answers to questions about how much we do or don't know about organizational change, will determine how work actually is designed in organizations—now, and in the years to come.

REFERENCES

Gyllenhammar, P. G. *People at work.* Reading, Mass.: Addison-Wesley, 1977.

Lawler, E. E., III. Strategies for improving the quality of work life. *American Psychologist,* 1982, **37,** 486–493.

———. The new plant revolution. *Organizational Dynamics,* Winter 1978, 2–12.

Locke, E. A. The case against legislating quality of work life. *Personnel Administrator,* May 1976, 19–21.

Lupton, T. Efficiency and the quality of worklife: The technology of reconciliation. *Organizational Dynamics,* Autumn 1975, 68–80.

Macy, B. A., & Mirvis, P. H. Measuring the quality of work and organizational effectiveness in behavioral-economic terms. *Administrative Science Quarterly,* 1976, **21,** 212–226.

Oldham, G. E. The motivational strategies used by supervisors: Relationships to effectiveness indicators. *Organizational Behavior and Human Performance,* 1976, **15,** 66–86.

Walton, R. E. The diffusion of new work structures: Explaining why success didn't take. *Organizational Dynamics,* Winter 1975, 3–22.

———. Work innovations at Topeka: After six years. *Journal of Applied Behavioral Science,* 1977, **13,** 422–433.